Writers' & Artists' YEARBOOK 2026

Praise for the *Yearbook*

"So much of interest, and so much that the budding writer needs explained.
Martina Cole

"The writers' Bible.
Susan Hill

"Read this book very carefully. Treasure it. Keep it beside you.
Rachel Joyce

"An indispensable companion for anyone seriously committed to the profession of author.
David Lodge

"Essential reading ... the A-Z of how to survive in publishing.
Kate Mosse

"When you're looking to get published, it's your bible.
Patrick Ness

"Everything you need to know about the business of being a writer.
Lawrence Norfolk

"Even established writers can feel as though they're climbing a mountain. Think of the *Writers' & Artists' Yearbook* as your sherpa.
Ian Rankin

"Get a copy of the *Yearbook*. It's the key that will help you unlock the world of publishing.
Samantha Shannon

"Every writer can remember her first copy of the *Writers' & Artists' Yearbook*.
Rose Tremain

Writers' & Artists' YEARBOOK 2026

ONE HUNDRED AND NINETEENTH EDITION

THE ESSENTIAL GUIDE TO THE MEDIA AND PUBLISHING INDUSTRIES

The perfect companion for writers of fiction and non-fiction,
poets, playwrights, journalists, and commercial artists

B L O O M S B U R Y   Y E A R B O O K S
LONDON • OXFORD • NEW YORK • NEW DELHI • SYDNEY

BLOOMSBURY YEARBOOKS
Bloomsbury Publishing Plc
50 Bedford Square, London, WC1B 3DP, UK
Bloomsbury Publishing Ireland Limited,
29 Earlsfort Terrace, Dublin 2, D02 AY28, Ireland

BLOOMSBURY, BLOOMSBURY YEARBOOKS, WRITERS' & ARTISTS' and the Diana logo are trademarks of Bloomsbury Publishing Plc

First published in Great Britain 1906
This edition published 2025

A catalogue record for this book is available from the British Library

ISBN: PB: 978-1-3994-2124-9; eBook: 978-1-3994-2123-2

2 4 6 8 10 9 7 5 3 1

Typeset by RefineCatch Limited, Bungay, Suffolk
Printed and bound in Great Britain by CPI Group (UK) Ltd, Croydon, CRO 4YY

MIX
Paper | Supporting responsible forestry
FSC www.fsc.org FSC® C013604

Writers' & Artists' team
Editor Alysoun Owen
Assistant editor Eden Phillips Harrington
Articles copy-editor Lisa Carden
Listings editors Lisa Carden, Rebecca Collins, Lauren MacGowan
Editorial assistant Alice Glasspool
Editorial assistance Sophia Blackwell (poetry), Kathryn Alley, Zara Relphman, Emily Camera
Production controller Rachel Murphy

Contents

A note from the Editor vii
Foreword by Naomi Alderman ix

Newspapers and magazines
Introduction 1
How to write features for the national and regional press – Georgina Fuller 3
The hidden art of B2B journalism – Blake Evans-Pritchard 7
Setting up and editing a new magazine – Ed Needham 11

Listings
National newspapers UK and Ireland 15
Regional newspapers UK and Ireland 24
Magazines UK and Ireland 36
Syndicates, news and press agencies 87

Books
Introduction 89

The publishing process
The publishing year: the highs, lows and trends – Tom Tivnan 94
Working with your editor: the author–editor relationship – Željka Marošević 99
Getting books to market: how books are sold – David Wightman 102
What every author needs to know about PR to sell more books – Hannah Hargrave 105
How bookshops can help sell your book – Carrie Morris 109
Assistive technology for visually impaired people – Bridget Norman 113
More options for more people: inclusivity and opening up the industry – Aki Schilz 114

Listings
Book publishers UK and Ireland 118
Book publishers overseas 190
Audio providers and distributors 223
Book packagers 225

Routes to publication
Becoming a bestselling author: my writing story – Peter James 228
My rocky road trip to writing success – Sarah Clarke 232
Keeping the writing dream alive – S.J. Watson 236
Getting your debut into print: the path to publication – Jennie Godfrey 238
Alphabet alchemy: turning letters into gold – Owen Sheers 241
Real people write books – Samantha Shannon 243
Writing across forms: my publishing routes to success – Rob Gittins 245
If at first you don't succeed … keep trying – Jessica Irena Smith 249

The writing craft
Reading as a writer – Cathy Rentzenbrink 254
Writing for readers – Rachel McLean 257
Writing successful dialogue – Angela Clarke 260
The importance of story development – Greg Mosse 264
The art and craft of literary translation – Jianan Qian 268
Ghosting: writing other people's stories – Gillian Stern 272

Writing for different genres
Writing thrilling fiction – Paula Hawkins 278
Ever wanted to write a saga? – Di Redmond 282
Writing Regency romances – Katy Moran 285
Tropes in romantic fiction – Sue Moorcroft 289
Reigniting the past: writing historical fiction – Annie Garthwaite 293
Writing and publishing short stories – Paul McVeigh 297
Keeping it short: putting together a short-story collection – Vanessa Onwuemezi 300
How to be a literary fiction writer – Rowan Hisayo Buchanan 304
Weaving fact into fiction – Jo Browning Wroe 308
Writing about the natural world – Sophie Pavelle 311
Pitching your travel ideas: books and articles – Jen and Sim Benson 316

Poetry
Introduction 321
Poems for the page and on stage – Raymond Antrobus 322
The portfolio poet – Sophia Blackwell 324
Being a poet and a publisher – Aaron Kent 329
Making poetry comics – Chrissy Williams 331
Getting your poetry out there – Neil Astley 334
Perseverance in getting poetry published – Pascale Petit 340
Becoming a lyricist – Kathryn Williams 344

Listings
Poetry organisations 349

Screen and audio

Introduction 357
Getting your screenplay noticed – Robert Taylor 358
Successful screenwriting – Anna Symon 362
A way with words: writing comedy – Ian Martin 365
Can you make a living writing comedy? Yes, but… – Dave Cohen 368
Creating compelling characters for TV – Kira-Anne Pelican 372
Writing series for television – Russell Lewis 376
Getting your audiobook published – Laura Smith 380
Audio dramatist or novelist? – Jonathan Myerson 384
Writing for videogames: a guide for the curious – Chris Bateman 387

Listings

Television and radio 391

Theatre

Introduction 399
Getting your script noticed – James McDermott 400
Play with fire: fighting the writing demons that hold you back – Carmen Marcus 404
How to write for the theatre – Gill Kirk 408

Listings

Theatre producers 412

Literary agents

Introduction 425
What a debut novelist should expect from an agent – Sallyanne Sweeney 426
Your non-fiction proposal for agents and publishers – Rebecca Carter 429
What a literary agent can do for you – Sarah Such 433
A day in the life of a literary agent – Charlotte Seymour 438
Going your own way: Do you need an agent? – Emma Denny 441
What does a good submission look like? – Eve White 444
Querying an agent: top tips about submission – Catherine Cho 449

Listings

Literary agents UK and Ireland 452
Literary agents overseas 483

Art and illustration

Introduction 501
Being a book cover illustrator – Laura Barrett 502
Illustrating non-fiction books – Frances Moffatt 506
Creating comics – Hannah Berry 511

Listings

Art agents and commercial art studios 516

Societies, prizes and festivals

Introduction 523
The winning touch: the impact of winning an award – Ingrid Persaud 524
Festival fun: your guide to why, how and what – Adam Hamdy 527
At a crossroads? How to choose the best writer development initiative – Julia Forster 531

Listings

Societies, associations and clubs 535
Prizes and awards 570
Grants, bursaries and fellowships 623
Festivals and conferences for writers, artists and readers 630
Writers' retreats and creative writing courses 646
Libraries 660

Self-publishing and indie authors

Introduction 671
Paid-for publishing services: *Is it a steal?* 672
Understanding book design – Catherine Lutman 675
In praise of fanfic – Hari Patience-Davies 680
Harnessing the power of BookTok and social media to promote your writing – Rosie Hewlett 685
ISBNs: what you need to know 689
Indexing – Society of Indexers 692

Listings

Publishing services for independent authors 694

Law and copyright

UK copyright law and publishing rights – Lynette Owen 703
A legal lexicon 711
Protecting your content: piracy and IP – MUSO 712
Copyright Licensing Agency 714
Authors' Licensing and Collecting Society 716
DACS (Design and Artists Copyright Society) 718
Publishers' Licensing Services 719

Financial advice and support

Managing your finances: a guide for writers – Jonathan and Louise Ford 721
National Insurance contributions – Sarah Bradford 732
Public Lending Right 741
Society of Authors 746
Writers' Guild of Great Britain (WGGB) 749

Indexes

Subject indexes 753
Listings index 781

A note from the Editor

The Editor welcomes readers to this edition of the *Writers' & Artists' Yearbook*

Welcome to the latest edition of the *Yearbook*. Here you will find (I hope) all you need to set you on your way as you create, shape, develop and refine your work and prepare it for publication or performance. Whether you are a writer (poet, novelist, screenwriter, playwright, journalist, games writer or podcaster) or an illustrator, this book exists to answer your how and who and when and where questions about the writing and publishing process and the opportunities open to you. The 80 plus articles, as well as thousands of listings with contacts from across the media industry, provide a comprehensive survey and access to what can sometimes appear to be an impenetrable world.

The advice within the articles covers a wide spectrum of genres and forms and reflects the diverse experiences of the contributors who have successfully found their own routes into getting their work noticed by agents, commissioning editors, producers and – importantly – readers. The breadth of content is a valuable and consistent feature of each edition of this book. This year, we have a record number of new articles which together deliver a mix of inspirational support and practical advice to those just starting out and for more seasoned creatives too.

Although these days there are more platforms, formats and ways to get your books to readers than ever before (take a look at these sections in particular: *Self-publishing and indie authors*, which starts on page 671 and *Societies, prizes and festivals* on page 523), getting a publishing deal can still seem a remote fantasy to most. In her article on page 114, *More options for more people: inclusivity and opening up the industry*, Aki Schilz suggests how that fantasy might become more of a reality. In a similar vein, Julia Forster considers how support can be found, in *At a crossroads? How to choose the best writer development initiative* (on page 531). A recipient of funding to support her writing, Pascale Petit shares her story in *Perseverance in getting poetry published* on page 340. New, too, to the *Poetry* section is *Becoming a lyricist* by Kathryn Williams (page 344).

In his annual round-up of *The publishing year: the highs, lows and trends* (on page 94), Tom Tivnan provides an invaluable digest of the good news from the last twelve months and considers some of the challenges ahead for the industry. Fiction has performed well at the tills, partly fuelled by reader and author enthusiasm for BookTok. In her article, *Harnessing the power of BookTok and social media to promote your writing* on page 685, Rosie Hewlett shares her tips.

For the budding writer for film, TV and audio, there are two new pieces from established screenwriter and screen editor respectively: *Getting your screenplay noticed* by Robert Taylor (page 358) and *Creating compelling characters for TV* by Kira-Anne Pelican (page 372). If making readers laugh is your intention, turn to page 368 for Dave Cohen's *Can you make a living writing comedy? Yes, but …*

The *Books* section, which starts on page 89, is full of wise words from bestselling authors; but we are reminded that once upon a time they too were debut writers looking for their lucky break. It is divided into four sub-sections to help you navigate the content. 'The publishing process' includes a new article from Jonathan Cape Editorial Director Željka

Maroševič on *Working with your editor: the author–editor relationship* (page 99) and pieces on promotion and selling. 'Routes to publication' includes *Getting your debut into print: the path to publication* (page 238) by Jennie Godfrey and in 'Writing for different genres', there are three new pieces which demonstrate the wide range of advice between these covers. *Keeping it short: putting together a short-story collection* by Vanessa Onwuemezi is on page 300, *How to be a literary fiction writer* by Rowan Hisayo Buchanan appears on page 304 and on page 311 is Sophie Pavelle's *Writing about the natural world*. For advice on hooking an agent, take a look at *What does a good submission look like?* by Eve White on page 444.

If you would like to write for the theatre, then award-winner Carmen Marcus will tell you how she started in *Play with fire: fighting the writing demons that hold you back* (page 404). 'Who needs your story …?' asks Carmen. The answer is readers and audiences do and that's what this *Yearbook* has existed over these many years (119 years to be precise) and why it continues to be a trusted friend to writers and illustrators of all backgrounds. And it's why, as Naomi Alderman entreats you in her *Foreword* on page ix, 'This book is for when you're ready to go into battle'. So ignore the demon whispering 'imposter' into your ear and take a chance by daring to share your work. Alderman reiterates: 'Make your work, I say to you. Make your work.'

Do it and let this book be your guide.

Alysoun Owen
Editor

All articles, listings and other material in this yearbook are reviewed and updated every year in consultation with the bodies, organisations, companies and individuals that we select for inclusion. To the best of our knowledge the websites, emails and other contact details are correct at the time of going to press.

Short story competition

The annual *Writers' & Artists' Yearbook* Short Story Competition offers published and aspiring writers the chance to win a place on an Arvon Residential Writing Week (worth £985). In addition, the winner's story will be published on the Writers & Artists website.

To enter the competition, submit a short story (for adults) of no more than 2,000 words, on the theme of 'play' by 13 February 2026 to waybcompetitions@bloomsbury.com. For full details, terms and conditions, and to find out more about how to submit your entry, visit www.writersandartists.co.uk/competitions.

For advice on short stories, see *Writing and publishing short stories* by Paul McVeigh on page 297 and *Keeping it short: putting together a short-story collection* by Vanessa Onwuemezi on page 300.

ARVON is the UK's home of creative writing, offering a wide range of in-person and online courses led by acclaimed writers. From poetry and fiction to screenwriting and memoir, their courses cater to writers of all levels, providing expert guidance, inspiration, and a supportive community. Alongside an extensive online programme of Writing Days, Weeks, Months, and Masterclasses, Arvon hosts immersive Residential Writing Courses in three historic countryside houses. Here, writers can step away from daily life to focus on their craft and make real progress on their projects.

Foreword

Naomi Alderman

When you buy this book, you know you're a writer. Not just buy it, of course. When you take it out of the library. When you sit perusing it in a reference section, when you borrow a friend's copy, when you mark it up, when you photograph or screenshot the pages, when you make decisions, when you use this book to create your battle plan, that's when you know you're a writer.

People say: writers write. And that's true enough. Sitting with a notebook, figuring out what word wants to follow along from the one you just put down, walking and thinking out your story, sitting in the loo to type a few words into your writing app before the feeling goes away, running home to get the perfect sentence down… yes, all of those are really what make you a writer. You can absolutely write and not show it to anyone. But I don't know, it's not really for me. I really, truly wanted my words seen and read, discussed and loved and hated and not kept quietly in a drawer.

This is a book for when you're ready to go into battle.

I wrote for years without showing anyone. Can I advise not doing that? I started trying to write a novel when I was 14, finally managing to finish a draft of a book in my summer holidays between my first and second years of university when I was 19. I showed it to a couple of friends who had an argument about it in front of me. One said: 'the dialogue is crappy.' The other said: 'no, there's just too much dialogue.' In the end, they compromised and presented me with their synthesised view. 'Too much crappy dialogue.' I felt I'd been told what I always feared: that actually I was a terrible writer, that there was no real point in this worthless hobby of mine. I kept on scribbling in notebooks and on my laptop but I didn't show anyone else anything I'd written until I was 26 years old.

Look, I don't say 'battle' lightly. It is relentlessly hard to take those words you started writing for your own satisfaction and enjoyment and to expose them to the absolute certainty of at least some rejection, misunderstanding, even outright mockery.

For me, it took quite literally witnessing the World Trade Center towers falling on 9/11. I was working at a law firm in Manhattan; I saw the towers fall with my own eyes, from our conference room window. I thought – not immediately but over the days and weeks that followed – that there were probably people in those buildings who were thinking what I was thinking: 'I'll just do this job for another few years and then I'll write that novel I've always meant to write.'

And then, that was that. Death sometimes gives you not a second to look behind and say 'oh, but I meant to…'. It doesn't wait. When that's it, that's it.

So I bought my copy of the *Writers' & Artists' Yearbook*. I applied to a Creative Writing Master's. I got in. I worked on my novel there. I was sick of letting myself be cowed by the world. Enough of being small. Make your work, I said to myself, make your work.

I applied for residencies and grants and prizes I found in these pages. I got rejected by a lot of them, but there were a few acceptances. I ended up as a writer in residence for a long hot summer in Arizona with no air-conditioning where I was staying. There was air-conditioning in the library, though, which was a good incentive to spend as much time as possible there, writing. I finished my book. I found an agent. She sent it to publishers. Here I am: books and games and film/TV projects and radio series to my name.

Here I am, doing the thing I was meant to do, which I almost missed because of taking 'too much crappy dialogue' much, much too seriously.

Listen, if you want it, come and take it. A career as a writer happens in two ways at once: by hard work and by chance. You write the things you want to write, you keep working on them until you think they're as good as you can make them. You send them to people and organisations and opportunities listed in this book. You keep on and on doing that. And then it's almost chance what happens, who finds your work and loves it, you don't control it. All you can do is to keep on making the work. No one is going to come asking you for it. But there are people who want to find whoever is writing the next brilliant thing. That might be you. You don't find out until you try.

Make your work, I say to you. Make your work.

You'll get slapped in the face from time to time, sure. But the sting of the slap is how you know you've stopped sitting your own life out. It's how you know you're in the real battle.

Naomi Alderman is an award-winning novelist, TV producer and videogames creator. She is the author of the bestselling *The Power* (Penguin Books 2017), winner of the Women's Prize for Fiction and since adapted for TV by Amazon Prime. Her other books (all also published by Penguin) include *The Future* (2023), *The Liars' Gospel* (2013), *The Lessons* (2010) and *Disobedience* (2006) and the forthcoming non-fiction book about the information crisis: *Don't Burn Anyone At The Stake Today*. She is the co-creator of the fitness game and audio adventure *Zombies, Run!*, which has more than 10 million players. Naomi writes and presents *Human Intelligence*, the history of thinkers from Socrates to Mary Wollstonecraft to Malcolm X on BBC Radio 4. She is Professor of Creative Writing at Bath Spa University and a Fellow of the Royal Society of Literature.

Newspapers and magazines
Introduction

Over the last quarter century, we have seen a steady decline in the consumption of traditional print media. Each year more print newspapers and magazines have reduced their frequency and size, while increasing their cover prices. According to *PressGazette* (https://pressgazette.co.uk), the total regional daily circulations of newspapers fell by 16% in 2024. The figure for non-dailies was a little better at 14%. Ofcom reported similar results for the nationals, in print at least.

People will always want to read the news, whether it be on paper or online. Digital subscriptions to regional papers, according to the same study by *PressGazette*, remained stable in 2024, and that gives hope. The media we use for transmitting and receiving news is changing but that does not mean that it is in decline overall. Just as there will always be consumers of news, there will always be writers, journalists and photographers who want to capture the news as it breaks, to be the first, or to be the most talked about, to comment and discuss, and encourage healthy debate.

For magazines, a general shift from physical copies to digital platforms have seen some longstanding publications reach the end of the road: the loss of *The Lady* in April 2025 after 140 years in print is a case in point.

Print media has been forced to diversify and expand into the digital realm to survive. Encouragingly, we have seen new news agencies spring up recently, internationally at least, with the birth of sites such as *Ground News* and *Flipboard*. Luxury and independent magazines in particular are making a comeback. *i-D*, relaunched in March 2025 by a conglomerate owned by the supermodel Karlie Kloss, emblematic of the interest and knowing nostalgia that Gen Z readers, in particular, have for print magazines.

Getting started

What's the best starting point for someone looking to have their work placed, in print or online? If you know the name of the publication you'd like to be featured in, you should find it within the following pages. If not, turn to the subject indexes on page 753 to find titles that might be of interest. Buy the latest phyiscal edition or download it from the newspaper's or magazine's website to see what is featured and the style, tone and approach of commissioned pieces. Knowing what an editor is looking for will help you select which of your articles, poems, essays, reviews or interviews might really hit the spot.

Study the market

- It is an editor's job to know what readers want and to see that they get it. Thus, freelance contributions must be tailored to fit a specific market; subject, theme, treatment and length must meet the editor's requirements.
- Before sending in a pitch, an article or feature, always look at the editorial requirements of the publication: the subjects covered by the publication as well as the approach, treatment, style and typical length of pieces.

Check with the editor first

• Before submitting material to any newspaper or magazine, it is advisable to first contact the relevant editor. A quick telephone call or email will establish the name of the relevant commissioning editor.

• It is not advisable to send illustrations 'on spec'; check with the editor first.

Understand how the market works

• It is worth considering using an agent to syndicate material. Most agents operate on an international basis and are aware of current market requirements. See listings for *Syndicates, news and press agencies* on page 87.

• The larger newspapers and magazines buy many of their stories, and the smaller papers buy general articles, through well-known syndicates.

• For the supply of news, most of the larger UK and overseas newspapers depend on their own staff and press agencies. The most important overseas newspapers have permanent representatives in the UK who keep them supplied with news and articles. While many overseas newspapers and magazines have a London office, it is usual for freelance contributions to be submitted to the headquarters' editorial office overseas.

Payment

• Many newspapers and magazines are reluctant to state a standard rate, since the value of a contribution may be dependent not upon length but upon the standing of the writer or the information supplied. Many other periodicals prefer to state 'by negotiation' or 'by arrangement', rather than giving precise payment information.

Listings in this section:

- *National newspapers UK and Ireland*, page 15
- *Regional newspapers UK and Ireland*, page 24
- *Magazines UK and Ireland*, page 36
- *Syndicates, news and press agencies*, page 87

How to write features for the national and regional press

Freelance journalist Georgina Fuller describes the appeal and variety of feature-writing, as well as the financial and commissioning challenges that make determination, flexibility and resilience essential attributes for a freelancer. She gives valuable tips on how to get started and how to pitch your piece to an editor for the best chance of success.

If you have ever watched an episode of the HBO hit show 'Sex and the City', you might think that freelance journalists spend their days going to glitzy parties, chain-smoking their way through work deadlines, and wearing fabulous shoes. Well, I've been freelance for over 15 years now and I'm here to tell you, it's more grit than glam – more frantic pitching, existential dread and chasing invoices than Manolo's, brunch and cocktails. Having said that, there is still little else I would rather do. 'Writing is the only thing that, when I do it, I don't feel I should be doing something else,' as the great Gloria Steinem once said.

Over the years, I have written for everyone from *Tatler* to *Take a Break*, but the process itself – pitching, writing, editing – is much the same, regardless of the publication you are writing for. The digital age has changed the face of journalism in many ways over the last decade or so. Topical news stories are published on a digital-first basis now and many publications pay less for online articles than they do for print pieces (see **Money matters** overleaf). This is probably partly due to the ever-changing news cycle, the many-headed Hydra that is social media, and the fact that journalism has become increasingly focused on clickbait rather than long reads. That's not to say the job of a freelance journalist has changed greatly. The skills required are still much the same – thinking of a different angle on a topical story, sourcing case studies, turning clean copy around quickly – though now it's also essential to have a basic understanding of SEO (search engine optimisation) and to know how to insert a few hyperlinks.

When I first went freelance, in about 2008, any publication I pitched to usually had a decent-sized editorial team – with a sub-editor, a picture desk, staff writers and an editorial assistant, as well as various editors handling news, features, art and so on. Nowadays, many publications have had their budgets slashed as the cost-of-living crisis bites and are running on a skeleton staff. This means, essentially, that freelancers are expected to do more for less – to source pictures, write headlines and sub their own work. It has also made it harder and harder to get commissions and generate work, as staff writers who are already on the payroll are cheaper than freelancers.

So what options are available to aspiring freelance journalists today? The good news is that newspapers and magazines are always looking for fresh voices, opinion pieces and a new take on a topical issue. The bad news is it's become harder and harder to make a living from freelance journalism. This is partly because there are a growing number of bloggers, influencers and chancers who will write for free, but also because – around the early 2000s or even the late '90s – freelance rates crashed and burned.

Starting out

Some publications seem to take the 'free' in 'freelance' quite literally and think that they can get away without paying a writer for their work. I would avoid doing this at all costs if you are looking to make a career out of it. Making a living as a freelancer is hard. If you are starting from scratch, it is pretty much essential that you have another form of income; this could be something related to freelance journalism, such as corporate communications, PR or blogging. Unless of course you have a trust fund or a famous surname (and the two, naturally, often go hand in hand). Not only is the pay lousy, it's also very precarious; many titles run on a pay-on-publication basis or they over-commission and then offer a paltry 'kill fee' (the term they use when a piece gets scrapped or doesn't make the cut) that is less than the rate you were commissioned to write the piece for. Furthermore, many magazines now expect you to sign away all your 'rights' to a piece, which means they can syndicate it out to other titles in their publishing group without paying you for the privilege. For those reasons, I would always advise anyone starting out on a freelance career to build on or capitalise on a niche area because, whatever it is – beekeeping, gong baths, white-water rafting – there will be a magazine for it. If you can write, and there's something you know a bit about – a quirky subject or hobby, or something 'zeitgeisty' such as the world of dating apps – that is a potential source of income.

My background was in business magazines and HR, so that was my main source of income when I started out as a freelancer. I then moved into writing more for consumer titles on family, parenting and, subsequently, mid-life (I've written about everything from *Peppa Pig* to the gentrification of the Cotswolds and how Black fathers are under-represented in the media). Some freelancers start out in the regional press, although that too has seen some seismic changes in recent years. In 2024, the *Press Gazette* estimated that at least 293 local newspapers had closed since 2005; the advent of social media, decline in advertising revenues and an evolving younger population of readers are all contributing factors.[1] Many local newspapers offer work experience, though, so that could be a great way of getting your foot in the door. Having local knowledge isn't always essential, but having a good eye for a story, a flexible attitude and a dogged determination *is*.

Bitching pitching: how to place a piece in a national newspaper

OK … you've had a brilliant idea for an article. How do you place it in a national newspaper or magazine? Firstly, you need to find the right editor to pitch it to, so do your research, know your stuff and the publications you'd like to write for. If you can pitch it for a specific page or slot, that's even better. Don't expect any favours! Here are some important rules to follow:

- **Hone it down.** Be sure to hone your pitch down to four or five sentences or points so that it's concise and easy to understand. You should be able to sum up your story in a single sentence. Think about the 'who, what, where, when and why,' and make sure you cover the basics.
- **Make it relevant.** Check that your pitch passes the 'so what' test. Remember, editors don't owe you anything and just because something is of interest to you, it may not be to them. So make it relevant, timely and interesting. Think of the headline, 'sell' and crux of the article.

1. https://pressgazette.co.uk/publishers/regional-newspapers/local-newspaper-closures-uk-2022-to-2024/

• **Show a topical link.** Tag your pitch to a recent news story, survey or topic to give it extra currency, and make it as easy and succinct as possible so that the editor 'gets it'. Pre-empt any questions with relevant stats, figures and reports.
• **Include pictures.** Always include suitable pictures, ideally hi-res landscape pics (which are better for print) in jpeg format. If you have interviewed any case studies, it's almost essential to include headshots.
• **Follow up.** Editors get hundreds of emails a day, so make sure you follow up at least once, to check if they have read it. If it's a No, ask them what else they might be interested in receiving pitches on.

Money matters

Jon Harris, chairman of the National Association of Press Agencies and managing director of Manchester-based news agency Cavendish Press, wrote in the *Press Gazette* in 2022 that the UK's national newspapers were in a 'time warp' when it came to fees. 'Even my own daughter once made more money doing a night's babysitting than I did covering a murder trial,' he said.

Payment rates can vary hugely depending on the title and, sadly, some have hardly gone up since I first started freelancing.[2] The benchmark set by the National Union of Journalists (NUJ; see page 547) used to be £250 per 1,000 words for features, but the focus on digital-first journalism has eclipsed this on many national newspapers. National newspapers typically pay between 25p and 50p a word, although many offer a standard rate for either a one-page or double-page spread (DPS). This can vary according to which section of the newspaper the article will appear in; the *Daily Mail*, for example, might pay £1,000 for a double-page spread for its *Femail* magazine, while its health pages pay £600–900. *Grazia* magazine paid £450 for a 900-word print feature in 2020, while *Grazia Daily* paid £200 for an 800-word feature in 2023. Regional newspapers can pay an abysmal £60 per 1000-word feature or up to £120 a day.

Day rates for shifts at regional papers can vary significantly, while standard day rates on the nationals for news are often lower. *The Times* paid £120 for a page lead and £58.50 for a shorter story in 2023, while the *Sun* paid £110–150. One freelance colleague who writes regularly for women's weekly magazines pointed out that the rate had gone down considerably – from £500 for a DPS in 2019 to around £300 in 2023: 'Nothing ever seems to go up and, if you make a fuss, it's suggested that there is always someone else willing to do it for less,' she said.

And finally...

If all of that hasn't put you off, I am here to tell you that being a freelance journalist can be the most rewarding, fun and varied job you will ever have. It's a job that has taken me from interviewing ex-offenders in the most deprived part of Glasgow to interviewing celebrities on their houseboats in Chelsea and stately houses in the Home Counties. While the pay might be abysmal, the perks (travel, press do's, freebies) can be great fun. But you do have to be tenacious, resilient and, of course, an excellent writer; the competition is

[2] Sources: NUJ, *Freelancing for Journalists* podcast (https://podcasts.apple.com/gb/podcast/freelancing-for-journalists/id1511920418) and my fellow journalists.

fierce and you have to learn not to take it personally if your pitch isn't picked up. It's not all strutting around the streets of New York in a tutu (although I once did that with a clipboard and microphone in Covent Garden ...). Good luck!

Georgina Fuller is a freelance journalist, editor and media consultant with over 20 years' experience, who has had bylines in the *Daily Telegraph*, *Guardian*, *The Times*, *Daily Mail*, *Observer*, *i Paper*, *Daily Express*, *Red*, *Tatler*, *Marie Claire*, *Grazia*, *Prima*, *Good Housekeeping*, *Woman*, *Woman's Own* and *Take a Break* magazine. She also writes a column for her local paper, the *Stratford Herald*. Georgina has lectured on journalism at several well-known universities, and she offers 1:1 or team media consultancy and training to small businesses. See her website www.georginafuller.co.uk for more information. Follow her on X @GeorgieR30.

See also...

- *Pitching your travel ideas: books and articles*, page 316

The hidden art of B2B journalism

Blake Evans-Pritchard describes how writing for the specialist trade press can be both intellectually stimulating and highly lucrative. He sheds light on B2B and its place in the market, with essential advice and top tips on how to establish yourself in this doubly rewarding field.

The collapse of Archegos, a US hedge fund, in 2021 was one of the biggest financial scandals of the past ten years. In just two days, South Korean-born Bill Hwang managed to lose a staggering 20 billion US dollars. Few individuals in history have blown through so much cash in such a short period of time. The incident left a number of prominent investment banks reeling. Financial journalists were all over the story. But some of the best reporting lay not within the pages of mainstream newspapers; it was the trade press that had the technical expertise and the resources to understand what was really going on. Within weeks of the Archegos collapse, I was pleasantly surprised to spot, right on the front page of the *Financial Times*, a story that came directly from the B2B magazine I was writing for. The *Financial Times* was even good enough to credit us as the source.

Admittedly, I can't really take credit for this particular story. I was working in Hong Kong at the time and, although Bill Hwang was originally from Asia, the most exciting action was taking place in the USA and Europe. I think that, out of the 135 articles about Archegos that we eventually published, I was able to contribute just one. Still, it was hugely satisfying to be at the centre of such a significant story, and to be one of those few journalists who had the close contacts and technical nous to really get to the heart of what was going on. This is what writing for the trade press is all about – having the knowledge and understanding that more mainstream journalists simply don't have the time, inclination or opportunity to match. Done well, this kind of journalism can be hugely lucrative too.

What is the B2B trade press – and why write for it?

B2B stands for 'business-to-business'. Put simply, B2B journalism is about writing specifically for businesses, so that they can take more informed and better decisions in the work that they do. This is different from business-to-consumer (B2C) journalism, which sees the public as the target audience. Let's illustrate this distinction with an example. Travel magazines such as *Condé Nast Traveller* or *Wanderlust*, which you can purchase in most British supermarkets, have as their core focus the individual traveller. Their articles do not dwell on how the travel industry works, but on how readers can get the most out of their travel experiences. These would be classed as B2C magazines.

Contrast this to *Travel Weekly* or *Travel Bulletin*. Each of these publications exist to serve the needs of the travel industry itself, preferring articles about the latest big tour company merger rather than a first-hand account of trekking in Antarctica. This would be B2B journalism. My background is in financial journalism, but B2B journalism is not just limited to this area. Healthcare periodicals for the medical profession, agricultural journals for farmers, fashion magazines for the clothing sector – all of these would also be considered B2B.

There are two main reasons why you might want to look to the B2B sector as an outlet for your writing. The first is cerebral. It can be hugely rewarding to be one of an elite group of journalists who understand the minute intricacies of a niche – though hugely important

– story. I have attended many media receptions organised by banks where some of the most important people at the event have migrated towards my corner of the room, simply because they know they will be able to have a more informed and interesting discussion about a subject they are really passionate about. The second reason for considering this avenue of writing is financial. In all my years of professional writing, both for mainstream and trade publications, I have always been able to earn more as a B2B journalist. Now that I am a freelancer, I find myself using my B2B earnings to supplement the other writing that I want to pursue but which invariably does not pay as much. We'll get on to the specifics of financials in a bit, but the logic is clear: B2B publications tend to pay more than less-specialist media because the readers that they serve are using the knowledge they find within articles to advance their business or their career. This provides a very important clue as to how to succeed in the B2B world.

Starting out

One of the most important pieces of advice for any aspiring journalist is: 'Know your readers'. This is doubly important when it comes to writing for B2B publications. Readers of B2B publications are prepared to fork out hefty subscription fees in the belief that they will get access to information they simply can't find elsewhere. As a B2B writer, you need to be able to provide that information. But how do you set about acquiring the knowledge base you need to market yourself convincingly as an industry expert? There are no quick-and-easy short cuts, unfortunately – but persistence, good preparation and a decent contact book can take you a long way.

Many years ago, before I had carved out a niche for myself as a B2B writer, I approached a British pensions magazine to ask if they would be interested in me writing for them. I had never written about the pensions industry before, but I had spotted an opportunity: a lot of news was emerging from the European Union, but no one was systematically covering its impact on the pensions industry. My optimistic approach resulted in a monthly column and a lasting freelance relationship with the publication. Understanding what readers want to learn about, and therefore what might interest potential editors, is crucial. It's simple enough to get this information – just go out there and ask them. One of the great things about B2B journalism is that many of the consumers of articles are often also the sources of such stories. Every single B2B interview I have these days ends with the question: 'So what else do you want to know about?'. This invariably leads to at least one or two good story ideas that I can work on at a later date.

Start by choosing your niche, based on what interests you and what magazines are available on the market. *Writers' & Artists' Yearbook* is a good starting place, but there are other ways of researching the sector too. Type 'trade magazines' into Google (avoid 'B2B publications' as a search term, as this can be confused with other uses of the word). When you feel confident enough in your chosen subject, approach an editor you want to work for and ask whether they ever take freelance contributions. At this stage, it is a good idea to suggest a few articles that you could start work on. The best way to catch the editor's eye is with an idea for an in-depth feature on something topical. The daily news churn will most likely be handled in-house.

In your pitches, be as specific as possible. A good tip is to try and focus on how companies are responding to a particular trend or development in the market. For example, an investment publication might be interested in an in-depth story on at how asset managers are reassessing their China strategy in a post-Covid world – with the promise that you would be able to speak to a handful of them. The editor might be less interested in a more general pitch about how much money is flowing into and out of the country (readers can gain this insight from the less specialist publications that they also regularly read). As long as you have been suitably convincing in your introductory letter, and have presented yourself as something of an authority on a particular industry, there is a good chance that the editor will be interested. There is a shortage of good B2B journalists out there, and most specialist publications are only too happy to take good freelance copy.

The relationship with the commissioning editor is key. In every approach, make sure that you display a high level of professionalism and knowledge of the market. Trade publications have a highly symbiotic relationship with readers. The last thing that an editor wants is an uninformed hack speaking to subscribers. If you have the enthusiasm and interest to pursue this, the trade press should not be overlooked. Once you have established a solid relationship as an expert in the field, editors should be chasing you to work for them, rather than the other way round. Remember: you do not have to become a top expert in your chosen field; you just have to acquire enough knowledge to convince your sources (and your editor) that you are.

Let's talk financials

So how much can a B2B journalist expect to earn for a particular article? Well, as with all forms of writing, the answer is: it depends. However, as you gain more confidence and experience within the B2B space, you will learn that you can command a much higher rate than when you first started out and can quickly leave behind those publications that are not prepared to pay top dollar. These days I find myself being much choosier than I used to be about who I write for.

I am generally happy to accept 75p per word. This means that, for a 2,000-word article, I would be able to charge around £1,500. Such a piece would typically take me around three days of total work, including interviews, to put together. Of course, not all publications pay so generously, and I sometimes accept 35p per word. The rate paid often depends on how specialist the writing has to be, and on how many others are capable of producing such copy. I would rarely accept less than 35p per word. The important thing is to feel your way around the market; as you gain confidence, you can start pushing for higher remuneration. If you're good and consistently deliver meaningful value to your readers, you'll be able to get it.

Top tips for B2B journalism:

- Study the market carefully before settling on your niche. Is this a sector in which you will be able to develop a lasting interest? What publications currently serve this industry? Is there enough scope within the sector for you to develop a regular income stream?
- Speak to readers and sources as much as you possibly can. They are usually only too happy to talk about a subject they are passionate about, and you need to learn from them.
- Remember to end every interview with the question: 'So, what else do you want to know about?'
- Make sure you demonstrate a high level of expertise at all times, both when communicating with your editor and when interviewing sources.
- Avoid asking uninformed questions. Sources will quickly tire of a lazy journalist who hasn't done their homework properly and displays a lack of understanding (or care) about the industry that they work for.

• Don't expect official spokespeople to understand the subject matter as well as you or your sources do. Spokespeople, especially within large organisations, regularly prioritise the mainstream press over trade publications. It can take skill and tact – and sometimes the helping hand of an inside source – to overcome this hurdle.
• Spend time cultivating a personal relationship with the editor(s) you want to write for. Once you have established a solid relationship as an expert in the field, editors should be chasing you to work for them rather than the other way round.
• And, finally, make sure that you enjoy the work. It will show in your copy. Industry leaders are passionate about what they do. You need to be too.

Blake Evans-Pritchard is Editor of *ESG Investor*, a B2B publication focused on corporate stewardship and sustainable investment. He was previously Hong Kong bureau chief for *Risk.net*, a global publication covering the derivatives markets and risk management within financial institutions. He has also served as Editor-in-Chief of *InsuranceAsia News*, another B2B publication. He is currently based in Barcelona.

Setting up and editing a new magazine

Ed Needham shares his experience and outlines the essential steps, decisions and realities involved in publishing a new magazine as a solo operation, and gives practical advice on how to turn your concept into a successful venture in today's changing digital industry.

I have spent much of my adult life working as a journalist and editor in magazines. I edited *FHM* in its million-selling heyday in the '90s, and launched and edited that magazine in the United States. Also in the USA, I was the managing editor at *Rolling Stone* and editor-in-chief at *Maxim*, then the biggest men's magazine in the world. I've established a successful online publishing and marketing company, and developed magazines for other companies. But, over the last decade or so, the magazine as a fact of life – a glossy, portable, affordable luxury, object of desire and trusted source of guidance – has fallen badly out of fashion, evicted from so many of the gaps it used to fill in people's lives by the mobile phone. That one gadget has changed the fortunes of the industry calamitously. Readers and advertising have wandered off. Titles have closed. And by 2017 I found myself looking for a job, in a market where positions for top editors had become reserved for candidates with far more modest salary expectations than mine.

But a couple of interesting developments also emerged from the magazine industry's change of life: 1) many of the special skills and physical processes that used to require an army of talent had been replaced by affordable software; 2) while legacy magazine publishers were struggling for sustenance at a diminishing waterhole, there was still plenty of margin for people operating in niche markets and who didn't have a heavy payroll or central London floorspace to maintain. Perhaps I could publish my own magazine? And to keep the costs really low, perhaps I could do the whole thing on my own?

I found an envelope and did a few sums on the back of it. I produced a dummy – a trial issue – to see whether one person could write and edit an entire magazine (and then another one in short order – the revelation that Issue Two comes hard on the heels of Issue One routinely comes as a shock to people 'having a go' at magazines). I had it printed to see what it would look like, liked it, and in 2018 launched *Strong Words*, a magazine about books (see page 80). It appears six times a year, and each issue has reviews of over 100 titles, as well as interviews and features that send readers into an ecstasy of book-buying, trying authors, genres and categories of books they wouldn't previously have dreamt of dabbling in. And it does so entertainingly – people like to be informed and amused by reviews, not lectured gravely on how important something is. There is no sad head-shaking nor acts of critical violence; if I find a book disappointing, I don't cover it, but I think the days of the snooty, disdainful review to showcase the critic's cleverness are nearly over. *Strong Words* is for people who want to read more, not less. So why waste valuable space urging people not to buy a book? Even though it requires my attention all seven days of the week, I've proved it can be done. And here are some of the things I've learned, if you'd like to have a go yourself.

1. Do some initial thought experiments

I was taught that the first question to ask when embarking on a new magazine project was 'Who's it for?' But the people asking that question used to be big magazine companies whose starting point was identifying which market to shove themselves into next. Now I think you need to answer two different questions first: 1) 'Why am I doing it?' and 2) 'Where's the money coming from?' If you can answer those two questions honestly, rather than as a delusional pipe dream, you'll have sketched a foundation for your project. My answer to 1) was that I needed to earn a living – but with a view to eventually also applying my model to established magazines that might benefit from my approach to costs. My answer to 2) was initially the Bank of Ed Needham and then through subscriptions. Not advertising – at first, that's another cost. But until you can answer those questions with confidence, you can't go to the next square.

2. Who's it for?

Identify your market. Why does anyone need your magazine? Bear in mind that the younger consumers can easily imagine reaching the end of their lives without ever once touching one. I chose a print product because I understand them, and they have a credibility that online doesn't; it's like the difference between a house and a picture of a house. Neither did I have the time to do print *and* online to an acceptable standard. I chose to write about books because the UK is the world's bookiest nation (no other country publishes as many books per capita), yet there is no consistently reliable source for book buyers to find out what's new.

There are the highbrow journals and the broadsheets, but all too often they make books feel like homework, whereas most people buy books for pleasure. The internet is a formidable marketing machine, but it rarely leaves a person thinking, 'That's the book for me.' If anyone is going to appreciate the special magic of ink on paper, it's book buyers. Books are a great untapped reservoir of the new and the useful, the funny and the gossipy, endless revelation about just how dysfunctional our planet and its population is. And that is the stuff of life – something people have a gluttonous appetite for.

3. The practicalities

If you haven't made a magazine before, familiarise yourself with InDesign, the universal page-making software from Adobe, for which you pay a license fee. Work out how many pages you want – it should be a multiple of eight, plus four more for the cover. Make a flatplan, i.e. decide, before you start, what is going on every page and in what order. The only bit of the process I can't do is design, so my original concept for *Strong Words* was to pay a designer friend to establish a template, which I could re-use with different content each issue, thus keeping design costs low. But I do still need a designer for a couple of weeks each issue.

You're going to need content and pictures, which – unless you know people keen to work for nothing – you either have to produce yourself or pay for. Helping yourself from the internet is not advisable. You might get away with it, or you might end up in court. I get my stock pictures from Shutterstock (www.shutterstock.com), more specific images such as archive news images from Alamy (www.alamy.com), and I use press-approved images from the books I write about, where possible.

As for copy, I produce it all myself – it amounts to reading the equivalent of *War and Peace* each week (about 1,500 pages) and writing the equivalent of *The Great Gatsby* each issue (about 45,000 words). I cut the copy to fit, write the headlines, write the display copy (the various other bits, like captions) check the spellings and punctuation and prices. You need a cover – traditionally known as the most important page in a magazine. If you're selling your publication in shops, you need a bar code; these are easy to buy (see www.axicon.com), but before that you need an ISSN number … If I can get one, you can.

You may want to trademark your name; do it yourself at www.gov.uk/how-to-register-a-trade-mark (apply in class 09 for digital, class 16 for print). Don't pay a third party. And ignore the avalanche of scam letters that follow straight after.

4. Print it

I'd always thought this was the big barrier to a solo operation. You used to have to order the paper, and well in advance. If you wanted special paper, even more in advance. You usually had to buy quite a lot of it. It required middlemen. Now you can print a single copy. This was where I began to see what was possible: someone mentioned a business called Newspaper Club (www.newspaperclub.com) who print on newsprint, and so the first three issues of *Strong Words* came as a newspaper. You just upload your files, choose your paper quality, and pay.

My original marketing plan was to print loads and give them away … then everyone would faint with delight and subscribe on the spot. When I discovered that news-stands couldn't cope with a tabloid newsprint magazine, because it didn't fit their racks, I switched to a conventional A4 format, and used a company called Mixam (https://mixam.co.uk). Note: if you're sending your magazine out by post, you need to know how much it's going to weigh before you print it. Postage costs are brutal, so you want to keep them down but still ensure a decent paper stock. Printers' websites enable you to calculate the weight of an issue. This is a nasty shock to any budget (… keep smelling salts handy). And don't forget to factor in the weight of the envelope. Mixam provided great quality, but I needed specific delivery dates so now I use The Magazine Printing Company (www.magprint.co.uk), who also give stunning quality and invaluable customer service. Upload the files, approve them, send. It is mind-blowingly easy.

5. Distribution

I thought this would be a big barrier too, but no. I use a third-party company called Webscribe (www.webscribe.co.uk) to run the subscription fulfilment, so they take the money and send the issues out – I don't have to handle credit cards and customer data, all that tricky stuff. If you want to sell in shops, third-party companies will look after that too; I used one called MMS (www.mmslondon.co.uk) and sold in independents and in WHSmith travel outlets at railways and airports (you have to pay an annual fee per outlet). When travel fell out of favour during lockdown, I switched to subscription only, and the poor Smith's staff weren't always sure where to rack *Strong Words*, so I'd sometimes find it shoved somewhere inappropriate like gardening, so I'm not sure I'd go back.

And now for some difficult news. Congratulations for getting this far, but you have only reached the foot of the mountain, because the biggest challenge is …

6. Marketing

I think you can divide people into two groups: people who make things and people who sell things. Few excel at both. Persuading someone to buy your product is not a skill that emerges naturally from learning how to produce magazines. This is the main reason why people have business partners – to overcome this skill set schism. But those magazines aren't going to sell themselves and, having made such a thing of beauty, it's heartbreaking to see them not find new homes.

I wish I could reveal the golden key to marketing serenity, but it hasn't been revealed to me yet. This is what I think I know. There are two steps: 1) make people aware of the magazine; 2) persuade them to subscribe. The tools at your disposal are: social media; conventional media (I find the former better for step one, the latter for step two); newsletters, podcasts, events, influential people (someone once recommended focusing on your 1,000 most influential customers first, rather than scatter-gunning your efforts in a frantic marketing orgy). Make sure everyone you have ever met knows what you are doing. Somehow make yourself a topic of conversation. Explain how your product helps people. Trade favours. Most of all, get on with it and find out what works for you, and spend as much time on selling as on making.

Your project may be an act of supreme folly or it may transform the media landscape, but if you don't give it your everything, it WILL fail, and you will never find out. Looking forward to seeing you all on my subscription list soon. Good luck.

Ed Needham is an editor and journalist, and publisher of *Strong Words* magazine which he launched in 2018, published by his own company De Pentonville Media Ltd. His former roles include Editor, then Editor-in-Chief, of *FHM* in the UK and USA, 1997–2002, Managing Editor of *Rolling Stone*, 2002–04, Editor-in-Chief of *Maxim*, 2004–06, and founder and Editor-in-Chief of *Coach* magazine, 2015–16. For more information see www.strong-words.co.uk. Follow Strong Words on X @StrongWordsMag.

National newspapers UK and Ireland

This section includes listings for national newspapers available in print, in both print and online, and as online-only news websites. The country code for phoning UK offices from overseas is +44.

BBC News

email haveyoursay@bbc.co.uk
website www.bbc.co.uk/news
Facebook www.facebook.com/bbcnews
X @BBCNews
Ceo Deborah Turness

Online only. The website contains international and regional news coverage as well as entertainment, sport, science and political news. Founded 1997.

Business Post

2nd Floor, Block B, The Merrion Centre, Merrion Road, Dublin D04 H2H4, Republic of Ireland
tel +353 (0)1 602 6000
email info@businesspost.ie
website www.businesspost.ie
Facebook www.facebook.com/businessposthq
X @businessposthq
Editor Daniel McConnell
Weekly Sun €4.90

Features on financial, economic and political topics. Also lifestyle, media and science articles. Illustrations: colour and b&w photos, graphics and cartoons. Payment: by negotiation. Founded 1989.

Business Editor Lorcan Allen
Managing Editor Gillian Neilis
Political Editor Michael Brennan

City AM

6th Floor, 107 Cheapside, London EC2V 6DN
tel 020-343 1490
website www.cityam.com
Facebook www.facebook.com/cityam
X @cityam
Editor Christian May
Daily Mon–Fri free (digital), Tues, Wed, Thurs (print)

Financial and business newspaper. Covers the latest economic, political and business news as well as comment, sport and lifestyle features. Founded 2006.

Comment & Features Editor Alys Denby
Life & Style Editor Steve Dinneen
Head of Video and Social Emmanuel Nwosu
Managing Editor Rupert Hargreaves
Sports Editor Frank Dalleres
UK Editor Jon Robinson

The Conversation

4th Floor, Shropshire House, 11–20 Capper Street, London WC1E 6JA
email uk-editorial@theconversation.com
website https://theconversation.com/uk/
Facebook www.facebook.com/ConversationUK
X @ConversationUK
Editor Stephen Khan

An online-only independent source of news and views, sourced from the academic and research community and delivered direct to the public. Founded 2011.

Arts & Cultural Editor Naomi Joseph
Deputy Editor Stephen Harris
Education & Young People Editor Grace Allen
Environment & Energy Editor Jack Marley
Senior Arts & Culture Editor Anna Walker
Senior Business Editor Sarah Reid
Senior Environment Editor Anna Turns
Senior Health Editor Clint Witchalls
Senior International Affairs Editor Jonathan Este
Senior Politics Editor Laura Hood
Senior Science Editor Miriam Frankel

Daily Express

One Canada Square, Canary Wharf, London E14 5AP
tel 020-7293 3000
email news.desk@express.co.uk
website www.express.co.uk
Facebook www.facebook.com/DailyExpress
X @Daily_Express
Editor-in-Chief Tom Hunt
Daily Mon–Fri £1.70, Sat £2.40
Supplements **Daily Express Saturday Magazine**

Exclusive news and striking photos. Leader page articles (600 words). Facts preferred to opinions. Payment: according to value. Founded 1900.

Head of Features Matt Nixson
Environment Editor Steph Spyro
Lifestyle & Travel Editor Sarra Gray
Political Editor David Maddox
Sports Editor Mike Ryder

Daily Express Saturday Magazine

Weekly Sat free with paper

Daily Mail

Northcliffe House, 2 Derry Street, London W8 5TT
tel 020-7938 6000
email news@dailymail.co.uk
website www.dailymail.co.uk
Facebook www.facebook.com/DailyMail
X @MailOnline
Editor Ted Verity
Daily Mon–Fri £1.10, Sat £1.60
Supplements **Weekend**

News, celebrity news, sport, leisure and topical stories of general interest. Payment: according to value. Founded 1896.

City Editor Alex Brummer
Executive Editor of Features Dominic Midgley
Literary Editor Sandra Parsons
Mail Online Money Editor Lee Boyce
News Editor Ben Rossington
Political Editor Jason Groves
Sports Editor Matt Gatward
Travel Editor Mark Palmer

MailOnline
tel 020-7938 6000
email tips@dailymail.com

The online platform for the *Daily Mail*. Founded 2003.

Daily Mirror

One Canada Square, Canary Wharf, London E14 5AP
tel 020-7293 3000
email mirrornews@mirror.co.uk
website www.mirror.co.uk
Facebook www.facebook.com/DailyMirror
X @DailyMirror
Editor Caroline Waterston
Daily Mon–Fri £1.80, Sat £2.50
Supplements **We Love TV, Life Magazine**

Top payment for exclusive news and news pictures. Freelance articles used and ideas bought: send synopsis only. Unusual pictures and those giving a new angle on the news are welcomed. Also cartoons. Founded 1903.

Associate Editor Kevin Maguire
Business Editor Graham Hiscott
Head of News Dominic Herbert
Political Editor Lizzy Buchan
Sports Editor Thomas Bristow

Daily Record

55 Douglas Street, Glasgow G2 7NP
tel 0141 309 3251
email reporters@dailyrecord.co.uk
website www.dailyrecord.co.uk
Facebook www.facebook.com/TheScottishDailyRecord
X @Daily_Record
Editor David Dick
Daily Mon–Fri £1.70 Sat £2.40
Supplements **Saturday, Seven Days, Living, TV Record, Road Record, Recruitment Record, The Brief**

Topical articles, from 300–700 words. Exclusive stories of Scottish interest and exclusive colour photos. Founded 1895.

Assistant Live News Editor Douglas Barrie
Assistant Live News Editor Emma O'Neill
Assistant Live News Editor Peter Davidson
Assistant Live Sports Editor Liam Bryce
Live Sports Editor Gavin Berry

Saturday
Weekly Sat free with paper

Lifestyle magazine and entertainment guide. Reviews, travel features, shopping, personalities and colour illustrations. Payment: by arrangement.

Daily Star

One Canada Square, Canary Wharf, London E14 5AP
tel 020-8612 7373
email news@dailystar.co.uk
website www.dailystar.co.uk
Facebook www.facebook.com/thedailystar
X @DailyStar
Editor Denis Mann
Daily Mon–Fri £1.10, Sat £1.80
Supplements **Hot TV, Seriously Football**

Hard news exclusives, commanding substantial payment. Major interviews with big-star personalities, short features, series based on people rather than things and picture features. Illustrations: line and half-tone. Payment: by negotiation. Founded 1978.

Associate Editor Star Online Andrew Gilpin
Daily Star Online Editor Ben Rankin
News Editor Steve Hughes
Sports Editor Michael Ham

Daily Star Sunday

One Canada Square, Canary Wharf, London E14 5AP
tel 020-8612 7373
website www.dailystar.co.uk/sunday
Editor Denis Mann
Weekly Sun £2.10
Supplements **OK! Extra**

Opportunities for freelancers. Founded 2002.

Daily Telegraph

111 Buckingham Palace Road, London SW1W 0DT
tel 020-7931 2000
email dtnews@telegraph.co.uk
website www.telegraph.co.uk
Facebook www.facebook.com/telegraph.co.uk
X @Telegraph
Editor Chris Evans
Daily Mon–Fri £3.50, Sat £4.50
Supplements **Gardening, Cars, Property, Culture, Sport, Telegraph Magazine, Travel, Your Money**

Articles on a wide range of subjects of topical interest considered. Preliminary letter and synopsis required. Length: 700–1,000 words. Payment: by arrangement. Founded 1855.

Assistant Editor Adam Sills
Breaking News Editor Allister Heath
Fashion Editor Lisa Armstrong
Health Editor Laura Donnelly
Home News Editor Bill Gardner
Political Editor Ben Riley-Smith

Telegraph Magazine
Editor Lisa Markwell
Weekly Sat free with paper

Short profiles (about 1,600 words). Articles of topical interest. Preliminary study of the magazine essential. Illustrations: all types. Payment: by arrangement. Founded 1964.

Telegraph Online
email dtnews@telegraph.co.uk
website www.telegraph.co.uk

Readers need to set up a monthly subscription after 30 days free access to view full articles. Founded 1994.

Managing Director Will Lewis

Financial Times
Bracken House, 1 Friday Street, London EC4M 9BT
tel 020-7873 3000
email ean@ft.com
website www.ft.com
Facebook www.facebook.com/financialtimes
X @FinancialTimes
Editor Roula Khalaf
Daily Mon–Fri £3.70, Sat £5.10
Supplements **Companies, FTfm, FT Special Reports, FT Executive Appointments, FT Weekend Magazine, House and Home, FT Money, How To Spend It, FT Wealth, Life & Arts**

One of the world's leading business news organisations, the *FT* provides news, commentary and analysis. Founded 1888.

Deputy Editor Patrick Jenkins
Economics Editor Sam Fleming
Finance & Markets Editor Arash Massoudi
FT Weekend Editor Janine Gibson
House & Home Editor Lucy Watson
International Business Editor Peggy Hollinger
News Editor Tom Braithwaite
Political Editor George Parker

Guardian
Kings Place, 90 York Way, London N1 9GU
tel 020-3353 2000
email national@theguardian.com
website www.theguardian.com
Facebook www.facebook.com/theguardian
X @guardian
Editor Katharine Viner
Daily Mon–Fri £3, Sat £4
Supplements **Sport, G2, Film & Music, The Guide, Weekend, Review, Money, Work & Careers, Travel, Family, Cook**

Articles, taken from outside contributors, are available for free up to a limit, feature and specialist pages are the only exception. Illustrations: news and features photos. Payment: apply for rates. See contributors guidelines on website. Founded 1821.

Books Editor Charlotte Northedge
Business Editor John Collingridge
City Editor Anna Isaac
Deputy Editor Owen Gibson
Economics Editor Larry Elliott
Education Editor Richard Adams
Fashion Editor Jess Cartner-Morley
Head of National News Fay Schlesinger
Head of Travel Andy Pietrasik
Health Editor Andrew Gregory
Music Editor Ben Beaumont-Thomas
Political Editor Pippa Crerar

Weekend
Weekly Sat free with paper

Features on world affairs, major profiles, food and drink, home life, the arts, travel and leisure. Also good reportage on social and political subjects. Illustrations: photos, line drawings and cartoons. Payment: apply for rates.

theguardian.com/uk
website www.theguardian.com/uk

Free website where the *Guardian* and the *Observer* publish all their current and archived content. Currently gives access to over three million stories. Although the service is free, readers are invited to make a donation. There are also US and Australian editions of the website. Founded 2013.

Herald
Herald & Times Group, 125 Fullarton Drive, Glasgow East Investment Park, Glasgow G32 8FG
tel 0141 302 7002
email news@theherald.co.uk
website www.heraldscotland.com
Facebook www.facebook.com/heraldscotland
X @heraldscotland
Editor Catherine Salmond
Daily Mon–Fri £2.00, Sat £2.40

News and stories about Scotland, the UK and the world. Opportunities for freelancers with quality contacts. Founded 1783.

Arts Editor Keith Bruce
Deputy Editor Garry Scott
Foreign Affairs Editor David Pratt
Group Business Editor Ian McConnell
Head of Content Gregor Kyle
Head of Print Alan Simpson
Political Editor Tom Gordon

Herald on Sunday
Herald & Times Group, 125 Fullarton Drive, Glasgow East Investment Park, Glasgow G32 8FG
tel 0141 302 7000
email news@theherald.co.uk
website www.heraldscotland.com
Editor Catherine Salmond
Weekly Sun £2.40
Supplements **Sport, Scottish Life Magazine**

News and stories about Scotland, the UK and the world. Opportunities for freelancers with quality contacts. Founded 2018.

i Paper

9 Derry Street, London W8 5HY
tel 020-3615 6020
email stories@inews.co.uk
website https://inews.co.uk/
Facebook www.facebook.com/theipaper
X @theipaper
Editor Oly Duff
Weekly Mon–Fri £1, Saturday £1.80

Originally the sister paper to the *Independent* which is online only. Founded 2010.

Arts Editor Sarah Carsen
Breaking News Editor Zoe Drewett
Deputy Editor Amy Iggulden
Economics Editor David Parsley
Head of News Mark Davies
Managing Editor Tal Gottesman
Opinion Editor Rupert Hawksley
Sports Editor Ally McKay
World Editor Emma Reynolds

i Weekend

9 Derry Street, London W8 5HY
tel 020-3615 6020
email stories@inews.co.uk
website https://inews.co.uk/
Editor Hanna Tavner
Weekly Sat £1.80

Weekend newspaper of the weekly i. Founded 2012.

Independent

Northcliffe House, 2 Derry Street, London W8 5HF
tel 020-7005 2000
email newsdesk@independent.co.uk
website www.independent.co.uk
Facebook www.facebook.com/TheIndependentOnline
X @independent
Editor Geordie Greig

Online only. Occasional freelance contributions. Preliminary letter advisable. Payment: by arrangement. Founded 1986.

Deputy Editor Chloe Hubbard
Deputy Editor David Marley
Executive Editor Philippa Jenkins
Head of Culture & Lifestyle Patrick Smith
Managing Editor Richard Best
Sports Editor Jack Rathborn

Irish Examiner

Linn Dubh, Assumption Road, Blackpool, Cork T23 RCH6, Republic of Ireland
tel +353 (0)21 427 2722 (newsroom)
email news@examiner.ie
website www.irishexaminer.com
Facebook www.facebook.com/IrishExaminer
Instagram @irish_examiner
Editor Tom Fitzpatrick
Daily Mon–Fri €2.60, Sat €4.20

Features. Material mostly commissioned. Length: 1,200 words. Payment: by arrangement. Founded 1841.

News Editor Deirdre O'Shaughnessy
Sports Editor Tony Leen
Head of Features Vickie Maye
Business Editor Alan Healy
Head of Editorial Development Sheila Reilly
Managing Editor John O'Mahony
Assistant Editor (Legal) Jill O'Sullivan
Assistant Editor (Production) David O'Mahony
Books Editor Michael Moynihan
Head of Visual Media Jim Coughlan
Digital Projects Editor Dolan O'Hagan

Irish Independent

Independent House, 27–32 Talbot Street, Dublin D01 X2E1, Republic of Ireland
tel +353 (0)1 705 5333
email info@independent.ie
website www.independent.ie
Facebook www.facebook.com/independent.ie
X @Independent_ie
Editor Cormac Bourke
Daily Mon–Fri €2.70, Sat €4.20

Special articles on topical or general subjects. Length: 700–1,000 words. Payment: editor's estimate of value. Founded 1905.

Business Editor Donal O'Donovan
Group Head of News Kevin Doyle
Group Head of Sport David Courtney

Irish Times

Irish Times Building, 24–28 Tara Street, Dublin D02 CX89, Republic of Ireland
email newsdesk@irishtimes.com
website www.irishtimes.com
Facebook www.facebook.com/irishtimes
X @IrishTimes
Editor Ruadhán Mac Cormaic
Daily Mon–Fri €2.60, Sat €4.20
Supplements **The Irish Times Magazine, The Ticket (Sat), Health + Family (Tue), Business (Daily), Sport (Mon, Wed, Sat)**

Mainly staff-written. Specialist contributions (800–2,000 words). Illustrations: photos and line drawings. Founded 1859.

Book Editor Martyn Doyle
Culture Editor Liam Stebbing
Editor of The Irish Times Magazine Ciara Kenny
News Editor Simon Carswell

BreakingNews.ie

website www.breakingnews.ie
Editor Michael McAleer

Mail on Sunday

Northcliffe House, 2 Derry Street, London W8 5TT
tel 020-7938 6000
email news@mailonsunday.co.uk
website www.mailonsunday.co.uk
Editor David Dillon
Weekly Sun £2.20
Supplements **You, EVENT**

Articles. Illustrations: line, half-tone and cartoons. Payment: by arrangement. Founded 1982.
Arts Editor Gordon Smith
Business Editor Ruth Sutherland
Literary Editor Susanna Gross
Political Editor Glen Owen
Sports Editor Alison Kervin

Financial Mail on Sunday
tel 020-7938 6984
Weekly Sunday free with paper

City, industry, business and personal finance. News stories 1,500+ words. Full-colour illustrations and photography commissioned.

You
Editor Jackie Annesley
Weekly Sat free with paper

Women's interest features: 500–2,500 words. Illustrations: full colour and b&w drawings, also colour photos. Payment: by arrangement.

Metro
Northcote House, 2 Derry Street, London W8 5TT
tel 020-3615 0600
email news.london@ukmetro.co.uk
website https://metro.co.uk/
Facebook www.facebook.com/metroUK
X @metroUK
Editor Deborah Arthurs
Daily Mon–Fri free

Sister paper to the *Daily Mail* (page 15). Distributed freely on mainline trains, Tube trains and buses and in hospitals and stations in and around selected locations in the UK. Founded 1999.
Features Editor Kylie Martin
Food Editor Chloe Scott
Lifestyle Editor Rachel Moss
News Editor Rory McKeown
Social Editor Cameron Clark

Morning Star
People's Press Printing Society Ltd, Ruskin House, 23 Coombe Road, Croydon CR0 1BDS
tel 020-8510 0815
email enquiries@peoples-press.com
website www.morningstaronline.co.uk
Editor Ben Chacko
Daily Mon–Fri £1.50, Sat–Sun £2

Newspaper for the Labour movement. Articles of general interest. Illustrations: photos, cartoons and drawings. Founded 1930.
News Editor Will Stone
Sports Editor Bella Katz

The National
125 Fullarton Drive, Glasgow G32 8FG
tel 0141 302 7007
email reporters@thenational.scot
website www.thenational.scot
Facebook www.facebook.com/thenationalnewspaperscotland
X @ScotNational
Editor Laura Webster
Daily Mon–Sat £1.50, Sun £2.70

Scottish newspaper owned by Newsquest and the first daily newspaper in Scotland to support Scottish independence. Founded 2014.
Content Editor Xander Elliards
Community Editor Shona Craven
Foreign Affairs Editor Davi Pratt
Political Reporter Hamish Morrison

The New European
22 Highbury Grove, Islington, London N5 2EF
tel 020-8959 1175
email contactus@tnepublishing.com
website www.theneweuropean.co.uk
Facebook www.facebook.com/theneweuropean
X @TheNewEuropean
Editor Steve Anglesey
Weekly Thurs £3.95

Covers British and European politics and culture. Writers include Alastair Campbell, Patience Wheatcroft, Matthew d'Ancona, Bonnie Greer, Paul Mason and James Ball. Founded 2016.
Associate Editor Suna Erdem
Digital Editor Jono Read

The Observer
Kings Place, 90 York Way, London N1 9GU
tel 020-3353 2000
email observer.news@observer.co.uk
website www.theguardian.com/observer
Editor Lucy Rock
Weekly Sun £3.80
Supplements **Observer Magazine, New Review, Sport, Observer Food Monthly**

Some articles and illustrations commissioned. Payment: by arrangement. Founded 1791.
Arts Editor Sarah Donaldson
Assistant Editor & Comment Editor Robert Yates
Fashion Editor Jo Jones
Literary Editor Lisa O'Kelly
New Review Editor Jane Ferguson
Observer Food Monthly Editor Allan Jenkins
Political Editor Toby Helm
Readers' Editor Elisabeth Ribbans

Observer Magazine
tel 020-3353 2000
email magazine@observer.co.uk
Editor Harriet Green
Weekly Sun free with paper
Commissioned features. Length: 2,000–3,000 words. Illustrations: first-class colour and b&w photos. Payment: NUJ rates; see website for details.

Pink News
Wisteria Grange Barn, Pikes End, Pinner, London HA5 2EX

email news@pinknews.co.uk
website www.thepinknews.com
Facebook www.facebook.com/pinknews
X @pinknews
Instagram @pinknews
Editor Benjamin Cohen

Online only UK-based newspaper marketed to the lesbian, gay, bisexual, transgender, queer and questioning community worldwide. For freelance opportunities see website: https://careers.thepinknews.com/en-GB/connect. Founded 2005.

The Poke

email info@thepoke.co.uk
website www.thepoke.co.uk
Facebook www.facebook.com/PokeHQ
X @ThePoke
Instagram @thepokeuk

Online only. A satirical and topical news source. Founded 2002.

politics.co.uk

Senate Media Ltd, 4 Croxted Mews, Croxted Road, London SE24 9DA
tel 020-3758 9407
email editorial@politics.co.uk
website www.politics.co.uk
Facebook www.facebook.com/politicscoukofficial
X @politics_co_uk
Editor Josh Self

Online only. See website for details on how to submit articles or drawings and animations. Founded 2002.

Scotland on Sunday

83 Princes Street, Edinburgh EH2 2ER
email reception@scotsman.com
website www.scotsman.com
Editor Neil McIntosn
Weekly Sun £2.50

Features on all subjects, not necessarily Scottish. Payment: varies. Founded 1988.

Spectrum Magazine

Weekly Sun free with paper

Scotsman

83 Princes Street, Edinburgh EH2 2ER
email newsdeskts@scotsman.com
website www.scotsman.com
Facebook www.facebook.com/TheScotsmanNewspaper
X @TheScotsman
Editor Alan Young
Daily Mon–Fri £2.60, Sat £3
Supplements **Saturday Magazine, Critique, Property, Motoring, Recruitment**

Considers articles on political, economic and general themes which add substantially to current information. Prepared to commission topical and controversial series from proved authorities. Length: 800–1,000 words. Illustrations: outstanding news pictures and cartoons. Payment: by arrangement. Founded 1817.

Arts & Books Editor Roger Cox
Political Editor Alistair Grant
Sports Editor Mark Atkinson

Scottish Sun

Aurora, 120 Bothwell Street, Glasgow G2 7JS
tel 0141 420 5200
email scottishsunletters@the-sun.co.uk
website www.thescottishsun.co.uk
Facebook www.facebook.com/thescottishsun
X @ScottishSun
Editor Gill Smith
Daily Mon–Fri £1.10, Sat £1.80, Sun £1.50
Supplements **Fabulous**

Scottish edition of the *Sun*. Illustrations: transparencies, colour prints, b&w prints and colour cartoons. Payment: by arrangement. Founded 1985.

Socialist Worker

PO Box 74955, London E16 9EJ
tel 020-7840 5600
email reports@socialistworker.co.uk
website https://socialistworker.co.uk/
Facebook www.facebook.com/SocialistWorkerBritain
X @socialistworker
Editor Charlie Kimber
Weekly Sat £1

A revolutionary socialist newspaper produced by the Socialist Workers Party. Founded 1968.

Sun

1 London Bridge Place, London SE1 9GF
tel 020-7782 4100
email exclusive@the-sun.co.uk
website www.thesun.co.uk
Facebook www.facebook.com/thesun
X @TheSun
Editor Victoria Newton
Daily Mon–Fri £1.10, Sat £1.50
Supplements **Cashflow, TV Magazine**

Takes freelance material, including cartoons. Payment: by negotiation. Founded 1969.

Deputy Editor James Slack
Bizarre Editor Ellie Henman
Business Editor Ashley Armstrong
Head of Sport Content Shaun Curtis
Political Editor Harry Cole
Travel Editor Lisa Minot
TV Editor Rod McPhee

Sun on Sunday

1 London Bridge Place, London SE1 9GF
tel 020-7782 4100
email exclusive@the-sun.co.uk
website www.thesun.co.uk

Editor Victoria Newton
Weekly Sun £1.80
Supplements **Fabulous**

Takes freelance material. Founded 2012.

Sunday Express

Northern & Shell Building, 10 Lower Thames Street, London EC4R 6EN
tel 020-8612 7000
email sundaynews@express.co.uk
website www.express.co.uk/news/sunday
Editor David Wooding
Weekly Sun £2.80
Supplements **Property, Review, S, Sport, Travel, Finance**

Exclusive news stories, photos, personality profiles and features of controversial or lively interest. Length: 800–1,000 words. Payment: top rates. Founded 1918.

Business & Finance Editor Geoff Ho
Health Editor Lucy Johnston
Literary Editor Charlotte Heathcote
Political Editor David Williamson
Sports Editor Scott Wilson
Television Editor David Stephenson

Sunday Independent

27–32 Talbot Street, Dublin D01 X2E1, Republic of Ireland
tel +353 (0)1 705 5333
email info@independent.ie
website www.independent.ie
Editor Alan English
Weekly Sun €4

Special articles. Length: according to subject. Illustrations: topical or general interest and cartoons. Payment: at editor's valuation. Founded 1905.

Sunday Mail

1 Central Quay, Glasgow G3 8DA
tel 0141 309 3232
email reporters@sundaymail.co.uk
London office One Canada Square, Canary Wharf, London E14 5AP
website www.dailyrecord.co.uk
Editor Lorna Hughes
Weekly Sun £2.90
Supplements **Entertainment, Fun on Sunday, Jobsplus!, 7-Days, Right at Home**

Exclusive stories and pictures of national and Scottish interest. Also cartoons. Payment: above average. Founded 1982.

Sunday Mirror

One Canada Square, Canary Wharf, London E14 5AP
tel 020-7293 3000
email scoops@sundaymirror.co.uk
website www.mirror.co.uk
Editor James Saville
Weekly Sun £2.80
Supplements **Notebook, Holidays & Getaways**

Concentrates on human interest news features, social documentaries, dramatic news and feature photos. Ideas, as well as articles, bought. Payment: high, especially for exclusives. Founded 1963.

Deputy Editor James Scott
Political Editor Nigel Nelson
Sports Editor Nick Cherrie

Sunday National

125 Fullarton Drive, Glasgow G32 8FG
tel 0141 302 7007
email reporters@thenational.scot
website www.thenational.scot
Facebook www.facebook.com/thenationalnewspaperscotland
X @ScotNational
Editor Laura Webster
Weekly Sun £2.70

Scottish Sunday newspaper owned by Newsquest. Replaced the *Sunday Herald*. Sister paper of *The National* (page 19). Founded 2018.

Sunday People

One Canada Square, Canary Wharf, London E14 5AP
tel 020-7293 3842
email feedback@people.co.uk
website www.mirror.co.uk/all-about/sunday-people
Editor Gemma Aldridge
Weekly Sun £2.80
Supplements **Take it Easy**

Exclusive news and feature stories needed. Investigative and campaigning issues. Features and human interest stories as specialty. Strong sports following. Payment: rates high, even for tips that lead to published news stories. Founded 1881.

Take it Easy

Editor Samantha Cope
Weekly Free with paper

Sunday Post

Spiers View, 50 High Craighall Road, Glasgow G4 9UD
tel (01382) 223131
email news@sundaypost.com
website www.sundaypost.com
Facebook www.facebook.com/SundayPostUK
X @sunday_post
Editor Dave Lord
Weekly Sun £2.70
Supplements **Travel & Homes, TV & Entertainment**

Human interest, topical, domestic, humorous and exclusive news. Payment: on acceptance. Founded 1914.

P.S.

tel (01382) 223131
Monthly Free with paper

General interest articles. Length: 1,000–2,000 words. Illustrations: colour transparencies. Payment: varies. Founded 2019.

Sunday Telegraph

111 Buckingham Palace Road, London SW1W 0DT
tel 020-7931 2000
email stnews@telegraph.co.uk
website www.telegraph.co.uk
Editor Allister Heath
Weekly Sun £3
Supplements **Business Reporter, Life, It's Your Money, Sport, Stella, Discover**

Occasional freelance material accepted. Founded 1961.

The Sunday Times

The News Building, 1 London Bridge Place, London SE1 9GF
tel 020-7782 5000
email newsdesk@sunday-times.co.uk
website www.thetimes.co.uk
Facebook www.facebook.com/timesandsundaytimes
X @thesundaytimes
Editor Ben Taylor
Weekly Sun £3.50
Supplements **Appointments, Business, Culture, Driving, Home, Money, News Review, Sport, Style, The Sunday Times Magazine, Travel**

Special articles by authoritative writers on politics, literature, art, drama, music, finance, science and topical matters. Payment: top rate for exclusive features. Founded 1822.

Deputy Editor Krissi Murison
Economics Editor David Smith
Literary Editor Robin Millen
Political Editor Caroline Wheeler
Sports Editor Tom Clarke
TV Editor James Jackson

The Sunday Times Magazine

tel 020-7782 5000
Editor Martin Hemming
Weekly Sun free with paper

Articles and pictures. Illustrations: colour and b&w photos. Payment: by negotiation.

Tes (The Times Educational Supplement)

70 Gray's Inn Road, London WC1X 8NH
tel 020-3194 3000
email newsdesk@tes.com
email features@tes.com
website www.tes.com
X @tes
Editor Jon Severs
Daily £3.50 (£19 per quarter, £40 per year for the first year, £59 per year thereafter)

Publishes daily online articles on educational subjects: the latest news, analysis and teaching and learning research for those who work in schools. Specialist knowledge required and ideas should be emailed to the relevant sector editor. Payment: by arrangement. Founded 1910.

Tess (The Times Educational Supplement Scotland)

70 Gray's Inn Road, London WC1X 8NH
email henry.hepburn@tes.com
website www.tes.com/magazine/hub/scotland
X @TesScotland
Scotland Editor Henry Hepburn
Daily See website for subscription options

Publishes online articles on education subjects. Looking for articles on education, preferably 600–800 words, written with special knowledge or experience. News items about Scottish educational affairs, especially those affecting schools. Payment: by arrangement. Founded 1965.

THE (Times Higher Education)

26 Red Lion Square, London WC1R 4HQ
email john.gill@timeshighereducation.com
website www.timeshighereducation.co.uk
Facebook www.facebook.com/timeshighereducation
X @timeshighered
Editor John Gill
Weekly £5

Publishes articles on higher education written with special knowledge or experience, or articles dealing with academic topics. Also news items. Illustrations: suitable photos and drawings of educational interest. Payment: by arrangement. Founded 1971.

Thomson Reuters

Five Canada Square, Canary Wharf, London E14 5AQ
website www.reuters.com
Facebook www.facebook.com/reuters
X @reuters
Instagram @reuters
Editor-in-Chief Alessandra Galloni

Online news platform. Provides business, financial, national and international news directly to consumers. Founded 1851.

The Times

The News Building, 1 London Bridge Street, London SE1 9GF
tel 020-7782 5000
email home.news@thetimes.co.uk
website www.thetimes.co.uk
Facebook www.facebook.com/timesandsundaytimes
X @thetimes
Editor Tony Gallagher
Daily Mon–Fri £2.80, Sat £4
Supplements **Books, Crème, Football Handbook, The Game, The Knowledge, Money, Times 2, Times Law, The Times Magazine, Times Sport, Travel, Arts and Entertainment, Fashion, Saturday Review, Technology, Weekend**

Outside contributions from experts in subjects of current interest, focus on first-hand experiences.

Contact appropriate section editor. Length: 1,200+ words. Founded 1785.

Business Editor Richard Fletcher
Education Editor Nicola Woolcock
Foreign Editor Ben Hoyle
Health Editor Eleanor Hayward
Literary Editor Robbie Millen
Political Editor Caroline Wheeler
Travel Editor Liz Edwards

The Times Magazine

Weekly Sat free with paper

Features. Illustrated.

Timesonline

website www.thetimes.co.uk

Subscription website containing news from *The Times* and *The Sunday Times*. Founded 1999.

TLS (The Times Literary Supplement)

The News Building, 1 London Bridge Street, London SE1 9GF
tel 020-7782 6000
email queries@the-tls.co.uk
website www.the-tls.co.uk
Facebook www.facebook.com/TheTLS
X @the.tls
Editor Martin Ivens
Weekly £4.50

Will consider poems for publication, literary discoveries and articles on literary and cultural affairs. Payment: by arrangement. Founded 1902.

Tortoise

website www.tortoisemedia.com
Facebook www.facebook.com/agathathetortoise
X @tortoise
Instagram @tortoise
Editor & Founder James Harding

Online only British news service. Founded 2019.

The Voice

Unit 1, Bricklayers Arms, Mandela Way, London SE1 5SR
tel 020-7510 0340
email newsdesk@thevoicemediagroup.co.uk
website www.voice-online.co.uk
Facebook www.facebook.com/voicenews
X @TheVoiceNews
Editor Lester Holloway
Monthly £3

Weekly newspaper for Black Britons. Includes news, features, arts, sport and a jobs and business section. Illustrations: colour and b&w photos. Founded 1982.

Lifestyle, Arts & Entertainment Editor Joel Campbell
News Editor Vic Motune
Sports & Features Editor Rodney Hinds

Wales on Sunday

6 Park Street, Cardiff CF10 1XR
tel 029-2024 3604
email newsdesk@walesonline.co.uk
website www.walesonline.co.uk
Facebook www.facebook.com/WalesOnline
X @walesonline
Editors David James, Chiara Rinaldi
Weekly Sun £2.50
Supplements **Life on Sunday, Sport on Sunday**

National Sunday newspaper of Wales offering comprehensive news, features and entertainment coverage at the weekend, with a particular focus on events in Wales. Accepts general interest articles, preferably with a Welsh connection. Founded 1989.

Lifestyle Editor Kathryn Williams
Head of Sport Jon Doel

Weekly Gleaner

GV Media Group Limited, 6th Floor, Northern & Shell Tower, 4 Selsdon Way, London E14 9GL
tel 020-7510 0340
email george.ruddock@gvmedia.co.uk
website www.jamaica-gleaner.com
Facebook www.facebook.com/GleanerJamaica
X @JamaicaGleaner
Editor Moya Thomas
Weekly: Thurs £1.20

Offshoot of the *Daily Gleaner*, the oldest operating newspaper in the English-speaking Caribbean. Newspaper for the UK Black British/Caribbean community, available in most of the major cities, including London, Birmingham, Manchester, Liverpool, Nottingham, Leicester, Bristol and Leeds. Content covers news, analytical viewpoints, art, entertainment, sports and various lifestyle feature supplements. Founded 1951.

Regional newspapers UK and Ireland

Regional newspapers are listed in alphabetical order under region. The list is not exhaustive. Over recent years, it has become increasingly difficult for freelance writers to have pitches accepted or commissions requested by regional news companies. The listings below include those papers that may still be accepting work from freelance writers.

BELFAST

Belfast Telegraph

Belfast Telegraph House, 33 Clarendon Road, Clarendon Dock, Belfast BT1 3BG
tel 028-9026 4000
email newseditor@belfasttelegraph.co.uk
website www.belfasttelegraph.co.uk
Facebook www.facebook.com/belfasttelegraph
X @beltel
Editor Eoin Brannigan
Daily Mon–Sat £1.60

An independent news and media publication. Any material relating to Northern Ireland. Payment: by negotiation. Founded 1870.

Irish News

Fountain Centre, College Street, Belfast BT1 6ET
tel 028-9032 2226
email newsdesk@irishnews.com
website www.irishnews.com
Facebook www.facebook.com/IrishNewsLtd
X @irish_news
Editor Chris Sherrard
Daily Mon–Sat £1.40

News and articles of interest to a Northern Ireland readership. Founded 1855.

News Letter

Suites 302–303, Glandore, Arthur House, 41 Arthur Street, Belfast BT1 4GB
tel 028-3839 5577
email newsdesk@newsletter.co.uk
website www.newsletter.co.uk/news
Facebook www.facebook.com/belfastnewsletter
X @News_Letter
Editor Ben Lowry
Daily Mon–Fri £1.80, Sat £2.50

Pro-Union. Founded 1737.

Sunday Life

Belfast Telegraph House, 33 Clarendon Road, Clarendon Dock, Belfast BT1 3BG
tel 028-9026 4000
email slnews@sundaylife.co.uk
website www.belfasttelegraph.co.uk/sunday-life
Editor Eoin Brannigan
Weekly Sun £2.40

Items of interest to Northern Ireland Sunday tabloid readers. Illustrations: colour and b&w pictures and graphics. Payment: by arrangement. Founded 1988.

CHANNEL ISLANDS

Jersey Evening Post

PO Box 582, Five Oaks, St Saviour, Jersey JE4 8XQ
tel (01534) 611611
email news@jerseyeveningpost.com
website https://jerseyeveningpost.com/
Facebook www.facebook.com/jerseyeveningpost
X @jepnews
Editor Andy Sibcy
Daily Mon–Sat £1.30

News and features with a Channel Islands angle. Length: 1,000 words (articles/features) and 300 words (news). Illustrations: colour and b&w. Founded 1890.

CORK

Echo

Linn Dubh, Assumption Road, Blackpool, Cork T23, Republic of Ireland
email news@eecho.ie
website www.eveningecho.ie
Facebook www.facebook.com/echolivecork
X @echolivecork
Editor Gráinne McGuinness
Daily Mon–Sat €2.10

Articles, features and news for the area. Illustrations: colour prints. Founded 1892.

DUBLIN

Dublin Gazette

Top Floor, Unit E7, Nutgrove Office Park, Meadow Park Avenue, Rathfarnham D14 F3F4, Republic of Ireland
website https://dublingazette.com/
Facebook www.facebook.com/dublingazettenewspapers
X @dublingazette
Editor P.J. Cunningham
Weekly Thurs free

Publishes City, Fingal, West and South editions. Founded 1689.

EAST ANGLIA

Cambridge Independent
Iliffe Media Ltd, Winship Road, Milton, Cambridge CB24 6PP
tel (01223) 320320
email newsdesk@iliffemedia.co.uk
website www.cambridgeindependent.co.uk
Facebook www.facebook.com/cambridgeindependent
X @cambridgeindy
Instagram @cambridgeindependent
Editor Paul Brackley
Weekly Wed £2.30 (or annual subscription £54.89)

News, culture, science, education, business and sport from Cambridge and surrounding area. Founded 1815.

Cambridge News
Winslip Road, Milton, Cambridge CB4 6PP
email newsdesk@cambridge-news.co.uk
website www.cambridge-news.co.uk
Facebook www.facebook.com/cambridgeshirelive
X @CambsLive
Editor Anna Starnes
Daily Mon–Sat £2.45

News, views and sport. Illustrations: colour prints, b&w and colour graphics. Payment: by negotiation. Founded 1888.

East Anglian Daily Times
Hyde Park House, Crown Street, Ipswich IP1 3LH
tel (01473) 230023
email newsroom@archant.co.uk
website www.eadt.co.uk
Facebook www.facebook.com/eadt24
X @eadt24
Editor Liz Nice
Daily Mon–Fri £1.05, Sat £2

Features of East Anglian interest, preferably with pictures. Length: 500 words. Illustrations: NUJ rates. Payment: negotiable. Founded 1874.

Eastern Daily Press
Prospect House, Rouen Road, Norwich NR1 1RE
tel (01603) 628311
website www.edp24.co.uk
Facebook www.facebook.com/edp24
X @edp24
Editor Richard Porritt
Daily Mon–Fri £1.35, Sat £2.40

Limited market for articles of East Anglian interest not exceeding 650 words. Founded 1870.

Ipswich Star
Hyde Park House, Crown Street, Ipswich IP1 3LH
tel (01473) 230023
website www.ipswichstar.co.uk
Facebook www.facebook.com/ipswichstar24
X @ipswichstar24
Editor Liz Nice
Daily Mon–Fri £1

Local news from the Ipswich area. Founded 1885.

Norwich Evening News
Prospect House, Rouen Road, Norwich NR1 1RE
tel (01603) 628311
website www.eveningnews24.co.uk
Facebook www.facebook.com/NorwichEveningNews
X @EveningNews
Editor Richard Porritt
Daily Mon–Sat £1

Interested in local news-based features. Length: up to 650 words. Payment: agreed rates. Founded 1882.

EAST MIDLANDS

Burton Mail
Unit 1–2, Milton House, Worthington Way, Burton upon Trent, Staffs. DE14 1BQ
tel (01283) 510075
email editorial@burtonmail.co.uk
website www.burtonmail.co.uk
Facebook www.facebook.com/BurtonNews
X @BurtonMailNews
Daily Mon–Sat £2.30

Features, news and articles of interest to Burton and south Derbyshire readers. Length: 400–500 words. Illustrations: colour and b&w. Payment: by negotiation. Founded 1898.

Chronicle & Echo, Northampton
Northamptonshire Newspapers Ltd, 400 Pavilion Drive, Northampton NN4 7PA
tel (01604) 467032
email editor@northantsnews.co.uk
website www.northamptonchron.co.uk
Facebook www.facebook.com/northamptonchron
X @ChronandEcho
Editor David Summers
Weekly Thurs £2.30

Articles, features and news – mostly commissioned – of interest to the Northampton area. Length: varies. Payment: by negotiation. Founded 1931.

Derby Telegraph
2 Siddals Road, Derby DE1 2PB
tel (01332) 411888
website www.derbytelegraph.co.uk
Facebook www.facebook.com/derbyshirelive
X @Derbyshire_live
Editor George Allen
Daily Mon–Sat £2

Articles and news of local interest. Payment: by negotiation. Founded 1879.

Leicester Mercury

c/o 3rd floor, City Gate, Tollhouse Hill,
Nottingham NG1 5FS
tel 0344 406 0910
website www.leicestermercury.co.uk
Facebook www.facebook.com/leicestershirelive
X @LeicsLive
Editor Linda Steelyard
Daily Mon–Sat £2

Occasional articles, features and news. Submit ideas to editor first. Length/payment: by negotiation. Founded 1874.

Nottingham Post

3rd Floor, City Gate, Tollhouse Hill,
Nottingham NG1 5FS
tel 0115 948 2000
email newsdesk@nottinghampostgroup.co.uk
website www.nottinghampost.com
Facebook www.facebook.com/Nottinghamshirelive
X @NottsLive
Editor Natalie Fahy
Daily Mon–Sat £2.35

Material on local issues considered. Founded 1878.

Peterborough Telegraph

c/o Brightfields Business Hub, Bakewell Road,
Peterborough PE2 6XU
tel (01733) 455600
email news@peterboroughtoday.co.uk
website www.peterboroughtoday.co.uk
Facebook www.facebook.com/peterboroughtoday
X @peterboroughtel
Weekly Thurs £1.70

Local news. Founded 1948.

LONDON

London Standard

Alphabeta, 14–18 Finsbury Square,
London EC2A 1AH
email news@standard.co.uk
website www.standard.co.uk
Facebook www.facebook.com/eveningstandard
X @standardnews
Editor-in-Chief Dylan Jones
Weekly Thurs Free

News and comment on the city of London. Founded 1827.

ES-Magazine

Editor Ben Cobb
Twice weekly Thurs and Fri free with paper

Feature ideas, exclusively about London. Illustrations: all types. Payment: by negotiation.

Homes & Property

email homesandproperty@standard.co.uk
Editor Prudence Ivey
Weekly Wed free with paper

UK property. Payment: by negotiation.

This Is London

website www.standard.co.uk

Online news website for *London Evening Standard*.

Social Spider

The Mill, 7–11 Coppermill Lane,
Walthamstow E17 7HA
tel 020-8521 7956
email hello@socialspider.com
website www.socialspidercommunitynews.co.uk
Editor David Floyd
Weekly or monthly Free

A group of free local newspapers serving London. Uses a social enterprise model and is not-for-profit The aim is to make independent local news accessible to everyone. Publications include: *Barnet Post* (weekly, online and print), *EC1 Echo* (bi-monthly, online), *Enfield Dispatch* (monthly, online and print), *Haringey Community Press* (monthly, online), *Newham Voices* (monthly, online and print) and *Waltham Forest Echo* (monthly, online and print). Founded 2003.

NORTH EAST

Berwick Advertiser

North East Head Office,
North East Business & Innovation Centre (BIC),
Warfield Enterprise Park East, Sunderland SR5 2TA
tel (01289) 334686
email Berwick.advertiser@nationalworld.com
website www.northumberlandgazette.co.uk
Facebook www.facebook.com/BAdvertiser
X @BAdvertiser
Editor Ian Smith
Weekly Thurs £1.60

News, sport and features. Founded 1808.

The Chronicle

2nd Floor, Eldon Court, Percy Street,
Newcastle upon Tyne NE1 7JB
tel 0191 201 6446
email ec.news@ncjmedia.co.uk
website www.chroniclelive.co.uk
Facebook www.facebook.com/NewcastleChronicle
X @ChronicleLive
Editor Sophie Barley
Daily Mon–Sat £1.85, Sun £3.10

News, photos and features covering almost every subject of interest to readers in Tyne & Wear, Northumberland and Durham. Payment: by prior arrangement. Founded 1858.

Darlington and Stockton Times

PO Box 14, Priestgate, Darlington DL1 1NF
tel (01325) 381313

email newsdesk@nne.co.uk
website www.darlingtonandstocktontimes.co.uk
Facebook www.facebook.com/darlingtonstocktontimes
X @DAndSTimes
Editor Hannah Chapman
Weekly Fri £1.80

Local news. Check website. Founded 1847.

Durham Advertiser

PO Box 14, Priestgate, Darlington DL1 1NF
tel 0191 384 4600
email newsdesk@nne.co.uk
website www.thenorthernecho.co.uk/news/local/northdurham/durham
Facebook www.facebook.com/durhamadvertiser
Editor Gavin Foster
Weekly Fri 80p

Local news and views. Founded 1814.

Hartlepool Mail

New Clarence House, Wesley Square, Hartlepool TS24 8BX
tel (01429) 225644
email mail.news@northeast-press.co.uk
website www.hartlepoolmail.co.uk
Facebook www.facebook.com/hartlepoolmailnews
X @HPoolMail
Editor Gavin Ledwith
Daily Mon–Sat £1.50

Features of local interest. Length: 500 words. Illustrations: colour, b&w photos and line. Payment: by negotiation. Founded 1877.

The Journal

Eldon Court, Percy Street, Newcastle upon Tyne NE1 7JB
tel 0191 201 6446
email ec.news@ncjmedia.co.uk
website www.chroniclelive.co.uk
Facebook www.facebook.com/NewcastleChronicle
X @ChronicleLive
Editor Graeme Whitfield
Daily Mon–Fri £2.40, Sat £2.90

News, sport items and features of topical interest considered. Payment: by arrangement.

The Northern Echo

Suite 10, 2nd Floor, Coniscliffe House, 5–7 Coniscliffe Road, Darlington, County Durham DL3 7EE
tel (01325) 381313
email newsdesk@nee.co.uk
website www.thenorthernecho.co.uk
Facebook www.facebook.com/thenorthernecho
X @TheNorthernEcho
Editor Gavin Foster
Daily Mon–Fri £1.15, Sat £1.70

Articles of interest to the North East; all material commissioned. Preliminary study of newspaper advisable. Length: 800–1,000 words. Illustrations: line, half-tone and colour – mostly commissioned. Payment: by negotiation. Founded 1870.

The Shields Gazette

Chapel Row, South Shields, Tyne and Wear NE33 1BL
tel 0191 455 4661
website www.shieldsgazette.com
Facebook www.facebook.com/shieldsgazette
X @shieldsgazette
Instagram @shields_gazette
Editor Liam Kennedy
Daily Mon–Sat £1.20

News from the Shields area. Founded 1855.

Sunday Sun

Eldon Court, Percy Street, Newcastle upon Tyne NE1 7JB
tel 0191 201 6201
email scoop.sundaysun@ncjmedia.co.uk
website www.chroniclelive.co.uk/all-about/sunday-sun
Facebook www.facebook.com/NewcastleChronicle
X @ChronicleLive
Weekly Sun £3.10

Topical and human interest articles on current issues. Particularly welcomed are features of family appeal and local news stories. Length: 200–700 words. Illustrations: photos. Payment: normal lineage rates or by arrangement. Founded 1919.

Sunderland Echo

North East Business & Innovation Centre, Westfield Enterprise Park East, Sunderland SR5 2TA
tel 0191 501 5800
email echo.news@northeast-press.co.uk
website www.sunderlandecho.com
Facebook www.facebook.com/sunderlandechoonline
X @SunderlandEcho
Editor Ross Robertson
Daily Mon–Sat £1.20

Local news, features and articles. Length: 500 words. Illustrations: colour and b&w photos, line and cartoons. Payment: by negotiation. Founded 1875.

Teeside Gazette

PO Box 1378, Newcastle upon Tyne NE99 5FF
email news@gazettemedia.co.uk
website www.gazettelive.co.uk
Facebook www.facebook.com/Teessidelive
X @TeessideLive
Editor Matt McKenzie
Daily Mon–Fri £1.55, Sat–Sun £2.40

News, topical and lifestyle features. Length: 600–800 words. Illustrations: line, half-tone, colour, graphics and cartoons. Payment: scale rate or by agreement for illustrations. Founded 1869.

NORTH WEST

Blackpool Gazette

Stuart House, 89 Caxton Road, Fulwood,
Preston PR2 9ZB
tel (01253) 400888
email editorial@blackpoolgazette.co.uk
website www.blackpoolgazette.co.uk
Facebook www.facebook.com/blackpoolgazette
X @the_gazette
Editor Vanessa Simms
Daily Mon–Sat £1.30

Local news and articles, photos. Length: varies. Payment: on merit. Founded 1929.

Bolton News

Suite A, 1st Floor, Knowsley House, Knowsley Street,
Bolton BL1 2AH
tel (01204) 522345
email newsdesk@nqw.co.uk
website www.theboltonnews.co.uk
Facebook www.facebook.com/theboltonnews
X @TheBoltonNews
Instagram @the_bolton_news
Editor Richard Duggan
Daily Mon–Sat £1

Founded 1867.

The Chester Chronicle

Maple House, Park West, Sealand Road,
Chester CH1 4RN
tel (01244) 606455
email newsroom@cheshirenews.co.uk
website www.chesterchronicle.co.uk
Facebook www.facebook.com/CheshireLive
X @CheshireLive
Editor Michael Green
Weekly Thurs £2.35

Local news and features. Founded 1775.

Lancashire Post

Stuart House, 89 Caxton Road, Fulwood, Preston,
Lancs PR2 9ZB
tel (01772) 838134
email lep.newsdesk@lep.co.uk
website www.lep.co.uk
Facebook www.facebook.com/lancashireeveningpost
X @leponline
Editor Vanessa Simms
Daily Mon–Sat £1.30

Topical articles on all subjects. Area of interest: Wigan to Lake District, Lancs and coast. Length: 600–900 words. Illustrations: colour and b&w photos, cartoons. Payment: by arrangement. Founded 1886.

Lancashire Telegraph

Suite 2, Freckleton Business Centre,
Freckleton Street, Blackburn, Lancs BB2 2AL
tel (01254) 678678
email lancsnews@nqnw.co.uk
website www.lancashiretelegraph.co.uk
Facebook www.facebook.com/lancashiretelegraph
X @lancstelegraph
Editor Richard Duggan
Daily Mon–Sat 95p

Will consider general news items from east Lancashire. Payment: by arrangement. Founded 1886.

Liverpool Echo

5 St Paul's Square, Liverpool LS3 9SJ
tel 0151 472 2453
website www.liverpoolecho.co.uk
Facebook www.facebook.com/theliverpoolecho
X @LivEchonews
Editor Maria Breslin
Daily Mon–Fri £1.90, Sat £2.30, Sun £2.30

Local interest articles 600–800 words. Also cartoons. Payment: according to merit with special rates for exceptional material. Founded 1879.

The Mail

Newspaper House, 1 Wainwrights Yard,
Kendal LA9 4DP
tel (01229) 840150
email news.em@newsquest.co.uk
website www.nwemail.co.uk
Facebook www.facebook.com/northwesteveningmail
Editor Joy Yates
Daily Mon–Fri 95p, Sat £1

Articles, features and news. Length: 500 words. Covering the whole of south Cumbria. Illustrations: colour photos and occasional artwork. Founded 1898.

Manchester Evening News

Mitchell Henry House, Hollinwood Avenue,
Chadderton, Oldham OL9 8EF
tel 0161 832 7200
email newsdesk@men-news.co.uk
website www.manchestereveningnews.co.uk
Facebook www.facebook.com/ManchesterEveningNews
X @MENNewsdesk
Editor Sarah Lester
Daily Mon–Fri £1.90, Sat £2.20, Sun £2.30

Feature articles of up to 1,000 words, topical or general interest and illustrated where appropriate, should be addressed to the Features Editor. Payment: on acceptance. Founded 1868.

The Mill

email info@millmediaco.uk
website https://manchestermill.co.uk/
Facebook www.facebook.com/themanchestermill
X @ManchesterMill
Bluesky @manchestermill.bsky.social
Instagram @themanchestermill
Editor Joshie Herrmann
Online only

Also known as *The Manchester Mill*, publishes one in-depth article via email and the web daily to paying members and a weekly digest email to those who subscribe for free. Sister publications are *The Tribune* in Sheffield and *The Post* in Liverpool. Founded 2020.

News and Star (Carlisle)

CN Group, Newspaper House, Dalston Road, Carlisle CA2 5UA
tel (01228) 612617
website www.newsandstar.co.uk
Facebook www.facebook.com/newsandstar
X @newsandstar
Editor Joy Yates
Daily Mon–Thurs, Sat £1, Fri 90p

Founded 1910.

Southport Reporter

4A Post Office Avenue, Southport PR9 0US
tel 0846 324 4195
email news24@southportreporter.com
website www.southportreporter.com
Facebook www.facebook.com/SouthportReporter
X @SouthportReport
Editor Patrick Trollope

Online only. An independent news and information online newspaper. Founded 1999.

SCOTLAND

The Courier

D.C. Thomson & Co. Ltd, 2 Albert Square, Dundee DD1 1DD
tel (01382) 575291
London office 185 Fleet Street, London EC4A 2HS
tel 020-7400 1030
website www.thecourier.co.uk
Facebook www.facebook.com/thecourieruk
X @thecourieruk
Editor David Clegg
Daily Mon–Fri £2, Sat £2.30
Supplements **Motoring, What's On, Food and Drink, Weekend, Beautiful Homes, Perfect Weddings, Farming, quarterly Farm Focus.**

Publishes three daily editions and covers local news for Perthshire, Fife, Angus and Dundee. Founded 1810.

Dundee Evening Telegraph

D.C. Thomson & Co. Ltd, 2 Albert Square, Dundee DD1 1DD
tel (01382) 575452
email newsdesk@eveningtelegraph.co.uk
website www.thecourier.co.uk
Facebook www.facebook.com/eveningtele
X @Evening_Tele
Editor Dave Lloyd
Daily Mon–Sat £1.10

Founded 1877.

Evening Express (Aberdeen)

Aberdeen Journals Ltd, 1 Marischal Square, Broad Street, Aberdeen AB10 1BL
tel (01224) 343033
email ee.news@ajl.co.uk
website www.pressandjournal.co.uk
Facebook www.facebook.com/EveningExpressAberdeen
X @eveningexpress
Editor Craig Walker
Daily Mon–Sat £1.20

Evening paper. Illustrations: colour and b&w. Payment: by arrangement. Founded 1879.

Evening News (Edinburgh)

83 Princes Street, Edinburgh EH2 2ER
tel 0131 370 0828
email newsen@edinburghnews.com
website www.edinburghnews.scotsman.com
Facebook www.facebook.com/edinburgh.evening.news
X @edinburghpaper
Editor Helen Gourlay
Digital Editor Rhoda Morrison
Daily Mon–Sat £1.30

Features on current affairs, preferably in relation to the circulation area. Also interested in local historical articles, subjects of general interest, community groups, health, beauty and fashion. Founded 1873.

Glasgow Evening Times

Herald & Times Group, 125 Fullarton Drive, Glasgow East Investment Park, Glasgow G32 8FG
tel 0141 302 7000
website www.glasgowtimes.co.uk
Facebook www.facebook.com/glasgowtimes
X @TheEveningTimes
Editor Stacey Mullen
Daily Mon–Sat £1

Founded 1876.

Greenock Telegraph

2 Crawfurd Street, Greenock PA15 1LH
tel (01475) 558904
email editorial@greenocktelegraph.co.uk
website www.greenocktelegraph.co.uk
Facebook www.facebook.com/greenocktelegraph
X @greenocktele
Editor David Goodwin
Daily Mon–Sat 90p, Sat £1.20

News and features from the area in and around Greenock. Founded 1857.

Inverness Courier

3rd Floor, 1–5 Bank Street, Inverness IV1 1DY
tel (01463) 246575
email newsdesk@hnmedia.co.uk
website www.inverness-courier.co.uk
Facebook www.facebook.com/invernesscourier

X @InvCourier
Editor Andrew Dixon
Twice weekly Tues, Fri £1.60

Articles of Highland interest only. Unsolicited material accepted. Illustrations: colour and b&w photos. Payment: by arrangement. Founded 1817.

Paisley Daily Express

One Central Quay, Glasgow G3 8DA
tel 0141 309 3555
email pde@reachplc.com
website www.dailyrecord.co.uk/all-about/paisley
Facebook www.facebook.com/paisleydailyexpress
X @PDEofficial
Editor John Hutcheson
Daily Mon–Sat £2

Articles of Paisley interest only. Considers unsolicited material. Founded 1874.

Press and Journal

5th Floor, 1 Marischal Square, Broad Street, Aberdeen AB10 1BL
tel (01224) 343311
email pj.newsdesk@ajl.co.uk
website www.pressandjournal.co.uk
Facebook www.facebook.com/ThePressandJournal
X @pressjournal
Editor Craig Walker
Daily Mon–Fri £2.10, Sat £2.45, Sun £2.70

Contributions of Scottish interest. Illustrations: half-tone. Payment: by arrangement. Founded 1747.

SOUTH EAST

The Argus

33 Bond Street, Brighton, East Sussex BN1 1RD
tel (01273) 021400
email editor@theargus.co.uk
website www.theargus.co.uk
Facebook www.facebook.com/brightonargus
X @brightonargus
Editor Arron Hendy
Daily Mon–Sat £1.10

News from Brighton and surrounding area. Founded 1880.

Banbury Guardian

c/o Regus Milton Keynes, Atterbury Lakes, Fairburn Drive, Milton Keynes MK10 9RG
tel 07803 506319
email editorial@banburyguardian.co.uk
website www.banburyguardian.co.uk
Facebook www.facebook.com/banburyguardian
X @banburynews
Editor Phil Hubble
Daily Mon–Sat £1.60

Local news and features. Founded 1838.

Echo

Echo House, Howard Chase, Basildon SS14 3BE
tel (01268) 522792
email echonews@nqe.com
website www.echo-news.co.uk
Facebook www.facebook.com/echo.essex
X @Essex_Echo
Editor Sean Davies
Daily Mon–Fri 95p

Most content is written by staff. Only interested in local material. Payment: by arrangement. Founded 1969.

Essex Chronicle

Kestrel House, Hedgerows Business Park, Chelmsford CM2 5PF
tel (01245) 602730
email newsdesk@essexlive.news
website www.essexlive.news/news
X @essexlive
Editor Katrina Chilver
Weekly Thurs £1.90

Local news and features for Essex. Founded 1764.

Hampshire Chronicle

5 Upper Brook St, Winchester SO23 8AL
tel (01962) 860836
email newsdesk@hampshirechronicle.co.uk
website www.hampshirechronicle.co.uk
Facebook www.facebook.com/hampshire.chronicle
X @hantschronicle
Editor Kimberley Barber
Weekly Thurs £1.60

News from the county of Hampshire. Founded 1772.

Isle of Wight County Press

Innovation Centre, St Cross Business Park, Newport, Isle of Wight PO30 5WB
tel (01983) 259003
email editor@iwcp.co.uk
website www.countypress.co.uk
Facebook www.facebook.com/iwcponline
X @iwcponline
Editor Lori Little
Weekly Fri £1.30

Articles and news of local interest. Founded 1884.

Kent and Sussex Courier

Courier House, 80–84 Calverley Road, Tunbridge Wells TN1 2UN
tel (01892) 239042
email kentlivenewsdesk@reachplc.com
website www.kentlive.news
Facebook www.facebook.com/kentlivenews
X @kentlivenews
Editor Lucy Thorne
Weekly Fri £2.40

Local news, articles and features. Founded 1872.

Medway Messenger
Medway House, Ginsbury Close,
Sir Thomas Longley Road, Medway City Estate,
Strood, Kent ME2 4DU
tel (01634) 227800
email medwaymessenger@thekmgroup.co.uk
website www.kentonline.co.uk
Facebook www.facebook.com/MedwayMessenger
X @MedwayMessenger
Editor Matt Ramsden
Weekly Thurs £2

Local news and sport. Illustrations: line and half-tone. Founded 1855.

The News, Portsmouth
100 Lakeside, North Harbour, Portsmouth PO6 3EN
tel 023-9262 2118
email newsdesk@thenews.co.uk
website www.portsmouth.co.uk
Facebook www.facebook.com/portsmouthnews
X @portsmouthnews
Editor Kelly Brown
Daily Mon–Fri £1.20, Sat £1.30

Articles of local relevance. Payment: by arrangement. Founded 1873.

Oxford Mail
5 King's Meadow, Ferry Hinksey Road, Osney Mead, Oxford OX2 0DP
tel (01865) 425262
email news@nqo.com
website www.oxfordmail.co.uk
Facebook www.facebook.com/oxfordmail
X @TheOxfordMail
Editor Andrew Colley
Daily Mon–Sat £1

Local news. Founded 1928.

The Oxford Times
5 King's Meadow, Ferry Hinksey Road, Osney Mead, Oxford OX2 0DP
tel (01865) 425262
email news@nqo.com
website www.oxfordtimes.co.uk
Facebook www.facebook.com/TheOxfordTimes
X @oxfordtimes
Editor Andrew Colley
Weekly Thurs £1.70

Local weekly newspaper for Oxford. The team is also responsible for the daily *Oxford Mail* and weeklies *Bicester Advertiser*, *Witney Gazette* and the *Herald* series. Founded 1862.

Reading Chronicle
2–10 Bridge Street, Reading RG1 2LU
tel 0118 955 3333
email news@readingchronicle.co.uk
website www.readingchronicle.co.uk
Facebook www.facebook.com/readingchronicle
X @rdgchronicle
Editor Katie French
Weekly Thurs £1.10

News and comment for Reading. Founded 1825.

Southern Daily Echo
Ocean Village Innovation Centre, Ocean Way, Southampton SO14 3JZ
tel 023-8042 4777
email newsdesk@dailyecho.co.uk
website www.dailyecho.co.uk
Facebook www.facebook.com/dailyecho
X @dailyecho
Editor Ben Fishwick
Daily Mon–Fri £1.05, Sat £1.15

News, articles, features and sport. Length: varies. Illustrations: line, half-tone, colour and cartoons. Payment: NUJ rates. Founded 1888.

Stratford Herald
Guild House, Guild Street, Stratford-upon-Avon, Warwickshire CV37 6RP
tel (01789) 266261
email news@stratford-herald.com
website www.stratford-herald.com
Facebook www.facebook.com/stratfordherald
X @heraldnewspaper
Editor Andy Veale
Weekly Thurs £1.10

Local news and features. Founded 1860.

Swindon Advertiser
Richmond House, Unit 1 and 2, Edison Park, Swindon SN3 3RB
tel (01793) 528144
email newsdesk@swindonadvertiser.co.uk
website www.swindonadvertiser.co.uk
Facebook www.facebook.com/swindonadvertiser
X @swindonadver
Editor Daniel Chipperfield
Daily Mon–Fri 95p, Sat 90p

Local news and information only. Considers unsolicited material. Founded 1854.

SOUTH WEST

Bournemouth Daily Echo
Richmond Hill, Bournemouth BH2 6HH
tel (01202) 554601
email newsdesk@bournemouthecho.co.uk
website www.bournemouthecho.co.uk
Facebook www.facebook.com/bournemouthdailyecho
X @bournemouthecho
Editor James Johnson
Daily Mon–Fri £1.05, Sat £1.15

Local news. Founded 1900.

The Bristol Cable

The Station, Silver Street, Bristol BS1 2AG
tel 07533 718547
email info@thebristolcable.org
website https://thebristolcable.org/
Facebook www.facebook.com/thebristolcable
X @TheBristolCable
Instagram @thebristolcable
Quarterly Free

An independent media company providing local news through independent investigative journalism, in a quarterly print publication and website. A cooperative, owned by its members, who pay a monthly fee. For writing opportunities: https://thebristolcable.org/got-a-story/. Founded 2014.

Bristol Post

Temple Way, Bristol BS2 0BU
tel 0117 934 3000
email bristolpostnews@localworld.co.uk
website www.bristolpost.co.uk
Facebook www.facebook.com/bristolpost
X @BristolLive
Editor Pete Gavan
Daily Mon–Thurs £2.40, Fri £2.80

Takes freelance news and articles. Payment: by arrangement. Founded 1932.

Cornish Guardian

1st Floor, Princess Court, 23 Princess Street, Plymouth PL1 2EX
tel (01872) 271451
email jeff.reines@reachplc.com
website www.cornwalllive.com
Facebook www.facebook.com/cornwalllivenews
X @CornwallLive
Editor Scott Harrison
Weekly Wed £1.60

Items of interest for Cornwall. Founded 1901.

Cornishman

1st Floor, Princess Court, 23 Princess Street, Plymouth PL1 2EX
tel (01872) 271451
email jeff.reines@reachplc.com
website www.cornwalllive.com
Facebook www.facebook.com/cornwalllivenews
X @cornishmanpaper
Editor Scott Harrison
Weekly Thurs £1.80

Local news and features. Founded 1878.

Dorset Echo

Fleet House, Hampshire Road, Weymouth DT4 9XD
tel (01305) 830930
email newsdesk@dorsetecho.co.uk
website www.dorsetecho.co.uk
Facebook www.facebook.com/dorsetecho
X @Dorsetecho
Editor Diarmuid MacDonagh
Daily Mon–Fri 70p, Sat 75p

News and occasional features, length: 1,000–2,000 words. Illustrations: b&w photos. Payment: by negotiation. Founded 1921.

Express & Echo

Heron Road Sowton, Exeter EX2 7NF
tel (01392) 442211
email echonews@expressandecho.co.uk
website www.devonlive.com
Facebook www.facebook.com/devonlivenews
X @DevonLiveNews
Editor Alex Richards
Weekly Thurs £1.90

Features and news of local interest. Length: 500–800 words (features), up to 400 words (news). Illustrations: colour. Payment: lineage rates for text and illustrations by negotiation. Founded 1904.

Gloucester Citizen

Suite 121C, 1st Floor, Gloucester Quays, St Ann Way, Gloucester GL1 5SH
tel (01452) 689320
email gloslivenews@reachplc.com
website www.gloucestershirelive.co.uk
Facebook www.facebook.com/GlosLiveOnline
X @GlosLiveOnline
Editor Michael Greenwood
Weekly Thurs £2.40

Local news, business, entertainment, property, motors and sport for Gloucester, Stroud and the Forest of Dean. Founded 1876.

Gloucestershire Echo

Suite 121C, 1st Floor, Gloucester Quays, St Ann Way, Gloucester GL1 5SH
tel (01242) 689320
email gloslivenews@reachplc.com
website www.gloucestershirelive.co.uk
Facebook www.facebook.com/GlosLiveOnline
X @GlosLiveOnline
Editor Jenni Phillips
Weekly Thurs £1.80

Local news, business, entertainment, property, motors and sport for Cheltenham, Cotswolds and Tewkesbury. Founded 1873.

The Herald

tel (01752) 765500
email news@plymouthherald.co.uk
website www.plymouthlive.com
Facebook www.facebook.com/plymouthlive
X @plymouth_live
Editor Catherine Salmond
Daily Mon–Fri £2.25, Sat £2.35

Local news. Will consider unsolicited material and ideas for articles and features. Illustrations: colour and b&w prints. Founded 1895.

Herald Express
Harmsworth House, Barton Hill Road, Torquay, Devon TQ2 8JN
tel (01752) 293084
website www.devonlive.com
Editor Andy Phelan
Weekly Thurs £1.80

News and articles about Torquay. Founded 1925.

Hereford Times
Stirling House, Unit 23, 1st Floor, Centenary Park, Skylon Central, Hereford HR2 6FJ
tel (01432) 274413
email news@herefordtimes.com
website www.herefordtimes.com
Facebook www.facebook.com/herefordtimes
X @HerefordTimes
Editor Alicia Kelly
Weekly Thurs £1.70

Local news and sports. Correspondence by email only. Founded 1832.

Voice
The Tindle Suite, Webb's House, Liskear, Cornwall PL14 6AH
tel 0333 305 3000
email news@voicenewspapers.co.uk
website www.voicenewspapers.co.uk
Weekly Wed £2.50

Available in print and digital formats and published across Cornwall: *Bodmin Voice*, *Newquay Voice*, *Penzance Voice*, *Saltash Voice*, *St Austell Voice* and *Truro Voice*. Founded 2001.

Western Daily Press
Yeovil Innovation Centre, Barracks Close, Copse Road, Yeovil BA22 8RN
tel (01935) 709735
website www.somersetlive.co.uk
Facebook www.facebook.com/WesternDaily
X @SomersetLive
Editor Gavin Thompson
Daily Mon–Fri £2.15, Sat £3.15

National, international or west country topics for features or news items, from established journalists, with or without illustrations. Payment: by negotiation. Founded 1858.

Western Morning News
One Canada Square, London E14 5AB
tel 020-7293 3000
email wmnnewsdesk@reachplc.com
website www.devonlive.com, www.cornwalllive.com
Facebook www.facebook.com/devonlivenews
X @WMNew
Editor Charlie Elder
Daily: Mon–Fri £2.10, Sat £3.10

Articles with illustrations considered on West Country subjects. Founded 1860.

WALES

Cambrian News
7 Cefn Llan Science Park, Aberystwyth SY23 3AH
tel (01970) 615000
email edit@cambrian-news.co.uk
website www.cambrian-news.co.uk
Facebook www.facebook.com/CambrianNews
X @CambrianNews
Editor Dylan Davies
Weekly Wed £1.50

Payment for freelance articles and pictures by arrangement. Founded 1860.

Daily Post
Bryn Eirias, Colwyn Bay LL29 8BF
tel (01492) 584321
email welshnews@dailypost.co.uk
website www.dailypost.co.uk
Facebook www.facebook.com/northwaleslive/
X @northwaleslive
Editor Dion Jones
Daily Mon–Fri £1.90, Sat £2.30

Local news. Founded 1855.

The Leader
NWN Media Ltd, Mold Business Park, Wrexham Road, Mold CH7 1XY
tel (01352) 707707
website www.leaderlive.co.uk
Facebook www.facebook.com/LeaderLive
X @leaderlive
Editor Susan Perry
Daily Mon–Fri £1

Local news, articles and features. Founded 1973.

South Wales Argus
1st Floor, Chartist Tower, Upper Dock Street, Newport NP20 1DW
tel (01633) 810000
email newsdesk@gwent-wales.co.uk
website www.southwalesargus.co.uk
Facebook www.facebook.com/southwalesargus
X @southwalesargus
Editor Gavin Thompson
Daily Mon–Sat 95p

News and features of relevance to Gwent. Limited paid freelance opportunities but community submissions are welcome. Length: 500–600 words (features) and 350 words (news). Illustrations: colour prints and transparencies. Founded 1892.

South Wales Echo
6 Park Street, Cardiff CF10 1XR
tel 029-2024 3600
email newsdesk@walesonline.co.uk
website www.walesonline.co.uk
X @walesonline

Editor Tryst Williams
Daily Mon–Fri £2.35, Sat £2.65

Evening paper: news, sport, features, showbiz, news features and personality interviews. Length: up to 700 words. Illustrations: photos and cartoons. Payment: by negotiation. Founded 1884.

South Wales Evening Post

220 High Street, Swansea SA1 1NW
tel (01792) 555520
email postnews@mediawales.co.uk
website www.walesonline.co.uk
X @WalesOnline
Editor Jonathan Roberts
Daily Mon–Sat £2

Swansea news and views. Founded 1893.

WEST MIDLANDS

The Asian Today

6A Olton Wharf, Richmond Road, Solihull B92 7RN
tel 0121 314 2892
email info@theasiantoday.com
website www.theasiantoday.com
Facebook www.facebook.com/theasiantoday
X @theasiantoday
Instagram @theasiantoday
Editor Zakia Yousaf
Monthly Free

A community newspaper for the Midlands providing the region's South-Asian community access to news stories and current events. Founded 2002.

Coventry Telegraph

c/o Floor 5, 3 Brindley Place, Birmingham B1 2JB
tel 024-7663 3633
email news@coventrytelegraph.net
website www.coventrytelegraph.net
Facebook www.facebook.com/livecoventry
X @live_coventry
Editor Graeme Brown
Daily Mon–Sat £2.35

Topical, illustrated articles with a Coventry or Warwickshire interest. Length: up to 600 words. Payment: by arrangement. Founded 1891.

Express & Star

8th Floor, Mander House, Mander Centre, Wolverhampton WV1 3NB
tel (01902) 485123
email newsdesk@expressandstar.co.uk
website www.expressandstar.com
Facebook www.facebook.com/expressandstar
X @expressandstar
Editor-in-Chief Mark Drew
Daily Mon–Fri £1.20, Sat £1.40

Local news and articles for Wolverhampton and surrounded area. Founded 1874.

Sentinel

Staffordshire Sentinel News & Media Ltd, Sentinel House, Bethesda Street, Hanley, Stoke-on-Trent ST1 3GN
tel (01782) 864100
email newsdesk@thesentinel.co.uk
website www.stokesentinel.co.uk
Facebook www.facebook.com/stokeontrentlive
X @SotLive
Editor Marc Waddington
Daily Mon–Fri £1.80, Sat £1.90

Articles and features of topical interest to north Staffordshire and south Cheshire. Illustrations: colour and b&w. Payment: by arrangement. Founded 1873.

Shropshire Star

Grosvenor House, Suite 304, Central Park, Hollinswood Road, Telford TF2 9TW
tel (01952) 421555
website www.shropshirestar.com
Facebook www.facebook.com/ShropshireStar
X @ShropshireStar
Editor Mark Drew
Daily Mon–Fri £1.20, Sat £1.40

News and features. No unsolicited material; write to Features Editor with outline of ideas. Payment: by arrangement. Founded 1964.

Sunday Mercury

Weaman Street, Birmingham B4 6AY
tel 0121 234 5567
website www.birminghamlive.co.uk
Editor Graeme Brown
Weekly Sun £3

Local news or features. Illustrations: colour and b&w. Payment varies. Founded 1918.

Worcester News

Rear 1st Floor Office, Redhill House, 227 London Road, Worcester WR5 2JG
tel (01905) 748200
website www.worcesternews.co.uk
Facebook www.facebook.com/theworcesternews
X @worcesternews
Editor Alicia Kelly
Daily Mon–Sat 95p

Local and national news, sport and features. Will consider unsolicited material. Welcomes ideas for articles and features. Length: 800 words (features) and 300 words (news). Illustrations: colour jpg files. Payment: by negotiation. Founded 1935.

YORKSHIRE/HUMBERSIDE

Grimsby Telegraph

80 Cleethorpe Road, Grimsby DN31 3EH
tel 020-7293 3000

email newsdesk@grimsbytelegraph.co.uk
website www.thisisgrimsby.co.uk
Facebook www.facebook.com/grimsbylive
X @GrimsbyLive
Editor Jamie Macaskill
Daily Mon–Sat £2.25

Considers general interest articles. Illustrations: line, half-tone, colour and cartoons. Payment: by arrangement. Founded 1897.

Halifax Courier

The Fire Station, Dean Clough Mills, Halifax HX3 5AX
tel (01422) 260208
email editor@halifaxcourier.co.uk
website www.halifaxcourier.co.uk
Facebook www.facebook.com/HalifaxCourier
X @HXCourier
Editor Chris Lever
Weekly Fri £1.90

Local news. Founded 1853.

Huddersfield Daily Examiner

Pennine Business Park, Longbow Close, Bradley Road, Huddersfield HD2 1GQ
tel (01484) 437712
email editorial@examiner.co.uk
website www.examinerlive.co.uk
X @YorkshireLive
Editor Wayne Ankers
Daily Mon–Fri £2.40, Sat £2.80

No contributions required at present. Founded 1851.

Hull Daily Mail

Blundell's Corner, Beverley Road, Hull HU3 1XS
tel (01482) 315016
email news@hulldailymail.co.uk
website www.hulldailymail.co.uk
Facebook www.facebook.com/hulllive
X @hulllive
Editor Neil Hodgkinson
Daily Mon–Sat £2

Local news and articles. Founded 1885.

Lincolnshire Echo

Ground Floor, Witham Wharf, Brayford Wharf East, Lincoln LN5 7AY
tel (01522) 804300
website www.lincolnshirelive.co.uk
Facebook www.facebook.com/LincsLive
X @LincsLive
Editor Sam DImmer
Weekly Thurs £2.30

Local news from Lincolnshire. Founded 1893.

The Press

Newsquest York, PO Box 29, 84–86 Walmgate, York YO1 9YN
tel (01904) 567131
email newsdesk@thepress.co.uk
website www.yorkpress.co.uk
Facebook www.facebook.com/thepressyork
X @yorkpress
Editor Nigel Burton
Daily Mon–Fri £1, Sat £1.15

Articles of local interest. Length: 500–1,000 words. Illustrations: line and half-tone. Payment: by arrangement. Founded 1882.

The Scarborough News

tel (01723) 860161
website www.thescarboroughnews.co.uk
Facebook www.facebook.com/thescarboroughnews
X @TheScarboroNews
North Yorkshire Content Editor Duncan Atkins
Weekly Thurs £2.10

Also publishes daily news on website. Founded 1882.

Scunthorpe Telegraph

4–5 Park Square, Scunthorpe DN15 6JH
tel (01724) 709067
email newsdesk@scunthorpetelegraph.co.uk
website www.scunthorpetelegraph.co.uk
Facebook www.facebook.com/scunthorpelive
X @ScunthorpeLive
Editor Jamie Macaskill
Weekly Thurs £2.30

Local news and features. Founded 1937.

Telegraph & Argus

The West Wing, New Hall Way, Bradford, West Yorkshire BD5 8FF
tel (01274) 729511
email newsdesk@telegraphandargus.co.uk
website www.thetelegraphandargus.co.uk
Facebook www.facebook.com/telegraphandargus
X @Bradford_TandA
Editor Nigel Burton
Daily Mon–Fri £1, Sat £1.15

Locally relevant ews and articles. Length: up to 1,000 words. Illustrations: line, half-tone and colour. Payment by negotiation. Founded 1868.

Yorkshire Post

No1 Leeds, 26 Whitehall Road, Leeds LS12 1BE
tel 0113 243 2701
website www.yorkshirepost.co.uk
Facebook www.facebook.com/yorkshirepost.newspaper
X @yorkshirepost
Editor James Mitchinson
Daily Mon–Fri £1.80, Sat £3.50

Authoritative, well-written articles on subjects of general, literary or industrial interests. Founded 1754.

Magazines UK and Ireland

Listings for regional newspapers start on page 24 and for national newspapers on page 15. For quick reference, magazines are listed by subject area starting on page 753. If you do have a piece placed with a magazine or journal, read any contract or licence agreement carefully: retaining copyright over your own writing is important and you should understand what you are agreeing to.

Abridged

email abridged@ymail.com
website www.abridged.zone
Facebook www.facebook.com/people/Abridged/
Bluesky @abridgedmagazine.bsky.social
Instagram @abridgedmagazine
Curatorial Editor/Project Coordinator Gregory McCartney, *Project Editor* Susanna Galbraith
Free

Contemporary or experimental poetry with occasional accompanying contemporary visual arts exhibitions and online projects. Themed issues: see social media feeds for upcoming themes prior to submitting. Payment: by arrangement. Founded 2004.

Accountancy Age

Contentive, Scale Space, 58 Wood Lane, London W12 7RZ
website www.accountancyage.com
X @AccountancyAge
Editor Aaran Fronda
Online

Articles of accounting, financial and business interest. Freelance assignments commissioned. Payment: by arrangement. Founded 1969.

Accounting & Business

Association of Chartered Certified Accountants, The Adelphi, 1–11 John Adam Street, London WC2N 6AU
tel 020-7059 5000
email info@accaglobal.com
website https://abmagazine.accaglobal.com/uk/en.html
Editor-in-Chief Jo Malvern
Online Free

Journal of the Association of Chartered Certified Accountants. Features accountancy, finance and business topics of relevance to accountants and finance directors. Illustrated. Founded 1998.

Acumen Literary Journal

4 Thornhill Bridge Wharf, Caledonian Wharf, London N1 0RU
email acumeneditor@gmail.com
email hello@acumen-poetry.co.uk
website https://acumen-poetry.co.uk/submissions-guide
Editor Danielle Hope
3 p.a. £7, £19 p.a.

Poetry, poetry in translation, plus relevant literary and critical articles, and reviews of poetry books. For submissions: by post, please ensure sufficient postage and include sae; online submissions should be sent via the website. Check website or magazine for submission guidelines. Books for review should be sent to Andrew Geary, 25 Southbrook Drive, Cheshunt EN8 0QJ; email acumenreviews@gmail.com. Payment: none. Founded 1985.

Aeroplane Monthly

Key Publishing Group, Units 1–4, Gwash Way Industrial Estate, Ryhall Road, Stamford, Lincs. PE9 1XP
email ben.dunnell@keypublishing.com
website www.key.aero/aeroplanemonthly
Monthly £5.99

Articles and photos relating to historical aviation and aircraft preservation. Length: up to 5,000 words. Illustrations: line, colour. Payment: by arrangement. Founded 1973.

Aesthetica Magazine

21 New Street, York YO1 8RA
email info@aestheticamagazine.com
website www.aestheticamagazine.com
X @AestheticaMag
Instagram @aestheticamag
Editor Cherie Federico
Bi-monthly £6.95

Visual art, design and photography. Also produces a number of awards, exhibitions and events focused on talent development in art, photography, literature and film: the Aesthetica Short Film Festival, Art Prize, Future Now Symposium and Creative Writing Award. Founded 2002.

Africa: St Patrick's Missions

St Patrick's Missionary Society, Kiltegan, Co. Wicklow W91 Y022, Republic of Ireland
tel +353 (0)59 647 3600
email editor@spms.ie
website www.spms.org
Facebook www.facebook.com/AfricaMagazineKiltegan
Editor Loretta Brennan
8 p.a. €15 p.a.

Articles of missionary and topical religious interest. Length: up to 1,000 words. Illustrations: colour.

Africa Confidential

3rd Floor, 45 Albemarle Street, London W1S 4JL
email andrew@africa-confidential.com
website www.africa-confidential.com
X @Africa_Conf
Deputy Editor Andrew Weir
Fortnightly £1,019 p.a. (print and online), £876 p.a. (online only)

News and analysis of political and economic developments in Africa. Unsolicited contributions welcomed, but must be exclusive and not published elsewhere. Length: 1,200-word features, 500-word pointers. No illustrations. Payment: by arrangement. Founded 1960.

African Business

IC Publications Ltd, 7 Coldbath Square, London EC1R 4LQ
tel 020-7841 3210
email info@icpublications.com
website https://african.business
Facebook www.facebook.com/AfricanBusinessMagazine
Monthly From £67 p.a.

Articles on business, economic and financial topics of interest to business professionals, ministers and officials concerned with African affairs. Length: 1,000–1,400 words; shorter coverage 500 words. Illustrations: by arrangement. Payment: by arrangement for both words and illustrations. Founded 1978.

AIR International

Key Publishing Ltd, PO Box 100, Stamford, Lincs. PE9 1XQ
tel (01780) 755131
email airint@keypublishing.com
website www.airinternational.com
Editor Glenn Sands
Monthly £64.99 p.a. (as part of Key Aero)

Technical articles on aircraft; features on topical aviation subjects – civil and military. Length: up to 3,000 words. Illustrations: by arrangement. Payment: by arrangement. Founded 1971.

The Alchemy Spoon

email alchemyspoonpoetry@gmail.com
website www.alchemyspoon.org/guidelines.html
Facebook www.facebook.com/thealchemyspoon
Instagram @alchemy_spoon
Editorial Team Roger Bloor, Mary Mulholland, Diana Cant
3 p.a.

Online poetry magazine. See website for information on forthcoming submissions windows and themes: up to three poems may be submitted at one time by new and established poets. Submissions from 'new phase' poets, who have come to poetry later in life, particularly welcome. Founded 2020.

Allegro Poetry

email allegropoetry@gmail.com
website www.allegropoetry.org
Editor Sally Long
2 p.a. Free

Online journal of contemporary poetry. Published twice a year, in March (general issue) and September (themed issue) respectively. See website for information on forthcoming submission windows and full details. Previously published work is not accepted. Payment: none. Founded 2014.

And Other Poems

email editor.andotherpoems@gmail.com
website https://andotherpoems.com/submissions/
X @And_OtherPoems
Bluesky @andotherpoems.bsky.social
Instagram @and_otherpoems
Editors Tom Bailey, Laurie Ogden
3 p.a.

Online poetry magazine. Open for submissions three times per year (January, May and September) via a website form. Submissions are free. Accepts previously unpublished poems from new and established writers, and also welcomes simultaneous submissions. All themes, forms and styles are considered. Founded by Josephine Corcoran in 2012.

Andromeda Magazine

email info@andromedamagazine.com
website https://andromedamagazine.com
Facebook www.facebook.com/andromedamag
Instagram @andromedaliterary

Literary magazine for new and established writers. Monthly short story competition for authors of general fiction, fantasy and sci-fi. (Small entrance fee charged.)

Angling Times

Bauer Media Group, Media House, Lynch Wood, Peterborough Business Park, Peterborough PE2 6EA
tel (01733) 395097
email newsdesk@anglingtimes.co.uk
website www.anglingtimes.co.uk
Facebook www.facebook.com/anglingtimes
X @angling_times
News Editor Freddie Sandford
Weekly £2.75

Articles, pictures, news stories, on all forms of angling. Illustrations: line, half-tone, colour. Payment: by arrangement. Founded 1953.

Anthropocene

email anthropocenepoetry@gmail.com
website www.anthropocenepoetry.org
X @anthro_poetry
Editor Charlie Baylis

Online poetry journal. New poems every Wednesday and Sunday. Expedited submissions open all year round.

Apollo

22 Old Queen Street, London SW1H 9HP
tel 020-7961 0150
email ed@apollomag.com
website www.apollo-magazine.com
Editor Edward Behrens
Monthly £7.95

Scholarly and topical articles of c. 2,000–3,000 words on art, architecture, ceramics, photography, furniture, armour, glass, sculpture and any subject connected with art, museums and collecting. Interviews with collectors, leading international artists and cultural leaders. Exhibition and book reviews, articles on current developments in the culture sector, regular columns on the art market. Illustrations: colour. Payment: by arrangement. Founded 1925.

The Architects' Journal

emap Publishing Ltd, 4th Floor, Harmsworth House, 15 Bouverie Street, London EC4Y 8DP
tel 020-3953 2600
email emily.booth@emap.com
website www.architectsjournal.co.uk
Instagram @architectsjournal
Editor Emily Booth
Monthly From £290 p.a.

Articles (mainly technical) on architecture, planning and building, accepted only with prior agreement of synopsis. Illustrations: by arrangement. Payment: by arrangement. Founded 1895.

The Architectural Review

emap Publishing Ltd, 4th Floor, Harmsworth House, 15 Bouverie Street, London EC4Y 8DP
tel 020-3033 2741
email editorial@architectural-review.com
website www.architectural-review.com
Instagram @thearchitecturalreview
Editor Manon Mollard
Monthly From £190 p.a.

Articles on architecture and the allied arts (urbanism, design, theory, history, technology). Writers must be thoroughly qualified. Length: up to 3,000 words. Illustrations: by arrangement. Payment: by arrangement. Founded 1896.

Architecture Today

Built Environment and Architecture Media, 2–6 Boundary Row, London SE1 8HP
tel 020-3714 4240
email editorial@architecturetoday.co.uk
website www.architecturetoday.co.uk
X @Arch_Today
Editor Isabel Allen
10 p.a. Circulated free of charge to architects; subscription options available

Mostly commissioned articles and features on contemporary European architecture. Length: 200–800 words. Illustrations: colour. Payment: by negotiation. Founded 1989.

Art Monthly

Peveril Garden Studios, 140 Great Dover Street, London SE1 4GW
tel 020-7240 0389
email info@artmonthly.co.uk
website www.artmonthly.co.uk
X @ArtMonthly
Instagram @art_monthly_uk
Editor Patricia Bickers
10 p.a. £9.50 (inc. p&p)

Features on modern and contemporary visual artists and art history, art theory and art-related issues; exhibition and book reviews. All material commissioned. Length: 750–1,500 words. Illustrations: by arrangement. Payment: by arrangement; none for photos. Founded 1976.

The Art Newspaper

17 Hanover Square, London W1S 1BN
tel 020-3586 8054
email info@theartnewspaper.com
website www.theartnewspaper.com
Instagram @theartnewspaper.official
11 p.a. From £70 p.a.

International coverage of visual art, news, politics, law, exhibitions with some feature pages. Length: 200–1,000 words. Illustrations: by arrangement. Payment: by arrangement. Founded 1990.

Art Quarterly

Art Fund, 2 Granary Square, London N1C 4BH
tel 020-7225 4800
email artquarterly@artfund.org
website www.artfund.org/pages/art-quarterly
Editor Helen Sumpter
Quarterly Free to Art Fund members with National Art Pass

Magazine of Art Fund, the national charity for art, which supports museums and galleries across the UK. Features information about what's on in UK galleries and museums. Also includes in-depth features, interviews and conversations about art and artists, exhibition previews and reviews, opinion by writers, critics, commentators and experts in the field, and updates on the impact of Art Fund's charitable programme.

ArtReview and ArtReview Asia

1 Honduras Street, London EC1Y 0TH
tel 020-7490 8138

email office@artreview.com
website www.artreview.com
Facebook www.facebook.com/ArtReview.Magazine
X @ArtReview_
Editor Mark Rappolt
ArtReview 9 p.a. £45 p.a. (print and online); ArtReview Asia 4 p.a. £25 p.a. (print and online)

Contemporary art features and reviews. Proposals welcome. Illustrations: colour. Payment: £350 per 1,000 words. Founded 1949.

Artists & Illustrators

The Chelsea Magazine Company, 111 Buckingham Palace Road, London SW1 0DT
tel 020-7349 3700
email info@artistsandillustrators.co.uk
website www.artistsandillustrators.co.uk
X @AandImagazine
Instagram @aandimagazine
Editor Niki Browes
13 p.a. From £39.95 p.a.

Practical and inspirational articles for amateur and semi-professional artists. Length: 500–1,500 words. Illustrations: hi-res digital images, hand-drawn illustrations. Payment: by arrangement. Founded 1986.

Astronomy Now

Pole Star Publications, PO Box 175, Tonbridge, Kent TN10 4ZY
email editorial2025@astronomynow.com
website https://astronomynow.com
Facebook www.facebook.com/astronomynow
X @astronomynow
Editor Keith Cooper
Monthly £6.49

Specialises in translating exciting astronomy research into articles for the lay reader. Also covers amateur astronomy with equipment reviews and observing notes. Submit article pitches via email. Length: 800–2,000 words. Payment: by arrangement. Founded 1987.

Asylum

c/o PCCS Books, Wyastone Business Park, Wyastone Leys, Monmouth NP25 3SR
tel (01600) 891509
email editors@asylummagazine.org
website https://asylummagazine.org
X @AsylumMagUK
Bluesky @asylummagazine.bsky.social
Instagram @Asylummagazine
Editor H. Spandler
Quarterly Subscriptions from £10 p.a.

Critical, radical and alternative perspectives on mental health, madness, neurodiversity, mental health systems and social movements. Open submissions (articles, poems, stories, illustrations etc). Contributions especially welcomed from service users, ex-users or survivors, carers, activists and frontline mental health workers. Founded 1986 as *Asylum*, the magazine for democratic psychiatry.

Atrium

email atriumpoetrysubmissions@gmail.com
website https://atriumpoetry.com
Facebook www.facebook.com/AtriumPoetry
X @Atrium_Poetry
Bluesky @atriumpoetry.bsky.social
Editors Holly Magill, Claire Walker

Worcestershire- and Wales-based based poetry webzine. Poems published on Tuesdays and Fridays each week. Up to three poems of up to 50 lines may be submitted at once; see website for full details. Payment: none. Founded 2017.

Attitude

Stream Publishing Limited, The Cowshed, Ladycross Farm, Hollow Lane, Dormansland, Surrey RH7 6PB
email attitude@attitude.co.uk
website www.attitude.co.uk
X @AttitudeMag
Editor-in-Chief Cliff Joannou, *Content Editor* Jamie Tabberer
13 p.a. £10

Men's style magazine aimed primarily, but not exclusively, at gay men. Covers style/fashion, interviews, reviews, celebrities, humour. Illustrations: by arrangement. Payment: by arrangement. Founded 1994.

The Author

24 Bedford Row, London WC1R 4EH
tel 020-7373 6642
email theauthor@societyofauthors.org
website https://societyofauthors.org/News/The-Author
Facebook www.facebook.com/TheSocietyofAuthors
X @Soc_of_Authors
Bluesky @societyofauthors.bsky.social
Instagram @thesocietyofauthors
Editor James McConnachie
Quarterly Membership publication

Commissioned articles from 800–1,500 words on any subject related to the craft, legal, commercial or technical side of authorship. Little scope for the freelance writer: preliminary email advisable. Artwork and illustrations: by arrangement. Payment: by arrangement. Founded 1890.

Aviation News

Key Publishing Group, Units 1–4, Gwash Way Industrial Estate, Ryhall Road, Stamford, Lincs. PE9 1XP
tel (01780) 755131
email josef.campion@keypublishing.com
website www.aviation-news.co.uk
X @AvNewsMag

Editor Josef Campion
Monthly £5.60

Covers all aspects of aviation. Many articles commissioned. Payment: by arrangement. Founded 1972.

AW (Athletics Weekly)

National World Publishing Limited, Suite E3, Joseph's Well, Hanover Walk, Leeds LS3 1AB
email euan.crumley@athleticsweekly.com
website www.athleticsweekly.com
Facebook www.facebook.com/athleticsweekly
X @athleticsweekly
Instagram @athletics.weekly
Editorial Director Euan Crumley
Monthly £9.99

News and features on track and field athletics, road running, cross country, fell running and race walking. Material mostly commissioned. Length: 300–1,500 words. Illustrations: by arrangement. Payment: varies. Founded 1945.

BackTrack

Pendragon Publishing, PO Box 3, Easingwold, York YO61 3YS
tel (01347) 824397
email pendragonpublishing@btinternet.com
website www.pendragonpublishing.co.uk
Editor Michael Blakemore
Monthly £5.85

British railway history from 1820s to 1980s. Welcomes ideas from writers and photographers. Articles must be well researched, authoritative and accompanied by illustrations. Length: 3,000–5,000 words (main features), 500–3,000 words (articles). Illustrations: colour and b&w. Payment: £30 per 1,000 words; £18.50 colour image, £10 b&w. Founded 1986.

Bad Lilies

website www.badlilies.uk/submit
X @BadLilies
Instagram @badlilies
Editors Kathryn Gray, Andrew Neilson

Digital poetry journal. Welcomes up to six previously unpublished poems per author during submission windows (see website and social media for updates on these). Simultaneous submissions from both new and established authors also accepted. Payment: none.

The Banker

FT Specialist, Bracken House, 1 Friday Street, London EC4M 9BT
tel 020-7873 3000
email silvia.pavoni@ft.com
website www.thebanker.com
Editor Silvia Pavoni
Monthly From £1,000 p.a.

Global coverage of retail banking, corporate banking, banking technology, transaction services, investment banking and capital markets, regulation, sustainable finance and Top 1,000 World Bank rankings. Founded 1928.

Baptist Times

Baptist House, PO Box 44,129 Broadway, Didcot, Oxon OX11 8RT
tel (01235) 517677
email editor@baptisttimes.co.uk
website www.baptisttimes.co.uk
X @baptisttimes
Editor Paul Hobson
Online

Religious or social affairs, news, features and reviews. Founded 1855.

BBC Countryfile Magazine

Our Media Ltd, Eagle House, Colston Avenue, Bristol BS1 1EN
tel 0117 927 9009
email editor@countryfile.com
website www.countryfile.com
X @BBCCountryfile
Editor Paul McGuinness
Monthly £5.99

Articles and features on making the most of the UK's countryside, and the lives of its rural communities.

BBC Gardeners' World Magazine

Immediate Media Co. Ltd, Vineyard House, 44 Brook Green, London W6 7BT
tel 020-7150 5770
email magazine@gardenersworld.com
website www.gardenersworld.com
X @GWmag
Editor Kevin Smith
Monthly £7.50

Advice, support and features for gardeners of all levels of expertise. Fully illustrated. Does not accept speculative features.

BBC History Magazine

Immediate Media Co. Ltd, Eagle House, Colston Avenue, Bristol BS1 1EN
email historymagazine@historyextra.com
website www.historyextra.com
Facebook www.facebook.com/historyextra
X @historyextra
Editor Rob Attar
Monthly £7.50

Popular history writing on a wide range of topics, from Ancient Egypt to the Second World War. Contents include feature spreads, book reviews, opinion and news. Contributors include Mary Beard, Tracy Borman, Dan Snow and Michael Wood. Illustrated. Founded 2000.

BBC Music Magazine

Our Media Ltd, Eagle House, Colston Avenue, Bristol BS1 1EN
email music@classical-music.com
website www.classical-music.com
X @MusicMagazine
Editor Charlotte Smith
Monthly £7.99

Reviews and articles on all aspects of classical music. Also interviews with leading practitioners, information on technical equipment and forthcoming tours. Founded 1992.

BBC Science Focus

Immediate Media Co. Ltd, Eagle House, Colston Avenue, Bristol BS1 1EN
tel 0117 314 8779
email jason.goodyer@immediate.co.uk
email joe.eden@immediate.co.uk
website www.sciencefocus.com
X @sciencefocus
Editor Daniel Bennett, *Commissioning Editor* Jason Goodyer, *Art Editor* Joe Eden
Monthly £5.99

Articles from popular scientists and leading academics, as well as news. Submissions accepted for articles only from experienced and previously published science writers: send 2–8pp overview along with feature pitch form provided on the website to the first email address above. Photography and illustration submissions also accepted: see website for full specifications. Founded 1992.

BBC Sky at Night Magazine

Our Media Ltd, Eagle House, Bristol BS1 1EN
email chris.bramley@ourmedia.co.uk
email ezzy.pearson@ourmedia.co.uk
website www.skyatnightmagazine.com
X @skyatnightmag
Editor Chris Bramley, *Features Editor* Ezzy Pearson, *Online Editor* Iain Todd
Monthly £6.99

Space science (planets, stars, galaxies, cosmology), the experience of dark skies and astronomy tourism (UK and international). Also practical astronomy (from casual stargazing to astrophotography), astronomy equipment (telescopes, binoculars, cameras, mounts and accessories) the history of astronomy and the commercial space industry. Runs full editions monthly in print, digital and Apple News, as well as shorter 'special' editions monthly on Apple News. Founded 2005

BBC Top Gear

BBC Broadcast Centre, 201 Wood Lane, London W12 7TQ
email editor@bbctopgearmagazine.com
website www.topgear.com
X @BBC_TopGear
Editor Jack Rix
13 p.a. £5.99

Articles and photographic features on motoring, lifestyle and cars. Founded 1993.

BBC Wildlife Magazine

Our Media Ltd, Eagle House, Colston Avenue, Bristol BS1 1EN
email wildlifemagazine@ourmedia.co.uk
website www.discoverwildlife.com
X @WildlifeMag
Editor Paul McGuinness
Monthly £5.50

Consumer natural history magazine. Expert-written articles and features, along with award-winning photography. Founded 1963 as *Animals Magazine*.

Bella

Bauer Media, The Lantern, 75 Hampstead Road, London NW1 2PL
tel 020-7241 8000
email bella.mag@bauermedia.co.uk
website www.bellamagazine.co.uk
X @bellamagazineUK
Instagram @bellamagazineuk
Editor Rachel Jones
Weekly £1.70

Women's magazine with celebrity interviews, exclusive photos, real-life stories, high-street fashion, diet advice, health, food and travel. Payment: by arrangement. Founded 1987.

Best

Hearst UK, House of Hearst, 30 Panton Street, London SW1Y 4AJ
tel 020-7339 4500
email nicola.dawson@hearst.co.uk
Facebook www.facebook.com/bestmagazine
X @BestMagOfficial
Instagram @bestmagofficia
Editor-in-Chief Siobhan Wykes, *Editor* Nicola Dawson
Weekly £1.99

Unsolicited work not accepted, but always willing to look at ideas/outlines. Payment: by agreement. Founded 1987.

BFS Horizons

The British Fantasy Society, The Apex, 2 Sheriffs Orchard, Coventry CV1 3PP
email bfshorizons@britishfantasysociety.org
email poetry@britishfantasysociety.org
website www.britishfantasysociety.org
Fiction Editor Pete W. Sutton, *Poetry Editor* Ian Hunter

Official publication of the British Fantasy Society, focusing on fiction and poetry across a broad fantasy genre, including weird fiction, horror and science fiction. Length: stories of up to 5,000 words (ideally);

poems of no more than 36 lines. See website for full guidelines and house style guide. Payment: £20 per story (flat rate).

BFS Journal

The British Fantasy Society, 37 Coley Avenue, Reading RG1 6LL
email bfsjournal@britishfantasysociety.org
website https://britishfantasysociety.org/submission-guidelines

Official publication of the British Fantasy Society, focusing on features, non-fiction and academic articles, including interviews, opinion pieces and biographies. Contact on email above with outline first. Length: preferably 2,500–6,000 words. Payment: £20.

The Big Issue

43 Bath Street, Glasgow G2 1HW (editorial office)
tel 0141 352 7260
email editorial@thebigissue.com
website www.bigissue.com
X @BigIssue
Editor Paul McNamee
Weekly £4

Features, current affairs, reviews, interviews – of general interest and on social issues. Length: 1,000 words (features). No short stories or poetry. Illustrations: colour and b&w photos and line. Payment: by arrangement. Founded 1991.

Bike

Bauer Media Group, Media House, Lynch Wood, Peterborough Business Park, Peterborough PE2 6EA
tel (01733) 468099
email mike.armitage@bauermedia.co.uk
website www.bikemagazine.co.uk
Editor Mike Armitage
Monthly £5.75

Motorcycle articles, features, news. Length: articles/features 1,000–3,000 words. Illustrations: colour and b&w photos. Payment: by arrangement. Founded 1971.

Bird Watching

Bauer Media Group, Media House, Lynch Wood, Peterborough Business Park, Peterborough PE2 6EA
tel (01733) 468201
email birdwatching@bauermedia.co.uk
website www.birdwatching.co.uk
X @BirdWatchingMag
Editor Matt Merritt
13 p.a. £5.99

Broad range of bird-related features and photography, particularly looking at bird behaviour, bird news, reviews and UK birdwatching sites. Limited number of overseas features. Emphasis on providing accurate information in entertaining ways. Send synopsis first. Length: up to 1,200 words. Illustrations: by arrangement. Payment: by negotiation. Founded 1986.

Birdwatch

The Maltings, West Street, Bourne PE10 9PH
email editorial@birdwatch.co.uk
website www.birdguides.com
Facebook www.facebook.com/birdwatchmagazine
Head of Content Josh Jones
Monthly £6.99

Topical articles on all aspects of British and Irish birds and birding, including conservation, identification, sites and habitats and equipment, as well as overseas destinations. Length: 700–1,500 words. Illustrations: hi-res jpgs (300 dpi at 1,500 pixels min. width) of wild British and European birds considered; submit full-size images via email or file-sharing site. Artwork: by negotiation. Payment: by arrangement. Founded 1991.

Black Beauty & Hair

Hawker Publications, Lombard Business Park, 12 Deer Park Road, Wimbledon, London SW19 3TL
tel 020-7720 2108
email info@blackbeautyandhair.com
website www.blackbeautyandhair.com
Facebook www.facebook.com/BlackBeautyandHair
X @BlackBeautyMag
Instagram @blackbeautymag
Editor-in-Chief Irene Shelley
Bi-monthly £5

Beauty and style articles relating specifically to women of colour; celebrity features. True-life stories and salon features. Length: approx. 1,000 words. Illustrations: by arrangement. Payment: by arrangement. Founded 1982.

Blithe Spirit

email bhsjournal@fastmail.org
website http://britishhaikusociety.org.uk/journal/
Editor Iliyana Stoyanova
Quarterly Free to members

Journal of the British Haiku Society: c. 90pp. Includes original poems (from Society members only), articles and reviews. Four submission windows (see website for up-to-date details); poems must not have appeared, or be under consideration, elsewhere.

Boat International

41–47 Hartfield Road, London SW19 3RQ
tel 020-8545 9330
email support@boatinternational.com
website www.boatinternational.com
X @boatint
Editor-in-Chief Stewart Campbell
12 p.a. From £46 p.a.

News and features on superyachts and the lifestyles of those who own them. Also yacht listings in a brokerage section and reviews. Founded 1983.

The Book Collector

(incorporating Bibliographical Notes and Queries)
PO Box 1163, St Albans AL1 9WS
email editor@thebookcollector.co.uk
website www.thebookcollector.co.uk
Facebook www.facebook.com/TheBookCollectorUK/
Instagram @thebookcollectoruk
Online From £60 p.a.

Articles, biographical and bibliographical, on the collection and study of printed books and MSS. Payment: for reviews only. Founded 1952.

Booklaunch

12 Wellfield Avenue, London N10 2EA
email editor@booklaunch.london
website www.booklaunch.london
Facebook www.facebook.com/booklaunch.london
Instagram @booklaunchlondon
Publisher Dr Stephen Games, *Assistant Editor* Maggie Bawden
6 p.a. £7.95; subscription options available

Largest print-run (51,000+) book-related magazine in the UK. Preference for non-mass-market titles (independent, academic and self-pub) and non-fiction. Tabloid format, max. 1,500 words per page. Contents include extracts, features and interviews on literary culture, coverage of linguistics and language curiosities, and quizzes with book prizes. Display advertising available by arrangement. Co-published with Envelope Books. Payment: none. Founded 2018.

Books Ireland

Unit 9, 78 Furze Road, Dublin D18 C6V6, Republic of Ireland
tel +353 (0)1 293 3568
email ruth@wordwell.ie
website www.booksirelandmagazine.com
Instagram @booksirelandmag
Editor Ruth McKee
Online

Reviews of Irish-interest and Irish-author books, as well as articles of interest to librarians, booksellers and readers. Length: 800–1,400 words. Founded 1976 (print); fully digital as of 2019.

The Bookseller

The Stage Media Company Ltd, 47 Bermondsey Street, London SE1 3XT
tel 020-3403 1818
email tom.tivnan@thebookseller.com
website www.thebookseller.com
X @thebookseller
Editor Philip Jones, *Managing Editor* Tom Tivnan
Weekly £5.95

Long-established magazine of the UK book industry magazine, featuring news, analysis, bestseller charts, interviews, previews of forthcoming titles and jobs in the industry, as well as in-depth coverage of international book fairs including Frankfurt, Bologna and Beijing. While outside contributions are welcomed, most of the journal's contents are commissioned. Length: c. 1,000–1,500 words. Payment: by arrangement. Founded 1858.

Breathe

GMC Publications Ltd, 86 High Street, Lewes BN7 1XN
tel (01273) 477374
email hello@breathemagazine.com
website www.breathemagazine.com/submissions
Publisher Jonathan Grogan
9 p.a. £6.99

Mindfulness magazine aiming to help readers achieve a healthier life across five key areas: wellbeing, living, creativity, mindfulness and escape. Submissions welcomed from experienced or new writers, and from illustrators. See website for specific requirements for each type of potential contributor. Founded 2016.

Briefly Write

email submissions@brieflywrite.com
website https://brieflywrite.com
X @BrieflyWrite
Editors Daniel Clark, Elinor Bell-Clark
2 p.a. Online only

Online magazine for bold and succinct flash fiction and poetry. Also runs free-to-enter fiction and poetry competitions, and features book reviews and reading challenges. Founded 2020.

British Birds

email editor@britishbirds.co.uk
website www.britishbirds.co.uk
Facebook www.facebook.com/britishbirdsmagazine
X @britishbirds
Bluesky @britishbirds.bsky.social
Editor Stephen Menzie
Monthly £7.50

Publishes major papers on bird identification, behaviour, conservation, distribution, ecology, movements, status and taxonomy with official reports on: rare breeding birds, scarce migrants and rare birds in Britain. Payment: token. Founded 1907.

British Chess Magazine

Albany House, Shute End, Wokingham, Berks. RG40 1BJ
email support@britishchessmagazine.co.uk
website www.britishchessmagazine.co.uk
Monthly £8 (print), £5.50 (digital)

Authoritative reports and commentary on the UK and overseas chess world. Payment: by arrangement. Founded 1881.

British Medical Journal

BMJ Publishing Group, BMA House, Tavistock Square, London WC1H 9JR
tel 020-7387 4410

email editor@bmj.com
website www.bmj.com
Editor-in-Chief Dr Kamran Abbasi
Weekly Free to members of BMA; see website for subscription details

Medical and related articles. Payment: by arrangement. Founded 1840.

Broadcast

Media Business Insight, 12 Essex Street, London WC2R 3AA
tel 020-8102 0900
email chris.curtis@broadcastnow.co.uk
website www.broadcastnow.co.uk
Editor-in-Chief Chris Curtis
Weekly From £384 p.a.

For people working or interested in the UK and international broadcast industry. News, features, analysis and opinions across a variety of platforms. Covers the latest developments in programming, commissioning, digital, technology and post-production. Founded 1973 as *Broadcast* monthly magazine.

Building

Assemble Media Group, 64 High St, Wanstead, London E11 2RJ
email chloe.mcculloch@building.co.uk
website www.building.co.uk
Editorial Director Chloë McCulloch
49 p.a. From £210 p.a.

Covers all aspects of the construction industry and built environment, from architecture to property development. Sectors include housing, commercial property, education and health buildings, and infrastructure. Will consider articles on the built environment in the UK and abroad; including news, comment, analysis and photos. Payment: by arrangement. Founded 1843.

Building Design

Assemble Media Group, 64 High St, Wanstead, London E11 2RJ
website www.bdonline.co.uk
Facebook www.facebook.com/BDmagazine
X @BDonline
Editorial Director Chloë McCulloch, *Architectural Editor* Ben Flatman
Annual subscriptions from £115 p.a.

Daily online newspaper and magazine. News and features on all aspects of architecture and urban design. Plus annual *World Architecture (WA) 100* printed magazine, the authoritative survey of world's largest architects. Founded 1970.

Bulletin

The Poetry Book Society, Milburn House, Dean Street, Newcastle Upon Tyne NE1 1L
email enquiries@poetrybooksociety.co.uk
website www.poetrybooks.co.uk
X @PoetryBookSoc
Instagram @poetrybooksociety
4 p.a. £9.99

In-depth reviews, interviews with international poets and extensive listings. Produced by The Poetry Book Society.

The Burlington Magazine

14–16 Duke's Road, London WC1H 9SZ
tel 020-7388 8157
email editorial@burlington.org.uk
website www.burlington.org.uk
Editor Christopher Baker
12 p.a. £25

Academic journal dealing with the history and criticism of art; book and exhibition reviews; publishes free-access online journal on contemporary art, *Burlington Contemporary*, with reviews of exhibitions and books. Submissions must offer new research; potential contributors must have specialist knowledge of the subjects treated. Length: 500–5,000 words. Illustrations: colour images. Payment: by arrangement. Founded 1903.

Buses

Key Publishing Ltd, Foundry Road, Stamford, Lincs. PE9 2PP
tel (01780) 755131
Consultant Editor Alan Millar, Fairways, Charleton, Colinsburgh, Leven KY9 1HG
tel (01333) 340637
email alan.millar@keypublishing.com
website www.keybuses.com
Monthly £5.70

Articles of interest to both road passenger transport operators and bus enthusiasts. Preliminary enquiry essential. Illustrations: digital (first preference), colour transparencies, half-tone, line maps. Payment: by arrangement. Founded 1949.

Business & Accountancy Daily

Croner-i, 240 Blackfriars Road, London SE1 8BU
tel 07779 907915 (senior reporter)
email sara.white@croneri.co.uk
email william.drysdale@croneri.co.uk
website www.accountancydaily.co
X @accountancylive
Editor Sara White, *Reporter* Will Drysdale
Daily online news service; free for registered readers

Articles, opinion and twice-daily newsletters on business, tax, finance, HR, accounting, audit, corporate governance, sustainability and charities, targeted at accountants, tax advisers, finance professionals in practice or industry, and C-suite executives and business owners. All news leads and feature proposals to be submitted by email in the form of a brief synopsis. No commercial advertising or sponsorship. Founded 1889.

Business Traveller

Blackburn House, Blackburn Road,
West Hampstead, London NW6 1RZ
tel 020-7821 2700
email editorial@businesstraveller.com
website www.businesstraveller.com
Editor Tamsin Cocks
10 p.a. £4.99

Articles, features and news on consumer travel aimed at individual frequent international business travellers. Submit ideas with recent clippings/links and a CV. Length: varies. Illustrations: colour for destinations features. Payment: by arrangement. Founded 1976.

Butcher's Dog

Lipman 130, Northumbria University, Newcastle NE1 8ST
email hello@butchersdogmagazine.co.uk
website www.butchersdogmagazine.co.uk
Facebook www.facebook.com/butchersdogpoetry
Instagram @butchersdogpublishing
Managing Editor Dr Jo Clement
2 p.a. £6.99

Bi-annual poetry magazine founded and published in North-East England. Aims to print outstanding poems by diverse writers with distinctive voices from across the UK and ROI, regardless of their career stage. Submissions accepted during open calls digitally via the homepage. Unpublished and original work only, although translations are welcome as long as the author has granted permission in advance. Payment: none, but contributors receive free copies. Tip-jar option. Founded 2012.

Campaign

Haymarket Ltd, Bridge House, 69 London Road, Twickenham TW1 3SP
tel 020-8267 8032
email maisie.mccabe@haymarket.com
website www.campaignlive.co.uk
UK Editor Maisie McCabe
Monthly & online Subscription packages on request

News and articles covering the whole of the mass communications field, particularly advertising in all its forms, marketing and the media. Features should not exceed 2,000 words. News items also welcome. Payment: by arrangement. Founded 1968.

Car

Bauer Media Group, Media House, Lynch Wood, Peterborough Business Park, Peterborough PE2 6EA
tel (01733) 468379
email car@bauermedia.co.uk
website www.carmagazine.co.uk
Editor Ben Miller
Monthly See website for subscription options

Top-grade journalistic features on car driving, car people and cars. Length: 1,000–2,500 words. Illustrations: by arrangement. Payment: by arrangement. Founded 1962.

Car Mechanics

Kelsey Publishing Ltd., The Granary, Downs Court, Yalding Hill, Yalding, Maidstone, Kent ME18 6AL
email cm.ed@kelsey.co.uk
website www.carmechanicsmag.co.uk
Facebook www.facebook.com/Car-Mechanics-123672554385156
Monthly £4.99

Practical articles on maintaining, repairing and uprating modern cars for DIY plus the motor trade. Always interested in finding new talent for this rather specialised market, but study a recent copy before submitting ideas or features. Email outlining feature recommended. Illustrations: line drawings, colour prints, digital images. Supply package of text and pictures. Payment: by arrangement. Founded 1958.

Caravan Magazine

Warners Group Publications Plc, The Maltings, West Street, Bourne, Lincs. PE10 9PH
tel (01778) 391000
email caravan@warnersgroup.co.uk
Facebook www.facebook.com/Caravanmag
Monthly From £39.99 p.a.

Lively articles based on real experience of touring caravanning, particularly welcomed if well illustrated by photos provided by the author or from regional Tourist Boards, attractions etc. Payment: by arrangement. Founded 1933.

The Caterer

Jacobs Media Group, 52 Grosvenor Gardens, London SW1W 0AU
tel 020-7881 4803
email info@caterer.com
website www.thecaterer.com
Editor James Stagg, *Deputy Editor* Caroline Baldwin, *News Editor* Sophie Witts
Weekly From £54.99 p.a. (some content remains free)

Multimedia brand for the UK hospitality industry. In print and online, offers content, job news and a digital platform for hotel, restaurant, food service, and pub and bar operators across the country. Article length: up to 1,500 words. Illustrations: by arrangement. Payment: by arrangement. Founded 1878.

The Catholic Herald

8 Cromwell Place, London SW7 2JN / 9 West 57th Street, New York, NY 10019
tel 020 7082 6529 / 020 3882 9432
email editor@catholicherald.co.uk
website www.catholicherald.co.uk
Facebook www.facebook.com/CatholicHeraldMagazine

X @CatholicHerald
Editor Serenhedd James
Weekly From £49.99 p.a.

Independent magazine covering national and international affairs from a Catholic/Christian viewpoint as well as church news, comment, arts reviews, travel, etc. Length: articles 800–1,200 words. Illustrations: colour. Payment: by arrangement. Founded 1888.

Catholic Pictorial

St Margaret Clitherow Centre, Croxteth Drive, Liverpool L17 1AA
tel 0151 522 1007
email CatholicPic@rcaol.org.uk
website www.catholicpic.co.uk
Editor Harriet Anwyl
Monthly Free

News and photo features (maximum 450 words plus illustration) on Merseyside, regional and national Catholic interest only. Payment: by arrangement. Founded 1961.

Ceramic Review

63 Great Russell Street, London WC1B 3BF
tel 020-7183 5583
email editorial@ceramicreview.com
website www.ceramicreview.com
Facebook www.facebook.com/ceramicreview
X @ceramicreview
Instagram @ceramicreview
YouTube www.youtube.com/@CeramicReviewmagazine
Editor Karen Bray
6 p.a. £9.99, £49.95 p.a. (print), £20.99 p.a. (digital)

International magazine containing critical features, reviews and practical information on all forms of ceramics and clay art and craft. Also looks at the role of ceramics within contemporary culture. Welcomes article proposals – critical, profile, technical, historical or experiential. Feature articles run from 800 to 1,500 words and must include large, hi-res images. Payment: offered at current rates on publication. Founded 1970.

Chat

Future Publishing Ltd, 121–141 Westbourne Terrace, London W2 6JR
email kate.williams@futurenet.com
website www.lifedeathprizes.com
Facebook www.facebook.com/ChatMagazine
Editor Kate Williams
Weekly £1.35

Tabloid for women. Includes readers' letters, tips and true-life features. Payment: by arrangement. Founded 1985.

Church of England Newspaper

Political and Religious Intelligence Ltd, 14 Great College Street, London SW1P 3RX
tel 020-7878 1001
email cen@churchnewspaper.com
website www.churchnewspaper.com
X @churchnewspaper
Editor Andrew Carey
Weekly £75 p.a. (print and digital)

Anglican news and articles relating the Christian faith to everyday life. Evangelical basis; almost exclusively commissioned articles. Prior study of paper desirable. Length: up to 1,000 words. Illustrations: by arrangement. Payment: by arrangement. Founded 1828.

Church Times

3rd Floor, Invicta House, 110 Golden Lane, London EC1Y 0TG
tel 020-7776 1060
email editor@churchtimes.co.uk
website www.churchtimes.co.uk
X @ChurchTimes
Editor Sarah Meyrick
Weekly £3.30

Articles on religious topics are considered. No verse or fiction. Length: up to 1,000 words. Illustrations: news photos, sent promptly. Payment: by arrangement. Negotiated rates for illustrations. Founded 1863.

Classic Boat Magazine

The Chelsea Magazine Company, 111 Buckingham Palace Road, London SW1W 0DT
email cb@chelseamagazines.com
website www.classicboat.co.uk
Facebook www.facebook.com/ClassicBoat
Contact Steffan Meyric-Hughes
Monthly £4.99

Cruising and technical features, restorations, events, new boat reviews, practical guides, maritime history and news. Study of magazine essential: read three to four back issues and send for contributors' guidelines. Length: 500–2,000 words. Illustrations: colour and b&w photos; line drawings of hulls. Payment: £75–£100 per published page. Founded 1987.

Classic Cars

H. Bauer Publishing, Media House, Lynch Wood, Peterborough Business Park, Peterborough PE2 6EA
tel (01733) 468000
email classic.cars@bauermedia.co.uk
website www.classiccarsmagazine.co.uk
Facebook www.facebook.com/classiccarsmagazine
Group Editor Phil Bell
Monthly From £5.99

Specialist articles on older cars and related events. Length: from 150–4,000 words (subject to prior contract). Photography: classic car event photography on spec; feature photography on commission basis. Payment: by negotiation. Founded 1973.

Classical Music

St Jude's Church, Dulwich Road, London SE24 0PB
tel 020-7338 5454
email florence.lockheart@classical-music.uk
website www.classical-music.uk
X @ClassicalMusic_
Editor Florence Lockheart
Quarterly From £55 p.a.

News, opinion, features on the classical music business. All material commissioned. Illustrations: colour photos and line; colour covers. Payment: minimum £150 per 1,000 words. Founded 1976.

Climber

email info@climber.co.uk
website www.climber.co.uk
X @climbermagazine
Instagram @climbermag
6 p.a. £5.99, or from £30 p.a.

Articles on all aspects of rock climbing/mountaineering in Great Britain and abroad, and on related subjects. Study of magazine essential. Length: 1,300–3,000 words. Illustrations: by arrangement. Payment: by arrangement. Founded 1962.

Closer

Bauer Media, The Lantern, 75 Hampstead Road, London NW1 2PL
email closer@closermag.co.uk
website www.closeronline.co.uk
Instagram @closeronline
Weekly £2.80

Women's celebrity magazine with real-life stories, lifestyle, fashion, beauty and TV entertainment and listings sections. Payment: by negotiation. Founded 2005.

Coin News

Token Publishing Ltd, 8 Oaktree Place, Manaton Close, Matford Business Park, Exeter, Devon EX2 8WA
tel (01404) 46972
email info@tokenpublishing.com
website www.tokenpublishing.com
Monthly £4.95

Articles of high standard on coins, tokens, paper money. Send text in digital form. Length: up to 2,000 words. Payment: by arrangement. Founded 1983.

Commercial Motor

1st Floor, Chancery House, St Nicholas Way, Sutton, Surrey SM1 1JB
tel 020-8912 2163
email george.barrow@roadtransport.com
website www.commercialmotor.com
X @Comm_Motor
Contact George Barrow
Weekly From £99.99 p.a.

Technical and road transport articles only. Length: up to 1,500 words. Illustrations: drawings and photos. Payment: by arrangement. Founded 1905.

Community Care

Chancery House, St Nicholas Way, Sutton, Surrey SM1 1J
tel 07917 183203
email communitycare@markallengroup.com
website www.communitycare.co.uk
Editor Mithran Samuel

Online magazine site with articles, features and news covering the Social Services sector. Founded 1974 (as print edition).

Computer Weekly

Informa TechTarget, 240 Blackfriars Road, London SE1 8BF
email cw-news@computerweekly.com
website www.computerweekly.com
Facebook www.facebook.com/computerweekly
X @computerweekly
Bluesky @computerweekly.bsky.social
Editor Bryan Glick
Weekly Free to registered subscribers

Feature articles on IT-related topics for business/industry users. Length: 1,200 words. Illustrations: colour photos. Payment: £250 per 1,000 words. Founded 1966.

Computeractive

Future Publishing Ltd, Quay House, The Ambury, Bath BA1 1UA
Facebook www.facebook.com/computeractive
Group Editor Daniel Booth
Fortnightly £3.20

Computing magazine offering plain-English advice for PCs, tablets, phones and the internet, as well as product reviews and technology news. Founded 1998.

Condé Nast Traveller

The Condé Nast Publications Ltd, The Adelphi, 1–11 John Adam Street, London WC2N 6HT
email cntraveller@condenast.co.uk
website www.cntraveller.com
Senior Features Editor Lydia Bell
Monthly £5.99

Lavishly photographed articles on all aspects of travel, featuring exotic destinations and those close to home. Specialist pieces include food and wine, motoring, health, foreign correspondents, travel news, hotels. Illustrations: colour. Payment: by arrangement. Founded 1997.

Cõnfingō Magazine

249 Burton Road, Didsbury M20 2WA
email tim@confingopublishing.uk
website www.confingopublishing.uk/submissions
Facebook www.facebook.com/confingopublishing
Instagram @confingopublishing
2 p.a. £7

Welcomes submissions of original and previously unpublished poetry, new short fiction and art. Stories should be less than 5,000 words but can be of any style or genre. Up to three poems can be submitted at once. Accepted work is published in a biannual print magazine. Payment: £30 for accepted work.

Cosmopolitan

Hearst UK, House of Hearst, 30 Panton Street, London SW1Y 4AJ
tel 020-7439 5000
email jennifer.savin@hearst.co.uk
website www.cosmopolitan.co.uk
X @CosmopolitanUK
Editor-in-Chief Claire Hodgson, *Features Editor* Jennifer Savin
Monthly £2.99

Commissioned material only. Payment: by arrangement. Illustrated. Founded 1972.

Cotswold Life

Redhill House, 227 London Road, Worcester WR5 2JG
tel 07834 104843
email candia.mckormack@cotswoldlife.co.uk
website www.cotswoldlife.co.uk
Facebook www.facebook.com/cotswoldlife
X @cotswoldlife
Instagram @cotswoldlife
Editor Candia McKormack
Monthly £5.49

Articles on the Cotswolds, including places of interest, high-profile personalities, local events, arts, history, interiors, fashion and food. Founded 1967.

Country Homes and Interiors

Future Publishing Ltd, 121–141 Westbourne Terrace, London W2 6JR
tel 020-3148 5000
email countryhomes@futurenet.com
website www.homesandgardens.com/country
Facebook www.facebook.com/countryhomesandinteriors
Instagram @countryhomesmag
Editor Andréa Childs
Monthly £5.50

Articles on country homes and gardens, interiors, food, lifestyle. Payment: by arrangement. Founded 1986.

Country Life

Future Publishing Ltd, 121–141 Westbourne Terrace, London W2 6JR
tel 0330 390 6102
email rosie.paterson@futurenet.com
website www.countrylife.co.uk
X @Countrylifemag
Editor Mark Hedges, *Deputy Editor* Kate Green, *Managing/Features Editor* Paula Lester, *Digital Content Director and Travel Editor* Rosie Paterson
Weekly £5

Illustrated journal chiefly concerned with British country life, social history, architecture and the fine arts, natural history, agriculture, gardening and sport. Length: c. 1,000 or 1,300 words (articles). Illustrations: mainly colour photos. Payment: according to merit. Print editorial team can be contacted via the email address above. Founded 1897.

Country Living

Hearst UK, House of Hearst, 30 Panton Street, London SW1Y 4AJ
tel 020-7439 5000
email laura.silverman@hearst.co.uk
website www.countryliving.co.uk
X @countrylivinguk
Monthly £5.99

Home-interest magazine with a country lifestyle theme, covering interiors, gardens, crafts, food, wildlife, rural and green issues. Unsolicited material not accepted. Illustrations: by arrangement. Payment: by arrangement. Founded 1985.

Country Walking

Bauer Consumer Media, Media House, Lynch Wood, Peterborough Business Park, Peterborough PE2 6EA
tel (01733) 468205
email sara.mattick@bauermedia.co.uk
website www.walk1000miles.co.uk
Head of Content Nick Hallissey
13 p.a. £5.99

Features. Length: 1,000 words on average. Illustrations: digital images. Payment: by arrangement. Founded 1987.

The Crank

email contact@thecrankmag.com
website www.thecrankmag.com
X @TheCrank11
Editor Humphrey Astley
3 p.a. Online only

Literary magazine 'with a contrarian bent'. Specialises in poetry but also features prose on commission. Submissions open year-round: up to five unpublished poems can be sent via email (author names should not be included). Founded 2020.

Crannóg

email hello@crannogmagazine.com
website https://crannogmagazine.com/submit
Facebook www.facebook.com/crannogmagazine
Instagram @crannogmagazine
Editors Tony O'Dwyer, Ger Burke, Jarlath Fahy
2 p.a. €10

Poetry and fiction from Irish and international contributors, plus interviews with authors on their writing life. Published bi-annually in March and September: submission windows are the month of

November for the March issue and the month of May for the September issue. See website for further information. Contributor's fee paid. Founded 2002.

Critical Quarterly

email cs-journals@wiley.com
website https://onlinelibrary.wiley.com/journal/14678705
Editor Colin MacCabe
Quarterly From £45 p.a.

Fiction, poems, literary criticism. Length: 2,000–5,000 words. Study magazine before submitting MSS. Payment: by arrangement. Founded 1959.

Crow & Cross Keys

email crowcrosskeys@gmail.com
website https://crowcrosskeys.com/submit/
Instagram @crowcrosskeys
Editor-in-Chief Elou Carroll

Online literary magazine looking for poetry, flash fiction and short stories with a speculative edge. Specialises in the gothic, horror, folk and fairy tales. See website for full submission details. New work is preferred but reprints and simultaneous submissions will be considered.

Crystal Magazine

3 Bowness Avenue, Prenton, Birkenhead CH43 0SD
tel 0151 608 9736
email christinecrystal@hotmail.com
website www.christinecrystal.blogspot.com
Editor Christine Carr
6 p.a. £21 p.a. (UK), £32.70 p.a. (overseas); sample £2

Includes stories, poems, articles (including Wordsmithing and Word Wise), letters and news. See website for full submission details and competitions. Current competition: Write a Sonnet. Closes 1 November 2025.

Intended for subscribers (Crystallites) but non-Crystallites may send work and purchase the copy it appears in for £3.50. Founded 2001.

Cumbria and Lakeland Walker

Dalesman Publications Ltd, The Gatehouse, Skipton Castle, Skipton, North Yorkshire BD23 1AL
tel (01756) 701381
email Mick@dalesman.co.uk
website www.cumbriamagazine.co.uk
Instagram @cumbria_lakelandwalker
Editor Mick Smith
Monthly £3.99

Articles of rural interest concerning the people and landscapes of the Lake District and surrounding county of Cumbria. Short length preferred; articles should be of a journalistic nature and no more than 1,200 words. Illustrations: first-class photos, illustrations. Payment: £70 per 1,000 words. Pictures extra. Founded 1947; New series 1951.

Custom Car

Assignment Media, PO Box 8632, Burton on Trent DE14 9PR
tel (01283) 742970
email enquiries@assignment-media.co.uk
Facebook www.facebook.com/CustomCarMagazine
Four-weekly £5.99

Hot rods, customs and drag racing. Length: by arrangement. Payment: by arrangement. Founded 1970.

Cycling Weekly

Future Publishing, Unit 415, Eskdale Rd, Winnersh Triangle, Reading RG41 5RA
tel (01225) 442244
email cycling@futurenet.com
website www.cyclingweekly.com
Facebook www.facebook.com/CyclingWeekly
X @cyclingweekly
Editor Simon Richardson, *News and Features Editor* Vern Pitt
Weekly £4.50

Racing, fitness, features and technical reviews. Illustrations: topical cycling racing photos considered; cartoons. Length: not exceeding 2,000 words. Payment: by arrangement. Founded 1891.

Cyphers

3 Selskar Terrace, Ranelagh, Dublin D06 DW66, Republic of Ireland
tel +353 (0)1 497 8866
website www.cyphers.ie
Editor Eiléan Ní Chuilleanáin
2 p.a. €16 p.a. See website for international rates.

Poems, fiction, translations. Submissions cannot be returned unless accompanied by postage (Irish stamps). Email submissions are not accepted. Payment: €35 to €50 per page. Founded 1975.

Darts World

email admin@dartsworld.com
website www.dartsworld.com
X @Darts_World
Publisher and Managing Editor C.J. Harris-Hulme
Monthly £4

Articles and stories with darts theme. Illustrations: half-tone, cartoons. Payment: negotiable per 1,000 words; illustrations by arrangement. Founded 1972.

The Dawntreader

24 Forest Houses, Cookworthy Moor, Halwill, Beaworthy, Devon EX21 5UU
email dawnidp@indigodreams.co.uk
website www.indigodreamspublishing.com
X @IndigoDreamsPub
Editor Dawn Bauling
Quarterly £5, £19 p.a.

Poetry, short stories and articles up to 1,000 words encompassing themes of the mystic, myth, legend, landscape, nature and love. New writers welcome. Lively feedback pages. Payment: none. Email submission preferred. Founded 2007.

Decanter

Future Publishing Ltd, 121–141 Westbourne Terrace, London W2 6JR
email editor@decanter.com
website www.decanter.com
Magazine Editor Amy Wislocki, *Editor, Decanter.com* Lisa Riley, *Editor, Decanter Premium* Georgie Hindle
Monthly £6.99

Articles and features on wines, wine travel and food-related topics. Welcomes ideas for articles and features. Length: 1,000–1,800 words. Illustrations: colour. Payment: £300 per 1,000 words. Founded 1975.

Delayed Gratification

email hello@slow-journalism.com
website www.slow-journalism.com/faqs
Facebook www.facebook.com/delayedgratification
Bluesky @dgquarterly.bsky.social
Instagram @dgquarterly
Co-editors Rob Orchard, Marcus Webb
4 p.a. £12

Long-form journalism, photo features and infographics. Aims to offer a reflective, informed and considered look over the previous quarter, as part of its 'slow journalism' ethos. Each cover is illustrated by a piece of original artwork: previous cover artists include Ai Weiwei and Grayson Perry. Authors and illustrators can submit pitches via the email address above. Founded 2011.

delicious.

10 Kennington Park Place, London SE11 4AS
email info@deliciousmagazine.co.uk
website www.deliciousmagazine.co.uk
Facebook www.facebook.com/deliciousmagazineuk/
X @deliciousmag
Instagram @deliciousmag
Editorial Director Laura Rowe
Monthly £5.99

Articles on food, recipes, skills, trends, chefs, sustainability, food waste, producers, food issues, humour, wine and ingredients. Founded 2003.

Descent: The magazine of underground exploration

Stalactite Publishing, PO Box 297, Kendal LA9 9GQ
email editor@descentmagazine.co.uk
website www.descentmagazine.co.uk
Facebook www.facebook.com/DescentCavingMagazine
Instagram @descentcavingmagazine
Editor Chris Scaife
Bi-monthly £8.45

Articles, features and news on all aspects of cave and mine sport exploration, including history. Submissions must match magazine style. Length: up to 2,500 words (articles/features), up to 1,000 words (news). Illustrations: colour. Payment: on consideration of material based on area filled. Founded 1969.

Devon Life

email catherine.courtenay@devonlife.co.uk
website www.devonlife.co.uk
Editor Catherine Courtenay
12 p.a. £5.49

Articles on all aspects of Devon, including inspiring people, places, walks, local events, arts, history and food. Unsolicited ideas welcome: 'ideal' features of 1,200 words, with a selection of eight to ten good-quality, high-resolution images. Founded 1963.

The Dickensian

The Dickens Fellowship,
The Charles Dickens Museum, 48 Doughty Street, London WC1N 2LX
email DickensianEditor@dickensfellowship.org
email C.waters@kent.ac.uk
website www.dickensfellowship.org/dickensian
Editor Professor Emerita Catherine Waters
3 p.a. From £14 p.a. (online access), £19 p.a. (UK individuals, print and online), £29 p.a. (UK institutions); £21 p.a. (overseas individuals, print and online), £32 p.a. (overseas institutions); reduced rate for Dickens Fellowship members

Welcomes articles (max. 5,000 words) on all aspects of Dickens's life, works and character. Send contributions by email attachment to the Editor. See website for house-style conventions and specifications for any photographic material. Payment: none. Founded 1905.

Digital Camera

Future Publishing Ltd, Quay House, The Ambury, Bath BA1 1UA
tel (01225) 442244
email digitalcamera@futurenet.com
website www.digitalcameraworld.com/uk
Instagram @digitalcameramag
Editor Niall Hampton
Monthly £5.99

Digital photography magazine containing practical guides, inspiring images, techniques and tips for capturing great photos, plus how to perfect them on a computer. Also includes reviews of the latest cameras, accessories and image-editing software.

DIVA

email editorial@diva-magazine.com
website www.diva-magazine.com
Facebook www.facebook.com/divamagazine
X @divamagazine

Instagram @divamagazine
Editor-in-Chief Roxy Bourdillon
Monthly £4.95

Features on LGBTQ+ women and non-binary people's culture, community, opinion and lifestyle. Length: 400–2,000 words. Illustrations: colour. Payment: by arrangement. Founded 1994.

Dogs Today

The Old Print House, 62 High Street, Chobham, Surrey GU24 8AA
tel (01276) 402599
email enquiries@dogstodaymagazine.co.uk
website www.dogstodaymagazine.co.uk
Facebook www.facebook.com/DogsTodayMagazine
Instagram @officialdogstoday
Monthly £5.99

Study of magazine essential before submitting ideas. Interested in human interest dog stories, celebrity interviews, holiday features and anything unusual – all must be entertaining and informative and accompanied by illustrations. Length: 800–1,200 words. Illustrations: colour, preferably digital. Payment: by arrangement. Founded 1990.

Drapers

4th Floor, Harmsworth House, 15 Bouverie Street, London EC4Y 8DP
tel 020-3033 2770
email Jill.geoghegan@emap.com
website www.drapersonline.com
Facebook www.facebook.com/Drapersonline
Instagram @drapersonline
Editor Jill Geoghan
From £292 p.a.

Online only. Business editorial aimed at fashion retailers, large and small, and all who supply them. Illustrations: colour and b&w photos. Payment: by negotiation. Founded 1887.

Dream Catcher

Stairwell Books, 161 Lowther Street, York YO31 7LZ
tel (01904) 733767
email hannah@stairwellbooks.com
website www.dreamcatchermagazine.co.uk/submissions
Facebook www.facebook.com/DreamCatcherLiteraryArtsMag
X @literaryartsmag
Editor Hannah Stone
2 p.a. £10

International literary and arts journal. Welcomes poetry, short stories (optimum length of 2,000 words), artwork, interviews and reviews; please see website for full submissions information. Each issue features a selected artist whose work is reproduced on the cover and inside. Promotes reading and workshops across the UK. Founded 1996 by Paul Sutherland.

The Dublin Review

PO Box 7948, Dublin 1, Republic of Ireland
tel +353 (0)1 678 8627
email enquiry@thedublinreview.com
website https://thedublinreview.com/submissions/
Editor Brendan Barrington
Quarterly €11.75 (UK), €9.50 (IRE)

Essays, memoir, reportage and fiction. Payment: by arrangement. Founded 2000.

Early Music

Faculty of Music, University of Cambridge, 11 West Road, Cambridge CB3 9DP
email earlymusic@oxfordjournals.org
website https://em.oxfordjournals.org
X @EarlyMus
Editors Alan Howard, Elizabeth Eva Leach, Stephen Rose
Quarterly £108 p.a. (individual, print)

Lively, informative and scholarly articles on aspects of medieval, renaissance, baroque and classical music. Payment: by arrangement. Illustrations: line, half-tone, colour. Founded 1973.

Economica

STICERD, London School of Economics, Houghton Street, London WC2A 2AE
tel 020-7955 7855
website https://onlinelibrary.wiley.com/journal/14680335
Editors Timothy Besley, Wouter denHaan, Maitreesh Ghatak, Rachel Ngai, Henry Overman and Catherine Thomas
Quarterly From £66 p.a. (other subscription rates on application)

Learned journal covering the fields of economics, economic history and statistics. Payment: none. Founded 1921; New series 1934.

The Economist

1–11 John Adam Street, London WC2N 6HT
tel 020-7576 8000
website www.economist.com
Facebook www.facebook.com/TheEconomist
X @TheEconomist
Editor-in-Chief Zanny Minton Beddoes
Weekly £9.99

Staff-written articles. Founded 1843.

Educate

National Education Union, Hamilton House, Mabledon Place, London WC1H 9BD
tel 020-7380 4708
email educate@neu.org.uk
website https://neu.org.uk/latest/union-journals/educate-magazine
Editor Max Watson
6 p.a. Free to NEU members

Articles, features and news of interest to all those involved in the education sector. Email outline in the first instance. Length: 500 words (single page), 1,000 (double page). Payment: NUJ rates to NUJ members. Founded 2019.

Electrical Review

SJP Business Media Ltd, 2nd Floor,
123 Cannon Street, London EC4N 5AU
tel 020-7062 2526
email jordano@sjpbusinessmedia.com
website www.electricalreview.co.uk
Managing Editor Jordan O'Brien
Monthly Free (restricted qualification; see website for details); subscriptions also available

Technical and business articles on electrical and control engineering; outside contributions considered. Good-quality imagery an advantage. Electrical news welcomed. Payment: according to merit. Founded 1872.

ELLE (UK)

Hearst UK, House of Hearst, 30 Panton Street,
London SW1Y 4AJ
tel 020-7150 7000
email Hannah.nathanson@elleuk.com
website www.elleuk.com
Facebook www.facebook.com/Ellemagazine
Instagram @elleuk
Editor-in-Chief Kenya Hunt, *Features Director* Hannah Nathanson
Monthly £7.99

Commissioned material only. Illustrations: colour. Payment: by arrangement. Founded 1985.

Embroidery magazine

email embroideryeditorial@warnersgroup.co.uk
website https://embroiderymagazine.co.uk/writing-for-embroidery/
Editor Claire Waring
6 p.a. £6.99

News and illustrated features on all aspects of embroidery and contemporary textiles in art, design, craft, illustration, fashion, interiors and world textiles. Features on internationally renowned artists, makers and designers working with modern textiles, stitch and embroidery. News covering exhibitions, books and products, plus event listings, book and exhibition reviews and opportunities. Contributors should familiarise themselves with the publication before contacting the editor with ideas. Max length: features, 1,000 words; reviews, 500 words. See website for forthcoming deadlines. Published every two months from January each year. Founded 1932.

Empire

Bauer Media Group, The Lantern,
75 Hampstead Road, London NW1 2PL
website www.empireonline.com
Facebook www.facebook.com/empiremagazine
Instagram @empiremagazine
Editor Nick de Semlyen
13 p.a. £7.50

Guide to film on all its platforms: articles, features, news. Length: various. Illustrations: colour and b&w photos. Payment: approx. £300 per 1,000 words; varies for illustrations. Founded 1989.

Energy Engineering

Media Culture Ltd, Pure Offices, Plato Close,
Leamington Spa, Warks. CV34 6WE
tel (01926) 671338
email steve@energyengineering.co.uk
website https://energyengineering.co.uk
Managing Editor Steve Welch
6 p.a. From £65 p.a.

Features and news for those engaged in technology, manufacturing and management. Contributions considered on all aspects of engineering. Illustrations: colour. Founded 1866.

The Engineer

Mark Allen Group, St Jude's Church, Dulwich Road,
London SE24 0PB
tel 020-7970 4437
email jon.excell@markallengroup.com
website www.theengineer.co.uk
X @TheEngineerUK
Editor Jon Excell
Monthly Price on application (free in some instances)

Features and news on innovation and technology, including profiles, analysis. Length: up to 800 words (news), 1,000 words (features). Illustrations: by arrangement. Payment: by negotiation.
Founded 1856.

Engineering in Miniature

Warners Group Publications Plc, The Maltings,
West Street, Bourne, Lincs. PE10 9PH
tel (01778) 391000
website www.world-of-railways.co.uk
Publisher (Railways) Steve Cole
Monthly From £3.99

Articles on all aspects of model engineering; technical articles preferred. Payment: by arrangement, depending on pages published. Founded 1979.

The English Garden

111 Buckingham Palace Road, London SW1W 0D
tel 020-7349 3700
email theenglishgarden@chelseamagazines.com
website www.theenglishgarden.co.uk
Facebook www.facebook.com/theenglishgardenmagazine
X @TEGmagazine
Editor Clare Foggett
13 p.a. £5.99

Features on gardens in the UK and Ireland, plants, practical gardening advice and garden design. Length:

800–1,200 words. Illustrations: colour photos and botanical artwork. Payment: by arrangement. Founded 1997.

Erotic Review

email info@ermagazine.com
website www.ermagazine.com
X @EroticReviewMag
Instagram @eroticreview
Editor Lucy Roeber, *Deputy Editor* Saskia Vogel; *Design* Studio Frith; Guest Art Editor in each issue
2 p.a., £20

Biannual literary and art journal in print. Publishes longer, considered pieces that explore desire: essays, fiction, long reviews, poetry and art collections. Not accepting submissions at present, but updates can be found online and in the free monthly newsletter. Starting a literary salon during 2025; plans are also in place for online submissions and an annual literary prize. Founded 1995; relaunched 2024.

Esquire

Hearst UK, House of Hearst, 30 Panton Street, London SW1Y 4AJ
tel 020-7439 5601
website www.esquire.com/uk
X @EsquireUK
Instagram @ukesquire
4 p.a. £7

Quality men's general interest magazine – articles, features, short stories. Length: various. Illustrations: colour and b&w photos, line. Payment: by arrangement. Founded 1991.

The Face

email hello@theface.com
website https://theface.com
Instagram @thefacemagazine
Editor-in-Chief Matthew Whitehouse
Quarterly £9.95

Style, music, culture and society. Founded 1980; relaunched 2019.

Family Tree

Warners Group Publications Plc, The Maltings, West Street, Bourne, Lincs. PE10 9PH
tel (01778) 395050
email editorial@family-tree.co.uk
website www.family-tree.co.uk
Facebook www.facebook.com/familytreemaguk
X @familytreemaguk
Editor Helen Tovey
Monthly £5.99

Features on family history, genealogy and related topics. Payment: by arrangement. Founded 1984.

Farmers Weekly

Quadrant House, The Quadrant, Sutton, Surrey SM2 5AS
tel 020-8057 8500
email farmersweekly@markallengroup.com
website www.fwi.co.uk
Editor Andrew Meredith
Weekly From £43 quarterly

Commissions freelance contributors to write articles; willing to consider pitches. Founded 1934.

Fictive Dream

email fictivedream@gmail.com
website https://fictivedream.com
Bluesky @fictivedream.bsky.social
Instagram @fictive.dream
Editor Laura Black

Online magazine publishing short fiction across three categories: microfiction (up to 400 words); flash fiction (up to 1,000 words), and short stories (no more than 2,500 words). Open for submissions all year round.

The Field

Future Publishing Ltd, 121–141 Westbourne Terrace, Paddington, London W2 6JR
tel 0330 390 6609
email field.secretary@futurenet.com
website www.thefield.co.uk
Facebook www.facebook.com/TheFieldMagazine
X @TheFieldmag
Instagram @thefieldmagazine
Editor Alexandra Henton
Monthly £6.99

Specific, topical and informed features on the British countryside and country pursuits, including natural history, fieldsports, gardening, rural conservation, food and drink and country lifestyle. Overseas subjects considered but opportunities for such articles are limited. No fiction. Articles of 800–2,000 words by outside contributors considered; also topical 'shorts' of 200–300 words on all countryside matters. Illustrations: commissioned. Also accepts colour photos of a high standard. Payment: by arrangement. Founded 1853.

Firewords

email info@firewords.co.uk
website https://firewords.co.uk
Instagram @firewordsmag
Editors Dan Burgess, Jen Scott
2 p.a. £9 inc. delivery

Short stories, poetry and illustration: issues are (loosely) themed, so check website for forthcoming themes and specifications. Original work preferred, but previously published pieces may be considered: prospective authors should indicate if their material has appeared elsewhere. Payment: none. Founded 2014.

Fishing News

Kelsey Publishing Ltd, The Granary, Downs Court, Yalding Hill, Yalding, Maidstone, Kent ME18 6AL

tel (01959) 543747
email fishingnews.ed@kelsey.co.uk
website www.fishingnews.co.uk
X @YourFishingNews
Editor Andy Read
Weekly From £36.50 per quarter

News and features on all aspects of the commercial fishing industry. Length: up to 1,000 words (features), up to 500 words (news). Illustrations: by arrangement. Payment: negotiable. Founded 1913.

Flash: The International Short-Short Story Magazine

International Flash Fiction Association (IFFA), Division of Communication, Screen and Performance, School for the Creative Industries, University of Chester, Parkgate Road, Chester CH1 4BJ
email flash.magazine@chester.ac.uk
website www1.chester.ac.uk/flash-magazine
Facebook www.facebook.com/groups/28291339826/
Editors Dr Peter Blair, Dr Ashley Chantler
Bi-annual Online open access. Back issues available to purchase in hard copy.

Quality stories of up to 360 words (title included); see website for submission guidelines. Suggestions for articles of up to 360 words considered.
Founded 2008.

Flora

124 City Road, London EC1V 2NX
tel 020-7235 6235
email info@flora-magazine.com
website https://flora-magazine.com
Bluesky @floramagazineuk
Editor Nina Tucknott
Bi-monthly £6.95

Flower arranging and floristry; also features flower-related crafts and flower arrangers' gardens. Unsolicited enquiries and suggestions welcome on any of these subjects. Send brief synopsis together with sample illustrations. Payment: by arrangement. Founded 1974.

Fly Fishing & Fly Tying

Mortons Media Group, Media Centre, Mortons Way, Horncastle, Lincs, LN9 6JR
tel (01507) 529529
email editor@mortons.co.uk
website www.flyfishing-and-flytying.co.uk
Facebook www.facebook.com/Fly-Fishing-Fly-Tying-Magazine
X @FFFTmag
Instagram @flyfishingandflytyingmagazine
Editor Mark Bowler
12 p.a. £4.99

Fly-fishing and fly-tying articles, fishery features, limited short stories, fishing travel. Length: by arrangement. Illustrations: colour photos. Payment: by arrangement. Founded 1990.

Folding Rock

email info@foldingrock.com
website https://foldingrock.com/submit-your-work/
Facebook www.facebook.com/FoldingRockMag
Instagram @foldingrockmag
Co-founder and Editorial Director (fiction) Rob Harries, *Co-founder and Editorial Director (non-fiction)* Kathryn Tann
3 p.a. £13; subscriptions also available from £24 p.a.

Accepts original fiction, creative non-fiction, literary criticism and art/photography to fit a designated theme. Submissions are rolling and accepted via an online submissions form on the website (submission guidelines and deadlines for each theme are also available on the website). Payment: flat fee of £360 for all accepted pieces. Print and digital editions available. Founded 2024.

Fortean Times

Diamond Publishing Ltd, 4th Floor, Harmsworth House, 13–15 Bouverie Street, London EC4Y 8DP
email drsutton@forteantimes.com
website www.forteantimes.com
Facebook www.facebook.com/ForteanTimes
X @forteantimes
Editor David Sutton
13 p.a. £4.99

Journal of strange phenomena, experiences, related subjects and philosophies. Includes articles, features, news, reviews. Length: 500–5,000 words; longer by arrangement. Illustrations: by arrangement. Payment: by negotiation. Founded 1973.

Forty20

tel 0113 225 9797
email editorial@forty-20.com
Facebook www.facebook.com/forty20magazine
X @forty20magazine
Monthly £4.25

Independent illustrated rugby league magazine, available nationally. Features interviews and articles on rugby league both in the UK and overseas and at a variety of levels. Articles and images welcome via email.

FourFourTwo

Future Publishing Ltd, 121–141 Westbourne Terrace, London W2 6JR
email fourfourtwo@futurenet.com
website www.fourfourtwo.com
Editor James Andrew
13 p.a. £5.99

Football interviews, in-depth features, issues pieces, odd and witty material. Length: 2,000–3,000 (features), 100–1,500 words (Up Front pieces).

Illustrations: colour transparencies and artwork, b&w prints. Payment: £200 per 1,000 words. Founded 1994.

fourteen poems

email hello@14poems.com
website www.fourteenpoems.com
X @fourteenpoems
Instagram @14poems
3 p.a. £7.50, £25 p.a. (4-issue subscription)

London-based poetry journal, featuring 14 LGBTQ+ poets per issue. Rolling submissions window but check website for any forthcoming deadlines. Up to five poems may be submitted at any one time in a single Word document or pdf. Payment: £25 per poem published.

The Friend

173 Euston Road, London NW1 2BJ
tel 020-7663 1010
email editorial@thefriend.org
website www.thefriend.org
Editor Simon Joseph Jones
Weekly Subscription available

Material of interest to Quakers and like-minded people; spiritual, political, social, economic, environmental or cultural, considered from outside contributors. Length: up to 1,200 words. Illustrations: b&w or colour photographs and line drawings by email preferred. Payment: not usually but will negotiate a small fee with professional writers. Founded 1843.

Frieze

1 Surrey Street, London WC2R 2ND
tel 020-3372 6111
website www.frieze.com
Senior Editor Terence Trouillot
8 p.a. £9.95

European contemporary art and culture including essays, reviews, columns and listings. Frieze Art Fair is held every October in Regent's Park, London, featuring over 150 of the most exciting contemporary art galleries in the world. Founded 1991.

The Frogmore Papers

21 Mildmay Road, Lewes, East Sussex BN7 1PJ
email frogmorepress@gmail.com
website www.frogmorepress.co.uk/submission-guidelines/
Editor Jeremy Page
2 p.a. £5

Long-established poetry and prose magazine. Two submission windows per year: 1–31 October for the March issue and 1–30 April for the September issue. Submissions from UK-based writers should be made by post, but overseas writers may contribute via email. Send no more than four to six poems at one time; short stories should be no more than 2,000 words. Familiarity with the magazine advised; also see website for further guidance. Founded 1983.

FT Adviser

Bracken House, 1 Friday Street, London EC4M 9BT
tel 020-7775 3000
email simoney.kyriakou@ft.com
website www.ftadviser.com
Editor Simoney Kyriakou
Online Free (after registering)

Topical personal finance news and features. Length: variable. Payment: by arrangement. Founded 1987.

The Furrow

St Patrick's College, Maynooth,
Co. Kildare W23 TW77, Republic of Ireland
tel +353 (0)1 708 3741
email editor.furrow@spcm.ie
website www.thefurrow.ie
Editor Rev. Pádraig Corkery
Monthly €6

Religious, pastoral, theological and social articles. Length: up to 3,500 words. Articles are available through JSTOR and from the Secretary at The Furrow office. Illustrations: line, half-tone. Payment: average €20 per page (450 words). Founded 1950.

Garden Answers

Bauer Media Group, Media House, Lynch Wood, Peterborough Business Park, Peterborough PE2 6EA
tel (01733) 468000
email gardenanswers@bauermedia.co.uk
website www.gardenanswersmagazine.co.uk
X @GardenAnswers
Monthly £5.50

Some commissioned features and articles on all aspects of gardening. Reader garden photo and interview packages considered. Study of magazine essential. Approach by email with examples of published work. Length: approx. 750 words. Illustrations: digital images and artwork. Payment: by negotiation. Founded 1982.

Garden News

Bauer Media Group, Media House, Lynch Wood, Peterborough Business Park, Peterborough PE2 6EA
tel (01733) 468000
email gn.letters@bauermedia.co.uk
website www.gardennewsmagazine.co.uk
Facebook www.facebook.com/GardenNewsOfficial
Instagram @gardennewsmagazine
Weekly £2.99

Up-to-date information on everything to do with plants, growing and gardening. Payment: by negotiation. Founded 1958.

Gay Times

Room 2.03, 133 Whitechapel High Street,
London E1 7QA

tel 020-7424 7400
email editorial@gaytimes.co.uk
website www.gaytimes.co.uk
Instagram @gaytimesmag
Editorial Director Megan Wallace
Monthly

Digital magazine featuring diverse LGBTQ+ talent. Includes features and interviews on celebrity, gay lifestyle, health, parenting, music, film, technology, current affairs, opinion, culture, art, style and grooming. Length: up to 2,000 words. Payment: by arrangement. Founded 1984.

Geographical

Unit 3, Boleyn Business Suite,
Hever Castle Golf Club, Hever Road, Edenbridge,
Kent TN8 7NP
email graeme@geographical.co.uk
website www.geographical.co.uk
Facebook www.facebook.com/GeographicalMagazine
Instagram @geographical_magazine
Editor Graeme Gourlay
Monthly From £39.99

Magazine of the Royal Geographical Society (with the Institute of British Geographers). Covers culture, wildlife, environment, science and travel. Illustrations: top-quality hi-res digital files, vintage material. Payment: by negotiation. Founded 1935.

The Ghastling

email theghastlingpress@gmail.com
website https://theghastling.com/submit
Instagram @theghastling
Editor and Founder Rebecca Parfitt
Biannual £12 (inc. p&p)

Short-story magazine dedicated to the macabre; describes itself 'as a modern-day Penny Dreadful'. See social media for forthcoming submissions windows. Simultaneous submissions not accepted. Artwork can be emailed to the editor, but both artists and authors are recommended to familiarise themselves with the magazine's content before contacting. Founded 2014.

Gibbons Stamp Monthly

Gibbons Stamp Monthly Stanley Gibbons Baldwins Ltd, Suite 4, Endeavour House,
Crow Arch Lane Ringwood BH24 1HP
tel (01425) 481042
email dshepherd@stanleygibbons.co.uk
website www.stanleygibbons.com/publishing/gibbons-stamp-monthly
X @GSM_Magazine
Editor Dean Shepherd
Monthly £5.35

Articles on philatelic topics. Contact the Editor first. Length: 500–2,500 words. Illustrations: photos, line, stamps or covers. Payment: by arrangement. Founded 1890.

Glamour

The Condé Nast Publications Ltd, The Adelphi,
1–11 John Adam Street, London WC2N 6HT
email glamoureditorialmagazine@condenast.co.uk
website www.glamourmagazine.co.uk
Global Editorial Director Samantha Barry
Principally online but occasional print editions from £2

Fashion, beauty, real-life features and celebrity news aimed at women aged 18–34. Feature ideas welcome; approach with brief outline. Length: 500–800 words. Payment: by arrangement. Founded 2001.

Golf Monthly

Future Publishing Ltd, Unit 415, Winnersh Triangle,
Eskdale Road, Winnersh RG41 5TU
tel (01225) 442244
email golfmonthly@futurenet.com
website www.golfmonthly.com
Editor Neil Tappin, *Features Editor* Nick Bonfield
Monthly From £5.50

Original articles on golf considered (not reports), golf clinics, handy hints. See website for information on pitch submissions. Illustrations: by arrangement. Payment: by arrangement. Founded 1911.

Good Food

Immediate Media Co. Ltd, Vineyard House,
44 Brook Green, London W6 7BT
email enquiries@bbcgoodfoodmagazine.com
website www.bbcgoodfood.com
X @bbcgoodfood
Group Magazines Editor Keith Kendrick
Monthly £6.75

Inspiration for everyday, weekend and seasonal cooking for cooks of all levels. Features recipes from many BBC TV chefs as well as other leading food writers, along with an extensive range of hints, tips and features. Founded 1989.

Good Housekeeping

Hearst UK, House of Hearst, 30 Panton Street,
London SW1Y 4AJ
email goodh.mail@hearst.co.uk
website www.goodhousekeeping.com/uk
Editor-in-Chief Jane Bruton, *Features Editor* Bethan Rose Jenkins
Monthly £6.99

Articles on topics of interest to women. No unsolicited features or stories accepted. Homes, fashion, beauty and food covered by staff writers. Illustrations: commissioned. Payment: magazine standards. Founded 1922.

GQ

The Condé Nast Publications Ltd, The Adelphi,
1–11 John Adam Street, London WC2N 6HT
tel 020-7851 1800
website www.gq-magazine.co.uk
X @BritishGQ

Instagram @britishgq
Deputy Global Editorial Director Adam Baidawi, *Features Editor* Oliver Franklin-Wallis, *Design Director* Kevin Fay, *Editorial Associate* Rebecca Dolan
Monthly £4.99

Style, fashion and general interest magazine for men. Illustrations: b&w and colour photos, line drawings, cartoons. Payment: by arrangement. Founded 1988.

Granta

12 Addison Avenue, London W11 4QR
tel 020-7605 1360
email editorial@granta.com
website www.granta.com, https://granta.submittable.com/submit
X @GrantaMag
Bluesky @grantamag.bsky.social
Editor Thomas Meaney
Quarterly £14.99

Original literary fiction, poetry, non-fiction, memoir, reportage and photography. Study magazine before submitting work. No academic essays or reviews. Note that submissions are accepted only via online submissions system (see above). Length: determined by content. Illustrations: photos and original artwork. Payment: by arrangement. Founded 1889; reconceived 1979.

Grazia

Bauer Media, The Lantern, 75 Hampstead Road, London NW1 2PL
email anna.silverman@graziamagazine.co.uk
website https://graziadaily.co.uk
X @graziauk
Editor-in-Chief Hattie Brett, *Features Director* Anna Silverman
Fortnightly £3.75

Women's magazine with the latest trends, gossip, fashion and news in bite-size pieces.

The Great Outdoors Magazine

Kelsey Publishing Ltd, The Granary, Downs Court, Yalding Hill, Yalding, Maidstone, Kent ME18 6AL
tel (01959) 541444
email david.lintern@kelsey.co.uk
website www.thegreatoutdoorsmag.com/magazine/about/
Commissioning Editor David Lintern
13 p.a. £5.25

Articles on walking or lightweight camping in specific areas, mainly in the UK, preferably illustrated with photography. See website for further information and contact details for digital and print features. Payment: by arrangement. Founded 1978.

The Grocer

William Reed Publishing Ltd, Broadfield Park, Crawley, West Sussex RH11 9RT
tel (01293) 613400
website www.thegrocer.co.uk
Facebook www.facebook.com/TheGrocer
X @TheGrocer
Editor-in-Chief Adam Leyland
Weekly From £335 p.a.

Trade journal: articles, news or illustrations of general interest to the grocery and provision trades. Payment: by arrangement. Founded 1861.

Grow Your Own

Artichoke Media Ltd, Jubilee House, 92 Lincoln Road, Peterborough, Cambs PE1 2SN
email laura.hillier@artichokehq.com
website www.growfruitandveg.co.uk
Editor Laura Hillier
Monthly £6.99

Aimed at kitchen gardeners of all levels of expertise. Will consider unsolicited material. Welcomes ideas for articles and features. Length: 1,000 words (articles), 1,500 words (features), 200 words (news). Illustrations: by arrangement. Payment: varies.

Guitarist

Future Publishing Ltd, Quay House, The Ambury, Bath BA1 1UA
tel (01225) 442244
website www.musicradar.com/guitarist
Editor Jamie Dickson
13 p.a. £7.49

Aims to improve readers' knowledge of the guitar, help them make the right buying choices and assist them in becoming a better player. Ideas for articles welcome. Founded 1984.

Gutter

23 Esmond Street, Glasgow G3 8SN
email contactguttermagazine@gmail.com
website www.guttermag.co.uk
X @Gutter_Magazine
Instagram @Gutter_Magazine
Managing Editor Malachy Tallack, *Co-Editors* Colin Begg, Henry Bell. *Editors-at-Large* Katy Hastie, Ryan Vance, Cal Bannerman, April Hill, *Prose Reviews Editor* Katie Goh, *Poetry Reviews Editor* Sean Wai Keung
2 p.a. £10 Subscriptions from £10; see website for options

New Scottish and international poetry, prose and reviews. Invites submissions of up to 2,500 words of fiction or non-fiction and up to 100 lines of poetry (submissions windows open in spring and autumn). Seeks provocative work that challenges, reimagines or undermines the individual or collective status quo. Mentorship and workshop programmes also available: see website for more information. Founded 2009.

H&E naturist

Hawk Editorial Ltd, PO Box 545, Hull HU9 9JF
tel (01482) 342000
email editor@henaturist.net
website www.henaturist.net
Editor Paul Rouse
Monthly £5.95

Articles on naturist travel, clubs, beaches and naturist lifestyle experiences from the UK and beyond. Length: 800–1,200 words. Illustrations: digital images featuring naturists in natural settings; also photos, letters and features with naturist theme. Payment: by negotiation but guidelines for contributors and basic payment rates available on request. Founded 1902 as *Vim*.

Harper's Bazaar

Hearst UK, House of Hearst, 30 Panton Street, London SW1Y 4AJ
tel 020-7439 5000
website www.harpersbazaar.co.uk
Instagram @bazaaruk
Editor-in-Chief Lydia Slater, *Features and Special Projects Director* Helena Lee
Monthly £5.25

Features, fashion, beauty, art, theatre, films, travel, interior decoration – some commissioned. Founded 1867.

Heat

Bauer Media, The Lantern, 75 Hampstead Road, London NW1 2PL
email heatEd@heatmag.com
website www.heatworld.com
Weekly £2.90

Features and news on entertainment and popular media. Founded 1999.

hedgerow: a journal of small poems

email hedgerowsubmission@gmail.com
website https://hedgerowhaiku.com
Editor Caroline Skanne
Quarterly £12 inc. postage (UK and US), £15 inc. postage (Europe and Canada), £18 (RoW)

Short-poetry journal dedicated to publishing an eclectic mix of new and established voices across the spectrum of the short poem, with particular attention to the constantly evolving forms of English-language haiku and related works. Includes original poems, photographs and artwork. Four submission windows (see website for up-to-date details).

Two sections are available to read for free online: hedgerow: young voices (haiku and related short poems by poets under the age of 16); hedgerow: vines (collaborative poems, sequences, linked forms & articles). Founded 2014.

Hello!

230 Blackfriars Road, London SE1 8NW
tel 020-7667 8700
website www.hellomagazine.com/our-team
X @hellomag
Editor Chief Content Officer Sophie Vokes-Dudgeon
Weekly £3.99

News-based features – showbusiness, celebrity, royalty; exclusive interviews. Illustrated. Payment: by arrangement. See website for full editor list. Founded 1988.

Here Comes Everyone

email raef@hcemagazine.com
website www.hcemagazine.com
Facebook www.facebook.com/HCEmagazine
X @HereComesEvery1
Editor Raef Boylan
3 p.a. £5

Original prose, poetry, non-fiction and art written to fit a theme. Submissions are accepted via online submissions form on the website (see above; submissions guidelines available here too). Current and past issues can be purchased in print and digital forms, and an archive of older issues can also be previewed online. Founded 2012.

Hi-Fi News

AVTech Media Ltd, Enterprise House, Enterprise Way, Edenbridge, Kent TN8 6HF
tel 0844 848 8822
email paul.miller@hifinews.com
website www.hifinews.com
Editor Paul Miller
Monthly £5.99

Articles on all aspects of high-quality sound recording and reproduction; also extensive record review section and supporting musical feature articles. Audio matter is essentially technical, but should be presented in a manner suitable for music lovers interested in the nature of sound. Length: 2,000–3,000 words. Illustrations: by arrangement. Payment: by arrangement. Founded 1956.

High Life

Cedar Communications Ltd, 9th Floor, Bankside 3, 90–100 Southwark Street, London SE1 0SW
tel 020-7550 8000
email high.life@cedarcom.co.uk
website https://bahighlife.com/
Bi-monthly

Online consumer magazine for British Airways passengers. Articles on entertainment, travel, fashion, business, sport and lifestyle. Founded 1973.

Hinterland

The Enterprise Centre, University of East Anglia, Norwich NR4 7TJ
email hello@hinterlandnonfiction.com
website www.hinterlandnonfiction.com/submissions
Facebook www.facebook.com/hinterlandnonfiction
Bluesky @hinterlandnf.bsky.social

Instagram @hinterlandnonfiction
Editors Freya Dean, Andrew Kenrick, Yin F Lim,
Designer Tom Hutchings
3 p.a. £12

Print and digital magazine of creative non-fiction. Showcases the best new writing from around the world across fields including memoir, essay, travel and food writing, reportage and biography. Two to three submissions windows per year: see social media for updates. Submissions must be made via Submittable: see website for full details. All material must be new and previously unpublished but can be self-contained extracts from longer/forthcoming works. Founded 2018.

History Today

2nd Floor (North), 55 Goswell Road,
London EC1V 7EN
tel 020-3219 7810
email submissions@historytoday.com
website www.historytoday.com
Editors Rhys Griffiths, Kate Wiles
Monthly £7.50

History in the widest sense – cultural, political, economic, social, biography, relating past to present; global history as well as British. Length: 3,000–3,500 words (feature articles); 1,600–2,200 words (mid-length features); 1,000 words (news/views and book reviews). Do not send original material until publication is agreed. Accepts freelance contributions dealing with genuinely new historical research. Payment: by arrangement. Founded 1951.

Homes & Gardens

Future Publishing Ltd, 121–141 Westbourne Terrace,
London W2 6JR
tel 020-3148 5000
email HomesAndGardens@futurenet.com
website www.homesandgardens.com
X @homesandgardens
Global Brand Director Sarah Spiteri
Monthly £5.99

Articles on home interest or design, particularly well-designed British interiors (snapshots should be submitted). Length: 900–1,000 words (articles). Illustrations: all types. Payment: by arrangement. Founded 1919.

Horse & Hound

Future Publishing Ltd, Unit 415, Winnersh Triangle,
Eskdale Road, Winnersh RG41 5TU
email pippa.roome@futurenet.com
website www.horseandhound.co.uk
Facebook www.facebook.com/horseandhound
X @horseandhound
Instagram @horseandhound
Editor-in-Chief Sarah Jenkins, *Magazine Editor* Pippa Roome, *Website Editor* Carol Phillips
Weekly £3.25

News, reports, features and opinion, covering all areas of equestrianism, particularly the Olympic disciplines of eventing, showjumping and dressage, plus showing and hunting. Payment: by arrangement. Founded 1884.

Horse & Rider

DJ Murphy Publishers Ltd, Olive Studio,
Grange Road, Tilford, Farnham, Surrey GU10 2DQ
tel (01428) 601020
email editor@djmurphy.co.uk
website www.horseandrideruk.com
Instagram @horseandrideruk
Editor-in-Chief Louise Kittle
Monthly £4.75

Covers all forms of equestrian activity at home and abroad. Good writing and technical accuracy essential. Length: 1,500–2,000 words. Illustrations: photos and drawings, the latter usually commissioned. Payment: by arrangement. Founded 1959.

Hortus

Upland Mansion, Upland Arms,
Carmarthen SA32 8DZ
tel 07889 138010 (editorial), 07943 724726 (sales/subs)
email d.a.wheeler@hotmail.com (editorial)
email all@hortus.co.uk (sales)
website www.hortus.co.uk
Editor David Wheeler
Quarterly £42 plus postage

Articles on decorative horticulture: plants, gardens, history, design, literature, people; book reviews. Length: 1,500–5,000 words, longer by arrangement. Illustrations: line, half-tone and wood-engravings. Payment: by arrangement. Founded 1987.

Hot Press

100 Capel Street, Dublin 1, Republic of Ireland
tel +353 (0)1 241 1500
email editorial@hotpress.ie
website www.hotpress.com
X @hotpress
Editor Niall Stokes
Fortnightly €6

High-quality, investigative stories, or punchily written offbeat pieces, of interest to 16–39 year-olds, including politics, music, sport, sex, and religion. Length: varies. Illustrations: colour with some b&w. Payment: by arrangement. Founded 1977.

House & Garden

The Condé Nast Publications, The Adelphi,
1–11 John Adam Street, London WC2N 6HT
email houseandgarden@condenast.co.uk
website www.houseandgarden.co.uk
Editor Hatta Byng
Monthly £4.99

Articles (always commissioned), on subjects relating to domestic architecture, interior decorating, furnishing, gardens and gardening, exhibitions, travel, food and wine.

Icon Magazine

Media 10, Crown House, 151 High Road, Loughton, Essex IG10 4LF
tel 020-3235 5200
email submissions@icon-magazine.co.uk
website www.iconeye.com
Facebook www.facebook.com/iconeye
Instagram @iconeye
Editor Jessica-Christin Hametner
Monthly From £40 p.a.

Articles on architecture and design culture, including projects and practitioners. Founded 2003.

i-D

New North Place, London, EC2A 4JA
email editorial@i-d.co
website https://i-d.co
Instagram @i_d
Editor-in-Chief Thom Bettridge
Biannual £20

Identity, style and culture, as well as fashion, music, art and film. Founded 1980; relaunched 2025.

Ideal Home

Future Publishing Ltd, 121–141 Westbourne Terrace, London W2 6JR
tel 020-3148 5000
email ideal_home@futurenet.com
website www.idealhome.co.uk
Instagram @idealhomeuk
Editor-in-Chief Heather Young
Monthly £5.99

Lifestyle magazine, articles usually commissioned. Contributors advised to study editorial content before submitting material. Illustrations: usually commissioned. Payment: according to material. Founded 1920.

The Idler

Great Western Studios, 65 Alfred Road, London W2 5EU
tel 020-3176 7907
email mail@idler.co.uk
email art@idler.co.uk
website www.idler.co.uk
Founder Tom Hodgkinson, *Art Director* Alice Smith
7 p.a. £9.50

Magazine dedicated to 'the art of living'. Includes a range of features and articles on topics from film to music, business and eating out, as well as readers' letters and diary pieces. Also runs online courses and stages live events in London. Unsolicited material rarely commissioned, but ideas may be emailed to the Editor. Illustrators may send their portfolio to the Art Director via the second email address given above. Founded 1993.

Index on Censorship

3rd Floor, 86–90 Paul Street, London EC2A 4NE
email info@indexoncensorship.org
website www.indexoncensorship.org
X @IndexCensorship
Bluesky @indexoncensorship.org.bsky.social
Editor Sarah Dawood
Quarterly £13

Articles of up to 3,000 words dealing with all aspects of free speech and political censorship. Illustrations: b&w, cartoons. Payment: £240 per 1,000 words. Founded 1972.

Ink Sweat & Tears

email enquiries@inksweatandtears.co.uk
website https://inksweatandtears.co.uk/
Facebook www.facebook.com/InkSweatandTears
X @InkSweatTears
Instagram @insta.inksweatandtears
Editor Helen Ivory, *Publisher* Kate Birch
Online

Poetry, short prose, word & image and filmpoem webzine. Accepts previously unpublished submissions of up to 750 words. Publishes something new every day. Has a paid editing internship programme for writers from the Black, Asian, Latinx and other global majority communities and a 'Pick of the Month' feature voted for by readers.

Publishes both new and more established writers and welcomes submissions of well-written reviews. Founded 2007.

Inkfish Magazine

email inkfishmagazine@gmail.com
website https://inkfishmag.com/submit
Facebook www.facebook.com/inkfishmagazine
X @inkfishmagazine
Instagram @inkfishmagazine
Editors and Founders Kate Horsley, Peter McAllister

Online literary journal. Accepts submissions of flash fiction, short stories, poetry and non-fiction. Also accepts visual art for its illustrations, cover art and gifs. Standard submissions are free but expedited submissions are available for a small fee (currently £3). Simultaneous submissions considered. Payment: none.

Inside Soap

Hearst UK, House of Hearst, 30 Panton Street, London SW1Y 4AJ
tel 020-7439 5000
email editor@insidesoap.co.uk
website www.insidesoap.co.uk
Facebook www.facebook.com/insidesoap
X @InsideSoapMag
Associate Editor Laura-Jayne Tyler
Weekly £4.50

Gossip and celebrity interviews with soap and popular TV characters on terrestrial and satellite channels. Submit ideas by email in first instance. Payment: by arrangement.

Insurance Age

InfoPro Digital Services, 133 Houndsditch,
London EC3A 7BX
tel 020-7316 9458
email emmanuel.kenning@infopro-digital.com
website www.insuranceage.co.uk
News Editor Emmanuel Kenning
10 p.a. £655 p.a.

News, features, research and rankings on general insurance and the regional broker market covering commercial lines, personal lines, regulation, people, opinion and technology. Payment: by arrangement. Founded 1979.

InterMedia

International Institute of Communications,
Suite 107, 238 Merton High Street, Wimbledon,
London SW19 1AU
email enquiries@iicom.org
website www.iicom.org
Editor Russell Seekins
Quarterly Available free on IIC website

International journal concerned with policies, events, trends and research in the field of communications, broadcasting, telecommunications and associated issues, particularly cultural and social. Founded 1970.

International Affairs

The Royal Institute of International Affairs,
Chatham House, 10 St James's Square,
London SW1Y 4LE
tel 020-7957 5728
email JMaher@chathamhouse.org
website www.chathamhouse.org/publications/international-affairs-journal, https://academic.oup.com/ia/pages/Author_Guidelines
Editors-in-Chief Professor Rita Floyd, Professor Asaf Siniver, *Managing Editor* Joanne Maher
6 issues p.a. From £119 p.a.

Peer-reviewed academic articles on international affairs; up to 40 books reviewed in each issue. Unsolicited articles welcome; submissions on ScholarOne: mc.manuscriptcentral.com/inta. Article length: 7,000–10,000 words. Illustrations: none. Payment: by arrangement. Founded 1922.

Investors' Chronicle

Bracken House, 1 Friday Street, London EC4M 9BT
tel 020-7873 3000
website www.investorschronicle.co.uk
Editor Rosie Carr
Weekly £5.99

Journal covering investment and personal finance. Occasional outside contributions for features are accepted. Payment: by arrangement. Founded 1860.

Ireland's Own

Channing House, Upper Rowe Street,
Wexford Y35 TH2A, Republic of Ireland
tel +353 (0)1 705 5454
email info@irelandsown.ie
email submissions@irelandsown.ie
website www.irelandsown.ie
Editor Seán Nolan, *Editor Monthly Editions* Shea Tomkins
Weekly €2.60, Monthly specials €3.80

Short stories: non-experimental, traditional with an Irish orientation (1,800–2,000 words); articles of interest to Irish readers at home and abroad (750–800 words); general and literary articles (750–800 words). Monthly special bumper editions, each devoted to a particular seasonal topic. Suggestions for new features considered. Payment: varies according to quality and length. Founded 1902.

Irish Arts Review

Tower 3, Fumbally Court, Fumbally Lane,
Dublin D08 TXY8, Republic of Ireland
tel +353 (0)1 676 6711
email editorial@irishartsreview.com
website www.irishartsreview.com
X @IrishArtsReview
Editor Brigid Mulcahy
Quarterly €75 p.a. (UK and Europe), €90 p.a. (US), €110 p.a. (RoW)

Magazine committed to promoting Irish art and heritage with articles on Irish painting, design, sculpture, architecture, photography and the decorative arts, and heritage. To submit information on Irish Art Exhibitions overseas, email: production@irishartsreview.com. Founded 1984.

Irish Farmers Journal

Irish Farm Centre, Bluebell, Dublin D12 YXW5,
Republic of Ireland
tel +353 (0)1 419 9500
email edit@farmersjournal.ie
website www.farmersjournal.ie
Editor Jack Kennedy
Weekly From €9.99 per month

Readable, technical articles on any aspect of farming. Length: 700–1,000 words. Payment: by arrangement. Illustrated. Founded 1948.

Irish Medical Times

Corville Road, Roscrea, Co. Tipperary, E53 H224,
Republic of Ireland
tel +353 (0)8 7928 815
email editor@imt.ie
website www.imt.ie
Editor Terence Cosgrave
Weekly Free to medical professionals, otherwise €298 p.a. (Republic of Ireland), €434 p.a. (UK)

Medical articles. Opinion column length: 850–1,000 words. Founded 1967.

Irish Pages: A Journal of Contemporary Writing

129 Ormeau Road, Belfast BT7 1SH
tel 028-9043 4800
email editor@irishpages.org
website www.irishpages.org
X @irishpages
Instagram @irishpages
General Editor Chris Agee, *Irish Language Editor* Róisín Costello, *Scottish Editor* Kathleen Jamie, *Scottish Gaelic Editor* Meg Bateman
Bi-annual €39

Poetry, fiction, essays, creative non-fiction, memoir, essay reviews, nature writing, translated work, literary journalism, and other autobiographical, historical and scientific writing of literary distinction. Publishes in equal measure writing from Ireland and overseas. Accepts unsolicited submissions by post only. Payment: pays only for certain commissions and occasional serial rights. Founded 2002.

Jane's Defence Weekly

Sentinel House, 163 Brighton Road, Coulsdon, Surrey CR5 2YH
tel 020-3253 2100
website www.janes.com
X @JanesINTEL
Weekly From £634 p.a.

International defence news; military equipment; budget analysis, industry, military technology, business, political, defence market intelligence. Illustrations: colour. Payment: by arrangement. Founded 1984.

Jewish Chronicle

915 High Road, London N12 8QJ
tel 020-7415 1500
email editor@thejc.com
website www.thejc.com
X @JewishChron
Editor Daniel Schwammenthal
Weekly £3.20

Authentic and exclusive news stories and articles of Jewish interest from 500–1,500 words are considered. Includes a lively arts and leisure section and regular travel pages. Illustrations: of Jewish interest, either topical or feature. Payment: by arrangement. Founded 1841.

Jewish Telegraph

Holland House, 12 Holland Road, Manchester M8 4AA
tel 0161 740 9321
email manchester@jewishtelegraph.com
The Gatehouse Business Centre, Chapel Allerton, Leeds LS7 4RF
tel 0113 295 6000
email leeds@jewishtelegraph.com
120 Childwall Road, Liverpool L15 6WU
tel 0151 475 6666
email liverpool@jewishtelegraph.com
May Terrace, Giffnock, Glasgow G46 6LD
tel 0141 621 4422
email glasgow@jewishtelegraph.com
website www.jewishtelegraph.com
Facebook www.facebook.com/jewishtelegraph
X @JewishTelegraph
Editor Paul Harris
Weekly 95p

Non-fiction articles of Jewish interest, Exclusive Jewish news stories and pictures, international, national and local. Length: 500–750 words. Illustrations: line, half-tone, cartoons. Payment: by arrangement. Founded 1950.

Kerrang!

Wasted Talent, 14 Charles II Street, London SW1Y 4QU
email feedback@kerrang.com
website www.kerrang.com
Instagram @kerrangmagazine
4 p.a. £4.99

News, reviews and interviews; music with attitude. All material commissioned. Illustrations: colour. Payment: by arrangement. Founded 1981.

Kitchen Garden

Mortons Media Group Ltd, Media Centre, Morton Way, Horncastle, Lincs. LN9 6JR
tel (01507) 529396
email SOtt@mortons.co.uk
website www.kitchengarden.co.uk
Facebook www.facebook.com/KitchenGardenMag
Instagram @GrowWithKG
Editor Steve Ott
Monthly £6.50

Magazine for people with a passion for growing their own vegetables, fruit and herbs. Includes practical tips and inspirational ideas. Specially commissions most material but welcomes ideas for articles and features. Length: 700–2,000 (articles/features). Illustrations: all commissioned. Payment: varies. Founded 1997.

The Lake

email poetry@thelakepoetry.co.uk
website www.thelakepoetry.co.uk
X @thelakepoetry
Bluesky @thelakepoetry.bsky.social

Online poetry magazine. Contributors may submit up to five poems within the body of an email or attach one Word document with 'Poetry Submission' in the subject line; a short third-person biography (50 words max) should also be included. Accepts some previously published poems and is open to simultaneous submissions under certain conditions; see website for details.

The Lancet

125 London Wall, London EC2Y 5AS
tel 020-7424 4922
email editorial@lancet.com
website www.thelancet.com
X @TheLancet
Editor-in-Chief Dr Richard Horton
Weekly From £214 p.a.

Research papers, review articles, editorials, correspondence and commentaries on international medicine, medical research and policy. Material may be submitted directly through a dedicated online system. Founded 1823.

LandScape Magazine

Bauer Media, Media House, Lynch Wood, Peterborough PE2 6EA
tel (01733) 468000
email landscape@bauermedia.co.uk
website www.landscapemagazine.co.uk
Editor Rachel Hawkins
Monthly £5.99

Seasonal content covering gardening, cookery, history and heritage, craft, travel, walks and country matters.

The Lawyer

79 Wells Street, London W1T 3QN
tel 020-7970 4000
email editorial@thelawyer.com
website www.thelawyer.com
Instagram @thelawyermag
Editor Catrin Griffiths
Weekly Subscription options available

News, articles, features and views relevant to the legal profession. Length: 600–900 words. Illustrations: as agreed. Payment: by arrangement. Founded 1987.

Leisure Painter & The Artist

Warners Group Publications plc, West Street, Bourne, Lincs. PE10 9PH
tel (01778) 391000
email leisurepainterletters@tapc.co.uk
website www.painters-online.co.uk
Editors Ingrid Lyon, Jane Stroud
12 p.a. £7.99

Practical, instructional articles on painting for all amateur and professional artists. Illustrations: line, half-tone, colour. Payment: by arrangement. Founded 1931 and 1967 respectively.

LGC (Local Government Chronicle)

4th Floor, Harmsworth House, 15 Bouverie Street, London EC4Y 8DP
email lgcnews@emap.com
website www.lgcplus.com
Editor Sarah Calkin
Weekly From £336 p.a.

Aimed at senior managers in local government. Covers politics, management issues, social services, education, regeneration, industrial relations and personnel, plus public sector finance and Scottish and Welsh local government. Length: 1,000 words (features). Illustrations: b&w and colour, cartoons. Payment: by arrangement. Founded 1855.

Life and Work: The Magazine of the Church of Scotland

121 George Street, Edinburgh EH2 4YN
tel 0131 225 5722
email magazine@lifeandwork.org
website www.lifeandwork.org
Editor Lynne McNeil
Monthly £3.50 (print), £2.99 (digital download)

Articles not exceeding 1,000 words and news; occasional stories and poetry. Study the magazine and contact the Editor first. Illustrations: photos and colour illustrations. Payment: by arrangement.

The Lincoln Review

email lincolnrevieweditors@gmail.com
website www.lincolnreview.org
Instagram @lincolnreview
Editor-in-Chief Alison Smith

International literary journal published annually by the University of Lincoln's Creative Writing Programme. Considers a range of submissions, including fiction, poetry, translations, art and creative non-fiction from established and new authors, particularly those from under-represented backgrounds. See website for full list. General submissions open between 1 September and 1 March annually. Founded 2019.

The Linguist

The Chartered Institute of Linguists, Thanet House, 231 Strand, London WC2R 1DA
tel 020-7940 3100
email linguist.editor@ciol.org.uk
website www.ciol.org.uk
Editor Miranda Moore
Bi-monthly Free online to CIOL members; other subscription options are available

Articles of interest to professional linguists in translating, interpreting and teaching fields. Most contributors have special knowledge of the subjects with which they deal. Articles usually contributed, but payment by arrangement. Length: 800–2,000 words.

Literary Review

44 Lexington Street, London W1F 0LW
tel 020-7437 9392
email editorial@literaryreview.co.uk
website www.literaryreview.co.uk
Facebook www.facebook.com/LiteraryReviewLondon
X @lit_review

Instagram @lit_review
Editor Nancy Sladek
Monthly (double issue December/January) £5.50

Reviews, articles of cultural interest, interviews and profiles. Material mostly commissioned. Length: articles and reviews 800–1,500 words. Illustrations: by arrangement. Payment: by arrangement; none for illustrations. Founded 1979.

Litro

180 Piccadilly, London W1J 9HF
email info@litro.co.uk
website www.litromagazine.com
Bluesky @litromagazine.bsky.social
Instagram @litromedia
Founder Eric Akoto FRSA
Quarterly £44 p.a.

Print and online literary magazine featuring fiction, non-fiction, reviews, articles of cultural interest, interviews, profiles and a monthly short story competition. Length: short stories, 2,500 words; articles and reviews, 800–1,500 words. Illustrations: line and b&w photos. Founded 2006.

Little White Lies

TCO London, Unit 2H, Zetland House,
109–123 Clifton Street, London EC2A 4LD
tel 020-7729 3675
email hello@tcolondon.com
website https://lwlies.com/
Instagram @lwlies
Editor David Jenkins
5 p.a. From £28 p.a.

Independent movie magazine that features cutting-edge writing, illustration and photography to get under the skin of cinema. Also explores the worlds of music, art, politics and pop culture as part of its mission to reshape the debate across the movie landscape. Length: various. Illustrations and photography. Payment: varies for illustration, articles and reviews. Founded 2005.

Living Plantfully

email editor@livingplantfully.co.uk
website www.livingplantfully.co.uk
Facebook www.facebook.com/livemoreplantfully
X @LivePlantfully
Editor Lindsey Harrad

Online magazine embracing food, nutrition, health and wellness, growing and gardening, sustainability and eco issues, focusing on a holistic plant-centred lifestyle. Guest contributions and collaborations are welcome; contact the editor for guidelines.

London Grip

email editor@londongrip.co.uk
email poetry@londongrip.co.uk
website http://londongrip.co.uk/
Facebook www.facebook.com/londongrip
X @LondonGrip
Instagram @londongrip
Founder Patricia Morris, *Editor* Stephen McGrath (reviews and articles), *Poetry Editor* Michael Bartholomew-Biggs

International online cultural magazine. The usual submission windows for poetry are January, April, July and October; reviews may be submitted at any time. Founded 2007.

The London Magazine: A Review of Literature and the Arts

Administration 11 Queen's Gate, London SW7 5EL
email info@thelondonmagazine.org
website https://thelondonmagazine.org/submission-guidelines/
X @TheLondonMag
Bluesky @thelondonmagazine.bsky.social
Instagram @thelondonmagazine
Editor Steven O'Brien, *Managing Editor* Jamie Cameron
Bi-monthly From £45 p.a.

The UK's oldest literary magazine. Publishes poems, short stories, essays, critical articles, interviews, reviews and more in bimonthly print issues online. See website for submission guidelines and information on submission windows. Payment: on acceptance. Founded 1732.

London Review of Books

28 Little Russell Street, London WC1A 2HN
tel 020-7209 1101
email edit@lrb.co.uk
website www.lrb.co.uk
X @LRB
Editors Jean McNicol, Alice Spawls, *Consulting Editor* Mary-Kay Wilmers
Fortnightly £6.99

Features, essays, poems. Payment: by arrangement. Founded 1979.

Long Poem Magazine

20 Spencer Rise, London NW5 1AP
email longpoemmagazine@gmail.com
website www.longpoemmagazine.org.uk
Facebook www.facebook.com/groups/longpoemmagazine
X @LongPoemMag
Editor Linda Black, *Deputy Editor* Claire Crowther
2 p.a. £13.50 (UK, inc. p&p), £27 p.a.

Published in May and October each year. Offers a wide range of poetry, including sequences and translations, plus one essay per issue on an aspect of the long poem. Also publishes online reviews and essays on the poetic practice, by invitation. See website for up-to-date details of current submission windows. Send no more than two original, unpublished poems of at least 75 lines each inside the dates indicated, by email only. Simultaneous submissions not accepted. Contributors should familiarise themselves with the magazine before sending in material. Founded 2008.

Magma Poetry

23 Pine Walk, Carshalton SM5 4ES
email info@magmapoetry.com
website https://magmapoetry.com, https://magmapoetry.submittable.com/submit
X @magmapoetry
Chair Lisa Kelly
3 p.a. £8.50 (inc. p&p), £22 p.a. (inc. p&p)

Magazine of contemporary poetry and writing about poetry including reviews, each issue of which has a different editor and theme (see website for details). Features new and established writers: recent contributors include Jason Allen-Paisant, Raymond Antrobus, Malika Booker, David Harsent, Luke Kennard, Fran Lock and Joelle Taylor. Previously unpublished poems are welcome via Submittable (see above) or (from UK writers only) by post, but potential contributors should check the website first for calls for submission and any specific requirements.

Management Today

Bridge House, 69 London Road, Twickenham, TW1 3SP
email claire.warren@haymarket.com
website www.managementtoday.co.uk
Editor-in-Chief Claire Warren
4 p.a. plus digital content Subscription options available, some upon application

Company profiles and analysis, features up to 3,000 words. Payment: by arrangement. Founded 1966.

Marketing Week

Floor M, 10 York Road, London SE1 7ND
tel 020-7970 4000
email lucy.tesseras@xeim.com
website www.marketingweek.co.uk
Editor-in-Chief Russell Parsons, *Managing Editor* Lucy Tesseras
Weekly From £455 p.a.

Aimed at marketing management. Accepts occasional features and analysis, but no bylined pieces. Length: 1,000–2,000 words. Payment: by arrangement. Founded 1978.

MBUK (Mountain Biking UK)

Our Media Ltd, 1st Floor, Eagle House, Bristol BS1 4ST
tel 0117 927 9009
email mbuk@ourmedia.co.uk
website www.mbuk.com
Group Editor James Costley-White
Every 4 weeks £6.99

Magazine for mountain bike enthusiasts with features, reviews, news and world and domestic racing coverage.

MCN (Motor Cycle News)

Bauer Media Group, Media House, Lynch Wood, Peterborough Business Park, Peterborough PE2 6EA
tel (01733) 468000
email emma.franklin@motorcyclenews.com
website www.motorcyclenews.com
Group Editor Richard Newland, *Magazine Editor* Emma Franklin
Weekly From £79.99 p.a.

Leading authority on all things motorbike – both in print and online – from riding the latest models to in-depth news investigations, up-to-the-minute sports news and insight. Adheres to strict modern journalism standards, with full fact-checking and unique angles on all stories sourced and developed through an extensive network of industry contacts and biking community relationships. Founded 1955.

Medal News

Token Publishing Ltd, 8 Oaktree Place, Manaton Close, Matford Business Park, Exeter, Devon EX2 8WA
tel (01404) 46972
email info@tokenpublishing.com
website www.tokenpublishing.com
10 p.a. £4.95

Well-researched articles on military history with a bias towards medals. Send text in digital form. Length: up to 2,000 words. Illustrations: if possible. Payment: by arrangement; none for illustrations. Founded 1989.

Men's Health

Hearst UK, House of Hearst, 30 Panton Street, London SW1Y 4AJ
email contact@menshealth.co.uk
website www.menshealth.co.uk
Editor-in-Chief Claire Sanderson, *Features Editor* Daniel Davies
10 p.a. £5.99

Active pursuits, grooming, fitness, fashion, sex, career and general men's interest issues. Length 1,000–4,000 words. Ideas welcome. No unsolicited MSS. Payment: by arrangement. Founded 1994.

Methodist Recorder

1 Merchant Street, London E3 4LY
tel 020-7793 0033
email editorial@methodistrecorder.co.uk
website www.methodistrecorder.co.uk
X @MethRecorder
Weekly £4.70

Methodist newspaper; ecumenically involved. Limited opportunities for freelance contributors. Preliminary contact advised. Founded 1861.

MMM (The Motorhomers' Magazine)

Warners Group Publications Plc, The Maltings, West Street, Bourne, Lincs. PE10 9PH

tel (01778) 391000
email danielattwood@warnersgroup.co.uk
website www.outandaboutlive.co.uk
Head of Content, Outdoor Leisure Daniel Attwood
Every four weeks £7.99

Articles including motorcaravan travel, owner reports and DIY. Length: up to 2,500 words. Illustrations: line, half-tone, colour prints and transparencies, high-quality digital. Payment: by arrangement. Founded 1966 as *Motor Caravan and Camping*.

Model Engineer & Workshop

Mortons Media Group Ltd, Media Centre,
Morton Way, Horncastle, Lincs. LN9 6JR
tel (01507) 529589
email MEWeditor@mortons.co.uk
website www.model-engineer.co.uk
Editor Neil Wyatt
Fortnightly £5.95

Detailed description of the construction of engineering models, small workshop equipment, machine tools and small electrical and mechanical devices; articles on small power engineering, mechanics, electricity, workshop methods, clocks and experiments. Relevant event reporting and visits. Illustrations: line, half-tone, colour. Payment: up to £50 per page. Founded 1898.

Modern Poetry in Translation

The Queen's College, Oxford OX1 4AW
email editor@mptmagazine.com
website www.modernpoetryintranslation.com
Instagram @modernpoetryintranslation
3 p.a. £29 p.a.

Features the work of established and emerging poets and translators from around the world. Welcomes translated work that has not been published previously; contemporary pieces preferred. Up to six poems may be submitted. Potential contributors should familiarise themselves with the magazine before sending their work. See website to submit, for full guidelines and to keep up to date with open calls. Founded 1965.

Mojo

Bauer Media, The Lantern, 75 Hampstead Road,
London NW1 2PL
email mojo@bauermedia.co.uk
email danny.eccleston@bauermedia.co.uk
website www.mojo4music.com
Editor-in-Chief John Mulvey, *Senior Editor* Danny Eccleston
Monthly £8.75

Serious rock music magazine: interviews, news and reviews of books, live shows and albums. Send pitches to the senior editor. Length: up to 10,000 words. Illustrations: by arrangement. Payment: by arrangement. Founded 1993.

MoneyWeek

Future plc, 121–141 Westbourne Terrace,
London W2 6JR
tel 020-3890 4060
email editor@moneyweek.com
website https://moneyweek.com
X @MoneyWeek
Editor Andrew Van Sickle
Weekly From £32.99 p.a.

Economic analysis, investment recommendations and market tips, as well as in-depth looks at national and international politics. Founded 2000.

Motor Boat and Yachting

Future Publishing Ltd, Quay House, The Ambury,
Bath BA1 1UA
email hugo.andreae@futurenet.com
website www.mby.com
Editor Hugo Andreae
Monthly £5.99

Specialist magazine about production motor boats of 30–100ft. Stories about buying, maintaining, refitting and/or cruising on motor boats welcomed. Features up to 2,500 words considered. Payment: varies. Illustrations: hi-res photos. Founded 1904.

The Motorship

Mercator Media Ltd, Spinnaker House,
Waterside Gardens, Fareham, Hants PO16 8SD
tel (01329) 825335
email editor@motorship.com
website www.motorship.com
Facebook www.facebook.com/TheMotorship
X @Motorship
Editor David Stevenson
11 p.a. Free three-month trial; subscription options thereafter

News, information and insight for marine technology professionals. Founded 1920 as *The Motor Ship*.

Mslexia

PO Box 656, Newcastle upon Tyne NE99 1PZ
tel 0191 204 8860
email postbag@mslexia.co.uk
website https://mslexia.co.uk/submit-your-work/
X @Mslexia
Founder and Editor Debbie Taylor
Quarterly £8.95

Magazine for women writers which combines features and advice about writing with new fiction and poetry by women. Accepts submissions via email and post across a range of genres, including fiction, non-fiction, poetry, and article and review proposals. See website for specific requirements for each category. Illustrations: by commission only; email submissions welcome. Payment: by negotiation. Founded 1998.

Music Teacher

MA Education, St Jude's Church, Dulwich Road, London SE24 0PB
email phil.croydon@markallengroup.com
website https://musicteachermagazine.co.uk/
X @MusicTeacherMag
Editor Phil Croydon
Monthly From £88 p.a.

Information and articles for classroom music teachers and private/peripatetic instrumental teachers, including reviews of books, music, software and other music education resources. Articles and illustrations must both have a teaching, as well as a musical, interest. Length: articles 400–2,000 words. Payment: by arrangement. Founded 1908.

Music Week

Future Publishing, 121–141 Westbourne Terrace, London W2 6JR
tel 0330 390 6751
website www.musicweek.com
Editor-in-Chief George Garner
Monthly £11.99

News and features on all aspects of producing, manufacturing, marketing and retailing music, plus the live music business and all other aspects of the music industry. Payment: by negotiation. Founded 1959.

Musical Opinion

1 Exford Road, London SE12 9HD
tel 020-8857 1582
email robertmw7@hotmail.co.uk
website www.musicalopinion.com
Editor Robert Matthew-Walker
Bi-monthly £32 p.a.

Suggestions for contributions of musical interest, scholastic, educational, anniversaries and ethnic. DVD, CD, opera, festival, book, music reviews. Illustrations: by arrangement. Founded 1877.

My Weekly

D.C. Thomson & Co. Ltd, 2 Albert Square, Dundee DD1 1DD
tel (01382) 223131
email myweekly@dcthomson.co.uk
website www.myweekly.co.uk
X @My_Weekly
Editor Susan Watson, *Fiction Editor* Kirstyn Smith
Weekly £2.59

Modern women's magazine aimed at 50+ age group. No unsolicited MSS considered. Send ideas or pitches to editor. Illustrations: colour. Payment: by negotiation. Founded 1910.

The National Trust Magazine

The National Trust, Heelis, Kemble Drive, Swindon SN2 2NA
tel (01793) 817716
email magazine@nationaltrust.org.uk
website www.nationaltrust.org.uk
Editor Sally Palmer
3 p.a. Free to members or £6.50

Lifestyle title with focus on the National Trust, encompassing interiors, gardens, food, UK travel, wildlife, environment, topical features and celebrity content. No unsolicited articles. Length: 1,000 words (features), 200 words (news). Illustrations: colour transparencies and artwork. Payment: by arrangement; picture library rates. Founded 1932.

Nature

Springer Nature, The Macmillan Building, 4 Crinan Street, London N1 9XW
tel 020-7833 4000
email nature@nature.com
website www.nature.com/nature
Editor-in-Chief Dr Magdalena Skipper
Weekly £199 p.a.

Devoted to scientific matters and to their bearing upon public affairs. All contributors of articles have specialised knowledge of the subjects with which they deal. Illustrations: full colour. Founded 1869.

NB Magazine

Studio 104, Leather Factory, 1 Brook Lane, Holt, Wilts. BA14 6RL
tel (01225) 302266
email madeleine@nbmagazine.co.uk
website https://nbmagazine.co.uk
Managing Director Alistair Giles, *Editor* Madeleine Knowles
4 p.a. Book and magazine subscriptions from £20 per quarter (UK, including p&p)

Literary magazine aimed at avid readers and book groups, which includes a variety of author interviews and a selection of book reviews. A diverse range of genres are covered within the magazine, and readers' voices and opinions are represented.

New Humanist

Unit A, 39 Moreland Street, London EC1V 8BB
tel 020-7324 3060
email editor@newhumanist.org.uk
website https://newhumanist.org.uk
Facebook www.facebook.com/NewHumanist
X @NewHumanist
Bluesky @newhumanist.bsky.social
Editor Niki Seth-Smith
Quarterly £27 p.a. (print), £10 p.a. (digital)

Articles on current affairs, philosophy, science, the arts, literature, religion and humanism. Length: 750–4,000 words. Illustrations: colour photos. Payment: 10–20p per word. Founded 1885.

New Internationalist

The Old Music Hall, 106–108 Cowley Road, Oxford OX4 1JE

tel (01865) 403345
email amy.hall@newint.org
email ni@newint.org
website https://newint.org/misc/editorial-submissions-form
X @newint
Contact Amy Hall
Bi-monthly From £32.85 p.a.

World issues, ranging from food to feminism to peace and the environment; one subject examined in each issue. Length: up to 2,000 words. Illustrations: by arrangement. Payment: by arrangement. Founded 1973.

New Law Journal

Lexis House, 30 Farringdon Street, London EC4A 4HH
tel 0330 161 1234
email jan.miller@lexisnexis.co.uk
website www.newlawjournal.co.uk
X @newlawjournal
Editor Jan Miller
48 p.a. £710 p.a.

Articles and news on all aspects of civil litigation and dispute resolution. Length: up to 1,900 words. Payment: by arrangement.

New Scientist

25 Bedford Street, London WC2E 9ES
tel 020-7611 1202
email claudia.canavan@newscientist.com
email alison.flood@newscientist.com
website www.newscientist.com/freelancers
Editor-in-Chief Catherine de Lange, *Head of Features* Claudia Canavan, *Comment and Culture Editor* Alison Flood
Weekly £6.95

Authoritative articles of topical importance on all aspects of science and technology. Pitches, ideas and reviews welcomed (see email addresses above). Potential contributors should study recent copies of the magazine. Illustrations: by arrangement. Founded 1956.

New Statesman

(formerly New Statesman & Society)
12–13 Essex Street, London WC2R 3AA
tel 020-7936 6400
email editorial@newstatesman.co.uk
website www.newstatesman.co.uk
Editor Tom McTague
Weekly £5.95

Interested in news, reportage and analysis of current political and social issues at home and overseas, plus book reviews, general articles and coverage of the arts, environment and science seen from the perspective of the British Left but written in a stylish, witty and unpredictable way. Length: strictly according to the value of the piece. Illustrations: commissioned for specific articles, although artists' samples considered for future reference; occasional cartoons. Payment: by agreement. Founded 1913.

New Theatre Quarterly

email m.shevtsova@gold.ac.uk
website www.cambridge.org/core/journals/new-theatre-quarterly
Editors Professor Maria Shevtsova, Dr Philippa Burt
Quarterly £342 p.a.

Articles, interviews, documentation, reference material covering all aspects of live theatre across the world. An informed, factual and serious approach essential. Generous editorial assistance to authors; refereed journal. Payment: by arrangement. Founded 1985; as *Theatre Quarterly* 1971.

New Welsh Review

The Old Surgery, Napier St, Cardigan SA43 1ED
tel 07890 968246
email newwelshreviewessays@yahoo.com
website www.newwelshreview.com
X @newwelshreview
Editor Gwen Davies
3 p.a. From £10

Literary magazine featuring stories, creative non-fiction, illustration and photography. Submissions accepted via email. See website for information on New Welsh Writing Awards and *New Welsh Rarebyte* (books). Illustrations: colour. Payment: £100 for stories of c. 2,500 words, £150 for non-fiction pieces of c. 2,500. Illustrations paid by arrangement. Founded 1988.

NME (New Musical Express)

(incorporating Melody Maker)
email editors@nme.com
website www.nme.com
Facebook www.facebook.com/nmemagazine
X @nme
Online only

Music news, features and album reviews. Length: by arrangement. Illustrations: hi-res images. Payment: by arrangement. Founded 1952.

The North

Campo House, 54 Campo Lane, Sheffield S1 2EG
email office@poetrybusiness.co.uk
website https://poetrybusiness.co.uk/the-north-magazine
Instagram @poetrybusiness
Editors Ann Sansom, Peter Sansom
2 p.a. £12

Contemporary poetry from new and established writers, as well as book reviews, critical articles and a range of features. Up to six poems may be submitted online only; full information on submission windows given on the website.

Northern Gravy

email info@northerngravy.com
website https://northerngravy.com/submissions
X @NorthGravy
Instagram @northerngravy
Poetry Editor Ralph Dartford, *Fiction Editor* Nick Jones, *Children's Editor* Jonny Syer
1 p.a. (print), 6 p.a. (online)

Literary periodical from the North of England. Accepts submissions for fiction, poetry and 'kid lit' (middle grade and YA) from writers based in the UK or Ireland. Length: 2,000 words (fiction and children's literature); 40 lines max. (poetry). Payment: £100. See X/Twitter for information on forthcoming submission windows. Founded 2020.

Nursery World

MA Education, St Jude's Church, Dulwich Road, London SE24 0PB
tel 020-8501 6693
email karen.faux@markallengroup.com
website www.nurseryworld.co.uk
Editor Karen Faux
Fortnightly From £11 per month

For all grades of primary school, nursery and childcare staff, nannies, foster parents and all those concerned with the care of expectant mothers, babies and young children. Authoritative and informative articles, 800 or 1,300 words, and photos on all aspects of child welfare and early education, from 0–8 years, in the UK. Practical ideas, policy news and career advice. No short stories. Illustrations: by arrangement. Payment: by arrangement.

Nursing Times

emap Publishing Limited, 4th Floor, Harmsworth House, 15 Bouverie Street, London EC4Y 8DP
tel 020-3953 2707
email steve.ford@emap.com
website www.nursingtimes.net
X @NursingTimes
Bluesky @nursingtimes.bsky.social
Instagram @nursingtimes
Editor Steve Ford, *Senior Clinical Editor* Denise Eaton, *News and Features Editor* Gemma Mitchell, *Producton Editor* Sam Gournay, *Online Editor* Charlotte Thomas
Monthly From £29 per quarter

News, features, opinion and journal articles on clinical practice, nursing education, nursing policy including workforce and regulation. All fields of nursing covered, including adult, children's, mental health and learning disabilities, plus social care and midwifery. Emerging areas of focus include sustainability, diversity and inclusion, and technology. Illustrated articles not longer than 2,000 words. Press day: first or last Friday of the month. Illustrations: photos, line. Payment: NUJ rates; by arrangement for illustrations. Founded 1905.

OK!

Reach plc, Northern & Shell Building, 10 Lower Thames Street, London EC3R 6EN
website www.ok.co.uk/home
Editor-in-Chief Caroline Waterston
Weekly £4.40

Exclusive celebrity interviews and photographs. Submit ideas in writing. Length: 1,000 words. Illustrations: colour. Payment: by arrangement. Founded 1993.

The Oldie

Moray House, 23–31 Great Titchfield Street, London W1W 7PA
tel 020-7436 8801
email editorial@theoldie.co.uk
website www.theoldie.co.uk
Editor Harry Mount
Monthly £5.50

General interest magazine reflecting attitudes of older people but aimed at a wider audience. Features (600–1,000 words) on all subjects, as well as articles for specific sections. Potential contributors should familiarise themselves with the magazine prior to submitting work. See website for further guidelines. No poetry. Illustrations: welcomes b&w and colour cartoons. Payment: by arrangement. Founded 1992.

Olive

Immediate Media Co. Ltd, Vineyard House, 44 Brook Green, London W6 7BT
tel 020-7150 5000
email alex.crossley@immediate.co.uk
website www.olivemagazine.com
Facebook www.facebook.com/olivemagazine
X @olivemagazine
Digital Editor Alex Crossley, *Reviews and E-commerce Editor* Lucy Roxburgh
Monthly £6.25

Upmarket food magazine which aims to encourage readers to cook, eat and explore. Each edition includes a range of recipes for both everyday and weekend cooking, as well as information on techniques, trends and tips; restaurant recommendations across the UK; and foodie-inspired travel ideas from around the world. Founded 2003.

Opera

Rivermead, 6 Lower Teddington Road, Hampton Wick KT1 4ER
tel 020-8563 8893
email editor@opera.co.uk
website www.opera.co.uk
X @operamagazine
Instagram @opera_magazine
Editor John Allison
13 p.a. £7.95

Reviews of opera from the UK and around the world, including profiles of opera's greatest performers and a comprehensive calendar of productions and events. Length: up to 2,000 words. Illustrations: photos. Payment: by arrangement. Founded 1950.

Opera Now

Mark Allen Group, St Jude's Church, Dulwich Road, London SE24 0PB
tel 020-7333 1701
email Hattie.Butterworth@markallengroup.com
website www.gramophone.co.uk/opera-now
Facebook www.facebook.com/operanow
Instagram @operanowmagazine
Editor Hattie Butterworth
4 p.a. £9.95

Articles, news, reviews on opera. All material commissioned only. Length: 150–1,500 words. Illustrations: by arrangement. Founded 1989.

oranges journal

email submissions@orangesjournal.com
website www.orangesjournal.com/submissions
X @orangesjournal
Instagram @orangesjournal
Founder/Editor-in-Chief Jade Green, *Editors* Kasandra Ferguson, Jordan Reddington, Yaminah Reid-Morgan, Lukas Kofoed Reimann

Intersectional feminist journal that aims to provide a platform for marginalised writers. Accepts short stories and flash fiction as well as articles and essays on mental health and wellbeing. See website for full details and submission requirements; submission windows will be announced on social media. Founded 2022.

Orbis International Literary Journal

17 Greenhow Avenue, West Kirby, Wirral CH48 5EL
tel 0151 625 1446
email carolebaldock@hotmail.com
website www.orbisjournal.com
Editor Carole Baldock
Quarterly £6, £20 p.a. (UK); £12, £42 p.a. (RoW). Introductory offer: 4 issues as pdfs, plus one print back copy of magazine for £12 (UK).

Literary magazine; provides feedback with proofs. Publishes poetry, fiction (1,000 words maximum), flash fiction, non-fiction, and translations. UK submissions: four poems; include C5-sized sae. Overseas: two submissions via email. *Word Masala* (Yogesh Patel) and *Orbis* Prize of the Year £200 & £25 x 2 runners-up. Each issue: Readers' Award of £50, plus £50 split between four runners-up. And subscribers receive the Xtra *Kudos* Newsletter. Founded 1969.

Our Dogs

Unit 1.01 Boat Shed, 12 Exchange Quay, Salford M5 3EQ
tel 0161 709 4550
email alismith@ourdogs.co.uk
email editorial@ourdogs.co.uk
website www.ourdogs.co.uk
Facebook www.facebook.com/www.ourdogs.co.uk
X @OURDOGSNEWS
Editor Alison Smith
Weekly £5.75

Articles and news on the breeding and showing of pedigree dogs worldwide. Unsolicited material not accepted. Founded 1895.

Oxford Poetry

c/o Partus Press Ltd, 266 Banbury Road, Oxford OX2 7DL
email editors@oxfordpoetry.co.uk
website www.oxfordpoetry.com
X @OxfordPoetry
Instagram @oxford_poetry
Editor-in-Chief Luke Allan, *Managing Editor* Vala Thorodds, *Reviews Editor* Rowland Bagnall
2 p.a. £20 (inc. p&p)

Previously unpublished poems (in English) and translations, both unsolicited and commissioned; also interviews, articles and reviews. Submissions via the website only. Founded 1910.

Oxford Review of Books

Radcliffe Humanities Building, Radcliffe Observatory Quarter, Woodstock Road, Oxford OX2 6GG
email orbeditor@gmail.com
website www.the-orb.org
Editors-in-Chief Georgie Walker, Juan Fueyo-Gomez, *Editors* Imogen Drake, Shreya Khullar, Taneesha Datta
3 p.a. £7.50

Long-form book reviews, interviews, cultural essays and poetry. Print edition three times a year, with releases in January, April and October. Published both online and in print: rolling submission window for online pieces; submissions for print should be made three weeks before the start of Oxford terms. Pitches should demonstrate contemporary relevance; prefer books released within one to two months of the magazine's print dates. Welcomes submissions from all; no fees. Founded 2017.

Panorama: The Journal of Travel, Place and Nature

email enquiries@panoramajournal.org
website https://panoramajournal.org
Facebook www.facebook.com/panoramajournal.org
X @Panorama_J
Instagram @panorama_journal
Director and Editor-in-Chief Matthew Webb
Online 3 p.a.

Online literary journal featuring literary-themed contemporary works of non-fiction, fiction and poetry about travel and the world; illustrations, photo essays and film stills also welcomed. Accepts submissions from experienced writers and emerging voices, with a special interest in global perspectives. See website above for submission notes; calls for themes also appear online and on social media. Payment: none. Founded 2016.

The Passionfruit Review

email editor@passionfruitreview.com
website https://passionfruitreview.com/submissions/
Instagram @Passionfruitlit
Editor Katherine Parsons
Monthly Free

Online journal dedicated primarily to love poetry, but short fiction, prose and visual art on the theme are also accepted occasionally. Up to three poems may be submitted at one time; no restrictions on length. Prose (including prose poetry, creative non-fiction and flash fiction): up to 1,000 words. Simultaneous submissions considered. Founded 2022.

PC Pro

Future Publishing Ltd, Quay House, The Ambury, Bath BA1 1UA
email editor@pcpro.co.uk
Facebook www.facebook.com/pcpro
X @pcpro
Editor-in-Chief Tim Danton
Monthly £6.99

Expert advice and insights from IT professionals, plus in-depth reviews and group tests, aimed at IT pros and enthusiasts. Email feature pitches to editor@pcpro.co.uk but only after reading the magazine first. Founded 1994.

Pennine Platform

PO Box 754, Wakefield WF4 4BP
email editor@pennineplatform.com
website https://pennineplatform.com/submissions/
X @PenninePlatform
Editor Julia Deakin
2 p.a. £18 p.a.

Literary magazine featuring poetry and occasional articles; does not currently carry reviews. Forward-looking, with an international reach. Welcomes submissions of three to six poems in February and September (to be published the following month). Postal submissions preferred from UK; email from overseas. Founded 1973.

The People's Friend

D.C. Thomson & Co. Ltd, 2 Albert Square, Dundee DD1 1DD
tel (01382) 223131
email pfeditor@dcthomson.co.uk
email lcrichton@dcthomson.co.uk
website www.thepeoplesfriend.co.uk
Facebook www.facebook.com/PeoplesFriendMagazine
X @TheFriendMag
Editor Stuart Johnstone, *Fiction Editor* Lucy Crichton
Weekly £2.50

Fiction magazine for women of all ages. Serials (60,000–70,000 words) and complete stories (1,000–4,000 words) of strong romantic and emotional appeal. Includes knitting and cookery. No preliminary letter required; send material for the attention of the Editor. Illustrations: colour. Payment: on acceptance. Founded 1869.

Period Living

Future Publishing Ltd, Quay House, The Ambury, Bath BA1 1UA
email period.living@futurenet.com
Facebook www.facebook.com/periodlivingmagazine
X @PeriodLivingMag
Instagram @period_living
Monthly £5.25

Articles and features on decoration, furnishings, renovation of period homes; gardens, crafts, decorating in a period style. Illustrated. Payment: by arrangement. Founded 1990.

The Photographer

BIPP, The Artistry House, 16 Winckley Square, Preston PR1 3JJ
tel (01772) 367 968
email editor@bipp.com
website www.bipp.com
Quarterly free to all members of British Institute of Professional Photography or £7.50

Journal of the British Institute of Professional Photography. Authoritative reviews, news, views and high-quality photographs. Founded 1922 as the *Record of Photography*.

PN Review

(formerly Poetry Nation)
Carcanet Press Ltd, Main Library, The University of Manchester, Oxford Road, Manchester M13 9PP
tel 0161 834 8730
email submissions@carcanet.co.uk
website www.pnreview.co.uk
Editors Michael Schmidt, John McAuliffe, Andrew Latimer
6 p.a. £9.99

Poems, essays, reviews, translations. Submissions by e-mail (subscribers); otherwise by post only. Payment: by arrangement. Founded 1973

Poetry Ireland Review/Iris Éigse Éireann

Poetry Ireland, 3 Great Denmark Street, Dublin 1, D01 NV63, Republic of Ireland
tel +353 (0)1 678 9815
email publications@poetryireland.ie
website www.poetryireland.ie, www.poetryireland.ie/writers/submission-to-pir
Publications Manager Paul Lenehan
3 p.a. €15.50

Poetry. Features and articles by arrangement. Payment: minimum €50 plus a copy of the magazine in which work appears. Submissions can be made by post but Submittable is preferred; see address above. Founded 1981.

Poetry London

Goldsmiths, University of London, New Cross, London SE14 6NW
tel 020-7919 7171
email admin@poetrylondon.co.uk
website www.poetrylondon.co.uk
Facebook www.facebook.com/poetrylondon
X @Poetry_London
Poetry Editor Niall Campbell, *Reviews Editor* Isabelle Baafi, *Managing Editor* Aminata Sow
3 p.a. From £25 p.a.

Poems of the highest standard, articles/reviews on any aspect of contemporary poetry. Contributors must be knowledgeable about contemporary poetry. Payment: £30 minimum. Founded 1988.

The Poetry Review

The Poetry Society, 22 Betterton Street, London WC2H 9BX
tel 020-7420 9880
email poetryreview@poetrysociety.org.uk
website https://poetrysociety.org.uk/publications-section/the-poetry-review/submissions-guidelines
Editor Wayne Holloway-Smith

Poems, features and reviews. Preliminary study of magazine essential. Payment: by arrangement. Founded 1912.

Poetry Wales

Suite 6, 4 Derwen Road, Bridgend CF31 1LH
tel (01656) 663018
email info@poetrywales.co.uk
website www.poetrywales.co.uk
Facebook www.facebook.com/poetrywales
Instagram @poetrywales
Editor Zoë Brigley
3 p.a. From £39 p.a., inc. postage (or from £20 p.a./£2 per month for concessions)

National poetry magazine of Wales, publishing contemporary poetry, features and reviews. Calls for submissions two to three times per year: see website for submissions guidelines. Potential contributors can sign up to the newsletter for updates on submission windows. Payment: £20/page for poems. Founded 1965.

The Political Quarterly

Wiley-Blackwell, 9600 Garsington Road, Oxford OX4 2DQ
tel (01865) 776868
website www.politicalquarterly.org.uk
X @po_qu
Editors Deborah Mabbett, Ben Jackson
4 p.a. From £13 p.a.

Topical aspects of national and international politics and public administration; takes a progressive, but not a party, point of view. See website for submissions information. Length: average 5,000 words. Payment: by arrangement. Founded 1930.

PR Week

Haymarket Ltd, Bridge House, 69 London Road, Twickenham TW1 3SP
tel 020-8267 5000
email siobhan.holt@haymarket.com
website www.prweek.com
X @prweekuknews
UK Editor John Harrington, *UK News Editor* Siobhan Holt
Bi-monthly Subscription offers available upon application

News and features on public relations. Length: approx. 800–3,000 words. Payment: by arrangement. Send pitches to the news editor. Founded 1984.

Practical Boat Owner

Future Publishing Ltd, Quay House, The Ambury, Bath BA1 1UA
tel 0330 390 6467
email pbo@futurenet.com
website www.pbo.co.uk
Facebook www.facebook.com/practicalboatownermag
X @p_b_o
Instagram @practical_boat_owner
Editor Katy Stickland
Monthly £5.25

Boating magazine: sail and power. Hints, tips and practical articles for cruising skippers. Send full text and high-res images: see pbo.co.uk/submission_guide for details. Illustrations: photos or drawings. Payment: by negotiation. Founded 1967.

Practical Caravan

Future Publishing Ltd, Quay House, The Ambury, Bath BA1 1UA
email practical.caravan@futurenet.com
website www.practicalcaravan.com
X @pcaravan
Editor-in-Chief Sarah Wakely, *Deputy Editor* Paul Critcher
Every four weeks £6.75

Caravan-related travelogues, caravan site reviews; travel writing for existing regular series; technical and DIY matters. Illustrations: colour. Payment: negotiable. Founded 1967.

Practical Fishkeeping

Warners Group Publications Plc, The Maltings, West Street, Bourne, Lincs. PE10 9PH
tel (01778) 391194
email editorial@practicalfishkeeping.co.uk
website www.practicalfishkeeping.co.uk
X @PFKmagazine
12 p.a. £5.99

Practical fishkeeping in tropical and coldwater aquaria and ponds. Heavy emphasis on inspiration and involvement. Good colour photography always needed, and used. No verse or humour, no personal biographical accounts of fishkeeping unless practical. Payment: by arrangement. Founded 1966.

The Practising Midwife

Saturn House, Mercury Rise, Altham Industrial Park, Altham, Lancs. BB5 5BY
email info@all4maternity.com
website www.all4maternity.com/about-us/the-practising-midwife-writing-for-us
X @TPM_Journal
Editor-in-Chief Dr Alys Einion, *Managing Editor* Jayne Purdy
Bimonthly

Disseminates evidence-based material to a wide professional audience. Research and review papers, viewpoints and news items pertaining to midwifery, maternity care, women's health and neonatal health with both a national and an international perspective. All articles submitted are peer-reviewed anonymously. See website for full submissions details. Illustrations: hi-res digital images. Payment: by arrangement. Founded 1997.

Premier Woman Alive

(formerly Christian Woman)
Premier Christian Communications Ltd, Unit 6, April Court, Sybron Way, Crowborough TN6 3DZ
email womanalive@premier.org.uk
website www.womanalive.co.uk
Facebook www.facebook.com/womanalivemagazine
X @WomanAliveUK
Instagram @womanaliveuk
Editor Tola-Doll Fisher
Monthly From £35 p.a.

Aimed at women aged 35 upwards. Celebrity interviews, topical features. Explores modern issues facing women within the context of Christian faith, profiles of women in interesting occupations, Christian testimonies and real-life stories, fashion, beauty, travel, health, crafts. Length: 500–1200 words. Payment: by arrangement. Founded 1982.

Press Gazette

40 Hatton Garden, London EC1N 8EB
tel 020-7936 6433
email pged@pressgazette.co.uk
website https://pressgazette.co.uk
X @pressgazette
Editor-in-Chief Dominic Ponsford
Weekly Online only

News and features of interest to journalists and others working in the media. Length: 1,200 words (features), 300 words (news). Payment: by arrangement. Founded 1965.

Pride

1 Garratt Lane, London SW18 4AQ
tel 020-8870 3755
email editor@pridemagazine.com
website https://pridemagazine.com
Instagram @pridemaguk
Monthly £3

Lifestyle magazine incorporating fashion and beauty, travel, food and entertaining articles for the woman of colour. Length: 1,000–3,000 words. Illustrations: by arrangement. Payment: by arrangement. Founded 1991; relaunched 1997.

Prima

Hearst UK, House of Hearst, 30 Panton Street, London SW1Y 4AJ
tel 020-7312 3815
email prima@hearst.co.uk
website www.prima.co.uk
Facebook www.facebook.com/primamagazine
Instagram @primamag
Editor Jo Checkley
Monthly £5.50

Articles on fashion, home, crafts, health and beauty, cookery; features. Founded 1986.

Private Eye

6 Carlisle Street, London W1D 3BN
tel 020-7437 4017
email strobes@private-eye.co.uk
website www.private-eye.co.uk
Facebook www.facebook.com/PrivateEyeNews
X @PrivateEyeNews
Bluesky @privateeyenews.bsky.social
Instagram @PrivateEyeNews
Editor Ian Hislop
Fortnightly £2.99

News and current affairs. Satire. Illustrations and cartoons: colour or b&w. Payment: by arrangement. Founded 1961.

Prole

email submissionspoetry@prolebooks.co.uk
email submissionsprose@prolebooks.co.uk
website https://prolebooks.co.uk
Facebook www.facebook.com/people/Prole/100041257775797
X @Prolebooks
Editors Brett Evans, Phil Robertson
2 p.a. (June/December) £10

Submissions of poetry, short fiction and creative non-fiction (7,500 words max) and photographic cover art welcome (see website for submission guidelines). Annual poetry competition. Payment: profit share. Founded 2010.

Propel Magazine

PO Box 78744, London N11 9FG
email info@propelmagazine.co.uk
website www.propelmagazine.co.uk
Instagram @propelmagazine

Editor-in-Chief Anthony Anaxagorou
6 p.a. £11.99

Magazine featuring poets that are yet to publish a full collection. Guest editor for each issue. Six submission windows for previously unpublished work per year: subscribe to mailing list for more information on forthcoming dates. Founded 2022.

Prospect Magazine

2 Queen Anne's Gate, London, SW1H 9AA
tel 020-7255 1344
email alona.ferber@prospect-magazine.co.uk
website www.prospectmagazine.co.uk
Instagram @prospect_magazine
Editor Alan Rusbridger, *Senior Editor* Alona Ferber
Monthly £8.99

Political and cultural magazine. Essays, features, special reports, reviews, short stories, opinions/ analysis. Length: 3,000–6,000 words (essays, special reports, short stories), 1,000 words (opinions). Illustrations: by arrangement. Payment: by negotiation. See website for full submission information. Founded 1995.

Psychologies

Kelsey Publishing Ltd, The Granary, Downs Court, Yalding Hill, Yalding, Maidstone, Kent ME18 6AL
tel (01959) 541444
email letters@psychologies.co.uk
website www.psychologies.co.uk/contact-team
Instagram @psychologiesmagazine
Editor-in-Chief Sally Saunders
Monthly £5.25

Women's magazine with a focus on how to flourish, improving mental health and helping readers create the life they want on their terms. Features cover relationships, family and parenting, personality behaviour, health, wellbeing, beauty, society and social trends, travel, spirituality and sex. Welcomes new ideas by email which fit into one of these areas, and suggestions should offer a combination of psychological insight and practical advice. Brief pitches accepted by email but do not send full unsolicited features. Original French edition founded 1970; UK edition founded 2005.

Pulsar Poetry Webzine

90 Beechwood Drive, Camelford, Cornwall PL32 9NB
email pulsar.ed@btinternet.com
website www.pulsarpoetry.com
Editor David Pike

Webzine, prefers publishing hard-hitting poems and poetry book reviews. Submissions may be sent via email with up to three unpublished poems. Poets retain copyright of their poems. Selected poems are published on the website. Payment: none. Does not accept simultaneous submissions. Founded 1995, online since 2009.

Pulse

Cogora, 1 Giltspur Street, London EC1A 9DD
email sofialind@cogora.com
website www.pulsetoday.co.uk
X @pulsetoday
Editor-in-Chief Jaimie Kaffash, *Editor* Sofia Lind
Online

Articles and photos of direct interest to GPs. Purely clinical material can be accepted only from medically qualified authors. Length: 600–1,200 words. Illustrations: by arrangement. Payment: by arrangement. Founded 1959.

Pushing Out the Boat

email info@pushingouttheboat.co.uk
website www.pushingouttheboat.co.uk
Facebook www.facebook.com/pushingouttheboat
X @POTBmag
Instagram @potbmag
Biennial See website for pricing details

North-East Scotland's magazine of new writing and visual arts. Features new prose, poetry and art from both the local area and the wider world, all selected (anonymously) from online submissions. Current edition published May 2025; next submissions open July–September 2026. The full-colour A4 print magazine (also available to view online) is run as a not-for-profit charity by volunteers. POTB's costs are met by sales revenue, plus events.

RA Magazine

Royal Academy of Arts, Burlington House, Piccadilly, London W1J 0BD
tel 020-7300 5820
email ramagazine@royalacademy.org.uk
website www.royalacademy.org.uk/ra-magazine
Editor Sam Phillips
Quarterly £7.95, £32 p.a.

Visual arts and culture articles relating to the Royal Academy of Arts and the wider British and international arts scene. Length: 150–2,500 words. Illustrations: consult the Editor. Payment: average £500 per 1,000 words; illustrations by negotiation. Founded 1983.

Radio Times

Immediate Media Co. Ltd, Vineyard House, 44 Brook Green, London W6 7BT
tel 020-7150 5429
email editor@radiotimes.com
website www.radiotimes.com
Editor Shem Law
Weekly £4.95

Articles and interviews that preview the week's programmes on British TV and radio as well as on-demand programming. All articles are specially commissioned – ideas and synopses are welcomed but not unsolicited MSS. Length: 600–2,500 words.

Illustrations: mostly in colour; photos, graphic designs or drawings. Payment: by arrangement. Founded 1923.

RAIL

Bauer Media Group, Media House, Lynch Wood, Peterborough Business Park, Peterborough PE2 6EA
tel (01733) 468000
email david.stubbings@bauermedia.co.uk
website www.railmagazine.com
Facebook www.facebook.com/Railmagazine
X @RAIL
Editor Dickon Ross, *Content Editor (news)* David Stubbings
Fortnightly From £120 p.a.

News and in-depth features on current UK railway operations. Length: 1,000–3,000 words (features), 250–400 words (news). Illustrations: by arrangement. Payment: by arrangement. Founded 1981.

Railway Gazette International

1st Floor, Chancery House, St Nicholas Way, Sutton, Surrey SM1 4JB
tel 020-8652 5200
email editor@railwaygazette.com
website www.railwaygazette.com
X @railwaygazette
Bluesky @railwaygazette.com.bsky.social
Instagram @railwaygazette
Executive Editor Nick Kingsley, *Head of News & Online* Andrew Grantham
Monthly £180 p.a.

Covers management, engineering, operation and finance of railway, metro and light rail transport worldwide. Articles of business interest on these subjects are considered and paid for if accepted. No 'enthusiast', heritage or modelling oriented articles. Email to discuss proposals. Illustrated articles, of 1,000–2,000 words, are preferred. Founded 1835.

The Railway Magazine

Media Centre, Morton Way, Horncastle, Lincs. LN9 6JR
tel (01507) 529589
email railway@mortons.co.uk
website www.railwaymagazine.co.uk
Instagram @therailwaymagazine
Editor Paul Bickerdyke, *Deputy Editor* Gareth Evans
Monthly £5.60

Illustrated magazine dealing with all railway subjects; no fiction or verse. Articles from 1,000–3,000 words accompanied by photos. Preliminary email or letter desirable. Illustrations: digital; b&w and colour scans. Payment: by arrangement. Founded 1897.

Reach Poetry

Indigo Dreams Publishing Ltd, 24 Forest Houses, Halwill, Beaworthy, Devon EX21 5UU
email publishing@indigodreams.co.uk
website www.indigodreamspublishing.com
X @IndigoDreamsPub
Editor Ronnie Goodyer
Monthly £5, £57 p.a.

UK's long-running monthly poetry magazine still in print. Unpublished and original poetry. Magazine subscribers submit up to two poems per month for consideration by post (include sae for reply) or email (preferred). New poets encouraged. Features lively subscribers' letters and votes pages. Four winners of Readers' Votes have their subscriptions increased. Founded 1998.

Record Collector

Diamond Publishing Ltd, 4th Floor, Harmsworth House, 13–15 Bouverie Street, London EC4Y 8DP
email paul.lester@metropolis.co.uk
website www.recordcollectormag.com
Instagram @recordcollectormag
Editor Paul Lester
Monthly £7.50

Covers all areas of music, with the focus on collectable releases and the reissues market. Specially commissions most material but will consider unsolicited material. Welcomes ideas for articles and features. Length: 2,000 words for articles/features; 200 words for news. Illustrations: all commissioned. Payment: negotiable. Founded 1980.

Red

House of Hearst, 30 Panton Street, Leicester Square, London SW1Y 4AJ
tel 020-7150 7600
email red@redmagazine.co.uk
website www.redonline.co.uk
X @RedMagDaily
Editor-in-Chief Sarah Tomczak
Monthly £5.99

High-quality articles on topics of interest to women aged 25–45: humour, memoirs, interviews and well-researched investigative features. Approach with ideas in writing in first instance. Length: 900 words upwards. Illustrations: by arrangement. Payment: by arrangement. Founded 1998.

Red Pepper

44–48 Shepherdess Walk, London N1 7JP
website www.redpepper.org.uk/get-involved/write-for-us/
Facebook www.facebook.com/redpeppermagazine
X @redpeppermag
Instagram @redpeppermagazine
Edited by An editorial collective
4 p.a. Subscribers may choose how much to pay

Independent radical magazine run by an editorial collective: news and features and debates on politics, culture and everyday life, written by and of interest to the feminist, green and international radical Left.

Material for inclusion in print mostly commissioned. Length: online 650-1200 words; print 500–2,000 words. Illustrations: by arrangement. Payment: £62 flat fee for online; up to £90 for print. See website for full information for editorial contact and pitching details, which vary per subject/topic. Founded 1994.

Reform

(published by United Reformed Church)
86 Tavistock Place, London WC1H 9RT
tel 020-7916 8630
email reform@urc.org.uk
website www.reform-magazine.co.uk
Editor Stephen Tomkins
10 p.a. From £18 p.a.

Explores theology, ethics, personal spirituality and Christian perspectives on social and current affairs. Offers articles about Christian ideas from a range of viewpoints, as well as interviews and reviews. Published by the United Reformed Church but has readers from all Christian denominations, as well as readers from other faiths and from no faith tradition. Illustrations: graphic artists/illustrators. Payment: by arrangement. Founded 1972.

Resurgence & Ecologist

The Resurgence Trust, The Resurgence Centre, Fore Street, Hartland, Bideford, Devon EX39 6AB
tel (01237) 441293
email editorial@resurgence.org
website www.resurgence.org
Facebook www.facebook.com/Resurgencetrust
Instagram @resurgencetrus
Editor Susan Clark
6 p.a. £6.95

Interested in environment and social justice investigations and features, green living advice and ideas, grassroots activism projects, artist profiles and reviews. Proposal first in most cases. Payment: various. See website for further guidance. Founded 1966 as *Resurgence*.

Retail Week

William Reed Ltd, Broadfield Park, Crawley RH11 9RT
email content@retail-week.com
website www.retail-week.com
X @retailweek
Editor-in-Chief Charlotte Hardie, *Executive Editor* George MacDonald, *Features Editor* Ellis Hawthorne
Weekly From £529 p.a.

Features and news stories on all aspects of retail management. Length: up to 1,400 words. Illustrations: colour photos. Payment: by arrangement. Founded 1988.

The Rialto

c/o 74 Britannia Road, Norwich NR1 4HS
email info@therialto.co.uk
website www.therialto.co.uk
Editor Michael Mackmin
2 p.a. £9, £25 p.a.

Mainly poetry, some commissioned prose. New poems welcome via Submittable (see website for details). Payment by arrangement. Also publishes poetry pamphlets and books (inquire before submitting) and runs competitions. Founded 1984.

Rouleur

New Wing, Somerset House, London WC2R 1LA
email info@rouleur.cc
website www.rouleur.cc
Instagram @rouleurmagazine
Editor Ed Pickering
8 p.a. £13

Cycling magazine and multi-channel offering, with international editions. Includes features, analysis, photography and race news, as well as tech and kit reviews.

Royal National Institute of Blind People (RNIB)

105 Judd Street, London WC1H 9NE
tel 0303 123 9999
email helpline@rnib.org.uk
website www.rnib.org.uk
X @RNIB

Publishes a variety of titles in a range of formats for adults and young people who have sight loss.

Rugby World

Future Publishing Ltd, 121-141 Westbourne Terrace, Paddington, London W2 6QA
tel 0330 390 6479
email josh.graham@futurenet.com
website www.rugbyworld.com
X @Rugbyworldmag
Editor Joe Robinson, *Content Editor* Josh Graham
Monthly £6.49

Features and exclusive news stories on rugby. Length: approx. 1,200 words. Illustrations: by arrangement. Payment: by arrangement. Founded 1960.

Runner's World

Hearst UK, House of Hearst, 30 Panton Street, London SW1Y 4AJ
tel 020-7339 4400
email editorial@runnersworld.co.uk
website www.runnersworld.com/uk
Facebook www.facebook.com/runnersworlduk
X @runnersworlduk
Editor-in-Chief Andy Dixon, *Deputy Editor* Joe Mackie
Monthly £6.99

Articles on running, health and fitness, and nutrition. Payment: by arrangement. Founded 1979.

Saga Magazine

3 Pancras Square, London N1C 4AG
email editor@saga.co.uk
website www.saga.co.uk/magazine
Instagram @sagamagazineuk
Editorial Director Louise Robinson
Monthly From £29.95 p.a.

General interest magazine aimed at the intelligent, literate 50+ reader. Wide range of articles from human interest, real-life stories, intriguing overseas interest (not travel), some natural history, celebrity interviews, photographic book extracts – all subjects are considered in this general interest title. Articles mostly commissioned or written in-house, but genuine exclusives welcome. Illustrations: colour, digital media; mainly commissioned but top-quality photo feature suggestions sometimes accepted. Payment: competitive rate, by negotiation. Founded 1984.

Sailing Today with Yachts & Yachting

The Chelsea Magazine Company,
111 Buckingham Palace Road, London SW1W 0DT
email sam.jefferson@chelseamagazines.com
website www.yachtsandyachting.co.uk
Facebook www.facebook.com/sailingtoday
Editor Georgie Corlett-Pitt
Monthly £5.50

Technical sailing and related lifestyle articles. Illustrations: line, half-tone, colour. Payment: by arrangement. Founded 1947.

Sainsbury's magazine

7C3, 77, Farringdon Road, London EC1M 3JU
tel 020-7775 777
email feedback@sainsburysmagazine.co.uk
website www.sainsburysmagazine.co.uk, www.seven.co.uk
Content Director Helena Lang, *Editorial Lead* Christine Faughlin
Monthly £3.95

Features: food and drink, health, travel; all material commissioned; no unsolicited material. Length: up to 1,500 words. Illustrations: colour and b&w photos and line illustrations. Payment: varies. Founded 1993.

School Libraries in View/SLG Newsletter

School Libraries Group,
CILIP: The Library and Information Association, Room 150, British Library, 96 Euston Road, London NW1 2DB
email treasurer.slg@cilip.org.uk
website www.cilip.org.uk
X @CILIPSLG
Instagram @cilipslg
Editor Newsletter Editor Barbara Band, School Libraries in View *Editor* Charlotte Cole

Newsletter published every half term to CILIP SLG members only. *School Libraries in View* published annually – Open Access.

Scientific Computing World

4 Signet Court, Cambridge CB5 8LA
tel (01223) 275464
email editor.scw@europascience.com
website www.scientific-computing.com
Editor Robert Roe
6 p.a. Free to qualifying subscribers, other subscription rates apply (see website)

Features on hardware and software developments for the scientific community, plus news articles and reviews. Length: 800–2,000 words. Illustrations: by arrangement. Payment: by negotiation. Founded 1994.

The Scots Magazine

D.C. Thomson & Co. Ltd, 2 Albert Square, Dundee DD1 1DD
tel (01382) 223131
email mail@scotsmagazine.com
website www.scotsmagazine.com
Editor-in-Chief Robert Wight
Monthly £4.99

Articles on all subjects of Scottish interest, but authors must also be Scottish. Illustrations: colour and b&w photos. Unsolicited material considered but preliminary enquiries advised. Payment: on acceptance. Founded 1739.

The Scottish Farmer

Newsquest Scotland, 125 Fullerton Drive, Glasgow G32 8FG
tel 0141 302 7732 , 07803 970225
email j.sleigh@thesf.co.uk
website www.thescottishfarmer.co.uk
Editor John Sleigh
Weekly From £58 p.a.

Articles on agricultural subjects. Length: 1,000–1,500 words. Illustrations: by arrangement. Payment: by arrangement. Founded 1893.

Scottish Field

Fettes Park, 496 Ferry Road, Edinburgh EH5 2DL
tel 0131 551 1000
email editor@scottishfield.co.uk
website www.scottishfield.co.uk
Facebook www.facebook.com/scottishfield
X @ScottishField
Editor Richard Bath
Monthly £5.50

Scottish lifestyle magazine: interiors, food, travel, wildlife, heritage, general lifestyle. Length of article accepted: 1,200 words. Founded 1903.

Screen Daily

Media Business Insight, Essex Street,
London WC2R 3AA
tel 020-8102 0900
email matt.mueller@screendaily.com
website www.screendaily.com
Instagram @screendaily
Editor Matt Mueller
Monthly From £193 p.a.

News and features on the international film business. No unsolicited material. Length: variable. Payment: by arrangement.

Sea Angler

Kelsey Publishing Ltd, The Granary, Downs Court, Yalding Hill, Yalding, Maidstone, Kent ME18 6AL
website www.seaangler.co.uk
Facebook www.facebook.com/seaanglermag
Editor David Mitchell
13 p.a. £4.75

Topical articles on all aspects of sea-fishing around the British Isles. Illustrations: colour. Payment: by arrangement. Founded 1972.

Sea Breezes

The Office, Strenaby Farm,
Lonan Church Road, Laxey, Isle of Man IM4 7JX
tel (01624) 863672
website www.seabreezes.co.im
Editor Captain Peter Corrin
Monthly £6.70

Factual articles on ships and the sea past and present, preferably illustrated. Length: up to 4,000 words. Illustrations: by arrangement. Payment: by arrangement. Founded 1919.

Seen and Heard

Nagalro, 3rd Floor, 86–90 Paul Street,
London EC2A 4NE
tel 07498 186980
email mail@rodneynoon.co.uk
website www.nagalro.com/journal/default.aspx
Editor Rodney Noon
Quarterly £35 p.a.

Professional journal of Nagalro, the professional association of children's guardians, family court advisers and independent social workers. Publishes high-quality articles and academic papers on issues relating to the professional practice of child-protection social workers, child abuse and protection, adoption and the law relating to children. Potential contributors are advised to contact the editor initially with proposals. Payment: on publication, ranging from £50 to £100.

The Sewing Directory

1 Pound Terrace, Wellington, Somerset TA21 8BY
tel (01823) 978137
email julie@thesewingdirectory.net
website www.thesewingdirectory.co.uk
Facebook www.facebook.com/thesewingdirectory
X @sewingdirectory
Instagram @sewingdirectory
Content Editor Julie Briggs

Online and local (searchable by UK counties) directory of UK sewing businesses – sewing courses, fabric shops and sewing groups. Plus free sewing projects, sewing features and technique guides. Payment: by arrangement. Founded 2010.

SFX Magazine

Future Publishing Ltd, Quay House, The Ambury, Bath BA1 1UA
tel (01225) 442244
email darren.scott@futurenet.com
website www.gamesradar.com/sfx
Facebook www.facebook.com/SFXmagazine
Instagram @sfxmagazine
Editor Darren Scott
13 p.a. Subscription offers available

Sci-fi and fantasy magazine covering TV, films, DVDs, books, comics, games and collectables. Founded 1995.

Ships Monthly

Kelsey Publishing Ltd, The Granary, Downs Court, Yalding Hill, Yalding, Maidstone, Kent ME18 6AL
tel (01959) 541444
email ships.monthly@btinternet.com
website www.shipsmonthly.com
Editor Nicholas Leach
Monthly £4.99

Illustrated articles of shipping and maritime interest – both mercantile and naval, preferably of 20th- and 21st-century ships. Well-researched, factual material only. No short stories or poetry. 'Notes for contributors' available. Mainly commissioned material; preliminary letter or email essential. Illustrations: half-tone and line, colour transparencies, prints and digital images via email, DVD or CD. Payment: by arrangement. Founded 1966.

Shooter Literary Magazine

98 Muswell Hill Road, London N10 3JR
email shooterlitmag@gmail.com
website www.shooterlitmag.com
Facebook www.facebook.com/ShooterLiteraryMagazine
X @ShooterLitMag
Instagram @ShooterLitMag
Editor Melanie Sykes-White
2 p.a. £15, £25 p.a.

Submissions of short fiction and non-fiction (2,000–6,000 words) and poetry welcome. Annual story and poetry competitions. Rolling monthly flash fiction/non-fiction competition. Editing services available. See website for guidelines, current theme and deadline information. Payment: £25 for prose, £5 for poetry, plus complimentary issue. Founded 2015.

Shoreline of Infinity

email contact@shorelineofinfinity.com
website www.shorelineofinfinity.com
X @shoreinf
Co-founder, Editor-in-Chief, Editor Emeritus Noel Chidwick
3 p.a. £9.50 (print)

Science fiction and fantasy science fiction stories, poetry, author interviews, articles and reviews. Based in Edinburgh, Scotland, but with a worldwide readership and contributor base. Invites submissions of short stories and poetry, both originals and translations into English, specifically: original and previously unpublished fiction of up to 6,000 words; up to six original and previously unpublished poems per issue. Contributors should indicate any translation rights issues in their cover note. Payment: 2p/word for stories and articles. Copies for contributors; any additional copies at discount rates. Check website for submission window openings. Founded 2014.

Sight and Sound

BFI, 21 Stephen Street, London W1T 1LN
tel 020-7255 1444
email isabel.stevens@bfi.org.uk
website www.bfi.org.uk/sightandsound
X @SightSoundmag
Editor-in-Chief Mike Williams, *Managing Editor* Isabel Stevens, *Reviews Editor* Katie McCabe
Monthly £6.50

Features, interviews and essays on world cinema; theatrical reviews; book reviews; DVD reviews; festival reports. Length: 1,000–5,000 words. Contact Managing Editor in the first instance. Illustrations and photography: by arrangement. Payment: by arrangement. Founded 1932.

Slightly Foxed

53 Hoxton Square, London N1 6PB
tel 020-7033 0258
email office@foxedquarterly.com
website www.foxedquarterly.com
Facebook www.facebook.com/foxedquarterly
X @foxedquarterly
Instagram @foxedquarterly
Publisher/Co-editor Gail Pirkis
Quarterly Single issue £14.50 (UK and Republic of Ireland), £16.50 (RoW); annual subscription £56 p.a. (UK and Ireland), £64 p.a. (Overseas)

Independent-minded quarterly magazine that introduces its readers to books that are no longer new and fashionable but have enduring appeal. Each issue contains 96pp of recommendations for books of lasting interest, old and new, both fiction and non-fiction. Unsolicited submissions are welcome; see website for guidelines. Founded 2004.

Snowflake Magazine

tel 0115 648 9573
email info@snowflakeculture.com
website www.snowflakeculture.com/submit-guidelines
Bluesky @snowflakemag.bsky.social
Instagram @Snowflake_Magazine
4 p.a. £9.99 (print), £2.99 (digital)

Quarterly literary and arts magazine that focuses on providing up-and-coming LGBTQ+ creators an entrance to, or boost within, the artistic community through a professional publication. Accepts submissions of fiction, poetry, art, essays, interviews, photographs and more from anyone who identifies as LGBTQ+. Ecological focus: magazine and shipping materials are made using predominantly recycled paper and soy-based inks. See website for full guidelines, submission windows, current themes and prompts.

Songwriting and Composing

30 Brantwood, Chester le Street, Co. Durham DH2 2UL
tel 0330 2020 760
email gisc@songwriters-guild.co.uk
website www.songwriters-guild.co.uk
Quarterly Free to members

Magazine of the Guild of International Songwriters and Composers. Profiles/stories, song assessments, articles, contacts relating to songwriting, music publishing, recording and the music industry. Illustrations: collaboration register. Payment: by arrangement. Founded 1986.

The Spectator

22 Old Queen Street, London SW1H 9HP
tel 020-7961 0200
email editor@spectator.co.uk
website www.spectator.co.uk
Instagram @spectator1828
Editor Michael Gove
Weekly £5.95

Articles on current affairs, politics, the arts; book reviews. Illustrations: by arrangement. Payment: on merit. Founded 1828.

Spellbinder Magazine

email spellbinder.contact@gmail.com
website www.spellbindermag.com/submission-guidelines/
Facebook www.facebook.com/spellbindermag
Instagram @spellbindermag
Editor-in-Chief Amber Natalie Kennedy
Quarterly

Inclusive and diverse print and online literary and art magazine. Welcomes submissions from writers of all levels of experience, particularly those early in their literary careers. Considers previously unpublished works of poetry, fiction, non-fiction, drama and visual art. See website for full submissions guidelines and windows.

Square Mile

7 Wingate Business Exchange,
64-66 Wingate Square, London SW4 0AF
tel 020-3970 0330
website https://squaremile.com
X @SQUAREMILE_COM
Instagram @squaremile
Editorial Director Mark Hedley
Monthly Free

Luxury lifestyle magazine aimed at men working and living in the City of London. Founded 2005.

The Stage

Stage House, 47 Bermondsey Street, London SE1 3XT
tel 020-7403 1818
email alistair@thestage.co.uk
website www.thestage.co.uk
Instagram @thestageuk
Editor Alistair Smith, *Features Editor* Georgia Snow
Weekly From £99 p.a.

Original and interesting articles on the theatre and performing arts industry may be sent for the Editor's consideration. Features range in length from 800 to 3,000 words. Payment: by arrangement.
Founded 1880.

Stamp Magazine

David Hall Publishing, 1st Floor, Nene House, Sopwith Way, Daventry NN11 8EA
email Guy.Thomas@dhpub.co.uk
website www.stampmagazine.co.uk
Editor Guy Thomas
13 p.a. £5.35

Informative articles and exclusive news items on stamp collecting and postal history. Preliminary letter. Payment: by arrangement. Illustrations: by arrangement. Founded 1934.

Stand Magazine

School of English, University of Leeds, Leeds LS2 9JT
tel 0113 233 4794
email engstand@leeds.ac.uk
website www.standmagazine.org
Managing Editor John Whale, *Editors* Hannah Copley, Kathryn Jenner, Ian Fairley
4 p.a. From £16 p.a. (online), £35 p.a. (print)

Poetry, short stories, translations, literary criticism. Submissions should be made via email. Will consider only original, previously unpublished material; potential contributors should familiarise themselves with the magazine first. Poetry submissions should be of four to six poems max; fiction should be no more than 3,000 words. Founded 1952.

The Stinging Fly

PO Box 6016, Dublin 1, Republic of Ireland
email editor@stingingfly.org
website https://stingingfly.org/submissions/
Facebook www.facebook.com/StingingFly
X @stingingfly
Editor Lisa McInerney
2 p.a. €33 p.a. (UK)

Publishes and promotes the best new Irish and international writing. Submissions of new, previously unpublished fiction, non-fiction and poetry welcomed: see website for guidelines, forthcoming submissions windows and payment information. Founded 1997.

The Strad

Newsquest Media Group, 4th Floor,
Queens House. 55–56 Lincoln's Inn Fields,
London WC2A 3LJ
tel 020-7618 3095
email thestrad@thestrad.com
website www.thestrad.com
Facebook www.facebook.com/thestrad
X @TheStradMag
Instagram @the_strad_
Editor Emma Baker
12 p.a. plus occasional supplements £5.95

Features, news and reviews for stringed instrument players, teachers, makers and enthusiasts – both professional and amateur. Specially commissions most material but will consider unsolicited material. Welcomes ideas for articles and features. Length: 1,000–2,250 (articles/features), 100–150 (news). Illustrations: by arrangement. Payment: £150–£350 (articles/features), varies for news. Founded 1890.

Streetcake Magazine

email streetcakemagazine@gmail.com
website www.streetcakemagazine.com
Facebook www.facebook.com/streetcakemag
Instagram @streetcakemagazine
Editors Trini Decombe, Nikky Dudley
4/6 p.a. Optional donation

Experimental writing magazine. See website for submissions windows: considers poems, visual poems and fiction (up to 2,500 words). Innovative perspectives, forms and imagery particularly welcome. Responses usually received within six weeks.

Strong Words

email info@strong-words.co.uk
website www.strong-words.co.uk
X @strongwordsmag
Instagram @strongwordsmag
Editor Ed Needham
6 p.a. £45 p.a.

Book reviews, author interviews and features on new books, trends, backlist titles and tips on how to write in various genres. Very limited options for outside contributions, but any pitches and information about new books for possible review can be sent via email. Academic essays or reviews not accepted.

Stuff

Kelsey Media, The Granary, Downs Court, Yalding Hill, Yalding, Kent ME18 6AL
email stuff.ed@kelsey.co.uk
website www.stuff.tv
X @StuffTV
Bluesky @stufftv.bsky.social
Instagram @stuffmag
Editor-in-Chief Dan Grabham
Monthly £5.99 and online

Articles on technology, games, films, lifestyle. Features and reviews. Payment: by negotiation. Founded 1996.

Style at Home

Future Publishing Ltd, 121–141 Westbourne Terrace, London W2 6JR
email styleathome@futurenet.com
website www.housetohome.co.uk/styleathome
Facebook www.facebook.com/StyleAtHomeMag
Instagram @styleathomemag
Editor Heather Young
Monthly £3.99

Interiors magazine aimed at those interested in updating, styling and decorating their home. Regular articles showing transformed rooms as well as step-by-step projects, shopping ideas and a recipe section.

Stylist

D.C. Thomson & Co. Ltd, 185 Fleet Street, London EC4A 2HS
tel 020-7611 9700
email stories@stylist.co.uk
website www.stylist.co.uk
Instagram @stylistmagazine
Editorial Director Lisa Smosarski, *Features Director* Hannah Keegan
12 p.a. From £2.99 per month

Women's interest magazine that covers topics from fashion and beauty to books, travel, money and women in the news. Email synopses of feature ideas to the address above. Also extensive online presence. Founded 2009.

The Tablet

1 King Street Cloisters, Clifton Walk, London W6 0GY
tel 020-8748 8484
email thetablet@thetablet.co.uk
website www.thetablet.co.uk
X @The_Tablet
Editor Brendan Walsh
Weekly £6

Catholic weekly: religion, philosophy, politics, society, books and arts. International coverage. Freelance work commissioned: do not send unsolicited material. Length: various. Illustrations: cartoons and photos. Payment: by arrangement. Founded 1840.

Take a Break

Bauer Media, The Lantern, 75 Hampstead Road, London NW1 2PL
tel 020-7241 8000
email tab.features@bauer.co.uk
website www.takeabreak.co.uk
Instagram @takeabreak.mag
Weekly £1.35

Lively, illustrated tabloid women's weekly. True-life features, health and beauty, family; lots of puzzles. Payment: by arrangement. Founded 1990.

Take a Break's Take a Puzzle

Bauer Media, The Lantern, 75 Hampstead Road, London NW1 2PL
email take.puzzle@bauer.co.uk
website www.puzzlemagazines.co.uk/takeapuzzle
Monthly £3.50

Puzzles. Fresh ideas always welcome. Illustrations: by arrangement. Payment: from £25 per puzzle, £30–£90 for picture puzzles and for illustrations not an integral part of a puzzle. Founded 1991.

Tate Etc

Tate, Millbank, London SW1P 4RG
tel 020-7887 8724
email enrico.tassi@tate.org.uk
email figgy.guyver@tate.org.uk
website www.tate.org.uk/tate-etc
X @TateEtcMag
Deputy Editor Enrico Tassi, *Assistant Editor* Figgy Guyver, *Editorial Assistant* Safi Bugel
4 p.a. £34 p.a. (UK)

Independent visual arts magazine: features, interviews, previews and opinion pieces. Length: up to 3,000 words but always commissioned. Illustrations: by arrangement. Payment: negotiable.

Tatler

The Condé Nast Publications Ltd, The Adelphi, 1–11 John Adam Street, London WC2N 6HT
website www.tatler.com
X @Tatlermagazine
Editor Richard Dennen
Monthly £5.99

Smart society magazine favouring sharp articles, profiles, fashion and the arts. Illustrations: colour, b&w, but all commissioned. Founded 1709.

Taxation

Lexis House, 30 Farringdon Street, London EC4A 4HH
tel 020-8212 1949

email taxation@lexisnexis.co.uk
website www.taxation.co.uk
X @Taxation
Editor-in-Chief Andrew Hubbard
48 issues p.a. £655 p.a.

Updating and advice concerning UK tax law and practice for accountants and tax experts. All articles written by professionals. Founded 1927.

Tears in the Fence

Flats, Durweston Mill, Mill Lane, Durweston, Blandford Forum, Dorset DT11 0QD
email tearsinthefence@gmail.com
website https://tearsinthefence.com
X @TearsInTheFence
Editor David Caddy
Bi-annual £12 per issue, or £30 for three issues/£50 for six issues

Socially aware literary magazine with an international outlook and author base. Includes regular columnists as well as critical reviews of recent books and essays on English and American poets, flash fiction, translations and interviews. See website for up-to-date information on forthcoming submission windows. Submissions of original, unpublished work should be made by email to the address above in the body of the message and as an attachment.

Television

RTS, 3 Dorset Rise, London EC4Y 8EH
tel 020-7822 2810
email publications@rts.org.uk
website www.rts.org.uk
Editor Steve Clarke
Monthly

Articles on all aspects of TV and related content sectors including the people, programmes, politics and media policy. Coverage of RTS events. Payment: by arrangement. Founded 1928.

Tempo

Cambridge University Press,
The Edinburgh Building, Shaftesbury Road,
Cambridge CB2 8RU
email tempoeditor@cambridge.org
website https://www.cambridge.org/core/journals/tempo
Editor Professor Christopher Fox
Quarterly From £233 p.a.

Authoritative articles on contemporary music. Length: 4,000–6,000 words. Illustrations: music type, occasional photographic or musical supplements. Payment: by arrangement. Founded 1939.

Today's Golfer

Bauer Media Group, Media House, Lynch Wood, Peterborough Business Park, Peterborough PE2 6EA
tel (01733) 468000
email chris.jones@bauermedia.co.uk
website www.todaysgolfer.co.uk
Facebook www.facebook.com/TodaysGolferBauer
X @TheTodaysGolfer
Editor Chris Jones
13 p.a. From £3.00 per month

Specialist features and articles on golf instruction, equipment and courses. Founded 1988.

Top Santé

Kelsey Publishing Ltd, The Granary, Downs Court, Yalding Hill, Yalding, Maidstone, Kent ME18 6AL
tel (01959) 541444
website www.topsante.co.uk
X @topsanteuk
Instagram @topsanteuk
Editor Katy Sunnassee
13 p.a. £5.25

Features and news on all aspects of health, wellbeing, fitness and beauty. Ideas welcome. Founded 1993.

Trail

Bauer Consumer Media, Media House,
Lynch Wood, Peterborough Business Park,
Peterborough PE2 6EA
tel (01733) 468363
email trail@bauermedia.co.uk
website www.livefortheoutdoors.com/magazines/trail/
Facebook www.facebook.com/Trailmagazine
Editor Oli Reed
Monthly £5.60

Outdoor activity magazine focusing mainly on high-level walking with some scrambling and climbing. Some opportunities for freelancers; ideas welcome.

Trout & Salmon

Time Well Spent Group Limited, Jubilee House,
92 Lincoln Road, Peterborough PE1 2SN
tel (01371) 851890
email editorial@twsgroup.com
website www.troutandsalmon.com
Instagram @troutandsalmon
Editor Andrew Flitcroft
13 p.a. £6.99

Articles of good quality with strong trout or salmon angling interest. Length: 400–2,000 words, accompanied if possible by good quality colour photographs. Illustrations: by arrangement. Founded 1955.

Truck & Driver

DVV Media International Ltd, 1st Floor,
Chancery House, St Nicholas Way, Sutton,
Surrey SM1 1JB
tel 020-8912 2131
email contact@truckanddriver.co.uk
website www.truckanddriver.co.uk
X @TRUCKNDRIVER
Editor Andy Stewart
Monthly From £57 p.a.

News, articles on trucks, personalities and features of interest to truck drivers. Words and picture packages preferred. Preferred feature length: 500-1,500 words. Payment: negotiable. Founded 1984.

TV Times Magazine

Future Publishing Ltd, 121–141 Westbourne Terrace, London W2 6JR
tel 020-3148 5615
website www.whatsontv.co.uk/tv-times
Instagram @tvtimesmagazine
Weekly £2.90

Features with an affinity to ITV, BBC1, BBC2, Channels 4 and 5, satellite and digital channels, as well as radio personalities and TV generally. Length: by arrangement. Photographs: commissioned only. Payment: by arrangement. Founded 1955.

The Vegan

The Vegan Society, Donald Watson House, 21 Hylton Street, Birmingham B18 6HJ
tel 0121 523 1730
email editor@vegansociety.com
website www.vegansociety.com
Editor Elena Orde
Quarterly £3, free to members

Articles on health, nutrition, cookery, vegan lifestyles, land use, climate change, animal rights. Length: approx. 1,000 words. Illustrations: photos, foods, animals, livestock systems, crops, people, events; colour for cover. Payment: £150–£500 per piece. Founded 1944.

Vegan Food & Living

Anthem Publishing, 1 Widcombe Parade, Bath BA2 4JT
tel (01225) 489984
email holly.jackson@anthem.co.uk
website www.veganfoodandliving.com/contact
Facebook www.facebook.com/veganfoodandliving
X @veganfoodliving
Instagram @veganfoodandliving
Editor Holly Jackson
Monthly £6.49

Plant-based recipes (70 per month), along with features on cooking techniques, vegan ethics and sustainable living. Also nutrition advice, and guides for gourmet travellers. Founded 2015.

Viz

Diamond Publishing, 4th Floor, Harmsworth House, 13–15 Bouverie Street, London EC4Y 8DP
email viz@viz.co.uk
website www.viz.co.uk
Facebook www.facebook.com/VizComic
10 p.a. £3.99

Cartoons, spoof tabloid articles, spoof advertisements. Illustrations: half-tone, line, cartoons. Payment: by arrangement. Founded 1979.

Vogue

The Condé Nast Publications Ltd, The Adelphi, 1–11 John Adam Street, London WC2N 6HT
website www.vogue.co.uk
X @BritishVogue
Head of Editorial Content Chioma Nnadi
Monthly Price varies, depending on special offers

Fashion, beauty, health, decorating, art, theatre, films, literature, music, travel, food and wine. Length: articles from 1,000 words. Illustrated. Founded 1916.

Waitrose Food

Dentsu Creative, 10 Triton Street, Regents Place, London NW1 3BF
tel 020-7565 3236
email waitrose.food@dentsu.com
Editor Jessica Gunn
Monthly £3.75 (free to MyWaitrose members)

In-house magazine of Waitrose & Partners. Features seasonal recipes, menu ideas, interviews, lifestyle and travel.

walk

The Ramblers, 13 Dirty Lane, London SE1 9PA
tel 020-3961 3300
email walkmag@ramblers.org.uk
website www.ramblers.org.uk/current-walk-issue
Facebook www.facebook.com/ramblers
X @RamblersGB
Instagram @ramblersgb
Editor Elyssa Campbell-Barr
Quarterly Free to members

Magazine of the Ramblers, Britain's walking charity. Articles on walking, access to countryside and related issues, and interviews. Material mostly commissioned. Length: up to 1,500 words. Illustrations: colour photos, preferably hi-res, digitally supplied. Payment: by agreement. Founded 1935.

Wallpaper*

Future Publishing Ltd, 121–141 Westbourne Terrace, London W2 6JR
website www.wallpaper.com
X @wallpapermag
Instagram @wallpapermag
Editor-in-Chief Bill Prince
12 p.a. £10

International media brand covering architecture, design, art, travel, entertaining, beauty and grooming, transport, technology, fashion, and watches and jewellery. Brand extensions include an in-house creative agency, an interior design service, and a digital learning programme in collaboration with Parsons School of Design. Founded 1996.

Wanderlust

Capital House, 25 Chapel Street, London NW1 5DH
email submissions@wanderlust.co.uk
website www.wanderlustmagazine.com

Editor-in-Chief George Kipouros
6 p.a. From £7.95

Features on independent, adventure and special-interest travel. See website for contributor guidelines. Length: up to 2,500 words. Illustrations: hi-res digital. Payment: by arrangement. Founded 1993.

The War Cry

The Salvation Army, 1 Champion Park,
London SE5 8FJ
email warcry@salvationarmy.org.uk
website www.salvationarmy.org.uk/warcry
Facebook www.facebook.com/TheWarCryUK
X @TheWarCryUK
Weekly

Voluntary contributions: human interest stories of personal Christian faith. Founded 1879.

Wasafiri

School of English and Drama,
Queen Mary University of London, Mile End Road,
London E1 4NS
email wasafiri@qmul.ac.uk
website www.wasafiri.org
Editor and Publishing Director Sana Goyal
4 p.a. £12.50

International contemporary literature. Accepts submissions for fiction, poetry, articles and interviews; see website for details. Founded 1984.

Waterways World

Waterways World Ltd, 151 Station Street,
Burton-on-Trent DE14 1BG
tel (01283) 742950
email editorial@waterwaysworld.com
website www.waterwaysworld.com
X @waterwaysworld
Editor Bobby Cowling
Monthly £4.99

Feature articles on all aspects of inland waterways in Britain and abroad, including historical material; factual and technical articles preferred. No short stories or poetry. See website for notes for potential contributors (under the contact section). Illustrations: by arrangement. Payment: by arrangement. Founded 1972.

The Week

Future Publishing Ltd, Quay House, The Ambury,
Bath BA1 1UA
email editorialadmin@theweek.co.uk
website www.theweek.co.uk
Weekly From £51 p.a. (special offers may be available)

Magazine that distils the best from the British and foreign press into 44pp, including news, art, science, business, property and leisure. Founded 1995.

Wet Grain

18/3 Marchmont Road, Edinburgh EH9 1HZ
email wetgrainpoetry@protonmail.com
website https://wetgrainpoetry.co.uk/submit
Facebook www.facebook.com/WetGrain
Instagram @wetgrainpoetry
Editors Patrick Romero McCafferty, Christian Lemay; also Guest Editors
1 p.a. From £7

Annual print poetry magazine based in Edinburgh. See website for information on current guest editors and for submission window dates. Potential contributors may submit up to four poems in a Word document via email (names should not be included); familiarity with the magazine encouraged. Simultaneous submission welcomed. Founded 2019.

What's On TV

Future Publishing Ltd, 121–141 Westbourne Terrace,
London W2 6JR
tel 020-3148 5573
website www.whattowatch.com
Facebook www.facebook.com/whatsontvuk
Weekly 85p

Features on TV programmes and personalities. All material commissioned. Length: up to 250 words. Illustrations: colour and b&w photos. Payment: by agreement. Founded 1991.

Woman

Future Publishing Ltd, 121–141 Westbourne Terrace,
London W2 6JR
tel 020-3148 5000
email woman@futurenet.com
website www.womanmagazine.co.uk
Instagram @woman.maguk
Group Editor Hannah Fernando
Weekly £2.30

News, celebrity and real-life features, of no more than 1,000 words. Particular interest in celebrity and diet exclusives. Digital images only. Read magazine prior to submission. Fiction not published. Payment: by negotiation. Founded 1937.

woman&home

Future Publishing Ltd, 121–141 Westbourne Terrace,
London W2 6JR
email ella.dove@futurenet.com
website www.womanandhome.com
Group Editor Hannah Fernando, *Features Editor* Ella Dove
Monthly £5.99

Centres on the personal and home interests of the lively minded mature, modern woman. Articles dealing with fashion, beauty, leisure pursuits, gardening, home style; features on topical issues, people and places. Fiction: complete stories from 3,000–4,500 words in length. Illustrations: by arrangement. Non-commissioned work is not accepted and cannot be returned. Founded 1926.

Woman's Own

Future Publishing Ltd, 121–141 Westbourne Terrace, London W2 6JR
tel 020-3148 5000
email womansown@futurenet.com
Facebook www.facebook.com/womansownmagazine
Editor Kira Agass, *Features Editor* Cher Heasmer
Weekly £2.30

Modern women's magazine aimed at the 35–50 age group. No unsolicited features. Payment: by arrangement. Founded 1932.

Woman's Weekly

Future Publishing Ltd, 121–141 Westbourne Terrace, London W2 6JR
tel 020-3148 5000
email ella.dove@futurenet.com
website www.womansweekly.com
Facebook www.facebook.com/WomansWeekly
Editor Geoffrey Palmer, *Features Editor* Ella Dove
Weekly £2.40

Lively family-interest magazine. Unsolicited short stories currently not accepted. Celebrity and strong human interest features, health, finance and consumer features, plus beauty, diet, travel, homes, craft, knitting, gardening and cookery; also inspirational and entertaining personal stories. Illustrations: full-colour fiction illustrations, small sketches and photos. Payment: by arrangement. Founded 1911.

The World of Interiors

The Condé Nast Publications Ltd, The Adelphi, 1–11 John Adam Street, London WC2N 6HT
tel 020-7851 1800
email ariadne.fletcher@condenast.co.uk
website www.worldofinteriors.co.uk
X @wofinteriors
Editor-in-Chief Hamish Bowles
Monthly £4.99

All material commissioned: send photographs/synopsis for article ideas. Length: 1,000–1,500 words. Illustrations: by arrangement. Founded 1981.

World Soccer

Kelsey Publishing Ltd, The Granary, Downs Court, Yalding Hill, Yalding, Maidstone, Kent ME18 6AL
tel (01959) 541444
email WOS.ed@kelsey.co.uk
website www.worldsoccer.com
Editor Stephen Fishlock
Monthly £5.99

Articles, features, news concerning football, its personalities and worldwide development. Length: 600–2,000 words. Payment: by arrangement. Founded 1960.

The World Today

Chatham House, 10 St James's Square, London SW1Y 4LE
tel 020-7957 5712
email MHiggins@chathamhouse.org
website www.chathamhouse.org/publications/the-world-today
Instagram @theworldtodaymag
Editor Mike Higgins
6 p.a. From £43 p.a. (student rate from £32)

Analysis of international issues and current events by journalists, diplomats, politicians and academics. Length: 1,200–1,500 words. Payment: nominal. Founded 1945.

Writing Magazine

Warners Group Publications Plc, 5th Floor, 31–32 Park Row, Leeds LS1 5JD
tel 0113 200 2929
email tjackson@warnersgroup.co.uk
website www.writers-online.co.uk
Facebook www.facebook.com/writingmagazine
X @writingmagazine
Content Editor Tina Jackson
Monthly £5.99

Articles on all aspects of writing. Length: 800–2,000 words. Payment: by arrangement. Founded 1992. In addition, *Writers' News* (now part of *Writing Magazine*) features news, competitions and market information. Length: up to 350 words. Payment: by arrangement. Founded 1989.

Yachting Monthly

Future Publishing Ltd, Quay House, The Ambury, Bath BA1 1UA
tel 0330 390 3933
email yachtingmonthly@futurenet.com
website www.yachtingmonthly.com
Editor Theo Stocker
Monthly £5.99

Articles on all aspects of seamanship, navigation, the handling of sailing craft, and their design, construction and equipment. Well-written narrative accounts of cruises in yachts. Contributors should read the magazine to understand where their submission might fit before contacting the editorial team, who can advise on what any requirements will be. Illustrations: colour photos. Payment: quoted on acceptance. Founded 1906.

Yachting World

Future Publishing Ltd, Quay House, The Ambury, Bath BA1 1UA
tel (01225) 442244
email yachting.world@futurenet.com
website www.yachtingworld.com
Editor Helen Fretter
Monthly £5.75

Practical and inspirational articles of an original nature, dealing with sailing yachts, both cruising and racing, for the experienced and knowledgeable sailor/owner. Length: 1,500–2,000 words. Illustrations: digital files, drawings. Payment: varies. Founded 1894.

The Yorkshire Dalesman

Country Publications Limited, The Gatehouse, Skipton Castle, Skipton, North Yorkshire BD23 1AL
tel (01756) 693479
email mick@dalesman.co.uk
website www.dalesman.co.uk
Facebook www.facebook.com/yorkshire.dalesman
Instagram @dalesmanmagazine
Editor Mick Smith
Monthly £3.90

Articles and stories of genuine interest concerning Yorkshire (1,000 to 1,200 words). Payment: £70 per 1,000 words plus extra for usable photos/illustrations. Founded 1939.

Your Dog Magazine

Warners Group Publications Plc, The Maltings, West Street, Bourne, Lincs. PE10 9PH
email editorial@yourdog.co.uk
website www.yourdog.co.uk
Facebook www.facebook.com/yourdogmagazine
X @yourdog
Monthly £4.99

Articles and information of interest to dog lovers; features on all aspects of pet dogs. Length: approx. 800–1,500 words. Payment: by arrangement. Founded 1994.

Your Horse Magazine

Kelsey Media Ltd, The Granary, Downs Court, Yalding Hill, Yalding, Maidstone, Kent ME18 6AL
email yh.ed@kelsey.co.uk
website www.yourhorse.co.uk
Facebook www.facebook.com/YourHorse
Magazine Editor Julie Harding, *Digital Editor* Aimi Clark
13 issues p.a. £4.75

Practical horse care, riding advice and inspirational interviews, features and real-life articles for riders, owners and horse lovers to enjoy. Send feature ideas with examples of previous published writing. Welcomes ideas for articles and features. Length: 1,500 words. Payment: (approx.) £130 per 1,000 words. Founded 1983.

Syndicates, news and press agencies

Before submitting material, you are strongly advised to make preliminary enquiries and to ascertain terms of work. Strictly speaking, syndication is the selling and reselling of previously published work although some news and press agencies handle original material.

Neil Bradley Studio

tel 07814 526808
email enquire@neilbradleystudio.co.uk
Director Neil Bradley

Supplies cartoons to national and regional press; emphasis placed on variety and topicality with work based on current media listings. Daily single frame and strip cartoons. Founded 1981.

Bulls Presstjänst AB

Augustendalsvägen 51, 131 52 Nacka Strand, Sweden
tel +46 8-55520600
email info@bulls.se
website www.bullspress.com

Market: newspapers, magazines, weeklies and advertising agencies across Northern Europe. Syndicates human-interest picture stories; topical and well-illustrated background articles and series; photographic features dealing with science, people, personalities, glamour; genre pictures for advertising; condensations and serialisations of bestselling fiction and non-fiction; cartoons, comic strips, film and TV rights, merchandising and newspaper graphics online.

DMG Media Licensing

Northcliffe House, 9 Derry Street, London W8 5HY
tel 020-7566 0360
website www.solosyndication.co.uk
Director of Licensing & Syndication William Gardiner

Worldwide syndication of newspaper features, photos, cartoons, puzzles and strips. Represents the international syndication of Associated Newspapers Ltd (*Daily Mail*, *Mail on Sunday*, the *i* newspaper, Mail+, *Metro*), *New Scientist*, Andrews McMeel Syndication (US) and Creators Syndicate (US) in Great Britain and Ireland, Africa and the Middle East. Formerly Solo Syndication.

Europress Features (UK)

18 St Chad's Road, Didsbury,
Nr Manchester M20 4WH
tel 0161 445 2945
email europressmedia@yahoo.com

Representation of newspapers and magazines in Europe, Australia and the US. Syndication of top-flight features with exclusive illustrations – human interest stories – showbusiness personalities. 30–35% commission on sales of material successfully accepted; 40% on exclusive illustrations.

Foresight News

Centaur Media Plc, 10 York Road, London SE1 7ND
tel 020-7970 4293
email editorial@foresightnews.co.uk
website www.foresightnews.com
X @ForesightNewsUK
Publisher Nicole Wilkins

Offers an extensive, fully searchable database featuring thousands of forthcoming events and news from across the UK and around the world, spanning a variety of sectors including politics, business, crime and home affairs, health, entertainment and sport.

Guardian Licensing

Kings Place, 90 York Way, London N1 9GU
tel 020-3353 2539
email licensing@theguardian.com
website https://licensing.theguardian.com
Head of Licensing Ross Paterson

International syndication services of news and features from the *Guardian* and theguardian.com. Unable to syndicate content which has not been published in its own titles. All permission requests to be submitted via online form.

Hayters Teamwork

47 Dean Street, London W1D 5BE
tel 020-7183 6727
email sport@hayters.com
website www.hayters.com
Facebook www.facebook.com/HaytersTV
Instagram @haytersTV

Sports news, features and data supplied to all branches of the media. Commission: negotiable according to merit. Founded 1955.

Headliners

tel 0191 231 4394
email enquiries@headliners.org
website www.headliners.org
Facebook www.facebook.com/HeadlinersUK
Instagram @headlinersuk

UK-wide journalism and multi-media charity. Offers young people aged 8–18 years the opportunity to write on issues of importance to them for newspapers, radio and TV. Founded 1995.

Independent Radio News (IRN)

The Harley Buidling, 77–79 New Cavendish Street,
London W1W 6XB

tel 020-7485 9800
email news@irn.co.uk
website www.irn.co.uk
X @IRNRadioNews
Managing Director Tim Molloy

National and international news.

PA Media

The Point, 37 North Wharf Road, London W2 1AF
website https://pa.media/
Facebook www.facebook.com/PAMediaGroupUK
X @PA

Provider of multimedia content and services, and the national news agency for the UK and Ireland. Has offices in several key locations (see website). Customers include major national, regional and international media and digital brands, as well as businesses and public sector organisations. Services include: news wire and digital ready-to-publish articles, pictures; video; data APIs; hosted live blogs; graphics; listings pages; social media curation; and page production. Part of the PA Media Group of specialist media companies. Founded 1868.

The Puzzle House

Ivy Cottage, Battlesea Green, Stradbroke, Suffolk IP21 5NE
tel (01379) 384656
email enquiries@thepuzzlehouse.co.uk
website www.thepuzzlehouse.co.uk
Partners Roy Preston & Sue Preston

Supplies original crosswords, quizzes and puzzles of all types. Commissions taken on any topic, with all age ranges catered for. Wide selection of puzzles available for one-off usage. Founded 1988.

Rann Media

120 Molesworth Street, North Adelaide, SA 5006 Australia
tel +61 (0)4 1883 2512
website www.rann.com.au
Managing Director Chris Rann

Professional PR, press releases, special newsletters, commercial and political intelligence, media monitoring. Welcomes approaches from organisations requiring PR representation or press release distribution. Founded 1982.

Sirius Media Services Ltd

37 Lower Brook Street, Ipswich IP4 1AQ
tel (01449) 833834
email info@siriusmedia.co.uk
website www.siriusmedia.co.uk

Crosswords, puzzles and quizzes, and Zygolex.

The Telegraph – Content Licensing & Syndication

Telegraph Media Group Holdings Limited, 111 Buckingham Palace Road, London SW1W 0DT
email syndication@telegraph.co.uk
website www.telegraph.co.uk/syndication/

Digital platforms, data aggregation, newswire services. News, features, photography and graphics, video, worldwide distribution and representation. Content licensing packages available for both print and all other media platforms.

WENN

78 York Street, London W1H 1DP
tel 020-7607 2757
email enquiries@wenn.com
website www.wenn.com

Provides the world's media with up-to-the-minute entertainment news and photos. Founded 1989.

Books

Introduction

UNESCO estimates that at least 2.2 million books are published worldwide every year. That's a lot of books. However, this is likely to be a vast underestimate. Figures available online vary from one million to four million. With the democratisation of the publishing industry, meaning that anyone can now be an author, this number will keep on growing. Ignited by the appearance of Amazon's Kindle Direct Publishing platform in 2007, further fuelled by the explosion of new software and platforms allowing writers to design, typeset, record and distribute their own books as ebooks, audio or physical copies, the publishing fire burns as bright as ever. It seems that every time a new technology has rumbled along, so have fears of the decline, and even death, of the traditional book. It hasn't happened yet, and even with the Artificial Intelligence (AI) tsunami fast approaching, those who love to read and write remain optimistic for the future.

New authors picking up the *Yearbook* for the first time may feel overwhelmed by the choices presented to them in the advice articles and listings in this section and elsewhere. The traditional route of finding an agent and securing a publishing deal still exists, but it is not the only path. The market is much more competitive than it used to be with independent authors proving that they can, in some cases, reach as many readers as the 'Big Five' publishers who have dominated the landscape for decades. The choice between finding a publisher or going it alone isn't necessarily an either/or scenario. Some writers choose a hybrid model: taking parallel routes to publishing with different projects, matching the approach to the text. Others might start on one route, and switch to another.

If an author does decide to take the traditional route, even then, there is a wide choice, from the 'kitchen table' not-for-profit, niche publisher on a remote Scottish island to the city-based sprawling organisation with imprints in every conceivable genre and offices all over the world, and marketing budgets to match. The publisher listings in the *Yearbook* reflect this diverse landscape, with micro-publishers sitting alongside the giants. What all publishers, big, small and medium have in common is a desire to publish the books their readers want, knowing that just as a one-size-fits-all doesn't apply to authors, it doesn't apply to readers either.

Authors looking at these listings to help them find the publishing solution that best fits their latest offering should choose what feels right, right now, and be prepared to flex and change in the years to come. There is just one thing they should keep steady – their optimism.

***

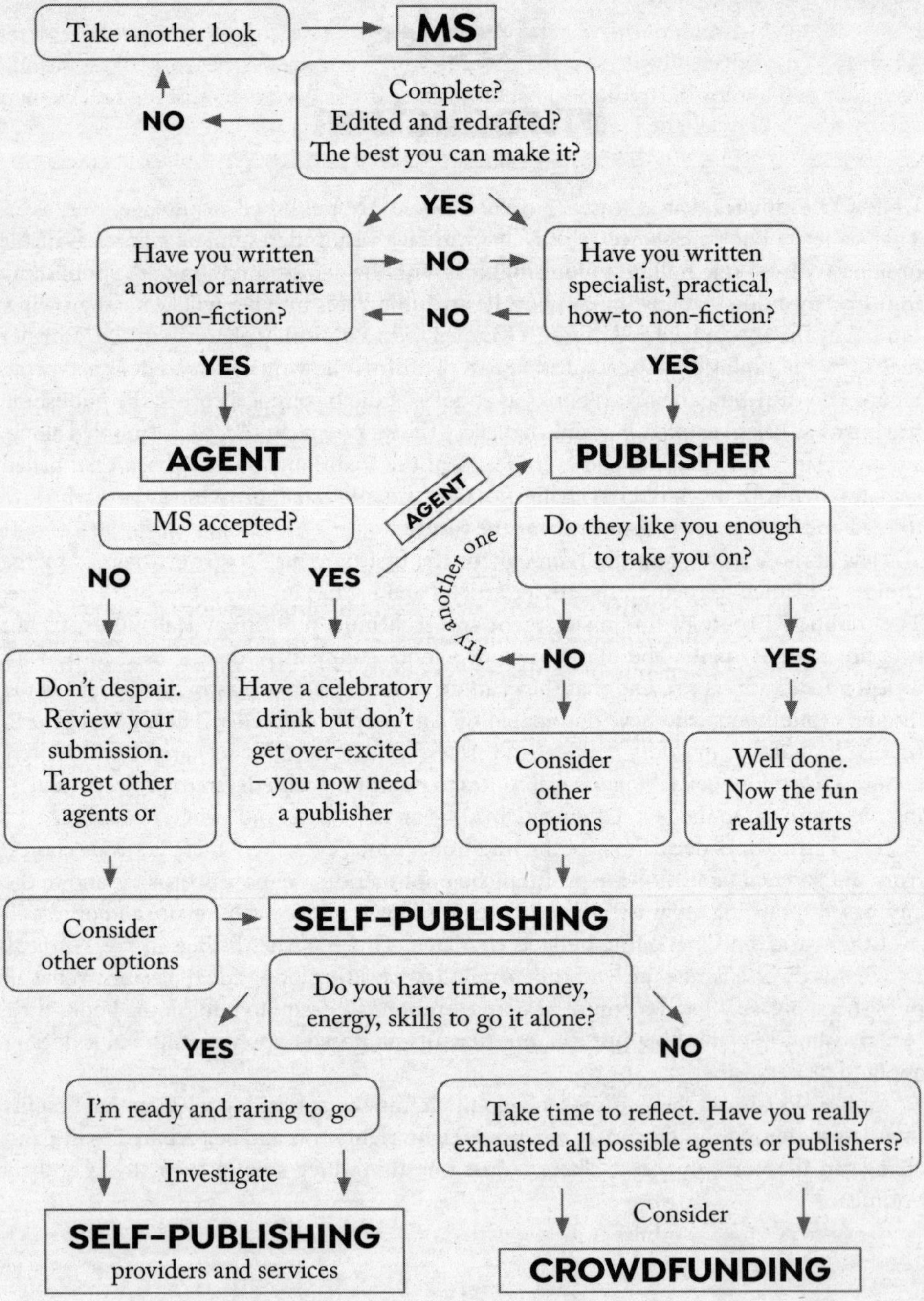

Deciding which route to take to get your book published

How to get published

The combined wisdom of the writers of the articles in this *Yearbook* provide some of the best practical advice you will need to negotiate your way through the world of publishing. Whether you opt for the traditional route via an agent or the self-publishing model, there are key things it would be useful to consider before you begin.

How can you give yourself the best chance of success whichever route you take?

1. Know your market

• Is there a readership for your book? Explore the intended market so you are sure that your publishing idea is of potential interest to an agent, publisher or reader.
• Know your competition and the latest trends: look in bookshops, at online ebook stores and book review sites, take an interest in publishing stories in the media and read lots.

2. Agent, publisher or self-publishing?

• Decide if you want to try and get a literary agent and be published by an established publisher. Self-publishing in print and digital can be a viable alternative.
• If you opt for the agent/publisher route, note that many publishers, particularly of fiction, will only consider material submitted through a literary agent. See page 425.
• For information about self-publishing, consult the *Self-publishing and indie authors* section of the *Yearbook* starting on page 671.

3. Choose the right publisher, agent or self-publishing provider

• Study the entries in this *Yearbook*, examine publishers' lists and websites; look in libraries and bookshops for the names of publishers which might be interested in your work.
• Consult the *Children's Writers' & Artists' Yearbook 2026* (Bloomsbury 2025) for in-depth coverage of writing and publishing for the children's and young adult markets.
• Authors should not pay publishers for the publication of their work. There are many companies that can help you self-publish your book, but you will need to make sure you know what it is the company will actually do and agree any fees in advance.

4. Prepare your material well

• It is understandable that writers, in their eagerness to get their work published, will send their manuscript out in a raw state. Do not send your manuscript to a literary agent or publisher and do not self-publish your script until it is *ready* to be seen and is as good as it can be. Have as your mantra: edit, review, revise and then edit again.

5. Approach a publisher or literary agent in the way they prefer

• Submit your work to the right person within the publishing company or literary agency. Most agents will expect to see a synopsis and up to three sample chapters or the complete manuscript. Publishers' and literary agents' websites give guidance on how to submit material.
• Always keep a copy of your manuscript. Whilst reasonable care will be taken of material in the possession of a publisher or agent, responsibility cannot be accepted if material is lost or damaged.

6. Write a convincing cover letter or email

• It will be your first contact with an agent or publisher and needs to make them take notice of your book for the right reasons.

• What is the USP (unique selling point) of the material you are submitting? Do you have an original, authorial 'voice', or an amazingly brilliant idea for a series? If, after checking out the market, you think you have something original to offer, be confident in what you have written and be convincing when you offer it around.

7. Network

• Talk to others who write in the same genre or share a similar readership by attending conferences and book or writers' groups. Consider doing a course – see *Writers' retreats and creative writing courses* on page 646.
• Go to a festival and be inspired. There are numerous literature festivals held throughout the year at which authors appear (see *Festival fun* on page 527).

8. Don't give up!

• Be prepared to wait for a decision on your work. Editors and agents are very busy people so be patient when waiting for a response. Don't pester them too soon.
• Even after an editor has read your work, there are many other people involved before a manuscript is acquired for publication. People from the sales, marketing, publicity, rights and other departments all have to be convinced that the book is right for their list and will sell.
• The harsh reality of submitting a manuscript to a publisher or literary agent is that you have to be prepared for rejection. But many successful authors have received such rejections at some time so you are in good company.
• Have patience and persevere. If the conventional route doesn't produce the results you were hoping for, consider self-publishing as a viable alternative.

Listings in this section:

- *Book publishers UK and Ireland*, page 118
- *Book publishers overseas*, page 190
- *Audio providers and distributors*, page 223
- *Book packagers*, page 225

The publishing process

The publishing year: the highs, lows and trends

The turbulence in the wider world over the past 12 months has been just as visible in publishing, as Tom Tivnan explains here. Meta or meta? Read on to find out more.

I am writing this in late March 2025 so almost inevitably – and with weary resignation – I begin this look at the British books landscape with the dismaying state of geopolitics. How much, you may reasonably ask, can the ructions across Western democracies have to do with authors' present or future prospects? Well, quite a bit already and there is the potential for much more.

The sledgehammer that Donald Trump has taken to global norms has made the book industry on both sides of the Atlantic wary, with far-reaching ramifications to contend with. The most obvious is the current tariff wars between the US and its closest allies which, if they spill over to include books, would be disastrous for an industry whose model – and authors' earnings – rely so much on friction-free international exports and rights trading.

While the shenanigans in the White House and, say, the rise of the nationalist AfD party in the 2025 German elections may seem remote to scribblers in Blighty, I should underscore that publishing is a conglomeratised, worldwide business and that eight of the top ten general book publishers in Britain, worth 62% of all UK bookshop sales in 2024, are owned by US or continental Europe-based multinationals (only fifth-placed Bloomsbury and number nine Usborne are home-headquartered). What happens in those countries will have at the very least an indirect effect on what British editors commission.

It can't happen here?

The cultural wars that have underpinned Trump's second coming and the ascent of the hard-right across Europe have made publishing a trickier proposition. Book bans of 'woke' titles are on the rise in the US, a worrying trend that has filtered over to the British Isles. The number of attempts to remove books from UK school libraries hit such a height in late 2024 that the Society of Authors issued a joint statement with several library organisations urging the government to fight these censorship efforts. There were numerous coordinated far-right protests at libraries across Ireland in 2024, several of which escalated into protestors assaulting staff and destroying books (titles with LGBTQ+ themes were targeted in particular).

There have been chilling attacks on free speech in America and a big Trumpian test case in this arena arrived in March 2025 with *Careless People*, the memoir/exposé of Mark Zuckerberg's Meta (the parent of Facebook and Instagram, among others) by its former director of global public policy, Sarah Wynn-Williams. In the US, Meta won a temporary halt to publication as a judge prohibited publisher Flatiron and Wynn-Williams from distributing or promoting the book on the grounds that the author may have violated a 'non-disparagement' clause in her Meta contract. Pan Macmillan, Flatiron's sister company and *Careless People*'s UK house, forged ahead with publication – Pan Mac need not follow US court decisions – and the book became a British bestseller at launch.

The final outcome for *Careless People* in the US will be determined in the months to come but one suspects that Meta was concerned less about Wynn-Williams' allegations of sexual harassment and other inappropriate behaviour than her contention that the tech company had Trump operatives embedded during his first presidential campaign and allowed them to use Facebook, in particular, to help him win (Wynn-Williams left Meta in 2018, so the book does not cover the 2020 or 2024 elections). But it is not necessarily the final outcome that matters so much. Even if it wins its case, Flatiron will have paid a sizable amount in lawyers' fees simply because it was releasing a book critical of one of the president's most ardent tech-bro billionaire supporters.

The industry seems up for battling to preserve free speech: the US's 'Big Five' publishers – Penguin Random House (PRH), Macmillan, Hachette, HarperCollins and Simon & Schuster – have filed a series of joint lawsuits in 2024 and 2025 against American states that are instituting book bans in schools and libraries. But publishing is a business with relatively low profit margins and the political climate raises the spectre of indirect as well as direct censorship: how many titles will publishers pass on because their subject matter means the fight to get them to market will prove too costly?

Fantastic fiction

The good news for short story writers and novelists is that this is the most fecund time for fiction in the history of British letters, at least in terms of sales. Just over £552m worth of fiction was shifted through industry sales monitor Nielsen BookScan in 2024, obliterating the record (set in the previous year) by some £50m. For the first time since accurate records began, the five bestselling books in Britain in a calendar year were all fiction, as were nine of the top ten and 32 of the top 50. And, at time of writing, 2025 fiction sales are running a blistering 15% ahead of 2024; the sector should eclipse the £600m mark by 2025's end and there is the slim possibility of fiction outselling non-fiction for the first time. This is fiction's golden age. What a time to be alive.

I have mentioned the main driver of this surge, BookTok – users enthusing about books and authors on the TikTok app – in the past few *Writers' & Artists' Yearbooks* and each time I have wondered how long the trend might last. It shows no signs of flagging as the sub-genres BookTok benefits most (science fiction and fantasy (SFF), romance, horror and, to some extent, crime) all hit record or near-record levels in 2024 and have started 2025 in even better shape. And it is not just that BookTokers sing the praises of books and the sales just magically happen; there is a virtuous circle of bookshops, particularly WHSmith and Waterstones, promoting the TikTok titles in store and publishers increasing their output into BookTokkable areas. This has led to new SFF and romance imprints sprouting up over the past couple years, usually led by young (or young at heart) editors whose remits are to find the new voices that will appeal to the TikTok generation. Just a smattering of these include Vicky Leech Mateos heading up SFF specialist Bloomsbury Archer, Claire Simmonds launching (on Valentine's Day 2025) the Cornerstone romance list Evermore and Anne Perry kickstarting Quercus' fantasy arm, Arcadia.

There is a feeling among some in the industry that we are at 'peak imprint' – that there are too many of these entities popping up which mean nothing for consumers. (And if they do mean nothing to you: imprints are subdivisions of publishing houses with their own logos, often with subject-specific focuses.) There is something in that: even bookish non-industry people might struggle to name more than a few imprints as the author is the only brand that really matters for readers – Richard Osman is the draw, for example, not that he is published under PRH's Viking list. But imprints do resonate with the media, authors and agents. Thus for the editors, a new imprint can serve as a sort of shorthand to help them bring together a community of authors with a shared mission and purpose.

USA! USA! USA!

One of the noticeable things about the TikTok surge, and particularly in SFF and romance, is just how American it is. Eleven of the top 15 SFF writers in the UK last year were all Americans or US-based, led by romantasy (romance + fantasy) superstar Sarah J. Maas, whose £13.2m through BookScan meant she was the second-bestselling author in Britain in 2024, trailing only children's legend Julia Donaldson. Romance has a few more home-grown TikTok stars, such as the pseudonymous Hannah Grace, but with the likes of Colleen Hoover, Ana Huang, Emily Henry and Laurie Gilmore ruling the top of the charts, nearly £2 in every £3 spent on a romance book in the UK in 2024 was American-authored.

This leads us back to politics. Again, at this writing (and, goodness me, how rapidly things can change in Trump's America), TikTok is under a reprieve from its ban from the Apple and Android US app stores as Congress is trying to force it to divest itself from Chinese ownership. An American buyer is likely to be found, but whatever the outcome, the app may change and potentially its millions of book influencers may decide to go elsewhere. If so, what would happen to the biggest cash cow the fiction market has ever seen?

Freed agents

A change to the industry ecosystem over the last year or so has been the huge swathe of agents waving goodbye to bigger firms and setting out on their own. A mere sampling includes (deep breath): children's specialist Gemma Cooper leaving The Bent Agency to form Gemma Cooper Literary; YMU Literary managing director Amanda Harris departing to create Maven Literary Management (Harris won the British Book Awards Literary Agent of the Year 2025 for her YMU work); United Agents duo Seren Adams and Kat Aitken starting up Lexington Literary; ex-Darley Anderson colleagues Tanera Simons and Laura Heathfield opening Greenstone Literary; and Marilia Savvides stepping out from the 42 MP umbrella to found The Plot Agency. The trend is so hot that publishers are crossing the aisle to get into the act, such as former HarperCollins Ireland boss Conor Nagle setting up Dublin's The Nagle Agency and ex-David Fickling Books and Usborne publicist Carolyn May McGlone launching her Oxfordshire-based May Literary Agency.

This flurry of openings has far exceeded the usual crop rotation of new agencies launching/others folding. What is more interesting is that this is happening in an era where many smaller agencies are also joining bigger firms – such as sole traders Charlie Brotherstone, Emily Sweet and Jack Ramm all bringing their outfits into the Aevitas Creative Management fold – and the alphabet soup of Hollywood mega-agencies (CAA, UTA, WME) swooping into London to acquire companies and bolster existing UK offices.

So what's happening? There is a post-Covid-19 aspect to this. The remote/hybrid-working world that has emerged after the pandemic showed that agencies do not need a swish (and expensive) London office to succeed. So the cost barrier for agents going solo is lower. Remote working is also unquestionably why quite a few of these openings are out of the London publishing bubble, such as Emma Layfield's Manchester-based Children's Agency North and Emma Shercliff's Suffolk-headquartered Laxfield Literary Associates.

Big agencies always say their scale helps authors – that a massive in-house translation rights department along with a fleet of bespoke books-to-screen agents in Tinsel Town gives them an edge to sell clients' books across the world. Which has some validity, but smaller agencies have long outsourced these roles to freelancers or sub-agents. And there are quite a few new entrants here, too, like Mary Darby (ex-Darley Anderson) and Jemma McDonagh (former joint MD of The Marsh Agency) launching specialist translation rights outfits (the model is that they mainly do not represent authors directly but other agencies' entire rosters, which they sell to publishers outside the Anglophone world).

Given all this, we should underscore that it is tough to launch a new agency in cash-flow terms. Agents tend to bring their authors with them to their new homes but previously done deals remain, in most cases, on the prior agency's books. So, many new agencies are starting at zero and it could be months before any revenue comes in. Still, the ultimate rewards may be worth the risk. Plus, agenting has a relatively flat organisational structure: some of the bigger firms have managing directors or Ceos, but most are simply a collection of agents working under an umbrella. The greatest attribute an agent can have is that when their submission emails hit editors' inboxes, a response comes quickly. If an agent has reached the point in their career where the speed of that response stems from building their name and contacts, and not necessarily that they work for a huge firm, then why wouldn't they roll the dice and set up their own shop?

AI owes you, or owns you?

I close with the issue that has convulsed the books world, and may prove to be the most seismic development since moveable type: artificial intelligence (AI). AI is evolving at a breakneck pace, one that over the past 12 months has seen almost daily advances, eye-popping outrages and 'did-not-see-that-coming' moments. A Florida-based firm, Spines, launched, promising to release 8,000 titles in 2025 as it says its AI-driven model shrinks the usual six-to-18 months publishing process to a fortnight. Academic giants like SAGE, Taylor & Francis and Wiley made deals with tech firms for their backlists to train chatbots and other AI tools, much to the despair of many of their authors. The Netherlands' biggest house, the Simon & Schuster-owned Veen Bosch & Keuning, announced it would start trialling AI translations, sending shockwaves through the translators' community. And on and on.

Amid this, class action lawsuits rumble on between authors and the tech companies, about what the UK Publishers Association Ceo Dan Conway has called 'the great copyright heist': AI companies using authors' work without compensation to train their large language models. The current controversy as I write this is the revelation from legal filings that Meta (hmm … that name again) had used millions of pirated works to train its Llama 3 system rather than licensing content because, as one of the company's research scientists wrote in an internal email, paying for authors' works would be 'unreasonably expensive'. A side note: the most recent Society of Authors data says the average author in Britain earns £7,000 annually from their writing.

The industry is fighting back with lawsuits, representations to governments and public campaigning. This is not some neo-Luddite posturing: creators and publishers just want to be adequately compensated for their copyright-protected work. And the trade is putting forth other interesting plans to survive in an AI world, such as the movement to have

AI-altered, -enhanced or -created works to be clearly labelled for consumers, like GM foods are now.

Is the trade hopeful for a positive outcome? Guardedly, but the problem is, you guessed it, with politics. Legislators across the world seem to be siding with the Bond villains, I mean, tech industry. A February 2025 Paris AI summit with world leaders, while offering some kernels of hope, left many in the creative industries dismayed that their concerns were being sidelined for the great god progress (the current US government, represented at that summit by Vice President J.D. Vance, was disdainful of the EU's attempt at any AI regulation). A huge backlash from the UK creative industries over Keir Starmer's AI plans announced in early 2025 – which contained an 'opt-out' measure that essentially meant AI firms would be free to mine copyrighted content until a creator actually noticed their work was being used – forced a rethink of policy. And so it goes. The battle for control of authors' works will be long, uphill and against largely unsympathetic governments and Silicon Valley's billions. Is it unwinnable? Stay tuned.

Tom Tivnan is Managing Editor of *The Bookseller*. Tom was a freelance writer and his work has appeared in the *Glasgow Herald*, the *Independent*, the *Daily Telegraph* and the *Times Literary Supplement*. Before joining *The Bookseller* in 2007, he worked as a bookseller for Blackwell's in the UK and for Barnes & Noble in the USA. He wrote the text for *Tattooed by the Family Business* (Pavilion 2010) and his debut novel is *The Esquimaux* (Silvertail 2017). Follow him on X @tomtivnan.

Working with your editor: the author–editor relationship

Having a book acquired by a large publishing house is the absolute dream of many aspiring authors. But what happens after that? Read on to find out how Željka Marošević of Jonathan Cape works with her authors from proposal to publication.

I often think my job title of 'editor' is a misleading one. It conjures up an image of a person working away at a text silently and alone. While this is a key component of what I do, and I love to work with a writer to shape their text, watching how over multiple drafts a book changes and becomes a more defined and clearer version of itself, it tends to overlook the fact that there are three parts to an editor's job: acquiring, editing and publishing.

I'm editorial director of Jonathan Cape (an imprint of Vintage, which is part of Penguin Random House), where I publish writers including Samantha Harvey, Brandon Taylor and Amy Key. I work within a small team of editors to acquire the books that we will publish on the Cape list. Usually, books come in the form of submissions from agents which I read to decide whether they would work on the Cape list. It's important to make that distinction. I read plenty of fine books on submission, books that are interesting or entertaining, or that I can tell will sell lots of copies. But if it doesn't feel like a book that will fit the identity of our list and be best served by it, I have to let it go.

This is something I try to reassure writers about all the time. Rejection really is a bit like dating: it's not you, it's me. What makes a Cape book? Frustratingly, you only know it when you see (or rather read) it. Broadly speaking, there is an attention to craft, the writing is distinctive and the thinking is expert and, quite often, groundbreaking. Frequently, there are original things happening with form. Cape is home to some of the world's leading writers, from Ian McEwan and Salman Rushdie to Anne Enright and Ocean Vuong. When I'm reading a submission, I am wondering whether the writer could be a future star. Simply put, are they doing something new I haven't seen before and/or are they doing something lots of people try to do, but doing it better than everyone else? Usually, it's a combination of the two, delivered with confidence and control. The next questions are can I see a career for them? And do I want to read their books forever?

I'm also weighing up whether I am the right editor for the book. I'm asking myself: do I already have ideas for how I would edit this book? Would I be confident in transforming this Word document into a hardback readers want to buy? Can I imagine myself telling everyone I know about how much this book excites me? I know it's affirming for an author when an editor wants to publish them, but it's perhaps underappreciated how much editors want the books they make offers on, and how good it feels when an author chooses you. This never changes, however many books you acquire. You're always chasing the thrill of the perfect match.

Usually in the process of acquiring a book I've got to know the author a little – often agents arrange author meetings during an auction and this is a chance to talk about my 'vision' for a book. It's very normal, especially for non-fiction proposals but also for fiction, that I will have ideas for shaping the book and I will want to discuss these with the author to check we are on the same page. I always like to be honest at the outset about what editorial work a book needs so that I can check that the author and I share the same ideas about the book and we'll work well together. Discussing 'comp titles' (a term we use in publishing which means published books that are comparable) can be useful at this point as it allows you to talk about different approaches to structure or genre, with clear examples of readership. For both fiction and non-fiction, it's really helpful when authors have thought about where their book will sit in the market. Or, to take it out of industry-speak, when an author can talk about similar books they love or were inspired by, or share the books they think theirs is in conversation with. I love to know who my author's touchstones are so that I can get closer to understanding their writing and we can develop a shorthand for how we talk about it.

My aim when I sit down to edit a book is to be the Platonic ideal of a reader. I am the most loving and supportive reader the writer will ever have, and I am always on their side. My belief in them is unwavering. It's important to establish that at the beginning because I want my writers to feel completely held as they do the hard and important work of wrestling with their manuscript to ensure it meets its potential. When I edit, I pay absolute attention and try to notice everything before another, less forgiving, reader does.

If the writer's job is to pull a reader into the world of their book and take them on a journey, my job is to notice every time a reader is spat back out into the real world. Sometimes the issue is structural: for example, the beginning might not be clear; a character disappears halfway through the book; one of the storylines is undeveloped so the book feels unbalanced, and sometimes it's on a line level: a scene is reported when it should be dramatized; dialogue isn't working hard enough; we need more or less detail about a character. I realised long ago that it doesn't help to have an ego; instead I ask annoying, sometimes obvious questions at the risk of sounding stupid because I want to make sure we have interrogated everything before that other, less sympathetic, reader does.

While this might sound gruelling, I've found the better a writer, the more they want to be edited. Often writers will say, 'I was hoping you wouldn't notice that, but I'm glad you did' or 'I can't believe you noticed that, it's exactly where I was struggling'. I don't tell the writer what to do or write the book for them, but I create the conditions for the book to come into its own by way of the writer's talents. Typically there will be at least two rounds of structural edits followed by a line edit and this will happen on a Word document, sometimes on paper but more likely on screen, in Track Changes, accompanied by an editorial letter, emails, phone calls and meetings. There might be quick check-ins as the writer is taking in the edits, either by email, phone or text. It's an involving process for both author and editor but hugely rewarding to watch the book click into place and to read the final draft, recognising the book is complete. Then the book is handed over to our brilliant managing editorial team to be copy-edited for grammar, punctuation and continuity, before being typeset and proofread.

To be an editor, you must somehow be a perfect, impossible mix of introvert and extrovert. Introvert: able to spend vast stretches of time reading and editing alone. Extrovert: while all the above is going on, the publishing of the book is happening. This is all the things I'm doing in-house to champion the book and set its publication up for success. Just as when I'm editing, I act as number one fan and founding member of the author's fan club. I keep enthusing about the book's specialness to my publicity, marketing and sales colleagues, as well as to every industry person I meet. This is formalised into meetings where, for example, I 'position' the book (establish a unique one-line pitch), present it at our design meeting so a cover can be designed, 'launch' it so our sales colleagues know how to talk about it to retailers, and represent it in meetings with publicity and marketing as a campaign is built around the book. I am the first advocate for the book and, as the book's publisher, I need to inspire an army of advocates who will go out into the world and build a readership. As I do this, all of the editorial conversations I've had with the author are at the front of my mind to make sure we're taking the author's wishes and intentions into account.

By the time it comes to publication, the author is part of a wide network of people working on behalf of their book, which has led out from their agent and editor to design and production, publicity and marketing, sales reps and online metadata specialists, and even further to booksellers, reviewers, prize judges and festival organisers. If I've performed my role well, each of them will understand why the book matters and how best to apply their expertise in finding readers for it.

I publish authors who are writing their first book, others who are writing their twentieth – and every stage in between. Some things are constant. Even a prize-winning, garlanded author cares deeply about what you think of their new book, and how it is received by readers. Their tenth book deserves as much care and attention as their first. Every time a writer delivers a new book, it's still my responsibility to assess it on its own terms and to work out what makes it special and unique in their oeuvre. I need to make a case for publishing it, remind my colleagues that they love the author's writing, and come up with ideas to bring fresh readers to their work. Finally and perhaps most crucially, every writer needs time to write, whether they are in demand and successful or struggling and blocked. When they are in between books and in writing mode, I still have work to do.

I chivvy them along. I collaborate with my team to keep engagements to only the truly beneficial. I send photos when I see commuters reading their books on the tube. I take them for lunch. I read their newest articles and Substacks. I hand their books to friends and authors. I meet up with their agents. I talk to them to work out what they want to write, not what they think they should. I keep emailing them to check on progress. I set deadlines, and forgive missed ones. I keep the faith. In short, I remain their devoted, number one fan.

Željka Marošević is Editorial Director of Jonathan Cape. She has edited some of the most popular and influential writers in the world, in both fiction and non-fiction.

Getting books to market: how books are sold

David Wightman, of Global Book Sales, describes the various parts, people and processes, skills and systems within the world of book sales that interlink to bring a book from publisher to customer, and what makes this a fascinating, challenging and satisfying area of work.

I've always been excited about sales and wanted to set up a company where the focus is on maximising the sales of every book that we represent. My company, Global Book Sales, has the distribution network in place to be able to supply books to any customer in the world, and we have skilled and passionate sales teams persuading booksellers that they should stock our publishers' books.

Who sells to whom, how and where?

Selling a book globally is a complicated process, but most publishers have excellent systems in place to ensure they maximise the sales of each book in every country. The process starts with setting up *metadata* for a new title; this includes information such as ISBN, title, author, format, price, publication date, number of pages, etc. This metadata is then added to databases owned by bibliographic agencies, such as Nielsen in the UK, who are then responsible for disseminating that information to customers globally.

Once the metadata is available, the publisher's sales teams kick into action. Key account managers and sales representatives will pre-sell new titles to their customers three to nine months prior to publication. This is a long *sell-in* period, but during that time the distributor will be recording any orders that come in for each book. These orders are known in the UK as *dues* and in the USA as *backorders*. The number of dues a new title has will help to determine how many copies the publisher will print in the initial run.

The aim of the publisher's sales team is to make sure the book is available for the consumer to buy on the date the book is published. This may mean that there are copies in stock at an independent bookshop or a branch of Waterstones, or that it is available to order easily through an online bookseller. When the book is published (or in the run-up to publication) then a publisher's publicity team and the author take over, to alert the consumer that the book is available to buy and persuade them that it's worth reading.

Day-to-day activity of a sales manager

Working with sales partners, distributors and agents

Global Book Sales has partnerships in place for book distribution with Macmillan Distribution (MDL) in the UK and Ingram Publishers Services LLC in the USA. Stock of our publishers' books are stored in both locations and this gives us the capability of supplying any customer quickly and cost-efficiently with any book they want to order, wherever they are located across the world.

We also have a network of sales agents across the world that sells new titles to customers in different countries. Each territory may have a slightly different way of working but the principles of the 'sell in' remain the same. To successfully sell a book in advance, the sales agent or representative needs accurate metadata, strong visual sales material, good information on what the book is about and who its audience is, and finally to know why this book stands out above the thousands of other books that will publish at the same time.

The opportunities

The traditional high-street book trade is still important for book sales, but it has declined in recent years, with some independent bookshops closing down and smaller bookshop chains either closing or being swallowed up by larger rivals. However, there is now a huge range of online booksellers, museums, galleries, gift shops, clothes retailers, music shops and toy shops that all want to sell books as part of their range. Publishers are becoming very strategic in what they publish, and they are increasingly expanding into non-book items such as games and toys to increase their overall customer base.

These opportunities to sell outside of the traditional bookshops are also evident in a number of export markets. Concept stores in Scandinavia are now selling many books and this is also happening in China, Hong Kong, Singapore, Korea and Taiwan where demand for quality books, particularly in areas such as art, photography and design, are very strong. Marketing and publicising new books using social media is now both easy and relatively cheap to do. Authors who have a large number of followers on X or TikTok can alert potential readers that their book is now available to buy. This can have a huge impact on book sales.

The challenges

One of the biggest challenges publishers face is shipping books between countries quickly and cost-efficiently. There are reduced number of commercial flights, and this has driven

Definitions

- **Distribution**

  All publishers of print books have a distribution facility: the warehouse where published books are stored. From here, the books are sent out to customers. The distributor is responsible for invoicing the customer for their book order and collecting the money.

- **Key accounts**

  These are the main customers for books, including chain booksellers, wholesalers, online retailers and supermarkets. UK examples are WHSmith, Waterstones, Gardners, Amazon and Tesco. Key accounts expect to buy new books six to nine months prior to publication.

- **Sales rep/representative**

  A sales rep is a member of the publisher's sales team who visits independent bookshops and other accounts, such as museums and galleries, to sell new titles. Reps tend to sell a book three to five months prior to publication. They sell to customers using AIs (advance information sheets), catalogues or promotional samples (*blads*).

- **Stock control/inventory management**

  Bookshops want a range of books that they think they can sell during a given period. Many have automated systems (EPOS, electronic point of sale) that generate re-orders when a book is sold. Distributors and wholesalers have sophisticated systems that enable them to process orders and get books out to shops quickly; reducing the need for shops to hold significant levels of stock of any one title.

- **Wholesaler**

  Similar to a distributor, it handles books from lots of publishers. Gardners is the biggest wholesaler in the UK; they claim to have over 500,000 different titles in stock at any one time. The benefit of a wholesaler is that any bookshop or retailer that wants to sell books can easily source all the titles from one place.

up the price of moving books by air, almost to the point that it's not profitable to do so anymore. Shipping times for sea-freight have also increased. The UK leaving the European Union has added to the cost of sending books to Europe and the price of paper is also increasing, which puts further pressure on publisher's margins.

Finances, margins, discounting and terms

In the UK, books are mostly sold at a trade discount off the RRP (recommended retail price). Each publisher will set its own discount in agreement with their customers. The range of trade discounts can vary significantly, from around 25% to 60%. Academic and education books tend to be sold at lower discounts than more consumer, mass-market titles. The average discount for more general titles is from 45% to 50%.

Sale-or-return, and how it works

In the UK, books are sold on a sale-or-return basis. This means that any trade customer (not individuals) can buy books from a publisher and return them if they don't sell them. This means that the risk of publishing and paying to print a book rests with the publisher. For export markets, books are still sold on a sale-or-return basis but, in practice, returns are low from export customers. These customers tend to buy in a less speculative way because they are also responsible for paying the cost of shipping these books from the UK, plus any additional import taxes and duties. Publishers will often have return allowances for export customers but this allowance is rarely fully used.

In the UK, the book and publishing industry have agreed some rules which means that a customer cannot return a book within three months of buying it and not after 15 months. The books should also be returned in a saleable condition. These restrictions don't apply in other countries, in particular the USA, where there are no such restrictions.

How do publishers know how well their books are selling?

Publishers can subscribe to Nielsen BookScan (https://online.nielsenbookscan.net) which records sales of books through the tills of a range of UK booksellers. Alternatively, a publisher can check to see on a daily basis how many copies of a book are being sent out by their warehouse. With these sales figures, you do need to factor in any potential returns – whereas the Nielsen figures record firm sales.

Working with marketing

Marketing departments are responsible for providing the sales team with what they need to sell a book to a buyer. They also provide regular updates of any marketing and publicity that may be happening to promote a particular title. This information can then be passed on by the sales team to their individual buyers. Marketing departments produce *AIs* (advance information sheets) for individual new books; some will produce six-monthly catalogues featuring the publisher's spring and autumn titles. For lead titles they often provide bound proofs and *blads* (samples). The typical 'lead time' for a book is five to six months; it takes this time for the various sales teams around the world to be briefed about the book, provided with the information to sell the book, and then to contact their customers in order to sell the book to them.

David Wightman is Managing Director of Global Book Sales (www.globalbooksales.co.uk), an independent sales and distribution company that works with publishers to sell their titles across the world. He was previously Group International Sales Director at Bloomsbury Publishing, Sales, Marketing and Rights Director at A&C Black Publishers, and UK Academic Sales Manager at Oxford University Press.

What every author needs to know about PR to sell more books

Congratulations, you've written a book! But typing 'The End' is just the start of your creative journey. Freelance book publicist Hannah Hargrave reveals how it's never too early to start work on your PR strategy. Whether you are self-publishing or launching a title with the support of a big publishing house, all authors can use PR (public relations) to sell more books.

Authors often overlook, misunderstand and undervalue the role of PR in publishing. While most publishers have in-house publicists, they can only achieve so much for each book. These days, authors are encouraged to increase their own chances of publicity. Promotion is an essential skill for all writers and it often involves a huge amount of work, most of which goes unseen and – with newspapers slashing their budgets as well as their books coverage – unpaid. I have worked in book PR for almost 20 years and have experience managing challenging and high-profile campaigns in-house and as a freelancer for some of the largest UK publishers as well as smaller, independent presses. I've worked with a whole variety of authors from celebrities and bestsellers (including Goldie Hawn and Ozzy Osbourne) to debut and self-published writers, covering a multitude of genres. But perhaps the key question for us to address at this point is …

What, exactly, is PR?

There is an element of mystery surrounding what a book publicist does (I'm not sure my own family fully understand what I do!), and my day-to-day activities vary dramatically depending on who my clients are and what stage of their campaign I am at. I could be escorting authors to book signings, talking to TV producers about current authors, researching specialist media contacts, scanning the newspapers for news hooks, packaging proof copies to post to bloggers, updating agents on progress, submitting books for awards or creating digital content to share on TikTok. I've been privileged to sit alongside Nile Rodgers during an interview on *Later with Jools Holland*, but I've also had to keep a long queue of unhappy fans entertained for over two hours while they waited for an A-list star to turn up to a book signing. It's wonderfully varied and exhausting, but very rewarding.

It's important for authors to understand what PR is, and how it differs from publicity, marketing and advertising. Publicity is a set of promotional activities with a focus on media coverage, coming under the wider 'umbrella' of PR. There is so much more to PR, from crisis management to brand awareness to building credibility, but given the distinct similarities between publicity and PR, we can view them in the same way that we consider advertising to be a part of marketing.

In between book publishing roles, I worked in the BBC press office for two years, starting shortly after the Jimmy Savile scandal broke. I was responsible for corporate communications with a range of external stakeholders, from MPs to the leaders of national arts organisations. This experience equipped me with a solid set of crisis-management skills, and I provide my authors with media training. By identifying potential risks in their narrative and supporting them with detailed briefing notes ahead of interviews, they feel supported and confident enough to share their story with journalists. If your book includes anything controversial that might generate negative reviews or legal challenges, you will need to prepare accordingly. A book I worked on in 2021 ended up being cancelled when I raised concerns over the potential for defamation claims. Had the author and publisher invested in a thorough legal read at an earlier stage, this could have been avoided.

My current role: what does a self-employed PR do?

My job is to generate excitement and interest from readers in a new book through media engagement: offering review copies to established critics, distributing press releases describing the book, pitching features articles, approaching radio and television programmes about author interviews, managing book events with bookshops and literary festivals, and engaging in social-media promotion. I've been freelance since 2015, which has afforded me greater freedom and control over the books on which I work. Throughout my years of experience, I have built up a robust contact list within niche genres.

The most recent available figures indicate that between 180,000 to 200,000 books are published traditionally every year in the UK. Add to that more than 750,000 self-published books (according to the Writers' Guild of Great Britain), and you get a sense of how fierce the competition can be for publicity coverage. Preparation is, therefore, crucial to ensure you get the best results.

Publicists start planning their campaigns four to six months in advance of a book launching and big publishing houses typically start discussions on PR and marketing a year ahead of publication. I even advise writers to consider how they plan to promote a book while they are still writing it, as it's crucial to spend time considering who your audience is and how you will reach them.

As a brand strategist, I also help position authors as leaders or experts in their field. Establishing them as an authority on their subject matter can lead to new opportunities in the media, such as op-eds or events. By including PR in their promotional toolkit, authors can reach new audiences, build credibility and contribute to increased sales of their book. For example, I recently worked with an award-winning TV producer who wanted to promote her self-published novel. I knew that her incredible career working on well-known programmes would interest the media, so – even though she was unknown as an author – I persuaded a leading women's magazine to interview her about her writing and several literary festivals to add her to their programmes.

It's important to understand that PR focuses on unpaid strategies to promote a book. It relies on someone influential (a journalist or reviewer) engaging with the book purely because they think it is right for their audience, rather than paying for it. Established media outlets have cultivated their reputations and built trust among their own audiences. By encouraging them to champion a book, I transfer the trust their audience has in them, to the author. Marketing, in contrast, involves advertising, partnership promotions or other paid tactics to gain exposure.

While many authors still regard a review in a broadsheet newspaper as the ultimate success measure for their book, there are so many more ways to reach readers. Review space has been shrinking in the national press for several years, but promotional opportunities online have been expanding. Sometimes a review on a book blog will get you in front of more potential readers than a review in print. The astronomical rise in how much social media influences book buyers has also led to the lines between PR and marketing becoming blurred. Readers can now share their views with a global reading community. It is essential for all book PRs to understand the different digital platforms and be skilled in creating content. Unlike traditional reviewers who are employed by a newspaper, online book reviewers often charge for their services through collaborations or paid reviews, making working with them marketing rather than PR. Authors need to remember that reviews achieved without a financial exchange are considered more credible by readers and are therefore more valuable.

Last year I worked with an author to launch her debut fiction novel, published through a small independent publisher. We knew that trying to get the book covered in the national press would be almost impossible, so together we created a digital publicity blitz, building relationships with book bloggers, submitting the book for a raft of indie-friendly awards and creating fun viral content: video trailers, interactive character quizzes and book club resources. Word of mouth continues to boost book-buying decisions and by generating a buzz online, the novel became an Amazon bestseller.

How can PR benefit self-published and traditionally published authors?

Self-published authors have irrevocably changed the industry, but they face huge challenges when it comes to PR. Most literary editors, and even some bloggers, won't consider reviewing a self-published title, no matter how good it is. A big-name author will always be an easier sell when pitching for media opportunities. Self-published authors often go into the publicity process inexperienced and unprepared, underestimating the time required to promote their book and holding unrealistic expectations. Indie authors also face book distribution challenges which can prevent them from finding space in bookshops. A freelance publicist can use their contacts to make sure that the right people know about your book and give you more credibility as an author.

Traditionally published authors can also benefit from hiring a freelancer. Typically, authors will have a dedicated in-house publicist, but they are often swamped with new book launches, juggling multiple authors with a limited budget. Publishers expect their authors to do some of the promotional work themselves, and this can be daunting. Freelancers can provide authors with the time, advice and support they need to make a bigger splash. Authors will usually foot the bill for this external support, but I am regularly commissioned by publishers where they require assistance with campaigns. Fees will vary depending on the length and challenges of project, as well as the experience of the publicist you hire.

While I am passionate about running successful PR campaigns and see the advantages in investing in one, there are notable downsides. Sadly, I don't own a magic publicity wand that can guarantee coverage. Publicists cannot control the media or guarantee increased sales. There's nothing more frustrating than having a big radio interview cancelled at the last minute due to a breaking news story. Book reviewers are inundated with proof copies, and often share photographs on social media of towering piles of books that are competing for a handful of review spaces. I know that for every pitch I send, a journalist will have received several others that same hour. And when a review is secured, a publicist can't control if it will be negative. The only way you can 'demand' that something gets published is by paying for it as advertising space.

How can authors help with PR?

Whether hiring a professional or not, authors play a significant role in a successful publicity campaign. If you are self-publishing, invest your time and money in making sure your book package is right. Only well-edited books with strong covers will be considered seriously by reviewers. In addition:

• **Work with your publicist.** It's vital that you develop a trusting relationship with them. Publicists are incredibly hard working, often putting in many hours behind the scenes. As experts with a wealth of experience and good relationships with journalists, it's a good idea to listen to our advice – even if it's not what you want to hear.

• **Manage your expectations.** Ask yourself the difficult questions: why should a reader care about your book? Why would an editor select an extract from your book or request an article from you over any other writer? Have you seen a book like yours reviewed in *The Times*?

• **What stories do you have to tell beyond 'I've written a book'?** Consider how to create additional content beyond reviews. Is your book inspired by anything from your own life, for example? Journalists are interested in compelling human stories, and if your story isn't timely or interesting, it's not going to be strong enough.

• **Develop your online presence.** Journalists will make a judgment on a book's potential by the size and activity of an author's audience. What do reviewers see when they visit your website? Do you have an active and engaged social media platform that shares valuable content?

Unlike advertising, where there is a clear return on investment, it can be difficult to quantify the results yielded by PR. But if you're going to go to the trouble of writing a book, it makes sense to create a plan to get it into the hands of readers. A freelance PR will use their experience, connections and knowledge to separate your book from the thousands of others hitting the bookshelves. By harnessing the power of PR, you can target the audiences who will ultimately buy your book.

Hannah Hargrave is an award-winning publicist who worked in-house for Little, Brown Book Group, Ryland Peters & Small and the BBC before going freelance. Recent clients include Summersdale (Hachette), Darton, Longman and Todd, SCM Press and Deixis Press. Visit www.hargraveprandevents.weebly.com for more information. Follow her on X @HannahHargrave8.

How bookshops can help sell your book

Carrie Morris is co-owner of the award-winning Booka Bookshops. In this article, she explains how bookshops and authors can work together most effectively to sell and promote the best new writing.

I run, with my husband Tim, the independent Booka Bookshop in Oswestry, a market town on the English/Welsh border. We began trading in October 2009 and six years later was named UK & Ireland Independent Bookshop of the Year at *The Bookseller* Industry Awards. In October 2023, we opened our second shop in Bridgnorth. We are passionate about bookselling and putting the right book into the right readers' hands. Our key aim is to create a book-buying experience that can't be replicated online, providing personal service in an environment that encourages 'discoverability'. Our events programme is wide and varied as we try to capture new audiences and widen our reach locally and regionally. We work with schools on a regular basis to organise author visits and book fairs.

Our philosophy

Bookshops and authors are interdependent: in short, they help each other to succeed.

Booka is proud of its independent status and with that, the curation of titles it decides to showcase. Independent bookshops hand-select every title on their shelves with passion, instinct, knowledge and an understanding of their particular community and customer base. They have to work very hard in challenging circumstances to remain on the High Street; needing to sell books to survive and thrive. We must add value to the customer experience and to keep surprising readers by offering the element of discovery.

One of the most thrilling parts of being a bookseller is finding a new author with a new story – one that immediately enthralls, entrances and excites. This can develop a ripple effect as booksellers chat with each other, with publishers and – perhaps most importantly – with customers: 'guess what's coming…' or 'I've just read the most amazing proof, it's about…' This is where the 'buzz about books' begins to build. It's what we do, and we do it well. We are always looking ahead, anticipating the next little gem that we can hand-sell to our customers. Today, these 'whispers' don't just take place in the shop. They happen across our social media platforms and are communicated through e-newsletters.

There is a vibrancy and purposefulness in everything we do as booksellers in order to promote books. At Booka, it is all about creating theatre around a book. We start with our windows. Martha, our amazing window artist, works her magic to make book buyers stop, stand and stare. It is a more beautiful and organic version of a poster on the Underground. This image is also beamed via our social media to our followers – those who don't live close to us physically, but are part of our online community. Even though we are a physical bookshop and rooted in our local community, we can still influence readers' buying decisions nationally and globally. We send books worldwide and among our loyal online customer base have collectors who are often looking for signed first editions. If a debut title is receiving a lot of attention and we promote it for pre-order, that can kickstart sales before publication.

Working with debut authors

Developing a relationship with your local independent bookshop or shops should be a key part of any new author's strategy. Events play a key role in that and are intrinsic to what we do at Booka. We host events of all shapes and sizes and, although the large events are exciting, often the most rewarding are those we do with debut authors in the intimacy of the bookshop.

Case study: Jessie Burton, *The Miniaturist*

Jessie Burton, author of *The Miniaturist* (Picador 2014), had her first event outside London at our Oswestry shop. There was an incredible feeling about Jessie and her book throughout the trade, and that proved to be correct: *The Miniaturist* was the fastest selling debut of the 2010s, going onto win prizes and be adapted for TV. Jessie has since followed it up with several other books that we joyfully put into the hands of readers.

Top tips for new authors

- Don't just rely on your publisher to promote your book; be as proactive as you can.
- Become a regular bookshop customer.
- Introduce yourself by popping into your local bookshop and/or bookshops in the location your book is set (it might be best to call ahead and make an appointment as bookshops are busy places).
- Use your visit to get a feel for the type of books the shop sells.
- Drop off a proof and document this by taking photos.
- Get active on social media and tag the bookshop.
- Offer to attend a book club to talk about your book.
- Be prepared – your book might not be right for every bookshop.

Case study: Annie Garthwaite, *Cecily*

Annie is one of our favourite local authors. She lives near our Bridgnorth shop and contacted us when her book *Cecily* was published in hardback (Viking 2021). It is a historical fiction title that is steeped in place. Annie's publishing schedule was compromised by the ongoing difficulties posed by the pandemic, but she did not let this defeat her. She contacted and visited as many independent bookshops as she could, talking to booksellers about her book with a passion that was contagious. She harnessed the power of her social media – documenting her travels, her events and the numerous displays of *Cecily* in bookshops. It was through her determination and hard work that *Cecily* became a word-of-mouth bestseller and a favourite among independent bookshops. Annie now has a strong network of bookshops throughout the country who were waiting avidly for the sequel, *The King's Mother*, which published in July 2024. The Booka team are huge fans of *Cecily* and *The King's Mother* and we planned a launch event at our Bridgnorth shop with an eye-catching window display from our resident window artist. We also promoted pre-orders for signed, dedicated copies in the run-up to publication.

The power of the pre-order

In recent years, the excitement around pre-orders has increased dramatically and can help to build sales prior to publication. At Booka, we have worked closely with a few local authors to promote exclusive pre-orders, with Annie being just one of them.

Case study: Rebecca Struthers, *The Hands of Time*

Rebecca is an award-winning designer, watchmaker, historian and the first person in British history to earn a PhD in horology. We worked together to promote pre-orders of signed dedicated copies of her book prior to its hardback publication date. *The Hands of Time* (Hodder & Stoughton 2023) is a niche book with a specific customer base. We might have expected to sell around ten copies through the shop over several months but thanks to our joint efforts, ended up selling over 250 copies before publication. And as a result of the strong relationship we built and the excitement from Rebecca's followers, within the first year we have sold over 500 copies.

This is a perfect example of how a bookshop can transform an author's book sales, particularly a specialist title, if the communication, the package and the willingness on both sides to make it work are in place. It also relied heavily on the strong relationship we have built with the publishers, who helped to facilitate this success story by putting the author and bookshop in touch.

Children's books

Children's books are a huge part of our offer across both our bookshop locations. We have a dedicated children's team and actively promote our 'Book Services for Schools' with a vibrant booklet. Taking authors into schools, coordinating book fairs, hosting a programme of children's events and running children's book clubs is part and parcel of our everyday operation. Additionally, we select a 'Children's Choice' Book of the Month and promote the Booksellers Association's Indie Children's Book of the Month.

The combined strength of these individual elements allows us to showcase a wide range of books suitable for readers from 0–99 years old. Ultimately, the focus is on books we are passionate about. We give them space in the shop, write accompanying reviews, promote on our website and (as noted above) use our e-newsletter to communicate with our wider reading community.

Brilliant book launches

If you've developed a good relationship with a local independent bookshop, work with them to plan a 'launch' event so that your book gets off to the best possible start. Think about the content of your book and what would work best in terms of 'theming'. It's also worth asking your publisher if they can help: perhaps they could sponsor the wine or point-of-sale materials, such as bookmarks, pin badges or tote bags. Decide on an appropriate format: you could appear in conversation, for example, or give a short talk. One less formal option is to introduce your book, give a reading and then do a book-signing (to encourage audience members to buy). Work hard to encourage potential audience members to attend the launch, but also invite family and friends to create a 'ready-made audience'. Re-post and share any social media from the hosting bookshop.

As an aside, it's worth investing the time in developing your own audience and curating an active social media presence. Clare Mackintosh does this exceptionally well with her newsletter, where she communicates regularly with her readers to build excitement about any new books. Creating content is a huge part of being an author.

Self-published authors

Getting your book onto the shelves of a bookshop can be difficult at the best of times: most independents are small and shelf space is at a premium. Here are some ways that self-published authors can reach an audience, however.

• Make sure your book is available through Gardners (www.gardners.com) – they are a leading wholesaler of books (most bookshops use Gardners and the main publishers/distributors to source their books).
• Booksellers are not editors and with the all-consuming demands of running a business, they don't have time to read every single book and give feedback to authors. Booksellers rely on review coverage, meeting with publisher reps, *The Bookseller* magazine, social media, a knowledge of their local reading community and instinct.
• Email is probably the best way to introduce yourself and your book to a bookshop. It then gives them time to consider whether the book is of interest to them and their customers.
• Leave a 'no-strings-attached' copy of your book and be polite and friendly when dropping it off.
• Think about the features of your book that make it commercial and marketable. How can a bookshop use those to showcase and sell it to their customers? Is it set locally, perhaps, or does it cover a particular event from local history.
• Find a guide from the Booksellers Association of more tips and advice: www.booksellers.org.uk/Industry-Info/Industry-Info/Getting-your-book-stocked-in-a-high-street-bookshop

Case study: Dave Andrews

Over the years, we have worked with various local writers and one of our collaborations has been with an author called Dave Andrews. He is a passionate writer and has worked extensively with Oswestry Library and is their writer-in-residence. He and his partner have also been loyal Booka customers since we opened. Dave started out writing local history titles, which he sold to raise money for charity, and we supported him by selling copies of these books. Over the last couple of years, he has begun writing crime fiction set locally. Dave is very proactive and has promoted the book locally mainly through print media and driving local customers into Booka to purchase copies.

We decided to read one of his crime fiction titles in our bookclub and invited Dave along to the meeting to chat to readers about the first book in the series and its forthcoming sequel. This is a great way to build readership and is another an example of a mutually beneficial relationship for both the author and bookshop.

The result

That's the alchemy of independent bookshops – working collaboratively with an author to sell their book and developing a readership which will continue to thrive. When the author and bookshop share the same ethos and understand the role they each play in the journey of the book from creation to consumption, magical things can happen and many books can be sold. Building a trusted relationship with a bookshop is key to this and the best relationships are those that foster mutual respect and appreciation of both parties.

Carrie Morris and her husband Tim own and run the award-winning independent Booka Bookshops in Oswestry and Bridgnorth, Shropshire. Find out about author events, as well as how to purchase signed copies and to sign up to their newsletter, at: www.bookabookshop.co.uk.

See also ...

• *Reigniting the past: writing historical fiction*, page 293

Assistive technology for visually impaired people

Bridget Norman considers the questions that visually impaired professionals might want to think about in terms of access, either when presented with a new tool to master, or when choosing which tool is needed to realise a specific creative objective.

When determining how to access a given program:

• What will you be using it for? Editing spoken word audio or music, for example?

• Are people like you already using it for that purpose and have they shared their challenges and/or 'workarounds'?

• Will this tool work with your screen reader or magnification software?

• Are there any bolt-on programmes that could sit alongside the main tool to improve its functionality for you, such as increasing the range of keyboard shortcuts available?

• Customising: what are the accessibility settings within the tool itself; could they be helpful?

• What technical support is available to users of the tool?

• Consider version compatibility between both the tool itself, the device operating system (such as Windows or Mac iOS) and any additional assistive software like a text-to-speech reader. JAWS for Windows (https://support.freedomscientific.com/Downloads/JAWS), is an example of this. This interrelationship is vital: it needs to balance optimum function with the most recent and therefore most supported and secure version.

When selecting which technical tool to use for a specific purpose:

What are the software tools that will deliver your key need? Investigate, compare program offerings and trial for free where you can; research experiences of others who share your requirements; consider affordability. Choose what feels right for you.

If moving to new software, what are your most used key commands and how are they ascribed in the new system's language? Do they work? You can often create new keyboard shortcuts if something is missing, provided it has not already been assigned to another function.

If a program is not currently usable, what are your other options? Are there any practical alternatives that might work for the purpose you want within your existing tech 'house of cards' i.e. interdependent programmes? If that tool is essential – it is an employer-specific database, various scripting services are available to code for enabling a screen reader to work with the programme.

Update software with caution

Once you have a system that works well for you and your needs, you will want to keep it that way. Updating one element can undermine the careful structures and resources you have set up. The newest version of an application may not necessarily be a step forward in terms of accessibility e.g. existing commands may have been reassigned or cease to exist.

Bridget Norman has worked across the audio broadcast and publishing industries, including as Custom Audio Manager for Penguin Random House Children's.

More options for more people: inclusivity and opening up the industry

While a dream industry for many, getting into publishing or getting published can be a nightmare without the right connections. And that's not right. In this article, Aki Schilz explains why inclusion and diversity programmes should be about a lot more than lip service.

For years now, there have been rumblings about what diversity and inclusion mean, why they are important, and how we should be talking about them in the publishing community.

In the 1970s the pioneering activist Naseem Khan wrote a landmark report, 'The Arts Britain Ignores', kickstarting a series of well-overdue conversations of what the cultural sector was doing to offer genuine representation of the incredible array of talent within the UK. The report advocated for a new approach to work by Black and Asian artists, boldly re-centring what the 'establishment' had hitherto dismissed or disqualified as somehow belonging on the outskirts of 'real art'.

Naseem's powerful memoir, *Everywhere is Somewhere*, is a book I was lucky enough to find her a publisher for just weeks before her death. She chose the mighty Bluemoose Books, whose Manifesto (which includes the rather delicious phrase 'we see ourselves as a delicatessen as opposed to a supermarket') resonated strongly with her independent spirit. In them, she – an Indian-German woman who had dedicated her life to building inclusive cultures – had found a place for her writing that felt like home. This is the fight we find ourselves in: for all writers to have somewhere for their writing that feels like home.

There are so many examples of publishing industry people and organisations doing 'the right things' since the arrival of Naseem's report, pushing open doors for writers who had been left waiting while others seemed to waltz in. Publishers like HopeRoad, Jacaranda, OWN IT! and Cassava Republic Press. Organisations and collectives working to redress the balance like DipNet (now rebranded as Equip), Words of Colour, Speaking Volumes. Chapters within publishing houses like Thrive at Hachette, and indeed entire divisions like Dialogue Books, whose strapline is 'Innovation, Inspiration, Inclusion'. More recently, we've had the Working Class Writers' Prize, the Curae Prize for writers with caring responsibilities, the Barbellion Prize for ill and disabled writers, as well as the ESEA (East and South East Asian) Lit Fest and a windfall £5m of investment to build a regional writing centre that, for once, is based in the North (and by those based there, not those flown out there from Bloomsbury).

The list goes on.

So aren't we already 'doing diversity'? Maybe we're even doing too much diversity! And why should writers care?

Well, firstly we're definitely not doing too much.

Where are we now?

First, and despite all of the hard work over the years, the latest reports present a fairly gloomy picture about the progress made. Ethnic minority representation in the UK publishing workforce has reduced by two percentage points from 17% to 15%, with a specific decline in numbers of Asian and British Asian staff, and over two-thirds of staff come from 'professional' backgrounds – a marker used to track socio-economic household status. In other words, a minority of those in publishing are what would be considered working class. And, as with other sectors, we have an unspoken ageism problem: 15% of those in publishing are over the age of 55.

In terms of creative output, in a survey conducted by the *New York Times*, 95% of the 8,000 titles published by major houses since 1950 were by white authors. And in the UK a recent survey concluded that global majority (Black, Asian and other previously labelled 'ethnic minority' writers) are earning less money from writing, with smaller advances. The 2024 'Reflecting Realities' report from CLPE shows that, for the first time in seven years, the percentage of global majority characters featured in children's books has dropped.

The idea that the writing industry is tipped towards marginalised writers is, despite what you might read from certain detractors, simply not true.

And second, yes, you should absolutely care, because when we talk about the future of publishing, we're talking about the world into which you might be dreaming of publishing your writing: how will you be treated? Will you be paid fairly? How will you be protected from exploitation, intellectual property theft, from harm? Who will be your readers? Your editor? Your marketing team?

Towards inclusion, and the missing puzzle piece

At the heart of it, this is a question about how all writers, from all backgrounds, can be given a fair shot. And how all editors, marketers and publicists can work with all writers with confidence and skill to bring their stories to life. We need to nurture the best writing for the future, and the most resilient and most creative writers, who feel properly valued and met where they are.

Here's another stat that is vital to this conversation. A recent report by *The Bookseller*, the publishing industry's primary media platform, found that 54% of debut authors felt the publication process negatively affected their mental health. Despite promises of forthcoming cross-sector support, there are to date no industry-wide best practice guidelines for author care. This affects all writers, but the brunt of the impact will fall on those without additional support in the early stages of development: disproportionately, this will be those writers who continue to be under-represented.

The publishing industry is full of talent, energy and ideas. The cultural economy is one of the only areas to have seen growth in a time of shrinking budgets and swingeing cuts. But it's also highly competitive, full of overworked and underpaid people, reliant on precedent but desperate for the new (can you see the paradox?). It can be cut-throat, and it's unequally weighted. Some writers get huge advances; some get none (the average advance currently sits at £6,000). Some writers make a living comfortably; most don't (the average professional writing income is £10,000 per annum). Yet the industry keeps pushing the narrative that success looks like a huge, shiny book deal and a magical guaranteed career for life. Which means that failure is … everything else.

And that's toxic to writers' wellbeing. There are so many ways to be a writer, and so many ways to nurture an inclusive, thriving literary culture. We can't build this if we don't think, carefully and hard, about author care. And about creative wellbeing in general.

So ... how do we make change happen?

At The Literary Consultancy we subscribe to the Social Model, a model from disability justice which tells us that it isn't a person's physical limitations, but rather societal barriers that 'disable' people by excluding them and actively preventing them from being able to thrive. This can be applied across all things that might be considered experiential 'limitations', from class and sexuality to age, geographic isolation, gender, illness, ethnicity and neurodivergence.

Systems of power built to cater only for certain demographics cannot be dismantled by diversity programmes alone. What we need is systemic change. And we need legacy: new approaches, behaviours and habits that are inheritable and enshrined. And within these systems, we need support for those fighting the good fight, and support for writers who are facing increasing pressure to become author brands. You are not a brand! You are a creative soul. And that soul needs nourishing and protecting.

Self-care is not about how a bubble bath will revolutionise your life (a mindfulness habit is not going to lift you out of poverty, or get you a book deal). Self-care is about insisting on proper boundaries, building community through solidarity, understanding that you cannot always produce, produce, produce: you must also take time to imagine, to dream and to rest. And, self-care is also saying: yes, I am a writer. Yes, what I have to say is important. Yes, I deserve this.

Changing behaviours; changing culture

Culture is a set of behaviours.

If we can change behaviours, we can change culture.

Behaviours run along tracks. There are the things that the industry needs to do (systemic behaviours) and there are things that writers can do (individual behaviours).

Three things organisations can do (show an open door; nurture talent)

1. Salary transparency. In 2017, I conducted a study that found that fewer than 10% of all job ads on two of the major publishing recruitment platforms included a salary. When I looked only at entry-level jobs, this dropped to 4%.

Why do it? Putting a salary or salary band on a job ad increases the number of applications by up to 60%, and will increase the diversity of your applicant pool.

2. Author starter packs. During our Ethical Editing training for corporate publishers, I noticed that when I asked whether there was a clear process for how publishers would work with an author from start to finish, most said yes. But when I asked whether they had this written down anywhere as a policy or protocol, the majority admitted they did not.

Why do it? By being clear about how you will work with an author, from initial meeting to how many edits to what the author care protocol is, you can manage their expectations, provide clear parameters and tangible reassurance. Just like good job descriptions enumerate benefits, be clear about what's on offer, and make sure your authors feel like they are part of the internal culture of your organisation – because they are.

3. Accessibility notices. If you are hosting something, whether in person or online, include a clear accessibility notice that shows what access measures are (and aren't) in place. Digital does not necessarily mean accessible! A simple tick box can help and is the most honest way to show up front if something has: wheelchair access, ramps, audio loop, BSL, quiet spaces, prayer spaces, comfort breaks, live or automated captions, distressing content, and so on. The same goes for working with an author one to one. What kind of adjustments are available? Is there an Access Rider they can use?

Why do it? One in five people in the United Kingdom has a disability. And anyone can have an access requirement. Don't leave it to your community to come to you. Tell them what you're doing to make sure they are comfortable and included. And yes, publishers, this includes not having seizure-inducing flashing imagery in your promotional videos for social media.

Three things writers can do (stay creative, build resilience and community)

1. Demand transparency. Whether this is about accessibility, terms and conditions, the details of your working relationship with your agent or publisher or something else, don't be afraid to ask. I was once asked to chair a panel for an event and there was no mention of fee in the invitation. As a fair pay advocate I queried this, and the organisers offered me a fee. I asked if the other panellists were being paid. 'Well, they didn't ask,' was the response. I said I would do it only if all of us were paid. After some negotiation, we all received the same fee.

2. Sell your story, not your soul. I believe in this one so much I have designed a TLC workshop about it! As a writer, remember that you don't owe anyone your soul. Whilst I've already admitted the idea of an 'author brand' makes me feel cynical, what I do believe in is the power of an author 'avatar': who you are as a writer does not have to be who you are as a person. There might be important divergences which protect you from unnecessary or painful disclosure. Even with good intentions, the line between, for example, wanting 'own voices' stories to exploiting writers' lived experiences is dangerously thin. Take the power back!

3. Pay it forwards. When I am sent a proof copy by a publisher, I write the title down in a spreadsheet and, when the paperback is published, buy a copy to give to someone as a present. This way, I make sure the author gets a tiny something back. As a writer, you are part of a wider ecology. Be active in that ecology! Swap skills, offer to beta read, write an online review for your writer friends (the magic number for Am*z** is 50 reviews for the algorithm to start recommending it to others!) etc. If you were helped by someone in your writing life, when you can, and however you can, pay it forwards.

The future

Together, we can make change happen. But it needs all of us to be on board, working together, for each other and for a better future. A future in which the greatest, bravest writing is encouraged and celebrated, in which writers are sustained and nourished according to their needs and desires, and in which literature is valued as an art, a social act and a soul-nourishing force.

Just as I am proud to stand on the shoulders of giants, I am confident that the future is being created by minds far greater than mine, and I look forward to seeing it, living in it, and benefiting from the great art that its writers will produce. Here's to literature that is bold, innovative and empathetic, that takes risks and that changes the world.

A consultant, writer and editor, **Aki Schilz** is also Director of The Literary Consultancy, which has to date supported 13,000 writers through its editing, mentoring and events services. Find out more at: https://literaryconsultancy.co.uk. Aki is on X @akischilz and Bluesky @akischilz.bsky.social.

Book publishers UK and Ireland

There are changes to listings in this section every year. We aim to provide a comprehensive list of publishing imprints, the name or brand under which a specific set of titles are sold by a publisher. Any one publisher might have several imprints; for example Bloomsbury publishes cookery books under the Absolute Press imprint and nautical books under Adlard Coles. The imprint usually appears on the spine of a book. Imprints are included either under a publisher's main entry or in some cases as entries themselves. Information is provided in a way that is of most use to a reader.

The subject indexes, which start on page 753 list publishers and imprints for different genres and forms of writing. The listings that follow are updated by the *Writers' & Artists'* editors based on information supplied by those listed. Increasingly, some legitimate publishers are offering paid-for editorial services in addition to their standard publishing model; please check carefully what they offer. Our section *Self-publishing and indie authors*, on page 694, provides advice on this.

The country code for phoning UK offices from overseas is +44.

sae = self-addressed envelope   MS = manuscript (MSS = manuscripts)

*Member of the Publishers Association or Publishing Scotland

†Member of the Publishers Ireland

‡Member of the Independent Publishers Guild

Some of the smaller companies listed are also members of the Indie Press Network, formed in 2023 to represent publishers with five or fewer employees (see also page 557).

AA Publishing

Grove House, Lutyens Close, Basingstoke, Hants. RG24 8AG
email contact@ratedtrips.com
website www.ratedtrips.com/books
X @theaa_lifestyle

Atlases, maps, leisure interests, travel including City Packs and AA Guides. Founded 1910.

Acair*

An Tosgan, 54 Seaforth Road, Stornoway, Isle of Lewis HS1 2SD
email info@acairbooks.com
website https://acairbooks.com/
Facebook www.facebook.com/acairbooks
X @acairbooks

Scottish Gaelic children's books and a wide range of titles in Scottish Gaelic and English. Founded 1977.

ACC Art Books‡

Riverside House, Dock Lane, Melton, Woodbridge, Suffolk IP12 1PE
tel (01394) 389950
email uksales@accartbooks.com
website www.accartbooks.com/uk
Facebook www.facebook.com/ACCArtBooks
X @ACCArtBooks
Instagram @accartbooks_
Publisher James Smith

Publisher and distributor of books on art, photography, decorative arts, fashion, gardening, design and architecture. Founded 1966.

Ad Hoc Fiction

6 Old Tarnwell, Stanton Drew, Bristol BS39 4EA
email jude@adhocfiction.com
website www.adhocfiction.com
X @AdHocFiction
Director Jude Higgins

Award-winning small, independent publisher of short-form fiction. Publishes anthologies of fiction from the thrice-yearly Bath Flash Fiction Award (page 598) and the Bath Short Story Award. Publishes single-author collections of flash fictions, novellas-in-flash, guidebooks on writing flash fiction and anthologies of stories from participants at the Flash Fiction Festival. Founded 2015.

Afsana Press

37 Conrad House, Matthias Road, London N16 8LJ
tel 07453 918505
email publisher@afsanapress.uk
website www.afsana-press.com
Facebook www.facebook.com/afsanapress/
X @afsana_press
Instagram @afsana_press
Co-publisher/Managing Director Aleksandra Markovic, *Co-publisher/Editor* Goran Baba Ali

A small, independent press of fiction and literary non-fiction. Considers any genre, but prefers literary. Particularly interested in authors in exile. Facilitates a free Writers' Collective to help profile the work of like-minded authors. Founded 2021.

Agenda Publishing‡
PO Box 185, Newcastle upon Tyne NE20 2DH
tel 0191 495 7330
email enquiries@agendapub.com
website www.agendapub.com
Facebook www.facebook.com/agendapub
X @agendapub
Publisher & Managing Director Steven Gerrard

Independent publisher of books in economics, politics, philosophy, human geography and sustainability for students and lecturers worldwide. Founded 2016.

Allison & Busby‡
11 Wardour Mews, London W1F 8AN
tel 020-3950 7834
email susie@allisonandbusby.com
website www.allisonandbusby.com
Facebook www.facebook.com/allisonandbusbybooks
X @allisonandbusby
Publishing Director Susie Dunlop, *Publishing Manager* Lesley Crooks

Fiction and general non-fiction. Fiction genres include: romance, historical, crime and mysteries and contemporary. Non-fiction genres include: biography and history. No unsolicited MSS. Founded 1967.

Alma Books
60 High Street, Wimbledon Village, London SW19 5EE
website www.almabooks.com, www.almaclassics.com
Directors Alessandro Gallenzi, Elisabetta Minervini

Contemporary literary fiction. Non-fiction: European classics, poetry, drama, art, literary criticism, biography and autobiography, essays, humanities and social sciences. No unsolicited MSS. Series include: Alma Classics, Alma Junior. Around 50% English-language originals, 50% translations. Founded 2005.

Amazon Publishing
email amazonpublishing-pr@amazon.com
website https://amazonpublishing.amazon.com/
Facebook www.facebook.com/amazonpublishing
X @amazonpub
Head of Publishing UK and Germany Eion Purcell

The full-service publishing arm of Amazon. See website for editorial contacts and genres of each imprint. Imprints include: Amazon Crossing, Amazon Crossing Kids, AmazonEncore, Amazon Original Stories, 47North, Lake Union Publishing, Little A, Mindy's Book Studio, Montlake, Skyscape, Thomas & Mercer, TOPPLE Books and Two Lions. Currently not accepting unsolicited MSS. Also provides a self-publishing platform via Kindle Direct Publishing (page 697). Founded 2009.

Amber Books‡
United House, North Road, London N7 9DP
tel 020-7520 7600
email enquiries@amberbooks.co.uk
website www.amberbooks.co.uk
Facebook www.facebook.com/amberbooks
X @amberbooks
Instagram @amberbooksltd
Chairman Stasz Gnych, *Managing Director* Sara McKie, *Editorial Director* Charles Catton

Illustrated non-fiction for adults and children. Subjects include: photography, travel, gift books, military technology, military history, general history, humour, music, survival, natural history and family reference. Works include: encyclopaedias and highly illustrated reference. Opportunities for freelancers. Founded 1989.

Amberley Publishing‡
The Hill, Stroud, Glos. GL5 4EP
tel (01453) 847800
email info@amberley-books.com
website www.amberley-books.com
Facebook www.facebook.com/amberleybooks
X @amberleybooks
Ceo Nick Hayward

General history/non-fiction and local interest; specialisations include transport (railways, road transport, canals, maritime), industry, sport, biography and military history. Owns Quiller Publishing (page 172) and Icon Books (page 151). Founded 2008.

Amgueddfa Cymru – Museum Wales‡
Cathays Park, Cardiff CF10 3NP
tel 029-2057 3235
email post@museumwales.ac.uk
website www.museumwales.ac.uk
X @AmgueddfaBooks
Head of Publishing Mari Gordon

Trade and special interest books based on the Welsh national collections and research of Amgueddfa Cymru, Wales's national museums. For adults, schools and children, in both Welsh and English. Founded 1907.

And Other Stories*
Central Library, Surrey Street, Sheffield S1 1XZ
email info@andotherstories.org
website www.andotherstories.org
Facebook www.facebook.com/AndOtherStoriesBooks
X @andothertweets
Instagram @andotherpics
Publisher Stefan Tobler

Contemporary literary fiction and non-fiction from around the world. Has an open submissions policy, but strict submissions guidelines are available on the website. Submissions not complying with these guidelines will be disregarded. Founded 2011.

Andersen Press*
6 Coptic Street, London WC1A 1NH
tel 020-7840 8701

email anderseneditorial@penguinrandomhouse.co.uk
website www.andersenpress.co.uk
Facebook www.facebook.com/andersenpress
X @andersonpress
Instagram @andersonpress
Managing Director Mark Hendle, *Publisher* Klaus Flugge

Children's books: picture books, fiction for 5–8 and 9–12 years and YA fiction. Founded 1976.

Angry Robot Books

Unit 11, Shepperton House, 89 Shepperton Road, London N1 3DF
tel 020-3813 6940
email incoming@angryrobots.com
website www.angryrobotbooks.com
Facebook www.facebook.com/angryrobotbooks
X @angryrobotbooks
Publisher Eleanor Teasdale

Modern adult sci-fi and fantasy with a speculative slant. Crime fiction imprint: Datura Books. Part of Watkins Media. Founded 2009.

Anness Publishing Ltd

Blaby Road, Wigston, Leicester LE18 4SE
email info@anness.com
website www.annesspublishing.com
Managing Director Paul Anness, *Publisher* Joanna Lorenz

Practical illustrated books on cookery, fine art, military and transport, lifestyle, crafts, hobbies, reference, gardening, health, new age, children's classics and non-fiction. Imprints include: Armadillo, Hermes House, Lorenz Books, Peony Press, Practical Pictures, Snake River Press and Southwater. Founded 1988.

Apa Publications‡

7 Bell Yard, London WC2A 2JR
tel 020-7403 0284
website www.insightguides.com, www.roughguides.com
Facebook www.facebook.com/InsightGuides, www.facebook.com/RoughGuides
X @InsightGuides, @RoughGuides
Instagram @insightguides, @roughguides
Managing Director Agnieszka Mizak, *Head of Publishing* Sarah Clark

Publishers of Rough Guides and Insight Guides for travel and language products, and related digital content. Founded 1970.

Appletree Press†

Roycroft House, 164 Malone Road, Belfast BT9 5LL
tel 028-9024 3074
email editorial@appletree.ie
website www.appletree.ie

Gift books, guidebooks, history, Irish interest, Scottish interest, photography, sport and travel. Founded 1974.

Arachne Press

100 Grierson Road, London SE23 1NX
email cherry@arachnepress.com
website https://arachnepress.com/
Bluesky @arachnepress.bsky.social
Instagram @arachnepress
Threads @arachnepress
Director Cherry Potts

Small, independent publisher of short fiction, poetry and select non-fiction for adults. Expanding children's fiction list. Particular interest in LGBTQ+, Global majority, disabled and older women writers. Currently only open to anthology calls. Founded 2012.

Arc Publications

Nanholme Mill, Shaw Wood Road, Todmorden OL14 6DA
tel (01706) 812338
email info@arcpublications.co.uk
website www.arcpublications.co.uk
Facebook www.facebook.com/arcpublications
X @arc_poetry
Founder & Managing Editor Tony Ward, *Publisher & Editor of Arc Music* Angela Jarman, *Editors* James Byrne, Jean Boase-Beier

Contemporary poetry and neglected work from the past: poetry from the UK and Ireland, world poetry in English, bilingual translations mainly from the smaller languages (individual poets and anthologies) and occasional books on music and musicians. Imprints: Arc Publications and Arc Music. Refer to website for current publication list/catalogue and submissions policy. Founded 1969.

Arkbound*‡

Rogart Street Campus, 4 Rogart Street, Glasgow G40 2AA
tel 0117 290 0386, 0871 268 9869
email hello@arkbound.com
website https://arkbound.com/

Fiction and non-fiction, focused on important social or environmental issues. Supports authors from disadvantaged and diverse backgrounds. Also enables people and other publishers to publish books through its dedicated crowdpublishing website, Crowdbound (page 133). Based in England and Scotland, operating on behalf of the Arkbound Foundation charity. Founded as a social enterprise with the support of the King's Trust. Founded 2015.

Ashmolean Museum Publications

Beaumont Street, Oxford OX1 2PH
tel (01865) 288070
email dec.mccarthy@ashmus.ox.ac.uk
website www.ashmolean.org
Contact Declan McCarthy

Exhibition catalogues, fine and applied art of Europe and Asia, archaeology, history and numismatics. Photographic archive and picture library. Museum founded 1683.

Books

Atlantic Books*‡
Ormond House, 26–27 Boswell Street,
London WC1N 3JZ
tel 020-7269 1610
email enquiries@atlantic-books.co.uk
website https://atlantic-books.co.uk/
Facebook www.facebook.com/AtlanticBooks
X @atlanticbooks
Instagram @atlanticbooks
Managing Director & Publisher Drummond Moir

Literary fiction, thrillers, history, current affairs, politics, sport, biography and memoir. Strictly no unsolicited submissions or proposals. Imprints: Allen & Unwin, Atlantic Books, Corvus and Grove Press. Founded 2000.

Aureus Publishing
Castle Court, Castle-upon-Alun, St Bride's Major,
Vale of Glamorgan CF32 0TN
tel 07500 89923
email aureuspublishing@gmail.com
website www.aureus.co.uk
Facebook www.facebook.com/AureusPublishing
X @AureusPublish
Instagram @aureuspublishing
Director Meuryn Hughes

Rock and pop, autobiography, biography and sport. Submissions: email synopsis and brief description of proposal. Founded 1993.

Aurora Metro‡
80 Hill Rise, Richmond TW10 6UB
tel 020-8948 1427
email submissions@aurorametro.com
website www.aurorametro.com
Facebook www.facebook.com/AuroraMetroBooks
X @aurorametro
Managing Director Cheryl Robson

Adult fiction, YA fiction, biography, drama (including plays for young people), non-fiction, theatre, cookery and translation. Submissions: send synopsis and three chapters. Runs a biennial competition for women novelists (odd years): Virginia Prize for Fiction. Entry fee for submission of either an adult or YA novel. Imprints: Amber Lane Press, Aurora Metro Books, River Light Press and Supernova Books. Founded 1990.

Authentic Media‡
PO Box 6326, Bletchley, Milton Keynes MK1 9GG
tel (01908) 268500
email info@authenticmedia.co.uk
website www.authenticmedia.co.uk
Facebook www.facebook.com/authenticmedia
X @authenticmedia
Instagram @authentic_media
Ceo Adam Betteridge

Biblical studies, Christian theology, ethics, history, mission, commentaries, Christian biographies, devotionals, children's books and Bibles. Imprints: Authentic and Paternoster. Founded 2001.

Avery Hill Publishing
67 Trumpington Road, London E7 9EH
website https://averyhillpublishing.com/
Facebook www.facebook.com/averyhillpublishing
Instagram @averyhillpublishing
Director Ricky Miller, *Head of Marketing & Production* Katriona Chapman

Graphic novels, comics and art books. Currently not accepting unsolicited submissions. Founded 2012.

Avon – see HarperCollins Publishers

Award Publications
The Old Riding School, The Welbeck Estate,
Worksop, Notts. S80 3LR
tel (01909) 478170
email info@awardpublications.co.uk
Facebook www.facebook.com/awardpublications
Instagram @award.books

Picture story books, fiction, early learning, information and activity books for 0–12 years. No unsolicited material. Refer to social media sites for details of submission windows. Founded 1972.

Bad Betty Press
Cobden Place, Unit 5, Cobden Chambers,
Pelham Street, Nottingham NG1 3ED
email info@badbettypress.com
website www.badbettypress.com
Facebook www.facebook.com/badbettypress
X @badbettypress
Instagram @badbettypress
Editor/Director Amy Acre, *Artistic Director* Jake Wild Hall, *Pamphlet imprint Little Betty, Editors* Anja Konig, Vanessa Kisuule

Award-winning independent publisher of new poetry and curator of live literature events across the UK. Submission windows in June (pamphlets) and July (collections). Founded 2017.

Little Betty
Collections and anthologies.

Bad Press Ink
The Studio, High Turney Shield, Hexham NE47 8AW
tel (01434) 345529
website www.badpress.ink
Facebook www.facebook.com/BADPRESS.iNKPublishing
X @badpressink
Directors & Commissioning Editors Pat Blayney, Iain Parke

Independent publisher of alternative, cult and niche lifestyle fiction. Run by authors for authors, interested in edgy fiction with a distinctive voice including crime, horror and urban subjects. Actively looking for new and unpublished talent. Submissions test available on website. Founded 2018.

Banshee Press

email bansheelit@gmail.com
website https://bansheepress.org/
Facebook www.facebook.com/bansheelit
X @bansheelit
Bluesky @bansheepress.bsky.social
Instagram @bansheepress
Director Eimear Ryan, *Poetry Editor* Jessica Traynor

Small independent Irish publisher of a print literary journal *Banshee*, as well as a select list of books. Publishes contemporary writing in all forms. Open to enquiries and proposals from contributors to the journal, particularly those who have not yet published a book-length work. Occasionally opens for unsolicited submissions, check website for details. Founded 2014.

Barbican Press

1 Ashenden Road, London E5 0DP
tel 07507 554731
email martin@barbicanpress.com
website https://barbicanpress.com/
X @barbicanpress1
Instagram @barbicanpress
Directors Martin Goodman, James Thornton

A small independent micro-publisher of poetry, drama, writing for children, translations and non-fiction, including issues-driven memoir and vivid tales of maritime communities. Founded 2009.

Barrington Stoke*

18 Walker Street, Edinburgh EH3 7LP
tel 0131 392 9400
email barringtonstoke@harpercollins.co.uk
website www.barringtonstoke.co.uk

Short fiction and non-fiction for children, specially adapted and presented for reluctant, struggling and dyslexic readers. Includes books for ages 5 to YA, with reading ages of 6–9. No unsolicited submissions. All work is commissioned from well-known authors and adapted for reluctant readers. Imprint of HarperCollins Publishers. Founded 1998.

BBC Books – see Ebury Publishing

Bearded Badger Publishing

33 High Street, Belper, Derbyshire DE56 1GF
tel 07470 458761
email paulh@beardedbadgerpublishing.com
website www.beardedbadgerpublishing.com
Facebook www.facebook.com/beardedbadgerpublishing
Instagram @bearded_badger_publishing
Managing Director Paul Handley

Independent publishing company with a mission to publish high-quality literature across all genres, with an initial focus on publishing writers with a link to the often-overlooked East Midlands region. Founded 2020.

Bedford Square Publishers*‡

14 Bedford Square, London WC1B 3JA
email info@bedfordsquarepublishers.co.uk
website https://bedfordsquarepublishers.co.uk/
Facebook www.facebook.com/bedfordsq.publishers
X @bedsqpublishers
Managing Director Jamie Hodder-Williams, *Commercial Director* Laura Fletcher, *Publisher* Carolyn Mays

An independent publisher of fiction and non-fiction. Subjects include wellness, smart-thinking and literary fiction. Founded 2022.

No Exit Press

Crime and thrillers, spy fiction.

Betimes Books†

email contact@betimesbooks.com
website https://betimesbooks.com/
Facebook www.facebook.com/betimesbooks
X @BetimesBooks
Instagram @betimesbooksnow
Directors Tanja Slijepčević, John Sheil, Maria Tirelli

Not-for-profit literary press. Founded 2020.

Bennion Kearny‡

6 Woodside, Churnet View Road, Oakamoor, Staffs. ST10 3AE
tel (01538) 703591
email info@bennionkearny.com
website www.bennionkearny.com
Publisher James Lumsden-Cook

Non-fiction: academic, professional, popular, niche and practical titles. All subjects considered. See website for submission details. Publishes titles both nationally and internationally. Imprints: Bennion Kearny, Dark River, Hawksmoor Publishing and Oakamoor Publishing. Founded 2008.

Berghahn Books‡

3 Newtec Place, Magdalen Road, Oxford OX4 1RE
email info@berghahnbooks.com
website www.berghahnbooks.com
Facebook www.facebook.com/BerghahnBooks
X @berghahnbooks
Instagram @berghahnbooks
Managing Director Vivian Berghahn

An independent publisher of scholarly books and journals in the humanities and social sciences. Publishes up to 150 new book titles and 60 paperback editions a year alongside a journals portfolio, spanning history, social and cultural anthropology, archaeology, migration studies, environmental studies and film studies. Founded 1994.

Birlinn*‡

West Newington House, 10 Newington Road, Edinburgh EH9 1QS
tel 0131 668 4371
email info@birlinn.co.uk
website www.birlinn.co.uk
Facebook www.facebook.com/birlinnbooks
X @BirlinnBooks
Instagram @birlinnbooks
Managing Director Hugh Andrew

Independent publisher of Scottish fiction and non-fiction and works by Scottish authors. Founded 1992.

Arena Sport

Football, rugby, golf, running and cycling.

BC Books

Quality illustrated books for young readers.

Birlinn

Scottish history, local interest/history, Scottish humour, guides, military, adventure, history, archaeology, sport and general non-fiction.

John Donald

Academic history books and biographies.

Polygon

Classic and modern literary fiction, poetry, music and film titles.

Biteback Publishing‡

Millbank Tower, 21–24 Millbank, London SW1P 4QP
email info@bitebackpublishing.com
website www.bitebackpublishing.com
Facebook www.facebook.com/BitebackPublishing
X @bitebackpub
Instagram @bitebackpub
Publisher James Stephens, *Editorial Director* Olivia Beattie, *Publicity Director* Suzanne Sangster

Political and current affairs, history, memoir, espionage, sport and general non-fiction. Founded 2009.

Bitter Lemon Press‡

47 Wilmington Square, London WC1X 0ET
email books@bitterlemonpress.com
website www.bitterlemonpress.com
Facebook www.facebook.com/bitterlemonpress
X @bitterlemonpub

Publishes crime fiction that exposes the darker side of countries such as Argentina, Cuba, Mexico, Belgium, France, Germany, Italy, the Netherlands, Poland, Spain, Switzerland, Turkey, India, Iraq, New Zealand, Australia and the USA. Founded 2015.

Wilmington Press

Culture and society.

Black & White Publishing*

Nautical House, 104 Commercial Street, Edinburgh EH6 6NF
tel 0131 625 4500
email mail@blackandwhitepublishing.com
website www.blackandwhitepublishing.com
Publishing Director Alison McBride

Non-fiction: general, sport, cookery, lifestyle, biography, humour and crime. Fiction: women's fiction, contemporary, historical, psychological thrillers and crime. See website for latest submission guidelines. Part of the Adult Trade Division of Bonnier Books. Founded 1999.

Ink Road

YA fiction.

Black Bee Books

Bryn Heulog, Talley, Llandeilo SA19 7YH
email info@blackbeebooks.wales
website www.blackbeebooks.wales
X @BlackBeeBooks

Fiction and non-fiction, YA and adult, from under-represented voices, including LGBTQ+ authors. Currently looking to work with authors that reflect the wide range of communities in Wales, especially under-represented voices. See website for details. Founded 2020.

Black Cat Poetry Press

1 Cross Street, Maidstone ME14 2SL
tel 07528 603405
email contact@blackcatpress.co.uk
website www.blackcatpress.co.uk
X @theblackcatpp
Instagram @theblackcatpoetrypress
Editors Satya Bosman, Catherine Balaq

Provides opportunities for poets to publish pamphlets. The window for submission is October each year. To date, has published debut pamphlets/collections for five poets and published eight poets in a debut nature anthology. Regularly hosts competitions which are free to enter. Founded 2022.

Black Dog Press

The Maple Building, 39–51 Highgate Road, London NW5 1RT
tel 020-8371 4000
email office@blackdogonline.com
website www.blackdogonline.com
X @blackdogpress
Instagram @blackdogpress

Contemporary art, design, photography and music. Founded 1995.

Blackstaff Press

Colourpoint House, Jubilee Business Park, 21 Jubilee Road, Newtownards, Co. Down BT23 4YH
tel 028-9182 0505 (within the UK), +353 (0)48 9182 6339 (Republic of Ireland)

email info@blackstaffpress.com
website www.blackstaffpress.com
Facebook www.facebook.com/Blackstaffpressni
X @BlackstaffNI

Local interest titles, particularly memoir, history and humour. See website for submission guidelines before sending material. Owned by Colourpoint Creative. Founded 1971.

John Blake Publishing*

Victoria House, Bloomsbury Square,
London WC1B 4DA
tel 020-3770 8888
email hello@bonnierbooks.co.uk
website www.bonnierbooks.co.uk/imprints/john-blake-publishing
X @jblakebooks
Instagram @johnblakebooks
Publisher Matthew Phillips

A commercial non-fiction imprint that publishes a mix of real-life stories, biographies, true crime, alternative histories, gift and humour. An imprint of Bonnier Books UK. Founded 1991.

Blink Publishing*

Victoria House, Bloomsbury Square,
London WC1B 4DA
tel 020-3770 8888
email hello@bonnierbooks.co.uk
website www.bonnierbooks.co.uk/imprints/blink-publishing
X @blinkpublishing
Instagram @blinkpublishing
Publisher Matthew Phillips

Commercial adult non-fiction. An imprint of Bonnier Books UK. Founded 2014.

Bloodaxe Books

Eastburn, South Park, Hexham,
Northumberland NE46 1BS
tel (01434) 611581
email editor@bloodaxebooks.com
website www.bloodaxebooks.com
Editor Neil Astley

Poetry. Check submissions guidelines on website and send sample of up to a dozen poems with sae only if the submission fits the guidelines. No email submissions or correspondence. Founded 1978.

Bloodhound Books

9 Hills Road, Cambridge CB2 1GE
email info@bloodhoundbooks.com
website www.bloodhoundbooks.com
Facebook www.facebook.com/BloodhoundBooks
X @BloodhoundBook
Founders Fred Freeman, Betsy Reavley

A digital-focused publisher of commercial and literary fiction: psychological, thrillers, crime, historical, romance and women's fiction. Accepts unsolicited MSS. Owned by US-based marketing tech company Open Road Media (OR/M). Founded 2014.

Bloomsbury Publishing*‡

50 Bedford Square, London WC1B 3DP
tel 020-7631 5600
website www.bloomsbury.com
Facebook www.facebook.com/BloomsburyPublishing
X @BloomsburyBooks
Bluesky @BloomsburyPublishing
Instagram @bloomsburypublishing
Founder & Chief Executive Nigel Newton

Independent publisher with authors who have won the Nobel, Pulitzer and Booker prizes. Offices in London, New York (page 205), New Delhi, Oxford and Sydney (page 190). MSS must normally be channelled through literary agents, with the exception of academic and professional titles. Founded 1986.

BLOOMSBURY CONSUMER DIVISION

Managing Director Ian Hudson

Imprints: Absolute Press, Apollo, Aria, Bloomsbury Children's Books, Bloomsbury Circus, Bloomsbury Press, Bloomsbury Tonic (wellbeing), Head of Zeus (page 149) and Raven Books.

Bloomsbury Adult Trade Publishing

Adult Editor-in-Chief Paul Baggaley, *Head of Trade Division* Alexis Kirschbaum (non-fiction, literary fiction & poetry), *Publishing Directors* Ian Marshall (non-fiction), Emma Herdman (fiction), *Head of General Division* Katy Follain (commercial fiction & non-fiction, crime & sci-fi/fantasy), *Publishing Directors* Alison Hennessey (Raven Books), Darcy Nicholson (commercial fiction), Vicky Leech Mateos (sci-fi & fantasy), *Head of Lifestyle Division* Rowan Yapp (illustrated & cookery), *Poetry Editor* Kayo Chingonyi, *Bloomsbury Tonic Editor* Mireille Harper (wellbeing list)

Fiction and non-fiction, including graphic novels and some titles printed in a dyslexia-friendly format.

Bloomsbury Children's Books

Publishing Director & International Editor-in-Chief Rebecca McNally

Children's fiction and non-fiction, graphic novels. No unsolicited MSS.

Bloomsbury Education

Head of Education Helen Diamond, *Editorial Director* Hannah Rolls (educational fiction & poetry), *Commissioning Editor* Joanna Ramsay (early years & CPD), *Commissioning Editor* Emily Evans (primary & CPD)

Educational fiction and non-fiction, children's poetry, teacher resource books and CPD titles. Imprints: Andrew Brodie and Featherstone Education.

BLOOMSBURY ACADEMIC AND PROFESSIONAL DIVISION

website www.bloomsbury.com/academic, www.bloomsburyprofessional.com

Managing Director Jenny Ridout
Scholarly and educational content in the arts, humanities and social sciences, law, business and management and study skills. Imprints: The Arden Shakespeare, British Film Institute, Fairchild Books, Hart Publishing, I.B. Tauris, Methuen Drama, The RSC Shakespeare, Rowman & Littlefield, T&T Clark and Zed Books.

Bloomsbury Digital Resources
Managing Director Kathryn Earle
Award-winning digital platform publisher across the visual and performing arts, humanities and social sciences, including Drama Online, Bloomsbury Collections, Bloomsbury Fashion Central, Bloomsbury Video Library and Bloomsbury Visual Arts.

Bloomsbury Special Interest
Non-fiction: arts and crafts, natural history, military history, sport and wellbeing, business, politics, history, popular science, philosophy, religion and reference. Imprints: Adlard Coles, Bloomsbury Sport, Bloomsbury Continuum, Bloomsbury Wildlife, Bloomsbury Yearbooks, Green Books, Green Tree, Christopher Helm, Herbert Press, Osprey Games, Osprey Publishing (page 166), Sigma and Philip Wilson Publishers (page 188).

Blue Diode Publishing
30 Lochend Road, Edinburgh EH6 8BS
email bluedioderob@gmail.com
website www.bluediode.co.uk
Facebook www.facebook.com/bluediodepress
X @DiodeBlue
Founder Rob A. Mackenzie

Anthologies and poetry collections. Founded 2018.

Blue Guides
Unit 2, Old Brewery Road, Wiveliscombe TA4 2PW
tel 020-8144 3509
email editorial@blueguides.com
website www.blueguides.com
Facebook www.facebook.com/blueguides
X @blueguides
Instagram @blueguides

Detailed guidebooks with a focus on history, art and architecture for the independent traveller. Founded 1918.

Blue Danube
Central European literature in translation.

Bluemoose Books
25 Sackville Street, Hebden Bridge HX7 7DJ
email kevin@bluemoosebooks.com
website www.bluemoosebooks.com
X @ofmooseandmen
Publisher Kevin Duffy

Literary fiction. No children's, YA or poetry. Founded 2006.

Bodleian Library Publishing‡
Broad Street, Oxford OX1 3BG
tel (01865) 283850
email publishing@bodleian.ox.ac.uk
website www.bodleianshop.co.uk
Facebook www.facebook.com/bodleianlibraries
X @BodPublishing
Instagram @bodleianlibrarypublishing
Head of Publishing Samuel Fanous

Illustrated titles related to the library. Library founded 1602.

The Bodley Head – see Vintage

Boldwood Books‡
23 Bowerdean Street, London SW6 3TN
email info@boldwoodbooks.com
website www.boldwoodbooks.com
Facebook www.facebook.com/TheBoldBookClub
X @BoldwoodBooks
Instagram @theboldwoodbookclub
Ceo & Founder Amanda Ridout, *Publishing/Sales & Marketing Director* Nia Beynon, *Publisher* Caroline Ridding, *Publishing Director* Sarah Ritherdon, *Publishing Director* Isobel Akenhead

Commercial fiction: crime, mystery, thrillers, historical fiction, saga, women's fiction, romance and book club fiction. Founded 2019.

Bonnier Books UK*‡
Victoria House, Bloomsbury Square, London WC1B 4DA
tel 020-3770 8888
email hello@bonnierbooks.co.uk
website www.bonnierbooks.co.uk
Facebook www.facebook.com/bonnierbooksuk
X @bonnierbooks_UK
Ceos Sarah Benton, Jonathan Perdoni, *Managing Director of Black & White Publishing Group* Tim Whiting, *Managing Director of Zaffre Publishing Group* Sarah Benton, *Managing Director of Children's Trade* Helen Wicks, *Editor-at-Large* Carole Tonkinson

A wide variety of genres for different ages including crime, reading group fiction, memoir, self-help, activity and reference. Publishers of a number of imprints. Adult trade: Black & White Publishing (page 123), John Blake (page 124), Blink (page 124), Echo Publishing (page 191), Embla Books, Eriu, Heligo Books, Ithaka, Lagom, Leap, Manilla Press (page 159), Nine Eight Books, Twelve Point Audio and Zaffre (page 188). Children's trade: Autumn Publishing, Big Picture Press, Hatch Press, Hot Key Books (page 151), Igloo Books (page 151), Piccadilly Press (page 170), Studio Press (page 180), Templar (page 182). Founded 2015.

The Book Guild
Unit E2 Airfield Business Park, Harrison Road, Market Harborough, Leics. LE16 7UL

tel 0116 279 2299
email info@bookguild.co.uk
website www.bookguild.co.uk
Facebook www.facebook.com/thebookguild
X @BookGuild
Instagram @thebookguildpublishing
Managing Director Alex Thompson, *Operations Director* Chloe May

Fiction, children's and non-fiction. See website for submission guidelines. The Book Guild is part of Troubador Publishing. Founded 1996.

Bookouture*

Carmelite House, 50 Victoria Embankment, London EC4Y 0DZ
email pitch@bookouture.com
website www.bookouture.com
Facebook www.facebook.com/bookouture
X @bookouture
Instagram @bookouture
Managing Director Jenny Geras

A digital imprint publishing commercial fiction across all genres including sci-fi and fantasy. Welcomes submissions via the website. Part of Hachette UK. Founded 2012.

Thread

website www.thread-books.com
Facebook www.facebook.com/threadbooks
X @threadbooks
Instagram @threadbooks

Books by leading experts across a range of non-fiction topics including self-development, personal finance, parenting, nutrition and fitness, popular psychology and inspirational memoir.

Books on the Hill Press

20 Hill Road, Clevedon, Somerset BS21 7NZ
email info@booksonthehill.co.uk
website www.booksonthehill.co.uk
Facebook www.facebook.com/booksonthehill
X @booksonthehill
Instagram @booksonthehill
Publisher Alistair Sims

Dyslexia-friendly books for adults and children. Also a bookshop. Founded 2019.

Boydell & Brewer‡

PO Box 9, Woodbridge, Suffolk IP12 3DF
tel (01394) 610600
email editorial@boydell.co.uk
website www.boydellandbrewer.com
Ceo Tom Clark

Independent academic publisher of medieval studies, early modern and modern history, maritime history, literature, archaeology, art history, music and Hispanic studies. Imprints include: Boydell Press, D. S. Brewer, Camden House, James Currey, Tamesis Books and University of Rochester Press. No unsolicited MSS. See website for submission guidelines. Founded 1969.

Bradt Travel Guides‡

31A High Street, Chesham, Bucks. HP5 1BW
tel (01753) 893444
email info@bradtguides.com
website www.bradtguides.com
X @BradtGuides
Managing Director Adrian Phillips, *Commissioning Editor* Claire Strange

Travel and wildlife guides with emphasis on unusual destinations and ethical/positive travel. Travel narratives and travel anthologies. For submission guidelines see website. Contract publishing imprint: Journey Books (page 697). Founded 1974.

Breakdown Press

1 Berwick Street, Soho, London W1F 0DR
email editors@breakdownpress.com
website www.breakdownpress.com
X @breakdownpress
Instagram @breakdownpress
Publishers Simon Hacking, Josh Palmano, Tom Oldham

Contemporary comics. For submission guidelines see website. Founded 2012.

The Bright Press

3rd Floor Queensberry House, 106 Queens Road, Brighton BN1 3XF
tel (01273) 727268
website www.quartoknows.com/Bright-Press

Illustrated books on science, lifestyle, culture, craft and adult activity. Part of the Quarto Group Publishing UK. Founded 2018.

Brilliant Publications‡

Unit 10, Sparrow Hall Farm, Edlesborough, Dunstable LU6 2ES
tel (01525) 222292
email info@brilliantpublications.co.uk
website www.brilliantpublications.co.uk
Facebook www.facebook.com/Brilliant.Publications
X @Brilliantpub, @BrillCreative
Managing Director Priscilla Hannaford

Easy-to-use educational resources, featuring engaging approaches to learning, across a wide range of curriculum areas, including English, foreign languages, maths, art and design, thinking skills and PSHE. No children's picture books, non-fiction books or one-off fiction books. See guidelines on website before sending proposal. Founded 1993.

Bristol University Press/Policy Press*‡

University of Bristol, 1–9 Old Park Hill, Clifton, Bristol BS2 8BB
tel 0117 374 6645

email bup-info@bristol.ac.uk
website www.policypress.co.uk, www.bristoluniversitypress.co.uk
Facebook www.facebook.com/PolicyPress
X @policypress, @BrisUniPress
Ceo Alison Shaw, *Journals Director* Julia Mortimer, *Sales & Marketing Director* Jo Greig, *Editorial Director* Victoria Pittman

Bristol University Press specialises in politics and international relations, sociology, human geography, business and management, economics and law. Policy Press specialises in social and public policy, criminology, social work and social welfare. Bristol University Press founded 2016, Policy Press founded 1996.

British Film Institute – see Bloomsbury Publishing

British Library Publishing‡

Publishing Office, The British Library, 96 Euston Road, London NW1 2DB
tel 020-7412 7294
email publishing_sales@bl.uk
website https://shop.bl.uk/pages/british-library-publishing

Publishes around 50 books a year: classic crime, sci-fi, weird fiction and women's fiction, art, maps, manuscripts, history, literature and facsimiles. Founded 1979.

The British Museum Press

Great Russell Street, London WC1B 3DG
tel 020-7323 8000
email publicity@britishmuseum.org
website www.britishmuseum.org/publishing
Head of Publishing Claudia Bloch

Illustrated books for general readers, families, academics and students, inspired by the collections of the British Museum. Titles range across the fine and decorative arts, history, archaeology and world cultures. Founded 1973.

Broken Sleep Books

PO Box 10, Llandysul SA44 9BG
email aaron@brokensleepbooks.com
website www.brokensleepbooks.com
Facebook www.facebook.com/brokensleepbooks
X @brokensleep
Bluesky @brokensleepbooks.bsky.social
Instagram @brokensleepbooks
Director & Publisher Aaron Kent

A working-class indie publisher striving for greater access to the arts and degentrification of publishing. Publishes prose and poetry pamphlets and collections from a diverse range of writers. Founded 2018.

Brown, Son & Ferguson*

Unit 1A, 426 Drumoyne Road, Glasgow G51 4DA
tel 0141 883 0141
email info@skipper.co.uk
website www.skipper.co.uk
Editorial Directors Richard Brown, Wendy Brown

Nautical books, ships stationery and plays. Founded 1832.

Bryntirion Press

North Wales Office, 31 Holyhead Road, Bangor, Gwynedd LL57 2EU
tel (01656) 655886
email office@emw.org.uk
website www.emw.org.uk/bryntirion
Publications Officer Stefan Job

Formerly Evangelical Press of Wales. Theology and religion (in English and Welsh). Founded 1955.

Burning Chair Publishing

61 Bridge Street, Kington HR5 3DJ
email info@burningchairpublishing.com
website www.burningchairpublishing.com
Facebook www.facebook.com/BurningChairPublishing
X @Burning_Chair
Directors Simon Finnie, Peter Oxley

Mystery, thriller, suspense, crime, action and adventure, sci-fi, fantasy (including urban fantasy and YA), paranormal, horror and historical fiction. Currently closed to submissions. Check social media for submissions windows. Founded 2018.

Burning Eye Books

email editor@burningeye.co.uk
website www.burningeye.co.uk
Facebook www.facebook.com/burningeyebooks
Instagram @burningeyebooks
Managing Partner Clive Birnie

An independent publisher of prose and poetry from spoken word artists. No unsolicited submissions. Founded 2011.

Buster Books – see Michael O'Mara Books

Calon Books

University of Wales Press, University Registry, King Edward VII, Avenue, Cathays Par, Cardiff CF10 3NS
website www.uwp.co.uk/calon
Director Natalie Williams

Non-fiction books with a Welsh interest, ranging from food to folklore, music to memoir, travel and nature writing. Books aimed at a general readership, with a link to Wales or to Welsh history and culture. Books do not have to be entirely focused on Wales and submissions from authors of all nationalities and backgrounds are welcome. See website for submissions policy. Trade non-fiction imprint of the University of Wales Press. Founded 2021.

Books

Cambridge University Press & Assessment*‡
University Printing House, Shaftesbury Road, Cambridge CB2 8BS
tel (01223) 358331
email directcs@cambridge.org
website www.cambridge.org
Facebook www.facebook.com/CambridgeUniversityPress
X @CambridgeUP
Chief Executive Peter Phillips, *Managing Directors* Mandy Hill (academic), Jill Duffy (UK education), Rod Smith (international education)

Academic: anthropology and archaeology, art history, astronomy, biological sciences, classical studies, computer science, dictionaries, earth sciences, economics, engineering, history, language and literature, law, mathematics, medical sciences, music, philosophy, physical sciences, politics, psychology, reference, technology, social sciences, theology and religion. Education: ELT, educational (primary, secondary, tertiary) and e-learning products. Journals: humanities, social sciences, science, technical and medical. Founded 1534.

Campbell – see Pan Macmillan

Canbury Press‡
14 Beresford Road, Kingston upon Thames, Surrey KT2 6LR
email info@canburypress.com
website www.canburypress.com
Facebook www.facebook.com/canburypress
X @canburypress
Instagram @canburypress
Director Martin Hickman

Modern non-fiction books. Politics, philosophy, health, environment, biography and technology. Non-fiction submissions (synopsis and two chapters) welcome by email to submissions@canburypress.com. Strictly no fiction. Founded 2013.

Candy Jar Books
Mackintosh House, 136 Newport Road, Cardiff CF24 1DJ
tel 029-2115 7202
email submissions@candyjarbooks.co.uk
website www.candy-jar.co.uk/books
Facebook www.facebook.com/CandyJarLimited
X @Candy_Jar
Head of Publishing Shaun Russell

Children's, YA, cult media, biography, general non-fiction, military history and fantasy. Publishes about 30 titles per year. Unsolicited material welcome; submissions form on website. No children's picture books. Partner imprint of Jelly Bean Self-Publishing. Founded 2010.

The Canelo Group
Unit 9, 5th Floor, Cargo Works, 1–2 Hatfields, London SE1 9PG
email hello@canelo.co
website www.canelo.co
Facebook www.facebook.com/canelobooks
X @canelo_co
Managing Director Iain Millar, *Publishing Directors* Louise Cullen, Keshini Naidoo, Martina O'Sullivan, *Editorial Director* Emily Bedford

Commercial fiction and narrative non-fiction. Favoured fiction genres include romance, saga, action, adventure, thriller, crime/mystery, espionage and suspense. Divisions/imprints: Canelo Publishing, Canelo Crime, Hera Books (page 149). Canelo acquired by DK in 2024. Founded 2015.

Canongate Books*‡
14 High Street, Edinburgh EH1 1TE
tel 0131 557 5111
email info@canongate.co.uk
Alternative address Eardley House, 4 Uxbridge Street, London W8 7SY
website www.canongate.co.uk
Facebook www.facebook.com/canongate
X @canongatebooks
Instagram @canongatebooks
Ceo Jamie Byng

Adult general non-fiction and fiction, literary fiction, translated fiction, memoir, politics, popular science, humour, travel, popular culture, history and biography. Submissions via agents. Founded 1973.

Canongate Audio
Head of Audio Joanna Lord, *Senior Audio & Online Executive* Gaia Poggiogalli
Canongate titles in audio.

Canterbury Press – see Hymns Ancient and Modern

Jonathan Cape – see Vintage

Carcanet Press*‡
Main Library, University of Manchester, Oxford Road, Manchester M139PP
tel 0161 834 8730
email info@carcanet.co.uk
website www.carcanet.co.uk
Facebook www.facebook.com/CarcanetPress
Bluesky @carcanet.bsky.social
Instagram @carcanetpress
Managing Director Michael Schmidt

Poetry and translations. Imprints: Carcanet Poetry, Carcanet Classics and Lives and Letters. Founded 1969.

Cassava Republic Press
Studio C11, Mainyard Studios, 94 Wallis Road, London E9 5LN

email info@cassavarepublic.biz
website https://cassavarepublic.biz/
Facebook www.facebook.com/CassavaRepublic
X @cassavarepublic
Instagram @cassavarepublicpress
Publishing Director Bibi Bakare-Yusuf

Contemporary Black and African writing. Aims to bring high-quality fiction and non-fiction for adults and children to a global audience. Has offices in Abuja and London. Founded 2006.

Catholic Truth Society‡

42–46 Harleyford Road, London SE11 5AY
tel 020-7640 0042
email p.finaldi@ctsbooks.org
website www.ctsbooks.org
Facebook www.facebook.com/ctspublishers
X @ctspublishers
Instagram @ctspublishers
Ceo & Publisher Pierpaolo Finaldi

General books of Roman Catholic and Christian interest, liturgical books, missals, bibles, prayer books, children's books and booklets of doctrinal, historical, devotional or social interest. MSS of 10,000–20,000 words with up to six illustrations considered for publication as booklets. Founded 1868.

CB Editions

email info@cbeditions.com
website www.cbeditions.com
Founder Charles Boyle

Short fiction, poetry and translations. Founded 2007.

Cengage Learning*

Cheriton House, Andover SP10 5BE
tel (01264) 332424
email emeahepublishing@cengage.com
website www.cengage.uk

Actively commissioning print and digital content for further education and higher education courses in the following disciplines: IT, computer science and computer applications; accounting, finance and economics; marketing; international business; human resource management; operations management; strategic management; organisational behaviour; business information systems; quantitative methods; psychology; hairdressing and beauty therapy. Submit content-writing interest either by email or post. Founded 2007.

Century – see Cornerstone

CGI Publishing

Saffron House, 6–10 Kirby Street, London EC1N 8TS
tel 020-7612 4741
email publishing@cgi.org.uk
website www.cgi.org.uk/shop
Publisher Saqib Lal Saleem

Publishing company of the Chartered Governance Institute UK & Ireland specialising in professional books, study texts for qualifications and online technical content for the governance and compliance market. Founded 1981.

Chapman Publishing

4 Broughton Place, Edinburgh EH1 3RX
tel 0131 557 2207
email chapman-pub@blueyonder.co.uk
website www.chapman-pub.co.uk
Editor Dr Joy Hendry

Includes the *Chapman New Writing* and the *Chapman Wild Women* series, poetry and drama. No unsolicited MS. Founded 1986.

Charco Press*

Office 59, 44–46 Morningside Road,
Edinburgh EH10 4BF
email info@charcopress.com
website https://charcopress.com/
Facebook www.facebook.com/CharcoPress
X @CharcoPress
Instagram @charcopress

Cntemporary Latin American literature in translation. Founded 2017.

Chatto & Windus/Hogarth – see Vintage

Chicken House

2 Palmer Street, Frome, Somerset BA11 1DS
tel (01373) 454488
email hello@chickenhousebooks.com
website www.chickenhousebooks.com
X @chickenhsebooks
Instagram @chickenhousebooks
Managing Director & Publisher Barry Cunningham,
Deputy Managing Director Rachel Hickman

Fiction for 7+ years and YA. No unsolicited MSS. See website for details of *The Times*/Chicken House Children's Fiction Competition for unpublished writers. Part of Scholastic. Founded 2000.

Child's Play (International)

Ashworth Road, Bridgemead, Swindon,
Wilts. SN5 7YD
tel (01793) 616286
email office@childs-play.com
website www.childs-play.com
Facebook www.facebook.com/ChildsPlayBooks
Bluesky @childsplaybooks.bsky.social
Instagram @childsplaybooks
Chair Adriana Twinn, *Publisher* Neil Burden

Children's educational books: board, picture, activity and play books; fiction and non-fiction. Founded 1972.

Choc Lit – see Joffe Books

Christian Education

Suite 5–6, Pure Offices Ltd, 1 Devon Way, Longbridge Technology Park, Birmingham B31 2TS
tel 0121 472 4242
email sales@christianeducation.org.uk
website https://shop.christianeducation.org.uk/, www.retoday.org.uk
Facebook www.facebook.com/RETodayServices
X @IBRAbibleread

Incorporating RE Today Services and International Bible Reading Association. Publications and services for teachers and other professionals in religious education including *REtoday* magazine, curriculum booklets and classroom resources. Also publishes bible reading materials. Founded 2001.

Churchwarden Publications

The Carriage House, Ningwood Manor, Ningwood, Isle of Wight PO30 4NJ
tel (01983) 761389
email enquiries@churchwardenbooks.co.uk
website www.churchwardenbooks.co.uk
Editor Nicholas Oulton

Care and administration of churches and parishes, in particular *The Churchwarden's Yearbook*. An imprint of Gresham Books. Founded 1986.

Cicada Books*

Studio 31A, Archway Studios, Bickerton House, 25–27 Bickerton Road, London N19 5J
email info@cicadabooks.co.uk
website www.cicadabooks.co.uk
X @cicadabooks
Instagram @cicadabooks

Independent publisher of award-winning, highly illustrated children's books, specialising in non-fiction, picture books and graphic novels. Publishes 10–12 titles per year. Founded 2009.

Cicerone‡

Juniper House, Murley Moss Business Park, Oxenholme Road, Kendal, Cumbria LA9 7RL
tel (01539) 562069
email info@cicerone.co.uk
website www.cicerone.co.uk
Facebook www.facebook.com/ciceronepress
X @ciceronepress
Instagram @ciceronepress
Publishing Director Joe Williams

Guidebooks for walking, trekking, mountaineering, climbing and cycling in Britain, Europe and worldwide. Founded 1969.

Cico Books – see Ryland Peters & Small

Cinnamon Press

Lytchett House, 13 Freeland Park, Wareham Road, Poole, Dorset BH16 6FA
email info@cinnamonpress.com
website https://cinnamonpress.com/

An independent not-for-profit publisher of poetry, fiction and creative non-fiction. MSS sent to the office will be recycled. Runs a regular competition for poets and prose writers, the Cinnamon Press Poetry Collection Award. Please see website for submissions and competitions. Founded 2005.

Cipher Press

203 Ryan House, 12 Smeed Road, London E3 2PE
website www.cipherpress.co.uk
X @cipherpress
Publishers Jack Thompson, Ellis K.

An independent press publishing books by queer and trans writers from the UK and beyond. Interested in fiction and creative non-fiction that explores LGBTQ+ experience in new ways. Open to any genre, as long as it fits somewhere within the literary bracket. Founded in 2020.

Claret Press‡

51 Iveley Road, London SW4 0EN
tel 07736 71692
email contact@claretpress.com
website www.claretpress.com
Facebook www.facebook.com/ClaretPublisher
Bluesky @claretpress.bsky.social
Instagram @claretpress
Founder & Editor-in-Chief Katie Isbester

Fiction and creative non-fiction. Flexible about genre, favouring deeply interesting and engaging narratives, often with a political edge. Founded 2015.

Ayebia Clarke Publishing Ltd

7 Syringa Walk, Banbury, Oxon OX16 1FR
email ayebia@ayebia.co.uk
website www.ayebia.co.uk
Managing Director Rebecca Nana Ayebia Clarke

An award-winning independent publisher of specialist African and Caribbean writing. Publishes both fiction and non-fiction, including novels, poetry, short stories, biographies, autobiographies, literary criticism and books on subjects such the immigrant condition in the world. Founded 2003.

James Clarke & Co.‡

PO Box 60, Cambridge CB1 2NT
tel (01223) 350865
email publishing@jamesclarke.co.uk
website www.jamesclarke.co
Facebook www.facebook.com/JamesClarkeandCo
X @JamesClarkeLtd
Instagram @lutterworthpress/
Managing Director Adrian Brink

Academic theology, philosophy, history and biography, biblical studies and reference books. Sister imprint of The Lutterworth Press. Founded 1859.

Cló Iar-Chonnacht Teo†

Indreabhán, Co. Galway H91 CHO1, Republic of Ireland

tel +353 (0)91 593 307
email eolas@cic.ie
website www.cic.ie
Facebook www.facebook.com/cloiarchonnacht
X @cloiarchonnacht
Instagram @cloiarchonnacht

Irish-language: novels, short stories, plays, poetry, songs and history; audio (writers reading from their works in Irish and English), downloads and bilingual books. Promotes the translation of contemporary Irish fiction and poetry into other languages. Founded 1985.

Collective Ink

Unit 11, Shepperton House, 89 Shepperton Road, London N1 3DF
email office@collectiveinkbooks.com
website www.collectiveinkbooks.com
Directors Etan Ilfeld, Vicky Hartley

Formerly John Hunt Publishing, publishes a range of non-fiction and fiction genres including culture, politics, spirituality, Christianity, history and fiction titles for adults and children. See the website for submission procedure. Imprints are divided under various divisions. Mind, Body & Spirit: 6th Books, Axis Mundi Books, Ayni Books, Dodona Books, Mantra Books, O-Books, Psyche Books, Soul Rocks Books. Non-Fiction: Business Books, Earth Books, Essentia Books, Iff Books, Liberalis Books. Transformation: Changemakers Books. Christianity: Christian Alternative Books, Circle Books. History: Chronos Books. Books For Writers: Compass Books. Fiction: Cosmic Egg Books, Roundfire Books, Top Hat Books. Children and YA: Lodestone Books, Our Street Books. Paganism: Moon Books. Culture and politics: Zer0 Books. Founded 2001.

Colourpoint Creative†

Colourpoint House, Jubilee Business Park, 21 Jubilee Road, Newtownards, Co. Down BT23 4YH
tel 028-9182 0505 (within UK), +353 (0)48 9182 0505 (Republic of Ireland)
email sales@colourpoint.co.uk
website www.colourpoint.co.uk
X @colourpoint
Publisher Malcolm Johnston, *Head of Educational Publishing* Wesley Johnston

Transport (covering the whole of the British Isles), railways, buses, road and aviation. Educational textbooks and resources. Full submission by email only including details of proposal, sample chapter/section, qualification/experience in the topic, full contact details. Imprints: Blackstaff Press (page 123) and Colourpoint Educationa. Founded 1993.

Columba Books

Unit 3B, Block 3, Bracken Business Park, Bracken Road, Sandyford, Dublin D18 K277, Republic of Ireland
tel +353 (0)1 687 4096
email info@columba.ie
website www.columbabooks.com
Facebook www.facebook.com/columbabooks
X @columbabooks
Instagram @columa_books
Publisher & Managing Director Garry O'Sullivan

Religion (Roman Catholic and Anglican) including pastoral handbooks, spirituality, theology, liturgy and prayer. Also counselling and self-help. Founded 1984.

Comma Press*

Studio 510A, 5th Floor, Hope Mill, 113 Pollard Street, Manchester M4 7JA
email info@commapress.co.uk
website https://commapress.co.uk/
Facebook www.facebook.com/CommaPressMcr
Bluesky @commondeerpress.bsky.social
Founder & Ceo Ra Page

A not-for-profit publishing initiative dedicated to promoting new writing with an emphasis on the short story and translated fiction. One of the Arts Council's National Portfolio Organisations (NPOs) since 2012. For submissions see 'resources' section of the website. Founded 2002.

Concord Theatricals

Aldwych House, 71–91 Aldwych, London WC2B 4HN
tel 020-7054 7200
email customerservices@concordtheatricals.co.uk
website www.concordtheatricals.co.uk
Facebook www.facebook.com/concordukshows
X @concordukshows
Instagram @concordukshows

A licensing, publishing, recording and producing company comprising R&H Theatricals, Samuel French and Tams-Witmark. As well as licensing shows to perform, sells an extensive range of scripts and theatre books. More information on play and musical submissions can be found on the website. Founded 1830.

Cōnfingō Publishing

249 Burton Road, Didsbury, Manchester M20 2WA
email tim@confingopublishing.uk
website www.confingopublishing.uk
Facebook www.facebook.com/confingopublishing
X @confingo
Bluesky @confingopublishing.bsky.social
Instagram @configopublishing

Independent publisher of new fiction, translated fiction, photography/art. Poetry imprint: Carmenta. *Magazine Confingo* published twice a year, featuring fiction, poetry and art. Founded 2014.

Constable & Robinson – see Little, Brown Book Group

Cork University Press†

Boole Library, University College Cork,
College Road, Cork T12 ND89, Republic of Ireland
tel +353 (0)21 490 2980
email corkuniversitypress@ucc.ie
website www.corkuniversitypress.com
Head of Publishing Sinéad Neville

Irish literature, history, cultural studies, landscape studies, medieval studies, English literature, musicology, poetry and translations. Founded 1925.

Cornerstone*

One Embassy Gardens, 8 Viaduct Gardens,
London SW11 7BW
tel 020-7139 3000
website www.penguin.co.uk/company/publishers/cornerstone
Managing Director Venetia Butterfield

No unsolicited MSS accepted. Part of Penguin Random House UK. Founded 1999.

Century Fiction

tel 020-7840 8394
Publisher Selina Walker, *Publishing Directors* Ben Brusey (non-fiction), Emily Griffin (fiction), *Senior Commissioning Editor* Susannah Hamilton (fiction)

Commercial hardback and paperback fiction and non-fiction.

Cornerstone Non Fiction

Publishing Director Ben Brusey, *Editorial Director* Zennor Compton

Commercial hardback and paperback non-fiction.

Cornerstone Press

tel 020-7840 8793
Publisher Helen Conford, *Associate Publisher* Nigel Wilcockson, *Publishing Director* Rowan Borchers, *Senior Commissioning Editor* Kate Craigie, *Editor* Danai Denga

Non-fiction: big ideas with practical applications across business, economics, smart thinking, psychology, self-development, health, popular science, religion and spirituality, family and relationships.

Del Rey

tel 020-7139 3690
Publishing Director Claire Simmonds, *Editorial Director* Sam Bradbury

Fiction: adult and YA crossover sci-fi, fantasy and horror.

Evermore

Publishing Director Claire Simmonds, *Commissioning Editor* Jess Muscio

Fiction: romance.

Hutchinson Heinemann

tel 020-7139 8384
Publisher Helen Conford, *Associate Publisher* Nigel Wilcockson, *Publishing Directors* Ailah Ahmed (fiction), Rowan Borchers (non-fiction), *Editorial Director* James Pulford (non-fiction), *Senior Commissioning Editor* Amy Batley, *Commissioning Editors* Linda Mohamed (fiction), Vanessa Phan (non-fiction)

Fiction: literary, book club and translated fiction. Non-Fiction: history, politics, memoir, current affairs, reportage, humour, art and culture.

Inklore

Publishing Director Claire Simmonds, *Editorial Director* Kate Mchale, *Editor* Clara Heathcock

Fiction: graphic novels and manga.

#Merky Books

tel 020-7840 8454
Publisher Helen Conford, *Editorial Director* Joelle Owusu-Sekyere, *Editor* Danai Denga

Fiction: literary fiction, commercial fiction, genre fiction and poetry. Non-fiction: art and culture, narrative non-fiction, sport, popular culture, personal development, science and memoir.

Council for British Archaeology

92 Micklegate, York YO1 6JX
tel (01904) 671417
email info@archaeologyuk.org
website www.archaeologyuk.org
Facebook www.facebook.com/Archaeologyuk
X @archaeologyuk

British archaeology: academic, practical handbooks and general interest archaeology. Publishes *British Archaeology* magazine. Founded 1944.

Country Books

38 Pulla Hill Drive, Storrington,
West Sussex RH20 3LS
tel 07889 234964
email jonathan@spiralpublishing.com
email office@spiralpublishing.com
website www.spiral-books.com, www.countrybooks.biz, www.sussexbooks.co.uk

Local history (new and facsimile reprints), family history, autobiography, general non-fiction, novels, fairy tales, customs and folklore. Books for the National Trust, Chatsworth House, Peak District NPA and Derbyshire County Council. Part of Spiral Publishing and incorporating Ashridge Press. Founded 1985.

Countryside Books‡

3 Catherine Road, Newbury, Berks. RG14 7NA
tel (01635) 43816
email info@countrysidebooks.co.uk
website www.countrysidebooks.co.uk
Facebook www.facebook.com/CountrysideBooks
X @countrysidebook
Instagram @countrysidebooks
Partners Nicholas Battle, Suzanne Battle, Alex Batho

Books of local or regional interest, usually on a county basis: walking, outdoor activities, also heritage, aviation, railways and architecture. Founded 1976.

Cranthorpe Millner Publishers‡

9 Hills Road, Cambridge CB2 1GE
tel 020-3441 9212
email enquiries@cranthorpemillner.com
website www.cranthorpemillner.com
Facebook www.facebook.com/CranthorpeMillner
X @CranthorpeMillner
Instagram @cranthorpemillner
Managing Director Kirsty Jackson

Fiction and non-fiction: memoir, celeb autobiographies, history, sci-fi, YA, historical fiction, crime/thriller and literary fiction. Founded 2018.

CRC Press – see Taylor & Francis Group

Crescent Moon Publishing

11 Eastfield House, Woodford Road, Maidstone, Kent ME16 9BX
tel (01622) 729593
email cresmopub@yahoo.co.uk
website www.crmoon.com
Director Jeremy Robinson, *Editors* C. Hughes, B.D. Barnacle

Literature, poetry, arts, cultural studies, media, cinema and feminism. Submit sample chapters or six poems plus sae, not complete MSS. Founded 1988.

Cressrelles Publishing

10 Station Road Industrial Estate, Colwall, Malvern, Herefordshire WR13 6RN
tel (01684) 540154
email simon@cressrelles.co.uk
website https://cressrelles.co.uk/
Director Simon Smith

General publishing. Founded 1973.

J. Garnet Miller

Plays and theatre textbooks.

Kenyon-Deane

Plays and drama textbooks for amateur dramatic societies. Plays for women.

New Playwrights' Network

General plays for the amateur, one-act and full length.

Crowdbound

4 Rogart Street, Glasgow G40 2AA
tel (01415) 724602
email info@crowdbound.org
website www.crowdbound.org
Facebook www.facebook.com/ArkboundFoundation
X @ArkboundUK
Contact Perla Llosa

A crowdpublishing platform that enables authors and other publishers to raise funds to launch their books, with match funding opportunities and addition of Gift Aid also available. Seeks to support books and projects that cover social and/or environmental themes. Anyone can apply and if eligible a campaign can be started for free, with no cost at any stage of the process. It is run under the ambit of the Arkbound Foundation, a literature charity based in Bristol and Glasgow. Founded 2022.

Crown House Publishing*‡

Crown Buildings, Bancyfelin, Carmarthen SA33 5ND
tel (01267) 211345
email books@crownhouse.co.uk
website www.crownhouse.co.uk
Facebook www.facebook.com/CrownHousePub
X @CrownHousePub
Bluesky @crownhousepub.bsky.social
Instagram @crownhousepub
Directors David Bowman, Karen Bowman

Award-winning independent publisher specialising in the areas of education, coaching, business training and development, leadership, NLP, hypnotherapy, psychotherapy, self-help, personal growth and children's books. Founded 1998.

Independent Thinking Press

email books@independentthinkingpress.com
website www.independentthinkingpress.com

CPD books and resources for teachers and school leaders, including business, training and development, coaching, health and wellbeing, NLP, hypnosis, counselling and psychotherapy. Publishes a range of children's books.

The Crowood Press

The Stable Block, Ramsbury, Marlborough, Wilts. SN8 2HR
tel (01672) 520320
email enquiries@crowood.com
website www.crowood.com
Director Mollie Broadhead

Art, architecture, craft, general interest and hobbies, home and garden, military history, sport, performing arts, motoring and transport. Imprints include: Airlife Publishing (aviation, technical and general, military, military history), J.A. Allen (equestrian), Robert Hale (non-fiction) and N.A.G. Press (horology and gemmology). Founded 1982.

Dahlia Books

108 Spencefield Lane, Leicester LE5 6HF
email f.shaikh@dahliapublishing.co.uk
website www.dahliapublishing.co.uk
X @dahliabooks
Contact F. Shaikh

Small independent press of contemporary, original short fiction, including single-author short story and flash fiction collections. See submission guidelines on website. Champions of regional and diverse voices. Founded 2010.

Darf Publishers

277 West End Lane, London NW6 1QS
tel 020-7431 7009
email enquiry@darfpublishers.co.uk
website www.darfpublishers.co.uk
Facebook www.facebook.com/DarfPublishers
X @DarfPublishers
Director Ghassan Fergiani, *Editor* Ghazi Gheblawi

Focuses on diversity and inclusion. Publishes and reprints historical, geographic and classical works in English about the Middle East, North Africa and the UK. Also contemporary works of fiction, non-fiction and children's books in translation. Recent published works from Arabic (Libya, Yemen, Sudan, Eritrea), Italian, German, and Japanese with plans for writers from other European countries, South America, Asia and Africa. Founded 1981.

Darton, Longman and Todd‡

1 Spencer Court, 140–142 Wandsworth High Street, London SW18 4JJ
tel 020-8875 0155
email editorial@darton-longman-todd.co.uk
website www.darton-longman-todd.co.uk
Facebook www.facebook.com/darton-longman-todd-publishing
X @dlt_books
Instagram @dlt_books
Editorial Director David Moloney

Spirituality, prayer and meditation, self-help and personal growth, biography; political, environmental and social issues. Founded 1959.

Daunt Books

207–209, Kentish Town Road, London NW5 2JU
email publishing@dauntbooks.co.uk
website www.dauntbookspublishing.co.uk
X @dauntbookspub
Bluesky @dauntbookspub.bsky.social
Instagram @dauntbookspub
Publisher Marigold Atkey, *Editor* Dredhëza Maloku

An independent publisher of new writing in English and in translation: literary fiction (novels and short stories) and narrative non-fiction (essays, memoir). Also publishes modern classics. Not currently accepting unsolicited submissions. Check website for submission details. Founded 2010.

David & Charles‡

Tourism House, Pynes Hill, Exeter, Devon EX2 5WS
tel (01392) 790650
email hello@davidandcharles.com
website www.davidandcharles.com
Facebook www.facebook.com/dandcbooks
Instagram @dandcbooks
Managing Director James Woollam, *Publishing Director* Ame Verso

Special interest: craft, art, wellbeing and automotive. Submissions via email. For submissions guidelines see website. Imprints: David and Charles, Verbena, Veloce. Founded 1960.

DB Publishing

29 Clarence Road, Nottingham NG9 5HY
tel 07914 647382
email steve.caron@dbpublishing.co.uk
website www.dbpublishing.co.uk
Managing Director Steve Caron

Primarily: football, sport, local history and heritage. Will consider fiction. Unsolicited MSS welcome. Preliminary letter essential. Imprint of JMB Media. Founded 2009.

Dead Ink Books

Northern Lights, 5 Mann Street, Liverpool L8 5AF
email nathan@deadinkbooks.com
website https://deadinkbooks.com/
Director Nathan Connolly, *Publishing Manager* Harriet Hirschman

Literary publisher supported by Arts Council England. Published books have three times made the shortlist for the Saboteur Awards, the longlists for both the *Guardian*'s First Book Award and Not the Booker Prize, and the longlist for the Edge Hill Short Story Award. Founded 2017.

Dedalus*

24 St Judith's Lane, Sawtry, Cambs. PE28 5XE
tel (01487) 832382
email info@dedalusbooks.com
website www.dedalusbooks.com
Chairman Margaret Jull Costa, *Publisher* Eric Lane, *Editorial* Timothy Lane

Original fiction in English and in translation; 12–14 titles a year. Imprints: City Noir, Dark Masters Literary Biography, Dedalus Africa, Dedalus Concept, Dedalus Euro Shorts, Dedalus Europe Contemporary Fiction, Dedalus European Classics, Original English Language Fiction in Paperback, Young Dedalus. Founded 1983.

Dedalus Press

13 Moyclare Road, Baldoyle, Dublin D13 K1C2, Republic of Ireland
email editor@dedaluspress.com
website www.dedaluspress.com
Facebook www.facebook.com/DedalusPressPoetry
X @dedaluspress
Directors Raffaela Tranchino, Pat Boran

Contemporary Irish poetry and poetry in translation. Also publishes occasional prose titles by poets, or books that survey or explore aspects of the world of poetry. Imprint: Dedalus Ireland. Founded 1985.

Deixis Press

483 Green Lanes, London N13 4BS
email info@deixis.press
website https://deixis.press/
Facebook www.facebook.com/DeixisPress

X @deixispress
Instagram @deixispress
Director Angel Belsey

A small independent publisher of literary fiction and beautifully-crafted genre fiction including horror, sci-fi, historical and thrillers. Subscribe to newsletter to hear about open submissions periods. Founded 2021.

Richard Dennis Publications

The New Chapel, Shepton Beauchamp, Ilminster, Somerset TA19 0JT
tel (01460) 240044
email books@richarddennispublications.com
website www.richarddennispublications.com

Books for collectors specialising in ceramics, glass, illustration, sculpture and facsimile editions of early catalogues. Founded 1978.

Dialect Press

23 Chandos Road, Stroud, Glos. GL5 3QT
tel 07951 327639
email juliette.morton@dialect.org.uk
website www.dialect.org.uk
X @dialectwriters
Instagram @dialectwriters
Founding Director Juliette Morton, *Director* Emma Kernahan

A small independent press publishing collaborative writing by writers and artists working in rural and edgeland spaces. Founded 2020.

DIRT

Environmental poetry written in collaboration and inspired by climate science. Printed on unbleached, compostable paper with vegetable inks, each pamphlet is supplied with a bag of seeds so that the work can be planted and return to the earth.

Dialogue*

Carmelite House, 50 Victoria Embankment, London EC4Y 0DZ
website www.dialoguebooks.co.uk
Facebook www.facebook.com/DialoguePublishing
X @dialoguepub
Instagram @dialoguepublishing
Managing Director Sharmaine Lovegrove

Originally an English language bookshop in Berlin, publishes within LGBTQ+, disabled, working-class, Black, Asian and marginalised communities across fiction, non-fiction, literary and commercial. A division under the name Dialogue within the John Murray Group. Founded 2017.

Dialogue Books

Editorial Director Hannah Chukwu, *Editorial Assistant* Adriano Noble

Literary fiction, non-fiction and poetry.

Renegade Books

Publisher Christina Demostheonous, *Editor* Alexa Allen-Batifoulier

Radical, commercial non-fiction.

Diamond Books

10 Bailiffs Close, Axbridge, Somerset BS26 2AZ
tel 07788 448344
email info@diamondbooks.co.uk
website www.diamondbooks.co.uk
Facebook www.facebook.com/diamondcrimepublishing
X @diamond_crime
Instagram @diamond_crime_publishing
Directors Steve Timmins, Phil Rowlands, Jeff Dowson

Small independent publisher created by writers to provide a platform for new and established crime writers. For submissions, see website. Founded 2021.

Discovery Walking Guides

10 Tennyson Close, Northampton NN15 7HJ
tel (01604) 244869
email ask.discovery@ntlworld.com
website www.dwgwalking.co.uk
Chairman Rosamund C. Brawn

Publishes *Walk!* walking guidebooks for UK and European destinations; *Tour & Trail Super-Durable* large-scale maps for outdoor adventures; *Bus & Touring* maps; and *Drive* touring maps. Premium content provider to 3G phone/tablet gps apps for digital mapping and hiking adventures. Publishing in conventional book/map format along with digital platforms. Welcomes project proposals from technologically (gps) proficient walking writers. Founded 1994.

DK*

(formerly Dorling Kindersley)
20 Vauxhall Bridge Road, London SW1V 2SA
tel 020-7139 2000
website www.dk.com
Facebook www.facebook.com/dkbooks.uk
X @dkbooks
Bluesky @dkbooks.bsky.social
Instagram @dkbooks
Ceo Paul Kelly

Illustrated and narrative books for adults and children. Also, children's fiction. Non-fiction: travel, licensing, reference, education, gardening, wellbeing, self-development and food and drink. Part of Penguin Random House UK. Founded 1974.

DK Flip

Chapter books, early middle grade, middle grade, teen, graphic and YA.

DK RED

Publisher Liz Gough

Author-driven lifestyle and narrative non-fiction.

Do Books‡

Hackney Downs Studios, 1.2, 17 Amhurst Terrace, London E8 2BT
tel 07957 597540
email info@thedobook.co
website https://thedobook.co
X @dobookco
Instagram @dobookco
Founder & Publisher Miranda West, *Rights Manager* Anya Glazer, *Editor* Jess Fry

Concise guides by experts who have spoken at The DO Lectures across business, design, wellbeing and sustainable living to inspire action and positive change. Founded 2013.

Dodo Ink

Red Rose Villa, Church Street, Scothern, Lincoln LN2 2UA
email dodopublishingco@gmail.com
website www.dodoink.com
Facebook www.facebook.com/Dodo-Ink-775175252560383
X @DodoInk
Managing Director Sam Mills, *Editorial Director* Thom Cuell

An independent press of daring literary fiction. Publishes two to three novels a year. No unsolicited MSS by post. See the website for submission guidelines. Founded 2015.

The Dovecote Press

Holdscroft Farm, Marshwood, Bridport DT6 5QL
tel 07753 632237
email office@dovecotepress.com
website www.dovecotepress.com
Editorial Director David Burnett

Books of local interest: natural history, architecture and history. Founded 1974.

dp books‡

Acre House, 11–15 William Road, London NW1 3ER
email contact@digital-publishers.com
website www.digital-publishers.com/en
Facebook www.facebook.com/61563957447220
Instagram @dp_books_uk
Publishing Director James Faktor

Commercial adult fiction as backlist and frontlist. Founded 2024.

Dref Wen

28 Church Road, Whitchurch, Cardiff CF14 2EA
tel 029-2061 7860
website www.drefwen.com
Facebook www.facebook.com/drefwen
X @dref_wen
Instagram @drefwen
Directors Roger Boore, Anne Boore, Gwilym Boore, Alun Boore, Rhys Boore

Welsh-language publisher. Original Welsh-language novels for children and adult learners. Original, adaptations and translations of foreign and English-language full-colour picture story books for children. Educational material for primary/secondary school children in Wales and England. Founded 1970.

Duckworth Books‡

1 Golden Court, Richmond TW9 1EU
email info@duckworthbooks.com
website www.duckworthbooks.co.uk
X @Duckbooks
Instagram @duck_books
Managing Director Peter Duncan

Biography and memoir, popular science, history, popular psychology, nature and travel writing as well as fiction, including historical and literary. Founded 1898.

Farrago

Series-led humorous fiction including mystery and cosy crime, social comedy and satire, sci-fi and fantasy.

September

Intelligent, transformational books in literature and art.

Dynasty Press

c/o Lucraft, Hodgson & Dawes LLP, 19 New Road, Brighton BN1 1UF
tel 020-8675 3435
email admin@dynastypresslondon.co.uk
website www.dynastypress.co.uk
Contact David Hornsby

Books about royalty, dynasties and people of influence. Founded 2008.

Ebury Publishing*

One, Embassy Gardens, 8 Viaduct Gardens, Nine Elms, London SW11 7BW
tel 020-7139-3000
website www.penguin.co.uk/company/publishers/ebury
X @EburyPublishing
Instagram @eburybooks
Managing Director Joel Rickett, *Divisional Publisher* Andrew Goodfellow

Non-fiction publisher. Part of Penguin Random House UK. Founded 1961.

BBC Books

Publishing Director Albert DePetrillo

Non-fiction with a BBC connection: history, natural history, science, cookery, lifestyle and pop culture.

Ebury Entertainment

Publishing Director Charlotte Hardman, *Senior Editorial Director* Lorna Russell

Imprint: Ebury Spotlight. Autobiography, memoir, TV, sport and popular culture books.

Books

Ebury Food
Publishing Director Laura Higginson Stephanie Milner
Imprint: Ebury Press. Food and cookery.

Ebury Lifestyle
Publishing Director Laura Higginson
Imprints: Ebury Press and Pop Press. Creativity, wellbeing, home and gardening, fashion and beauty, hobbies, craft and gift humour.

Ebury Partnerships
Publishing Director Elizabeth Bond
Gift, branded and bespoke books across food and drink, health and lifestyle, museums and galleries, and entrepreneurs and business pioneers.

Ebury Self
Instagram @eburyselfbooks
Publishing Director Olivia Morris
Imprints: Happy Place Books, Rider and Vermilion. Parenting and relationships, personal development and popular psychology, spirituality and wellbeing, diet and health.

Ebury Smart
Publishing Directors Robyn Drury, Jamie Joseph
Imprints: WH Allen, Ebury Edge, Ebury Press, Flight Books and Witness Books. Memoir, history, politics, current affairs, science, technology, business and performance.

Edinburgh University Press*‡
13 Infirmary Street, Edinburgh EH1 1LT
tel 0131 650 4218
email editorial@eup.ed.ac.uk
website www.edinburghuniversitypress.com, www.euppublishing.com
Facebook www.facebook.com/EdinburghUP
X @EdinburghUP
Bluesky @edinburghup.bsky.social
Head of Publishing Sarah McDonald

Academic publishers of scholarly books and journals: art and visual culture, classics and ancient history, film and television studies, history, Islamic and Middle-Eastern studies, language and linguistics, law, literary studies, philosophy, politics and Scottish studies. Trade: Scottish history, Islamic and Middle-Eastern studies, art and visual culture. See website for submission guidelines. Founded 1949.

The Educational Company of Ireland
12 Ballymount Road, Walkinstown, Dublin D12 R25C, Republic of Ireland
tel +353 (0)1 450 0611
email info@edco.ie
website www.edco.ie
Facebook www.facebook.com/edcoireland
X @edco_ie

Educational publisher of all subjects in English or Irish language. A member of the Smurfit Kappa Group. Founded 1910.

Eglantyne Books
Club Room, Conway Hall, 25 Red Lion Square, London WC1R 4RL
tel 020-7831 9905
email olivia@eglantynebooks.com
website https://eglantynebooks.com/
X @eglantyne_books
Instagram @eglantyne_books
Publishers Robert Temple, Olivia Temple, Eric Wright

New titles and reprints of rare titles: modern literature, world literature, early modern history and modern history. Also publishes original reprints of English Civil War pamphlets. Other areas include: Egyptology, classical studies, short stories, anthologies and poetry in translation. Founded 2021.

Eland Publishing
61 Exmouth Market, London EC1R 4QL
tel 020-7833 0762
email info@travelbooks.co.uk
website www.travelbooks.co.uk
Directors Rose Baring, John Hatt, Barnaby Rogerson

Classic travel literature. No unsolicited MSS. Email in first instance. Founded 1982.

Elephant Press
Forge Lodge, Ashburnham, Battle, East Sussex TN33 9PH
tel 07775 600618
email books@elephantpress.co.uk
website www.elephantpress.co.uk
Co-founders Clare Whistler, Raphael Whittle

A small press of eco poetry books.

Edward Elgar Publishing‡
The Lypiatts, 15 Lansdown Road, Cheltenham, Glos. GL50 2JA
tel (01242) 226934
email info@e-elgar.co.uk
website www.e-elgar.com
Facebook www.facebook.com/EdwardElgarPublishing
X @elgarpublishing
Instagram @elgar_publishing
Managing Director Tim Williams

Economics, business, law, public and social policy. Founded 1986.

Elliott & Thompson‡
2 John Street, London WC1N 2ES
tel 020-3405 0310
email info@eandtbooks.com
website www.eandtbooks.com
X @eandtbooks
Bluesky @eandtbooks.bsky.social
Instagram @elliottandthompson
Chairman Lorne Forsyth, *Publisher* Katie Bond, *Publishing Director* Sarah Rigby

Award-winning independent publisher of narrative non-fiction, history, nature writing, biography, geopolitics, popular science, smart thinking and intelligent giftbooks. Open to submissions via the website. Founded 2009.

Elsevier*

The Boulevard, Langford Lane, Kidlington, Oxford OX5 1GB
tel (01865) 843000
website www.elsevier.com
Facebook www.facebook.com/ElsevierConnect
X @ElsevierConnect
Ceo Kumsal Bayazit

Academic and professional reference books; scientific, technical and medical products and services (books, journals and electronic information). No unsolicited MSS, but synopses and project proposals welcome. Imprints include: Academic Press, Architectural Press, Bailliere Tindall, Butterworth-Heinemann, Churchill Livingstone, Digital Press, Elsevier, Elsevier Advanced Technology, Focal Press, Gulf Professional Press, JAI, Made Simple Books, Morgan Kauffman, Mosby, Newnes, North-Holland, Pergamon, Saunders and Woodhead Publishing. Division of RELX Corp., Amsterdam. Founded 1986.

Elsewhen Press

Alnpete Limited, PO Box 757, Dartford, Kent DA2 7TQ
tel 07956 237041
email info@elsewhen.co.uk
website https://elsewhen.press
Facebook www.facebook.com/ElsewhenPress
Bluesky @elsewhen.press.bsky.social
Instagram @elsewhenpress
Managing Director Alison Buck, *Editorial Director* Peter Buck

Small independent publisher of speculative fiction (including sci-fi, fantasy, paranormal, horror and alternative history), for ages YA upwards. Digital-first publisher. For submission guidelines see website. Founded 2011.

The Emma Press‡

Jewellery Quarter, Birmingham B18 6HQ
email hello@theemmapress.com
website https://theemmapress.com/
Facebook www.facebook.com/TheEmmaPress
Bluesky @theemmapress.bsky.social
Instagram @theemmapress
Director Emma Dai'an Wright

Publishes single-author books and pamphlets in poetry and prose – including short stories, novellas, essays and translations. Their children's chapter books and poetry collections include CLiPPA award-winning titles. No unsolicited MSS. There are regular calls for poetry and prose, check website for details. Founded 2012.

Encyclopaedia Britannica (UK)

2nd Floor, Unity Wharf, 13 Mill Street, London SE1 2BH
tel 020-7500 7800
email enqbol@britannica.co.uk
website www.britannica.co.uk
Facebook www.facebook.com/BritannicaUK
X @Britannica_UK
Instagram @digital_learning_britannica

Global digital educational publisher of instructional products used in schools, universities, homes, libraries and in the workplace. Founded 1999.

Enitharmon Editions

Rear Barn Upper Adhurst Industrial Park, London Road, Petersfield, Hants. GU31 5AE
tel 020-7430 0844
email info@enitharmon.co.uk
website www.enitharmon.co.uk
Directors Stephen Stuart-Smith, Isabel Brittain

Artists' books and prints, poetry, including fine editions. Some literary criticism, fiction and translations. No unsolicited MSS. No freelance editors or proofreaders required. Founded 1967.

Equinox Publishing‡

Office 415, The Workstation, 15 Paternoster Row, Sheffield S1 2BX
website www.equinoxpub.com, www.marionboyars.co.uk, www.prospectbooks.co.uk
Facebook www.facebook.com/equinox.publishing.ltd
X @EQUINOXPUB
Managing Director Janet Joyce

Publishes academic books and journals in the humanities as well as a trade list for music and food history. Founded 2003.

Prospect Books

Food history. Accepting submissions.

Everyman's Library

50 Albemarle Street, London W1S 4BD
tel 020-7493 4361
email books@everyman.uk.com
email guides@everyman.uk.com
website www.everymanslibrary.co.uk
Facebook www.facebook.com/everymanslibrary
X @EverymansLib

Everyman's Library (clothbound reprints of the classics), *Everyman Pocket Classics*, *Everyman's Library Children's Classics*, *Everyman's Library Pocket Poets*, *Everyman Guides* and P.G. Wodehouse. Publishes fiction novels, non-fiction and poetry. No unsolicited submissions. Imprint of Knopf Doubleday Publishing Group. Founded 1905.

Everything with Words

5th Floor, 30–31 Furnival Street, London EC4A 1JQ
tel 020-8771 2974
email info@everythingwithwords.com
website www.everythingwithwords.com
Editor Mikka Haugaard

Literary fiction for children, YA and adult. Accepts unsolicited MSS. Send synopsis, brief bio and first 50 pages to info@everythingwithwords.com. Founded 2016.

University of Exeter Press

Reed Hall, Streatham Drive, Exeter, Devon EX4 4QR
tel 0845 468 0415
email info@exeterpress.co.uk
website www.exeterpress.co.uk
Facebook www.facebook.com/UniversityofExeterPress
X @UExeterPress
Bluesky @uexeterpress.bsky.social
Instagram @uexeterpress
Publisher Nigel Massen

Academic and scholarly books on international relations, film history, performance studies, linguistics, folklore and local history (Exeter and the south west). Founded 1958.

Helen Exley

16 Chalk Hill, Watford, Herts. WD19 4BG
tel (01923) 474480
website www.helenexleygiftbooks.com
Facebook www.facebook.com/helenexleylondon
X @helen_exley
Ceo Helen Exley

Popular colour gift books for an international market. No unsolicited MSS. Founded 1976.

Eye Books

29A Barrow Street, Much Wenlock, Shrops. TF13 6EN
tel 020-3239 3027
email dan@eye-books.com
website www.eye-books.com
X @EyeAndLightning
Publisher Will Atkinson

Commercial narrative non-fiction with particular emphasis on business, travel and 'ordinary people doing extraordinary things'. Imprints: Eye Books and Lightning Books (page 155). Founded 1996.

Faber & Faber*‡

The Bindery, 51 Hatton Garden, London EC1N 8HN
tel 020-7927 3800
website www.faber.co.uk
Facebook www.facebook.com/FaberBooks
X @FaberBooks
Publishers Alex Bowler (adult), Leah Thaxton (children's)

Independent publisher of fiction, non-fiction, poetry, drama, film, graphic novels and children's books. Founded 1929.

Fabian Society

61 Petty France, London SW1H 9EU
tel 020-7227 4900
email info@fabians.org.uk
website www.fabians.org.uk
Facebook www.facebook.com/fabiansociety
X @thefabians
Bluesky @thefabians.bsky.social
Editorial contacts Kate Murray, Iggy Wood

Current affairs, political thought, economics, education, environment, foreign affairs and social policy. Founded 1884.

Fahrenheit Press

85–97 Bayham Street, London NW1 0AG
website www.fahrenheit-press.com
Facebook www.facebook.com/FahrenheitPress
X @fahrenheitpress
Founder Chris McVeigh

An independent publisher of crime fiction, publishing approx. 50 books per year. Open submissions policy. Imprints: Fahrenheit Editions (limited edition hardbacks), Fahrenheit Press (traditional crime fiction) and Fahrenheit 13 (hard-boiled noir and experimental crime fiction). Founded 2015.

Fairlight Books‡

Summertown Pavilion, 18–24 Middle Way, Oxford OX2 7LG
email submissions@fairlightbooks.com
website www.fairlightbooks.co.uk
Facebook www.facebook.com/FairlightBooks
X @fairlightbooks
Instagram @fairlightbooks

Literary fiction, particularly novellas (the Fairlight Moderns) and online short stories. Founded 2017.

CJ Fallon

Ground Floor, Block B, Liffey Valley Office Campus, Dublin D22 X0Y3, Republic of Ireland
tel +353 (0)1 616 6400
email editorial@cjfallon.ie
website www.cjfallon.ie
Executive Director Brian Gilsenan

Educational textbooks. Founded 1927.

Farshore Books – see HarperCollins Publishers

Fernhurst Books‡

The Windmill, Mill Lane, Harbury, Leamington Spa, Warwickshire CV33 9HP
tel (01926) 337488
email fernhurst@fernhurstbooks.com
website www.fernhurstbooks.com
Facebook www.facebook.com/fernhurstbooks
X @FernhurstBooks
Instagram @fernhurstbooks
Publisher Jeremy Atkins

Non-fiction: how-to guides, narrative non-fiction and illustrated. Subjects covered include: sailing, surfing, canoeing, kayaking, stand up paddleboarding, swimming, diving and fishing. Founded 1979.

David Fickling Books‡

31 Beaumont Street, Oxford OX1 2NP
tel (01865) 339000
website www.davidficklingbooks.com
Facebook www.facebook.com/davidficklingbooks
X @DFB_storyhouse
Bluesky @dfbstoryhouse.bsky.social
Instagram @dfb_storyhouse
Publisher David Fickling, *Publishing Director* Liz Cross

Independent publisher of picture books, novels and non-fiction for all ages, as well as graphic novels. Currently not accepting unsolicited MSS. Founded 1999.

Fig Tree – see Penguin General

Fighting High

23 Hitchin Road, Stotfold, Hitchin, Herts. SG5 4HP
tel 07936 415843
email fightinghigh@btinternet.com
website www.fightinghigh.com
Facebook www.facebook.com/groups/24337176057
X @FightingHigh
Founder Steve Darlow

Non-fiction books that focus on human endeavour, particularly in a historical military setting. For submission guidelines see website. Founded 2009.

Fincham Press

University of Roehampton, School of Humanities, Fincham Building, Roehampton Lane, London SW15 5PH
email finchampress@roehampton.ac.uk
website https://estore.roehampton.ac.uk/product-catalogue/fincham-press
Facebook www.facebook.com/finchampress
X @finchampress

Titles are commissioned, edited and published by a team based in English and creative writing, part of the School of Humanities and Social Sciences. Creative writing anthologies, a journalism anthology. Founded 2014.

Findhorn Press

305A, The Park, Findhorn, Findhorn, Moray IV36 3TE
email sabine@findhornpress.com
website www.innertraditions.com/imprints/findhorn-press

Mind, body & spirit, spirituality, holistic health, self-help and nature. Founded 1971.

Fircone Books

The Holme, Church Road, Eardisley, Herefordshire HR3 6NJ
tel (01544) 327182
email info@firconebooks.com
website www.firconebooks.com
Facebook www.facebook.com/firconebooks
Directors Richard Wheeler, Su Wheeler

Illustrated books on church art and architecture. Founded 2009.

Firefly Press*

Britannia House, Caerphilly Business Park, Van Road, Caerphilly CF83 3GG
email hello@fireflypress.co.uk
website www.fireflypress.co.uk
Facebook www.facebook.com/FireflyPress
X @fireflypress
Bluesky @fireflypress.bsky.social
Publisher Penny Thomas

Fiction for 5–19 years. Founded 2013.

Fitzcarraldo Editions

A103 Fuel Tank, 8–12 Creekside, London SE8 3DX
email info@fitzcarraldoeditions.com
website www.fitzcarraldoeditions.com
X @FitzcarraldoEds
Instagram @fitzcarraldoeditions

An independent publisher of contemporary fiction and long-form essays. Focuses on ambitious, imaginative and innovative writing, both in translation and in the English language. Founded 2014.

5mBooks‡

Lings, Great Easton, Essex CM6 2HH
email hello@5mbooks.com
website www.5mbooks.com
Publishing Director Jeremy Toynbee

Independent publisher of books for professionals, students and general readers. Topics covered: veterinary medicine, companion animals, aquaculture and agriculture/smallholding. Imprints: Nottingham University Press and Unbreaking. Founded 2020.

Flame Tree Publishing‡

6 Melbray Mews, Fulham, London SW6 3NS
tel 020-7751 9650
email info@flametreepublishing.com
website www.flametreepublishing.com, www.flametreepress.com
Publisher & Founder Nick Wells, *Executive Editor* Don D'Auria

Art, music, lifestyle and fiction. Accepts unsolicited MSS for fiction imprint Flame Tree Press (horror and suspense, sci-fi and fantasy). No YA titles. Short story submission windows for thematic anthologies. Founded 1992.

Flapjack Press

Chiffon Way, Salford M3 6AB
email mail@flapjackpress.co.uk
website https://flapjackpress.co.uk/
Facebook www.facebook.com/groups/flapjackpress
X @FlapjackPress
Director Paul Neads

Performance poetry, poetry-theatre, playscripts and art collections for adults and children. Currently closed to submissions. Founded 2007.

Fleming Publications

9/2 Fleming House, 134 Renfrew Street, Glasgow G3 6ST
tel 0141 328 1935
email info@ettadunn.com
website www.flemingpublications.com
Managing Editor Etta Dunn

Fiction, non-fiction, poetry, history, biography, photography and self-help. Founded 2012.

Flipped Eye Publishing‡

3rd Floor, 86–90 Paull Street, London EC2A 4NE
email books@flippedeye.net
website https://flippedeye.net/
Facebook www.facebook.com/flipped.eye.publishing
X @flippedeye
Instagram @flippedeye
Director Nii Ayikwei Parkes, *Editorial Director* Mitchell Albert, *Senior Editors, Poetry* Jacob Sam-La Rose, Niall O'Sullivan

Publishes an eclectic catalogue of fiction, non-fiction and poetry. Founded 2001.

Floris Books*

Canal Court, 40 Craiglockhart Avenue, Edinburgh EH14 1LT
email floris@florisbooks.co.uk
website www.florisbooks.co.uk
Facebook www.facebook.com/FlorisBooks
X @FlorisBooks
Bluesky @florisbooks.bsky.social
Commissioning Editors Sally Polson, Eleanor Collins

Religion and philosophy; holistic health and organics; mind, body & spirit; crafts and parenting. Children's books: board books, picture books and story anthologies. See website for submission details. Founded 1976.

Kelpies

website www.discoverkelpies.co.uk
Facebook www.facebook.com/DiscoverKelpies
X @DiscoverKelpies

Contemporary Scottish fiction: board books (1–3 years), picture books (3–6 years), young readers series (6–8 years) and novels (8–15 years). Annual Kelpies Prize.

Flying Eye Books

27 Westgate Street, London E8 3RL
tel 020-7033 4430
email subs@flyingeyebooks.com
email gnsubs@flyingeyebooks.com
website www.flyingeyebooks.com
Facebook www.facebook.com/flyingeyebooks
X @flyingeyebooks
Bluesky @flyingeyebooks.bsky.social
Instagram @flyingeyebooks

Children's board books, picture books, illustrated non-fiction, graphic readers, comics and graphic novels. Founded 2013.

Fly on the Wall Press

56 High Lea Road, New Mills, Derbyshire SK22 3DP
email flyonthewallpress@hotmail.com
website www.flyonthewallpress.co.uk
Facebook www.facebook.com/flyonthewallpress
X @fly_press
Bluesky @flyonthewallpress.bsky.social
Instagram @flyonthewallpress
Threads @flyonthewallpress
Managing Director Isabelle Kenyon

Politically engaged novels, short fiction and poetry. Small Press of the Year Winner (North) in 2024, British Book Awards. Check website for summer reading periods. Submissions: direct or via agent. Founded 2018.

Folens Publishers

Hibernian Industrial Estate, Greenhills Road, Tallaght, Dublin D24 DH05, Republic of Ireland
tel +353 (0)1 413 7200
email info@folens.ie
website www.folens.ie
Facebook www.facebook.com/FolensIreland
X @FolensIreland
Instagram @folenseducation
Chairman David Moffitt

Educational (primary, secondary). Founded 1958.

Fonthill Media

Millview House, Toadsmoor Road, Stroud, Glos. GL5 2TB
tel (01453) 886959
email office@fonthillmedia.com
website www.fonthillmedia.com
Facebook www.facebook.com/fonthillmedia
X @fonthillmedia
Publisher & Ceo Alan Sutton

General history. Specialisations include biography, military history, aviation history, naval and maritime history, regional and local history, transport (railway, canal, road) history, social history, sports history, ancient history and archaeology. US imprints: American History House, America Through Time and Fonthill. Founded 2011.

Footnote Press

email info@footnotepress.com
website https://footnotepress.com/
Facebook www.facebook.com/wearefootnote
X @WeAreFootnote
Instagram @wearefootnote
Founder & Managing Director Vidisha Biswas

Politically engaging fiction and non-fiction, including history, current affairs, philosophy, memoir, situational reportage and the environment. Founded 2022.

W. Foulsham & Co.

The Old Barrel Store, Brewery Courtyard, Draymans Lane, Marlow, Bucks. SL7 2FF
tel (01628) 400600
email annemarie.howe@foulsham.com
website www.foulsham.com
Contact Annemarie Howe

Life issues; mind, body & spirit; health, therapies and lifestyle; popular philosophy and practical psychology; food and drink and parenting. Digital publishing: content management systems and data, iGuides travel, nutrition, self-help, gardening and cookery. Founded 1819.

Quantum

Mind, body & spirit; popular philosophy and practical psychology.

Four Courts Press

7 Malpas Street, Dublin D08 YD81, Republic of Ireland
tel +353 (0)1 453 4668
email info@fourcourtspress.ie
website www.fourcourtspress.ie
Managing Director Martin Healy, *Publisher* Martin Fanning

Academic books in the humanities, especially history, Celtic and medieval studies, art and local studies. Founded 1970.

Free Association Books

1 Angel Cottages, Milespit Hill, London NW7 1RD
email freeassociationbooks@gmail.com
website www.freeassociationpublishing.com
X @Fab_Publishing
Director Trevor E. Brown, *Publishing Director* Alice Solomons, *Marketing & Editorial Consultant* Lisa Findley

Social sciences, psychoanalysis, psychotherapy, counselling, cultural studies, social welfare, addiction studies, child and adolescent studies, mental health, parenting and health studies. No poetry, fiction or memoir. Founded 1984.

From You To Me

Studio 100, The Old Leather Factory, Glove Factory Studios, Holt, Wilts. BA14 6RJ
tel (01225) 866225
email hello@fromyoutome.com
website www.fromyoutome.com
Facebook www.facebook.com/fromyoutome
Instagram @fromyoutome_ltd
Founder Neil Caxon, *Publisher* Helen Stephens

Bespoke and illustrated gift books. Authors and illustrators see Work With Me page on the website for details of current opportunities. Founded 2009.

Gaia Books – see Octopus Publishing Group

The Gallery Press

Loughcrew, Oldcastle, Co. Meath A82 N225, Republic of Ireland
tel +353 (0)49 854 1779
email books@gallerypress.com
website www.gallerypress.com
Facebook www.facebook.com/thegallerypress
X @TheGalleryPress
Instagram @thegallerypress
Directors Peter Fallon, Jean Fallon

Publishes the work of writers who are Irish by birth, residence or citizenship (or who have applied for citizenship). Poetry, plays and prose. See website for submission guidelines. Only accepts postal submissions. Imprint: Gallery Books. Founded 1970.

Galley Beggar Press

37 Dover Street, Norwich NR2 3LG
email info@galleybeggar.co.uk
website www.galleybeggar.co.uk
X @GalleyBeggars
Bluesky @galleybeggars.bsky.social
Co-directors Eloise Millar, Sam Jordison

Independent publisher of literary fiction and non-fiction as novels and short stories. When submitting a MS, provide proof that you have read another book published by Galley Beggar Press. Prefers completed MS in pdf or Word. One submission per author. No poetry or children's. Founded 2011.

Gallic Books – see Pushkin Press

J. Garnet Miller – see Cressrelles Publishing

Garnet Publishing‡

8 Southern Court, South Street, Reading RG1 4QS
tel 0118 959 7847
email info@garnetpublishing.co.uk
website www.garnetpublishing.co.uk
Facebook www.facebook.com/Garnetpub
X @Garnetpub

Trade non-fiction pertaining to the Middle East: art and architecture, cookery, culture, current affairs, history, photography, political and social issues, religion, travel and general. Accepts unsolicited material. Founded 1991.

Ithaca Press

website www.ithacapress.co.uk

Academic books with a focus on Middle Eastern studies. Accepts unsolicited MSS.

Periscope

website www.periscopebooks.co.uk

Literary fiction and trade non-fiction from around the world: biography, crime fiction, current affairs, historical fiction, literary translations, memoir, political and social issues, popular history, popular science, reportage, general literary fiction and general trade non-fiction. Accepts unsolicited material.

Gemini Books Group

Marine House, Tide Mill Way, Woodbridge, Suffolk IP12 1AP
email customerservice@geminibooks.com
website www.geminibooks.com
Instagram @geminibooksgroup
Founder & Managing Director Marcus E. Leaver, *Publishers* Dan Graham, Lisa Dyer

Illustrated non-fiction books for children and adults. Founded 2023.

Ghost Orchid Press

13 California Road, St Ives PE27 6SJ
email info@ghostorchidpress.com
website https://ghostorchidpress.com
X @ghostorchidpress
Bluesky @ghostorchidpress.bsky.social
Instagram @ghostorchidpress
Director Antonia Ward

An independent publisher of horror, gothic and supernatural fiction. Novels, novellas and anthologies by authors from a wide range of backgrounds including LGBTQ+. Established 2021.

Gibson Square‡

128 City Road, London EC1V 2NX
tel 020-7096 1100
email info@gibsonsquare.com
website www.gibsonsquare.com
Facebook www.facebook.com/gibson.square
Publisher Martin Rynja

Non-fiction: general non-fiction, biography, current affairs, philosophy, politics, cultural criticism, psychology, history, travel and art history. Some fiction. See website for guidelines or email to receive an automated response. Submission by email only. Founded 2001.

Gill†

Hume Avenue, Park West, Dublin D12 YV96, Republic of Ireland
tel +353 (0)1 500 9500
email sales@gill.ie
website www.gill.ie
Chief Executive Officer Margaret Burns

An independent publisher and distributor. Founded 1856.

Gill Books

website www.gillbooks.ie
Facebook www.facebook.com/gillbooks
X @gillbooks

Trade publishing. Irish interest: biography, cookery, children's, wellness, history, politics, current affairs, reference, lifestyle and fiction.

Gill Education

website www.gilleducation.ie, www.gillexplore.ie

Primary and post-primary publisher. Working with educators to create books and resources, tailored to the Irish market. Also supplies Irish schools with a range of literacy and numeracy resources.

Gingko

4 Molasses Row, London SW11 3UX
tel 020-3637 9730
email gingko@gingko.org.uk
website www.gingko.org.uk
X @gingkolibrary
Instagram @gingko_org
Founder & Ceo Barbara Schwepcke

Works with scholars of diverse backgrounds and research interests to increase understanding of the Middle East, West Asia and North Africa through conferences, public events and cultural programmes. Publishes academic books on the history, art history and religions of the MENA region. See website for submission guidelines. Founded 2014.

Globe Law and Business‡

3 Mylor Close, Horsell, Woking, Surrey GU21 4DD
email sian@globelawandbusiness.com
website www.globelawandbusiness.com
Managing Director Sian O'Neill, *Chairman* Jim Smith, *Marketing Manager* Nicola Hornsby, *Managing Editor* Lauren Simpson, *Commissioning Editor* Alex Davies, *Head of Digital Publishing* Steve Savory

Professional law books. Titles available online via content platform, Globe Law Online. Practical and accessible legal content for practising professionals. Most authors from the Magic Circle and top commercial firms. Welcomes ideas for potential new titles in the core areas of law and law firm management. Founded 2005.

Goat Star Books*

76 Dron House, Adelina Grove, London E1 3AB
tel 07812 101664
email goatstarbooks@gmail.com
website https://goatstarbooks.com/
X @goatstarbooks
Instagram @goatstarbooks
Managing Director Rafael Cruz, *Editor-at-Large* Kevin Harrison

English/Spanish poetry translations. Founded 2021.

Godsfield Press – see Octopus Publishing Group

Goldsmiths Press

Room 108, Deptford Town Hall, New Cross, London SE14 6NW
tel 020-7919 7258
email goldsmithspress@gold.ac.uk
website www.gold.ac.uk/goldsmiths-press
X @goldsmithspress
Director Sarah Kember

Academic and trade publisher of non-fiction. An Open Access monograph publisher. Founded 2016.

Graffeg‡

24 Stradey Park Business Centre, Mwrwg Road, Llangennech, Llanelli SA14 8YP
tel (01554) 824000
email croeso@graffeg.com
website https://graffeg.com/
Facebook www.facebook.com/graffegbooks
X @graffeg_books
Instagram @graffegbooks
Founder Peter Gill

Non-fiction illustrated books about food, art, music, culture and heritage, architecture, gardens, photography, sport and lifestyle, and illustrated fiction for children. Open to submissions – see website for guidelines. Founded 2003.

Bird Eye Books

Photography and art.

Cadno

Middle-grade and YA fiction in English and Welsh.

Graffeg Bach

Welsh language children's fiction.

Granta Books‡

12 Addison Avenue, London W11 4QR
tel 020-7605 1360
website www.granta.com
Facebook www.facebook.com/grantamag
X @GrantaBooks
Instagram @granta_magazine
Publisher Sigrid Rausing

Literary fiction, graphic novels, memoir, nature writing, cultural criticism and travel. No submissions except via a reputable literary agent. An imprint of Granta Publications. Founded 1982.

Green Print – see Merlin Press

Gresham Books

The Carriage House, Ningwood Manor, Ningwood, Isle of Wight PO30 4NJ
tel (01983) 761389
email info@gresham-books.co.uk
website www.gresham-books.co.uk
Facebook www.facebook.com/GreshamBooks
X @greshambooks
Managing Director Nicholas Oulton

Hymn books, prayer books, service books, school histories, diaries, journals and other bespoke publications. Imprint: Churchwarden Publications (page 130). Founded 1979.

The Gresham Publishing Company

31 Six Harmony Row, Glasgow G51 3BA
tel 0141 375 1996
email info@waverley-books.co.uk
website www.waverley-books.co.uk
Facebook www.facebook.com/WaverleyBooks
X @WaverleyBooks
Instagram @waverleybooks
Publishers Ron Grosset, Liz Small

General trade and Scottish interest books. Founded 2013.

Geddes & Grosset

tel 0141 375 1998
email info@geddesandgrosset.co.uk
website www.geddesandgrosset.com

Mass market reference, English language learning, health and wellbeing. Founded 1988.

Waverley Books

Books of Scottish interest, food and drink, fiction and humour.

Grub Street Publishing

4 Rainham Close, London SW11 6SS
tel 020-7924 3966, 020-7738 1008
email post@grubstreet.co.uk
website www.grubstreet.co.uk
Facebook www.facebook.com/grubstreetpublishing
X @grub_street
Instagram @grubstreetpublishinguk
Principals John B. Davies, Anne Dolamore

Adult non-fiction: military history, aviation history and cookery. Founded 1982.

Guild of Master Craftsman Publications

166 High Street, Lewes, East Sussex BN7 1XU
tel (01273) 477374
email jonathanb@thegmcgroup.com
website www.gmcbooks.com
X @GMCbooks
Instagram @gmcpublications
Managing Director Jonathan Phillips, *Publisher* Jonathan Bailey

Leisure and hobby project books with a focus on woodworking. Craft subjects include: needlecraft, paper crafts, forest schooling and jewellery-making. Founded 1979.

Ammonite Press

website www.ammonitepress.com
X @AmmonitePress
Publisher Jonathan Bailey

Highly illustrated non-fiction for the international market including mindfulness journals, escape puzzle books and other gift books featuring illustration, infographics and photography on pop culture, pop reference, biography and history. Practical photography titles written by professional photographers provide authoritative guides to technique and equipment.

Button Books

website www.buttonbooks.co.uk

Publishes design-led children's books including award-winning non-fiction, round-cornered board books, wipe-clean flash cards, hardbacks with poster jackets, activity books with stickers and picture books with pop-out animals to make.

Guillemot Press

email editor@guillemotpress.co.uk
website www.guillemotpress.co.uk
Facebook www.facebook.com/guillemotpress
Bluesky @guillemotpress.bsky.social
Instagram @guillemotpress
Founders Luke Thompson, Sarah Cave

A small independent publisher of poetry and non-fiction, often in pamphlet form and illustrated, as well as postcards, box sets and other objects. Founded 2016.

Guinness World Records

Ground Floor, The Rookery, 2 Dyott Street, London WC1A 1DE
tel 020-7891 4567
website www.guinnessworldrecords.com
Facebook www.facebook.com/GuinnessWR
X @GWR
Instagram @guinnessworldrecords
Editor-in-Chief Craig Glenday

Guinness World Records, *GWR Gamer's Edition*, TV and brand licensing, records processing. No unsolicited MSS. A Jim Pattison Group company. Founded 1954.

Guppy Publishing*

Bracken Hill, Cotswold Road, Oxford OX2 9JG
tel 07884 068983
email bella@guppybooks.co.uk
website www.guppybooks.co.uk
Facebook www.facebook.com/guppybooks
X @guppybooks
Bluesky @guppybooks.bsky.social
Instagram @guppypublishing
Director Bella Pearson

Children's and YA fiction for 5–18 years. Illustrated books for newly emerging readers, fiction for middle-grade readers and novels for YA. Poetry, prose and graphic novels. No unsolicited submissions outside the Guppy Open Submission Competition (run annually in May). Founded 2019.

Hachette Children's Trade*

Carmelite House, 50 Victoria Embankment, London EC4Y 0DZ
tel 020-3122 6000
email editorial@hachettechildrens.co.uk
website www.hachettechildrens.co.uk
Facebook www.facebook.com/hachettechildrens
X @HachetteKids
Instagram @hachettechildrens
Ceo Hilary Murray Hill

Baby and preschool books, picture books, illustrated gift, fiction, non-fiction, series fiction, books for the school and library market and licensed publishing. Imprints include: Hodder Children's Books, Laurence King Children's Books, Little, Brown Books for Young Readers, Orchard Books, Orion Children's Books, Quercus Children's Books, Pat-a-Cake, Franklin Watts, Wayland Books, Welbeck Children's Books and Wren & Rook. Owner of Enid Blyton Entertainment. Generally only accepts submissions sent via an agent. Occasionally holds periods of open submissions for a limited time or a specific genre. See social media channels for details. Founded 1986.

Hachette Learning*

Carmelite House, 50 Victoria Embankment, London EC4Y 0DZ
tel (01235) 827720
website www.hoddereducation.co.uk, www.galorepark.co.uk, www.risingstars-uk.com
Ceo Seshni Jacobs

School and college publishing. Imprints: Galore Park, Hodder Education, Rising Stars and RS Assessment. Part of Hachette UK. Founded 1960.

Hachette UK*

Carmelite House, 50 Victoria Embankment, London EC4Y 0DZ
tel 020-3122 6000
website www.hachette.co.uk
Facebook www.facebook.com/pages/Hachette-UK
X @hachetteUK
Ceo David Shelley, *Deputy Ceo* Richard Kitson, *Ceo Adult Trade* Katie Espiner, *Ceo Education* Seshni Jacobs, *Managing Director, Children's Trade* Ruth Alltimes

Hachette UK comprises three publishing divisions: Adult Trade, Children's Trade and Education. Hachette group companies: Bookouture (page 126), Hachette Australia (page 191), Hachette Book Publishing India; Hachette Children's Trade (above), Hachette Ireland, Hachette Learning (above), Hachette New Zealand (page 199), Headline Publishing Group (page 149), Hodder & Stoughton (page 150), Little, Brown Book Group (page 156), John Murray Group (page 161), Octopus Publishing Group (page 164) and Orion Publishing Group (page 165). Founded 1986.

Hadean Press‡

59A Cavendish Street Keighley, West Yorkshire BD21 3RB
email info@hadeanpress.com
website https://hadean.press/
Facebook www.facebook.com/hadeanpress
Instagram @hadeanpress
Managing & Editorial Director Erzebet Barthold

A small press producing titles in modern occultism, publishing academic and independent scholarship in the areas of folklore, folk magic and spellbooks. Founded 2008.

Halban Publishers‡

176 Goldhurst Terrace, London NW6 3HN
tel 020-7692 5541
email books@halbanpublishers.com
website www.halbanpublishers.com
Facebook www.facebook.com/HalbanPublishers
X @Halban_Publishers
Instagram @halban_publishers
Directors Martine Halban, Peter Halban

General fiction and non-fiction, history and biography, Jewish subjects and Middle East. No unsolicited MSS considered; preliminary letter or email essential. Founded 1986.

Halcyon Publishing

40 Crompton Avenue, Glasgow G44 5TH
website https://halcyonpublishing.co.uk/
X @HalcyonPublish1
Instagram @halcyonpublishing
Founders Rob MacDonald, Adam Bushby

Publisher of books that tell real stories about real (non-fiction) football. Founded 2021.

Ockley Books

Sports.

Halsgrove Publishing

Halsgrove House, Ryelands Business Park, Bagley Road, Wellington, Somerset TA21 9PZ
tel (01823) 653777
email sales@halsgrove.com
website www.halsgrove.com
Facebook www.facebook.com/Halsgrove.Publishing
X @Halsgrove
Directors Guy Puglsey, Steven Pugsley

Regional books for local-interest readers in the UK. Illustrated books on individual artists. Imprints: Community Histories, Halsgrove, Halstar, Halswood, HPiXZ, Ryelands. Founded 1986.

Hamish Hamilton – see Penguin General

Hamlyn – see Octopus Publishing Group

Happy Yak

2nd Floor, 1 Triptych Place, London SE1 9SH
tel 020-7000 8084
website www.quartoknows.com/happy-yak
Instagram @happyyakbooks
Associate Publisher Rhiannon Findlay

Preschool, picture books and illustrated non-fiction for children from birth upwards, with a focus on fun, accessible content and contemporary illustration. A children's imprint of Quarto Group Publishing UK. Founded 2021.

Hardie Grant UK

5th and 6th Floors, Pentagon House, 52–54 Southwark Street, London SE1 1UN
tel 020-7601 7500
email info@hardiegrant.co.uk
website www.hardiegrant.com/uk
Founders Sandy Grant, Fiona Hardie

Non-fiction, categories include: food and drink, gift and humour, craft, gardening, wellness, interiors and pop culture. Founded 1994.

Harlequin UK*

HarperCollins Publishers, 1 London Bridge Street, London SE1 9EF
tel 0844 844 1351
website www.millsandboon.co.uk
Facebook www.facebook.com/millsandboon
X @MillsandBoon
Executive Publisher of Mills & Boon UK Lisa Milton, *Executive Editor of Harlequin/Mills & Boon Series* Bryony Green

Part of HarperCollins Publishers. Founded 1908.

Mills & Boon Historical

Senior Editor Carly Byrne
Historical romance fiction.

Mills & Boon Medical

Senior Editor Sheila Hodgson
Contemporary romance fiction in a medical setting.

Mills & Boon Modern Romance

Senior Editor Flo Nicoll
Contemporary romances – luxury and passion.

Mills & Boon True Love

Senior Editor Sheila Hodgson
Contemporary romances – emotion and escapism.

HarperCollins Publishers*

The News Building, 1 London Bridge Street, London SE1 9GF
tel 020-8741 7070
Alternative address 1 Robroyston Gate, Robroyston, Glasgow G33 1JN
tel 0141 772 3200
website www.harpercollins.co.uk
Facebook www.facebook.com/HarperCollinsPublishersUK
X @HarperCollinsUK
Ceo Charlie Redmayne

For adults: fiction (commercial and literary) and non-fiction. Subjects include history; celebrity memoirs and biographies; popular science; mind, body & spirit; and dictionaries, maps and reference. All fiction and trade non-fiction must be submitted through an agent. Owned by News Corporation. Founded 1817.

HARPERCOLLINS (ADULT COMMERCIAL PUBLISHING)

HarperFiction

Managing Director & Publisher Frankie Gray, *Publishers* David Brawn, Lynne Drew, Julia Wisdom,

Publishing Directors Martha Ashby, Charlotte Brabbin, Kate Bradley, Chris Smith
General, historical fiction, women's fiction, crime and thrillers.

The Borough Press
Publisher Beth Coates
Literary fiction.

Hemlock Press
Publisher Julia Wisdom
Cime, mystery and thrillers.

Harper Voyager
Publisher Natasha Bardon
Fantasy and sci-fi.

Magpie
Publisher Natasha Bardon
YA fantasy and sci-fi.

Harper NonFiction
Managing Director & Publisher Sarah Emsley, *Publisher (Mudlark and Smart Thinking)* Joel Simmons, *Publishing Director (Mudlark and Smart Thinking)* Huw Armstrong, *Publisher (Entertainment)* Katya Shipster, *Publishing Director (Entertainment)* Ajda Vucicevic, *Editor-at-Large, Sports* Jonathan Taylor, *Publisher (Element, Thorsons and Gift &IP)* Jane Storrock, *Publishing Director (Element, Thorsons and Gift & IP)* Tom Asker
Autobiographies, entertainment, sports, true crime, history, business, politics, science, cookery, lifestyle and culture. Imprints: Mudlark and Smart Thinking, Sport and Entertainment, Element, Thorsons and Gift & IP.

HarperNorth
Managing Director & Publisher Sarah Emsley, *Publisher* Genevieve Pegg
Fiction: general, historical, crime and thrillers. Non-fiction: autobiographies, memoir, politics, history, sport, nature writing, smart-thinking.

Avon
Publisher Helen Huthwaite
General fiction, crime and thrillers, women's fiction.

One More Chapter
Publisher Charlotte Ledger
Digital-first commercial fiction.

Collins
website www.collins.co.uk
Managing Director Alex Beecroft
Children's fiction and non-fiction. Education publisher for UK and international school curriculums, revision and home learning support. Reference publishing, including dictionaries and atlases. Imprints include: A–Z, the National Trust and Times Books. Children's imprints include: Barrington Stoke and Rocket Bird Books.

Farshore Books
website www.farshore.com
Managing Director & Publisher Cally Poplak
Children's fiction, YA, graphic novels, picture books, non-fiction, film/TV, toy and gaming. Imprints include: Electric Monkey, Expanse and Red Shed.

4th Estate
Managing Director & Publisher David Roth-Ey, *Publishing Directors* Louise Haines, Michelle Kane, Kishani Widyaratna
Fiction, literary fiction, current affairs, popular science, biography, humour, travel, cookery, art, music, memoir, popular culture, self-improvement and essays. Imprints include: Monument Books.

William Collins
Managing Director & Publisher David Roth-Ey, *Publishing Directors* Arabella Pike (history, politics, current affairs, biography), Myles Archibald (natural history, science)
Science, history, art, politics and current affairs, biography, business, religion and natural history.

HarperCollins Audio
Group Technology & Digital Director Joanna Surman, *Audio Publishing Director* Fionnuala Barrett
Trade fiction and non-fiction audiobooks for children, as well as standalone audio projects. Publishes in excess of 75,000 audiobooks each year.

HarperCollins Children's Books
Managing Director & Publisher Cally Poplak
Children's fiction, YA fiction, graphic novels, picture books and non-fiction. Also film/TV tie-in brands. Imprints: Harper Fire and Kumusha.

Harper360
Publishes all HarperCollins Publishers books worldwide.

HQ
website www.hqstories.co.uk
Managing Director & Publisher Lisa Milton, *Fiction Publishers* Kate Mills (commercial & historical), Manpreet Grewal (crime & book club), *Non-fiction Publishing Directors* Louise McKeever, Danielle Pender
Fiction: commercial fiction, crime and thrillers, women's fiction, historical and book club. Non-fiction: memoir, cookery, self-help and wellbeing, and smart thinking.

HQ Digital
Publishing Director Georgina Green
Digital-first commercial fiction list, general, crime and thrillers, women's fiction, psychological thrillers, saga.

Pavilion Books
website www.pavilionbooks.com
Publishing Director Laura Russell

Food and drink, craft, hobbies, health and wellbeing, lifestyle and gift. Imprints include: Collins & Brown, Pavilion, Portico and Robson. Formerly Anova Books Group. Founded 2013.

Akan Books
Publisher Manpreet Grewal

Fiction: crime and thriller, psychological suspense, romance, historical, contemporary/book club and family drama. Non-fiction: self-help, smart thinking, memoir and parenting. Accepting unagented submissions from authors from ethnic minority backgrounds, authors who identify as working class and authors with disabilities. Visit akanbooks.co.uk for more information.

Mills & Boon
Executive Editor Bryony Green

Imprint of Harlequin (UK).

Times Books
The Times puzzle books.

Harriman House
3 Viceroy Court, Bedford Road, Petersfield, Hants GU32 3LJ
tel (01730) 233870
email contact@harriman-house.com
email commissioning@harriman-house.com
website www.harriman.house

Non-fiction books: business and finance, creative marketing, smart thinking and lifestyle. For submission guidelines see website. Imprint of Pan Macmillan. Founded 1992.

Hart Publishing – see Bloomsbury Publishing

Harvill Secker – see Vintage

Hashtag Press
10 Bankfields, Headcorn, Kent TN27 9RA
email submissions@hashtagpress.co.uk
website www.hashtagpress.co.uk
Facebook www.facebook.com/hashtagbooks
X @hastag_press
Founders Abiola Bello, Helen Lewis

A female-led, award-winning independent publisher of diverse and inclusive stories and writers. Founder of The Diverse Book Awards. Children's, middle-grade and YA fiction. Has open submissions for imprints a few times a year. Submission guidelines see website. Founded 2016.

Hashtag BLAK
email info@hashtagblak.co.uk
website www.hashtagblak.co.uk
X @hashtag_BLAK

Supported by Arts Council England. An imprint for under-represented voices telling stories about love.

Haunt Publishing*
email boo@hauntpublishing.com
website www.hauntpublishing.com
Facebook www.facebook.com/HauntPublish
X @HauntPublishing
Bluesky hauntpublishing.bsky.social
Instagram @hauntpublishing
Director & Managing Editor Rebecca Wojturska

Independent publisher of traditional and contemporary Gothic, horror and dark fiction. Keen to work with global and under-represented voices. Publishes novels, novellas, short story collections, anthologies and poetry collections. Founded 2019.

Haus Publishing
4 Cinnamon Row, Plantation Wharf, London SW11 3TW
tel 020-3637 9729
email haus@hauspublishing.com
website https://hauspublishing.com/
X @HausPublishing
Editor Ed Doxey

History, biography, memoir and current affairs. Founded 2003.

Hawthorn Press‡
Hawthorn House, 1 Lansdown Lane, Stroud, Glos. GL5 1BJ
tel (01453) 757040
email info@hawthornpress.com
website www.hawthornpress.com
Facebook www.facebook.com/HawthornPress
X @HawthornPressUK
Bluesky @hawthornp.bsky.social
Instagram @hawthornpress
Director Martin Large

A small, ethically aware press. Series include *Early Years*, *Steiner/Waldorf Education*, *Crafts*, *Storytelling* and *Parenting*. Founded 1981.

Hay House Publishers
Crawford Corner, 1st Floor, 91–93 Baker Street, London W1U 6QQ
tel 020-3927 7290
email info@hayhouse.co.uk
website www.hayhouse.co.uk
Facebook www.facebook.com/HayHouse
X @HayHouseUK
Managing Director & Publisher Michelle Pilley

Self-help (including mind, body & spirit), business, spirituality, personal development, health and wellness. For submissions use website only. Founded 1984.

Haynes Publishing
Sparkford, Yeovil, Somerset BA22 7JJ
tel (01963) 440635
website www.haynes.co.uk
Facebook www.facebook.com/haynesmanuals

X @haynesmanuals
Chairman Eddie Bell, *Chief Executive* J. Haynes

Practical lifestyle manuals for the home, motorsport, space, military, aviation, entertainment and leisure activities. Founded 1960.

Hazel Press

website https://hazelpress.co.uk/
Publisher & Editor Sara Hudston

Independent publisher of short books of poetry, essays and interdisciplinary titles. Contact can be made via website. Founded 2020.

Head of Zeus – see Bloomsbury Publishing

Headline Publishing Group*

Carmelite House, 50 Victoria Embankment, London EC4Y 0DZ
tel 020-3122 6000
email enquiries@hachette.co.uk
website www.headline.co.uk
X @headlinepg
Managing Director Mari Evans

Commercial and literary fiction and popular non-fiction including autobiography, biography, food and wine, gardening, fashion, music, health and wellbeing, history, popular science, sport and TV tie-ins. Imprints include: Headline, Headline Accent, Headline Eternal, Headline Home, Headline Press, Headline Review, Headline Welbeck Non-fiction, Mountain Leopard Press, OH, Tinder Press, Welbeck (page 187) and Wildfire. Part of Hachette UK. Founded 1986.

Headpress

email headoffice@headpress.com
website www.headpress.com
Facebook www.facebook.com/HEADPRESSPUB
X @headpress
Instagram @headpress
Publisher David Kerekes

Cult film, strange music, pulp literature, fanzines, conspiracy theories, sex and gender, occult and folklore, true crime and pop culture in general. Founded 1992.

Héloïse Press

4 Pretoria Road, Canterbury CT1 1QL
tel (01227) 500382
email a.marti@heloisepress.com
website www.heloisepress.com
Facebook www.facebook.com/Heloisepress
X @heloisepress
Instagram @pressheloise
Publisher & Director Aina Marti-Balcells

Contemporary literary fiction by women (prose only). See website for submission details. Founded 2021.

Henley Hall Press‡

Woofferton Grange, Brimfield, Ludlow, Shrops. SY8 4NP
tel 07984 585861
email susanne@henleyhallpress.co.uk
website www.henleyhallpress.co.uk
X @HenleyHallPress
Contact Susanne Lumsden

An independent non-fiction publisher. Categories include farming, topical affairs, gardening, history and biography. Launch title *On Plan & Proportion* by award-winning garden designer George Carter. Founded 2019.

Henningham Family Press

130 Sandringham Road, London E8 2HJ
tel 07976 843290
website https://henninghamfamilypress.com/
Facebook www.facebook.com/HenninghamPress
Instagram @henninghampress
Publishers David Henningham, Ping Henningham

Makes artists' books by hand that are collected by libraries and museums. Since 2018 the studio has sold fiction paperbacks in bookshops. Novels have been shortlisted for The Goldsmith's Prize, Republic of Consciousness Prize, British Book Awards and longlisted for The Walter Scott Prize. Founded 2006.

Hera Books

Canelo Digital Publishing Limited, 20 Vauxhall Bridge Road, London, SW1V 2S
email submissions@herabooks.com
website www.herabooks.com
Publishing Director Keshini Naidoo

Independent commercial fiction publisher. Crime and thriller, romance, saga and general fiction. No poetry, children's books, non-fiction or illustrated books. Send a one-page synopsis and the whole MS in Word to submissions email. Part of The Canelo Group. Founded 2018.

Nick Hern Books‡

The Glasshouse, 49A Goldhawk Road, London W12 8QP
tel 020-8749 4953
email info@nickhernbooks.co.uk
website www.nickhernbooks.co.uk
Facebook www.facebook.com/NickHernBooks
X @NickHernBooks
Instagram @nickhernbooks
Publisher Nick Hern, *Managing Director* Matt Applewhite

Plays and practical books on creative disciplines including writing, directing and performance. Also license published plays for amateur and educational performance. Submissions for plays should include details of the project and its planned production; submissions for books should include a synopsis and sample chapter. Founded 1988.

Hesperus Press

13 Staines Road, Hounslow TW4 5DJ
tel 020-7436 0943
email publishing@hesperus.press
website https://hesperus.press/
Facebook www.facebook.com/hesperuspress
X @HesperusPress
Instagram @hesperuspress/

Three imprints. Hesperus Classics introduces older works of literature. Hesperus Minor publishes well-loved children's books from the past. Hesperus Nova showcases contemporary literature. Founded 2001.

The History Press‡

97 St Georges Place, Cheltenham, Glos. GL50 3QB
tel (01242) 895310
website www.thehistorypress.co.uk
Facebook www.facebook.com/TheHistoryPress
X @TheHistoryPress
Instagram @thehistorypressuk
Managing Director Gareth Swain, *Publishing Director* Laura Perehinec

Local history, genealogy, military history. Imprints: The History Press, Spellmount, Tempus and THP Ireland. Founded 2008.

Hobeck Books

24 Brookside Business Park, Stone, Staffs. ST15 0RZ
email hobeckbooks@gmail.com
website www.hobeck.net
Facebook www.facebook.com/Hobeckbooks10
X @hobeckbooks
Bluesky @hobeckbooks.bsky.social
Instagram @hobeckbooks
Directors Rebecca Collins, Adrian Hobart

Crime, thrillers, mystery and suspense. Titles have been shortlisted for Bloody Scotland and the CWA Daggers. For submission guidelines see website. Also hosts a weekly podcast called the Hobcast Book Show for writers and readers. Runs the four-times-a-year Henshaw Press Short Story Competition (page 601) and publishes the winning stories in an anthology. Founded 2019.

Hodder & Stoughton*

Carmelite House, 50 Victoria Embankment, London EC4Y 0DZ
tel 020-3122 6777
website www.hodder.co.uk
Facebook www.facebook.com/hodderbooks
X @hodderbooks
Instagram @hodderbooks
Ceo Katie Espiner

Commercial and literary fiction; biography and autobiography, history, humour, travel, lifestyle and cookery. Also mind, body & spirit and other general interest non-fiction and audio. No unsolicited MSS or synopses. Publishes under Coronet, Hodder & Stoughton, Hodderscape, Sceptre and Yellow Kite. Part of Hachette UK. Founded 1960.

Hodder & Stoughton Audio

Audio Publisher Dominic Gribben

Fiction and non-fiction audiobooks from within the Hodder group. Also commissions and publishes original audiobook content and podcasts.

Holland House Books*

47 Greenham Road, Newbury, Berks. RG14 7HY
email contact@hhousebooks.com
website www.hhousebooks.com
Senior Editor Robert Peett

Literary fiction and non-fiction. Happy to read traditional and experimental work. Submissions welcome from agents and authors, but check website or send query email first. Founded 2012.

Honno (Welsh Women's Press)‡

D41 Hugh Owen Building, Penglais Campus, Aberystwyth University, Aberystwyth SY23 3DY
tel (01970) 623150
email submissions@honno.co.uk
website www.honno.co.uk
Facebook www.facebook.com/honnopress
X @honno

Literature written by women born or living in Wales or women with a significant Welsh connection. All subjects considered – fiction, non-fiction and autobiographies. No poetry or works for children. Honno is a community cooperative. Founded 1986.

HopeRoad

West Brompton Delivery Office, 256A Fulham Road, London SW10 9LZ
email rosemarie@hoperoadpublishing.com
website www.hoperoadpublishing.com
Facebook www.facebook.com/HopeRoadPublishing
X @hoperoadpublish
Instagram @hoperoadpublishing
Director & Publisher Rosemarie Hudson

Fiction for adults and YA from and about Africa, Asia and the Caribbean. Founded 2010.

Small Axes

Editor Pete Ayrton

Out-of-print post-colonial classics. Founded 2019.

Hopscotch

St Jude's Church, Dulwich Road, London SE24 0PB
tel 020-7501 6736
email orders@hopscotchbooks.com
website www.hopscotchbooks.com
Associate Publisher Angela Morano Shaw

Teaching resources for primary school teachers. A division of McGraw-Hill Education. Founded 1997.

Practical Pre-School Books

website www.practicalpreschoolbooks.com

Early years teaching resources.

Hot Key Books

Victoria House, Bloomsbury Square,
London WC1B 4DA
tel 020-3770 8888
email hello@bonnierbooks.co.uk
website www.bonnierbooks.co.uk/imprints/hot-key-books
X @HotKeyBooksYA
Executive Publisher Emma Matthewson

Literary teen and YA fiction, some books also suitable for an adult audience. An imprint of Bonnier Books UK. Founded 2012.

House of Riviera‡

email info@houseofriviera.com
website www.houseofriviera.com
Facebook www.facebook.com/riviera
X @rivierabooks
Instagram @rivierabooks
Publishing executives Gemma Harris, Justin Jones

A new independent publisher of commercial fiction. Open to agented and unagented submissions from debut and accomplished authors. Part of Riviera Artists Agency. Founded 2024.

Howgate Publishing‡

Station House, North Street, Havant,
Hants. PO9 1QU
email info@howgatepublishing.com
website www.howgatepublishing.com
X @kirstin_howgate
Publisher & Director Kirstin Howgate

Military training, education and narrative books. Shortlisted for the 2023 Independent Publisher Awards – Nick Robinson Newcomer Award. Submission guidelines and bookshop available on website. Founded 2015.

Hurst Publishers‡

New Wing, Somerset House, Strand,
London WC2R 1LA
website www.hurstpublishers.com/about
Facebook www.facebook.com/hurstpublishersFB
X @hurstpublishers
Bluesky @hurstpublishers.bsky.social
Instagram @hurstpublishers
Publishing Director Michael Dwyer, *Senior Editor* Lara Weisweiller-Wu

An independently owned, non-fiction press. Publishes approx. 90 new titles per year in history, politics, sociology, war studies. Founded 1969.

Hutchinson Heinemann – see Cornerstone

Hymns Ancient and Modern*‡

13A Hellesdon Park Road, Norwich,
Norfolk NR6 5DR
website www.hymnsam.co.uk/the-business/book-publishing
Publishing Director Christine Smith

Theological and reference books and contemporary theology for both students and clergy. Founded 1929.

Canterbury Press

Norwich Books and Music, 13A Hellesdon Park Road,
Norwich NR6 5DR
tel (01603) 785925
website www.canterburypress.co.uk
X @canterburypress

Hymnals, popular religious writing, spirituality and liturgy.

Church House Publishing

website www.chpublishing.co.uk
X @CHPublishingUK

Publisher of the Church of England – church resources, stationery and Common Worship.

The Revised English Hymnal

Imprint for the publication of a completely new and updated edition of the English Hymnal.

Saint Andrew Press

website www.standrewpress.hymns.co.uk
X @standrewpress

Publisher of the Church of Scotland.

SCM Press

website www.scmpress.co.uk
X @SCM_Press
Associate Publisher David Shervington

Academic theology.

Icon Books‡

The Omnibus Business Centre, 39–41 North Road,
London N7 9DP
tel 020-7697 9695
email info@iconbooks.com
website www.iconbooks.com
Ceo Nick Hayward

Popular, upmarket non-fiction: literature, history, philosophy, politics, psychology, sociology, sport, humour, science, current affairs, music and economics. Will consider unsolicited MSS (adult non-fiction only). Owned by Amberly Publishing. Founded 1992.

Igloo Books

Cottage Farm, Mears Ashby Road, Sywell,
Northants. NN6 0BJ
tel (01604) 741116
email customerservices@igloobooks.com
website www.igloobooks.com
X @igloo_books

Children's books: licensed books, novelty, board, picture, activity and education. Adult books: cookery, lifestyle, gift, trivia and non-fiction. Not currently accepting submissions. Founded 2005.

Ignite Books

58 Wolverhampton Street, Willenhall,
West Midlands WV13 2NL
email hello@ignitebooks.co.uk
website https://ignitebooks.co.uk/
Bluesky @ignitebooks.bsky.social

A small independent press publishing one or two books a year, mostly memoir. Two books have been longlisted for the Polari Prize, another featured on BBC Radio 6. Does not have a specific submissions window and are unable to take on 99% of the MSS. Founded 2018.

Imprint Academic

PO Box 200, Exeter, Devon EX5 5YX
tel (01392) 851550
email graham@imprint.co.uk
website www.imprint.co.uk
X @ImprintAcademic
Bluesky @imprintacademic.bsky.social
Instagram @imprint.academic
Publisher Keith Sutherland, *Assistant Publisher* Emma McInnes, *Managing Editor* Graham Horswell

Books and journals in politics, society, philosophy and psychology for both academic and general readers. Book series include *St Andrews Studies in Philosophy and Public Affairs*, *British Idealist Studies*, *Societas* (essays in political and cultural criticism) and the *Library of Scottish Philosophy*. Also publishes under Amphora Press (biography and general historical interest titles). Unsolicited MSS, synopses and ideas welcome by completing the online form on the website. Founded 1980.

Indigo Dreams Publishing

24 Forest Houses, Halwill, Beaworthy,
Devon EX21 5UU
email indigodreamspublishing@gmail.com
website www.indigodreamspublishing.com
X @IndigoDreamsPub
Editors Ronnie Goodyer, Dawn Bauling

Main subject areas: poetry anthologies, collections, competitions, monthly poetry magazine and one quarterly poetry and prose magazine. New and experienced writers welcome. Founded 2010.

The Indigo Press

50 Albemarle Street, Mayfair, London W1S 4BD
email publish@theindigopress.com
website www.theindigopress.com
Facebook www.facebook.com/theindigopress
X @PressIndigoThe
Instagram @theindigopress
Founder & Publisher Susie Nicklin

An independent publisher of contemporary fiction and non-fiction with a focus on internationalism, feminism and social justice. No unsolicited submissions – see website for guidelines. Founded 2018.

Influx Press

The Greenhouse, 49 Green Lanes, London N16 9BU
email hello@influxpress.com
website www.influxpress.com
X @InfluxPress
Instagram @influxpress
Directors Gary Budden

Award-winning literary and experimental fiction. Imprint: New Ruins. Founded 2012.

Inkandescent

Flat 4, 60 Cambridge Gardens, London W10 6HR
tel 07956 478512
email justin@inkandescent.co.uk
website www.inkandescent.co.uk
Facebook www.facebook.com/InkandescentPublishing
X @inkandescentUK
Instagram @inkandescentuk
Threads @inkandescentuk
Publisher Justin David, *Editor* Nathan Evans

Focuses on writers under-represented in mainstream publishing. Publishes fiction, non-fiction and poetry. Also produces Bold Queer Poetry Soirée. Founded 2016.

Inspired Quill

email info@inspired-quill.com
website www.inspired-quill.com
Facebook www.facebook.com/inspiredquill
X @inspiredquill
Instagram @inspiredquill
Publisher Sara-Jayne Slack

Independent non-profit press. Focuses on inclusive publishing in both fiction (novels and short stories) and non-fiction. Fiction genres include: crime, LGBTQ+, steam punk, historical, new adult, sci-fi and fantasy. Non-fiction genres include: wellness, women's issues, LGBTQ+, general non-fiction and social justice. As a social enterprise, the company pledges profit percentages to charity, runs subsidised workshops and mentoring schemes, and donates books to community-led initiatives. Founded 2011.

Institute of Public Administration

57–61 Lansdowne Road, Ballsbridge,
Dublin D04 TC62, Republic of Ireland
tel +353 (0)1 240 3600
email information@ipa.ie
website www.ipa.ie
Head of Communications John Paul Owens

Government, economics, politics, law, public management, health, education, social policy and administrative history. Founded 1957.

IOP Publishing*‡

No. 2, The Distillery Glassfields, Avon Street,
Bristol BS2 0GR
tel 0117 929 7481

email customerservices@ioppublishing.org
website https://ioppublishing.org/
X @IOPPublishing
Bluesky @ioppublishing.bsky.social
Instagram @ioppublishing
Threads @ioppublishing

A subsidiary of the Institute of Physics. Publishes journals, books, conference proceedings, magazines and science news websites. Non-fiction: physics, materials science, biosciences, astronomy and astrophysics, environmental sciences, mathematics and education. Also publishes on behalf of other scientific organisations. Founded 1874.

Irish Academic Press†

Merrion Press, Tuckmill House, 10 George's Street, Newbridge, Co. Kildare W12 PX39, Republic of Ireland
tel +353 (0)45 432497
email info@merrionpress.ie
website www.merrionpress.ie
Publisher Conor Graham, *Commissioning Editor* Síne Quinn, *Production Manager* Wendy Logue, *Marketing Manager* Ciara Kinsella

General and non-fiction publisher with a focus on Irish history, politics, biography, memoir, current affairs, literature, culture, arts and heritage. Imprint: Merrion Press. Founded 1974.

The Irish Pages Press/Cló An Mhíl Bhuí†

129 Ormeau Road, Belfast BT7 1SH
tel 028-9043 4800
email editor@irishpages.org
website https://irishpages.org/
Facebook www.facebook.com/IrishPages
X @irishpages
Instagram @irishpages
Editor Chris Agee

Publishes poetry, essays, memoir and general non-fiction (including graphic novels), in both English and Irish. Founded 2002.

ISF Publishing

PO Box 81251, London NW2 9XN
email info@idriesshahfoundation.org
website www.idriesshahfoundation.org
Facebook www.facebook.com/idriesshah
X @idriesshah
Instagram @idriesshah

Publisher of the work of Idries Shah, translator of key works of Eastern Sufi classical literature. Founded 2014.

Ithaca Press – see Garnet Publishing

IWM (Imperial War Museums) Publishing‡

Lambeth Road, London SE1 6HZ
tel 020-7416 5000
email contact@iwm.org.uk
website www.iwm.org.uk
Facebook www.facebook.com/iwm.london
X @I_W_M

Titles published draw on the expertise and archives of the museum, produced both in-house and in partnership with other publishers. Founded 1917.

Jacaranda Books*‡

27 Old Gloucester Street, London WC1N 3AX
tel 020-8133 4841
email office@jacarandabooksartmusic.co.uk
website www.jacarandabooksartmusic.co.uk
Facebook www.facebook.com/jacarandabooks
X @jacarandabooks
Founder & Publisher Valerie Brandes

Award-winning, Black-owned independent publisher of literary and genre fiction, and non-fiction. Dedicated to promoting and celebrating diverse storytelling in all forms, and to directly addressing the ongoing lack of inclusion in the book trade. Interested in writing from the perspective of the Global South. Publishers of the *Twenty in 2020* and *A Quick Ting On* series. Founded 2012.

Jane's

163 Brighton Road, Coulsdon, Surrey CR5 2YH
tel 020-3159 3255
email communications@janes.com
website www.janes.com

Military books: systems and weapons, threat intelligence, defence, forecasts and budgets, sustainment and procurement. Founded 1898.

Jantar Publishing

82 St Mildreds Road, London SE12 0RF
email Alex@jantarpublishing.com
website www.jantarpublishing.com
Facebook www.facebook.com/JantarPublishing
X @JantarBooks
Instagram @jantarbooks
Founder Michael Tate

Independent publisher of European literature and poetry. Titles have been shortlisted for the EBRB Prize and the Warwick Women in Translation Prize as well as winning a number of English PEN Translation awards. Founded 2011.

Joffe Books‡

111 Shoreditch High Street, Hackney, London E1 6JN
email office@joffebooks.com
website www.joffebooks.com
Facebook www.facebook.com/joffebooks
X @joffebooks
Publisher Jasper Joffe

Independent award-winning publisher of crime thrillers, mysteries, historical, romcom, saga and psychological fiction. Accepts submissions from authors and agents, see website for guidelines.

Encourages submissions from under-represented backgrounds. Offers an annual prize for new crime writers of colour, the Joffe Prize for Crime Writers of Colour (page 611). Imprints include: Choc Lit (romance), Lume Books (fiction and non-fiction) and Ostara Classics. Founded 2014.

Jordan Publishing

21 St Thomas Street, Bristol BS1 6JS
website www.lexisnexis.co.uk/products/jordan-publishing.html
Facebook www.facebook.com/LexisNexisUK
X @lexisnexisuk
Instagram @lexisnexis.uk

Practical information for practising lawyers and other professionals including textbooks, looseleafs, journals, court reference works and news services. Supplies software to law firms in the form of digital service PracticePlus, which combines step-by-step workflows, practice notes, automated court forms and links to core reference works. The company works with partners in key areas, such as the APIL series of guides. Owned by LexisNexis. Founded 1863.

Kelpies – see Floris Books

Kenilworth Press – see Quiller Publishing

Laurence King Publishing*

Carmelite House, 50 Victoria Embankment, London EC4Y 0DZ
tel 020-3122 6000
email commissioning@laurenceking.com
website www.laurenceking.com
Facebook www.facebook/LaurenceKingPublishing
X @laurencekingpub
Instagram @laurencekingpub
Publishing Directors Elen Jones, Philip Contos

Publishes over 120 titles each year in the illustrated mainstream, children's and gifting markets, on topics including architecture, art, design, fashion, film, photography and popular culture. Imprint of The Orion Publishing Group. Founded 1976.

Jessica Kingsley Publishers – see John Murray Group

Kitchen Press*

1 Windsor Place, Dundee DD2 1BG
tel 07951 451571
website www.kitchenpress.co.uk
Facebook www.facebook.com/kitchenpress
X @Kitchen_Press
Instagram @kitchenpress

Independent publisher of food writing, particularly restaurant cookery. Founded 2011.

Knight Errant Press*

13 Glenbervie Drive, Larbert FK5 4NP
email knighterrantpress@outlook.com
website www.knighterrantpress.com
X @KnightErrantPub
Instagram @knighterrantpress
Publisher Nathaniel Kunitsky

A queer micro press with a focus on LGBTQ+ and intersectional storytelling and creators. Publishes stories written by and about LGBTQ+ people, working-class people, people with disabilities as well as migrants and the displaced. Publishes fiction (long and short form), flash fiction, non-fiction, graphic novels and occasionally poetry in all genres with a lean towards sci-fi and fantasy and horror. Founded 2017.

Kogan Page*‡

2nd Floor, 45 Gee Street, London EC1V 3RS
tel 020-7278 0433
website www.koganpage.com
Facebook www.facebook.com/KoganPage
X @Koganpage
Instagram @koganpage
Managing Director Helen Kogan, *Publishing Director* Chris Cudmore

Independent global publisher of business books, digital solutions and content with over 1,000 titles in print. Key subject areas: accounting, finance and banking; business and management; digital and technology; human resources, learning and development; marketing and communications; risk and compliance; skills, careers and employability; and logistics, supply chain and operations. Founded 1967.

Korero Press‡

157 Mornington Road, London E11 3DT
tel 07906 314098
email contact@koreropress.com
website www.koreropress.com
Facebook www.facebook.com/koreropress
X @KoreroPress
Instagram @koreropress

Art and design books: illustration, pop culture and comic books. Founded 2013.

Kube Publishing‡

Markfield Conference Centre, Ratby Lane, Markfield, Leics. LE67 9SY
email info@kubepublishing.com
website www.kubepublishing.com
Facebook www.facebook.com/KubePublishing
X @kube_publishing
Instagram @kubepublishing
Managing Director Haris Ahmad

Publishes books of a Muslim interest. Founded 2006.

Kyle Books

Carmelite House, 50 Victoria Embankment, London EC4Y 0DZ

tel 020-3122 6000
email general.enquiries@kylebooks.co.uk
website www.kylebooks.co.uk
X @Kyle_Books
Publisher Joanna Copestick

Food and drink; health, beauty and style; reference; gardening; design; and mind, body & spirit. Part of Octopus Publishing Group. Founded 1990.

Peter Lang‡

John Eccles House, Science Park,
Robert Robinson Ave, Littlemore, Oxford OX4 4GP
tel (01865) 502124
email oxford@peterlang.com
website www.peterlang.com
Facebook www.facebook.com/PeterLangPublishers
X @PeterLangOxford
Ceo, Peter Lang Publishing Group Arnaud Béglé

Humanities and social sciences. Print, digital and Open Access. All forms of scholarly research as well as textbooks, readers and student guides. Welcomes submissions from prospective authors. Part of the international Peter Lang Publishing Group. Founded 2006.

Lantana Publishing

Clavier House, 21 Fifth Road, Newbury RG14 6DN
email info@lantanapublishing.com
website https://lantanapublishing.com/
Facebook www.facebook.com/lantanapublishing
X @lantanapub
Instagram @lantana_publishing
Ceo Alice Curry, *Commissioning Editor* Katrina Gutierrez

Children's book publisher and social enterprise, publishing inclusive books by authors from under-represented groups from around the world. Looking for inclusive picture books for babies and toddlers, and fiction and non-fiction for 5–8 years and 9–12 years. Authors should send full MS, illustrators their portfolio and link to their website and author-illustrators a complete book dummy. See submissions page on website. Founded 2014.

Lawrence & Wishart

Central Books Building, Freshwater Road,
Chadwell Heath RM8 1RX
tel 020-8597 0090
email lw@lwbooks.co.uk
website www.lwbooks.co.uk
Facebook www.facebook.com/lwbooks
X @lw_books
Instagram @lawrencewishart_
Book Editor Jumanah Younis

Cultural studies, current affairs, history, socialism and Marxism, political philosophy, politics and popular culture. Founded 1936.

Leamington Books*

32 Leamington Terrace, Edinburgh EH10 4JL
email peter@leamingtonbooks.com
website https://leamingtonbooks.com/
Facebook www.facebook.com/leamingtonbooks
X @leamingtonbooks
Instagram @leamingtonbooks
Managing Editor Peter Burnett

Independent press with a backlist of fiction, non-fiction, crime, anthology and poetry. Imprints: Garrison, Gothic World Literature Editions, Leamington Books, Pierpoint and The Magic Road. Also has a poetry imprint. Founded 2020.

Legend Press‡

3rd Floor, 86–90 Paul Street, London EC2A 4NE
tel 020-8127 0793
email info@legendtimesgroup.co.uk
website www.legendpress.co.uk
Facebook www.facebook.com/LegendTimesGroup
X @legend_press
Bluesky @legendpress.bsky.social
Instagram @legend_press
Managing Director Tom Chalmers

Mainstream literary and commercial fiction. Associated publishers include: Buckingham University Press, Hero Press and New Generation Publishing. Submissions can be sent to submissions@legendtimesgroup.co.uk. Founded 2005.

LexisNexis

Lexis House, 30 Farringdon Street,
London EC4A 4HH
tel 0330 161 1234
email customer.services@lexisnexis.co.uk
website www.lexisnexis.co.uk
Facebook www.facebook.com/lexisnexisuk
X @lexisnexisuk
Instagram @lexisnexis.uk

Formerly LexisNexis Butterworths. Division of Reed Elsevier (UK). Founded 1974.

Lightning Books

29A Barrow Street, Much Wenlock,
Shrops. TF13 6EN
tel 020-3239 3027
email dan@lightning-books.com
website www.lightning-books.com
X @EyeAndLightning
Publisher Dan Hiscocks

Literary and commercial fiction, particularly interested in writers under-represented by traditional publishers. See also Eye Books (page 139). Founded 2015.

The Lilliput Press†

62–63 Sitric Road, Arbour Hill, Dublin D07 AE27,
Republic of Ireland

tel +353 (0)1 671 1647
email publicity@lilliputpress.ie
website www.lilliputpress.ie
Facebook www.facebook.com/thelilliputpress
X @LilliputPress
Instagram @lilliputpress
Managing Director Antony T. Farrell

General and Irish literature: essays, memoir, biography/autobiography, poetry, fiction and criticism; Irish history; philosophy; Joycean contemporary culture; nature and environment. Founded 1984.

Frances Lincoln

1 Triptych Place, London SE1 9SH
tel 020-7700 6700
email philip.cooper@quarto.com
website www.quarto.com/Frances-Lincoln
Publisher Philip Cooper

Illustrated books on gardening, art, culture and the history of London. Imprint of Quarto Group Publishing. Founded 1977.

Little, Brown Book Group

50 Victoria Embankment, London EC4Y 0DZ
tel 020-3122 7000
email info@littlebrown.co.uk
website www.littlebrown.co.uk
X @LittleBrownUK
Ceo Charlie King, *Deputy Managing Director* Cath Burke

Fiction and general non-fiction. No unsolicited MSS. Part of Hachette UK. Founded 1988.

Abacus

Publisher Richard Beswick (non-fiction), *Executive Publisher* Clare Smith (fiction)

Literary fiction, politics, biography, crime fiction and general fiction.

Atom

website www.atombooks.co.uk
Deputy Publisher Sarah Castleton

Teen fiction with a fantastical edge.

Blackfriars

website www.blackfriarsbooks.com
Executive Publisher Clare Smith (literary fiction)

Digital.

The Bridge Street Press

Publisher Sameer Rahim

Literary non-fiction.

Constable & Robinson

Publishing Director Andreas Campomar (non-fiction)

Fiction, non-fiction, psychology, humour, brief histories and how-to books.

Corsair

X @CorsairBooks
Publisher James Gurbutt

Literary fiction.

Fleet

Literary fiction and narrative non-fiction.

Little, Brown Audio

email sarah.shrubb@littlebrown.co.uk
X @HachetteAudioUK
Audio Publisher Sarah Shrubb

Titles from Little, Brown's bestselling authors. Publishes approx. 400 audiobooks per year.

Orbit

website www.orbitbooks.com
Publisher Anna Jackson

Sci-fi and fantasy.

Piatkus Constable & Robinson

website www.piatkus.co.uk
Executive Publisher Zoe Bohm (non-fiction), *Publisher* Gina Luck

Fiction and general non-fiction.

Robinson

Publisher Emma Smith

An imprint of three parts: a major commercial non-fiction list, market-leading Robinson Psychology and the practical how-to and cookery list.

Sphere

Executive Publisher Lucy Malagoni (fiction), *Publisher* Kelly Ellis (non-fiction)

Fiction and non-fiction.

Virago

website www.virago.co.uk
Publisher Sarah Savitt

Women's literary fiction and non-fiction.

Little Tiger Press

1 Coda Studios, 189 Munster Road,
London SW6 6AW
tel 020-7385 6333
email contact@littletiger.co.uk
website www.littletiger.co.uk
Publishing Director Thomas Truong, *Publisher* Jude Evans, *Editorial Director (Picture Book Studio)* Steph Stansbie, *Editorial Director (Caterpillar Studio)* Patricia Hegarty, *Editorial Director (Bespoke Studio)* Sam Sweeney, *Associate Editorial Director (Liontree Studio)* Becky Davies, *Editorial Director (Fiction Studio)* Lauren Ace

Children's books: board books, novelty board books, picture books, activity books, children's fiction, YA fiction and non-fiction. Founded 1987.

Little Toller Books

Pineapple Lane, Bridport, Dorset DT6 5HZ
email adrian@littletoller.co.uk
website www.littletoller.co.uk
Facebook www.facebook.com/littletoller
X @littletoller

A family-run publisher of non-fiction about place, nature and culture. Publisher of the *Nature Classics* series. Also publishes the online journal *The Clearing*. Founded 2008.

Liverpool University Press‡

4 Cambridge Street, Liverpool L69 7ZU
tel 0151 794 2233
email lup@liv.ac.uk
website www.liverpooluniversitypress.co.uk
Bluesky @livunipress.bsky.social
Chief Executive Anthony Cond

Publishes approx. 200 books a year and 50 journals, specialising in modern languages, history, literary studies and earth sciences. Founded 1899.

Logaston Press

The Holme, Church Road, Eardisley, Herefordshire HR3 6NJ
tel (01544) 327182
email info@logastonpress.co.uk
website www.logastonpress.co.uk
X @LogastonPress
Proprietors Richard Wheeler, Su Wheeler

History, social history, archaeology and guides to Herefordshire, Worcestershire, Shropshire, rural West Midlands and Mid-Wales. Welcomes submission of ideas relevant to this geographical area: send synopsis first. Founded 1985.

LOM ART

16 Lion Yard, Tremadoc Road, London SW4 7NQ
tel 020-7720 8643
email enquiries@mombooks.com
website www.mombooks.com/lom
Facebook www.facebook.com/MichaelOMaraBooks
X @OMaraBooks
Managing Director Lesley O'Mara

Illustrated non-fiction for children and adults. Publishes approx. ten titles a year. Submissions including sae will be returned by post. Imprint of Michael O'Mara Books. Founded 2015.

Lonely Planet Publications

2nd Floor, 186 City Road, London, EC1V 2NT
email recruiting_contributors@lonelyplanet.com
website www.lonelyplanet.com
Facebook www.facebook.com/lonelyplanet
X @lonelyplanet
Instagram @lonelyplanet
Ceo Luis Cabrera

A travel media company. Publishes 900 titles in 14 languages in over 150 countries. Offices in USA, UK, Australia, Ireland, India and China. Founded 1973.

Loudhailer Books

13 Lyminster Avenue, Brighton BN1 8JL
tel 01273 921569
email info@loudhailerbooks.com
website www.loudhailerbooks.com
Facebook www.facebook.com/loudhailerbooks
X @LoudhailerBooks
Instagram @loudhailerbooks
Publisher David Haviland

Fiction, non-fiction and poetry. Accepts submissions from authors, either directly or via a literary agent. For fiction, send a synopsis and the first three chapters. For non-fiction, send a brief proposal including a synopsis, author profile and sample material. Founded 2009.

Luath Press*‡

543/2 Castlehill, The Royal Mile, Edinburgh EH1 2ND
tel 0131 225 4326
email gavin.macdougall@luath.co.uk
website www.luath.co.uk
Facebook www.facebook.com/LuathPress
X @LuathPress
Instagram @luathpress
Director Gavin MacDougall

Modern fiction, history, travel guides, art, poetry, politics and humour in English, Scots and Scottish Gaelic. Over 800 titles in print, mostly with a Scottish connection. Submission guidelines: see website. Founded 1981.

Lucent Dreaming‡

103 Bute Street, Cardiff CF10 5AD
email dreaminglucent@gmail.com
website https://lucentdreaming.com/
Facebook www.facebook.com/LucentDreaming
X @LucentDreaming
Instagram @lucentdreaming
Co-founder & Director Jannat Ahmed, *Fictional Editor* Samiha Meah

Book and magazine publisher. Publishes poetry collections, novels and anthologies. Founded 2017.

Lume Books – see Joffe Books

Luna Press Publishing*

149/4 Morrison Street, Edinburgh EH3 8AG
email lunapress@outlook.com
website www.lunapresspublishing.com
Facebook www.facebook.com/lunapress8
Director Francesca Barbini

Fantasy, dark fantasy and sci-fi (no children's) in fiction and academia. Fiction: novels, novellas, graphic novels, collections and anthologies. Academia

Books

Lunare is the non-fiction, academic branch, dealing with sci-fi and fantasy and non-genre. Publication comes through academic papers, proceedings, calls for papers and PhDs. Non-fiction non-genre by invite only. Now running regular open submission days – check website for details. Submissions email: submissionsluna@outlook.com. Founded 2015.

Lund Humphries‡

Second Home Spitalfields, 68–80 Hanbury Street, London E1 5JL
email info@lundhumphries.com
website www.lundhumphries.com
Facebook www.facebook.com/LHArtBooks
X @LHArtBooks
Instagram @lhartbooks
Managing Director Lucy Myers

Independent publishing imprint of quality art and architecture books. Founded 1895.

Lurid Editions

email contact@lurideditions.com
website www.lurideditions.com
Instagram @lurid_editions
Director D.M. Withers

Queer literature from the 20th and 21st centuries. Founded 2022.

The Lutterworth Press

PO Box 60, Cambridge CB1 2NT
tel (01223) 350865
email publishing@lutterworth.com
website www.lutterworth.com, www.lutterworthpress.wordpress.com
Facebook www.facebook.com/JamesClarkeandCo
X @LuttPress
Instagram @luttpress
Managing Director Adrian Brink

Independent publisher, originally founded as the Religious Tract Society and publisher of *The Boy's Own Paper* and *The Girl's Own Paper*. Now a publisher of educational and adult non-fiction including: history, biography, literature and criticism, science, philosophy, art and art history, biblical studies, theology, mission, religious studies and collecting. Imprints: Acorn Editions, James Clarke & Co (page 130) and Patrick Hardy Books. Founded 1799.

Mabecron Books

3 Briston Orchard, St Mellion, Saltash, Cornwall PL12 6RQ
tel (01579) 350885
email ronjohns@mabecronbooks.co.uk
website www.mabecronbooks.co.uk
X @mabecronbooks

Children's picture books and books with a Cornish or West Country subject. Linked to bookshops in Falmouth, St Ives and Padstow. Founded 1998.

McGraw-Hill Education*

email emea_schools_intl@mheducation.com
website www.mheducation.co.uk
Facebook www.facebook.com/mheducationemea
X @mhe_emea

Educational publisher and digital solution provider for primary and secondary education in English language arts, maths, science and other subject areas, including intervention and learning support. Founded 1988.

MACK

Studios E + B, Emperor House, Dragonfly Place, London SE4 2FL
020-7442 2190
email info@mackbooks.co.uk
website https://mackbooks.co.uk/
Facebook www.facebook.com/mackpublishing
Instagram @mack_publishing
Founder Michael Mack, *Commissioning Editor* Louis Rogers

Independent publisher of award-winning books on contemporary art, critical theory, film, and architecture. Submissions window open three times a year, for visual arts projects, text-based books, and architecture books. Founded 2010.

Macmillan Education – see Springer Nature

McNidder & Grace*

Market Place, Jedburgh Scotland TD8 6AP
tel 07788 219370
website https://mcnidderandgrace.com/
Publishing Director Caroline Peden Smith, *Publisher* Andrew Peden Smith

Non-fiction and fiction titles for adults. With a particular emphasis on popular culture, the non-fiction list includes books on photography, art, music, biography, history, country pursuits and, more recently, health and wellbeing in partnership with BBC Radio 2's Janey Lee Grace. Publishes the *Railway Journeys in Art Poster to Poster* series in collaboration with the National Railway Museum and Swann Galleries, New York. Fiction list consists mainly of crime and thrillers, including *Torquil MacLeod Malmö* series. Founded 2011.

Major Books

UCL Base KX, 103c Camley Street, London N1C 4PF
email contact@major-books.com
website https://major-books.com/
Instagram @majorbooks.uk
Founders Pascal Nguyen, Kim Tran

Independent press translating Vietnamese literature into English. Titles span from national classics to contemporary writing. Founded 2024.

Management Books 2000

36 Western Road, Oxford OX1 4LG
tel (01865) 600738

website www.mb2000.com
Directors N. Dale-Harris, R. Hartman

Practical books for working managers and business professionals: management, business and life skills, and sponsored titles. Unsolicited MSS, synopses and ideas for books welcome. Founded 1993.

Manchester University Press‡

176 Waterloo Place, Oxford Road,
Manchester M13 9GP
email mup@manchester.ac.uk
website www.manchesteruniversitypress.co.uk
X @manchesterup
Bluesky @manchesterup.bsky.social
Instagram @manchester_university_press
Chief Executive Simon Ross

Non-fiction: history, literary criticism, popular culture, politics, global affairs, economics and art history. Works of academic scholarship: anthropology, archaeology and heritage, art, architecture and visual culture, economics and business, film, media and music, history, human geography, international relations, law, literature and theatre, methods and guides, philosophy and critical theory, politics, religion and sociology. Textbooks and monographs. Subscription and Open Access journals. Founded 1904.

Mandrake of Oxford

PO Box 250, Oxford OX1 1AP
tel (01865) 243671
email mandrake@mandrake.uk.net
website www.mandrake.uk.net
Director Mogg Morgan

Art, biography, classic crime studies, fiction, Indology, magic, witchcraft, philosophy and religion. Query letters only. Founded 1986.

Mango Books

18 Soho Square, London W1D 3QL
tel 020-7060 4142
email adam@mangobooks.co.uk
website www.mangobooks.co.uk

Non-fiction for lovers of crime, detection and mystery. Imprints: Blue Lamp Books and Little Wing. Founded 2017.

Manilla Press*

Victoria House, Bloomsbury Square,
London WC1B 4DA
tel 020-3770 8888
email hello@bonnierbooks.co.uk
website www.bonnierbooks.co.uk/imprints/manilla-press
Instagram @manilla_press
Publishers Margaret Stead, Sophie Orme

Boutique literary imprint of fiction and non-fiction. The imprint is named after Nedre Manilla: the Bonnier family home on the outskirts of Stockholm. An imprint of Bonnier Books UK. Founded 2020.

Mantra Lingua

Global House, 303 Ballards Lane, London N12 8NP
tel 020-8445 5123
email info@mantralingua.com
website https://uk.mantralingua.com/
Facebook www.facebook.com/Mantralingua
X @mantralingua
Managing Director Robene Dutta

Bilingual picture books and educational resources for UK, US, Swedish and German audiences. Looking for illustrators with ability to draw racially diverse faces and authors and storytellers with ability to interpret or imagine modern city lives. Commission and royalty-based relationships with print runs covering between ten and 15 language editions. Founded 2002.

Maverick House†

Unit 33, The Business Centre,
Stadium Business Park, Ballycoolin Road,
Dublin D11 HY40, Republic of Ireland
email info@maverickhouse.com
website www.maverickhouse.com
Facebook www.facebook.com/maverickhouse
X @maverickhouse
Instagram @maverickhouse
Managing Director Jean Harrington

Publishes socially and politically relevant non-fiction books. Publishes books on true-crime, terrorism, sport, memoirs, biographies and environmental issues. Founded 2002.

Kevin Mayhew

Fengate Farm, Rattlesden, Suffolk IP30 0SZ
tel (01284) 374495
email info@kevinmayhew.com
website www.kevinmayhew.com
Facebook www.facebook.com/KevinMayhewPublishers
X @kevinmayhew
Director Barbara Mayhew

Christianity: prayer and spirituality, pastoral care, preaching, liturgy worship, children's, youth work, drama, instant art and education. Music: hymns, organ and choral, contemporary worship, tutors, piano and instrumental. Submissions guidelines on website. Founded 1976.

Medina Publishing

50 High Street, Cowes, Isle of Wight PO31 7RR
tel (01983) 300044
email info@medinapublishing.com
website www.medinapublishing.com
Facebook www.facebook.com/medinabooks
Instagram @medinapublishing
Director Peter Harrigan

An independent publisher based on the Isle of Wight. Publishes a diverse range of academic and trade books on social, political and cultural topics. Founded 2008.

Arabian Publishing
email info@arabian-publishing.com

Dedicated to producing engaging titles on the Arabian Peninsula.

Mensch Publishing
51 Northchurch Road, London N1 4EE
tel 07793 264455
website www.menschpublishing.com
Publisher Richard Charkin

Books for the general reader. Founded 2018.

Mentor Books
43 Furze Road, Sandyford Industrial Estate, Dublin D18 PN30, Republic of Ireland
tel +353 (0)1 295 2112
email admin@mentorbooks.ie
website www.mentorbooks.ie

General: non-fiction, humour, biographies, politics, crime, history and guidebooks. Educational (secondary): languages, history, geography, business, maths and sciences. No unsolicited MSS. Founded 1979.

The Mercier Press†
82 Ballyhooley Road, St Lukes, Cork T23 Y3V2, Republic of Ireland
email info@mercierpress.ie
website www.mercierpress.ie
Facebook www.facebook.com/MercierPress
X @MercierBooks
General Manager Mary Feehan

Irish literature, folklore, history and politics; humour; academic and current affairs; health; mind, body & spirit; general non-fiction; and children's. Founded 1944.

Merlin Press
Central Books Building, Freshwater Road, London RM8 1RX
tel 020-8590 9700, 020-8590 9700
email info@merlinpress.co.uk
website www.merlinpress.co.uk
Managing Director Anthony Zurbrugg

Radical history and social studies. Letters/synopses only. Founded 1957.

Green Print
Green politics and the environment.

Merrell Publishers
70 Cowcross Street, London EC1M 6EJ
email hugh.merrell@merrellpublishers.com
website www.merrellpublishers.com
Publisher Hugh Merrell

Illustrated books on all aspects of visual culture, including art, architecture, photography, garden design, interior design, product design and books specially developed for institutions, foundations, corporations and private collectors. Unsolicited carefully prepared proposals welcomed via email. Founded 1989.

Metro Publications‡
Flat B, 24 Ainsworth Road, London E9 7LP
tel 020-8533 7777
email info@metropublications.com
website www.metropublications.com
X @metrolondon
Instagram @metropublications

London guidebooks. Founded 2007.

Mills & Boon – see Harlequin UK

Milo Books
The Old Weighbridge, Station Rd, Wrea Green, Preston, Lancs. PR4 2PHY
tel (01772) 672900
email info@milobooks.com
website www.milobooks.com
Publisher Peter Walsh

True crime, sport and current affairs. Founded 1997.

Mirror Books
One Canada Square, Canary Wharf, London E14 5AP
tel 020-7293 3740
email mirrorbooks@reachplc.com
website www.mirrorbooks.co.uk
Facebook www.facebook.com/mirrorbooksuk
X @themirrorbooks
Instagram @mirror.books
Managing Director Steve Hanrahan

Non-fiction: memoir, crime, nostalgia, personalities and celebrities. Accepts submissions online: mirrorbooks.co.uk/pages/submissions. Founded 2016.

Mitchell Beazley – see Octopus Publishing Group

Moonflower‡
Unit 303, The Pill Box, 115 Coventry Road, London E2 6GH
tel 020-8054 8111
email hello@moonflowerbooks.co.uk
website www.moonflowerbooks.co.uk
X @moonflowerbooks
Instagram @moonflower_books
Managing Director Jack Jewers, *Publisher* Christi Daugherty, *Editorial & Communications Director* Emma Warin

Independent publisher of commercial fiction. Adult fiction: crime, women's, historical, fantasy and thrillers. For submissions guidelines see website. Founded 2020.

Morrigan Book Company/City of Dublin Press

email morriganbooks@gmail.com
website http://conankennedy.com/
Publishers Gerry Kennedy, Hilary Kennedy

Non-fiction: general Irish interest, biography, history, local history, folklore and mythology. Morrigan Book Company founded 1979. City of Dublin Press founded 1982.

Mud Pie

Leckford Road, Oxford OX2 6HY
tel 07985 935320
email info@mudpiebooks.com
website www.mudpiebooks.com
Facebook www.facebook.com/Mud-Pie-Books-665982096919314
X @mudpiebooks
Founder & Director Tony Morris

An independent specialist online publisher of Buddhist writing, Buddhist blogs and books. Founded 2016.

Muddy Pearl*

email books@muddypearl.com
website https://muddypearl.com/
Facebook www.facebook.com/muddypearl
X @muddypearlbooks
Instagram @muddypearlbooks
Director Richard Heald, *Publishing Director* Stephanie Heald

An independent publisher of Christian books based in Edinburgh. Topics include: family, work, technology, love, loss, belief and faith. Founded 2013.

Murdoch Books‡

Ormond House, 26–27 Boswell Street, London WC1N 3JZ
tel 020-8785 5995
email info@murdochbooks.co.uk
website www.murdochbooks.co.uk
X @murdochbooksuk
Instagram @murdockbooks_uk
Publisher (UK) Céline Hughes

Non-fiction: cookery, homes and interiors, gardening, self-help, environment, physical and mental wellbeing. Owned by Australian publisher Allen & Unwin. Founded 1991.

John Murray Group*

Carmelite House, 50 Victoria Embankment, London EC4Y 0DZ
tel 020-3122 6777
website www.johnmurraypress.co.uk
Facebook www.facebook.com/johnmurraybooks
X @johnmurraypress
Managing Director Nick Davies

No unsolicited MSS without preliminary letter. Part of Hachette UK. Divisions include Dialogue (page 135) and Quercus Publishing (page 172). Founded 1768.

Basic Books

Publishing Director Joe Zigmond

History, biography, science, current affairs, philosophy and economics.

Jessica Kingsley Publishers

Managing Director Sanphy Thomas

Autism and neurodiversity, gender diversity and sexuality, inclusive teaching and learning, mental health, counselling and other therapies, social care and health professions. The Singing Dragon imprint includes books on alternative health and wellbeing as well as the Handspring list.

John Murray

Executive Publisher (Baskerville, Dialogue, John Murray, John Murray One) Jocasta Hamilton

Quality literary fiction and non-fiction: science, business, travel, history, reference, biography and memoir. The JM Originals imprint publishes distinctive new voices.

John Murray Business

Editorial Director Holly Bennion

Coaching and leadership, personal development and popular psychology, smart thinking, business, finance and economics.

John Murray Languages

Head of Digital Learning Claire Lipscomb

Home to learning brands including Teach Yourself, Michel Thomas language courses, and Brewers and Chambers reference.

John Murray One

Publishing Director Iain Campbell

Self-help, popular psychology and health; wealth; lifestyle; and mind, body & spirit.

Sheldon Press

Editorial Director Victoria Roddam

Imprint of John Murray Learning. Physical and mental health, parenting, psychology and emotional wellbeing.

Muswell Press‡

72 Cromwell Avenue, London N6 5HQ
email team@muswell-press.co.uk
website www.muswell-press.co.uk
Facebook www.facebook.com/MuswellPress/
X @MuswellPress
Instagram @muswellpress
Directors Kate Beal, Sarah Beal, *Editor-at-Large* Matt Bates

Independent publisher of contemporary fiction, crime, biography and travel. The queer list republishes forgotten gay classics. Founded 2008.

Myriad Editions‡

59 Lansdowne Place, Brighton BN3 1FL
email info@myriadeditions.com
website www.myriadeditions.com
Facebook www.facebook.com/myriadeditionspublishers
X @MyriadEditions
Instagram @myriad_editions

Independent publisher of literary fiction, crime written by women, graphic novels and feminist non-fiction. Merged with New Internationalist in 2017 as part of a joint plan to expand and embrace diversity. Founded 1993.

Natural History Museum Publishing

Cromwell Road, London SW7 5BD
tel 020-7942 5336
email publishing@nhm.ac.uk
website www.nhm.ac.uk/publishing
Head of Publishing Colin Ziegler

Natural history, life sciences, earth sciences, wildlife photography, art of natural history and books for children. Founded 1881.

Neem Tree Press

95A Ridgmount Gardens, London WC1E 7AZ
tel 020-7993 5581
website www.neemtreepress.com
Facebook www.facebook.com/neemtreepress
X @neemtreepress
Instagram @neemtreepress
Ceo & Publisher Archna Sharma, *Coo* Alison Savage, *Senior Editor* Cecilia Bennett

Fiction, non-fiction and children's and YA books including translation and short stories. See website for submission guidelines. Imprint of Boundless. Founded 2013.

New Island Books†

10 Richview Office Park, Clonskeagh, Dublin D14 V8C4, Republic of Ireland
tel +353 (0)1 278 4225
email info@newisland.ie
website www.newisland.ie
Facebook www.facebook.com/NewIslandBooks
X @NewIslandBooks
Publisher Djinn von Noorden, *Managing Director* Mariel Deegan, *Commissioning Editor* Aoife K. Walsh

Fiction, poetry, drama, humour, biography, current affairs, history and memoir/personal essay. Unsolicited submissions during open call only. See social media platforms for notice of open submission call. Founded 1992.

The New Menard Press

tel 07831 051453
email info@thenewmenardpress.com
website www.thenewmenardpress.com
Facebook www.facebook.com/TheNewMenardPress
X @thenewmenardpress
Instagram @thenew_menardpress
Managing Director Elte Rausch, *Marketing & Publicity* Alexander Spears

The Menard Press began as a magazine founded by Anthony Rudolf in 1969 and published its first chapbook in 1971. Before it closed in 2009, it published more than 150 titles. The New Menard Press is the UK imprint of indie-press HetMoet. Founded 2018.

New Welsh Rarebyte

PO Box 170, Aberystwyth, Ceredigion SY23 1WZ
tel (01970) 628410
website www.newwelshreview.com
Facebook www.facebook.com/NewWelshReview
X @newwelshreview
Instagram @newwelshreview
Editor Gwen Davies

Publish prize-winners from the annual New Welsh Writing Awards, the writer development initiative run by New Welsh Review since 2015, which seeks prose works of 5,000–30,000 words on a different theme each year. See *New Welsh Reader* (page 68) or website for more information. Founded 2015.

Nine Arches Press

Studio 221, Zellig Gibb Street, Deritend, Birmingham B9 4AT
email mail@ninearchespress.com
website www.ninearchespress.com
X @NineArchesPress
Instagram @ninearchespress
Editorial Director Jane Commane

Independent publisher of poetry. Founded 2008.

Nine Pens

email poetsdirectory@gmail.com
website www.ninepens.co.uk
X @nine_pens
Editor Colin Bancroft

A small poetry press based in the North Pennines. Provides opportunities for new and emerging poets to get their work into print through pamphlet series and Nine Series anthologies. Founded 2020.

Nobrow – see Flying Eye Books

No Exit Press – see Bedford Square Publishers

Nordisk Books

81 Harbour Street, Whitstable CT5 1AE
tel 07437 202582
email info@nordiskbooks.com
website www.nordiskbooks.com
Facebook www.facebook.com/nordiskbooks
X @nordiskbooks
Instagram @nordisk_books
Director Duncan J. Lewis

Books

Modern and contemporary fiction from the Nordic countries. Publishes a wide range of literary titles from across the Scandinavian peninsular and beyond. No crime. Founded 2016.

Northodox Press

8 Maiden Greve, Malton YO17 7BE
email submissions@northodox.co.uk
website www.northodox.co.uk
Facebook www.facebook.com/northodoxpress
X @northodoxpress
Instagram @northodoxpressofficial
Contacts James Keane, Ted O'Connor, Amy Leacy

Represents authentic northern voices and caters to readers of literary and genre fiction. Genres: literary, sci-fi, fantasy, historical and YA/middle-grade fiction. Publishes authors born or living in the north of England (Cheshire, Cumbria, County Durham, Greater Manchester, Lancashire, Merseyside, Northumberland, Tyne & Wear and Yorkshire). See website for submissions guidelines. Part of the Northern Fiction Alliance. Founded 2020.

W.W. Norton & Co.‡

15 Carlisle Street, London W1D 3BS
tel 020-7323 1579
email Crussell1@wwnorton.com
website www.wwnorton.co.uk
X @wwnortonuk
Instagram @wwnortonuk
Managing Director John Donovan

English and American literature, economics, music, psychology, science, politics and current affairs, biography and memoir, food and drink, technology, history, arts, lifestyle. Founded 1980.

Nosy Crow*‡

Wheat Wharf, 27A Shad Thames, London SE1 2XZ
tel 020-7089 7575
email hello@nosycrow.com
website www.nosycrow.com
Facebook www.facebook.com/NosyCrow
X @nosycrow
Instagram @nosycrow
Group Ceo Kate Wilson, *Publishing Directors* Kirsty Stanfield (fiction), Louise Bolongaro (picture books), Rachel Kellehar (non-fiction, preschool & activity)

Independent publisher of child-focused, parent-friendly children's books. Publishes in partnership with The National Trust and The British Museum. Founded 2010.

Nourish Books

Unit 11, Shepperton House, 89 Shepperton Road, London N1 3DF
tel 020-3813 6940
email enquiries@watkinspublishing.com
website https://nourishbooks.com/
Facebook www.facebook.com/nourishbooks
X @nourishbooks

A modern cookery list with a focus on cookery from authentic dishes to ethical recipes. Part of Watkins Media. Watkins Media, founded 1893.

Oak Tree Press†

Suite 309, NSC Campus, Mahon, Cork T12 XY2N, Republic of Ireland
tel +353 (0)21 230 7022
email info@oaktreepress.com
website https://oaktreepress.ie/
Directors Axel Neefs, Pierre Delroisse, *Publisher* Brian O'Kane

Business management, enterprise, law, accountancy and finance. Special emphasis on titles for small business owner/managers. Now part of Corporate Group, Brussels. Founded 1991.

Nubooks

Ebooks.

The O'Brien Press†

12 Terenure Road East, Rathgar, Dublin D06 HD27, Republic of Ireland
tel +353 (0)1 492 3333
email books@obrien.ie
website obrien.ie
Facebook www.facebook.com/TheOBrienPress
Bluesky @theobrienpress.bsky.social
Instagram @theobrienpress
Directors Ivan O'Brien, Kunak McGann

Adult: biography, politics, history, travel, food, drink, sport, humour and reference. No poetry or academic. Children: illustrated fiction (ages 3+, 5+, 6+, 8+) and also novels (10+ and YA) in the genres of contemporary, historical and fantasy. Also publishes children's non-fiction. Unsolicited MSS (sample chapters only), synopses and ideas for books welcome. Submissions will not be returned. Further information on website. Founded 1974.

Ockham Publishing Group‡

Bishop's Court, 29 Albyn Place, Aberdeen AB10 1YL
email info@ockham-publishing.com
website www.ockham-publishing.com
Facebook www.facebook.com/ockhampublishing
X @vulpine_press
Instagram @vulpine_press
Publisher Rob Johnson, *Editorial Director* Sarah Hembrow

Publishes various books for the popular market across four imprints. Founded 2015.

Hypatia Press

Publisher David G McAfee

Irreligious and atheist titles.

Level Up Publishing

Publisher Conor Kostick

LitRPG and GameLit titles.

Ockham Publishing
Publisher Rob Johnson
Popular science and popular philosophy.

Vulpine Press
Publisher Sarah Hembrow
Fiction and non-fiction.

Octopus Publishing Group*
Carmelite House, 50 Victoria Embankment, London EC4Y 0DZ
tel 020-3122 6000
email info@octopusbooks.co.uk
email publisher@octopusbooks.co.uk (submissions)
website www.octopusbooks.co.uk
Managing Director Anna Bond

Part of Hachette UK. Imprints below, also Summersdale Publishers (page 180) and Kyle Books (page 154). Founded 1998.

Aster
Publisher Stephanie Jackson
Food, drink, wellbeing and lifestyle.

Brazen
Publisher Romily Morgan
Non-fiction and fiction.

Cassell
Publisher Trevor Davies
Popular culture, sport, music, pets and gift/humour.

Conran Octopus
Publisher Alison Starling
Illustrated books, particularly lifestyle, cookery and gardening.

Gaia Books
Publisher Stephanie Jackson
Nature and country life.

Godsfield Press
email publisher@godsfieldpress.com
Publisher Stephane Jackson
Mind, body & spirit.

Hamlyn
Publisher Stephanie Jackson
Food, drink, home, garden, health and parenting.

Ilex
Publisher Alison Starling
Illustrated books on practical art, photography, craft and books exploring visual culture.

Mitchell Beazley
Publisher Alison Starling
Quality illustrated books on food and drink, home and garden, the outdoors, fashion and design.

Monoray
Publisher Jake Lingwood
Memoir, current affairs, music, modern history, health and big ideas.

Philip's
email publisher@philips-maps.co.uk
Publishing Director Sarah Bailey
Atlases, maps and astronomy.

Pyramid
email bountybooksinfo-bp@bountybooks.co.uk
Group Custom Publisher Lucy Pessell
Mind, body & spirit; gift and humour; cookery; craft and reference.

Radar
Publisher Briony Gowlett
Popular culture.

Short Books
Publisher Joanna Copestick
Popular non-fiction.

Offord Books
6A Norman Road, Hove BN3 4LS
email offordbooks@gmail.com
website www.offordroadbooks.co.uk
Facebook www.facebook.com/offordbooks
X @offordbooks
Editor Martha Sprackland

Publishers of poetry books and pamphlets that have won or been shortlisted for accolades including the Ledbury Forte Award, the Forward Prize for Best First Collection and the T.S. Eliot Prize. Founded 2017.

Old Barn Books*‡
Warren Barn, Bedham Lane, Fittleworth, West Sussex RH20 1JW
email ruth@oldbarnbooks.com
website www.oldbarnbooks.com
Facebook www.facebook.com/oldbarnbooks
X @oldbarnbooks
Instagram @oldbarnbooks

Independent publisher of picture books, gift books and teen and YA fiction. Interested in the natural world and promoting empathy. No unsolicited submissions. Founded 2015.

Old Pond Publishing
20–22 Wenlock Road, London N1 7GU
email info@foxchapelpublishing.co.uk
website www.foxchapelpublishing.co.uk

Specialist publisher of agriculture, trucking, machinery and practical farming books. Owned by Fox Chapel Publishers International. Founded 1997.

The Oleander Press
16 Orchard Street, Cambridge CB1 1JT
tel (01638) 500784
website www.oleanderpress.com
Managing Director Dr Jane Doyle

Travel, language, crime, general fiction, history, reference and classics. No unsolicited MSS. Founded 1960.

Michael O'Mara Books*‡

16 Lion Yard, Tremadoc Road, London SW4 7NQ
tel 020-7720 8643
email enquiries@mombooks.com
email publicity@mombooks.com
website www.mombooks.com
Facebook www.facebook.com/MichaelOMaraBooks
X @OMaraBooks
Instagram @omarabooks
Chairman Michael O'Mara, *Managing Director* Lesley O'Mara

General non-fiction: biography, autobiography, history, lifestyle and humour. See website for submission guidelines. Imprints: Buster Books, LOM ART (page 157), O'Mara Books. Founded 1985.

Buster Books

website www.mombooks.com/buster
Facebook www.facebook.com/BusterBooks
X @BusterBooks
Instagram @buster_books

Activity, novelty, picture books, fiction and non-fiction for children.

O'Mara Books

Inspiring and creative adult non-fiction.

Omnibus Press/Wise Music Group

14–15 Berners Street, London W1T 3LJ
tel 020-3929 9047
email david.barraclough@wisemusic.com
website https://omnibuspress.com/
X @omnibuspress
Chief Editor David Barraclough

Music biographies, autobiographies, illustrated books and books about music. Founded 1976.

On Stream Publications

Currabaha, Cloghroe, Blarney, Cork T23 EW08, Republic of Ireland
tel +353 (0)21 438 5798
email info@onstream.ie
website www.onstream.ie
Owner Rosalind Crowley

Cookery, wine, travel, human interest non-fiction, local history, academic and practical books. Founded 1986.

Oneworld Publications*

10 Bloomsbury Street, London WC1B 3SR
tel 020-7307 8900
email info@oneworld-publications.com
website www.oneworld-publications.com
Facebook www.facebook.com/oneworldpublications
X @OneworldNews, @PointBlankCrime, @RocktheBoatNews
Instagram @oneworldpublications, @rocktheboatnews
Directors & Publishers Juliet Mabey, Novin Dootstdar

Fiction and general non-fiction: current affairs, politics, history, Middle East, popular science, philosophy, psychology, green issues, world religions and Islamic studies; literary fiction with a focus on diverse voices and great stories, upmarket book club fiction, crime/suspense novels and fiction in translation, plus children's and YA fiction. No unsolicited fiction MSS; email or send non-fiction proposals via website. Imprints: Magpie, Point Blank Crime and Rock the Boat. Founded 1986.

Orbit – see Little, Brown Book Group

Orenda Books

16 Carson Road, West Dulwich, London SE21 8HU
tel 020-8355 4643
email info@orendabooks.co.uk
website www.orendabooks.co.uk
Facebook www.facebook.com/orendabooks
X @OrendaBooks
Instagram @orendabooks
Publisher Karen Sullivan, *Editorial Director* West Camel

Award-winning independent publisher specialising in literary fiction, with a heavy emphasis on crime thrillers, about half in translation. Founded 2014.

Open Borders Press

Publisher Christopher MacLehose

Literary fiction and non-fiction in translation, launched 2024.

The Orion Publishing Group*

Carmelite House, 50 Victoria Embankment, London EC4Y 0DZ
tel 020-3122 6444
website www.orionbooks.co.uk
Managing Director Anna Valentine

No unsolicited MSS; approach in writing in first instance. Imprints listed below. See also Laurence King Publishing (page 154). Part of Hachette UK. Founded 1992.

Gollancz

Sci-fi, fantasy and horror.

Orion Audio

Senior Audio Manager Paul Stark

Adult fiction and non-fiction.

Orion Dash

Digital-first commercial imprint of the Orion Publishing Group.

Orion Fiction

Trade and mass market fiction.

Orion Ignite

Non-fiction in the areas of smart-thinking, self-improvement, psychology, business and business narrative, finance, economics, health and life-optimisation.

Orion Spring
Wellbeing, health and lifestyle non-fiction.

Phoenix
Literary fiction and memoir.

Seven Dials
Trade and mass market: cookery, memoir and autobiography, gift and humour, personal development and parenting, lifestyle, diet and fitness.

SF Gateway
Classic sci-fi, crime and horror.

Trapeze
Trade and mass market fiction: reading group, crime and thriller, women's fiction. Trade and mass market non-fiction: memoir and autobiography, lifestyle, gift and humour, popular psychology and entertainment.

Weidenfeld & Nicholson
Literary and translated fiction. Non-fiction: history, memoir, ideas-driven books, popular science, biography, sport, business, diaries and narrative non-fiction.

White Rabbit
Music: memoir, history, fiction and limited editions.

Orphans Publishing
3 Arrow Close, Leominster Enterprise Park, Leominster, Herefordshire HR6 0LD
email books@orphanspublishing.co.uk
website www.orphanspublishing.co.uk
Facebook www.facebook.com/orphanspublishing
Instagram @orphanspublishing

An independent, family-run publisher of non-fiction including infographics books, illustrated gardening histories, biographies and memoirs. To submit, please send synopsis and letter introducing yourself. Founded 2015.

Ortac Press‡
1 Cumberland Gardens, London WC1X 9AF
email hello@ortacpress.com
website www.ortacpress.com
Bluesky @ortacpress.bsky.social
Instagram @ortacpress
Managing Director & Publisher Henry Rowley

Publishes non-fiction and novels on art, culture, music and social science. See website for submission guidelines. Founded 2021.

Osprey Publishing*
Kemp House, Chawley Park, Cumnor Hill, Oxford OX2 9PH
tel 020-7631 5600
email info@ospreypublishing.com
website https://ospreypublishing.com/
Facebook www.facebook.com/ospreypublishing
X @OspreyBooks
Instagram @ospreypublishing
Editorial Director Marcus Cowper

Military history with 3,000 titles in print on a wide range of military history subjects from ancient times to the modern day. Owned by Bloomsbury Publishing. Founded 1968.

Out-Spoken Press
PO Box 74744, London N11 9FG
email press@outspokenldn.com
website www.outspokenldn.com
X @outspoken_press
Instagram @outspoken_press
Editor Anthony Anaxagorou

Independent publisher of poetry and critical writing. Provides a platform for compelling writing from voices under-represented in mainstream publishing. Founded 2015.

Oversteps Books
6 Halwell House, South Pool, Nr Kingsbridge, Devon TQ7 2RX
tel (01548) 531969
email alwynmarriage@overstepsbooks.com
website www.overstepsbooks.com
Director & Managing Editor Alwyn Marriage

Poetry. Check website for submission windows and details of how to submit. Poems must be either major competition winners or previously published. Founded 1992.

Oxford University Press*
Great Clarendon Street, Oxford OX2 6DP
tel (01865) 556767
email enquiry@oup.com
website https://corp.oup.com/
Facebook www.facebook.com/OUPAcademic
X @OxUniPress
Instagram @oxunipress
Ceo Nigel Portwood

Archaeology, architecture, art, bibles, bibliography, children's books (fiction, non-fiction and picture books), commerce, current affairs, dictionaries, drama, economics, educational (foundation, primary, secondary, technical and university), encyclopaedias, ELT, essays, foreign language learning, general history, hymn and service books, journals, law, medical, music, philosophy, political economy, prayer books, reference, science, sociology, theology and religion. Also publishers of the *Grove Dictionaries of Music & Art*. Founded 1478.

P&H Books
email info@poniesandhorsesbooks.com
website www.poniesandhorsesbooks.com
Publisher Rob Westwood

Independent publisher founded as Ponies and Horses Books. Fiction and non-fiction. Genres: comedy, literary, satire, biography, memoir and essays. Founded 2014.

Palgrave Macmillan – see Springer Nature

Pan Macmillan*
6 Briset Street, Farringdon, London EC1M 5NR
tel 020-7038 5000
email publicity@macmillan.com
website www.panmacmillan.com
Facebook ww.facebook.com/panmacmillanbooks
X @panmacmillan
Ceo Joanna Prior

Novels, literary, crime, thrillers, romance, sci-fi, fantasy and horror, autobiography, biography, business, gift books, health and beauty, history, humour, natural history, travel, philosophy, politics, world affairs, theatre, film, gardening, cookery and popular reference. Founded 1843.

Bluebird
Non-fiction: personal development, environment, inspirational memoir, parenting, cookery, feminism and creativity.

Campbell
Early learning, pop-up, novelty and board books for the preschool market.

Kingfisher
Children's illustrated non-fiction.

Macmillan
Hardback fiction and non-fiction.

Macmillan Audio
Audio.

Macmillan Business
Business.

Macmillan Children's Books
Children's books.

Macmillan Collector's Library
Fiction classics in high-quality binding. Non-fiction: poetry, short stories and children's books.

Mantle
Fiction: crime, thriller, general and literary. Non-fiction: narrative non-fiction and memoir.

One Boat
Non-fiction: climate change and environmental issues.

Pan
Commercial fiction and non-fiction.

Picador
Literary international fiction, non-fiction and poetry.

Tor
website https://torpublishinggroup.com/imprints/tor-books/
Facebook www.facebook.com/torbooks
X @torbooks
Instagram @torbooks
Sci-fi and fantasy.

Two Hoots
Illustrated children's books.

Parthian Books
The Old Surgery, Napier Street, Cardigan SA43 1ED
email info@parthianbooks.com
website www.parthianbooks.com
Facebook www.facebook.com/parthianbooks
X @parthianbooks
Bluesky @parthianbooks.bsky.social
Instagram @parthian_books
Publishing Editor Susie Wildsmith

Independent publisher of poetry, literary fiction, creative non-fiction and translations that reflect a diverse and contemporary Wales and wider world. See website for submission opportunities and guidelines. Founded 1993.

Pavilion Books – see HarperCollins Publishers

Pavilion Poetry
Liverpool University Press, 4 Cambridge Street, Liverpool L69 7ZU
email lup@liverpool.ac.uk
website www.liverpooluniversitypress.co.uk/topic/imprints/pavilion-poetry
X @PavilionPoetry

Publishes contemporary poetry from British and international poets. An imprint of Liverpool University Press. Founded 2014.

Pearson UK*
80 Strand, London WC2R 0RL
email schools@longman.co.uk
website www.pearsoned.co.uk
Facebook www.facebook.com/pearsonplc.uk
X @Pearson_UK
Instagram @pearsonhighereducation
Ceo Andy Bird

Consists of five divisions: Virtual Learning, Higher Education, English Language Learning, Workforce Skills and Assessment and Qualifications. Founded 1998.

Peepal Tree Press*
17 King's Ave, Burley, Leeds LS6 1QS
tel 0113 245 1703
email contact@peepaltreepress.com
website www.peepaltreepress.com
Facebook www.facebook.com/peepaltreepress
X @peepaltreepress
Founder & Managing Editor Jeremy Poynting

Leading independent publisher of Caribbean and Black British writing. Fiction, poetry and non-fiction, including the *Caribbean Modern Classics* series. Notable prizes include the Costa Novel and Book of the Year Awards, the T.S. Eliot Prize, and the Jhalak Prize. Publishes approx. 15 books per year. Since February 2024 Peepal Tree Press has managed the day-to-day operation of HopeRoad (page 150). Founded 1985.

P8tech

6 Woodside, Churnet View Road, Oakamoor, Staffs. ST10 3AE
tel (01538) 703591
email info@P8tech.com
website www.P8tech.com

IT, AI and computer-related books. Specialises in Oracle, OneStream and Java. Founded 2012.

Peirene Press

The Studio, 10 Palace Yard Mews, Bath BA1 2NH
website www.peirenepress.com
X @PeirenePress
Instagram @peirenepress
Publishers James Tookey, Stella Sabin

Independent publisher of translations including literary fiction. The Stevns Translation Prize (page 607) is an annual award for early career translators, run in collaboration with Two Lines Press in the USA, focusing on a different language every year. For details see website. Accepts MS submissions and pitches from translators and international agents via the website. Founded 2008.

Pelagic‡

20–22 Wenlock Road, London N1 7GU
tel 0845 468 0415
email info@pelagicpublishing.com
website www.pelagicpublishing.com
Facebook www.facebook.com/pelagicpublishing
X @pelagicpublish
Bluesky @pelagic.bsky.social
Instagram @pelagicpublishing
Publisher Nigel Massen

Academic and trade books on natural history, ecology, conservation, data analysis, sustainability and environmental science. Founded 2010.

Pen & Sword Books

George House,
Unit 12–13 Beevor Street Industrial Estate,
Beevor Street, Barnsley, South Yorkshire S71 1HN
tel (01226) 734555, (01226) 734222
email editorialoffice@pen-and-sword.co.uk
website www.pen-and-sword.co.uk
Managing Director Charles Hewitt, *Publisher* Jonathan Wright, *Commissioning Editors* Phil Sidnell, Sarah-Beth Watkins, Michael Leventhal, Julian Mannering, Rob Gardiner, Martin Mace, Tara Moran, Rob Green

Military history, aviation history, naval and maritime, general history, local history, family history, transport, social history, archaeology, natural history, gardening, space, science, sports, hobbies, retro video games, movie history and biographies. Imprints: After the Battle, Leo Cooper, Frontline Books, Greenhill, Pen & Sword Archaeology, Pen & Sword Aviation, Pen & Sword Digital, Pen & Sword Discovery, Pen & Sword Military, Pen & Sword Naval & Maritime, Pen & Sword Social History, Pen & Sword Transport, Remember When, Seaforth and White Owl. Founded 1990.

Penguin General*

20 Vauxhall Bridge Road, London SW1V 2SA
tel 020-7010 3000
website www.penguin.co.uk/about/publishing-houses/penguin-general
Managing Director Preena Gadher

No unsolicited MSS or synopses. Part of Penguin Random House UK. Penguin Books founded 1855.

Fig Tree

X @figtreepenguin
Instagram @penguinfigtree
Publishing Director Helen Garnons-Williams, *Assistant Editor* Ella Harold

Literary fiction, reading group fiction, narrative non-fiction and memoir.

Hamish Hamilton

Publishing Director Simon Prosser, *Editorial Director* Hermione Thompson, *Assistant Editor* Ruby Fatimilehin

Literary fiction, translated fiction, nature writing, biography and memoir and political non-fiction.

Penguin Life

Publishing Director Pippa Wright, *Editorial Director* Emily Robertson, *Commissioning Editors* Amy McWalters, Jamie Birkett, *Editorial Assistant* Sana Al-Raimi

Wellness, general health, parenting and psychotherapy. Mind, body & spirit and alternative therapies.

Sandycove

Publisher Michael Mcloughlin, *Deputy Publisher* Patricia Deevy, *Editorial Director* Brendan Barrington

Titles with an Irish focus.

Viking Fiction

Publishing Director Harriet Bourton, *Publisher* Isabel Wall, *Editorial Director* Rosa Schierenberg, *Senior Commissioning Editor* Vikki Moynes, *Editor* Edward Kirke

Fiction: commercial, literary and book club fiction. Non-fiction: memoir and narrative non-fiction.

Viking Non-Fiction

Publishing Director Daniel Crewe, *Editorial Director* Connor Brown, *Senior Commissioning Editor* Shyam Kumar, *Commissioning Editor* Greg Clowes, *Editorial Assistant* Alexandra Mulholland

Modern history, biography, memoir, culture, current affairs, popular culture, sport, history, literature, politics, narrative non-fiction, reportage and travel.

Penguin Michael Joseph*

One Embassy Gardens, 8 Viaduct Gardens, London SW11 7AY
tel 020-7010 3000
website www.penguin.co.uk/company/publishers/penguin-michael-joseph
Managing Director Louise Moore, *Publishing Director* Maxine Hitchcock (fiction), *Publishing Directors* Rowland White, Dan Bunyard (non-fiction)

General and women's fiction, crime, thriller, cookery, celebrity memoir and wellbeing. Part of Penguin Random House UK. Founded 1935.

Penguin Press*

1 Embassy Gardens, 8 Viaduct Gardens, Nine Elms, London SW11 7B
tel 020-7010 3000
website www.penguin.co.uk/about/publishing-houses/penguin-press
Managing Director Stefan McGrath

Incorporates the non-fiction imprint Allen Lane, the innovative Particular Books, the newly revitalised Pelican imprint, new poetry and the world of Penguin Classics. No unsolicited MSS. Part of Penguin Random House UK (see below). Founded 1997.

Allen Lane

Non-fiction: history, science, politics, economics, philosophy, psychology, language and current affairs.

Particular Books

Non-fiction: history, science, politics, travel, biography and memoirs, current affairs and photography.

Pelican

Non-fiction: history, science, politics, economics and finance, philosophy, psychology, language and current affairs.

Penguin Classics

Classic literature, poetry, drama, biography and memoir.

Penguin Random House Children's UK*

One Embassy Gardens, 8 Viaduct Gardens, London SW11 7BW
tel 020-7139 3000
website www.penguin.co.uk/company/publishers/penguin-random-house-children-s
X @PenguinKids
Instagram @randomhousekids
Managing Director Francesca Dow

Books for toddlers to YA. Formats: board books, activity books, picture books, graphic novels, novels and non-fiction. Imprints: Alfred A. Knopf Books for Young Readers, Bright Matter Books, Crown Books for Young Readers, Delacorte Press, Delacorte Romance, Doubleday Books for Young Readers, Dragonfly, Ember, Joy Revolution, Labyrinth Road, Little Golden Books, Make Me A World, Princeton Review, Random House Books for Young Readers, Random House Graphic, Random House Studio, Rodale Kids, and Yearling Books. Part of Penguin Random House UK. Founded 1925.

Penguin Random House UK*

One Embassy Gardens, 8 Viaduct Gardens, London SW11 7BW
tel 020-7139 3000
website www.penguin.co.uk
Facebook www.facebook.com/PenguinRandomHouse
X @PenguinUKBooks
Ceo Tom Weldon

Penguin Random House UK publishing divisions: Cornerstone (page 132), DK (page 135), Ebury Press (page 137), Penguin General (page 168), Penguin Michael Joseph (above), Penguin Press (above), Penguin Random House Children's UK (see above), Penguin Random House UK Audio (see below), Transworld (page 183) and Vintage (page 186). Founded 2013.

Penguin Random House UK Audio

Penguin Studios, One Embassy Gardens, 8 Viaduct Gardens, London SE11 7BW
email audiopublicity1@penguinrandomhouse.co.uk
website www.penguin.co.uk/about/publishing-houses/audio

Fiction: classic and contemporary. Non-fiction: autobiography, poetry and drama. Founded 2013.

Persephone Books

8 Edgar Buildings, Bath BA1 2EE
tel (01225) 425050
email info@persephonebooks.co.uk
website www.persephonebooks.co.uk
Instagram @persephonebooks
Managing Director Francesca Beauman

Reprints of neglected fiction and non-fiction, mostly by women writers and mid-20th century. Founded 1999.

Perspective Books

The Old Vicarage, Doncaster, South Yorkshire DN6 9JF
email contact@perspectivesbooks.com
website www.perspectivesbooks.com
Facebook www.facebook.com/IntegrityMediaUK
Contact Grant Budge

Multi-genre fiction and non-fiction. Especially interested in autobiographies and memoirs dealing with significant life challenges. Welcomes approaches from agents and authors, including first-time authors of original material. All submissions should include a cover letter, synopsis and first three chapters. Founded 2020.

Phaidon Press

2 Cooperage Yard, London E15 2GR
tel 020-7843 1000
email enquiries@phaidon.com
website www.phaidon.com
Facebook www.facebook.com/phaidoncom
X @phaidonpress
Instagram @phaidonpress
Ceo Bob Miller, *Vice-President & Publisher* Deborah Aaronson, *Associate Publisher, Children's Books* Maya Gartner

Visual arts, art, architecture, fashion, photography, lifestyle, culture, food, travel and illustrated books for children. Has over 1,500 titles in print. Founded 1923.

Philip's – see Octopus Publishing Group

Phoenix Publishing House

Unit 2, Brookstone House, 6 Elthorne Road, London N19 4AG
tel 020-8442 1376
email hello@firingthemind.com
website www.firingthemind.com
Facebook www.facebook.com/firingthemind
X @firingthemind
Instagram @firingthemind
Publisher Kate Pearce

Independent publisher of mental health publishing for professionals. For submission guidelines see website. Founded 2018.

Piatkus Constable & Robinson – see Little, Brown Book Group

Piccadilly Press*

Victoria House, Bloomsbury Square, London WC1B 4DA
tel 020-3770 8888
email hello@bonnierbooks.co.uk
website www.bonnierbooks.co.uk/imprints/piccadilly-press
Facebook www.facebook.com/piccadillypressbooks
X @PiccadillyPress
Instagram @piccadillypress
Editorial Director Ruth Bennett

Publishes books primarily for readers 5–12 years. Titles can be standalone stories or part of a series. Imprint of Bonnier Books UK. Founded 1983.

Pimlico – see Vintage

Plexus Publishing

26 Dafforne Road, London SW17 8TZ
tel 020-767 7126
email editorialassistant@plexusbooks.com
website www.plexusbooks.com
X @plexusbooks
Instagram @plexusbooks

Film, music, biography, popular culture, fashion and gift. Imprint: Eel Pie. Founded 1973.

Pluto Press‡

New Wing, Somerset House, Strand, London WC2R 1LA
tel 020-8348 2724
email pluto@plutobooks.com
website www.plutobooks.com
Facebook www.facebook.com/plutopress
X @plutopress
Instagram @plutopress
Editorial Director David Castle, *Senior Commissioning Editor* David Shulman

An independent, political publisher of radical non-fiction: politics, economics, history, race, international relations, gender and sexuality. Book proposals should be emailed to submissions@plutobooks.com. Founded 1969.

Policy Press – see Bristol University Press/ Policy Press

Polity Press‡

65 Bridge Street, Cambridge CB2 1UR
tel (01223) 324315
website www.politybooks.com
Facebook www.facebook.com/politypress
X @politypress
Bluesky @politybooks.bsky.social
Instagram @politypress

Publisher of academic books in social sciences and humanities and non-fiction books for general readers. Academic subjects include: politics, sociology, history, philosophy, media and cultural studies, literary studies, feminism, political economy, geography, environmental studies and anthropology. Founded 1984.

Poolbeg Press

Grange Hill, Baldoyle, County Dublin D13 N539, Republic of Ireland
tel +353 (0)1 806 3825
email info@poolbeg.com
website www.poolbeg.com
Directors Kieran Devlin, Barbara Devlin

Popular fiction, non-fiction and current affairs. Imprint: Poolbeg. Founded 1976.

Portland Press*

1 Naroji Street, London WC1X 0GB
email editorial@portlandpress.com
website https://portlandpress.com/
Facebook www.facebook.com/portlandpresspublishing
X @PPPublishing

Science publishing. Owned by the Biochemical Society. Founded 1990.

Prestel Publishing

1st Floor, 15 Adeline Place, London WC1B 3AJ
tel 020-7323 5004
email ahansen@prestel-uk.co.uk
website www.prestel.com
Facebook www.facebook.com/PrestelPublishing
X @Prestel_pub
Instagram @prestel_publishing
Vice-President Andrew Hansen

Pop culture, major exhibition catalogues and artist retrospectives. Art, architecture, photography, fashion, lifestyle, design and children's books. Book submissions: submissions@prestel-uk.co.uk. Press enquiries: publicity@prestel-uk.co.uk. Founded 1924.

Princeton University Press – Europe*‡

99 Banbury Road, Oxford OX2 6JX
tel (01993) 814500
website www.press.princeton.edu
Facebook www.facebook.com/PrincetonUniversityPress
X @PrincetonUPress
Editor for Humanities Ben Tate, *Publisher for Sciences* Ingrid Gnerlich, *Senior Editor for Social Science* Rebecca Brennan, *Associate Editor for Economics & Political Science* Hannah Paul

Academic publishing for the social sciences, humanities and sciences. Founded 1999.

Profile Books*‡

29 Cloth Fair, London EC1A 7JQ
tel 020-7841 6300
email info@profilebooks.com
website https://profilebooks.com/
Facebook www.facebook.com/profile.books
Instagram @profilebooks
Managing Director Rebecca Gray

General non-fiction: history, biography, current affairs, popular science, politics, business, management and humour. Publishes books for *The Economist*. No unsolicited MSS. Founded 1996.

The Economist

Publishes workplace guides and the *Economist Edge* series.

Pursuit

Books related to the subject of cycling.

Souvenir Press

Publisher Rebecca Gray
Non-fiction, especially practical and expert advice, spiritual, gift and memoir. No unsolicited MSS.

Wellcome Collection

Publishes history, memoir, psychology, medicine and science.

Prototype

71 Oriel Road, London E9 5SG
website https://prototypepublishing.co.uk/
Facebook www.facebook.com/prototypepubs
X @prototypepubs
Instagram @prototypepubs
Founder Jess Chandler

Fiction, poetry, anthologies and interdisciplinary projects. Publishes new voices in free-form contemporary literature. Imprints: House Sparrow Press and Test Centre. Founded 2019.

Pure Indigo

Publishing Department, 17 The Herons, Cottenham, Cambridge CB24 8XX
tel 07981 395258
email ashley.martin@pureindigo.co.uk
website www.pureindigo.co.uk/publishing
Commissioning Editor Ashley Martin

Children's books: develops innovative junior series fiction in-house. Also develops software products that complement the product range. Sometimes authors and illustrators are commissioned to complete project-based work. Currently closed to submissions. Founded 2005.

Pushkin Press‡

New Wing, Somerset House, Strand, London WC2R 1LA
email books@pushkinpress.com
website www.pushkinpress.com
Facebook www.facebook.com/PushkinPress
X @pushkinpress
Publisher Adam Freudenheim, *Publishing Director* Laura Macaulay, *Senior Commissioning Editor* Daniel Seton

Contemporary fiction and non-fiction, classics crime/thrillers and children's books. Graphic novels. Imprints: Pushkin Children's Books, Pushkin ONE, Pushkin Press, Pushkin Press Classics and Pushkin Vertigo. Founded 1997.

Pyramid – see Octopus Publishing Group

Quadrant Books

Suite 2, 7 Dyer Street, Cirencester, Gloucs. GL7 2PF
tel 020-3290 0290
email info@quadrant-books.com
website www.quadrant-books.com
X @BooksQuadrant
Publisher Antonia Tingle, *Editor-in-Chief* Peter Jacobs

Contemporary fiction, crime, mystery, historical, romance, speculative fiction and non-fiction. Founded 2020.

Quantum – see W. Foulsham & Co.

Quartet Books*

27 Goodge Street, London W1T 2LD
tel 020-7636 3992

Books

email info@quartetbooks.co.uk
website www.quartetbooks.co.uk
Facebook www.facebook.com/quartetbooks
X @quartetbooks

Independent publisher with a tradition of pursuing an alternative to mainstream publishing. Publishes books by women in the areas of literary and crime fiction, biography and autobiography, health, culture, politics, handbooks, literary criticism, the arts, psychology and self-help. Accepting submissions, see website. Founded 1978.

Quarto Group Publishing UK‡

1 Triptych Place, 2nd Floor, 185 Park Street, London SE1 9BL
tel 020-7700 9000
website www.quarto.com
Ceo Alison Goff, *Managing Director* Karine Marko

The UK division of The Quarto Group includes: Aurum, Design Eye, Carnival, Frances Lincoln (page 156), France Lincoln Children's Books, Happy Yak (page 146), Holler, Ivy Kids, Ivy Press, Kaddo, Leaping Hare Press, Quarto Publishing, The Bright Press, White Lion Publishing, Wide Eyed Editions (page 187) and words & pictures. General adult non-fiction, illustrated and non-illustrated: history, sport, entertainment, biography, autobiography, military, gardening, architecture, environment, interiors, photography, art, walking and climbing, design and landscape, gift, interiors, food and drink, lifestyle and craft. Children's picture books and general children's non-fiction. Founded 1976.

Quercus Publishing

Carmelite House, 50 Victoria Embankment, London EC4Y 0DZ
tel 020-3122 6000
website www.quercusbooks.co.uk
Instagram @quercusbooks
Managing Director Jon Butler

Fiction and non-fiction. Imprints: Arcadia, Greenfinch, MacLehose Press, Quercus Fiction, Quercus Non-Fiction and riverrun. Part of the John Murray Group. Founded 2005.

Quiller Publishing‡

12 The Hill, Merrywalks, Stroud, Glous. GL5 4EP
tel (01453) 847800
email info@quillerbooks.com
website www.quillerpublishing.com
Ceo Nick Hayward

Owned by Amberley Publishing. Founded 2001.

Kenilworth Press

Equestrian (riding, training, dressage, eventing, show jumping, driving and polo). Publisher of BHS official publications and exclusive distributor for The Pony Club.

Quiller

Biographies, history, food and drink, sport, art and photography, humour and gift books. Also specialist practical books on country pursuits including dog training, fishing, shooting, stalking, gamekeeping, deer, falconry, natural history and gardening.

Radio Society of Great Britain*

3 Abbey Court, Fraser Road, Priory Business Park, Bedford MK44 3WH
website https://rsgb.org/
Facebook www.facebook.com/theresgb
X @thersgb

Books for the amateur radio community. Founded 1913.

Ransom Publishing*‡

Unit 7, Brocklands Farm, West Meon GU32 1JN
tel (01730) 829091
email orders@ransom.co.uk
website www.ransom.co.uk
Managing Director Jenny Ertle, *Creative Director* Steve Rickard

Children's fiction and non-fiction, phonics and school reading programmes, and books for children and adults who are reluctant or struggling readers. Also publishes books in a dyslexia-friendly format. Range covers high interest age/low reading age titles, quick reads and reading schemes. Currently not accepting unsolicited submissions. Founded 1995.

Raven Books

Publishes fiction and non-fiction for children 8–14 years.

Reaktion Books

Unit 32 Waterside, 44–48 Wharf Road, London N1 7UX
tel 020-7253 4965
email info@reaktionbooks.co.uk
website www.reaktionbooks.co.uk
Facebook www.facebook.com/ReaktionBooks
Instagram @reaktionbooks
Publisher Michael R. Leaman

Non-fiction: art, architecture, design and photography, popular science, food, history, nature, film, music, philosophy, economics and politics. Publishes around 100 books a year. Founded 1985.

Red Planet Books

Dove House, Tregoniggie Industrial Estate, Falmouth, Cornwall TR11 4SN
email info@redplanetbooks.co.uk
website https://redplanetmusicbooks.com/
Facebook www.facebook.com/RedPlanetBooks
X @RedPlanetZone
Instagram @redplanetbooks
Founder Mark Neeter

Independent publisher of books about music. Founded 2017.

Renard Press*‡

124 City Road, London EC1V 2NX
tel 020-8050 2928
email info@renardpress.com
website www.renardpress.com
Facebook www.facebook.com/therenardpress
X @renardpress
Bluesky @renardpress.bsky.social
Instagram @renardpress
Publisher Will Dady

Classics and contemporary literary fiction, non-fiction, poetry and theatre titles. Imprints: Hay Press (commercial and genre fiction), Haywood Books (hybrid publishing of fiction and poetry) and Renard Press. Founded 2020.

Repeater Books

Shepperton House Unit 11, 89 Shepperton Road, London N1 3DF
email enquiries@repeaterbooks.com
website https://repeaterbooks.com/
Facebook www.facebook.com/rsepeaterbooks
X @RepeaterBooks
Directors Etan Ilfeld, Vicky Hartley

Books with new and radical ideas: counter-culture, critical theory, politics, music, popular culture and current affairs. Part of Watkins Media. Founded 2014.

Revenge Ink

6D Lowick Close, Hazel Grove, Stockport SK7 5ED
email amita@revengeink.com
website www.revengeink.com
Director Amita Mukerjee, *Editor* Gopal Mukerjee

Adult fiction. Prefers unsolicited, first-time novelists or established writers seeking a new outlet for edgier material. Considers original and creative poetry. Publishes approx. seven titles a year. Does not publish children's fiction or non-fiction titles such as cookery, gardens and how-to books. For submission guidelines see website. Send short sample and query first, preferably by email. Founded 2007.

Ringwood Publishing*

0/1 314 Meadowside Quay Walk, Glasgow G11 6AY
email mail@ringwoodpublishing.com
website www.ringwoodpublishing.com
X @RingwoodPublish
Ceo Sandy Jamieson

Scottish fiction and non-fiction: politics, football, religion, money, sex and crime. Founded 1997.

Romaunce Books

76 Cottrell Road, Bristol BS5 6TN
tel 020-3286 8686
email toni@romaunce.com
website www.romaunce.com
Facebook www.facebook.com/romaunce
X @Romaunce
Instagram @romaunce
Publisher Antonia Tingle

Romantic and historical fiction: historical romance, contemporary romance, romantic comedy, erotic romance and memoirs. Founded 2017.

George Ronald

71 Oakdale Drive, Heald Green, Cheadle, Cheshire SK8 3SN
tel (07814) 164740
email sales@grbooks.com
website www.grbooks.com
Manager D. Smith

Religion, specialising in the Bahá'í Faith. Founded 1939.

Route

PO Box 167, Pontefract, West Yorkshire WF8 4WW
tel (01977) 793442
email info@route-online.com
website www.route-online.com
Facebook www.facebook.com/routebook
X @Route_News
Instagram @route_books
Contacts Ian Daley, Isabel Galán

Memoir, cultural non-fiction and biography, with a strong interest in music books. Occasional fiction. Unsolicited MSS discouraged, book proposals in first instance. Founded 2000.

Routledge – see Taylor & Francis Group

Royal Collection Trust

York House, St James's Palace, London SW1A 1BQ
tel 020-7839 1377
website www.rct.uk/about/publishing
Facebook www.facebook.com/royalcollectiontrust
X @rct
Instagram @royalcollectiontrust
Head of Publishing Kate Owen, *Manager Editor* Polly Fellows, *Commissioning & Development Editor* Anjali Bulley

Trade books, exhibition catalogues, guides and children's books with a focus on royal residences and their works of art. Also produces scholarly catalogues raisonnés. Contact details on website. Founded 1993.

Royal National Institute of Blind People (RNIB)*

Midgate House, Midgate, Peterborough, Cambs. PE1 1TN
tel 0303 123 9999
email helpline@rnib.org.uk
website www.rnib.org.uk
Facebook www.facebook.com/rnibuk
X @rnib
Instagram @rnib

Magazines, catalogues and books for blind and partially sighted people, to support daily living, leisure, learning and employment reading needs. Includes the charity's flagship Talking Books service, providing more than 30,000 fiction and non-fiction titles to borrow free of charge for adults and children with sight loss. Formats: braille, audio and large/clear print. Founded 1868.

Ruby Tuesday Books‡

6 Newlands Road, Tunbridge Wells, Kent TN4 9AT
tel (01892) 557767
email shan@rubytuesdaybooks.com
website www.rubytuesdaybooks.com
X @RubyTuesdaybks
Bluesky @rubytuesdaybooks.bsky.social
Instagram @rubytuesdaybks
Publishers Ruth Owen, Shan White

Children's books for ages 0 to 16 years, with over 150 in print. See website for submission guidelines. Founded 2008.

Ryland Peters & Small

20–21 Jockey's Fields, London WC1R 4BW
tel 020-7025 2200
email info@rylandpeters.com
website https://rylandpeters.com/
Facebook www.facebook.com/rylandpetersandsmall
X @rylandpeters
Instagram @rylandpetersandsmall
Managing Director David Peters

Illustrated books: food, drink, home and garden, gift, babies and children. Founded 1995.

Cico Books

Lifestyle and interiors; crafts; health; and mind, body & spirit.

Rymour Books*

45 Needless Road, Perth PH2 0LE
tel 07535 698829
website www.rymour.co.uk
X @rymourbooks
Publisher Dr Ian Spring

An award-winning small independent publisher of mostly Scottish authors or books with a Scottish theme. All genres considered, including humour. Founded 2020.

Hog's Back

Academic books on Scottish history or literature.

SAGE Publishing*‡

1 Oliver's Yard, 55 City Road, London EC1Y 1SP
tel 020-7324 8500
email info@sagepub.co.uk
website www.sagepublishing.com
Facebook www.facebook.com/SAGEPublishing
X @SAGE_Publishing
Instagram @sage_publishing

Journals, books and library products for the educational, scholarly and professional markets. Founded 1965.

St David's Press

PO Box 733, Cardiff CF14 7ZY
tel 029-2021 8187
email post@st-davids-press.wales
website www.st-davids-press.wales
Facebook www.facebook.com/StDavidsPress
X @StDavidsPress
Instagram @stdavidspress

Sport, leisure and popular culture, including rugby, football, cricket, boxing, horse racing, cycling, athletics, walking and music. Also general titles of a Welsh and/or Celtic interest. Founded 2002.

St Pauls Publishing

St Pauls, Westminster Cathedral, Morpeth Terrace, Victoria, London SW1P 1EP
tel 020-7828 5582
email editor@stpauls.org.uk
website www.stpauls.org.uk
Facebook www.facebook.com/stpaulsbookshopuk
X @stpaulsuk
Instagram @stpaulsuk

Theology, ethics, spirituality, biography, education, general books of Roman Catholic and Christian interest. Founded 1948.

Salmon Poetry

The Salmon Bookshop & Literary Centre, Main Street, Ennistymon, County Clare V95 XD35, Republic of Ireland
tel +353 (0)85 231 8909
email info@salmonpoetry.com
website www.salmonpoetry.com
Editor Jessica Lendennie

Alternative voices in Irish literature, specialises in the promotion of new poets, particularly women. Has published over 700 volumes. Founded 1981.

Salt Publishing‡

12 Norwich Road, Cromer, Norfolk NR27 0AX
email sales@saltpublishing.com
website www.saltpublishing.com
Bluesky @saltpublishing.bsky.social
Instagram @saltpublishing
Publishing Directors Christopher Hamilton-Emery, Jennifer Hamilton-Emery

Award-winning independent publisher of fiction and poetry. Home of the annual Best British Short Story anthology. Founded 1999.

Sans. PRESS

email submissionsanspress@gmail.com
website www.sanspress.com
Facebook www.facebook.com/sans.press
X @PressSans
Instagram @sans.press
Editors Paula Dias Garcia, Sam Agar, Marc Clohessy, Aran Kelly

Limerick-based small independent publisher of literary short stories. Publish bi-annual themed collections of fresh and weird stories, inspired by magical realism and speculative fiction. Supported by the Arts Council of Ireland. Founded 2020.

Sapere Books‡

24 Trafalgar Road, Ilkley LS29 8HH
website www.saperebooks.com
Facebook www.facebook.com/saperebooks
X @SapereBooks
Instagram @saperebooks
Editorial Director Amy Durant

A digital-first publisher of historical fiction (including crime, mysteries, thrillers, romance and sagas), action and adventure (military, naval and aviation fiction), crime fiction, mysteries, thrillers and history. Not currently open for submissions but remains open to publishing backlist books that may have gone out of print. Founded 2018.

Saqi Books*‡

Gable House, 18–24 Turnham Green Terrace, London W4 1QP
tel 020-7221 9347
email lynn@saqibooks.com
website www.saqibooks.com
Facebook www.facebook.com/SaqiBooks
X @SaqiBooks
Bluesky @saqibooks.bsky.social
Instagram @saqibooks
Publisher Lynn Gaspard, *Associate Publisher* Simon Liebesney, *Editorial Director* Elizabeth Briggs

Independent publisher of global trade and academic books on the Middle East and North Africa. Also translates new and classic Arabic literature. Subjects include: art, photography, cookery, language, literature and philosophy, history and current affairs. Founded 1978.

Telegram

New and classic international literature.

Westbourne Press

Alternative, progressive perspective on the leading issues of our time.

Saraband*‡

email hermes@saraband.net
website www.saraband.net
Facebook www.facebook.com/sarabandbks
X @sarabandbooks
Instagram @sarabandbooks

Nature and environmental writing, memoir, history and local interest non-fiction (especially on Scotland and the north of England). Also literary and historical fiction, occasionally in translation. Founded 1994.

Contraband

Literary noir and dark fiction.

Schofield & Sims*

7 Mariner Cour, Wakefield, West Yorkshire WF4 3FL
tel (01484) 607080
email editorial@schofieldandsims.co.uk
website www.schofieldandsims.co.uk

Educational: nursery, infants and primary, also posters. Founded 1901.

Scholastic*

Euston House, 1 London Bridge, London SE1 9BG
tel 020-7756 7756
website www.scholastic.co.uk
Facebook www.facebook.com/Scholastic
X @scholasticuk
President & Ceo Peter Warwick

Children's fiction, non-fiction: picture books and education resources for primary schools. Owned by Scholastic Inc. Founded 1964.

Scholastic Children's Books

tel 020-7756 7761
email submissions@scholastic.co.uk
website www.scholastic.co.uk
X @scholasticuk
Fiction Publisher Lauren Fortune, *Non-Fiction Publisher & Licensing* Elizabeth Scoggins, *Editorial Director, Illustrated Books* Sophie Cashell

Activity books, novelty books, picture books, fiction for 5–12 years, teenage fiction, series fiction and film/TV tie-ins. Imprints: Alison Green Books, Klutz and Scholastic. No unsolicited MSS. Unsolicited illustrations are accepted, but do not send any original artwork as it will not be returned.

Scholastic Educational Resources

Thorney Leys Business Park, Unit 18F, Witney, Oxfordshire OX28 4GE
tel (01993) 893456
Publishing Director Rachel Morgan

Professional books, classroom materials, home learning books and online resources for primary teachers. GCSE support material.

Science Museum Group

Publishing Department, Science Museum, Enterprises, Exhibition Road, London SW7 2DD
tel 0870 870 4771
website www.sciencemuseumgroup.org.uk

Science, technology, engineering, medicine and mathematics. Adult and children's non-fiction (licensed). Museum guides and exhibition books. Founded 1857.

SCM Press – see Hymns Ancient and Modern

Scorpius Books

10 Erle Havard Road, West Bergholt, Essex CO6 3LH
website www.scorpiusbooks.com
Facebook www.facebook.com/scorpiusbooks.com

Instagram @scorpiusbooks
Threads @scorpiusbooks
Publisher & Founder Jacqueline Kibby

Fantasy, horror, paranormal and general fiction. Publisher of dyslexia-friendly fiction for adults. See website for submission guidelines. Regional Small Press of the Year 2024. Founded 2020.

Scotland Street Press*

100 Willowbrae Avenue, Edinburgh EH8 7HU
email info@scotlandstreetpress.com
website www.scotlandstreetpress.com
Facebook www.facebook.com/ScotStreetPress
X @scotstreetpress
Instagram @scotstreetpress
Founder & Ceo Jean Fraser

Biography, literary fiction and poetry. Submissions window in February. Allow three to six months for a response. Founded 2014.

Scottish Mountaineering Press*

16 Union Road, Inverness IV2 3JY
email mail@scottishmountaineeringpress.com
website https://scottishmountaineeringpress.com/
Facebook www.facebook.com/scottishmountaineeringpress
Director Susan Jensen, Iain Young, John Hall, Chris Ravey, Brian Whitworth

Guidebooks, fiction and non-fiction about Scottish nature, including poetry. Subsidiary of the Scottish Mountaineering Trust, a charity. All profits are channelled into the Trust. Founded 1990.

Scratch Books

website www.scratch-books.co.uk
X @scratch_books
Instagram @scratch_books_uk
Publisher Tom Conaghan

Short stories. Publishes two books a year. Publishes the *Reverse Engineering* series. Runs the biannual Scratch A4 competition. Founded 2022.

Scribe*

2 John Street, London WC1N 2ES
tel 020-3405 4218
email info@scribepub.co.uk
website https://scribepublications.co.uk/
Facebook www.facebook.com/ScribePublicationsUk
X @scribeukbooks
Instagram @scribe_uk

An award-winning independent publisher. Publishes a range of fiction and non-fiction for the general reader. Does not accept submissions. Founded 1976.

Scribble

Picture books.

Scripture Union

Trinity House, Opal Court, Fox Milne, Milton Keynes MK15 0DF
tel (01908) 856000
email hello@scriptureunion.org.uk
website www.scriptureunion.org.uk
Facebook www.facebook.com/scriptureunionews
X @SUEnglandWales
National Director Dave Newton

Christian books and bible reading materials for people of all ages. Educational and worship resources for churches. Children's fiction and non-fiction and adult non-fiction. Founded 1867.

Search Press‡

Wellwood, North Farm Road, Tunbridge Wells, Kent TN2 3DR
tel (01892) 510850
email searchpress@searchpress.com
website www.searchpress.com, www.bookmarkedhub.com
Facebook www.facebook.com/SearchPress
Instagram @searchpress
Managing Director Martin de la Bédoyère, *Publishing Director* Samantha Warrington

An independent, award-winning, family-owned art and craft book publisher. Founded 1970.

SelfMadeHero

139 Pancras Road, London NW1 1UN
email info@selfmadehero.com
website www.selfmadehero.com
Facebook www.facebook.com/selfmadehero
X @selfmadehero
Bluesky @selfmadehero.bsky.social
Instagram @selfmadehero
Managing Director & Publisher Emma Hayley

Graphic novels and visual narratives in literary fiction, biography, classic adaptation, sci-fi, horror, crime and humour. Founded 2007.

September Publishing

tel 020-3637 0116
email info@septemberpublishing.org
website www.septemberpublishing.org
Facebook www.facebook.com/SeptemberPublishing
X @septemberbooks
Instagram @septemberpublishing
Publisher Hannah MacDonald

Non-fiction: illustrated and narrative adult books, including memoir and biography, travel, humour, art, graphic novels and politics. Founded 2013.

Seren

Suite 6, 4 Derwen Road, Bridgend CF31 1LH
tel (01656) 663018
email seren@serenbooks.com
website www.serenbooks.com
Ceo Bronwen Price

Poetry, fiction, literary criticism, biography and art – mostly with relevance to Wales. Founded 1981.

Severn House

Eardley House, 4 Uxbridge Street, London W8 7SY
tel 020-7467 0840
email info@severnhouse.com
website www.severnhouse.com
Facebook www.facebook.com/severnhouse
X @severnhouse
Bluesky @severnhouse.bsky.social
Instagram @severnhouseimprint
Publisher Joanne Grant

Adult genres for the library market: mysteries, thrillers, detective, horror, romance, sci-fi and fantasy. Visit website for submissions guidelines. Imprint of Canongate Books. Founded 1974.

Shearsman Books‡

PO Box 4239, Swindon SN3 9FN
tel 0330 113 6514
email editor@shearsman.com
website www.shearsman.com
Facebook www.facebook.com/Shearsman-Books-272720625528
X @ShearsmanBooks
Editor & Publisher Tony Frazer

Contemporary poetry in English and in translation. Founded 2003.

Sheldon Press – see John Murray Group

Sheldrake Press

PO Box 74852, London SW12 2DX
tel 020-8675 1767
email enquiries@sheldrakepress.co.uk
website www.sheldrakepress.co.uk, www.sheldrakepress.com
X @SheldrakePress
Publisher J.S. Rigge

History and art, travel, architecture, cookery, music; humour; and stationery. Founded 1979.

Shepheard-Walwyn (Publishers)

Suite 108. 4. Little Portland Street London W1W 7JB
tel 020-8241 5927
email books@shepheardwalwyn.com
website www.shepheardwalwyn.com, www.ethicaleconomics.org.uk
Facebook www.facebook.com/ShepheardWalwynPublishers
X @SWPublishing
Instagram @swpublishers
Director K. Toth

History, biography, political economy, perennial philosophy, women's studies, social, environmental and climate issues. Publishing partner of The School of Philosophy and Economic Science, London. Also hosts a podcast: wwwshepheardwalwyn.podbean.com. Founded 1971.

Short Books – see Octopus Publishing Group

Sigma Press

Stobart House, Pontyclerc, Penybanc Road, Ammanford, Carmarthenshire SA18 3HP
tel (01269) 593100
email info@sigmapress.co.uk
website www.sigmapress.co.uk
Facebook www.facebook.com/sigmawalkingbooks
X @Sigma_Press
Directors Nigel Evans, Jane Evans

Leisure: country walking, cycling, regional heritage, ecology, folklore and biographies. Founded 1979.

Silvertail Books

Beauchamp House, 402–403 Stourport Road, Kidderminster DY11 7BG
email editor@silvertailbooks.com
website www.silvertailbooks.com
X @silvertailbooks
Publisher Humfrey Hunter

Independent publisher of commercial fiction and non-fiction. Especially likes publishing newsworthy non-fiction and fiction that tells captivating stories. No children's books. Founded 2012.

Simon & Schuster UK*

222 Gray's Inn Road, London WC1X 8HB
tel 020-7316 1900
email enquiries@simonandschuster.co.uk
website www.simonandschuster.co.uk
Facebook www.facebook.com/simonschusterUK
X @simonschusteruk
Ceo Perminder Mann, *Managing Directors* Suzanne Baboneau (adult), Rachel Denwood (children's), *Publishing Directors* Clare Hey (adult), Holly Harris (non-fiction), Sophie Missing (Scribner), Ravi Mirchandani (Summit), Ali Dougal (children's), *Deputy Publishing Directors* Katherine Armstrong (adult crime & thriller), Kris Doyle (non-fiction), Michelle Signore (Gallery)

Adult non-fiction: history, biography, current affairs, science, self-help, political, popular culture, sports books, memoirs and illustrated titles. Adult fiction: mass-market, literary fiction, historical fiction, commercial women's fiction, sci-fi and fantasy and general fiction. Children's and YA fiction, picture books, novelty, pop-up and licensed character. Founded 1986.

Children's Books

Books for all ages, across all genres, including picture books, chapter books, novels for 8–12 years, YA and non-fiction.

Gallery Books

Non-fiction: popular culture and general non-fiction.

Little Simon UK

Contact Jane Buckley
Board and novelty books for 0–5-year-olds from a mix of new and established authors. Also oversees in-house IP projects.

Scribner

Literary fiction and non-fiction.

Simon & Schuster Audio

website www.simonandschuster.co.uk/audio
Publisher Alice Twomey
Fiction, children's, YA and non-fiction audiobooks.

Sincere Corkscrew

email sincerecorkscrew@gmail.com
website https://sincerecorkscrew.neocities.org/
Editor-in-Chief Ian Macartney

Independent publisher of short prose. For submissions, email postal address and instructions on how to submit will be sent by post. Founded 2021.

Siri Scientific Press

Arrow Mill, Queensway, Castleton,
Rochdale OL11 2YW
tel 07770 796913
email books@siriscientificpress.co.uk
website www.siriscientificpress.co.uk
Facebook www.facebook.com/Siri-Scientific-Press-134567006626977
Publishing Consultant David Penney

Specialist natural history books including academic monographs, compiled edited volumes, photographic atlases, field guides and more general works. Specialises in works on entomology, arachnology and palaeontology, but will also consider other topics. Debut authors welcome. Founded 2008.

Skein Press†

Talbot Mews, Vernon Grove,
Rathgar Dublin D06 W9K5, Republic of Ireland
email info@skeinpress.com
website www.skeinpress.com
X @skeinpress
Editors Gráinne O'Toole, Nidhi Zak/Aria Eipe

Curates and publishes thought-provoking stories not commonly featured in the literary arts in Ireland. Founded 2017.

SmashBear Publishing

118 Canterbury Road, Folkestone CT19 5PF
tel 07826 856019
email info@smashbearpublishing.co.uk
website www.smashbearpublishing.com
Facebook www.facebook.com/smashbearpublishing/
X @SmashBearPH
Instagram @smashbearpublishing
Managing Director & Publisher Loredana Carini, *Publisher* Bianca Carini, *Acquisitions Manager & Commissioning Editor* Ellee Cooper, *Commissioning Editor* Ren Dooley

Publishes novels of 60,000+ words in fantasy, urban fantasy, horror and paranormal romance. Also publishes short story anthologies to raise money for Women's Aid. Founded 2020.

Colin Smythe

38 Mill Lane, Gerrards Cross, Bucks. SL9 8BA
tel (01753) 886000
email info@colinsmythe.co.uk
website www.colinsmythe.co.uk
Director Colin Smythe

Irish biography, phaleristics, heraldry, Irish literature and literary criticism and Irish history. Imprints include: Dolmen Press and Van Duren Publishers. Founded 1966.

Snowbooks

email info@snowbooks.com
website www.snowbooks.com
Directors Emma Barnes (managing), Rob Jones

Genre fiction: steampunk, fantasy, sci-fi and horror. General non-fiction. See website for submission guidelines; not currently accepting submissions. No postal submissions or calls. Founded 2003.

Society for Promoting Christian Knowledge (SPCK)‡

36 Causton Street, London SW1P 4ST
tel 020-7592 3900
email spck@spck.org.uk
website www.spckpublishing.co.uk
Facebook www.facebook.com/SPCK-publishing
X @SPCKpublishing
Instagram @spck_publishing
Ceo Sam Richardson

Theology, bibles, history, contemporary culture, children's picture books and fiction, biography, liturgy, prayer, spirituality, biblical studies, educational resources, social and ethical issues, mission, gospel and culture. Founded 1698.

IVP

Theology and academic, commentaries, biblical studies, contemporary culture.

Marylebone House

Commercial and literary fiction.

Society of Genealogists

40 Wharf Road, London N1 7GS
tel 020-7251 8799
email sales@sog.org.uk
website www.sog.org.uk

Local and family history books, software and magazines plus extensive library facilities. Founded 1911.

Somerville Press

Dromore, Bantry, Co. Cork P75 NY22,
Republic of Ireland
tel +353 (0)28 32873
email somervillepress@gmail.com
website www.somervillepress.com
Directors Andrew Russell, Jane Russell

Irish interest: fiction and non-fiction. Founded 2008.

Sparsile Books*

PO Box 2861, Glasgow G61 9ED
tel 07938 864485
email enquiries@sparsilebooks.com
website www.sparsilebooks.com
Facebook www.facebook.com/sparsilebooks
X @sparsileb
Publisher James Campbell

Contemporary fiction and non-fiction, literary fiction, biography, history, general science and memoir. Open periodically for submissions, check website for details. Founded 2018.

Sphere – see Little, Brown Book Group

Springer Nature*

4 Crinan Street, London N1 9XW
tel 020-7833 4000
website www.springernature.com
X @SpringerNature
Bluesky @springernature.bsky.social
Instagram @springernature
Ceo Frank Vrancken Peeters

Publishes research. Provides technology-enabled products, platforms and services for researchers. Founded 1842.

BMC

website www.biomedcentral.com

Global scientific, technical and medical portfolio, providing researchers in academia, scientific institutions and corporate R&D departments with content through innovative information, products and services.

Macmillan Education

email info@macmillaneducation.com
website www.macmillaneducation.com

Three divisions: Language Learning (ELT content and resources in Spanish and Chinese for certain regions), Schools Curriculum Division (materials to fit with the curricula of countries around the world) and Higher Education (university-level content across a wide range of subject areas).

Nature Portfolio

website www.nature.com

Publishes the journals *Nature* (founded 1869), *Nature Research*, *Nature Reviews* and *Nature Communications*. Also publishes Open Access journals including *Scientific Reports*.

Palgrave Macmillan

website www.palgrave.com

Books and journals in the humanities and social sciences.

SRL Publishing

email admin@srlpublishing.co.uk
website www.srlpublishing.co.uk
Facebook www.facebook.com/srlpublishing
X @srlpublishing
Instagram @srlpublishing
Publisher Stuart Debar

The world's first climate positive publisher, small independent press of fiction. Genres: YA, new adult, contemporary and crime/thriller. Non-fiction. Founded 2014.

Stainer & Bell

Victoria House, 23 Gruneisen Road, London N3 1LS
tel 020-8343 3303
email post@stainer.co.uk
website www.stainer.co.uk
Facebook www.facebook.com/stainerandbell
X @stainerandbell

Music and religious communication. Founded 1907.

Stairwell Books

161 Lowther Street, York YO31 7LZ
website www.stairwellbooks.co.uk
X @StairwellBooks
Bluesky @stairwellbooks.bsky.social
Founder Alen Gillott

Small press of genre and literary fiction, children's books and poetry. Founded 2005.

Stanley/Barker

71–75 Shelton Street, Covent Garden, London WC2H 9JQ
email info@stanleybarker.co.uk
website www.stanleybarker.co.uk
Founders Rachel Barker, Gregory Barker

Art and photography. Works with local organisations, schools and universities in the Midlands to offer young people the opportunity to learn about publishing. Also offers paid internships to students. Founded 2014.

Stenlake Publishing

54–58 Mill Square, Catrine, Ayrshire KA5 6RD
tel (01290) 552233
email sales@stenlake.co.uk
website www.stenlake.co.uk
Managing Director Richard Stenlake

Local history, Scottish language and literature especially Robert Burns, studio pottery, beekeeping, railways, transport, aviation, canals and mining covering Wales, Scotland, England, Northern Ireland, Isle of Man, Republic of Ireland and Zambia. Founded 1987.

Alloway Publishing

website www.allowaypublishing.co.uk

Books by ploughman poet, Robert Burns.

Oakwood Press

Railway and transport. Founded 1931.

Stewed Rhubarb Press

9 Anderson Terrace, Tarland, Aboyne AB34 4YH
email charlie@stewedrhubarb.org
website https://stewedrhubarb.org/
Facebook www.facebook.com/stewedrhubarb
X @stewedbooks
Director Duncan Lockerbie, *Head of Publishing Programme* Charlie Roy

Poetry anthologies, special collections and pamphlets. Founded 2018.

Storm Publishing

email hello@stormpublishing.co
website https://stormpublishing.co/
Facebook www.facebook.com/stormpublishingco
X @stormbooks_co
Managing Director Oliver Rhodes, *Deputy Managing Director* Claire Bord, *Publisher* Kathryn Taussig, *Editorial Directors* Emily Gowers, Vicky Blunden, *Commissioning Editor* Kate Smith

Independent publisher of crime, thrillers, mysteries, romance, contemporary and historical fiction. Full MSS can be submitted via website, no cover letter necessary. Founded 2022.

Strange Region

74 Pearl Street, Bedminster, Bristol BS3 3DL
email joe@strangeregion.co.uk
website www.strangeregion.com
X @strangeregion
Instagram @strangeregionpress
Publisher/Director Joe Vaughan

Writing by artists, novelists and poets, including in narrative form and plays. Aims to use publishing as a collaborative tool to celebrate writing as performance. Routinely open for unsolicited and unagented submissions. Founded 2022.

Studio Press*

Victoria House, Bloomsbury Square, London WC1B 4DA
tel 020-3770 8888
email hello@bonnierbooks.co.uk
website www.bonnierbooks.co.uk/imprints/studio-press
X @StudioPress
Managing Director Helen Wicks, *Head of Studio Press* Stephanie Milton

Pop culture trends and health, wellbeing and environmental issues. Publishing partner to major brands including Disney, Marvel and Harry Potter. Creators of the bestselling *Ultimate Football Heroes* series for children. An imprint of Bonnier Books UK. Founded 2015.

Summersdale Publishers

46 West Street, Chichester, West Sussex PO19 1RP
tel (01243) 771107
email submissions@summersdale.com
website www.summersdale.com
Managing Director Alastair Williams

Popular non-fiction, humour and gift books, travel writing and health and wellbeing. See website for guidelines. Imprints include: Summersdale and Vie. Owned by Octopus Publishing Group. Founded 1990.

Sunflower Books

PO Box 36160, London SW7 3WS
tel 020-7589 2377
email info@sunflowerbooks.co.uk
website www.sunflowerbooks.co.uk
Director P.A. Underwood

Travel guidebooks. Founded 1983.

Sweet Cherry Publishing*‡

Unit 4u18, The Book Brothers Business Park, Tolwell Road, Leicester LE4 1BR
tel 0116 253 6796
email info@sweetcherrypublishing.com
website www.sweetcherrypublishing.com
Facebook www.facebook.com/sweetcherrypublishing
X @sweetcherrypub
Instagram @sweetcherrypublishing
Director A. Thadha

Children's fiction series. Children's picture books, novelty books, gift books, board books, educational books and fiction series for all ages. Also welcomes YA novels and series. See website for submission guidelines. Founded 2011.

Cherry Stone Publishing

website www.cherrystonepublishing.com

Literary classics for a modern audience.

Clock Tower Publishing

Marginalised and diverse voices trade fiction, including standalone and series titles.

Every Cherry

Accessible books for the SEND community.

Swift Press‡

43 Drewstead Road, London SW16 1LY
tel 020-8265 2062
email info@swiftpress.com
website www.swiftpress.com
Facebook www.facebook.com/SwiftPressBooks
X @_swiftpress
Bluesky @swiftpress.bsky.social
Instagram @_swiftpress
Managing Director Diana Broccardo, *Editorial Director* Robin Baird-Smith, *Publisher* Mark Richards.

Independent publisher of fiction and non-fiction. Founded 2020.

Ta-Ha Publishers‡
tel 020-8670 1888
email editor@tahapublishers.com
website www.tahapublishers.com
Facebook www.facebook.com/tahapublishers
Instagram @tahapublishers
Managing Director Abia Afsar-Siddiqui

Family-run small independent Islamic publisher of books on Islamic themes, including the Quran, Islamic history, jurisprudence, comparative religion, contemporary issues, self-development, family life and children's books with Islamic cultural elements, often with illustrations. Founded 1980.

tall-lighthouse
email tall-lighthouse@yahoo.com
website https://tall-lighthouse.co.uk/
Director Les Robinson

An independent poetry press of full collections of poetry, pamphlets and anthologies with over 100 titles issued from more than 60 poets. Founded 1999.

Tangerine Press
c/o The Library, Station Road, New Malden, London KT3 6JF
email info@thetangerinepress.com
website https://thetangerinepress.com
X @tangerinepress
Instagram @tangerine_press
Publisher Michael Curran

New, neglected and innovative writing in handbound, hardcover limited editions, often in tandem with paperbacks. Also releases chapbooks, broadsides, vinyl records, artwork, screen prints, posters and ephemera. Founded 2006.

Taproot Books
website https://taprootpressuk.co.uk/
Facebook www.facebook.com/taprootpressUK
X @presstaproot
Instagram @taprootpress
Co-founders Daniela Silva, Patrick Jamieson

Literary fiction, non-fiction and poetry. Founded 2020.

Tarquin Publications
Suite 74, 17 Holywell Hill, St Albans AL1 1DT
tel (01727) 833866
email info@tarquinbooks.com
website www.tarquinbooks.com

Mathematics and mathematical models, puzzles, codes and logic. Also paper cutting, paper engineering and pop-up books for children. No unsolicited MSS, send suggestion or synopsis. Founded 1970.

Tartarus Press
Coverley House, Carlton, Leyburn, North Yorkshire DL8 4AY
website www.tartaruspress.com
Facebook www.facebook.com/tartarus.press.5
Directors R. B. Russell, Rosalind Rosalie Parker

A small independent press of collectable hardback limited editions of literary supernatural/strange/ horror fiction, also publishes other formats. Has been awarded five World Fantasy awards and a 'Stoker' from the Horror Writers Association. Founded 1990.

Taschen UK
5 Anderson Street, London SW3 3LU
tel 020-7845 8585
email contact-uk@taschen.com
website www.taschen.com
Facebook www.facebook.com/taschen
Instagram @taschen

Art, anthropology and aphrodisia. Founded 1980.

Tate Enterprises*‡
The Lodge, Millbank, London SW1P 4RG
email orders@tate.org.uk
website www.tate.org.uk/about-us/tate-publishing
Facebook www.facebook.com/tatebooks
X @tate_publishing
Instagram @tatepublishing
Publishing Director Tom Avery, *Merchandise Director* Rosey Blackmore

Exhibition catalogues, art books, children's books and merchandise for Tate in London, Liverpool and St Ives. Also product development, picture library and licensing. Founded 1911.

I.B. Tauris – see Bloomsbury Publishing

Taylor & Francis Group*
4 Park Square, Milton Park, Abingdon, Oxon OX14 4RN
tel 020-7017 6000
email enquiries@taylorandfrancis.com
website https://taylorandfrancis.com/
Ceo Penny Ladkin-Brand, *Managing Director, Books* Jeremy North

Academic and reference. Founded 1798.

CRC Press
Science: physics, mathematics, chemistry, electronics, natural history, pharmacology and drug metabolism, toxicology, technology, history of science, ergonomics, production engineering, remote sensing, geographic information systems and engineering.

Routledge
website www.routledge.com

Addiction, anthropology, animation, archaeology, architecture, art history, Asian studies, audio, business, behavioural science, civil engineering, classical studies, construction, counselling, criminology, development and environment, dictionaries, economics, education, film, gaming,

Books

geography, health, history, Japanese studies, law, leisure and recreation management, library science, language, linguistics, literary studies, media and culture, music, nursing, performance studies, philosophy, photography, politics, psychiatry, psychology, reference, social administration, social studies/sociology, social work, sports science, theatre and women's studies. Also directories, international relations, reference and yearbooks.

Templar Books

Victoria House, Bloomsbury Square,
London WC1B 4DA
tel 020-3770 8888
email hello@bonnierbooks.co.uk
website www.bonnierbooks.co.uk/imprints/templar-books
X @templarbooks
Publisher Sophie Hallam

Children's imprint. Series include the *Ology* series, *Jonny Duddle's Gigantosaurus* titles and the *Amazing Baby* range of board and novelty books. Imprint of Bonnier Books UK. Founded 1978.

Templar Poetry

58 Dale Road, Matlock, Derbyshire DE4 3NB
tel 07582 219078
email info@templarpoetry.com
website www.templarpoetry.com

An independent publisher of poetry and fiction. Founded 2005.

Thames & Hudson*‡

6–24 Britannia Street, London WC1X 9JD
tel 020-7845 5000
email submissions@thameshudson.co.uk
website www.thamesandhudson.com
Facebook www.facebook.com/thamesandhudson
X @thamesandhudson
Instagram @thamesandhudson
Ceo & Publisher Sophy Thompson

Illustrated non-fiction for adults and children: art and art history, architecture, photography, design, fashion, popular culture, history and archaeology. For submission guidelines see website. Founded 1949.

Thinkwell Books

7 Winsford Crescent, Little Bispham,
Thornton-Cleveleys, Lancs. FY5 1PS
tel 07940 933159
email thinkwellbooksuk@gmail.com
website https://thinkwellbooks.org/
Managing Editors Jeff Weston, Patricia Khan

Literary fiction, political and social works, sports journalism and commercial fiction. New authors and unsolicited MSS welcome. See website for details regarding submissions. Founded 2019.

Thistle Publishing

36 Great Smith Street, London SW1P 3BU
tel 020-7222 7574
email david@thistlepublishing.co.uk
website www.thistlepublishing.co.uk
Facebook www.facebook.com/ThistlePublishing
X @ThistleBooks
Ceo Sophie Long, *Publisher* David Haviland

Fiction and non-fiction. Accepts unsolicited submissions. Send three chapters and a synopsis by email. Founded 1996.

Thomson Reuters – Round Hall*

Spaces Office 313, 77 Sir John Rogerson's Quay,
Block C, Grand Canal Docklands, Dublin 2,
D02 VK60 Ireland
tel 0345 600 9355
website www.sweetandmaxwell.co.uk/roundhall
Directors A. Clarke, M. McCann

Law. Formerly The Round Hall Press. Acquired by Sweet & Maxwell in 1995. Now part of Thomson Reuters. Founded 1980.

3dtotal Publishing

29 Foregate Street, Worcester WR1 1DS
tel (01905) 29764
email support@3dtotal.com
website www.3dtotal.com
Facebook www.facebook.com/3dtotal
X @3dtotal
Instagram @3dtotal
Managing Director Tom Greenway

Art books for beginners, hobbyists and professionals. Founded 1999.

3TimesRebel

21 Durris Loan, Broughty Ferry, Dundee DD5 3BD
email info@3timesrebel.com
website www.3timesrebel.com
Facebook www.facebook.com/3timesrebel
X @3TimesRebel
Director Bibiana Mas Corbella

Translated fiction: women from minorities. Founded 2020.

ThunderPoint Publishing*

Bryn Heulog, Talley, Llandeilo SA19 7YH
email info@thunderpoint.co.uk
website www.thunderpoint.scot
X @thunderpointltd

Fiction and non-fiction. Books that reflect the wide range of communities in Scotland, especially under-represented voices. Adult and YA (age 15+). Submission guidelines on website. Founded 2012.

Tilted Axis Press

639 High Road, London N17 8AA
email info@tiltedaxispress.com
website www.tiltedaxispress.com

Facebook www.facebook.com/tiltedaxispress
X @tiltedaxispress

Books by Asian and African writers, translated into a variety of Englishes. Founded 2015.

Tiny Owl Publishing

366 Woodstock Road, Oxford OX2 8AE
email info@tinyowl.co.uk
website www.tinyowl.co.uk
Facebook www.facebook.com/tinyowlpublishing
X @TinyOwl_Books
Instagram @tiny_owl_publishing
Publisher Delaram Ghanimifard

An independent publisher of global children's literature. Picture books for ages 3–11. Aims to promote diversity and human rights values. Founded 2015.

Tippermuir Books*

3 Graham's Place, King Street, Perth PH2 8HZ
email wavmail@tippermuirbooks.co.uk
website http://tippermuirbooks.co.uk
Facebook www.facebook.com/people/Tippermuir-Books
X @tippermuirbooks
Instagram @tippermuirbooks
Directors Paul Philippou, Matthew Mackie, Rob Hands

Adult and children's fiction and non-fiction including poetry with a cultural and social importance. Submissions welcome. Founded 2009.

Titan Books

144 Southwark Street, London SE1 0UP
tel 020-7620 0200
website www.titanbooks.com
Facebook www.facebook.com/titan-books
X @titan_books
Directors Nick Landau, Vivian Cheung

Fiction: sci-fi, fantasy, horror, crime and YA crossover. Licensed fiction and non-fiction covering TV, film, gaming and popular culture. Graphic novels. No children's proposals or middle grade. All fiction submissions must come from an agent. Division of Titan Publishing Group. Founded 1981.

Tramp Press

email info@tramppress.com
email submissions@tramppress.com
website www.tramppress.com
Facebook www.facebook.com/tramppress
X @TrampPress
Founding Publishers Lisa Coen, Sarah Davis-Goff

Feminist press of fiction and narrative non-fiction. No poetry, children's books or work submitted from the USA or Canada. Founded 2014.

Transworld*

Penguin Random House, One Embassy Gardens, 8 Viaduct Gardens, London SW11 7BW
tel 020-7840 8400
website www.penguin.co.uk/transworld
Managing Director Kimberley Young, *Publishing Directors* Susanna Wadeson (non-fiction), Kirsty Dunseath (Doubleday, UK), *Publishers* Bill Scott-Kerr (Transworld), Sarah Adams (fiction & brand)

Non-fiction: autobiography, biography, business, current affairs, crime, health and diet, history, humour, memoir, military, music, natural history, personal development and self-help, science, travel and adventure. Fiction (commercial): crime, thrillers, contemporary, historical and saga fiction, sci-fi, horror and fantasy, literary and book club fiction. No unsolicited MSS accepted. Imprints: Bantam (UK), Doubleday (UK), Penguin and Torva. Part of Penguin Random House UK. Founded 1950.

Troika*

Troika Books Well House, Green Lane, Ardleigh, Colchester, Essex CO7 7PD
email info@troikabooks.com
website www.troikabooks.com
Publisher Martin West, *Publicity, Marketing & Editorial* Roy Johnson

Picture books, poetry and fiction with a focus on diversity for all ages. Founded 2012.

Trotman Indigo Publishing‡

18e Charles Street, Bath BA1 1HX
email info@trotman.co.uk
website https://trotman.co.uk/
Managing Director Sarah Cambell

Professional and educational publisher of books by contemporary careers education influencers. Founded 1969.

TSO (The Stationery Office)

18 Central Avenue, St Andrews Business Park, Norwich NR7 0HR
email customer.services@tso.co.uk
website www.tsoshop.co.uk
Publishing Director Lisa Daniels

Publishing and information management services: business, directories, pharmaceutical, professional, reference and *Learning to Drive*. Founded 1996.

Turas Press†

6–9 Trinity Street, Dublin 2, D02 EY47, Republic of Ireland
email admin@turaspress.ie
website https://turaspress.ie/
X @TurasPress
Instagram @turas_press
Founder & Director Liz McSkeane

Independent publisher of poetry and fiction for Irish and international readers. Poetry and literary fiction, in English. Does not publish translations or children's literature. The submissions window is open twice a year: March and September. See website for details. Founded 2017.

Two Rivers Press‡

7 Denmark Road, Reading, Berks. RG1 5PA
tel 0118 987 1452
email tworiverspress@gmail.com
website www.tworiverspress.com
Facebook www.facebook.com/tworiverspress
X @TwoRiversPress
Publisher Anne Nolan, *Editorial Director, Botanical Art Portfolios* Sally Mortimore, *Poetry Editor* Peter Robinson

Champions Reading and surrounding area's heritage and culture through contemporary and classic poetry, art and local interest books. Publishes an international *Botanical Art Portfolios* series. Founded 1994.

Two Windmills

Marine House, Tide Mill Way, Woodbridge, Suffolk IP12 1AP
tel (01394) 386651
email customerservice@twowindmills.com
website www.twowindmills.com
Instagram @twowindmills
Founder & Managing Director Marcus E. Leaver, *Publishers* Dan Graham, Steve Munnings

Children's activity, novelty, picture, reference, character, gift and early learning books. Founded 1999.

UCLan Publishing‡

The Media Factory, University of Central Lancashire, Preston PR1 2HE
email uclanpublishing@uclan.ac.uk
website https://uclanpublishing.com/
Facebook www.facebook.com/uclanpublishing
X @publishinguclan
Bluesky @uclanpublishing.bsky.social
Instagram @uclan_publishing
Publisher Hazel Holmes

Supporting students at the University of Central Lancashire, not-for-profit publishers of early years, middle-grade, teen and YA fiction. Currently closed to submissions. Founded 2010.

UCL Press*

University College London (UCL), Gower Street, London WC1E 6BT
email uclpresspublishing@ucl.ac.uk
website www.uclpress.co.uk
X @UCLPress
Bluesky @uclpress.bsky.social
Instagram @uclpress
Publisher Lara Speicher, *Commissioning Editors* Chris Penfold, Pat Gordon Smith, *Textbook Programme Manager* Dhara Snowden, *Journals Manager* Ian Caswell

Peer reviewed Open Access scholarly monographs, edited collections, textbooks, journals and other research outputs. Imprints UCL IOE Press and UCL Press. Submission guidelines, see website. Founded 2015.

UEA Publishing Project

Office AHB 3.11, Interdisciplinary Institute for the Humanities, University of East Anglia, Norwich NR4 7TJ
tel (01603) 593707
email publishing@uea.ac.uk
website www.ueapublishingproject.com/
Facebook www.facebook.com/ueapublishingproject
X @ueapublishing
Instagram @publishinguea
Managing Director Nathan Hamilton, *Editor* Brad Bigelow (Recovered Books series for Boiler House Press)

Operates commercially through micro-imprints. Boiler House Press specialises in fiction, poetry and non-fiction. Strangers Press focuses on literary translations and international writing. The UEA Publishing Project also provides an experiential learning resource for UEA students aiming to enhance participation in literature by opening up access to the publishing industry. Founded 2017.

Ulric Publishing

PO Box 55, Church Stretton, Shrops. SY6 6WR
tel (01694) 781354
email info@ulricpublishing.com
website www.ulricpublishing.com
Directors Ulric Woodhams, Elizabeth Oakes

Non-fiction military and motoring history. Licensing, bespoke bindings and publishing services. No unsolicited MSS. Visitors by appointment. Founded 1992.

Ulverscroft

The Green, Bradgate Road, Anstey, Leicester LE7 7FU
tel 0116 236 4325
email customersupport@ulverscroft.co.uk
website www.ulverscroft.co.uk
Facebook www.facebook.com/ulverscroft
X @UlverscroftLtd

Publisher and distributor of large print, digital and physical audiobooks. Founded 1964.

Unicorn Publishing Group

Charleston Studio, 1 Meadow Business Centre, Lewes BN8 5RW
tel (01273) 812066
email ian@unicornpublishing.org
website www.unicornpublishing.org
X @UnicornPubGroup
Instagram @unicornpubgroup
Directors Lord Strathcarron, Lucy Duckworth, Simon Perks, Ryan Gearing, David Breuer

Independent publisher with the Unicorn imprint specialising in the visual arts and cultural history. Submissions welcomed, see website for guidance. Founded 1985.

University College Dublin Press†
Room H103, Humanities Institute, Belfield,
Dublin D04 V1W8, Republic of Ireland
tel +353 (0)1 716 4680
email ucdpress@ucd.ie
website www.ucdpress.ie
X @UCDPress
Bluesky @ucdpress.bsky.social
Instagram @ucdpress
Publisher Noelle Moran

Academic trade: humanities, Irish studies, history and politics, literary studies, social sciences, sociology, music and food science, architecture, ecology, gender, migration and environmental studies. Founded 1995.

Merlin Unwin Books*
6 Rural Enterprise Centre, Eco Park Road, Ludlow, Shrops. SY8 1FF
tel (01584) 877456
email books@merlinunwin.co.uk
website www.merlinunwin.co.uk
Facebook www.facebook.com/merlinunwinbooks
X @merlinunwin
Instagram @merlinunwinbooks
Chairman Merlin Unwin, *Managing Director* Karen McCall

Countryside, wildlife, herbalist, fieldsports, sports, foraging, fishing and fly-tying books. Founded 1990.

Usborne Publishing‡
83–85 Saffron Hill, London EC1N 8RT
tel 020-7430 2800
email help@usborne.co.uk
website www.usborne.com
Facebook www.facebook.com/UsbornePublishing
X @usborne
Directors Nicola Usborne, *Publishing Director* Jenny Tyler (editorial)

An independent, family publisher of books for children of all ages, including baby, preschool, novelty, activity, non-fiction and fiction. Looking for imaginative children's fiction. No unsolicited MSS. Founded 1973.

Vallentine Mitchell
Catalyst House, 720 Centennial Court,
Centennial Park, Elstree WD6 3SY
tel 020-8292 5637
email info@vmbooks.com (general)
email editor@vmbooks.com (submissions)
website www.vmbooks.com
Directors Stewart Cass, A.E. Cass, H.J. Cass

International publisher of books of Jewish interest, both for the scholar and general reader. Subjects include Jewish history, culture and heritage, modern Jewish thought, Holocaust studies, Middle East studies, biography and reference. Founded 1949.

Valley Press
Woodend, The Crescent, Scarborough YO11 2PW
email hello@valleypressuk.com
website www.valleypressuk.com
Publisher Jamie McGarry

Poetry (collections, pamphlets and anthologies), fiction (novels and short stories) and non-fiction (memoirs, travel writing, journalism, music and art). Founded 2008.

Velocity Press
16 Long Meadow Close, West Wickham BR4 0EQ
tel 07595 823298
email info@velocitypress.uk
website https://velocitypress.uk/
Facebook www.facebook.com/velocitypressbooks
X @PressVelocity
Director Colin Steven

Electronic music and club culture non-fiction and fiction. Founded 2019.

Verso‡
6 Meard Street, London W1F 0EG
tel 020-7437 3546
email enquiries@verso.co.uk
website www.versobooks.com
Facebook www.facebook.com/VersoBks
X @versobooks
Instagram @versobooks
Managing Director Nicole Aschoff

Current affairs, politics, sociology, economics, history, philosophy and cultural studies. Founded 1970.

Vertebrate Publishing‡
Omega Court, 352 Cemetery Road, Sheffield S11 8FT
email info@adventurebooks.com
website www.adventurebooks.com
Facebook www.facebook.com/vertebratepublishing
X @VertebratePub
Instagram @vertebrate_publishing
Founder Jon Barton

Narratives and guidebooks inspired by the outdoors in areas of mountain biking, cycling, climbing, walking, running, outdoor swimming and travel. Awarded Small Press of the Year and Specialist Consumer Publisher of the Year in 2022. Founded 2004.

Verve Poetry Press
tel 07713 236205
email mail@vervepoetrypress.com
website https://vervepoetrypress.com/
X @VervePoetryPres
Instagram @verve.publisherofpoetry
Co-founders Stuart Bartholomew, Amerah Saleh

Poetry. Founded 2018.

Viking – see Penguin General

Vintage*

One Embassy Gardens, 8 Viaduct Gardens,
London SW11 7BW
tel 020-7139 3000
website www.penguin.co.uk/vintage

Fiction and non-fiction. No unsolicited MSS. Part of Penguin Random House UK. Founded 1954.

The Bodley Head

tel 020-7139 3824
X @TheBodleyHead
Publishing Director Stuart Williams, *Deputy Publishing Director* Will Hammond, *Editorial Director* Jorg Hensgen, *Paperback Editor* Alice Skinner, *Assistant Editor* Laura Reeves

Non-fiction: natural history, science, history, current affairs, politics, tech, big ideas, economics, autobiography and how to live.

Jonathan Cape

tel 020-7139 306
X @JonathanCape
Instagram @jonathancapebooks
Publishing Director Hannah Westland, *Deputy Publishing Director* Bea Hemming, *Editorial Directors* Željka Marošević, David Milner, *Associate Publishers* Dan Franklin (graphic novels), Robin Robertson (poetry), *Senior Commissioning Editor* Alex Russell, *Editorial Assistant* Louise Navarro-Cann, Leeza Isaeva

Non-fiction: biography and memoirs, current affairs, history, poetry, travel and politics. Fiction: general fiction and graphic novels.

Chatto & Windus/Hogarth

tel 020-7139 3695
Instagram @chattobooks
Publishing Director Becky Hardie, *Associate Publishing Director* Clara Farmer, *Editorial Director* Molly Slight, *Senior Editor* Victoria Murray-Browne, *Commissioning Editor* Kaiya Shang, *Assistant Editor* Rosanna Hildyard, *Poetry Editor* Sarah Howe, *Assistant Editor* Asia Choudhry

Non-fiction, fiction and poetry. No unsolicited MSS.

Classics and Catalogues

tel 020-7840 8895
Publishing Director Nicholas Skidmore, *Senior Editor* Charlotte Knight, *Assistant Editor* Orla Schätzlein

Classic editions.

Fern Press

tel 020-7139 3097
Instagram @fernpress_
Publishing Director Michal Shavit, *Editor* Sean Hayes

Fiction: literary. Non-fiction: memoir, history, ideas, popular science, psychology, philosophy, politics, popular culture, music, design, fashion and art. No unsolicited MSS.

Harvill

tel 020-7139 3457
X @harvillsecker
Instagram @harvillsecker
Publishing Director Elizabeth Foley, *Senior Commissioning Editor* Ellie Steel, *Assistant Editors* Sania Riaz, Christopher Sturtivant

English literature, crime, crossover fiction, world literature in translation, romance, fantasy and sci-fi. Non-fiction: history, current affairs, literary essays and music. No unsolicited MSS.

Pimlico

tel 020-7840 8836

History, biography and literature. Exclusively in paperback. No unsolicited MSS.

Yellow Jersey Press

tel 020-7840 8438
Senior Editorial Joe Pickering

Literary and prize-winning sports writing of all kinds. No unsolicited MSS.

University of Wales Press‡

University Registry, King Edward VII Avenue,
Cardiff CF10 3NS
tel 029-2037 6999
email press@press.wales.ac.uk
website www.uwp.co.uk,
www.gwasgprifysgolcymru.org
Director Natalie Williams

Non-fiction: academic, education and trade (Welsh and English). Specialises in the humanities and social sciences across a broad range of subjects: Welsh studies, European studies, literary criticism, history, political philosophy, Celtic and Medieval studies. Trade imprint: Calon Books (page 127). Founded 1922.

Walker Books*‡

87 Vauxhall Walk, London SE11 5HJ
tel 020-7793 0909
website www.walker.co.uk
Facebook www.facebook.com/walkerbooks
X @walkerbooksuk
Instagram @walkerbooksuk
Publishing Director Shannon Cullen

Children's: activity books, novelty books, picture books, fiction for ages 5–8 and 9–12, YA fiction, series fiction, film/TV tie-ins, plays, poetry, digital and audio. Imprints include: MITeen Press, MIT Kids Press, Walker Books, Walker Entertainment and Walker Studio. Founded 1980.

Watkins Publishing‡

Unit 11, Shepperton House, 89 Shepperton Road,
London N1 3DF
tel 020-3813 6940
email enquiries@watkinspublishing.com
website www.watkinspublishing.com
Facebook www.facebook.com/WatkinsPublishing
X @WatkinsWisdom
Editorial Director Ella Chappell, *Commissioning Editor* Sophie Blackman

Books

Wellbeing, personal development and esoteric books. Part of Watkins Media. Founded 1893.

The Waywiser Press

Christmas Cottage, Church Enstone,
Chipping Norton, Oxon OX7 4NN
tel (01608) 677492
website https://waywiser-press.com/
Facebook www.facebook.com/thewaywiserpress
X @Waywiserpress
Editor-in-Chief Philip Hoy

Small independent literary press of modern poetry and fiction. Sometimes publishes memoir, criticism and history. Founded 2001.

Weatherglass Press

20 Parklands Road, London SW16 6TE
email neil@weatherglassbooks.com
website https://weatherglassbooks.com/, https://weatherglass.substack.com/
Facebook www.facebook.com/WeatherglassBooks
X @weatherglassbks
Founders Neil Griffiths, Damian Lanigan

An independent press of literary fiction. Runs a bi-annual novella prize judged by Ali Smith. Founded 2021.

The Wee Book Company

website www.theweebookcompany.com
Facebook www.facebook.com/theweebookcompany
X @theweebookco
Director Susan Cohen

Modern non-fiction Scottish humour and children's fiction. Founded 2018.

Josef Weinberger Plays

12–14 Mortimer Street, London W1T 3JJ
tel 020-7580 2827
email shows@jwmail.co.uk
website www.josef-weinberger.com
Facebook www.facebook.com/josef-weinberger-plays
X @weinberger-plays

Stage plays only, in both acting and trade editions. Preliminary letter essential. Founded 1936.

Welbeck Publishing Group

Carmelite House, 50 Victoria Embankment,
London EC4Y 0DZ
tel 020-3122 7222
email enquiries@welbeckpublishing.com
website www.headline.co.uk/imprint/headline/welbeck

Non-fiction. Imprints include: Headline Welbeck non-fiction, Mountain Leopard Press and Orange Hippo. No unsolicited MSS. Synopses and ideas welcome, but no fiction or poetry. A division of the Headline Publishing Group. Founded 2019.

Welsh Academic Press

PO Box 733, Cardiff CF14 7ZY
tel 029-2021 8187
email post@welsh-academic-press.wales
website www.welsh-academic-press.wales
Facebook www.facebook.com/WelshAcademicPress
X @WelshAcadPress
Instagram @welshacademicpress

History, political studies, public affairs, education, medieval Welsh and Celtic studies, Scandinavian and Baltic studies. Founded 1994.

Whittet Books

1 St John's Lane, Stansted, Essex CM24 8JU
tel (01279) 815871
email mail@whittetbooks.com
website www.whittetbooks.com
Director & Publisher Shirley Greenall

Natural history, wildlife, countryside, poultry, livestock, horses and donkeys. Send outline by email. Founded 1976.

Wide Eyed Editions

2nd Floor, 1 Triptych Place, London SE1 9SH
tel 020-7700 9000
website www.quartoknows.com/Wide-Eyed-Editions
Publisher Georgia Buckthorn

Children's non-fiction. Imprint of Quarto Group Publishing UK. Founded 2014.

Wild Hunt Books‡

email info@wildhuntbooks.co.uk
website www.wildhuntbooks.co.uk
X @wildhuntbooks
Bluesky @wildhuntbooks.bsky.social
Instagram @wildhuntbooks_uk
Publisher & Editorial Director Ariell Cacciola

Literary and upmarket fiction with experimental narratives, plot and structure. Submission guidelines: accepts agented submissions throughout the year. Open submission windows are scheduled periodically. Founded 2020.

Wild Things Publishing

Freshford, Bath BA2 7WG
tel 07761 375717
email hello@wildthingspublishing.com
website www.wildthingspublishing.com
Facebook www.facebook.com/wildthingspublishing
X @wildswimming
Instagram @wildswimming
Founders Daniel Start, Tania Pascoe

Books (and apps) about nature. Founded 2011.

Wildthought Books

Box Wildthought, 245 Gladstone Street,
Nottingham NG7 6HX

email submissions@wildthoughtbooks.co.uk
website https://wildthoughtbooks.co.uk/
Facebook www.facebook.com/61574004987163
Instagram @wildthought_books
Co-founder Ronny Worsey

Independent publisher of fiction, non-fiction, handbooks and children's books. ee submissions page on website for guidelines and genres. Founded 2024.

John Wiley & Sons*

The Atrium, Southern Gate, Chichester, West Sussex PO19 8SQ
tel (01243) 779777
email customer@wiley.com
Alternative address 9600 Garsington Road, Oxford OX4 2DQ
tel (01865) 776868
website www.wiley.com
President & Ceo Matthew Kissner

Scientific, technical, medical and scholarly journals, encyclopaedias, books and online products and services. Also publishes professional/trade books, subscription products, training materials and online applications, websites and educational materials for undergraduate and graduate students and lifelong learners. Founded 1807.

Philip Wilson Publishers*‡

50 Bedford Square, London WC1B 3DP
email ContactPWP@bloomsbury.com
website www.bloomsbury.com/uk/discover/superpages/non-fiction/philip-wilson-publishers
Publisher Jayne Parsons

Fine and applied art, architecture, photography, collecting and museums. An imprint of Bloomsbury Publishing. Founded 1975.

Wooden Books

The Lawn, Walsham-le-Willows, Bury St Edmunds, Suffolk IP31 3AW
email woodenbooksoffice@gmail.com
Alternative address Red Brick Building, Glastonbury BA6 9FT
website www.woodenbooks.com
Facebook www.facebook.com/woodenbooks
Instagram @woodenbooks
Ceo John Martineau

Liberal arts, modern and ancient arts and sciences. Founded 1996.

Wrecking Ball Press

5 Theatre Mews, Egginton Street, Hull HU2 8DL
email editor@wreckingballpress.com
website www.wreckingballpress.com
Facebook www.facebook.com/wreckingballpress
X @wbphull
Editor Shane Rhodes

Independent publisher of contemporary cutting-edge literature including poetry. Founded 1997.

Yale University Press London‡

47 Bedford Square, London WC1B 3DP
tel 020-7079 4900
website www.yalebooks.co.uk
X @YaleBooks
Managing Director Heather McCallum, *Editorial Directors* Mark Eastment (art & architecture), Julian Loose (trade & academic)

Art, architecture, history, economics, political science, religion, history of science, biography, current affairs and music. Founded 1961.

Yellow Jersey Press – see Vintage

Zaffre*

Victoria House, Bloomsbury Square, London WC1B 4DA
tel 020-3770 8888
email hello@bonnierbooks.co.uk
website www.bonnierbooks.co.uk/imprints/zaffre
X @zaffrebooks
Managing Director Sarah Benton, *Publisher* Ben Willis

Commercial fiction: crime, thrillers, saga, women's and reading group. Part of the Adult Trade Division of Bonnier Books UK. Founded 2014.

Zambezi Publishing

22 Second Avenue, Camels Head, Plymouth PL2 2EQ
tel (01752) 367300
email info@zampub.com
website www.zampub.com
Contacts Sasha Fenton, Jan Budkowski

Mind, body & spirit. Founded 1998.

Zed Books – see Bloomsbury Publishing

ZigZag Education

Unit 3, Greenway Business Centre, Doncaster Road, Bristol BS10 5PY
tel 0117 950 3199
email submissions@publishmenow.co.uk
website www.zigzageducation.co.uk, www.publishmenow.co.uk
Development Director John-Lloyd Hagger, *Strategy Director* Mike Stephens

Secondary school teaching resources: English, maths, ICT, geography, history, science, business, politics, PE and media studies. Founded 1998.

CROWDFUNDED PUBLISHING

Crowdfunding, the raising of small investments from a wide pool of individuals to fund a project, can be a viable option for writers wishing to publish their work. The first publisher to use this model was London-based publisher Unbound, founded in 2011. Unbound is now an imprint of Boundless Publishing Group (https://unbound.com/). Other publishers and platforms that use crowdfunding as a way to raise funds include the following:

And Other Stories (page 119)
Cloudscape Comic Society (page 195)
Crowdbound (page 133)
Inkshares (page 210)

Indiegogo

website www.indiegogo.com

Acts as a 'launchpad' for creative ideas.

Kickstarter

website www.kickstarter.com

Helps artists, musicians, filmmakers, independent authors and designers find resources and support needed for a project.

Publishizer

website https://publishizer.com/

Books only. Authors submit a proposal and launch a pre-orders campaign. If a publisher signals interest, an exchange is initiated between author and publisher. Alternatively an author can approach a crowdfunding publisher to help raise finances with them. The publisher will critically assess their work before presenting it for funding opportunities and will publish and distribute the book. Some publishers seek investment from readers across their operation and not for a specific title.

SOCIAL ENTERPRISE PUBLISHING

Organisations with social enterprise at their heart offer publishing support – expertise and funding – to those who might not otherwise be published. These initiatives, many not-for-profit charitable operations, are motivated by social, community and environmental objectives rather than by money. There are an increasing number of social enterprise publishers in operation now, including the following:

Acair (page 118)
Arkbound (page 120)
Betimes Books (page 122)
Cinnamon Press (page 130)
Comma Press (page 131)
Cordite (page 191)
Dead Ink Books (page 134)
Fly on the Wall Press (page 141)
Freemantle (page 191)
Graywolf (page 208)
Héloïse Press (page 149)
Honno Ltd (Welsh Women's Press) (page 150)
Inspired Quill (page 152)
Invisible Publishing (page 196)
JewishGen Press (page 211)
Lantana Publishing (page 155)
Leamington Books (page 155)
McSweeney's Books (page 213)
Scottish Mountaineering Press (page 176)
Syndney University Press (page 193)
Tippermuir Books (page 183)
UCLan Publishing (page 184)
Wisdom Publications (page 222)

Book publishers overseas

Listings are given for book publishers in Australia (below), Canada (page 194), New Zealand (page 199), South Africa (page 201) and the USA (page 203).

MS = manuscript (MSS = manuscripts)
sae = self-addressed envelope

AUSTRALIA

**Member of the Australian Publishers Association*

ACER Press

19 Prospect Hill Road, Private Bag 55, Camberwell, VIC 3124
tel +61 (0)3 9277 5555
email proposals@acer.org
website www.acer.org/au
Facebook www.facebook.com/acer.edu.au
X @acereduau
Ceo Lisa Rodgers

Publisher of the Australian Council for Educational Research. Produces a range of books and assessments including professional resources for teachers, psychologists and special educational needs professionals. Founded 1930.

Affirm Press

28 Thistlethwaite Street, South Melbourne, VIC 3205
tel +61 (0)3 8695 9623
email info@affirmpress.com.au
website https://affirmpress.com.au/
Facebook www.facebook.com/affirmpress
X @affirmpress
Ceo & Publishing Director Martin Hughes

Non-fiction, fiction and young fiction. Owned by Simon & Schuster. Founded 2010.

Allen & Unwin*

83 Alexander Street, Crows Nest, NSW 2065
Postal address PO Box 8500, St Leonards, NSW 1590
tel +61 (0)2 8425 0100
website www.allenandunwin.com
Chairman Patrick Gallagher, *Ceo* Robert Gorman, *Publishing Directors* Jane Morrow (Murdock Books), Eva Mills (children & YA), Cate Paterson (Allen & Unwin and Atlantic Books)

General trade, including fiction and children's books, and broad-ranging non-fiction. Imprints: Albert Street Books, Allen & Unwin, Atlantic Books, Crows Nest, Inspired Living, Joan, Murdoch Books and Pier 9. Will consider unsolicited MSS but will only accept MSS through electronic Friday Pitch system. Founded 1990.

Bad Apple Press

Sydney: 33 Blacks Road, Arcadia, NSW 2159
email enquiry@badapplepress.com.au
website https://badapplepress.com.au/bad-apples/
Facebook www.facebook.com/ApplePressPublisher
X @PressApple
Co-founder & Publishing Manager Samantha Miles

Independent publisher of fiction and non-fiction. Founded 2018.

Black Inc Books*

Wurundjeri Country,
22–24 Northumberland Street Collingwood, VIC 3066
tel +61 (0)3 9486 0288
email enquiries@blackincbooks.com
website www.blackincbooks.com.au
Facebook www.facebook.com/blackincbooks
X @blackincbooks
Instagram @blackincbooks
Publishing Director Elisabeth Young

An independent publisher of non-fiction. History, politics, biography, criticism and current affairs. Imprints: La Trobe University Press books and the Quarterly Essay journal. Founded 2000.

Bloomsbury Publishing*

Level 6, 387 George Street, Sydney, NSW 2000
tel +61 (0)2 8820 4900
email au@bloomsbury.com
website www.bloomsbury.com/au
Facebook www.facebook.com/bloomsburypublishingaustralia
X @BloomsburySyd
Managing Director Cristina Cappelluto

Supports the worldwide publishing activities of Bloomsbury Publishing: caters for the Australia and New Zealand territories. See Bloomsbury Publishing (page 124). Bloomsbury Publishing founded 1986.

Cambridge University Press & Assessment Education Australia*

477 Williamstown Road, Private Bag 31, Port Melbourne, VIC 3207
tel +61 (0)3 8671 1400
email enquiries@cambridge.edu.au
website www.cambridge.org
Chief Executive Peter Phillips

Academic, educational, reference and ESL. Founded 1534.

Cengage Learning Australia*

Level 7, 80 Dorcas Street, South Melbourne, VIC 3205

tel +61 (0)3 9685 4111
website www.cengage.com.au

Educational books. Founded 2007.

Clan Destine Press*

website www.clandestinepress.net
Facebook www.facebook.com/LindysClanDestinePress
Bluesky @clandestinepress.bsky.social
Publisher Lindy Cameron

Genre fiction by Australian authors for adults and YA. Crime, mystery, historical fiction, thrillers, adventure, speculative fiction, fantasy, sci-fi, horror, urban fantasy, paranormal and steampunk. Founded 2010.

Cordite Books*

PO Box 58, Castlemaine, VIC 3450
email cordite@cordite.org.au
website https://corditebooks.org.au/
Facebook www.facebook.com/corditepublishing
X @corditepoetry

Not-for-profit poetry publisher. Founded 1997.

Echo Publishing*

6/69 Carlton Crescent, Summer Hill, NSW 2130
website www.echopublishing.com.au
Facebook www.facebook.com/echopublishingaustralia
X @echo_publishing
Bluesky
Instagram @echo_publishing
Publisher & Managing Director Juliet Rogers

Adult commercial fiction (all genres except sci-fi) and non-fiction. Open to submissions at various points throughout the year. See website for details. An imprint of Bonnier Books UK. Founded 1991.

ELK Publishing

PO Box 2828, Toowoomba, QLD 4350
tel +61 (0)4 0030 1675, +61 (0)4 7592 3670
email contactus@elk-publishing.com
website www.elk-publishing.com
Facebook www.facebook.com/elkpublishing
X @elkpublish
Instagram @elkpublishing
Founder & Ceo Selina Kucks

Independent publisher of children's and educational literature. Provides opportunities for unknown artists and illustrators to collaborate with in-house authors and offers internships to university students. Founded 2009.

Elsevier Australia*

Level 1, Tower 2, 475 Victoria Avenue, Chatswood, NSW 2067
tel +61 (0)2 9422 8500
email customerserviceau@elsevier.com
website www.elsevierhealth.com.au

Science, medical and technical books. Imprints: Academic Press, Butterworth-Heinemann, Churchill Livingstone, Endeavour, Excerpta Medica, Focal Press, The Lancet, MacLennan and Petty, MD Consult, Morgan Kauffman, Mosby, Saunders, Science Direct, Syngress. Founded 1972.

Exisle Publishing*

Unit 11, 201 Main Street, Gosford, NSW 2250
email sales@exislepublishing.com
website www.exislepublishing.com
Facebook www.facebook.com/ExislePublishing
X @ExisleBooks
Instagram @exislepublishing
Ceo Gareth St John Thomas

Independent publisher of non-fiction for adults and fiction and non-fiction for children. Imprint: EK Books. Founded 1991.

Freemantle Press*

PO Box 158, North Fremantle, WA 6159
tel +61 (0)8 9430 6331
email admin@fremantlepress.com.au
website https://fremantlepress.com.au/
Facebook www.facebook.com/FreemantlePress
X @FreemantlePress
Publisher Georgia Richter

A not-for-profit publisher of fiction, non-fiction, poetry and children's literature. Founded 1976.

Hachette Australia*

Level 17, 207 Kent Street, Sydney, NSW 2000
tel +61 (0)2 8248 0800
email reception@hachette.com.au
website www.hachette.com.au
Facebook www.facebook.com/HachetteAustralia
X @HachetteAus
Instagram @hachetteaus
Ceo Louise Stark

General, children's. Accepts MSS via website. Founded 1971.

HarperCollins Publishers (Australia)*

PO Box A565, Sydney South, NSW 1235
tel +61 (0)2 9952 5000
website www.harpercollins.com.au
Facebook www.facebook.com/HarperCollinsAustralia
X @HarperCollinsAU
Adult Books Publishing Directors Brigitta Doyle, Catherine Milne (fiction), Helen Littleton (non-fiction)

Literary fiction and non-fiction, popular fiction, children's, reference, biography, autobiography, current affairs, sport, lifestyle, health/self-help, humour, true crime, travel, Australiana, history, business, gift and religion. Founded 1989.

Lawbook

Level 6, 19 Harris Street, Pyrmont, NSW 2009
tel +61 (0)2 8587 7980
website www.thomsonreuters.com.au

Law. Part of Thomson Reuters. Founded 1985.

LexisNexis Australia*

Tower 2, 475–495 Victoria Avenue, Chatswood, NSW 2067
tel +61 (0)2 9422 2174
Postal address Level 9, Locked Bag 2222, Chatswood Delivery Centre, Chatswood, NSW 2067
website www.lexisnexis.com.au
Facebook www.facebook.com/lexisnexisaustralia
Instagram @lexisnexisaus

Accounting, business, legal, tax and commercial. Founded 1970.

McGraw-Hill Australia*

Level 33, 680 George Street, Sydney, NSW 2000
website www.mcgraw-hill.com.au
Facebook www.facebook.com/MHEducationANZ
X @MHeducationAU

Educational publisher: higher education, primary education and professional (including medical, general and reference). Division of the McGraw-Hill Companies. Founded 1964.

Major Street Publishing*

29 Haydens Road, Beaumaris, VIC 3193
email info@majorstreet.com.au
website https://majorstreet.com.au/
Facebook www.facebook.com/MajorStreetPublishing
X @MajorStreetPub
Publisher Lesley Williams

Leadership, business, entrepreneurship, career development, personal finance, personal development, share market and property investing, self-care, personal growth and motivation. Founded 2009.

Melbourne University Press*

Level 1, 715 Swanston Street, Carlton, VIC 3053
tel +61 (0)3 9035 3333
email mup-contact@unimelb.edu.au
website www.mup.com.au
Facebook www.facebook.com/MUPublishing
X @mupublishing
Bluesky @mupublishing.bsk.social
Publisher Foong Ling Kong

Non-fiction: trade, academic, history and society. Imprints: Melbourne University Press and Miegunyah Press. Publishes the journal *Meanjin*. Founded 1922.

New Holland Publishers*

PO Box 5062, South Turramurra, NSW 2074
tel +61 (0)2 8986 4700
email orders@newholland.com.au
website https://au.newhollandpublishers.com/

Illustrated non-fiction books on natural history, sports and hobbies, animals and pets, travel pictorial, reference, gardening, health and fitness, practical art, DIY, food and drink, outdoor pursuits, craft, humour, gift books. New proposals accepted, send CV, synopsis and sample chapters in first instance; sae essential. Founded 1955.

Pan Macmillan Australia*

Level 25, 1 Market Street, Sydney, NSW 2000
tel +61 (0)2 9285 9100
email pan.reception@macmillan.com.au
website www.panmacmillan.com.au
Facebook www.facebook.com/PanMacmillanAustralia
X @macmillanaus
Publishing Director Ingrid Ohlsson

Commercial and literary fiction, children's and YA fiction, non-fiction and character products, general non-fiction, sport, cookery and lifestyle. Founded 1843.

Penguin Random House Australia*

Sydney office Level 3, 100 Pacific Highway, North Sydney, NSW 2060
tel +61 (0)2 9954 9966
email information@penguinrandomhouse.com.au
Melbourne office Level 28, 2 Southbank Blvd, Southbank, VIC 3006
website www.penguinrandomhouse.com.au
X @PenguinBooksAus
Ceo Julie Burland, *Publishing Directors* Holly Toohey, Jess Malpass (Head of Launch)

General fiction, non-fiction, children's and illustrated. MS submissions for non-fiction accepted, unbound in hard copy addressed to Submissions Editor. Fiction submissions are only accepted from previously published authors, or authors represented by an agent or accompanied by a report from an accredited assessment service. Imprints: Arrow, Bantam, Ebury, Hamish Hamilton, William Heinemann, Michael Joseph, Knopf, Penguin, Viking and Vintage. Subsidiary of Bertelsmann AG. Founded 2013.

University of Queensland Press*

PO Box 6042, St Lucia, QLD 4067
tel +61 (0)7 3365 7244
email reception@uqp.com.au
website www.uqp.com.au
Facebook www.facebook.com/uqpofficial
X @UQPBooks
Instagram @uqpbooks

Fiction, non-fiction, poetry and First Nations writing. Founded 1948.

Rhiza Edge

PO Box 302, Chinchilla, QLD 4413
tel +61 (0)7 3245 1938
email editor@rhizaedge.com.au
website www.rhizaedge.com.au
Facebook www.facebook.com/rhizaedge

Issue-based stories for YA readers. Imprint of Wombat Books. Founded 2018.

Scholastic Australia*

76–80 Railway Crescent, Lisarow, Gosford, NSW 2250
tel +61 (0)2 4328 3555
website www.scholastic.com.au
Facebook www.facebook.com/ScolasticAustralia
X @scholasticAUS
Instagram @scolastic_au
Managing Director David Peagram

Children's fiction and non-fiction. Founded 1968.

Simon & Schuster (Australia)*

Office address Suite 19A, Level 1, Building C, 450 Miller Street, Cammeray, NSW 2062
Postal address PO Box 3047, Willoughby North, NSW 2068
tel +61 (0)2 9983 6600
email cservice@simonandschuster.com.au
website www.simonandschuster.com.au
Facebook www.facebook.com/SimonSchusterAU
X @simonschusterAU
Instagram @simonschusterau
Managing Director Dan Ruffino

Part of Paramount. Fiction, non-fiction and children's books. Imprints: Adams Media, Atria, Avid Reader Press, Free Press, Gallery, Howard, One Signal, Pocket, Scout Press, Scribner, Simon & Schuster, Tiller Press and Touchstone. Founded 1987.

Spinifex Press*

PO Box 105, Mission Beach, QLD 4852
tel +61 (0)4 1850 6645
email women@spinifexpress.com.au
Postal address PO Box 105, Mission Beach, QLD 4852
website www.spinifexpress.com.au
Facebook www.facebook.com/spinifexpress
X @spinifexpress
Instagram @spinifexpress
Managing Directors Susan Hawthorne, Renate Klein

An independent feminist press of fiction, non-fiction and poetry. Areas include: Indigenous, writing from Asia and Africa, lesbian books as well as women's health, violence against women, racism and cultural opportunism, ecology and economics, war and exile, prostitution and pornography. No AI training. No unsolicited MSS. Founded 1991.

Syndey University Press*

Level 1, Fisher Library F03, University of Sydney, NSW 2006
email sup.info@sydney.edu.au
website https://sydneyuniversitypress.com/
Facebook www.facebook.com/sydney-university-press
X @sydneyunipress
Instagram @sydenyunipress
Manager & Publisher Susan Murray

A not-for-profit, scholarly publisher of research-based books. Founded 1962.

Tale Publishing*

email talepublishing@gmail.com
website https://talepublishing.com/

A small publisher of anthologies, fiction and non-fiction that developed out of the Monash Writers Group. See website for submission windows. Member of the Small Press Network. Founded 2015.

UNSW Press*

University of New South Wales, Sydney, NSW 2052
tel +61 (0)2 8936 1400
email enquiries@unswpress.com.au
website https://unsw.press/
Ceo Kathy Bail

Academic and general non-fiction. Politics, history, indigenous history, popular science, environmental studies, art and design. Founded 1962.

UWA Publishing*

University of Western Australia, M419, 35 Stirling Highway, Crawley, WA 6009
tel +61 (0)8 6488 3670
email admin-uwap@uwa.edu.au
website www.uwap.uwa.edu.au
Facebook www.facebook.com/uwapublishing
Instagram @uwapublishing
Publishing Manager Kate Pickard

Fiction, general non-fiction, natural history and contemporary issues. Founded 1935.

John Wiley & Sons Australia*

Level 4, 600 Bourke Street, Melbourne, VIC 3000
tel +61 (0)8 0077 7474
email custservice@wiley.com
website www.wiley.com

Educational, technical, atlases, professional, reference and trade journals. Imprints: Capstone, For Dummies, Jacaranda, Jossey-Bass, Polity, John Wiley & Sons and Wiley-Blackwell. Founded 1807.

Wilkinson Publishing*

PO Box 24135, Melbourne, VIC 3001
email enquiries@wilkinsonpublishing.com.au
website www.wilkinsonpublishing.com.au
Facebook www.facebook.com/WilkinsonPublishing
X @WPBooks
Owner & Director Michael Wilkinson

A family-owned, independent publisher. Publishes art, biography, memoir, business, finance, children's, cookery, fiction, health, history, humour, personal development, philosophy and religion, poetry, politics, opinion, society, culture, sport and true crime. Founded 2005.

Wombat Books*

PO Box 302, Chinchilla, QLD 4413
tel +61 (0)7 3245 1938

email website@wombatrhiza.com.au
website www.wombatrhiza.com.au
Facebook www.facebook.com/wombatbooks
Publisher Rochelle Manners

An independent publisher of children's picture books and books for early readers. YA and adult imprint: Rhiza Edge (page 192). Founded 2009.

CANADA

**Member of the Canadian Publishers' Council*

†Member of the Association of Canadian Publishers

Annick Press†

665 Gerrard Street East, Toronto, ON M4M 1Y2
tel +1 416-221-4802
email annickpress@annickpress.com
website www.annickpress.com
Contact David Caron

Preschool, YA fiction and non-fiction. Publishes approx. 24 titles each year. For submission guidelines, authors and illustrators should visit website. Founded 1975.

Anvil Press†

PO Box 3008, Station Terminal, Vancouver, BC V6B 3X5
email info@anvilpress.com
website www.anvilpress.com
Facebook www.facebook.com/Anvil-Press-115437275199047
X @anvilpress
Publisher Brian Kaufman

Progressive, contemporary Canadian literature with an entrenched urban sensibility. Also poetry, fiction and non-fiction. Founded 1990.

ARP Books†

205–70 Arthur Street, Treaty 1 and Historic Métis, Homeland, Winnipeg, Manitoba R3B 1G7
email info@arpbooks.org
website https://arpbooks.org/

Founded as a workers' collective, publishing left-of-centre and Marxist-leaning books. Fiction and non-fiction. Founded 1996.

Arsenal Pulp Press†

#202–211 East Georgia Street, Vancouver, BC V6A 1Z6
tel +1 604-687-4233
email info@arsenalpulp.com
website https://arsenalpulp.com/About-Arsenal-Pulp-Press/
Facebook www.facebook.com/arsenalpulp
X @arsenalpulp
Bluesky @arsenalpulp.bsky.social
Instagram @arsenalpulp
Publisher Brian Lam

Literary fiction, graphic novels, non-fiction and poetry on social issues. Areas covered: gender studies; LGBTQ+ and BIPOC literature, regional history, cookery, alternative crafts and books in translation. Also children's and YA. Founded 1971.

Bayeux Arts†

2403, 510–6th Avenue, SE Calgary, AB T2G 1L7
email ashis.bayeux@gmail.com
website www.bayeux.com
X @Bayeux_Arts
Publisher Ashis Gupta

Non-fiction. Imprints: Gondolier (management and social sciences) and Odd Little Books (pocket-sized books by visual artists, dramatists, poets, puppeteers, playwrights and musicians). Founded 1994.

Between the Lines†

401 Richmond Street West, Studio 281, Toronto, ON M5V 3A8
tel +1 416-535-9914
email info@btlbooks.com
website https://btlbooks.com/
Facebook www.facebook.com/BTLbooks
X @BTLbooks
Instagram @bltbooks
Managing Editor Amanda Crocker

Non-fiction that highlights the struggles of Black, Indigenous and racialised communities, migrants, women, queer people and working-class people. Founded 1977.

Book*hug Press†

401 Richmond Street West, Suite 350, Toronto, ON M5V 3A8
tel +1 416-994-5804
website www.bookhugpress.ca
Facebook www.facebook.com/bookhugpress
X @bookhugpress
Bluesky @bookhugpress.bsky.social
Instagram @bookhugpress

Literary fiction, literary non-fiction, poetry and literature in translation. Founded 2004.

Breakwater Books†

PO Box 2188, St John's, NL A1C 6E6
tel +1 709-722-6680
email orders@breakwaterbooks.com
website https://breakwaterbooks.com/
Facebook www.facebook.com/breakwaterbooksltd
X @breakwaterbooks
President & Publisher Rebecca Rose

Fiction, non-fiction, poetry, drama, art, YA and children's books. Also cookery, guidebooks and educational resources. Founded 1973.

Brick Books†

487 King Street West, Kingston, Ontario, ON K7L 2X7

tel +1 613-701-1743
website www.brickbooks.ca
Facebook www.facebook.com/brickbooks
Instagram @brickbooks
Publisher Alayna Munce

Poetry. Publishes around eight books per year. Founded 1975.

Caitlin Press†

8100 Alderwood Road, Halfmoon Bay, BC V0N 1Y1
website https://caitlinpress.com/
Facebook www.facebook.com/caitlinbooks
X @caitlinpress
Instagram @caitlinpress.daggereditions
Publisher Vici Johstone

Fiction, non-fiction and poetry by Canadian authors with a majority being British Columbia-based. Interested in topics concerning British Columbia or by writers from the British Columbia Interior, stories about and by Canadian women and LGBTQ+ voices. Usually publishes 12 to 14 books, most of which are regional non-fiction (e.g., British Columbia history or exploration, industry, politics and contemporary creative non-fiction). The remaining titles are literary selections such as works of fiction, short fiction, poetry or prose. Founded 1977.

Dagger Editions

Literary fiction, non-fiction and poetry by and about queer women (those who identify as queer women, including trans people or anyone who includes this in their personal history).

The Charlton Press

645 Avenue, Lepine, Dorval, QC H9P 2R2
tel +1 416-962-2665
email info@charltonpress.com
website www.charltonpress.com

Collectables, numismatics and sportscard price catalogues. Founded 1952.

Cloudscape Comics†

website www.cloudscapecomics.com
Facebook www.facebook.com/cloudscape
X @cloudscapecomic
Instagram @cloudscapecomics
President Jeffrey Ellis

A graphic novel publisher and artist collective, made up of over 100 members of the comics community within British Columbia. As a registered non-profit organisation, proceeds from sales of books go towards providing developing artists with free drawing classes, studio space, a lending library and a small printing centre, as well as delivering public events, talks, demonstrations, art exhibitions and publishing more books. Founded 2007.

Douglas & McIntyre†

4437 Rondeview Road, PO Box 219, Madeira Park, BC V0N 2H0
tel +1 604-883-2730
email info@douglas-mcintyre.com
website www.douglas-mcintyre.com

Canadian biography, art and architecture, natural history, history, native studies and Canadian fiction. Unsolicited MSS accepted. Owned by Harbour Publishing. Founded 1971.

Dundurn Press†

1382 Queen Street E, Toronto, ON M4L 1C9
tel +1 416-214-5544
email submissions@dundurn.com
website www.dundurn.com
Facebook www.facebook.com/dundurnpress
X @dundurnpress
Instagram @dundurnpress
Managing Editor Elena Radic

Canadian history, fiction, non-fiction and YA fiction, mystery fiction, popular non-fiction and translations. Founded 1972.

ECW Press†

665 Gerrard Street E, Toronto, ON M4M 1Y2
tel +1 416-694-3348
email info@ecwpress.com
website www.ecwpress.com
Facebook www.facebook.com/ecwpress
X @ecwpress
Co-Publishers David Caron, Jack David, *Acquisitions Editors* Jen Knoch, Susan Renouf, Michael Holmes, Jennifer Smith, Jen Sookfong Lee

Popular culture, TV and film, sports, humour, general trade books, biographies, memoir, popular science and guidebooks. Founded 1979.

Fernwood Publishing†

2970 Oxford Street, Halifax, Nova Scotia, NS B3L 2W4
tel +1 902-857-1388
email info@fernpub.ca
website https://fernwoodpublishing.ca/
Facebook www.facebook.com/fernwood.publishing
X @fermpub
Instagram @fernpub
Editors Tanya Andrusieczko, Wayne Antony, Art Bouman, Jazz Cook

Critical non-fiction. Imprint: Roseway. Founded 1992.

Fitzhenry & Whiteside

209 Wicksteed Avenue, Unit 51, East York, ON M4G 0B1
tel +1 905-477-9700
email hdoll@fitzhenry.ca
website www.fitzhenry.ca
Facebook www.facebook.com/FitzWhits
X @FitzWhits

Trade, educational and children's books. Fiction and non-fiction (biography, environment, social studies and visual arts). Publishes first-time authors.

Emphasis is on Canadian authors and illustrators, subject or perspective. Will review MS/illustration packages from artists. Submit outline and copy of sample illustration. For illustrations only, send samples and promotional sheet. Founded 1966.

Goose Lane Editions†

500 Beaverbrook Court, Suite 330, Fredericton, NB E3B 5X4
tel +1 506-450-4251
email info@gooselane.com
website https://gooselane.com/
Facebook www.facebook.com/gooselaneeditions
X @goose_lane
Publisher Susanne Alexander

Fiction, non-fiction and poetry. Founded 1954.

Gordon Hill Press†

130 Dublin Street North, Guelph, ON N1H 4N4
website www.gordonhillpress.com
Facebook www.facebook.com/gordonhillpress
Instagram @gordon_hill_press
Managing Editor Shane Neilson

Poetry, fiction, non-fiction and literary criticism (especially concerning poetry). Founded 2019.

Guernica Editions†

1241 Marble Rock Road, Gananoque, ON K7G 2V4
website https://guernicaeditions.com/
Facebook www.facebook.com/guernicaed
X @guernica_ed
Instagram @guernicaeditions
Founder/Co-publisher Michael Mirolla, *Co-publisher* Connie Guzzo-McParland

Adult and YA fiction and non-fiction. Essays, poetry, memoirs and literary fiction that address social issues. Imprints: Guernica World Editions, MiroLand and 1366Books. Submission guidelines: please check website. Founded 1978.

Harlequin Enterprises*

PO Box 603, Fort Erie, ON L2A 5X3
tel +1 888-432-4879
email customer_ecare@harlequin.ca
website www.harlequin.com
Facebook www.facebook.com/harlequinbooks
X @harlequinbooks
Instagram @harlequinbooks
Publisher Craig Swinwood

Fiction for women, romance, inspirational fiction, African American fiction, action adventure, mystery. Imprints: Carina Adores, Harlequin Desire, Harlequin Heartwarming, Harlequin Historical, Harlequin Intrigue, Harlequin Medical Romance, Harlequin Presents, Harlequin Romance, Harlequin Romance Suspense, Harlequin Special Edition, Harlequin Special Releases, Love Inspires, Love Inspired Special Releases and Love Inspired Suspense. Founded 1949.

HarperCollins Publishers (Canada)*

22 Adelaide Street West, 41st Floor, Toronto, ON M5H 4E3
tel +1 416-975-9334
email hcOrder@harpercollins.com
website www.harpercollins.ca
Facebook www.facebook.com/HarperCollinsCanada
X @HarperCollinsCa

Literary fiction and non-fiction, history, politics, biography, spiritual and children's books. Founded 1989.

House of Anansi Press and Groundwood Books†

128 Sterling Road, Lower Level, Toronto, ON M6R 2B7
tel +1 416-363-4343
email publicity@houseofanansi.com
website https://houseofanansi.com/
Facebook www.facebook.com/houseofanansi
X @HouseofAnansi

House of Anansi Press is a publisher of literary fiction. Groundwood Books publishes children's and adult fiction, picture books, graphic novels and non-fiction. Founded 1967.

Inanna Publications and Education†

210 Founders College, York University, 4700 Keele Street, Toronto, ON M3J 1P3
tel +1 416-736-5356
email inanna.publications@inanna.ca
website www.inanna.ca
Facebook www.facebook.com/InannaPublications
X @inannapub

Feminist-inspired fiction, poetry and creative non-fiction. Founded 1978.

Invisible Publishing†

Suite 1, 289 Main Street, Picton, ON K0K 2T0
email info@invisiblepublishing.com
website https://invisiblepublishing.com/
Publisher Norm Nehmetallah

A not-for-profit publisher of contemporary fiction, graphic fiction, non-fiction and poetry. Areas include: pop culture biographies, experimental poetry and prose, with an emphasis on Canadian authors. Founded 2007.

Kids Can Press†

25 Dockside Drive, Toronto, ON M5A 0B5
tel +1 416-479-7000
email customerservice@kidscan.com
website www.kidscanpress.com
Facebook www.facebook.com/kidscanbooks
X @kidscanpress
Editorial Director Yasemin Uçar

Middle grade/YA books. Founded 1973.

Knopf Canada – see Penguin Random House Canada

LexisNexis Canada*

111 Gordon Baker Road, Suite 900, Toronto, ON M2H 3R1
tel +1 800-668-6481
email info@lexisnexis.ca
website www.lexisnexis.ca
Facebook www.facebook.com/lexisnexiscanada
X @lexisnexiscan

Law and accountancy. Division of Reed Elsevier. Founded 1979.

McGill-Queen's University Press†

1010 Sherbrooke Street West, Suite 1720, Montreal, QC H3A 2R7
tel +1 514-398-3750
email mqup@mcgill.ca
website www.mqup.ca
Managing Editor Kathleen Fraser, *Associate Managing Editor* Lisa Aitken

Academic, non-fiction and poetry. Founded 1969.

McGraw-Hill Canada*

300 Water Street, Whitby, Ontario, ON L1N 9B6
website www.mheducation.ca
Facebook www.facebook.com/mcgrawhillcanada
X @mcgraw_canada

Education and trade. Founded 1972.

Metonymy Press†

PO Box 143 BP Saint Dominique, Montréal, QC H2S 3K6
email publish@metonymypress.com
website https://metonymypress.com/
Facebook www.facebook.com/metonymypress
X @metonymypress
Instagram @metonymypress
Founders Ashley Fortier, Oliver Fulger

Based in Tio'tia:ke (Montreal), unceded Kanien'kehá:ka (Mohawk) territory. Literary fiction and non-fiction by emerging writers from queer, feminist and social justice communities. Founded 2014.

Nelson Education*

2005 Sheppard Ave E, Suite 700, Toronto, ON M2J 5B4
tel +1 416-752-9448
website www.nelson.com
Facebook www.facebook.com/NelsonClassroom
X @NelsonClassroom
Instagram @nelsonclassroom
President & Ceo Steve Brown

Education: K–12. Creator of digital platform, Edwin. Founded 1914.

NeWest Press†

8540, 109 Street, Edmonton, AB T6G 1E6
tel +1 780-432-9427
email info@newestpress.com
website www.newestpress.com
Facebook www.facebook.com/newestpress.page
X @newestpress
Instagram @newest.press
General Manager Matt Bowes

Fiction, drama, poetry and non-fiction. Founded 1977.

Nimbus Publishing

3660 Strawberry Hill, Halifax, NS B3K 5A9
tel +1 800-646-2879
website https://nimbus.ca/
Facebook www.facebook.com/nimbuspub
X @nimbuspub
Instagram @nimbuspub

Children's picture books and fiction, literary non-fiction, social and cultural history, nature photography, current events, biography, sports and cultural issues. Founded 1978.

Oberon Press

203–145 Spruce Street, Ottawa, ON K1R 6P1
tel +1 613-238-3275
email oberon@sympatico.ca
website www.oberonpress.ca

General fiction, short stories, poetry, some biographies, art and children's. Only publishes Canadian writers. Currently not accepting submissions. Founded 1985.

Oxford University Press, Canada*

8 Sampson Mews, Suite 204, Don Mills, ON M3C 0H5
tel +1 416-441-2941
website www.oupcanada.com

Education and academic. Founded 1586.

Palimpsest Press

1171 Eastlawn Ave., Windsor, ON N8S 3J1
email info@palimpsestpress.ca
website https://palimpsestpress.ca/about/
Publisher Aimée Parent Dunn

Poetry, literary fiction and non-fiction. Genres: poetics, cultural criticism, literary biography, essays and memoirs. Publishes work by poets who examine Canadian poetry and the Canadian cultural landscape. Committed to publishing at least 20% of titles written by authors living with disability. Founded 2000.

Anstruther Books

Poetry.

Pearson Canada*

26 Prince Andrew Place, North York, ON M3C 2T8
tel +1 800-361-6128

website www.pearson.com/ca/en.html
Facebook www.facebook.com/pearsonhighereducationCA
X @pearson
Instagram @pearsonhighereducation

Academic, technical, educational, children's and adult trade. Founded 1998.

Penguin Random House Canada*

320 Front Street West, Suite 1400, Toronto, ON M5V 3B6
tel +1 416-364-4449
website www.penguinrandomhouse.ca
Facebook www.facebook.com/penguinrandomca
X @penguinrandomca
Instagram @penguinrandomca
Ceo Kristin Cochrane

Literary fiction, commercial fiction, memoir, non-fiction (history, business, current events, sports), adult, children and YA. No unsolicited MSS; submissions via an agent only. Imprints: Appetite (Appetite by Random House), Double Day Canada (Anchor Canada, Bond Street Books and Doubleday Canada), Knopf Canada (Alchemy by Knopf Canada, Knopf Canada and Vintage Canada), McCelland & Stewart (Emblam Editions, McCelland & Stewart, Signal and Strange Light), Penguin Canada (Allen Lane, Hamish Hamilton, Penguin Canada and Viking), Random House Canada (Random House Canada and Vintage Canada). Subsidiary of Penguin Random House. Founded 2013.

Radiant Press

PO Box 33128, Cathedral PO, Regina, SK S4T 7X2
email info@radiantpress.ca
website www.radiantpress.ca
Facebook www.facebook.com/radiantpress
X @radiant_press
Instagram @radiantpress
Publisher & Managing Editor Debra Bell

Poetry, fiction and creative non-fiction by Canadian authors and artists, with a special emphasis on Saskatchewan. Founded 2017.

Ronsdale Press†

125A–1030 Denman Street, Vancouver, BC V6G 2M6
tel +1 604-738-4688
email info@ronsdalepress.com
website www.ronsdalepress.com
Facebook www.facebook.com/ronsdalepress
X @ronsdalepress
Publisher Wendy Atkinson

Publishes literary fiction, non-fiction, young reader chapter books and poetry. Founded 1988.

Second Story Press†

20 Maud Street, Suite 401, Toronto, ON M5V 2M5
tel +1 416-537-7850
email info@secondstorypress.ca
website https://secondstorypress.ca/
Facebook www.facebook.com/secondstorypress
X @secondstory
Instagram @_secondstory

Feminist-inspired fiction and non-fiction for adults, children and YA. Founded 2015.

Thompson Educational Publishing†

20 Ripley Avenue, Toronto, ON M6S 3N9
tel +1 416-766-2763
email info@thompsonbooks.com
website www.thompsonbooks.com

Social sciences. Founded 1989.

Thornapple Press†

email press@thornapplepress.ca
website https://thornapplepress.ca/
Facebook www.facebook.com/ThornapplePress
Founder Eve Rickert

Non-fiction about relationships, love, sexuality and relational ethics from under-represented perspectives including LGBTQ+, families, mental health, disability and related topics. Founded 2013.

University of Toronto Press

800 Bay Street, Mezzanine, Toronto, ON M5S 3A9
tel +1 416-978-2239
email publishing@utpress.utoronto.ca
website www.utorontopress.com
Facebook www.facebook.com/utpress
X @utpress
Vice President Antonia Pop

Non-fiction, monographs, textbooks and academic books, ESL/EFL, teacher reference, adult basic education and school texts. Imprints: Aevo, Irwin, New Jewish Press, Rotman and University of Toronto Press. Founded 1901.

Tundra Books

320 Front Street West, Suite 1400, Toronto, ON M5V 3B6
tel +1 416-364-4449
email submissions@tundrabooks.com
email art@tundrabooks.com
website www.penguinrandomhouse.ca/imprints/TU/tundra-books
Facebook www.facebook.com/tundrabooks
X @TundraBooks
Bluesky @tundrabooks,bsky.social

Children's and YA picture books and novels. A division of Penguin Random House Canada. Founded 1967.

Whitecap Books

209–314 West Cordova Street, Vancouver, BC V6B 1E8
tel +1 905-477-9700
website www.whitecap.ca
Facebook www.facebook.com/whitecapbooks

Books

X @whitecapbooks
Ceo Hollister F. Dol

Food, wine, gardening, health and wellbeing, regional history and regional guidebooks. Submissions must be sent by mail. Founded 1977.

NEW ZEALAND

**Member of the Publishers Association of New Zealand (PANZ)*

Auckland University Press*
University of Auckland, Private Bag 92019, Auckland 1142
tel +64 (0)9 373 7528
email press@auckland.ac.nz
website https://aucklanduniversitypress.co.nz
Director Sam Elworthy

Archaeology, architecture, art, biography, business, health, New Zealand history, Māori and Pacific studies, poetry, politics and law, science and natural history and social sciences. Founded 1966.

David Bateman Ltd*
Unit 2/5 Workspace Drive, Auckland 0618
tel +64 (0)9 415 7664
email info@bateman.co.nz
website www.batemanbooks.co.nz
Facebook www.facebook.com/batemanbooks
Instagram @batemanbooks

General trade: fiction, children's, craft, natural history, gardening, health, sport, cookery, history, travel, motoring, maritime history, business, art, humour and lifestyle. Founded 1979.

The Caxton Press
32 Lodestar Ave, Wigram, PO Box 36 411, Christchurch 8042
tel +64 (0)3 366 8516
email sales@caxton.co.nz
website www.caxton.co.nz
Managing Director Bridget Batchelor

Local history, tourist pictorial, Celtic spirituality and parent guides. Founded 1935.

The Cuba Press
Level 6, 138 Wakefield Street, Te Aro, Wellington 6011
email hello@thecubapress.nz
website www.thecubapress.nz
Facebook www.facebook.com/TheCubaPress
Instagram @thecubapress
Director Mary McCallum, *Publisher* Paul Stewart

Fiction (historical and crime), creative non-fiction, poetry, memoir, biography, social history, children's fiction and poetry, with Aotearoa New Zealand setting. Imprints: Ahoy! (children's books), Mākaro Press (literary fiction (page 200)) and Wayfarer (memoir). Founded 2018.

Dunmore Publishing
34 Ngake Street, Orakei, Auckland 1071
tel +64 (0)9 521 3121
email books@dunmore.co.nz
website www.dunmore.co.nz

Education secondary/tertiary texts and other, New Zealand society, history, health, economics, politics and general non-fiction. Founded 1970.

Edify*
PO Box 444, Whitianga 3542
tel +64 (0)9 972 9428
email orders@edify.co.nz
website www.edify.co.nz
Facebook www.facebook.com/edifynz
X @edifynz

Publishes in the New Zealand educational market. Exclusive representatives of Pearson and the educational publisher Sunshine Books. Founded 2013.

Hachette Aotearoa New Zealand*
PO Box 3255, Shortland Street, Auckland 1140
tel +64 (0)9 379 1480
email contact@hachette.co.nz
website www.hachette.co.nz
Facebook www.facebook.com/HachetteNZ
Managing Director Melanee Winde

International fiction and non-fiction. Local publishing includes children's and fiction titles. Founded 1970.

HarperCollins Publishers (New Zealand)*
Unit D, 63 Apollo Drive, Rosedale, Auckland 0632
tel +64 (0)9 443 9400
email publicity@harpercollins.co.nz
Postal address PO Box 1, Shortland Street, Auckland 1140
website www.harpercollins.co.nz
Facebook www.facebook.com/Harpercollinsnz
X @HarperNZ

Non-fiction titles by New Zealand authors. Submissions to: nz.submissions@harpercollins.co.nz. Founded 1989.

Huia Publishing*
PO Box 12–28, Thorndon, Wellington 6144
email info@huia.co.nz
website https://huia.co.nz/
Facebook www.facebook.com/huiapublishers
X @huiapublishers
Directors Eboni Waitere, Pania Tahau-Hodges

A Māori owned, independent publisher producing innovative and inspiring books and resources. Founded 1991.

Koa Press*

38 Courtenay Street, St Albans, Christchurch
tel +64 (0)21384608
email hello@koapress.co.nz
website www.koapress.co.nz
Instagram @koapress
Director Tonia Shuttleworth

Independent publisher of non-fiction lifestyle: cookbooks, floral/gardening, art and craft and interior. Founded 2021.

LexisNexis NZ

Level 13, SAP Tower, 151 Queen Street, Auckland 1010
email customersupport@lexisnexis.co.nz
website www.lexisnexis.co.nz
Facebook www.facebook.com/LexisNexisNZ
X @LexisNexis_NZ

Law, business and academic. Founded 1914.

Mākaro Press*

Level 6, 138 Wakefield Street, Te Aro, Wellington 6011
email kiaora@makaropressl.com
website https://makaropress.co.nz/
Facebook www.facebook.com/makaropress
X @makaropress
Publishers Mary McCallum, Paul Stewart

Literary fiction with Aotearoa setting. Imprint of The Cuba Press. Founded 2013.

Massey University Press*

Private Bag 102904, North Shore Mail Centre, Auckland 0745
email editorial@masseypress.ac.nz
website www.masseypress.ac.nz
Facebook www.facebook.com/masseyuniversitypress
X @masseyunipress
Instagram @masseyuniversitypress
Publisher Nicola Legat

History, design, art, biography and memoir, agricultural science, veterinary science, poetry, architecture, social issues and children's. Founded 2016.

New Zealand Council for Educational Research

Box 3237, Education House, 178–182 Willis Street, Wellington 6140
tel +64 (0)4 384 7939
email info@nzcer.org.nz
website www.nzcer.org.nz
Facebook www.facebook.com/nzcer
X @nzcer

Education, including educational policy and practice, early childhood education, educational achievement tests, Māori education, schooling for the future, curriculum and assessment. Founded 1934.

Odyssey Books

email contact@odysseybooks.com.au
website www.odysseybooks.com.au
Facebook www.facebook.com/odysseybooks
X @odysseybooks
Instagram @odysseybooks
Publisher Michelle Lovi

Fiction: action and adventure, fantasy, historical fiction, horror, mystery and crime, romance, sci-fi, urban fiction, children's and YA. Non-fiction: biographies and memoir, narrative non-fiction, Christian and cookery. Imprints: Ensorcellia, Odyssey Books and Publisher Obscura. Founded 2009.

Otago University Press*

PO Box 56, Dunedin 9016
tel +64 (0)3 479 8807
email university.press@otago.ac.nz
website www.otago.ac.nz/press
Facebook www.facebook.com/otagouniversitypress
X @otagounipress
Instagram @otagounipress
Publisher Sue Wootton

Non-fiction books on New Zealand and the Pacific, particularly history, natural history, Māori and Pacific. Other non-fiction: biography/memoir, poetry, literature and art. Also publishes Aotearoa, New Zealand's longest-running literary journal, *Landfall Tauraka*. Founded 1958.

Penguin Random House New Zealand*

Private Bag 102 902, North Shore, Auckland 0745
tel +64 (0)9 442 7400
email submissions@penguinrandomhouse.co.nz
website www.penguin.co.nz
Facebook www.facebook.com/PenguinBooksNewZealand
X @PenguinBooks_NZ
Instagram @penguinbooksnz
Publishing Grace Thomas

Adult and children's fiction and non-fiction. Imprints: Black Swan, Godwit, Penguin, Puffin Books and Vintage. Part of Penguin Random House. Founded 2013.

Te Herenga Waka University Press*

Victoria University of Wellington, PO Box 600, Wellington 6140
tel +64 (0)4 886 4543
email thwup@wgtn.ac.nz
website https://teherengawakapress.co.nz/
X @thwupbooks
Instagram @thwupbooks
Publisher Fergus Barrowman, *Publicist* Caoimhe McKeogh, *Editors* Ashleigh Young, Kyleigh Hodgson, Jasmine Sargent

Formerly Victoria University Press. Literary fiction and poetry, scholarly works on New Zealand history, sociology, law, Māori language, biography, memoir and essays. For submission guidelines, please see website. Founded 1974.

Ugly Hill Press*

website www.uglyhillpress.co.nz
Founder Deborah Coddington

A small independent publisher of art, photography, historical and social commentary. Founded 2022.

Viking Sevenseas NZ

201A Rosetta Road, Raumati Beach, Wellington 5032
tel +64 (0)4 902 8240
email vikingsevenseas@gmail.com
website https://vikingsevenseas.co.nz/

Natural history books on New Zealand only. Founded 1957.

SOUTH AFRICA

**Member of the Publishers' Association of South Africa*

Jonathan Ball Publishers*

PO Box 33977, Jeppestown 2043
tel +27 (0)21 469 8900
email gill.moodie@jonathanball.co.za
website www.jonathanball.co.za
Facebook www.facebook.com/jonathanballpublishers
X @JonathanBallPub
Instagram @jonathanballpublishers
Publisher Gill Moodie

South African biography, history, business, current affairs, investigative and narrative journalism. A division of Media24. Founded 1977.

Jonathan Ball

General publications, current affairs, politics, history, business and reference.

Delta Books

Military history.

Sunbird Publishers

Natural history.

Blackbird Books

email info@blackbirdbooks.africa
website https://blackbirdbooks.africa/
X @blackbirdbooks
Instagram @blackbirdbooks_africa
Publisher Thabiso Mahlape

Fiction and non-fiction about the African experience. Founded 2015.

Burnet Media

PO Box 53557, Kenilworth, Cape Town 7745
email info@burnetmedia.co.za
website www.burnetmedia.co.za
X @BurnetMedia
Publishing Manager Tim Richman

Independent publisher of non-fiction. Founded 2006.

Mercury

Non-fiction for the South African and international markets.

Two Dogs

Non-fiction focusing on contemporary and lifestyle for the South African market.

Cambridge University Press & Assessment, Africa*

Unit OW3A Old Warehouse Building, Black River Park, 2 Fir Street, Observatory, Cape Town 7925
tel +27 (0)21 412 7800
email cambridge-sa@cambridge.org
website www.cambridge.org
Publishing Director Johan Traut

Textbooks and literature for sub-Saharan African countries, as well as primary reading materials in 28 African languages. Founded 1534.

Delta Books – see Jonathan Ball Publishers

Juta and Company*

1st Floor, Sunclare Building, 21 Dreyer Street, Claremont 7708
tel +27 (0)21 659 2300
email orders@juta.co.za
website www.juta.co.za
Facebook www.facebook.com/JutaSouthAfrica
X @JutaZA
Instagram @jutasouthafrica
Ceo Brian Wafawarowa

Academic, education, agencies, learning, law and health. Founded 1853.

University of KwaZulu-Natal Press*

Private Bag X01, Scottsville, Pietermaritzburg, KwaZulu-Natal 3209
tel +27 (0)33 260 5226
email books@ukzn.ac.za
email press@ukzn.ac.za
website www.ukznpress.co.za
Facebook www.facebook.com/UKZNPress
X @UKZNPress
Instagram @ukznpress
Director Phindile Dlamini, *Production Editor* Susan Elliott

Southern African social, political and economic history, sociology, politics and political science, current affairs, literary criticism, gender studies, indigenous languages, cultural studies, education and biography. Founded 1947.

Macmillan Education South Africa

4th Floor, Building G, Hertford Office Park, 90 Bekker Road, Vorna Valley, Midrand 1685
tel +27 (0)11 731 3300

Postal address Private Bag X19, Northlands 2116
website www.macmillan.co.za
Managing Director Mandla Balisa

Educational titles. Founded 1843.

Maskew Miller Learning*

10 Freedom Way, Milnerton, Cape Town 7441
tel +27 (0)21 532 6000
email info@mml.co.za
website https://mml.co.za/

Learning materials, technologies and services for use in schools, TVET colleges, higher education institutions and in home and professional environments. Founded 2010.

NB Publishers*

12th Floor, Media24 Centre, 40 Heerengracht, Cape Town 8001
tel +27 (0)21 406 3033
email nb@nb.co.za
website www.nb.co.za

General: Afrikaans fiction, politics, children's and youth literature in all the country's languages, non-fiction. Imprints: Best Books, Human & Rousseau, Kwela, Lux Verbi, Pharos, Queillerie and Tafelberg. Founded 1950.

New Africa Books

Unit 13, Athlone Industrial Park, 10 Mymoena Crescent, Cape Town 7764
tel +27 (0)21 467 5860
email info@newafricabooks.co.za
website https://newafricabooks.com/
X @DavidPhilipPub
Instagram @newafricabooks
Contacts Dušanka Stojaković, Nerina van Wyngaarden Lindhout, Cheraldine Smit, Felicity Solomons

Award-winning independent publisher of picture books publishing approx. 60 titles per year. Fiction, non-fiction and comics with South African content in all South African languages. Imprints: David Philip and New Africa Books. Founded 1971.

Oxford University Press Southern Africa*

Vasco Boulevard, N1 City, Goodwood, Cape Town 7460
tel +27 (0)21 596 2300
email oxford.za@oup.com
website www.oxford.co.za
Facebook www.facebook.com/OxfordSASchools
Instagram @oxford_university_press_sa
Managing Director Africa Karen Simpson

Pre-primary education, primary education, secondary education, higher education, TVET, dictionaries, atlases, literature, children's books, home learning, reading schemes, ELT, online and offline learning solutions, professional development services. Produces educational material and support for Grade R to 12, TVET, higher education, and home learning in all official written South African languages. Founded 1586.

Pan Macmillan SA*

2nd Floor, 1 Jameson Avenue, Melrose Estate, Johannesburg 2196
tel +27 (0)11 684 0400
email roshni@panmacmillan.co.za
Postal address Private Bag X19, Northlands, Johannesburg 2116
website www.panmacmillan.co.za
Facebook www.facebook.com/panmacmillansa
X @panmacmillansa
Managing Director Terry Morris

Autobiography, biography, business, children's books, cookery and wine, crafts and hobbies, crime, environment, fiction (popular and literary), humour, inspiration, literature, business, reference, sport and stationery. Imprints: Guinness, Hachette Children's Books, Hinkler Books, Macmillan US, Pan KinderBoeke/Pan Children's Books, Pan Macmillan Australia, Pan Macmillan South Africa, Pan Macmillan UK, Priddy Books and Walker Books. Founded 1943.

Penguin Random House South Africa*

The Estuaries, No 4, Oxbow Crescent, Century Avenue, Century City 7441
email info@penguinrandomhouse.co.za
Postal address PO Box 1144, Cape Town 8000
tel +27 (0)21 460 5400
website www.penguinrandomhouse.co.za
Ceo Steve Connolly

General illustrated non-fiction, lifestyle, natural history, South African politics, sport, business, memoirs, contemporary fiction, literary fiction, local fiction, Afrikaans, children's books and religion. Imprints: Lapa, Luca, Penguin Fiction, Penguin Non-Fiction, Penguin Random House, Romanza, Struik Lifestyle, Struik Nature, Struik Travel & Heritage, Umuzi and Zebra Press. Part of Penguin Random House. Founded 2013.

Shuter and Shooter Publishers*

45 Willowton Rd, Willowton, Pietermaritzburg 3201
tel +27 (0)33 846 8700
email sales@shuters.com
website www.shuters.co.za
Facebook www.facebook.com/shuterandshooter
X @shuters

Core curriculum-based textbooks for use at foundation, intermediate, senior and FET phases. Supplementary readers in various languages, dictionaries, reading development kits and charts. Literature titles in English, isiXhosa, Sesotho, Sepedi, Setswana, Tshivenda, Xitsonga, Ndebele, isiZulu and Siswati. Founded 1925.

Unisa Press*
University of South Africa, PO Box 392, Unisa, Mackleneuk, Pretoria 0003
tel +27 (0)12 429 3182
email pietehc@unisa.ac.za
website www.unisa.ac.za/sites/corporate/default/Unisa-Press
Facebook www.facebook.com/UniversityofSouthAfrica
X @unisa
Instagram @universityofsouthafrica
Commissioning Editor Hetta Pieterse

All academic disciplines, African history, sustainable development, economics, the arts and the humanities generally. Imprint: UNISA. Email for MS submissions. Founded 1957.

Van Schaik Publishers*
PO Box 27678, Sunnyside, Pretoria 0132
tel +27 (0)12 342 2765
email JRead@vanschaiknet.com
website www.vanschaiknet.com
General Manager Julia Read

Textbooks for the higher education market in southern Africa. Founded 1915.

Wits University Press*
PO Wits, Johannesburg 2050
tel +27 (0)11 717 8700/1
email corina.vanderspoel@wits.ac.za
website www.witspress.co.za
Facebook www.facebook.com/witspress
Instagram @witspress

Academic and general non-fiction: art and heritage, political and social sciences, history and literary studies, playscripts and select textbooks. Founded 1922.

USA

**Member of the Association of American Publishers Inc.*

ABC-CLIO*
147 Castilian Drive, Santa Barbara, CA 93117
tel +1 805-968-1911
website www.abc-clio.com
Facebook www.facebook.com/ABCCLIO
X @ABC_CLIO

Academic resources for secondary and middle schools, colleges and universities, libraries and professionals (librarians, media specialists, teachers). Owned by Bloomsbury Publishing. Founded 1955.

Abingdon Press
810 12th Ave South, Nashville, TN 37203
tel +1 800-251-3320
website www.abingdonpress.com
Facebook www.facebook.com/AbingdonPress
X @AbingdonPress

General interest, professional, academic and reference, non-fiction and fiction, youth and children's non-fiction and Vacation Bible School, primarily directed to the religious market. Imprint of United Methodist Publishing House. United Methodist Publishing House founded 1789.

Harry N. Abrams
195 Broadway, 9th Floor, New York, NY 10007
tel +1 212-206-7715
email abrams@abramsbooks.com
website www.abramsbooks.com

Art and architecture, photography, natural sciences, performing arts and children's books. Imprints: Abrams, Abrams Appleseed, Abrams Books for Young Readers, Abrams ComicArts (imprints: Kana, Megascape and Surely Books), Abrams Fanfare, Abrams Image, Abrams Press, Amulet Books, Magic Cat, The Overlook Press and Taunton Press. Founded 1949.

Akashic Books
232 Third Street, Suite A115, Brooklyn, NY 11215
tel +1 718-643-9193
email info@akashicbooks.com
website www.akashicbooks.com
Facebook www.facebook.com/AkashicBooks
X @AkashicBooks
Publisher & Editor-in-Chief Johnny Temple, *Managing Editor* Johanna Ingalls

Independent publisher of urban literary fiction and political non-fiction. Founded 1997.

The University of Alabama Press
Box 870380, Tuscaloosa, AL 35487-0380
tel +1 205-348-5180
website www.uapress.ua.edu
Facebook www.facebook.com/UniversityALPress/about
X @univofalpress
Instagram @uniofalpress
Managing Editor Jon Berry

American and Southern history, African American studies, religion, rhetoric and communication, Judaic studies, literary criticism, anthropology and archaeology. Founded 1945.

Angry Gable Press
email angrygablepress@gmail.com
website www.angrygablepress.com
Facebook www.facebook.com/people/Angry-Gable-Press/100095404923226/
X @angrygablepress
Bluesky @angrygablepress.bsky.social
Instagram @angrygablepress

Niche speculative fiction and poetry that is experimental in technique, form, perspective and subject matter at the boundaries of the speculative. Welcomes a spectrum of aesthetics. Founded 2023.

Applause Theatre and Cinema Book Publishers

64 S. Main Street, Essex, CT 06246
tel +1 203-458-4500
email ApplauseSubmissions@rowman.com
website www.applausebooks.com
Facebook www.facebook.com/globepequot
X @ApplauseBooks
Publisher Chris Chappell

Performing arts. Part of Rowman and Littlefield. Founded 1980.

Arcade Publishing

11th Floor, 307 West 36th Street, New York, NY 10018
tel +1 212-643-6816
website www.arcadepub.com
Facebook www.facebook.com/SkyhorsePublishing
X @skyhorsepub
Instagram @skyhorsepub
Executive Editor Cal Barksdale

General trade. No unsolicited MSS. Imprint of Skyhorse Publishing. Founded 1988.

The University of Arkansas Press

McIlroy House, 105 N. McIlroy Avenue, Fayetteville, AR 72701
tel +1 479-575-7544
email info@uapress.com
website www.uapress.com
Facebook www.facebook.com/uarkpress
X @uarkpress
Instagram @uark
Director & Publisher Mike Bieker

Arkansas and regional history, poetry and literature, African American studies, food studies, sports studies, art and architecture. Home of the Miller Williams Poetry Prize, awarding publication and a cash prize for a new collections of poetry, and the Etel Adnan Poetry Prize for collections of poetry by writers of Arab heritage. Founded 1980.

Astra Publishing House

19 West 21st Street, #1201, New York, NY 10010
email info@bmkbooks.com
website https://astrapublishinghouse.com/imprints/astra-young-readers/
Facebook www.facebook.com/astrakidsbooks
X @astrakidsbooks
Instagram @astrakidsbooks
Publisher Betsy Wollheim

Fiction, non-fiction and poetry trade books for children and YA. Imprints: Astra House, Astra Young Readers, Calkins Creek, Daw Books (page 207), Hippo Park, Kane Press, minverva, mineditionUS, Toon Books and WordSong. Founded 1991.

Avery – see Penguin Publishing Group

Barefoot Books

23 Bradford Street, Concord, MA 01742
tel +1 617-576-0660
email help@barefootbooks.com
website www.barefootbooks.com
Facebook www.facebook.com/barefootbooks
X @BarefootBooks
Editorial Director Emma Parkin

Children's picture books, activity decks and board books: diverse, inclusive and global stories that build social-emotional and literacy skills. See website for submission guidelines. Founded 1993.

Basic Books Group*

1290 Avenue of the Americas, 5th Floor, New York, NY 10104
tel +1 212-346-1100
email Basic.Books@hbgusa.com
website www.basicbooks.com
Facebook www.facebook.com/BasicBooks
X @BasicBooks
Publisher Lara Heimert

History, science, natural history, sociology, psychology, biography, politics and African American studies. An imprint of Perseus Books, a Hachette Book Group company. Founded 1952.

Beacon Press

24 Farnsworth, Boston, MA 02110
tel +1 617-742-2110
website www.beacon.org
Director Gayatri Patnaik

General non-fiction in fields of religion, ethics, philosophy, current affairs, gender studies, environmental concerns, African American studies, anthropology and women's studies and nature. Founded 1854.

Bella Books

PO Box 10543, Tallahassee, FL 32302
tel +1 800-729-4992
email info@bellabooks.com
website www.bellabooks.com
Facebook www.facebook.com/bellabooks
X @bellabooks
Instagram @bellabooks

Lesbian fiction: mystery, romance and sci-fi. Founded 1973.

Bellevue Literary Press

90 Broad Street, Suite 2100 New York, NY 10004
website https://blpress.org/
Facebook www.facebook.com/bellevue.literary.press
X @bellevuepress
Instagram @bellevueliterarypress
Publisher & Editorial Director Erika Goldman, *Associate Editor* Laura Hart

Literary fiction and non-fiction in both the arts and sciences. Founded 2007.

Bloomsbury Publishing USA*
1385 Broadway, New York, NY 10018
tel +1 212-419-5300
email Contact-USA@bloomsbury.com
website www.bloomsbury.com/us
President Sabrina McCarthy

Supports the worldwide publishing activities of Bloomsbury Publishing: caters for the US market. For submission guidelines see website. Established in 1998 as an American subsidiary of Bloomsbury Publishing. Founded 1986.

Bold Strokes Books
648 South Cambridge Road, Building A, Johnsonville, NY 12094
email service@boldstrokesbooks.com
website www.boldstrokesbooks.com
Facebook www.facebook.com/BoldStrokesBooks/
X @boldstrokebooks
Bluesky @boldstrokesbooks.bsky.social
Instagram @boldstrokebooks
Publisher Len Barot

LGBTQ+ general and genre fiction. Genres: romance, mystery/intrigue, crime, erotica, speculative fiction (sci-fi/fantasy/horror), general fiction and YA fiction. Over 1,800 titles in print. For submission instructions see website. Founded 2004.

Soliloquy
YA fiction.

George Braziller
90 Broad Street, Suite 2100, New York, NY 10004
tel +1 212-260-9256
website https://georgebraziller.squarespace.com/
Facebook www.facebook.com/george-braziller-inc
X @BrazillerBooks
Publisher & Editorial Director Michael Braziller

Books about art, literary fiction and poetry. Founded 1955.

Burford Books
757 Warren Road, #4137, Ithaca, NY 14852
tel +1 607-319-4373
email pburford@burfordbooks.com
website www.burfordbooks.com
President Peter Burford

Outdoor activities: golf, sports, fitness, nature and travel. Founded 1997.

Cambridge University Press & Assessment*
1 Liberty Plaza, Floor 20, New York, NY 10006
tel +1 212-337-5000
email customer_service@cambridge.org
website www.cambridge.org
Chief Executive Peter Phillips

Academic and professional. Cambridge Learning (ELT, primary and secondary education). Founded 1534.

Candlewick Press*
99 Dover Street, Somerville, MA 02144
tel +1 617-661-3330
email bigbear@candlewick.com
website www.candlewick.com
Facebook www.facebook.com/candlewickpressbooks
X @candlewick
Bluesky @candlewickpress.bsky.social

Books for babies through YA: board books, picture books, novels, non-fiction, novelty books. Submit material through a literary agent. Subsidiary of Walker Books in the UK. Founded 1991.

Candlewick Entertainment
Media-related children's books, including film/TV tie-ins.

Candlewick Studio
Books for all ages.

C&R Press
812 Westwood Avenue Street D, Chattanooga, TN 37405
email info@crpress.org
website www.crpress.org
Facebook www.facebook.com/cr.press.lit
X @CRPress
Instagram @candrpress
Publisher & Editorial Director Andrew Ibis

Independent publisher of literary fiction, non-fiction and poetry. Solicited or agented queries only. Founded 2006.

Catapult Book Group
20 Jay Street, #704 Brooklyn, New York NY 10221
email contact@catapult.co
website https://books.catapult.co/
Facebook www.facebook.com/catapultstory
X @CatapultStory
Co-founder & Ceo Elizabeth Koch

Fiction and non-fiction. Offers writing classes taught by acclaimed emerging and established writers, produces a daily online magazine of narrative non-fiction and fiction and hosts an open online platform where writers can showcase their own writing, find resources, and get inspired. Imprints: Catapult, Counterpoint Press and Soft Skull Press. Founded 2015.

Center Street*
Hachette Book Group USA, 6100 Tower Cir #210, Franklin, TN 37067
email centerstreetpub@hbgusa.com
website www.centerstreet.com

Non-fiction: biography, business and leadership, health and fitness, family and relationships, inspirational, military, politics and government, self-help and social issues. Fiction. Books in Spanish. Imprint of Hachette Book Group. Founded 2005.

University of Chicago Press*

1427 East 60th Street, Chicago, IL 60637
tel +1 773-702-7700
website www.press.uchicago.edu, www.journals.uchicago.edu

Scholarly books and monographs (humanities, social sciences and sciences), general trade books, reference books and 80 scholarly journals. Founded 1891.

Chronicle Books

680 Second Street, San Francisco, CA 94107
tel +1 415-537-4200
email hello@chroniclebooks.com
website www.chroniclebooks.com, www.chroniclebooks.com/titles/kids-teens
Facebook www.facebook.com/ChronicleBooks
X @ChronicleBooks
Instagram @chroniclekidsbooks
Chairman & Ceo Nion McEvoy

Illustrated books and gift products in design, art, architecture, photography, food, lifestyle, pop culture and children's. Part of the McEvoy Group along with Princeton Architectural Press and Galison/Mudpuppy. Founded 1967.

City Lights Publishers*

261 Columbus Avenue, San Francisco CA 94133
tel +1 415-362-1901
website http://citylights.com/publishing/
Facebook www.facebook.com/CityLightsBooks
X @CityLightsBooks
Ceo Elaine Katzenberger

Fiction, poetry, memoirs, literary translations and non-fiction on vital social and political issues. Founded 1955.

Coffee House Press

79 13th Avenue NE, Suite 110, Minneapolis, MN 55413
tel +1 612-338-0125
email info@coffeehousepress.org
website www.coffeehousepress.org
Executive Editor Jeremy M. Davies

Literary fiction, essays, literature in translation and poetry. Founded 1984.

Columbia University Press*

61 West 62nd Street, New York, NY 10023
tel +1 212-459-0600
website https://cup.columbia.edu/
X @ColumbiaUP
Associate Provost & Director Jennifer Crewe, *Editorial Director* Christine Dunbar

General interest, scholarly and textbooks in the humanities, social sciences, sciences and professions; reference. Subjects include: African American and African diaspora studies, Asian studies, business, earth science and sustainability, economics, English and comparative literature, film and media studies, global and American history, international relations, journalism, life science, Middle Eastern studies, neuroscience, palaeontology, philosophy, political science and international relations, religion, sociology and social work. Publishes Asian literature in translation. Submission guidelines, see website. Founded 1893.

Concordia Publishing House

3558 South Jefferson Avenue, St Louis, MO 63118
tel +1 314-268-1000
website www.cph.org
Facebook www.facebook.com/concordiapublishing
X @concordiapub
Bluesky @concordiapub.bsky.social
President & Ceo Jonathan D. Schultz

Religious books, Lutheran perspective. Few unsolicited MSS accepted; query first. Founded 1869.

Cornell University Press

Sage House, 512 East State Street, Ithaca, NY 14850
tel +1 607-253-2338
email cupressinfo@cornell.edu
website www.cornellpress.cornell.edu
X @CornellPress
Bluesky @cornellupress.bsky.social
Instagram @cornelluniversitypress
Director Jane Bunker

Scholarly books. Founded 1869.

The Countryman Press

500 Fifth Avenue, New York, NY 10110
tel +1 212-354-5500
email countrymanpress@wwnorton.com
website www.countrymanpress.com
Facebook www.facebook.com/countrymanpress
X @countrymanpress
Instagram @countrymanpress

Outdoor recreation guides for anglers, hikers, cyclists, canoeists and kayakers. Also, cookery and lifestyle, US travel guides, New England non-fiction, how-to books, country living books, books on nature and the environment, classic reprints and general non-fiction. No unsolicited MSS. Division of W.W. Norton & Co. Founded 1973.

Crown Publishing Group*

1745 Broadway, New York, NY 10019
tel +1 212-366-2000
website https://crownpublishing.com/
Facebook www.facebook.com/crownpublishing
X @crownpublishing
Instagram @crownpublishing
President David Drake

Non-fiction: politics, current affairs, social justice, personal narrative, biography, history, economics, business, cultural criticism, science, social science and psychology. Imprints: Crown, Currency, Clarkson Potter and Ten Speed Press (page 220). One of four publishing groups within Penguin Random House. Founded 1933.

DAW Books*

1745 Broadway, New York, NY 10019
tel +1 212-366-2096
email daw@penguinrandomhouse.com
website https://astrapublishinghouse.com/imprints/daw-books/
Publisher Betsy Wollheim

Sci-fi, fantasy, horror and paranormal: originals and reprints. Imprint of Astra Publishing, which publishes under Penguin Random House. Founded 1971.

Dover Publications

1325 Franklin Ave, Ste 250, Garden City NY 11530
website https://store.doverpublications.com/
Facebook www.facebook.com/doverpublications
X @doverpubs
Instagram @doverpublications

Art, architecture, antiques, crafts, juvenile, food, history, folklore, literary classics, mystery, language, music, mathematics and science, nature, design and ready-to-use art. Founded 1941.

Elsevier (Clinical Solutions)

1600 John F. Kennedy Boulevard, Philadelphia, PA 19103-2398
tel +1 215-239-3900
website www.uk.elsevierhealth.com, www.elsevier.com/clinical-solutions

Medical books, journals and electrical healthcare solutions. No unsolicited MSS but synopses and project proposals welcome. Imprints: Bailliere Tindall, Churchill Livingstone, Elsevier, Mosby, Pergamon and Saunders. Founded 1880.

Europa Editions

27 Union Square West, Suite 302, New York, NY 10003
email info@europaeditions.com
website www.europaeditions.com
Facebook www.facebook.com/europaeditionsNYS
X @europaeditions
Instagram @europaeditions
Editor-in-Chief Michael Reynolds

An independent publisher of an eclectic mix of literary fiction. Founded 2005.

Farrar, Straus and Giroux

175 Varick Street, 9th Floor, New York, NY 10014
tel +1 212-741-6900
website https://us.macmillan.com/fsg/
Facebook www.facebook.com/fsgoriginals
X @FSOriginals
President Mitzi Angel

Literary fiction, autobiography, politics and non-fiction. Imprints: Auwa Books, FSG, FSG Originals, Hill and Wang, MCD and North Point Press. Part of Macmillan Publishers. Founded 1946.

Feather Proof Books

website www.featherproof.com
Facebook www.facebook.com/featherproof
X @featherproof
Publisher & Editor-in-Chief Jason Sommer, *Co-founder* Zach Dodson

Publishes literary fiction in the form of novels, short stories and poetry, and also non-fiction and post-, trans- and inter-genre tragicomedy. Founded 2005.

The Feminist Press

365 Fifth Avenue, Suite 5406, New York, NY 10016
website www.feministpress.org
Facebook www.facebook.com/feministpress
X @feministpress
Publisher Margot Atwell

Cutting-edge fiction, activist non-fiction, literature in translation, hybrid memoirs and children's books. Publishes 12 to 15 books a year. Founded 1970.

Flyaway Books

100 Witherspoon Street, Louisville, KY 40202–1396
tel +1 502-569-5000
website www.flyawaybooks.com
Facebook www.facebook.com/flyawaybooks
X @flyaway_books
Instagram @flyawaybooks1
President & Publisher David Dobson

Children's picture books with a social justice and spiritual angle. Division of Presbyterian Publishing Corp. Founded 1938.

Fonthill Media

2C Rose Lane, Charleston, SC 29403
tel +1 843-203-3432
email info@fonthillmedia.com
website www.fonthillmedia.com
Publisher & President (Charleston SC Office) Alan Sutton

General history: biography, military history, aviation history, naval and maritime history, regional and local history, transport history, social history, sports history, ancient history and archaeology. US imprints: American History House, America Through Time and Fonthill. Founded 2012.

Forest Avenue Press

PO Box 80134, Portland, OR 97280
website www.forestavenuepress.com
Facebook www.facebook.com/forestavenuepress
X @forestavepress
Instagram @forestavenuepress

Literary fiction and the occasional memoir. Founded 2012.

Forge – see Tor Publishing Group

Fulcrum Publishing

7333 W Jefferson Ave, Ste. 225, Lakewood, CO 80235
email orders@fulcrumbooks.com
website www.fulcrumbooks.com
Facebook www.facebook.com/Fulcrumbooks
X @fulcrumpublishing

Independent publisher of literary works exploring conservation, American culture, civics and the American West. Subjects include: science and nature, literature and storytelling, history, multicultural studies, and Native American and Hispanic cultures. Founded 1965.

Future Tense Books

PO Box 42416, Portland, OR 97242
website https://futuretensebooks.com/
Facebook www.facebook.com/groups/42894248151
X @futuretensebook
Editor & Publisher Kevin Sampsell

Independent publisher of edgy fiction by new writers. Founded 1990.

Getty Publications*

1200 Getty Center Drive, Suite 500, Los Angeles, CA 90049
tel +1 310-440-6536
email booknews@getty.edu
website www.getty.edu

Art, art history, architecture, classical art and archaeology and conservation. Founded 1983.

Gibbs Smith

570 N Sportsplex Drive, Kaysville, UT 84037
tel +1 800-835-4993
email info@gibbs-smith.com
website www.gibbs-smith.com
Facebook www.facebook.com/gibbssmithbooks
X @gibbssmithbooks
Instagram @gibbssmithbooks

An employee-owned, independent publisher of home reference, cookery, non-fiction and children's books. The Gibbs Smith Education division is the nation's leading publisher of state history programmes. All unsolicited queries, submissions and correspondence should be via email. Responds only to projects of interest. Founded 1969.

David R. Godine, Publisher

PO Box 40, Jaffrey NH 03452
tel +1 617-451-9600
website www.godine.com
Facebook www.facebook.com/davidgodinepublisher
X @GodinePub
Instagram @godinepub
Publisher David Alexander, *Editor* Celia Johnson

Fiction, non-fiction, poetry, biography, children's, essays, history, photography, art, typography, architecture, nature and gardening, music, cookery, words and writing and mysteries. No unsolicited MSS. Founded 1970.

Grand Central Publishing*

1290 6th Avenue, New York, NY 10104
tel +1 212-364-1100
email grandcentralpublishing@hbgusa.com
website www.grandcentralpublishing.com
Facebook www.facebook.com/grandcentralpub
X @grandcentralpub

Previously Warner Books. Division of Hachette Book Group. Founded 1970.

Graywolf Press

212 Third Avenue North, Suite 485, Minneapolis, MN 55401
tel +1 651-641-0077
email wolves@graywolfpress.org
website www.graywolfpress.org
X @graywolfpress
Director & Publisher Carmen Giménez

A not-for-profit publisher of poetry, non-fiction, literary fiction and works in translation. Founded 1974.

Grove Atlantic, Inc.

154 West 14th Street, 12 Floor, New York, NY 10011
tel +1 212-614-7850
email info@groveatlantic.com
website www.groveatlantic.com
Facebook www.facebook.com/groveatlantic
X @groveatlantic
Vice-President & Editorial Director Elisabeth Schmitz

Fiction, biography, autobiography, history, current affairs, social science, belles lettres and natural history. No unsolicited MSS. Imprints: Atlantic Monthly Press, Black Cat, Grove Press and Mysterious Press. Founded 1952.

Hachette Book Group*

1290 Avenue of the Americas, New York, NY 10104
tel +1 212-364-1100
website www.hachettebookgroup.com
Facebook www.facebook.com/HachetteUS
X @HachetteUS
Instagram @hachetteus
Chairman Michael Pietsch, *Ceo* David Shelley

Publishing groups: Basic Books Group (page 204); Grand Central Publishing (above); Hachette Books; Hachette Nashville; Little, Brown Audio; Little, Brown and Company (page 211); Little, Brown Books for Young Readers; Orbit; Running Press Group (page 217) and Workman Publishing (page 222). Imprints: Basic Books Group: Basic Books, Bold Type Books, PublicAffairs and Seal Press.

Grand Central: Balance, Forever, Forever Yours, Legacy Lit, Twelve and Vision. Hachette Books: Hachette Go. Hachette Nashville: Center Street, Ellie Claire, FaithWords, Worthy Books and WorthyKids. Little, Brown and Company: Back Bay Books, Little, Brown Spark, Mulholland Books and Voracious. Little, Brown Books for Young Readers: Christy Ottaviano Books, JIMMY Patterson, LB Kids and LBYR+. Orbit: Orbit Works and Redhook. Running Press Group: Avalon Travel, Black Dog & Leventhal, Moon Travel, Rick Steves, RP Studio, Running Press and Running Press Kids. Workman Publishing: Algonquin Books of Chapel Hill, Algonquin Young Readers, Artisan, Storey Publishing, Timber Press, Workman and Workan Calendars, Workman Kids. Founded 2006.

HarperCollins Publishers*

195 Broadway, New York, NY 10007
tel +1 212-207-700 0
website https://corporate.harpercollins.com/us/
X @HarperCollins
President & Ceo Brian Murray

Fiction, history, biography, poetry, science, travel, cookery, juvenile, educational, business, technical and religious. The company is composed of a number of brands within which there are various imprints. The Harper Group imprints: Broadside Books, Caedmon, Ecco, Harper, Harper Audio, Harper Business, Harper Influence, Harper Perennial and Harper Perennial Modern Classics. The HarperOne Group imprints: Amistad, HarperCollins Español, HarperOne, HarperVia and Martin Luther King Jr. Library. The Morrow Group imprints; Avon, Dey Street, Harper Voyager, Harvest, Mariner and William Morrow. HarperCollins Children's Books imprints: Allida, Amistad, Clarion Books, Greenwillow Books, Harper, Harper Alley, Heartdrum, Quill Tree Books, Storytide, Versify and Walden Pond Press. HarperCollins Christian Publishing imprints: Editorial CLIE, Emanate Books, Grupo Nelson, HarperChristian Resources, Magnolia Publications, Nelson Books, Thomas Nelson, Tommy Nelson, Vida, W Publishing Group, Westbow Press, Zondervan, Zondervan Academy, Zondervan Books and Zondervan Reflective. HarperCollins Focus imprints: Applesauce Press, Blink, Cider Mill Press, Harper Celebrate, HarperCollins Leadership, Harper Horizon, Harper Muse and Harper Select. Harlequin imprints: Hanover Square Press, MIRA, Park Row Books, Harlequin, Carina Press, Love Inspired Novels and Wordwide Mystery. Founded 1817.

Harpeth Road Press

PO Box 158184, Nashville, TN 37215
website www.harpethroad.com
Facebook www.facebook.com/harpethroad
X @harpethroad
Instagram @harpethroad
Founder Jenny Hale

Digital-first romantic fiction publishers. Currently accepting mainstream commercial romantic fiction (no erotica). Founded 2020.

Harvard University Press*

79 Garden Street, Cambridge, MA 02138
tel +1 617-495-2600
email contact_hup@harvard.edu
website www.hup.harvard.edu
Director George Andreou, *Editorial Director* Sharmila Sen

History, philosophy, literary criticism, politics, economics, sociology, music, science, classics, social sciences, behavioural sciences and law. Founded 1913.

Hippocrene Books

171 Madison Avenue, New York, NY 10016
tel +1 718-454-2366
email info@hippocrenebooks.com
website www.hippocrenebooks.com
Facebook www.facebook.com/hippocrene-books
X @hippocrenebooks

International cookery, foreign language dictionaries, travel, military history, Polonia and general trade. Founded 1971.

Histria Books

7181 N Hualapai Way Suite 130-86, Las Vegas, NV 89166
email info@histriabooks.com
website https://histriabooks.com/
Facebook www.facebook.com/HistriaBooks
X @histriabooks
Instagram @histriabooks
Director Kurt Brackob

Independent academic publisher of general interest books, fiction and literature, and children's books, as well as scholarly books in broad range of categories. Imprints: Addison & Highsmith, Center for Romanian Studies, Guadium, Histria Academic, Histria Kids, Prende Publishing and Vita Histria. Founded 1996.

Holiday House*

50 Broad Street, Ste 301, New York, NY 1000
tel +1 212-688-0085
email info@holidayhouse.com
website www.holidayhouse.com
Facebook www.facebook.com/HolidayHouseBks
X @holidayhousebks
Instagram @holidayhousebks

General children's books. Send entire MS. Only responds to projects of interest. Founded 1935.

Henry Holt and Company

120 Broadway, New York, NY 10271
tel +1 646-307-5095

website https://us.macmillan.com/henryholt/
Facebook www.facebook.com/HenryHoltandCompany
X @HenryHolt
Instagram @henryholtbooks

History, sports, politics, biography, memoir and novels. Imprints: Holt, Metropolitan Books, Andy Cohen Books and Holt Paperbacks. Imprint of Macmillan Publishers Inc. Founded 1866.

Johns Hopkins University Press*

2715 North Charles Street, Baltimore, MD 21218–4319
tel +1 410-516-6900
email tcl@press.jhu.edu
website www.press.jhu.edu
Facebook www.facebook.com/johnhopkinsuniversitypress
X @JHUPress
Instagram @hopkinspress
Director Barbara Kline Pope

History, literary studies, classics, environmental studies, biology, history of STEM, bioethics, public health and health policy, health and wellness, physics, astronomy, mathematics and education. Founded 1878.

Houghton Mifflin Harcourt

3 Park Avenue, Floor 19, New York, NY 10016
tel +1 212-598-5730
website www.hmhco.com
Facebook www.facebook.com/houghtonmifflinharcourt
X @hmhco
Instagram @houhtonmifflinharcourt
Ceo Jack Lynch

Educational content and solutions for K–12 teachers and students of all ages. Also reference, and fiction and non-fiction for adults and young readers. Divisions: Center for Model Schools (formerly ICLE), Heinemann and NWEA. Founded 1832.

Center for Model Schools

Dedicated to ensuring that every child attends a model school.

Heinemann

Provides professional resources and a provider of educational services for teachers, kindergarten through college.

NWEA

Provides assessment and learning solutions for educators.

Ig Publishing

PO Box 2547, New York, NY 10163
tel +1 718-797-0676
website www.igpub.com
Facebook www.facebook.com/ig-publishing
X @igpublishing
Publisher Elizabeth Clementson

Publishes literary fiction and political non-fiction. Founded 2002.

University of Illinois Press

1325 South Oak Street, Champaign, IL 61820
tel +1 217-333-0950
email uipress@uillinois.edu
website www.press.illinois.edu
Facebook www.facebook.com/universityofillinoispress
X @illinoispress
Bluesky @illinoispress.bsky.social
Instagram @illinoispress
Director Laurie Matheson

American studies (history, music, literature, religion), ethnic studies, labour studies, communications, regional studies, architecture, philosophy, women's studies, film, sports history, folklore and disability studies. For submission guidelines, see website. Founded 1918.

Indiana University Press

Herman B Wells Library 350, 1320 East 10th Street, Bloomington, IN 47405–3907
tel +1 812-855-8817
email iupress@indiana.edu
website https://iupress.org/
Director Gary Dunham

Humanities and social sciences: African, Jewish and Holocaust, Middle East, Russian and East European and women's and gender studies; film, history, music, palaeontology, philosophy and religion. Imprint: Quarry Books (regional publishing) and Red Lightning Books (trade publishing). Founded 1950.

Infobase Publishing

8 The Green, Suite 19225, Dover, DE 19901
tel +1 800-322-8755
website www.infobase.com/about
Facebook www.facebook.com/infobaseinc
X @infobaseinc
Instagram @infobaseinc

General reference books and services for colleges, libraries, schools and general public. Founded 1940.

Inkshares

95 Linden Street, Suite 6, Oakland, CA 94607
email hello@inkshares.com
website www.inkshares.com
Facebook www.facebook.com/inkshares
X @Inkshares
Co-founder & Ceo Adam Gomolin, *Co-founder & Cpo* Thad Woodman, *Co-founder* Larry Levitsky

A book publisher that has readers, not agents or editors, decide what is published. Publishes books that successfully hit a pre-order threshold on the company's platform, or win a contest run in partnership with an imprint on the platform. The process is as follows: authors pitch, readers pre-order, and the company publishes. Any author can submit a proposal for a book. Once the project goes live, readers support the project by pre-ordering copies of the book. Once the 750 pre-order goal is hit, the work is published: authors are assigned an editor, a designer and the company deals with printing, distribution, marketing and publicity once the MS is finished. Founded 2013.

Inner Traditions Bear & Company

PO Box 388, Rochester, VT 05767
tel +1 800-246-8648
email comcustomerservice@InnerTraditions.com
website www.innertraditions.com
Facebook www.facebook.com/ITIBco
X @InnerTraditions
Instagram @inner_traditions

Subjects include: spirituality, the occult, ancient mysteries, new science, holistic health and natural medicine. Founded 1975.

JewishGen Press

The Museum of Jewish Heritage, 36 Battery Place, New York, NY 10280
tel +1 781-367-3995
email press@jewishgen.org
website www.jewishgen.org/Yizkor/ybip.html
Director Joel Alpert, *Managing Editor* Peter Harris

Publishes books with Jewish content, Jewish History, Holocaust, Memorial (Yizkor) books of destroyed Jewish communities of Eastern Europe, Holocaust Memoirs, Jewish culture. Jewish education. Non-Profit. Publishing Division of JewishGen.org, the on-line web site dedicated to Jewish genealogy. Founded 2012.

Jolly Fish Press

2297 Waters Drive, Mendota Heights, MN 55120
tel +1 888-417-0195
email publicity@northstareditions.com
website https://northstareditions.com/jolly-fish-press/

Publishes new voices in middle-grade fiction. Imprint of North Star Editions. Founded 2011.

University Press of Kansas

2502 Westbrooke Circle, Lawrence, KS 66045–4444
tel +1 785-864-4154
email upress@ku.edu
website www.kansaspress.ku.edu
Facebook www.facebook.com/kansaspress
X @kansas_press
Bluesky @univpressofkansas.bsky.social
Instagram @kansas_press
Director Tim Paulson, *Assistant Director* Kelly Chrisman-Jacques, *Editor-in-Chief* Joyce Harrison, *Senior Editor* David Congdon

American history (political, social, cultural and environmental), military history, American political thought, American presidency studies, law, constitutional history and political science. Founded 1946.

Kensington Publishing

900 Third Avenue, 26th Floor, New York, NY 10022
website www.kensingtonbooks.com
Facebook www.facebook.com/kensingtonpublishing
X @kensingtonbooks
Instagram @kensingtonbooks
Ceo Steven Zacharius, *Publisher* Jackie Dinas, *Editor-in-Chief* John Scognamiglio

An independent, family-owned publisher of thrillers, romance, historical fiction, cosy mysteries, western, literary fiction, sci-fi and speculative fiction titles. Also publishes non-fiction, including true crime. Releases more than 300 fiction and non-fiction titles each year. Imprints: Citadel Press, Dafina, Erewhon Books, John Scognamiglio Books, Kensington Books, Kensington Cozies, Lyrical Press, Pinnacle and Zebra. Founded 1974.

Knopf Doubleday Publishing Group*

1745 Broadway, New York, NY 10019
tel +1 212-782-9000
website https://knopfdoubleday.com/
President & Publisher Maya Mavjee; *Executive Vice-Presidents & Publishers* Reagan Arthur (Knopf), Bill Thomas (Doubleday), *Senior Vice-President & Publisher* Lisa Lucas (Pantheon & Schoken)

A publishing group, one of four within Penguin Random House. Alfred A. Knopf was founded in 1915 and has long been known as a publisher of distinguished hardback fiction and non-fiction. Imprints: Doubleday, Everyman's Library, Knopf, KnopfCook, Pantheon, Schocken and Vintage. Founded in 2008.

Krause Publications*

5525 Joerns Drive, Suite 2, Stevens Point WI 544817
tel +1 715-445-2214
website www.krausebooks.com

Antiques and collectables, coins, stamps, automobiles, toys, trains, firearms, comics, records, sewing, ceramics, outdoors and hunting. Imprint of Penguin Random House. Founded 1952.

Little, Brown and Company

1290 Avenue of the Americas, New York, NY 10104
tel +1 212-364-1100
email lbpublicity.Generic@hbgusa.com
website www.littlebrown.com
Facebook www.facebook.com/littlebrownandcompany
X @littlebrown
President Sally Kim, *Editorial Director* Denise Roy

General literature, fiction, non-fiction, biography, history, trade paperbacks and children's. Founded 1837.

Algonquin Books
Literary fiction and non-fiction with a focus on underrepresented writers.

Back Bay Books
Fiction and non-fiction.

Little, Brown Spark
Publishes books for young people and adults. Looking for authors who are experts and thought leaders in the fields of health, lifestyle, psychology and science.

Mulholland Books
Suspense and crime.

Voracious
Non-fiction: cookery, self-help, current issues and interest.

Llewellyn Worldwide

2143 Wooddale Drive, Woodbury, MN 55125
tel +1 651-291-1970
email publicity@llewellyn.com
website www.llewellyn.com
Facebook www.facebook.com/LlewellynBooks
X @llewellynbooks
Instagram @llewellynbooks
President Sandra Weschcke

A publisher of new age and mind, body & spirit books, including self-help, holistic health, witchcraft, Wicca, astrology, tarot, paranormal and alternative spirituality titles. Founded 1901.

Blue Angel
Mind, body & spirit and New Age.

Llewellyn
Holistic and metaphysical.

Lo Scarabeo
Tarot cards and related products.

Lonely Planet

230 Franklin Road, Building 2B, Franklin, TN 37064
email pressusa@lonelyplanet.com
website www.lonelyplanet.com
Facebook www.facebook.com/lonelyplanet
X @lonelyplanet
Instagram @lonelyplanet

An international travel publisher of guidebooks and ebooks. Also produces a range of gift and reference titles, a website, a magazine and digital travel products and apps. Founded 1973.

The Lyons Press

246 Goose Lane, Guilford, CT 06437
tel +1 203-458-4500
website www.lyonspress.com, www.globepequot.com
Facebook www.facebook.com/lyonspress
X @lyons_press
Instagram @lyonspress

Fishing, hunting, sports, outdoor skills, history, military history, reference, true crime, entertainment and non-fiction. An imprint of Globe Pequot, the trade division of Rowman & Littlefield. Founded 1978.

McGraw-Hill Professional*

1325 Avenue of the Americas, 7th Floor, New York, NY 10019
website www.mhprofessional.com
Facebook www.facebook.com/mcgrawhilleducation
X @MHEducation
Ceo Simon Allen

Divisions and imprints: Business, Education and Test Prep, International Marine and Ragged Mountain Press, Medical and Open University Press. To find individual editorial contacts check website. Founded 1966.

Macmillan Publishers*

120 Broadway, New York, NY 10271
tel +1 646-307-5151
email press.inquiries@macmillanusa.com
website https://us.macmillan.com/
Facebook www.facebook.com/MacmillanUS
X @MacmillanUSA

Imprints for adults: Castle Point Books, Celadon Books, Farrar, Straus & Giroux (page 207), Flatiron Books, Henry Holt & Co. (page 209), Macmillan Audio, Metropolitan Books, Minotaur Books, Picador, Quick and Dirty Tips, St Martin's Essentials, St Martin's Griffin, St Martin's Press (page 217), St Martin's Publishing Group, Tor Publishing Group (page 220), Wednesday Books. For children: FSG Books for Young Readers, Feiwel & Friends, First Second, Holt Books for Young Readers, Kingfisher, Macmillan Children's Publishing Group, Neon Squid, Odd Dot, Priddy Books, Roaring Brook, Starscape/Tor Teen, Square Fish, Swoon Reads and Young Listeners. Founded 1843.

McPherson & Company

PO Box 1126, Kingston, NY 12402
tel +1 845-331-5807
email bmcphersonco@gmail.com
website www.mcphersonco.com
Facebook www.facebook.com/McPherson-and-Company
X @bookmaverick
Publisher Bruce R. McPherson

Literary fiction and non-fiction: art criticism, writings by artists, film-making. Occasional general titles (e.g., anthropology). No poetry. No unsolicited MSS. Query first. Imprints: Documentext, Saroff Books and Treacle Press. Founded 1974.

McSweeney's Books

PO Box 410987, San Francisco, CA 94141
website www.mcsweeneys.net
Facebook www.facebook.com/McSweeneys.Publishing
X @mcsweeneys
Bluesky @mcsweeneys.bsky.social
Instagram @mcswys
Threads @mcswys
Founder Dave Eggers

An independent not-for-profit publisher publishing ten books a year. Also publishes quarterly literary journal *Timony McSweeney's Quarterly Concern* and runs a daily humour website McSweeney's Internet Tendency. Founded 1998.

The University of Massachusetts Press*

New Africa House, 180 Infirmary Way, 4th Floor, Amherst, MA 01003-9289
email info@umpress.umass.edu
website www.umass.edu/umpress
Facebook www.facebook.com/umasspress
X @umasspress
Director Mary Dougherty, *Executive Editor* Matt Becker

Scholarly books and works of general interest: American studies and history, Black and ethnic studies, women's studies, cultural criticism, architecture and environmental design, literary criticism, poetry, fiction, philosophy, political science, sociology and books of regional interest. Founded 1964.

Melville House*

46 John Street, Brooklyn, NY 11201
tel +1 718-722-9204
email info@mhpbooks.com
website www.mhpbooks.com
Facebook www.facebook.com/melvillehouse
X @melvillehouse
Instagram @melvillehouse
Co-founders Valerie Merians, Dennis Johnson

An independent publisher founded by sculptor Valerie Merians and fiction writer/journalist Dennis Johnson in order to publish *Poetry After 9/11*. Publishes literary fiction and thought-provoking non-fiction. Founded 2001.

The University of Michigan Press

4190 Shapiro Library, 919 South, University Avenue, Ann Arbor, MI 48109-1185
tel +1 734-764-4388
email um.press@umich.edu
website www.press.umich.edu
Facebook www.facebook.com/universityofmichiganpress
X @UofMPress
Editorial Director Sara Jo Cohen

Scholarly and general interest works in literary and cultural theory, classics, history, theatre, women's studies, political science, law, American history, American studies, anthropology, economics and jazz. Also textbooks in English as a second language and regional trade titles. Founded 1930.

Microsoft Press Books

One Microsoft Way, Redmond, WA 98052–6399
tel +1 425-882-8080
email 4bkideas@pearson.com
website www.microsoftpressstore.com

IT books for home users, developers, professionals and educators. Published by Pearson. See the 'write for us' page for submission guidelines. Founded 1983.

Milkweed Editions

1011 Washington Avenue South, Suite 300, Minneapolis, MN 55415
tel +1 612-332-3192
website www.milkweed.org
Publisher & Ceo Daniel Slager, *Managing Editor* Lauren Langton Klein, *Editor* Morissa Young

Fiction, poetry, essays and the natural world. Founded 1979.

University of Missouri Press

113 Heinkel Building, 201 South 7th Street, Columbia, MO 65211
tel +1 573-882-7641
email upress@missouri.edu
website https://upress.missouri.edu/
Facebook www.facebook.com/umissouripress
Bluesky @umissouripress.bsky.social
Editor-in-Chief Andrew Davidson

US history (esp. 20th-century military, African American, women, sports, political/constitutional and early Republic), journalism, political science, Missouri and regional history and literary criticism (US and Mark Twain). Founded 1958.

The MIT Press

255 Main Street, 9th Floor, Cambridge, MA 02142
tel +1 617-253-5646
website https://mitpress.mit.edu/
Facebook www.facebook.com/mitpress
X @mitpress
Bluesky @mitpress.bsky.social

Art and architecture, cognitive sciences, philosophy, bioethics, computer science, culture, technology, design and visual culture, education and learning, economics, finance and business, environmental studies, urbanism and food studies, information science and communications, life sciences, neuroscience and trade science, linguistics, new media, game studies and digital humanities, medical and health sciences, physical sciences, mathematics and engineering, science, technology and society and sci-fi. Also, books of MIT and regional interest. Founded 1962.

University of Nebraska Press
1225 L Street, Suite 200, Lincoln, NE 68588-0630
email presswebmail@unl.edu
website www.nebraskapress.unl.edu
Facebook www.facebook.press/nebraskapress
X @univnebpress
Instagram @univnebpress

Scholarly and general-interest books, with more than 6,000 titles in print and an additional 140 new titles released each year. Imprints: The Backwater Press, Bison Books, Nebraska and Potomac Books (page 216). Also works in partnership with The Jewish Publication Society. Founded 1941.

Thomas Nelson Publisher*
PO Box 141000, Nashville, TN 37214
tel +1 800-251-4000
email publicity@thomasnelson.com
website www.thomasnelson.com

Bibles, religious, non-fiction and fiction general trade books for adults and children. Owned by HarperCollins Publishers. Founded 1798.

New Directions
80 Eighth Avenue New York, NY 10011
tel +1 212-255-0230
website www.ndbooks.com
Facebook www.facebook.com/ndbooks
X @newdirections
Instagram @ndpublishing
Ceo Barbara Epler

Independent publisher of literary fiction and poetry. Founded 1936.

New Harbinger Publications
5674 Shattuck Avenue, Oakland, CA 94609
tel +1 800-748-6273
email customerservice@newharbinger.com
website www.newharbinger.com
Facebook www.facebook.com/NewHarbinger
X @NewHarbinger
Instagram @newharbinger

Psychology, health, spirituality and personal growth. Imprints: Context Press, Impact Publishers, Instant Help Books, Non-Duality Press, New Harbinger and Reveal Press. For submission guidelines see website. Founded 1973.

University of New Mexico Press
1717 Roma NE, Albuquerque, NM 87106
tel +1 505-277-3495
email custserv@unm.edu
website www.unmpress.com
Director Stephen Hull, *Publishing Assistant* Abigail Vermette

Western history, anthropology and archaeology, Latin American studies, photography, multicultural literature, fiction and poetry. Founded 1929.

Noemi Press
website www.noemipress.org
Facebook www.facebook.com/noemi.press
X @noemi_press
Instagram @noemipressbooks
Publishers Antony Cody, Suzi F. Garcia

A literary arts publisher dedicated to publishing and promoting the work of emerging and established artists. Founded 2002.

The University of North Carolina Press*
116 South Boundary Street, Chapel Hill, NC 27514
tel +1 919-966-3561
website https://uncpress.org/
Facebook www.facebook.com/UNCPpress
X @UNC_Press

American history, American studies, Southern studies, European history, women's studies, Latin American studies, political science, anthropology and folklore, classics and regional trade. See website for editorial contacts. Founded 1922.

North Point Press – see Farrar, Straus and Giroux

W.W. Norton & Co.*
500 Fifth Avenue, New York, NY 10110
tel +1 212-354-5500
website www.wwnorton.com
Facebook www.facebook.com/wwnorton
X @wwnorton
Instagram @w.w.norton
Vice-President & Editor-in-Chief John Glusman

Narrative non-fiction and literary fiction, history, politics, science, biography, music and memoir. Founded 1923.

University of Oklahoma Press
2800 Venture Drive, Norman, OK 73069–8216
website www.oupress.com
Facebook www.facebook.com/oupress
X @oupress
Director Tony Roberts, *Editorial Director* Andrew Berzanskis

American West, American Indians, classics and political science. Founded 1928.

OR Books
40 Avenue C, New York, NY 10009
tel +1 212-514-6485
email info@orbooks.com
website www.orbooks.com
Facebook www.facebook.com/orbooks
X @orbooks
Instagram @or_books
Founders John Oakes, Colin Robinson

Publishes non-fiction, literature, history and politics, activism, society, the internet and the Middle East. Founded 2009.

Oxford University Press

198 Madison Avenue, New York, NY 10016
tel +1 212-726-6000
website https://global.oup.com/academic/
President Niko Pfund

Academic: scholarly, medicine, technology, science, humanities, law, music, trade and bibles. Education: ELT and ESL, dictionaries, higher education. Law, medicine and music. Also journals, online and reference. Publishes globally for a range of audiences, across a multitude of cultures, education systems and languages. Currently publishes more than 6,000 titles a year worldwide, in a variety of formats. Many of these titles are created specifically for local markets and are published by regional publishing branches. Founded 1586.

Pelican Publishing

990 N. Corporate Drive, Suite 100, New Orleans, LA 70123
tel +1 504-684-8976
email editorial@pelicanpub.com
website www.arcadiapublishing.com/pages/pelican-publishing
Publisher & President Scott Campbell

Gulf South cookery, biography, history, paranormal, children's and holiday. Founded 1926.

Penguin Publishing Group*

1745 Broadway, New York, NY 10019
tel +1 212-366-2000
website www.penguin.com
Facebook www.facebook.com/PenguinGroupUSA
X @penguinusa
Instagram @penguinusa
President Allison Dobson

A publishing group, one of four within Penguin Random House (see below). Imprints: Avery, Berkley Books, Dutton, Family Tree Books, Impact, KP, North Light Books, Pamela Dorman Books, Penguin Books, Penguin Classics, Penguin Press, Plume, Popular Woodworking Books, Portfolio, G.P. Putnam's Sons, Riverhead, Sentinel, Tarcher Perigee, Tiny Reparations Books, Viking Press and Writer's Digest Books (page 222). Founded 1935.

Penguin Random House*

1745 Broadway, New York, NY 10019
tel +1 212-782-9000
website www.penguinrandomhouse.com
X @PenguinUSA
Ceo Nihar Malaviya

Consists of over 300 independent imprints and brands, more than 15,000 new print titles a year. Adult and children's fiction and non-fiction. Imprints: Jonathan Cape (UK), Doubleday, Ebury, Hamish Hamilton, Alfred A. Knopf (US) and Viking. Also: DK (International), Plaza & Janés and Alfaguara (Spain) and Sudamericana (Argentina). See Crown Publishing Group (page 206), Knopf Doubleday Publishing Group (page 211), Penguin Publishing Group (above), Random House Publishing Group (page 217), Penguin Young Readers (below) and Random House Children's Books (page 216). Founded 2013.

Penguin Young Readers*

1745 Broadway, New York, NY 10019
tel +1 212-366-2000
website www.penguin.com/children
Facebook www.facebook.com/penguinkidsbooks
X @penguinkids
President Jen Loja

Publishes under a wide range of imprints and trademarks including: Kathy Dawson Books, Dial Books, Dutton, Grosset & Dunlap, Kokila, Nancy Paulsen Books, Penguin Workshop, Philomel, Puffin, G.P. Putnam's Sons, Razorbill, Speak, Viking and Frederick Warne. Penguin Young Readers is a division of Penguin Group, a Penguin Random House company. Founded 1935.

University of Pennsylvania Press*

3905 Spruce Street, Philadelphia, PA 19104–4112
tel +1 215-898-6261
email custserv@pobox.upenn.edu
website www.pennpress.org
Facebook www.facebook.com/PennPress
X @pennpress
Instagram @penn_press
Editor-in-Chief Walter Biggins

American and European history, African American studies, anthropology, Atlantic studies, architecture, cultural studies, ancient studies, human rights, literature, medieval and early modern studies, Jewish studies, religious studies, current affairs, politics and public policy, urban studies and Pennsylvania regional studies. Founded 1890.

Pennsylvania State University Press*

820 North University Drive, USB1, Suite C, University Park, PA 16802
tel +1 814-865-1327
website www.psupress.org
Facebook www.facebook.com/pennstateuniversitypress
Instagram @psupress
Executive Director David Aycock

Art history, literary criticism, religious studies, philosophy, political science, sociology, history, Latin American studies and medieval studies. See website for submission details. Founded 1956.

The Permanent Press

4170 Noyac Road, Sag Harbor, NY 11963
tel +1 631-725-1101

website www.thepermanentpress.com
Facebook www.facebook.com/ThePermanentPress
X @TPermanentPress
Publisher Judith Shepard

Literary fiction. Imprint: Second Chance Press. Founded 1978.

Potomac Books

1225 L St. STE 200, Lincoln, NE 68506
tel +1 402-472-3581
email presswebmail@unl.edu
website www.nebraskapress.unl.edu/potomac
Facebook www.facebook.com/PotomacBooks
X @PotomacBooks

National and international affairs, history (military and diplomatic), reference and biography. Imprint of University of Nebraska Press. Founded 1984.

powerHouse Books

32 Adams Street, Brooklyn, NY 11201
tel +1 718-666-3049
email madison@powerhousebooks.com
website www.powerhousebooks.com
Facebook www.facebook.com/pages/powerHouseBooksNY
X @powerhousebooks
Instagram @powerhousebooks
Ceo & Publisher Daniel Power

Fine art, documentary, pop culture, fashion and celebrity books. Check submissions page on website for submissions procedure. Founded 1995.

Press 53

560 N Trade Street, Ste 103,
Winston-Salem NC 27101
tel +1 336-770-5353
website www.press53.com
Facebook www.facebook.com/press53
Publisher & Editor-in-Chief Kevin Morgan Watson

An independent publisher of short stories and poetry, including their free, monthly 53-Word Story Contest open to writers around the world. Founded 2005.

Princeton University Press*

Postal address 41 William Street, Princeton, NJ 08540
tel +1 609-258-4900
website www.press.princeton.edu
Director Christie Henry

Scholarly and scientific books on all subjects. Founded 1905.

Puffin – see Penguin Young Readers

Quarto Publishing Group USA

142 West 36th Street, Fourth Floor, New York, NY 10018
tel +1 212-779-4972
website www.quarto.com
Facebook www.facebook.com/QuartoBooksUS
X @quartobooksus
Instagram @quartobooksus
Ceo C.K. Lau

Home improvement, gardening, practical arts and crafts, licensed children's books, transport, graphic arts, food and drink, sports, military history, Americana, health and body, lifestyle, pets and music. Imprints: becker&mayer!, becker&mayer! kids, Chartwell Books, Cool Springs Press, Epic Ink, Fair Winds Press, Harvard Common Press, Motorbooks, Quarry Books, Rock Point, Rockport Publishing and Voyageur Press. Details of the imprints can be found on the website. Founded 2004.

Quirk Books*

215 Church Street, Philadelphia, PA 19106
tel +1 215-627-3581
website www.quirkbooks.com
Facebook www.facebook.com/quirkbooks
X @quirkbooks
Instagram @quirkbooks
President David Borgenicht

Unconventional books for adults and children. Founded 2002.

Rand McNally

9550 W. Higgins, Rosemont, Illinois, Chicago, IL 60018
tel +1 847-329-8100
website www.randmcnally.com/publishing
Facebook www.facebook.com/randmcnally
X @randmcnally

Maps, guides, atlases, educational publications, globes and children's geographical titles and atlases in print and electronic formats. Founded 1856.

Random House Children's Books*

1745 Broadway, New York, NY 10019
tel +1 212-782-9000
website www.rhcbooks.com, www.randomhouse.com/teachers
President & Publisher Barbara Marcus

An English-language children's trade book publisher. Creates books for preschool children through YA readers, in all formats from board books to activity books to picture books, graphic novels, novels and non-fiction. Imprints: Alfred A. Knopf, Anne Schwartz Books, Beginner Books, Bright Matter Books, Crown, Delacourt Press, Double Day, Dr Seuss, Dragonfly Books, Ember, Golden Books, Joy Revolution, Labyrinth, Little Tiger, Make Me A World, Random House Books for Young Readers, Random House Graphic, Random House Studio, Rodale Kids, Step into Reading, The Princeton Review, Underlined, Wendy Lamb Books and Yearling Books. Part of Penguin Random House. Founded 1925.

Random House Publishing Group*
1745 Broadway, New York, NY 10019
tel +1 212-782-9000
website www.randomhousebooks.com
Facebook www.facebook.com/randomhouse
X @randomhouse
Instagram @randomhouse
President & Publisher Sanyu Dillon

A publishing group, one of four within Penguin Random House. Literary and commercial fiction, narrative non-fiction. Genres: history, science, politics, current affairs, biography, memoir, religion and business, culinary and lifestyle. Imprints: Ballantine Books, Bantam Books, Convergent Books, Del Rey, Delacorte Press, Dell, The Dial Press, Goop Press, Harmony Books, Hogarth, Ink Lore, Modern Library, One World, Random House, Random House Worlds, Roc Lit 101 and Rodale. Founded 1927.

Razorbill – see Penguin Young Readers

Rizzoli International Publications
49 West 27th Street, 4th Floor, New York, NY 10010
tel +1 212-387-3400
email publicity@rizzoliusa.com
website www.rizzoliusa.com
Facebook www.facebook.com/RizzoliNewYork
X @rizzoli_books
Instagram @rizzolibooks

Art, architecture, photography, fashion, gardening, design, gift books and cookery. Founded 1976.

Rocky Nook
1010 B Street, Ste 350, San Rafael, CA 94901
email info@rockynook.com
website https://rockynook.com/
Publisher Scott Cowlin, *Associate Publisher* Ted Waitt

A small, independent publisher of books on digital photography, imaging and workflow. Founded 2006.

Rodale Book Group
733 Third Avenue, New York, NY 10017
tel +1 212-573-0300
website www.randomhousebooks.com/imprint/rodale-books

General health, women's health, men's health, senior health, alternative health, fitness, healthy cookery, gardening, pets, spirituality/inspiration, trade health, biography, memoir, current affairs, science, parenting, organics, lifestyle, self-help, how-to and home arts. Imprint of Penguin Random House. Founded 1932.

Routledge
270 Madison Avenue, New York, NY 10016
tel +1 212-216-7800
website www.routledge.com
Facebook www.facebook.com/taylorandfrancisgroup
X @routledgebooks

Music, history, psychology and psychiatry, politics, business studies, philosophy, education, sociology, urban studies, religion, film, media, literary and cultural studies, reference, English language, linguistics, communication studies and journalism. Editorial office in the UK. Subsidiary of Taylor & Francis. Imprint: Routledge. Founded 1834.

Rowman & Littlefield – see Bloomsbury Publishing

Running Press Group
123 South Broad Street, Fl 27, Philadelphia, PA 19107
email perseus.promos@perseusbooks.com
website www.runningpress.com
Facebook www.facebook.com/runningpressbooks
X @running_press
Publisher Shannon Connors Fabricant

General non-fiction, TV, film, humour, history, children's fiction and non-fiction, food and wine, pop culture, lifestyle and illustrated gift books. Imprint of Hachette Book Group. Founded 1972.

Rutgers University Press
106 Somerset Street, Third Floor, New Brunswick, NJ 08901
tel +1 800-848-6224
website www.rutgersuniversitypress.org
Facebook www.facebook.com/rutgersunipress
X @rutgersupress
Bluesky @rutgersupress.bsky.social
Instagram @rutgersupress
Threads @rutgersupress
Director Micah Kleit, *Editorial Director* Nicole Solano

Women's studies, LGBTQ+ studies, anthropology, childhood studies, Latin American and Caribbean studies, higher education, human rights, television, film and media studies, communication, sociology, public health, history of medicine, Asian American studies, African American studies, American studies, Latinx studies, Jewish studies, religious studies and regional titles. Founded 1936.

St Martin's Press*
120 Broadway, New York, NY 10271
website https://us.macmillan.com/smp/

Trade, reference and college. No unsolicited MSS. Imprints: Castle Point Books, Minotaur Books, St Martin's Essentials, St Martin's Griffin and Wednesday's Books. Imprint of Macmillan Publishers. Founded 1952.

Santa Monica Press
PO Box 850, Solana Beach, CA 92075
tel +1 858-832-7906
email acquisitions@santamonicapress.com
website www.santamonicapress.com
X @santamonicapress
Instagram @santamonicapress1
Publisher Jeffrey Goldman

Modern non-fiction titles: pop culture, film, music, humour, biography, travel and sports, as well as regional titles focused on California. YA historical fiction and YA narrative non-fiction recently added to the list. Visit website to view author guidelines. Founded 1994.

Sasquatch Books

1904 Third Avenue, Suite 710, Seattle, WA 98101
tel +1 206-467-4300
email custserv@sasquatchbooks.com
website www.sasquatchbooks.com
Facebook www.facebook.com/SasquatchBooksSeattle
X @sasquatchbooks
Instagram @sasquatchbooks

Non-fiction children's. Will consider queries and proposals from authors and agents for new projects that fit into the company's West Coast regional publishing programme. Imprints: Little Bigfoot (children's), Sasquatch Adult and Spruce Books. Founded 1986.

Scholastic*

557 Broadway, New York, NY 10012
tel +1 212-343-6100
email news@scholastic.com
website www.scholastic.com
Facebook www.facebook.com/scholastic
X @scholastic

Children's, education and technology. Divisions: Scholastic Book Clubs, Scholastic Book Fairs, Scholastic Education, Scholastic Magazines and Scholastic Trade. Imprints include: Acorn, AFK (Away From Keyboard), Branches, Cartwheel Books, Chicken House, Graphix, Klutz, Little Shepherd Books, Orchard Books, Point, PUSH, Scholastic Early Learners, Scholastic en español, Scholastic Non-fiction, Scholastic Focus, Scholastic Paperbacks and Scholastic Press. Founded 1920.

Seal Press*

1290 Avenue of the Americas, 5th Floor, New York, NY 10104
tel +1 212-364-1100
email seal.presss@hbgusa.com
website www.sealpress.com
Facebook www.facebook.com/sealpress
X @SealPress
Instagram @sealpress

Publishes radical feminist, antiracist and LGBTQ+ non-fiction books. Seal Press is an imprint of Basic Books, itself an imprint of Hachette Book Group. Founded 1976.

Simon & Schuster*

1230 Avenue of the Americas, New York, NY 10020
tel +1 212-698-7000
website www.simonandschuster.com
Facebook www.facebook.com/simonandschuster
X @simonschuster
Instagram @simonandschuster
President & Publisher Jonathan Karp

General fiction and non-fiction. No unsolicited MSS. Founded 1924.

Adams Media

website www.simonandschusterpublishing.com/adamsmedia
Facebook www.facebook.com/adamsmediapublishing
Instagram @adams_media
Publisher Karen Cooper

Lifestyle books and other products.

Atria Books

Commercial and literary fiction, mysteries and thrillers, narrative non-fiction, memoir, politics, popular culture, science, personal development and spirituality. Imprints: Atria Books and Atria Trade Paperbacks, Emily Bestler Books, Beyond Words, Black Privilege Publishing, Howard Books, One Signal Publishers, Primero Sueño Press and Washington Square Press.

Avid Reader Press

website https://avidreaderpress.com/
Facebook www.facebook.com/avidreaderpress
X @AvidReaderPress
Instagram @avidreaderpress
Co-founders Jofie Ferrari-Adler, Ben Loehnen, *Editorial Director* Lauren Wein

Literary fiction.

Gallery Books

website https://simonandschusterpublishing.com/gallery-books/
Facebook www.facebook.com/gallerybooks
X @GalleryBooks
Instagram @gallerybooks
Publisher Jennifer Berstrom

Pop culture, thrillers and mysteries, romance and horror, memoirs, self-help and cultural commentary. Imprints: Gallery Books, Gallery 13, Lemonada, Scout Press and 13A.

Scribner

website www.simonandschusterpublishing.com/scribner
Facebook www.facebook.com/scribnerbooks
X @scribnerbooks
Instagram @scribnerbooks
Publisher Marysue Rucci

Literary fiction and poetry.

Simon Element

website www.simonelement.com
Facebook www.facebook.com/simonelement8
X @_SimonElement
Instagram @_simonelement
Managing Editor Jessie McNiel

Non-fiction: business, lifestyle, cookery, science, health. Imprints: Simon Element. Simon Acumen. Marysue Rucci Books.

Simon & Schuster

Publisher Sean Manning

Adult non-fiction (history, biography, current affairs and science), illustrated non-fiction, mass market fiction. Imprints: Saga Press, Summit Books and 37 Ink.

Simon & Schuster Children's Publishing Division*

1230 Avenue of the Americas, New York, NY 10020
tel +1 212-698-7200
website www.simonandschuster.com/kids
President & Publisher Jon Anderson

Preschool to YA, fiction and non-fiction, trade, library and mass market. Division of Simon & Schuster. Founded 1924.

Beach Lane Books

website www.simonandschusterpublishing.com/beach-lane
Publisher Allyn Johnston

Picture books.

Boynton Books

Board books by author and illustrator, Sandra Boynton.

Little Simon

website https://simonandschusterpublishing.com/little-simon/
Facebook www.facebook.com/simonkids
X @simonskids
Instagram @simonkids
Publisher Valerie Garfield

Books for young children.

Denene Millner Books

website https://simonandschusterpublishing.com/denenemillnerbooks/
Publisher Denene Millner

YA and children's books by Denene Milner.

Salaam Reads

email salaamreads@simonandschuster.com
website https://simonandschusterpublishing.com/salaam-reads/
Senior Editor Deeba Zargarpur

YA, middle-grade and young children's books that explore Muslim life. For submission guidelines, see website.

Simon Spotlight

website https://simonandschusterpublishing.com/simon-spotlight/
Editorial Director Siobhan Ciminera

Imprint for developing licensed properties and brands.

Skyhorse Publishing

307 West 36th Street, 11th Floor, New York, NY 10018
tel +1 212-643-6816
website www.skyhorsepublishing.com
Facebook www.facebook.com/SkyhorsePublishing
X @skyhorsepub
Instagram @skyhorsepub
President Tony Lyons

Outdoor sports, adventure, team sports, nature and country living. Also politics, true crime, history and military history, reference and humour (practical, literary and general trade). Imprints: Allworth Press and Arcade Publishing (page 204), Good Books, Night Shade Books, Sky Pony Press, Sports Publishing and Talos Press. Founded 2006.

Soho Press

853 Broadway, New York, NY 10003
tel +1 212-260-1900
email soho@sohopress.com
website www.sohopress.com
Facebook www.facebook.com/SohoPress
X @soho_press
Publisher Bronwen Hruska

Literary fiction, commercial fiction, mystery and memoir. Imprints: Soho Crime, Soho Press and Soho Teen. Founded 1986.

Sourcebooks

PO Box 4410, Naperville, IL 60567-4410
website www.sourcebooks.com
Publisher & Ceo Dominique Raccah

Independent publisher in a wide variety of genres including fiction, romance, children's, YA, gift/calendars and college-bound. Imprints include: Bloom Books, Cumberland House, Dawn Publications (Dawn Publications), Duo Press, Hometown World, Little Pickle Press, Poisoned Pen Press, Put Me In The Story, Simple Truths, Sourcebooks, Sourcebooks Casablanca, Sourcebooks Explore, Sourcebooks Fire, Sourcebooks Jabberwocky, Sourcebooks Kids, Sourcebooks Landmark, Sourcebooks Young Readers and Sourcebooks Wonderland. Founded 1987.

Stairway Press

1000 West Apache Trail, Suite 126, Apache Junction, AZ 85120
website https://stairwaypress.com/
Facebook www.facebook.com/stairwaypress
X @stairwaypress
Founder Ken Coffman

Literary books. Fiction: sci-fi, thriller, suspense, historical, adventure, thrillers, literary and short stories. Non-fiction: maths and science, politics, self-help, environmental and essays. Check website for submission guidelines. Founded 2005.

Stanford University Press*

485 Broadway, First Floor, Redwood City, CA 94063-3136
tel +1 650-723-9434
email information@sup.org
website www.sup.org
Facebook www.facebook.com/stanforduniversitypress
X @stanfordpress
Instagram @stanfordpress

Scholarly and general trade books in the humanities and social sciences, professional business, law, economics and management science and high-level textbooks. For submission guidelines, visit website. Imprints: Redwood Press, Stanford Business Books and Stanford University Press. Founded 1893.

Tachyon Publications

1459 18th Street, #139, San Francisco, CA 94107
tel +1 415-285-5615
email Tachyon@tachyonpublications.com
website https://tachyonpublications.com/
Facebook www.facebook.com/Tachyon-Publications
X @TachyonPub
Publisher Jacob Weisman

Smart sci-fi, fantasy and horror, as well as occasional mysteries, memoirs, YA and literary fiction. Founded 1995.

Ten Speed Press*

1745 Broadway, 10th Floor, New York, NY 10019
tel +1 510-559-1600
website https://crownpublishing.com/archives/imprint/ten-speed-press
Facebook www.facebook.com/crownpublishing
X @crownpublishing
Instagram @crownpublishing
Editor-in-Chief Molly Birnbaum

Career/business, cookery, practical non-fiction, health, women's interest, self-help, children's. Imprints: Watson-Guptill (art, design, and photography) and Lorena Jones Books (cookery and lifestyle). *PUNCH*, the James Beard Award-winning online magazine about wine, spirits, beer, and cocktails, is published in collaboration with Ten Speed Press. Imprint of the Crown Publishing Group. Founded 1971.

University of Tennessee Press

323 Hodges Library, 1015 Volunteer Blvd, Knoxville, TN 37996-1000
tel +1 865-974-3321
website www.utpress.org
X @utennpress
Director Katie Hannah

American studies: African American studies, Appalachian studies, history, religion, literature, historical archaeology, folklore, vernacular architecture and material culture. Founded 1940.

University of Texas Press*

3001 Lake Austin Blvd, 2.200 Stop E4800, Austin, TX 78703–4206
tel +1 800-252-3206
email info@utpress.utexas.edu
website https://utpress.utexas.edu/
Facebook www.facebook.com/utexaspress
X @utexaspress
Editor-in-Chief Casey Kittrell

Academic books and journals. Founded 1950.

Tin House

website https://tinhouse.com/
Facebook www.facebook.com/tinhouse
X @tin_house
Instagram @tin_house
Editorial Director Masie Cochran

Literary fiction, non-fiction and poetry. Also offers a workshop and seminar series and partner of a critically acclaimed podcast. Founded 1999.

Tor Publishing Group

120 Broadway, 22nd Floor, New York, NY 10271
tel +1 212-388-0100
email enquiries@tor.com
website https://torpublishinggroup.com/
Facebook www.facebook.com/torbooks
X @torbooks
Instagram @torbooks

Adult, YA and middle-grade. Genres: sci-fi, fantasy, mystery, thriller, horror, romance, magical realism, speculative fiction, humour and contemporary fiction. Founded 1980.

Bramble

website https://torpublishinggroup.com/imprints/bramble/
Facebook www.facebook.com/BrambleRomance
X @brambleromance
Instagram @brambleromance

Fantasy romance.

Forge

website https://torpublishinggroup.com/imprints/forge-books/
Facebook www.facebook.com/forgereads
X @forgereads
Instagram @forgereads

General fiction, both contemporary and historical, thrillers, mysteries and suspense, Westerns and Americana, military fiction and non-fiction.

Nightfire

website https://torpublishinggroup.com/imprints/tor-nightfire/
Facebook www.facebook.com/tornightfire
X @tornightfire
Instagram @tornightfire

Fantasy horror.

Tor
website https://torpublishinggroup.com/imprints/tor-books/
Facebook www.facebook.com/torbooks
X @torbooks
Instagram @torbooks

Sci-fi and fantasy.

Tordotcom Publishing
website https://torpublishinggroup.com/imprints/tordotcom/
Facebook www.facebook.com/tordotcompub
X @tordotcompub
Instagram @tordotcompub

Fantasy sci-fi.

Tupelo Press
PO Box 1767 North Adams, MA 01247
tel +1 413-664-9611
email contact@tupelopress.org
website www.tupelopress.org
Facebook www.facebook.com/tupelopress
X @tupelopress
Instagram @tupelopress
Publisher & Artistic Director Jeffrey Levine

Novels, literary fiction, poetry and creative non-fiction. Founded 1999.

Tuttle Publishing/Periplus Editions
Airport Business Park, 364 Innovation Drive, North Clarendon, VT 05759
tel +1 802-773-8930
email info@tuttlepublishing.com
website www.tuttlepublishing.com
Facebook www.facebook.com/tuttlebooks
X @tuttlebooks

Asian art, culture, cookery, gardening, Eastern philosophy, martial arts and health. Founded 1948.

Union Square & Co.
33 East 17th Street, New York, NY 10003
tel +1 800-367-9692
email editorial@sterlingpublishing.com
website www.unionsquareandco.com
Facebook www.facebook.com/UnionSqandCo
X @unionsqandco
Instagram @unionsqandco

Adult non-fiction and children's board books, picture books and non-fiction. Imprints: Boxer Books, EM & Friends, Flashkids, Hearst Books, Knock Knock, Puzzlewrright Press, Sparknotes, Sterling Ethos, Union Square & Co. and Union Square Kids. Part of the Hachette Book Group. Founded 1949

Unnamed Press | Smith & Taylor Classics
6040 N Figueroa St., Los Angeles, CA 90029
email info@unnamedpress.com
website www.unnamedpress.com
Facebook www.facebook.com/theunnamedpress
X @unnamedpress
Instagram @unnamedpress
Co-founders Chris Heiser, Olivia Taylor Smith,
Editors Chris Heiser, Brandon Taylor, Allison Miriam Woodnutt

Independent publisher of fiction and non-fiction. Puts an emphasis on debuts by women, under-represented voices and people of colour, as well as internationally focused speculative fiction, fantasy and translation. Aims to nurture emerging talent and partner with more established authors.
Founded 2014.

University of Washington Press
4333 Brooklyn Avenue NE, Seattle, WA 98105
Postal address Box 359570, Seattle, WA 98195-9570
tel +1 206-543-4050
website https://uwapress.uw.edu/
Facebook www.facebook.com/washingtonpress
Editorial Director Larin McLaughlin

American studies, anthropology, art history and visual culture, Asian American studies, Asian studies, critical ethnic studies, environmental history, Native American and Indigenous studies, nature and environment, gender and sexuality studies, Western history and Pacific Northwest history. Also publishes a broad range of books about the Pacific Northwest for general readers, often in partnership with regional museums, cultural organisations and local tribes.
Founded 1920.

WaterBrook Multnomah Publishing Group*
10807 New Allegiance Drive, Suite 500, Colorado Springs, CO 80921
tel +1 719-590-4999
email info@waterbrookmultnomah.com
website www.waterbrookmultnomah.com
Facebook www.facebook.com/WaterBrookMultnomah
X @WaterBrookPress
Instagram @waterbrookmultnomah

Fiction and non-fiction with a Christian perspective. No unsolicited MSS. Subsidiary of Penguin Random House. Founded 1996.

John Wiley & Sons*
111 River Street, Hoboken, NJ 07030
tel +1 201-748-6000
email info@wiley.com
website www.wiley.com
President & Ceo Matthew Kissner

Scientific, technical, medical and scholarly journals; encyclopaedias, books and online products and services; professional/trade books, subscription products, training materials and online applications and websites; and educational materials for undergraduate and graduate students and lifelong learners. Founded 1807.

Wisdom Publications

199 Elm Street, Somerville, MA 02144
website https://wisdomexperience.org/
Facebook www.facebook.com/wisdompubs
X @wisdompubs
Instagram @wisdompubs
Ceo Daniel Aitken, *Senior Editor* David Kittelstrom

Not-for-profit publisher of books and online courses on contemporary and classic Buddhism, mindfulness, and meditation.

Workman Publishing Company*

1290 Avenue of the Americas, New York, NY 10104
email info@workman.com
website www.workman.com
Facebook www.facebook.com/workmanpublishing
X @workmanpub
Instagram @workmanpub
Publisher Lia Ronnen

General non-fiction for adults and children. Imprints Algonquin, Algonquin Young Readers, Artisan, Page-a-Day, Storey Publishing, Timber Press, Workman, Workman Calendar and Workman Kids. Owned by Hachette Book Group. Founded 1968.

Writer's Digest Books

1745 Broadway New York, NY 10019
tel +1 212-782-9000
website www.writersdigest.com/wd-books
Facebook www.facebook.com/writersdigest
X @writersdigest
Instagram @writersdigest
Editor-in-Chief Amy Jones

Market directories, books and magazine for writers, photographers and songwriters. Imprint of Penguin Random House. Founded 1920.

Yale University Press*

PO Box 209040, New Haven, CT 06520-9040
tel +1 203-432-0960
UK office 47 Bedford Square, London WC1B 3DP
website www.yale.edu/yup
Director Niko Pfund

Scholarly, trade books and art books. Founded 1908.

Yen Press

150 W 30th Street, 19th floor, New York, NY 10001
email yenpress@hbgusa.com
website www.yenpress.com
Facebook www.facebook.com/yenpress
X @yenpress

Graphic novels and manga in all formats for all ages. Founded 2006.

Audio providers and distributors

Below are a list of suppliers who support the production of audio books for download and streaming. Where publishers have their own audio imprints, these are listed in their entries in the Book publishers section, starting on page 118.

Audible

email partners-uk@audible.co.uk
website www.audible.co.uk
X @audibleuk
Instagram @audible_uk

Producer and seller of digital audio entertainment, including fiction and non-fiction audiobooks for adults and children. Publishers interested in exploring business opportunities with Audible may email the address above, or find out more about turning print books into audiobooks at www.acx.com. Founded 1995; acquired by Amazon 2008.

Audio Factory

Unit 8, High Jarmany Rural Workshops,
Barton Saint David, Somerset TA11 6DA
email contact@audiofactory.co.uk
website www.audiofactory.co.uk
Facebook www.facebook.com/audiofactoryuk
Co-founders Dave Perry, Arran Dutton

Audiobook production company. Recommends narrators based on an author's brief, followed by an audition process at the end of which the author makes the final decision. Studio recording takes place over multiple sessions and is guided by a detailed plan created by producers with guidance and feedback from the author. The audiobook goes through editing, mixing, mastering and proofing before being delivered to the author or their chosen distributor.

Audiobook Creation Exchange (ACX)

email support-uk@acx.com
website https://www.acx.com
Facebook www.facebook.com/goacx
X @acx_com

Authors are invited to create a profile for their book, including a synopsis and a brief sample. If authors choose not to narrate for themselves, interested narrators will submit an audition tape reading from the sample; authors can then make an offer to their preferred narrator. Once the full audiobook is completed, ACX will distribute on the author's behalf to Audible, Amazon and iTunes and return monthly payments and sales reports. ACX take a percentage of earnings and narrators can be compensated either through a one-off payment or through a share of royalties.

Audiobooks.com

email acquisitions@audiobooks.com
website www.audiobooks.co.uk/
Facebook www.facebook.com/audiobookscom
X @audiobooks_com
Instagram @audiobooks_com

Subscription audiobook service offering a wide range of fiction and non-fiction genres, as well as some children's titles. Publishers interested in having their titles included in the company's library may get in touch via the email address above.

Author's Republic

email info@authorsrepublic.com
website https://authorsrepublic.com
Facebook www.facebook.com/authorsrepublic
X @authorsrepublc
Instagram @authorsrepublic

Global operation. Accepts completed audiobooks which are then distributed on the author's behalf to over 50 audiobook retailers, including Audible, Apple and Spotify. Also has audiobook production options (for a fee) and offers hints and tips about how to create and market an audiobook. The quality of all submissions is tested before they are distributed. All income from these retailers is combined into one monthly payment which is delivered alongside a sales report showing how many audiobooks an author is selling and where. Distribution services cost a percentage of all audiobook profits.

BookBeat

email info@bookbeat.com
website www.bookbeat.com/uk
X @BookBeatUK
Instagram @bookbeat

Digital streaming service for adult and children's audiobooks across a variety of fiction and non-fiction genres. Monthly subscription model (from £6.99). Owned by Bonnier. Founded 2017.

Creative Content Ltd

5th Floor, Watson House, 54–60 Baker Street,
London W1U 7BU
tel 07771 766838
email ali@creativecontentdigital.com
website www.creativecontentdigital.com
X @CCTheLowdown
Publisher Ali Muirden, *Editorial Director* Lorelei King

Publishes audio digital downloads, ebooks and print-on-demand books in the business, language improvement, self-improvement, lifestyle, crime fiction, classic fiction, sci-fi, short stories and YA genres. Founded 2008.

W. F. Howes Ltd

Unit 5, St George's House, Rearsby Business Park, Gaddesby Lane, Rearsby, Leicester LE7 4YH
tel (01664) 423000
email info@wfhowes.co.uk
website www.wfhowes.co.uk
X @wfhowes
Instagram @wfhowes

Audiobook publisher, distributing its content through all leading consumer and library vendors. Authors include bestselling writers such as Jilly Cooper, Val McDermid, Mark Dawson and David Nicholls. UK subsidiary of RBmedia. Founded 1999.

Isis Audio

7 Centremead, Osney Mead, Oxford OX2 0ES
email thereadinghouse@firstygroup.com
website https://thereadinghouse.co.uk
Facebook www.facebook.com/Isis.Soundings
X @Isisaudio
Instagram @isisaudio

Complete and unabridged audiobooks: fiction, non-fiction, autobiography, biography, crime, thrillers, family sagas, mysteries, romances.

Kobo

website www.kobo.com/gb/en
X @kobo

Audiobook streaming service, for a monthly fee. Offers fiction, non-fiction, adult, children's and YA titles.

Media Music Now

email support@mediamusicnow.com
website www.mediamusicnow.co.uk
Facebook www.facebook.com/mediamusicnow
X @MusicMediaNow
Co-founders Lee Pritchard, Adam Barber

Audio production company. Supplies royalty-free music and sound effects as well as voice-overs and narration. For the latter, authors submit a brief indicating their preferred choice of narrator from a catalogue. Once a narrator has accepted, production will begin, with the author being given the opportunity to review and make edits to a completed proof copy. If authors have already recorded an audiobook, it can be edited and/or polished as required. Completed audiobooks are returned to authors, who are responsible for organising distribution. Founded 2005.

Naxos AudioBooks

5 Wyllyotts Place, Potters Bar, Herts. EN6 2JD
tel (01707) 653326
email info@naxosaudiobooks.com
website www.naxosaudiobooks.com
X @NaxosAudioBooks
Managing Director Anthony Anderson

Recordings of classic literature, modern fiction, non-fiction, drama and poetry. Founded 1994.

Book packagers

Many illustrated and reference books are created by book packagers for mainstream publishers. They often have particular skills in book design and graphic content. In-house desk editors and art editors match up the expertise of specialist writers, artists and photographers, who are usually freelance.

Brown Bear Books

Unit 1/D, Leroy House, 436 Essex Road, London N1 3QP
tel 020-3176 8603
website www.windmillbooks.co.uk
Children's Publisher Anne O'Daly

Specialises in high-quality illustrated reference books and multi-volume sets for trade and educational markets. Opportunities for freelancers. Imprint of Windmill Books. Founded 1967.

Canopus Publishing

8 Foxcombe Road, Bath BA1 3ED
tel 07970 153217
email robin@canopusbooks.com
website www.canopusbooks.com
X @robin_rees
Director Robin Rees

Packager of books on astronomy, aerospace, photography and rock music. Publisher for the London Stereoscopic Company and Starmus. Founded 1999.

Diagram Visual Information

10 Athol Road, Sunderland SR2 8LW
tel 07841 043307
email info@diagramgroup.com
website www.diagramgroup.com
Director Jane Johnson

Research, writing, design and illustration of reference books, supplied as disks. Founded 1967.

Elwin Street Productions

10 Elwin Street, London E2 7BU
tel 020-7033 6706
email silvia@elwinstreet.com
website www.elwinstreet.com, www.modern-books.com
Director Silvia Langford, *Operations Manager* Claire Anouchian

Boutique co-edition publisher of adult illustrated non-fiction. Categories include: literary, culture and science, food, diet and wellness, creativity, lifestyle and gift. Founded 2001.

Global Blended Learning

Singleton Court, Wonastow Road, Monmouth NP25 5JA
tel 0845 5480261
email hello@globalblendedlearning.com
website www.globalblendedlearning.com

Primary, secondary academic education (geography, science and modern languages) and co-editions (travel guides, gardening and cookery). Multimedia (CD-Rom programming and animations). Opportunities for freelancers. Founded 1985.

Heart of Albion

Syringa Cottage, Chapel Street, Orston, Nottingham NG13 9NL
tel (01949) 850631
email albion@indigogroup.co.uk
website www.hoap.co.uk
Director Bob Trubshaw

Folklore, mythology, cultural studies and local history. Founded 1989.

Ivy Press

1 Triptych Place, Second Floor, London SE1 9SH
tel 020-77006 700
email ivypress@quarto.com
website www.quartoknows.com/Ivy-Press
X @QuartoExplores
Group Publisher Richard Green

Publishers of illustrated trade books on art, science, popular culture, design, children's non-fiction, natural history and conscious living. Opportunities for authors and freelancers. Part of the Quarto Group Publishing UK. Founded 1996.

Little People Books

The Home of BookBod, Knighton, Radnorshire LD7 1UP
tel (01547) 520925
email littlepeoplebooks@thehobb.tv
website www.littlepeoplebooks.co.uk
Director Grant Jessé

Packager of audio, children's educational textbooks and digital publications. Parent company: Grant Jessé UK. Founded 2018.

Market House Books

Kedua, Oving Road, Whitchurch, Aylesbury, Bucks. HP22 4ER
tel (01296) 484911
email books@mhbref.com
website www.markethousebooks.com
X @markethousebook

Directors Jonathan Law (editorial), Anne Kerr (production)

Book packagers with experience in producing reference books from small pocket dictionaries to large multi-volume colour encyclopaedias and from specialist academic reference books to popular books for crossword enthusiasts. Deals with publishers worldwide. Services offered include: start-to-finish project management, commissioning of writers and editors, writing and rewriting, editing and copy-editing, proofreading, checking of final pages, keyboarding, typesetting, page design and make-up, text conversion, data manipulation and database management. Founded 1970.

Orpheus Books Ltd

2 Hewlett Place, Cheltenham, Glos. GL52 6DQ
tel (01993) 774949
email info@orpheusbooks.com
website www.orpheusbooks.com, www.Q-files.com
Executive Directors Nicholas Harris, Sarah Hartley

Children's illustrated non-fiction/reference books and ebooks. Orpheus Books are the creators of Q-files.com, the online educational resource for schools and libraries. Founded 1993.

Storymix

The Wenta Business Centre Colne Way, Watford, Hertfordshire WD24 7ND
email jasmine@storymix.co.uk
website www.storymix.co.uk
Facebook www.facebook.com/storymixstudio
X @storymixstudio
Director Jasmine Richards

Multi-award-winning inclusive children's fiction studio. Works with publishers to create fiction for children, middle grade and YA. Offers paid collaboration opportunities to writers and illustrators of colour. Actively looking to add emerging and established talent who write children's or crossover fiction to our database of creatives. To apply: www.storymix.co.uk/write-for-us. Founded 2019.

Toucan Books

128 Aldersgate Street, Suite 106, London EC1A 4AE
tel 020-7250 3388
website www.toucanbooks.co.uk
Contact Ellen Dupont

International co-editions: editorial, design and production services. Non-fiction only. Founded 1985.

Windmill Books

Unit 1/D, Leroy House, 436 Essex Road, London N1 3QP
tel 020-3176 8603
website www.windmillbooks.co.uk
Children's Publisher Anne O'Daly

Publisher and packager of books and partworks for trade, promotional and international publishers. Opportunities for freelancers. Imprint: Brown Bear Books (page 225). Founded 2009.

Working Partners

9 Kingsway, 4th Floor, London WC2B 6XF
tel 020-7841 3939
email enquiries@workingpartnersltd.co.uk
website www.coolabi.com/books
Managing Director Chris Snowdon

Creators of children's and YA fiction. Genres include: animal fiction, fantasy, horror, historical, detective, magical and adventure. Unable to accept any submissions. Pays advance and royalty. Retains copyright on all works. Selects writers based on specific brief. Part of the Coolabi Group. Founded 1995.

Routes to publication

Becoming a bestselling author: my writing story

Peter James shares his first-hand experience of the ups and downs, false starts and challenges a writer may face along the route to success, and the value of passion and persistence – and chance moments of opportunity.

I am so pleased to have been invited to write this piece for the *Writers' & Artists' Yearbook*, not only because it was the place I turned to when I finished my first novel in 1967, but also because I want to share with all of you all to know that a successful writing career does not come overnight. Mine had many detours but I always kept my destination in mind.

I often get asked why I became a writer. I always wanted to be one, right from the age of seven, but I had very little self-confidence and never believed I would ever actually succeed. I kept a notebook by my bed and used to write my thoughts and ideas into it. I remember the very first entry, a great pearl of wisdom: 'Life is a bowl of custard – it's all right until you fall in.' When I went to my boarding school, Charterhouse, I had one English teacher, David Summerscale, who believed in me and encouraged me. He went on to become headmaster of Westminster School and we are still in touch today. At 15, I won a school poetry prize and then at 17, I won a BBC short story competition, and these both gave my confidence a boost – but I was still a troubled, uncertain kid. My housemaster, Ted Hartwell, turned out to be absolutely bang on prophetic in his leaving report for me: 'Enigmatic and unpredictable as ever, he fits into no conventional mould and has clearly taxed his tutors' powers of prophecy. I'm sure he will ultimately be successful, but I doubt if his talent will flower in a solicitor's office or even in a university setting. A literary career seems inevitable, but there may be some false starts.'

I guess it really started when my dad bought me a portable electric typewriter for my 17th birthday, along with a real battle-axe of a typing tutor, who would put sticky tabs on the keys to make them unreadable and then rap my fingers with a ruler if I looked down! I learned to touch-type within days out of sheer terror, and it has stood me in good stead ever since. Eighteen months later I set to work writing my first novel, *Ride Down A Rollercoaster*, in a garage converted into a bedsit on the Fulham Road, and when I finished I went straight out and bought *Writers' & Artists' Yearbook* so that I could send my manuscript off to literary agents. The replies I received said it was 'too American' and, instead of letting that deter me, I referred to the American section of the *Yearbook* and started sending copies to the States. After mailing countless letters, I finally received a reply from Kurt Helmer, a New York literary agent who said I showed 'real promise' and encouraged me to re-work the book and send him another draft. However, in the arrogance of youth, I insisted the second novel that I had written in the meantime, a zany sci-fi comedy, was much better. He didn't agree and asked me to return to the first book. Instead, now 21, I wrote a third. Again, he told me to go back to the first book, and again I ignored him.

During this time, I had been attending Ravensbourne Film School, after trying to get into Oxford. Although I got in on my second attempt, I turned down Oxford's offer as the idea of telling stories through film had got under my skin. However, after graduation from

Ravensbourne I realised how hard it is to get your first job in film without having a contact on the inside. Nor had I managed to publish a novel yet. On the advice of my Canadian uncle, I moved to Canada and got my first job in television as a gofer on a children's show called *Polka Dot Door*. Through a twist of fate, I had the chance to write an episode and, following the success of that first episode, was asked to take on the writing three days a week. I sent a letter to Kurt Helmer, my literary agent, sharing my excitement. He replied, 'You a**hole, never do both. Don't have a job writing television in the day and expect go home and to write a novel in the night.' He told me the only way I'd ever write a good novel was if I got a job in a factory and wrote after work. This proved to have been very good advice, after I went on to work on a 'movie-gone-wrong' in Spain called *Spanish Fly* (that I had had to help finance on my own credit card during production) starring Terry-Thomas and Lesley Philips. It was described by the eminent critic Barry Norman as 'the worst British film since the Second World War and the least funny British funny film ever made'. It was a critical and financial disaster and left me pretty much stoney broke.

So I joined the family business and started working in the factory of Cornelia James Glovemakers by day and writing at night. I read an article in *The Times* which said ever since the death of Ian Fleming, there had been a shortage of spy thrillers. I decided I could write one and it became my first published book, *Dead Letter Drop* (W.H. Allen 1981). I would love to say this was a shining start to my career as a published author, but it was, as my teacher had predicted, a false start. *Dead Letter Drop* sold around 1,800 copies and 1,500 of those were to libraries. I remember a particularly bad press interview where the journalist asked me how I had found Namibia, a location in my second published novel, and I couldn't answer … because I had never been. I vowed then to never write about something I had not fully researched and experienced. This was reinforced by a chance meeting with the author Elizabeth Buchan who told me, 'People who read are intelligent, they don't just want a story, they want to learn something. What can anyone learn from you about the world of spies? You are up against authors like John Le Carre who have backgrounds in the security services. You'll never be successful writing something you're not passionate about and can't research.' This was a real turning point for me in terms of how I approached my writing.

An unexpected lucky break came just a week later when my former wife and I were burgled after moving into a house in Brighton. Sussex Police arrived to take my statement and eagle-eyed detective, Mike Harris, noticed my books. He said that if I ever needed help with research I should let him know. This was the beginning of my long-term relationship with Sussex Police. Ever since, after years of earning their trust, I have been privileged to join officers on shifts, to go out in response and traffic patrol cars, attend raids, and some major crime scenes, as well as social events and I have been able to talk to officers about their experiences. I am regularly reminded of the breadth of life a police officer sees over their career, and the extraordinary situations they experience. I have been told many times over the years that I have 'become part of the furniture' in the station! So, at this point, I knew I needed to write a crime novel, but my protagonist still eluded me. It would be a few more years before I would meet the man who would inspire Roy Grace.

Writing from what I knew and what I was passionate about took a surprisingly supernatural turn after the death of the son of good friends in a car accident, soon after the death my own father. My friends consulted a medium to try and make contact with their son, and this gave me an idea: how the intense love between a mother and her son might continue, but with dangerous consequences, from beyond the grave. The result was my supernatural thriller, *Possession* (Gollancz 1988), and for the first time I experienced a bidding war, with every major publisher in the UK, as well as in the US and many countries around the world, vying for it. I had started to be called 'Britain's answer to Stephen King' in the press and I was encouraged by my publisher to write further horror books. But this would once again prove to be a false start, as the sales of horror books started a sharp decline in the 1990s.

Knowing I was keen to meet police officers with an interesting story to tell, my friends at Sussex Police invited me down to the station to chat with a young Detective Inspector called Dave Gaylor. I walked into his office and was surprised to see there were plastic crates all over the floor, piled with documents. When I asked if he was moving Dave explained that, in addition to being an active homicide investigator, he was also in charge of reviewing all the county's unsolved murders where there was still a perpetrator at large or someone alive who could benefit from a successful conclusion: 'I'm the last chance the victims have for justice, and I'm the last chance the families have for closure.' In talking to Dave I realised that he had the rare qualities that make a truly great homicide detective – that is to be calm, to have a high degree of emotional intelligence and empathy, and to be highly methodical yet, at the same time, open to creative, blue-sky thinking. Over the next few years, I switched from supernatural to psychological thrillers, putting policing more and more into my novels.

In 2002 Dave was promoted to Detective Chief Superintendent, and effectively became head of major crime for Sussex Police. My publishers, Pan Macmillan, approached me just and asked if I'd ever thought of creating a fictional detective as my central character. I went straight to Dave and asked him, 'Would you like to be a fictional cop?'. He loved the idea! Dave, my notebook and I spent many nights in Brighton pubs talking in detail about his life and police procedure. From this, we then worked out the plot of *Dead Simple* (Pan Macmillan 2005) together, with Dave ensuring that I was absolutely correct in my research. We've worked closely on every Roy Grace novel since and we've become great friends, with Dave being best man when my wife Lara and I married. Dave reads all my manuscripts to make sure they are entirely accurate in how I portray the way the police would approach a case. This was when I finally, and thankfully, got my writing career on the trajectory I had been hoping for. My first Roy Grace novel was published in 2005, my 20th Roy Grace novel, *One Of Us Is Dead*, came out in September 2024, and a smash hit ITV series, *Grace*, with John Simm playing Detective Superintendent Roy Grace, first aired in 2021 (with the sixth series now in production as of 2025). In addition, there have now been seven highly successful Roy Grace stage plays, the most recent, *Picture You Dead*.

I'm currently writing a book about writing, to be published in 2027. The most important lesson I can offer – and I hope that this has come across – is never to give up. If you believe you have a story to tell, keep going. Even when I was published for the first time, it was not the end of my struggles; in fact, it was still the beginning. Another lesson that I learned the hard way is that research is paramount and frequently bizarre. For example, when a character in *Dead Simple* got buried alive, I asked a funeral parlour to nail me into a coffin so that I could understand the experience and write about it in a convincing way. Too often an author who has spent years working on their writing is called an 'overnight success', and this is hardly ever accurate. Writers are craftspeople and we need to spend time making mistakes and honing our skills. I often liken writing to being a mechanic; the best way to learn is to take things apart and put them back together in your own way. Read and reread the bestselling novels in the genre you want to write, pick apart what makes them great novels, and apply that in your own work.

Good luck, and never let a false start send you off course.

Peter James is an international bestselling author and film producer. His crime thriller series featuring Detective Superintendent Roy Grace includes 20 consecutive *Sunday Times* Number one bestsellers (all published by Pan Macmillan), has sold over 23 million copies worldwide, and has been translated into 38 languages. He has won over 40 awards, including the WHSmith Best Crime Author of All Time Award and the Crime Writers' Association Diamond Dagger. Her Majesty Queen Camilla has announced that Detective Superintendent Roy Grace is her favourite fictional detective. Born in Brighton, he graduated from Ravensbourne Film School, and worked as a film producer and screenwriter for some years before starting to write novels. His first book, *Dead Letter Drop* (W.H. Allen), was published in 1981. His latest book is *One of Us Is Dead* (Macmillan 2024). Peter's *Roy Grace* novels are now a major ITV series, *Grace*, starring John Simm and Richie Campbell, and seven of his books have been adapted for the stage, which have grossed over £19 million at the box office to date. His website is www.peterjames.com; follow him on X and Instagram @peterjamesuk and TikTok @peterjamesauthor.

My rocky road trip to writing success

Sarah Clarke shares the ups and downs of her journey to becoming a published author and has valuable advice on how to give yourself the greatest chance of success as a writer.

As a child I always wanted to be an author, and I showed my propensity for the thriller genre from an embarrassingly young age. My mother still has a rather chilling poem I wrote, aged about ten, about a violent criminal in our local area, and I remember sneaking thrillers – P.D. James, Frederick Forsyth, Dick Francis – off my father's bookshelf when he wasn't looking. My love for the genre has never waned and I think my skills as a thriller writer have largely developed from being a thriller reader for so long.

I started my first novel when I finished university. I remember going to my local bookshop to buy the *Writers' & Artists' Yearbook* and methodically working through it to find the right publishers to submit to (this was before agents became the main route into publishing). But, with both the arrogance and impatience of youth, I sent off my query as soon as I'd finished my first three chapters and, funnily enough, a series of rejections followed. What's even worse is that I didn't learn from my mistake. After repeating the same error with two more books, and getting the same results, I decided to 'give up' novel writing. However, I did develop a career as a copywriter, so I got to practise my craft in a different way.

Fast forward 20 years, and in 2018 my youngest child started secondary school. This gave me more spare time and the perfect opportunity to resurrect my childhood dream. But still, I hesitated – the arrogance had gone and had taken my confidence with it. I knew the odds were heavily stacked against me and getting published felt impossible without any industry contacts or a host of writing prizes under my belt. But then two things happened: an ex-work colleague secured a two-book deal, and a friend's daughter got through multiple auditions to be cast in a West End show. These events made me realise that dreams can come true, but only if you commit to them fully. So I applied and was accepted for the Faber Academy 'Writing a Novel: First 15,000 Words' online course. And, to use the analogy of a journey, Faber Academy (see page 647) taught me how to drive.

Learning to drive

The Faber Academy course required a big-time commitment and high levels of self-motivation – as I imagine all similar courses do. As well as hitting chapter deadlines and completing additional writing tasks, we were expected to review each other's work and provide advice where we could. Luckily, though, it never felt like a chore. The course taught me lots of things within two specific categories: 1) novel-writing skills and 2) industry knowledge. By the time I finished writing my book in June 2019 – which later became my debut novel *A Mother Never Lies* (HQ Digital 2021) – I also had a clear set of instructions on how to navigate my journey, including a heavily edited cover letter and synopsis.

Setting off

As part of the course, I received detailed feedback on my first 15,000 words. My tutor's comments were incredibly positive, my optimism had grown exponentially, and I had started to believe my dream might actually come true. I joined X and followed all the right people. I read *The Bookseller* and gleaned information from industry websites. And then I submitted my book to six agents and crossed my fingers.

Hitting traffic

I should have been more prepared for how long the first stage of my journey would take. Agents explain on their websites that a response can take 12 weeks or longer – but I found it impossible to put it out of my mind. I checked my email multiple times a day and daydreamed about a spot on Graham Norton's radio show. The first rejection made me cry. By the third, I'd learned to swear instead. It was later that someone advised me to respond to every rejection by submitting to a new agent, and I now give that advice to anyone who asks. It is both distracting and empowering (it even beats swearing) and, in total, I submitted to 29 agents over eight months.

Navigating road bumps

Two months after I started querying, I received my first full manuscript request. I can still remember reading the email (it had gone into my junk folder, so always check that!) and responding with shaking fingers, my dream feeling so much closer to coming true. Over the following six months, I received a total of six full manuscript requests – including two asking for edits and resubmission – but my manuscript was ultimately rejected by each one. After those rejections, I never quite managed to swap tears for swear-words.

Hailing a cab

One agent asked me to work with a freelance editor to iron out the problems in my manuscript. I wasn't sure, as it would cost me a few hundred pounds and still offered no guarantee of success, but eventually I decided to go for it. And, while the revisions didn't lead directly to representation, I have never regretted having input from a professional editor. We live and breathe our books and it is an impossible task to step far enough away to make fresh or objective observations. And remember, that insight doesn't have to be something you pay for – joining writing groups can provide it too.

Pitstop

As for so many other people around the world, the pandemic turned life upside down for my family, and I chose to put my writing aspirations aside so that I could focus on the day-to-day of our 'new normal'. But when the pandemic appeared to be in retreat in the autumn of 2020 (oh, how wrong we were!) I resumed my journey, with a little help from Sophie Hannah's Dream Author coaching programme (see below).

Turning left (field)

One day in late 2020, I was scrolling through X when I paused on a familiar name. It was my sister-in-law's name, but it also belonged to a publishing professional. I dug a little deeper and found out that she was open to submissions from debut authors. It felt like destiny, and I quickly set about sending her my manuscript. And this is how I stumbled upon digital-first publishing.

Changing course

Initially I was excited purely because digital-first publishers accept manuscripts directly. After lots of failed attempts and oh-so-close misses, being able to circumvent agents felt like a positive step. But, as I learned more, digital-first publishing started to appeal for other reasons too. Although there is no advance, the royalties tend to be more generous than with traditional publishing. The process is quicker too, with some digital-first authors publishing two books a year or more – although this is flexible, with the publisher usually happy to fit around the author's schedule. And, while the ebook is the core focus for marketing activity, the book is released in paperback and audio formats too.

Tips for submitting to agents

- Record every submission with names, dates and details of whether and when you can chase for a response.
- Research agents fully before submitting and choose 30 possible targets.
- Split these agents into three categories (dream; very good; perfectly acceptable) and send your MS to an even spread of agents in small groups, e.g. six submissions at a time.
- Be grateful for any feedback and give yourself time to consider how best to apply it (remember that agents only provide this if they think your book has potential).
- Treat agent submissions like job interviews. If one is unsuccessful, it is because that agent isn't the right fit for you.

The final climb

I sent my manuscript to three digital-first publishers and in January 2021 I had positive responses from two. One of them was HQ Digital, an imprint of HarperCollins, which I was particularly excited about, but the commissioning editor wanted me to change one fundamental aspect of my story. So I spent the next month editing the manuscript, as well as writing synopses for two new book ideas. When I submitted at the end of February, I did so with my fingers *un*crossed; I had realised by then that luck wasn't the driving force behind these decisions.

Dream destination

Through various writing groups, such as my brilliant Faber Academy alumni group, I had heard the story many times of the author who battled through numerous rejections before finally finding representation and/or a book deal. But I never thought it would happen to me ... how could an agent or publisher possibly like my book if 29 others had not? So I feel like a fraud asking you to believe me now – but I hope that you do, because it does indeed happen. Resilience, tenacity and a confidence in your book and your writing talent are the tools you need for success.

Building a support network

Writing is a very personal experience, and it can be a lonely one, especially if you're dealing with rejections. Having a support network around you is important. As well as friends and family, I use the following support to keep me on track:

- Other authors. Before I was published, I was introduced to a local crime author. She gave me lots of useful advice and made me believe being an author was possible.
- Sophie Hannah's Dream Author coaching programme (https://dreamauthorcoaching.com). I signed up to Sophie's programme to help build my confidence after dozens of rejections and a pandemic. Sophie is an experienced thriller writer with a very positive message, and her programme made a big difference to my mindset.
- Virtual writing community. The Faber Academy alumni group plus X and Facebook writer groups have all helped me feel part of a community with similar fears and hopes.

Road trip

When I danced around my kitchen in March 2021, I thought I had arrived; I had been offered a three-book publishing deal with a brilliant publisher. But I soon realised that it was only the start of my journey. While I enjoyed the amazing high of reaching Number 39 in the UK Kindle charts, and reading reviews that were so lovely they brought tears to my eyes, I was also learning to cope with negative reviews, rollercoaster rankings and trying to write my second book to a tight deadline. I have now written five thrillers and learned something new with each one – and I hope this road trip is going to continue for a long while yet.

Sarah Clarke signed her first book deal in March 2021 at the age of 48, after a career as a copywriter, and has since become the bestselling author of six psychological thrillers published by HQ Digital: *A Mother Never Lies* (2021), *Every Little Secret* (2022), *My Perfect Friend* (2022), *The Ski Trip* (2023), *The Night She Dies* (2024) and *Someone In The Water* (2025). Follow Sarah on Instagram @sarahclarkewriter or see www.sarahclarkeauthor.com for more details.

See also...

- *Becoming a bestselling author: my writing story*, page 228
- *Writers' retreats and creative writing courses*, page 646

Keeping the writing dream alive

S.J. Watson proves why no writer should give up on their dream of being published one day.

I'm writing this in late March 2020, sitting not in my office but at a table I've set up in the bay window of my sitting room. From here I have a view of the garden – I can watch the birds as they flit from branch to branch and eventually settle at the feeder outside the window; I can chart the day's progress by the changing light. But the world has changed – suddenly I can move no further than I can see, other than in an emergency or to collect provisions and, even then, I must stay a minimum of two metres from anyone I may meet. A virus is tearing through the population, threatening to overwhelm us, and it must be slowed. Collectively, we're in lockdown.

And so, unable to travel, we temporarily escape our surroundings in other ways. We reach out to our friends on social media and through meet-up apps, checking in, lifting each other up. And we turn to stories – to our books and films, our TV shows and, yes, even our plays, as theatres stream recorded performances direct to our living rooms. Through words we bond, we are entertained and amused, offered ways to escape and expand. Never before has the importance of a shared story been more apparent.

Yet it has always been so. I grew up in the Black Country, an only child, gay. My childhood was far from unhappy, but it felt … limited, confusing. I turned to books at a very early age, visited the local library weekly, taking out and reading my allotted five books without fail. They were my escape, my life raft, and it wasn't long before I began to write stories of my own. Encouraged by teachers, I dreamt of one day seeing a book of mine on a shelf in a library or bookshop, of having the power to transport people as I had been transported. When asked what I wanted to be when I grew up, I replied, 'A writer!' – without hesitation, every time.

It took me a long time (or a long time to be a *published* writer, at least; I've been a writer my whole life, and the distinction is important). Seduced by the idea that I needed a sensible career alongside my writing, I studied physics and eventually worked in the NHS. But the writing was always there. I filled notebooks, I wrote stories and poems and started novels, I pushed forward. I vowed I wouldn't stop as long as my output was improving. My dream never left me.

The publishing side of things, though? That remained a mystery. I hoovered up as much advice as I could, yet much of it was conflicting, and the path to publication remained impossibly opaque. I read somewhere that one needed an agent to be published, then read somewhere else that to get an agent one needed to have been published. 'Win a prize!', they said, 'or no one will even look at your work. Get some short stories into magazines!', though no one told me how, or which magazines.

But then, one day, in a now-vanished bookshop in North London, I lifted down from the shelf an earlier version of the book you're holding now. And my eyes were opened. Here was a guide, a clear way through what had previously been misty and unclear – not only a reference guide that listed agents, publishers and other helpful organisations along with their contact details and preferences, but also a treasure trove of invaluable and inspirational articles and guides covering every stage of the writer's journey. Here, at last, was a beacon that could guide me through the choppy waters ahead. I kept it on hand the whole time and referred to it frequently for information, inspiration or support. And when, in my late thirties and ground down by working in an overstretched health service, I decided it was time my career took a back seat to my writing ambitions, it was *this* book that gave me the courage to drop to part-time at work and really go for it.

A definitive guide, in here you'll find everything you need. It won't write your book for you, quite, but it'll demystify the whole process of getting your book into the hands of readers, however you choose to do that, as well as illuminating the 'business' side of being a writer. There can be few published writers who haven't turned to the *Writers' & Artists' Yearbook* at some stage in their development, and many use it still. All writing is an act of optimism, including this foreword – I hope that, by the time you're reading it, the world will be in a different, better place. But we'll still need stories, perhaps more than ever. We'll always need stories. They make us human. They connect us – across space, across time. The only way to learn to write is by doing it, by practising, over and over … but for every other aspect of the world of publishing, we have this book.

Foreword from *Writers' & Artists' Yearbook 2021*

S.J. Watson is the award-winning author of the international bestsellers *Before I Go to Sleep* (Doubleday 2011), winner of the Crime Writers' Association Award for Best Debut Novel and the Galaxy National Book Award for Crime Thriller of the Year, and *Second Life* (Doubleday 2015). He was born in the Midlands and studied physics at Birmingham University, later working as an audiologist in the NHS, before enrolling on the first Faber Academy 'Writing a Novel' course in 2009. He now lives in Brighton. The film adaption of *Before I Go to Sleep*, directed by Rowan Joffe and starring Nicole Kidman and Colin Firth, was released in 2014. S.J. Watson's latest book, *Final Cut*, was published by Transworld in 2020. See www.sjwatson-books.com/ or join his newsletter community at https://sjwatson.substack.com.

Getting your debut into print: the path to publication

For many people, being published is a life-long dream. Making it happen, and coping with a rollercoaster of emotions along the way, is a genuine challenge. Novelist Jennie Godfrey explains how it was for her, offering invaluable advice along the way.

I had my nose in a book from a very young age. If you had asked me when I was eight years old what I wanted to be when I grew up, I would have definitely said 'an authoress' (I was obsessed with *The Famous Five* and Enid Blyton). My love of books only grew as I did and eventually I went on to study English at university, but coming from a working-class family in Yorkshire, being a writer didn't seem like something a person like me could do. I put the dream to one side and didn't come back to it again until my late forties.

By that stage, I had built a successful career in HR but was experiencing what I guess most people would call a midlife crisis. I was no longer happy or fulfilled in my profession and when a coach I was working with asked me whether I still wanted to be doing the role I was in, I didn't hesitate to say 'no'. This created a domino effect and led to me accepting voluntary redundancy and taking some time to decide what I wanted to do next. It turned out that writing a novel would be that next thing.

At the time, psychological thrillers were very popular (they still are, of course!) so I decided to have a go at writing one but abandoned it fairly quickly. Although I had a plot and the words were in the right order, I knew it wasn't living and breathing in the way it should be. It had no heart. Shortly after that, I had the idea for *The List of Suspicious Things* while out walking the dog and, somehow, I knew this was 'The One'. I began writing it that day.

I see the time during which I wrote *The List of Suspicious Things* as one of the happiest of my life. I used some of my redundancy money to go on a Curtis Brown Creative (CBC) three-month 'write your novel' course, which I found enormously helpful in understanding the more technical aspects to novel writing as well as the broader publishing industry. It also had the added benefit of getting feedback from my tutor and peers, which was invaluable. My tutor, the novelist Cathi Unsworth, was so encouraging: she gave me the confidence to keep going and to pursue being traditionally published.

Before I embarked on the whole endeavour, I imagined that the actual writing of it would be the hardest part of the process. I was so wrong. While writing the book was challenging, and difficult at times, it was also inspiring, rewarding and one of the most fulfilling things I have ever done. Even the difficult parts were wonderful, because ultimately I was learning and overcoming. In fact, the hardest part of the process for me was querying and submitting to agents. Not from a practical perspective, though: that bit I enjoyed, treating it like a 'work project'. With the help of the *Writer's & Artists' Yearbook* I found agents who represented the novels I write, along with their contact details and lots of excellent advice. But I found the waiting, and the subsequent rejections, more emotionally draining than I had anticipated.

I spent the first couple of weeks of querying repeatedly refreshing my email, constantly anxious, not sleeping, and jumping every time my phone made a noise. When agents I had queried were tweeting about TV programmes they were watching, I wanted to reply 'PLEASE READ MY BOOK'. I very quickly realised that I needed to take myself in hand. I didn't want to be that constantly anxious person and needed to find ways of dealing with the process. I look back now and can see so clearly that none of it is personal – agents need to know they can represent a book effectively in order to sell it to editors – but at the time I felt as though it was something to do with me!

Rejection is hard-wired into the writing experience and is actually part of the process (and for me, part of improving) but that doesn't make it easy to deal with, especially if, like me, you struggle with your mental health. My aforementioned tutor – the wonderful Cathi Unsworth – once said the following to me when I was crying in a crumpled heap about some savage critique of my work: 'The best writers are often the most sensitive people, and therefore paradoxically ill-equipped to deal with the life of a writer.'

I've heard it said that one of the most important things a writer can develop is a thick skin. I'm actually not sure I agree. It's my thin skin that helps me to see, understand and feel deeply, and translate that to the page. What I did have to develop, though, was a way of bouncing back from rejection and setbacks, and here are some of the ways I have learned to do that. This is by no means an exhaustive list, but it includes the things that have really worked for me.

1. Don't pretend you don't feel it

This has been a really important one for me to learn and is a life lesson as much as a writing lesson. When something hurts, I let myself acknowledge the hurt and feel it fully. I've found it's actually the only way it will pass ('the only way out is through'). Pretending I don't feel a certain way, or denying my feelings altogether, tends to lead to them coming out in other ways. My initial attempt at joining the CBC course that I eventually attended was rejected, and I felt it as viscerally as a punch in the stomach. I allowed myself to cry, curl up under the duvet and feel sorry for myself, and within two days I was revising my application and sending it in for the next intake.

2. Tell someone who 'gets it'

There is something unique about rejection when it comes to writing/art. I have heard it said, and in fact said myself (see above!), that 'it's not personal' or even 'it's just business'. But the truth is that it feels personal. I have a wonderful group-chat of writers who are at the same stage in our careers, and any time I feel upset/rejected/stuck, I know I can message them and they will understand. There's something so comforting about having someone really empathise with your experience.

3. Allow yourself time to grieve

Sometimes I just need to take a break. Eat lots of chocolate. Watch lots of trashy TV. One particular rejection still hurts when I think about it. After it, I had to be gentle with myself, and my emotions, until I felt strong enough to get back up again. And that's OK. Not everyone is made the same way, I just happen to be made of sensitive stuff and the more I accept that, the quicker I heal.

4. Write about it

While I was writing *The List of Suspicious Things*, I did *The Artist's Way* by Julia Cameron. It's a course (in the form of a book) to help unblock the creative process. Part of the work you do is the discipline of 'morning pages', which is writing, longhand, three pages of your thoughts/feelings/whatever comes up, first thing. I now do this every day and cannot recommend it enough. As writers, we tend to process things by writing them down (!) and this way of doing it means that you move through emotions and experiences quickly and have an opportunity to really understand them. Journaling and blogging work too.

5. Get back on the horse

Eventually, its time to learn from the experience and move on. I never know when that's going to be, or how long it will take, but there comes a point – always – where I am back at my keyboard, putting in the work, even if I don't feel at my creative best. And there is always something to learn from rejection (even if it is that the other person is wrong!). You can too. I promise you.

6. See it as part of the journey to finding the best home for your work

I found it really helped to look up the stories of some of my favourite books/creative works. Did you know *Line of Duty* was rejected many times before it found a home on BBC2? *Shuggie Bain*, the Booker Prize winner, was rejected by 20+ publishers, and both the hilarious *Stath Lets Flats* and *This Country* took years to get the green light. Seeing it as just part of the process just might help you to keep going.

Eventually I was lucky enough to find Nelle Andrew, the perfect agent for me. She actually found me as a result of the Curtis Brown Creative course. She contacted me at the beginning of 2021 after being sent an anthology of our work and asked to see what I had done so far. By then, I had written the whole thing and she read it overnight. We had a Zoom call the following week. I know writers are advised to have discussions with other agents too – if that's an option – but after our conversation, during which I got a real feel for how she works, I didn't hesitate to say 'yes' when she offered me representation.

For me, this was where the hard work really began. I spent a year editing the novel, with Nelle's expert editorial eye and guidance. I learned so much in that year. She and I call it my 'writing bootcamp' and I will be forever grateful for it. Nelle made me realise I was capable of more than I thought I was, and she made me a better writer. That's one of the reasons I always tell other writers 'don't be afraid of being edited'.

When the novel did go out on submission, we got our first offer after only eight hours. To say it was a whirlwind is an understatement. Within 48 hours I had signed with Hutchinson Heinemann (the literary imprint of Penguin Random House) and it is a decision I have celebrated every day since. The team there are incredibly talented and so behind the book that I often feel as though they care about it just as much as I do. While I had edits to do, they weren't extensive (thanks to 'writing bootcamp') and I could just see that every single one would make the book better.

The last year, during which the novel has been published in hardback and paperback, has been the best year of my life. I never dreamed that it would be as successful as it has been. The whole experience has been a joy (if very tiring!). I've had so much lovely feedback from readers, book bloggers and booksellers. There really is nothing like knowing your book has had an impact on somebody. I feel incredibly lucky.

Author and part-time bookseller, **Jennie Godfrey**'s debut novel, *The List of Suspicious Things*, is inspired by her childhood in West Yorkshire during the 1970s. A *Sunday Times* bestseller and instant hit, the book was shortlisted for the British Book Awards Debut Novel of the Year 2024. Her second novel is set in the 1980s and will be published in 2026.

Books

Alphabet alchemy: turning letters into gold

Owen Sheers reflects on the art of turning letters into words, and words into magic.

If you are holding this book, then you already have a writer's relationship with language. It's very likely that you have already experienced, to whatever degree, something of the addictive miracle and failure of trying to capture life in words. A miracle because, with the same letters of the alphabet with which we order a coffee or fire off a WhatsApp message, you have created something unique, something that has never existed before in the history of the universe – a new poem, article or short story. And a failure because – well, isn't that how we get better? By acknowledging what's worked in our writing, but also by being attuned to what hasn't. By going back to those few letters of the alphabet and trying again.

All of us have our own paths towards this experience: maybe there was a teacher who opened our minds to a certain story, a certain writer; a novel or a poem that transported us, leaving us wanting to know just how that magic happened; a film or a play that left you altered, so that you walked out a subtly, and yet also significantly, different person from the one who entered a couple of hours before.

For me, it began with words on the air, not the page … early memories of my mother singing ballads such as 'William and Dinah' and then, one day in the car, on an anthology tape of Anglo-Welsh poetry, the poet Dannie Abse reading his poem 'In the Theatre'. It wasn't a long poem but, as the best poems can, it took me a vast distance over a short space of speech. By the time Dannie was intoning the words of a brain-surgery patient suddenly awoken mid-surgery – *Leave my soul alone, leave my soul alone* – the poem had very much done the opposite. That most elusive of poetic calibrations – a crafted weighting of music, language, imagery and rhythm – had somehow altered my internal weather and left me wanting not just more, but also to try my own hand at this strange alchemy.

Encouraged by a succession of teachers in my local schools and a clutch of placings or prizes in young people's poetry competitions, I began my own journey into the miracles and failures of writing. One of those competitions, run by an early two-tents-down-by-the-river Hay Festival, offered the prize of a week's residential course at the beautiful Tŷ Newydd in Llanystumdwy, North Wales. The competition had been for short stories, but the only course I could attend was poetry. One afternoon, sitting in the Tŷ Newydd garden, one of the tutors, Gladys Mary Coles, scribbled down a list of poetry magazine titles on the back of my poem. 'Start sending your poems out,' she told me. 'See what happens.'

On returning home, when I unpacked I found that list of titles, written in faint pencil: *Envoi, Ambit, PN Review, Poetry Wales*. I'd seen the same titles on the shelves of Ty Newydd; I'd taken some of those magazines off those shelves, opened their pages to read the poems inside, seen the shapes of the black-printed words – each poem, as Glyn Maxwell says, the mark of 'a human presence.' And all of it felt so far away … so impossible.

But then I remembered a book I'd seen on my mother's desk: bright red with yellow writing – *Writers' & Artists' Yearbook*. I found the book and, inside, saw that the magazines in Gladys Mary's list had editors behind them, people with names and addresses. And so

I wrote to these people, sending them my poems in the way the *Yearbook* had advised me. And I waited … to see what would happen.

Which was, mostly, of course, that my poems were rejected. But nearly always politely and often with advice, suggestions – which is when I realised that the *Yearbook* hadn't just given me a way to find addresses, but also a way to find people who, like me, were in love with language and words and what they could do. The advice and suggestions some of those people gave made my poems better, and eventually some of them were printed – which in turn led me to more people, other editors and other writers, some of whom went on to guide me towards writing my first books. And at that point *Writers' & Artists' Yearbook* proved a vital resource once again – from researching agents to helping me understand the marks of a copy-editor on my manuscript.

This was all over 20 years ago now, and much has changed, of course. The internet offers myriad new ways to be published, or to find new voices and new work. But perhaps that makes a book like *Writers' & Artists' Yearbook* all the more useful, not less. In such a crowded, competitive landscape, a writer starting out on their individual journey needs a trusted map and compass more than ever. And this is what the book you're now holding offers you – a way of navigating your own path into writing, of finding the people behind those companies, web addresses and profiles who will help you on your way. It might be that, at first, these people will write back to you more often about the failures of your writing than about its miracles. But if they do, remember that such advice is no less valuable and, perhaps, even more so.

Owen Sheers is an award-winning novelist, poet and playwright. His books include *The Dust Diaries* (2005), *Resistance* (2008), *I Saw A Man* (2015) and *Pink Mist* (2013), all published by Faber & Faber. His poetry collections include *Skirrid Hill* (Faber & Faber 2005), which won a Somerset Maugham Award. In 2018 Owen was the winner of the Wilfred Owen Prize. His BBC film-poem to mark the 50th anniversary of the Aberfan disaster, *The Green Hollow*, won three BAFTA Cymru awards. His dramatic work include *Mametz* and *The Passion* for National Theatre Wales, and *The Two Worlds of Charlie F.*, winner of the Amnesty International Freedom of Expression Award at the 2021 Edinburgh Festival. A stage version of his verse drama *Pink Mist* was produced by Bristol Old Vic in 2015, and his one-man play *Unicorns, almost*, about the life and poetry of Second World War poet Keith Douglas, premiered at the Hay-on-Wye Festival of Literature in 2018. His first children's book *Drew, Moo and Bunny, Too* was published by Walker Books in 2023. Owen is Professor of Creative Writing at Swansea University. See his website www.owensheers.co.uk for more information and follow him on X @owensheers.

Real people write books

Samantha Shannon reflects on the unknowable and untraceable mystery of the published author from the perspective of the fledgling writer. She sheds light on what finally allowed her to 'illuminate every dark corner of publishing' and become a bestselling author herself.

Some years ago, I wrote my first story. I believe I was seven or eight years old. From what little I remember of it, it was about a princess who inherited the moon. The reason I know nothing else about this piece of my juvenilia is that I only printed one copy, and I sent that copy to a publishing house (don't do this). I used spotless paper and double-checked that the ink had dried. I stapled the pages together, sealed them in an envelope, and penned the address in my very best handwriting. My grandmother walked me down the street to the postbox and, together, we sent my little story to the only publisher I could recall off the top of my head.

For a long time, I forgot about that story. I have no proof that it existed; it survives as a cobweb in the corner of my memory. Still – for a short time – it was out in the world. I imagine someone heaved a sigh when it arrived as it did, bereft of an agent to represent it or a synopsis to describe it. Perhaps a kind-hearted editor would have sent me a reply, had they known I was a child with a vivid imagination and no idea how publishing worked – but they would have hit a dead end if they'd tried. I had sent no letter to introduce myself, nor included a self-addressed envelope. I'm not confident I even thought to include my name on the cover.

Perhaps it was because I never got an answer that in my young mind a silence grew around publishing. My impression of it was all shadow and clockwork. Perhaps machines created books. Perhaps they grew on trees. Either way, it was clear that little girls like me had no place in the process. I continued to write stories, but I set aside the notion that anyone would ever find them in a bookshop. The author became an abstract concept. I glossed over the names on my favourite books, for they belonged to ethereal beings whose lives were worlds away from mine.

Then a media storm around a certain author brought her name to my attention. People weren't just talking about a book but about its creator – about her life, her dreams, and how she had conjured a universe in a café and on trains. There was fierce interest in her personal story. She was telling marvellous tales, but she was not a clockwork toy, not a shadow. Reading about her reminded me of what I must have always known – that people wrote books. Real people. From then on, I plunged back in to writing ferociously, with a luminous dream: I was going to be an author.

When I was 15, I started a full-length novel. Once it was finished, I decided to try to get it published but found myself with as little knowledge of publishing as I'd possessed when I was a child. All I had gained was a suspicion that there were many more pieces in the jigsaw than one author and one story, and I had no sense of how to fit those pieces together. I turned to the internet, where I found a local freelance editor and paid her all of my saved-up pocket money to look at a few chapters. Countless websites sang to me, promising me they could publish my book if I paid them far more money than I had ever had. I had only a tenuous understanding of what an agent was. In short, I was overwhelmed.

When I found the *Writers' & Artists' Yearbook* it was like striking a match in the dark. After someone mentioned it to me in passing, I got my hands on a copy straight away. With every page I turned, I understood more about the trade that had flummoxed me since I was a child. Soon I was armed with the knowledge I needed to begin my journey.

Writers' & Artists' Yearbook does not come with a guarantee of publication. There is no formula to publishing, no code to crack, no single 'right answer' that will launch your book onto the shelves. I don't think I've ever heard exactly the same publication story twice. All writers are wayfarers, and there are many paths we travel on ... some longer than others. That novel I wrote when I was 15 never saw the light of day. Even though I followed agency guidelines, even though I used the right font and the right line spacing – it was not to be.

You might have a book like that. You might have several. Trying to get someone to see them can sometimes feel like knocking on a door that never opens. But, if there's one thing I can tell you from the other side, it's that each minute you spend writing is worthwhile. Every story whets your craft. Every story hones your ability to see a tale through to its end. I would not have written my debut novel, *The Bone Season* (Bloomsbury 2013), without having first written the one I had to put away.

I got my book deal when I was 20. I've now been in the industry for over ten years and have three bestsellers under my belt – yet there are still things I'm only just learning, things that take me by surprise. As with any vocation, getting to grips with being a writer is a lifelong process. But, by opening *Writers' & Artists' Yearbook*, you've taken your first step. This is your toolbox, your skeleton key, and the torch that will illuminate every dark corner of publishing. I wish you all the luck in the world.

Samantha Shannon is the *New York Times* and *Sunday Times* bestselling author of *The Bone Season* series (published by Bloomsbury): *The Bone Season* (2013), *The Mime Order* (2015), *The Song Rising* (2017), *The Mask Falling* (2021) and *The Dark Mirror* (2025), with two more instalments to come. Her books outside the series are *The Priory of the Orange Tree* (Bloomsbury 2019), a finalist for the Lambda Literary Awards 2020, and two prequels: *A Day of Fallen Night* (Bloomsbury 2023) and *Among the Burning Flowers* (September 2025). Samantha's work has been translated into 26 languages. See www.samanthashannon.co.uk for more information. Follow her on X and Instagram @say_shannon..

Writing across forms: my publishing routes to success

From radio to TV to novels, Rob Gittins' wealth of writing experience is extraordinary. In this article, he explains the importance of persistence and of never throwing away a good idea.

I always wanted to be a writer. But how to start? I didn't know anyone who wrote – certainly not for a living, which is what I decided, from an early age, that I wanted to do.

Then, I heard that the BBC would read radio plays if you sent them in. Television at that time seemed a closed shop, film and publishing even more so. So, I started writing and sending in radio plays, and the BBC did read them. And sent each and every one back for at least two years. One day, though, I got a phone call from a BBC producer to tell me that one of my plays had been accepted.

This wasn't exactly what you'd call a groundbreaking commission. It was a fifteen-minute drama which went out a quarter to midnight on a Friday night. To this day, I've never met anyone in the world who heard it, apart from me. My old mum came over to listen to it with me and fell asleep before the end. But it was the moment every writer wants, when someone says, we'll tell your story. And we'll pay you at the same time.

So – that was a start, but how to sustain it? I soon came to realise that original plays, for most screenwriters, are the passion projects that can sometimes take years (if not decades) to bring off.

For a professional screenwriter, the answer seemed obvious – series and serial drama. Week after week, these massive cruise liners floated through the schedules – *Casualty, The Bill, Coronation Street, EastEnders, Minder, The Sweeney*. The list seemed pretty much endless and, from what I could see from the credits, different writers seemed to write them too.

But whatever the show, series or serial, the main attraction wasn't just the need to make a living, although I don't believe anyone should apologise for that. All these different shows presented an opportunity to tell different types of stories, too.

Look at the challenge *The Bill* set writers in its early days. The writer comes up with the story, but there were two rules. First, we could never go into the personal lives of the characters. Second, nothing that happens in that episode can happen unless it's from the police's point of view. The audience can never be in possession of any information not available to the police themselves. So, all of a sudden everything a writer may have in mind about the way to tell a story – a bank job, perhaps – has to be rethought. The writer now has to find a different structure and a different approach that I probably would never have considered before.

I've written for series drama and for serial drama. The serial drama that I've been most involved in is *EastEnders*. I was first commissioned to write for it in 1986 and now, somewhat bewilderingly to me, I'm the longest-serving writer with over 350 episodes behind me.

The modern-day system of telling that story is relatively simple. Every three months or so, a group of about ten writers go away for a long weekend and play. And what we play is a sort of extended 'what if…?' game. What if X did this or Y did that? Flights of fancy, most destined never to see the light of day. But out of that, through a combination of one writer saying this and another saying that, something always emerges, which is also another useful lesson.

I've seen many writers crippled before they start because they believe everything they say has to be gold-plated. It never is. But there's something in there someone else might pick up, and all of a sudden there's a great story on the table even if no one can actually quite remember who came up with it in the first place. Nothing is ever too stupid to say. Nothing is ever wasted.

So, we've got some ideas from our three-month regular conference and the next thing we do is meet up once a month to work out how those stories play over the next few weeks. Then, there's the little matter of actually writing the script.

Briefly, I get a page or so of notes. That's what happens and it's set in stone. But how those story points happen, how you structure the episode, that's your choice. So, it's a strange combination of absolute freedom and total constraint.

Sometimes, on *EastEnders*, the rules go out of the window. I got a call one day from the then Executive Producer asking me if I wanted to write a special episode. It was going to be an hour long and would be devoted to the exit of a key character called Mel. I was intrigued to see how she would go, given that this character had already left the Square twice, the first time walking out on her wedding day and the second blowing up one of our key locations along the way.

I said yes, and send me the story doc. That doc came through: the title, 'Mel's Exit', was on the front and inside were five words – 'To be devised by writer'. So, suddenly, inside what can be a limiting medium you have total freedom to play.

There's the flip side too. It's inevitable that, on occasion, I'll be writing for characters I don't like, doing things I don't understand in a story I find unbelievable. Tough. You've still got to write it and you've got to make it work. Is that useful? I believe it is. Because it's down to craft again. Once you've brought off the seemingly impossible in one story, it makes you much more confident in tackling what also seems impossible in another.

Series drama offers more freedom than serial drama. In those types of drama – *Casualty, The Bill, Heartbeat, Vera* – the writer is given the world and the characters that inhabit it, but after that, everything's up for grabs. What do you want to do with these characters? How do you want to develop them? What situations do you want to put them in that test them in a way that maybe hasn't been done before?

Series drama also offers the chance to do something else. I carried around with me for a long time a story I really wanted to tell about a prisoner who breaks out of prison to try and repair a relationship with his wife. He's actually caught on his way out by a guard, who, because of problems in his own life, allows him to go. And I always knew the actor I wanted to play the prisoner and that was Ray Winstone,

I talked to lots of people about it and could never attract sufficient interest to get it made – and Ray Winstone seemed a pipe dream. Then *Casualty* asked if I wanted to write for them and what story did I want to tell? And I said, well, I've got a story about a prisoner …

I had to get the prisoner into hospital but that wasn't too difficult, I staged a prison riot which ended up with a few of the prisoners being treated in A&E, including my guy, and then basically played out the beats in my original story. And – the icing on the cake – the director then asked if I had any ideas as to who might play the guest lead and I said, er, Ray Winstone? And because this was the BBC and a flagship show asking (rather than me), Ray Winstone said yes.

The wider point is that you can tell all sorts of stories in series drama. The best of them can become a Trojan Horse, allowing you to smuggle in stories which you feel are important, and you might struggle to get produced elsewhere. But what happens when you can't get your stories on at all as a one-off, inside a series drama, on the radio, or wherever?

A great writer called Alan Plater once wrote his life story, but he wrote about the plays that hadn't been produced, the ideas that had never seen the light of day, because he believed that they're the ones that burn inside you.

I had a similar experience with my first novel, *Gimme Shelter* (Alcemi 2013). I had a central character I very much wanted to write about, and a world I wanted to explore, and I talked to the usual suspects in my world – producers, script editors, commissioners, broadcasters. Years went by and, with it, dozens of outlines.

After a while, I thought, I'll just write it. I'll write the story I want to write in the way I want, and I'll worry afterwards whether anyone will ever read it. It's the greatest thing about our world. You don't need permission. No one can stop you, apart from maybe yourself. The novel was published and was then optioned by one of the TV companies who had rejected the original outline.

But what if what's stopping you isn't just a problematic path to production or publication? What if it's something in the idea? In those cases, I find it really useful to almost literally put the idea down on the floor and walk round it. Experiment with the same idea, but from different points of view. Sometimes, if I put it down in the middle of a room, I can see options and possibilities on the edges.

That's related to something else I really believe – never throw anything away. That idea you had ten years ago but could never make work, may well marry up to a half-formed idea you had this morning and all of a sudden two half-formed ideas become something you can work with.

Just to illustrate that, well over thirty years ago I initiated a documentary film for ITV. I was fascinated by Dylan Thomas's time in America, and a broadcaster and I decided to make a film about it. We managed to find his lecture agent, John Malcolm Brinnin, his lover Liz Reitell, and the original cast members of *Under Milk Wood*, reuniting them all in New York for a reconstruction of Dylan's last US tour. As a documentary, it worked well.

The BBC then commissioned me to write a feature film version of the story. It seemed to have everything – a doomed and famous poet, a tragic end, an ill-fated love affair – but I just couldn't make it work. No matter how I tried to tell the story in dramatic form, it became a tale about a man who left home, behaved badly and then died. I ended up handing the commission back and writing it off as one that got away.

But remember what Alan Plater said? Those abandoned projects? The ones that burn inside? And remember points of view? Putting an idea down in the middle of a room and walking round it, trying to see the angles you hadn't seen before?

It took me the best part of thirty years to take that advice on board, but then I returned to the notes I'd made on that trip and found a reference I'd forgotten about.

Before Dylan went out to the US, he'd issued a writ against *Time* magazine. They'd written a profile of him which he'd decided was libellous. When *Time* heard he was coming back, they employed a private detective to shadow him, intending to dig up dirt which they could use in case his writ ever came to court.

And there it was. The solution. Dylan isn't the hero. The hero of this story is a private eye. This private eye is a man in crisis in his own life, but gradually he gets increasingly absorbed by the man he's tailing. He actually starts to read some of his poetry. He begins to find, in the chaotic life of the man he's shadowing, a way of resolving issues with his own.

We can't change history. Dylan was always going to die. But the private eye lives on and it's a changed man who lives on, a testament to the way an artist lives on too and changes other lives.

It's the same story. But by walking round the idea, seeing who else was on the edge of the tale, it became dramatic and life-affirming where before it was anything but. And that became another novel of mine called *The Poet and The Private Eye* (Y Lolfa Cy 2014).

Again, the lesson's clear – it's not just never throw an idea away, but keep walking around it, keep refreshing it. Somehow, you'll find a way through.

And hopefully – and unlike with me – it won't take you thirty years.

Rob Gittins is a screenwriter and novelist. The longest-serving writer on *EastEnders*, his other TV credits include *Casualty*, *The Bill* and *Vera*. He has also written prolifically for radio and is the author of 12 novels, the most recent of which is *Year Zero* (Hobeck 2025). For more information see www.robgittins.com. Follow him on X @Gittins2Rob.

See also ...

- *Successful screenwriting*, page 362
- *Writing series for television*, page 376
- *Audio dramatist or novelist?*, page 384

If at first you don't succeed ... keep trying

In this article, Jessica Irena Smith offers her refreshingly honest take on the highs and lows of the submissions process. The key to success? Resilience.

Growing up, it was never my intention to become a writer, but in 2009, after graduating with an MA in Glass from Sunderland University, I began writing for no other reason than I had an idea for a story – a middle grade, fantasy-adventure inspired by my time at the National Glass Centre. I was a self-employed glass artist and – to be honest – felt I needed a fallback plan in case the being an artist thing didn't work out (I know, I know – how could writing ever be a fallback plan?!). But although I'd thrown myself into writing, I'm ashamed to say I wasn't an avid reader. Never had been. Growing up, though my parents tried – they always read to me; we had a houseful of books – the closest I came was 'story tapes' in my younger years, and a *Point Horror* stage in my teens (not that there's anything wrong with *Point Horrors*. People can be sniffy about them, but I still maintain they taught me so much about pacing, plot and structure). While my sister was – still is – a speed-reading demon, devouring a book a day in the school holidays, I was making things: think Blue Peter's papier-mâché Tracy Island. Although my sister was forever recommending books, it wasn't until my twenties, and Carlos Ruiz Zafón's *The Shadow of the Wind*, that something happened: I fell in love with reading and never looked back.

But back to writing, and when I first began submitting to literary agents in 2009 – far too early, I realise now – I used a combination of my trusty *Writers' & Artists' Yearbook* and the internet. Many agency websites were pretty basic at that time, lacking the more detailed guidelines on offer now, and I made all the mistakes you read about in 'submission dos and don'ts': I addressed queries to the wrong agent (in one case, to one who was long dead!); forgot to attach my synopsis and sample chapters; even let the odd typo slip through the net. But despite my rookie errors – and, in my defence, they were relatively few – I was lucky enough in those early days to receive feedback from one agent, which spurred me on. And so, over the next few months, then years, I continued in an endless cycle of round after round of submissions. What kept me going was that I always got some interest, some full manuscript requests, though ultimately the feedback was much the same: close, but not close enough. After every round I'd wallow in self doubt, then rework my manuscript and begin the process all over again. I lost count of the number of drafts I went through, never mind how many rounds of submissions (it was a lot). I'd swing from wanting to give up (*surely if I'd been going to find an agent, I'd have found one by now?*), to knowing I couldn't (*I was too invested – the fact I was getting full manuscript requests had to mean something*). At one point, I even met with an agent, but – long story short – he didn't take me on, saying that, to sign an unknown debut on the strength of a single manuscript was 'too much of an eggs in one basket situation'.

Then, in 2016, I won a Northern Writers' Award. I'd read the stats on how many writers go on to be published after winning and – although a born pessimist – was hopeful. But even though the award was invaluable in so many ways – my 'coming out' as a writer, for one; no more writing in secret – and led to further full manuscript requests, I still didn't find representation. Early on, my sister had told me, somewhat bluntly, that no one ever gets their first book published. But I hadn't wanted to hear it: it was my children's book or nothing. I had no more ideas in me. I didn't want to have any more ideas. So I decided to give it one more shot and, in 2017, got a part-time job so I could write at times of year that were quieter for my glass business. And then, in 2018, something funny happened: having sworn I wouldn't write another thing if I didn't get anywhere with my children's novel, I began my first attempt at adult fiction, inspired by a Netflix docuseries, *The Keepers*. It wasn't easy, but I felt excited about writing in a way that I hadn't in a long time. In truth, I was probably always more suited to writing for adults: whereas with my children's novel I'd adopted the old adage of 'write what you know', with adult fiction I was writing what I loved: something dark and twisting (if Carlos Ruiz Zafón made me fall in love with reading, then it was Gillian Flynn who made me want to become a writer of adult fiction).

In 2019, my new work was longlisted for *Mslexia*'s novel-writing competition, and an extract from it published in a TLC/AM Heath-sponsored anthology. Then, in 2020, after having surgery a week before the first lockdown and using my recovery time to redraft my manuscript, I was invited to attend David Higham's Open Day for under-represented writers (which, thanks to Covid, became a virtual open week). Everything seemed to happen pretty quickly after that: I began my first round of submissions, one full manuscript request led to another, and I ended up with a pretty even spread of 'no thank yous'; agents who asked me to do some more work on my manuscript before they'd reconsider; and outright offers. I chatted with a number of agents, all of whom were lovely, before signing with Marina de Pass at The Soho Agency that summer. What made me pick Marina? She was generous with her time (our first meeting, over Zoom, lasted two hours), thoughtful (I felt she really got my manuscript), passionate and enthusiastic without being overly effusive, and clear about the fact she was offering me representation (after my earlier experience with my children's manuscript, I was looking for an upfront commitment, rather than someone asking me to do more work speculatively). I think I'm quite a low-maintenance client – I'm pretty self-contained, motivated and not prone to meltdowns – though I am an over-thinker and worrier; Marina is the perfect foil. After a few months of working on the manuscript together, she began submitting to editors and, in 2022, I signed a two-book deal with Headline. *The Summer She Vanished* came out in 2023, with my second book scheduled for 2024.

So, what are my tips for anyone trying to find an agent and publisher?

- First, the most obvious, the advice I ignored for so long: read, read, read. Reading, and reading widely, is key to strengthening your own writing.
- Second, when it comes to your manuscript, redraft, redraft, redraft. Also, print and read a hard copy. Then read the hard copy aloud. It's amazing how differently things read on a screen versus a printed page, and in your head versus out loud.
- Make sure your work really is as polished and typo-free as possible before submitting. If you do submit too early, though, it's not the end of the world – there's always a new agent to query.
- That said, pick carefully. There's no point wasting an agent's time if they don't represent your genre.
- There's lots of good advice online about writing query letters, but in a nutshell, have a template letter that's polished and tight, and which you can adapt to each agent.

• Don't be too hard on yourself. I'd tie myself in knots over the tiniest query-letter-related decision, or kick myself after I'd submitted, thinking I should I have said this or that (or that I shouldn't have said that or this). But, truth is, if an agent's interested, they're interested.
• Keeping track of submissions, especially after multiple rounds, can be tricky. I kept a table with the agent and agency name; the date I submitted; whether I'd received an acknowledgement of receipt; the particular agent's guidelines on response time – if given – along with how long to leave before chasing; whether or not I received a full manuscript request; and any extra notes or feedback. (Any rejections, I'd simply strike that row out. Any agents with the full manuscript, I'd highlight in red.)
• Try to build your writing CV: being short-listed – or long-listed – for writing competitions helps your work stand out from the crowd.
• Do follow up politely if the agent's guidelines say so, but also know when to give up. Early on, I spent a lot of time chasing queries and full manuscript requests, when the fact the agent hadn't got back to me really told me everything I needed to know.
• Feedback from agents is like gold dust. You don't have to agree with it, but don't be defensive about it. Most agents get hundreds of unsolicited submissions a week, so if an agent takes the time to give you feedback, view it as a win. When I look back, I realise how generous people in the industry were with their advice – they didn't need to be, but they took the time anyway.
• If you get a full manuscript request or offer, be sure to inform other agents you've submitted to: interest breeds other interest.
• Don't be afraid to make changes to your work, or start something new. There'll be edits to do if you're taken on by an agent and editor, so it's something you've got to get used to. Agents' and editors' knowledge and fresh eyes are invaluable – mine made excellent suggestions and flagged issues in my manuscript I'd missed, so not being too precious about your work is key.
• That said, you don't have to agree with all suggestions, but it's worth explaining why. Agents and editors are usually very reasonable, open-minded people – as long as you give a valid reason, they're more often than not willing to see things from another perspective.
• Don't be afraid to ask questions. When I got my book deal, I realised I'd been so focused on getting an agent, I knew relatively little about the actual publishing process. I wish I'd asked more.
• I think it was the great Anna Wintour who said we should never compare ourselves to others. She's absolutely right, but it's easier said than done; I still do it. When I didn't have an agent, it felt like everyone else did. Once I got an agent, it felt like everyone else had a publishing deal. Now that I have a publishing deal, it feels like not only do the world and his wife have one, but they're all doing way better than I am, and their books are way superior…
• Take time out if you need to. The submissions process can feel endless and punishing. Allow yourself to wallow – I did – then move on.

Would I have even started writing if I'd known how long it would take, or how hard it would be? I like to think so but, honestly, I really don't know. Looking back, I'd always viewed getting a publishing deal as the end goal. Now, I realise it's just the beginning. It goes without saying that having an idea for a story, and being able to write, are key to becoming an author. But resilience is also essential. So perhaps the most important piece of advice I can give, is keep trying. No doesn't mean no forever, it just means not right now.

Jessica Irena Smith is a glass artist from County Durham. Her debut novel, *The Summer She Vanished*, was published by Headline in 2023. *The Night of the Crash*, her second book, was published by Headline in 2024.

See also...

- *Becoming a bestselling author: my writing story*, page 228
- *Keeping the writing dream alive, page 236*

The writing craft

Reading as a writer

Cathy Rentzenbrink shares her lifelong passion for reading. She shows how it can open up new worlds and possibilities, providing an invaluable learning resource for aspiring writers as well as pleasure for the reader, and how studying the lives, work and technique of other authors can drive, inform and enhance your own individual practice.

I have always loved reading more than pretty much anything else. It enables exploration and escape, gives consolation and pleasure, and fuels my desire to know the world. I don't remember learning how to do it, so it doesn't feel like a skill I had to acquire, more like a gift bestowed by a benevolent fairy godmother. 'I will make this one a reader,' she said, as she waved her wand over my crib. Perhaps it was this way for you, too, or maybe you came to reading later in life. My dad only learnt to read as an adult, and it strengthens my gratitude for books and reading to know that what is a comfort and joy for me, is not always easy for everyone. So welcome, dear reader, no matter what your journey to this page has been. My mission today is to share with you that, as well as everything else it offers, reading is probably the single best thing you can do in the service of your writing.

If reading was my first love, then writing was hard on its heels. When asked what I wanted to do when I grew up, I would announce that I wanted to be a writer or a detective (the influence of all those Enid Blytons, I'm sure) and would be told not to be silly by my teachers. Luckily my parents were encouraging and I had books where children were always striking out on adventures, solving crimes, and ruling magical kingdoms.

This, perhaps, is the first thing reading can do for us as well as offering entertainment – it opens up alternative realities. If you are struggling to find your tribe, if you are surrounded by people who care less about words and stories than you do, then look for friends in books. As a child I loved Anne Shirley as much as if she existed in my real life and I could visit her at Green Gables. I've never really stopped imagining myself into books in this way and it is a great cure for loneliness. In addition to fiction, I have always loved books about writers – both memoir and biography – and I see now that I was looking for clues as to how writing could be done. I was looking for the granular details: what time someone got up; where they wrote; how they earned money; and how they transitioned between the states of aspiration and arrival. When I had a child, I wanted to read about how authors managed their childcare, and when my first book, *The Last Act of Love* (Picador 2015), came out I wanted to read about how they dealt with attention. This is all available to you, dear reader, this mentoring via what writers say about themselves. Consider it all as you forge your own path.

And engage with the process: read a novel and then seek out what the writer says about how they made it. Go to events in bookshops, libraries and festivals (see *Festivals and conferences for writers, artists and readers* on page 630). If you can see authors in the flesh – our scruffy shoes, our bitten nails – the prospect of joining the ranks becomes less intimidating. There is a vast amount of stuff, often free, that you can access online. I have taken huge inspiration over the years from Hilary Mantel; from her books, yes, but also from her Reith Lectures and her interviews with the *Paris Review* and the *Guardian*. This is about chemistry. Maya Angelou, Maggie O'Farrell and Kit de Waal all float my boat, but your search might lead you to a different writer. Experiment. Read around. Find your soulmates. They don't have to know you for a relationship to have a significant impact and influence on your work.

Some writers send me directly to the page. And this doesn't seem to have anything to do with the subject. When I read Maggie Nelson or Elena Ferrante then I yearn to wield my own pen. One of the things that makes me happiest is when people tell me that reading my books has encouraged them in their own practice. I go forth into my day with great joy that someone out there is opening a notebook and sharpening their pencil because of me.

The most useful way to learn about technique, the nuts-and-bolts stuff, is to look at what other writers do. What point of view they have chosen? How do they handle any time shifts? How have they selected the start and end point of their story? When I get stuck on a point like this, I will look for the answer on my bookshelves. If I'm struggling with handling the dialogue when there are lots of characters present, then I'll search out dinner party scenes. At the moment I'm considering writing a novel that happens largely in flashback, but when I tried this before I found it too hard. This time I am going to reread *The Secret History* by Donna Tartt, *Rebecca* by Daphne du Maurier and *The Confessions of Frannie Langton* by Sara Collins and carefully study exactly how it is done.

And I'm always on the lookout. I read a book for pleasure first, racing through, and then, if it fits the bill, I go back and read it again with forensic attention. How did they do it? How did they capture and then hold my attention? How did they make me care so much about that really quite unpleasant character? As well as doing this with a brilliant book, it can be useful to do it when a book has fallen short. Where did the author lose your interest? Where did the pace drop? What didn't quite ring true? If you were this book's editor, what would you suggest to make it better? Would it be less confusing if there were fewer characters? Does that relentless present tense get on your nerves? Is there too much back story? If so, how could you fix this?

A word of caution, though. Don't compare your work in progress with a finished book – that's like watching the Oscars from the sofa in your pyjamas and berating yourself for not being red-carpet-ready. If a book is good, and the author has done their job; it will read as though they sat down one day and it just flowed out in the time it takes you to read it. That is the magic trick of literature; we all sign up to suspend disbelief and allow the wizard to wave their wand – but, if you are going to write as well as read, you need to know just how much work is involved in that sleight of hand. A finished book has almost always involved gargantuan effort, sometimes years of wailing and gnashing of teeth and pulling out of hair and endless drafts, and then finally – finally – the writer got an agent who made suggestions, and an editor who worked on several drafts, and then a copy-editor and a proofreader made the manuscript the best version of itself it could be. I didn't always know this – I would allow myself to be swamped with despair and I'd down tools because I didn't see how I could ever measure up. Eventually I realised how futile it is to brood on the knowledge that I will never be as good as Julian Barnes or Bernardine Evaristo. How pointless! I don't want to be trying to sound like them, I want to be putting all my time and energy into trying to sound like *myself.*

When you get deep into your work-in-progress you might want to be careful about exposing yourself to new ideas. I do press pause on certain things every so often. When I was finishing my novel *Everyone is Still Alive* (Phoenix 2021) I stopped reading new fiction and confined myself to memoirs or rereading Agatha Christie and Georgette Heyer. Then, when the novel was safely dispatched to my editor, I went on a fiction binge to make up for lost time. Another tip is an occasional week or two of complete deprivation. If you can make your manuscript the most interesting thing in your life, if you have no other sources of distraction – no email, no Netflix, no books – then you'll have to get all your entertainment from your own words. This isn't terribly compatible with living a 21st-century life, but I find it pays great dividends every so often, especially at the start of a project when the green shoots are tender and need a bit of protection, and when I'm coming towards the end of a draft; at that stage I feel like a juggler with all the colourful balls of my own story up in the air and I'm ready to commit to dedicated concentration as I bring the novel to an end with a flourish. But most of the time I am reading and think you should be too. These days, I have to carve out and protect both writing and reading time so that I am not seduced by the easy, empty pleasure of the internet. I write in the mornings, before I have looked at my email, and then, unless I have an event, I firmly shut down my computer and phone in the evening and give myself up to someone else's book.

So, read. Because it's useful. Because it's pleasurable. Because books are the best that humanity has to offer. Because your life will be enlarged when you spend as much of it as you can engaged in long-form narrative. Because you will feel better than if you toss away your time on the internet. And because you can take it all back to your own work; then one day you will know the joy of having readers of your own, as well as being a reader, and maybe someone will tell you that your book has inspired them to start writing their own and you will fill up with a sense of meaning and purpose that makes it all worthwhile.

Cathy Rentzenbrink is the author of the memoir *The Last Act of Love* (2015), *How to Feel Better* (2017) and *Dear Reader: The Comfort and Joy of Books* (2020), all published by Picador. *Everyone is Still Alive* (Phoenix 2021) was her first novel. Her latest book is *Ordinary Time* (Phoenix 2024). Cathy has worked for The Reading Agency and Waterstones and regularly contributes to the media on all aspects of books and reading. She is President of the Budleigh Salterton Literary Festival. For more information see https://cathyreadsbooks.com. Follow her on X and Instagram @catrentzenbrink.

See also...

- *Festival fun: your guide to how, why and what,* page 527

Writing for readers

In this article, thriller-writer Rachel McLean asks one of the most fundamental questions for authors of all genres: who is your reader?

Who's going to read your book?

If you're poring over the pages of the *Writers' & Artists' Yearbook* – and you wouldn't be reading this if that weren't the case – then there's a very good chance that you're hoping an agent and or a publisher will read it. You may already have worked with an editor, or beta readers, or maybe a writing group. All those well-read people will get their eyes on your manuscript and will give you feedback.

But in all this, it's easy to lose sight of the most important person who will ever read your book, and that's the end reader. The person who strolls into a bookshop or clicks on an online store, who finds your books in amongst all the thousands (or more) on offer, peruses your book description, and decides that this is worth a few hours of their time.

If you write for this reader, then you're in with a much better chance of delighting agents, editors, beta readers and all the rest of them. And if readers love this book of yours, they'll want to read more. And that's how you build a career.

Like many budding authors, when I started out as a writer, I wrote a series of books that were what I wanted to read. I knew what interested me and when I couldn't find exactly that on the shelves, I wrote the books myself. I mean this literally: in 2017 I took four books on holiday, didn't enjoy any of them, and so spent the rest of the trip writing the first 20,000 words of what became my first published novel.

But I struggled to find readers. My first six books sold, but not in the quantities I needed if I was going to make a living from my writing. And that was my goal. So I changed my focus: writing not for me, or for my editor. But for readers. The next book I wrote is part of a story world that has sold over two million books, and launched my writing career. Writing for readers worked for me. So how do you do it?

The first step is to understand who your readers are. And who they aren't.

Writing for readers could mean that in the early stages of the publication process, you might not get the feedback you're expecting. I'm a member of a wonderful writers' group whose members write in very different genres from mine, and I've learned to cherry-pick which pieces of feedback I take into account. Only readers who love the kind of thing you write will get it. And if you're looking for an editor, publisher or agent, you need to find one who gets it, too. Don't send your manuscript to literary editors if you're writing genre fiction, however good your writing. And don't send it to someone who only represents children's authors if you're writing YA.

You can find your target readers in a whole host of places, depending on what genre you write in (and before you start identifying your ideal reader, please, please identify your genre). Crime readers (like mine) hang out in Facebook groups for people who love crime fiction, they listen to true crime podcasts and attend events like the annual crime writing festival in Harrogate. Romance readers might be on TikTok or Instagram talking about their new favourite read. And all of them will be on the reviews pages of Amazon, giving feedback on the books they love and the books they hate. (I'll come to that shortly.)

Talk to people who read books like yours. Ask them what they enjoy most about the genre, and what they find less appealing. When I was writing my first police procedural novel, I asked a question in a Facebook group for crime readers: did people enjoy reading about the detectives' personal lives, or did they prefer to focus on the case? The answer led to a series of sub-plots in my novels all about my protagonists' home lives, entwining them with the cases and giving my characters so much more depth.

Asking questions can give you an insight into what readers love. And so can reviews. The advice is mixed on whether you should read your own reviews, but do you read other authors'? They can be incredibly enlightening.

When I was writing my first DI Zoe Finch book, I took time to identify my comparable authors ('comps'): writers whose books were read by people I thought would enjoy my books. It's important to know who your comps are: if you're looking for a publishing deal, it shows you've done your research; and if you're an indie like me, it's essential for marketing. I read books by all my comps, to see what they'd done well (and what I would do differently: this isn't about aping anyone else). And I read their reviews, especially the five-star reviews and the one-star reviews. These don't tell me about the quality of their books so much (they were great books selling hundreds of thousands of copies) but about what readers expected from them. Understanding the elements of your genre that prompt a strong reaction from readers will help you understand what they want from your books.

So you've identified your comps, and I've already mentioned knowing what genre you write in. This is so important. Understanding your genre won't constrain you: in fact, it'll give you a framework to work within which then allows you to push at the boundaries of that framework and make it yours. But when you're starting out and have less confidence, that framework will help you write good books that people want to read. Writing a mystery? The crime has to be solved. A romance? You'll need a HEA (Happy Ever After), in most cases. Miss out these crucial elements, and you'll get bad reviews and low sales. Keep them in – and, even better, play around with them and make them yours – and you'll have a writing career.

I regularly peruse the charts in my genre. I want to know who's selling, who's dropping and who's new. I want to know what books everyone's talking about. I don't just look at the charts, though; I read the books as well. Not so I can copy them (that won't work, and it makes for a very dull life as a writer), but so I can understand what readers want to read, and how those trends are changing.

For example, my books always have prominent gay characters, because I'm gay. When I was starting out, this wasn't so common in crime writing, but as an indie author I didn't let that stop me. Now, things are different. Publishers are crying out for diverse casts of characters, written by authors who understand life from the point of view of people who may not have been written about in the past – and that isn't just about box-ticking. Hera Books, who are republished my Dorset Crime series in print over the course of 2024/25, prides itself on publishing mass-market fiction featuring diverse voices and characters. Right now, that's something that would help you find readers or get a deal, while five years ago it might not have. You can be yourself while also keeping readers happy.

So… you've immersed yourself in your genre, you've gained a solid understanding of what readers love, and you've written and published a book that's selling. What do you do next?

If you're like many, many writers, you dream of giving up your day job and making a living from your words. And one book won't make that happen. So you need to do it again. You need to write more books that readers will want to read, and you need to make sure they keep coming back for more.

Now you've got a book out there in the wild, you'll have reader feedback. Don't obsess about the one-star reviews (even the best books get them). But listen to what your readers say. If they contact you, do they tell you which was their favourite character? Why don't you ask them? Could you then give that character a bigger role in a future book? The DI in my first series had a sidekick who readers loved. So I moved him to Scotland and gave him a spinoff series. I never would have thought of that if it hadn't been for readers wanting to see more of him. Sure, you don't have to do everything your readers ask for. You're the creative, after all. But understanding what it is about your work that readers love will help you maximise sales of your next book, and the next, and the next…

Which is why it's so important, from the start, to do it your own way. Yes, know your genre. Yes, understand what your comps are doing that works. But take those elements and work them into your writing in a way that make you delight in your own stories, not just the readers. That way you'll want to keep on writing the books that keep people reading, rather than committing yourself to just another day job, and one without a pension or any employment rights…

Keep learning, keep improving your craft, and keep listening to readers: your own, and those of your comps. Identify the sweet spot between what you love writing, what readers love reading, and what sells. And that way, you'll have a sustainable writing career that means you can give up your day job. And your pension, if you get the business side right, will be your backlist.

Good luck, and keep writing!

Rachel McLean writes thrillers that make readers think. Her books include the *Detective Zoe Finch* series, the *Dorset Crime* series and the *Tanner and McBride* series: all are linked, and characters appear in multiple series. Visit her website to find out more: https://rachelmclean.com.

Writing successful dialogue

He looked anxious. 'I just don't know how to make my characters sound authentic?'
'Read Angela Clarke's article on dialogue,' she replied with a wink.

'Train was packed. Why can't people do their job?' He arrived in a flurry of layers, unpeeling a coat, scarf, rucksack onto the third, and empty seat at the table.

'Hi. Yeah,' she said half-rising, before thinking better of it. 'I...'

'Last thing I need. Mick's at it again.' He pointed at the untouched cake on the table. 'That for me?'

She nodded. 'Listen, we –'.

'Great. Thanks.' He pulled it toward him. 'He talked all through the meeting. And he kept us there till gone five. After all his talk about time keeping!' Crumbs of cake sprayed from his lips. 'I'm starving. What d'you want to do for tea?'

'I'm pregnant,' she said.

I shamelessly eavesdropped this conversation in a suburban Pret one rainy Tuesday afternoon. It is still my go-to example of how to write great dialogue. Both people came at the conversation with their own internal motives, aims and wants. They sound like real people talking – because they were. They cut across each other, interrupted. There is a rhythm – albeit, in this case, broken – to the conversation. The words ebb and flow, the tide of his frustration and annoyance washing in and over her, before she mic-drop stops him in his tracks with a propulsive inciting incident worthy of an on-page or on-screen scene. What happens next? Well, I don't know: I was too busy furiously scribbling notes. All writers are spies on occasion, gathering surveillance, information, hints and clues as to what is really going on. We're observers, nosy note-takers, collecting threads from the people and things around us, and weaving them into the new worlds and characters we construct. And dialogue is intrinsic to that.

Having cut my teeth on pithy newspaper columns that honed my sentence structure, and reined in my ramblings to a professionally tight word count, when I started to write my first book I was nonetheless intimidated. A commissioned memoir based on my own twenties spent working in London's fashion industry, I had managed to sell the non-fiction piece off a ten-chapter sample that didn't contain dialogue. This is because I didn't know how to write dialogue. I hadn't had to write any since some laughable attempts in secondary school. Sure, I could tell a good story, but the words of my GCSE English teacher still rang in my ears: 'Angela, your syntax structure, punctuation, grammar, your spelling – they're too poor for you to write professionally.' And punctuation, all those inverted commas, speech marks and semi-colons, they're all over dialogue, aren't they? They *are* dialogue. They were scary. My fear of dialogue had grown so large, I had talked myself (pun intended) into a corner. I was a writer, though, I knew that. I felt it deep inside: it didn't matter how many abortive attempts I'd had at writing a novel, or the number of rejections I'd collected, writing was a compulsion. It was also one of the only things I was really good at. But this storyteller had backed herself against the wall. It was me versus Speech. And as my fledgling panic fully had matured into some solid procrastination I was out of time. *Confessions of a Fashionista* was my first ever book deal. I had a deadline. I had a contract. I had to deliver. Ironically, I needed to give myself a good talking-to.

And I did. Obviously, or I wouldn't be here, sharing this with you. One memoir, four novels published, and numerous screenplays optioned and commissioned for UK television later, I now love dialogue. I think I always did. Nothing conveys with such ease, in fewer words, more about who your characters are, what they want, and what they need, than what they say. Or what they don't. Oh, the beauty of subtext – from Harold Pinter's on-stage silences, to Lee Child's on page: 'Reacher said nothing.' Dialogue works in the words on the page, and in the gaps in between the lines. Stylistically, it's fairly straightforward. So how did I get over my initial dialogue doubts? Facing my own pressing deadline, I eventually pulled the nearest novel down from my bookshelf and copied how they had done it. In books, that looks like a fresh indented line when a new, or the next, character speaks. All speech is enclosed in inverted commas, or speech marks: it doesn't matter which, as long as it is uniform throughout the manuscript. (You clever literary novelists can play with this form, opting for no speech marks but rather an indented dash etcetera, à la Sally Rooney – but be cautious. You don't want your beautiful manuscript rejected by an overzealous agent's intern on the first page, because they mistakenly believe you don't understand professional punctuation.)

Nine years into my writing career, when I came to try my hand at scripts, I utilised the same trick. I simply copied the accepted form and layout from an already produced screenplay (the BBC Writers' site handily has a free script library online you can take a look at: see www.bbc.co.uk/writers/scripts/).

But what about the actual words? How do you make your dialogue dance on the page or screen? How do you spruce up your speech to elevate your manuscript? Let's unpack the toolkit: let's face down your own dialogue demons. Let's get those words down (you can always fix them later).

Write what you know – aka write how people actually talk

It sounds obvious, but do your characters sound like real people? People very rarely talk in a grammatically correct, overly polite way, where they patiently wait for each other to finish.

'How are you today, Mrs Smith?'

'I am feeling very well today. Thank you. And you, how are you feeling, Mr Jones?'

That comes across as stilted, right? Perhaps it feels old fashioned, like it belongs in a novel published in the 1800s. It is also quite dull. Real people interject, cut over each other, as with my opening eavesdropped conversational gem. People have their own focus, aims and motivations in each conversation they come to. Even if it's as simplistic as one character – a patron – wanting their glass of wine to be refilled and to be left alone as soon as possible, and one character – a bartender – being bored and so wanting to flirt, there is a conflict at the heart of each exchange. And that gives you tension. And something for your reader or audience to become invested in. And, importantly, neither character is there simply to two-dimensionally service the plot or narrative arc of the other character.

Even if a character appears only briefly on your pages, they should be fully fleshed out, with their own desires and drives (ideally at odds with your protagonist's wants – even if it's low key). If you are redrafting or editing, watch for this. Often when we are telling ourselves the story (the first draft), we don't have the creative capacity to make every secondary character who is found on the page feel authentic. Go back: fix this. If all your characters sound like actual humans, you won't just bring them to life on the page, you will bring the whole world to life. You will make your reader or audience care.

Real people also don't tend to talk in huge chunks of exposition. Okay, arguably there are some people – mansplainers, I'm giving you side-eye – who do try to do this. I don't know about you, but if I meet one of those types of talker in my life, I try to avoid them. And trust me, you don't want your reader treating your characters like people they've been trapped in the kitchen with at parties; bored out of their brain and trying to escape their dull, dry conversation. It can be tempting to use dialogue to info dump on your readers, especially if it offers a convenient way to explain plot elements, but you'll suck all the life out your writing if you do. Find another way to show narrative or character elements you need to, rather than have a character tell them. You're a writer; you're better than that.

In reality, people speak in a natural, informal way. And simply writing how you talk is a good place to start with dialogue. Write speech as if you were telling your mate down the pub, or your partner before bed, put it into realistic words.

But do differentiate between how characters talk on the page. People sound different, dependent on myriad factors including – but not limited to – where they were born and grew up, their socioeconomic class, level of education, age, gender, status within that situation, and, importantly, to whom they are talking. A word of caution, though: be wary of tropes based on regional, national or socioeconomic dialects. If you don't have lived experience of the way a particular person may speak, avoid slipping into parodies or caricatures, and make sure your character's dialogue is grounded in authentic research. Keep bringing it back to how real people talk. You may well include intimate nicknames or slang when gossiping with your closest friend, but you would never use such casual or affectionate terms with your boss. Similarly, if you're trying to convince a bank manager to give you a business loan, it's probably best not to call them 'darling' or 'bruv'. Again, we are back to the aims and motivations of each character in a scene: ask yourself to whom are they speaking, and what do they want? In an ideal world, if you removed any tell-tale attributions, you should be able to demarcate between characters on the page just by reading what they say. They should feel like singular, distinctive people.

Craft a scene

You don't need to include every single bit of dialogue a person would say in real life. As the writer, you choose when your scene starts, and when we come in as readers. You decide who speaks, what they say, and when. It's time to flex that God complex. A good writer is always controlling which way a reader, or an audience, is looking. This is artistry, as well as art. As long as a reader can comprehend what is happening, you're fine to step away from a prosaic documentation of what someone may say. Avoid the mundane beats that would occur in real life. Instead of a reoccurring cop character, who interviews and investigates multiple witnesses and suspects in a crime novel, saying, 'Hello Mrs Mins, I'm DCI Blue,' you can merely write: I introduced myself (first person). Or The DCI introduced himself (third person). As with all writing, the more you can say with the fewest words the better. If you are repeating information the reader already knows, there's no need to write it out again in full in dialogue. This is not a factual witness statement for court. In our imagined crime novel, if DCI Blue is asked to report their findings to their boss, we don't have to recap it in the dialogue for the reader. We can simply write: I updated the guv on our progress. Readers are smart. They will fill in the gaps. You don't need to remind them of something that has already happened (especially within a short space of reading time): and if you do, you run the risk of your dialogue feeling repetitive, which is turgid to wade through. Get those editing scissors out and snip off any bit of (unintentionally) clumsy chat.

Read it out loud

Once you have worked on sharpening up your dialogue, a great way to test whether it's working is to read it out loud. If an element of the speech is not how a real person would talk, chances are the words will sound strange in your mouth. Is the chat flat? Does it sound too formal? Too long? Too uninterrupted? Do your characters all sound the same? Try recording yourself speaking the dialogue on your phone and listening to it back. It's often easier to hear if the rhythm and pace is off with a piece (brains are clever things – when you are reading in your own head, they paper over the cracks on the page). Or co-opt some volunteers to read different characters' parts out loud. Listen to how they sound.

And thus, we are back at the beginning of this piece, clandestinely recording the patterns, beats and cadence of conversations taking part around us. Fundamentally, as with much writing, the kernel of crafting successful dialogue lies in our ability to listen. Hear that? It's the sound of your manuscript levelling up.

Angela Clarke is a novelist and a screenwriter. She is the author of the bestselling crime thrillers *The Anniversary Party* (Hachette 2025), *On My Life* (Hachette 2019), *Trust Me* (HarperCollins 2017), *Watch Me* (HarperCollins 2016) and *Follow Me* (HarperCollins 2015). She also wrote the humorous memoir *Confessions of a Fashionista* (Penguin Random House 2013). *Follow Me* was named Amazon's Rising Star Debut January 2016, longlisted for the Crime Writer's Association Dagger in the Library 2016, and shortlisted for the Dead Good Page Turner Award 2016. Angela is currently working on several new television developments: her screen credits as a writer include *JoJo & Gran Gran* (CBBC, series 2) and *The Break* (BBC Studios/BBC 3, series 5). A sufferer of hypermobile Ehlers-Danlos syndrome (hEDS), Angela is passionate about bringing marginalised voices into the creative industries. Follow her on Instagram @theangelaclarke.

See also...

- *Successful screenwriting*, page 362

The importance of story development

Scriptwriter and crime author Greg Mosse shares his thoughts on how story development helps shape and support his novels, drawing the reader through from prologue to epilogue and solving a mystery along the way.

Over twenty-five years ago, my wife, Kate Mosse, was beginning the research for a historical adventure novel that would finally be published to huge acclaim in 2005 with the dynamic one-word title *Labyrinth*. She wanted to share the writing process, building a community of readers – and aspiring writers – in advance of publication. I helped her create a website – mosselabyrinth.co.uk – which grew, over time, to 1,400 pages of hyperlinked webpages on history, inspiration, key locations, character studies, favourite books and more.

Back then, just before the turn of the millennium, Kate was also working with the telecoms company Orange as sponsors for the Women's Prize for Fiction. They took an interest in the *Labyrinth* online project – it was, after all, something quite unique a quarter of a century ago – and provided funds to create a 3D, online world that internet users could explore virtually. We also provided a range of inspirational story ideas and prompts, ran writing competitions and generally invited people to be part of a bigger conversation about the interlinked nature of reading and writing.

Neither Kate nor I, though, thought that the 'sharing' should end there – we didn't want it to remain in the virtual word. Reading is a tactile, physical, 'in-the-moment' experience. Even before *Labyrinth* was published, Kate spoke at an important launch event at the Institute of Contemporary Arts on the Mall and I followed it up with a series of free monthly writing workshops in the delightful plush-red ICA cinema.

I had worked as a reader and editor for several London publishers and had experience of the industry in Paris, too, alongside freelance work in international organisations and businesses as an interpreter and translator. Before that, I gained a degree in Drama and English from Goldsmiths, University of London. I read widely in three languages. But it wasn't these qualifications that made the workshops a success.

So what did? A technique for which I didn't yet have a name.

> It was a cold Wednesday in the last week of February, towards the end of the afternoon. In the West Sussex village of Framlington, a Norman church sat squat and, if truth be told, a little neglected, at the end of a narrow lane. It had no special architectural features, no historical oddities, but it had served sixty generations of local people in their weekly devotions and important life-changing ceremonies. Their births, marriages and deaths – hatch, match and despatch.
>
> Today was despatch.

These are the opening lines of chapter one of my first mystery novel, *Murder at Church Lodge* (Hodder & Stoughton 2023). I was encouraged to write it by the superb London agent Luigi Bonomi who saw me working in another workshop – just before the first lockdown in February 2020 – with aspiring writers at a festival and suggested: 'You should write cosy crime. I think you'd be good at it.' A few weeks later, I sent him 20,000 words and asked: 'Is this what you mean?'

At this time, I had, over many years, been a writer of plays and musicals and one wonderful thing about writing for the stage is the fact that you can produce your own work. You can put on your shows and people give you money for the pleasure of sitting and watching the actors 'selling' your words across the footlights. You don't have to confront the 'gatekeepers' that are necessary in big businesses. There's no acquisitions meeting that you will never witness with your own eyes, at the heart of a major conglomerate, where the fate of your typescript is decided.

Plays are not like novels and films and TV shows. You can't flit about from place to place on stage, from one moment in time to another – or, rather, you can, but you risk your show becoming very bitty, annoying and hard to follow. Plays are mostly a sequence of static scenes that drill down into character and motivation through intense dialogue. Luigi's encouragement to write a cosy crime novel gave me a joyous freedom.

That said, as a consequence of his notes – I can summarise them as: 'Yes, but ...' – I started again. The lines I've quoted above are from my reworking, more or less exactly where I began for a second time, in 1972 in my imagination and memory; at that time, I was eleven years old, living in poverty in a sad village in southwest Sussex, experiencing strikes and power cuts and dismal English food. But it wasn't the eleven-year-old me at the heart of the mystery:

> Maisie Cooper went ahead and took up a position by the lychgate. At five-foot-eight, she had a slim figure, short curly hair, good complexion, large brown eyes, and was dressed in her light-blue travelling clothes because her brother's death had come as a surprise.

Because *Murder at Church Lodge* is a mystery novel, it's not a spoiler to reveal that there is more to Maisie's brother's death than meets the eye. We know from the title that someone has been unlawfully killed. But, later on, when I had my first complete draft, I realised something that worried me as a dramatist. A key protagonist in *Murder at Church Lodge* was missing from the drama: the first victim, Maisie's brother Stephen.

> **Prologue**
> It was early, soon after dawn, and the kitchen at Church Lodge was bitter. The stone flagstones were so cold that Stephen could feel the ache through the worn soles of his threadbare slippers. He couldn't face another cup of black tea so he was drinking cold water, fresh from the iron tap over the enormous butler sink, using a dimpled pint pot he had 'borrowed' from the pub. There was nothing to eat but a rather dreadful dehydrated ready meal.
>
> He pulled his notebook towards him – actually a cheap school exercise book bought at Woolworth's in town. He opened it in the middle and pulled out two folded sheets, eight lined pages, wondering where to begin.

I decided that Stephen should write Maisie a letter that would go on a roundabout journey from Sussex to Paris, where she lives and works, and then back again, just in time to resolve the mystery of his last moments in the Epilogue. In that way, his voice appears both on the page and as part of the reader's imagination.

At that same precise juncture in the evolution of my novel, Luigi came up with his own excellent addition, a device that helped give shape and strength to the story. He suggested developing the intrigue of the theft of valuables from the crypt of the cathedral with:

... a sumptuously illuminated and illustrated devotional book. Created in the early sixteenth century, it was an ecclesiastical commentary on the 'seven deadly sins' and the 'seven holy virtues'.

Then, he went on, the novel could be divided into sections, each one titled with a different 'sin'. The idea worked beautifully, requiring just a few tweaks to the narrative to fit.

These techniques – bookending with a Prologue and Epilogue, titled internal sections – have become characteristics of my series. In the subsequent volumes, too – *Murder at Bunting Manor*, *Murder at the Theatre* and *Murder at Bitling Fair* – they helped to mould to my imagination while I was writing, and also supported the reader's enjoyment with a recognisable pattern.

Perhaps you've noticed that these ideas – putting Stephen on the page, introducing the devotional book – are about adding things, not criticising or taking away?

The workshop technique that I employed all those years ago at the ICA, without knowing its name, I now refer to as 'story development'. It is the foundation of the theatre script programme that I run in the West End, on stage at the Criterion Theatre. It underpinned the MA in Creative Writing that I wrote and taught, validated by the University of Sussex, and my open-access Southbank Centre Creative Writing School. It relies on a very particular mindset of positivity and growth that says, simply:

Given this interesting thing happening now, it would be great if this other compelling thing happened later, as a consequence, and even better if this third intriguing thing happened earlier to set them both up.

It sounds simple because it is. My story-development workshops teach and practise ten or 12 fundamentally productive aspects of narrative creation that the participants are usually aware of but seldom – if ever – articulate. By saying them out loud, I hope to help each writer to grow their story into a dynamic sequence of falling dominos, with a crescendo of intensity leading to a dramatic conclusion where all the narrative questions are answered.

> 'What did you say?' said Nigel Bacon.
> 'Shut up, Nigel,' said Derek. 'This is nothing to do with you.'
> 'Or is it?' said Maisie.
> This time the silence took on a completely different quality, then someone moved. Was it because they were preparing to make a break for it? Maisie thought Jack had the same idea and once more spoke with the quiet voice of authority.
> 'Stay quite still, if you please, all of you.'
> Maisie looked round. Who hadn't yet spoken? No one. It was time for the final push.

Helping Kate with the mosselabyrinth.co.uk project kickstarted a phase of life in which I have spent some time almost every day thinking about story development. The technique has transformed my 'internal critic' from a negative commentator into a demanding but supportive voice, always wanting me to find new, intricate connections of cause and effect, character and motivation.

Years ago, I worked with a novelist who, once their first draft was finally complete, unexpectedly apologised:

'I'm sorry I took so long. All the time I was writing, it felt like I was laboriously carving every word in stone.'

Miraculously, though, once they had reached 'The End', the writer became able to edit the story quickly and efficiently, making it tighter and more fluent over several drafts.

I write with a kind of tunnel vision, pausing after fifty or so pages to review what I've got: timeline; consistency of characterisation; clues; pace, and so on. I do the same after 100 pages, from the beginning, then again at 150, 200, 250, after which there's nothing left for me to put down except the way in which everything I've already set up plays out in a plausible, satisfying – but also surprising – climax.

> Maisie folded the letter and put it away, fetched her mackintosh and went outside, locking the heavy front door behind her. She crossed the road and paused outside the pub, looking in through the smoky windows at Jack and Mohammed, chatting and sharing a basket of chips by the light of a candle in a jam jar. Just then, Jack turned his head and saw her, his face softening, half rising from his chair.
>
> With a rush of pleasure, Maisie pushed open the door and went inside.

I write because I enjoy writing. That's important because, when I show my second draft to the genius I married, Kate Mosse, and she tells me positive ways to make it better, that needs to be a blessing not a curse. Ditto when I show draft three to Luigi. Ditto when I show draft four to my editor. Ditto when the copy-editor finds useful tweaks in draft five.

I am very lucky to do what I do, so I take every opportunity I am offered to promote the story-development method in workshops at every festival I am invited to attend. Whatever you are writing – cosy crime, historical, romance, adventure, literary or even thrillers like my 2037 cli-fi trilogy *The Coming Darkness* – I hope to meet you at one of them, soon.

Greg Mosse is a 'writer and encourager of writers' with twenty-five plays and musicals on his CV. Founder and leader of the Criterion New Writing script-development programme in London's West End, he is the author of an ongoing series of cosy crime novels, *The Maisie Cooper Mysteries* published by Hodder, and a trilogy of future cli-fi thrillers, *The Coming Darkness*, *The Coming Storm* and *The Coming Fire* (Moonflower Publishing).

See also...

- *How to write for the theatre*, page 408

The art and craft of literary translation

Jianan Qian sheds light on the challenges and intricacies of literary translation, sharing her experience and valuable advice for would-be translators on how to get started, hone your skills and get your translated works published.

Perhaps you may think that, since your Italian is good enough to get you around coffee shops and grocery stores, you could perhaps try translating some Italian poems or short stories into English. You are not alone in displaying such misplaced confidence. So before you do anything hasty, let's take a closer look at the concept of literary translation.

What is literary translation?

How do you translate 'in bocca al lupo', the Italian idiom that literally means 'in the mouth of the wolf'? The phrase originates from a theatre setting and is used to wish a performer good luck before a performance. So that's easy – you immediately come up with its English equivalent, 'break a leg'. Now let me add a bit of context: someone says 'in bocca al lupo' to his classmate before a school exam. Would you still translate it as 'break a leg'? In that case Italians might respond with that strange expression 'crepi il lupo', literally 'the wolf shall die', and you may find a perfect alternative – 'knock em' dead' or (in the USA) 'kick the exam's ass'. Very good. And now let's add even more to the previous context. In the story, it is an Italian student who uses that phrase to wish a Chinese international student good luck before an exam, and the latter doesn't seem to understand the idiom. Would you still translate the phrase as 'knock em' dead'? I would either retain the expression in Italian or use its literal translation 'in the mouth of the wolf' if the Chinese student understands what every Italian word means.

Perhaps this gives you a sense of where I am headed. Literary translation is more than Google translation plus human editing. Because every language functions differently, one of our biggest challenges as literary translators is to create something in the target language that will evoke similar feelings in the reader as the original but without deviating too far away. Then again, we translators have to carefully define what we mean by 'similar' and 'too far' in every individual case. Tone, atmosphere, character, humour, irony, metaphor and rhythm must all stay in our minds as we chew over every word choice.

If you speak a language other than English, try translating the famous opening of Shakespeare's *Richard III* – 'Now is the winter of our discontent/ Made glorious summer by this sun of York' – into that language. How would you manage to retain the political connotations within its simple and yet powerful syntax? If you are already attempting to solve any of these puzzles, welcome to our rabbit hole.

Getting started

This first glimpse into literary translation may make you wonder whether it's necessary to be an expert in both the source and target languages to translate. Ideally, a literary translator demonstrates a deep knowledge of the languages and cultures on both sides. If you deal with a more complicated text – such as Dante Alighieri's *Divine Comedy* from the 15th century or Cao Xueqin's *Dream of the Red Chamber* from the 18th century – additional knowledge is a must .

But there are practical solutions too. You can work with a co-translator if you feel the need to. In today's English-speaking world, Richard Pevear and Larissa Volokhonsky are perhaps the best-known collaborative literary translators, whose translations of Tolstoy, Dostoevsky, Chekhov and Gogol have won numerous awards and recognitions. Volokhonsky is a native speaker of Russian, whereas Pevear, a native English speaker, does not read Russian. Usually, that is how collaborative translation works. The native speaker of the source language closely studies the original text and attempts a first draft marked with her notes of the author's literary style. The English speaker then edits the draft, weighing every change with the co-translator to make sure their rendition stays true to the original and also connects to the English-speaking audience. While translating contemporary Chinese author Zhu Yue's story collections into English, I also work with a wonderful co-translator, Alyssa Asquith. Alyssa is not only a native English speaker but also a fabulous fantasy writer. Like the famous Argentine author Jorge Louis Borges, Zhu Yue mixes the real and the fantastic, fact with fiction. Working collaboratively, Alyssa and I are able to render the stories of Zhu Yue's mind-blowing stories vividly on the page. Then again, the majority of literary translators work solo and, in that case, maintaining a humble mind and doing lots of research are key to keeping mistakes in check.

Selecting your work

What to translate? Normally we don't jump into translating foreign literature overnight. Perhaps when studying Korean at university you read Ae-ran Kim's stories for a class and have been in love with them ever since? Maybe you attended a reading of another literary translator from the same language who mentioned the names of the most important literary journals in that language? The bottom line is that you must translate something that you genuinely enjoy reading. Then you can use the internet to check whether the piece or book has been previously translated. If it hasn't, find the contacts of the author to ask for permission. Some authors have their own Facebook pages or websites, others can be reached through the universities they work at or the journals they have published their works in. It's necessary to ask the authors to sign an agreement that allows you to translate and submit the works to the publishers. If you are new in your career, ask for permission to translate a single story/poem/essay first. Win trust through your good work and then your dream authors will be delighted to work with you.

As a general practice, literary works enter the public domain 70 years after the death of their authors. In that case, you do not need permission from the author or the agent. But keep in mind that many of those authors have had previous translations published. If you want to do a new translation, make sure you can persuade the publisher why your version is going to be better. You learn and grow as you translate. But it is always a good idea to prepare yourself with some handy techniques, such as how to sneak in necessary cultural contexts without complicating the sentences. Several schools offer literary translation classes; these two institutions, in particular, come with stellar recommendations:

- University of East Anglia, MA Literary Translation (www.uea.ac.uk/course/postgraduate/ma-literary-translation)
- University of Iowa, MFA in Literary Translation (https://translation.uiowa.edu/; Iowa's program is fully funded, if money is a concern.)

I took translation classes at Iowa while doing an MFA in fiction there. Each of the students in the class worked from a different language. As a group, we started with the English translation and discussed the translation issues that we spotted on the page (for example, where the diction was not consistent or an expression seemed to be confusing). The translator was invited to explain the problems she had met and, in talking about how to solve those specific issues, the professor taught us both useful techniques and fundamental principles in literary translation. Taking translation classes at Iowa was a life-changing experience for me.

One particularly helpful way of learning translation skills is to study good translations vis-à-vis the original text. I pored over every small change Ken Liu makes in translating the 2016 Hugo Prize-winning story *Folding Beijing* from Chinese to English. His every choice – breaking paragraphs, converting indirect speeches to direct quotations in certain cases, clarifying the physical spaces – taught me something important.

After translation

Congratulations – you have finished the translation and revised the manuscript. But your job is not done yet. Unless you are hired by the author only to produce the translation, you must get your translated works published. Submission can be overwhelming – you will face a lot of rejection before you make things happen. But here is a wonderful tip I have received from a fiction classmate: devote half a day every week to submit your works. Try starting with the journals where your favourite authors first published their works. Although not all literary journals accept translation, it never hurts to try. Chances are that most journals accept translation, so long as the stories/poems are good. Some of the best journals that are dedicated to translations include:

- *Asymptote* (www.asymptotejournal.com)
- *Exchanges* (https://exchanges.uiowa.edu)
- *Samovar* (http://samovar.strangehorizons.com)
- *Two Lines* (www.catranslation.org/journal/#display-tile)

When you have your entire manuscript ready, then it is time to contact publishers. Translators usually find that independent presses, such as New Directions, Archipelago Books, Open Letter Books, And Other Stories and Action Books, are more friendly. Different presses have different reading times. You may want to bookmark their websites and revisit them frequently.

Making a living

Another rule of thumb is always to keep your day job. Literary authors are not well paid, and translators even worse. Besides, it is a fact that the English-speaking world does not read much literature in translation, which means the market can be small. In recent years, however, things are slowly but surely changing. The Booker Prize launched its first International Prize, for literature in translation (see page 586) in 2016, when Korean author Han Kang and her English translator Deborah Smith shared the £50,000 award. In the USA, literary translators can apply for fellowships such as the National Endowment for the Arts and PEN/Heim Translation Fund. Note: those fellowships are very competitive. The American Literary Translators Association (ALTA; https://literarytranslators.org) is arguably the largest professional community for literary translators in the USA; you should definitely check out their conferences and mentorship programs. Translators across the world also exchange information and ideas in this Facebook group: Literary Translation (www.facebook.com/groups/351836658289669).

It is very rare for translators to get royalties (except for the books in the public domain), but you must make sure you get paid for the published book. Sadly, it is still a norm that some books do not even include the translator's name on their covers. You must fight for the credit that you deserve. Money talk can be depressing for literary translators, but there is light at the end of the tunnel. More and more universities around the globe are launching literary translation programs, which means more teaching jobs. Writers may experience writers' block, but translators do not. Translators never run out of books that they can't wait to share with a bigger audience.

Literary translation also pays off in different ways. As Italian author Elena Ferrante writes (via translator Ann Goldstein) in I*ncidental Inventions* (Europa 2019), 'My only heroes are translators. [...] Translators transport nations into other nations. They are the first to reckon with distant modes of feelings. Even their mistakes are evidence of a positive force. Translation is our salvation. It draws us out of the well in which, entirely by chance, we are born.' Ferrante's words deeply resonate with me. Translation teaches me that sometimes I have to move away so I can get closer. The most beautiful souls I have ever met in my life are mostly literary translators. They are altruistic, compassionate, knowledgeable and deeply curious. Whenever I find myself inundated with disturbing news, and feeling hopeless about the future, their friendship inspires and guides me, reminding me of the best of humanity.

Jianan Qian is a writer and translator. She has published four books in her native language Chinese, with her latest essay collection, *A Future that I Do Not Want to Have* listed by Douban as Top 10 Chinese non-fiction in 2019. In English, her works have appeared in the *New York Times*, *Granta*, the *O. Henry Prize Stories* and elsewhere. She has translated five books from English to Chinese, the latest being a story collection by Shirley Jackson. Her English translations with co-translator Alyssa Asquith of Chinese author Zhu Yue's stories have widely appeared in American journals such as the *Washington Square Review*, the *Portland Review* and *Margins*.

Ghosting: writing other people's stories

Behind many big sellers is ... a great ghostwriter. In this article, Gillian Stern explains how she became a ghostwriter, shining a light on the practicalities and pitfalls of the role along the way.

Make no mistake: ghostwriters fuel the publishing industry. We are the best-kept secret that is no secret, especially since J.R. Moehringer stepped into the limelight in a brilliant article, 'Notes from Prince Harry's ghostwriter' (*The New Yorker*, 8 May 2023), that allowed ghostwriters to emerge from the publishing underworld and enjoy a brief moment of collective recognition. Yes, I thought. That's what I do. That's how I feel and yes, yes, that's exactly how it works.

We all know that there are books out there – many of them bestselling – by authors who are well known for their particular skill or place in society, that they could never have created without considerable input from someone who can write. And – again – make no mistake, this is often not because the famous person has insisted they write their memoir, but because publishers have seen a place in the market for their book and have then needed someone who can write, to write it.

There's nothing wrong with this. I have ghosted for people who are at the very top of their tree, world-famous and celebrated; and I have ghosted books for unknown people with extraordinary stories. What they all have in common is that none of them is skilled in the art of writing a book. Why should they be? They've been busy leading their book-worthy lives. And just in case you think they aren't, every single person I have ghosted for has been humble about putting a book out there – excited, cooperative, available (give or take) and intensely grateful. And it's for this reason, that I refer to them, with no problem at all, as the author.

I am often asked how I became a ghostwriter and I am more often asked when I am going to write my own book. I started my professional life in academic publishing before moving over to the commercial side of things, becoming a structural editor of fiction and non-fiction. It was when a publisher handed me a tortuously wooden manuscript by someone extremely famous (signing non-disclosure agreements means I am not allowed to disclose who I am ghosting before, during and after) and asked me to edit it and I handed it back, saying I absolutely couldn't, that I saw a different way forward. I offered to spend time with the extremely famous person to re-work the material, set the original script aside and re-wrote it. This memoir went on to become a *Sunday Times* bestseller, and I was officially a ghostwriter.

I guess I am what you might call a reactive ghostwriter, in that I am generally commissioned to write, having been approached by an agent or publisher. I will be invited to meet with the author, to see how well we fit together. I have walked into some interviews and there has been no connection or, as the interview has progressed, it's become clear that our outlooks are too different; and I have walked into others and known instantly that this is going to work. Not that this means I am going to get the job, as the author needs to feel it too. And like them, I need to be careful about what I accept. I am going to be spending a great deal of time with them, investing emotionally in them, burying myself in the process, and so I write someone's story only if I can imagine myself into their voice, into being them.

I have, from time to time, been more proactive, coming across an interesting story, or in one case, following someone on X because I liked their daily posting and then contacting him to ask if he was interested in writing a book. When he replied telling me no, but come and have tea, and here's a memory stick (yes, back in the day) containing over 475,000 words of journal entries spanning twenty or so years, I set to work, drafting a proposal, finding him an agent and the rest – how I wish I could tell you who this is – is a massive chart-topping success.

Talking of which – no clues, obviously – the question of ghostwriting novels is one that can present challenges to some, readers and ghostwriters alike. I have once helped a celebrity rewrite her novel but she had had a very good go at it first – the plot, characters and sensibility were all pretty impressive for a debut novelist – and my role was more like a structural editor, with a bit of rewriting. To me, that was ok – really just a little more input than I give for most novelists I edit. However, when I have been asked by publishers to ghostwrite a novel for a celebrity from scratch, I have declined. There's something straightforward about helping write their memoir or their factual story, for reasons mentioned above, but as I come across so many talented novelists who can't get their novels published, I have an issue with a celebrity somehow jumping that queue simply because they are famous and then not actually writing the novel. Also, if I could write a novel, I would write my own.

Broadly, to be a ghostwriter, you need to:

- Tuck yourself away. First and foremost, you need to park any ego you might have. This is not about you, however seductive the intimacy of the process may suggest. And believe me, when those WhatsApps come pinging in, the author, the great star, loved by millions, disclosing information 'no one else in the word knows', it's tempting to come back with yours. But, when you are sitting with them and they are revealing their greatest disappointments, their deepest passions, you do not come back with yours, however exciting you may want to appear. I look back in horror at the transcripts of one of my first jobs in which I had limited time with this world-class sportsman and I spoke more than he did, even though I had never even played his sport. He was so charming and so charismatic, that I must have thought: he wants to know all about me, this is about both of us. He didn't. It wasn't. Remember: it's all about them.
- Listen. Once you accept a job, and if a body of material such as broadcasts, diaries, letters etc. exists, you need to listen, watch and read as much as you can. I tape interviews and as I settle into the job, I stick in my headphones at any opportunity and listen. This I enjoy, hearing how they talk, taking in the words they use, their favourite expressions, the timbre of their voice.
- Zip yourself in. And when you can hear them, you need to become them, inhabiting them. You need to see the world around them, the world inside them, from their point of view. It's a strange intimacy, becoming them, and it always takes a while but when I get there, I know the book is going to sing.
- Be empathetic and non-judgmental. I have had authors tell me things that are intensely personal, things that may not end up hitting the page. Equally, I have had authors tell me

things that I would never do or say or think, but it's not my place to judge and so I have taught myself not to.

• Be trustworthy. It's beyond tempting to talk about things you and the author discuss. If I sign an NDA, I always ask if it's ok I tell my family that I am working with the author and, while I have learned not to betray the author's trust, it helps that I can at least talk broadly at home about my work.

• Be robust. I have written elsewhere about the lack of pastoral care for ghostwriters from agents and publishers. As ghostwriters, we are often exposed to trauma or difficulties the author has experienced and the emotional toll on us can be overwhelming. We are not trained therapists, we can't talk to anyone about what we are experiencing and yet there is no industry support for us. I have worked with publishers who do ask how I am doing, but to be honest, most of the interaction with them is about delivery deadlines. I recommend swimming, and you too will need to find a way of discharging your emotions.

• Write well, and true. As tempting as it can be, do not insert yourself into what goes on the page. Be as true to the author as you can possibly be. Accept any changes and suggestions they make with good grace. It's their book.

• Remain calm and collected. When you hand the manuscript over to the publisher, you are more or less toast. Ghosts exist in this sort of murky world of acceptance and denial – totally necessary to get the book written but then cast aside once we have delivered. And while this is understandable – we aren't publishers – I try and mark the moment of delivery with some sort of treat or celebration. Later, when the author is all over the TV talking about how they wrote their book, turn it off. They will never mention you. You know they can't mention you. But you don't want to be there for that.

• Know when it is time to move on. Of course, your relationship with the author cannot be cast aside as easily as the publishers cast you aside. I have formed many (appropriately) intimate connections and both of us have suffered from separation anxiety. After all, you've pretty much been their (untrained) therapist and you will have been a part of their life, let in to this thrilling confidence that can make you feel special and chosen. But there comes a moment when you know it's time to move on. The WhatsApps reduce, the need to be in touch lessens and the book comes out and it's over. You are not friends – it's been a transactional relationship – and will never recover that thrilling intensity. Get over it and move on to the next exciting job.

At its core, being a ghostwriter is a terrific job and if you can get a good gig, go for it. If you aren't already a journalist, or have ties to the publishing industry, my advice would be to:

• Keep up-to-date with what sort of books are selling by looking at industry trends and what publishers are looking for.

• Read a lot and decide what you think makes a compelling memoir or story.

• Write, feeling your way in to someone's life. Maybe take someone near to you and write a piece in their voice, focusing in on an incident that brings them fully alive on the page. Or, look at the life of someone you admire and imagine yourself writing a piece from their point of view. Practise tucking yourself away and inhabiting them.

• Go to book events, visit bookshops regularly to ask what is selling. Booksellers are a great source of information about what readers are reading and that they might want to see on the shelves in the future. Go on social media and see who's influencing what.

• School yourself in how to write an outline. There are resources online to help, so practise writing them, including a rationale for the book, a brief summary of chapters and some sample writing.
• Be open and flexible. If you approach someone or they approach you, and their story is interesting but they can't pay you, if you are in a position to be able to work with them, do so. You can always, later down the line, agree that you will recoup that part of your fee once a book deal is done.
• Ask for advice. The Ghostwriting Agency (www.theghostwritersagency.com) or United Ghostwriters (www.unitedghostwriters.co.uk) are good places to start.

And just to be clear, I am not a frustrated writer who can't get my 'own' books published. I have no aspirations to write a novel and I do not have an interesting enough life for a memoir. I have no desire to see my name on the front of a book when the story belongs to someone else. I just get this intense buzz and satisfaction from bringing interesting stories to life, in capturing someone else's voice so convincingly, they hear themselves come off the page. I like being mired in the messy complexities of others, and ghostwriting definitely delivers on that front.

Gillian Stern has ghostwritten several bestselling memoirs, some of which have gone on to win awards or be adapted for the stage. She combines this with her work as a structural editor for fiction and non-fiction for many leading agents and publishers. She is known for her passion for discovering and supporting debut novelists. Gillian has been a judge for The Lucy Cavendish Fiction Prize and Nero Book Awards. Contact her at gillybethstern@hotmail.com or follow her on X @gillybethstern.

Writing for different genres

Writing thrilling fiction

Bestselling author Paula Hawkins explores the essential elements and creative process involved in the art of thriller-writing, revealing some of the key tools inside 'the crime novelist's box of tricks', and has valuable, practical tips and encouragement for aspiring crime writers.

Where to begin? With a concept, maybe? There are zombies on this runaway train! Or perhaps a devastating opening line: 'Once the queen's head is severed, he walks away'.[1] Some novelists begin at the end and work backwards, reverse-engineering their plots so that events flow neatly and inexorably to the end they started from. Others talk about beginning with a single image for which they have no context whatsoever, only the strong sense that they *must* write about it. A novel can begin anywhere.

This is how it starts for me: someone is telling a story, about something that happened to them, or to someone they know. It's usually something terrible or tragic or frightening, and I find myself grasping at some small detail of this story, latching onto it, turning it over in my mind, examining it from different angles, wondering: but *then what*? What became of the person at the heart of that terrible story? *Who* did they become?

Character

My stories start with character. But characters don't arrive in the imagination fully formed; they start off as one peculiar characteristic, one particular trait. To use an obvious example, I might know that this character drinks too much – so much, in fact, that she can't remember what she did last night, or with whom. Immediately you begin thinking about a person like that, questions arise: why is she like this? What happened to her? Did her drinking become problematic gradually, or was there one major trigger? And what does it mean for her day to day? How does she cope? Does she cope? Do her friends help her, or have they tired of her now? And what of her sense of self?

Now we're getting somewhere. But in order to really get somewhere, we need to go somewhere. What I mean by that is a character isn't enough: I need something else, some other element, to get her moving. It's usually a location: a commuter train, say, trundling through suburbia. Or a cold, black river winding its way through a village, or a neglected houseboat, half-sinking into the sludgy waters of a London canal. A character on her own is an intriguing idea, but a character plus a location is the beginning of a story.

I believe quite strongly that there are no right or wrong ways to write crime novels (or indeed any kind of novel). Moreover, I sometimes think that following too slavishly the advice of others can hinder more than it helps. But I also believe there are certain elements which are essential to a thrilling psychological suspense novel, and right up at or near the top of the list is a compelling character – hopefully, a whole cast of compelling characters. I like to write about outsiders, about people who don't quite fit. They aren't doing as they're told, they're failing somehow to live up to expectations, they struggle. They're rarely *good*, but they aren't bad either. They are frequently frustrating – indeed they are often labelled 'unlikable'. I don't care about that. I don't expect readers of crime fiction to come to my novels to make friends. What I want is for them to find people who are psychologically true, people whose actions – however ill-advised – make sense in context. So, let's

[1] *The Mirror and the Light*, Hilary Mantel (Fourth Estate 2020)

say, in the context of this particular woman's day or week or life. We know why Rachel drinks. If we were Rachel, we might drink too.

Voice

What *you* find compelling in a protagonist might be quite different: you might focus on humour, or a good heart, someone a reader will fall in love with. You need to find characters who chime with your own unique voice.

You also need to find the characters' voices; maybe try writing them from various perspectives, to see what feels most comfortable. At times I have started off in third person and found myself, almost without noticing, switching to first. If you do that, take notice. You may not want to switch points of view, but you might want to move *closer* to a different point of view if the character demands it. First-person narratives have their detractors – and they are perhaps overused in a certain sort of psychological thriller – but there is no denying their immediacy or the fierce attraction of allowing your readers direct access to your central character's deepest, darkest, most discomforting, strange, horrifying, funny or moving thoughts and feelings. What first-person narration lacks, of course, is distance. And that can be a problem for the thriller writer. If the reader has access to a character's every thought and feeling, then there is no place to hide. And hiding things – concealing by sleight of hand certain pertinent facts – is a key tool in the crime novelist's box of tricks.

Structure

If character is the aspect of a story readers consciously cling to – the one they most clearly remember – then structure has a more subtle effect, yet it is key to what makes the experience of reading a novel satisfying. Do you need to use flashbacks, or separate out timelines? Is the narrative divided into sections, and what is the effect of this? I want to achieve a moment when it dawns upon the reader that the story is being told in this way for a very particular reason – a moment of realisation that should make them sit back and smile and think, 'Oh, I see. This is where she's taking me.'

A strong structure is invaluable to a writer: it will help you through your story; you will start to know what needs to come next, what to reveal next, because it will fit into the framework you've been building. It becomes your guide, too. There's no handbook for this, no template. Every novel is different, and each has its own requirements. For me, finding the right way to tell a story is often the trickiest bit of the writing process. In *The Girl on the Train* (Doubleday 2015), I had the gift of the commute – the perfect vehicle to give the early part of the novel a rhythm. As Rachel travelled back and forth every morning and every evening, I invited the reader onto the train to sit with her, and within a page or two they knew exactly where they were: sitting in a train carriage, running through the grubby outskirts of London, looking out of the window.

The construction of *A Slow Fire Burning* (Penguin 2022) felt quite different. I imagined the crime at the heart of this novel having the effect of a stone thrown into water, causing a ripple effect, and I tried to recreate that effect in some ways in how I told the story – in the way the characters were introduced and how they encountered each other. But it is notable that this ripple effect idea was not something I thought about at the beginning of the writing process. When I wrote the early scenes, I had no idea what the novel would end up looking like. I think it's rarely possible to visualise the shape of your novel at its outset. But whether you are a writer who plots out each chapter in detail, the sort who starts out with no idea whatsoever where they are going, or you're somewhere in between, the likelihood is that at some point during the process (for me it's generally around half way to two-thirds through) you will have to draw up some sort of schematic to help with that visualisation.

This might be as simple as a list of key points in a Word document; it might be a complicated hunt-the-serial-killer style board, complete with bits of string and photographs. When you stand back and look at this plan, it should help you notice patterns in your story, gauge the shape of your characters' arcs, and spot any imbalances there might be. Are there periods where the pace slackens? Are there sections where there is perhaps too much action? Sometimes you need to pause for a moment, allow the reader to take a breath. If your subject matter is very dark, you might want to allow some light in.

As I mentioned above, some people are planners and others are not; I think most of us are somewhere in between. Even if you are a plotter, my advice would be to leave plenty of room for manoeuvre, especially in early drafts. Give yourself space for surprises. I have always found that the best, most exciting, most joyful writing happens when I am in the thick of a novel, when my mind starts to make connections I hadn't conceived of at the outset, when twists and turns start to occur to me in a way they had not before, when suddenly the way ahead is clear and I start to understand more fully what the novel is really about. Don't plot so tightly that you do not allow yourself the freedom and excitement of a spontaneous twist in the road.

Twisting

Twists, while we're on the subject, can be overdone. Often what people describe as twists are not twists at all – they are simply shocking revelations thrown into the final third of a novel. Such revelations may have their place, but a real twist is more than just a surprise; a twist wrongfoots you; it makes you gasp and sit up and re-evaluate everything you have read up unto that point. Gillian Flynn did it in *Gone Girl* (Crown Publishing 2012), Ian McEwan did it in *Atonement* (Jonathan Cape 2001), Louise Doughty managed a killer twist on the very last page of *Apple Tree Yard* (Faber & Faber 2014). Good twists are earned: they will surprise you, but as a reader you will also have the sense that, had you been paying very careful attention, you might have been able to see this coming. A twist is not a bolt from the blue, it is a filter which changes the complexion of everything that has gone before.

A few other tips:

• **Share your work** when you're starting out – not with everyone, just with one or two select readers who share your taste in books. It's daunting to show your writing to anyone in the early stages, but I urge you to do so. Be sure to avoid what happened to me: I never progressed because I didn't seek feedback. I had no idea whether people would engage with the characters I was writing or whether they found my story intriguing – because I didn't ask. This meant that the only voice I had to listen to was the one in my head, telling me that this was no good, that it wasn't working. So I would give up on the work in progress and move on to the next: write, doubt, abandon, repeat.

• **Treat writing like a job** (even if it's not your job). There may be people who can afford to search for the ideal writer's room, who have the luxury of lounging about, waiting for the muse to appear, but I don't think many of them are working novelists. If you are serious about finishing a novel, you have to find a way to carve out time in your day (or at least your week) to write regularly. I know it's easy for a childless full-time novelist to say that, but it is the truth as I see it. Writing a novel is hard work and it takes a long time: there are no hacks and no shortcuts; it's a slog. It is also rewarding – rarely financially, admittedly, but creatively it can be enormously so.

• **Learn from the best.** By that I mean learn from what you think is best, what you love. Think for a moment about how painters learn to paint: they study the work of painters they admire, they copy it, they scrutinize it – and not just the effect but the paint itself, the brushstrokes on the canvas. Think about why you love your favourite novelists; what is it about their sentences that attracts you?

• **Beware word counts.** Writing 2,000 words a day might work for some writers, but it won't work for them all the time. A high word-count target can look dispiriting if you are struggling through a difficult point in your book. Give yourself a different goal – say, five sentences. Not five average sentences, but five brilliantly crafted sentences, the ones that bring a smile to your face when you're editing. Then maybe tomorrow you'll write 2,000 words…

• **Find your creative place** – the place where you feel most energized, where you fizz with ideas. It might be an actual place, or a time of day, or a particular group of people, or one like-minded friend. Where are you when you have your best ideas? Who are you with? What makes you feel inspired? Keep returning to that place; keep mining it for more.

• **Stay faithful to the stories in your head.** Don't allow yourself to be swayed by fashion, because fashions can change from month to month, while writing and publishing a book takes years. Big success stories, like *The Girl on the Train*, are often born out of a kind of alchemy – a combination of the right book at the right time, the right agent, editor, publisher, the right marketing strategy. Most of those things you cannot control, so focus on the things you can: your characters and your plot and your sentences on the page.

Good luck!

Paula Hawkins worked as a journalist for 15 years before she started writing fiction. She is the author of international bestseller *The Girl on the Train* (Doubleday 2015), which has sold 23 million copies worldwide and has been adapted into a major motion picture. *The Girl on the Train*, *Into the Water* (Doubleday 2018) and *A Slow Fire Burning* (Doubleday, 2021) were *Sunday Times* and *New York Times* Number one bestsellers. Paula's most recent novel, *The Blue Hour*, was published in October 2024 and was a *Sunday Times* bestseller. Paula was born in Zimbabwe and now splits her time between London and Edinburgh. For more information see http://paulahawkinsbooks.com. Follow her on Instagram @paulahawkins2010.

Ever wanted to write a saga?

Bestselling author Di Redmond (aka Daisy Styles) outlines the key elements required for a successful saga, and shares her insights into the market, character and demands of this popular genre.

Be prepared for the long haul!

A saga, by definition, is a genre of literature which chronicles the life of a family, interconnecting dramatic events over a long period of time – think *The Crown*, *The Archers* and *Coronation Street*. The saga as an art form is as old as the Norse myths, but more recently writers like Jeffrey Archer, Maeve Binchy, Danielle Steele, Anne Tyler and Catherine Cookson (to name but a few) have put them firmly at the top of the bestseller list. The key ingredients of any successful saga are: background content (e.g. the Napoleonic Wars, the Victorians, the Second World War); the pace of the writing; the accuracy to historical detail; and the strength of the core characters who hold the entire structure tightly together.

A series can run from two to six books, with each book usually having a word count of 100,000 words, roughly 40 chapters, and with a swift turnaround from the end of one book to the start of the next. The public appetite for sagas is surprisingly voracious … I know this for certain from my 'Daisy Styles' Facebook page (I had to take Daisy Styles as a nom de plume, since my real name – I'm proud to say – is often associated with writing *Bob the Builder*!). People who buy sagas (mostly women) regularly treat themselves to a new paperback whilst doing their weekly shop in any of the big supermarkets – Tesco, Asda, Sainsburys, Morrisons. They sell cheaply – usually on offer at two for £7 – thereby undercutting regular bookshop prices. With a short shelf life of about 12 weeks, the books have their popularity ratings flagged up beside the titles; these are based on the success of their sales figures and run from Number one bestseller to Number 20. Believe me, these books virtually fly off the shelf! As they sell, their numbers are regularly topped up until a batch of newly published sagas arrive, immediately replacing the previous batch; it's a case of 'out with the old and in with the new' – a never-ending cycle.

Sagas follow a seasonal pattern; mine covered *Bomb Girl Brides* (Penguin 2018) and *Christmas with the Bomb Girls* (Penguin 2017), but for other seasons the sagas might have covered springtime and rationing, or summertime and evacuees. Saga readers are a dedicated fan base – hence the ever-hungry market – and their loyalty and dedication is such that they each build up their own personal library of favourite authors, and (touchingly) they're hot on ordering the next saga – the very one the author is in the process of writing – well in advance on Amazon. They also like to keep in touch with their saga author on Facebook, relishing details of work in progress, deadlines, edits, research and travel related to the forthcoming book. It's almost as if you were having a baby!

A fan base can also be very exacting; get a fact wrong, such as confusing Prime Minister Chamberlain's Second World War timeline with Prime Minister Churchill's, and you'll know about it. As they respect you, they in turn expect you to respect the territory – which is where research comes in …

The research

When I launched into my saga-writing career, I spent more time researching the period than I did writing the book. I had to back up almost every paragraph I wrote with hard facts and it nearly drove me crazy. Was I writing a history text or a novel? With the plotline rapidly unfolding in my head, and my fabulous characters champing at the bit, I was as eager to get cracking as they were, but I felt thwarted at every turn. I was constantly checking and re-checking references in my mounting pile of history books and endlessly on a search engine. When it came to googling 'how to build a bomb' for a spy plotline, a good friend advised me to always insert a date – 1941 or 1944 for example – otherwise I would have a Special Branch officer knocking on my front door!

After decorating my study walls with a printout of Second World War's timeline, I decided I was going to go for it – otherwise I would never meet my deadline. Though I was nervous, I told myself that wherever I felt uncertain about a date I would leave a blank and address the problem at the end of the working day, rather than spend the entire working day thumbing through history books. I'm happy to say, it worked. As the story unrolled and my fabulous *Bomb Girls* stepped out of the woodwork, I became more and more familiar with the dreaded timeline. At the drop of a hat I could have told you when the Canadians joined the war ('God love 'em', as the nation chorused), when the Yanks bombed Pearl Harbor, how to slaughter a pig, build an air-raid shelter, read Morse code, and the price of nylons on the black market. The moral of the story is not to get bogged down by facts, which I know are very important and must be respected, but there has to come a point when you have to let the writing flow, secure in the knowledge that if you make a mistake you can go back and rectify it later.

The setting

Once you've got your timeframe, you have to establish exactly where your saga will be played out. When I was asked by my agent if I might be interested in writing a saga series, my mind immediately flew to Lancashire where I was brought up and where, as a child, I rambled for miles across the moors – sometimes coming across a crumbling ruin of a mill which locals told me had been a munitions factory. During wartime the locations of these sites were kept top secret, for fear of spies reporting their whereabouts to the Luftwaffe who would unquestionably bomb both the site and the workers to kingdom come. I'd considered writing about land girls, nurses on the front line, WRNS, Special Ops, Women's Auxiliary Air Force (WAAF) and the Auxiliary Territorial Services (ATS), but memories of that dark ruin defined my choice – I'd write about conscripted women building bombs in a former cotton mill on Pendle Moor.

The core characters

It's vital that your core group of characters can pack a punch! My *Bomb Girls* were all very different characters; the lead girl was savvy and a brilliant cook, the second shy and bookish, the third poor and bullied and the fourth sexy and a bit of a comedian, whilst the fifth girl was posh. Though vastly different in every respect, they complemented each other in rather surprising and unexpected ways, stirring up plots and complications because of their intrinsic differences. Conscription was a great leveller, bringing together the rich and the poor, forcing them to live under the same roof whether they liked it or not. Poor girls, used to an outside privy and an old water pump, couldn't believe the luxury of having hot and cold running water in their domestic lodgings and a flush toilet too, whilst the rich girls were appalled at the thought of sharing a bathroom and queueing for the toilet.

In my enthusiasm I went for five women and thereby created a problem for myself; not that the women were a problem – all of them were fantastic to write for – but five characters going off in different directions is just too many to juggle. My advice is to keep your core group down to three or four; it's a more manageable number, especially as the characters develop and become stronger than you originally anticipated (a little mouse of a girl can grow into a lion when she's building bombs to fight Hitler!). The environment in which these women worked round-the-clock shifts fed them propaganda that didn't just strengthen their muscles to do the gruelling hard work, but strengthened their mindset too. The women who entered the factory at the start of the war had changed into very different women by the time they left at the end.

Location, location ...

The setting for saga-based novels is important for both the reader and the writer. Big old industrial towns like Glasgow, Manchester, Liverpool, Leeds, Sheffield, Bristol and Birmingham bring their own history – cotton and woollen mills, docks, steelworks, shipyards and harbours. Added to which, there's a war raging, bombs are falling, men dying, telegrams arriving, sweethearts grieving, and innocent children being evacuated. It's drama upon drama; at the heart of any saga there are irrefutable facts. In every reader's family there will be someone who lived through the war and has a story to tell – a true and cherished story which they are proud to pass on to the next generation.

When it came to writing *The Wartime Midwives* (Penguin 2019), my love of the Lake District lured me further north; on visiting Grange-over-Sands, Cartmel, Kendal and the whole breathtaking sweep of Morecambe Bay and the Irish Sea I knew that it was the perfect place to set a secluded mother and baby home. For *Engine Girls*, I chose Nottingham for my location, close to Derby and the industrial Midlands it's an area where many iconic wartime aircraft were built by conscripted women during World War Two.

A word of warning

Although Catherine Cookson – queen of the saga – made a fortune from her books, it would be insincere of me to suggest you're going to get rich from this genre. You will get royalties when you've paid off your publisher's advance, but the royalty payment depends on how big your sales are and if the book goes to a reprint. The plus side is that sagas don't stop with one publication; the demand will grow, and so will your fan base, as your books become a regular feature on the supermarket shelves.

If you have an agent, approach them with an outline of your characters, location and an exact timeframe (be warned – taking on the entire six years of the war is huge, so focus on a section of the Second World War you want to work around, such as after Dunkirk, before Pearl Harbor, or during the Blitz). Your agent may ask you to write three sample chapters and then present to a number of publishers known to be on the lookout for a new saga series. If you haven't got an agent, you should do extensive research on the publishers that have a particular interest in the genre (there are a lot), then submit your outline and three sample chapters to the editor of that department.

If you love writing on a broad canvas, about a pivotal point in history with a possible cast of thousands, and you can keep a convoluted plot line running over 100,000 words, this is the one for you!

Di Redmond, under the pen name Daisy Styles, is the author of the bestselling *Bomb Girls* and *Engine Girls* series published by Penguin. Di is also a prolific writer, writing for children's television, stage and radio, and is an established celebrity ghostwriter. She has published over 120 books and is the Audio-Visual Director on ALCS's Board of Directors.

Writing Regency romances

Katy Moran uncovers the captivating character and appeal of Regency romance, its evolution and popularity as a genre, and the creative possibilities it offers a writer. She shares her recommended reading and insights for aspiring romantic novelists.

Sunlight glanced in through the window, striking the bookshelves in my parents' home office. Thrillers by James Clavell jostled with 30-year-old textbooks and *Readers' Digest* volumes passed down from my grandparents. I thought I'd long since read every book in this house, but I was wrong. It was the yellow Pan Macmillan logo that first caught my eye, followed by the battered taupe spine. I pulled out a well-thumbed paperback edition of *The Toll-Gate*, raising an eyebrow at the front cover: a red-headed woman locked in an embrace with a tall, masterful man. Georgette Heyer? I'd never heard of her. I never looked back, either – swept away by Captain Jack Staple, a bored war-hero with a twinkling sense of humour and a fine-tuned appreciation of the ridiculous. The redhead was Nell, a gloriously competent orphan left to run a crumbling estate and outwit her grasping cousin. Having so far evaded his family's best efforts to see him married off, Jack says to his mother that he doesn't mean to offer marriage to any girl who doesn't give him a leveller. Although 'If one *did*,' he added thoughtfully, 'it's Lombard Street to a China orange that you wouldn't take to her.' Heyer lays her cards on the table the moment Jack meets Nell for the first time: 'He stood as though stunned, for he had received his leveller at last.'

I came to love Heyer's books, craving her sparkling wit in times of crisis, and the satisfaction of a happy ending. Nowadays my relationship with her novels is more nuanced, complicated by instances of antisemitism and racism, or age gaps between heroes and heroines that I can no longer view as romantic – even if they do reflect a darker side of the Georgian period that it might be easier to forget. Romance as a genre can so often be dismissed, and it's my belief that critiquing Heyer's work in this way isn't to judge her unfairly by the standards of our time. She was the grand dame of Regency romance, and her work is worthy of critical discussion.

What's the appeal of the Regency, anyway? If you don't already know your curricles from your top boots, I hope my enthusiasm will be infectious. Officially, this period began in 1811 when a spoiled and complex man became de facto ruler in place of his incapacitated father. It ended in 1820 when King George III died, and the Prince Regent became George IV. Researching, I fell headlong into a compelling world of progress, discovery, glamorous ballrooms and giddy excess. It was also a time when our economy was still tied to the illegal slave trade and men could be hanged for the crime of having sex with another man. We were next door to a bloody theatre of war on the continent, a drama extended to provincial British towns when the redcoats passed by – so memorably brought to life by Jane Austen's Lydia Bennet and the scoundrel Mr Wickham.

The Regency took place against a backdrop that must have been, by turns, exhilarating and terrifying to live through. As Regency romance author Catherine Kullmann points out, during this period calls for political reform and emancipation intensify – and the fashion was wearable too. Our heroes and heroines look gorgeous in a way we can relate to: we don't have to get past ruffs or powdered wigs. But even in a Regency romcom or soothing comfort-read, brutal social mores create a backdrop of peril that doesn't exist now, with the course of many a young woman's life being dependent on success or failure in her first Season, when a single malicious rumour could condemn her to life as a disempowered unmarried daughter. A man whose heart led him to other men might find himself on the gallows. In the Regency, the dramatic stakes are anything but trivial.

Georgette Heyer ignited my fascination with the Regency; she's the reason I started scribbling plot diagrams in a notebook one day. But how on earth could I do justice to this era? Over time, I came to realise what my predecessors already understood. As bestselling historical romance author Lynne Connolly puts it, 'The Regency was a historical period, but many authors deviate from the historical reality to create their own Regencyland.' It's true – whether this Regencyland is a place of ebulliant escapism, like that of Julia Quinn or tenured Shakespeare professor Eloisa James, where handsome young noblemen proliferate (with all their own teeth), or one where dragons appear as part of a glorious magical backdrop, as they do in Stephanie Burgis's glittering romcom *Scales and Sensibility* (2021).

When sketching out my own Regencyland I followed not only Heyer, and all the other Regency romance authors who had gone before me, but also the Diana Wynne Jones novels of my childhood. I took a sideways step into a history almost like our own but not quite, creating a Napoleonic alternate universe where a mutinous Cornwall echoes the previous century's Jacobite rebellion in Scotland and the French have outwitted the British navy, mounting a successful invasion. I was hurrying after a hero, Crow, Earl of Lamorna, who at first glance looked very much like Wynne Jones' mercurial Chrestomanci. Tall, dark-haired and arrogant, Crow is capable of visiting violence upon his enemies and tenderness on those he loves in (more or less) equal measure. My Cornish-island dwelling heroine, Hester Harewood, is a capable sailor and a practical young woman who is about to take Crow down by several pegs. In *Game of Hearts* (Head of Zeus 2017), Crow first meets Hester in a none too patient frame of mind. After rescuing his rebellious young brother from occupation soldiers, by ruining his captor at dice, he encounters a young woman washed up on a beach:

> 'You're coming back to London with me.' All Crow could do was hope she wouldn't give him any trouble.
>
> She stared at him, incredulous. 'Am I, indeed?'
>
> 'Yes.' Crow reached for his hip flask and contented himself with a scalding shot of the 1811 Le Courvoisier, before holding the flask to Miss Harewood's lips. Somewhat to his surprise, she didn't protest against the cognac, but took a swallow and straightened herself to her full height, tall and queenly in a sodden gown, and Crow could not escape the notion that he had met his match.
>
> 'Take another drink, my lord,' said Miss Harewood. 'You look as though you need it.'[1]

Crow has received his leveller and he knows it. A fictional war throws Hester and Crow together, but it's the strict social rules of the true Regency that raise the stakes, because Hester has no female chaperone. Crow might offer Hester his protection but, alone as she is, even being in his presence is enough to ruin her. Around the time that I first drafted this scene, I was watching the first series of *Outlander*, based on Diana Gabaldon's passionate timeslip romances. I had no idea then whether the story I was writing for my own

[1] From *Game of Hearts* (Head of Zeus) © Katy Moran 2017

pleasure would ever be published, but I remember thinking that if it ever was, given the alternate history, it would need to be picked up by an editor with an eye for something as different as it was swashbuckling and romantic. Sure enough, the book that became *Game of Hearts* was signed by Rosie de Courcy, who years earlier bought UK rights to *Outlander* and became Diana Gabaldon's editor in the UK.

Writing the book of your heart without regard to genre and then seeing it published is only one way into Regency romance. Since Georgette Heyer published *Regency Buck* in 1935, the genre has evolved with spectacular invention. As a first port of call, I'd advise anyone interested in writing Regency romance to read it widely – including books published recently. Read Regency romances first published in the States, too, where the market is not only larger but different. UK-based authors Emily Royal, Emily Windsor and Virginia Heath have found great success across the pond with their joy-filled romances and romcoms. Vanessa Riley is from the US and writes award-winning examples of the genre with sparkling heroines, shining a light on the hidden histories of women of colour. Here in the UK, Audrey Harrison, Penny Hampson and Fenella Miller all successfully self-publish in this category. Sophie Irwin is an exciting voice in UK Regency romcom with the *Sunday Times* bestselling *A Lady's Guide to Fortune-Hunting* (HarperCollins 2022), and Jane Lark writes passionate Regency romance. Felicity George's *A Lady's Risk* is a delightful Regency romance that has a classic feel.

K.J. Charles writes in a variety of periods including the Regency, and her witty, escapist, subversive and sexy m/m romances have a huge and devoted worldwide following of fans, as do those of well-loved romance author Alexis Hall, who writes sparkling and witty queer Regency romance. Jenni Fletcher's *How to Lose an Earl in Ten Weeks* (Penguin 2021) was published for the YA market but has also found a wider readership – which is no surprise given the appeal of the Regency genre, and Fletcher's uplifting take on it. Amita Murray's new Regency series is about the daughters of an English earl and his Indian mistress. This breathtaking romantic adventure opens with *Unladylike Lessons in Love* (HarperCollins 2023), starring a heroine who dares to break the mould. And, as Amita says, 'there's all the usual witty banter and runaway horses and suppressed passion of a Regency but in a way that allows room understand the impact of colonial history'. Another relative newcomer is Emma Orchard, with *The Second Lady Silverwood*, a passionate, romance with deeply authentic emotional weight and Heyer's wit.

So … read! Read as much in the genre as you can, and in doing so you'll understand who your own ideal readers will be. As a reader, do you enjoy on-page sex or do you find it off-putting? As a writer, do you relish exploring human chemistry to that extent or might you prefer to show the heat of attraction between your characters in smaller gestures, leaving sex behind closed doors? The more we read, the sooner we understand what we're best placed to create. Over the years I've been developing as a writer, a particular piece of wisdom from Alan Garner has come to take on deeper meaning for me: 'If the other fellow can do it, let him.' Is there a special niche within Regency romance that you can explore like no one else?

There are other questions to consider too. Do stories like yours tend to be published independently (self-published) or traditionally? If you're aiming at the traditional market, you should research which publishers and agents deal with the sort of novel that you want to write – and the book in your hands now is the perfect place to start. If you're unpublished or new to the genre, I'd strongly recommend joining the Romantic Novelists' Association (RNA; see page 567). Not only is it a great way of meeting fellow romantic novelists, but they also curate and run the New Writers' Scheme, which aims to support emerging writers. Philippa Carey spent three years refining the craft of writing Regency romance within this scheme and found success submitting to The *People's Friend* magazine. And, taking a broader look at routes to market: Catherine Tinley made an unsolicited submission to Harlequin Mills & Boon and secured a deal for *Waltzing with the Earl* (2017), which went on to win a prestigious award; Jasmina Svenna has had several pocket novels published with *My Weekly* (Jasmina advises that, at 50,000 words or fewer, pocket novels are ideal for writers who aren't sure if they can manage anything longer, and that the best submission format is three chapters and a synopsis, with the third chapter ending on a dramatic cliffhanger). Submission guidelines and all other details can be found at www.myweekly.co.uk/2023/08/18/calling-all-fiction-writers.

If you want to write Regency romance, then welcome to the ballroom. You'll be in for an exhilarating time – reading and writing books that can challenge stereotype just as much as they comfort readers in our hour of need.

After a career in publishing, **Katy Moran** began writing books for young adults. She is the author of the Regency romance trilogy for adults, published by Head of Zeus: *Game of Hearts* (2017), *Wicked by Design* (2022) and *Scandalous Alchemy* (2022). *My Lady's Secrets* (2024) is a fast-paced standalone Regency romance. You can find out more at katymoran.co.uk and follow her on X @KatyjaMoran.

See also...

- *Ever wanted to write a saga?*, page 282
- *Reading as a writer*, page 254
- *Going my own way: Do you need an agent?*, page 441

Tropes in romantic fiction

If you're hoping to move f*rom rags to riches* with the help of a *character on a mission* in your work in progress, look no further: here, Sue Moorcroft explains the power of tropes in romantic fiction.

I used to save up to buy the *Writers' & Artists' Yearbook* every year – except once, when I managed to get it for £1 from a book club and then cancelled my membership immediately. Evening after evening, I'd comb the pages, pen in hand, asterisking magazines that took short stories and, for my novels, editors and agents open to submissions. Beside any I fancied but which were not open to unsolicited approach, I drew a sad face. (And I probably submitted anyway.) I'd also pore over the articles about authors' publishing journeys, hoping the alchemy of perseverance, learning, skill, talent and pragmatism that led to their success would rub off on me.

Now, further on by hundreds of magazine short stories and around twenty-five novels, *Writers' & Artists'* has approached me via my agent Juliet Pickering of Blake Friedmann to write one of those pieces. I'm delighted to accept the brief of investigating tropes in romantic fiction, as I do think that analysing your romance and knowing how to recognise and label all its many facets can illuminate the way.

What is a trope?

A trope is a recognisable situation that adds strength to your book – a creative signpost, a storytelling convention that's characteristic of the genre. It can relate to theme, message, setting, character journey or, commonly, an aspect of the plot. It doesn't matter whether your romantic protagonists are straight, gay, non-binary or from different cultures, planets or species, tropes are relevant. Don't worry if you hear doubters suggest that a trope must be a cliché. No, it must not. No imagination, ingenuity or originality is sacrificed, because tropes provide the bones of your story, but not the complete, beautiful, unique whole that you create. Tropes can be found in everything from Shakespeare to romantasy.

How could utilising tropes work for you?

Tropes can keep you focused as you write. It's surprising how character dynamics might waver if you're not sure what's beneath your story's skin. For example, if you understand that you're writing a second-chance romance, you'll recognise the need to create good reasons for the relationship to have foundered first time around, and to find a way for your characters to get over those hurdles in a credible way when they plunge into a new love story.

In the same way that publishers highlight tropes such as enemies to lovers to let readers know what they're getting and enable them to choose their favourite kind of story, an awareness of tropes allows you, the author, to speak the same language as editors or agents. In a submission, a covering letter or the synopsis can mention specific tropes to convey aspects of the plot, signal that you know what you've written and that you're writing with the market in mind.

Romance readers and reviewers use trope hashtags on social media to tell each other what to expect and make it possible to easily locate the kind of story they like to read. #FakeDate, #RightPersonWrongTime and #ForcedProximity are just a few. You can use similar hashtags, too, to let readers know you're writing to please and satisfy them. Some tropes even become the title of a book, so keen are publishers to find the readers who love exactly what that author writes.

But don't forget that tropes are perfect for using in combination. See my example under the next heading of how I put over a plot to my editor that contained several tropes, each building on the other, and then try it for yourself.

Plot tropes

A few books into my relationship with Avon Books UK, part of HarperCollins, I wanted to give my editor an idea of the novel that became *A Christmas Gift*. I said something like, 'She and he were unlikely teenage buddies who had a massive quarrel, and then he disappeared. They meet again as adults. He's gone from rags to riches while she's gone from riches to rags. I'm setting it in a rock school.' My editor said 'Yes' on the spot. Why? Not just because I'd provided the premise and an interesting setting in four sentences, but because other tropes were indicated, and they'd assist in marketing, blurb and tagline – not just *rags to riches* and its subversion, *riches to rags*; but *friends to lovers* becoming *enemies to lovers*; *second-chance romance*; and *rock school*.

And I could include *impossible love*, because every good romance holds that moment when it seems as if there's no future for the couple . . . until the author proves that there is.

Character tropes

I love mentally categorising my characters. I think of a *reluctant hero/ine* as one of the main characters who was on her or his way to do something when my plot got in the way and made them stay around – and fall in love. *The adventurer* might be involved in something that s/he has to exhibit flexible morals to allow, but I always let their fundamental decency shine through because in the end they do what's right – and they do it for love. The message that *love conquers all* allows me to present these characters as quirky rather than unpleasant. I often create a *character with a mission*. Maybe they need to trace lost family or look after a relative but it's personal to them, it informs their character, their past and future, and it fuels their journey through the book, becoming a significant part of the novel's story arc.

I find it helpful to have a kind of headline tag for my major characters, the stronger the better. I wouldn't want *earth mother* or *boy-next-door* to be another way of saying *domestic drudge* or *mouse*.

Along with deciding on *your* type, if your characters are going to find a happy ending together, it's vital to consider *their* type. You might do this via *opposites attract*. How will a single parent mix it up with a workaholic? How will your loner cope with a party animal? There's huge potential for flying sparks, conflicts, obstacles and misunderstandings, though sooner or later you will have to find a way to get them together and make their future look rosy. You might prefer what I used to term *a match made in heaven*, but which hashtaggers and BookTokers have updated to *instalove*. Your couple are just so perfect for each other . . . so you need to find ways to keep them apart (or risk a short and boring book). Are their lifestyles and commitments hard to align? Are they on opposite sides of a fence that's fundamentally important to them both? Maybe one is passionately opposed to the bulldozing of a local landmark and the other's job is . . . to demolish it.

Settings

I think of setting as falling into two categories – location and type.

Locations can be huge draws for readers. They might love the cosiness of a *seaside village* setting with an atmosphere of beaches, funfairs, lighthouses, sea trips, the cries of gulls and tang of salt on the air. With that comes the potential for tourists and out-of-towners to arrive and create choices and dilemmas for locals, such as villagers no longer being able to afford stone cottages because incomers have snapped them up. On the other hand, seaside village settings are perfect for new starts and escapes from towns and cities. I created *The Skye Sisters* trilogy around a seaside village on the Isle of Skye specifically to give the sisters somewhere remote for their escape from the past.

Type of setting relates to books set around a season or event. Many of my books are either summer or winter . . . often characterised as a *beach read* or *Christmas romance*, or simply a *seasonal read* or *holiday romance*. The latter is a lovely umbrella term for romances encompassing special days or events in every culture.

The right trope

Consider your genre when creating your tropes. *Class divides* work well in historical romance or sagas. However, in contemporary romance, an aristocrat falling for a mill worker is less likely to make modern characters reach for the smelling salts and more likely to result in a nuanced examination of what equality means today, and how respect can be earned. *Enforced proximity* might apply to anything from being stranded together in a broken-down car to being part of an arranged marriage. Attitudes vary enormously not just from period to period but from culture to culture and world to world.

Even the way you express a trope on social media might be affected by what you write. A *reformed rake* in a Regency romance could be a *bad boy* in a romcom.

Is there a 'wrong' trope?

Again, there are a couple of things to separate here. I'd avoid outdated tropes. For instance, my feminist principles don't like the *damsel in distress* trope, particularly if she's rescued by the *guy who wears the white hat*. Even period romances tend to be written with contemporary reader sensibilities in mind, so female characters are just as strong as their male counterparts, even if they have to show their strengths despite the restrictions and realities of the days in which they lived. Also, not all couples are heterosexual. I could suggest a balancing *dude in distress*, but that cuts out non-binary characters. Romantic fiction is an inclusive genre, because love's for everybody.

I also think there are tropes that need careful handling. I can easily read a book where *the bet* is based on the characters wagering between themselves, with a meaningful (and plot-worthy, appropriate) forfeit for the loser. Then, both characters know what they're letting themselves in for and the forfeit can further a romance between them. But where Character A makes a play for Character B to win a bet of which B has no knowledge ... I assume A to be unkind, and the author would have to work hard to convince me that s/he had a good motive. But that's possible, because people do *bad things for good reasons*.

I hope that I've given you food for thought, or just clarity of thought on the advantages of being able to analyse your own work. As I touched on earlier, tropes are just the helpful bones beneath your story's skin of nuanced characterisation and clever plots, convincing relationships, deep back stories, family dynamics, brilliant dialogue and beautiful imagery.

Many of the tropes I've mentioned you'll recognise as labels that we use in everyday life. This is because a romance is an account of how characters experience real life and find love along the way. That's the essence of the genre – that Character A meets Character B and they fall in love. In another genre, A might meet B and become their stalker or abduct them and another set of tropes might apply.

I'll leave you to do your own research as to current tropes and how they might fit your work, and therefore your plotting, characterisation, setting, themes, marketing, and posts on social media. Opinions vary as to the best or catchiest names and these need constant updating as fashions and tastes change.

But studying the market is second nature to successful, commercial writers of romance, anyway. Romantic fiction is a lively, bestselling, ever-evolving genre of which it's a joy to be a part. That's no *dark secret*.

Sue Moorcroft is President of the Romantic Novelists' Association (RNA) and a million-copy *Sunday Times* bestselling author of women's fiction. She writes contemporary romantic fiction with occasionally unexpected themes. Her books – many of which are set in the fictional village of Middledip – include *Let It Snow* (Avon 2019), *The Christmas Love Letters* (Avon 2023) and *An Italian Island Summer* (Avon 2023). Her latest book is the third in the *Skye Sisters Trilogy: Over the Sea to Skye* (Avon 2025). For more information see www.suemoorcroft.com. Follow her on Instagram @suemoorcroftauthor and X @SueMoorcroft.

See also...

- *The Romantic Novelists' Association*, page 567
- *Writing successful dialogue*, page 260

Reigniting the past: writing historical fiction

Annie Garthwaite's novels, *Cecily* (Penguin 2021) and *The King's Mother* (Penguin 2024) were born out of a lifelong interest in the women of the Wars of the Roses. Her greatest ambition (and most fearful challenge), she says, has been to make these long-dead matriarchs live for today's readers. Here she offers some of the lessons she learned from writing their story.

'Cecily who?' This was the most common response I got when I told people I was writing a novel about Cecily Neville. I soon learnt that I needed to explain: 'Richard III's mother,' I'd say, then wait for the spark of recognition to light their faces. It usually didn't take long. Most people know something about Richard – the King in the Carpark, the hunchback tyrant, Shakespeare's villain. I'm not here to defend Richard's reputation; think of him what you will, most people know his name and have an opinion. Of Cecily, however, few have any opinion at all. And it's this very thing that, to my mind, made her a ripe subject for fiction. Cecily is one of those women – a giant in her time – who has slipped through the net of history, ignored by the (mostly male) writers who, over centuries, have curated our understanding of the civil wars that tore 15th-century England apart.

My interest in the Wars of the Roses began when I was a teenager, but it took years of reading and study for me to realise how large a part Cecily played in them. The only major protagonist to live through the wars from beginning to end, Cecily was England's most powerful lady, close to the centre of political power and driving the action much more decisively than you might imagine. By the time I was in my twenties, the desire to tell her story was burning hot within me. And that brings me to my first piece of advice: if you're setting out to write historical fiction, choose a character that you simply can't *not* write about. You're going to be spending a lot of time with them, so you have to want it badly.

Find the obsession

Historical fiction is hard, a long haul, and the depth of research required to do it well will shock you – it shocks me still. From that first spark of interest in Cecily, it took me the best part of 40 years to reach the point where I could start to write her story. Admittedly, a business career and 'life' got in the way but, even if they hadn't, the time spent in research and preparation would have been measured in years rather than months. Throughout those years – my twenties, thirties and forties – when I wasn't working I was reading constantly, attending conferences and talks, and delving deep into the controversies surrounding Cecily and her family. So, unless you're 100% committed to your character's story – obsessed by it even – stop now. This is a serious undertaking. Writing historical fiction isn't just an act of imaginative creation, it's *work*. Sign up or sign out.

The obsession thing was never hard for me. Cecily set her teeth in my flesh early and wasn't letting go. And, to be fair, the research was a joy. One of the things that has pleased me most since Cecily was published is that real historians (people who make their living by studying the past) have recognised the level of research that informs it. That means a lot to me. I've always felt a responsibility to root out the likely truth of Cecily's life from the dark soil of known fact. But here comes the next hard lesson: once you've completed that tireless preparatory research – once you understand the physical, political, religious and emotional 'scape' your character lives in and can navigate it as confidently as they can – you need to look *beyond* it. Somewhere deep within their history you'll find their story.

Find the story

For me, walking within Cecily's 'scape' meant coming to understand the complex twists and turns of the wars and the motivations of the key players. It also meant grappling with European as well as English politics, and being familiar with the role of women in medieval society – from their experiences of childbirth to their rights under the law. It meant knowing the fashions of the times in music, literature and clothes, from Burgundian waistlines to the depth and texture of Italian velvets. It meant bending my post-reformation sensibilities around the arcane practices and beliefs of the medieval catholic church, and appreciating that, within the medieval mind, religious conviction could live side by side with a belief in witchcraft, sorcery and astrology.

As I've said before, this was a work of many years. But, in the end, everything I'd learned was only – as the much-lamented Dame Hilary Mantel described such things – 'furniture': vital if you want to create a world, tedious if described in detail. Just because you know how a 15th-century door handle works, you don't need to describe it; just give us the satisfying thud as the door is slammed. The truth is, everything you will have learned in your research is 'just' history – political, social, cultural or decorative. And although that history is utterly vital, fascinating, revelatory and occasionally mind-blowing, it isn't a story. It's the *starting* point for your work, not its conclusion.

If readers want to read history, they'll read history books. They should. Your appeal is to readers who have chosen fiction, whose first hunger is for propulsive narrative and compelling characters. In the reader of historical fiction, I believe, the need for emotional engagement is at least equal to, if not greater than, intellectual curiosity. Your readers will want to walk through your character's 'scape' with you, take in its scents and sounds, and experience its dramas first-hand. E.L. Doctorow described perfectly the difference between the historian and the novelist: 'The historian,' he said, 'will tell you what happened. The novelist will tell you what it felt like.'

So I stick by my guns; your primary responsibility as a writer of historical fiction is to find your character's compelling story. It must be one that, though set within an arcane, long-ago world, will be comprehensible to today's audience. To be so, it must appeal to the human mind and heart. Let me explain through example: there are two ways to describe what *Cecily* is about. First and most obviously, it's about the matriarch of the house of York during the Wars of the Roses. Now, that's a fine description, accurate and succinct so far as it goes, but hardly revelatory. More meaningfully, my book is about how women exercise power in a world where men hold most of the power cards. It's about what a woman might do to protect her family and future. It's about what happens to a person when they reach for power rather than let themselves be destroyed by it. It's about matters that preoccupy us today but set in a world and time that lets us view those matters through a new lens. Someone interested in 15th-century history might buy the book based on the first description; someone interested in life and story will be attracted by the second. And here's a universal truth you need to grasp, because it will directly impact on your sales: there are many more people interested in life than in history.

At the heart of every great story, of course, sits the protagonist – the character who drives the action and whose fate, ultimately, matters most. In my first book that's obviously Cecily. Who might it be for you? To write successfully, you'll need to know them (and everyone with whom they interact) at least as well as you know yourself. Once you've learned their story and 'scape', your next challenge is to uncover their nature – their ambition, motivation and emotional range.

Know your characters

I was given a head start in this regard by an inspiring teacher. Keith Hill taught history like it happened yesterday and, while others of his ilk were stuffing kid's heads with dates and facts, he asked the most important questions: 'So why do you think she did that?' he'd ask. 'What was in his mind when…?' My A level result wasn't that impressive; I was a bit woolly on dates – but I was very strong on character motivation!

I think this is the most important advice I have to offer any aspiring writer of historical fiction: know your history, but understand your character. History, after all, will only tell us so much. Here I must quote Hilary Mantel again (what can I say? She was a genius, and her *Wolf Hall* trilogy is a landmark in historical fiction). Hilary pointed out that what we know of the past from history is incomplete; there's a great deal we're ignorant of, or that's been misrepresented or forgotten. 'History,' she says, 'is no more the past than a map is a journey.' To find your character, pick up the imperfect map and take the journey with them. Walk it in their shoes. Your hard-won knowledge of their world – from its politics to its door handles – will help you find the route, but it's the days on the road together that will unlock the secrets of their personality.

For me, Mantel's greatest achievement is that her novels are peopled with characters who live and breathe, who are simultaneously of their time and all time, who are both distant and familiar. And it's particularly impressive that she's achieved this with characters so 'famous' (quite the reverse of my own Cecily) that they've almost become caricatures: Henry the lusty and frustrated king, Anne Boleyn the vixen queen and, of course, Thomas Cromwell, the thuggish Machiavel who brought down the church for money. In Mantel's hands their personalities and their motivations stretch; they become multidimensional, sometimes contradictory – just as people are. Cromwell is ruthless enough to see his enemies hang, but takes in beggars and stray cats. He is rigorously pragmatic, but motivated by profound faith. He is at the same time arrogant and fearful; he remembers every one of his personal hurts. In short, he is utterly human, completely relatable.

To create characters of such authenticity we have to put our own sensibilities aside and adopt theirs. Sometimes I find, when I'm writing Cecily, that her dialogue spins out almost without my intervention… ('Ouch!' – I'll find myself thinking, as she lets fly some verbal barb – 'That's a terrible thing to say!'. 'I don't care,' she replies. 'I speak as I find.' I can almost see the shrug of her silk-laden shoulders.) This is when you know it's working – when dialogue falls from your pen, or when you can't help but weep at your character's disasters or grin at their triumphs. When the grief you feel at the loss of them is as fresh as if they'd died this morning.

But, before I turn whimsical, let me share with you some Cromwellian wisdom: 'Choose your prince', he advises in *Wolf Hall* (Fourth Estate 2009). And I advise: choose your characters and hitch your wagon firmly to their star. Stay with them, walk with them, lay down in the dust and weep with them if the occasion demands it. Make it your business to put flesh on their bones and breath in their lungs, by understanding the three things that shape us all: our history, our 'scape' and our nature.

Annie Garthwaite grew is the acclaimed author of two novels that bring the women of the Wars of the Roses to life. *Cecily* (Viking, Penguin 2021) was named a 'top pick' by *The Times* and *Sunday Times*, a 'Best Book of 2021' by independent bookshops and Waterstones, and has recently been optioned for television. *The King's Mother* (Viking, Penguin 2024) was named 'Book of the Month' by *The Times* immediately upon publication. Annie came to writing after a 30-year international business career, determined to cast light on a female history so often overlooked. She is currently working on her third novel, also for Viking, Penguin. Find more on www.anniegarthwaite.com. Follow her on Instagram and X @anniegarthwaite, Bluesky @anniegarthwaite.bsky.social, and on Facebook @anniegarthwaitewriter.

See also...

- *Weaving fact into fiction*, page 308

Writing and publishing short stories

Paul McVeigh describes what he has learned about the world of short stories, stressing the value of performing one's work live and hearing it performed. He has tips on the practicalities, as well as the rewards and opportunities, of competitions and radio commissions catering for this demanding and alluring art form.

I had given up writing for a few years – due to a mixture of rejection and, getting older, needing the financial security of a job, especially as I was living in that beautiful, big, bank-account vampire called London. In a final attempt at the whole writing dream, I thought to kick-start the old writing engine by going along to a one-day course. The tutor mentioned she was reading a short story that night at a live event in Soho. I went along and, unexpectedly, fell in love with short stories.

Since that night, I've read stories at events, had stories read on BBC radio and even 'performed' one on TV for Sky Arts, as well as being published in newspapers, journals and anthologies. I also became involved in producing short story events such as Word Factory – described by the *Guardian* as 'the national organisation for excellence in the short story' – and co-founding the London Short Story Festival. At the same time, I became a reader for small prizes and eventually a judge for bigger ones – the Royal Society of Literature's V.S. Pritchard Short Story Prize, the Edge Hill Short Story Award and the Dylan Thomas Prize. For this article, I'll try to condense as much of what I've learned judging, performing, producing events, publishing and reading short stories as I can possibly fit in. Let's start with a short-story avenue that little has been written about. Here goes ...

Live events

I know that some people, for numerous reasons, hate reading their work live. If you like the idea, or if you could push yourself, give it a go. It can be a little like the difference between traditional poetry and performance poetry – some writers love it as an art in itself, with publication as an added pleasure rather than the purpose. Some writers appear like actors or performers; at a reading there will be those who write solely to be seen and heard, while others try out ideas or hone a piece before submitting for publication. It's a small but vibrant scene that enables you to meet other writers for community support and gain potential book buyers for the future. And, in my case, it was where my agent saw and signed me. Listening to the work of others, like reading, makes you a better writer – either because you learn tricks and tools of the trade or because you learn what *not* to do.

Even if you don't continue to do live reading for its art, think of it as excellent practice for when that publishing deal happens and you're asked to read from your collection (or novel) at a literary event or festival. If you're good at reading from your work, and can engage or electrify the audience, word travels – not only will you be asked back but you'll also be asked to attend other events. The opposite can happen too, so it's worth starting in a small and supportive environment where the stakes are low.

Top tip: even if you don't want to read your work at an event, read it out loud to yourself. It's one of the best pieces of editing advice I ever received and it gives you some of the benefits that live readings provide. If you stumble in a sentence, so will your reader; you also get a real feel for rhythm. In addition, if you can bear it, get someone else to read your work to you; see where they stumble. When reading our own work, we often read what we intended to write and with the inflection we desire, whereas a new reader reads out what you have actually written – just what's on the page.

Short stories for radio

Live events provide a good arena to start thinking about writing short stories for radio. In the rush for publication, writing for radio is often forgotten, and the irony is that radio is probably the largest commissioner of short stories in the UK and Ireland. Put BBC Radio 4 Short Story in your search bar and you will find a treasure trove of recordings read by our greatest performers. You can listen to stories from some of the best short story writers the world has to offer. Don't forget, Radio 4 is also the home to the BBC National Short Story Award (see page 598), offering £15,000 for the winner, so once you've honed your style to the platform you can send a story in. On the website you'll find past winning stories and also those shortlisted, as well as specially-commissioned stories celebrating the art of the short story.

These stories, like those at live events, are also written to be read out and listened to, and there is a vocal performance (usually by professional actors and only occasionally by the author). But there aren't the visual cues we get from watching a reading. This sounds obvious, I know, but it requires a recalibration of your writing – it's a style that sits in between writing to be read and writing to be read out.

Here are some useful tips given to me by my first radio producer, Heather Larmour. Firstly, it pays to be mindful that radio slots tend to be in the afternoon (… think parents listening with children in the car on the school run). You can tackle serious issues, but don't be too bleak or depressing, and strong language wouldn't be encouraged. Consider how intimate the radio experience is – this makes your words so much more powerful and potentially shocking than they would be in written form. And using fast dialogue is fine on the page, but it can be difficult to read out and confusing to the listener; remember there will be only one reader and not a cast (you are not writing a play). Do you live or are you from a region? There are BBC studios all around the UK, each of which commission work, so you might have more of a fighting chance with your local studio than by trying to get noticed in London, say – simply due to the number of writers hoping for that spot. The great news is that you can earn up to £500 for a new story. Doesn't sound like a lot to you? Compare it to the fact that the average debut novelist gets less than £1000 for their 120,000-word opus.

Top tip: short stories for the radio are 2,100 words, give or take a word of two. This is much shorter than you'd expect; the slots are 15 minutes but, with intro and outro music, and credits, it comes in under that time. So give it a try – you might be one of those writers who is relieved by the very achievable word count (similar to the length of this article, for comparison) but it's quite a task to conjure a world, a character or three, and take the listener on a satisfying journey in such a short time. Even if it's not your thing, it's a good challenge. Which brings me to the question …

How short is a short story?

Stories for the radio slots mentioned above are the shortest example I've heard of for what is traditionally accepted as a short story. In the UK and Ireland, a lot of journals and competitions use the 3,000-word mark. Why? Market forces would be my guess. From the admin side, they are quicker to read, saving your first readers and editors (often unpaid or, at best, poorly paid) precious time; also, you can fit more of these in your magazine. And there's the much-debated argument that, these days, readers' attention is harder to keep – so-called 'swipe culture' – made worse by the amount of free content online. There are those who do take longer stories, such as the aforementioned BBC award which takes stories up to 8,000 words (although this will be heavily edited when aired), so have a look around if that's your bag.

Some writers also think they'll write short stories because they are easy, or easier, than writing a novel. It may take you less time … but easier? Most short-story writers will tell you that a great short story takes a novel's worth of thinking. Every word counts, and so much needs to be conveyed in such a short space, that each sentence has to do a lot of work covering at least a couple of these elements: hint at back story, reveal character, further the plot, create tension … Think about the Hemingway story 'Iceberg Theory'; in the short story you are reading just the surface, the tip of the iceberg that can be seen, but nine tenths of its mass is unseen, below the surface, below the words.

Awards, competitions and prizes

I've been a reader and judge for awards, competitions and prizes. The odds are as tough as submitting for publication – sometimes worse, as there may only be one winner. If it's so tough, why try? Well, the benefits can be career-making; even being shortlisted can lead to success. A writer who was shortlisted for the *Sunday Times* Audible Short Story Award a couple of years ago landed a six-figure, multi-book deal from it. The awards themselves can be lucrative too. The *Sunday Times* prize money comes in at a whopping £30,000. Not bad for a short story, eh? Apart from these biggies, there are lots of small and mid-sized competitions that not only offer prize money but also the chance of publication, as they print the shortlisted stories in an anthology. Some are free to enter but others can ask for a fee. Though some writers get cross about this, the entrance fee goes towards the administration as well as paying the readers and judges.

Top tip: to paraphrase Stephen King, to be a good writer you have to be a good reader. Every writing class I've been to tells you the same thing: read, read, read. Anthologies are a great place to start – they can hold a large number of stories, usually in a 'best of' collection, so you also know you are reading what are considered to be prime examples by readers and the industry. You can also read free stories in the *New Yorker*; these are newly written and by the best writers in the field today. The *Paris Review* also has an interview series free online in which the greatest of modern and 'classic' writers, such as Hemingway and Fitzgerald, have discussed their craft.

Good luck!

Paul McVeigh began his writing career in Belfast as a playwright, and has written comedy, short stories and flash fiction, as well as a novel, *The Good Son* (Salt Publishing 2015) which won the Polari First Book Prize and the McCrea Literary Award. His work has been performed on radio, stage and TV, and his short stories published in anthologies, newspapers and literary journals. Paul has been the judge for several international literary prizes and his work has been translated into seven languages. He co-founded the London Short Story Festival, is Associate Director at the Word Factory, and was Head of Literature for the Arts Council of Northern Ireland. Paul's debut short story collection *I Hear You* (Salt Publishing 2025) contains all the stories that he had commissioned by BBC Radio 4. See his website https://paulmcveighwriter.com for more information.

Keeping it short: putting together a short-story collection

Writing high-quality short stories is a genuine skill. In this article, the award-winning Vanessa Onwuemezi explains how she started writing this genre, and shares some vital lessons she learned on the way to publication.

I didn't grow up wanting to be a writer. In the time between childhood and leaving university with a bachelor's degree in Biological Sciences, I had tried on many personas for size; I'd had a go at figure skating, acting, dreamt of being a classical musician or an athlete, and had just about settled on becoming a doctor. After a brief work experience in a hospital, I knew that this wasn't going to happen either.

My journey to becoming a published author was a convoluted one, as you're beginning to see. If I could pinpoint a 'beginning' to this story, it was in a secondhand shop in Pimlico where, having gone to buy clothes, I left with a copy of *Orlando* by Virginia Woolf that changed the way I thought about literature forever.

It was still years before I would put pen to paper. I worked as a visual merchandiser for John Lewis. I moved to Paris. I had the words of a story bubbling to the surface of my mind during this time. On my return to London, living with my parents, I bought a large sketchbook and wrote my first short story in it.

Stories are important in life as well as in literature and it's important to remember the first story you ever knew – your own. I think that we write our own story into everything and cherishing it helps you to remember why you began writing in the first place. When you encounter challenges and disappointment, keep finding joy in the craft.

Starting to write the short story form

After that first short story, the short form continued to enchant me as I took my writing more seriously. I enrolled for a Creative Writing MA at Birkbeck and while there wrote and read lots of short stories. I was exposed to writers such as Julio Cortázar, George Saunders, Flannery O'Connor and discovered favourites of my own – such as Jayne Anne Phillips and Denis Johnson – who were working with the short form.

To some writers, short stories are a useful testing ground for ideas that will eventually go into a novel; for others, they are the training wheels, so to speak, to help a writer move on to a longer form. These are all legitimate, but I've only ever written short stories because I felt inspired to write

Creative Writing MA: learn to write by writing, reading and listening ...

Learning to write is a process that is never done. So, if you are still on your way to being published, know that you have this in common with all writers, we are all learners.

During my MA at Birkbeck, I learned to write and edit, and also some other very important things:

- Support each other. I left that course with a group of writer friends and we read and critiqued each other's work. We also supported each other through the ups and downs of rejection. We read short stories and essays by writers and kept the love of writing alive.
- Remember why you write. Go back to the beginning of the story and remind yourself why you began to write in the first place; this will help you to let go of any bad feeling and competitiveness.
- Feedback tells you how people read. Not only does feedback tell you what is and isn't working in a story, but it also reveals what people pay attention to when they're reading, and gives clues as to how narrative works in the mind.

them. I wrote for the fun of seeing what I could do, and how much I could develop my skill in writing them. I enjoyed imitating writers that I admired and I think that we can enjoy writing without concern for originality, or the development of 'a voice': that will come in time.

Eventually, my writing style took on its own flavour and the stories I wrote circled more tightly around the existential questions that I have always asked myself. I had written three stories I was happy with and had four more stories in mind, and thought that this would be enough to make a short story collection when they were finished.

In 2019, my story 'At the Heart of Things' won *The White Review* Short Story Prize. It was a real honour to win and the windfall of a bit of money was very helpful. It also brought my work to an audience beyond my immediate writing peers, and with that some attention from agents. I didn't yet have a finished collection, but realised after a few initial conversations with agents that I had to get back to writing before any of them would seriously consider representing me.

This was the third time I had entered *The White Review* prize. I had entered many other prizes too and although not getting anywhere can feel frustrating, it teaches you the value of persistence. Due to the nature of the form, there are many prizes that cater to short stories and which are good for the visibility of both authors and publishers. But remember that they're not everything, and are not the measure of the worth of your work.

Putting together a collection

A short-story collection, in publishing terms, will typically contain about ten pieces, with some combination of story length. How the collection is organised will be down to the writer and editor's choice about what the collection is about, as well other considerations such as the audience and publisher. This being said, there is variation. It's good to read a range of collections to get a sense of what they tend to have in common.

My short-story collection, *Dark Neighbourhood*, is made up of seven stories and is a relatively short book if we consider the number of pages alone. But I felt that as the stories are very dense in style, each word counted for more. The stories are literary and they come together in one collection because they share a style, a mood and a particular way of looking at characters.

It might have been enough for the stories to be united by nothing but their style, but I wanted to go one step further to bring them together. I repeated certain phrases across the stories, or used the name of a character in one story as a street name in another. I diagrammed all of these linkages to keep track of them. It wasn't crucial that the reader notice

Entering prizes: know your work

Where does your work fit in the writing landscape? This will help you to find your way towards publishers, agents and prizes that will appreciate your work. When looking for the prizes to enter I considered the following:

- Do I like the stories? I read the winning stories to see if their style chimed with my work, if it didn't, I didn't enter, however prestigious. Once I'd identified a few prizes that I respected, which means I really liked the work that won the prize, I entered those prizes year on year.
- Have previous winners been published, where? Follow the trail of previous winners, even if you don't enter the prize; it can help you to find the kinds of publishers you would like to publish with.
- Again, prizes are not the measure of your work. Not winning them does not mean your work is unpublishable and that agents and publishers won't love it. Remember that prizes reflect the judges' tastes and not the tastes of everyone in the publishing world, which is much broader.

all of the them but rather that they might feel as if they'd read certain lines or seen certain images before, like déjà vu.

Whatever genre of fiction you write, understanding why you have put your stories together into one collection will be your best guide to organising them. You may have composed your stories over a number of years and now are deciding which to include and which to leave out – your writing style may have changed over that time too, which is another important consideration. Or you may have written under a theme and now need to decide what order to put them in.

Once *Dark Neighbourhood* was complete, I sent it out to the agents that had been in touch after I won *The White Review* Prize, and almost all of them replied to say that the collection wasn't for them. I did feel some despondency after that flurry of 'no's, but reminded myself that this was just the start, and many authors published today will tell you that their journey began with a paper trail of rejections.

I think that it's important to have faith in your work before anyone in publishing takes an interest in it. Being certain that your work is worth publishing will save you a lot of anxiety, frustration and doubt as you know that you'll be okay either way. Even if one particular work has to be left in a drawer for a while, you don't need to wait to be told that your work is good enough: if you know it is worthwhile, then it is. When an email from your future agent or publisher lands in your inbox it will feel natural because, in fact, you are already an author.

One day not long after my rejections, an agent got in touch with me. I hadn't submitted my work to them, but they were a colleague of another agent who had read my collection. *Dark Neighbourhood* was bought by Fitzcarraldo Editions in 2021 and published that same year after a only a brief period of editing. I put the minimal need for changes down to having such a supportive and talented group of writer friends from whom I have learned a lot about editing my own work, and who were

Tips on how to organise your collection

The collection is a microcosm, a little world you are creating, a world with its own assumptions, preoccupations and rules. The stories in your collection need to reflect each other, to show some affinity with each other to be part of the same world with the same rules. For example, you won't be pairing science fiction with a domestic drama which has no science fiction elements.

- You can't control what order your reader will read in, but how do *you* read short story collections? Front to back for many, so consider this when you make decisions.
- Your stories should share similarities in style even if there is some progression in style throughout the collection.
- Why do you like your favourite collection? How does it make you feel and what do you value in it?
- Think about your favourite album. How does one song progress to another? There are many ways to organise your stories, such as by emotional register, rhythm or mood.
- Get the work off the computer. Print it out, write out the titles, put them onto Post-its and move them around.

Submitting a short-story collection to agents

1. As you would with any other book, follow the submission guidelines of the agency you are submitting to.

2. Unless the guidelines rule it out, you can include extras that express what your work is about. I included a recording of me reading one of the stories, and in my email to the agent, an epilogue for the collection that I felt unified the stories.

3. What brings these stories together? Let them know about the world you have created.

4. Read the agent's list of clients. Submit both to agents who represent other short-story writers, and those who may not, but whose taste resonates with your work.

5. Some may tell you that 'short stories don't sell'. They might be a *harder* sell, but agents and publishers do sell them.

the first readers and editors of *Dark Neighbourhood*. I also owe them a debt of gratitude for continually reminding me why I write in the first place – because I like to feel the world expand.

Vanessa Onwuemezi is a London-based writer. Winner of *The White Review* Short Story Prize in 2019, her book *Dark Neighbourhood* was published by Fitzcarraldo Editions in 2021 and was named one of the *Guardian*'s Best Books of 2021. Her work has appeared in literary and art magazines including *Granta*, *i* and *Art Review*. She was the inaugural writer-in-residence at the Roberts Institute of Art, 2023, and Scholar of Note at the American Library in Paris, 2024. Follow her on Instagram @vanessa_onwuemezi

How to be a literary fiction writer

'Literary fiction' is often regarded as the gold standard for authors. But what actually is it? In this article, Rowan Hisayo Buchanan explores what it means for her, and what she's learned while writing.

Ingredients: 2 cups verbs, 3 cups nouns, 7 cups tea, adverbs and adjectives to taste. Bake at 180 degrees for one to seven years.

I wish the 'How To' for a novel was as clear as the recipe for a stack of Anna Jones pancakes. Though on a tough writing day, I do recommend those pancakes. They are raggedy at the edges and sweet with apple and crunchy from pecan. If it were possible to give you the seven easy steps, I'd hand them over readily.

Maybe my first piece of advice is that literary fiction has no easy 'how to' guide or set of rules.

Sometimes, when I am asked, 'what do you write?', I release the words 'literary fiction' reluctantly. I worry that I sound like a terrible snob – as if I am claiming that my work is somehow superior to crime, romance, horror, historical and science fiction. In fact, literary fiction often borrows from those places. Ursula K. Le Guin described her work as fantasy and science fiction. It was. She wrote about space travel, alien races and fantasy kingdoms. Her work is also deeply literary. I recommend her essay, 'The Carrier Bag Theory of Fiction' to readers and writers of all stripes. Kazuo Ishiguro's writing about Nazi collaborators, King Arthur and clones won the Nobel Prize in Literature. I'd tremble at the thought that someone might think I was trying to put my work above such legends.

And in any case, while my work has always been marketed as literary fiction. My third novel, *The Sleep Watcher* (Sceptre 2023), owes a great debt to crime fiction. After all, it begins with a character confessing that she did something terrible and you don't find out what until the end.

So what do we mean, then, by describing work as 'literary fiction'? We mean that, even if it borrows from other places, it doesn't have to slot neatly into another genre. (Hence no rulebook!) We might also mean a concern for language and character. That's not to say that writers on other shelves cannot care for these things. But these are the benchmarks against which literary fiction is usually judged, rather than how terrifying the killer was or how sexy the love interest.

If I cannot give you an ingredient list, what simple advice can I offer? On language – never describe anyone's eyes as the colour of a jewel unless the narrator has a predilection for jewellery or geology. Also, please note, it is quite hard to see someone's eye colour from across the room. On character – I have never met anyone wholly good or wholly evil. They may exist. Nonetheless, a book populated by only the very good and the very bad is likely to feel a little thin.

I have taught for Faber, Granta, Cambridge and elsewhere. On those courses, we spend many weeks thinking about craft. But here I'm going to offer the advice that comes up in my one-to-one tutorials. The advice I give to the stuck, the nervous, those trying to figure out if being a writer is even possible for them.

Read as much as you can

Read widely. Read across genres. Read slim books and doorstops. Read things that were written 200 years ago. Read things that came out today. This is how you will refine your taste, and your taste is what will become your voice.

Try not to think of evaluating a novel as equivalent to reviewing kitchen roll on Amazon. This isn't about how many stars you'd give the author. It's about the choices they made. If you loved a book, then narrow in on what you loved about it. Was it the dialogue? The sense of plot? The formal playfulness? If you hated a book, think about why you hated it. What choices did that writer make that you would not? Is there something that you'd salvage?

Write as often as your life allows

When I was writing my first book, *Harmless Like You* (Sceptre 2016), I told myself I had to write 250 words a day. Every day. 250 words is not long. It's half a double-spaced page. Even on days that I felt blocked, I could get out that much. Some days, it took me hours with many breaks for cups of gingery tea and assorted morsels from the fridge. On others, I breezed past without even noticing the word count ticking by. When I tell students that I chose 250 as my number, many are surprised by the meagreness. They assume you'd have to have a lot of those breezy days. But if you write 250 words every single day without fail for a year, you'll have 91,250 words. 70k–80k is usually considered a 'normal' novel length.

It's not actually the number that matters, though. The number is a trick – a trick to get you to sit down and write. To make you get there on bad days and good, busy days and slow days. Because if you go to your desk every day, two things happen. The first is that words pile up. They become something book-like. The second is that the book is always with you. It's with you when you shower, when you are eavesdropping in restaurants, when you're admiring the scarf of a stranger, or planning a meal. Sometimes the connection feels direct. You think yes, that is the scarf that character would wear. Sometimes it feels out of nowhere. One minute you're trying to stop your dog from investigating an abandoned chicken bone and the next you've decided to kill off a character's father. But your subconscious is working all the time.

Does it have to be every day? I don't think so. Every day makes your life easier, but we don't write novels because they are easy. If your situation means you can only slip to your desk once a week, then revel in that once a week. If you can get a whole week to binge every now and then, with months in between in which your bones are too exhausted, then fill yourself up with words when you can.

Every night as I lie in bed, I try to dream my way into my book, because no one can take that away from me.

Remember that a good book is better than a fast book

There are some excellent books that have been written in a fever. However, it is not their speed that makes them brilliant. Nowhere on the spine, front cover or blurb of a book does it tell you if the author took seven years or seven days. Your readers will not think you should have got on with it. Take the time to be with your book to figure out what it needs.

My third novel, *The Sleep Watcher* (Sceptre 2023), is about a teenage girl who loses the ability to sleep and begins to have out-of-body experiences instead. She cannot fly or move at super speed. She is just trapped in her house and her village. Because of this, she is forced to confront something that she has been trying not to know about her father – the man who taught her to sing and cut her vegetables, who always championed her. I knew the novel had to be claustrophobic. It's a novel about being unable to look away. She had to be a teenager. And yet I was stuck. Each time I tried to write it in her teenage voice, I found myself floundering – asking what word would a teenager use? But there is no generic teenager. Then I tried an adult narrator, who felt patronising, smug even, and too distant. I kept writing and rewriting the first three chapters. Friends would ask what I was working on and, for a year, I'd feel a tickle of shame. Yes, still that novel. No, still at the beginning. And then it clicked. I realized the narrator had to be the main character, Kit, as an adult. Then I asked myself why would her adult-self tell this story? And I realized it was a confession. After that, I knew exactly how to tell the story.

I am so grateful I gave myself the time to figure that out. That I didn't force myself to be done for the sake of it. It is easy to be impatient but you and your books will have your whole lives to be together.

Write the story only you can tell

Perhaps you've heard the advice to write what you know. Or the furious rebuke that this is a smotherer of imagination. This is a variation on that advice. I cannot take credit for it. It was told to me over a decade ago, by the novelist Steven Wright, when I was living in Madison, Wisconsin, and dreaming up my first novel. It is cold in my memory and I'm in the passenger seat of his car. It has either just snowed or it is about to snow and the wind is blowing hard over the lake. I am trying to figure out what it is that I have to write about. I'm wearing the thick blue parka my parents bought me when I told them I was moving away to somewhere where people regularly got frostbite.

I was working on a novel. It had relationships, misunderstandings, a reveal. And it felt dead. I was aping what I thought a novel should be – the difference between birdsong and the sound of our washing machine finishing. I was stuck and it was Steve who asked me, 'What is the novel only you can write?' I didn't have an answer. Then my mother was struck by a sudden sickness. I was terrified. She was far away and I couldn't help her. I didn't write immediately. But after that, I started to wonder what my life would have been like without her in it. I knew that there were times in my childhood where she had very much wished she could leave.

And it is from here that *Harmless Like You* emerged, a novel about a Japanese artist in New York in the 1960s and 70s who abandons her child and about how and why that happened. My mother also grew up in New York at that time. She is half-Chinese and half-Japanese whereas my character, Yuki, is Japanese. My mother did not abandon me. I had to imagine my way into what would have had to be different. And I had to do plenty of research to get the era right. I ran it past many readers who had been there at the time. There was much I did not know that I needed to find out in order to write the novel.

Still, that novel felt deeply connected to questions that live in me to this day. How do you find belonging? What does it mean if people can't place you easily? Can art help you connect? Why does love guide people to dark places? I'm not the only person with these questions, but *Harmless Like You* feels truly mine. It remains deeply connected to my particular way of living in the world. And it was this novel that found me my first readers.

What are your 'What ifs...'? Your passions? Your niche interests? These are what you will bring.

Remember you're in it for the love

If not love, then passion. Many people spend their whole lives not writing a single short story. You aren't a failure if you don't write a novel. No one is making you do it. It is hard, yes. But if the difficulty ever starts to feel too much, the answer is almost always to find your way back to that love. Maybe reread the book that most inspires you. Maybe go to the town that you wanted to wrap into words. Bathe in a different form of art – cinema, painting, music – and think about how you can take the way they make you feel and bake them into language. Plunge into the slick and sweat of a club, the feeling of a night whose heat gets into your bones. And remember the uncapturable feeing you nonetheless wanted to trap inside language. You will know your own loves best.

Write.

Just that.

Rowan Hisayo Buchanan is the award-winning author of three novels, *Harmless Like You* (2016) – which won the Author's Club First Novel Award, *Starling Days* (2019) and *The Sleep Watcher* (2023) – all published by Sceptre. She is a Fellow of the Royal Society of Literature. Follow her on Instagram @rowanhisa.

Weaving fact into fiction

Jo Browning Wroe tells how the story for her debut novel came into being, woven around the personal experience of those deeply affected by a true-life disaster. She describes what she learned in the process of collecting and immersing herself in historical facts to craft her fictional characters and narrative.

As a debut novelist, I only have one experience to draw on for this piece about weaving real events into fiction. I was a novice; I was conscious that I had to pay close and careful attention to what I was trying to do and how I went about it.

The idea for my novel *A Terrible Kindness* (Faber & Faber 2022) started with me reading an account, in some 50-year-old conference papers, for the annual gathering of the UK funeral industry. I was in Cambridge University Library, researching a different project. The account was written by the man who had co-ordinated the extraordinary voluntary operation carried out by embalmers from all over the UK following the Aberfan disaster of 1966, when a coal tip thundered down a mountainside burying a primary school and killing most of its children. I was floored by the heroic kindness called upon from people because of their profession, how they stood shoulder to shoulder with a community at the outer limits of human distress. I was pulled in as if by power suction and, with no agent, let alone publisher, I was soon flying to Belfast to meet the author of that account.

Breaking his silence of fifty years, he talked with me for hours about his experience. I was left wanting to honour his and his colleagues' contribution, whilst respecting the people of Aberfan. I would never have taken it upon myself to write a story from the perspective of someone from the village, but to try and crawl under the skin of someone who went to help, because they had a skill that nobody ever wants to need, felt worth a try. So this is the story of how I went about it – and the important things I've learned. My book begins and ends in Aberfan; in between are 17 years of my protagonist's life – as a boarding boy chorister in Cambridge, a trainee embalmer, and someone living with undiagnosed PTSD. I had a lot to find out, consider and apply.

I sought out people whose lived experience was relevant to my characters, I prepared questions and then, whenever possible, I travelled to where they were, or occasionally we spoke on the phone. One way or another, I interviewed them. Lots of them … embalmers who had been in Aberfan, press photographers and news reporters, former Cambridge choristers, current-day choristers, choirmasters, therapists. I had prepared a lot of questions.

And here's the most important thing I learned early on: too many questions can seriously get in the way of the best material. Constantly pulling the conversation back to an agenda I'd drawn up when I didn't know what I didn't know could so easily close down valuable recollections and reflections. Whilst there were many particular and important things I needed to find out, I learned to leave those until the end. It became my priority to create a space in which people could talk freely about their experience in the way that came naturally to them. All sorts of things came out that I could never ever have anticipated or thought to have asked about – elements that became vital threads in my woven story. The specificity of these memories was so often the gold I was hoping for; details to surprise and move readers, pulling them into the story. I stopped thinking of these meetings as interviews and started thinking of them as *listenings*.

I have alluded already to the many specific and practical questions that really did need answering. To write about the experience of being a chorister in the 1950s, I needed to know how their days panned out, what they sang, when they sang, how they rehearsed, how they managed all the other schoolwork, what mealtimes and bedtimes were like. And what initially felt like more of a challenge was that I was writing from the point of view of an embalmer – a profession and process about which I knew little.

The men who had been to Aberfan were generous with their time, dredging up memories that couldn't have been easy to reconnect with, and I remain hugely indebted to them for the opening section of the story. When I started writing in earnest and questions quickly started stacking up, I was uncomfortable going back to bother them for more detail. They had breathed life into my imagining of the disaster from an embalmer's point of view and it felt inappropriate to pester them for practical questions. So, in order to avoid anachronisms, I found someone who had been an embalmer during the 1960s, but who hadn't attended the disaster. He was happy for me to email him questions whenever they arose and was astonishingly quick and detailed in his response.

Even before I went into the mortuary to watch this, I'd had three visits with a young, third-generation embalmer, and it was these encounters that were most responsible for me shifting my emphasis from 'interviews' to 'listenings'. He not only shared factual details with me but, unexpectedly and unasked, he talked about the emotional and psychological cost of coming into work each day to face the very thing the rest of us work so hard to ignore. He had 'looked after' two beloved family members within a short space of time; it was simply too much and resulted in time off work. This self-imposed expectation, of needing to step up and embalm loved ones, became an important part of William's story. So many of William's experiences and struggles originated in this way, from real people, which I then wove into the life of my character.

My interviews with former choristers reminded me that humans may share experiences with others, but they actually *experience* and remember them differently. I spoke with one former chorister who had entered the choir school three years later than other boys. He was talented and was fast-tracked to soloist. I asked one of his contemporaries, a gentle, kind soul, how the rest of them had felt about this. He said, as far as he could remember, they all felt it was 'jolly well done to him', that he had a marvellous voice. The chorister in question said it was awful and that he was beaten up every day for a week. The idea of a chorister arriving late to their cohort, but with prodigious talent, caught my attention and became part of William's story also.

I spent hours with another former chorister who, though likeable and hugely talented, was badly beaten at school for his bad behaviour. When I started talking to him, it was to find out the specifics of a chorister's day – but by the time I had finished I had found the character of Martin, William's best friend, who became essential to the story. A few months later, after the ten year-old Martin was well-rooted in my novel, the same man unexpectedly came to lead a rehearsal of my choir because our director was away. He was a phenomenal teacher – the atmosphere was electric. I dashed home to try and capture these moments, and decided I wanted the adult version of this character in my story too.

Clearly these listenings are the bedrock of my story – real events, memories and feelings that I wove into a fictional narrative with what I hope is emotional truth. Of course, I also read all I could, trawled the internet for articles and images and tracked down old documentaries; writers develop an insatiable hunger for their subject matter. I also listened endlessly to recordings of the music I featured. My final edit was done in a slightly feverish manner with Allegri's 'Miserere mei' playing loudly.

My experience tells me that if I find out what I need to know – the factual stuff, and the stories from the people who matter – it will sit in my unconscious ready to spark, trigger and inform my imagination as I write. It's also true that there will be things I didn't find out that would have helped, and I will have got some things wrong. But I've done my best.

And what about Aberfan? I started by saying that I didn't set out to write about the disaster per se, but about outsiders who went in to help and left again, each to deal with their own personal aftermath. But of course, I was apprehensive about entering such tender territory. I visited Aberfan several times, wandering round on my own and once escorted by someone who'd grown up there during the '60s and '70s. Later, I shared the relevant passages with this person, and they then showed it to one of the survivors, someone I never met and who asked not to be quoted. I've been asked if I ever considered making up a disaster. I didn't. What drew me to this story was completely rooted in one particular place, time and event. To have invented a situation would have diluted both the power of the story and the tribute I wanted to pay.

I'll end with the dedication from the book: *For the embalmers who went to Aberfan and for the people they went to help.*

Jo Browning Wroe has an MA in Creative Writing from the University of East Anglia. Her debut novel, *A Terrible Kindness*, published by Faber & Faber in 2022, was a *Sunday Times* bestseller, has been translated into several languages, was shortlisted for the Bridport Peggy Chapman-Andrews First Novel Award and the RSL Christopher Bland Prize, longlisted for the Prix du Roman Fnac and was a Richard and Judy Pick. Follow her on X @JoBrowningWroe.

Writing about the natural world

Nature writing is one of the most popular genres within non-fiction. In this article, Sophie Pavelle explains how she found her way to writing about the natural world, as well as her unexpected journey to publication.

I never wanted to be an author. A writer, maybe, in passing. I suppose I have always written – from stacks of unread journals to postcards and school essays. The art of correspondence was demonstrated to me by my mother, who, over the decade she lived in the States with my father, drafted weekly handwritten letters to her parents in England. Email did not exist. Even now, 25 years later and back in the UK, her writing keeps friends and family abroad close. I remember falling asleep to the sound of her fluid touch-typing.

Keeping options open

I was fortunate to be raised in a family where books, music and imaginative play were valued alongside maths and biology. Where my brother nosedived into physical books, I found escapism in audiobooks (or rather, story tapes!). I would listen to the worlds built by Jane Austen, Enid Blyton, Dick King-Smith, Roald Dahl, J.R.R. Tolkien and J.K. Rowling to the point where I could recite every line.

Always obsessed with stories…but never thought about being an author. The title of 'author' implies a kind of coveted, glamorous role to society. I wrongly assumed that to write about nature, travel, science and climate change was a position afforded only to those of a certain age, expertise and intellect – perhaps even gender. As I turn 30, on the cusp of publishing my second book with Bloomsbury, I still squirm when someone asks me what I do for work, dismissing my achievements, deflecting the attention. As ever, acknowledging this profession to myself is a work in progress.

At school I was ok at many things, interested in everything, but felt pressured to excel at something. Although they didn't seem the right fit at the time, this broad sweep of occupations (sport, outdoor adventure, piano, stories, school, animals) led me to study Zoology (BSc) at the University of Bristol. I loved the natural world, but I wanted to keep my options open.

Build a varied portfolio

Following my undergraduate degree, I studied for a Master's in Science Communication (MSc) at the University of the West of England. By then I had cycled through a maddening variety of career moves, ranging from the military to physiotherapy, veterinary medicine and environmental law, until I finally arrived at a perfect interface: the opportunity to blend science and creativity in a vocation that felt increasingly urgent and purposeful in a noisy, misinformed world. It turns out that ending up writing about the natural world by way of chance, with a medley of different interests behind you, can be just as useful as realising a long-held dream.

During my MSc, I compiled a writing portfolio: mainly coursework, reports and essays, but also the odd opinion piece and article that I volunteered to write for independent nature blogs, environmental charity websites and magazines. The plan was that I could present this portfolio as part of a job application or networking opportunity. The subject matter was deliberately varied. I enjoyed the practice of writing in different tones, for different audiences and different editors. I continue to challenge myself to write in different styles: commentaries, features, fiction, academic and news. Writing is like a muscle – it needs a varied training plan in which to flex and strengthen.

You never know who's reading

Writing for something or someone always has value – even if the text remains private and the reader stays in your head. It keeps you motivated and focused. And when you share your work, you never know who might end up reading it.

My debut opinion piece was published by *Metro* – a commentary on the 2019 State of Nature Report. I was intimidated but honest, reporting my concern on learning that one in seven species risked extinction from the UK at the time, how biodiversity is in freefall with the rising climate emergency, how helpless I feel. But I also wrote about hope and positive action. The future of our planet requires all hands on deck, all fingers to the pen, the page, the keyboard.

Two days later, a commissioning editor from Hodder & Stoughton emailed me, referencing that article, asking whether I had considered writing a book, and if so, what's the story?

The proposal

And so started the publishing rollercoaster. I drew up a formal proposal for Hodder & Stoughton, dissecting an idea that came from nowhere, who I was writing for, why me, why now. I proposed the concept of what became *Forget Me Not* (Bloomsbury 2022): narrative non-fiction, first person, telling the story of ten underdog British species vulnerable to climate change.

It turned out Hodder & Stoughton weren't looking for a narrative piece and they wished me luck in placing the idea elsewhere. I was crushed, but grateful for the experience. Book proposals are a fantastic exercise. You interrogate your own idea, demonstrating your expertise and ability in writing about the natural world. Each publisher has their own in-house template, but the essentials are often the same and can be practised anytime: a synopsis, chapter outline, sample text, your target market/readership and competitors, your credibility as the proposed author.

Dealing with rejection

Keen to be fuelled (not floored) by defeat, I tried Bloomsbury, knowing their legacy in specialist non-fiction titles. The story in my head needed a narrator, and I had faith that my voice mattered in this crowded genre. The natural world is changing rapidly, and more human perspectives are required. I found out the email of a commissioning editor, and sent a short, to-the-point message introducing myself and my rejected proposal, asking if they were interested. We had lunch in London the following week.

To agent or not to agent?

Nobody tells you how to write a book. One author's process is another's nightmare. An agent can help navigate the rocky terrain. As soon as my commission was green-lit, I looked ahead at the two-year wait until publication which would feature travelling, research, writing, editing and production – and felt out of my depth. As a 25-year-old (at the time) with barely any professional experience and no family members or friends in the industry, I wanted guidance so started researching and emailing literary agencies.

Already having a book commission was a useful hook. My agent at Curtis Brown signed with me halfway through the writing process of *Forget Me Not* and has been an invaluable port of call. She provides a keen editorial eye, and prompts questions and conversations I never considered. Writing is notorious for being a solo occupation and, at times, lonely. A good agent can become a trusted colleague.

Write without fear

I think about Tom Albrighton's line 'write without fear, edit without mercy' almost daily. Writing about the natural world is daunting – not least the imposter syndrome that lurks in the background.

Conveying the truth of nature's past, present and uncertain future is a vast science communication challenge – but one that is necessary to rise to. Having a level of fear about the task ahead can motivate impactful storytelling. Small doses of fear can clarify our minds and offer solutions. Writing always scares me, but it electrifies me as well. Like embarking on an expedition, or physical feat, feeling my brain work and heart beat tells me I'm doing something that matters. At your desk and in the field, there is merit in being animal: instinct and intuition are your ally in the endless writing days.

Travel and adventure as agents of pace

Writing about the natural world is an undertaking as engrossing as it is overwhelming. This genre that has the potential to be dense and layered with infinite topics to explore, constant distractions and intricacies that risk losing the reader. Since writing my second book, *To Have or To Hold* (Bloomsbury 2025), my focus has benefitted from choosing a topic to dive into – symbiosis – versus the broad sweep of natural history that *Forget Me Not* explored.

Nature is anything but passive, and inspires me to try and emulate its dynamism. To address nature's fragility demands active, galvanizing prose. And I find that travel, movement and 'place' offers one solution to the potential problem of pace.

This is nothing new. Works by Nan Shepherd, Mary Oliver, Robert Macfarlane, Robin Wall Kimmerer and Amy-Jane Beer, for example, all pivot on personal reflections that arise from time spent in nature, adventure and periods of isolation. They remind us how headspace exists everywhere, from rivers to ridges.

Prose (be it fiction or otherwise) can flourish from even the briefest of encounters with a species, a sunset, a storm, another person. It's easy to assume these anecdotes cost weeks and money. Those of you who, like me, are writing books around full-time work and life, can achieve much of your field research goals in a well-planned day on location: taking notes, recording voice memos, taking pictures of what you see, hear, smell, think and feel. You can never gather too much material. Your reader will want to know.

Choosing to travel by low-carbon means (where possible) adds drama that can joyfully disrupt more serious narrative passages, offering the reader (and you!) a breather from gritty environmental truths – as well as advocating a greener way to collect your material. I also discovered that moving physically through a landscape by foot or bicycle, rain or shine, helps deepen my connection.

A narrator as travel guide invites the reader to feel part of the journey. Isn't that one of the reasons we escape into books in the first place?

Humour as a secret weapon

If you're reading a book about climate change, species loss and environmental damage, would you expect to laugh? You should. Studies have repeatedly hallmarked the significance of humour in improving information recall and attentiveness.

Humour can disarm a curious, concerned reader, inviting them further into your world. As science communicators, authors writing about nature are in a privileged position of responsibility: to encourage care for the environment, inform opinion and maybe even change behaviour. Adding levity as a tool to lighten tone and increase impact should not be underestimated.

Expert voices

Writing about the natural world is different for everyone. For me, with only a degree-level understanding and little-to-no naturalist experience, I turn to experts to supplement the gaps in my knowledge.

Finding them is easier than you think – you just need to be sure of your purpose in contacting them, staying polite and succinct. Take the time to research them before you send that first email, reference specific areas of their expertise that resonate with you and your project, and tell them how their work complements your aims. I find social media and LinkedIn good starting points, as well as author lists on peer-reviewed research papers, and university websites. If you have time, attending relevant events or conferences can introduce you to people who may have an otherwise low profile. From there, word-of-mouth recommendations can yield enormously helpful contacts.

Once interviews have been conducted, maintain those good working relationships. In some cases, you may be communicating research that's been a scientist's life's work, so I'd recommend giving them the opportunity to review their contribution to your manuscript. You never know when you might want to call on them again.

Break free of the echo chamber

When writing about nature, a key element of my research is reading non-nature books. To write well, is to read widely – not necessarily voraciously, but strategically. Think carefully about your target audience: what will they likely be reading in their spare time, not just in print, but online? What podcasts or radio shows might they enjoy listening to? What movies do they watch?

Cast your net widely. I follow online book clubs; which encourage me to read titles I never would have otherwise explored. If my goal is to reach readers for whom a book about nature might not usually be on their radar, then I need to understand their preferences and be inspired by their interests.

My latest book, *To Have or To Hold*, investigates nature's hidden relationships. To help me navigate their nuanced and volatile characteristics, I turned to novelists for help: from Jane Austen, D.H. Lawrence and Thomas Hardy to more modern writers like Carmen Maria Machado, Maggie O'Farrell and Anthony Doerr. Even screenwriters, like Phoebe Waller-Bridge, and songwriters, like Taylor Swift, have a had a lasting impact on me with their wordplay and storytelling. Their collective portrayals of human relationships, flaws and all, helped me untangle those in nature, better understand them, and identify parallels with us – the aim being to make the information somewhat more relatable and engaging (which is famously difficult, when writing about the natural world). Broadening your pool of resources that you draw upon creatively, is never time wasted.

Reading aloud

Reading my work aloud is a non-negotiable part of my review and creative process. There are always errors, stumbles, weak jokes and missing links that are only identified in speech – no matter how many times I or others have read the text.

Reading aloud is also a key part of forward planning in a manuscript's journey to publication. If the book is due to also be recorded as an audiobook, it's important you enjoy the way it sounds. I also have found that if I'm struggling to communicate a particularly complex piece of science, trying to explain it out loud (if only to the wall!), can assist in detangling the point.

Connect to nature

Taking time away from your manuscript is as beneficial as having someone else read and offer feedback. It's easy to tell yourself that a break from the manuscript is unproductive. But writing about the natural world especially requires those authors to have an ongoing connection to nature themselves, to give the story integrity and keep them in a balanced state of mind during the marathon of writing.

So, without hesitation, I suggest that now you've got here – seek some fresh air. Leave your phone behind. Then return to the page and see what you can do.

Sophie Pavelle is a writer, science communicator and author of two books: *Forget Me Not* (2022) and *To Have or To Hold* (2025), both published by Bloomsbury. Visit www.sophiepavelle.com to find out more.

Pitching your travel ideas: books and articles

Travel writing has never been more popular. In this article, Jen and Sim Benson offer invaluable advice about how to make sure your pitches for travel books and articles stand out from the crowd.

2024 marked a decade since the publication of our first book, *Wild Running: 150 Great Adventures on the Trails and Fells of Britain*. Writing that book, and getting it published, was our first big step towards making a career out of travel writing. And it changed everything. In the years since, we've gone from working for other people to being full-time writers, working for ourselves.

The process of creating *Wild Running* was an adventure in its own right. We spent a year travelling the country; seeking out the best routes; writing, reading and rewriting; and learning to take better photos by taking hundreds at a time, looking at them with a critical eye, and going back to try again. It was tough, and scary, and the book wasn't perfect. But it was our book, and holding it in our hands for the first time made every minute of struggle worthwhile.

Since then, we've been lucky enough to write many books and articles on travel and outdoor adventure, from family camping and walking with dogs to running and rock climbing in the mountains of Britain and Europe. We've learnt a lot, made mistakes, enjoyed some successes and experienced plenty of failures. It's hard work, and at times only just pays the bills, but we love what we do.

Even now we're more established, though, the work doesn't often come to us. As freelance travel writers, we're always on the lookout for new places and new experiences – or new ways of seeing familiar ones – to write about. Once we've had an idea, the next step is turning it into an exciting overview of an article or book that, hopefully, someone will pay us to write. This part is all about the pitch.

General tips for pitching travel writing

• Do your homework. Thoroughly research the publisher or publication's titles, subjects and writing styles and pitch accordingly. Find those that match your interests, skillset and writing style.

• Play to your strengths. Whether you want to write about extreme adventure sports, food or walking, find the titles and publishers that specialise in these areas. Readers tend to know their subjects well, so using the right terminology, and knowing who's who in the world you're writing about, are essential.

• Read and follow submission guidelines carefully. Each publication will have its own set of requirements, so be specific with your pitch and never send blanket versions.

• Proofread your pitch for spelling, punctuation, grammar and clichés. Then proofread it again. Wherever possible, close the document and step away from it for a few days and then come back to it with fresh eyes.

• Make it really clear why you're the best person to write this book or article. What's your unique blend of experience and skills that means you'll do a better job than anyone else?

• Use all your skills. Many publications like to include photography to illustrate a piece. While some will want to send out a professional photographer, if you're handy with a camera, you can take insider photos as you explore a place or undertake an adventure or activity. If you can also provide mapping/gpx files, illustrations etc. alongside your copy, this can add more value to your submission.

Pitching to magazines and newspapers

The print media world is fast and furious, and everyone's always on a deadline. When you're pitching to a magazine or newspaper, spend a moment imagining what an editor's day looks like. They'll probably receive dozens – if not hundreds – of emails pitching ideas for articles every day. So start off by making your email one they have to click on, drawing them in with a catchy subject line. Instead of calling it 'Article Proposal', pique their interest with a great title for your piece.

Again, read the submission guidelines carefully. Some larger publications have several editors and clearly specify who to send your pitch to. Don't be tempted to send a blanket email to all the editors, or even a bulk email to all relevant publications. If your pitch isn't specific and personalised to each publication, and directed to the right editor, it won't make it past the first filter.

Submission guidelines may also tell you what the publication is looking for, and what it isn't. As an example, some magazines love 'Top 10 best…' lists, whereas others specifically ask writers not to submit them. It's well worth re-reading submission guidelines even if you've written for a publication before, as they can – and do – change.

Keep pitches short and to the point. Remember, editors are busy people, so the best pitches capture a great idea in an engaging way and get it across in a couple of sentences. Include your suggested headline, a brief summary of the story, who or what will feature in your piece and why it should be covered now. Having a time limit – for example a festival, seasonal element, launch event or other reason to commission your piece right now – can all be helpful.

Find an angle on your place or story that's unusual but relevant and interesting to the publication's readers. Imagine you're taking a photo of an iconic building or view. You can stand where everyone else stands and get the same photo, or you can be inventive, zooming in or out on your subject, getting other people involved, or visit at an unusual time of day or time of year. As well as your main pitch, you could also include a couple of one-line suggestions for alternative stories or angles on your main story.

In the same way as avoiding reproducing the same 'view' on a place, try to avoid using clichés in your writing. Travel editors in particular will have read about many crystal-clear lakes, snow-capped mountains and spectacular sunsets, so giving them more of the same is unlikely to capture their interest. Instead, give them a story that explores a place or activity in a new way that they may not have considered before, using fresh, vibrant language.

Pitching books

Non-fiction books about travel and adventure are usually commissioned based on a proposal. Sometimes, especially if it's your first book, you'll also need to provide a writing sample, such as a completed chapter of your book. This gives you the opportunity to sell your brilliant idea, demonstrate your writing skills and showcase why you're the best person to write the book, direct to the commissioning editor.

Not all publishers accept unsolicited book proposals, but many do, including some of the larger publishers if you're writing in a more niche area. Find the 'submissions' page on the publishers' website and read the guidelines carefully. Then follow them to the word. Make your proposal as easy to say yes to as possible, ensuring you've included all the relevant information clearly and concisely.

What's in a proposal?

The specifics will vary somewhat depending on the publisher, but a proposal generally contains the following:

- A synopsis of the book, outlining your idea and getting across the 'feel' of your book.
- A chapter breakdown, showing you've planned out the topics you'll cover, and how they'll flow.
- Sample material, demonstrating your expertise in, and ability to write about the subject area. If you're pitching a photo-led book, include some examples of your photography work.
- Information about the intended market – who is the book for? – and how your book compares to the current competition, including what sets yours apart. You'll need to demonstrate that you've thoroughly researched other books out there in your area, and show there's a need and demand for your book in the market.
- Brief details about your background and qualifications to write the book, as well as your passion for the subject – why are you the best person for the job?

Whether you're pitching an idea for a book or an article, once you've clicked 'send', it's exciting (and a little nerve-wracking) waiting for a reply. If you've pitched to a newspaper or magazine, you'll usually hear if they want to commission your piece within a few days. A reply to a book pitch can take weeks or even months, though. In the past, we've assumed a publisher isn't interested in our book proposal, only to receive a surprise offer long after we'd given up hoping.

Bear in mind that it's very normal to simply hear nothing. Try to see this as the default – again, editors have a lot to juggle and it might just not be the right time for your story. Don't take it to heart and don't be put off. Try a different publication, a different angle or even just a different heading. Think of it as experimentation – what gets noticed, and what doesn't?

Sometimes, although increasingly rarely, you'll receive a rejection with feedback on what you could have done to improve your pitch. In our experience, these can be more challenging to deal with than getting no reply at all! If you can, try to look at feedback as advice rather than criticism. After all, your pitch was clearly good enough for the editor to spend time reading and replying to it.

Early on in our writing career, we received some fairly strongly worded feedback from an editor at a major newspaper who had actually approached us to write a piece. It had felt like an incredible opportunity, but the pressure was overwhelming and, with hindsight, we weren't ready to take it on. At the time, reading through the comments was heart-breaking, humiliating, and made us question our life choices. But in the end we chose to view it as personalised advice from someone at the top of the travel writing business. That advice has shaped our writing ever since, and, though it stung at the time, we're better writers for it.

If your pitch or proposal is commissioned – congratulations! This is when the really hard work begins, but it's also when you can look forward to the incredible feeling of finally seeing your idea made a reality in print.

Editors at magazines and newspapers will usually come back to you with a word count, deadline and fee for you to agree, and then it's up to you to write the piece and submit it on time. Books are a little different. If a commissioning editor is interested in your initial proposal, they'll usually ask you for more details, including a suggested word count and timeline, and whether you'll be supplying other material such as images and maps. Once they have all the information they need, they'll take it along to an editorial meeting, where they'll present your proposal to the publishing team. If everyone's on board, they'll come back to you with an offer.

Once you've agreed to undertake the work, whether it's a 2,000-word article for a magazine or a 100,000-word book, now is the time to remember the most important rule of being a freelancer: be great to work with. As a travel writer, you'll often end up pitching ideas to the same editors time and time again. Being great to work with means they're more likely to open your email, and more likely to keep commissioning you. They might even start approaching you for work. As Neil Gaiman says in his book, *Art Matters*, freelancers keep getting work because: 1.) their work is good; 2.) they are easy to get along with; and 3.) they deliver the work on time. Did we mention editors are busy people? Being great to work with, hitting your brief and always filing on time means they're more likely to pick you next time. And, ultimately, that's the key to a building a long and successful travel writing career.

Jen and Sim Benson are outdoor adventure writers and photographers. They write a weekly walking column – *A Good Walk* – for *The Times* and are regular contributors to *Walk, Trail, Country Walking* and *Runner's World* magazines. Their books include *The Adventurer's Guide to Britain* (Bloomsbury 2018), *Wild Running* (Wild Things Publishing 2019), *Short Runs in Beautiful Places* (National Trust Books 2020), *100 Great Walks with Kids* (Bloomsbury 2021), *The Camping Bible* (Bloomsbury 2024), *Great British Walkies* (National Trust Books 2024) and *Smart Running* (Vertebrate 2024). Jen has also written *The Path We Run* detailing her account of completing her first 100-mile ultramarathon (Octopus Publishing Group 2024). Find out more at https://jenandsimbenson.co.uk/. Follow them on X and Instagram @jenandsim.

See also...

• *How to write features for the national and regional press*, page 3

Poetry
Introduction

Poetry has been an intrinsic and vital part of the UK's literary world for over 1,000 years. From Beowulf to Zephaniah, Byron to Duffy, poets have rocked the establishment, and continue to inspire and comfort readers. Meeting and sharing one's words has also – and always – been a hugely important part of the poetry world but for a while, it looked as if the pandemic had put paid to that. However, the resilience of the poetry community during lockdown, and in the five years since, has shown that the love of communicating in verse only got stronger during challenging times: well-established groups moved online and new ones sprang up. Many have returned stronger to in-person meetings and some operate both in person and online.

The listings in this section offer an excellent starting point for meeting and finding community with other poets, while the articles contain a range of inspiring, honest and uplifting advice on what works for some of today's published poets. Seamus Heaney (1939–2013) once described poetry as a threshold rather than a path: turn the page here and cross the threshold to what the future holds for you as a poet.

Listings in this section:

- *Where to get involved*, page 349
- *Where to get information*, page 350
- *Online resources*, page 351
- *Where to celebrate and perform poetry*, page 352
- *Where to write poetry*, page 354
- *Competitions*, page 355
- *Help for young poets and teachers*, page 355

Poems for the page and on stage

Raymond Antrobus celebrates poetry on the page and in performance, a passion he shares with fellow poet Anthony Anaxagorou. Here he records their views on writing and reading poetry in private and in public spaces, and what it can offer, particularly in times of change.

While London was in lockdown, I and my fellow poet Anthony Anaxagorou, curator of Out-Spoken and Out-Spoken Press, decided to choose four poems (by other poets) to read on Instagram live. We started this series and each week attracted between 300 and 400 viewers. We discussed the poems and why they resonated with us in those times of uncertainty.

At first, I was unsure of how this would be received. I was anxious that at times it felt more like exploiting the moment rather than living it but, after a month of these sessions, I could see how it was sharing the moment we're living in with people – giving a sort of fly-on-the-wall perspective to the kind of private discussions Anthony and I, as peers, have been having for years about the writing and reading of poetry. We found that these discussions helped give a wider dimension to the Audenesque anxieties of our times; the crucial element to it is that it is improvised, unrehearsed sharing.

For example, Anthony and I didn't know in advance which poems each of us was going to read; everything was revealed live, but there was often a natural relationship of some kind that happened between each of the poems. In the third episode we both happened to choose poems with animals and children in them, poems that ask questions rather than claim answers; in some there were tones of cynicism woven around sentimentality. Sometimes images even reoccurred within the poems we chose, and Anthony and I delighted in these mystic synchronicities.

I asked Anthony if he missed giving readings and performances. He said no – he prefers reading poetry alone and engaging with poems on the page to reading for an audience. Watching poetry readings online, I notice that a lot of poems do sound the same in the air even though they make different sounds and shapes on the page. There is an assumed poetry voice for every poem – a kind of jolting, careful reading where, even if the content has different tones, it is still read in that same kind of stately, over-pronounced voice.

Coming from the spoken word scene, I know that part of the craft is knowing how to surprise an audience beyond just the words; the voice and body also have agency, in the same way that line breaks and line length do on the page. In performance, monotony bores audiences – you see it – but this is craft talk for poems in performance, something rarely considered by poets who only think of the readers who come to them on the page.

Anthony's preference for engaging on his own with poems on the page is significant, because both of us started out on the London 'open mic' circuit. We both co-curate poetry nights (mine were Chill Pill and Keats House Poets Forum, and his was Out-Spoken). Anthony, as well as running a live night, also runs a publishing house (Out-Spoken Press). During lockdown I missed giving readings where you feel your poems connecting with audiences in real time, but I do also have an appreciation for quietly reading other people's poems privately on the page. I love geeking out about enjambments, voltas and how to create volume and surprise around the white space. I read poetry collections the way most people read novels; first poem to last poem fast, then going again – first poem to last poem – marking the poems that moved me.

For years Anthony has been the one person I know who has both that kind of sustained, intense relationship with poetry on the page and also comes from the stage. Polarising stage and page has always felt like a loaded issue to me, in the sense that the open mic and spoken word scene is a lot more diverse culturally than the literary scene. The dismissal of spoken word as low art, from the *Guardian* to *PN Review*, came with racial and class undertones; it's a kind of prejudice hidden in language, but it works both ways. Poets I know who also come from the spoken word scene say literary poets are too posh, that they write poems where you don't know if they're starting or finishing. I do understand that, but this is a discussion about the expectations of audience. Those poems that end quietly without declaring some kind of resolve or punch line are often expecting their audience to meet the poem halfway. This requires a different kind of listening – a kind of listening that engages subtly with meanings that are sometimes less immediate. Often there are no digressions or statements or opinions of the poet guiding the poem; it's more of a focusing-in on smaller moments or ideas.

Now, I don't want to privilege one style over the other. To pull off a quality spoken-word performance and a good page poem takes craft and talent. But talking to Anthony about performance has highlighted to me that, as we've grown older, our taste has developed and our expectations of poetry have changed. However, there is still a fundamental integrity in what we expect from poems, and that is a kind of widening curiosity and wonder about the world and our existence – an openness. I think an easier way to put it is: heart and imagination.

Even now, I remember the slam poems from my days in Slam. 'Gay Poem' by Keith Jarrett beat me in a national Slam championship final back in 2009. The poem is a conversation between the poem and the poet: the poem comes to life to ask the poet, 'Am I gay?' In spoken word, there is a lot of space for self-affirmation because of how active the body and voice is in the way poems are received. This poem stood out because it engages with the visibility and *invisibility* of the poet.

Other memorable poems from the London spoken word scene include Ross Sutherland's poem about how the language of customer service has changed over the centuries (Ross performs his dramatic poem in the dialect of each period of history between a customer and a shopkeeper) and Kae Tempest's poem 'Ballad of a Hero' about a soldier returning from war, which they performed at a reading commemorating the poet Christopher Logue. These live experiences are an important part of my poetry history as a reader and as a listener, so I can't privilege page over stage ... or vice versa. I acknowledge them as two different species of poetry that co-exist with my poetry eye and ear.

Raymond Antrobus is the author of *To Sweeten Bitter* (Out-Spoken Press 2017), *The Perseverance* (Penned in the Margins 2018), *All The Names Given* (Picador 2021) and *Signs, Music* (Picador 2024). His debut work of non-fiction, *An Investigation of Missing Sound*, will be published by Orion in 2025. His children's picture books are *Can Bears Ski?* (2021) and *Terrible Horses* (2024) both by Walker Books. In 2019, Raymond was the first poet awarded the Rathbones Folio Prize for best work of literature in any genre. Other accolades include the Ted Hughes Award, *Sunday Times* Young Writer of the Year Award and *Guardian* Poetry Book of the Year 2018. He is a Fellow of The Royal Society of Literature and Cave Canem, and was awarded an MBE for his services to literature. For more information see www.raymondantrobus.com.

The portfolio poet

Poet Sophia Blackwell explores the varied options, opportunities and combinations available to poets who are suited to the variety, creative freedom and independence of a portfolio career. She offers ideas and encouragement on the many ways to make a living and supplement your income while growing as a writer.

The idea of a poetry career is not exactly an oxymoron, but it's not straightforward either. This article might more aptly be called, 'How to make whatever money you can from poetry while doing other things you don't hate'. Poetry careers often involve a certain amount of juggling, and some people enjoy it more than others. You might be more of a portfolio poet than someone who moves linearly from one grant and project to another. Generally, portfolio poets:

- **Enjoy trying different things** and aren't daunted by the prospect of learning new skills.
- **Have a 'butterfly mind'** and jump from one task to another. They find it helpful to approach a task by doing a less urgent item on their to-do list and then returning to the original task.
- **Don't want to be tied down** to a rigorous publishing schedule – this isn't as problematic for poets as for commercial novelists, but some poets still find a strict timetable an unappealing prospect.
- **Like keeping their options open** by being able to do a variety of different things and enjoy being independent, with the creative freedoms that come with that.

There's a lot to be said for the portfolio approach in terms of future-proofing your career. You may be less negatively affected when a new editor at your publisher doesn't care for your work, or when the venue that hosts your readings closes, if you can return to one of the other projects you have on the back burner. Keeping your options open can provide a sense of control.

The idea of the poet as troubadour, traveller, teacher and entrepreneur is close to my heart. This is probably because it resembles my life to date more than the idea of working for a single academic institution or publisher. Like a lot of poets, I give lectures, teach workshops in schools and colleges, and edit manuscripts covering all genres from romance novels to business reports. I have run literary salons and been paid by hundreds of different festivals, colleges and organisations. For a decade, performing and hosting literary events made up at least 50% of my income from poetry. Historically, selling copies of my books at events has made up roughly a tenth of my yearly income from poetry. I have taken on commissions to create and run large poetry events in venues such as theatres, galleries and museums. I have given private poetry lessons and made radio shows and podcasts, some of which are funded by arts organisations. It would be hard to say what I enjoy doing the most, but there are hundreds of ways a poet can make a living and supplement the money they make from their writing.

Running writing groups or poetry classes

If you're thinking about running a comprehensive series of classes, it's best to be an experienced poet with a couple of published books to your name and a working knowledge of 20th- and 21st-century poetry. If you are not quite there yet, you can easily arrange to teach a few one-off classes as part of a bigger event taking place near you, either in a physical space or online. Literary festivals, libraries and arts venues (such as galleries and theatres), offer plenty of possibilities for an enthusiastic would-be educator to run an event over a weekend or during a quiet evening. These venues or their funders can pay you a modest fee, and one-off events of this kind can develop over time into a poetry course.

Once you have the outline of a poetry course, you can start running writing and feedback sessions in a library, cafe or pub, or online. If you feel you've created something unique, you can approach an organisation with an established reputation for teaching poetry. If they see the value of what you offer, they can give you space, help you monetise the course, and give it legitimacy by hosting it on their campus or in another venue connected to theirs. If you have an area of expertise, either in a particular style of poetry, another art form you can combine with poetry, or a theme or hobby that genuinely fascinates you, it is worth leaning into that and creating at least one spectacular workshop or short course that you feel can be best taught by you alone. It does not have to be unique, but ask yourself what you can offer that few others can.

The teaching route suits patient, tactful, well-read and confident people who communicate well and are prepared to engage with a vastly different range of abilities and personalities. Some of your students will be opinionated, some will be shy, and some will go on to create impressive projects that outdo your own poetic CV. A skilful teacher will have to address these very different sets of needs and personalities, and what each student hopes to get out of the class.

Running events for young writers

Some poets might find it especially rewarding to teach young people as part of youth groups, school activities and after-school clubs, which may be eligible for community or national arts funding. The focus of such a group may be on developing young people's performance skills and helping them to express themselves in writing. The teacher's literary knowledge would not need to be as high-level as someone wishing to teach intermediate or advanced adult poets, but they *would* need other skills suited to working with young people. Anyone thinking about working with children will need to arrange a DBS check (a background check of your criminal records); this is a requirement for going into schools, even if you're only planning on doing so now and then.

Editing a poetry magazine

Editing a poetry magazine can be a source of relatively steady income as well as prestige, but it is a full-time job, even if the hours may technically be part-time. As well as a strong artistic vision, this role requires business sense, people skills and experience of filling out funding applications. Jobs on established magazines are competitive and, because a lead editor or poetry editor is often in place for years, turnover is quite low. I am delighted to see new magazines spring up and succeed, even in today's challenging climate, but it's not for nothing that people say if you want to make a small fortune in publishing, you need a large one first. If you have a strong urge to launch a new publication but you are not sure about committing to something on this scale, try running a webzine online first. This will give you the flexibility to produce one-off print publications which can be paper zines, chapbooks or pamphlets with short selections from a poet you've discovered. This allows you to create a tailored publishing business on your own terms, without the non-negotiable publishing and proofreading schedule that a print magazine requires. Established poets can also work with magazines and literary organisations to provide funded mentorships to emerging, early-career poets whose work shows promise, and these mentorships will be funded by the magazine or organisation, who in turn are likely to be funded by the Arts Council or other charitable foundations.

Giving readings and performances

If your style has something in common with performance poetry or you're an established name, you can supplement your writing with performances. Some poets use it as their primary source of income or at least aspire to increase the percentage of the money they make from performing. One way of making a full-time career out of poetry is to make 50-minute (or longer) shows and tour your work, but this requires being as consummate a show-person as you are a writer, and eager to embrace the highs and lows of life on the road. This route requires focus, resilience and self-belief. I'd suggest you need 'thick skin' too; hardly any poets have that, so performance poets would be advised to invest in developing other forms of toughness, self-care and coping strategies for days on the road and nights in front of an audience. Writers, actors and comedians must maintain the difficult balance of remaining sensitive enough to make art and respond to the world around them, and tough enough to manage late nights on railway station platforms, solitary hotel breakfasts, poor reviews and the occasional social media pile-on. Performers do not have to be extroverts but, to fully enjoy the unprecedented options for self-expression provided by performance, they must firmly believe in what they are doing.

Commissions from local literary festivals

Many cities have their own literary or cultural festivals, and the organisers are likely to pass on part of their funding from the Arts Council or city council to a writer for a project that speaks to a place or theme relevant to that city. Mills, mines, markets, historical battles, theatre districts, Huguenot, Bangladeshi or Irish neighbourhoods can all be a source of inspiration. When putting together a pitch for an event like this, poets might theme their offering around an upcoming anniversary of an important day for the town or community. This approach suits the rigorous and organised, as these commissions are time-sensitive and require research. Local festival organisers will be looking for poets with a taste for combining their writing with visual and aural elements (video, film, audio soundscapes or dance). The poet might work on their own, with a group, or in partnership with another local artist or musician to create an immersive experience for the public to enjoy. Open-minded organisers will be looking for both types of event – the large-scale, multimedia type that's location-specific and might require music, projectors and lighting, and the small, flexible type that only requires a microphone and some willing participants and can be run anywhere from a library to a village green.

Events at local literary or community festivals

It is worth getting to know the organisers of your local festivals, as there is often funding for a poet to run a couple of hours of readings with their friends, an open mic or a poetry Slam. These smaller events are also attractive to hard-working festival organisers because they can be arranged at the last minute, aren't dependent on big-name artists and can work well to get audience members into a venue or fill an awkward-length slot between programmed events. Local literary festivals may also commission a writer to create a new poem or series of poems, or a printed pamphlet or anthology about the city or the festival's theme. If you are already inspired by the place where you live, look out for opportunities to share your location-specific writing with the community. Audiences enjoy hearing about the places they know, and that familiarity can be a powerful way to get them on your side.

Writing articles and editing manuscripts

Writing articles and editing manuscripts are much more than nice-to-have options for an aspiring writer. Journalism and editing are full-time careers, or should be, and they require a great deal of professional knowledge. However, most freelance copy-editors and journalists are already used to working with different newspapers and magazines, taking on various types of work, ghostwriting and generally adopting a portfolio approach to their careers, either out of choice or necessity. Experienced poets can also pick up reviewing work for poetry magazines, as these are keen to find appropriate reviewers for new books and to develop the next generation of poetry critics. Reviews editors generally want to diversify the voices in their reviews section, in terms of backgrounds, identities and geography. For example, reviewers from outside London or reviewers with a disability might fit the brief that a reviews editor is looking for, provided that the would-be reviewer can also write well and has a compelling understanding of the book or poet they are writing about. Look up 'Ledbury Poetry Critics' (https://ledburypoetry.org.uk/home/ledbury-poetry-critics), a national mentorship programme for poetry reviewers, which is aimed at encouraging new and diverse voices.

Writing in another genre alongside your poetry

Whole books and careers have been devoted to the other things you might write, not least the other titles in the *Writers' & Artists'* series. Most writers do try out more than one genre in their lifetime. There is significant overlap between poets and the following categories (though you might just as easily come across a romance author or graphic novelist who also writes poems):

• **Children's and young adult (YA) writers.** Poets often write books for young children, sometimes in verse and sometimes not. Fantasy and mythical themes are popular and reasonably paid options. Established prose writers for young adults, such as Sharon Creech, as well as poets who started out in spoken word and Slam, like Mahogany L. Browne, often turn their hands to young adult novels in verse.

• **Non-fiction authors.** Poets often have specialist interests and a way with words that makes them ideal candidates to write non-fiction books.

• **Playwrights.** The rhythm of page poetry, the staged nature of performance poetry, and the desire to create something ambitious and long-form from similar raw materials have led to interesting creations and collaborations over time. Full plays in verse have waxed and waned in popularity throughout the 20th century, but now performance poets are doubling back by creating extensive works of poetry-based theatre. Like poets, playwrights are aware of the measure, beat and timings of certain words. Poetry and playwriting have shared a long relationship, from T.S. Eliot's verse plays to the contemporary works of Mike Bartlett – who, as well as writing one play, *King Charles III*, in blank verse, writes his other playscripts in a singular way that indicates exactly how the lines should be paused and punctuated by the actors.

Even if the portfolio model of career is not for you, here are some ways of broadening your skillset that you may not have considered. There are plenty of online and in-person opportunities to help you master those that pique your interest:

• **Video, radio and podcasting.** This is ideal for creating live or recorded readings and reaching new and international audiences through digital channels.
• **Visual art.** If you have skills in this area, you can combine your poetry and artistic abilities. You might design and illustrate your own chapbook, or curate an exhibition that includes poetry and painting, photography or sculpture.
• **Comedy and/or acting.** Many comedians offer classes and sometimes private tutoring. Even if you don't see yourself as the next Edinburgh award-winner, cracking a couple of jokes before a reading can be a real icebreaker.

Taking on projects for a variety of different clients can be seductive for a creative person, and it can be a positive thing in terms of your growth as a writer and strengthening different parts of your portfolio.

Sophia Blackwell is a performance poet with three published collections. Her poetry has been anthologised by Bloodaxe, Nine Arches and the Emma Press among others, and her most recent collection was longlisted for the Polari Prize. She is also the author of a novel and of the *Writers' & Artists' Poetry Writers' Handbook* (Bloomsbury 2022). Sophia makes podcasts and radio shows for London-based station Resonance FM. Notable gigs include five times at Glastonbury on the Poetry&Words Stage, Women of the World (WOW) Festival at the South Bank and headlining a national tour with Hammer and Tongue. For more information, see www.sophiablackwell.co.uk. Follow her on X @sophiablackwell.

See also ...

Can you make a living writing comedy? Yes, but ..., page 368

Being a poet and a publisher

Aaron Kent urges writers to build and engage in a supportive, collaborative, nurturing community in which to grow creatively, with the many opportunities, challenges and encouragement this will provide. As both poet and publisher, he explains that finding the right places to share your work but, above all, enjoying the act of creating, are key.

I grew up unaware that the arts were a career option – I assumed that was just something rich people did in their spare time rather than a viable ambition. It was a field where the gates had been securely shut and not one where individuals of low socioeconomic status stood a chance of entering, particularly as allowing us in threatened the system they had created to benefit themselves. Eventually I learnt that you *could* have a career in the arts, but you had to have either connections or money – both things that weren't prevalent outside of the middle and upper classes. This sounds frustrating because it is, because gentrification works for those people, and disseminating the arts more widely threatens the boundaries already set. Fortunately, there is a pathway that degentrifies the industry, one that dismantles gates and offers solutions: it's called community.

'Community', as a word, can be looked down upon by artists who already find themselves with a readership and a practice, but it's important to remember that community can exist as an idea that holds inclusion at its core. What those who already sit beyond the gated walls tend to ignore is that they reside in a community – a community that boasts exclusion at its heart; one that is defined by who it keeps out, and the hierarchies it presents. I cling, firmly, to the working-class motto: It's not about rising above your community, it's about rising with it. And that is a sentiment the gatekeepers don't like, because they lose control over who can access the arts. So, first and foremost, my advice is to build a community or engage as part of one. When you're involved this way, you'll find people keen to celebrate your successes and console you in your struggles, and you can offer the same. You'll find artistic growth in the collaboration of admiring others' work, and your work will grow from active and passive engagement with the work of others.

Now that technology is so prevalent, this collaboration doesn't have to be something that happens purely in person – you can create these gatherings and connections anywhere. There are artists I talk to in time zones across the world whose friendship has helped me to become a better author. Stuart McPherson, for example, is my assistant editor at Broken Sleep Books (www.brokensleepbooks.com) and my closest friend. We began our friendship in 2012 online as part of a poetry forum and remained in touch but not to any extent before finally meeting in 2021. There are a multitude of poets and artists I connect with over WhatsApp, social media and email. These are people who see opportunities to share with each other, who cast an eye over each other's work, who boost each other when we need it. This is a connection that money can't buy, because it is built and grounded in selflessness, and it doesn't shut the gates to people on the basis of pre-existing capabilities.

I was 16 when I first wrote a poem. I was 27 before I wrote a poem I liked. Between 16 and 24 I didn't really read any poetry; I was raised in the second most deprived area of Northern Europe, Redruth in Cornwall, and my English teacher was just happy if a dozen or so students actually did any work in class – so there was no inspirational 'Dead Poets Society' education. My parents didn't have an education beyond secondary school, and education wasn't an aspirational thing, it was just a chore to complete as part of the journey to adulthood. So, when I dropped out of my A-levels and worked full-time as a barista maestro, I had no literary platform to work from, and no real desire to engage with one. But I continued to write, and write poorly, because I had no community; there was nobody whose work I read, and therefore I felt no ambition to improve, as I now do when reading poetry by Luke Lankester. There was nobody pushing me beyond my boundaries and encouraging me to grow artistically, the way Azad Ashim Sharma now does ... nobody, like Andre Bagoo, Martha Sprackland, Andrew McMillan, whose encouragement helped me to believe in myself. And so, writing by myself, with no readers, no ambition, no drive, I stagnated into work that existed as just another chore. If you're writing because you're purely interested in the response – whether that's a review, publication or money – then the act of creation becomes no more than a task designed to achieve something else. The fundamental part of art, for me at least, is to enjoy the creating of art – to get a boost from putting ink to paper or fingers to a keyboard or paint to a canvas. If creating something has lifted your morale and made you proud, or happy, or understand yourself at a deeper level, then the work is a success, regardless of how it is received later.

Through Broken Sleep Books we get over 6,000 submissions a year, so I read a lot of cover letters and bios, and I see a noticeable difference between somebody who has sent their work to every possible magazine and journal hoping for publication, and somebody who has a clear idea of the type of journal they want to be published by. There's a perception that collecting acceptances is more valuable than it actually is. The key is to ensure proper research with regards to submissions, finding places that fit with your work and who publish writers you want to be positioned alongside. This is all part of that community I've spoken of – remember, it's harder to feel a part of anything if you're trying to be a part of *everything*. Art that situates itself with intention and care is more likely to benefit from the work it resides with than art that exists purely to attain a name to put in a covering letter.

Finally, one of the most important parts of my practice has been to engage in what I call 'creative sorbet'. This means that when I hit a wall and think I can no longer create or write, I move to a different artistic form – whether that's painting, or playing my bass guitar, or learning a difficult recipe. By engaging your creative practice elsewhere, you take your mind off that artistic block and stimulate different artistic muscles. It doesn't matter, to me, if my painting is good or not; what matters is that I created something using a different skillset and then, when I return to writing, those things I learnt about myself and my practice are brought back with me. It also means you immerse yourself in different creative practitioners. The US painter Barnett Newman is currently more important to my writing than many writers are, because his art makes me reconsider how I write.

These reasons, and more, matter because if you've enjoyed the act of creating and got something out of it, if you've got people around you to share in the highs and lows, who challenge you, and you've achieved something before the art has entered the world, then you've won the battle – regardless of the result. If you've got *this* in place, then the rejections matter less and the successes taste sweeter.

Aaron Kent is a working-class writer, stroke survivor and insomniac from Cornwall. His second collection, *The Working Classic*, is available from the87press. He has read his poetry for the BBC, the Shakespeare Birthplace Trust, and Stroke Association, had work published in various journals including *The Poetry Review*, *Poetry London*, and *The Rialto*, and is an Arvon tutor. Follow him on Bluesky @godzillakent.bsky.social, X and Instagram @godzillakent.

Making poetry comics

Poet and comic book writer Chrissy Williams talks about creating poetry comics – an exciting hybrid art form that combines the lyricism of poetry with the visual dynamism of comics – and thinks about what delights they might yield.

I used to edit a magazine called *Poetry Digest* that was published on cupcakes. The poetry had to be eaten before any actual digesting could happen. It was delicious. It was also a reminder that experience is ephemeral, and our engagement with art is worth savouring, literally.

I've always been interested in messing about with art. As a writer and editor of both poems and comics, it feels inevitable that I'd get drawn into mashing together the two art forms at some point, to see what they could offer each other. As with all hybrid art forms, poetry comics take a little from each side, but ultimately create something that is new, different and wholly their own.

Poems are, usually, made of words. Some poems are designed primarily for the ears, and some are designed primarily for the eyes. As they make the poem, poets decide whether it will live on a page, and how much they want to engage with the words visually. Some poems can be structured very elaborately or formally. Some can be a stream of free-flowing text. Some can look like a spray of isolated words, scattered across the page like blossom. Some can be considered visual artworks in and of themselves.

The words in a poem are sometimes straightforward – purely descriptive or narrative – and at other times more complex. Poems can use words to capture or enact complicated moments, or thoughts, or ideas, about experience or about language itself. William Carlos Williams said a poem is 'a machine made of words'. Mark Yakich said: 'a poem helps the mind play.'

Comics are, usually, made of pictures. More specifically, comics are visual sequences. They often include text as captions or dialogue, but if all you're reading in a comic is the words, you're missing the point. The pictures must also be read, both individually and in relation to each other. As Eddie Campbell said: 'The drawing is the story; it doesn't illustrate it.' If the text and the art are just repeating each other, it's a bad comic.

The art of comics is one of aesthetics, of course – of looking at someone's work and saying 'blimey, that is gorgeous', but it's also one of playing with how we interpret images in sequence, and of letting our brains fill in the blanks between panels.

Let's take, for example, a comic that is two panels long. Panel one shows a cat with her eyes closed. Panel two features the same cat, with her eyes open. You can easily infer that an action has taken place in between these two static images – the cat has opened her eyes.

What happens when we make those panel transitions a little more complicated, or more abstract? What happens if you add a panel between the two cats of a star exploding? What happens if the first cat is instead followed by a drawing of the Titanic? What if we see three panels in a row where the cat is simply keeping its eyes closed, but we are zooming closer in with every panel? Where does your brain go in any of those gaps between panels? Our brains are machines made for trying to make connections. The sparking of thought is the only real remit for art.

Poetry often works this way, too. Look at these lines from Ezra Pound's classic 1913 imagist poem, 'In a Station of the Metro'. Think about the work your brain is doing in piecing together a single image from the juxtaposition of these two images, one in each line:

The apparition of these faces in the crowd;
Petals on a wet, black bough.

Juxtaposition is an important tool for providing context, helping us rethink the things we take for granted. In poetry comics, a medium that pivots directly around the relationship between art and text, juxtaposition is fundamental.

That comics are made of sequential art means they are almost always narrative. The nature of sequence propels us inevitably forward. So what happens when you lean into comics' more abstract communicative capabilities? And what happens when you allow a poem's communication and image-building to come from a wordless source?

Poetry comics are a tremendous vehicle for evoking the sorts of messy impulses that drive us all to be creative in the first place. They liberate the poet in us from the constraints of language. They liberate the artist in us from straightforward narrative. They can take us somewhere much stranger, much more quickly. American poet and artist Bianca Stone describes poetry comics as having a 'perplexing but also entertaining ability to wed mystery with meaning'.

Where is the best place to start, then, with something so seemingly mysterious? Well, first, you can see what other people have already done, to provide a little context. I co-edited an introduction to poetry comics with artist Tom Humberstone in 2015 called *Over The Line*, which still serves as a useful showcase. The now defunct American journal *Ink Brick* is also excellent. It might be useful to brush up on your comics and poetry skills individually too. Scott McCloud's *Understanding Comics* is a how-to guide for comics written in the same medium. Guides to writing poetry range from the very practical *Writing Poems* by Peter Sansom, to the more lyrical *Making Your Own Days* by Kenneth Koch, or even *Strong Words*, an anthology of modern poets' statements and essays.

How you approach the physical process of making your own poetry comics will depend on whether you are a poet or an artist and how confident you are in your abilities in both mediums. It is possible to start from the writing side without being an artist. Kenneth Koch drew poetry comics by hand-writing words into hand-drawn misshapen panel squares, deliberately drawing attention to the function of art and ability as part of his process.

It is also possible to start from the drawing side without generating any words yourself. In *A Humument* (although not self-identified as poetry comics), Tom Raworth painted and drew over pages of an existing book, isolating individual words and creating new artworks, usually viewed in sequence, to create a sort of poetry comic experience from reworked found materials.

Collage is a useful tool when it comes to poetry comics, especially (but not only) when you are starting out. The art of collaging gives you permission to work with existing materials and reconfigure them in thought-provoking and interesting ways. It frees you up from having to create the raw ideas yourself, and lets you focus on the process instead. You ideally need to use out-of-copyright material, though, or else have the artist's permission to use their work.

You can also look for someone to collaborate with. I personally have the drawing ability of a bee, so have almost always collaborated with other artists. Small book press and indie comics fairs and conventions are a great way to see contemporary poets' and artists' work and meet potential creative partners. You can also scour through existing anthologies and social media, or go along to other live events, such as poetry readings and comic book signings. Local libraries, bookshops and comic book shops are a great place to begin.

A collaborative poetry comic will usually start with a script, which contains as much or as little detail as is desired. I have sometimes provided a script with more prosaic detail in it than a film script, and at other times given just a single word or line of poetry, from which the artist mapped out the entire work themselves. It's important to have a chat about expectations with your collaborator (even if it's just your own tortured psyche) to make sure everyone's on the same theoretical page.

Once a script exists, in whatever form, the artist will create some sketches to map out roughly how the page or pages will flow. Inking usually follows, or fixing in place if collaging – some process of making the work more solid and permanent. Colour is often a wholly separate stage of its own. What would 'adding colour' mean to a poem, I wonder?

Lettering – that is, adding the layer of text – usually happens last in mainstream comics, after all the artwork is complete. In children's picture books, however, lettering sometimes happens first: the artist is given a blank page with text of the correct size and shape on it, that they can move around as they wish, knowing the exact dimensions they have to accommodate in their art. In a collage or poetry comics collaboration, the words and the pictures are sometimes inextricable from each other.

The last part of any creative process is an editorial one – seeing what can be improved upon or removed completely. An important part of comics work comes from recognising what is being carried best by the words or the pictures at any given moment, and deleting anything that feels like a needless repetition of the other.

Like all good collaborations, you get to make up your own rules. Poetry comics is still a relatively new area that anyone could walk into and make their own. It is massively open to interpretation of subject, form, process and effect – and that's what makes it so exciting. As comics critic Eileen Gonzales has said: 'Given the deliberately abstract nature of poetry comics, it doesn't matter where you start. The fact that you start at all is what matters.'

Chrissy Williams is a poet, editor and comic book writer based in London. Her writing has been featured on BBC radio and television, and her full poetry collections are *Bear* (Bloodaxe 2017) and *Low* (Bloodaxe 2021). Her debut comic *Golden Rage* came out from Image Comics in 2022, and is described as '*Battle Royale* meets *The Golden Girls*'. As an editor, she is best known for her work on *Die*, *The Wicked + The Divine* and *Superfreaks*. She edits the online poetry journal *Perverse*, and has run numerous poetry comics workshops over the years. She co-edited *Over the Line: An Introduction to Poetry Comics* (Sidekick Books) with Tom Humberstone in 2015, about which Alan Moore said 'I really can't recommend this venture highly enough'.

Getting your poetry out there

Neil Astley knows that you need talent, passion, patience and dedication to become a published poet. He gives valuable advice on the possibilities, pitfalls and rewards that any budding poet might encounter.

Are you a poet – yet?

This article assumes that you have a potential readership or audience for your poetry, and that where you need guidance is in how to reach all those readers. But most poets just starting out believe that. There is, however, *no* readership for poets who *think* they are ready to publish but whose work isn't really *there* yet. It is essential to read other poets' works, to absorb yourself in their writing: this is what will help get you published and will make you a better writer. People either have talent or they don't, and no amount of self-promotion and/or even education in the way of poetry workshops or MA courses will make you a poet if you don't have an insatiable passion for *reading* poetry (not just your own) and an original way of writing it. But if you've been drawn to poetry, and have *read* as much poetry as you can get hold of, I'd say you're halfway there.

A poet's reading list

One of the poets I publish, Hannah Lowe, was an English teacher who'd always loved poetry but wasn't familiar with the full range of contemporary poetry until her mother gave her a copy of the Bloodaxe anthology *Staying Alive* as a birthday present. That book made her think that *she* could write poetry. With other younger poets writing now, the process has often been the other way round; maybe they've read Simon Armitage, Carol Ann Duffy, Seamus Heaney and Philip Larkin, but they haven't read their Shakespeare, Donne, Keats, Wordsworth, Coleridge, Browning, Dickinson, Frost, Yeats, Auden and Eliot, all essential reading for anyone who wants to write poetry.

Without that groundwork reading, your own work will go nowhere. But all is not lost. If you really do have a gift for poetry, but life circumstances have been such as to make your reading patchy, stop thinking of getting your work out there now, and for the next year, just read and reread judiciously without thinking of writing. Start with the *Norton Anthology of Poetry* (W.W. Norton, 6th edn 2018) and the *Penguin Book of English Verse* (Penguin 2004), and get hold of books by the major figures they include; then *The Rattle Bag* (Faber & Faber 1982, 2005), *Emergency Kit* (Faber & Faber 2004) and the *Staying Alive* anthology series (Bloodaxe Books 2002, 2004, 2011 and 2020) and read more by the poets who most appeal to you. When you come back to writing, a year or more later, both you and your poetry will have changed. The poems you had wanted to get out there earlier will go in the bin, and you'll be writing poetry that should interest other readers.

Getting critical feedback

Next you need feedback. If you can find a good writing group or workshop in your area, that can be helpful. Even if you disagree with other people's comments on your work, their feedback should still show what aspects of your poems don't work for other readers. Later, once you've been working on your poetry for at least a year or two, it would be helpful to go on one of the writing courses (which are more week-long workshops than taught courses as such) run by the Arvon Foundation at three centres in England, or by Tŷ Newydd in Wales or Moniack Mhor in Scotland. Or contact the Poetry School in London (https://poetryschool.com) which offers online tuition, downloads, workshops and summer schools. There are also part-time MA courses run by numerous universities and colleges throughout Britain, but I don't think those are right for relative beginners; to gain full benefit from such courses (which cost thousands of pounds in fees) I think you need to have been writing seriously for at least five years. (See page 646 for a list.)

You can also start sending out poems to magazines; their websites will say whether you should submit online or if you need to send half a dozen poems with a stamped addressed envelope for their possible return. It won't be hard to get poems taken by the smallest of the magazines. The real challenge will be in sending work to the long-standing, leading poetry or literary magazines edited by significant poets or critics. These might include *Acumen*, *Granta*, *Iota*, *The London Magazine*, *Magma Poetry*, *The North*, *Orbis*, *PN Review*, *Poetry London*, *The Poetry Review*, *Poetry Wales* or *The Rialto*. There are also literary and cultural journals that publish poems, but these are much harder for new writers to break into, such as the *London Review of Books* and the *Times Literary Supplement*; somewhat perversely, you may find you have more luck with the political press: the *Morning Star*, *New Statesman* and the *Spectator* all publish newcomers as well as established poets.

Just as important as getting poems accepted is getting them rejected, especially if that includes getting a note back from an editor with a comment on your submission that makes something click. You may think that what you're writing now is great, but there will be flaws. There are always improvements that can be made that make all the difference between a half good poem and a really good one. Poets judging poetry competitions talk about 'the wrong note', a line or phrase in a poem that sticks out as not belonging there or needing to be changed even with just one word added or a phrase taken out, and they can't give the prize to that poem because readers will see it too, but the poet is too close to the work and isn't aware of it.

Poetry magazines

Acumen
See page 36

The Dark Horse
www.thedarkhorsemagazine.com

The London Magazine
See page 64

Magma Poetry
See page 65

The North
https://poetrybusiness.co.uk/the-north-magazine/

PN Review
See page 71

Poetry London
See page 72

The Poetry Review
See page 72

Poetry Wales
See page 72

The Rialto
See page 76

For a fuller list see www.bloodaxebooks.com/links.

See also *Magazines UK and Ireland* starting on page 36 and *Poetry organisations* on page 349.

To submit or not to submit?

So the first lesson in how to get your poetry out there is *not* to send it out, or not yet. Put it in a drawer for six months and come back to it; with that amount of distance from the work, you should be able to fix that 'wrong note' and also make the whole poem read more smoothly. Also – and this is absolutely essential – read the poem aloud. As you're writing it, and when you think you've finished it, and when you come back to it months later. Again, poets who haven't done this all talk about only realising what doesn't work in a poem when they were reading it aloud to an audience; trying not to let their expression show that they've just read a bum line at the live event, but rushing home afterwards to correct it. And if you do all your writing on a computer, print out your poems, and read through and edit them on paper. What may look right on a computer screen will often not *feel* right on paper, and then you'll see what needs to be edited. This is also where magazine rejections are helpful: six months later, going back to the poem you thought was your best but which kept being returned, you see the 'wrong note', fix the problem, send it out, and the poem is taken right away.

Don't submit to magazines unless you're familiar with the kind of work each one publishes. They are all different, and you will not be able to publish much unless you research the field and send to those whose output you like and respect. If you live in or can get to London, Edinburgh or Manchester, spend a day in the National Poetry Library at the Southbank Centre, the Scottish Poetry Library or the Manchester Poetry Library and read the latest issues of the current magazines, and afterwards take out subscriptions to those you like most. Familiarity with the work of other poets is an important part of that process: if you're expecting others to read your work, you should read theirs too and learn from it; and support the magazines which support you. Join the Poetry Society and you'll receive *The Poetry Review* and *Poetry News* every quarter; join the Poetry Book Society and you'll receive their four Choices over the course of the year with the PBS *Bulletin* (including highly illuminating pieces by the poets about their books). The National Poetry Library also has two websites: www.nationalpoetrylibrary.org.uk, which includes listings of all the current print and online magazines, and http://poetrymagazines.org.uk, which has an archive covering many of the leading journals where you can read their back issues.

You can familiarise yourself with the editorial taste of online magazines much more easily. Some magazines publish both print and online editions, while others that started out as print have gone over completely to online publication. But so much poetry is published online now – and online imprints come and go – that readers and writers alike find it hard to see the wood for the trees, an appropriate metaphor to use here given that the cost and labour involved in printing and distributing magazines used to discourage poorly edited publications from flourishing. For a list of significant webzines which currently publish poetry, see the box overleaf. These are the webzines (some quite new, not all exclusively poetry) picked out by poets I've consulted as the places where they'd most like to see their work, and where the younger poets in particular go to read their peers. It's worth adding that they also want their work to be featured or discussed in several webzines which don't take submissions, notably *The Quietus* (http://thequietus.com) and *Wild Court* (http://wildcourt.co.uk). And the ultimate accolade is getting your poems into America's *Poetry* magazine, with all the work it publishes being added to a historic online archive that goes back to 1912. The recently established reciprocal publication by *Poetry* and *The Poetry Review* of selections by US and UK poets has helped make this less of a pipe dream for British poets.

Get noticed through competitions and performance

Building up a coherent body of work can take years. As your work matures, so your confidence grows, and you start getting more and more poems taken by magazines and perhaps win prizes in poetry competitions. And some of the poetry competitions are worth trying, but as with the magazines, don't submit blindly; do your research. Just as you can almost predict which poets will win each year's poetry prizes from who the judges are, or what kind of work the combination of judges on each prize's judging panel is likely to favour, so it is with the poetry competitions. And the timing of their deadlines is such that you can't usually submit the same poems to more than one of the main poetry competitions in any one year. So check out the main competitions and submit to those judged by the poets you admire. As well as the Poetry Society's National Poetry Competition, these might include the Bridport, Cheltenham, Ledbury, Manchester, *Mslexia* (women only) and *Poetry London* competitions. (See *Competitions* on page 355 under *Poetry organisations.*)

Popular webzines

And Other Poems
http://andotherpoems.com

Atrium
https://atriumpoetry.com

Bad Lilies
www.badlilies.uk

The Fortnightly Review
http://fortnightlyreview.substack.com

Ink Sweat and Tears
www.inksweatandtears.co.uk

The Lake
www.thelakepoetry.co.uk

London Grip
http://londongrip.co.uk

Pulsar Poetry
www.pulsarpoetry.com

The recent growth of festivals and venues with open mic slots has given new writers opportunities to read their work in public; and you don't have to be a performance poet for your work to go down well with audiences, you just have to read strong work and read it well. Don't overrun your time slot and give a straightforward presentation of your work, which means a short introduction only, use your 'natural' voice and don't adopt the highly mannered whining delivery style favoured by poets who should know better.

Once you've published widely in magazines and are starting to do readings, you'll be at the stage of seeking out a small press willing to publish a pamphlet or chapbook (15 to 20 poems). Most pamphlets are sold at readings, and having a pamphlet to give to organisers and to sell at events can lead to more opportunities to read your work. And finally – we're talking about years now – you might have a book-length manuscript (typescript) of around 50 poems which you think worthy of publication. But the chances of having this taken up by one of the 'big ten' leading poetry imprints (Bloodaxe, Bloomsbury, Cape, Carcanet, Chatto, Corsair, Faber, Granta, Penguin and Picador) are exceedingly slim. Apart from the big trade publishers, which don't consider unsolicited submissions except from literary agents, we all receive *thousands* of submissions every year, but the annual output of first collections from *all* ten imprints is rarely more than a dozen books *in total*. Much wiser to try the smaller poetry presses you'll find listed in this *Yearbook*, and you won't

Poetry publishers

THE BIG TEN

Bloodaxe Books
See page 124

Bloomsbury Publishing
See page 124

Jonathan Cape
See page 186

Carcanet
See page 128

Chatto & Windus
See page 186

Corsair
See page 156

Faber & Faber
See page 139

Granta Books
See page 57

Penguin
See page 169

Picador
See page 167

SMALLER PRESSES

Arc Publications
See page 120

Blue Diode
See page 125

Broken Sleep Books
See page 127

Burning Eye Books
See page 127

Cinnamon Press
See page 130

Dedalus Press
See page 134

The Emma Press
See page 138

Eyewear Publishing/The Black Spring Press Group
https://blackspringpressgroup.com

flipped eye publishing
See page 141

The Gallery Press
(Ireland) See page 142

Nine Arches Press
See page 162

Out-Spoken Press
See page 166

Pavilion Poetry
See page 167

Peepal Tree Press
See page 167

Salmon Poetry
See page 174

Seren
See page 176

Shearsman Books
See page 177

Smith|Doorstop Books
www.poetrybusiness.co.uk/smith-doorstop

Templar Poetry
See page 182

the87press
www.the87press.co.uk

Valley Press
See page 185

Verve Poetry Press
See page 185

The Waywiser Press
See page 187

For a fuller list of poetry publishers visit www.bloodaxebooks.com/links.

need an agent to do this. The only poets with agents are writers who are also novelists, journalists or playwrights. Don't think of ebooks as any kind of solution. Ebooks don't give poets the massive readership reached by writers of thrillers or romance, amounting to just 4% of total poetry sales.

Poets, beware!

Finally, a word of warning. There are certain firms which charge poets to publish their work or which require payment for copies of anthologies in which your work appears as a condition of publication. Poets starting out are particularly susceptible to what is known as vanity publishing. Reputable publishers or magazines of any size will pay authors for their work, usually with royalties in the case of books. If you are asked to pay for the production of your book by a publisher who sends you a flattering 'reader's report' on your work, try asking a local printer to give you an estimate for printing a few hundred copies of your book. The likelihood is that the cost will be considerably lower, and if you want your work to be read by friends, colleagues and people in your local community, the circulation you can achieve by this DIY method will be more effective. The normal arrangements for publishing also involve the author receiving complimentary copies of a book or a free contributor's copy of a magazine or anthology. If you're asked to pay to see your own work in print, you are paying to have it published. For more information see the advice offered by the Society of Authors (https://societyofauthors.org/vanity-publishing/).

If you're unable to get your book published but are confident of selling enough copies at readings, there are effective ways of self-publication covered by other articles in this *Yearbook*. As an alternative to local printers, a number of poets use the self-publishing website www.lulu.com, which offers a distribution channel in addition to well-produced books and ebooks.

Neil Astley is the Editor of publisher Bloodaxe Books, which he founded in 1978. His own books include novels, poetry collections and anthologies, most notably the Bloodaxe *Staying Alive* series: *Staying Alive* (2002), *Being Alive* (2004), *Being Human* (2011) and *Staying Human* (2020). He has edited four collaborations with Pamela Robertson-Pearce, *Soul Food* (2007), *Soul Feast* (2024) and the DVD-books *In Person: 30 Poets* (2008) and *In Person: World Poets* (2017). His novels are *The End of My Tether* (Scribner 2002), which was shortlisted for the Whitbread First Novel Award, and *The Sheep Who Changed the World* (Flambard Press 2005).

Perseverance in getting poetry published

Finding the time, space and inspiration to write poetry is challenging enough, but being published can feel like another mountain to climb. In this article, Pascale Petit amply illustrates the power of persistence.

I believe that everyone can write poetry. If I can, anyone can. I had no literary education, no mentor and had attended no creative writing courses. I may have talent, but what I definitely do have in abundance is tenacity. I needed perseverance because I had to wait until I was 44 to find a publisher for my first collection. All that's required to start is a sense of wonder and love of words; what it takes to get somewhere is perseverance. I now have nine collections, one novel and two pamphlets, have won a few prizes and I'm with my dream publisher, Bloodaxe. I look back amazed at my younger self, the person who thought she would never get there.

Improve your craft

One of the reasons it took me so long to be published was I didn't have enough craft to make my lines sing with power and clarity. There are shortcuts to learning craft – plenty of creative writing courses on offer – but one crucial habit you must acquire for the long haul is to read, read, read. I read contemporary UK poets, American authors, everyone writing in English. I read poets in translation, and I read some of the classics I missed out on by going to art school instead of university to study English – creative writing courses weren't much of a thing back then.

My first break came when I became an editor of the then-fledgling magazine *Poetry London*. Submissions flooded in and I quickly learnt not what makes a good poem, because that's difficult to define, but what makes a poem bad – it's easy to spot the ones with clichéd and tired language. I say this aware that it's hard to use fresh language, just as it's hard to write a good poem. I discovered what makes a fine poem even better when I corresponded with top names and saw how they revised at proof stage. Selima Hill cut her poems to the essential bones. Sharon Olds re-lineated every line, changed tenses and word choices. I realised the necessity of meticulous revision.

Seek encouragement

Whether it's from a magazine editor or a poet whose work you admire, cherish words of encouragement that come your way. Editors mean it when they ask you to send again, even if they did reject your current batch. Les Murray encouraged me before I published my first collection, and I drew on his affirmation when others were disheartening. I wasn't writing what was fashionable, so it was challenging to break into the scene. But I trusted his opinion, so stuck it out. Write what you must write and not what you think you should write. Lead the fashion, don't follow it. Pin notes of praise, not rejection slips, on the wall next to your desk, to keep faith with your art.

Enter competitions

Do enter competitions, but choose them carefully. I entered many before my first win. Some have serious prize rewards, and this can help you survive financially, as happened when I won the Manchester Poetry Prize with a £10,000 cheque for five poems. Check before you send – are the judges poets you respect and whose opinions you value? Even a commendation builds confidence and adds a valuable line to your profile. Publishers keep an eye out for the winners, and occasionally offer publication, or at least might remember your name when you send them your manuscript. You will be motivated by any success, and gain an energy boost for your writing.

Carve out regular writing time

Try different times of day and night and see what is most productive for you. I wrote my first collection, *Heart of a Deer*, at night when I was sleepless. My best time now is early morning before breakfast, when my head is still half in dreams and before the day imposes. I don't just write in that time, though; I also trawl for poems and artworks to inspire me, and collect them either as notes or photos on my iPhone. I keep several notebooks nearby and it's surprising how often I find abandoned drafts in them that spring to life. I store files of discarded poems from previous collections, and these too can spark a new poem. All of these activities are what I call 'trying to write' time – each is as valid as attempting to pen a new poem from thin air. This space I protect for writing keeps me on an even keel when rejections arrive because there's always the hope the new ones will be better.

Don't give up on your bad poems

Bad poems lead to good poems, so don't despair when you're not writing well. The best poems are little miracles, gifts from the ether. I love those of mine that come easily, but most evolve from initial wrong starts. Those failures are your imagination reconfiguring itself to make something new, ploughing through possible approaches. They are pre-poem material as you find fresh ways to recreate the world and your life through that difficult medium – words.

Apply for funding for writing time

I don't have family backing or a secure income, so I've been lucky that six of my collections have been supported by grants, either from Arts Council England, the Society of Authors or the Royal Literary Fund. For the first two, you don't have to have published a book, but for the RLF you need to have two books published (not self-published) and they assess if you are eligible for financial support based on quality and hardship. They are a lifesaver for authors (they don't offer grants for writing but for financial difficulty). It is hard to receive funding from ACE because so many creatives apply. My last ACE grant was to complete *Mama Amazonica* and travel to the Peruvian Amazon for research – it took three attempts before I succeeded. Each time they rejected it, they gave the reason 'other applications preferred', which meant I could re-apply. Persistence paid off.

Apply for funding for research and travel

As well as family griefs, my books explore place; several are based in the Amazon rainforest, while *Tiger Girl* is set in national parks of central India. I have a deep interest in Earth's wild places and this has led me to thrilling locations. I could not afford to do these trips without funding – I earn my living from freelance work, much of which is tutoring and mentoring. But I have to find a balance between teaching and my own creative time, and this is where grants have been invaluable. I have stayed in the Camargue to study its wildlife and I've seen a wild jaguar in his rainforest, wild tigers in Bandhavgarh as well as in other

Indian national parks. While it is possible to imagine these places, what being in them has given me is sensory detail – how a pristine rainforest smells and sounds. And although I was looking for tigers in India, what fed into many poems in *Tiger Girl* was the unexpected profusion of extraordinary birds.

Passion and single-mindedness

Three of my collections were written in Paris, as for many years I was teaching term-length courses at Tate Modern and the Poetry School, so to make space for my own writing I'd spend monthly retreats between terms there, renting a room and working every day. The location is resonant for me because it's my birth city and I lived there as a child, then returned to visit my dying father decades later. The Latin Quarter, where he lived, never fails to inspire. I'd avoid meeting friends, focused on the task of drafting twenty poems during each stay. It took discipline to be so prolific while there. Not everyone is cut out to be a poet; it requires solitude and a willingness to prioritise your art.

Build your profile

Publishers will rarely consider your manuscript unless you have magazine publications. Aim for the best: *The Poetry Review*, *Poetry London*, *PN Review*, *The Rialto*, *Granta*, *The North*, *Magma*, and smaller but well-edited online magazines. Try sending to the ultimate journal, *Poetry*, at the Poetry Foundation in Chicago. These, as well as competition placings and readings at festivals and events, assure the publisher that you have a growing readership, and that they'll be able to sell your books to recoup production costs. A profile also shows that you're serious and are forming a unique identifiable style, which is another quality publishers like. No one else can write the way you do, so concentrate on developing your voice with passion and dedication, and it will show. Another way to get ahead is to publish a pamphlet of between twenty and thirty pages. Plenty of little presses run pamphlet competitions. This shorter form gives you a trial run and something to sell at readings.

Managing disappointments

The life of a poet is emotionally precarious. Rejection from a magazine editor or a publisher is upsetting. It's essential to remember how inundated they are with submissions. They may have liked your poems, but not enough, or they may have their quota on that theme already. When I was poetry editor at *Poetry London*, I sometimes didn't take poems because they didn't fit into the space left for that issue, so I know first-hand that it's not always about quality. I've often been rejected myself, and have found it's advisable to send several batches out at the same time to different magazines, so if one comes back there are still others out, keeping me hopeful. If a poem gets rejected too often, I will see if I can improve it. Recycling lines that are most alive for a new poem is also a good antidote to discouragement. When it comes to manuscript submissions, it helps to bear in mind just how many submissions the publisher gets, and how few debut poets they publish each year – the odds are not favourable, but it's always worth trying.

Find a mentor

I have mentored a lot of poets. Some have paid privately for my help, while others received mentoring as part of a package they've won. I work with mentees towards the development of their craft and editing skills. With advanced poets, we discuss their manuscript – its order, structure, spine (the best poems) and I suggest which poems to leave out and which to keep. I wish I'd had this help. You can apply to the Arts Council to fund your mentoring – many emerging poets do this as part of their project. Approach mentors before you apply, so you can quote realistic budgets. Ask your dream mentor first, and if they are too busy, ask someone else who seems a good fit.

The long haul

What if the prestigious magazines repeatedly reject your poems? Don't give up! Your work may not be to an editor's taste, but editors come and go. I first published poems in *The Poetry Review* in 1985 – but then, when my work became more personal, they dropped me. I had to wait years before I could get in again. The more poets you read, the more you will evolve. Magazines survive on subscriptions, so if you can, subscribe to a few, and you'll also get an idea of where you can see yours fitting in. If you want people to read your poems when they are published in them, you should read theirs – it's a reciprocal process.

Editors of presses might change too, so be aware of what's going on, follow them on social media, and keep improving your poems. I sent my first manuscript to Bloodaxe, and was rejected with a thoughtful letter from Neil Astley. But I tried him with my seventh, and got in. Editors change their minds, or maybe my style evolved. Join classes at the Poetry School, where you'll not only have tutors' advice, but meet contemporaries at the same stage as you. Find a poetry buddy with whom you can exchange and critique poems. Above all, enjoy writing and write what brings you joy. Don't forget to play – poetry is a pleasurable art, and pleasure is what the reader seeks when they read yours. Good luck.

Pascale Petit is a French-born British poet. She has written nine collections of poetry, four of which have been nominated for the T.S. Eliot Prize; the most recent is *Beast* (Bloodaxe Books 2025). *Mama Amazonica* (Bloodaxe Books 2017), her seventh, won the Ondaatje Prize and Laurel Prize. Her debut novel, *My Hummingbird Father*, was published in 2024 by Salt. Find out more at www.pascalepetit.co.uk.

Becoming a lyricist

All writers have their own creative process, and in this article Kathryn Williams explains how, for her, inspiration takes shape.

I am a singer-songwriter. It took me a long time to admit that when asked what I did for a living by a taxi driver, because I thought it sounded silly. But yes, that is what I am and I have been releasing records since 1998. I've been nominated for various awards and had chart positions but never been a big star; instead I just forged my own path of creativity and have been lucky enough to still be hanging on in one way or another. To date, I've made 17 albums, written a novel, hosted a podcast and sell my paintings. I'm telling you this so you won't judge how untidy my house is. I've got things to do, and I tend to 'crop-rotate' between different arts.

I've been writing words down since I was 10 years old, and am still doing so 40 years on. Lyrics echo in my head with a tune attached; I write words down in my phone or sketchbook and return to them later, taking the scraps and gluing things together into a new story or image.

I've written a piece and then matched the rhythm of the text for a song. The sonorous sound of the word in my head and its rhythm informs the melody that will emerge. Words in songwriting are defined and utilised by shapes, rhymes and rhythms. Of course meaning is important, but there is a sensuous instinct when I write; the map of how the song will move in the music comes from interlocking pieces, hooks, reoccurring motifs. If you have a verse, for instance, once that shape is there with a framework, you know you can fill in that framework with the second verse. I would think about the journey of the song – the meaning, the story – but the frame for the rhythm and the word length would be there to slot that in from the first verse.

Things aren't fixed in the process of songwriting; songs can come all sorts of ways. Sometimes it's the other way round. I'll be playing my guitar or singing to myself and the melody will be there, but not the words. I've heard many songwriters talking about not 'owning' their songs and that they are gifts. I definitely have that with melodies. I think maybe I have an aerial that picks up a radio station called Inspiration. When a song falls into you like that, it's a case of being ready to receive. My job is to note it down and make sense of it later. I will have a feeling of what the song is about, though. It's like someone walking towards me in the mist – a vague shadow or outline. In these instances, I sing words, made-up noises – 'Oo ahh doo ship bop boo' – random things in the melody. Sometimes the first words that appear may remain because they have the same 'feeling' that the melody is suggesting, and strangely they can have a big impact on the meaning of the song. When songs come this way, it is about remaining in a semi-dream state, as if you've just woken up but the dreaming still makes sense. You need to be flexible and led by the song rather than try to wrestle it into a rigid, solid form.

Almost everything I've done in music is self taught; at times it's felt like fumbling around in the dark for a light switch. In the past, when asked, I would not talk about the process because I thought I didn't have one. I was embarrassed that I didn't know enough about the mechanics of why I wrote. I was just driven to write and sing. If you're reading this, presumably it's because you either want to write lyrics and need some encouragement, you want to know how I write lyrics or you like people talking about their creative process. You should know, then, that there's no Eureka moment. Or least not for me. The voices of inspiration and of my creative muse speak softly. They tap on my shoulder very lightly, asking me to look again at something. It's a first small spark rather than a roaring fire, but you have to be ready to listen for it. And you need the time and space for it to come to you. I often tell participants on my writing courses that when you begin a song, you should walk quietly into the woods. If you are shouting 'hello, I'm here looking for a song! Where are you?', stamping your feet and waving your arms around, the first thing that will happen is nothing. Songs, poems, melodies are shy animals. They will run for the hills.

But if you walk quietly, listening for a noise, looking for a small shadow, noticing a shaft of light falling diagonally back there behind a tree, you might start to be quiet enough, to be out of the way enough, for these shy things to come forward. This might just be a twitch in your stomach, a humming feeling in your chest, a gear change in writing faster or an automatic feeling that things are flowing. 'But I'm not in a forest, I'm sitting at my desk with a pen,' I hear you say. Talking a lot about the creative process can become an impediment that takes us further away from how we actually work, so I'm going to talk to you as honestly as I can about a new song I wrote and how it came to be.

'Sea of Shadows'

One morning, I was sitting with a cup of tea after both my sons had left for school/college and my husband had left for work. I noticed on photo memories on socials a picture of my son: he was 19 by then but in the photo he was around 6. As I looked at the image, feelings came flooding in about time passing. My heart felt heavy at the realisation that those times had gone, even though they had been hard. I picked up my guitar and started strumming. How was I going to convey all this? I started to describe what was in the picture. Louis was dressed up for World Book Day: he had wanted to go as a minor character from an *Octonauts* book.

> 'Dressed up as the sea of shadows, with a red nose, and black clothes. And you had to tell them who you were, 'cause they didn't know at the book show.'

So World Book Day turned into 'book show' because the shape and rhythm held better with the phrase ''cause they didn't know'.

The next part of the song, which is sort of the chorus, came in a bit of a dream vision, imagining Louis was protected by a sheriff's star that he used to wear. It is me as mother voice telling him not to be afraid of who he is (Louis struggled at school and has been diagnosed with dyslexia, ADHD and autism): 'don't forget who you are, you can wear your mysteries, like a sheriff's star, don't forget who you are wearing mysteries with an open heart.'

I worked with scribbles of phrases around that imagery, lots of lines, sentences, lists. I would circle things that felt good, better, best and try them with a melody that was forming until both sort of slotted in. Then I knew I had the framework because I had the shape of the verse and the chorus. I took a break, filled the dishwasher, started putting clothes away. I picked up one of Louis' T-shirts and sort of time-travelled to the present day. I stopped what I was doing and started the second verse: 'wearing an MF Doom cartoon t-shirt' (the item I had picked up), 'you're out the door fast, every weekend, I never know where you're going but when you're hungry you come home'. At this point, I felt self-conscious. I wasn't sure if what I was doing was good because it felt very real and I could hear my own voice in it. This is a crucial point in all types of creative work: doubt sets in. I would say it is good to listen to yourself, but momentum is key. Let yourself be two people: the creator while you are in this mode; and the editor later, otherwise you halt the flow. Now I had the chorus but I wanted to tweak it a bit to relate to this new time-travelling forward. 'You don't explain where you are, so I'll wear your mysteries like a sheriff's star, don't explain where you are, why apologise for an open heart': this time it's me wearing the star.

This is all I had going into the studio to do a demo. I was still a little embarrassed by it, because it was so close to me. I played it to my producer, Leo, and guitarist, Neill, and they encouraged me to finish it, so we sat round a kitchen table where they chipped in while we wrote the last verse. I was able to explain that I wanted to finish the song by going right back in time again to Louis as a baby and the last verse goes: 'you're always on my mind and I love it when you smile, it takes me back in time like a dream, to when you used to fit inside me, now your shoes are size 13.' We wrestled with these lines and it was in the discussion about placement that I knew I wanted the humour of the shoe size to be the pay-off line. (I did give both Leo and Neill writing credits as: 1) I wouldn't have finished without their encouragement; and 2) they helped me finish the song.) As an aside, co-writing with people you trust can be a good way of finding out what you want – or not. A suggestion of how something could be can give you a whole new pathway through the song or it can reaffirm what you don't want. Both are helpful shortcuts. Even explaining a song idea to someone can solidify what were just vague thoughts before.

Finally I wanted to shift the chorus again to relate better to the last verse. I should say that this is not normally how a chorus works in a song: it usually remains the same and it's the verses that change.

The final chorus was as follows: 'we all grow into who we are, wearing mysteries like we are deputies, don't forget who you are, why apologise for an open heart'. I'd written a list of everything associated with the sheriff's star to see if I could unlock something and when the word 'deputy' came up, it felt really poignant: it touched on the idea of the stars of the show and their sidekicks and being a deputy of who we are rather than the sheriff of ourselves. It tied into the changing dynamics in families and relationships.

This song was then recorded almost immediately in the studio and I didn't have time to process it until I heard it back. With a huge lump in my throat, I realised I had captured something really meaningful to me.

The spark was the photo, which gave me the momentum to begin; the break was the reflection after the framework had been established, the openness to co-writing and sharing that helped finish the song. The holding-off of my unease and embarrassment of it being too much in my voice or too personal until it was made was keeping the editor in me at bay while the song was in flow.

I hope this helps you see that songs can come in so many ways and myriad varieties.

Things to note

You don't need to play an instrument to write a song. You have one: your voice. Did you know that Ewan MacColl, who wrote 'The First Time Ever I Saw Your Face' and 'Dirty Old Town', didn't write them on an instrument?

Singing acapella is such a great way to write songs. You aren't tied down to any chord structure or progression; you can beat out a rhythm at a table; you can walk along and hum ideas to yourself. Probably the first bits of music we hear are a singular voice when we are being sung to as babies or children by our parents. Stop reading this piece for a moment and hum or sing a little tune to yourself. It's free. Similarly you can play on a piano with one finger for notes, strum a guitar and find chord shapes (that's what I did). Explore a little. There is a freedom in not having any rules and you may well come up with something unique. Not knowing and exploring is such an important part of creating. So is being able to laugh if it's awful. If you sing a terrible tune and then laugh, I would call that a win.

There is a difference between poetry and lyric writing. When I was making a Christmas album with Carol Ann Duffy, she said to me that 'poetry has its own music, whereas lyrics are put to music'. The words are attached to a melody that evokes more emotion as a result of that connection. Words are sung. The shape and sound of the words become something that needs to slot in to the rhythm of the song, and sound right and feel right in the mouth. I've realised over time that the right-shaped word is more important than the right definition. This is what scan is all about. When you sing a line in a song, there might be a bit that you realise you trip over; perhaps it has a clunky, odd shape to sing. So you need to find the next best word with a shape that feels and flows right with the music.

Exercises that can spark writing

I use some of the following exercises in groups and also for my own work.

Picturing

Write down what you see in a photograph, postcard, painting, film etc. In short, write the image in words.

Journalism

Note down what time it is now and what's happening. Factual journalistic writing is a great way of starting to define the exterior world before dipping into internal thoughts and feelings. Some examples are 'Famous Blue Raincoat' by Leonard Cohen ('It's four in the morning, the end of December / I'm writing you now to see if you're better') or Bob Dylan's 'Tangled Up in Blue' ('Early one morning the sun was shining I was laying in bed').

Change of place

Go to different locations – park, shopping centre, seaside, train station – and write down what you see. For example, how is the light different? What is the food like on holiday? How do you feel in different environments? You'll notice people act differently; maybe you do too.

One-way conversations/confessions

Write a letter. It can be addressed to someone you know, living or dead. It can be something you know you will never say or send. It could be a letter to a younger you or a future you.

Imaginary word Tetris

Hum a tune with made-up words, record it (on a phone), listen back a few times and see if you can slot in real words like blocks and make sense of the automatic.

List-writing

Think of a subject – a door, say, or a window or heart. Write a list of related words as quickly as you can in a short space of time. Don't try and be poetic; make it like a shopping list. You'll be amazed by what will emerge from the constraints. Be specific. Specificity will begin to take you past the usual shorthand, less about what everyone notices and more about your personal connections and observations.

Co-writing

Find someone to write with, either on a writing course/retreat or a friend or family member. You can have really good fun and it can open up new ways to connect. I started out writing songs in secret on my own in my bedroom, desperate for no one to hear them (what a strange thought, I now realise). Today, I do a lot of co-writing with artists and other writers and this can be a great way to motivate yourself and plan writing time. The benefits of co-writing are the conversations that you have together, where you're hearing things out loud, circling in on a good idea or subject. This all helps the song become clear because you are explaining to each other what you mean and chipping in with better words, rhymes and images.

Finally, I've realised that my own personal way of seeing things and the real specifics I plant in my songs are what make things ring true. You don't have to include diary entries or real-life things, but do observe detail so that you're moving away from cliché. It's that which seems to help connect me to the listener.

There is only one me and there is only one you and there is a duty to be true to that and value what each of us brings to the world. I was riddled with anxiety, self-doubt and embarrassed by my own singular voice for so many years. But that voice is, in the end, my/your biggest strength, so don't be afraid to write and sing your own way, the way it comes out of you. When you feel as though you've made something you're proud of, let people hear what you have created.

Kathryn Williams is a singer-songwriter. A Mercury Music Prize nominee, she writes with musical artists around the world and was the only female included in the top ten list of Liverpool songwriters of all time. She has also written a novel, *The Ormering Tide* (Wrecking Ball Press 2021), run writing residential courses for the Arvon foundation and Creative Scotland, and was a judge on the 2016 British Poetry Society's Ted Hughes Award. See www.kathrynwilliams.co.uk to find out more.

Poetry organisations

Below are some organisations which provide budding poets with opportunities to explore, extend and share their work.

WHERE TO GET INVOLVED

A range of organisations – from local groups to larger professional bodies – exist for emerging and established poets to access support or to learn more about others' work. A concise selection appears below.

The British Haiku Society

16 Croft Gardens, Andover, Hampshire SP10 2RH
email britishhaiku@gmail.com
website www.britishhaikusociety.org.uk
Facebook www.facebook.com/thebritishhaikusociety
Instagram @britishhaikusociety
President Iliyana Stoyanova, *General Secretary & Treasurer* Paul Hickey, *Membership Secretary* Julie Williamson, *Editor, Blithe Spirit* Iliyana Stoyanova, *Editor, the brief* Maya Daneva, *Communications Officer* Jenny Shepherd

Pioneers the appreciation and writing of haiku and kindred forms of verse in the UK. Currently there are around 400 BHS members from 27 countries. Members receive a quarterly journal, *Blithe Spirit*, an annual members' anthology and a newsletter. Runs the annual British Haiku Society Awards in three categories: haiku, tanka and haibun; publishes books concerning haiku and related matters; and is active in promoting the teaching of haiku in schools and colleges. Founded 1990.

Literature Wales

Tŷ Newydd Writing Centre, Llanystumdwy, Cricieth, Gwynedd LL52 0LW
tel (01766) 522811
email post@literaturewales.org
website www.literaturewales.org
Instagram @llencymru_litwales
Executive Director Claire Furlong, *Artistic Director* Leusa Llewelyn

National company for the development of literature in Wales. Working to inspire communities, develop writers and celebrate Wales' literary culture. Activities include the Wales Book of the Year Award, the National Poet of Wales, Children's Laureate Wales and Bardd Plant Cymru schemes, creative writing courses at Tŷ Newydd Writing Centre, and various writer-development initiatives. The organisation is a member of the Arts Council of Wales' Arts Portfolio Wales.

The Poetry Book Society

Milburn House, Dean Street, Newcastle Upon Tyne NE1 1LF
tel 0191 230 8100
email enquiries@poetrybooksociety.co.uk
website www.poetrybooks.co.uk
Facebook www.facebook.com/poetrybooksoc
Instagram @poetrybooksociety

Book club for readers of poetry founded in 1953 by T.S. Eliot. Every quarter, their expert poet selectors choose one outstanding new poetry publication (the PBS Choice), and recommend up to six books to deliver to PBS members across the globe. Also produces a lively quarterly poetry magazine, the *Bulletin*, which includes in-depth reviews, interviews with international poets and extensive listings. Members also enjoy 25% off all book orders and access to a lively poetry community with nationwide events.

The Poetry Business

Campo House, 54 Campo Lane, Sheffield S1 2EG
tel 0114 438 4074
email office@poetrybusiness.co.uk
website www.poetrybusiness.co.uk

Publishes books, pamphlets and audio under its Smith|Doorstop imprint; runs the literary magazine, *The North*. Also organises an international Book & Pamphlet competition, Writing Days, online workshops and runs an advanced writing school for published poets. Founded 1986.

Poetry Ireland

(Temporary office) 3 Great Denmark Street, Dublin 1, D01 NV63, Republic of Ireland
tel +353 (0)1 678 9815
email info@poetryireland.ie
website www.poetryireland.ie
Director Liz Kelly, *Publications Manager* Paul Lenehan

Committed to achieving excellence in the reading, writing and performance of poetry throughout the island of Ireland. Receives support from The Arts Council (An Chomhairle Ealaíon) and The Arts Council of Northern Ireland and enjoys partnerships with arts centres, festivals, schools, colleges and bookshops at home and abroad. Creates performance and publication opportunities for poets at all stages of their careers. Publishes *Poetry Ireland Review* three times a year, *Trumpet* once a year and an online journal of work by early career poets who participate in the Introductions/Ceadlínte programme.

The Poetry Society

22 Betterton Street, London WC2H 9BX
tel 020-7420 9880

email info@poetrysociety.org.uk
website www.poetrysociety.org.uk
Instagram @thepoetrysociety

Established over a century ago to promote a more general recognition and appreciation of poets and poetry, the Society has more than 3,000 members. Supports education initiatives, commissioning and publishing programmes, and a calendar of performances, readings and competitions.

Offers advice and information to all, with exclusive offers and discounts available to members. Every quarter, members receive copies of *The Poetry Review* and the Society's newsletter, *Poetry News*. Also publishes education resources; organises events including an Annual Lecture and National Poetry Day celebrations; runs Poetry Prescription, a critical appraisal service available to members for £40 and non-members for £50; and provides an education advisory and training service, as well as school and youth memberships.

Competitions include the annual National Poetry Competition, with a first prize of £5,000, and the Foyle Young Poets of the Year Award. Founded 1909.

The Seamus Heaney Centre at Queen's

Queen's University Belfast, 38–40 University Road, Belfast BT7 1N
tel 028-9097 1077
email shc@qub.ac.uk
website www.seamusheaneycentre.com
Director Professor Glenn Patterson

The Centre's new building opened in 2024 and hosts a permanent exhibition, literary archives and a programme of talks, readings and performances throughout the year, primarily to support the work of students studying Poetry and Creative Writing at Queen's University. The Centre has an outreach programme, a prestigious Poetry Summer School, and awards an annual First Collection Poetry Prize. The current Seamus Heaney Professor of Poetry is Nick Laird. Founded 2003 with director Ciaran Carson.

Survivors' Poetry

95 Wick Hall, Furze Hill, Hove BN3 1NG
tel (01273) 202876
email drsimonjenner@gmail.com
Director Simon Jenner

National charity and survivor-led arts group which coordinates artistic activities using poetry to make connections between creativity and mental health.

Tower Poetry

Christ Church, Oxford OX1 1DP
tel 07849 625906
email tower.poetry@chch.ox.ac.uk
website www.chch.ox.ac.uk/towerpoetry
Facebook www.facebook.com/towerpoetry
X @towerpoetry
Instagram @towerpoetry

Exists to encourage and challenge everyone who reads or writes poetry. Funded by a generous bequest to Christ Church, Oxford, by the late Christopher Tower, the aims of Tower Poetry are to stimulate an enjoyment and critical appreciation of poetry, particularly among young people in education, and to challenge people to write their own poetry.

The Write-on Group

email writeon.galway@gmail.com
website www.write-on.ie
Facebook www.facebook.com/WriteonGalway
Chairperson Frank Fahy

Not-for-profit online international writing group dedicated to creative writing, including short stories, novels, poems, and songs. Meets exclusively on Zoom and welcomes writers from around the world to share their work and support one another. Projects go beyond the written word: up-to-date technology and multimedia is used to showcase members' writing through video and audio recordings, films, documentaries, illustrations and professional presentations. Funded by member donations. Publishes annual anthologies and other collaborative works. All writers are welcome: see website for more information.

WHERE TO GET INFORMATION

Your local library is a good first port of call and should have information about the poetry scene in the area. Many libraries are actively involved in spreading the word about poetry as well as having modern poetry available for loan.

Arts Council England

tel 0161 934 4317
email enquiries@artscouncil.org.uk
website www.artscouncil.org.uk
Instagram @aceagrams

National development agency for the arts in England, providing funding for a range of arts and cultural activities. It supports creative writing including poetry, fiction, storytelling, spoken word, digital work, writing for children and literary translation. Also funds a range of publishers and magazines as well as providing grants to individual writers. Contact the enquiries team for more information on funding support and advice.

Arts Council of Wales

Bute Place, Cardiff CF10 5AL
tel 0845 873 4900
email information@arts.wales
website https://arts.wales
Facebook www.facebook.com/celfyddydau
Instagram @celfcymruarts

Independent charity with three regional offices; its principal sponsor is the Welsh Government. It is the country's funding and development agency for the arts, supporting and developing high-quality arts activities. Its funding schemes offer opportunities for arts organisations and individuals in Wales to apply, through a competitive process, for funding towards a clearly defined arts-related project. Founded by Royal Charter 1994.

Manchester Poetry Library

Manchester Metropolitan University,
Grosvenor Building, Cavendish Street,
Manchester M15 6BG
email poetrylibrary@mmu.ac.uk
website www.mmu.ac.uk/poetry-library
Instagram @mcrpoetrylibrary
Director Becky Swain

Public poetry library: free and open to all. Aims to expand access to poetry and to encourage the writing of it at all levels, from primary school to professional publication. Core collection includes 19th- to 21st-century poetry in English from around the world, as well as poetry in translation. Audio and print versions available. Runs events that celebrate the role of local communities and languages.

National Association of Writers' Groups

Old Vicarage, Scammonden, Huddersfield HD3 3FT
email info@nawg.co.uk
website www.nawg.co.uk

Aims to bring cohesion and fellowship to isolated writers' groups and individuals, promoting the study and art of writing in all its aspects. There are many affiliated groups and associate (individual) members across the UK.

National Poetry Library

Level 5, Royal Festival Hall, Southbank Centre,
London SE1 8XX
tel 020-7921 0943
email info@poetrylibrary.org.uk
website www.nationalpoetrylibrary.org.uk
Facebook www.facebook.com/NationalPoetryLibrary
Instagram @nationalpoetrylibrary
Membership Free with two forms of ID, one photographic and the other showing a UK address

Largest public collection of modern poetry in the world, open to everyone and free to join (see website for details). Members can borrow from the extensive loan collections, including audio items and ebooks can be loaned at distance. The extensive collection of current poetry magazines gives a window into the breadth of poetry in the UK and beyond. The library runs regular live readings, a programme of exhibitions and children's events throughout the year. Its website features publishers' information, poetry news and a list of UK-wide events.

Northern Poetry Library

Morpeth Library,
Morpeth Sports and Leisure Centre,
Gas House Lane,
Morpeth Northumberland NE61 1SR
tel 01670 620391
email mylibrary@northumberland.gov.uk
website http://northernpoetrylibrary.org.uk

Largest collection of contemporary poetry outside London, housing over 15,000 titles and magazines covering poetry published since 1945. Founded 1968.

Scottish Poetry Library

5 Crichton's Close, Canongate, Edinburgh EH8 8DT
tel 0131 557 2876
website www.scottishpoetrylibrary.org.uk
Facebook www.facebook.com/scottishpoetrylibrary
Instagram @splscotland
Director Asif Khan

Houses over 45,000 poetry-related items: books, magazines, pamphlets, recordings and the Edwin Morgan Archive (featuring rare works by Morgan and others). The core of the collection is contemporary and classic poetry written in Scotland – Scots, Gaelic and English – but classic Scottish poetry as well as contemporary works from almost every part of the world are also available. All resources, advice and information are readily accessible, free of charge. The SPL has its own shop and holds regular exhibitions and poetry events, including reading and writing groups and outreach projects throughout the nation; see website for details. Closed Friday to Sunday. Founded 1984.

ONLINE RESOURCES

There is a wealth of information available for poets at the click of a mouse; the suggestions below are a good starting point.

The Poetry Archive

email admin@poetryarchive.org
website www.poetryarchive.org
Facebook www.facebook.com/PoetryArchive
X @PoetryArchive
Instagram @thepoetryarchive

World's premier online collection of recordings of poets reading their work. Over 700 authors featured. Features the voices of contemporary English-language poets as well as those from the past, including C. Day Lewis, Paul Farley and Dorothea Smartt. The Archive is added to regularly. Funded by donation; a membership scheme is available to help keep collections freely accessible.

The Poetry Kit

email info@poetrykit.org
website www.poetrykit.org
X @thepoetrykit

Collates a wide variety of poetry-related information, including events, competitions, courses and more for an international readership.

Poetry Space

email susan@poetryspace.co.uk
website www.poetryspace.co.uk

Specialist publisher of poetry and short stories, as well as news and features, edited by Susan Jane Sims. Operates as a social enterprise with all profits being used to publish online and in print, and to hold events to widen participation in poetry. Submissions of poems, stories, novel extracts, photographs and artwork accepted all year for Young Writers' and Artists' Space (18s and under; work by under-16s particularly welcomed).

Poets and Writers

website www.pw.org
Facebook www.facebook.com/poetsandwriters/
Instagram @poetswritersinc

US-based online magazine and e-newsletter on the craft and business of writing.

Write Out Loud

email info@writeoutloud.net
website www.writeoutloud.net
Instagram @wolpoetry

Poetry news, features and reviews, with comprehensive listings of poetry events, publications, festivals and competitions. Members may post poems, join discussions, add their profile, etc. 50,000+ monthly users.

WHERE TO CELEBRATE POETRY

Festival information should be available from Arts Council England offices (see page 539). See also *Festivals and conferences for writers, artists and readers* on page 630. As well as the list below, major poetry festivals each year include Aldeburgh and Cheltenham. Poetry also often features prominently at the Glastonbury and Latitude Festivals.

The British Council

British Council Customer Service UK, Bridgewater House, 58 Whitworth Street, Manchester M1 6BB
tel 0161 957 7755
email uk-literature@britishcouncil.org
website https://literature.britishcouncil.org
Instagram @britishcouncil

Information on events, authors and projects.

Canterbury Festival

Festival House, 8 Orange Street, Canterbury, Kent CT1 2JA
tel (01227) 452853
email info@canterburyfestival.co.uk
website https://canterburyfestival.co.uk
Takes place 17 October–1 November 2025, 16–30 October 2026

Showcases the best in performing arts, including classical and contemporary music, theatre, circus, comedy, talks and family events. Also runs year-round public engagement projects to inspire creativity in people of all ages.

Ledbury Poetry Festival

The Barrett Browning Institute, Homend, Ledbury HR8 2AA
tel (01531) 634156
email director@poetry-festival.co.uk
website www.poetry-festival.co.uk
Artistic Director Chloe Garner
Takes place June, July and throughout the year

The UK's biggest celebration of poetry and spoken word, attended by poets from all over the world. Established and upcoming talents take part in a wide variety of events, from masterclasses, walks, talks and films through to breakfasts, music, exhibitions and bike rides. International Poetry Competition launches every February.

WHERE TO PERFORM

Poetry evenings are held all over the UK and the suggestions listed below are worth checking out. Others can be found by visiting your local library or your Arts Council office, or by visiting the What's On section of the Poetry Society website (https://poetrysociety.org.uk/events/). The Poetry Library (www.nationalpoetrylibrary.org.uk/events-exhibitions) is also an excellent source for upcoming poetry events. Also look out for local groups at which members can share their work.

Allographic

tel 07904 488009
email press@allographic.co.uk
Facebook www.facebook.com/allographica
Bluesky @allographica.bsky.social
Instagram @allographica
Contact Fay Roberts

Cambridge-based live or Zoom events with new and upcoming names from the spoken word scene and a set of workshops for aspirant poets, storytellers and other writers and performers. Also produces a range of publications, from anthologies to books and pamphlets, that can be purchased online.

Apples and Snakes

The Albany, Douglas Way, London SE8 4AG
tel 07496 393793
email info@applesandsnakes.org
website www.applesandsnakes.org
Instagram @applesandsnakes

Exists to support poets at all stages of their careers. Runs regular live events and artist development programmes across the country, working collaboratively to ensure that unheard voices become heard. Founded 1982.

Book Slam

email elliott@bookslam.com
website www.bookslam.com
Contact Elliott Jack

Founded with the aim of returning literature to the heart of popular culture and open to authors, poets, singer-songwriters and comedians. Various venues; see website for details.

Café Writers Norwich

Louis Marchesi, Tombland, Norwich NR3 1HF
email info@cafewriters.co.uk
website www.cafewriters.co.uk
X @cafewriters
Instagram @cafe.writers
Contacts Ramona Herdman, Julia Webb, Stuart Charlesworth, Anne Bailey, Jenny Pagdin

Readings of poetry and prose in a relaxed and welcoming atmosphere, on the second Monday of every month. Open mic slots available. Some events on Zoom.

Coffee House Poetry

email coffpoetry@aol.com
website www.coffeehousepoetry.org

Readings, courses, classes and the annual Troubadour International Poetry Prize.

Genesis Poetry Slam

Genesis Cinema, 93–95 Mile End Road, London E1 4UJ
email poetry@genesis-cinema.co.uk
Facebook www.facebook.com/GenesisSlam
Instagram @genesispoetryslam
Contact Laurie Eaves

Three-round poetry slam. Usually held the first Thursday of every month (check social media for latest listings). Slots should be booked via the email above.

Jawdance

Rich Mix, 35–47 Bethnal Green Road, London E1 6LA
email info@applesandsnakes.org
website https://applesandsnakes.org/event/jawdance/
Facebook www.facebook.com/applesandsnakes
Host Yomi Sode

Poetry, film and music night, currently every third Wednesday of the month. Check website for details.

Kent & Sussex Poetry Society

email kentandsussexpoetry@gmail.com
website www.kentandsussexpoetry.com

Local group with national reputation. Organises monthly poetry readings (some online), workshops and an annual poetry competition.

Loud Poets (I Am Loud CIC)

email hello@iamloud.co
website www.iamloud.co
Facebook www.facebook.com/iamloudpro
Bluesky https://iamloudpro.bsky.social
Instagram @iamloudpro
YouTube www.youtube.com/c/IAmLoud
Staff Kevin Mclean, Mark Gallie, Dr Katie Ailes

Spoken word poetry organisation. Monthly Loud Poets showcases in Edinburgh feature a curated selection of spoken word talent performing with live music; annual Slam Series features regional heats across Scotland and England, culminating in a Grand Slam Final with a £3,000 cash prize. Also hosts twice-monthly open mics in Edinburgh and facilitates in-person and digital writing and performance workshops. See YouTube channel for hundreds of videos of spoken word performances, video podcasts, workshops and other resources. Founded 2014.

Out-Spoken

Southbank Centre, Belvedere Road, London SE1 8XX
email info@outspokenldn.com
website www.outspokenldn.com
Facebook www.facebook.com/outspokenLDN
X @OutSpokenLDN
Instagram @outspokenldn

Monthly poetry and live music event. See website or social media accounts for forthcoming dates and start times. Also runs Out-Spoken Press, publishing poetry and non-fiction; and Out-Spoken Academy, offering mentoring and writer development.

Poets' Café

South Street Arts Centre, 21 South Street, Reading RG1 4QU
email info@poetscafereading.co.uk
website www.poetscafereading.co.uk
Hosts Vic Pickup, Katherine Meehan

Reading's longest-running poetry platform, organised and hosted by The Poetry Society's Reading Stanza. Held on the second Friday of each month, this event consists of an open mic section and a full reading by an established poet at South Street Arts Centre in Reading. Also runs Reading Stanza, a monthly online feedback session. See website for details.

Polari

email polariprize@gmail.com
website www.polarisalon.com
X @polarisalon
Instagram @polarisalon
Contact Paul Burston

Multi-award-winning LGBTQ+ literary salon, which also goes on tour: see website for forthcoming events. Focuses on established authors but has some pre-arranged spots per event for up-and-coming LGBTQ+ writers. Based at the British Library, but see website for full details of event locations.

Rainbow Poetry Recitals

2 Old Farm Court, Shoreham BN43 5FE
tel (01273) 465423
email rainbow.poetry@hotmail.co.uk
Administrator Hugh Hellicar

Poetry meetings and recitals at two branches in London and four in Sussex. Poetry appreciation and members' poems. Magazine available on request. Founded 1994.

Shortlands Poetry Circle

tel 020-8464 9810
email shortlands@poetrypf.co.uk
website www.poetrypf.co.uk/shortlands.html

Meets twice a month during term time and one meeting per calendar month online. Visitors welcome. Check venue before attending: most meetings take place at Ripley Arts Centre, 24 Sundridge Avenue, Bromley BR1 2PX, but check before attending. Founded 1911.

SoapBox Spoken Word CIC

tel 07879 353396
email amy@getonthesoapbox.co.uk
website www.getonthesoapbox.co.uk
Facebook www.facebook.com/getonthesoapbox
X @getonthesoapbox
Contact Amy Wragg

Uses spoken word as a tool to benefit people and communities. Delivers workshops, community groups, open mics, booked events, networking and professional development opportunities for poets, performers & writers. Also published a 'print-only' handmade zine, featuring original poetry from members, available to purchase through a postal subscription service. Based in Ipswich (Suffolk); not available digitally.

Ver Poets

tel (01582) 715817
email gregsmith480@gmail.com
website https://verpoets.wixsite.com/verpoets
Facebook www.facebook.com/Ver_poets
Secretary Gregory Smith
Membership £15 p.a. UK; £20 p.a. overseas; £10 p.a. students

Encourages the writing and study of poetry. Holds evening meetings and daytime workshops in the St Albans area, as well as workshops via Zoom. Holds members' competitions and the annual Open Competition. Founded 1966.

WHERE TO WRITE POETRY

Arvon

Lumb Bank – The Ted Hughes Arvon Centre, Heptonstall, Hebden Bridge, West Yorkshire HX7 6DF
tel (01422) 843714
email lumbbank@arvon.org
Totleigh Barton, Sheepwash, Beaworthy, Devon EX21 5NS
tel (01409) 231338
email totleighbarton@arvon.org
The Hurst – The John Osborne Arvon Centre, Clunton, Craven Arms, Shrops. SY7 0JA
tel (01588) 640658
email thehurst@arvon.org
website www.arvon.org

Hosts residential creative writing courses and retreats in three rural writing houses. With the opportunity to live and work with professional writers, participants transform their writing through workshops, one-to-one tutorials, time and space to write. Five-day courses and shorter courses are available in a wide range of genres, including writing for children and young adults, fiction, poetry, theatre and creative non-fiction. An online programme of writing courses, masterclasses and live readings also runs year-round. Grants and concessions are available to help with course fees. Founded 1968.

Cannon Poets

22 Margaret Grove, Harborne, Birmingham B17 9JH
email martin@cannonpoets.org.uk
email greg@cannonpoets.org.uk
Meets at The Moseley Exchange, The Post Office Building, 149–153 Alcester Road, Moseley, Birmingham B13 8JP usually on the first Sunday of each alternate month at 2pm. Zoom meetings on the first Sunday of each intermediate month at 3pm.
website www.cannonpoets.org.uk
Facebook www.facebook.com/CannonPoetsBirmingham
Honorary Secretary Martin Underwood, *Editor, The Cannon's Mouth* Greg Cox

Cannon Poets have met monthly since 1983. The group encourages poetry writing through: workshops run by members or visitors; break-out groups where poems are subjected to scrutiny by supportive peer groups; ten-minute slots where members read a selection of their poems to the whole group; publication of its journal, *The Cannon's Mouth* (email poetry and poetry-related submissions to greg@cannonpoets.org.uk).

Cannon Poets' annual poetry competition, Sonnet or Not, invites poems of just 14 lines in length. See website for full details.

City Lit

1–10 Keeley Street, London WC2B 4BA
tel 020-7831 7831

email writing@citylit.ac.uk
website www.citylit.ac.uk
Facebook www.facebook.com/CityLit

Offers classes and courses (online and in-person) on poetry appreciation and writing for children, as well as a wide range of other topics.

The Poetry School

Ground Floor, 1 City Square, Park Row,
Leeds LS1 2ES
website www.poetryschool.com
Instagram @thepoetryschool

Teaches the art and craft of writing poetry, with courses in Leeds, London and around the UK, ranging from evening classes, small seminars and individual tutorials, to one-day workshops, year-long courses and an accredited MA. Activities for beginners to advanced writers, with classes happening face-to-face and online. Three termly programmes a year, plus professional skills development projects and CAMPUS, a social network for poets.

Tŷ Newydd Writing Centre

Llanystumdwy, Cricieth, Gwynedd LL52 0LW
tel (01766) 522811
email tynewydd@literaturewales.org
website www.tynewydd.wales
Instagram @canolfantynewydd

Runs residential writing courses encompassing a wide variety of genres and caters for all levels, from beginners to published poets. All the courses are tutored by established writers. Writing retreats are also available; see website for full details, including prices.

Wey Poets (Surrey Poetry Centre)

Friends Meeting House, 3 Ward Street,
Guildford GU1 4LH
email owen.osler@btinternet.com
email bb_singleton@hotmail.com
website www.weypoets.com
Contacts Belinda Singleton, Owen Osler

Long-standing group. New members/visitors and enquiries very welcome. Supportive workshops third Wednesday of the month, September to June. Additional speaker events first Wednesday in September, November, March, April and May. See current programme or web for samples of programme and poems. 2026 is the group's 50th anniversary in its present form; latest anthology will be published, among other events. Members include published poets.

COMPETITIONS

There are now hundreds of competitions to enter. As a rule, as the value of the prize increases, so does the prestige associated with winning. The Poetry Library publishes a list of competitions online (www.nationalpoetrylibrary.org.uk/write-publish/competitions). See also *Prizes and awards* on page 570.

Literary prizes are given annually to published poets and as such are non-competitive.

HELP FOR YOUNG POETS AND TEACHERS

National Association of Writers in Education (NAWE)

Tower House, Mill Lane, off Askham Fields Lane,
Askham Bryan, York YO23 3FS
tel 0330 333 5909
email admin@nawe.co.uk
website www.nawe.co.uk

Advocates for creative writing: enhancing knowledge and understanding of the subject, supporting writers and good practice in teaching and facilitation in all settings. NAWE promotes creative writing as both a distinct discipline and an essential element in education generally. Its membership is national and international and includes those working in Higher Education, freelance writers working in schools and community contexts, and the teachers and other professionals who work with them. It runs a national directory of professional members offering workshops, talks and other services, produces a fortnightly opportunities bulletin and holds an annual national conference. Professional Membership includes public liability insurance cover.

Professional Graduate Membership is available for university creative writing students who have recently graduated and aims to support the move from student to working as a professional writer in education and the community, offering the benefits of Professional Membership at a discounted rate.

Poetry Society Education

The Poetry Society, 22 Betterton Street,
London WC2H 9BX
tel 020-7420 9880
email educationadmin@poetrysociety.org.uk
website www.poetrysociety.org.uk
X @poetryeducation
Instagram @thepoetrysociety

An arm of The Poetry Society, one of the UK's leading poetry organisations, aiming to facilitate exciting and innovative education work. For over 30 years it has been introducing poets into classrooms, providing free downloadable learning resources and producing accessible publications for pupils. It develops projects and schemes to keep poetry flourishing in schools, libraries and workplaces, giving work to hundreds of poets and allowing thousands of children and adults to experience poetry for themselves.

Through projects such as the Foyle Young Poets of the Year Award and Young Poets Network, The

Poetry Society gives offers talent-development opportunities and exposure to young writers and performers. A network for poets and teachers, Cloud Chamber, is free to join and provides opportunities to share knowledge and best practice. Schools membership and Youth membership offer a range of benefits, including quarterly Poetry Society publications, books and posters.

Young Poets Network

email educationadmin@poetrysociety.org.uk
website https://ypn.poetrysociety.org.uk
Facebook www.facebook.com/YoungPoetsNetwork
X @youngpoetsnet

Free online platform from The Poetry Society comprising features about reading, writing and performing poetry, plus new work by young poets and regular writing challenges. Open to anyone under the age of 25.

YOUNG POETRY COMPETITIONS

Children's competitions are included in the competition list provided by the Poetry Library: this is free online at www.nationalpoetrylibrary.org.uk/write-publish/competitions.

Foyle Young Poets of the Year Award

The Poetry Society, 22 Betterton Street,
London WC2H 9BX
tel 020-7420 9880
email fyp@poetrysociety.org.uk
website https://foyleyoungpoets.org
Facebook www.facebook.com/thepoetrysociety
X @PoetrySociety
Bluesky @poetrysociety.bsky.social
Instagram @thepoetrysociety

Annual competition for writers aged 11–17. Prizes include books, mentoring and talent development opportunities, such as publication and performance. Deadline 31 July. Free to enter. Founded 2001.

Christopher Tower Poetry Competition

Christ Church, Oxford OX1 1DP
tel 07849 625906
email tower.poetry@chch.ox.ac.uk
website www.chch.ox.ac.uk/towerpoetry
X @TowerPoetry

Annual poetry competition (open from October to February) from Christ Church, Oxford, aimed at students aged between 16 and 18 in UK schools and colleges. The poems should be no longer than 48 lines, on a different chosen theme each year. Free to enter. Prizes: £5,000 (1st), £3,000 (2nd), £1,500 (3rd). There will also be ten commended awards of £500 each.

See also...

• *Publishers of poetry*, page 777

Further reading

Addonizio, Kim, *Ordinary Genius: A Guide for the Poet Within* (W.W. Norton 2012)
Bell, Jo and Jane Commane, *How to Be a Poet: A 21st-Century Guide to Writing Well* (Nine Arches Press 2017)
Bell, Jo and guests: *52: Write a Poem a Week – Start Now, Keep Going* (Nine Arches Press 2015)
Blackwell, Sophia, *Writers' & Artists' Poetry Writers' Handbook* (Bloomsbury, 2022)
Chisholm, Alison, *A Practical Guide to Poetry Forms* (Compass Books 2014)
Fairfax, John and John Moat, *The Way to Write* (Penguin Books, 2nd edn revised 1998)
Greene, Roland et al., *Princeton Encyclopedia of Poetry and Poetics* (Princeton University Press, 4th edn 2012)
Hamilton, Ian and Jeremy Noel-Tod, *The Oxford Companion to Modern Poetry in English* (Oxford University Press, 2nd edn 2014)
Kowit, Steve, *In the Palm of Your Hand: A Poet's Portable Workshop* (Tilbury House, 2nd edn 2019)
Maxwell, Glyn, *On Poetry* (Oberon Books 2017)
Oliver, Mary, *Rules for the Dance: Handbook for Writing and Reading Metrical Verse* (Houghton Mifflin 1998)
Padel, Ruth, *52 Ways of Looking at a Poem: A Poem for Every Week of the Year* (Vintage 2004)
Padel, Ruth, *The Poem and the Journey: 60 Poems for the Journey of Life* (Vintage 2008)
Roberts, Philip Davies, *How Poetry Works* (Penguin Books, 2nd edn 2000)
Sampson, Fiona, *Poetry Writing: The Expert Guide* (Robert Hale 2009)
Sansom, Peter, *Writing Poems* (Bloodaxe 1993, repr. 1997)
Whitworth, John, *Writing Poetry* (A&C Black, 2nd edn 2006)

Screen and audio
Introduction

In 2023, Ofcom reported that Brits watch, on average, four hours and 31 minutes of video content a day. This was a small 2% increase on the previous year, but the consumption of live, broadcast TV was actually down. Instead, viewers are turning to on-demand services (up 29%) and video-sharing platforms (up 12%) for entertainment, which is most likely due to the increased capabilities for apps on family Smart TVs. In the same report, Netflix was named the most popular streaming service (accounting for more than half of all on-demand viewing), while YouTube leads for video-sharing platforms.

There is some overlap between broadcasting and streaming, with almost all broadcasters having their own platforms alongside relationships with other streaming services. An awareness of the content that is most popular on these services is key to understanding the types of projects that they are looking for and a great source of inspiration for budding screenwriters. Broadcasters are increasingly looking at how they can strengthen the offering on their own video-on-demand services, such as iPlayer and ITVX.

Live radio (including both analogue AM/FM and online) is seeing growth across the board, especially at commercial stations. The number of weekly radio listeners in the first quarter of 2024 was the highest it's been for two decades at just under 50 million. Of listeners aged 15 and above, over 70% tuned into a commercial station, while 55% listened to one of the BBC's stations. The popularity of audio broadcasting does not stop at the radio – with half of all UK adults listening to a streaming service like Spotify and BBC Sounds at least once a week, while the demand for podcasts has doubled in the last five years.

This means there are opportunities aplenty for writers for screen and audio, with the broadcasters themselves proving to be a valuable starting point for guidance. Their websites include contact details for commissioning editors and information on the content they are most interested in, reflecting genre and demographic trends in television and radio more widely. Many broadcasters run initiatives for aspiring creatives that include competitions, workshops, training and longer development programmes, all of which make the process of pitching television and radio projects more transparent and accessible.

There are also a variety of societies that exist to promote television and radio broadcasting, and the creators working within them. They share relevant information and guidance, facilitate opportunities for networking, and run workshops and other events. For more societies that support film, theatre and television creatives see page 549.

Listings in this section:

- *Regulation*, page 391
- *Television*, page 391
- *Streaming services*, page 395
- *Radio*, page 397

Getting your screenplay noticed

Writing an outstanding screenplay is one thing; getting it noticed by the right people quite another. In this article, Robert Taylor explains how he (and his hero) would go about it.

'O for a Muse of fire, that would ascend
The brightest heaven of invention,
A kingdom for a stage, princes to act
And monarchs to behold the swelling scene!'

Over the years, I've asked several agents how they know a screenplay is one they are willing to spend weeks, or even months representing, one on which they are prepared to stake their reputation. Some said: 'believable characters ... authentic dialogue ... intriguing premise ...'. Others said: 'fresh ... original ... it says something ... a voice'. But you know this. You've read all the books, have some sort of film school degree perhaps, have written a couple of screenplays while logging up 3,000 of Malcolm Gladwell's 10,000 hours. Just like the thousands of other aspiring screenwriters out there.

A couple of agents said the screenplay 'resonated with me ... it touched me'. Or 'Honestly, I don't know ... I just know'.

If one is to make that leap from amateur to professional writer, or is in that liminal phase between emerging writer and established writer, how does one write a screenplay that touches or resonates or makes someone say '... I just know ...?'

The first important lesson the aspiring writer must understand is that, as Steven Pressman put it so pithily (and wrote a book called), no one wants to read your s***. And Pressman is right; no one wants to read it. So how do we get them to read our s***?

'Write, dear boy, just write.'

'Bang your head against a keyboard till it bleeds.'

Well, it works for some.

'What's this guy's motivation?' screams the actor, the director, the producer, the agent.

'What is your motivation for writing this screenplay?' I ask.

One popular theory has it that writers write in order to make sense of the world, to bring order out of the chaos, to resolve inner turmoil. And doesn't every agent or producer also want to make sense of the world, to bring order out of the chaos? We all know that great screenplays are about something (plot) but are really about something else (call it theme). You are writing a screenplay to tell a story you can sell but you are really writing it to – for example – plead for justice in an unjust world. That's a motivation for writing. But can we go deeper, take it down another level? Pressman says great screenplays return us to Eden, back to the Garden, regain us our Paradise Lost. Pretty hi-falutin'. Or is it? Surely, at heart, the cosiest of cosies, the screwiest of screwballs, the rommest of coms rewards virtue, casts out sinners, brings justice to an unjust world? Isn't this the beginning of it all, that deepest place in all our psyches, that part of the collective unconscious which will touch, will resonate, which will ... 'I don't know ...'

Whatever your motivation, articulate it. Know why you are really writing your screenplay.

Art imitates life. Sometimes it's the other way around. For screenwriters, I believe life is art and art is life. A screenplay is the story of a hero's journey and the writer's journey.

There are plenty of good screenwriting manuals out there. Field, McKee, Snyder et al. All compulsory reading. But the one book that I – and most professional screenwriters I know – lean on is Vogler's *The Writer's Journey*. The 12-stage hero's journey provides a structured story template for your protagonist's journey and during the process of writing the screenplay, your journey will mirror your hero's. You and your hero embark on the journey. Together.

Your screenplay has a hero with a back story; you, the writer have a backstory which will inform your screenplay, your protagonist's journey, every step of the way. Art and life. Writer and hero.

Your hero is going about their business; perhaps they are happy, more likely they are not. As are you. This is the first of the 12 stages: **the Ordinary World**. Like your hero, you are ready for change. Ready to write.

You get your killer idea. The one! This is your **Call to Adventure**. But you are overcome by doubts. One hundred pages of screenplay? One hundred minutes of film? What agent will read this dross? What producer will produce it? Get outta town! You **Refuse the Call**.

Some years ago, I wanted to write a screenplay. It was based on a true story about a potato farmer who won a 550-mile footrace from Melbourne to Sydney and became (briefly) a national hero. Doubts and fears set in. Who would be interested in a story about some forgotten old geezer winning a footrace? (Plenty, as it turned out.) I abandoned the idea. For weeks. For months. But it wouldn't go away and I returned to it. It ticked all the boxes for a great story except one: the protagonist was a 63-year-old nobody. A loser. But at its heart was a man who was silently screaming at an uncaring, unjust universe for love and validation, for some confirmation that his puny, unfulfilled life was actually worth something. I no longer wanted to write this story; I *needed* to write it. I didn't know it then but I do now: I wanted to take an audience back to the Garden where the innocent, the pure and the just are rewarded. So I wrote it. And it got made and when it screened on TV, it damn near knocked the final of *Strictly* off its perch. The final! There will always be unticked boxes, but look to the positives in your idea and when the want to write becomes the need to write, write.

You're ready to write: you have **Crossed the First Threshold**. You know the drill, you know the boxes you've got to tick: protagonist, clear dramatic goal, conflict, high stakes, plot points with consequences, character transformation/arc etc etc. You've written all the scenes on cards and put them up on the structure board.

You write your first draft: you have **Approached the Innermost Cave**. You read it. You'll probably cringe. You've brought this baby into the world, bawling and screaming, and all you want to do is push it back in the womb and wish you could shove yourself back in there as well. These fears are probably unfounded. As Hemingway said: 'the first draft of anything is s***'. And who's going to argue with Papa?

So begins the rewrite(s). Do not return to page one and start writing. That's not a rewrite; it's a polish. Instead, revisit the idea, logline, tagline, synopsis. Some years ago I worked with John Collee (*Master and Commander*, *Happy Feet* et al.) on an original screenplay of mine. Whenever John got stuck, or prior to each pass, he rewrote his one-page synopsis. One goal of rewriting is focus and the one-pager is a terrific focusing tool.

Return to the structure board. Does it still hold up? Almost certainly there will be changes. Two very useful exercises here. Way back when, an American writer called Brion

Gysin developed the 'cut-up' method by which a writer takes a great tranche of writing, randomly cuts it up and then shuffles and reorders it. William Burroughs used it when writing *The Naked Lunch* et al. Davids Bowie and Byrne wrote some of their lyrics this way. Shuffle your structure board cards and put them back on the structure board. Maybe some guiding, cosmic force is called into play (or not!), but I guarantee the results will surprise, illuminate and inspire. Using the structure board cards, work backwards from final scene to first. If the narrative logic works backwards, you've got yourself a solid structure.

So you've put your protagonist through hell. You've put yourself through hell. You've rewritten and polished, you've logged up another 1,500 of Gladwell's hours. But now you have to face **The Ordeal.**

Or not. Putting a screenplay out prematurely may harm or even kill your nascent career. You need feedback, you need professional coverage. Check out this website: https://screencraft.org/blog/top-5-best-screenplay-coverage-services-improve-your-script.

In my view, the fees are incredibly reasonable for the coverage they provide.

The Ordeal is your protagonist's dark night of the soul, the all is lost scene. You've done all the above and you send out dozens of enquiry letters. Months later and one agent agrees to read it. But it's a no. All is lost. Can it ever get worse? (Yes, it can. Wait till your screenplay is shot and they've hired an inappropriate director, miscast a major character, and a subplot is ruined by bad weather and lack of funds. Ha!)

Really, there's not much more you can do other that put it in the bottom drawer. (Never, never trash your screenplay. You may cannibalise elements for another screenplay or one day it may be neither ahead of, nor behind the curve, but bang on it.)

In your screenplay, your protagonist has an epiphany, is transformed, resurrected. S/he returns to the fray ready to slay dragons. What is your epiphany? Has this experience transformed you? Or are you defeated by the ordeal and ready to give up?

For me the epiphany came in the form of self-awareness when the pain of not writing became greater than the pain of writing. That is when you know you are a writer.

Robert McKee says protagonists are 'wilful' and will go to 'the end of the line' to achieve their dramatic goal. So it is with the writer. So, back to the structure board and the keyboard? Another well-crafted screenplay. Another round of query letters. If that's what it takes, yes.

Or.

You could take a look at The Black List (https://blcklst.com). They assess screenplays and the website also hosts screenplays. They boast that producers, directors, agents and managers scour their lists for projects. The 2025 film *Flight Risk*, starring Mark Wahlberg and Michelle Dockery, was found on The Black List. They're LA-based but if your screenplay has international appeal, it's worth checking them out.

Or.

It is worth remembering that it is producers, not agents who buy/option/commission screenplays. A screenwriting friend, a sci-fi/horror maven, works at a production company specialising in low budget sci-fi/horror productions. Another friend is a writer for Nickelodeon. The show he worked on (he told me with no trace of irony) was #1 in the 4–6 year-old demographic. He was envious that I had written two feature films; I was envious that he had a steady paycheck. He's a showrunner at Disney now and has met *a lot* of producers at Disney. Another contact works at a distribution company. He travels the world, attending film festivals (Cannes, Berlin, Venice, Sundance etc), buying titles for local distribution. He has the phone numbers of hundreds – hundreds – of producers.

All three began as interns. To become a successful screenwriter of feature films, you need to play the long game. If I had my time again, I would have interned. Multiple times if necessary.

Did you know that the BBC and other content providers hold an annual event at which they showcase their current productions and outline what they're looking for in the future? Producers are invited to attend. (Interns can wangle an invite.) A roomful of producers! Meet them. Establish relationships.

There are two lessons here: first, it is more fulfilling to work within the industry while you hone your craft; second, chaining yourself to your keyboard and writing hundreds of query letters to agents is not the only way to get noticed.

The hero of your screenplay has her epiphany. Transformed and resurrected, she **Returns with the Magic Elixir**. By asking an agent or producer to read your screenplay, you are asking them to invest their time or money. Reward them for their investment, share the magic elixir of your hero's and your writer's journey. Take them back to the Garden.

They still may not want to read your s***. But they're more likely to.

Robert Taylor's original feature screenplay *Muggers* premiered at Cannes in 1999 and was nominated for the Australian Writers' Guild's Best Original screenplay award. A second original feature screenplay, *Cliffy*, premiered on ABC TV (Australia) in 2013 to critical and popular acclaim and outstanding ratings. He has optioned, sold, or been assigned a further 12 feature film scripts in the US, the UK and Australia to Oscar-nominated and Palme d'Or-, Golden Lion- and Golden Globe-winning producers. These include *Stealing America* and *All I Want*. He also has written two novels (as R.B. Taylor), *St Barlaam's Day* (2020) and *The Great Pockes* (2021).

Successful screenwriting

Anna Symon suggests what it takes to forge a career as a screenwriter. She gives practical advice on how to develop the skills and traits needed to succeed in this creative, collaborative and competitive field.

How do you become a professional screenwriter? Unfortunately, there is no one answer, and there's certainly no recognised career path. Some writers come from fiction or the theatre. Others arrive from film and television production, having previously worked as, say, a script editor or documentarian (as I myself did). But, increasingly, plenty of screenwriters do seem to be coming straight to the medium, without any previous story-telling or writing experience. This could be because, with the proliferation of television streaming platforms, there is such a thirst for new content.

Although the field will always be hugely competitive, there are definitely more opportunities out there. However, before you start, I believe you need to work out if you have a writer's soul. What do I mean by this? It's hard to sum up in a word or two but all the good writers I know care deeply and are curious about the world around them. Sometimes this curiosity is deeply buried, sometimes it's right on the surface. But it manifests as an interest in scratching below the veneer of life, a compulsion to examine widely held truths, and to express a point of view. I think it makes us a fun bunch of people to hang out with, because we like to question what we see around us, make sense of the world or simply enjoy observing its complexity and absurdity. If that rings a bell and you want to scratch that itch, the next step is to sit down (or stand up) and write. And that's when you need stamina.

There's no shortcut to a career in screenwriting. The craft of telling stories appears deceptively straightforward because we are all so story-literate. Our world is flush with narrative: not just in entertainment, but in advertising and social media, as well as in the stories we constantly tell ourselves about our own lives. So we know what stories are, and can recognise good ones, but learning how to create them successfully takes time. You need to practise as hard as you would at a piano if you wanted to be a concert pianist. They say it takes ten years to become an overnight success and I think, in screenwriting, that's true. It was certainly true for me. The good news is that the ten years honing your craft can be very rewarding. They are certainly some of the most fun times I've had in my life. It's the time when you are reading books, watching films, reading scripts, trying to absorb what everyone else is doing, while all the time writing your own stuff. Perhaps thinking about whether you have a voice and, if you do, what it is? I wouldn't worry too much about that. Write from the heart, lay down the story as you see it, and leave it to others to discover your voice. I truly believe that, with enough time and effort, the majority of screenwriting skills can be learnt. If you think in an interesting way, and have something to say, you can learn the nuts and bolts of how to put a screenplay together.

For some lucky new screenwriters, they'll get off to a flying start and get paid while they are still learning their craft – although they will then make their mistakes in public (which can test the ego). For others, at the start of their writing journey, they are penning spec scripts, unpaid and largely unnoticed, each one hopefully better than the last until, one day, they find that people ask to read their work and then pay for it. (It should be said that all professional writers will have their work reviewed, so you have to find a way to deal with public criticism, which can feel incredibly exposing.)

If 'a career' means getting paid for your writing, then in fiction that means getting published. In television and film, it means getting a project into 'development'. You may well make a healthy living as a full-time, paid screenwriter (particularly in film) for quite a long time before you get a project green lit and on screen. It can be a long haul, otherwise known as 'development hell', trying to get something made. This is a paid process, as scripts go back and forth from broadcaster to producer to writer, with a pile of notes and tweaks along the way. There's a reason for the much-quoted saying: 'Writing is re-writing.' Be prepared for more voices and stakeholders than you would expect commenting on your work – and don't become a screenwriter unless you genuinely enjoy collaboration with other creatives. Professional input from script editors, directors and producers can, and should, massively improve your work. However, at times it can feel like your insides are being scraped with a rusty blade. Get used to it.

If, given all this, you still want to write screenplays there are a few steps you can take along the way to give yourself the best chance. Firstly, I would recommend signing up for as much good quality training as you can afford. I did an MA in Screenwriting and it went a long way towards demystifying both the craft and the business. The course had links with the industry, so it was a first shot at meeting producers and agents and learning how I could turn what I had written into a commercial proposition that a broadcaster would want to finance and an audience would want to watch. More importantly, it was the first time I met a whole cohort of others on the same journey as me. I found my tribe. It was also an opportunity for us all to find people to read and critique our work, to develop that thick skin for what was coming down the road. There were a few people on the course who genuinely couldn't take criticism of their work, however constructively it was offered, and for those people it was useful to discover that screenwriting was not right for them.

The second step comes out of the first, and it is to find a smart, sensitive first reader of your work. This person doesn't have to be a writer, but it should be someone who will be honest with you and whose creative opinion you value. It does feel extremely exposing to have someone question work that took you so long to create, but having fresh eyes on it is essential. It means that when you sit down to write another draft, as you must if you're serious about it, you'll have a sense of where its strengths and weaknesses are – which parts are intriguing, which bits a little slow. Quite often the most useful feedback is to learn which scenes or sequences don't really make sense yet – even if they do to you. 'It's not on the page yet' is a common note given. This means that, despite the fact you feel you have expressed a particular storyline or character point, it is not 'landing' for the reader. If the reader doesn't 'get it', nor will an audience. It needs more work ...

In that sense your first reader is your best friend, who will protect you from harsher criticism from the outside world. Listen to them … carefully. Try not to be too defensive or write off their notes as them just not 'getting' you. You don't have to alter anything. But you may find that what they pick up on is an area of the script that you weren't quite sure about yourself, a problem you thought you had solved but in your heart of hearts knew wasn't working. Let the criticism settle and then buoy yourself up to tackle the problem head on in your next pass. On the other hand, the reader's thoughts may be inexplicable to you – a real surprise. In that case, I'd suggest finding another reader if you can. Listen carefully to them too. If they come up with a similar point, then I'd suggest you try and do some work on that area of the script.

Try out a few readers if you can. See who you are in tune with – but by that I don't mean the person who simply says: 'Amazing, I loved it'. However evolved a script is, there is always something to talk about. Sometimes the most useful thing is simply to discuss the script with someone who has read it. It forces you to articulate what you are trying to express as your work develops. If you feel really stuck, with lots of contradictory thoughts on your work, and are not sure if something's there yet, I'd suggest sending it to a professional script editor. Make sure you have done everything you possibly can to get the script to this stage, so you don't waste your money getting notes you could have given yourself.

Finally, don't send your work out into the world too soon. If you are looking for an agent, or you have met a producer, and you have that precious email address and their invitation to send in a script, pause a moment. Think carefully. This person would not have suggested you send something in unless they intend to read it. Contrary to popular opinion, everyone is looking for new talent, new voices. There is no reason that new voice won't be yours, but the field is very competitive. You are new and therefore a risk. There are lots of talented writers out there already, with long track records. Your work has to have the potential to be as good as theirs … or better. So you need to seriously impress at this point. You almost certainly won't get another chance with this particular person. So, force yourself to look at your script again; if there is a character that you think is still rather two-dimensional or a plot point that feels coincidental, your reader will pick that up too. If, on the other hand, you read through your script one final time and you genuinely feel there is nothing more you can do to improve it, then you are ready to hit 'send'. Good luck!

Anna Symon's scriptwriting credits include the ITV series *Joan* (2024), the adaptation of Sarah Perry's *The Essex Serpent* for Apple TV (2022), the BBC series *Mrs Wilson* (2018), the ITV series *Deep Water* (2019) and Channel 4's *Indian Summers* (2015–16). She is a graduate of the Channel 4 Screenwriting Programme and previously worked as a producer/director in current affairs and documentaries. Follow her on X @AnnaSymon.

See also...

- *Writing across forms: my publishing routes to success*, page 245

A way with words: writing comedy

Ian Martin tells how, over time, thanks to such essentials as tenacity and serendipity, his job description widened from humble hack to writer and screenwriter. He has firm advice and encouragement for fellow writers as he shares what he has learned along the way.

Congratulations, you're a WRITER! Even when you're starting out and are nowhere close to making a living from it, identifying as a 'writer' is empowering. It's more than a job description. It's motivational. A declaration of intent, a glorious definition of *you*. And *me*. Yeah, get *us* ... we're part of a global community that includes Nobel laureates, Pulitzer Prize winners and Oscar-bagging screenwriters. Dazzling company.

Yeah, it feels great to big ourselves up. However ... let's embrace reality, put things into perspective and – counterpoint – 'ensmallen' ourselves. In the spirit of those gladiator-slaves whispering '*memento mori*' in the ears of Roman generals, let me remind you of what we actually do, physically. We type for a living, all of us. And this is no less inclusive – nearly every writer these days taps at a keyboard. Outcomes vary. At this very moment a poet is coaxing words from some plasmic thoughtfield, through her brain, along her fingers and onto the page. Simultaneously, a copywriter somewhere is knocking out 400 words about a foot spa. They're both writers, although obviously the copywriter's earning more.

I've typed for a living since 1973 when, as a gormless 20 year-old, I started work as a junior reporter for a local paper in County Durham. That newspaper, like thousands of others, is long gone – bought up as part of a job lot by freesheet publishers, then amalgamated with other papers, 'value-engineered' down to a skeleton staff, then entirely deboned and discarded. Local journalism, once an unshakeable keystone of community life, providing essential scrutiny of local government affairs, has never recovered from the blunt trauma of the internet and its ruthless harvesting of small ads. Half a century on, though, I can still feel the thrill of my first byline in print. Oh my days ... the smell of the newsprint. The thud as a massive sheaf of fat broadsheets landed on the reception desk. And there it was – my name just above the fold, a ragged little yard-high tower of '***by Ian Martin***'. It's never left me, that narcissistic urge to shine, to see my name or hear it. 'I'm a writer', we say, which is really just shorthand for 'I'm an insufferable show-off'.

Life was so insanely different then – I sometimes marvel at my luck. In those days you could be taken on by one of the old newspaper groups, trained in journalism law, sub-editing, shorthand, all the craft skills. The three years of my indentureship taught me how to write a narrative; they don't call them news stories for nothing. Incidentally, the three big storytelling principles of soap operas are exactly those used in journalism, and indeed, in all writing: 1) HEAT – who's angry with whom, why, and what will they do now? 2) TOPSPIN – a touch of velocity just before ad breaks and credits, to keep the viewer wanting more. News stories also need snappy intros to pull the reader in; those clickbait one-liners, like 'You Won't Believe What This Once-Handsome Child Star Looks Like Now, He's Horrific!!!' are the apotheosis of topspin. Of course, you won't click on the link, you're not a monster. Nevertheless, a tiny part of you wants to see what a haunted, middle-aged 40-stone human tragedy looks like. And 3) PIPEWORK – fill the casual viewer/reader in as subtly as possible with background info. Exposition, we call it now. For we are *writers*.

What my journalism training *didn't* teach me was the First Law of Journalism. As a trainee reporter I'd assumed it was something like 'Always speak truth to power' or 'Give voice to the powerless'. Then I encountered the fearsome might of sub-editors and learned that the First Law of Journalism was FILL THE SPACE. Seems quaint now, the idea of casting off a word count to fit an outline on paper. Imagine … finite space. Little did we know that the global connectivity of science fiction – the telly somehow hooked up to a telephone so flat and small you could slip it into a pocket – would actually happen. Now, life before the internet is unthinkable. And it has proved vitally important for writing opportunities; anyone can set up a blog, or a newsletter, or a website, or a podcast. (It's proved invaluable for time-wasting too – that integral part of a writer's life. In the old days, we had to stare out of a window.)

I've been a hack all my life. I was in (massively unprofitable) bands for years, and I juggled that with magazine stints. Really not making enough to make ends meet, especially with a young family. We were permanently skint. I'd fallen into architectural journalism by accident – we had to sell the car, and I needed a job I could get the bus to. And even when I went fully freelance in the early '80s we stayed badly overdrawn, but were kept afloat, just, by a silly satirical column I wrote in an architecture magazine for 27 years. And here's the rub. I know there may be people reading this, writers who are losing faith in themselves, without the confidence to approach commissioning editors or producers or agents, and I am here to tell you that the greatest gift an aspiring writer can have is tenacity. Never, ever, ever give up. If you think you're good enough to make a living as a writer, back yourself and keep going. Keep at it, I implore you. Make yourself unignorable.

I always wanted to be a writer and I always wanted to be funny. In every steady hack job I had, I ended up writing a silly column. I'd been writing that piss-taking one about architecture for a decade before it was noticed by a features editor at a national newspaper, who invited me to write something with a similar tone about arts and culture. Oh, I was well chuffed. Every Friday it appeared. For about ten weeks, until it didn't. They decided it was a poor fit and I was dropped there and then, like lead from a shot tower. Reader, my feelings were hurt. But vengeance burned in my heart. It throbbed in my veins. They were right, by the way. The column was, in retrospect, rubbish. Overthought and overwrought. Nevertheless, how DARE they deny me a ventilation shaft for my brilliance? How DARE they snatch away my byline? Once a hack, always a hack.

This was in 1999, when both our children had left home for university. It felt rather like early retirement. Also – stroke of luck – my brother had just been made redundant. Together we started a weekly online satirical website ('martian.fm – from the north of the heart'). I wrote the words; Paul did the artwork and everything else, including actually making it happen. Nobody was paying us, and I spent two or three days a week writing stuff for it. Still, it was the most hilarious of times – me and my bro down in the cellar with a bottle of scotch and each other as the only audience. Week in, week out for three years, congratulating ourselves on our excoriating website so niche it was cult, and so cult it was months before the readership was into three figures. There were times when it seemed utterly absurd, shrieking into the void. The feature that took the most time every week was 'Hansard Late', a fictitious record of rowdy drunken evening proceedings in the Commons, MC'd by a very sweary, very angry Scottish Speaker.

Then the email arrived. I thought it was a prank at first. It apparently came from comedy genius Armando Iannucci, who needlessly explained that he'd produced *The Day Today* and *Knowing Me, Knowing You* and who said 'I like your stuff. It makes me laugh'. Would I be interested in chucking some jokes at a Channel 4 thing he was putting together? It did seem quite an *elaborate* prank …

And so my screenwriting career began, a few days after my 50th birthday. After the Channel 4 thing (a young Olivia Colman read out my 'Controversial Swearing Rap Millionaires – Court Appearances', my first TV credit), I went on to do a bit of radio stuff before Iannucci invited me to a swearing pass on the first three *The Thick of It* scripts. I got mythologised as the show's 'swearing consultant', but – for the record – all the writers wrote swears; I didn't just do swears, I became a full member of the writing team. The first 'alt' (alteration) of mine that got through actually removed a swear: 'He's f**king useless' became 'He's as useless as a marzipan dildo'. I've been working with Iannucci pretty much every year since. But if I hadn't been writing martian.fm he'd almost certainly never have noticed me, and I wonder how my 21st century would have turned out.

Anyway, look – in screenwriting terms I'm nowhere *near* the top of my profession. League Division 3 or 4, say. I am now a 'writer', but I'll always be a hack. And, like all old hacks, I have quite a good sense of how much space I have left in this piece and had better start stuffing it with advice:

- **Keep going**. My screenwriting career started late, and only then because I couldn't bear not to keep showing off. I wasn't washed up at 50, so there's no need for anyone to be. Also, duh, you can't be a writer if you don't write. Even if it's just for your own amusement, even if you're just giggling with mates on X, even if it's a terrible diary that'll never be read by anyone … **write**. Every day. You're not going to get worse, are you?
- **Welcome the criticism, love the notes**. The hardest thing about exposing your work to others for the first time is people not unconditionally loving it. Get over it. Get over yourself. In time you will *love* criticism – the more destructive the better; all writing needs to be stress-tested. Notes are your friends. People will give notes and it will make your thing better, which is what you want (unless you're deranged). You might not understand at first why other people say this or that isn't working, but – come on – if it isn't working for them, it isn't working. Fix it.
- **Get an agent**. I know, it's a conundrum. If you haven't had anything published or broadcast, you're less of a catch; you stand more chance of getting noticed if you have an agent. Find the ones who specialise in what you write; pitch yourself. How to find an agent? I dunno … maybe get some sort of writers' and artists' yearbook or whatever.
- **Join a union.** This isn't just about you, it's about us. The stronger the union, the stronger the union member.

Good luck. We all need it. However hard you work at it, you still need to catch a break. Serendipity is what we call it, for we are *writers*.

Ian Martin is an Emmy award-winning comedy writer and producer. His screen credits include the BAFTA-winning BBC series *The Thick of It*; BAFTA-nominated *The Death of Stalin* (National Society of Film Critics Award, Best Screenplay); the multi-Emmy award-winning *Veep* (for which he won an Emmy and two Writers' Guild of America awards) and HBO's *Avenue 5*. He also wrote for the Oscar-nominated *In The Loop*. His comedy-drama *The Hartlepool Spy* won the Tinniswood Award for Best Radio Drama in 2020. His books include *Epic Space* (Unbound 2017), *The Coalition Chronicles* (Faber & Faber 2011), *So You Think You Can Be Prime Minister* (Bloomsbury 2024) and *Unhinged: A Parody* (Bloomsbury 2024).

Can you make a living writing comedy? Yes, but ...

Funny? Good. Proactive? Better. Obsessed? Even better. In this article, Dave Cohen offers his suggestions for breaking into the world of comedy writing.

Doors opening …

For the first three decades as a comedy writer for TV and radio, there was only one piece of advice guaranteed to confer an immediate advantage over your competitors. All you needed was to be a white middle-class man.

Lucky me.

That's changed. There's never been a better time for anyone to choose a comedy writing career. Whatever your background, you're invited to participate.

Doors closing …

However, there are far fewer opportunities. Across Britain and the US, the old commissioning model is broken. Around the world and on social media, unscripted comedy is king. It's never been harder to pick up a commission for a radio or TV show.

Doors opening …

That said, it's never been cheaper or easier to make your own projects. You can create and sell your own funny stuff via podcasts, sketches, TikTok videos, you name it, without having to talk to a single gatekeeper. Fancy writing a novel? Your life story? There's nobody and nothing apart from your credit card limit to stop you.

Doors closing …

Unfortunately, just because you build it, that doesn't mean they will come.

As I gaze towards the middle horizon like a misty-eyed grandpa in a Private Health Plan advert contemplating the infinite pleasures of my forthcoming retirement (less money, more back pain, intimations of mortality), I'm aware that it's a lot harder to make a living from writing funny than when I started out 40 years ago.

I can't offer easy solutions. I can tell you what's out there, and what you can do to improve your chances of achieving success.

1. Write jokes

What do the following top writers have in common: Georgia Pritchett (*Succession*, *The Thick of It*), Simon Blackwell (*Back*, *Breeders*, *The Personal History of David Copperfield*), Mark Burton (*Madagascar*, *Shaun the Sheep*) and John O'Farrell (*Chicken Run*, *Mrs Doubtfire The Musical*)?

The answer is they all achieved their first professional credits writing one-line topical jokes for BBC shows. The BBC still exists (just), as do a number of radio shows that anyone can send jokes to. The competition is fierce and the odds are stacked against you, which doesn't mean you should refuse to engage.

And don't be put off by the word 'topical'. You don't need to understand the geopolitical implications of the latest international trade agreement, but you can spot when a politician or celebrity is being grandiose, or controlling, or crap at lying.

What is a joke?

Immanuel Kant described humour as the pricking of pomposity. George Orwell called every joke 'a tiny revolution'. A joke is a surprise and can best be described as 'something that goes against expectation'.

'Every joke,' said the great British comedy writer Denis Norden, 'is a momentary removal of sympathy'. Note the importance of the word 'momentary' there. Having exposed the fool with a harsh, unsympathetic truth, we're ready to forgive them.

The landscape has changed over the decades. Shows without jokes are feted as comic masterpieces, while narrative comedies have been so cut back that most funny audience shows are now either panel games or stand-up specials.

Gags are still needed for these and for online comedy performers, though. In recent years the most successful have emerged through YouTube and TikTok. They have millions of fans but the need for content is insatiable and many online performers blaze briefly before burning out. Everyone needs material. If you can develop a name as a joke writer, you'll soon be in demand.

It's incredible how little information there is out there about how to write topical comedy. I mean come on, the internet. There's more information on 'How do I fix the sound on my Bush TV?' than about writing for TV shows. The most up-to-date blogs on that subject are more than eight years old.

Write jokes. Every day if you can. It's time to step outside of your comfort zone, stop using clichés like comfort zone, and keep writing. Build a habit. Isn't that how we become good at anything?

2. Don't write a script – yet

Unlike the advice on joke writing, there are 432 million blogs telling you how to write sitcoms and screenplays. I'm guilty of contributing my share.

There's reams of information. Loads of it is really good. Why is this? It's because even the premier-league professional writers with dozens of credits can't sell anything in LA or London. The only way they can stay working in the business is by offering advice on what they've learned about how to become a scriptwriter.

Here's the quickest and most proven way to become a professional comedy scriptwriter: write jokes (See '1. Write jokes' above). I know, you've already decided that's not the route you're going to take, and nothing I say will persuade you otherwise. Here then, is a brief explanation of how to become a sitcom writer, screenwriter, novelist – everything, everywhere, all at once ...

3. Go on then, write the script

It starts with an idea. Loads of them. Be curious about the world. Read more. Find things that interest you. Imagine taking the thoughts you have about stories or articles you read to unusual places.

When you come up with a concept, spend time thinking about it. Does it excite you? At this stage, you can do anything with it. Imagine you're in a maze. If you reach a dead end, re-trace your steps and try a new path. Also:

- Don't fall in love with the first idea. Be prepared to adapt or change it or put it to one side.
- Don't throw anything away. It may come in handy again when you least expect it.

Screen and audio

• What's it about? Who's it about? Describe it using a cliché. Where is it set? Why are you writing it? Why now?

All scripts are about four things:

• A character taking a journey.
• The world.
• A goal.
• Obstacles met along the way.

Have you got any of those yet? Try putting them together in 25 words. You may not get close but don't worry, this is only the first step.

In drama, the obstacle is a baddy. In comedy, the protagonist's worst enemy is staring back at them from the mirror.

4. Meet people

The three questions I'm asked most frequently by new writers are:

• 'Where do you get your ideas from?' (See '2. Don't write a script – Yet' above)
• 'How do I get an agent?'
• and the biggie: 'Which font should I write my scripts in?' (Sorry, don't know.)

Let's remove one word from the second question and ask instead: *Do* I get an agent?

The answer is, not necessarily. Agents perform several great tasks for writers: they read your contracts carefully and secure you the best deal. They hear when producers are looking for writers on new shows and will ensure your name is added to the shortlist.

They help set up meetings. Give you credibility. 'Call my agent' isn't only a fab French TV show, it's a phrase you can utter that tells the listener you should be taken seriously.

Agents don't get you work. Work gets you an agent. And what you need now is work. Writing credits. How do you get those? See '1. Write jokes' above.

Now isn't the time to be talking to agents. The people you need to be meeting are producers and script editors.

You can do it. Get your scripts and ideas out there. Pick up knowledge of your industry. It's not difficult. This book is an excellent place to start. I love it and hope your copy becomes as dog-eared with over-use as many of my old ones did.

Who do you know? Write out a list. You'll be surprised. There are many comedy websites who'll be happy to help you: British Comedy Guide, The Comedy Crowd, Chortle. Contact the Writers' Guild of Great Britain (WGGB), Society of Authors, Alliance of Independent Authors. Don't bombard them but if you want to find out useful information, don't be afraid to establish polite contact.

Others you don't know as yet might have a presence on social media. Don't barge in but again, don't be afraid to ask intelligent questions. If you're going to be on social media, think about how you can be present. Write topical jokes if you can. Be a funny, interesting person. See what observations people are making and search for a different angle.

What's the best way to approach producers? Start with the BBC. Most people think of the BBC as a giant homogenous conglomerate. In our comedy world, though, it's a few diminutive sub-departments that are known to encourage new writers: Comedy, Radio (Sounds), Kids' TV, Writers (formerly Writers Room). Comedy production is a tiny industry and, while it's incredibly hard to get anything made, there are a few gatekeepers at the BBC who are actively looking for people like you.

TV and radio producers are only an email away. It's not difficult to find out how to contact them. If you enjoyed a show they made, tell them what you liked about it. Mention you have some scripts already written and that you'd like to meet for an informal chat.

You're not asking to pitch your script to them at this stage. (Not least because the answer would be 'no'.) You're making a connection – meeting someone who can give you inside information and who, some time down the line, may be able to give you work.

A lot of this involves two difficult actions for the typical writer. First, it asks you to step out of your introvert shell – the thing, as we all know, that made us want to be writers in the first place. The second is to think about your career like a professional. Imagine this as a five-, ten-, 20-year plan. People say 'It's not a sprint, it's a marathon', but it's actually both. Gags are the instant hit that get you noticed, but you're going to need more stamina to turn your bigger ideas into working projects.

If you want to be a writer, you must participate in an industry. You may achieve your dream of quitting the day job and spending your life doing what you love. You still need to turn up at the office occasionally. Be nice to strangers. Make deals and sign contracts.

5. Do it because you love it

Everybody's passionate nowadays. Two seconds on Google was enough to tell me that IKEA are passionate about 'life at home', while Phoenix Group are passionate about 'understanding what's important to our customers, colleagues and society'. Yet not passionate enough to tell us what they do, which is sell insurance.

My favourite is that McCain, of Oven-Ready Chips fame, are passionate about potatoes. Me too, mate. Now there's a product I can get behind.

I'd love to say that the key to success is keep going, to never give up on the dream, and that as long as you have talent then persistence and passion will get you there in the end, but there's no guarantee.

Obsession: now that's different. That's what you need in your approach to comedy, more than passion. I'm not sure if that's something you can cultivate, or if you have to be born with it.

And that brings us back to where we started. Becoming a paid, successful comedy writer is hard. Much harder than when I started out. You might never get there. But if you're obsessed, then what will interest you most is the process.

I've had meetings and plaudits, close calls and disappointments, five-star reviews and absolute stinkers. Through all this time, one thing has kept me going: every day I wake up excited and ask 'how can I become a better writer?'

Nothing else matters. Apart from the plaudits. I love them.

Dave Cohen is a multi-award-winning BBC comedy writer best known for his hugely popular song lyrics for *Horrible Histories*, which has won multiple BAFTAs. In November 2024, the show received a Special BAFTA in recognition of its cultural and social impact over the years. Dave works with new comedy writers to help them improve their craft. He has independently published two novels: *Stand Up, Barry Goldman* (2021) and *Barry Goldman: The Wilderness Years* (2023). Find him at www.davecohen.org.uk.

See also ...

- *What a literary agent can do for you*, page 433
- *Society of Authors*, page 746
- *Writers' Guild of Great Britain (WGGB)*, page 749

Creating compelling characters for TV

Every successful TV show has a great story, but it also has compelling characters. Heroes and villains alike, they're what makes the audience keep coming back for more. In this article, Kira-Anne Pelican explains the key components of truly multidimensional characters.

Thinking about creating a new series for television, but not sure where to start? Start with your characters. They don't just drive the story; they are the story. Even if you naturally gravitate towards plot, it won't be story events that get your series commissioned, but strong characters in an interesting situation making fascinating decisions under pressure. No one watches *Love Island* to see Mallorca. It is the characters who we connect with, the characters who we remember, and the characters who keep us yearning to see more. But what's the best way of creating characters that keep your audiences coming back for more? What is so special about some roles that they attract the best cast?

Most characters start from a hunch about a person that you'd love to see on screen. It's often useful to reflect why you've had a particular idea – and why now – so that you can develop this further for your story. Ideas for characters often speak to us because they feel particularly urgent or timely. What is it about the idea for your character that resonates? Does the role reflect struggles, perspectives or voices that feel especially timely? Maybe it embodies a challenge many people are facing today, or perhaps it brings a fresh viewpoint – like the character Alma from BBC sitcom *Alma's Not Normal*, whose optimism is shaped by her experience in the care system. Creating characters that speak to contemporary audiences is equally important when developing historical shows. Have a think about why their viewpoints feel timely today and what it is that you're intending to say through these.

The most engaging protagonists are believable, which means that they're multidimensional, complex and flawed. One way to think about creating multidimensional characters is via personality theory. The Big Five model of personality reminds us that people aren't one dimensional and that we all have a range of traits that fall under the following dimensions: extraversion, agreeableness, neuroticism, conscientiousness and openness. Extraversion describes the degree to which a character is more outward- or inward-facing. An extraverted character might be charismatic and outgoing, while an introverted one may be more thoughtful, serious and reserved. Agreeableness determines how warm and co-operative a character is in their relationships, while neuroticism describes how emotionally reactive or anxious they tend to be. Conscientious characters are dutiful, disciplined and determined, whereas those lacking this trait tend to be unreliable, disorganised and impulsive. The final category describes the degree to which a character is open-minded. Characters high in openness are usually imaginative and adventurous, while those low in it tend to be more traditional, resisting change and clinging to routine. Consider where your characters fall on each of these spectrums of personality in order to ensure they're multidimensional.

The most memorable characters stay with us long after a show ends – but what makes them unforgettable? Some captivate with their bold, larger-than-life personalities, like Tanya McQuoid (from HBO's drama *The White Lotus*), whose mix of impulsiveness, neuroticism and vulnerability makes her wonderfully tragic, darkly humorous and deeply flawed. Others leave a quieter but lasting impact through their relatability, drawing us in with their authenticity. The more time we spend with them, the more they feel like part of our lives.

With their distinctive mix of traits, great characters often embody striking contradictions. Sherlock Holmes is brilliant and highly open yet socially difficult, while Tanya McQuoid is desperate for connection but drives people away. The most compelling characters aren't just multidimensional – they have tensions within them that create complexity and intrigue. So, what makes your characters stand out? Do some demand attention with their wit and energy, or will they linger in your audience's mind through quiet emotional depth? How might their contradictions shape their journey – do you have an extravert who struggles with intimacy, or a meticulous planner who yearns for spontaneity? Consider how your characters' opposing traits may drive their decisions and the way they navigate the world.

Beyond ensuring that your characters feel believable, flaws make characters truly engaging. A character's central flaw often hints at an interesting backstory and drives the way they self-sabotage. In the BBC comedy *Amandaland*, the protagonist's flaw is her belief that her current life and reduced circumstances are just a temporary setback until she returns to the wealthier existence she feels entitled to. This sense of superiority leads her to undermine her relationships, seeing people as stepping stones rather than genuine connections. A strong flaw adds dramatic tension – your audience should hope your character overcomes their flaw, while also fearing they won't. What are your main characters' flaws? How do these cause them to sabotage their own success or happiness? And how does this create obstacles on their journey?

Just as flaws make characters more compelling, so do their hidden depths when they unfold over time. As these layers emerge, they will deepen your characters' complexity and offer greater insight into their motivations – often tied to their backstories. Unveiling these hidden depths also makes for compelling viewing, strengthening your audience's connection with your characters as they get to know them more intimately. Consider what hidden depths work best for your characters and what other sides may come out under pressure. Do they carry a secret that changes everything, or completely transforms your audience's understanding of them, once revealed?

These hidden depths help keep your audience emotionally invested in your characters, but it's equally important to consider how you want them to feel about your characters. Your viewers need to care enough to stay engaged, even when countless distractions in real life compete for their attention. One way to achieve this is by creating a character that audiences genuinely like, someone who is trustworthy, kind, positive and funny – qualities that we appreciate in a good friend. Another approach is to make your character relatable, allowing viewers to see themselves in the way they navigate familiar situations. These characters offer a sense of shared experience, allowing audiences to live vicariously through them, subconsciously learning how to handle challenges they may not have faced themselves. Other characters seize our attention because they're fascinating. Think of Walter White from US drama *Breaking Bad*: what makes him so compelling? Is it his unpredictability, his moral descent, or the tension between his actions and our expectations? As humans, we are wired to anticipate behaviour, constantly trying to predict how those around us will act. When a character defies our expectations, they command our attention. How do your characters surprise the audience and what does this tell us about them?

Another compelling aspect of a character is their emotional journey. When characters transform over time, some overcome their flaws while others become more deeply entrenched in them. Take the character Donny Dunn from British black comedy *Baby Reindeer* as an example. Initially presented as a well-meaning bartender caught off guard by Martha's relentless attention, Donny's quiet vulnerability is gradually overtaken by a turbulent mix of guilt, shame and self-sabotage – elements that force him to confront painful truths about his past and reshape his future. At the same time, these elements make for compulsive viewing. As you develop your characters, consider how their evolution transforms their identity and deepens the emotional investment of your audience.

While many TV characters undergo significant emotional transformations, not all characters evolve in the same way. Some, like Catherine Cawood from *Happy Valley*, remain largely unchanged on the surface, but keep audiences engaged through their emotional depth and consistency. Catherine's complex blend of resilience, grief and duty makes her compelling, even though her core values and personality remain steady throughout the series. Consider whether your characters' arcs involve transformation, or whether their power lies in their consistency. Does their emotional journey stem from their reactions to external events, or are they unyielding, offering a sense of stability and predictability amidst chaos? Both types of characters can be deeply engaging, as long as their internal landscape is rich enough to connect with the audience.

Keeping your audience invested in your characters over multiple episodes is crucial in any TV series. One effective way to do this is by creating throughlines that tie directly to the plot. For example, in the Apple TV drama *Severance*, the central plot revolves around the characters' struggle between their severed work and personal lives, with each character's journey to uncover the truth about the process providing an ongoing throughline. The mystery behind the severance process isn't just a plot device, but rather the driving force behind the characters' decisions and motivations, keeping the audience invested as the stakes rise. So, what are your characters striving for, and how does this drive their actions throughout the series? Consider how their pursuit of their goals keeps your audience hooked, both through any plot twists and emotional depth.

Equally important are the relationships your characters navigate. Whether they are romantic, professional or platonic, the dynamics between characters often provide the most compelling drama and tension. Think about how your characters' relationships evolve: do they form alliances, only to see them crumble, or do they experience moments of vulnerability that change the way they view one another? In *The White Lotus*, the shifting power dynamics between guests and staff create intrigue and tension, with characters constantly testing each other's boundaries. How can you use relationship dynamics to add layers to your characters, and what impact do these ever-changing connections have on their personal growth?

Pulling this all together, creating compelling characters for TV is never an arbitrary process. It begins with a gut instinct about a character or group of characters that feels just right for the moment. That spark, however, is only the starting point. To truly resonate with audiences, your characters must be fully developed: layered with complexity, shaped by flaws that drive them to self-sabotage, and rooted in rich backstories. Consider how their unique traits and interpersonal dynamics will forge an emotional connection with viewers. Rather than simply hoping your characters captivate, determine how you want your audiences to feel about them, then showcase these specific qualities that bring about these feelings in action on your pages.

If you find yourself stuck, try assembling a character dossier – a personal working document that helps you flesh out every nuance of your characters. This dossier isn't the same as the character profiles you'll include in your series bible; it's simply a tool for you to develop and refine your characters, complete with visual references, backstory details and notes on relationships and throughlines. Drawing on real-life observations of people and gathering headshots of actors – or even images of people who you feel resemble your characters – can add extra inspiration and help bring your character to life. By collecting visual references that reflect the personalities, appearances or energies you envision for your characters, you'll probably find that you can better understand their physical presence and emotional nuances, making them feel more real and grounded as you write. You won't need every detail from the outset, but you must have enough substance to show that your series idea has legs – so that when your characters walk onto the screen, they feel alive, real and unforgettable.

Kira-Anne Pelican is the author of *The Science of Writing Characters* (Bloomsbury Academic 2020), an educator and script editor. She specialises in helping writers create more engaging characters through insights from psychology and teaches character development workshops at organisations including BBC Writers, Cambridge University, Roadmap Writers, Story Academy and the London Screenwriters' Festival. As a script editor, she works for organisations including RSA and the BFI as well as independent writers and producers. Her websites are www.filmscribe.co.uk and www.charactermasterclass.com.

Writing series for television

Scriptwriter Russell Lewis has tough-talking advice about making your way into the competitive and collaborative business of writing for television, and describes how, when that break comes, you can succeed if you give it your all and never stop learning.

The first rule of Write Club is: you do not talk about Write Club.

The stock reply to the question, 'What advice would you give to someone who wanted to be a television writer?' is, of course, 'Don't' Seriously. Develop another ambition. Become the fluffer for a tiger-mating program, or a teething ring for rattlesnakes. But you've invested in a copy of *Writers' & Artists' Yearbook*, so you must believe that it's something you want to do – you crazy, idealistic little fool! Let's see if I can put you off.

It's difficult to catch a break and find a way into the industry – but then, you know that, or you wouldn't be reading this. No short cuts or magic formulae lie within the body of this article, only some vestigial amount of fellow feeling. We have all been there. Every writer you like has been there, and every writer you detest. They have all been on the same journey. There is only graft, and patience, and frustration, and more patience, and anger, and even more patience, and very, very occasionally, a bit of luck. And that's just to get a foot in the door. So, why do it at all? Well – let's be honest, it beats working for a living … Who was it said: 'Find the thing you love, and let it kill you'? Those who answered Madeleine Elster, go to the back of the class.

However, I promise you, if you have talent then somewhere, amongst all the pain and patience and frustration and anger and more patience, something will happen. You will get better at what you're doing. And 'getting better at what you're doing' is a process without end. Every day is a school day. You know that scene or line of dialogue that yesterday was a line in the sand that you scratched out with your own blood and sweat, and which you swore to defend against all comers to your last breath? Today, you will decide that you don't need it. You will find a more elegant and infinitely more economical way to make the same point, or a better one, or decide that you don't need it at all, and the piece will be improved a thousandfold by its excision. Very likely, your good colleagues will have been telling you this – or something like it – for some time. They couldn't tell you exactly what needed to be done, but they just knew they were bumping on something around that section. But – *here's the important bit* – you absolutely had to walk that lonely moonlit mile yourself to get to the moment of epiphany. That's the drug. That's what keeps us coming back for more. It's the Devil's candy – we know we shouldn't but, like the beat-up old ex-con in every heist movie, we keep coming back for one … last … job.

You will hear your peers (and others) talk self-mockingly about 'Writer Monkeys'. It's okay when we do it, but the 'others' aren't allowed to disparage. I'm proud to be a Writer Monkey, and you should be, too. Because it's a slight misnomer. What we actually are is the 'Problem-Solving Ape'. A script – any script – is, at its most basic level, a sequence of problems and solutions. In the first instance – be they physical, emotional or moral – those problems are intentional points of plot and narrative, the building blocks of story. Bring me the broomstick of the Wicked Witch of the West. What's a saloon bar owner to do with two letters of transit? What did he mean, 'Rosebud'? What should Sophie choose, and how can she live with that choice? How could anyone? Resolving those problems, answering those questions – while maintaining the established integrity of the imagined world in which they exist, and retaining the audience's interest in the solution – is more than half the job. I suppose it's what the late, great William Goldman called 'the spine'. Find the spine of your story, and all else follows. (Seriously, if you want to do this, read Goldman; let *Adventures in the Screen Trade* (Warner Books 1983) become your Bible.) Another way of putting it is, 'What's it about?'. When you begin, you may not have that answer down pat. You may not know. You may have a vague idea, a mood you want to catch, a feeling. Some things we wish to express are so gossamer and fragile that they're nigh on impossible to nail down straight out of the traps. In part, the process of writing is an uncovering – a chipping away at the block of marble to discover the form that lies within.

But back to the advice … Outside of the 'soaps', long-form drama series with high volume and turnover where a writer can develop their chops are few. The BBC has its writing scheme – and that's a way in for some. That route leads, typically – in the first instance – to continuing drama, a.k.a. the aforementioned 'soap'. And that's terrific. There are many fantastic talents who have come through that forcing ground – some of my favourite writers. I started with drama on a variation of the same, a show called *The Bill*, which was then a bi-weekly policier. The difference between that show and the current continuous dramas is that *The Bill* wasn't storylined; the 'episodes' were essentially 22-minute playlets. You could take it pretty much anywhere you wanted to go, provided you stuck to the one Golden Rule (and we only had one rule) – everything had to be seen from a police point of view. Otherwise, you could do what you liked.

It took me about a year to get through the door on that show. I'd been turned down, repeatedly. I'd come from a performing background – and that kind of weighed against being taken seriously – but the greatest bit of good luck that ever came my way arrived in the shape of a young woman by the name of Gina Cronk (insert Hollywood Recognition Applause here). Gina had been working in Reception, but – like your faithful correspondent – had ambition and ideas above her station. She'd just been made up from assistant script editor to script editor and consequently was looking to fill her flight roster with her own writers. If that hadn't happened, I would never have been seen and may have never got started. I don't doubt that the spec half-script I put in was pretty awful, but she saw something in there and gave me a break. I owe her pretty much everything.

The other thing the BBC's Writersroom has (at least at the time of writing) is a brilliant resource of scripts that you can download and read at your leisure, by people who really know what they're doing. Read every play, script and screenplay you can get your hands on. *That's* how you learn to know your way around a script. You watch the shows, and you read the scripts. See what was dropped; see what was added. Take note of who the script editor was. If it's a recent show, odds are that the script editor is still a script editor and hasn't ascended to the purple of Producerdom. Get in touch with them. If you're local, offer to buy them a cup of tea in a brightly lit public place and throw yourself upon their mercy. Beg, weep, grovel, offer whatever inducements you both consider legal, acceptable and, moreover, physically possible to get them to clue you in to what's going on in their department and the wider industry. They will know far better than anyone which shows are crewing up, which are looking for writers, what's in development, which of the afternoon dramas have a slot. If you are not local, try to do the same thing, initially, via email. Become pen pals, but (useful tip) – *don't be weird*. And remember – TV doesn't have to be your first port of call. A well-received fringe play or radio play can open just as many doors as the spec script. Get a rehearsed reading together. Invite agents and script editors and producers – especially agents – because representation is important. It will help get you in the room; after that you're on your own.

When that break comes, be ready to throw everything you've got at it. If you're pitching for a slot on an existing show, find the gap in the internal market. Know that show inside out. If everyone else is turning left, you turn right. Nothing to frighten the horses – you're not there to reinvent the wheel – but there will be characters who have been a bit under-served, or a coming curve that you can get ahead of. Furthermore, leave your pride and ego at the door; they're surplus to requirements. No matter how much you privately disagree, you will attend to the notes you are given diligently and with utmost dispatch, as if they were the Word of God. If that means you have to go a couple of nights without sleep to make the production deadline, then that is what you will do. This is not your great oeuvre or *meisterwerk*; this is episode 5, series 3, of whatever it might be. SERVE THE SHOW. Cut the throat of your favourite lines and characters and scenes if ordered to do so, without flinching or a moment's remorse. Stay light on your feet as production issues arise which will inevitably impact your script. Don't be precious about any of it. You've just lost the most important location? Write around it. *One of the regulars has had an accident and won't be available to shoot scenes 3, 24, 55A, 57 and 103B tomorrow … however, another character is available. Oh, and the first assistant director says the schedule is still 'over' and they won't be able to make the day; the request is to amalgamate scenes 55A and 57 while losing a page from their current page-count of three. We'll also have to cut 103B – and fold in the important information into scene 24. And, by the way, we're going to need it by close of play … today.*

Here's my modern heresy: I don't believe you can teach someone how to write. I think the snake-oil salesmen who tell you they can are exactly that. You can learn how to write – and you never stop learning – but that's a different thing. We learn by *doing*. You can no more teach someone to write than you can teach them to think or feel. You can provide them with a supportive environment, a creative soft space where they can stumble and fall frequently and safely. You can be a sounding board who offers thoughts about their work – a new angle, a different approach to a narrative problem or a way to rework the plot. But these are creative and editorial conversations you can expect to have all the time with your colleagues – commissioners, executives, producers, directors, actors – and especially, above all else, your editor. The good ones are worth their weight in diamonds and will save your arse more times than you can thank them, without it becoming an embarrassment – and really, you *do* need to thank them. So will many of the others on that list; because … (all together now) television – or film, radio or theatre – is a collaborative medium. This places the writer (who, you will remember, 'does not play well with others') in something of a cleft stick.

To illustrate this dichotomy, I keep two messages on my wall. The first reads, 'Television is a collaborative medium'. The second reads, 'COLLABORATORS WILL BE SHOT!' As Morgan Freeman's Detective Somerset observes at the end of the film *Se7en*: 'I agree with the second part's.

In the beginning was the word. Stay limber.

Oh, and the second rule of Write Club is ...?

Russell Lewis began his career as a child actor. His earlier TV credits included episodes of *Perfect Scoundrels*, *Taggart*, *The Bill*, *Wycliffe*, *Inspector Morse*, *Kavanagh QC*, *Spooks* and *Lewis*. He wrote for *Between the Lines* (1992), winner of the Writers' Guild of Great Britain TV Original Drama Series Award, and *Murphy's Law* (2003). He also co-wrote three of the *Sharpe* films. Russell devised and has written every script for all nine series of *Endeavour*, the last of which transmitted in Spring 2023, and he adapted five of the Peter James' books featuring DS Roy Grace for *Grace* on ITV starring John Simm. The first was transmitted in 2021 and the following four in 2022.

See also...

- *Successful screenwriting*, page 362

Getting your audiobook published

Laura Smith shares her knowledge of the audio publishing world, with options and advice on how to create a high-quality product, safeguard your rights as an author and tap into the potential of this increasingly popular format.

Over the past 15 years the audiobook market has been transformed. Audio is the fastest-growing part of the publishing industry, with new listeners, publishers, retailers and authors coming to the format each year. With things moving quickly, it can be hard to navigate what is best for you and your book. But if you get your audiobook publication right, you unlock a new pool of potential fans and another stream of revenue to reward you for the hard slog of writing your book. So here's what you need to know.

Understanding the audiobook market

The audiobook market comprises three main elements:

1. Digital audiobooks for consumers, accessed through Amazon, Audible, Apple, Kobo, Google, Spotify and a host of other large platforms. Smaller independent retailers are also innovating and establishing themselves in the market. The digital retail space is by far the biggest part of the market by revenue.
2. E-lending in public libraries. There are various platforms used in libraries across different territories, notably OverDrive (the Libby app; www.overdrive.com) and BorrowBox (www.borrowbox.com).
3. Physical CDs: bought by public libraries for loaning. This is still essential for libraries, and a good source of revenue for authors. There is also still a small market for CDs in consumer stores, but it is now small and selective, and mostly sold through online retailers such as Amazon.

Each part of the market has a broadly different demographic and, with new listeners coming to the format each year, the 'average listener' is constantly changing. But all you need to know is that the audiobook market holds a section of people who don't read books. Yes! As crazy as it sounds to us book-folk, some people just don't. But before you write them off, consider the millions of people who listen to podcasts, radio or music for hours each day. Some are migrating to long-form and discovering that they *do* have time for audiobooks. An audiobook could be their gateway drug into your back catalogue.

There is also a portion of the population who love great storytelling but are unable to read physical books, for a variety of reasons. Making your books accessible to *all* people can only be a good thing for your readership and your sales.

So how are people listening? The majority of audiobook fans listen through a smartphone or smart speaker, and they buy or borrow books through apps such as Audible (www.audible.co.uk), Spotify (https://open.spotify.com/), Audiobooks.com (www.audiobooks.co.uk), Apple Books (www.apple.com/uk/apple-books) or library lending apps. Visibility within each app is crucial to the success of your book, and we'll cover more on that later.

Know your rights

Before your work can become an audiobook you need to figure out who will publish it; so it is important that you pay attention to your audio rights. Whether you are self-published, represented by a literary agent, or work directly with a publisher – be clear on who owns your rights, for how long and in which territories. Crucially, establish *when* your audiobook will be published. For most books, the best time to publish an audiobook is at the same time as the ebook and print edition. An audiobook takes several months to plan and produce, so if your publisher doesn't have a plan for your audiobook six months ahead of the ebook release, you need to start asking questions.

If you are represented by a literary agent, they should explore the options for audio publishing when your book goes out on submission. Is it more lucrative for you to retain the rights and sell to an independent audio publisher? What plans does the publisher have creatively for your audiobook, and how will they bring it to market? If you raise and discuss these things at an early stage, you are more likely to get a clear plan for your audiobook.

If you are an indie author, you could consider recording and publishing the audiobook yourself, but this option is high risk. There is a significant financial investment needed up front; the recording needs to be high-quality or you risk poor reviews that damage sales. Without the clout of a large publisher, you may not get best terms or marketing placements needed to attract listeners to your book in a competitive marketplace. Audible's ACX scheme (www.acx.com) offers a way in for authors but, before committing to one retailer in a rapidly evolving market, look carefully at the terms, returns policy and exclusivity agreements they offer.

Many self-published authors choose to publish their ebooks and paperbacks independently but work with an audio publisher (such as W.F. Howes Ltd, who have an imprint called QUEST that caters for indie and Kindle authors) to publish their audiobook and distribute more widely across all retailer platforms and global markets.

Finding your voice

Once you have decided on your route to market, you will be faced with the most important decision for your book: who should read it – or more accurately, who is the best person to perform your work for the listener? Well, the overwhelming majority of audiobook listeners prefer to listen to a professional audiobook narrator or actor, rather than the author. So, unless you are reading your memoir and have broadcasting or acting experience, you probably aren't the right voice for the job.

For most listeners, the narrator's voice is the deciding factor in how they rate a book. The skill and nuance of the best audiobook narrators can elevate your work to a new level and create something truly special for you and your fans. Audiobook narration is extremely difficult – it takes training and preparation, and there are many successful actors who would admit they cannot do it. The most skilled narrators are able to create atmosphere, tension, comedic timing, *and* embody a full cast of characters for 12 hours with minimal mistakes.

When it comes to casting, it is important to cast authentically. For example, if your book is a first-person narrative from the perspective of a young Scottish woman, that's the voice you need to cast. If you have a dual narrative, time slip or some other narrative set-up, consider more than one voice to bring your story to life. If you have thoughts about characterisation, accents or unusual pronunciations, share these with your publisher or recording partner as soon as possible. Preparation for the audiobook recording takes time, and everyone across the recording team needs to know if you imagine your protagonist having a Yorkshire accent that you didn't mention anywhere in the text!

You may wonder whether you need a celebrity voice to get audiobook sales. In most cases the answer is no. Some narrators have a fan base among audiobook listeners, so it is worth browsing the reviews to see who is best rated in your category. But it is more important to get the right voice for your character, with a high-quality recording, a thorough edit and a proof-listen.

Visual impact

Next you will need to consider artwork. The dimensions for an audiobook cover are different to those for print, with the jacket presented as a square rather than a rectangle, owing historically to the shape of a CD cover. To potential listeners, who will see your book cover in an app on their smartphone as a digital 'stamp', only a square thumbnail will be visible. When consulting on cover artwork with your designer or publisher, ask how it will be adapted for audio and whether it is bold and simple enough to make an impact as a thumbnail.

Marketing

As your publication date approaches, you will need to bring listeners to your book. If you are working with a publisher, ask them about their marketing plan and how you can help. Do they have marketing and PR strategy specifically for audio, and how does it differ from their ebook and print campaign?

If you have an established readership, think about how you usually reach them. Perhaps you have a large mailing list or an active Facebook community. And if you have a significant social media following, what content can your publisher provide to share with them? Be open with ideas and suggestions that suit your readership. If you have a budget for advertising, make sure your ads are carefully targeted to reach potential listeners.

Once your book is published, encourage reviews. Reviews and ratings can make or break the success of your audiobook, change how visible it is within retailer algorithms and offer useful feedback. The more positive reviews you get, the more likely your audiobook will be to get selected for retailer spotlights and promotions.

Writing for audio

If you know your work has a future as an audiobook, please bear this in mind as you write. You may love using infographics or detailed lists in your books, but these won't work when read aloud. If necessary, consider adaptations or rewrites for visual sections of your book. Try reading troublesome pages out loud to yourself or have someone read them to you. It is surprising how well you can evaluate your writing by doing this, and it is a great way to hear how your book will work in audio.

Do you have an established audience and love the audio format? Then why not explore an audio-first project? A story told entirely through sound is ripe with creative possibilities. As the market changes, the lines between audiobook, audio documentary, podcast and audio drama are merging – with exciting results. If you have a compelling story to tell, it might find a home as an audio exclusive. At W.F. Howes we recently launched WFH ORIGINAL, an imprint for audio-first projects which are commissioned, developed and tailored to the audio format. As the audio market evolves, there are more opportunities for writers in this area, whether through publishers, studios or production companies.

What next?

Armed with more information about the audio publishing world, you can consider what is right for your work. Reflect on what matters to you the most, be it keeping financial risk to a minimum, having full creative control, or having a high-cost, full-cast studio production. Ask questions, get feedback and enjoy listening to the finished product.

Laura Smith is Acquisitions Manager at W.F. Howes, the UK's leading independent audiobook publisher. Over the past 14 years she has worked across commissioning, contracts, casting, marketing and sales of audiobooks. Laura has acquired and published audiobooks across fiction, non-fiction and children's categories, including books by Marian Keyes, Val McDermid, Sally Rooney, Chris Brookmyre, Gregg Hurwitz, Hilary Mantel and L.J. Ross. She oversees a team acquiring audiobook rights from agents and publishers, as well as running the WFH ORIGINAL imprint, comprising works commissioned and produced exclusively for audiobook format. For more information see www.wfhowes.co.uk.

See also...

- *Audio providers and distributors*, page 223
- *Audio dramatist or novelist?*, page 384

Audio dramatist or novelist?

Writer Jonathan Myerson describes what has drawn him towards audio drama, how closely this form of storytelling relates to the art of a novelist, and where it differs. He explains the freedom offered by audio drama, plus its dangers and demands, and outlines crucial elements for success.

As a chain-reader of fiction since my teenage years, I am not quite sure how I became a dramatist. But then again, I'm not surprised that audio drama has become my chosen form – I've dabbled in TV drama (too melodramatic), film (too much second-guessing) and even animation (still can't even draw stick men), but it is audio drama that I keep coming back to. I have also written novels, which is probably the one *un*surprising element in that spectrum: there's a clear affinity between a story told on the page and a story conveyed purely in sound.

To begin with, both the novel and the audio drama take shape only in the reader's or listener's mind. The well-worn maxim that 'the pictures are better on radio' rings equally true for the novel, whose scenes exist in that netherworld between the actual and the imagined, forcing the reader-audience to add the missing elements. And audio dramas, like novels, must tread the thin line between what the character might observe and what the story demands. A novelist – any good novelist, anyway – includes only the elements which are crucial for the given scene. Anything else – as we all discover when editing our own prose – is just typing.

This is also the stricture which a good audio dramatist must obey. Back when the BBC believed younger audiences craved an alternative soap to *The Archers*, I wrote for a drama called *Citizens*. It taught me one glorious lesson: very sporadically would you be reminded that one character (it was the landlord of the pub, I think) was in a wheelchair. For most scenes it was wholly irrelevant and therefore not mentioned (not even as a sound effect). A novelist would do the same. But in any other storytelling form, it would be inescapable in every frame, and would inevitably misdirect the audience's attention constantly.

Perhaps this is why so many of our great novelists have turned simultaneously to audio drama – William Trevor, Rose Tremain and Hilary Mantel, for instance – and so many audio dramatists have tried their hand at novels – recently and most notably Rachel Joyce. In fact, the latter's breakout bestseller, *The Unlikely Pilgrimage of Harold Fry*, started life as a (somewhat shorter) play for BBC Radio 4. Apart from the budget-busting range of eras and locations available to audio dramas and novels, both forms crucially enable the writer to tell you only what they want you to focus on – leaving you to pour your own imaginative fuel onto the rest.

I'll admit that, when I started writing my first novel after more than a decade as a dramatist, I went through a period of shock. I was accustomed to simply typing terse scene-settings (maybe 'deck of freighter during force eight storm' or 'the characters stroll through an autumnal forest glade') and leaving it to the crew to execute my demands. Suddenly, with no production staff, I was going to have to bring all of this to life myself, to find the precise and most convincing sequence of words to make it real. And then my second realisation: this wouldn't be simply 'Sound Effects Disc 37B' or a studio manager waltzing across crisp packets. No, here my words were free to evoke exactly what it feels like for the characters to endure that storm or breathe the leafy mist coming in on that October air.

It would all be about the characters' response to these surroundings. Their perspective would be my liberation.

And perspective brings us back to that crucial element of audio drama storytelling: just as many novels are written either in the first person or in close third person, audio dramas thrive on that same intense bond between listener and central character. If asked to define the role of the modern novel, I would say it's a 300-page exploration of What It's Like to Be X (whether X is a woman of 60 who has just discovered her husband's secret love child or X is a mixed-race teen on a West London estate where it's all about to kick off). At their most successful, audio dramas perform the same function. Sure, you can choose to bounce around between different characters in different places, but any audio drama gains hugely from a central pivot - the sort of viewpoint you'd take for granted in a novel. Emile Zola defined art as 'a corner of creation seen through a temperament' and that ticks the audio drama boxes just as neatly.

As always in the writing game, though, there's no such thing as a free lunch. That central temperament will also do its best to pull you down the fatal primrose path for audio drama writers: the internal monologue. Many novels thrive on this kind of commentary, but at this point drama and prose must part ways. For me, the internal monologue is the enemy of live drama, and any play must feel *live*, must hum with the danger of *now*, with the unknowingness of its characters. And that's why the internal monologue is the dramatist's sworn enemy. For so many seemingly good reasons, voice-over will feel like the solution to all your problems: anything which you cannot convey in sound can instantly get itself described. What's more, it's your chance to speak directly and unimpeded to the audience. But characters in drama, unlike prose fiction, must always be up against a ticking clock and, as soon as a character has unlimited and unopposed time to unleash their thoughts and reflections, that clock stops ticking.

So my advice on the 'narratorly voice-over' is: Handle With Extreme Caution. That direct channel into the mind and feelings of the protagonist, that self-dissecting honesty, will erode any genuine suspense. If the central character understands himself, why does the audience need to even try? Imagine if the curtain went up on the latest production of *Hamlet* and the title character strode to the front of the stage and announced he has an issue with getting things done, is probably a bit confused about his sexuality, and let's not even talk about his mother issues. Would you bother to watch the ensuing four hours? No, you watch the five acts in order to work all this out for yourself.

Worse than self-knowledge, a voice-over becomes a safety net underlying your plot, because however bad things turn out, this character is still able to tell us about what happened, and how they have come to terms with those events. When I fulminate about voice-overs, people throw something like *Sunset Boulevard* back at me (non-spoiler alert: Scene 1 reveals William Holden's corpse floating in the swimming pool and the rest of the film unravels his journey to that point), but even that trades on a Zen-like resignation in Holden's narration. He survived, he's down with it, and you don't need to worry.

So how then to ensure that the audio drama remains your protagonist's story? How to generate that solidity of POV? It's not easy, but now we come full circle back to the novelist's skill set. Any novelist writing in first or close third person takes for granted that their protagonist appears in every scene. Yes, in a shorter drama that can make the plotting tricky, but you can always contrive the setting and 'agenda' of your scenes so that everything is revealed (though beware those faux voice-overs: the Therapist's Couch, the Endlessly Patient Best Friend!). Once you have finagled your plotting to tell it all through action involving your protagonist, the coherence and focus of your play is assured. The listener is now freed to walk a single, ribbon-like journey – and we're back to Harold Fry.

Of course, in this sense, a protagonist is not always a single person. In 1998 Bruce Springsteen agreed to play a concert in East Germany, behind the Berlin Wall. My play, *Born in the GDR*, dramatises how three young people first had the crazy idea of asking him, and how they squeezed the whole scheme past the Stasi and then staged a concert in front of what is still the largest audience ever in Europe. Those three people, as a joint enterprise, are the protagonist – one or more of them is in every scene. They are the ribbon; they are the temperament through whom we view this particular corner of creation.

In fact, many of my plays – because they dramatise actual events – have demanded this approach. In my trilogy of plays about *The Clintons*, Bill and/or Hillary is in every scene; it was their show, their unfolding. We never jump to the other side's POV. What happens is happening to them. Or think sideways: Anthony Minghella's *Cigarettes and Chocolate* explores the mystery of why the pivotal character has stopped speaking. The result is a brilliant set of agonised, one-sided conversations with a woman who won't reply. The other characters can say what they want, but they are still talking to someone – it's not just narration into a convenient theatrical void. And the clock remains ticking ... until, at the last, she reveals the reason for her silence.

And why stop there? We now all carry a device engineered for self-advertisement and this hands the audio dramatist a sledgehammer with which to demolish the fourth wall entirely. My podcast serial *That Was Then* has the central character secretly recording everything – for her own safety, as much as anything – into her phone, both the events and her follow-up diary. In fact, we even recorded it on location on an iPhone in order to generate that kind of scratchy, amateurish recording (but Apple outwitted us, and the quality was barely distinguishable from the BBC's best in-house microphones). But the protagonist's need to hide the recordings from everyone, including her own family, kept that clock ticking loudly; the drama remains set firmly in the now.

So I am often asked, how do you know if your next idea is a novel or an audio drama? And the truthful answer is, I don't know. In so many respects, they're the same thing and ask the same from their audiences – but don't forget that they make slightly different demands on the writer.

A word on words: throughout this piece I have used the term 'audio drama'. Now that podcasts have reinvented this particular wheel, 'radio drama' seems old-fashioned. Nowadays audio dramas are sometimes called 'scripted podcasts', but I find that dull and unwieldy. Certainly, someday soon, podcast providers will be creating more hours of audio drama than the BBC – and the Corporation is the only reason still to call it 'radio' drama.

Jonathan Myerson is the author of over 50 individual dramas for the BBC, as well as episodes of series *Westway* and *Citizens*. For TV, he has written episodes of *The Bill*, *EastEnders* and *Holby City*. His audio drama series include *The Republicans*, *Doctor Zhivago* and *Number 10* (winner of the Writers' Guild Award for Best Radio Drama). His most recent podcasts are *Nazis: The Road To Power* and *Nuremberg*, both multi-episode dramatic retellings for BBC Sounds, and *That Was Then*, a scripted 15-episode drama. Jonathan has been nominated for an Oscar and won a BAFTA in 1999 for his animated film of *The Canterbury Tales*. He consults for www.finishyournovel.org.

Writing for videogames: a guide for the curious

Chris Bateman shines a light on videogame writing, its nature and challenges, and has essential advice for anyone hoping to build a career in the rewarding and creative world of game narrative and design.

So you've played a few videogames, and marvelled at the production values and the intensity of the experience, but were perhaps a little underwhelmed by the stories you've encountered. Like any writer, you can't resist a creative challenge and you know that with the right tools you could do a better job. The question is: what do you need to create a videogame narrative? How do you begin? Where do you go to make it happen?

Let's start with the bucket of cold water – you will not end up writing for videogames if it's just an idle fancy; it takes a real commitment to work in games writing and – make no mistake – this is the toughest medium to work in. But at the same time, working on a game story, helping a team bring characters into beautifully animated life and working with voice actors to give a soul to those animations, can be hugely rewarding. Working on an animated movie or TV show carries the same emotional payoff, is substantially easier, and gives more creative control to the writing team, but if you're dedicated to your dream of writing for games, or don't think anything else would quite satisfy your creative needs, videogame writing is a path you can take.

Getting started

So how do you get the opportunity? As with most jobs, you frustratingly need to have prior experience to get hired. If you've already written novels, short stories, radio plays, screenplays, stage plays or anything of the kind, you can try fishing for work with that experience but you're likely to come up against a certain resistance from game developers. One way around this, especially if you're a writer with time to invest in career-building, is to lend your support to indie games (i.e. low-budget projects) that are advertising on sites like Game Developer (www.gamedeveloper.com) or via social media asking for help. They may be willing to take on a writer (typically unpaid) and in return you can get experience working in games. It's not a glamorous way to start, but gaining experience seldom is.

If you have a little money to invest in your career, consider attending one of the major industry events like Develop in Brighton or GDC in San Francisco (see box for details), where you can hear from experienced game writers and get networking. This was more or less how my company, International Hobo, built up clients in the early years, although admittedly I'd already worked on several critically acclaimed games at that point. You can also go to these events and set up meetings with developers to talk about what you can offer. There's usually a meeting app provided with the ticket, and there are also third-party options, like MeetToMatch (www.meettomatch.com), which are often worth the extra cost.

How game projects begin

Let's say you've found a developer willing to work with you. Now is the time to pitch that screenplay you wrote as a dynamite basis for a videogame, right? Sorry, no. Videogames are never made from screenplays (we don't even have a standard format for one!) and very few start as story concepts either. If you want to make your own glossy digital masterpiece for games consoles, you'd better have a few million in your back pocket to fund production. Otherwise, accept that your job as game writer is to assist a development team to get the most out of the game they're making, by helping them discover opportunities to get more out of characters or settings or theme (a subtlety many game developers tend to overlook).

Typically, a game begins as either a prototype, showing off what the game is like, or as a concept document – a short pitch for a game. Concept documents are quite similar to the proposals that a book publisher or agent expects to be submitted (and often written after the manuscript is completed). Laying out the story in broad strokes is part of the concept and so can be an element of the documentation from the very beginning – although, in practice, writers seldom get attached to projects this early. This, however, is short-sightedness on the part of developers, who actually could use your input at this stage. You can pitch your services to companies in this way – but expect scepticism if you can't show evidence that you have a handle on how stories in games work.

How do you build up your understanding of the workings of videogame? The easiest way is to play games. You can learn a lot from playing videogames, but don't just play the latest releases or you'll end up playing solely what are called AAA games (i.e. multi-million-dollar blockbusters) and, as a writer trying to break into games, you won't be working on these. Play older games, play new games made on a low budget, and play games from wildly different genres. While you're networking, you can even ask game developers which games they rate for clever use of story materials ... you'll get plenty of suggestions! Another option is to watch online videos of other people playing games. Some game writers will cluck their tongues at this suggestion, but you don't need to be able to play a certain kind

Networking opportunities

Develop Conference
www.developconference.com
Europe's leading convention and expo for those working in game development. Held annually in Brighton for three days in July.

Game Development Conference (GDC)
www.gdconf.com
The world's largest professional gaming industry event, incorporating The Independent Games Festival and The Game Developers Choice Awards. Takes place over five days every March in San Francisco.

Gamescom
www.gamescom.global
Europe's largest expo, and a good networking opportunity. Held in August each year in Cologne.

International Game Developers Association (IGDA)
https://igda.org
US-based with a global network of over 150 chapters and Special Interest Groups (SIGs) with individual members from all fields of game development: programmers and producers, designers and artists, writers and other experts.

WGA – Writers Guild of America
www.wga.org
Union that represents writers for film, TV and games, combining WGA West and WGA East. Like the WGGB, its UK equivalent, the WGA honours writers for games in its annual awards.

WGGB – Writers' Guild of Great Britain
https://writersguild.org.uk
Union that supports UK-based writers, including games writers, with a useful guide *Writing for Videogames* on its site. See page 749.

of game to work on its story, you just have to be able to appreciate how it works; other people's player experiences can be just as useful for this (in some cases, more useful) because games are not played in the same ways by all players.

Narrative design

In the early 2000s, when I was setting up International Hobo, my colleagues and I conceived of our job as 'narrative design'. It's a term that has now crept out into the industry thanks to the International Game Developers Association, for which I set up the Game Writing Special Interest Group (you might want to check this out as a helpful community for game writers at all stages of their careers; see box). Narrative design is the intersection of game design and writing: it's about putting a player into the centre of your story or, perhaps more accurately, about turning a story inside-out so that it can work when the central character is (nearly) beyond your control. A player isn't an actor, so you'll need to provide reasons for them to take on the role provided – or alternatively give them opportunities to mess around with the world.

There are several key aspects of narrative design you'll need to consider:

1. Dialogue

You'll need to decide if your focus will just be on dialogue – in which case, expect the scenarios to be almost entirely dictated to you, and prepare to work with a low level of creative influence – or if you're going to get involved with narrative design. This means having a hand in the structuring of the game materials, which in turn means understanding game design as well as writing. Woe betide the conventional screenwriter who thinks they will 'fix' videogames by making them more like movies!

2. Cut scenes and voice actors

Almost everything you want to do to make a conventional narrative work is too expensive. You will struggle to get much budget for animated sequences (called *cut scenes*, or *FMV* – full motion videos) and if you're having to tell your story in this way you're working in the wrong medium. Talking heads (i.e. voice actors providing dialogue to animated characters in the game) is a powerful and relatively cost-effective tool, but the moment you need one of the characters to be animated in a specific way (say, banging their fist on a table for emphasis) you're draining money from the budget. As a writer, words are your greatest tool so use them to great effect. If the game has voice recording (most mid-budget or higher games do) the voice actors will be able to 'sell' your dialogue to the player without you having to specify animations for emphasis. If it doesn't, well, then you get an even greater opportunity to make every word count, because it's your text being read directly by the players. Either way, don't use more lines than you need to advance the narrative.

3. Narrative spaces

The other key element of narrative design is location: games typically flow through environments and, as a writer, you can use your grasp of locations to great effect in discussions with the developer. As always, though, every location costs money to make and, unlike for film or TV, you can't just nip out with a location crew if you need footage; everything has to be painstakingly built by the team. That means nothing should go into the game that isn't absolutely necessary, and ideally you shouldn't be creating more locations than are needed.

Theatre is a much better guide than film in this regard. The playwright has to think about how it works on stage; you don't have an entire set put up just for an actor to say two lines and walk off. In a game, every location has to earn its time. Unlike theatre sets, however, videogame environments are typically vast open spaces; that gives you the opportunity to paint in stories, without text or dialogue, by using environmental storytelling. You won't get the budget to show, say, a werewolf tearing apart a village, but you can show the aftermath and let the player piece together the back story from what they can find.

4. World-building

Some games, particularly computer role-playing games, also rely on a depth of lore – and the need for the associated texts can be a way for a writer to get added to a project. World-building is part of the writer's toolkit, and while few game developers will let you put together the world for their game single-handed, they may well be delighted for you to write short texts that fill in the substance of their setting. I won't lie to you – this may involve a great deal of writing descriptions for weaponry, but I have to say I found it very rewarding to paint a picture of a fantasy world solely from the swords, shields, jewellery and clothing players will encounter. There's a challenge here that no other medium will give you.

Part of the team

Ultimately, writing for games is about working in a team in which different professionals have a hand in making everything happen. The most important thing you can do, as a writer, when you join a developer is to acknowledge that the programmers and artists are the ones who are actually making the game – your job is to help bring out the best in what they're doing. If you can place yourself in the service of a developer, your writing can take videogames to another level. That's what keeps me going. There are always new ways to tell stories in games, and it's my pleasure and honour to work with developers to help them discover the right one for their project.

Chris Bateman is a game designer, technology ethicist and founder of the award-winning creative consultancy International Hobo. He is best known for the games *Discworld Noir* and *Ghost Master* and his book *Game Writing: Narrative Skills for Videogames* (Cengage Learning 2007, 2nd edition Bloomsbury 2021). His other books include *Imaginary Games* (2011) and *Chaos Ethics* (2014), both published by Zero Books, and *The Virtuous Cyborg* (Eyewear Publishing 2018). Chris has an MSc in Artificial Intelligence/Cognitive Science and a PhD in game aesthetics, and has worked on over 80 published games. He was a member of the thinking group for the Digital Futures Commission, and sits on the editorial board for the *International Journal of Play*.
He writes 3-minute reflections on contemporary problems at *Stranger Worlds and How To Live In Them* (https://strangerworlds.substack.com). Find out more about him at his company's blog (https://blog.ihobo.com).

Television and radio

The information in this section has been compiled as a general guide for writers, artists, agents and publishers to the major companies and key contacts within the broadcasting industry. As personnel, corporate structures and commissioning guidelines can change frequently, readers are encouraged to check the websites of companies for the most up-to-date information.

REGULATION

Advertising Standards Authority

Castle House, 37–45 Paul Street, London EC2A 4LS
tel 020-7492 2222
website www.asa.org.uk
Facebook www.facebook.com/adauthority
X @ASA_UK
Chief Executive Guy Parker

The UK's independent regulator of advertising across all media. Its work includes acting on complaints and taking action against misleading, harmful or offensive advertisements.

Ofcom

Riverside House, 2A Southwark Bridge Road, London SE1 9HA
tel 020-7981 3000, 0300 123 3000
website www.ofcom.org.uk
Facebook www.facebook.com/ofcom
X @Ofcom
Instagram @ofcom.org.uk
Chief Executive Melanie Dawes

Accountable to parliament. Exists to further the interests of consumers by balancing choice and competition with the duty to encourage plurality, protect viewers and listeners, promote diversity in the media and ensure full and fair competition between communications providers.

TELEVISION

There are five major TV broadcasters operating in the UK: the BBC, ITV, Channel 4 (S4C in Wales), Channel 5 and Sky. In Ireland, RTÉ is the country's public service broadcaster.

The BBC

BBC Broadcasting House, Portland Place, London W1A 1AA
website www.bbc.co.uk

The BBC is the world's largest broadcasting organisation, with a remit to provide programmes that inform, educate and entertain. Established by a Royal Charter, the BBC is a public service broadcaster funded by a licence fee. Income from the licence fee is used to provide services including:

- eight national TV channels plus regional and local programming
- ten national radio stations
- 39 local radio stations
- two national radio services each in Scotland, Wales and Northern Ireland
- BBC World Service.

Anyone in the UK who watches or records TV programmes (whether via TV, online, mobile phone, games console, digital box, etc), or watches or downloads any BBC programmes from BBC iPlayer, needs a TV licence. The Government sets the level of the licence fee. The annual cost is £174.50. For full details of which services require a TV licence, visit: www.tvlicensing.co.uk.

Governance

BBC Board

The BBC is governed by a board. Tim Davie, Director-General, sits on the board alongside other BBC executive and non-executive members. More information is available at: www.bbc.co.uk/aboutthebbc.

Ofcom

External regulation of the BBC is carried out by Ofcom.

What does the BBC do?

The following provides a selective overview of the BBC's main services and key contact information we consider most relevant to our readership.

Television

The BBC's eight national TV channels provide entertainment, news, current affairs and arts programming for the whole of the UK: BBC One, BBC Two, BBC Three, BBC Four, CBeebies, BBC News and BBC Parliament.

Chief Content Officer Charlotte Moore
Controller, Youth Audiences, iPlayer & BBC Three Fiona Campbell
Controller, iPlayer & Channels Dan McGolpin
Director, Children's & Education Patricia Hidalgo Reina
Head, BBC Sport Philip Bernie

BBC Content

BBC's online services include news, sport, weather, CBBC, CBeebies, BBC iPlayer and the school learning and revision site, BBC Bitesize. Sites are developed to provide audiences with access to content on a variety of devices including tablets, smartphones and computers.

Access to the BBC's radio and TV programme archives is available through BBC iPlayer.

News Group

BBC News incorporates network news (the newsroom, news programmes, political programmes, and the weather team), English Regions and Global News.

Ceo, News & Current Affairs Deborah Turness

Nations

The Nations division is one of the largest divisions in the BBC, with staff working for the BBC in England, Scotland, Wales and Northern Ireland. The division produces a range of content across TV, radio and online for audiences locally, across all of the UK and globally.

Director, Nations Rhodri Talfan Davies

BBC Studios

BBC Studios works with British writers, directors and programme-makers to create content every year through production bases in the UK and in partnership with countries around the world.

Ceo Tom Fussell

BBC Studioworks

A wholly owned subsidiary of the BBC. Works with media companies to create and manage content across all genres for a diverse range of broadcasters and platforms, including ITV, Channel 4 and Sky, as well as the BBC.

Ceo Andrew Moultrie

BBC World Service Group

Incorporates BBC World Service and BBC Global News and includes the BBC World News Television Channel, the BBC's international-facing online news services in English, BBC Monitoring Service and BBC Media Action (the BBC's international development charity).

Director, BBC World Service Liliane Landor

Commissioning

For full details of editorial guidelines, commissioning, production and delivery guidelines, and how to submit a proposal, see www.bbc.co.uk/commissioning.

Developing and producing programmes is complex and requires substantial knowledge of production and broadcasting. PiCos (www.bbc.co.uk/commissioning/picos) is the BBC's pitching and commissioning system designed for UK-based production companies to submit content proposals to the BBC. Individuals and members of the public cannot use PiCos. If you are a member of the public with an idea, see www.bbc.co.uk/commissioning/talent.

Who's who in commissioning?

Television (genre commissioning)

Chief Content Officer Charlotte Moore

Children's

Head of Commissioning & Acquisitions Kate Morton (0–6 years), Sarah Muller (7–12 years)

Comedy

Director of Comedy Jon Petrie, *Head of Comedy* Tanya Qureshi, *Head of Development* Roya Eslami, *Commissioning Editors* Ben Caudell, Seb Barwell, Gregor Sharp, Emma Lawson

Daytime and Early Peak

Head of Daytime & Early Peak Commissioning Rob Unsworth, *Commissioning Editors* Lindsay Bradbury, Neil McCallum, Rachel Platt, Julie Shaw, Muslim Alim, Helen Munson

Drama

Director of Drama Lindsay Salt, *Head of Development* Sami El-Hadi, *Head of Business, Scripted* Geraldine Atlee, *Senior Commissioning Editor* Lucy Richer, *Commissioning Editors* Jo McClellan, Gaynor Holmes, Rebecca Ferguson, Nawful Faizullah, Danielle Scott-Haughton, Nick Lambon

Entertainment

Head of Commissioning Kalpna Patel-Knight, *Commissioning Executive* Jamie Dodds, *Senior Commissioning Editor* Jo Wallace, *Commissioning Editors* Ruby Kuraishe, Katie Taylor, Pinki Chambers, Sarah Clay, Clodagh O'Donoghue, Neil McCallum, Chantal Boyle

Factual

Director of Unscripted Kate Phillips, *Heads of Commissioning* Suzy Klein (Arts & Classical Music), Clare Sillery (Documentaries), Jack Bootle (Specialist Factual), Catherine Catton (Factual Entertainment & Events), Jonathan Rothery (Popular Music)

BBC Nations

Director, Nations Rhodri Talfan Davies

BBC Cymru Wales *Director* Rhuanedd Richards, *Senior Head of Commissioning* Nick Andrews, *Commissioners* Christina Macaulay, Julian Carey, Sian Harris, *Commissioning Executive* Paul Forde

BBC Scotland *Director* Hayley Valentine, *Head of Commissioning* Louise Thornton, *Commissioners* Heather Kane-Darling, David Harron, Tony Nellany, Gavin Smith, Steve Allen

BBC Northern Ireland *Senior Head of Content Commissioning* Eddie Doyle, *Commissioning Executives* Fiona Keane, Justin Binding, Karen Kirby, Mary McKeagney

BBC Writers

website www.bbc.co.uk/writers
Facebook www.facebook.com/BBCWriters
X/Twitter @bbcwritersroom
Instagram @bbcwriters

BBC Writers seeks to discover, develop and champion new and experienced writers across the UK. Unsolicited submissions are accepted as part of

Open Call script submission windows, announced on the BBC Writers Opportunities page. Shortlisted writers are offered a development programme through either the Voices or Drama Room groups which include expert masterclasses, workshops and networking opportunities to provide participants with core tools and knowledge to write for broadcast television.

BBC Writers also offers other bespoke development programmes including the Writers' Access Group for d/Deaf, disabled and neurodivergent writers and the Pilot scheme for credited/agented writers. The BBC Writers blog provides a wealth of behind-the-scenes commentary from writers and producers who have worked on BBC TV and radio programmes: www.bbc.co.uk/writers/blogs.

Education and training

The BBC has adopted a recruitment system called BBC Careers. It allows candidates to apply for trainee schemes, work experience, apprenticeships and jobs. To learn about the BBC's recruitment processes visit the website at www.careers.bbc.co.uk.

BBC Academy

website www.bbc.co.uk/academy

A free, online learning resource providing practical advice and information working in TV, radio and online.

Channel 4

124–126 Horseferry Road, London SW1P 2TX
tel 0345 076 0191
website www.channel4.com
Facebook www.facebook.com/Channel4
X @Channel4
Instagram @channel4

A publicly-owned television network freely available to all in the UK. Its commercially-funded, publicly-owned structure enables all profit generated to be directly reinvested back into its public service remit. As a publisher–broadcaster, Channel 4 commissions UK content from the independent production sector and currently works with over 300 creative companies across the UK every year. Provides a digital streaming service, All 4, and a network of six television channels, aiming to create change by representing unheard voices and reinventing entertainment.

Management team

Chief Executive Alex Mahon, *Chief Content Officer* Ian Katz, *Director of People* Kirstin Furber

Commissioning

Information about commissioning and related processes and guidelines can be found at www.channel4.com/4producers. Email addresses for most individuals named below can be found on the relevant parts of the website.

Comedy

Head of Comedy Charlie Perkins, *Senior Commissioning Editor* Andy Bereton, *Commissioning Editors* Laura Riseam, Joe Hullait

Lifestyle

Head of Lifestyle Jo Street, *Senior Commissioning Editors* Clemency Green, Jayne Stranger, *Commissioning Executives* Jasper Hone, Barry Agnew

Documentaries and Factual Entertainment

Head of Documentaries and Factual Entertainment Alisa Pomeroy, *Senior Commissioning Editors* Sacha Miroeff, Madonna Benjamin, Anna Miralis, *Commissioning Editors* Ian Dunkley, Tim Hancock, Rita Daniels, *Commissioning Executive* Simon Lee

Drama

Director of Drama Ollie Madden, *Commissioning Editors* Gemma Boswell, Gwawr Lloyd, Rebecca Holdsworth, *Commissioning Executives* Louise Donald, Danyele Seignoret

News and Current Affairs

Head of News & Current Affairs Louisa Compton, *Commissioning Editors* Adam Vandermark, Nevine Mabro, Joanne Potts, Janine Thomas

Reality and Entertainment

Head of Reality and Entertainment Steven Handley, *Head of Live Events* Tom Beck, *Senior Commissioning Editor* Vivienne Molokwu, *Commissioning Editors* Lee McMurray, Cimran Shah, Genna Gibson

Specialist Factual

Head of Specialist Factual Shaminder Nahal, *Commissioning Editors* Jonah Weston, Emily Shields

Sport

Head of Sport Peter Andrews, *Commissioning Editor* Joe Blake-Turner, *Commissioning Executive* Antonia Howard-Taylor

4Skills

website https://careers.channel4.com/4skills

Through 4Skills, Channel 4 aims to help people who want to work in the broadcasting industry gain experience, qualifications and career development. There are a range of options including apprenticeships, work experience, training, events and workshops.

Channel 5

17–29 Hawley Crescent, Camden Town, London NW1 8TT
tel 020-3580 3600
website www.channel5.com
Facebook www.facebook.com/channel5uk
X @channel5_tv
Instagram @channel5_tv
Director of Programming Ben Frow

Brands include Channel 5, 5Star, 5Select and 5USA, and an on-demand service, My5. Channel 5 works with independent production companies to provide its programmes.

Commissioning

Drama

Deputy Chief Content Officer Sebastian Cardwell, *Commissioning Editors* Paul Testar, Greg Barnett

Factual, Factual Entertainment, News and Current Affairs (Unscripted)

Commissioning Editors Guy Davies (Factual), Lucy Willis (Factual), Adrian Padmore (Factual, Factual Entertainment, Specialist Factual), Dan Louw (Factual, Factual Entertainment, Specialist Factual), Denise Seneviratne (Factual), Kit Morey (Popular Factual), Greg Barnett (Factual, Factual Entertainment)

Acquisitions

Senior Acquisitions Managers Cherry Yeandle, *Senior Director* Anna-Belen Dunlop

Children's Programming: Milkshake!

Senior Vice President Kids & Family Louise Bucknole

ITV Plc

White City, White City Place, 201 Wood Lane, London W12 7RU
website www.itv.com, www.itvplc.com
Facebook www.facebook.com/itv
X @ITV
Instagram @itv
Chief Executive Carolyn McCall, *Chairman* Andrew Cosslett, *Managing Director of Media & Entertainment* Kevin Lygo, *Managing Director of Commercial* Kelly Williams, *Managing Director of ITV Studios* Julian Bellamy

The ITV network is responsible for the commissioning, scheduling and marketing of network programmes on ITV and its digital channel portfolio including ITV2, ITV3, ITV4 and ITVBe. In addition to TV broadcasting services, ITV also delivers programming via a number of platforms, including ITVX which is the home for children's programming.

ITV Studios

https://itvstudios.com

The UK's largest production company produces over 7,000 hours of original content annually. ITV Studios produces programming for the ITV network's own channels as well as other UK broadcasters. ITV also has an international production business which produces for broadcasters around the world.

Commissioning

ITV's commissioning areas include comedy, current affairs, daytime, drama, entertainment, factual entertainment and sport. Information, FAQs and guidelines for commissioning can be found at www.itv.com/commissioning.

Current Affairs

Controller of Current Affairs Tom Giles

Drama and Comedy

Director of Drama Polly Hill, *Head of Scripted Comedy* Nana Hughes, *Senior Commissioner* Helen Ziegler, *Commissioner* Huw Kennair Jones, *Assistant Commissioner* Callum Dziedzic

Entertainment and Daytime

Head of Entertainment Katie Rawcliffe, *Commissioners* Gemma John-Lewis, David Smyth, *Commissioning Editors* Louise Major, Lily Wilson, Kevin O'Brien, Joe Mace, Paula Thomas, *Assistant Commissioner* Leanne Clarke

Factual Entertainment

Head of Factual Entertainment Sue Murphy, *Controller* Jo Clinton-Davis, *Commissioner* Kate Teckman, Satmohan Panesar

Reality

Commissioning Editors Amanda Stavri, Peter Tierney

Sport

Director of Sport Niall Sloane, *Assistant Commissioner* Richard Botchway

Recruitment, training and work experience

Information about training schemes, work experience and recruitment at ITV can be found at www.itvjobs.com, including details of ITV Academy, a traineeship scheme which enables people seeking experience in the TV industry to gain training and knowledge.

ITV Network regions

The ITV Network is made up of the following regions:

ITV Anglia www.itv.com/news/anglia

ITV Border www.itv.com/news/border

ITV Calendar www.itv.com/calendar

ITV Central www.itv.com/news/central

ITV Granada www.itv.com/news/granada

ITV London www.itv.com/news/london

ITV Meridian www.itv.com/news/meridian

ITV TyneTees www.itv.com/news/tyne-tees

ITV Wales www.itv.com/news/wales

ITV West Country www.itv.com/news/westcountry

STV Group www.stv.tv (Scotland)

UTV www.itv.com/news/utv (Northern Ireland)

Channel TV www.itv.com/news/channel

RTÉ

Donnybrook, Dublin 4, Republic of Ireland
tel +353 (0)1 208 3111
email info@rte.ie
website www.rte.ie
Facebook www.facebook.com/ExploreRTE
X @rte
Instagram @explorerte
Director General Kevin Bakhurst

RTÉ (Raidio Teilifis Éireann) is Ireland's national public service broadcaster. A leader in Irish media, it provides comprehensive, free-to-air multimedia services.

Commissioning

RTÉ works in partnership with independent producers to create many of Ireland's favourite TV programmes. It commissions content in seven groups: drama, entertainment, music and comedy, factual, arts and culture, Cláracha Gaeilge (Irish programs), and sport and young people's programmes. Full details of commissioning guidelines, specifications and submissions can be found at www.rte.ie/commissioning.

Director of Content Jim Jenning, *Deputy Director of Content* Niamh O'Connor, *Head of Arts & Culture* Grainne McAleer, *Head of Cláracha Gaeilge* Niamh Ní Churnáin, *Head of Drama* David Crean, *Group Head of Entertainment & Music* Alan Tyler, *Group Head of Factual* Sean Mac Giolla Phadraig, *Group Head of Sport* Declan McBennett, *Head of Children's & Young People's Content* Suzanne Kelly

S4C

Canolfan S4C Yr Egin, Carmarthen SA31 3EQ
tel 0370 600 4141
email gwifren@s4c.cymru
website www.s4c.cymru/en
Facebook www.facebook.com/S4C
X @S4C
Instagram @s4c
Chief Operating Officer Elin Morris, *Chief Content Officer* Llion Iwan, *Head of Film and Drama* Gwenllian Gravelle, *Head of Unscripted* Iwan England, *Head of Sports* Sue Butler, *Head of Documentaries and Specialist Factual* Llinos Wynne, *Head of Entertainment and Factual Entertainment* Beth Angell, *Commissioners* Sharen Griffith (News and Current Affairs), Sioned Geraint (Education and Children's), Guto Rhun (Young Audiences)

S4C is a Welsh-language television channel which transmits live from 6 a.m. until late at night, and features news, drama, documentaries, music, entertainment, sport and children's programmes. Shows are available to stream 24 hours a day on the S4C app. An online service called Hansh is aimed mainly at 16–34 year olds. Independent production companies produce most of the programmes; the BBC also produces for the channel. See website for full details of commissioning and production guidelines and personnel.

STREAMING SERVICES

Amazon Prime

website www.amazon.co.uk/gp/video/primesignup, https://press.amazonmgmstudios.com/gb/en
Facebook www.facebook.com/PrimeVideo
X @PrimeVideoUK
Instagram @primevideouk
Heads of Amazon MGM Studios Mike Hopkins, Jennifer Salke, *Head of International Originals* James Farrell

Amazon Prime streams to countries around the world. Its original content includes film, television shows and live coverage of events and sport. All Amazon Prime original content is acquired and created by Amazon MGM Studios.

Amazon MGM Studios does not accept submissions but their IMDbPro service gives subscribers access to industry contacts, in-development projects looking for creatives, casting notices, and box office trends and insights. More information can be found at: https://pro.imdb.com.

Apple TV+

website www.apple.com/uk/apple-tv-plus
Facebook www.facebook.com/appletv
X @AppleTV
Instagram @appletv
Creative Director, Europe, Worldwide Video Jay Hunt

Original commissioned and acquired content focuses on scripted film and television across a range of genres, including children's, as well as sport, documentaries and talk shows.

Disney+

website www.disneyplus.com/en-gb
Facebook www.facebook.com/DisneyPlusUK
X @DisneyPlusUK
Instagram @disneyplusuk
President of Disney+ Alisa Bowen, *Vice President, Europe* Karl Holmes

Disney's digital streaming service primarily distributes original films and television series produced by Walt Disney Studios and Walt Disney Television, with dedicated hubs for Disney, Pixar, Marvel, Star Wars, National Geographic and Star. Star also streams films and television shows produced by Disney-owned production companies.

EE TV

81 Newgate Street, London EC1A 7AJ
tel 020-7356 5000
website www.bt.com/tv
Head of EE TV Maryann Varsamides

Formerly BT. Alongside their mobile and internet services, EE TV offers subscription television services in the UK which provide on-demand content, entertainment channels and live sports channels.

Freesat

23–24 Newman Street, London W1T 1PJ
tel 0345 313 0051
website www.freesat.co.uk
Facebook www.facebook.com/freesat
X @freesat_tv
Ceo Jonathan Thompson

Freesat is a British free-to-air satellite television service, made up of over 100 channels, which also provides access to online streaming platforms. A joint venture between the BBC, ITV, Channel 4 and Channel 5.

Hulu

website https://press.hulu.com/corporate
Facebook www.facebook.com/hulu
X @hulu
Instagram @hulu
President Joe Early

An American-only streaming service that incorporates both live channels and on-demand television and film. Original content is available to watch in the UK through Disney+.

Netflix

website https://media.netflix.com/en
Facebook www.facebook.com/NetflixUK
X @NetflixUK
Instagram @netflixuk
Co-Ceos Ted Sarandos, Greg Peters, *Vice President, Content for Europe* Larry Tanz

Netflix was the world's first digital streaming service and now reaches more than 190 coutries and shares content in 50 languages. Netflix's original film and television shows cover all genres, including children's and YA.

Paramount+

17–29 Hawley Crescent, London NW1 8TT
website www.paramountplus.com
Facebook www.facebook.com/ParamountPlusUK
X @ParamountPlusUK
Instagram @paramountplusuk
Regional Lead, UK Sarah Rose, *Chief Content Officer, UK* Ben Frow

A streaming service comprised of classic and new content from Paramout's portfolio of brands and channels. Across film and television, the platform features scripted content, documentaries, reality shows, music, sport and news. Children's channel Nickelodeon's content is also featured.

Sky

Grant Way, Isleworth TW7 5QD
tel 0330 100 0333
website www.skygroup.sky
Facebook www.facebook.com/sky
X @skytv
Instagram @skytv
Group Chief Executive Officer Dana Strong, *Ceo of Sky Studios and Chief Content Officer* Cécile Frot-Coutaz, *Commissioning Editors* Hayley Reynolds (Factual), Phillip Edgar-Jones (Entertainment and Arts), Lucy Murphy (Kids), Julia Stuart (Cinema), Katherine Butler (Drama), Alex Moody (Comedy)

Sky is a British telecommunications company which provides a range of television and internet services in the UK, including entertainment, news and sport. It owns a number of subsidiaries including NOW TV. Through Sky Studios they produce original films and television shows throughout Europe. Full details of commissioning guidelines and contacts can be found at www.skygroup.sky/skystudios/commissioning.

Virgin Media

tel 0345 454 1111
website www.virginmedia.com
Facebook www.facebook.com/virginmedia
X @virginmedia
Instagram @virginmedia
Ceo Lutz Schüler

Virgin Media provides a range of television and internet services throughout the UK. Virgin TV is the largest cable television provider in the country.

YouView

2nd Floor, Aldgate Tower, 2 Leman Street, London E1 8FA
email info@youview.com
website www.youview.com
Ceo Riccardo Balestiero

YouView is a hybrid television platform in the UK, developed by a partnership of telecommunications operators and broadcasters including the BBC, ITV, Channel 4 and Channel 5.

ORGANISATIONS CONNECTED TO TELEVISION BROADCASTING

BARB

4th Floor, 114 St Martin's Lane, London WC2N 4BE
email enquiries@barb.co.uk
website www.barb.co.uk
X @BarbAudiences
Chief Executive Justin Sampson

The Broadcasters Audience Research Board is the official source of viewing figures in the UK. Shares what people are watching and how, providing insights into trends and most viewed shows.

Ipsos MORI

3 Thomas More Square, London E1W 1YW
tel 020-3059 5000
website www.ipsos.com/en-uk
X @IpsosUK
Instagram @ipsos_uk
Ceo Ben Page

One of the UK's leading research companies; conducts surveys for a wide range of major organisations (such as BARB and RAJAR), as well as for other market research agencies.

Pact – see page 549

Public Media Alliance

Room 02.101, Lawrence Stenhouse Building, University of East Anglia, Norwich NR4 7TJ
tel (01603) 592335
email info@publicmediaalliance.org
website www.publicmediaalliance.org
Facebook www.facebook.com/publicmediaalliance
X @PublicMediaPMA
Ceo Kristian Porter

World's largest association of public broadcasters. Provides advocacy, support, knowledge exchange, research and training opportunities for public media worldwide.

Royal Television Society

3 Dorset Rise, London EC4Y 8EN
tel 020-7822 2810
email info@rts.org.uk
website www.rts.org.uk
X @RTS_media
Instagram @royaltelevisionsociety
Ceo Theresa Wise

An educational charity promoting the art and science of television and the leading forum for discussion and debate on all aspects of the TV community. Runs events, masterclasses and workshops, and provides training and bursaries.

RADIO

A number of radio stations are broadcast in both analogue and digital, whilst some broadcast in digital alone. Digital radio (DAB – digital audio broadcasting) is available through digital radio sets, car radios, online, and on games consoles and mobile devices such as smartphones and tablets. Radio provision in the UK is comprised of public service radio programming provided by the BBC and programming provided by independent, commercial stations.

BBC Radio

The BBC operates 10 national radio stations offering music and speech programming for the whole of the UK: Radio 1, Radio 1 Xtra, Radio 2, Radio 3, Radio 4, Radio 4 Extra, Radio 5 Live, Radio 5 Live Sports Extra, Radio 6 Music and Asian Network. In addition, there are 39 regional/local radio stations and two national radio services each in Scotland, Wales and Northern Ireland. The BBC Sounds website and app host all of the BBC's live radio stations alongside a catalogue of BBC programmes, interviews, podcasts and playlists available to stream.

Commissioning

For full details of commissioning and delivery guidelines, see www.bbc.co.uk/commissioning/radio.

Radio 1/1Xtra/Asian Network *Head of Radio 1* Aled Haydn Jones, *Head of Radio 1 Xtra* Dari Samuels, *Head of Asian Network* Ahmed Hussai

Radio 2 *Head* Helen Thomas, *Commissioning Editor* Robert Gallacher

Radio 3 *Director, Speech Audio* Sam Jackson, *Head of Content Commissioning* Jeremy Evans

Radio 4/4 Extra *Controller* Mohit Bakaya, *Commissioning Editors* Rhian Roberts (Podcasts and Formats), Alison Hindell (Drama & Fiction), Julia McKenzie (Comedy & Entertainment), Dan Clarke (Factual), Matthew Dodd (Arts), Hugh Levinson (Reactive Factual)

Radio 5 Live/5 Live Sports Extra *Controller* Heidi Dawson, *Commissioning Editor* Richard Maddock

Radio 6 Music *Head* Sam Moy

World Service *Controller* Jon Zilkha, *Commissioning Editors* Gwenan Roberts, Simon Pitts, Jon Manel (Podcasts)

Commercial radio

There are over 350 commercial radio stations operating in the UK, most of which serve a local area or region. A number of commercial radio stations operate nationally, including Classic FM, Absolute Radio, talkSPORT and LBC. The majority of commercial radio stations are owned by one of three groups.

Bauer Media

website www.bauermedia.co.uk

Global Radio

website https://global.com/radio

News UK

website www.news.co.uk

ORGANISATIONS CONNECTED TO RADIO BROADCASTING

Media.info

website https://media.info/uk

This website provides detailed listings of UK radio stations alongside information about TV, newspapers, magazines and media ownership in the UK.

The Radio Academy

Suite 303, The Pill Box, 115 Coventry Road, London E2 6GH
email info@radioacademy.org
website www.radioacademy.org
Facebook www.facebook.com/radioacademy
X @radioacademy
Instagram @radioacademy
Chair Helen Thomas

The Radio Academy is a registered charity with branches across the UK dedicated to the promotion of excellence in radio broadcasting and production. Runs the annual Audio and Radio Industry Awards (ARIAS), which celebrate content and creativity in the industry.

Radiocentre

15 Alfred Place, London WC1E 7EB
tel 020-7010 0600
website www.radiocentre.org
X @Radiocentre
Ceo Matt Payton

Radiocentre is the voice of UK commercial radio. Works with government, policy makers and regulators, and provides a forum for industry-wide debate and discussion.

RAJAR

15 Alfred Place, London WC1E 7EB
tel 020-7395 0630
website www.rajar.co.uk
X @RAJARLtd
Ceo Jerry Hill

Radio Joint Audience Research is the official body in charge of measuring radio audiences in the UK. It is jointly owned by the BBC and the Radiocentre on behalf of the commercial sector.

Theatre
Introduction

The British theatre scene is one of the world's great cultural draws. From London's Theatreland, to historic Stratford-upon-Avon and excellent regional theatres, the industry is experiencing remarkable growth, contributing over £4.4bn to the UK economy in 2024 and helping to sustain over 230,000 workers and creatives.

In the last year, the West End saw over 17.1 million theatregoers, which surpasses pre-pandemic levels by 11%, according to The Society of London Theatre's report *The West End: The Theatre Capital of the World* published in April 2025. Other players in the 'experience' market are struggling to attract paying punters (cinema attendance dropped by 28%, for instance), but the West End continues to thrive, attracting 2.5 million more attendees than Premier League football matches.

Though this paints an encouraging picture of a buoyant theatre scene, looking at the industry more broadly, the UK's main subsidised theatres, which include the National Theatre on London's Southbank, opened only 229 original productions in 2024. This is a drop of 31% compared to a decade ago – blame is placed firmly on rising costs and significant cuts to funding both at a governmental and local level. These are sobering statistics, but it's not unusual to see fluctuation in total production numbers overall. Though there may be fewer new shows, more theatres are putting on larger-scale productions, or running tours and West End runs for longer.

Many theatre companies welcome new work from writers of all levels of experience, as well as those that run talent-development programmes for aspiring authors, dramaturgs and directors. Our listings are a helpful resource to discover various types of theatre companies and their respective remits. Many of those that specialise in new writing are based in London (for example, Hampstead Theatre, Royal Court, Bush Theatre, Soho Theatre), but also include the Royal Exchange Manchester, Everyman Theatre Liverpool, Leeds Playhouse, etc. Regional repertory theatre companies are based in towns and cities across the country and may produce new plays as part of their repertoire. Commercial production companies and independent producers typically are unsubsidised, profit-making theatre producers who may occasionally be interested in new plays to take on tour or to present in the West End. Small- or middle-scale touring companies explore or promote specific themes or may be geared towards particular audiences.

You may also be able to find independent theatre producers who could be keen to collaborate, especially at the start of their careers, or consider drama schools or amateur companies, both of which sometimes develop and produce new work. See the *Actors' & Performers' Yearbook* (Bloomsbury; published annually in October) for further information. Break a leg!

Listings in this section:

- *Theatre producers – London*, page 412
- *Theatre producers – Regional*, page 415
- *Touring companies*, page 421

Getting your script noticed

James McDermott describes how an aspiring new playwright can grow into their craft and find their own unique writing voice. He has advice on how to develop valuable skills, techniques, passion and perseverance and to make full use of beneficial resources, opportunities and connections to bring your work onto the stage.

The world of writing and of theatre can seem intimidating to the new playwright. As an early-career writer based outside of London, here is my advice on how to get started, how to make regional work and how to write your 'calling card' script: that script that will get you noticed.

Growing up queer in rural Norfolk, I didn't feel engaged with the dramas played out at the local cinemas and theatres; LGBTQ+ stories based in the East of England were rarely staged or screened. So, aged 18, I started writing the plays I needed to see in the world, which asserted and celebrated experiences like mine. In all your work, and especially in the first script you create and submit, I'd advise you to write what you love and what you feel impelled to write. If *you* don't feel a deep connection to your work, then a producer-director and ultimately your audience might not either. Writing something that audiences will get excited about is your goal.

I realised pretty quickly that, if I wanted to be a dramatist, I couldn't simply sit down at a laptop and write a great script – just as an aspiring musician can't sit down at a piano and crack out a symphony overnight. If you want to be a musician, you have to study music, learn and practise chords. If you want to be a scriptwriter, you have to watch, read and study other scripts, talk to writers, learn and practise dramaturgy – the dramatist's equivalent of chords. So, between 2012 and 2016, I studied for a BA then an MA in Scriptwriting at the University of East Anglia under playwrights Steve Waters and Timberlake Wertenbaker. Among many other things, they taught me that drama derives from the Greek word 'draein' which means 'to do' or 'to take action': drama is about a hero taking action to try and do something. If a hero could just do what they wanted, there would be no story – the story is in the struggle – and so the hero encounters internal and external obstacles they have to overcome in order to achieve their goal. In trying to overcome these obstacles, the hero is changed. Ensure your protagonist is in action, overcoming internal and external obstacles, in pursuit of achieving their objective.

At that time I was also introduced to the fundamentals of **five-act dramatic structure**, which now underpins my writing and teaching. In short, most Western dramatic stories can be broken down into five acts. In Act One, we meet heroes in trouble who want something to make life better: three little pigs are homeless, so they want to build houses and live happily ever after. In Act Two, things initially go well for the heroes as they pursue their want: three little pigs go their separate ways, gather different materials and build their own houses. It's important for things to go well, so that there's something for the heroes to lose in Act Three when things go badly as obstacles gather strength: the wolf arrives and blows down one of the houses. In Act Four, things get worse, and it looks like the heroes will never overcome the obstacles to get what they want unless they can change: the wolf blows down a second house, and the three little pigs look set to be killed unless they can work together to defeat the wolf. In Act Five, the heroes do or don't change, do or don't overcome the obstacles, and do or don't get what they want: the three little pigs learn to work together, defeat the wolf and live happily ever after in one house. This model acts as a torch for me when I'm trying to find my way in and out of planning, writing and rewriting drama.

It's important to stress – you don't have to study scriptwriting at university. That academic approach to creative training isn't for everyone and courses in tertiary education can be incredibly expensive; I had a student loan to support me during my BA and was lucky enough to receive a bursary from UEA to fund my MA. Instead, there are several great books on scriptwriting craft you could study: John Yorke's *Into The Woods: How Stories Work and Why We Tell Them* (Penguin 2014) and Russell T. Davies' *Doctor Who: The Writer's Tale* (BBC Books 2008) have proved invaluable to me. I also participated in several free scriptwriting groups run by theatres across the country: in London, I attended the Royal Court Writers Group, Soho Theatre's Writers Lab and Hampstead Theatre's Inspire Programme; in the East of England, I attended Menagerie Theatre's Young Writer's Programme and Mercury Theatre's Playwrights Group. Taking part in these groups gave me the space and time to learn how to craft, write and **workshop** new scripts under the tutelage of professional playwrights, create new connections and begin collaborations with theatres and artists across the country. This was invaluable for me as a theatre-maker based in East Anglia.

During my time at UEA, I wrote my **'calling card' script**. It was a solo play called *Rubber Ring* about a sexually confused Norfolk teenager desperate to get to London to find his hero Morrissey and to find himself. That play was a real declaration of who I am as a person and as a writer; it was queer, camp, sassy, vulnerable, East Anglian and full of both low- and highbrow pop cultural references. In short, my voice on the page sounded like my speaking voice and the voice in my head. In my own practice, I see my 'voice' as a writer as mapping the movement of my mind on the page, as well as documenting all those things that are manifest in my speaking voice: my accent, dialect, rhythm, insecurities, obsessions and sense of humour. Don't worry about making your writing just smart, serious or funny: try and put all of the beautiful mess of yourself onto the page. Many people are clever, sincere and humorous in similar ways, but only *your* mind moves in the distinct way it does, only *your* speaking voice sounds as it does. Mapping both of those things on the page feels like a good step towards ensuring your writing voice is uniquely yours.

Writing a script and not hearing it is like writing a song and not playing it. So, having written your script, try it out in front of an audience. Look out for the annual Open Call on the BBC Writersroom website (www.bbc.co.uk/writers). It was there I saw a call out for ten-minute extracts from comedy plays to be produced by Velvet Trumpet theatre company at a **scratch night**, an evening where several writers try out new work in front of an audience. I submitted the first ten pages of *Rubber Ring* and it was selected for performance at the Southwark Playhouse. Seeing and hearing the work in front of a live audience taught me how and where the play was and wasn't working. Before sending out your script in its entirety, I recommend trying out extracts in front of an audience to see if it's 'singing'; keep an eye out for the numerous scratch nights and script development opportunities listed on BBC Writersroom and on the London Playwrights Blog (https://londonplaywrightsblog.com). These are both great sources of information and support for the emerging playwright. Taking part in these scratch nights also allows you to connect with and potentially collaborate with the many new writers, actors, directors, producers and agents who attend.

The short extract of *Rubber Ring* went down well and Velvet Trumpet asked to read the rest of the play. They went on to produce the show at the Pleasance Islington before touring it nationwide. A month or two before the show was scheduled to be staged, I emailed lots of people I wanted to work with or learn from and invited them to see the show. These included agents I'd like to represent my work, literary managers of theatres I'd love to write for, and actors, writers and directors whose practice I admired. Many ignored my emails, several politely declined my invitation, but some said yes and came along to see the play, including Micheline Steinberg Associates who became my first agent and several artistic directors in East Anglia who went on to commission new work from me.

Definitions

- The **calling card script** is the one that gets you noticed within the industry. It's the sample that you hope will entice agents, production and theatre companies and lead to commissions.
- A **scratch night** is a chance to test your script-in-progress to see what works and what doesn't in order to help you rewrite and refine it.
- **Workshopping** a script typically involves actors performing the latest version of your script at a table read or staged read-through.

When you have that initial calling card script staged, or even scratched or workshopped, don't be shy about emailing those people you want to work with and learn from and inviting them along. Make sure you don't send a generic email to everybody; write an authentic honest email explaining why you'd like that particular person to give up their time and engage with your work. Emailing people you admire can feel daunting but, as an anxious queer working-class writer, I remember a piece of advice I was once given: The straight middle-class people who dominate the industry might not think twice about emailing anybody. So, if you aren't from that background, the only way you change your life and the industry is by stepping up and reaching out.

With a produced play and an MA under my belt, I then approached several of my local theatres to ask if I could set up a scriptwriting course in their buildings (... the swagger of being in your early twenties!). Several said yes, including the ever-supportive Norwich Theatre Royal where I have now taught scriptwriting for six years. This gave me a creative part-time day job to support my writing. It also allowed me to create, for other local writers, an inexpensive course I wish had existed when I was starting out. Reading, thinking and talking about writing all day also helped me to understand my craft better. If you want to learn how to do something, teach it. Leading writing groups in my local theatres also meant that, as a kind of writer in residence, I was a first port of call if one of those venues needed a new play written.

If you're a scriptwriter outside London, connect with your local theatres. Offer to teach there or send them your plays. For so many venues, funding depends on engaging with local talent – so they want and need you. Like a business card, that calling card script leads to other work: 'Rubber Ring' helped me secure an agent, a play text publisher (Samuel French), and several other productions including *Time and Tide* (Park Theatre), *Robin Good: The Politico-Panto* (Norwich Playhouse) and *Ghosted* (Out There Festival).

I wish you the very best of luck with your scriptwriting. Write the work you love and need to see. The harder you work, the luckier you'll get. Never give up.

James McDermott is a scriptwriter, poet and creative writing teacher based in East Anglia. His published plays include *Jab*, *Time & Tide* and *Rubber Ring* (all Samuel French; 2024, 2020, 2019) and the poetry collections *Manatomy* (Burning Eye Books 2020) and *Wild Life* (Nine Arches Press 2023). His latest poetry collection is *Father Myself* (Nine Arches Press 2025). James has written episodes of *EastEnders* and plays for BBC Radio 4. He is a lecturer in scriptwriting at the University of East Anglia and an Arvon writing tutor. For more information see https://jamesmcdermottwriter.weebly.com.

See also...

- *Theatre producers*, page 412
- *Writers' retreats and creative writing courses*, page 646

Play with fire: fighting the writing demons that hold you back

Carmen Marcus, winner of the Faber New Play Award for *And the Earth Opened Up Under Her* (a working-class reimagining of the Persephone and Demeter myth), shares her advice on how to defeat writing demons.

Consider this your practical guide to the demons you will meet if you want to get a play commissioned (I suspect this is why playwrights are obsessed with ghosts, phantoms and pucks).

Demon #1: The Imp Osta

When that spark of a play first ignites in your head, it will attract the Imp Osta. This tricky demon will tell you all the reasons why you, specifically you, should not write a play! It will go for your deepest insecurities. The Imp likes to tell me that theatre belongs to myth, listing the gods: Aeschylus, Shakespeare, Chekhov, Beckett, Churchill. Osta says: 'Who do you think you are? Who needs your story when we have the glory of theatre's mighty inheritance? You are a middle-aged, working-class mother, a lapsed Catholic from the wrong schools, and theatre doesn't want or need you.' Harsh. But theatre does want and need my story – and yours too. In her book *A Director Prepares* (Routledge 2001), Anne Bogart says, 'the inherited myths lose their value' because our society is always undergoing change and 'in that moment new myths are needed to encompass who we are becoming'. So, we need new stories to witness the change, especially from voices we aren't used to hearing on stage.

Slay tactics

When I made the transition from novel to theatre, I went back to the books – the classics and the contemporaries – and asked:

- What has changed?
- Whose story is missing?

The only way to defeat Osta is to find the absences and write into them. The industry is changing. The Writers' Guild of Great Britain's New Play Commission Scheme helped me and many under-represented writers make new work and today theatres across the country offer development schemes for writers that prioritise missing voices. It's important to connect to those theatres because you cannot defeat this or any of the writing demons alone – let me introduce the next one …

Demon #2: Lo Nellie

Lo Nellie will tell you that she didn't need any help to get to where she is, she did it all by herself in a garret, on a typewriter built from tears. Writing for theatre is a collaborative process. You will need other people at every stage to get commissioned.

I want to outline for you the different types of relationships I've had at different stages of my career to help you build your own connection strategy.

Emerging writer relationships

At this stage you might have a premise, maybe a work in progress but not a finished a piece. This is the time to link with local writers' groups.

I worked with Writers' Block North East (WBNE), New Writing North and Tees Women Poets (TWP). WBNE provided mentoring, deadlines and links to agents. New Writing North gave me a development grant for my poetry and an award for my novel. TWP provided performance skills. All these connections played their part in getting my work seen, securing an agent and the publication of my first novel, *How Saints Die* (Vintage 2018). That's four development agencies that got me through multiple brutal rejections; a campaign to challenge bias against working-class writers; being dumped by one agent and all the attendant crying. In addition, I have a group of trusted, demon-slaying writer-buddies, and we champion one another. Identify the groups and people in your area, get the help you need.

Mid-career sideways moves

A writer's career does not move progressively upward; we are operating in a funding-dependent industry that is still coming to terms with its internal biases and structural barriers for under-represented voices. Moving sideways is still moving, especially when your life changes. In 2020 my young child began to show autistic traits, and my mother was diagnosed with dementia and then – Pandemic! Whilst theatre was on enforced leave, two of the UK's most brilliant directors set up a free online group, bringing speakers from every aspect of theatre to share their knowledge. If you find yourself in a mid-career crisis, look for opportunities beyond your field, build connections and learn new skills. Theatre makers are some of the most generous people I've met: even now you can find Mark Ravenhill's incredible wisdom for free on X @MarkRavenhill2 – see *101 Notes on Playwriting*. By moving sideways, I was ready when an opportunity came up.

Be ready for your big break

Big Breaks can't happen if cultural organisations don't know you exist! I went to my local council's online cultural partnership meetings so that when the incredible national touring group Pilot Theatre arrived with their project 'Northern Girls' and wanted to work with a local writer, I was finally in the right place at the right time. Weird coincidence warning: in my first chat with the Artistic Director, Esther Richardson, we discovered that not only had we attended the same Catholic primary school, but we had already shared the stage in a nativity play there. It was a sign! This strong, longstanding relationship with Pilot led to us making a joint pitch to the Writers' Guild of Great Britain, who commissioned my first play, *And the Earth Opened Up Under Her*, which would go on to win the Faber New Play Award.

If I hadn't built those local community connections, I wouldn't have developed the relationship with Pilot Theatre, who continue to support me with the play's next steps and will mentor me on my Developing Your Creative Practice ACE Award.

Slay tactics

Ask yourself:

- Where am I now?
- What can I offer?
- Where do I want to be?
- What support do I need?

Identify the people, venues and support organisations in your region who can help. Make a case for what you have to offer, and what you need to thrive and reach out. Don't be shy.

And don't slay Lo Nellie, because she exists to protect your time: sometimes it needs to be just you and the story, and she'll be there to insist you take a tea break.

Lo Nellie also has a word of warning about writing relationships. She says some groups are all talk and no writing; some people will take more than they give. She is right. When you enter a creative relationship, it must always make you feel excited; you should feel stretched not stagnated, safe not vulnerable, nurtured not drained. Protect yourself, your time, your ideas and your work – because to get commissioned, you need to be writing exciting new work and that's when our third demon shows up.

Demon #3: The Baron Stan d'Still

What scares me most about writing for theatre is the fortress of its history and its icons, from Aristotle to Peter Brook. It's intimidating! Stan d'Still asks 'How can you possibly offer anything new to this form, when you have all the disadvantages of being northern, a woman and alive?' Stan d'Still is a collector of dead things and believes that tradition, convention and the quest for the 'original' is the goal of theatre. But he's wrong.

Slay tactics

To defeat the Baron, I went in search of my own traditions. I summoned the sea gods from the oral storytelling practices of my fisherman father. I reconnected with the Irish ghost stories my mum told me, and the ceílí house tradition she recreated in our home where there is no hierarchy between the performer and audience. My story traditions are interested in making magic circles, creating a field of receptivity. This is achieved when the story builds radial connections between speaker, listeners, the time of telling and the place of telling. This is what all theatre does, but discovering my story roots made me feel that I deserved a space here too.

As with Lo Nellie, you don't need to slay Stan – he's already dead – but you do need to ensure that your work remains alive by asking questions like:

- What are your story roots? (You don't need ancient roots or family traditions; your influences can come from music, TV, film etc.)
- What are the limits of these traditions for your work?
- What are the possibilities of these traditions for your work?
- How can I adapt and cross-pollinate my influences with theatre traditions? (That's how I got to a working-class reimagining of Persephone and Demeter.)

One of the most important lessons from the oral tradition is to speak your work out loud at every stage. I got the chance to test out a new hybrid play-poem at a poetry night. You don't need funding, venues or validation to do this. Make opportunities to read your work out loud, either to yourself or in front of family or peers, in your home or at Scratch nights. This way, you will find out if you are creating that field of receptivity – the magic connection between your words, people, time and the space – and if your work is alive, you will feel it!

And to do all this deep work you need to face down …

Demon #4: Madame Rumpere

Rumpere is also a writer: she writes To Do Lists, appointment schedules, the Post-it that says the wigglybob under the sink needs fixing. Rumpere tells your kids not to wash their hands, so they get the sickness bug bang on your deadline. She is Dame Distraction. Lady of the List. Princess Competing Priorities. Ms Intrusive Thoughts. She will do anything to get between you and your writing and social media has made her a monster.

Web Services for
Writers & Artists
Website Design
Every author needs a website for books, bio, events, and contact details.
Starting from £50 per month.
SEO
Boost your Google ranking and sell more books with Search Engine Optimisation.
Starting from £175 per month.
LOYAL UK
WEB SOLUTIONS
www.LoyalWebSolutions.co.uk
team@LoyalWebSolutions.co.uk

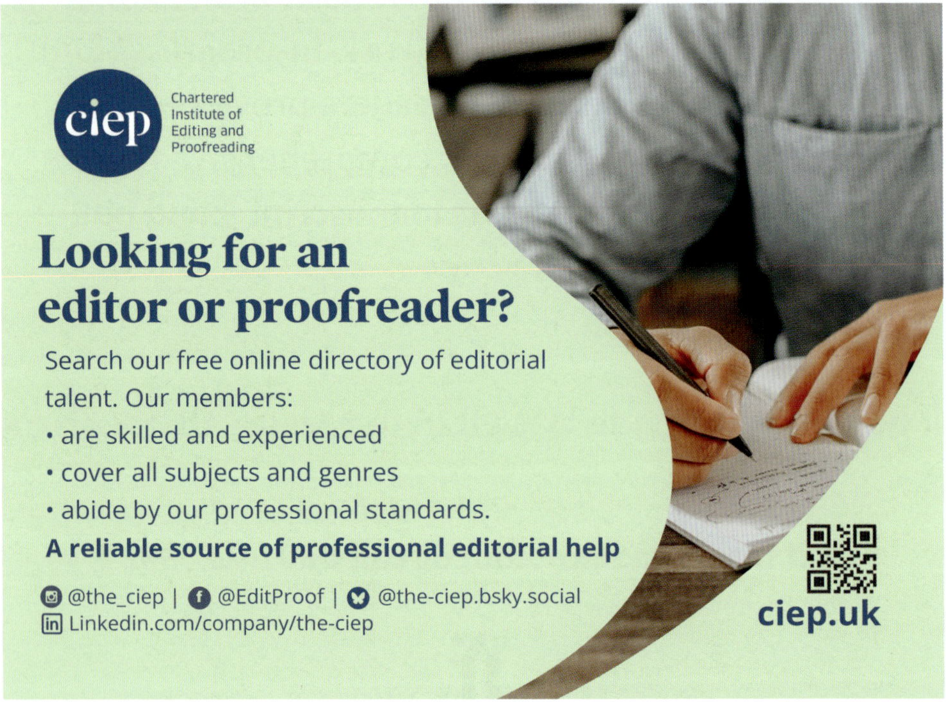
ciep
Chartered Institute of Editing and Proofreading
Looking for an editor or proofreader?
Search our free online directory of editorial talent. Our members:
• are skilled and experienced
• cover all subjects and genres
• abide by our professional standards.
A reliable source of professional editorial help
@the_ciep | @EditProof | @the-ciep.bsky.social
Linkedin.com/company/the-ciep
ciep.uk

Slay tactics

In a workshop I delivered for the Rebecca Swift Foundation recently, I asked a group of writers what would happen if we allowed interruptions to shape our work? Working in a fragmentary way is not new – sometimes only fragments survive, as with Sappho, and yet there is still power in broken things. In *The Common Reader* (The Hogarth Press Ltd 1932), Virginia Woolf tells us: 'The proper stuff of fiction' does not exist; 'everything is the proper stuff of fiction, every feeling, every thought; every quality of brain and spirit is drawn upon; no perception comes amiss.' So why do we filter out the interruptions when they could be part of the story? I don't fight Rumpere. I work with interruption because it is life. In *The Years* (Fitzcarraldo Editions 2022), Annie Ernaux seeks 'the mass of floating speech, that hubbub that tirelessly ferries the wordings and rewordings of what we are and what we must be, think, believe, fear, and hope' to write her 'common time'. Theatre is interruption – ritual interrupted – the rupture of the inevitable, the predictable, the expected by desires and dreams and impulses. I had to accept this when writing *And the Earth Opened Up Under Her*. I had to write around and in response to the hubbub of life, integrating new information about violence against women and girls, and adapting my working patterns and writing forms around my family's needs. It felt like playing with fire, but it was the only way to avoid burnout. And yes, it is frustrating. And no, it isn't easy – but what choice do we have if those without the privilege of protected space and time are to tell their story?

I've accepted that writing is many things – it is a 'mass', as Ernaux says, and it is also the call and response between the writer, their life and their time. I'm saying that these broken pieces are the work. I'm saying it's okay to feel it's a lot to cope with. I'm saying there's one more demon…

Demon #5: You

If you write, you're possessed. My demon is howling, furred and snouted and speaks with my mother's Donegal ripple, 'Never lose your imagination'. It wakes me at 4am with ideas, licks up after rejection and won't give up a story-scent. Tell me yours …

Carmen Marcus is an award-winning author, playwright and performance poet. Find out more about her work at carmenmarcus.co.uk and follow her on Instagram @carmenmarcuswrites.

See also ...

Being a poet and a publisher, page 329

How to write for the theatre

Gill Kirk shares her tried-and-tested formula for anyone drawn to writing for stage and screen, with advice on developing valuable connections, knowledge and skills, and embracing the challenge without losing the fun.

Writing for theatre – how is it done? Like anything else, there's a trick. There are five things you need. Keep those in mind, and you can't go far wrong.

The five essentials

First: a passion for human connection.
Second: acceptance that to do anything well, you must commit to constantly improving your craft; art is no exception.
Third: heck – just goddamned playfulness.
Fourth: 'abundance' in self-help lingo, i.e. a furious refusal to be stingy and an embarrassing belief in creative incontinence.
Fifth: *dahlings*, it's theatre! You must understand a little (or even better, a lot) of our industry's economics.

You've already sussed that they're all equally important. Connect, build your craft, be playful, be abundant, be economically realistic. Interdependent, these five essentials nourish each other. Take care of them all and at the very least you'll enjoy yourself in the wonderful world of writing for theatre. (Worst? You might become a millionaire. Be careful …).

1. Passion for connection

What's that all about? In common with its cousins (circus, live music, stand-up and magic), theatre's where artifice, effort and creativity meet to go wild. Here, we surrender to the moment: anything could happen. You – the audience – are part of it. Because that's who theatre is for. If you want to see creations of yours on stage (oh, yes, you do!), with people paying to watch, you must take – and keep – people with you. Great connection-making is smart.

The best playwrights are passionate about connecting with other humans. They won't tell you what to feel, but will present a human in a predicament, so that you snag your heart on the jagged nails of their character. They won't bore, but *lure* you through their maze, 'til your Werther's Originals are forgotten loot, and you're unrecognisable from the 'you' of 7pm.

When you think 'I have this play I want to write …', first put yourself in the audience's seat. Imagine how you would love this story to unfold. Remember what delights you in theatre, what frustrates and even bores you. If your imagination's rusty, just loiter outside when an audience comes out – it's horribly educational. Or learn how to review plays (*don't* ever abuse this position; think carefully when you praise a show or warn an audience).

You need maximum audience contact, but that's not the only connection you need. Actors, directors, stage managers, venue teams and other writers will all fuel you through this exciting experience. Playwrights are questioning souls, and we're hard on ourselves. We need others to learn from and make our work better, to share the downs and the ups. If you have these connections when you write, you will also improve your connection with yourself. And that will make you a better writer, too.

How can you make theatre connections?

Find online and real-life communities – writers' groups (especially those doing readings with actors). Use this book: see *Film, theatre and television* (page 549) and *Writers' organisations* (page 561). Don't assume small theatres can't work with writers; many offer incredible opportunities you won't get in larger spaces. Build connections through social media, if you're that way inclined. And above all, *meet* people. I'm a long-term single parent, free-lancing outside London – I know this can be hard. But the theatre connections I've made have been life-changing.

I've a photo on my phone of a gang of my mates at night, laughing and pointing at an illuminated poster, and it's my name on the poster they're pointing at – because it's in lights. And behind that picture sprawls a criss-cross of connections made over the last 12 years. In 2011, I met a director at a 24 Hour Play (https://24hourplays.org) show. In 2019, I ran a workshop for her theatre company, because my day job is in strategic communications, and we agreed they should stop looking so hard for stories – it was exhausting and the fun had leaked a little, all over the floor. Almost too late, I realised this was advice I should take myself, and headed off on holiday to Pitlochry. I promised myself I would not write. Nor would I go to the lovely theatre there – instead, I would just *live*.

But what normal human being can do a day-long walk and NOT invent a story? I didn't write it down, I just recorded it on my phone … every minute or so. On the last night of the holidays, I caved in and visited the theatre, and, incredibly, the actor from a 2010 one-man short play of mine was in the cast. A chatty front of house staffer noticed that I appeared to know someone in the show and persuaded me to buy a ticket, stay after and say hello (what a salesman!). So I did, and the actor said nice things about my writing, and told me that there were great writers' opportunities there; why didn't I drop the new work team a wee line…? I sent them the bonkers collection of ideas from that day-long walk – and they offered me a residency.

I applied for grants to cover the costs (Society of Authors, Peggy Ramsay Foundation – see page 746 and page 627) and had ten amazing days in Pitlochry to develop the show. A few months later, my small local theatre gave me space for a day and a night to run a workshop and 'script in hand'. A kindly West End producer I'd met through two local writers, as well as an actor-director from a writers' group, gathered together a cast and crew. We would pay them through £5 tickets and what was left of the grant funding. The producer then spotted an opportunity to show the play at the New Wimbledon Theatre; we applied and won the slot. But then Covid arrived … I lost my team, and assumed I'd lost the New Wimbledon. I asked everyone for help; they helped, but I couldn't find a new director or producer. Then I asked a woman I'd only ever met on X: Maybe she knew people who'd want this great opportunity – a theatre, a script? And yes, she knew someone: herself. With incredible energy, she found a team and got the show on the road.

A week before our London show, I was working for a friend at a posh event he was running. There, I met the editor of a local culture mag. She ran a piece on me and the play. Months later, an old copy of that mag lay on a cafe table, when this *Yearbook*'s editor came to my town. And here we are – you couldn't (I didn't) make it up. Of course, at times I've hidden away, and said no to stuff. But look where the yeses can get you. This is why connection matters.

2. Improving your craft

Before my work got on stage, I'd done no formal learning about scripts or stories. It was writers, directors and actors who taught me so much, by having me in rehearsals, doing readings, sharing work and feedback. Then, thanks to script development with Bath's Theatre Royal and a run at Bath's Rondo Theatre, my second script won me a place on the incredible 4Screenwriting programme run by Channel 4 (they select 12 writers from thousands of entrants). Here I realised that, to write an hour of TV, I needed solid craft guidelines and I taught myself story structure. I use this every day, beyond scriptwriting, as a professional communicator and non-professional parent. There are a billion books on story structure, but you can see my 'easy-to-remember' guide (using 1970s kids' TV icon *Mr Benn*) on my blog at https://gillkirk.com/2014/01/20/and-as-if-by-magic-the-story-structure-appeared.

I rework every single script with other people. If it's not a commissioned work, I pay a dramaturg and/or gather a group of actors I've met through small readings and scratch nights (again, promising sources of crowdfunder cash or copious offers of new connections, cake and coffee). You cannot do this alone.

3. Playfulness

Why are we here … to bore? Who are we here for … us?

'Of course not, Gill!', I hear you roar. 'We want to transport people. Challenge, tease, excite, soothe, calm, provoke.' Excellent news.

This doesn't need much explaining. Just don't take yourself too seriously, even when writing the most gothic grimness. This is play. What you make and present is a gift. Keep a place inside yourself that's light. It will make everything else (craft, connection, abundance and economics) much more fun. If you haven't already, check out Elizabeth Gilbert's *Big Magic* (Riverhead Books 2015), *Impro* (Methuen Drama 2007) by Keith Johnstone and *The Games People Play* (Penguin Life 2016) by Eric Berne. And if you can't do that, as Nina says in Anthony Minghella's *Truly, Madly, Deeply*, 'Say "bum" and "Trotsky" twice a day before meals.'

4. Abundance

Abundance? Why? Answer: so you can kill your darlings. What?! How horrible. No, how wonderful! As you see with connection and play and craft, a good playwright has to be generous and know when to give things away. Don't hold back. Get it out. Share so you can improve, then write another one.

I often found (especially at the start) that collaborators would ask, 'Why's this character even here?' 'What does this line mean?' Then I'd realise: we were looking at 'legacy text' – cold leftovers from the first draft that I couldn't bear to bin. But a play isn't for the writer. After a few years, you realise there's a whole universe of people, places and circumstances inside you who've never yet met a stage and that's OK. They're still useful – they have opinions about people and stuff; they might help you grow new worlds. But if you are 'mean' (afraid) with your writing, if you hold too tight, and find it too hard to take feedback (or to give it well), you harm your craft. It's a paradox, but, in short, don't worry about getting it right. Just get it written. Lots of it. Then expose it to air. This will improve your craft.

5. Economics

If you think theatre tickets are expensive, try actually making theatre. Now that's expensive – and ticket sales rarely cover the costs. It means everyone is underpaid and people give too much of their time for free. Don't exploit them. This thing we do is a huge privilege. That means working-class writers – especially women – are rare; it's hard to write, unpaid, when your priorities are caring, clothing, housing. So, no matter your personal circumstances, when you build connections with commissioners who can pay for scripts (companies, venues, producers) talk to them about money. Ask about their writing budgets and funds for everything else; ask what grants are available. Check the WGGB (Writers' Guild of Great Britain; see page 749) writers' fee levels and Equity's rates cards (www.equity.org.uk) and work out how much your five-person show will cost to rehearse and put on before you write it (don't forget director, stage manager, crew, insurance, space …). And don't let money get you down. Theatre economics are always tough, yet we make magic all the time. We crowdfund. We cry at Arts Councils. And do amazing things on the cheap. But it's part of your job to understand how it works – you're creating employment for others.

Alongside this, know that playwriting isn't likely to be your only career. The myth of the full-time, well-fed playwright comes from an age when the curse of inherited wealth meant a chap just had to find something to do. Remember, doing other paid work feeds your imagination and connection, so that you can be the writer that you're going to be. Yes, a playwright is a many-splendoured thing.

How to work in theatre? Connect, play, be abundant, build craft, know the economics. From your first five-minute creation, you are a playwright, joining a very wonderful fellowship. In the last week, I've workshopped with 70 year-old and 20 year-old first-timers, seen a friend's new show, gloom-Zoomed with the new and 'famous', and – best of all – a mate of mine from a HighTide (https://hightide.org.uk) workshop a decade ago just won the Women's Prize. Welcome to the fold.

Gill Kirk is a scriptwriter and playwright whose theatre work includes *Skin in the Game* (New Wimbledon Theatre), *Passion* (Vaults Festival, Tobacco Factory Bristol and Aberdeen Dance Live) and *Glitter Knickers* (Bath Rondo). On screen, she was most recently the narrative consultant on HBO's recently acquired feature documentary, *The Contestant*. She's currently working on a novel and a non-fiction guide to everyday communication for a kinder life. Her day job is as a public affairs strategic communicator. For more of her ideas and insights on writing, visit https://gillkirk.com, or follow her on Bluesky @gillkirk.bsky.social.

See also...

- *The importance of story development*, page 264
- *Prizes and awards*, page 570

Theatre producers

This list is divided into metropolitan theatres (below), regional theatres (page 415) and touring companies (page 421). See also *Literary agents for television, film, radio and theatre* on page 779.

LONDON

Almeida Theatre

Almeida Street, London N1 1TA
email info@almeida.co.uk
website https://almeida.co.uk
Instagram @almeida_theatre
Artistic Director Rupert Goold, *Executive Director* Denise Wood, *Head of Programming & Literary* Stephanie Bain, *Director of Participation and Work for Young People* Dani Parr

Stages approx. six shows per year, both new work (such as *The Secret Life of Bees*) and reimagined classics. Does not accept unsolicited scripts.

Opportunities for young people include the Young Company (for aspiring actors), Young Designers and a Youth Advisory Board. Also works with schools in a variety of ways, including free tickets, bespoke workshops, career tasters and teacher training. Founded 1980.

The Bridge Theatre

3 Potters Fields Park, London SE1 2SG
tel 0333 320 0052
email info@bridgetheatre.co.uk
website www.bridgetheatre.co.uk
Founders Nicholas Hytner, Nick Starr

Home of the London Theatre Company. Focuses on the commissioning and production of new shows, as well as staging the occasional classic. Founded 2017.

Bush Theatre

7 Uxbridge Road, London W12 8LJ
tel 020-8743 3584 (admin)
email info@bushtheatre.co.uk
website www.bushtheatre.co.uk/artists/
X @bushtheatre
Artistic Director Taio Lawson

Home to hundreds of groundbreaking premieres since its inception in 1972 – many of them Bush commissions – and has hosted guest productions by leading companies and artists from around the world. Check the website for submissions windows and full guidelines, including information on unsolicited submissions. Founded 1972.

Donmar Warehouse

41 Earlham Street, Seven Dials, London WC2H 9LX UK
email office@donmarwarehouse.com
website www.donmarwarehouse.com
X @DonmarWarehouse
Instagram @donmarwarehouse
Artistic Director Tim Sheader, *Executive Director* Henny Finch, *Associate Director (Literary)* Craig Gilbert

Independent producing house. Recent productions include *The Cherry Orchard, Watch on the Rhine* and *Trouble in Butetown.*

Works with new writers through training programmes but does not accept unsolicited scripts. Authors may invite Donmar staff to see their plays by contacting them on the above email, at least four weeks before the production opens. Also works with young audiences via its LOCAL programme, schools partnerships and school performances. Founded 1977.

Finborough Theatre

118 Finborough Road, London SW10 9ED
tel 020-7244 7439
email literaryteam@finboroughtheatre.co.uk
website https://finboroughtheatre.co.uk/literary/
Facebook www.facebook.com/FinboroughTheatre
X @finborough
Instagram @finboroughtheatre
Artistic Director Neil McPherson

Presents new writing, revivals of neglected plays from 1800 onwards, music theatre and UK premieres of foreign work. Unsolicited scripts are accepted, but see literary policy on website before sending. Founded 1980.

Hampstead Theatre

Eton Avenue, London NW3 3EU
tel 020-7722 9301
email info@hampsteadtheatre.com
website www.hampsteadtheatre.com
Facebook www.facebook.com/hampsteadtheatre
Instagram @hampstead_theatre
Producer and Chief Executive Greg Ripley-Duggan

Designed with writers in mind, allowing for flexible staging within an intimate main house auditorium and a second studio space. Accepts full-length plays from agented and unagented UK-based writers throughout the year.

Jermyn Street Theatre

16B Jermyn Street, London SW1Y 6ST
email info@jermynstreettheatre.co.uk
website www.jermynstreettheatre.co.uk/work-with-us/
Facebook www.facebook.com/JSTheatre
Instagram @jermynstreettheatre

Artistic Director Stella Powell-Jones, *Executive Director and Co-founder* Penny Horner, *Executive Producer* David Doyle

Programmed and receiving house in central London. Stages new plays (by writers such as Esther Freud and Stephen Berkoff), revivals (Ibsen, Coward and Sondheim, for example), new versions of European classics and high-quality musicals, as well as one-off musical and literary events. Collaborates with theatres around the world, and over recent years has expanded into online work and theatre-on-film.

Does not accept unsolicited scripts; production proposals preferred. Works mostly with mid-career or established authors, but open to emerging voices. Synopses should be emailed in the first instance. Winner of Fringe Theatre of the Year 2021 at *The Stage* Awards. Founded 1994.

Bill Kenwright Ltd

BKL House, 1 Venice Walk, London W2 1RR
tel 020-7446 6200
email info@kenwright.com
website www.kenwright.com
X @BKL_Productions
Chief Executive David Gilbery, *Executive Producers* Julius Green, Jeremy Meadow

Award-winning prolific commercial theatre and film production company, presenting revivals and new works for the West End, international and regional theatres. Productions include *The Lightning Thief*, *Blood Brothers*, *Heathers*, and *Boys from the Black Stuff*.

Kiln Theatre

269 Kilburn High Road, London NW6 7JR
tel 020-7372 6611
email info@kilntheatre.com
website https://kilntheatre.com
Instagram @kilntheatre
Artistic Director Amit Sharma

Presents at least six productions per year, aiming to provoke debate and engage the audience. Many of these are commissioned and written specifically for the theatre, or are programmed in collaboration with national or international companies. Unable to accept unsolicited submissions. Founded 1980 as the Tricycle Theatre.

King's Head Theatre

115 Upper Street, London N1 1QN
tel 020-7226 8561
email info@kingsheadtheatre.com
website www.kingsheadtheatre.com
Instagram @kingsheadtheatre
Executive Producer and Acting Ceo Sofi Berenger

Off-West End theatre producing opera, LGBTQ+ plays and revivals. Founded 1970.

Lyric Hammersmith

Lyric Square, King Street, London W6 0QL
tel 020-8741 6850
email enquiries@lyric.co.uk
website https://lyric.co.uk
Instagram @lyrichammersmith
Artistic Director Rachel O'Riordan, *Executive Director* Amy Belson

West London's largest producing and receiving theatre. Unsolicited scripts for in-house productions not accepted. Founded 1895.

Neal Street Productions Ltd

1st Floor, 26–28 Neal Street, London WC2H 9QQ
tel 020-7240 8890
email post@nealstreetproductions.com
website www.nealstreetproductions.com
Instagram @nealstreetproductions
Co-Directors Sam Mendes, Pippa Harris, Nicolas Brown, *Executive Producer* Julie Pastor, *Head of Development* Lola Oliyide

Film, TV and theatre producer of new work and revivals. No unsolicited scripts or treatments; work accepted only via an agent. Founded 2003.

The Old Red Lion Theatre

418 St John Street, London EC1V 4NJ
tel 020-7837 7816
email info@oldredliontheatre.co.uk
website www.oldredliontheatre.co.uk
Facebook www.facebook.com/oldredliontheatre/
Instagram @orltheatre
Executive Director Damien Devine, *Artistic Director* Jack Robinson

Interested in contemporary pieces, especially from unproduced writers. No funding: incoming production company pays to rent the theatre. All submissions should be sent via email. Founded 1977.

Orange Tree Theatre

1 Clarence Street, Richmond, Surrey TW9 2SA
tel 020-8940 0141
email literary@orangetreetheatre.co.uk
website www.orangetreetheatre.co.uk
Facebook www.facebook.com/OrangeTreeTheatre
Instagram @orangetreetheatre
Artistic Director and Joint Ceo Tom Littler, *Executive Director and Joint Ceo* Hannah Streeter

Producing theatre presenting a mixture of new work, contemporary revivals and rediscoveries in an intimate in-the-round space. Unsolicited work is not accepted but writers should visit the website for up-to-date information about opportunities. Enquiries can be addressed to the Literary Associate at the email address above. Founded 1971; present theatre opened 1991.

The Questors Theatre

12 Mattock Lane, London W5 5BQ
email enquiries@questors.org.uk
website www.questors.org.uk
Facebook www.facebook.com/questorstheatre

X @questorstheatre
Instagram @questors_theatre
Executive Director Michael Eppy

Largest independent community theatre in Europe. Produces 15–20 shows a year, specialising in modern and classical world drama. Visiting productions hosted too. Also runs a youth theatre group, QYT, for young people aged between five and 18, as well as summer workshops. No unsolicited scripts. Founded 1929.

Royal Court Theatre

(English Stage Company Ltd)
Sloane Square, London SW1W 8AS
tel 020-7565 5050
email literary@royalcourttheatre.com
website https://royalcourttheatre.com/playwriting
X @royalcourt
Artistic Director David Byrne, *Executive Director* Will Young, *Senior Dramaturg and Associate Playwright* Gillian Greer

Programmes new plays that ask bold questions about today's world: these should be original in form or theme and unlikely to be produced elsewhere. Submissions accepted all year round using online submissions portal only. Authors with access needs should contact the theatre via the email address above. Founded 1870.

Royal National Theatre

South Bank, London SE1 9PX
tel 020-7452 3333
email scripts@nationaltheatre.org.uk
website www.nationaltheatre.org.uk
X @NationalTheatre
Artistic Director Indhu Rubasingham, *New Work Administrator* Sarah Clarke

New Work Department considers submissions from the UK and Ireland. No synopses, treatments or hard copy submissions; full-length scripts (minimum playing time one hour) can be emailed as pdfs. Founded 1962.

@sohoplace

4 Soho Place, Charing Cross Road, London W1D 3BG
email info@sohoplace.org
website https://sohoplace.org/
X @sohoplacelondon
Instagram @sohoplace
Founder and Producer Nica Burns

Flexible 602-seat in-the-round auditorium with programming that aims to push theatre boundaries. The first new-build West End Theatre for 50 years. Productions staged since opening include new revivals, such as *Medea* and *As You Like It*, and world premieres, such as *Brokeback Mountain* and *The Little Big Things*. Founded 2022.

Soho Theatre

21 Dean Street, London W1D 3NE
tel 020-7478 0100
website https://sohotheatre.com/about-us/team/
website https://sohotheatre.com/walthamstow-about/
Instagram @sohotheatre
Executive Director Mark Godfrey, *Head of Theatre* David Luff, *Head of Comedy* Steve Lock, *Head of Creative Engagement* Jessica Draper

Produces and co-produces new plays, presents the best emerging theatre companies and comedians, and works with artists in a variety of ways. Has a range of artist and talent development and participation programmes – Writers' Lab offers support for new writers over a nine-month three-draft process – and two new writing awards, including the biennial Verity Bargate Award for emerging playwrights. Submissions can be made via the website address above. Founded 1972; sister site, Soho Theatre Walthamstow, opened in May 2025.

Theatre Royal, Stratford East

Gerry Raffles Square, London E15 1BN
tel 020-8534 7374
website www.stratfordeast.com
X @stratfordeast
Artistic Director Lisa Spirling

Middle-scale producing theatre. Specialises in new writing, including developing contemporary British musicals. Welcomes new plays that are unproduced, full in length, and which relate to its diverse multicultural, Black and Asian audience. Founded 1884.

Unicorn Theatre

147 Tooley Street, London SE1 2HZ
tel 020-7645 0560
email hello@unicorntheatre.com
website www.unicorntheatre.com
Facebook www.facebook.com/unicorntheatre
X @unicorn_theatre
Instagram @unicorn_theatre
Artistic Director Rachel Bagshaw, *Executive Director* Rebekah Jones

Produces a year-round programme of theatre for children and young people under 21. In-house productions of full-length plays with professional casts are staged across two auditoria, alongside visiting companies and education work. Rarely commissions plays from writers who are new to it, but it is keen to hear from writers who are interested in working with the theatre in the future. Do not send unsolicited MSS, but submit a short statement describing why you would like to write for the Unicorn along with a CV or a summary of your relevant experience. Founded 1949 as Caryl Jenner Mobile Theatre.

White Bear Theatre Club
138 Kennington Park Road, London SE11 4DJ
tel 07985 500697
email info@whitebeartheatre.co.uk
website https://whitebeartheatre.co.uk
Facebook www.facebook.com/WhiteBearTheatre
X @WhiteBearTheatr
Instagram @whitebeartheatre
Artistic Director Michael Kingsbury

Metropolitan new writing theatre company. Welcomes scripts from new writers: send queries to whitebearliterary@gmail.com. Founded 1988.

Young Vic Theatre Company
66 The Cut, London SE1 8LZ
tel 020-7922 2922
email programming@youngvic.org
website www.youngvic.org/about-us/get-in-touch
Facebook www.facebook.com/youngvictheatre
X @youngvictheatre
Instagram @youngvictheatre
Artistic Director Nadia Fall, *Executive Director* Lucy Pattison

Leading London producing theatre. Unsolicited scripts are not accepted. Artists can invite members of the artistic team to see their work via a form on the website. Founded 1969.

REGIONAL

Abbey Theatre Amharclann na Mainistreach
26 Lower Abbey Street, Dublin D01 K0F1, Republic of Ireland
tel +353 (0)1 887 2200
email info@abbeytheatre.ie
website www.abbeytheatre.ie
X @AbbeyTheatre
Artistic Director Caitríona McLaughlin, *Executive Director* Mark O'Brien, *Literary and New Work Director* Ruth McGowan

Ireland's national theatre. Commissions and produces new Irish writing and contemporary productions from the canon, alongside hosting and presenting work by other Irish and international artists and companies. Founded 1904.

Yvonne Arnaud Theatre Management Ltd
Millbrook, Guildford, Surrey GU1 3UX
tel (01483) 440077
email yat@yvonne-arnaud.co.uk
website www.yvonne-arnaud.co.uk
X @YvonneArnaud
Director and Chief Executive Joanna Read

Presenting and producing theatre which also makes its own productions. Runs creative learning and community activities throughout the year. Founded 1965.

The Belgrade Theatre
Belgrade Square, Coventry CV1 1GS
tel 024-7625 6431
email developmentadmin@belgrade.co.uk
website www.belgrade.co.uk
Bluesky @belgradetheatre.bsky.social
Creative Director Corey Campbell, *Ceo* Laura Elliot

Repertory theatre producing drama, comedy and musicals. Does not accept unsolicited scripts; email short synopses first to the address above. Runs a series of training development opportunities, including its Springboard initiative. Founded 1958.

Birmingham Repertory Theatre
Broad Street, Birmingham B1 2EP
tel 0121 236 4455
email stage.door@birmingham-rep.co.uk
website www.birmingham-rep.co.uk/take-part/
Facebook www.facebook.com/BirminghamRep
Instagram @therepbirmingham
Artistic Director Joe Murphy

Only producing theatre in Birmingham and the oldest building-based theatre company in the UK. Over the last 15 years The Rep has produced more than 130 new plays as well as presenting over 60 productions on its three stages every year; many of its productions have toured nationally and internationally. Its learning and outreach programme is one of the largest and most diverse in the UK and continues today with a youth theatre and the Rep Foundry programme.

See website for forthcoming opportunities in youth theatre, talent development and a programme of workshops and masterclasses throughout the year. These include Feedback Fridays, which give scriptwriters from the West Midlands the opportunity to receive valuable support and feedback on their work from The Rep's in-house directors every two months. Founded 1913.

The Bootleg Theatre Company
23 Burgess Green, Bishopdown, Salisbury, Wilts. SP1 3EL
tel (01722) 421476
email colinburden281@gmail.com
website www.bootlegtheatre.com/tearawayfilms
Contact Colin Burden

New writing theatre company whose recent productions include *Girls Allowed* by Trevor Suthers, *A Rainy Night in Soho* by Stephen Giles, and *The Squeaky Clean* by Roger Goldsmith. Also produces compilation productions of monologues/duologues: these have included *15 Minutes of Fame*, *Tales from The Street* and *Parting Shots*. Founded 1985.

Bristol Old Vic
King Street, Bristol BS1 4ED
tel 0117 949 3993

email programming@bristololdvic.org.uk
website https://bristololdvic.org.uk/for-artists
Facebook www.facebook.com/BristolOldVic
Instagram @bristololdvic1766
Artistic Director Nancy Medina, *Executive Director* Charlotte Geeves

Oldest theatre auditorium in UK (opened in 1766). See website for more details on submission windows and related requirements. The Bristol Old Vic company was founded 1946.

Chichester Festival Theatre

Oaklands Park, Chichester, West Sussex PO19 6AP
tel (01243) 784437
email leap.mailbox@cft.org.uk
email hello@cft.org.uk
website www.cft.org.uk
Instagram @chichesterft
Executive Director Kathy Bourne, *Artistic Director* Justin Audibert

Stages annual Summer Festival Season from April–October in the Festival and Minerva Theatres together with a year-round education programme, winter touring programme and youth theatre Christmas show. Does not accept unsolicited scripts. The Learning, Education and Participation (LEAP) department runs a programme of events for all ages, including workshops, performances, talks and tours. Founded 1962.

Contact Theatre Company

Oxford Road, Manchester M15 6JA
tel 0161 274 0600
website https://contactmcr.com
Instagram @contactmcr
Chief Executive Director Jack Dale-Dowd

Multidisciplinary arts organisation focused on working with and for young people aged 13 years and above. Offers a range of free projects, from writing to music and drama, including the Contact Young Company ensemble. Founded 1972.

Creation Theatre Company

tel (01865) 766266
email boxoffice@creationtheatre.co.uk
website www.creationtheatre.co.uk
Facebook www.facebook.com/CreationTheatre
X @creationtheatre
Instagram @creationtheatre
Ceo and Artistic Director Dr Helen Eastman

Award-winning producing theatre company, specialising in site-specific and digital theatre in extraordinary locations. Also runs drama classes during term-time for ages 5–19 and theatre & creativity workshops during the school holidays in Oxford. Does not accept unsolicited manuscripts.

Curve

Rutland Street, Leicester LE1 1SB
tel 0116 242 3560
email artistdevelopment@curvetheatre.co.uk
website www.curveonline.co.uk/artists/artist-development
X @CurveLeicester
Chief Executive Chris Stafford, *Artistic Director* Nikolai Foster

Regional producing theatre company. Artist-development opportunities include Curve Connect, First Fridays (offering publicly bookable meetings with senior Curve staff) and a yearly New Work Festival with opportunities for artists at all levels of their career. Founded 2008.

Derby Theatre

15 Theatre Walk, St Peter's Quarter, Derby DE1 2NF
email creatives@derbyplayhouse.co.uk
website www.derbytheatre.co.uk
Facebook www.facebook.com/DerbyTheatre
X @DerbyTheatre
Artistic Director and Chief Executive Sarah Brigham, *Creative Learning Director* Caroline Barth

Regional producing and receiving theatre. Offers opportunities for theatre-makers in the region. Founded 1975.

Druid

The Druid Building, Flood Street, Galway H91 PWX5, Republic of Ireland
tel +353 (0)91 568 660
email info@druid.ie
website www.druid.ie
X @druidtheatre
Bluesky @druidtheatre.bsky.social
Instagram @druidtheatre
Artistic Director Garry Hynes, *Executive Director* Anneliese Davidsen, *Producer* Brian Fenton

Leading Irish touring theatre company, led by Tony Award-winner, Garry Hynes. Produces a wide range of plays, with an emphasis on new Irish writing and the Irish canon. Annual submission window for scripts and annual series of rehearsed readings of new plays (see website for details). Tours nationally and internationally. Founded 1975.

The Dukes

Moor Lane, Lancaster LA1 1QE
tel (01524) 598500
email ask@dukes-lancaster.org
website https://dukes-lancaster.org
Instagram @thedukeslancaster
Chief Executive Chris Lawson

Producing theatre and cultural centre. The Lancaster Writing Prize is open to young writers aged between 12 to 18. See website for information about the theatre's forthcoming productions and programming approach. Founded 1971.

Dundee Rep and Scottish Dance Theatre Limited

Tay Square, Dundee DD1 1PB
tel (01382) 227684

email info@dundeereptheatre.co.uk
website www.dundeereptheatre.co.uk
X @DundeeRep
Artistic Director (Dundee Rep) & Joint Ceo Andrew Panton, *Executive Director & Joint Ceo* Liam Sinclair

Regional repertory theatre company with resident ensemble. Mix of classics, musicals and new commissions. Founded 1982.

Everyman Theatre Cheltenham

7 Regent Street, Cheltenham, Glos. GL50 1HQ
tel (01242) 512515
email admin@everymantheatre.org.uk
website www.everymantheatre.org.uk
X @Everymanchelt
Creative Director Paul Milton

Regional presenting and producing theatre promoting a wide range of plays. Small-scale experimental, youth and educational work encouraged in The Studio Theatre. Contact the Creative Director before submitting material. Founded 1891.

Exeter Northcott Theatre

Stocker Road, Exeter,
Devon EX4 4QB / Barnfield Theatre, Exeter EX1 1SN
tel (01392) 722417
email info@exeternorthcott.co.uk
website www.exeternorthcott.co.uk
Facebook www.facebook.com/ExeterNorthcottTheatre
X @ExeterNorthcott
Instagram @exeternorthcott
Joint Ceos Emma Stephenson, Kelly Johnson, Martin Berry

Offers a varied programme of in-house and touring productions at Exeter Northcott and the Barnfield Theatres, along with creative opportunities for young people, communities, and emerging artists. South-West playwrights may use their free Elevate membership to access exclusive opportunities, and submit work during an annual script submission window.

Harrogate Theatre

Oxford Street, Harrogate, North Yorkshire HG1 1QF
tel (01423) 502710
email info@harrogatetheatre.co.uk
website www.harrogatetheatre.co.uk/get-involved/artistic-development/
Instagram @harrogatetheatre
Chief Executive David Bown, *Head of Creative Engagement* Hannah Draper

Predominantly a receiving house; rarely produces productions in-house. Unsolicited scripts not accepted, but see website for information on artist development hub. Founded 1900.

HOME

2 Tony Wilson Place, First Street,
Manchester M15 4FN
tel 0161 200 1500
email info@homemcr.org
website www.homemcr.org
Instagram @homemcr
Executive Director & Joint Ceo Karen O'Neill, *Interim Creative Director & Joint Ceo* Sita McIntosh

Purpose-built centre for international contemporary art, theatre and film. Hosts drama, dance, film and contemporary visual art with a strong focus on international work, new commissions and talent development. Founded 2015.

Leeds Playhouse

Playhouse Square, Quarry Hill, Leeds LS2 7UP
tel 0113 213 7700
website https://leedsplayhouse.org.uk
Instagram @leedsplayhouse
Chief Executive Shawab Iqbal, *Artistic Director* Tom Wright

Seeks out the best companies and artists to create theatre in the heart of Yorkshire. Its artistic development programme, Furnace, discovers and supports new voices, while developing work with established practitioners. It provides a creative space for writers, directors, companies and individual theatre-makers to refine their practice at all stages of their career. The Playhouse Connect team works with more than 12,000 people every year reaching out to refugee communities, young people, students, older people and people with learning challenges. Founded 1990.

Live Theatre

Broad Chare, Quayside,
Newcastle upon Tyne NE1 3DQ
tel 0191 232 1232
email info@live.org.uk
website www.live.org.uk
website https://www.live.org.uk/children-young-people/schools-teachers
Instagram @livetheatrenewcastle
Executive Director & Joint Ceo Jacqui Kell, *Artistic Director & Joint Ceo* Jack McNamara

New writing theatre company and venue. Stages three to six productions per year of new writing, plus touring plays from other new writing companies. The Live Youth Theatre programme is free and open to young people between the ages of ten and 25. CPD and INSET support for teachers is also available. Founded 1986.

Liverpool Everyman and Playhouse

Liverpool and Merseyside Theatres Trust Ltd,
5–11 Hope Street, Liverpool L1 9BH
tel 0151 709 4776
email newworks@everymanplayhouse.com
website www.everymanplayhouse.com/script-submissions
Facebook www.facebook.com/everymanplayhouse

Instagram @liveveryplay
Chief Executive Mark Da Vanzo, *Creative Director* Nathan Powell, *New Works Associate* Tommo Fowler

Produces and presents new plays, revivals, adaptations and comedy across two buildings. Develops original work by writers based within the Liverpool city region and the North West, via writing programmes and annual script submission window. See website for further details of opportunities available through New Works. Founded 1964.

Mercury Theatre Colchester

Balkerne Gate, Colchester, Essex CO1 1PT
tel (01206) 577006
email info@mercurytheatre.co.uk
website www.mercurytheatre.co.uk
X @mercurytheatre
Executive Producer Tracey Childs, *Executive Director* Steve Mannix, *Creative Director* Ryan McBryde

Active producing theatre in East Anglia, aiming to put theatre at the heart of the community it serves and to make work in Colchester that reaches audiences regionally and nationally. Runs a comprehensive Creative Learning & Talent programme to support artists and theatre-makers at all stages of their development. Founded 1972.

The New Theatre: Dublin

The New Theatre, Temple Bar, 43 East Essex Street, Dublin D02 XH92, Republic of Ireland
tel +353 (0)1 670 3361
email info@thenewtheatre.com
website www.thenewtheatre.com
Instagram @thenewtheatre
Artistic Director Anthony Fox, *Dramaturgs* Stephen Murray, Dee Burke, Jessica Traynor

Innovative theatre supporting plays by new Irish writers and others whose work deals with issues pertaining to contemporary Irish society. Seats 66 people. Welcomes scripts from new writers. Founded 1997.

New Vic Theatre

Etruria Road, Newcastle under Lyme ST5 0JG
tel (01782) 717954
email admin@newvictheatre.org.uk
website www.newvictheatre.org.uk
Facebook www.facebook.com/NewVicTheatreStaffordshire#
Artistic Director Theresa Heskins, *Managing Director* Fiona Wallace

Europe's first purpose-built theatre-in-the-round, presenting drama, contemporary and new plays, comedy and a range of one-night concerts. Also runs the award-winning Borderlines community programme and creative learning opportunities for those aged four and upward. Does not accept unsolicited scripts. Founded 1986.

The New Wolsey Theatre

Civic Drive, Ipswich, Suffolk IP1 2AS
tel (01473) 295900
email info@wolseytheatre.co.uk
website www.wolseytheatre.co.uk
Facebook www.facebook.com/NewWolsey
X @NewWolsey
Instagram @newwolsey
Chief Executive/Artistic Director Douglas Rintoul, *Head of Creative Communities* Tony Casement

Mixed producing/receiving house, staging four to five produced or co-produced productions a year, often specialising in actor-musician productions. Alongside these productions, there is talent development support for professionals in or from East Anglia, as well as a vibrant Youth Theatre and the delivery of creative projects with schools and communities. Founded 2000.

Northern Stage (Theatrical Productions) Ltd

Barras Bridge, Newcastle upon Tyne NE1 7RH
tel 0191 242 7210
email info@northernstage.co.uk
website www.northernstage.co.uk
X @northernstage
Artistic Director Natalie Ibu, *Executive Director* Kate Denby

The largest producing theatre company in the North-East of England. Presents local, national and international theatre across three stages and runs an extensive participation programme.

Nottingham Playhouse

Nottingham Playhouse Trust Ltd, Wellington Circus, Nottingham NG1 5AF
tel 0115 941 9419
website https://nottinghamplayhouse.co.uk/get-involved/young-people
X @NottmPlayhouse
Artistic Director Adam Penford, *Chief Executive* Stephanie Sirr

Seeks to nurture new writers from the East Midlands primarily through its Artist Development programme, Amplify. Also offers a range of groups and youth theatres for young people aged two and above; see website for full details. Founded 1963.

Octagon Theatre

Howell Croft South, Bolton BL1 1SB
tel (01204) 520661
email literary@octagonbolton.co.uk
website www.octagonbolton.co.uk
X @octagontheatre
Chief Executive Roddy Gauld, *Artistic Director* Lotte Wakeham

Fully flexible professional theatre, which reopened in summer 2021 following extensive refurbishment.

Year-round programme of own productions and visiting companies, including a studio theatre for creative engagement, family theatre, new work and emerging artists.

Queen's Theatre, Hornchurch

Billet Lane, Hornchurch, Essex RM11 1QT
tel (01708) 443333
email info@queens-theatre.co.uk
website www.queens-theatre.co.uk
website www.queens-theatre.co.uk/get-involved/youth-theatre
X @QueensTheatre

Regional theatre working in outer East London, Essex and beyond. Each annual programme includes home-grown theatre, visiting live entertainment and learning and participation projects.

Royal Exchange Theatre Company Ltd

St Ann's Square, Manchester M2 7DH
tel 0161 833 9833
email suzanne.bell@royalexchange.co.uk
website www.royalexchange.co.uk/create-participate
website www.writeaplay.co.uk
Facebook www.facebook.com/rx
Instagram @rxtheatre
Creative Director and Deputy Ceo Selina Cartmell

Varied programme of major classics, new plays, musicals, contemporary British and European drama. Focus on new writing, writer development, creative collaborations and community participation. See website for forthcoming script submission windows for writers based in the North West. Facilitates and delivers the Bruntwood Prize for Playwriting biennially (see second website listed above). Founded 1976.

Royal Lyceum Theatre Company

30B Grindlay Street, Edinburgh EH3 9AX
tel 0131 248 4800
email info@lyceum.org.uk
website www.lyceum.org.uk
X @lyceumtheatre
Artistic Director David Greig

Producing theatre with a diverse year-round programme of classic, contemporary and new drama. Interested in the work of Scottish writers. Founded 1883.

Royal Shakespeare Company

The Royal Shakespeare Theatre, Waterside, Stratford-upon-Avon, Warks. CV37 6BB
tel (01789) 296655
email newwork@rsc.org.uk
website www.rsc.org.uk/about-us/new-plays-and-writers
Facebook www.facebook.com/thersc
X @TheRSC
Instagram @thersc
Co-artistic Directors Daniel Evans, Tamara Harvey

Produces new work by contemporary writers on all three of the company's permanent stages: the Royal Shakespeare Theatre, the Swan Theatre and The Other Place, in Stratford-Upon-Avon in Warwickshire. This programme of new plays, musicals, adaptations and translations sits alongside the work of Shakespeare and his contemporaries and contemporary revivals of modern classics. The company produces work regularly in London and tours nationally. The New Work department does not accept unsolicited scripts but rather seeks out writers for commission and monitors writers in production in the UK and internationally. Writers are welcome to invite the New Work Department to attend readings, showcases or productions by emailing the address above. Founded 1961.

Salisbury Playhouse

Malthouse Lane, Salisbury, Wilts. SP2 7RA
tel (01722) 320117, (01722) 320333 (box office)
email info@wiltshirecreative.co.uk
website www.wiltshirecreative.co.uk
Facebook www.facebook.com/wiltscreative
Instagram @wiltscreative
Artistic Director Gareth Machin

Regional producing and presenting theatre with a broad programme of classical and contemporary plays, as part of Wiltshire Creative. Does not accept unsolicited scripts. The Playhouse is committed to a programme of original drama with a particular focus on South-West writers. Check website for current information on script submission. Founded 1976.

Shakespeare North Playhouse

Prospero Place, Prescot L34 3AB
tel 0151 433 7156
email artists@shakespearenorthplayhouse.co.uk
website https://shakespearenorthplayhouse.co.uk/get-involved/artists/
X @ShakespeareNP
Instagram @shakespearenorthplayhouse
Ceo and Creative Director Lisa Allen

Performances (theatre, music, comedy), workshops, events and activities inspired by Shakespeare but relevant to modern audiences. The venue's seventeenth-century-style Cockpit Theatre seats 450 spectators, and can be configured into two formations: end-on and in-the-round. The venue is also home to a fully-accessible outdoor performance garden funded by the Ken Dodd Charitable Foundation, exhibition gallery, 60-seater studio theatre, learning centre, events spaces, and a cafe and bar with outdoor piazza.

Committed to working with local artists in order to develop innovative, diverse work: contact the Culture and Learning team via the email above with information in the first instance (see website for guidance). Unsolicited scripts not accepted. Named Theatre Building of the Year at *The Stage* Awards 2023. Founded 2022.

Sheffield Theatres

(Crucible, Tanya Moiseiwitsch Playhouse & Lyceum)
55 Norfolk Street, Sheffield S1 1DA
tel 0114 249 5999
website www.sheffieldtheatres.co.uk
Facebook www.facebook.com/shefftheatres
X @crucibletheatre
Instagram @sheffieldtheatres
Artistic Director Elizabeth Newman

Large-scale producing house with distinctive thrust stage; mid-scale flexible space; Victorian proscenium arch theatre used mainly for touring productions.

Sherman Theatre

Senghennydd Road, Cardiff CF24 4YE
tel 029-2064 6900
email scripts@shermantheatre.co.uk
website www.shermantheatre.co.uk/theatre-makers
Instagram @shermantheatre
Chief Executive Julia Barry, *Artistic Director* Joe Murphy

Produces new work and revivals. Seeks to stage high-quality and innovative drama with a local, national or international perspective. Develops work by Welsh and Wales-based writers, both in English and Welsh. Participatory work with youth theatres, community engagement, and mentorship of new artists. Check website for information on forthcoming submission windows for unsolicited scripts (typically two per year). Founded 2007.

Show of Strength Theatre Company Ltd

tel 0117 953 5976
email info@showofstrength.org.uk
website www.showofstrength.org.uk
Facebook www.facebook.com/showofstrength
X @Showofstrength
Instagram @showofstrengthtc
Creative Producer Sheila Hannon

Small-scale company committed to producing new and unperformed work. Unsolicited scripts not accepted. Founded 1986.

Stephen Joseph Theatre

Westborough, Scarborough,
North Yorkshire YO11 1JW
tel (01723) 370540
email scripts@sjt.uk.com
website www.sjt.uk.com/aboutus/new_writing
Bluesky @thesjt.bsky.social
Artistic Director / Joint Ceo Paul Robinson, *Executive Director / Joint Ceo* Caroline Routh

Regional repertory theatre company presenting approx. five productions a year, many of which are premieres. Unsolicited scripts accepted from represented and unrepresented writers; see website for details. Founded 1996.

Swansea Grand Theatre

Singleton Street, Swansea SA1 3QJ
tel (01792) 475715
email swansea.grandmarketing@swansea.gov.uk
website www.swanseagrand.co.uk
Facebook www.facebook.com/swanseagrandtheatre
X @swanseagrand
Instagram @swanseagrandinsta

Regional receiving theatre.

Theatr Clwyd

Raikes Lane, Mold, Flintshire CH7 1YA
tel (01352) 344101
email writers@theatrclwyd.com
website www.theatrclwyd.com
Instagram @theatrclwyd
Executive Director Liam Evans-Ford, *Artistic Director* Kate Wasserberg

Largest producing theatre in Wales, creating up to 14 productions each year in English, Welsh and bilingually. Productions are a mix of classic plays, contemporary revivals, musicals and new writing. Will consider plays by writers, particularly Welsh, Wales-based or with Welsh themes, and usually offers 6 writing residencies each year. No literary department, so authors should expect to wait for a response to unsolicited scripts.

Theatre Royal Bath

Sawclose, Bath BA1 1ET
tel (01225) 448815
website www.theatreroyal.org.uk
Facebook www.facebook.com/TheatreRoyalBath
Director Danny Moar

One of the oldest theatres in Britain. Comprises three auditoria: the Main House, the Ustinov Studio Theatre and the Egg Theatre for children and young people. Founded 1805.

Theatre Royal Plymouth

Royal Parade, Plymouth PL1 2TR
tel (01752) 668282
email info@theatreroyal.com
website www.theatreroyal.com
Facebook www.facebook.com/theatreroyalplymouth
X @TRPlymouth
Instagram @theatreroyalplymouth
Chief Executive Officer & Executive Producer James Mackenzie-Blackman

Registered charity and the largest regional producing theatre in the UK housing three theatres – The Lyric, The Drum and The Lab. Delivers outreach work to engage young people and communities in Plymouth and beyond. Its production and learning centre, TR2, offers set, costume, prop-making and rehearsal facilities. Runs an Artist Development programme to support artists and creatives from the South West, helping individuals and companies to develop new work, connect and collaborate.

Theatre Royal Windsor

32 Thames Street, Windsor, Berks. SL4 1PS
tel (01753) 863444
email info@theatreroyalwindsor.co.uk
website www.theatreroyalwindsor.co.uk
Facebook www.facebook.com/TheatreWindsor/
X @TheatreWindsor
Director Anne-Marie Woodley

Regional producing theatre presenting a wide range of productions, from classics to new plays. Founded 1902.

Traverse Theatre

10 Cambridge Street, Edinburgh EH1 2ED
tel 0131 228 3223
website www.traverse.co.uk
X @traversetheatre
Artistic Director Gareth Nicholls

Annual programme of creative writing and talent development opportunities, including workshops, casting calls and networking events – see website for further details. Founded 1963.

Visible Fictions

Suite 325/327, 4th Floor, 11 Bothwell Street, Glasgow G2 6LY
email laura@visiblefictions.co.uk
website https://visiblefictions.co.uk
X @visiblefictions
Artistic Director Dougie Irvine, *Producer* Laura Penny

Specialises in professional productions for young audiences and their families across a range of artforms, from theatre to film, puppetry to immersive experiences. Also works in creative learning settings – community, educational, institutional, and professional – to make bespoke projects to accompany and enhance artistic experiences of young audiences. Founded 1991.

Watford Palace Theatre

20 Clarendon Road, Watford, Herts. WD17 1JZ
tel (01923) 225671
website www.watfordpalacetheatre.co.uk
X @watfordpalace
Instagram @watfordpalace
Ceo & Director of Programming Steve Marmion, *Executive Director* Jamie Arden

Regional theatre. Produces and co-produces seasonally, both classic and contemporary drama and new writing. Accepts unsolicited scripts from Hertfordshire-based writers. Founded 1908.

York Theatre Royal

St Leonard's Place, York YO1 7HD
tel (01904) 658162
website www.yorktheatreroyal.co.uk
Facebook www.facebook.com/yorktheatreroyal
X @yorktheatre
Instagram @yorktheatreroyal
Creative Director Juliet Forster

Repertory productions, tours. Founded 1744.

TOURING COMPANIES

Actors Touring Company

email atc@atctheatre.com
website www.atctheatre.com
Facebook www.facebook.com/actorstouringcompany
Instagram @actorstouringcompanyatc
Artistic Director Matthew Xia

Small- to medium-scale touring company producing international new writing and new plays by global and global majority writers, for audiences in the UK and internationally. Does not accept unsolicited scripts.

Boundless Theatre

12 South Norwood Hill, London SE25 6AB
tel 020-7072 0140
email hello@boundlesstheatre.org.uk
website www.boundlesstheatre.org.uk
website https://boundlessdrama.club/welcome
Instagram @boundlessabound

Creates new plays with and for audiences aged 15–25 years. Tours the UK and internationally. Resources, exclusive deals, workshops and more are available to members of the Boundless Drama Club, a community of young creatives.

Eastern Angles Theatre Company

Eastern Angles Centre, Gatacre Road, Ipswich IP1 2LQ
tel (01473) 218202
email admin@easternangles.co.uk
website www.easternangles.co.uk
Facebook www.facebook.com/EasternAnglesTheatreCompany
X @easternangles
Instagram @easternangles
Artistic Director Jake Smith, *General Manager* Jess Baker

Touring company producing new work with a regional theme. Stages three to four productions per year. Also runs a community, arts and heritage hub in Ipswich with a satellite venue in Peterborough. Welcomes scripts from new writers in the East of England region. Founded 1982.

Graeae Theatre Company

Bradbury Studios, 138 Kingsland Road, London E2 8DY
tel 020-7613 6900
email literary@graeae.org
website https://graeae.org/get-involved/new-writing/
Facebook www.facebook.com/graeae
X @graeae

Instagram @graeaetheatrecompany
Joint Ceo & Artistic Director Jenny Sealey OBE, *Joint Ceo & Executive Director* Kevin Walsh, *Literary Manager* Josh Elliott

Small- to mid-scale touring company placing Deaf and disabled artists centre stage. Welcomes scripts from Deaf and disabled writers; see website. Founded 1980.

Headlong Theatre

3rd Floor, 207 Waterloo Road, London SE1 8XD
tel 020-7633 2090
email info@headlong.co.uk
website https://headlong.co.uk
Instagram @headlongtheatre
Artistic Director Holly Race Roughan, *Executive Director* Lisa Maguire, *Literary Manager* Frank Peschier

Mid- to large-scale touring company presenting a provocative mix of new writing, reimagined classics and influential twentieth-century plays.

Hull Truck Theatre Co. Ltd

50 Ferensway, Hull HU2 8LB
tel (01482) 224800
email admin@hulltruck.co.uk
website www.hulltruck.co.uk
X @HullTruck
Artistic Director Mark Babych, *Executive Director* Janthi Mills-Ward

Producing and receiving theatre with a national reputation for new writing. Premieres of new plays, including own commissions, have included works by Tanika Gupta, Amanda Whittington, Mike Kenny, Deborah McAndrew, James Graham and Richard Bean. Founded 1971.

The London Bubble

(Bubble Theatre Company)
5 Elephant Lane, London SE16 4JD
tel 020-7237 4434
email admin@londonbubble.org.uk
website www.londonbubble.org.uk
Instagram @bubbletheatre
Co-Ceos Lucy Bradshaw, Marie Vickers

Aims to provide the artistic direction, skills, environment and resources to create inspirational, inclusive and involving theatre for the local community and beyond. Also runs a number of groups for children and young people as well as an adult drama group.

M6 Theatre Company

Studio Theatre, Hamer C.P. School,
Albert Royds Street, Rochdale, Lancs. OL16 2SU
tel (01706) 355898
email admin@m6theatre.co.uk
website https://m6theatre.co.uk
Facebook www.facebook.com/M6Theatre
Instagram @m6theatre
Artistic Director Gilly Baskeyfield

Touring theatre company specialising in creating and delivering innovative theatre for young audiences. Founded 1977.

New Perspectives Theatre Company

Park Lane Business Centre, Park Lane, Basford, Nottingham NG6 0DW
tel 0115 927 2334
email info@newperspectives.co.uk
website www.newperspectives.co.uk
Facebook www.facebook.com/newperspectivestheatrecompany
X @NPtheatre
Artistic Director Angharad Jones

Touring theatre company, staging a minimum of two productions. The company tours new writing to theatres, arts centres, festivals and rural village halls around the country. Founded 1973.

Paines Plough

Stockroom, 38 Mayton Street, London N7 6QR
tel 020-7240 4533
email office@painesplough.com
website https://painesplough.com/get-involved/invite-us
Facebook www.facebook.com/painesploughHQ
Instagram @painesplough
Joint Artistic Directors Katie Posner, Charlotte Bennett

Commissions and produces new plays by British and Irish playwrights. Tours at least six plays per year nationally for small- and mid-scale theatres. Seeks original plays that engage with the contemporary world and are written in a distinctive voice. Founded 1974.

Proteus Theatre Company

Proteus Creation Space, Council Road, Basingstoke, Hants RG21 3DH
tel (01256) 354541
email info@proteustheatre.com
website www.proteustheatre.com
Instagram @proteustheatre
Artistic Director and Chief Executive Mary Swan

Small-scale touring company particularly committed to new writing and new work, education and community collaborations. Produces up to three touring shows per year plus community projects. Founded 1981.

Red Ladder Theatre Company

3 St Peter's Buildings, York Street, Leeds LS9 8AJ
tel 0113 245 5311
email info@redladder.co.uk
website www.redladder.co.uk
Facebook www.facebook.com/RedLadderTheatre
X @redladder
Instagram @redladdertheatrecompany

Artistic Director Cheryl Martin, *Creative Producer and Programmer* Alice Barber, *Executive Producer* Chris Lloyd

Theatre performances with a dissenting, often working-class voice. National touring of theatre venues and community spaces. Commits to reading at least the first ten pages of every script sent to the company, discussed at monthly creative team meetings (see redladder.co.uk for details), and commissions one or two new plays each year. Runs free theatre-training programmes for over-18s. Founded 1968.

Sphinx Theatre Company

email info@sphinxtheatre.co.uk
website www.sphinxtheatre.co.uk
X @Sphinxtheatre
Artistic Director Sue Parrish

Specialises in writing, directing and developing roles for women. Accepts unsolicited scripts via email. Founded 1974 as The Women's Theatre Group; relaunched as Sphinx Theatre Company 1990.

Talawa Theatre Company

Fairfield Halls, Park Lane, Croydon CR9 1DG
tel 020-7251 6644
email contact@talawa.com
website www.talawa.com
Facebook www.facebook.com/TalawaTheatreCompany
X @TalawaTheatreCo
Instagram @talawatc
Artistic Director & Joint Ceo Michael Buffong, *Executive Director & Joint Ceo* Carolyn ML Forsyth

Champions and platforms Black writers in the UK. Annual programmes for artists include the Introductory Writers' Group, Script Submission Service, Creating Routes, Talawa Young People's Theatre programme for emerging theatre-makers aged 18–25 and Talawa Firsts festival of new work. Founded 1986.

Theatre Centre

1 Town Barn Road, Crawley RH11 7XG
tel (01293) 304377
email admin@theatre-centre.co.uk
website www.theatre-centre.co.uk
Facebook www.facebook.com/TheatreCentreUK
X @TClive
Instagram @theatrecentre
Artistic Director Eleanor Manners, *Executive Director and Ceo* Emma Rees

Young people's theatre company producing plays and workshops which tour nationally across the UK. Productions are staged in schools, arts centres and other venues. Keen to nurture new and established talent, encouraging all writers to consider writing for young audiences. Also runs creative projects and manages writing awards: see website for details. Founded 1953.

Literary agents
Introduction

'Have you got an agent yet?'

It is the first question many would-be writers are asked when they reveal to their trusted few that they have written a book. The question is harmless. For many being asked will be exciting, eager to share their dream agent list like a prized fantasy football team. For others, it may be flippant. Irritating even. It makes it seem so easy.

You may perhaps be nursing the wound of recent rejection. 'I'm trying', you might say, or 'I don't know how to get one'.

Literary agents feel out of reach to many, hidden behind contact forms, submission guidelines and perpetual rejection emails. In this section of the *Yearbook*, we hope to prove that agents are very much open for business and hungry for new talent. We will provide you with the tips and tricks agents want you to know, to make your manuscript as appealing a proposition as possible, turning your submission into a coveted offer of representation.

The articles in this section will contest that literary agencies are overwhelmed with submissions, racking up thousands upon thousands in a single calendar year. Many have introduced ways to combat this with the online submission forms or strict guidelines. This is not to create unnecessary obstacles for authors. It is to help streamline the process for the agents, providing submissions in a way they prefer to tackle and read them. For fiction, the most common guidelines ask for a covering 'letter' (usually pasted into the body of an email), short one- to two-page synopsis and the first three chapters, but it does not mean an agent will read them in that exact order. Some will jump straight to your writing sample, without so much as a glance at your covering letter, not wanting to spoil the surprise of what may lie within the work itself. Others will review your letter, checking your book is compatible with their existing client list and something that matches their current wish list.

Agents will quickly know if you are a good fit for them or not. They will also check if you have followed the submission guidelines. Showing zero respect for the guidelines is a surefire way to be rejected immediately. Agents are looking for individuals who they can work with for many years to come, which involves trust, respect and professionalism. Treat the submission of your manuscript with the same care and attention you would when applying for a new job; it requires time and it requires precision. Agents cannot spend lots of time pouring over individual submissions, so your first impression counts.

Agents want you. Agents need you. They do not make any money unless their clients are writing books and getting publishing deals, so if you have a manuscript you are confident is ready, put your best foot (or should we say 'opening chapters') forward and read on, there are many great agents to discover, one of whom may well be *the* one.

Listings in this section:

- *Literary agents UK and Ireland*, page 452
- *Literary agents overseas*, page 483

What a debut novelist should expect from an agent

Sallyanne Sweeney explains what a literary agent's job entails, and the range of roles that may include as they work closely with, and for, an author to ensure the best possible outcome for a debut novel.

Congratulations! You've beaten the slush pile. You have a literary agent. Dream realised, job done, right?

Signing to an agency is an exciting time both for authors and agents. One of the best parts of my job is taking on a new client – that fizz of anticipation mixed with a slight trepidation, as now the work really begins. You may well be wondering what happens next, and it's okay not to know what to expect at this stage; your agent is there to guide you through everything that lies ahead. You may have been in the position of choosing between multiple offers of representation or you may have found 'the one' on your first try. Either way, it's a good idea to meet your new agent or at least have a phone conversation before accepting their offer. This is your chance to ask about their process and discuss expectations – and if you don't feel comfortable asking these questions, are they the right agent for you?

The debut

When I started working in publishing, the submissions pile tended to tower precariously in the office corner, gathering dust. Since then, the attitude towards debuts has completely shifted (and, thankfully for everyone, electronic submissions have become the norm). Publishers have proven they can launch debuts into the world as major brands, with marketing campaigns to match. The competition between agents to sign talented new authors is fierce, and for good reason: Nielsen BookScan recorded more debut novels in the top 150 fiction titles published in 2020 than in 2019, with sales of the top 10 debutants up 151%.

No two paths to publication are the same and my relationship with clients differs according to their individual needs and styles. Last year, I sold five debut novelists across children's and adult fiction. With one of these authors, the period from their joining the agency to agreeing a publication deal was a matter of weeks, after a contracted round of edits and a swift auction. With another, we had been working together for five years by the time I sold her manuscript, so her 'debut' was actually the second novel I'd 'gone on submission' with. Many debut novels are anything but. Sometimes that first book will be published later; more often than not, it remains in a drawer.

Below are the key elements the agent will bring to your new partnership.

1. The edit

By the time of securing an agent, you will have already revised and honed your manuscript, sometimes over multiple drafts. The bad news: you need to be prepared for several more. The good news: this time, you're not working alone.

An agent will work with you to get the manuscript into as polished a state as possible for submission. This creative back-and-forth is one of the most rewarding (and time-consuming) aspects of my job. It's a vital investment from your agent and one that will hopefully pay off – remember, you have one chance to make a winning first impression on publishers. I start with the 'big picture' or structural edits, homing in on how to get the best out of the story and characters, and identifying what might not be working as well as it could be. The final stage focuses on a line edit and looking for anything that might have been missed in previous drafts. How many rounds come in between completely depends on the individual manuscript.

Your agent should share your vision and ambition for your book and want to work with you to make it the best it can be. You don't have to agree with, or implement, all these edits, but they should serve as a useful guide through your revisions. I'm always happy for an author to find their own solutions to my editorial concerns; the magic is often in the unexpected and I love when an author thinks around the issue and elevates their work in a way I could never have anticipated.

2. The sale

While my client is working on their edits, I'll be progressing things behind the scenes, discussing the manuscript with editors and finessing both the pitch and the submission list.

Passion sells and, in the same way you might rush to tell all your friends and family about a wonderful book you've just read, I want to be 'going on submission' feeling excited about pressing a manuscript into the hands of editors I think will love it. This entails knowing editors' tastes, keeping in constant touch about what publishers are buying and looking for, researching the market, looking at trends, and reading recently published titles. You won't necessarily be aware of all of this going on as you're working on edits, but it's a good idea to keep your agent informed of your progress so that they can plan their timing for submission. Once you've both signed off on the final manuscript, you're ready to go.

Most authors find being on submission tough. You've now done everything you can, and your manuscript is out of your hands. I'd advise trying to keep yourself occupied while waiting on news, whether that's throwing yourself into your next book or scrubbing your skirting boards, as is one client's habit – whatever it takes! It can be a nerve-wracking time for agents, too. At Mulcahy Sweeney Associates we are extremely selective about new authors we take on because we want to maintain our high success rate in sales. An agent's reputation is on the line with each submission and we want editors to respond quickly and positively to every manuscript from our agency, ideally to immediately call and tell us they love it as much as we do (and make us a compelling offer at the same time).

3. The deal

Hopefully, you'll have one or multiple publishers wishing to acquire your debut novel and your agent will guide you through this process. My job is to get the best deal for my author, thinking strategically beyond this first book to look ahead at the author's career as a whole. This means not only orchestrating a competitive auction to secure the optimal advance, royalties and rights, but also matchmaking the author with the right editor and ensuring the commitment of the full publishing team for the book.

When you have accepted a publisher offer, your agent will cast a forensic eye over the finer detail of the contract. This is the less glamorous side of agenting, but no less important – examining the small print (for example, negotiating favourable high discount, reversion and option clauses) and worrying about the minutiae of the deal – so that the author doesn't have to.

4. Rights

Along the way, an agent will be thinking about subsidiary rights – in particular, US, translation and dramatic rights – ensuring that they build momentum after that primary deal. This initial energy surrounding a title can create ripples around the world that lead to a wave of international offers, which in turn maintains that buzz at home. To try to achieve this, I'll regularly discuss forthcoming projects with literary scouts (employed by international publishers to flag up the 'hot' titles in the English language markets) and our co-agents, and pitch to international publishers or production companies myself at the London, Bologna and Frankfurt book fairs.

5. Advocacy

An agent's job doesn't end once you have a publisher on board (or indeed, many publishers around the world). As my clients' foremost champion, I stay involved throughout the whole publication process and beyond, bringing my own ideas and experience and making sure things flow as smoothly as possible. As a debut author, you may not know which concerns are worth raising and which are standard practice. What do you do if you hate your cover or the publisher's proposed title, if no copies have shown up at a scheduled event, or if your signature advance is nowhere to be seen? Your agent can tell you what's acceptable – or not – and advocate on your behalf so that your relationship with the publisher stays purely creative.

6. The long game

What happens when (… whisper it …) things go wrong? If your debut novel doesn't sell, or it does but isn't the success you'd hoped for? Your agent should be there in bad times as well as good, as your creative and business partner throughout your whole career and not just your debut. As great as it is to get immediate offers on a book, I find immense satisfaction in securing a harder-fought deal for an author. Agents get rejected too (and it hurts!), but when I believe in a book I will persist in fighting for it. Sometimes, if I think we just haven't found the right match yet and there hasn't been a common editorial concern flagged in the responses, I'll start a second submission round; one such novel on my list ended up selling at auction and winning awards, after being rejected across the board in its first publisher outing. In some instances, this might first entail a further round of edits with the author, after going through the publisher feedback together. Or, in what's a tougher call, you and your agent might decide that it's time to move on to your next novel … which might be the one that sets the world alight.

What can an author do throughout this whole journey? Keep the faith and keep writing. Most authors with long careers will work with different publishers and editors along the way but usually with the same agent. Your debut should be only the very beginning of this long and successful partnership.

Sallyanne Sweeney started her career at Watson, Little Ltd, where she became a director in 2011. In 2013 she joined Mulcahy Associates, part of the MMBcreative group, and since 2021 has been a director of the renamed Mulcahy Sweeney Associates. Sallyanne was Chair of the Children's Agents' Circle 2014–18. See https://mmbcreative.com/agents/sallyanne-sweeney for more information and follow her on X @sallyanne_s.

Your non-fiction proposal for agents and publishers

Literary agent Rebecca Carter describes the potential impact of a well-crafted book proposal for turning your non-fiction idea into a published book. She explains the essential components and qualities of a book proposal, what agents and publishers are looking for, and the guiding role an agent plays in this key step towards publication.

Dreams and reality

Before getting down to the practicalities, let's start with some dreams ... because all writing, and therefore publishing, begins with the imagination. As a literary agent, I dream of submitting a non-fiction proposal to a publisher in which my short pitch (over the phone or in a covering letter) is so compelling that the editor drops everything to read the proposal as soon as it reaches their inbox. They skip lunch; they cancel meetings; the proposal is so unputdownable, so thrillingly original, so in tune with the zeitgeist that the editor tells their colleagues they simply must read it immediately. The colleagues share the editor's enthusiasm, the acquisitions process is fast-tracked and, by the end of the day (okay, maybe by the next morning), the publisher has put in an offer. Within 24 hours I have a ten-way auction up and running, and by the end of the week the author has the book deal of their dreams.

Such dream-like events do occasionally happen. This is because the majority of non-fiction is sold on short, easy-to-read proposals.[1] The advantage of a proposal is that it can be read in a lunch break and shared rapidly with others. Editors can't read 300-page novels over lunch, and it's easier to persuade their colleagues to prioritise reading 30 pages over 300 pages that will entail giving up more of their evening or weekend (publishers have little time to read submissions during working hours). However, the advantageous brevity of a proposal is also its disadvantage, as it has to achieve a great deal in a few pages. The best proposals make you feel you have already read the future book in miniature, without diminishing your desire to read the whole book as soon as it can be delivered. Many times I have seen a proposal set not just the UK publishing scene alight, but the international one too, securing deals in America and in translation in a matter of days.

Submitting a non-fiction proposal to a literary agent

Writing such a document will inevitably seem daunting. As a literary agent, a crucial part of my time is spent helping the writers I represent find the best structure and voice for their proposals. It is rare for me to submit a proposal to a publisher without carefully workshopping it with the writer, sometimes over a number of weeks or months. By making the process collaborative, and breaking it down into manageable chunks, I try to dispel any fear. I roleplay the reader, stress-testing the proposal both as a potential publisher and a potential book buyer. But if you're not lucky enough to be contacted out of the blue by a literary agent offering proposal-writing help, due to the up-front strength of your

1. My use of the word 'majority' here is pretty unscientific; I have consulted no statistics but have simply gone by experience. Also, I'm referring to a very specific type of non-fiction proposal, i.e. the narrative kind submitted to general trade rather than to academic or specialist publishers.

particular story or expertise, how do you persuade an agent to take on your non-fiction idea in the first place?

As I'm sure every agent contributing to this *Yearbook* will tell you, always consult the *submission criteria* on the agency's website and try to obey these as closely as possible. Most agencies ask for a complete non-fiction proposal, and possibly even a sample chapter or two. Although it's likely the proposal you submit to an agent will change substantially before it is submitted to a publisher, it still needs to be the best you can make it, without the agent's input. There are many (free and not-so-free) resources and courses on proposal-writing out there for you to find. It's worth researching them until you discover the common threads that are most useful to you personally. Even if you've already written all or a substantial part of your book, you might think of reverse-engineering it into a proposal so that it's quicker for the agent to grasp.

After that, spend lots of energy thinking up a great title and subtitle, and writing a *short pitch letter* that describes succinctly and arrestingly: 1) what the book is about; 2) why you are the best person to write it; 3) why it is timely and different from other books in the field; and 4) why you have chosen to approach this particular agent (perhaps because of the other authors they represent, or the type of book they say they are looking for). It may sound harsh, but I tend to know within three or four sentences of a pitch letter whether I'm interested enough in the author to take their email seriously and read their proposal. That's because I can immediately imagine myself pitching the book to publishers. The pitch letter does not need to be flashy and make big claims (it's probably better not to), but it needs to have a compelling confidence, and clarity of tone and purpose. I have taken on some authors who have simply written me a really good letter describing a proposal they would like to write, and asking if they can have a conversation with me about it. But I'm not recommending this strategy; these were mainly authors who had written books before and therefore had a track record. However, this illustrates how important your short pitch letter is. The proposal effectively confirms that you are capable of writing a long work of prose to realise your idea – or at least that you have the ambition and skills to become capable of it.

Why is your idea a book, and what kind of book is it?

There are some questions I ask myself when I'm considering whether to offer representation to a non-fiction writer (and if the proposal indicates that the writer already has a firm grasp of the answers to these, it always inspires confidence):

- Most importantly – will the subject matter sustain a book-length treatment, or would it work better as a long-form essay?
- If it passes the above 'Is it a book?' test, what *kind* of book is it?
- Does the writer understand the type of non-fiction they are trying to write, and the strategies they might use to engage their reader?
- Are the chapters separate, self-contained essays, or does the whole book have a strong narrative propulsion?
- Is it a book that a reader would dip into – or one they would devour from cover to cover?
- If the latter, how does the writer demonstrate that the narrative arc will be exciting?

I often like proposals which start with an extended piece of writing presenting an introductory story that relates to the book. This allows the writer to showcase both their storytelling abilities and the voice in which the book will be written. It immediately draws a reader into the world of the book, and signals to a potential publisher what 'genre' of non-fiction the book aspires to. It is harder to demonstrate these qualities with a more abstract description of what the book will be about. This is not to say that a proposal shouldn't have a more explanatory section that describes the author's vision for it, both in terms of its contents and its place in the bookshop. But you don't necessarily need to put that first. There are no absolute rules for ordering your proposal – you can be creative about it, allowing your material to guide you, whilst also making sure you say everything you need to.

How long should the proposal be? Again, allow the material to guide you – I've submitted proposals of 8,000 words and of 40,000. The *chapter summaries* are really important as they show if you have a strong sense of that crucial narrative arc: too short and they are boring and uninformative; too long and there's a danger the reader feels they are reading the chapter itself, but in a duller form than in the actual book.

Can you *afford* to write the book?

When I look at my non-fiction submissions, I am of course asking myself whether I think I can sell the proposal to a publisher – but I'm also wondering whether the author can realistically afford to write the book. This might seem counterintuitive: surely the agent's role is to get the author an advance that finances them to turn the proposal into a finished manuscript? But there are many factors to be considered here. The advance offered may not end up being that big, and even big advances are paid out in tranches on signature, delivery and publication. The book might require expensive research and illustration permissions, or travel to distant places. Even if the author can do the research from the comfort of their own home, it will require lots of time. Will the author be able to take enough time off from their day job not only to write the book but to promote it? Is their day job one that is complementary to the book project (perhaps giving them a ready-made platform from which to promote the book) or is it one that will impede it? If they don't have a day job, and the book advance isn't large, how are they going to live?

Books are costly to write – in time, money and emotion. Does the author understand this? Agents can only smooth the path so far; authorial doggedness and determination are a prerequisite. The delivery date given in a proposal needs to be realistic. There is nothing more stressful for a non-fiction author than the fear that the contract might be cancelled because of late delivery. After securing a deal for an author, I consider it part of my role to cheer them on and offer regular hydration as they steadily run the marathon of finishing the book.

Reality and dreams – full circle

For an author eager to get on and write a book, proposals can seem a bore. Why do you have to spend time describing your book when you just want to start researching and writing it? I sympathise! Why, I lament to myself, do I have to spend time persuading publishers to publish something when they should be able to see my author's native genius immediately? The truth is that proposals are more than just sales documents. They are the book in microcosm and, as such, they accomplish a lot of the book-writing work in advance. Authors often tell me they are grateful for time spent workshopping a proposal because it means that, when they start writing the book, they are not facing a blank page: they have the scaffolding in place to cling to as they climb. By the way, that doesn't mean writers can't redesign bits of the building if perhaps they discover, in the process of writing, that Chapter Two would be better as Chapter Four. A proposal should never be a prison.

I've mixed a lot of metaphors in this piece, so let's return to the dreams. Yes, I dream of ten-way auctions – but I also dream of the great satisfaction of simply finding a publisher for a book. Maybe the proposal is excellent but only one publisher wants it; that's all it takes for a book to exist and make an impact in the world, and for its ideas to enter someone else's imagination. It is thrilling for an agent to help a writer take their book idea from dream to reality. First, though, you have to write the proposal ...

Rebecca Carter has worked in publishing for 30 years, first as a book scout, then as an editor and publisher, and since 2012 as a literary agent. In January 2023 she set up independently as Rebecca Carter Literary. She represents fiction and non-fiction. In fiction, the focus is on literary fiction, crime and thriller novels. In non-fiction, the range of styles and subjects is wide, from creative non-fiction to more straightforward narrative non-fiction, from innovative history and biography to books on science, nature and the environment, culture and politics. See www.rebeccacarterliterary.com for more information. Follow her on Instagram @rebeccacarterliteraryagent and X @RebeccasBooks.

What a literary agent can do for you

Literary agent Sarah Such explains her role and the reasons why it's worth engaging an agent to represent you as an author in our multimedia world.

I founded Sarah Such Literary Agency in 2007 and my list of authors is wide-ranging and varied. It includes award-winners and bestsellers such as Jeffrey Boakye, Anne Charnock, Antony Johnston, Vina Jackson, internationally renowned artist Liliane Lijn, Caroline Sanderson, Nikhil Singh, Tony White, Mike Wendling as well as debut writers like Sabrina Pace-Humphreys and Hazell Ward. They are representative of my own broad reading tastes and publishing experience in both literary and commercial publishing.

I specifically look for distinct and original voices, and writers who are outstanding in their field. I help shape the long-term careers of authors who are often writing across genre and format. The offer of a publishing deal direct from an enthusiastic editor following a publisher's open submission can look enticing to a new author excited to be published for the first time, while the prospect of paying a literary agent commission for the whole lifetime of a work can be daunting. Typically, however, a good literary agent will negotiate considerably better financial terms for the author.

How a literary agent earns their commission

The reality is that a good literary agent should always earn their commission by adding value to every publishing deal they negotiate; as often as not, that means not only increasing an author's financial terms through bettering advances, nuanced negotiation and deals in numerous territories and formats, but also by ceding far fewer rights.

1. Finding the right publisher for your work

Reputable literary agents work solely by commission, to justify their time they can only take on authors when they feel strongly enough about a work, and when they think there is a good chance of placing a work with a publisher. It's quite possible that I will spend several months working editorially with an author prior to submission, and if the author's book is not placed, there is no payment due to me as agent.

So, from the outset, a literary agent will give serious thought not only to the traditional publishing potential for the work (what revisions are necessary, how to pitch the work, where it lies in the market place and submission to the right editor and publisher) but also to the work's potential in some, if not all, of the following areas: newspaper serial extracts, foreign rights (North America and translation), film, TV, theatre and radio (dramatic, documentary or serialisation), audiobook (one of the fastest growing areas of publishing, served by specialist audiobook publishers, such as W.F. Howes and Bolinda, as well as by traditional publishers), picturisation or graphic novel rights, and electronic version rights and merchandising rights. Whereas ebook rights, i.e. the verbatim text of the work (mirroring the print title) for the sole purpose of reading, are usually part of a traditional publishing contract, electronic version rights – or multimedia rights, as they are sometimes known – allow adaptations that include images, sounds and graphics.

I'll give some examples of what this means in practice. Over and above traditional publishing agreements, I have recently been in discussions about licensing the electronic adaptation rights to a graphic novel, which will allow for an interactive experience with both text and pictures. These are separate from ebook rights or film and television rights. Even in manuscript, some books are clearly filmic or have potential to tell a story in a different format. The film rights to Matthew De Abaitua's seminal artificial intelligence novel *The Red Men* (Snowbooks 2007; shortlisted for the Arthur C. Clarke Award) were acquired by Shynola Films before it was even published, as were virtual reality rights to another author's work before it was submitted. By contrast, the TV rights to cyber-thriller *The Exphoria Code* by Antony Johnston, the first in the Brigitte Sharp series, were acquired in 2020 by Red Planet Pictures three years after publication.

The popularity of podcasts and the listening experience, in addition to the increased global market for audiobooks, has led to publishers such as Audible commissioning Audible Originals (books commissioned specifically for audiobook listeners, that will only appear in print later). An example is the 2022 title *Secrets: What We Hide and Why* by Kit Caless, which was acquired exclusively as an Audible Original in five languages. The print and ebook editions will be published traditionally supported by an existing platform.

Another of my authors, Jeffrey Boakye, co-presents the award-winning BBC Radio 4 series *Add to Playlist* as well as having published both a children's book, Yoto Carnegie Greenaway Medal-longlisted, *Musical Truth* (Faber Children's 2021) and his adult non-fiction book about racism in the education system, *I Heard What You Said* (Picador 2022), an Amazon non-fiction Book of the Year 2022, with the TV rights optioned by Stigma Films. Working with a literary agent has aided Jeffrey in publishing effectively across both adult and children's books, format and genre.

Others are writing original film scripts, videogames and developing podcasts, a large growing area including rights that authors need to be sure not only of safeguarding but agreeing competitive deals. The writing life of an author can be a varied one over the course of a career, and part of the challenge is making good choices to sustain a long career in ever-altering landscapes and markets.

The starting point for any writer, therefore, should be to ensure that they value and take their own work seriously, either by finding a literary agent to advise them or, if unagented, by understanding exactly what they are signing up to, as well as the long-term implications of any publishing contract they enter into. Publishing contracts (in all their many varied forms) have become more complicated in a global market place, and choosing the right publisher for your work – crucially which rights are granted to a publisher – is one of the fundamental reasons why a writer needs an experienced literary agent to navigate increasingly complex waters. A poor publishing deal is frequently a lost opportunity, because it results in valuable rights that could be exploited separately (i.e. earn an author greater remuneration) being tied up as part of the publishing agreement.

An unagented author should think carefully before signing a publishing contract without either seeking advice from the Society of Authors (SoA; see page 746), who have an excellent contract vetting service for members where an author has a publishing contract in-hand, or from publishing industry contract experts such as Contracts People (www.contractspeople.co.uk) who are not literary agents but rather offer a contract service to review, advise and negotiate publishing contracts on a professional fee basis.

2. Negotiating deals

Most successful writers appoint a literary agent because a strong author/literary agent relationship plays a pivotal role for any writer serious about their work and long-term future in an ever-fluctuating industry where there are few guarantees. It is also done because a writer does not have time – nor often the inclination – to negotiate their own publishing deals, never mind numerous publishing deals in foreign languages throughout the world (when a book has a global market).

The impact that the Covid-19 pandemic (as well as Brexit) had on the global print publishing industry should not be underestimated. We saw rapid growth in online book sales and an increase in ebook and audiobook sales, particularly once VAT was removed from the price of ebooks, notwithstanding that post-pandemic, customer loyalty particularly to independent bookshops and buying locally has helped sustain the printed book market. This may well lead to literary agents pushing to negotiate stronger royalty positions for their authors in these areas where sales are increasing dramatically.

Agented contracts typically include clauses that review an author's key terms against prevailing industry standards, for example, so can allow for dramatic changes should they occur. The re-election of President Trump and fluctuation in export tariffs may affect authors' book sales in the US (though it is too early to know how exactly), while the impact of AI (artificial intelligence) to authors and the publishing industry is a matter of immense concern in terms of unauthorised use of authors' work. A good literary agent will help an author navigate challenging market situations and be careful to review any AI policy.

It is not unusual to receive high advance offers from specialist audiobook publishers for the audiobook rights alone. The audiobook market has grown dramatically in foreign markets, and can guarantee immense reach to listeners. The demand for books to option for TV and film, both fiction and non-fiction, has seldom been stronger with the popularity of BBC iPlayer and streaming services such as Apple TV+, Disney+, Netflix and Amazon Prime. Literary agents have close relationships with literary scouts and TV scouts, increasingly a realistic and important source of revenue to writers.

An author needs to be aware of the potential value of their work in different formats. As the publishing industry readjusts, also considering the increasing influence of social media platforms such as TikTok, it may be more necessary than ever to find a good literary agent to place work in a very competitive new publishing landscape. Literary agents spend time working editorially with writers honing their work and submission, and they have close relationships with editors and publishers, know their lists and what they are looking for.

3. Championing you as an author

The literary agent plays a key role in the publishing process by working to give voice to an author's work, initially through the submission process, but then primarily with the author's publisher and to the outside world, including media and readers. A writer can go from having a six-figure publishing deal at the dizzying heights of the publishing experience, with sizeable marketing budgets, to finding their next book is not acquired if sales figures are less than expected. Or, at a more mundane level, an author can find the simplest things – such as their editor leaving before their book is published – can impact their publication and longer-term relationship with a publisher. In the long trajectory of a writer's publishing life, having a literary agent who can champion a writer, voice their concerns with the publisher on their behalf, retrench in times of difficulty and help plan and shape their publishing career is vital for professional longevity.

4. Long-term support

As a minimum, working with a literary agent should result in considerably more favourable and industry-competitive contracts, and therefore substantially more earnings over the lifetime of a work. It ensures greater accountability from UK and/or US publishers, as agents work closely with their authors and their publishers throughout the publication process, and a direct relationship with foreign publishers, for example, where foreign rights are retained – since literary agents broker separate publishing deals with publishers in each separate territory. Some 12 years after the original UK publication, I agreed a repeat deal for the French rights to Vina Jackson's *Eighty Days* six-book series (Orion 2012; 2013). Books can have long lives in many territories. Ensuring that new deals are being brokered, that an author is issued payment promptly, and new opportunities are explored are all part of a literary agent's role. Unsurprisingly in challenging times, there has been a recent surge in demand for romance – and romantasy – and uplifting fiction, and for more experimental crime writing. For example, Unbound's international success with their re-issue of *Cain's Jawbone* has led to them acquiring Tony White's crossword-led novel *Phantom at the Feast*, the follow up to his *The Fountain in the Forest* (Faber 2018).

What an agent provides

Authors say they value Sarah's ...

'... passion and commitment .... I am thrilled by the opportunities and feel protected and supported going forward.'

Jeffrey Boakye, author of *Hold Tight* (Influx Press 2017), *Black, Listed* (Dialogue Books 2019), *Musical Truth* (Faber Children's 2021), *I Heard What You Said* (Picador 2022), *Musical World* (2023) and his *Kofi* series, all published by Faber Children's: *Kofi and the Rap Battle Summer* (2023), *Kofi and the Secret Radio Station* (2024) and *Kofi and the Brand New Vibe* (2025).

'... experience, tenacity, tranquillity, charm and professionalism. She conducts her business with the utmost integrity.'

Kit Caless, author of *Spoon's Carpets: An Appreciation* (Square Peg 2016, Vintage Digital 2016), and *Secrets: What We Hide and Why* (Audible Original 2022), co-publisher of Influx Press and a *Bookseller* Rising Star 2019.

'... help in shaping and developing my career. Thanks to her input I'm now in a situation where I can be a full-time writer, doing what I love, with deals in the UK, around Europe and also in the US. Over the years she has helped me make decisions that are business-smart but that also feel "right" for me.'

Louisa Leaman, author of *The Perfect Dress* (Transworld Digital 2019, Corgi 2020) and *Meant To Be* (Transworld Digital 2020, Corgi 2021)

'... rare combination of skills. Whenever I seek her opinion on my work, I know that she will always take time to give me the honest and thorough answer I need. She also applies the excellent market knowledge and broader cultural savviness, which is so essential to any writer working today.'

Caroline Sanderson, author of *A Rambling Fancy: In the footsteps of Jane Austen* (Cadogan Guides 2006) and *Someone Like Adele* (Omnibus 2012)

'... [role as] guide, philosopher, and friend. Her editorial input has been absolutely invaluable. She has managed always to tread that delicate line between being endlessly supportive and encouraging without giving false expectations, which from the perspective of the author (and authors are a needy bunch) is so vital.'

Heather Cooper, author of *Stealing Roses* (Allison & Busby 2019) and *Arresting Beauty* (Beachy Books Ltd 2023)

'... expertise to pitch to the right editors at the right time and in the most compelling way. When bids were coming in thick and fast and I was losing my head, Sarah was able to calmly talk me through each option so that we could pick the deal that was best for me. Publishing deals are much more complicated than I could have possibly imagined. Having an agent in your corner is so valuable.'

Hazell Ward, debut author of *The Game Is Murder* (Penguin Michael Joseph 2025)

More broadly, a literary agent works with their author to advise, shape and help plan their career. I signed the extraordinarily talented debut novelist Hazell Ward soon after meeting her at the Crime Writers' Association Awards dinner where she won the prestigious Short Story Dagger 2023 for a short story published by Honno Ltd who publish Welsh women writers. Her incredible debut crime novel *The Game Is Murder* (Penguin Michael Joseph 2025) caused a huge flurry with editors and was pre-empted for six figures in the UK within hours of submission, with deadlined pre-empts following fast in North America and numerous territories. These are atypical situations but the speed of the offer process is intense for debut writers without knowledge of the mores of publishing.

Confidential conversations and trust between author and literary agent are crucial to steer major decisions – such as moving from one publisher to another, or advising on shaping a career that traverses different genres and formats including fiction, non-fiction and children's books. It is also telling that publishing industry insiders who are also published writers nearly always appoint literary agents, even though they are wholly familiar with industry practice and publishing contracts. At times in any writer's career there can be concerns about how their work is being promoted or published by their publisher, or whether the publication date is optimum, or when an author needs more input or information; perhaps the author needs to go in a different writing direction altogether. Quite often an author may be successful in one area of publishing but yearns to write in another genre. The ability to navigate such decisions and aspects of the publishing process astutely is something that an author needs to be able to sustain in the longer term; at these times authors can benefit immensely from having a literary agent.

In all writers' careers there will be challenges as well as celebrations. It is the literary agent's role to champion, represent and lobby for the author, to get to the bottom of issues and to help even the most successful author navigate the many troughs and peaks of their publishing career.

Sarah Such founded Sarah Such Literary Agency in 2007. Her previous roles have included Publicity and Marketing Manager at Chatto & Windus, Publicity Director at Penguin Books UK, Commissioning Editor at 4th Estate, Senior Editor at Hodder & Stoughton and Editorial Director at Duckworth. She has been shortlisted for Literary Agent of the Year at the British Book Awards three times. Sarah was a judge for Mslexia's 2017 first novel competition and the London Short Story competition 2018. She was a panellist on the Royal Society of Literature's 2023 Careers in Literature event with King's College London. Follow her on X at @sarahsuch, Bluesky @sarahsuch.bsky.social, Instagram @sarahsuch1 and at https://sarahsuchliteraryagency.tumblr.com.

A day in the life of a literary agent

Charlotte Seymour reveals the many different strands of an agent's day-to-day work. She explains how fulfilling the role of literary matchmaker is and how being an author's champion requires endless perseverance – and makes for a full and often unpredictable day.

One of the best things about working as a literary agent is the variety that fills each and every day and night (I often wake up in the morning surrounded by my Kindle, which I use for reading submissions, a published novel I'm reading for pleasure and probably a cookery book too – always good for browsing if you can't get to sleep ...). It's a common misconception that people who work in publishing spend all day reading; in fact, most of us do all our reading at home in the evenings and at weekends – otherwise, books would simply never make it onto readers' shelves.

So exactly what do agents do in their daily work? Agents come in all shapes and sizes, and have varying interests and ways of working, but an agent is by necessity protean, acting as an author's reader, editor and mentor, their greatest champion and staunchest defender. Here are some of the key elements of my day-to-day work:

1. Discovering authors

Discovering and supporting writing is at the essence of what we do, and as with everything else about the job, we do it in a variety of ways. I always keep an eye on the unsolicited submissions coming in, for although the vast majority are blanket submissions, rather than being targeted to my personal interests, there are gems to be found from time to time. Existing clients and contacts will also often recommend writers to us.

There is an ever-growing number of creative writing courses and writers' festivals which agents are invited to attend, and while it's by no means a requirement of getting published to undertake a costly MA or similar qualification, such courses do offer writers access to industry professionals and vice versa. I try to visit local writers' groups and other book-related events, from launches to readings – you just never know who you might meet.

Finally, when it comes to non-fiction, I will regularly approach someone who is an expert in their field – whether a chef or a scientist – with a view to developing a proposal. So the process of finding new authors to work with is a very proactive one; occasionally, something special will land in your inbox, but, more often than not, you have to go out and find it for yourself!

2. Developing an author's work

Once I've signed up a new author, I will do whatever it takes to get the manuscript or proposal to the stage where I feel it is ready to show to editors. Sometimes it's a case of going through multiple drafts until the work feels as polished as I know how to make it. At other times, and with non-fiction in particular, you can take an idea and working proposal to editors and offer them more input on how they would shape and publish a project.

3. Submitting to editors

When the material is ready, I make an initial round of submissions to those publishing houses I think would be the best fit for the author. In some cases, a book will sell very quickly, in a pre-empt or at auction; in others, it's a question of persisting until you find the one editor who falls for the book. If that book doesn't work, rather than giving up, you think about why it didn't sell and then get working on something new with the author.

At Strand Bookstore in New York, I saw a tote bag for sale bearing the well-known feminist slogan 'Nevertheless she persisted', and I always think this sums up my job. As an agent, you need endless perseverance – and often a bit of luck.

4. Negotiating a publishing deal

When a publisher or several publishers offer for a book, I will negotiate the best possible publishing deal for the author, not just in terms of the money being offered but also the publisher's plans for how to edit, position and promote the book and the author. Sometimes, in an auction, we will choose a publisher who offers slightly less money than another but who is a better overall fit for the author.

5. The run-up to publication, and beyond

Getting a publishing deal for an author is a hugely exciting moment, but it's by no means the end of an agent's job. From the moment we have a signed contract, in the run-up to and following publication, I will be regularly checking in with the publisher to ensure that everything is on track, finding out how many copies are being printed, what coverage the publicist has lined up, how the book is performing, and so on. I will also be working with my colleagues and partner agents who sell foreign rights, and film and TV rights, to bring the work to as many other territories and platforms as possible.

6. Keeping up with editors and the book market

An agent is essentially a literary matchmaker, so we dedicate a lot of time to getting to know the individual editors who acquire in the genres we represent, and to understanding their tastes and interests. For those of us based in London and the UK, we can meet fairly easily at any time of year, and a week will rarely go by when I don't see an editor for coffee or visit their office to find out what they've been buying recently and tell them about the projects I have coming up.

I work with English-language publishers across the world as well, so the London Book Fair every spring is a good opportunity to meet with visiting editors; I will also spend a week in New York each year if I can. From time to time I meet with film and TV scouts and producers who are looking for content to adapt. Whoever I'm seeing and wherever we are, I am constantly championing my authors, even if the book in question won't be ready for another year.

Finally, in addition to keeping in touch with editors, I try to stay on top of the book market by reading reviews every week, making sure to read newly published books as well as those I'm working on and just spending time in bookshops, familiarising myself with what's new on the shelves. I go into a bookshop at least once a week, ostensibly for 'research purposes', though I often leave with something to add to the ever-growing pile!

Highs and lows

One of the best moments as an agent is when you can call an author to let them know you've found them a publisher – and the right publisher for them. After that, the point when it starts to feel more real is when you see the final cover, and of course when you get to hold a print copy for the first time. There are low moments too: brilliant books that you just can't sell, ideas that never quite come to fruition, disappointing sales and dashed expectations. For every peak there's usually a trough, and as an agent you have to weather the storms with and for your authors, as well as celebrating the successes.

The very unpredictability of the job is also one of the greatest joys: some books are instant hits and others are slow burners; reviews can be amazing and sales minuscule; 30 publishers might turn down a book and it goes on to win prizes. You never know quite what's around the corner – and it's thrilling.

A typical day ...

Some days, I'll be out and about quite a bit, meeting with editors and/or authors, and if I'm reading or editing, I usually work from home, but when I'm in the office, a typical day might go something like this:

Morning

• I get to work and answer any emails that have come in overnight. A publisher has sent a draft contract for a book they have acquired from me, so I will check that it accurately reflects what we've agreed and mark any amendments I want to make before sending back to the publisher.
• If I'm sending a new book out on submission, I'll check in with editors first to share the pitch if we haven't already spoken about it, or not recently.
• I might also check in with any editors who are considering other projects I have out on submission and set a deadline for offers on a book for which I've received a first bid.

Afternoon

• After lunch, I have a call with an author to discuss progress on their latest book, and then another call with our Film and TV agent to catch up on the projects she is representing for us.
• If I have time, towards the end of the day, I usually look at any unsolicited submissions that have come in by email. It's very rare that I will call in a full manuscript, but I have taken on several wonderful authors this way, and am always looking for more.

Evening

• Some weeks, my colleagues and I will have a book launch (or two) to attend; otherwise, it's a rare evening I won't be reading something!

Charlotte Seymour is a literary agent at Johnson & Alcock. She previously worked as an agent at Andrew Nurnberg Associates and as a literary scout at Eccles Fisher Associates. She was Secretary of the Association of Authors' Agents 2019–21 and a *Bookseller* Rising Star 2021.

This article first appeared on the author Sarah Pearse's website, https://sarahpearse.co.uk. Sarah's debut novel, *The Sanatorium*, was published in 2021, and became a No. 1 *Sunday Times* and a *New York Times* bestseller. Charlotte is her agent.

Going your own way: Do you need an agent?

While finding an agent is often seen as a key part of getting published, it's not the only way for authors to move forward. Emma Denny explains how being unagented has worked for her to date.

When people ask me for writing advice, I'm ready to go. I've got lists. I've got lists of lists. Want to know some practical tips for keeping track of notes or how to get into a routine? I've got you … most of the time.

But when people ask me about the business of writing – and more specifically, the business of publishing – I suddenly become a lot less useful. A good resource for accurate medieval names? I'm your guy. How to find an agent? Maybe not.

I'm a published author of two books with a third on the way, and I don't have an agent. As far as I can tell, this is a pretty unique situation to be in; at least it is at the time of writing this in 2024. When it comes to what is, for many people, the first step on their publishing journeys, I'm entirely inexperienced.

I don't have an agent, or been in the querying trenches. So how did I get here?

How I got a contract without an agent

The contract for my first novel, *One Night in Hartswood*, was the prize for a competition hosted by Mills & Boon and the Romantic Novelists' Association. The competition, called Romance Includes Everyone, was designed to champion queer romance. I submitted *Hartswood*, and – to my utter surprise – won. The prize, which had initially been for an ebook contract, was extended to cover hardback, paperback and audiobook. Everything started happening at once. I had no agent, no publishing connections, not even a sizable following of like-minded writers on X. It was a very surreal place to start one's writing career, especially when so much today seems to rest on having 20k+ followers.

It was part-way through the editing process for *Hartswood* that I mentioned to my editor that I had plotted two more books in the *Hartswood* series, taking the traditional romance route of giving key secondary characters their own stories. She fist-pumped the air, and a few months later I was contracted to write the next two books in the series.

My second book, *All The Painted Stars*, hit the shelves across the UK in March 2024. *Untitled Book Three* is currently in progress. And after that? That's where I'm unsure: I just don't know.

I've not had to contemplate getting an agent until now, when the end of my contract is in sight and I'm having to decide what happens next. For me, the agent question is somewhat of a moot point. To find an agent, I need a new, unpublished manuscript – something that doesn't exist yet. But when it comes to my fourth book, I'll need to start thinking more seriously about the matter.

What does your agent do?

An agent wears a lot of different hats, and no two authors will have exactly the same experience with their agent. For many people, an agent is employed largely to find and then vet contracts, being a champion for your manuscript. They're the person who finds you a publisher and, if you're lucky, encourages different publishers to battle it out against each other to land a deal with you. Not all publishers require you to have an agent, but a lot do: the Big Five publishing houses, for example, only take submissions via an agent. If your goal is to aim for one of them, then you may need an agent no matter what.

Some agents act more editorially, helping you with idea-generation and plot difficulties. They may even be your book's first professional editor. They can also help with structural advice, such as whether your book should be split into a series, or if it's the right length and style for the genre and market.

Your agent, in most cases, should be your book's main supporter. They're its biggest fan, and they want it to succeed.

Getting published without an agent

There are routes to publication which don't require you to have an agent. Many indie publishers accept unagented submissions, for example, as do some imprints like Mills & Boon.

Some of my best advice is to always keep an eye out for opportunities. Without an agent, the onus of finding them now falls on you. I heard about the Mills & Boon competition when they posted about it on their socials, and would never have known about it were I not following them.

There are quite literally thousands of indie publishers out there, and today most of them will have a presence on some form of social media. Find them, follow them, and turn on alerts: if they're opening submissions, they'll post about it. Find ones who publish books in the same genre as yours, and get ready to submit when the time comes.

Doing this also means you need to be ready to go at the drop of a hat. If a publisher's submission window opens for a month but your manuscript is only three pages long, you're going to be in trouble. Believe me: being in a position where you need to get an unfinished manuscript sent to a publisher in a limited window of time is a unique kind of hell. Ask me how I know.

Let's say you've followed the advice above, and you've managed to find a publisher without an agent. What next?

If you're based in the UK, I cannot overemphasize how much I recommend you join the Society of Authors. They offer truly invaluable advice to all their members, and – most importantly – you can contact them directly and their legal team will look over any contracts you've been given and advise you on how they would proceed. Aside from finding you that much-sought-after publishing contract, an agent ensures you're getting the best deal possible from it, detangling the dense legalese that many authors may not be familiar with. If you don't have an agent, having an expert provide you with legal counsel is a must.

This, in my experience, is the most vital step to take when you don't have an agent. Publishing contracts can be complicated if you're unfamiliar with them, and it's always worth those extra days to get yours checked out by a professional. Your publisher should be used to this, and should not try to prevent you seeking an independent legal opinion. If they do, then you've got a bigger problem, and it might be time to reassess your relationship with that publisher.

It's also important to prepare to be an advocate for yourself. Agents often act as an intermediary between yourself and your publisher, and without one you have to be prepared to be assertive in what you want and need for your book. If you're anything like me, you might struggle with this, but it's a hurdle you'll need to get over. Don't assume that you can't push back against your publisher if something isn't right or isn't achievable. At the end of the day, after all, you both want the same thing: a successful book that sells well.

Do you need an agent?

It's a complicated question, and only you can answer. I've spoken to friends, fellow writers, even sought legal advice, and the general answer is always the same: it's up to you, but you don't need one. If you've already got a contract, then a great deal of the agent's job is already done, and after signing that contract there's not a lot they can do for you. It's not all about money, but an agent does take a percentage of your royalties, and it's something to keep in mind if you're deciding whether or not you need to find one.

Everyone's journey in publishing is different, and many of us take unusual or less traditional routes. There is room in publishing – whether through entering a competition, like I did, or submitting to publishers who accept unagented authors – to make it on your own. It can be a tempting prospect, especially when seeing first-hand the trials and pains of those in the querying trenches.

There's a few reasons why you may choose not to find an agent. Maybe you want to retain full control over your journey, or already have the legal experience you need to navigate contract negotiations. You might not want to give up a percentage of your royalties. You might be aiming for indie publishers, who are less likely to require an agent in the first place. For me, the choice was never one I made actively: I saw a competition and I entered it. The question of finding an agent never factored into it, and most likely wouldn't have for a long time.

Would I do it differently?

Not having an agent has meant there's a lot of work I've had to do myself. I've had to push back on certain clauses in my contract, which can be difficult if you've not got a lot of experience advocating for yourself so readily. I've spent a lot of time waiting for legal advice from third parties, or encountering situations where I've sat back and thought 'would this whole thing be easier if I had an agent?'.

Because of my unique circumstances, the issue of finding an agent was one I hadn't even contemplated before I'd already signed a contract. Entering the Mills & Boon competition was a risk, one that I wouldn't usually take. Becoming a finalist was unexpected, and it forced me to finish my manuscript and get my things in order. There was no waiting around for inspiration to strike, no wringing my hands over the best notebook to outline in. It had to happen, and it had to happen fast. In truth, I suspect that getting to the stage where I had a completed manuscript to shop to agents would have taken me a small age without the looming threat of a deadline. It would have taken years.

Now I've been published, and am reaching the final stage of my contract, it's time for me to really sit down and think about what happens next. And honestly, what happens next is a nice, long holiday.

The question of finding an agent is one which, I think, is going to have to wait until manuscript number four is ready to roll.

Emma Denny writes queer historical romance fiction. The winner of the 2021 Mills & Boon Romance Includes Everyone competition, she is the author of *One Night in Hartswood* (2023) and *All the Painted Stars* (2024). Follow her on Instagram @emmadennywrites.

What does a good submission look like?

Finding an agent is top of many new writers' wish lists, but how might an agent find *them*? Read on to find out what leading literary agent Eve White is looking for.

My writers

I started Eve White Literary Agency 21 years ago and have loved every minute of it. One of the first things I learned was the importance of getting my details into the *Writers' & Artists' Yearbook* so that writers would be able to find me.

Andy Stanton was one of the very early clients who found me this way. In those days, writers had to print out their full manuscripts and post them to agents. The cost meant that they usually wrote to one agent at a time. Luckily for me, he got fed up after working through the A listings to no avail, and decided to turn to the Zs and work backwards. He came across me! I couldn't understand why he hadn't been snapped up – *You're a Bad Man, Mr Gum* was the funniest book I'd ever read. Andy has sold millions worldwide. He was asked to write the foreword to an edition of the *Yearbook* in which he mentioned how it changed his life. I'd like to add, 'Mine too, Andy!'

Not long after that, Rae Earl submitted her adult non-fiction *My Mad Fat Diary*, which also made me laugh out loud. We managed to get it published by Hodder and sold it to Channel 4. It's still streaming twelve years on.

Looking for clients

Once I had a roster of successful writers, I didn't have time to read submissions myself. In my view, you just can't put the search for new talent higher on your to-do list than looking after your current clients. So, I decided to search for freelance readers. I approached editors who had recently left publishing houses to go freelance and then created a website which clearly set out how to approach the agency with a submission. I made sure that the *Yearbook* directed people to this.

We still have three freelancers reading fiction, non-fiction and children's book submissions. Agents Ludo Cinelli, Steven Evans and I work closely with them, and they understand our tastes. For example, my fiction reader, Nicky Marcus, passed me three chapters of Yvvette Edwards's *A Cupboard Full of Coats*, having found it among a huge pile of submissions. We quickly requested the full manuscript, and I offered Yvvette representation. Nicky and I worked together on editing the novel, as we do with all our books to give writers the best possible chance of receiving an offer from a publisher. One year later, Yvvette was published by Oneworld and subsequently longlisted for The Booker Prize.

Submitting to agents

We've found so much wonderful talent in this way.

Now super successful, Ruth Warburton's first novel was for young adults and her experience looking for an agent taught her that you must write, rewrite and keep editing until your book is as good as it can possibly be. She joined a writers' group to get feedback and, as a result of that, what she eventually sent me was something that I couldn't put down.

Ruth went to the website as advised, took note of our guidelines and followed them. My reader passed the chapters on to me; I loved them and requested the full manuscript from Ruth. We then met, got on really well and she decided to accept my offer of representation. It was all very speedy.

Following five YA novels, published by Hodder Children's Books, Ruth has written ten thrillers under her pen name, Ruth Ware. These are published by Simon & Schuster in English and by 42 publishers in translation. Each novel has been a *New York Times* bestseller and over 10 million copies have been sold worldwide. Many of her books are under option with film and TV companies: a movie of *The Woman in Cabin 10* has now been made by Netflix starring Keira Knightley.

Ruth says: 'I think demonstrating your professionalism and attention to detail up front is an important part of the submission process, and following a given agent's procedures helps to show that. You'll hopefully be meeting deadlines and following publisher processes for the rest of your working life, after all. You might as well start off on the right foot!'

The competition

It is probably not helpful to dwell too much on the fact that we – and, we presume, other agencies – receive around 10,000 submissions a year. What you do need to remember, though, is that yours needs to stand out. So how do you do that?

First, when you make contact with an agent, tell them why you chose them. It might be that you like some of their clients' books, that you have read about their tastes or seen their wish list, or that you think there's a gap on their list which your work fills perfectly. Whatever the reason, show you have thought about your approach and are serious about finding representation and getting published. We advise a tailored approach where you reach out to a handful of agents in the first instance; don't send a generic email bcc'ing all agents on your list. If you want an agent to be enthusiastic about your submission, it helps to be polite and specific in your approach.

Given the mountain of submissions we receive, help agents to help you by being as clear and concise as possible and, as Ruth says, follow the guidelines. Each agency will have its own way of handling submissions, so make sure you read and understand them before you submit. For fiction, we ask for your first three chapters and a page-long synopsis in a single attachment. For non-fiction, however, we ask for a proposal, which includes some sample writing, and (where relevant) a CV. Let your writing do the work: stick to clear, easy-to-follow formatting and a reliable font such as Times New Roman (12pt).

The cover letter (or email)

The covering letter or email is a very important part of any submission. This is where you can pitch your novel, provide some context, show you are serious about writing and finding representation, and outline why you think you and the agent/agency would be a good fit. As readers, we are looking for something that leaps out at us: the subject matter, the promise of a fresh, distinct narrative voice, or – probably more than anything at this stage – a strong, premise with a great hook that will make us want to dive straight into your opening chapters. So, start with a short pitch: one or two enticing sentences that convey the question/dilemma/conflict at the heart of your story. It lets us know that you understand the essential ingredients that go into making a good story and that you've got a tight grasp on your own. Think along these lines: my protagonist (who you might describe using their primary traits, flaws and role in the story) has this goal/key want/need. But, when this thing happens, they must take this action before/because/otherwise this bad thing will happen.

Then briefly state the word count and genre of your novel and tell us why you're writing to us specifically. Now is your time to concisely show you've done your research and therefore understand why we might be the right agents for you. You might appreciate, say, the boutique, hands-on nature of our agency, or how editorial we are. Maybe we've got a track record in representing debut writers or perhaps we represent several writers of your particular genre.

Now you can elaborate a little more on the novel. Provide a couple more sentences describing the story and a few key themes that take you neatly into two or (max) three comparison titles. Comparison titles are a great way to let us know that you've got an awareness of the market and the kind of books yours might sit alongside. More than that, though, they act as a bit of a shortcut for us; a flavour of what we're about to dive into. Feel free to use film or TV series titles but again, keep it short: you don't need to go into too much detail about the plot at this stage, as it will be covered in your synopsis.

End with a few lines about yourself. You do not need to provide a detailed biography at this stage, but do mention anything that is relevant to the book and any writing or publishing experience you have had. For instance, you might tell us that you've been shortlisted in a writing competition or completed a writing course, or that you're a member of a writing group. If you can add anything about the authenticity you bring to this story – why only you could have written this book – make that front and centre. And if you have any accessibility requirements that you wish to make the agent aware of, do flag them here.

Synopsis

The synopsis is a technical document. We usually turn to it last, when something about the writing has piqued our interest, so that we can check where the story is going, that there's a logic to it and that the writer has a keen understanding of how to craft a plot.

The synopsis does not need to be written beautifully, but it does need to be easy to understand. You should be able to tell your story in a concise way. If you are finding that you can't, it might be that you aren't quite ready to submit. Perhaps there is an issue with your story or its structure, and you need to continue editing. If the plot outline is vague, or you find you are focusing on minutiae, backstory, character traits or themes, then it could be a sign that you haven't yet worked out the heart of your story. It is important to highlight the main characters only (having their names in capitals helps) and the plot should feel consequential, not sequential; that is, the narrative should read as if it's building, that events are leading on from one another with whys and wherefores. It shouldn't read like a list of events.

Kick things off with the hook from your cover letter and then cover the obvious: where and when is it set? Who's telling the story? Who's the protagonist? Who or what is the antagonist? What is your protagonist's conflict or dilemma? Who are the other key characters and why are they there? What are the other sources of conflict or obstacles that arise? What are the key turning points? What's the climax? How does it all get resolved? How does the protagonist (and possibly the other key characters) change? What are the key themes?

Your excerpt

Send only the amount of sample writing requested by the agent you are submitting to and, unless otherwise stated, your excerpt must be your opening chapters. You may be tempted to send later chapters because you think they're your best; if this is the case, and you feel your opening chapters aren't strong enough, it is likely that they need to be edited, reworked or perhaps even cut. We read as if we're buyers in a bookshop, picking up a book with an interesting cover and turning to the first page; your opening needs to stop us from putting the book down. When an agent sends a submission to a publisher, their interest needs to be grabbed from the very beginning.

We cannot teach you how to write or what to write about, but below are some tips on how to give your opening the best possible chance of standing out:

- Trust the reader and throw us straight into the action: no need for lengthy exposition. Introduce us to your character/s with some sort of conflict. That doesn't mean big and dramatic, necessarily; in fact, too much too soon can be off-putting. The conflict might derive from some sort of antagonistic force, whether it is something as globally catastrophic as a meteorite or as local as a bullying boss. Or it might take the form of an internal dilemma, like whether to leave a marriage.
- From the first page, we look for a distinct narrative voice: that's difficult to define, but we know it when we see it. It's about tone, wit, how succinct, lyrical or descriptive you are, the rhythm of your writing, how, when, why you elicit an emotional response, the nature of that response, the way you access the thoughts of your characters, your sentence structure, grammar, word choice, when and how you use metaphor and simile, whether you use colloquialisms, how you punctuate, whether you use short or long sentences, paragraphs, scenes, chapters, how much dialogue you use and how you use it. It's basically the way you write – everything that makes you unique as a writer.
- We appreciate clarity.

Also, help us focus on who and what is important:

- Ensure any description is essential. This will depend on the story you are telling and the way you are telling it, but think: is the thing, person or story you are describing moving the plot forward or giving the reader a new perspective on a character or event? If we're never going to encounter this person or thing again and they have no role in the plot, then only a short description is necessary. Use original or more unusual descriptions or, if you are describing someone with a well-used description such as 'emerald-green eyes', make sure there's a reason for it.
- Don't introduce us to too many characters too quickly. We don't have to meet the protagonist in the first scene, but it should be pretty early, otherwise we're left wondering who's worthy of our attention.
- Have a clear, consistent point of view (POV). Avoid changing POV too quickly, before we've managed to tune into whoever we're with. If you are going to have more than one perspective, keep them to separate sections or chapters.
- Give us a sense of momentum. There's got to be something driving the narrative forward; a dynamism that keeps us turning the page. The character's world and/or POV might be captivating, but we also need the feeling that something is going to happen.
- Avoid too much sex, swearing or violence too soon. It can come over as the author just looking for shock value.

• We won't stop reading if we see the odd typo, but do consider getting someone to proofread your submission. However many times you read it, you're bound to miss some errors in your own work.

Good luck

My favourite bit of this job is calling a new client to tell them that they will be published. I hope that, after all your hard work, this will happen for you.

Eve White is the founder of the Eve White Literary Agency, which represents writers of adult fiction and non-fiction as well as children's authors. Its clients include Ruth Ware, James Norbury and Andy Stanton. Find out more at https://evewhite.co.uk.

Querying an agent: top tips about submission

Catherine Cho offers valuable advice for new authors on the submission process, with five essential tips on how to prepare and submit the perfect query package for your book.

I have a lot of faith in the submissions process. It is how I've found nearly all of my authors – writers who just happened to send me a query email along with their first few chapters. But, as much as I want to read my submissions (or 'queries', as we say in the USA), it is often the last thing on my to-do list. Like most agents, my working day is focused on my clients, and so I read submissions in my free time – in the early morning hours, on the tube between meetings or in the evenings after my children have gone to bed. I know that the querying process can be incredibly frustrating and opaque. It's not a perfect process, but what I think is helpful to know is that I want to find a manuscript; I want to say yes.

It's common to hear about the sheer number of queries an agent receives, and it's true. I'm continually amazed by the number of people who write books. I receive over 100 queries a week, and there are agents who receive many more than this. I share this not to be discouraging but as a reminder that when you're preparing your query, you want to make sure that your work and query package is strong. I truly believe that if your book is compelling, then ultimately, it will find a home.

I do know what it's like to be on the other side of the screen. I'd always thought of myself as an agent first – writing was something of an accident. I wrote a memoir that was published in 2020; it was about my experience of postpartum psychosis after the birth of my son. I will never forget how vulnerable I felt putting so much of myself into a piece of work. As an agent, I try to remember that behind every submission, there is a story. I share these tips in the hope that it will give some insight into the querying (submission) process. It's a dream for me to fall in love with something I'm reading – and I feel that sense of possibility every time I open my submissions inbox.

1. Edit again ... and again

My first tip has to be about revision. The most important thing will always be the quality of the work. When you have finished your book, there is often a compulsion to send it out to agents straight away. This is completely natural; you've finished your work and you want someone to read it. However, it's important to resist this feeling and give yourself the space to read your book again, and revise. *Never* send out a first draft. A first impression is the most important one, and you'll need time and space away from your project to be able to read it with perspective. If you can, set the book away for a month or two, and then re-read it again. Edit it again.

The querying process is not the place to receive feedback. Sometimes we hear writers say that they will send out a project to see what agents will say about it, but this can be a very discouraging approach. It's a terrible feeling to send out a project that you know is probably not ready and, most of the time, agents will not give feedback. I often have writers ask me if I can give editorial advice, but I resist doing this unless I have a clear idea of what I think would improve the book. Firstly because it is subjective, but also because, if I'm not able to give a considered and thoughtful response to a manuscript, I don't think it's helpful for me to offer a quick reaction.

Remember that there will always be more edits after signing with an agent, and even more after receiving a publication offer. The best thing you can do for yourself ahead of the querying process is to make your manuscript as strong as it can be, so you feel confident that you're presenting your best work. When I finished my first draft, I was really excited to share it because I couldn't believe I'd finished. I wanted to share it with an agent, but I fought that urge and set it aside for several weeks. When I opened it again, I realised it wasn't ready, and so I redrafted. I think the version I eventually sent to my agent was my eleventh or twelfth draft. I would go on to do another three drafts with my agent, ones that completely took my book apart. Each time I felt I'd gone the furthest I could go – but we kept pushing, and the book kept getting better.

2. Make your opening page the best

The opening sentences of a book are so important in the querying process. I remember being at a conference panel and hearing an agent say that they often stopped reading at the first sentence – which is a terrifying thing to hear, but I think it illustrates how important it is. The strongest opening page or sentence is one that is immediate and distinctive.

As an agent, I remember reading the openings of my clients' books. I'm usually immediately drawn in by the first few lines, and if I don't want to stop reading, then I know that it's something for me. There are many resources about opening pages and scenes, but what is probably most helpful is to look at your favourite books and read their opening paragraphs. Imagine that you're browsing in a bookshop, you open a book that seems intriguing – what are you looking for from those first lines? What will draw you in?

I know that coming up with an opening is very difficult. As a writer, it's something I struggled with. The opening of my book changed multiple times. While I always knew how I wanted my book to be structured, I couldn't figure out the best place to *begin*. Initially I started with what I thought was the most exciting part of the memoir, as a kind of prologue, and then I changed it to something that was slower paced. Each time, it didn't feel quite right. My agent was the one who suggested moving a section from the mid-point of the book to the opening. She was right. This opening helped the book when it was on submission to editors, and it remained in place, word for word, when published.

3. Research

Research is your best friend when it comes to the querying process. Reading this *Yearbook* is already a great first step. It will put you ahead of many of the submissions we receive. It's important to research the agents you choose to submit to. There is no point in sending your picture book to an agent who doesn't represent children's books, or in sending a romantic comedy to an agent who specialises in thrillers.

An agent's taste is subjective (the entire industry is subjective) and so the goal is to find an agent who is looking for the book you've written. And these days, it's so easy to find out what an agent wants – most of us have a social media profile and manuscript wish lists that outline what we're looking for. I would also recommend looking at the acknowledgements section of your favourite authors, or of authors you feel write in the same space that you do, to see who represents them, because that can be a good indicator of someone who is on the lookout for a book like yours.

4. Perfect your query letter

Aside from the material itself, the query letter is the most important part of your submission. There are many opinions on best practices, but I would say the most important thing is that it should be clear and concise. On reading your letter I should have a clear understanding of what your book is and what it's about. That's why many agents will ask for a logline, which is a film industry term, but it's to say what your book is about in one or two sentences. People often tend to put *everything* into their first book, and so the narrative can become muddled or lacks a clear sense of narrative urgency.

So think: Do you know who your readership is? Do you know what books are similar to your own? I truly believe that a writer must also be a reader – it is a red flag for me when a writer says in a submission that they've never read anything like their own work before. There will always be some element of it you can find out there in the marketplace. If someone asks you, 'So, what's your book about?', see if you can describe it concisely: 'It's a book about X'. If you find yourself describing a lot of events that happen in the book: 'Well, this is a book where this happens, and then this happens, and it's about this …', perhaps it doesn't have the narrative drive you need to draw in a reader. This is true for non-fiction, memoir, as well as novels – a compelling book is one that is focused.

There was only one agent I had in mind to represent my book. Admittedly, I had a clear advantage because she was my colleague, so I didn't have to follow the traditional query process. However, I did have to convince her that I knew exactly what my book was about – it was one of the first things she asked me. It wasn't enough that it was a memoir about a difficult experience; I told her that, at the heart of it, my book was about identity and what happens when your identity is blown apart – how do you put yourself back together?

Read as many sample query letters as you can; many authors have generously shared theirs online as examples. When you're writing your query letter, first put as much as you can in, and then cut it down as much as possible. Give your draft letter to someone who has no idea what your book is about and then check: do they have an immediate understanding of what your book is about? I don't think any agent expects a polished sales document, but remember – the query letter is your way of presenting your work. There is a strong correlation between a well-crafted query letter and a compelling manuscript.

5. Focus on the writing process

It can sometimes feel like querying/submission is the most important thing, and that if you have an agent, that's everything. But, actually, signing with an agent is just the first step; finding an editor, finding a readership … there are many more steps in the publishing journey. I recommend that you focus on the process, focus on the writing. It is the best way to get a book published, if that is the goal, but publishing a book isn't the most effective end goal in itself. Storytelling is a craft, and the quality many successful authors share is that they write not to get published, but because they *have* to write. The writing is something that is completely in your control. And the more you write, the better you'll become.

Catherine Cho is a literary agent and the founder of Paper Literary which she founded in Spring 2021. After a background in law and public affairs, she started her publishing career in New York before moving to London. She has sold six- and seven-figure deals in the US and UK. Catherine is the author of *Inferno: A Memoir of Motherhood and Madness* (Bloomsbury Circus 2020), which was shortlisted for the *Sunday Times* Young Writer of the Year Award. For more information see www.paperliterary.com.

Literary agents UK and Ireland

The *Writers' & Artists' Yearbook*, along with the Association of Authors' Agents and the Society of Authors, do not recommend any literary agent who asks potential clients for a fee prior to reading a manuscript. We advise you to treat any such request with caution and to let us know if that agent appears in the listings below. It is assumed that all agents listed do *not* charge a 'reading fee'. Agents may charge additional costs later in the process but these should only arise once a book has been accepted by a publisher and the author is earning an income. We urge authors to make the distinction between upfront and additional charges. Authors should also check agents' websites before making an enquiry and should familiarise themselves with submission guidelines, agent preferences and manuscript formatting.

The country code for phoning UK offices from overseas is +44.

NOTE: Where an agency is named after a specific agent, they are listed in alphabetical order by surname, i.e. David Higham Associates can be found under H.

*Member of the Association of Authors' Agents
†Member of the Personal Managers' Association
sae = self-addressed envelope

A for Authors

email enquiries@aforauthors.co.uk
website https://aforauthors.co.uk
Facebook www.facebook.com/aforauthors
Agents Annette Crossland, Kirstie Long, *Associate Agent* Caroline Raeburn

Fiction only: commercial and literary, crime, thriller and historical. Email submissions only. Include a covering letter, brief synopsis, author bio and first three chapters as an attachment.

Authors include Awais Khan, A.A. Chaudhuri, Faiqa Mansab, Linda Stratmann, Shirin Amani Azari, N.N. Jehangir, Susie Green, Frank Britt, Ian Hawthorne, Rob Barrow, Lyndsay Russell, Chris Musto, Catherine Balavage, J.J. Thomas, Alan Gorevan. *Founded* 2014.

The Accidental Agency

email clare.gristtaylor@accidentalagency.co.uk
website www.accidentalagency.co.uk
Contact Clare Grist Taylor

Agency specialising in non-fiction for adults. Represents memoir, nature writing, history, current affairs, popular science and psychology, lifestyle and wellbeing, smart thinking, business/personal-professional development and humour/gift. *Commission* Home 15%, overseas 20%, film/TV 20%. Submissions should be made via the website. No fiction, academic texts, poetry or children's books.

Authors include Graham Allcott, Ellen Bradley, Roger Morgan-Grenville, Simon Morley, Diane Watt, Jessica Joelle Alexander, Sue Unerman, Kathryn Jacob, Amanda Goodall, Clare Paterson, Mark Edwards, Kate Kelland, Sara Ward, Laura Saetveit Miles. *Founded* 2019.

Aevitas Creative Management UK*

43 Great Ormond Street, London WC1N 3HZ
email ukenquiries@aevitascreative.com
website www.aevitascreative.com/acm-uk
X @AevitasUK
Ceo & Agent Toby Mundy, *Agents* Charlie Brotherstone, Charlie Viney, Clara Foster, Emily Sweet, Jack Ramm, Julie Finidori, Maria Cardona Serra, Morwenna Loughman, Valeria Huerta, Trevor Dolby

A management company that represents writers, speakers and brands. Wide range of genres represented including history, science, biography, autobiography, politics and current affairs, literary fiction, crime, thrillers and illustrated books. *Commission* Home 15%, USA/translation 20%. Submissions via website. No plays or poetry.

Clients include Stephen Bush, Clive Myrie, Daniel Finkelstein, Hannah Barnes, Marianna Spring, Chris Miller, George the Poet, the estate of A.A. Gill. *Founded* 2019.

The Agency (London)*

24 Pottery Lane, London W11 4LZ
tel 020-7727 1346
email childrensbooksubmissions@theagency.co.uk
website https://theagency.co.uk/childrens-books/childrens-home
X @TheAgencyBooks
Instagram @theagencybooks, @theagencyldn_

Represents picture books, including novelty books, fiction for all ages including YA fiction and series fiction. Works in conjunction with overseas agents. Also represents screenwriters, directors, playwrights and composers. *Commission* Home 15%, overseas 20%. Submission guidelines on website. *Founded* 1995.

Aitken Alexander Associates*

291 Gray's Inn Road, London WC1X 8QJ
tel 020-7373 8672
email reception@aitkenalexander.co.uk
website www.aitkenalexander.co.uk
Instagram @AitkenAlexander
Directors & Agents Clare Alexander, Lesley Thorne, Lisa Baker, Chris Wellbelove, Emma Paterson, *Agents* Harriet Moore, Monica MacSwan, *Film/TV/Stage Rights* Lesley Thorne, Alice de Abaitua

Fiction and non-fiction. *Commission* Home 15%, USA/translation 20%, film/TV 15%. Email submissions@aitkenalexander.co.uk with preliminary letter that includes a half-page synopsis and first three chapters or 50 pages. No plays. *Founded* 1976.

AMP Literary

email anna@ampliterary.co.uk
website www.ampliterary.co.uk
Bluesky @annapallai.bsky.social
Instagram @ampliterary
Founder Anna Pallai

Specialises in commercial non-fiction with a focus on bold female voices. With strong connections across various media platforms, from digital to TV, AMP develops ideas beyond print to maximise exposure. *Commission* Home 15%, USA 20%. Submissions to submissions@ampliterary.co.uk. Include a synopsis and at least three chapters.

Authors include Natasha Devon, Anita Mangan, Annalisa Barbieri, Nadine White, Nichi Hodgson, Ellen Jones. *Founded* 2016.

The Ampersand Agency*

Ryman's Cottages, Little Tew, Oxon OX7 4JJ
tel (01608) 683677, (01608) 683898
email submissions@theampersandagency.co.uk
website www.theampersandagency.co.uk
Contacts Peter Buckman, Jamie Cowen, Anne-Marie Doulton

Fiction and non-fiction. Contemporary and historical novels, literary, crime, thrillers, fantasy and science fiction. For non-fiction, interested in current affairs, history and popular science. *Commission* Home 15%, USA 15–20%, translation 20%, all other formats 15%. Consult the website for information on agents' preferences. Submit first three chapters (approx. 50 pages), synopsis and author bio. No poetry, self-help, books for young children or scripts (except for existing clients).

Clients include Tariq Ashkanani, Quentin Bates, Helen Black, Sharon Bolton, Ben Crane, Cora Harrison, Mark Hill, Tendai Huchu, Adrian Selby, Vikas Swarup, the estates of Georgette Heyer, Jin Yong, Angela Thirkell, Winifred Foley and John James. *Founded* 2003.

Darley Anderson and Associates*

Estelle House, 11 Eustace Road, London SW6 1JB
tel 020-7385 6652
website www.darleyanderson.com, www.darleyandersonchildrens.com
X @DA_Agency
Instagram @darleyanderson_agency
Agents Darley Anderson, Camilla Bolton, Clare Wallace, Jade Kavanagh, Rebeka Finch, *Rights* Georgia Fuller, Francesca Edwards, Ilaria Albani, Janice Tedder

Overseas associates AIG Talent & Literary Agency (LA); Catapult Dramatic Rights (London); WME (LA) and leading foreign Agents in selected territories. All commercial fiction and non-fiction. Special interests (fiction): all types of thrillers, crime and mystery, suspense, horror; all types of American and Irish novels; comic fiction; popular women's fiction, contemporary and historical romantic fiction, romcoms, romance, romantic fantasy and book club/ accessible literary fiction. Special interests (non-fiction): autobiographies, memoirs, sports books, popular psychology, self-help, diet, health, animals, interior design, gardening and religious books. *Commission* Home 15%, USA/translation 20%, film/ TV/radio 20%. Submitted via website form, include a covering letter, one-page synopsis and first three chapters. Return postage/sae essential for postal submission reply. See website for agent specialties. No poetry, novellas, academic books, scripts or screenplays.

Clients include Chris Carter, Lee Child, Martina Cole, John Connolly, Holly Craig, Margaret Dickinson, Tana French, T.M. Logan, Donna Marchetti, Annie Murray, B.A. Paris, Phaedra Patrick, K.L. Slater, Catherine Steadman, Tim Weaver. *Founded* 1988.

Apple Tree Literary*

tel 07515 876444
email max.edwards@appletreeliterary.com
website https://appletreeliterary.com
X @AppleTreeLit
Founder Max Edwards

Fiction and non-fiction for adults and YA. Interested in all fiction, but particularly keen on literary and speculative fiction of any type. Clients include a host of academics, journalists, memoirists and experts in the non-fiction space, and seeks those telling untold or unknown stories. Email submissions only to submissions@appletreeliterary.com. For fiction, send a covering email, with a one-page synopsis and first three chapters as attachments. For non-fiction, send a covering email that includes a book outline and author bio plus a proposal and/or sample chapter as an attachment. Does not represent children's fiction below YA, TV/ film scripts or poetry. *Founded* 2024.

Artellus*

30 Dorset House, Gloucester Place,
London NW1 5AD

tel 020-7935 6972
email submissions@artellusltd.co.uk
website www.artellusltd.co.uk
X @Artellus
Bluesky @artellusltd.bsky.social
Agents Leslie Gardner, Darryl Samaraweera, Jon Curzon, Gabriele Pantucci (Chairman)

Wide range of fiction, from literary to crime and genre fiction, plus non-fiction, in areas including history, current affairs, science, economics, investigative journalism, memoir, culture and food. Also interested in fine writers in translation. *Commission* Home 15%, direct sales to USA 20%, rest of world 20%. Submit a covering note with the first three chapters and synopsis. Postal submissions accepted with sae.

See the website for a full client list. *Founded* 1986.

ASH Literary*

email info@ashliterary.com
website www.ashliterary.com
X @ashliterary
Instagram @ashliterary
Agents Alice Sutherland-Hawes, Saffron Dodd, Paula Weiman

Represents fiction authors and illustrators covering picture books through to YA titles, including graphic novels. Interested in all genres. *Commission* Home 15%, translation/dramatisation 20%. Send first three chapters and synopsis through QueryManager or by email to submissions@ashliterary.com. Does not handle adult fiction or non-fiction.

Clients include Alex Falasa-Koya, Jess McGeachin, Harry Woodgate, Amy Leow, Jennifer Iacopelli, Ravena Guron, Katie Cottle. *Founded* 2020.

Kate Barker Literary Agency*

tel 020-7688 1638
email kate@katebarker.net
website www.katebarker.net

Fiction for adults including crime, thriller, suspense, women's fiction, historical and reading group fiction. Non-fiction including narrative non-fiction, popular psychology and science, smart thinking, business, history, memoir, biography, lifestyle and wellbeing. *Commission* Home 15%, overseas 20%, film/TV 20%. Submissions via the website. Does not represent sci-fi, fantasy or children's books. *Founded* 2016.

Bath Literary Agency*

5 Gloucester Road, Bath BA1 7BH
email john.mclay@btinternet.com
website www.bathliteraryagency.com
X @BathLitAgency
Instagram @bathlitagency
Agent Gill McLay

Specialist in fiction for children and YA. Also accepts adult fiction, non-fiction and author-illustrator submissions. *Commission* UK 15%, overseas 20%, film/TV 20%. For full submission details, refer to the website.

Clients include Jake Biggin, Conor Busuttil, Mariesa Dulak, Philippa Forrester, Dr Jess French, Joe Haddow, Demelsa Haughton, Ben Hoare, Laura James, Gill Lewis, Pippa Pixley, Luke Scriven, Dr Shini Somara, Anna Terreros-Martin, Paul Westmoreland. *Founded* 2011.

Bell Lomax Moreton Agency*

Suite C, Victory House, 131 Queensway, Petts Wood, Kent BR5 1DG
tel 020-7930 4447
email agency@bell-lomax.co.uk
website www.belllomaxmoreton.co.uk
X @BLM_Agency
Executives Paul Moreton, Lauren Gardner, Jo Bell, Katie Fulford, Justine Smith, John Baker, Lorna Hemingway, Julie Gourinchas, Callen Martin, Rory Jeffers, Sarah McDonnell

Will consider most fiction, non-fiction and children's (including picture books, middle grade and YA) book proposals. Submission guidelines on website. Physical submissions should be accompanied by sae for return and an email address for correspondence. Does not represent poetry, short stories or novellas, education textbooks, film scripts or stage plays. *Founded* 2000.

Lorella Belli Literary Agency (LBLA)*

Westbourne Studios, Unit 106, 242 Acklam Road, London W10 5JJ
tel 020-7727 8547
email info@lorellabelliagency.com
website www.lorellabelliagency.com
Facebook www.facebook.com/LorellaBelliLiteraryAgency
X @lblaUK
Bluesky @lorellabelliagency.bsky.social
Proprietor Lorella Belli

Full-service literary and management agency representing debut, award-winining and bestselling authors, as well as publishing clients worldwide. Works with film/TV and overseas associates; represents US literary agencies in the UK. Also sells translation, audio, film/TV and other rights on behalf of British publishers, literary agents and successful independent authors. Fiction and general non-fiction. Particularly interested in books which have international appeal, multicultural writing, books on Italy, accessible literary fiction, crime, mysteries, thrillers, psychological suspense, reading group fiction, women's romance, historicals, memoirs, personal development, popular history, wellness, popular science, current affairs, soft business and investigative journalism. *Commission* Home 15%, overseas/dramatic 20%. Send a query email introducing yourself and your work before submitting sample material. Only email submissions considered. May suggest revision. No children's, sci-fi, fantasy, academic, poetry, original scripts or short stories.

Clients include Nancy Barone, Ruth Dugdall, Joy Ellis, Lisa Hobman, Eowyn Ivey, Caroline James, Angela Marsons, Holly Martin, Nicola May, Tom Mead, Liz Mistry, Dreda Say Mitchell, Rick Mofina, Siddarth Shrikanth, Susie Tate. *Founded* 2002.

The Bent Agency*

Greyhound House, 23/24 George Street, Richmond TW9 1HY
email info@thebentagency.com
website www.thebentagency.com
Agents Nicola Barr, Molly Ker Hawn, Zoë Plant

Full-service literary agency with offices in the UK and USA. Represents a diverse range of genres including history, humour, lifestyle, inspiration, memoir, literary fiction, children's and commercial fiction. Only accepts email queries. See website for detailed query and submission guidelines.

Clients include Faridah Abike-Iyimide, B.B. Alston, Gary John Bishop, Stephanie Garber, Frances Hardinge, Guy Gavriel Kay, Beth Lincoln, Hilary McKay, Jo Spain, Martin Stewart, Louie Stowell, Angie Thomas, Jessica Townsend. *Founded* 2009.

Berlin Associates†

7 Tyers Gate, London SE1 3HX
tel 020-7836 1112
email agents@berlinassociates.com
website www.berlinassociates.com
X @berlinassocs
Instagram @berlinassociates
Agents Marc Berlin, Stacy Browne, Matt Connell, Alexandra Cory, Rachel Daniels, Yas Lewis, Charlie MacVicar, Julia Mills, Maddie O'Dwyer, Laura Reeve, Fiona Williams, Emily Wraith, Julia Wyatt

A boutique agency representing writers, directors, producers, designers, composers and below-the-line talent across theatre, film, TV, radio and new media. All genres represented. The majority of new clients are taken on through recommendation or invitation; however, if you would like your work to be considered for representation, email a CV along with a brief outline of your experience and the work you would like to submit for consideration to submissions@berlinassociates.com. Writers need to send a full-length writing sample alongside the covering letter. No prose/fiction. *Founded* 2003.

The bks Agency*

Penway Place, 2A Charing Cross Road, London WC2H 0FH
website www.thebksagency.com
Contacts Jason Bartholomew, Jessica Killingley, James Spackman, Joanna Kaliszewska

A literary management agency representing fiction and non-fiction authors. A division of the Midas Group. Non-fiction: history, politics, current affairs, biography, memoir, narrative non-fiction, business, personal development, general lifestyle and wellbeing, cookery, sport, music, culture and smart thinking. Fiction: crime, mystery, thriller, suspense, women's fiction, reading group fiction, literary fiction, graphic fiction/non-fiction, sci-fi and fantasy. Graphic fiction and non-fiction. Pitch ideas via the online form. See website for full guidelines. No poetry.

Authors include Noor Hibbert, Kate Dramis, Pete Wharmby, Amy Dowden, Vicky Renyal, Grace Koelma, Angharad Hampshire, Lucy Inglis, Nicola Whyte, Stephen McGinty, Eva Mozes Kor, Jane Cholmeley, Doro Globus, Jill Halfpenny, Greg Mosse. *Founded* 2018.

The Blair Partnership*

PO Box 7828, London W1A 4GE
tel 020-7504 2520
email info@theblairpartnership.com
website www.theblairpartnership.com
X @TBP_agency
Bluesky @tbpagency.bsky.social
Instagram @theblairpartnership_agency
Founding Partner & Agent Neil Blair, *Managing Director, Client Management* Rory Scarfe, *Agents* Hattie Grünewald, Rachel Petty, Emily Barrett, Ed Wood, *Associate Agent* Rhian Parry

Represents a range of people internationally from debut and established writers to broader talent across business, arts, politics, sport and lifestyle. Range of work spans fiction, non-fiction, digital, TV and film production. Considers all genres of fiction and non-fiction for adults, young readers and children. Will consider unsolicited MSS. Fiction: email the specific agent with a covering letter, one-page synopsis and first three chapters. Non-fiction: email a proposal document and writing sample. Not currently accepting screenplays, short stories or poetry.

Clients include Lizzy Dent, Earthling Ed, Sue Fortin, Henry Fraser, Tyson and Paris Fury, Dr Pippa Grange, Emma Hayes MBE, Sir Chris Hoy, Louise Jensen, Lee Lawrence, Luna McNamara, Nancy Tucker, Jon Sopel, J.K. Rowling, Stephanie Yeboah. *Founded* 2011.

Blake Friedmann Literary Agency*†

Ground Floor, 15 Highbury Place, London N5 1QP
tel 020-7387 0842
email info@blakefriedmann.co.uk
website https://blakefriedmann.co.uk
Bluesky @blakefriedmann.bsky.social
Instagram @BlakeFriedmannLiteraryAgency
Threads @BlakeFriedmannLiteraryAgency
Book Agents Isobel Dixon, Kate Burke, Juliet Pickering, Sian Ellis-Martin, *Film/TV Agents* Julian Friedmann, Conrad Williams

Fiction: crime, thrillers, women's fiction, historical fiction, speculative fiction and literary fiction; a broad range of non-fiction. Media Department handles film and TV rights, and represents scriptwriters, playwrights and directors. *Commission* Home 15%, overseas 20%. Email chosen agent directly at [firstname]@blakefriedmann.co.uk with introductory letter in body of the email. Fiction: attach a full synopsis and first three chapters (or first 10,000 words). Non-fiction: synopsis (500 words max), full chapter plan and two sample chapters (one of which should be the introduction/opening chapter). No books for children.

Authors include Graeme Armstrong, Bolu Babalola, Graeme Macrae Burnet, Edward Carey, Will Dean, David Gilman, Kerry Hudson, Peter James, Lucy Mangan, Joseph O'Connor, Sheila O'Flanagan, Monique Roffey. *Scriptwriters* include Andy Briggs, Marteinn Thorisson, Stuart Urban. *Founded* 1977.

The Book Bureau Literary Agency

7 Duncairn Avenue, Bray, Co. Wicklow A98 R293, Republic of Ireland
tel +353 (0)1 276 4996
email thebookbureau123@gmail.com
website http://thebookbureauliteraryagency.com
Managing Director Ger Nichol

Works with agents overseas. Sub-agents: The Rights People. Fiction only: general, thrillers, crime, Irish novels, literary fiction and women's commercial novels. *Commission* Home 15%, USA 20%, translation 25%. Send preliminary letter, synopsis and three sample chapters (single line spacing); return postage required. Email preferred. No horror, sci-fi, children's or poetry.

Clients include Ciara Geraghty, Patricia Gibney, Claire Allan, Amanda Robson, Sian O'Gorman, Dr Paula McGrath, Dr Ellen McWilliams, Dan Brotzel, Gillian Harvey, Nicola Gill, Barbara Leahy, Isobel Mahon. *Founded* 1998.

Alan Brodie Representation†

14 The Barbon Buildings, Red Lion Square, London WC1R 4QH
tel 020-7253 6226
email ABReception@alanbrodie.com
website www.alanbrodie.com
X @abragency
Managing Director Alan Brodie, *Agent* Victoria Williams

A dramatic literary agency specialising in writers for the stage and literary estates. Represented in all major countries. *Commission* Home 10%, overseas 15%. No unsolicited scripts; recommendation from known professional required. No prose, fiction or general MSS. *Founded* 1996.

Jenny Brown Associates*

42 The Causeway, Edinburgh EH15 3PZ
email submissions@jennybrownassociates.com
website https://jennybrownassociates.com
Contacts Jenny Brown, Lucy Juckes, Lisa Highton

Literary and women's fiction, crime writing and narrative non-fiction; writing and illustration for children, both fiction and non-fiction. Has a preference for working with writers or illustrators based in Scotland. *Commission* Home 15%, overseas/translation 20%. Submission by email with covering letter in body of the message. Include first three chapters and synopsis (fiction) or proposal and sample chapters (non-fiction) as attachments. No poetry, sci-fi, fantasy or academic.

Clients include Lin Anderson, Shaun Bythell, Christopher Edge, Gavin Francis, Alex Gray, Joanna Hickson, Ruth Hogan, Kathleen Jamie, Helen Kellock, Sally Magnusson, Sara Maitland, Jonathan Meres, Ann O'Loughlin, Malachy Tallack. *Founded* 2002.

Felicity Bryan Associates*

2A North Parade, Banbury Road, Oxford OX2 6LX
tel (01865) 513816
email agency@felicitybryan.com
website www.felicitybryan.com
Managing Director Catherine Clarke, *Agents* Caroline Wood, Carrie Plitt, Angelique Tran Van Sang, James Gill, *Associate Agent* Sally Holloway

Translation rights handled by Andrew Nurnberg Associates; works in conjunction with US agents. Literary and commercial upmarket fiction and general non-fiction, with emphasis on history, biography, science and nature. *Commission* Home 15%, overseas 20%. All submissions and queries through website. No high-concept sci-fi and fantasy (including romantasy), horror, erotica, graphic novels, scripts or poetry.

Authors include Karen Armstrong, Catherine Belton, Louis de Bernières, Jonathan Coe, Edmund de Waal, Reni Eddo-Lodge, Damon Galgut, Thomas Halliday, Tim Harford, Gill Hornby, Diarmaid MacCulloch, K. Patrick, James Rebanks, Jon Savage, Lucy Worsley. *Founded* 1988.

C&W Agency*

(previously Conville & Walsh)
Cunard House, 15 Regent Street, London SW1Y 4LR
tel 020-7393 4200
website www.cwagency.co.uk
X @CWAgencyUK
Instagram @CWAgencyUK
Agents Clare Conville, Susan Armstrong, Sophie Lambert, Emma Finn, Lucy Luck, Richard Pike, Sarah Ballard, Carrie Kania

Handles all genres of fiction, non-fiction and children's worldwide. *Commission* Home 15%, overseas 20%. Part of the Curtis Brown Group of Companies; simultaneous submission accepted. Send cover letter, first three chapters and synopsis by email to the agent you would like to consider your work. No picture books or dramatic works.

Fiction clients include Matt Haig, M.L. Stedman, Rachel Joyce, Kevin Barry, Andrew Michael Hurley, Joanna Cannon, Nathan Filer, D.B.C. Pierre, Jess Kidd, Miranda Cowley Heller, Alice Winn, Jenny

Colgan, Julian Barnes, Bridget Collins. *Non-fiction clients* include Dolly Alderton, Misha Glenny, Tim Spector, Christie Watson, Ben Wilson, Hallie Rubenhold. *Founded* 2000.

Georgina Capel Associates*

29 Wardour Street, London W1D 6PS
tel 020-7734 2414
email [firstname]@georginacapel.com
website https://georginacapel.com
Directors Georgina Capel, Rachel Conway, Irene Baldoni, *Film/TV Agent* Simon Shaps, *Agency Assistant* Polly Halladay

Literary and commercial fiction; broad range of non-fiction including history, biography, cookery, science and nature. *Commission* Home/overseas 15%. Accepts submissions by email (preferred) and post. Include a covering letter, synopsis and first three chapters. See website for full submission guidelines.

Clients include Garrett Carr, Julia Copus, Daisy Dunn, Victoria Hislop, Philip Hoare, Dan Jones, Ben Judah, Thea Lenarduzzi, Martin MacInnes, Ben Okri, Olivette Otele, Matt Ridley, Andrew Roberts, Minna Salami, Simon Sebag Montefiore. *Founded* 1999.

Rebecca Carter Literary*

email info@rebeccacarterliterary.com
website www.rebeccacarterliterary.com
X @RebeccasBooks
Bluesky @RebeccasBooks.bsky.social
Instagram @rebeccacarterliteraryagent
Director Rebecca Carter

Full-service agency with a broad international reach across the media industry. Literary fiction, crime and thriller. Narrative non-fiction with an emphasis on books that engage with the past and the issues of our times in an imaginative way. *Commission* Home 15%, overseas 20%, film/TV 20%. Consult website for submissions guidelines.

Authors include Alice Albinia, Josh Cohen, Elly Griffiths, Xiaolu Guo, Andrew Harding, Olivia Laing, Ferdia Lennon, Gavin McCrea, Charlie Porter, Nell Stevens, Rebecca Stott, Chris Summerfield, Leor Zmigrod. *Founded* 2022.

Casarotto Ramsay & Associates†

7 Savoy Court, Strand, London WC2R 0EX
tel 020-7287 4450
email info@casarotto.co.uk
website www.casarotto.co.uk

Works in conjunction with agents in USA and other overseas markets. Represents screenwriters, playwrights and dramatists as well as industry professionals in the film, TV and theatre industries. *Commission* 10%. Preliminary letter essential. *Founded* 1989.

Robert Caskie

tel 07900 431005
email robert@robertcaskie.com
website www.robertcaskie.com
X @rcaskie1

Represents a broad range of writers of fiction (particularly reading group and literary) and non-fiction (narrative, nature writing, memoir, politics and social issues). *Commission* Home 15%, overseas 20%. Email submissions@robertcaskie.com. For fiction: send an introductory email and the first three chapters. For non-fiction: send an introductory email, a detailed outline and a sample chapter. Does not represent children's, crime and thriller, YA, horror or sci-fi.

Authors include Louis Theroux, Sarah Winman, Libby Page, Emma Barnett, Sir Trevor McDonald, Lord Michael Cashman, Ilana Fox, Manda Scott, Kate Spicer, Lorraine Candy. *Founded* 2020.

The Catchpole Agency

53 Cranham Street, Oxford OX2 6DD
tel 07789 588070
email james@thecatchpoleagency.co.uk
website www.thecatchpoleagency.co.uk
Instagram @thecatchpoles
Proprietor James Catchpole

Agents for authors and illustrators of children's books from picture books through to YA novels, with a specialism in story-editing work. Email submissions@thecatchpoleagency.co.uk with a covering letter which includes a one- or two-sentence elevator pitch, the intended readership and a writing sample pasted directly into the body of the email.

Authors include Polly Dunbar, S.F. Said, Michelle Robinson, Emer Stamp, Sean Taylor, Eoin McLaughlin. *Founded* 1996.

Teresa Chris Literary Agency*

43 Musard Road, London W6 8NR
tel 020-7386 0633
email teresachris@litagency.co.uk
website www.teresachrisliteraryagency.co.uk
Director Teresa Chris

All fiction, especially crime, women's commercial, general and literary fiction. Representation in all overseas territories. *Commission* Home 10%, overseas 20%. Send an email with an introductory letter, synopsis and the first three chapters. Will only respond if interested. No sci-fi, horror, fantasy, short stories, poetry or academic books.

Clients include Dilly Court, Stephen Booth, Rory Clements, Julie Cohen, Kate Rhodes, M.A. Bennett. *Founded* 1988.

Anne Clark Literary Agency*

email submissions@anneclarkliteraryagency.co.uk
website www.anneclarkliteraryagency.co.uk
Facebook www.facebook.com/anneclarkliterary
X @AnneClarkLit
Bluesky @anneclarklit.bsky.social
Contact Anne Clark

Specialist in fiction, non-fiction and picture books for children and young adults. *Commission* Home 15%, overseas 20%. Submissions by email only. See website for details.

Clients include Mike Barfield, Anne Booth, Max Boucherat, Moira Butterfield, Lou Carter, Emily-Jane Clark, Patricia Forde, Pippa Goodhart, Cath Howe, Ruth Lauren, Ben Lerwill, Leah Mohammed, Rebecca Patterson, Lucy Rowland. *Founded* 2012.

Mary Clemmey Literary Agency*

6 Dunollie Road, London NW5 2XP
tel 020-7267 1290
email mcwords@googlemail.com
Agent Mary Clemmey

High-quality fiction and non-fiction with an international market. Works in conjunction with US agent. *Commission* Home 15%, overseas 20%, performance rights 15%. Approach by letter or email first. No unsolicited MSS. No children's books or sci-fi and fantasy. TV, film, radio and theatre scripts from existing clients only. *Founded* 1992.

Jonathan Clowes*†

tel 020-7722 7674
email admin@jonathanclowes.co.uk
website www.jonathanclowes.co.uk
Directors Ann Evans, Nemonie Craven Roderick

Literary and commercial fiction and non-fiction, film, TV, theatre (for existing clients) and radio. Email for general enquiries. Works in association with agents overseas. *Commission* Home 15%, overseas 20%. Send covering email with synopsis and first three chapters attached. Check agents' interests and availability before submitting.

Clients include Simon Critchley, Brian Freemantle, Francesca Hornak, Gruff Rhys, the literary estates of Doris Lessing, Elizabeth Jane Howard, Michael Baigent, Dr David Bellamy and Richard Leigh. *Founded* 1960.

Colwill & Peddle*

email submissions@colwillandpeddle.com
website www.colwillandpeddle.com
Bluesky @colwillandpeddle.bsky.social
Instagram @colwillandpeddle
Agents Charlotte Colwill, Kay Peddle, Milly Reilly, Donna Greaves

Works with a number of foreign, film and TV co-agents to sell the rights to clients' work internationally, in all formats and mediums. Seeking intimately drawn characters, unconventional settings and humour, with rich storytelling that interweaves cultural, political or historical context. Charlotte is looking for adult commercial and genre fiction, especially horror and crime, and children's fiction and non-fiction. Kay is looking for non-fiction: history, politics, essays, popular science, biography, memoir, travel, current affairs, cookery and food writing. Milly is looking for literary fiction, memoir, expert-led non-fiction, creative non-fiction, essays, food writing and cookery. Donna is looking for voice-led adult fiction and narrative non-fiction. *Commission* Home 15%, USA/overseas 20%. See website for detailed submission guidelines. Does not represent screenwriters, poets or picture books.

Authors include Kerri Andrews, Terri Apter, Emily P. Webber, Helen Graves, Gianni Washington, Harriett De Mesquita, Tom Ramsay, Tamsin Keilly, Annabel Sowemimo, Gabrielle de la Puente, Zarina Muhammad, Melek Erdal, Benjamina Ebuehi, Lucy Easthope. *Founded* 2022.

Coombs Moylett Maclean Literary Agency*

120 New Kings Road, London SW6 4LZ
tel 020-8740 0454
email info@cmm.agency
website https://cmm.agency
Instagram @cmmlitagency
Contacts Lisa Moylett, Jamie Maclean, Zoë Apostolides, Elena Langtry

Interested in well-written commercial fiction, particularly historical, crime, mystery, suspense, thrillers, women's fiction from chick-lit sagas to contemporary and literary fiction. Considers most non-fiction, particularly history, biography, current affairs, politics, how-to, true crime and popular science. *Commission* Home 15%, overseas 20%, film/TV 20%. Works with overseas agents. Whole books and manuscript submissions via post and/or email will not be accepted. Check the website for details on how to submit. Does not handle poetry, plays or scripts for film and TV, or children's.

Clients include Leye Adenle, Dr Sarah Woodhouse, Simon Brett, Ian Dunt, Jonathan Gash, John Gardner, Jonathon Green, Lisa Hall, Chrisopher Hart, Mark McCrum, Frankie McGowan, Catriona McPherson, Malachi O'Doherty. *Founded* 1997.

Gemma Cooper Literary*

email info@gemmacooperliterary.com
website www.gemmacooperliterary.com
X @gemma_cooper
Instagram @gemmacooperliterary
Founder & Literary Agent Gemma Cooper

Primary focus is children's and YA authors, and adult fiction in a few, select categories. Open to all genres in children's fiction. For adult fiction: cosy crime, smart contemporary crime with humour, and crime with a fantasy twist. Actively looking for something on the lighthearted side that is clever with an unusual or interesting hook. *Commission* Home 15%, overseas 20%, film/TV 20%. Submit by email to gemmaqueries@gemmacooperliterary.com. Include book title, short pitch, author bio and the first ten pages of the MS in the body of the email. For graphic novels or illustrated non-fiction: in addition to the above, include links to website or social media, if work is shared there, or attach up to five low-res images. Not seeking YA fantasy, but will consider light speculative with a twist. No contemporary adult fiction, adult non-fiction, literary novels, romance or poetry. Not interested in dark thriller, or crime that is gritty and includes gratuitous violence or child death.

Authors include B.B. Alston, Sophie Anderson, P.G. Bell, Abiola Bello, Claire Fayers, Beth Garrod, Siobhan McDermott, Katrina Charman, Sibéal Pounder, Sam Hay, Robin Stevens, Mo O'Hara, Jessica Townsend, Katy Watson, Freja Nicole Woolf. *Founded* 2024.

Creative Authors

11A Woodlawn Street, Whitstable, Kent CT5 1HQ
email write@creativeauthors.co.uk
website www.creativeauthors.co.uk
X @creativeauthors
Instagram @creativeauthors
Director Isabel Atherton

Fiction, non-fiction, humour, history, science, autobiography, biography, business, memoir, health, cookery, arts and crafts, crime, children's fiction, picture books and illustrators. *Commission* Home 15%, overseas 20%. Only accepts email submissions.

Authors and illustrators include Guojing, Ged Adamson, Zuza Zak, Dr Keith Souter, E.A. Hanks, Caroline Young, Tamara Sturtz-Filby, Kristen Bateman. *Founded* 2008.

Rupert Crew*

Southgate, 7 Linden Avenue, Dorchester DT1 1EJ
tel (01305) 260335
email info@rupertcrew.co.uk
website www.rupertcrew.co.uk
Facebook www.facebook.com/RupertCrew
Bluesky @rupertcrewltd.bsky.social
Instagram @rupertcrew
Managing Director Caroline Montgomery

International representation, handling accessible literary and commercial fiction and non-fiction for adult and children's (8+) markets. *Commission* Home 15%, overseas 20%, film/TV/radio 20%. No unsolicited MSS: see website for current submission guidelines policy. No picture books, plays, screenplays, poetry, journalism, sci-fi and fantasy or short stories. *Founded* 1927.

Julie Crisp Literary Agency*

email julieacrisp@gmail.com
website www.juliecrisp.co.uk
X @julieacrisp
Agent Julie Crisp

Actively looking for full-length adult historical fiction (including mythological retellings), crime/thrillers, book club fiction, horror, sci-fi and fantasy. *Commission* Home 15% UK, overseas/translation 20%, film/TV 20% Send submission via QueryManager. Include first three chapters, a synopsis, biography and covering letter.

Clients include E.J. Beaton, Heather Child, John Gwynne, Sam Hawke, Devin Madson, Den Patrick, C.T. Rwizi, Nick Setchfield, Dr Lucy Kissick, Kell Woods.

Cull & Co.*

website https://cullandco.com
X @CullandCoAgency
Ceo & Agent Tom J. Cull

Specialises in non-fiction and some fiction for adults. Works in conjunction with overseas agents in translation and dramatic rights. Wide range of genres represented including history, espionage, biography, autobiography, pop culture, sport, politics and current affairs. Occasional fiction including literary, crime and thrillers. Open to Spanish language writers and Latin American stories. *Commission* Home 15%, overseas 20%, film/TV 20%. Submissions via website. No plays or screenplays, poetry, children's books or YA.

Clients include Michael Smith, Rachel Lichtenstein, C.J. Schuler, Mary Novakovich, Seth Thevoz, Henry R. Schlesinger, Sarah-Louise Miller, Dan Collyns, Kathy Marks, Shafik Meghji, Ros Belford, Daniel Stables, George Harrison, T.J. Brearton, Christiana Spen. *Founded* 2017.

Curtis Brown*†

Cunard House, 15 Regent Street, London SW1Y 4LR
tel 020-7393 4400
email cb@curtisbrown.co.uk
website https://curtisbrown.co.uk/section/books, www.curtisbrowncreative.co.uk
X @CBGBooks, @cbcreative
Chair Jonny Geller, *Head of Books* Stephanie Thwaites, *Senior Agents* Sheila Crowley, Gordon Wise, *Agents* Davinia Andrew-Lynch, Felicity Blunt, Sabhbh Curran, Viola Hayden, Jonathan Lloyd, Alice Lutyens, Jess Molloy, Lucy Morris, Cathryn Summerhayes, *Heritage* Becky Brown, Norah Perkins, *Associates* Ciara Finan, Isobel Gahan, Rachel Goldblatt, Rosie Pierce, *Audio & Podcasts* Sophia MacAskill

Represents prominent writers of fiction and non-fiction, from winners of all major awards to international bestsellers and from debuts to literary estates. Also manages the international careers of authors, with strong relationships in translation and US markets as well as a growing European-language business. Offers full-service representation in film, TV, theatre, audio, events and other performance. In fiction, works across many genres, both literary and those aimed at a popular audience, and looks for strong voices and outstanding storytellers in general fiction, crime, thrillers, psychological suspense, speculative and historical fiction, YA and children's books. Non-fiction list includes leading commentators and thinkers, historians, biographers, social media influencers, lifestyle brands, scientists and writers of quality narrative non-fiction.

Commission Home 15–20%. See website and individual agent web pages for submission guidelines. *Founded* 1899.

Dark House Literary & Screen Agency

19 Tottenhall Road, London N13 6HY
tel 07812 004546
email submission@darkhouse.uk
website www.darkhouse.uk
X @DarkHouseAgency
Managing Director Andreas Charalambous

Represents the works of authors and creatives working within the horror and dark fantasy genres, including adult fiction, non-fiction, graphic novels, children's (with subtle horror themes) and YA. Also interested in screenplays for film and TV. Email submissions only. Fiction: attach a Word document that includes a brief synopsis and the first three chapters of the MS. Non-fiction: include a proposal, short synopsis and up-to-date CV. Does not represent works of poetry, picture books, theatrical scripts and any other genres except horror and dark fantasy. *Founded* 2023.

Caroline Davidson Literary Agency*

5 Queen Anne's Gardens, London W4 1TU
tel 020-8995 5768
email enquiries@cdla.co.uk
website www.cdla.co.uk

Handles exceptional novels, memoirs and non-fiction of originality and high quality. All submissions must be in hard copy; email submissions are not considered. For non-fiction, send letter with CV and detailed, well-thought-out book proposal, including chapter synopsis. For fiction, send letter, CV, three-line pitch, synopsis and the first 50 pages and last ten pages of text. No reply without large sae with correct return postage. Does not represent fantasy, horror, sci-fi and crime.

Authors include Emma Donoghue, Chris Greenhalgh, Richard Hobday, Helena Whitbread. *Founded* 1988.

Felix de Wolfe†

20 Old Compton Street, London W1D 4TW
tel 020-7242 5066
email info@felixdewolfe.com
website https://felixdewolfe.com
X @felixdewolfe
Instagram @felixdewolfe
Agents Caroline de Wolfe, Wendy Scozzaro, Rob Hughes, Dom Scozzaro

Theatre, films, TV, sound broadcasting and fiction. Works in conjunction with many overseas agencies. *Commission* Home 10–15%, overseas 20%. For fiction, send a CV/biography with a synopsis and the first 15 pages of your work. Not currently accepting unsolicited literary submissions. *Founded* 1947.

DHH Literary Agency*

23–27 Cecil Court, London WC2N 4EZ
tel 020-3954 5999
email enquiries@dhhliteraryagency.com
website www.dhhliteraryagency.com
Facebook www.facebook.com/dhhliteraryagency
X @dhhlitagency
Bluesky @dhhlitagency.bsky.social
Instagram @dhhlitagency
Agents David H. Headley, Broo Doherty, Harry Illingworth, Emily Glenister, Abi Fellows, Diana Beaumont

Represents fiction, women's commercial fiction, crime, thriller, literary fiction, speculative fiction, sci-fi and fantasy. Non-fiction special interests include narrative non-fiction, memoir, history, cookery, humour and social justice. Also children's and YA fiction. *Commission* UK 15%, overseas 15% (where a sub-agent is used 20%). Send informative preliminary email with first three chapters and synopsis. Consult website for correct email address for each agent. New authors welcome. No plays or scripts, poetry or short stories.

Authors include Stuart Turton, Jules Wake, M.W. Craven, Phillipa Ashley, Saima Mir, Natalie Marlow, Jon Ransom, Becca Day, Tom Hindle, Sunyi Dean, Stephen Moss, Sean Lusk, Daisy Buchanan, Claire McGowan, Lucy Vine. *Founded* 2008.

Diamond Kahn & Woods Literary Agency*

Office 378, Salisbury House, 29 Finsbury Circus, London EC2M 5QQ
tel 020-3514 6544
email info@dkwlitagency.co.uk
email submissions.ella@dkwlitagency.co.uk
email submissions.bryony@dkwlitagency.co.uk
website www.dkwlitagency.co.uk
Instagram @dkwliteraryagency
Agents Ella Diamond Kahn, Bryony Woods, Camille Burns

Literary and commercial fiction (including all major genres) and non-fiction for adults, plus children's, YA and crossover fiction. Interested in new writers. *Commission* Home 15%, USA/translation 20%. Ella and Bryony accept email submissions only. Send three chapters and synopsis to one agent. For Camille, please submit via QueryManager at https://querytracker.net/query/camille.

Clients include Joanne Burn, Daniel Aubrey, Chris Lloyd, David Owen, Caroline O'Donoghue, Sharon Gosling, Sylvia Bishop, Katharine Orton, Calum McSwiggan, Laura Jane Williams, Catriona Silvey, Jayne Cowie, Daisy May Johnson, Sandra Lawrence, Rebecca Orwin. *Founded* 2012.

Elise Dillsworth Agency

9 Grosvenor Road, Muswell Hill, London N10 2DR
email elise@elisedillsworthagency.com
website www.elisedillsworthagency.com
X @EliseDillsworth

Instagram @elise.dillsworth
Owner & Literary Agent Elise Dillsworth

Represents literary and general fiction and non-fiction in the areas of memoir, biography, travel and cookery, with a keen aim to reflect writing that is international. *Commission* Home 15%, overseas 20%. Send preliminary letter, synopsis and first three chapters (or approx. 50 pages). No postal submissions accepted. See website for full submission guidelines. Does not represent sci-fi, fantasy, plays, film/TV scripts or children's books.

Authors include Yvonne Battle-Felton, Maria Bradford, Karen Downs-Barton, Anthony Joseph, Kemi Olaperi Lawson, Foday Mannah, Yewande Omotoso, Noo Saro-Wiwa, Courtney Pine, Stephanie Victoire, Aisling Watters, the estates of Roy Heath, Diane Oliver and Ken Saro-Wiwa. *Founded* 2012.

Robert Dudley Agency

135A Bridge Street, Ashford, Kent TN25 5DP
tel 07879 426574
email info@robertdudleyagency.co.uk
website www.robertdudleyagency.co.uk
Proprietor Robert Dudley

Non-fiction only. Specialises in history, biography, sport, politics, military history and current affairs. *Commission* Home 15%, overseas 20%, film/TV/radio 20%. Will suggest revision. Email submissions only.

Authors include Edoardo Albert, Ben Barry, Michael Broers, Tim Bentinck, Prit Buttar, Ambrogio Caiani, Tim Hannigan, Kit Holden, Mungo Melvin, Adrian Phillips, Brian Holden Reid, Mary Colwell, Chris Sidwells, Martyn Whittock. *Founded* 2000.

DunnFogg*

PO Box 78047, London N4 9LP
email info@dunnfogg.co.uk
website https://dunnfogg.co.uk
Agents Ben Dunn, Jack Fogg

A full-service, independent literary agency. Fiction: literary, crime, book club, historical, sci-fi and fantasy. Non-fiction: memoir, narrative, sport, business, popular science, big ideas, music, food and media tie-in. *Commission* Home 15%, overseas 20%. Fiction: synopsis, brief biography and first three chapters or 50 pages of your novel. Non-fiction: pitch of the book, brief biography and sample chapter(s). No children's or YA.

Clients include Ben Benton, Buzz Baum, Kate Bryan, Daisy May Cooper, Andrew Cotter, Sophia Handschuh, Penny Lancaster, Barnaby Martin, Dan Schreiber, Meriel Schindler, David Shrigley, Paul Sexton, Ben Timberlake. *Founded* 2021.

Eddison Pearson*

West Hill House, 6 Swains Lane, London N6 6QS
tel 020-7700 7763
email enquiries@eddisonpearson.com
website www.eddisonpearson.com, https://eddisonpearson.blog
Contact Clare Pearson

Small, personally run agency. Children's and YA books, fiction, non-fiction and poetry. *Commission* Home 10–15%, overseas 15–20%. Enquiries and submissions by email only; email for up-to-date submission guidelines. May suggest revision.

Authors include Valerie Bloom, Sue Heap, Caroline Lawrence, Robert Muchamore, Mary Murphy, Megan Rix. *Founded* 1997.

Edwards Fuglewicz Literary Agency*

49 Great Ormond Street, London WC1N 3HZ
tel 020-7405 6725
Contacts Ros Edwards, Jill McCluskey, Mark Lacey

Literary and commercial fiction; non-fiction: biography and narrative non-fiction (including animal stories). *Commission* Home 15%, USA/translation 20%. No email submissions. No children's fiction, sci-fi or horror. *Founded* 1996.

Featherstone Cairns*

10 Willow Drive, Barnet, London EN5 2LQ
email hello@featherstonecairns.com
website www.featherstonecairns.com
Director Ruth Cairns

Specialises in adult non-fiction, but occasionally represents fiction and children's. Universally interested in all subject types, especially work that blurs the lines between commercial and literary. *Commission* Home 15%, overseas 20%. Email submissions only. For fiction, include a covering letter, synopsis and sample chapter. For non-fiction, include a proposal and sample chapter. *Founded* 2015.

Fillingham Weston Associates†

(formerly Janet Fillingham Associates)
20 Mortlake, 20 Mortlake High Street, London SW14 8JN
tel 020-8748 5594
website https://fillinghamweston.com
Agent Kate Weston, *Consultant* Janet Fillingham

Film, TV and theatre only. *Commission* Home 15%, overseas 15–20%. Strictly no unsolicited MSS; professional recommendation required. No books. *Founded* 1992.

Film Rights

(in association with Laurence Fitch)
11 Pandora Road, London NW6 1TS
tel 020-8001 3040
email information@filmrights.ltd.uk
email information@laurencefitch.com
website www.filmrights.ltd.uk, www.laurencefitch.com
Contact Brendan Davis

Incorporating The London Play Company. Represented in USA and abroad. Theatre, films, TV and sound broadcasting. *Commission* Home 10%, overseas 15%.

Clients include Carlo Ardito, John Chapman, Peter Coke, Ray Cooney OBE, Dave Freeman, John Graham, Robin Hawdon, Jeremy Lloyd (plays), Dawn Lowe-Watson, Glyn Robbins, Edward Taylor, the estates of Dodie Smith and Frank Baker, the literary estates of N.C. Hunter and Michael Pertwee. *Founded* 1935.

42*†

Palladium House, 7th Floor, 1–4 Argyll Street, London W1F 7TA
email info@42mp.com
website https://www.42mp.com/books
Instagram @42__mp
Agents Eugenie Furniss, Emily MacDonald

Full-service representation, including placing books with producers for adaptation in film, television, podcasting and other types of media. Authors are published in over 40 languages. Fiction: all types of thrillers, crime and mystery, historical fiction, speculative fiction, women's fiction and accessible literary/reading group fiction. Non-fiction: biography, history, memoir, investigative, popular psychology and a wide range of narrative non-fiction. *Commission* Home 15%, USA/translation 20%, film/TV 20%. See website for agent wish lists and contact information, as well as submission guidelines. No poetry, plays or academic books.

Authors include Catherine Bailey, Clare Balding, Julian Clary, Emily Maitlis, Abi Morgan, Callum McSorley, Celia Walden, Matthew Reilly, Keith Stuart, S.K. Tremayne, Adriana Trigiani. *Founded* 2019.

FRA*

(formerly Futerman, Rose & Associates)
91 St Leonards Road, London SW14 7BL
tel 020-8255 7755
email guy@futermanrose.co.uk
email seb@futermanrose.co.uk
website www.futermanrose.co.uk
Contacts Guy Rose, Seb Flatau

Non-fiction: biography (especially sport, music and politics), show business and current affairs; scripts for TV and film. *Commission* Home 15%, overseas 20%. No unsolicited MSS. Send a chapter breakdown and two or three sample chapters (non-fiction) or a sample section of the work (scripts). No children's, sci-fi or fantasy.

Clients include Larry Barker, Nicky Butler, Prof. Stephen Duckworth, Rt Hon. Sir Iain Duncan Smith MP, Paul Ferris, Rt Hon. Mark Francois MP, Keith Gillespie, Sir Mike Gooley, Dame Sara Khan, His Hon. Judge Chris Nicholson, Sir Tommy Steele, Paul Stinchcombe KC, Toyah Willcox, Graham Wilson, Simon Woodham. *Founded* 1984.

Fraser Ross Associates

42 Hadfast Road, Cousland, Midlothian EH22 2NZ
email agentlmfraser@gmail.com
email kjross@tiscali.co.uk
website www.fraserross.co.uk
Facebook www.facebook.com/fraserrossassociates
Instagram @fraserrossassociates
Threads @fraserrossassociates
Partners Lindsey Fraser, Kathryn Ross

Writing and illustration for children and adults. See website for client list and submission information. *Founded* 2002.

Frog Literary Agency

15 Queens Road, London SW14 8PH
tel 07712 660990
email hello@frogliterary.agency
website www.frogliterary.agency
X @frogliterary
Bluesky @frogliterary.bsky.social
Instagram @frogliterary
Managing Director Andrew James

UK's first literary agency solely dedicated to representing, championing, and providing a platform for queer voices in fiction and non-fiction writing. *Commission* Home 15%, US/overseas 20%, translation 20%. Submissions via email to submissions@frogliterary.agency with the covering letter in the body of the email. Fiction: include a one- to two-page synopsis, bio note and first three chapters. Non-fiction: include a proposal, biographical note, chapter breakdown and sample chapter for non-fiction. No children's, poetry, play or film scripts.

Authors include Charley Barnes, The Crooked Men, Emily Garside, Daniel Harding, Robert Hamberger, Emma Morgan, Daniel O'Shaughnessy, Kristiane Sherry, Jake Williams. *Founded* 2023.

Jüri Gabriel

35 Camberwell Grove, London SE5 8JA
tel 020-7703 6186
email jurigabriel35@gmail.com

Quality fiction and non-fiction; radio, TV and film, but selling these rights only in existing works by existing clients. *Commission* Home 10%, overseas 20%, performance rights 10%. Submit three sample chapters plus a one- to two-page synopsis and sae (if using snail mail) in the first instance. Will suggest revision where appropriate. No short stories, articles, verse or books for children.

Authors include Jack Allen, Gbontwi Anyetei, Nick Bradbury, Prof. Christopher Day, Paul Genney, Pat Gray, Mikka Haugaard, Robert Irwin, Richard Mankiewicz, David Miller, John Outram, Philip Roberts, Roger Storey, Fiona Subotsky, Sir Peter Thornton. *Founded* 1983.

David Godwin Associates (DGA)*

2nd Floor, 40 Rosebery Avenue, Clerkenwell, London EC1R 4RX
tel 020-7240 9992

email rachel@davidgodwinassociates.co.uk
website www.davidgodwinassociates.com
X @DGALitAgents
Instagram @DGALiterary
Directors David Godwin, Heather Godwin

Broad range of fiction and non-fiction with a strong focus on literary. Email submissions submissions@davidgodwinassociates.co.uk. Send first 30 pages with synopsis and cover letter.

Clients include Christina Lamb, Richard Holmes, Claire Tomalin, Jeremy Paxman, Vikram Seth, Arundhati Roy, William Dalrymple, Shehan Karunatilaka, Geetanjali Shree. *Founded* 1995.

Bill Goodall Literary Agency

26 Lower Road, Malvern, Worcs. WR14 4BX
email bill@billgoodall.co.uk
website www.billgoodall.co.uk
Facebook www.facebook.com/BGLitAgency
X @BGLitAgency
Bluesky @billgoodall.bsky.social
Owner & Director Bill Goodall

Adult fiction, including (but not exclusively) commercial, literary, crime and thriller, and general fiction. *Commission* Home 15%, overseas/translation 20%; film/TV Home 15%, overseas 20%. Send synopsis plus first three chapters or 50 pages, whichever is shorter, by email as Word attachments. No postal submissions. No sci-fi and fantasy, short stories, poetry or children's books.

Clients include Ian Moore, Tom Benjamin, Marius Gabriel, Conor Farrington, Joanne Kormylo, Anna and Jacqui Burns, Mandy Byatt, Leigh Russell, Sophie Morton-Thomas, Kevin Sullivan, James Brydon, Jez Pinfold. *Founded* 2018.

Graham Maw Christie*

37 Highbury Place, London N5 1QP
email enquiries@grahammawchristie.com
website www.grahammawchristie.com
X @litagencygmc
Bluesky @litagencygmc.bsky.social
Contacts Jane Graham Maw, Jennifer Christie, Amy O'Shea, Amandeep Singh

General non-fiction: autobiography/memoir, business/smart thinking, humour and gift, food and drink, craft, health and wellness, lifestyle, parenting, self-help/how-to, popular science/history/culture/reference. Considers some fiction. Email submissions only. Will suggest revisions. See website for submission guidelines. Also represents ghostwriters. No children's or poetry.

Authors include Louise Allen, Ruth Allen, Dr Sharon Blackie, Dr Natalie Cawley, Sally Coulthard, Milli Hill, Vex King, Kaushal, Tim James, Katie McKenna, Dr Clare Plumbly, Paulina Rowinska, Veganuary, Helen Villiers, Raynor Winn. *Founded* 2005.

Annette Green Authors' Agency

5 Henwoods Mount, Pembury, Tunbridge Wells TN2 4BH
tel (01892) 263252
email annette@annettegreenagency.co.uk
website www.annettegreenagency.co.uk
Partners Annette Green, David Smith

Fiction: literary, general, women's, historical, romance and fiction for older children. Non-fiction: popular culture, history and science. *Commission* Home 15%, overseas 20–25%. Preliminary email or letter, synopsis, sample chapter and sae essential. No picture books, dramatic scripts, poetry, sci-fi or fantasy.

Authors include Louis Barfe, Tim Bradford, Bill Broady, Katherine Clements, Terry Darlington, Elizabeth Haynes, Jane Kerr, Maria McCann, Adam Macqueen, Audrey Reimann, Katie Hutton, Rachael McGill, Julia Williams, Elizabeth Woodcraft. *Founded* 1998.

Christine Green Authors' Agent*

email info@christinegreen.co.uk
website www.christinegreen.co.uk
Contact Christine Green

Literary and commercial fiction, narrative (novelistic) non-fiction. General fiction welcome. *Commission* Home 15%, overseas 20%. Currently closed for submissions. No sci-fi or fantasy, travelogues, self-help, picture books, scripts or poetry.

Clients include Maeve Binchy, Mary Beckett, Ita Daly, Sairish Hussain, Ali Lewis, Gaile Parkin, Alice Redmond. *Founded* 1984.

Louise Greenberg Books*

The End House, Church Crescent, London N3 1BG
tel 020-8349 1179
email louisegreenberg@btinternet.com

Literary fiction and non-fiction. *Commission* Full-length MSS: home 15%, overseas 20%. New writers by recommendation only. No telephone enquiries. *Founded* 1997.

Greene & Heaton*

T18, West Wing, Somerset House, Strand, London WC2R 1LA
email submissions@greeneheaton.co.uk
email info@greeneheaton.co.uk
website https://greeneheaton.co.uk
X @GreeneandHeaton
Contacts Carol Heaton, Judith Murray, Antony Topping, Claudia Young, Laura Williams, Holly Faulks, Imogen Morrell, *Translation Rights Director* Kate Rizzo

A literary and media agency with a diverse range of clients. We work closely with our clients, where necessary or desired, to polish their proposals, edit their texts, and to give advice about positioning in the fast-changing publishing landscape. Handles all manner of activities from straightforward book representation and contract negotiation to film and TV adaptations. Fiction and non-fiction. *Commission*

Home 15%, USA/translation 20%, film/TV 20%. Email submissions accepted, but no reply guaranteed. Postal submissions not accepted. No original scripts for theatre, film or TV.

Clients include Lewis Goodall, Lucy Clarke, Marcus du Sautoy, Hugh Fearnley-Whittingstall, Joseph Knox, Clare Chambers, Andrew Taylor, Laura Shepherd-Robinson, Ruth Mancini, Sarah Waters, Sabine Durrant, Emma Flint, Stephen Sackur, the estates of C.J. Sansom and P.D. James. *Founded* 1963.

The Greenhouse Literary Agency

email info@greenhouseliterary.com
website www.greenhouseliterary.com
Director Chelsea Eberly, *Agent* Kristin Ostby

Children's fiction and non-fiction: illustrators who write picture books, middle grade, teen/YA and graphic novels. Some women's fiction. Submissions via QueryManager only; see website for submission guidelines. No poetry, short stories or film scripts.

Authors include Gavin Aung Than, Sarwat Chadda, Winifred Conkling, Andrea Contos, Alexandra Diaz, Bill Doyle, Theanne Griffith, Michelle Lam, Rebecca Mock, Kelis Rowe, Ali Standish, Emily Thiede, Ngozi Ukazu. *Founded* 2008.

Greenstone Literary*

email hello@greenstoneliterary.com
website www.greenstoneliterary.com
X @GreenstoneLit
Instagram @greenstoneliterary
Agents Laura Heathfield, Tanera Simons

Adult fiction and non-fiction. Specialists in commercial fiction across romance (including romantic fantasy), crime, thriller, historical and book club. Represents select non-fiction. Use submissions form on website. Include query letter, synopsis and opening three chapters (or first 50 pages) as individual Word docs or pdfs. No poetry, novellas or screenplays.

Authors include Beth O'Leary, Sally Page, Mandy Baggot, Ally Zetterberg, Sophie White, Tammye Huf, Emma Steele, Kate Smith, Laura Carter, Natalie Cooper, Katie Bohn, Elaine Hastings, Claire McCauley, Claire Kershaw, Claire Frost. *Founded* 2024.

Greyhound Literary*

6 Warwick Court, London WC1R 5DJ
email info@greyhoundliterary.co.uk
website www.greyhoundliterary.co.uk
Instagram @greyhoundliteraryagency
Founder Charlie Campbell, *Agents* Charlotte Atyeo, Salma Begum, Alexander Cochran, Sam Edenborough (Rights Director), Natalie Galustian, Dotti Irving, Philip Gwyn Jones, Julia Silk

Fiction and non-fiction for adults and children. Represents YA and some picture books for authors whose work is represented in other areas. *Commission* Home 15%, USA/film/TV 20%, translation 20%. Submissions via website. No plays, poetry or scripts.

Clients include Beach, S.J. Bennett, Eliza Chan, Yvvette Edwards, Robert Elms, Rebecca Front, Maisie Hill, Michael Holding, Vijay Khurana, Molly O'Neill, Bonnie Quinn, Lias Saoudi, Gemma Tizzard, Tade Thompson, the estate of Alan Rickman. *Founded* 2022.

David Grossman Literary Agency

9 Lamington Street, London W6 0HU
tel 020-8741 2860
email submissions@dglal.co.uk

Works in conjunction with agents in New York, Los Angeles, Europe, Japan and China. *Commission* Full-length MSS: home 10–15%, overseas 20% (including foreign agent's commission), performance rights 15%. No submissions by email without a preceding preliminary letter or message briefly describing the work and justifying its publication. *Founded* 1976.

Marianne Gunn O'Connor Literary, Film/TV Agency

Morrison Chambers, 32 Nassau Street, Dublin 2, Republic of Ireland
tel +353 (01) 677 9100
email submissions@mariannegunnoconnor.com
website www.mariannegunnoconnor.com
Contact Marianne Gunn O'Connor

Represents literary fiction, book club and psychological suspense and non-fiction authors with a focus on big ideas and narrative. No screenplays.

Clients include Christy Lefteri, Liz Nugent, Louise Nealon, Mike McCormack, Adrian Duncan, Edel Coffey, Sheila Armstrong, Anya Bergman, Catherine Prasifka, David McWilliams, Disha Bose, Nana Oforiatta Ayim, Sinead Moriarty, Claudia Carroll, Michael Harding. *Founded* 1996.

Gwyn Palmer Associates (Literary Agents)

email robertgwynpalmer@gmail.com
Contact Robert Gwyn Palmer

Non-fiction only, including (but not limited to) self-help, memoir and autobiography, history, cookery, economics, popular science, graphic design, architecture and design. *Commission* Home 15%. Make initial contact via email with an outline of the proposal. No fiction, poetry or children's.

Authors include Anthony Murphy (The Beefy Boys), Daniel Fryer, Ben Aldridge, Tom Goodwin, Sarah Stamford, Paul Farrell, Marcus Bawdon, Emma Armstrong, Adrian Waddington CBE, Alvin Carpio, J.T. White, Matt Kiely. *Founded* 2005.

The Hamilton Agency

12A Portland Road, London W11 4LA
email matthew@thehamiltonagency.co.uk
website https://thehamiltonagency.co.uk
X @MWHamilton
Founder & Agent Matthew Hamilton

Represents writers of literary and commercial non-fiction, with a particular interest in politics and culture, memoir, music and entertainment. Submissions via the website using the form provided. No queries by post or phone. Submissions via form on the website and must include a covering letter, short author bio and a brief synopsis. An excerpt or the full MS can be included at submission.

Authors Yaba Badoe, Nigel Biggar, Mike Brearley, Rose Boyt, John Crace, Andrew Doyle, Mary Harrington, Konstantin Kisin, Paul Mason, Benjamin Moser, Douglas Murray, Sarah Rainsford, Simple Minds, Louise Perry, A.N. Wilson. *Founded* 2019.

The Hanbury Agency, Literary Agents

Suite 103, Lower Marsh, London SE1 7AB
email enquiries@hanburyagency.com
website www.hanburyagency.com

Represents general fiction and non-fiction. See website for submission guidelines.

Authors include Tom Bergin, Simon Callow, Jane Glover, Roman Krznaric, Margarette Lincoln, Judith Lennox, Kate Raworth, Simon Sharpe, Charles Saumarez Smith, Jerry White, the estate of George Alagiah. *Founded* 1983.

Hardman & Swainson*

S106 New Wing, Somerset House,
London WC2R 1LA
tel 020-3701 7449
email submissions@hardmanswainson.com
website www.hardmanswainson.com
X @hardmanswainson
Directors Caroline Hardman, Joanna Swainson

Literary and commercial fiction, crime and thriller, women's, contemporary, historical and accessible literary. Non-fiction including memoir, biography, popular science, history and philosophy. *Commission* Home 15%, USA/translation 20%, film/TV 20%. Submissions by email only; check the website for details. Will work editorially with the author where appropriate. No poetry, screenplays, children's or picture books.

Clients include Dinah Jefferies, Liz Trenow, Ali McNamara, Giovanna Fletcher, Helen Fields, Sarah Turner, Daniel M. Davies, Oskar Jensen, Beth Kempton, B.P. Walter, Rebecca Wait. *Founded* 2012.

Antony Harwood

103 Walton Street, Oxford OX2 6EB
email mail@antonyharwood.com
website www.antonyharwood.com
Contacts Antony Harwood, Jo Williamson

General and genre fiction; general non-fiction. *Commission* Home 15%, overseas 20%. Will suggest revision.

Clients include Louise Doughty, Peter F. Hamilton, Alan Hollinghurst, A.L. Kennedy, Dorothy Koomson, Charlotte Levin, George Monbiot. *Founded* 2000.

The Haworth Agency†

Studio 103, Babel Studios, 158B Kentish Town Road, London NW5 2AG
tel 020-4551 2607
email info@haworthagency.co.uk
website www.haworthagency.co.uk
X @haworth_agency
Bluesky @thehaworthagency.bsky.social
Instagram @thehaworthagency
Agents Georgina Ruffhead, Catherine Goldstone, *Agents' Assistant* Katie Butler

Represents writers, directors and creatives for stage and screen. Email CV with a brief paragraph about yourself and your work. Include details of your credits and/or attached industry reference. Writers should have a play or script/screenplay of no fewer than 30 pages ready to submit on request. *Founded* 2021.

A.M. Heath & Co.*

6 Warwick Court, London WC1R 5DJ
tel 020-7242 2811
email enquiries@amheath.com
website www.amheath.com
Instagram @a.m.heath
Agents Julia Churchill (children's), Bill Hamilton, Victoria Hobbs, Tom Killingbeck, Jessica Lee, Oli Munson, Florence Rees, Rebecca Ritchie, Euan Thorneycroft, Anna Webber, *Rights Director* Alexandra McNicoll

Literary and commercial fiction and non-fiction, children's and film/TV. *Commission* Home 15%, USA/translation 20%, film/TV 20%. Digital submission via website. No screenplays, poetry or short stories except for collections.

Clients include Terry Deary, Samantha Harvey, Sarah Moss, Vaseem Khan, Katie Fforde, Annie Lord, Conn Iggulden, Cynan Jones, Maggie O'Farrell, Kamila Shamsie, Afua Hirsch, Zeinab Badawi, Tim Shipman, the estates of George Orwell and Hilary Mantel. *Founded* 1919.

HHB Agency*

11 Ingersoll Road, London W12 7BE
tel 020-7405 5525
email elly@hhbagency.com
website https://hhbagency.com
X @hhbagencyltd
Instagram @hhbagencyltd
Contact Elly James

Non-fiction: journalism, history and politics, contemporary autobiography and biography, original thinking, popular science, memoir, food and cookery. Fiction: women's commercial, book club, historical and thrillers. *Commission* 15%.

Authors include Nick Barratt, Charlotte Betts, Emma Burstall, Rory Cellan-Jones, Ben Chu, Suzanne Goldring, Molly Green, James Hanning, Mishal

Husain, Saliha Mahmood Ahmed, Louise Minchin, Dr Max Pemberton, Rosemary Shrager, Rachel Trethewey. *Founded* 2005.

Sophie Hicks Agency*

Providence Yard, Ezra Street, London E2 7RJ
email info@sophiehicksagency.com
website www.sophiehicksagency.com
X @SophieHicksAg
Agents Sophie Hicks, Sarah Williams

Adult fiction and non-fiction. Also handles children's books for 9+. Represented in all foreign markets. *Commission* Home/USA 15%, translation 20%. Email submissions only, see website for guidelines. No poetry, scripts or illustrated books.

Authors include Anne Cassidy, Lucy Coats, Eoin Colfer, Dan Davies, Ruth Fitzmaurice, Tristan Gooley, Tom Hodgkinson, Shahroo Izadi, Benedict Jacka, Signe Johansen, Emerald Fennell, Padraig Kenny, Andrew Meehan, Alex Smith, Tom Whipple. *Founded* 2014.

David Higham Associates*†

6th Floor, Waverley House, 7–12 Noel Street, London W1F 8GQ
tel 020-7434 5900
email dha@davidhigham.co.uk
website www.davidhigham.co.uk
Managing Director Lizzy Kremer, *Books* Veronique Baxter, Nicola Chang, Jemima Forrester, Stephanie Glencross, Georgia Glover, Andrew Gordon, Christabel McKinley, Caroline Walsh, Jessica Woollard, *Foreign Rights* Alice Howe, Allison Cole, Giulia Bernabe, Rachael Sharples, Anna Watkins, Sam Norman, Mariam Quraishi, Kathryn Williams, *Film/TV/Theatre* Nicky Lund, Clare Israel, Georgie Smith

Agents for the negotiation of all rights in literary and commercial fiction, and general non-fiction. Represented in all foreign markets either directly or through sub-agents. All genres, children's fiction and picture books, plays, film and TV scripts, offering a full service across all media. *Commission* Home 15%, USA/translation 20%, scripts 10%. See website for submissions policy.

Clients include Naomi Alderman, Belinda Bauer, J.M. Coetzee, Bernard Cornwell, Stephen Fry, Paula Hawkins, Mick Herron, Owen Jones, Damien Lewis, Robert Macfarlane, Carole Matthews, Val McDermid, Alexander McCall Smith. *Children's authors* include Michael Morpurgo, Cressida Cowell, Liz Pichon, Jacqueline Wilson, the estate of Roald Dahl. *Founded* 1935.

Holroyde Cartey*

email claire@holroydecartey.com
email penny@holroydecartey.com
website www.holroydecartey.com
Contacts Claire Cartey, Penny Holroyde

A literary and artistic agency representing a list of award-winning and bestselling authors and illustrators for the children's market. Welcomes submissions from debut and established authors. *Commission* Home 15%. See website for submission guidelines. Does not handle proposals for the adult market. *Founded* 2015.

Vanessa Holt*

59 Crescent Road, Leigh-on-Sea, Essex SS9 2PF
tel (01702) 473787
email v.holt791@btinternet.com

General fiction and non-fiction. Works in conjunction with foreign agencies and publishers in all markets. *Commission* Home 15%, overseas 20%, film/TV/radio 15%. No unsolicited MSS and submissions preferred by arrangement. No overseas submissions. *Founded* 1989.

Kate Hordern Literary Agency*

18 Mortimer Road, Clifton, Bristol BS8 4EY
tel (01179) 239368
email kate@khla.co.uk
email anne@khla.co.uk
website https://khla.co.uk
Agents Kate Hordern, Anne Williams

A small agency with an international reach representing a wide range of fiction and some non-fiction. See website for further details of what the agency is looking for. Submission by email only and include a pitch, a synopsis and the first three chapters. *Founded* 1999.

Valerie Hoskins Associates†

20 Charlotte Street, London W1T 2NA
tel 020-7637 4490
email info@vhassociates.co.uk
website https://vhassociates.co.uk
Proprietor Valerie Hoskins, *Agent* Rebecca Watson

Film, TV and radio; specialises in animation. Works in conjunction with US agents. *Commission* Home 12.5%, overseas max. 20%. No unsolicited MSS; preliminary letter and sae essential.

Clients include Joe Alexander, Andy Amfo, Catherine Williams, Tom Bradby, Guy Burt, Laurence Davey, Michelle Gayle, Matthew Graham, Julian Unthank, Henrietta Hardy, Sarah Louise Hawkins, Paul Mari, Jeff Povey, E.L. James. *Founded* 1983.

Clare Hulton Literary Agency*

email info@clarehulton.co.uk
website www.clarehulton.com
Instagram @clarehultonliteraryagency
Director Clare Hulton

Represents numerous bestselling and award-winning authors. Specialises in non-fiction especially cookery, health and fitness, parenting, music, self-help, true crime and memoir. Also has a small but growing fiction list. Submissions consisting of a synopsis and sample chapter should be sent by email. No fantasy, poetry, screenplays, YA or children's.

Authors include Kay and Kate Allinson, Jackie Kabler, Dan Toombs, James Haskell, Chloe Madeley, Amy Sheppard, Matt Roberts, Catherine Phipps, Kwoklyn Wan, Lesley-Ann Jones, Dr Liz O'Riordan, Robert Murphy, Lacey Ostermann, Sam and Dom Milner, Catherine Phipps. *Founded* 2012.

Independent Talent Group†

40 Whitfield Street, London W1T 2RH
tel 020-7636 6565
website www.independenttalent.com
Instagram @itg_Ltd

Specialises in scripts for film, theatre, TV and radio. Client base encompasses actors, directors, writers, producers and their production companies, below-the-line talent, casting directors, presenters, comedians and voice-over artists. No unsolicited material. Referral only; contact specific agent directly attaching CV and details about referral.

Janklow & Nesbit (UK)*

Holborn Town Hall, 193–197 High Holborn, London WC1V 7BD
tel 020-7243 2975
email submissions@janklow.co.uk
website https://janklowandnesbit.co.uk
X @JanklowUK
Instagram @janklownesbituk
Agents Will Francis, Claire Paterson Conrad, Julia Eagleton, Emma Leong, Hayley Steed, *Foreign Rights* Mairi Friesen-Escandell, Nathaniel Alcaraz-Stapleton, Ellis Hazelgrove, Maimy Suleiman, Janet Covindassamy

Represents a bestselling, global and award-winning range of commercial and literary fiction, non-fiction, children's, YA and poetry. Handles translation rights directly or through sub-agents in all territories. US rights handled by Janklow & Nesbit Associates in New York. Submission by email only. Include name, the title and the name of the agent the submission is for in the email subject line. For fiction, send informative covering letter, synopsis and first three sample chapters. For non-fiction, include a covering letter, full outline setting out the aims of each chapter and a sample chapter. For poetry, submit a short pitch and small sample of 3–5 poems. No plays or film/TV scripts. Does not currently have a dedicated children's agent.

Clients include Dr Rangan Chatterjee, Ed Yong, Jasper Fforde, Adam Rutherford, Mya-Rose Craig, Hannah Fry, Oliver Burkeman, Anne-Marie Imafidon, Michel Faber, Sunjeev Sahota, Lucy Cooke, Tsedal Neeley, Chukwuebuka Ibeh. *Founded* 2000.

Oscar Janson Smith Agency

53 Turnham Green Terrace, Chiswick, London W4 1RP
email oscar@oscarjansonsmith.com
website www.oscarjansonsmith.com
Instagram @oscarjansonsmith
Founder Oscar Janson Smith

Fiction, non-fiction, cookery and children's. Email submissions. Consult website for interests.

Clients include Niall Kirkland, Georgia Harrison, Moses Swaibu, Abby Rawlinson, Ro Mitchell, Sarah Asuquo, Grant Brydon, Emmanuel Asuquo, Elly Smart, Jay McGuiness. *Founded* 2023.

JFL Agency†

60 St. Martin's Lane, London WC2N 4JS
tel 020-3137 8182
email agents@jflagency.com
website www.jflagency.com
Agents Alison Finch, Dominic Lord, Gary Wild

TV, radio and film. *Commission* Home 10%. Initial contact by preliminary email to representation@jflagency.com; do not send scripts in the first instance. See website for further information. No novels, short stories or poetry.

Clients include Bill Dare, Ed Dyson, Jan Etherington, Sinead Fagan, Phil Ford, Rob Gittins, Gabby Hutchinson Crouch, Lisa McMullin, Julie Parsons, David Semple, James Serafinowicz, Pete Sinclair, Paul Smith, Fraser Steele. *Founded* 2011.

Johnson & Alcock*

West Wing, Somerset House, Strand, London WC2R 1LA
tel 020-7251 0125
website www.johnsonandalcock.co.uk
X @JohnsonAlcock
Instagram @johnsonandalcockliterary
Contacts Michael Alcock, Anna Power, Ed Wilson, Charlotte Seymour, Anna Dawson

Commercial and literary fiction, and non-fiction. *Commission* Home 15%, USA/translation/film 20%. Email relevant agent a brief covering letter, a synopsis and first 50 pages. For agent biographies and contact details see website. No plays or board/picture books. *Founded* 1956.

Tibor Jones & Associates

PO Box 74604, London SW2 9NH
email enquiries@tiborjones.com
website www.tiborjones.com
Contact Kevin Conroy Scott

Literary fiction and non-fiction, category fiction, music autobiographies and biographies. Send first five pages, synopsis and covering letter by email.

Authors include Wilbur Smith, Guillermo Arriaga, Deborah Curtis, Olafur Eliasson, Hala Jaber, Paul Lake, Hans Ulrich Obrist, Bernard Sumner, Christopher Winn. *Founded* 2007.

Jane Judd Literary Agency*

18 Belitha Villas, London N1 1PD
tel 020-7607 0273
website www.janejudd.com
X @janelitagent

General non-fiction and fiction. Works with agents in the USA and most other countries. *Commission* Home 10%, overseas 20%. No longer accepting new clients.

Authors include Jill Mansell, Anne O'Brien, John Brunner, David Winner, S.W. Perry, Michelle Birkby, Andy Dougan, Quentin Falk, Margaret Rooke, Margret Geraghty. *Founded* 1986.

Kane Literary Agency*

2 Dukes Avenue, London N10 2PT
tel 020-8351 9680
email submissionskaneliterary@gmail.com
website www.kaneliteraryagency.com
Director Yasmin Kane

Interested in discovering and launching the careers of debut writers. Literary and commercial fiction, children's fiction (middle grade to YA). Non-fiction: memoirs, metaphysics. *Commission* Home 15%, overseas 20%. Send submissions by email only; no submissions by post. For fiction, send a covering letter with the first three chapters and a synopsis; for non-fiction, send a covering letter and full book proposal plus two sample chapters. See website for further information. Currently closed to submissions.

Authors include Richard Butchins, Sarah Harris, Ruchita Misra, Min Day. *Founded* 2004.

Michelle Kass Associates*†

85 Charing Cross Road, London WC2H 0AA
tel 020-7439 1624
website www.michellekass.co.uk
Agents Michelle Kass, Rebecca Ferrin, Tishna Molla

Literary and commercial fiction. Scripts for film and TV. Works with agents around the world. *Commission* Home 10%, overseas 15–20%. No unsolicited material, phone in first instance. Sample material on request. No picture book or non-fiction. *Founded* 1991.

Keane Kataria Literary Agency

email info@keanekataria.co.uk
website www.keanekataria.co.uk
Partners Sara Keane, Kiran Kataria

Boutique agency representing commercial fiction and non-fiction. Women's commercial fiction (contemporary, historical, romantic comedy, saga), reading group fiction, historical fiction, cosy crime and narrative non-fiction. *Commission* Home 15%, USA/translation 20%. See website for current submission guidelines. No children's, YA, sci-fi, fantasy, thrillers, academic, short stories, poetry, plays or film/TV scripts.

Clients include Tommy Barnes, Jan Casey, Lucy Coleman, Lynne Francis, Helen Fripp, Claire Heywood, Jenny Kane, Judy Leigh, Gabrielle Malcolm, Rosie Meddon, Beth Moran, Amy Myers, Fiona Veitch Smith, Georgina Stewart, Alexandra Walsh. *Founded* 2014.

Ki Agency*†

Primrose Hill Business Centre,
110 Gloucester Avenue, London NW1 8HX
tel 020-3214 8287
email meg@ki-agency.co.uk
email fabienne@ki-agency.co.uk
email helen@ki-agency.co.uk
website www.ki-agency.co.uk
Bluesky @kiagency.bsky.social
Instagram @ki_agency_ltd
Managing Director Meg Davis, *Agents* Fabienne Schwizer, Helen Lane

Represents writers of fiction, non-fiction and screenplays for film or TV. Focus on genre fiction. See website for current submission guidelines. No children's or poetry.

Clients include M.R. Carey, Claire North, Angela Slatter, Daniel Church, John Allison, Matthew Feldman, K.C. Harper, Savannah Stephens, Jarom Strong, Olivia Jackson, Emma Sterner-Radley, Adam Roberts, Fiona Barnett, the estates of Fred Hoyle and Anne Perry. *Founded* 2011.

Knight Hall Agency†

Lower Ground Floor, 7 Mallow Street,
London EC1Y 8RQ
tel 020-3397 2901
email office@knighthallagency.com
website www.knighthallagency.com
Contacts Charlotte Knight, Samara Wash

Specialises in writers for stage, screen and radio/podcasts, and directors. *Commission* Home 10%, overseas 15%.

Clients include Simon Amstell, Simon Beaufoy, Jeremy Brock, Matthew Dunster, Jemima Khan, Francis Lee, Martin McDonagh, Simon Nye, Ol Parker, Ripley Parker, Lucy Prebble, Philip Ridley, Polly Stenham, Robert Thorogood, Laura Wade. *Founded* 1997.

Laxfield Literary Associates*

tel 07746 751820
email info@laxfieldliterary.com
website https://laxfieldliterary.com
Founder Emma Shercliff

Represents authors from Norfolk and Suffolk, and writers from under-represented backgrounds. Keen to receive work from authors based in Africa, the Caribbean, the Middle East and Ukraine. Translation rights, screen rights and permissions are handled by Blake Friedmann Literary Agency. Looking for literary and commercial fiction and non-fiction, particularly creative non-fiction, travel writing, memoir and nature writing. Email submissions only to submissions@laxfieldliterary.com. For fiction, include a covering letter, synopsis and the first three chapters. For non-fiction, include a covering letter with a CV, a one-page summary of the project, chapter outline and three sample chapters.

Submissions not open during the month of August. Does not represent plays, screenwriting, horror, high fantasy, children's or YA.

Clients include include Mstyslav Chernov, Brian Chikwava, Kalaf Epalanga, Heather Parry, Tom Shakespeare, Luke Wright, the estate of Victoria Amelina. *Founded* 2020.

LBA Books*

91 Great Russell Street, London WC1B 3PS
tel 020-7637 1234
email info@lbabooks.com
website www.lbabooks.com
X @LBA_Agency
Instagram @lba_litagency
Agents Luigi Bonomi, Amanda Preston, Louise Lamont, Hannah Schofield

Fiction and non-fiction. Keen to find new authors and help them develop their careers. Works with foreign agencies and has links with film and TV production companies. Fiction: commercial and literary fiction, thrillers, crime, psychological suspense, YA, children's, women's fiction, fantasy. Non-fiction: history, science, memoir, parenting, lifestyle, cookery and TV tie-in. *Commission* Home 15%, overseas 20%. Send preliminary letter, synopsis and first three chapters. No postal submissions. No poetry, short stories or screenplays.

Authors include Ben Miller, Lesley Kara, Simon Kernick, Lauren North, Susan Lewis, Ande Pliego, Mensun Bound, Natali Simmonds, Jane Monckton Smith, Alice Roberts, Simon Scarrow, Heidi Swain, Karen Swan, Nick Foulkes, Catherine Walsh. *Founded* 2005.

Susanna Lea Associates*

S78 South Wing, Somerset House, Strand, London WC2R 1LA
tel 020-7287 7757
email london@susannalea.com
website www.susannalea.com/about/london
X @SLALondon
Agents Susanna Lea, Thérèse Coen, Mark Kessler, Stephanie Cabot, Cara Lee Simpson

General fiction and non-fiction with international appeal. Send query letter, brief synopsis, the first three chapters and/or proposal by email. No plays, screenplays or poetry.

Authors include Alexandra Potter, Tom Service, Stella Duffy, Luke Harding, Carole Cadwalladr, Marc Levy, Alex Bell, Maria Kuzniar, Christine Pillainayagam, Dolen Perkins-Valdez, Jacqueline Bublitz, V.V. Ganeshananthan, Okechukwu Nzelu, Roxy Dunn. *Founded* 2000.

Barbara Levy Literary Agency*

64 Greenhill, Hampstead High Street, London NW3 5TZ
tel 020-7435 9046
email submissions@barbaralevyagency.com
website www.barbaralevyagency.com
Director Barbara Levy

Translation rights handled by the Buckman Agency; works in conjunction with US agents. Adult fiction and general non-fiction. Film and TV rights for existing clients only. *Commission* Full-length MSS: home 15%, overseas by arrangement. Preliminary letter with synopsis and sae essential, or by email. *Founded* 1986.

Lewinsohn Literary Agency*

58 Old Compton Street, London W1D 4UF
email queries@lewinsohnliterary.com
website www.lewinsohnliterary.com
Instagram @lewinsohnliterary
Agent & Director Becky Thomas

Translation rights handled by Blake Friedmann Literary Agency. Email submissions only. For fiction, send a covering letter, a synopsis, and 50 pages as a Word document. For non-fiction, include a covering letter, an introduction to the project, a basic chapter breakdown and a sample chapter. Ideally as a Word document, pdf will be accepted if the project is highly illustrated. No poetry collections, fantasy, historical or children's including YA.

Authors include Hollie McNish, Justin Myers, Sabrina Mahfouz, Gemma Cairney, Michael Pedersen, Will Burns, Carl Anka, Vanessa Kisuule, Cecilia Knapp, Richard Milward. *Founded* 2021.

Lexington Literary*

email [firstname]@lexingtonliterary.co.uk
website www.lexingtonliterary.co.uk
Instagram @lexingtonliterary
Agents Seren Adams, Kat Aitken

Adult fiction and non-fiction including novellas and some poetry. Interested in literary fiction with distinctive and bold new voices, and narrative non-fiction that tackle big ideas, history, science, politics, nature writing and true crime. Email individual agent directly. For Kat, send brief cover letter along with a biographical note and first three chapters of your work (fiction) or proposal (non-fiction). For Seren, send a sample and description of the project along with a brief biographical note. *Founded* 2024.

Limelight Celebrity Management*

10 Filmer Mews, 75 Filmer Road, London SW6 7BZ
tel 020-7384 9950
email mail@limelightmanagement.com
website www.limelightmanagement.com
Facebook www.facebook.com/LimelightCelebrityManagement
X @Fionalimelight
Contacts Fiona Lindsay, Maclean Lindsay

General fiction, crime, thrillers, historical, suspense, mystery and women's commercial fiction. Also non-fiction in the areas of arts and crafts, cookery, biography, autobiography, popular science, business, natural history, sport, travel and health. *Commission* Full-length and short MSS: home 15%, overseas 20%, TV/radio 10–20%. Will suggest revision where appropriate.

Clients include James Martin, Oz Clarke, Theo Randall, Linda Barker, Jinny Blom, Tara Ward, Jules Hudson, Tim Wonnacott, Salvatore Calabrese, Lesley Waters. *Founded* 1991.

Lindsay Literary Agency*

East Worldham House, Alton, Hants GU34 3AT
tel (01420) 831430
email info@lindsayliteraryagency.co.uk
website www.lindsayliteraryagency.co.uk
X @LindsayLit
Founder Becky Bagnell

Specialists in children's fiction and non-fiction, teen/YA, middle grade and picture books. *Commission* Home 15%, translation 20%. Send first three chapters, synopsis and covering letter by email, unless submitting a picture book which requires the submission of the full text. No submissions by post. Will suggest revision.

Authors include Pamela Butchart, Christina Collins, Donna David, James Davis, Louise Finch, Sam Gayton, Sital Gorasia Chapman, Ruth Hatfield, Larry Hayes, J.M. Joseph, Nicola Penfold, Beth O'Brien, Kate Peridot, Lui Sit, Daniel Tawse, Rachel Valentine, Sue Wallman, Joe Wilson. *Founded* 2008.

The Literary Office

71–75 Shelton Street, London WC2H 9JQ
tel 07910 267336
email jenny.todd@theliteraryoffice.com
website www.theliteraryoffice.com
Founder Jenny Todd

Represents literary and commercial fiction, non-fiction, YA, film and TV. Drawn to works of originality by inventive, relevant and multi-faceted writers and artists, and committed to developing long-term strategies for their careers. *Commission* Home 15%, overseas 20%. Submissions via website. Send covering letter, synopsis and three sample chapters. *Founded* 2021.

The Liverpool Literary Agency*

email submissions@liverpool-literary.agency
website www.liverpool-literary.agency
Bluesky @liverpool-lit.bsky.social
Threads @Liverpool_literary_
Agents Clare Coombes, Laura Bennett

Looking for adult fiction in all genres. Only accepting submissions from writers born, or currently living in, the north of England unless it's sci-fi or fantasy. Submissions should include a synopsis and the first three chapters by email, with an author bio included in the covering email. See website for further submission guidelines. Does not accept children's or middle-grade fiction, scripts, non-fiction, poetry, short stories or YA (unless specifically YA sci-fi and fantasy).

Authors include David Beckler, Steven Bernstein, Rachel Bowdler, Ania Card, Helen Glynn Jones, Alice James, John Maxwell, Caron McKinlay, K.N. Milde, Ashleigh Nugent, Helen Parusel, Zoe Richards, Michael Sellars, Emma Whitehall, Patricia Wilson. *Founded* 2020.

James Lockhart Agency

email james@jameslockhartagency.com
website www.jameslockhartagency.com
X @JMLockhart2
Agent James Macdonald Lockhart

General non-fiction and fiction. Represents writing which covers a broad range of genres including memoir, geography, economics, politics, history, nature writing, biography, science, travel and literary fiction. *Commission* Home 15%, overseas 20%. Email a covering letter and the first 30 pages. See website for full submission guidelines.

Authors include Amy Liptrot, Guy Shrubsole, Caspar Henderson, Julian Hoffman, Gwyneth Lewis. *Founded* 2023.

Andrew Lownie Literary Agency

36 Great Smith Street, London SW1P 3BU
tel 020-7222 7574
email andrew@andrewlownie.co.uk
website www.andrewlownie.co.uk
X @andrewlownie
Director Andrew Lownie

Handles non-fiction, working in association with a range of sub-agents around the world. Represents biography, history, reference, current affairs plus journalists and celebrities. Represents inspirational memoirs and ghostwriters. *Commission* Home/USA 15%, translation 20%, film 20%. Submissions should include synopsis, author profile, chapter summaries and sample material. Will suggest revision.

Authors include Jeremy Dronfield, Juliet Barker, Roger Crowley, Tom Devine, Robert Hutchinson, Lawrence James, Sean McMeekin, Daniel Tammet, *The Oxford Classical Dictionary*, *The Cambridge Guide to Literature in English*, the estates of Joyce Cary and Julian Maclaren-Ross. *Founded* 1988.

Luithlen Agency

88 Holmfield Road, Leicester LE2 1SB
tel 0116 273 8863
email penny@luithlenagency.com
website www.luithlenagency.com
Agent Penny Luithlen

Children's fiction, all ages up to YA. *Commission* Home 15%, overseas 20%, performance rights 15%. Currently no accepting submissions or new clients. *Founded* 1986.

Lutyens & Rubinstein*

17 Powis Mews, London W11 1JN
tel 020-7792 4855
email submissions@lutyensrubinstein.co.uk
website https://lutyensrubinstein.co.uk
Agents Sarah Lutyens, Felicity Rubinstein, Jane Finigan, Daisy Parente, Jenny Hewson

Fiction and non-fiction, commercial and literary. *Commission* Home 15%, overseas 20%. Send material by email with a covering letter and short synopsis. Submissions not accepted by hand or by post. *Founded* 1993.

David Luxton Associates*

23 Hillcourt Avenue, London N12 8EY
email admin@davidluxtonassociates.co.uk
website www.davidluxtonassociates.co.uk
X @DLuxAssociates
Instagram @davidluxtonassociates
Agents David Luxton, Nick Walters, Rebecca Winfield

Specialises in non-fiction, with a focus on sports writing. DLA also handles translation and subsidiary rights on behalf of its clients, including film, TV, podcast and performance rights. Submission by email only. Include a synopsis (300 words max), CV, chapter breakdown and sample chapter. Does not represent fiction, poetry, scripts or screenplays. *Founded* 2011.

Eunice McMullen

Low Ibbotsholme Cottage, Troutbeck Bridge, Windermere, Cumbria LA23 1HU
email eunice@eunicemcmullen.co.uk
website www.eunicemcmullen.co.uk
Director Eunice McMullen

All types of children's fiction, particularly picture books and older fiction. *Commission* Home 15%, overseas 15%. No unsolicited MSS.

Authors include Alison Friend, Charles Fuge, Cally Johnson Isaacs, James Mayhew, Momoko Abe, Mark McKinley. *Founded* 1992.

Marjacq Scripts*

The Space, 235 High Holborn, London WC1V 7DN
tel 020-7935 9499
email [firstname]@marjacq.com
website www.marjacq.com
X @MarjacqScripts
Agents Leah Middleton, Philip Patterson, Imogen Pelham, Catherine Pellegrino, Sandra Sawicka

Full-service agency. Handles all rights. In-house legal, foreign rights, book-to-screen and interactive media support. Commercial and literary fiction and non-fiction, crime, thrillers, horror, sci-fi, commercial women's fiction, romantic fiction, graphic novels, children's, history, lifestyle, contemporary issues and screenwriting. *Commission* Home 15%, overseas 20%, film 20%. Send first 50 pages with synopsis by email to appropriate agent. See website for further submission guidelines. No poetry or theatre.

Clients include Jimi Famurewa, Roopa Farooki, Helen FitzGerald, Annie Garthwaite, Finbar Hawkins, Marie Le Conte, Stuart MacBride, Amy McCaw, Nicola Martin, Syd Moore, Alex North, Gita Ralleigh, Yara Rodrigues Fowler, Suzanne Snow, Kassia St Clair. *Founded* 1973.

The Marsh Agency*

50 Albemarle Street, London W1S 4BD
tel 020-7493 4361
email hello@marsh-agency.co.uk
website www.marsh-agency.co.uk
X @TheMarshAgency
Managing Director Camilla Ferrier

Offers international representation to a wide range of writers, literary agents and publishing companies. No unsolicited submissions. *Founded* 1994.

Maven Literary Management*

email info@mavenliterary.com
website www.mavenliterary.com
Instagram @mavenliterary
Founder Amanda Harris

Represents award-winning journalists, world-leading academics, thought-leaders and spellbinding storytellers. Translation rights by Rachel Mills Agency and works with Speed Literary and Talent Management for film and TV rights. Adult fiction and non-fiction. Email submission only to submissions@mavenliterary.com. For fiction: covering letter in body of email with a one-page synopsis and first three chapters (around 10,000 words) attached as Word docs. Full manuscript on request. For non-fiction, covering letter with a full chapter outline and a sample chapter. Does not consider scripts or screenplays.

Clients include Dr Federica Amati, Gwyneth Archer, Rebecca Bainbridge, Sarah Berry, Adina Belloli, Kathryn Bruton, Emma Cowing, Paloma Faith, Professor Noel Fitzpatrick, Anna Haugh, Sarah Hiscox, Christina Kynigos, Marina Litvinenko, Poppy O'Neill, Sophie Scott. *Founded* 2025.

May Literary Agency*

email carolyn@mayliteraryagency.com
website www.mayliteraryagency.com
Instagram @mayliteraryagency
Agent Carolyn May McGlone

Fiction and non-fiction for all ages. Submissions currently closed. Does not represent sci-fi, horror, crime or cookery books. *Founded* 2024.

MBA Literary and Script Agents*†

62 Grafton Way, London W1T 5DW
tel 020-7387 2076
email submissions@mbalit.co.uk
website https://mbalit.co.uk
Instagram @mbaliteraryagents

Agents Diana Tyler, David Riding, Susan Smith, Sophie Gorell Barnes

Fiction, non-fiction and children's books. Foreign rights handled by Louisa Pritchard Associates. *Commission* Home 15%, overseas 20%, TV/theatre/radio 10%, film 15%. Submission by email only. Include the first three chapters and a synopsis as attachments and a covering letter in the body of the email. All attachments must be in Word, pdfs or Final Draft format. Not currently accepting unsolicited film and television submissions.

Clients include Sufiya Ahmed, Jeffrey Caine, Julian Jones, Rosanna Ley, Stef Penney, the estate of Anne McCaffrey. *Founded* 1971.

Jemma McDonagh Agency

email jemma@jmcagency.co.uk
website www.jmcagency.co.uk
Instagram @jemmamcdonaghagency.co.uk
Agent Jemma McDonagh

Boutique literary and rights agency. Adult fiction and non-fiction. *Commission* Home 15%, film/TV/translation 20%. Email submissions only. For non-fiction proposals, include a covering letter, full outline of the project and one sample chapter. For fiction, include a covering letter, full summary and the first three chapters or first 50 pages. *Founded* 2024.

Madeleine Milburn Literary, TV & Film Agency*

The Factory, 1 Park Hill, Clapham, London SW4 9NS
tel 020-7499 7550
email submissions@madeleinemilburn.com
website www.madeleinemilburn.co.uk
Facebook www.facebook.com/MadeleineMilburnLiteraryAgency
X @MMLitAgency, @agentmilburn
Instagram @madeleinemilburn
Directors Madeleine Milburn, Giles Milburn, *Director of Children's & YA* Chloe Seager, *Head of Books* Olivia Maidment, *Head of International Rights* Valentina Paulmichl, *Head of Film & TV* Hannah Ladds, *Literary Agents* Emma Bal, Rachel Yeoh, Jessica Leeke, Maddy Belton

Manages and develops the careers of global bestselling and award-winning authors of fiction and non-fiction in the UK and Commonwealth, USA, Canada and Europe. Handles all literary rights in international markets directly including film/TV/theatre/radio and digital. Represents prominent writers of literary fiction, book club, smart commercial, upmarket suspense, crime, thrillers, mystery, historical, romance, romcom, humour, action, fantasy, sci-fi, YA, children's, coming of age and film/TV tie-ins. Non-fiction list includes academics, historians, scientists, cookery writers, journalists, memoirists and activists. *Commission* Home 15%, USA/Canada/translation 20%, film/TV 20%. No submissions by post. See submission guidelines on website.

Authors include Gail Honeyman, C.L.Taylor, Nita Prose, Ashley Audrain, C.J. Tudor, Holly Bourne, Mark Edwards, Nick Newman, Hanako Footman, Charlotte Runcie, Lucy Jane Wood, Maithree Wijesekara, Katherine May, Corinne Fowler, Maikel Kuijpers. *Founded* 2012.

Rachel Mills Literary*

M27 South Wing, Somerset House, Strand, London WC2R 1LA
website www.rachelmillsliterary.co.uk
X @rmliterary
Bluesky @rmlagency.bsky.social
Instagram @rachelmillsliterary
Agents Rachel Mills, Nelle Andrew

Focused on fiction and non-fiction which can effect positive change, aimed at an upmarket, mainstream audience. Non-fiction: big ideas books, popular science, popular economics, popular psychology, narrative non-fiction, memoir, health, wellbeing, lifestyle, food, the environment, feminism and nature writing. Fiction: literary, commercial, upmarket female fiction, historical, suspense, thrillers, crime, romantasy and high concept. *Commission* Home 15%, overseas 20%, film/TV 20%. Send synopsis and first three chapters for fiction. For non-fiction send proposal and full biography. Consult website for individual agent's email addresses. Does not represent erotica, children's, sci-fi and fantasy, short stories, business, educational or academic books.

Authors include Bryony Gordon, Candice Carty-Williams, Jennie Godfrey, Sara Collins, Heidi Perks, Catherine Gray, Alice Vincent, Hassan Akkad, David Nutt, Peter Walker, Uju Asika, Claire Ratinon, Max La Manna, Joshua Fletcher. *Founded* 2019.

MMBcreative*

(Mulcahy Sweeney Associates Ltd)
165 Highlever Road, London W10 6PH
tel 020-3582 9379
email mulcahyadmin@mmbcreative.com
website https://mmbcreative.com/literary-agency/books
X @my_agent_secret
Instagram @myagentsecret
Contacts Ivan Mulcahy, Sallyanne Sweeney, Edwina de Charnace, Sidney Jones

Non-fiction, literary fiction, and certain genres which vary during the year. *Commission* Home 15%, Overseas/US 20%. See website for full list of submission email accounts and current guidelines.

Clients include Ha-Joon Chang, Juno Dawson, Ian Kelly, David Mitchell, Steven Lenton, Lisa McInerney, Sheena Demspey, Robert Webb, Dapo Adeola, Nathan Bryon, Brian Cox, Poppy Kuroki, James Roseman, Bridget Hourican, Africa Brooke. *Founded* 2016.

Morgan Green Creatives

157 Ribblesdale Road, London SW16 6SP
email kirsty@morgangreencreatives.com
website www.morgangreencreatives.com
Founder Kirsty McLachlan

Actively looking for fresh talent and to be challenged with new ideas, inspired and moved by great writing. Represents fiction, non-fiction and children's book writers. Submission by email which includes a covering letter within the body of the email, plus 30 pages of your work attached. Does not represent picture books for 0–5 year olds (other than for existing clients). *Founded* 2020.

Judith Murdoch Literary Agency

19 Chalcot Square, London NW1 8YA
tel 020-7722 4197
website www.judithmurdoch.co.uk
Contact Judith Murdoch

Full-length fiction only. Especially interested in commercial women's fiction and crime. *Commission* Home 15%, overseas 20%. Closed to new submissions. No sci-fi and fantasy, poetry, short stories or children's.

Clients include Diane Allen, Trisha Ashley, Frances Brody, Jill Childs, Rosie Clarke, Diney Costeloe, Norma Curtis, Kate Eastham, Juliet Greenwood, Faith Hogan, Emma Hornby, Ali Mercer, Elizabeth Morton, Kitty Neale. *Founded* 1993.

Mushens Entertainment*

email submissions@mushens-entertainment.com
website www.mushens-entertainment.com
X @MushensEnt, @mushenska, @lizadeblock, @Rachel_Neely_
Instagram @mushensentertainment
Contact Juliet Mushens, Liza DeBlock, Rachel Neely

Fiction and non-fiction. *Commission* Home 15%, overseas 20%. Send an email addressed to a specific agent. For fiction: use the subject line 'Fiction Submission: [Title of work]', the cover letter in the body of the email and a synopsis and the first three chapters or approx. 10,000–15,000 words as attachments. For non-fiction: use the subject line 'Non-Fiction Submission: [Title of work]', the cover letter in the body of the email and a proposal or the first 10,000–15,000 words attached. Does not represent picture books, middle grade or children's fiction younger than teen, novellas, short stories, poetry, screenplays, comics/graphic novels or erotica.

Authors include Richard Osman, Jessie Burton, Claire Douglas, Hannah Kaner, Jenny Saint, Saara El-Arifi, Stacey Halls, Abigail Dean, Elodie Harper, Lora Jones, Sue Hincenbergs, Fiona McPhillips, Carys Green, Pim Wangtechawat, Sally Abé. *Founded* 2020.

The Nagle Agency

email contact@thenagleagency.com
website www.thenagleagency.com
Founder Conor Nagle

Adult fiction and non-fiction. Submit via email: submissions@thenagleagency.com. Fiction: covering letter with synopsis and substantial sample of the work (5,000+ words). For short story collections, provide a minimum of three individual stories. Non-fiction: covering letter with synopsis of proposal and sample or supplementary material. No poetry or academic work. *Founded* 2024.

Kate Nash Literary Agency*

website https://katenashlit.co.uk
Facebook www.facebook.com/KateNashLiteraryAgency
X @KNLitAgency, @katenashagent, @justinnashlit, @litagentfran, @saskialeach_
Contacts Kate Nash, Justin Nash, Francesca Riccardi, Saskia Leach

Represents commercial, general, genre fiction and popular non-fiction. Open to approaches from both new and established authors. General fiction, book club, literary fiction, crime and thriller, historical fiction, romantic fiction, women's fiction, sci-fi and fantasy, YA and popular non-fiction. *Commission* Home/English language 15%, translation 20%, film/TV/other media 20%. See website for full submission guidelines. No poetry, drama, comedy, erotica, short stories or children's picture books.

Clients include P.R. Black, Heather Burnside, Alice Castle, Helena Dixon, Lesley Eames, Hannah Hendy, Jane Lovering, Leonie Mack, David Mark, Faith Martin, Lilac Mills, Andie Newton, Bella Osborne, Alex Shaw, Maggie Sullivan. *Founded* 2009.

The North Literary Agency

The Chapel, Market Place, Corbridge, Northumberland NE45 5AW
email hello@thenorthlitagency.com
website http://thenorthlitagency.com
Instagram @northlitagency
Threads @northlitagency
Agents Julie Fergusson, Allan Guthrie, Lina Langlee, Kevin Pocklington

Looking for all types of fiction and narrative non-fiction. Email a brief covering letter plus a synopsis (fiction) or proposal (non-fiction) and 15,000-word sample to submissions@thenorthlitagency.com. Check website for full submission guidelines. No academic writing, poetry, self-help, picture books or screenplays.

Clients include Andreina Cordani, Gavin Extence, David Fenne, J.M. Hall, Seth Insua, John Ironmonger, Jack Jackman, Andy Jones, Craig Robertson, Fiona Leitch, Ann Sei Lin, Doug Sinclair, Adam Southward, Nige Tassell, the estate of Paul Torday. *Founded* 2017.

Northbank Talent Management*

email info@northbanktalent.com
website www.northbanktalent.com
Facebook www.facebook.com/northbanktalent

X @northbanktalent
Instagram @northbanktalent
Agents Matthew Cole (Non-fiction), Elizabeth Counsell (Fiction)

A talent and literary agency representing thought leaders, broadcasters, writers and content creators across all media. Fiction: women's fiction, reading group fiction, crime, thrillers, literary fiction with a strong storyline, historical and speculative fiction. Non-fiction: politics, current affairs, memoir, celebrity, autobiography, biography, business, lifestyle, history, science, self-help and smart thinking. *Commission* Home 15%, overseas/rights in other media 20%. Send cover letter, synopsis and first three chapters as Word or Open Document attachments to either fiction@northbanktalent.com or nonfiction@northbanktalent.com. Aims to give initial response within two weeks. No poetry, academic books, plays, scripts or short stories. No children's without referral.

Authors include Brian Cox, Anthony Seldon, Damian Collins, Claire Hubard-Hall, Duncan Mavin, Caroline Wheeler, David Torrance, Rory Cormac, Tim Gregory, Bianca Gillam, Chloe Howarth, J.D. Kirk, Marion Todd, Megan Freeman, Veronika Dapunt. *Founded* 2006.

Andrew Nurnberg Associates*

43 Great Russell Street, London WC1B 3PD
tel 020-3327 0400
email info@nurnberg.co.uk
website www.andrewnurnberg.com
X @nurnberg_agency
Instagram @andrewnurnbergassociates
Managing Directors Jenny Savill, Doug Wallace

Represents adult and children's authors, agent and publisher clients in the fields of literary and commercial fiction, and general non-fiction for the sale of rights throughout the world via offices in the UK and overseas. *Founded* 1977.

Originate Literary Agency*

71–75 Shelton Street, Covent Garden, London WC2H 9JQ
email info@originateliterary.co.uk
website www.originateliterary.co.uk
X @OriginateLit
Instagram @originateliterary
Founder & Literary Agent Natalie Jerome

Actively looking for new voices who push boundaries and want to create change on a global stage. Represents a broad range of genres including YA, commercial fiction and non-fiction. *Commission* Home 15%, overseas 20%. Send a covering note including a brief biography and the first three chapters (for illustrated titles send sample spreads with the proposal) by email to originatesubmissions@originateliterary.co.uk. Does not represent academic and educational texts.

Clients include Anchal Seda, Amir Khan, Sir Lenny Henry (children's publishing), Maya Jordan, Rene Germain. *Founded* 2023.

Paper Lion

13 Grayham Road, New Malden, Surrey KT3 5HR
tel 07748 786199, (01276) 61322
email katyloffman@paperlionltd.com
email lesleypollinger@paperlionltd.com
website www.paperlionltd.com
Agents Katy Loffman, Lesley Pollinger

A cross-media literary agency. The client list includes award-winning authors and literary estates. Has a strong focus on the exploration of digital opportunities, and expertise in solving complex copyright, dramatic rights and literary issues from the present and past.

Clients include Max Allen, Diane Barker, Nick Drake-Knight, Stewart Ferris, Catherine Fisher, Bill D. Palmer, Saviour Pirotta, HopeRoad Ltd, the estates of authors including Grantley Dick-Read, Bruce Hobson, D.H. Lawrence, Ada Lovelace and John Wyndham. *Founded* 2017.

Paper Literary*

email submissions@paperliterary.com
website www.paperliterary.com
X @PaperLiterary
Agents Catherine Cho, Katie Greenstreet, *Associate Agent* Kiya Evans

Focused on storytelling with a vision of building author careers internationally. Represents upmarket and reading group fiction, speculative fiction, historical fiction, crime and thriller, YA fantasy and narrative non-fiction titles. *Commission* Home 15%, USA 20%, translation/book-to-film 20%. Send a query letter, synopsis and the first three chapters (up to 10,000 words) by email. Does not represent screenplays or dramatic works.

Authors include Sarah Underwood, Kate Fagan, Brooke Robinson, Tasha Coryell, Rosanna Pike, Katherine Blake, Natasha Siegel. *Founded* 2021.

PBJ Management†

22 Rathbone Street, London W1T 1LG
tel 020-7287 1112
email general@pbjmanagement.co.uk
website www.pbjmanagement.co.uk
Instagram @PBJManagement
Contacts Peter Bennett-Jones, Caroline Chignell

Represents writers, performers, presenters, podcasters, composers, directors, producers and DJs. Specialises in comedy. *Commission* Theatre 15%, film/TV/radio 15%.

Clients include Rowan Atkinson, Armando Iannucci, Eddie Izzard, Lenny Henry, Mawaan Rizwan, Simon Blackwell, Adam Buxton, Richard Ayoade, Tim Minchin, Tim Key, Nina Conti, Maisie Adam, Vic and Bob, Sally Phillips, James Acaster. *Founded* 1988.

Jonathan Pegg Literary Agency*

c/o Workshop, 47 Southgate Street,
Winchester SO23 9EH
tel (01962) 656101
email info@jonathanpegg.com
website https://jonathanpegg.com
Founder & Agent Jonathan Pegg

Specialises in full-length quality fiction and non-fiction. See website for genre categories represented. *Commission* Direct 15%, co-agented 20%. Email submission to submissions@jonathanpegg.com. For fiction, send an author bio note, synopsis plus three sample chapters. For non-fiction, include an author bio note, synopsis and proposal which includes a chapter plan and writing sample. Does not represent children's fiction, YA or pure fantasy.

Authors include Dr Nafeez Ahmed, Michael Blastland, Steve Bloomfield, Alex Brummer, Alex Christofi, Nick Davies, Dr Stuart Farrimond, Kaffe Fassett OBE, Zac Goldsmith, Robert Lacey, Tom McCarthy, General Sir Michael Rose, Jonathan and Angela Scott, Carolyn Steel, Prof. Sir David Spiegelhalter OBE. *Founded* 2008.

Pérez Literary & Entertainment*

49 Greek Street, London W1D 4EG
email assist@perezliterary.com
website www.perezliterary.com
X @perez_literary
Instagram @perezliterary
Managing Director Kristina Pérez

Represents a wide variety of fiction and non-fiction, from book club to horror to current affairs. *Commission* Home 15%, USA 15%, overseas 20–25%. Submission guidelines on website. *Founded* 2023.

Peters Fraser & Dunlop*

55 New Oxford Street, London WC1A 1BS
tel 020-7344 1000
email info@pfd.co.uk
website https://petersfraserdunlop.com
Facebook www.facebook.com/pfdagents
X @PFDAgents
Instagram @PFDAgents
Ceo Caroline Michel, *Literary Agents* Caroline Michel, Tim Bates, Samantha Brace, Kate Evans, Adam Gauntlett, Sarah Hornsley, Lucy Irvine, Annabel Merullo, Silvia Molteni, Fiona Petheram, Laurie Robertson, Daisy Chandley, Elizabeth Sheinkman, Lisette Verhagen, *Associate Agent* Kieron Fairweather, *Film & TV* Rosie Gurtovoy, Jonathan Sissons, *Broadcast & Live Events* Tris Payne, *Foreign Rights* Rebecca Wearmouth, Lucy Barry, Antonia Kasoulidou

Represents authors of fiction and non-fiction, presenters and public speakers throughout the world. Email submissions addressed to individual agents. Include covering letter, synopsis or outline and first three chapters as well as author biographies. See website for submission guidelines. Does not represent scriptwriters.

Authors include Jeanette Winterson, Simon Schama, Bear Grylls, Sir Michael Caine, Onjali Q. Raúf, Jamie Bartlett, Lesley Pearse, Rose Tremain, Niall Williams, Jamie Susskind, Kenya Hunt, Ruby Wax, the estate of Edna O'Brien. *Founded* 1924.

PEW Literary*

46 Lexington Street, London W1F 0LP
tel 020-7734 4464
email info@pewliterary.com
website www.pewliterary.com
X @pew_literary
Agents Patrick Walsh, Margaret Halton, Doug Young

Boutique agency with a strong list of prize-winning authors. Non-fiction and fiction. *Commission* Home 15%, overseas 20%, film/TV 20%. Submit a covering letter with a synopsis and first three chapters (fiction) or a proposal including an outline and sample chapter (non-fiction) by email to submissions@pewliterary.com. Postal submissions accepted. No poetry, children's picture books, plays film/TV scripts or academic titles.

Clients include Nick Harkaway, Luke Jennings, Keggie Carew, Laura Cumming, Jim al-Khalili, Tom Holland, Helen Castor, Andrea Wulf, Anita Anand, Gaia Vince, Simon Singh, Bill Browder, Mark Cocker, Peter Sarris. *Founded* 2016.

The Plot Agency*

email marilia@theplotagency.com
website www.theplotagency.com
X @mariliasavvides
Bluesky @mariliasavvides.bsky.social
Founder & Literary Agent Marilia Savvides

Fiction and non-fiction. *Commission* Home 15%, USA/translation 20%, film/TV 20%. Email submission only with covering letter in the body of the email. Include the first three chapters (fiction) or project (non-fiction) with a full synopsis. Current wish list can be found on the website. Does not accept fantasy, poetry, plays, academic books or short stories.

Authors include Jack Anderson, Natasha Bell, Joeli Brearley, Lauren Brown, Bexy Cameron, Paul Bradley Carr, Robyn Delvey, Katja Ivar, Hanna Jameson, Henry Lewis, Abigail Marsh, Jessica Moor, Eleanor Morton, Sherry Rankin, Amy Stewart. *Founded* 2024.

Portobello Literary*

email submissions@portobelloliterary.co.uk
website www.portobelloliterary.co.uk
Instagram @portyliterary
Founder Caro Clarke

Looking for unique and engaging writing that disrupts the status quo. Represents fiction: commercial and literary, all genres from speculative fiction and fantasy to gripping crime (specifically looking for queer fiction); and non-fiction: narrative, memoir, popular science, big ideas, travel, food writing and cookery books, nature, culture, essays, politics, queer culture and intersectional feminism. Email a synopsis, short bio and the first three chapters or 50 pages. Provide a chapter outline in addition for non-fiction. Not currently open for fiction submissions. No children's and YA.

Authors include Polly Atkin, Jenny Chamarette, Rachel Charlton-Dailey, Mona Dash, Joe Donnelly, Harry Josephine Giles, C.L. Hellisen, Russell Jones, Louise Kenward, Wenying Li, J.C. Niala, Andrés N. Ordorica, Alycia Pirmohamed, Wendy Pratt, Elspeth Wilson. *Founded* 2022.

Shelley Power Literary Agency*

33 Dumbrells Court, North End, Ditchling, East Sussex BN6 8TG
tel (01273) 844467
email sp@shelleypower.co.uk
Contact Shelley Power

General fiction and non-fiction. Works in conjunction with agents abroad. No longer accepting submissions. *Commission* Full-length MSS: home 12.5%, USA/translation 20%. Preliminary letter essential – may be sent by email. No children's books, YA, sci-fi, fantasy, short stories, poetry, screenplays or plays. *Founded* 1976.

RCW*

(formerly Rogers, Coleridge & White)
20 Powis Mews, London W11 1JN
tel 020-7221 3717
email info@rcwlitagency.com
website www.rcwlitagency.com
Instagram @rcwliteraryagency
Managing Director Peter Straus, *Deputy Managing Director* Georgia Garrett, *Directors* Nelka Bell, Sam Copeland, Stephen Edwards, Natasha Fairweather, Laurence Laluyaux, Zoë Waldie, Claire Wilson, Jon Wood, *Agents* Eleanor Birne, Cara Jones, Matthew Marland, Matthew Turner, Millie van Grutten

International representation for all genres of fiction, non-fiction, children's, YA and illustration. *Commission* Home 15%, USA 20%, translation 20%. See website for submissions information. Note that due to the volume of unsolicited queries, it is policy to respond (usually within six weeks) only if interested in the material. *Founded* 1967 as Deborah Rogers Ltd, 1989 as RCW Ltd.

Redhammer Management

website https://redhammer.info
X @Litopia
Agent Peter Cox

A boutique literary agency providing in-depth management for a restricted number of clients. Specialises in works with international book, film and TV potential. Participates in Pop-Up Submissions every Sunday; submit a title, brief description and first 700 words of the work. No radio or theatre scripts.

Clients include Rt. Hon. Norman Baker, Michelle Paver. *Founded* 2006.

The Lisa Richards Agency†

108 Upper Leeson Street, Dublin D04 E3E7, Republic of Ireland
tel +353 (0)1 637 5000
email info@lisarichards.ie
website www.lisarichards.ie
Contact Faith O'Grady

Handles fiction and general non-fiction. Overseas associate: The Marsh Agency for translation rights. *Commission* Ireland 10%, UK 15%, USA/translation 20%, film/TV 15%. Approach with proposal and sample chapter for non-fiction and three to four chapters and synopsis for fiction (sae essential).

Clients include Dr Marie Cassidy, Mick Clifford, Aoife Dooley, Austin Duffy, Christine Dwyer Hickey, Paul Howard, Gerry Hussey, Michelle McDonagh, Eve McDonnell, Frank McNally, Joanne McNally, Vicki Notaro, Hector O'Heochagain, Colm O'Regan, Gill Perdue. *Founded* 1998.

Richford Becklow Agency

2 Church Street, Peasenhall, Suffolk IP17 2HL
tel (01728) 660879
email lisa.eveleigh@richfordbecklow.co.uk
website www.richfordbecklow.com
Contact Lisa Eveleigh

Literary and commercial fiction and non-fiction. Historical fiction, saga, crime, romantic comedy, biography and memoir. *Commission* Home 15%, overseas 20%. Closed to submissions.

Authors include Hugo Barnacle, Stephen Buck, Ralph Fevre, R.P. Marshall, Carol McGrath, Adrienne Vaughan, Grace Wynne-Jones, the estate of Tony Slattery. *Founded* 2012.

Rocking Chair Books Literary Agency*

2 Rudgwick Terrace, St Stephens Close, London NW8 6BR
email representme@rockingchairbooks.com
website www.rockingchairbooks.com
X @rockingbooks
Contact Samar Hammam

Dedicated to original and page-turning books. Currently open for submissions. Focuses on adult commercial fiction, literary fiction, graphic novels and non-fiction. Also works with other agencies to represent their translation or English language rights, including MMBcreative and the Raya Agency. *Commission* Home 15%, translation/adaptation rights 20%. Submission by email only. No children's, YA or sci-fi (unless they are crossover).

Authors include Warsan Shire, Dominique Duong, Christina Fonthes, Brian Turner, Kay Medaglia,

Nydia Hetherington, Laura Coleman. *As co-agent alongside The Raya Agency for Arabic Literature in Translation:* Dima Wannous, Khaled Khalifa, Samar Yazbek, Hoda Barakat. *As co-agent alongside Anjali Singh Agency:* Devapriya Roy, Padma Viswanathan, Susan Abulhawa, Deena Mohammed. *Founded* 2013.

The Sayle Literary Agency*

1 Petersfield, Cambridge CB1 1BB
email info@sayleliteraryagency.com
website www.sayleliteraryagency.com
Proprietor & Agent Rachel Calder

Uses specialist co-agents to sell books in foreign language markets, in the USA and for film/TV. Translation rights handled by The Marsh Agency. Film and TV rights handled by Sayle Screen. US rights handled by Dunow, Carlson and Lerner. Fiction: general, literary and crime. Non-fiction: current affairs, social issues, travel, biographies and history. *Commission* Home 15%, USA/translation 20%. List is currently closed. No plays, poetry, textbooks, children's, technical, legal or medical books. *Founded* 1896.

Sayle Screen†

11 Jubilee Place, London SW3 3TD
tel 020-7823 3883
email info@saylescreen.com
website www.saylescreen.com
Agents Jane Villiers, Matthew Bates, Kelly Knatchbull, Eva Robinson

Specialises in scripts for film, TV, theatre and radio. Represents film, TV and theatre rights in fiction and non-fiction for The Sayle Literary Agency, Greene & Heaton and RCW. Works in conjunction with agents in New York and Los Angeles. In 2021, alongside The Artists' Partnership and Sara Putt Associates, Sayle Screen formed The Partnership Group representing above and below the line talent, behind and in front of the camera. Unable to consider unsolicited material unless recommended by producer, development executive or course tutor. Email a CV, covering letter and details of your referee or course tutor to submissions@saylescreen.com. Every submission carefully considered, but responds only to submissions it wishes to take further; not able to return material sent in. *Founded* 1896.

Linda Seifert Management†

c/o 1st Floor, Arthur Stanley House,
40–50 Tottenham Street, London W1T 4RN
tel 020-3327 1180
email contact@lindaseifert.com
website https://lindaseifert.com
X @lindaseifert
Agent Edward Hughes

Represents writers, directors and producers for film and TV. *Commission* Home 10%, overseas 20%. No book authors. Not currently accepting unsolicited submissions.

Clients include Stephen Volk, Paul Gerstenberger, Nathan Cockerill, Gavin Scott, Mark Bussell and Justin Sbresni, Adam Butcher, Tim Lebbon, Paul Staheli, Marco van Belle, Keith Storrier, Nancy Netherwood, Sandy Johnson, Simon Hynd, Emma Lindley, Paul Taylor. *Founded* 2002.

Seventh Agency

email info@seventhagency.co.uk
website www.seventhagency.co.uk
X @seventhagency_
Instagram @the_seventhagency
Agents Kemi Ogunsanwo, Joe Sedgewick, Lisa Goodrum, *Assistant* Lina Benosman

Specialises in fiction including literary, commercial, mystery/thriller, romance, historical, sci-fi and fantasy, New Adult and YA. Also represents children's middle-grade literature and select non-fiction. Fiction submissions welcome in the months of March and November. Non-fiction by invitation only. Consult website for specific details once the submission window is open. Not currently offering representation to scriptwriters.

Authors include Plestia Alaqad, Kenny Imafidon, Eric Collins, Mikaela Loach, Sharada Keats, Vasundra Tailor, Wenyan Lu, Yemi Dipeolu, Patrick Gallagher, Jeffrey Boadi, Verna Gao, Perri Drayton Shakes, Chidi-Ebere Onwuka. *Founded* 2024.

The Shaw Agency

website www.theshawagency.co.uk
X @KateJShaw
Instagram @agentkateshaw
Agent Kate Shaw

Interested in literary and commercial fiction, fact and fiction books for children (6+) and teens/YA, and narrative non-fiction. Submission by contact form on website. Include a cover letter of up to 300 words, the first six pages or approx. 3,000 words of the MS and a short synopsis of about 500 words (or in the case of non-fiction, a chapter plan and one sample chapter).

Clients include Lucy Adlington, Isabel Ashdown, Jasbinder Bilan, Lesley Lokko, Alan MacDonald, Mark Powers, Holly Smale, Isabel Thomas. *Founded* 2019.

Sheil Land Associates†

Room 9–25, LABS House, 15–19 Bloomsbury Way, London WC1A 2TH
tel 020-7405 9351
email info@sheilland.co.uk
website www.sheilland.co.uk
X @sheilland
Instagram @sheillandassociates
Agents UK & USA Sonia Land, Gaia Banks, Piers Blofeld, Ian Drury, Natalie Barracliffe, *Film/Theatre/TV* Lucy Fawcett, Rebecca Lyon, *Foreign Rights* Lauren Coleman

Literary and commercial fiction and non-fiction; adult and children's. Represents book club, commercial and literary fiction: thrillers, crime, romance, drama, sci-fi and fantasy and YA; and non-fiction: biography, politics, history, military history, gardening, travel, cookery and humour. *Commission* Home 15%, USA/translation 20%. Welcomes approaches from new clients to start or to develop their careers. Send cover letter, synopsis and first three chapters to submissions@sheilland.co.uk.

Clients include Peter Ackroyd, Pam Ayres, Steven Carroll, Nadine Dorries, Robert Fabbri, Janice Hallett, Graham Hancock, Susan Hill, Mark Lawrence, The Brothers McLeod, Gill Paul, Diane Setterfield, Julie Soto, the estate of Catherine Cookson. *Founded* 1962.

Caroline Sheldon Literary Agency – see RCW

Hannah Sheppard Literary Agency*

email enquiries@hs-la.com
website www.hs-la.com
Bluesky @hslanews.bsky.social
Instagram @HS_LA_News
Founder & Literary Agent Hannah Sheppard, *Associate Agent* Louise Buckley

Actively seeking new authors, particularly from under-represented groups. Current wish lists can be found on the website. Represents children's fiction (primarily across middle grade, teen and YA), commercial adult fiction (with a focus on crime/thriller, women's fiction and upmarket/book-club fiction) and a very small amount of non-fiction. *Commission* Home 15%, overseas 20%, film/TV 20%. Submission via form on website between the 1st and 7th of each month. No poetry, short story collections, novellas or screenplays.

Clients include Dee Benson, Jim Beckett, Sarah Bonner, Abi Elphinstone, Betty Firth, Keris Fox, Liam Higginson, Gabrielle Kent, Philippa Leathley, Gina Lees, Chris McGeorge, Kate Mallinder, Terri Nixon, Morgan Owen, Felicity Yeoh. *Founded* 2023.

Dorie Simmonds Agency*

email info@doriesimmonds.com
website https://doriesimmonds.com
Contact Dorie Simmonds

Children's fiction, general non-fiction and commercial fiction. *Commission* Home 15%, USA 15%, translation 20%. Email submissions only. Fiction: send the first chapter plus a full synopsis and a covering letter, with a brief CV. Non-fiction: send a detailed proposal, alongside the covering letter and CV. Full-length MS submission on request. Does not represent poetry or screenplays. *Founded* 1997.

Philippa Sitters Associates*

128 City Road, London EC1V 2NX
email ps@philippasitters.co.uk
website www.philippasitters.co.uk
X @PhilippaSitters
Bluesky @phi1ly.bsky.social
Instagram @psaliterary
Agent Philippa Sitters

Adult fiction across the literary-commercial spectrum. *Commission* Home 15%, US/translation/dramatic rights 20%. Send a covering letter by email, plus synopsis and first three chapters (or 30 pages) as Word doc attachments. Not interested in high fantasy, sci-fi, YA, middle-grade and children's books, poetry, scripts or mind, body & spirit.

Clients include Ashley Hickson-Lovence, Connor Hutchinson, Dani Garavelli, Davina Quinlivan, Dawn Watson, Holly Kyte, Jamie Lafferty, Kate Brook, Lottie Gross, Marc Millon, Margarita Montimore, Nick Trend, Rebecca Sarah Ley, Rebecca Struthers, Scott Bryan. *Founded* 2024.

The Soho Agency*†

16–17 Wardour Mews, 2nd Floor, London W1F 8AT
tel 020-7471 7900
email admin@thesohoagency.co.uk
website https://thesohoagency.co.uk
X @TheSohoAgencyUK
Instagram @thesohoagencyuk
Managing Director Rowan Lawton, *Agents* Mark Lucas, Julian Alexander, Araminta Whitley, Alice Saunders, Ben Clark, Sophie Laurimore, Helen Mumby, Carina Rizvi, Philippa Milnes-Smith (Children's and YA), Marina de Pass, *Associate Agent* Melissa Fontaine

Full-length commercial and literary fiction, non-fiction, fantasy, YA and children's books. Special interests (fiction): accessible literary fiction, character-led narrative, contemporary romance, crime, domestic dramas, historical, psychological suspense and thrillers, reading group fiction, romantic comedy and women's fiction. Special interests (non-fiction): big ideas, business, history, inspirational stories and people, leadership, memoir, philosophy and science. *Commission* Home 15%, USA/translation 20%. Representation in all markets. Unsolicited MSS considered. See website for further information about the clients and genres represented and essential information on submissions. No postal submissions. No poetry or textbooks.

Clients include Tom Bradby, Poorna Bell, Frank Gardner, Tim Peake, Bettany Hughes, Lindsey Kelk, Sophie Kinsella, Kate Mosse, Henry Marsh, Chris Riddell, Lauren Child, Michael Robotham, Nigel Slater, Alison Weir. *Founded* 2019.

Spring Literary

email submissions@springliterary.com
website www.springliterary.com
Instagram @springliterary
Agent Neil Dunnicliffe

Specialises in children's and YA writing and illustration. Searching for beautiful, entertaining, funny and thought-provoking books for children from picture books up to YA fiction. Send covering letter by email only. As attachments include: a one-page synopsis and sample chapters up to 10,000 words (fiction); a synopsis, short CV and three sample sections/chapters (non-fiction); one to three full book texts (picture book authors); or a portfolio of up to ten images (illustrators).

Clients include Sarah Massini, Sam Usher, Ross Collins, Pam Smy, Mick Jackson, David Melling, Rose Blake, Matt Sewell, Maisie Paradise Shearring. *Founded* 2022.

Elaine Steel Writers' Agent*†

49 Greek Street, London W1D 4EG
tel (01273) 739022
email es@elainesteel.com
website www.elainesteel.com
Contact Elaine Steel

Represents screen, radio, theatre and book writers. Does not read unsolicited material. Any consideration for representation must be by email and accompanied by a CV together with a short outline of the work to be submitted.

Authors include Gwyneth Hughes, Penny Woolcock, James Lovelock, Michael Eaton, Ian Kennedy Martin, Pearse Elliott, Brian Keenan. *Founded* 1986.

Abner Stein*

Suite 137, China Works, 100 Black Prince Road, London SE1 7SJ
tel 020-7373 0456
email info@abnerstein.co.uk
website www.abnerstein.co.uk
Contacts Caspian Dennis, Sandy Violette

Fiction, general non-fiction and children's. *Commission* Home 15%, overseas 20%. Not taking on any new clients at present.

Micheline Steinberg Associates†

Studio 315, ScreenWorks, 22 Highbury Grove, London N5 2ER
email info@steinplays.com
website www.steinplays.com
X @SteinbergAssocs2
Bluesky @SteinbergAssocs.bsky.social
Agent Micheline Steinberg, *Literary Associate* Helen MacAuley

Represents writers/directors for theatre, opera, musicals, television, film, radio and animation, as well as writer-directors, translators and librettists. Media rights in fiction and non-fiction on behalf of book agents, including Watson, Little and and Paper Lion. Also works in association with agents overseas. *Commission* Home 10%, with associates 15–20%. No unsolicited submissions. Industry recommendation preferred. No poetry or prose (except for current clients).

Authors include David K. Barnes, Julie Jones, Jonathan Larkin, Susie McKenna, Glyn Maxwell, Robin Norton-Hale, Debbie Owen, Mark Robertson, Danny Spring, Jane Upton, Steve Waters, Sarah Woods, the estates of Don Taylor, Snoo Wilson and John Wyndham. *Founded* 1987.

Rochelle Stevens & Co†

2 Terretts Place, Upper Street, London N1 1QZ
tel 020-7359 3900
email info@rochellestevens.com
website https://rochellestevens.com
Directors Rochelle Stevens, Frances Arnold

Scripts for TV, theatre and radio. *Commission* Home 10%. Recommendation from industry professional required. Email to introduce yourself and include your CV and the recommendation. Will request a writing sample if interested. Does not accept book submissions. *Founded* 1984.

Sarah Such Literary Agency

38 Church Road, Barnes, London SW13 9HN
tel 020-8741 2107
email info@sarah-such.com
website https://sarahsuchliteraryagency.tumblr.com
X @sarahsuch
Bluesky @sarahsuch.bsky.social
Instagram @sarahsuch1
Director Sarah Such

High-quality literary and commercial non-fiction and fiction for adults, young adults and children. Always looking for exciting new writers with originality and verve. Translation representation: The Buckman Agency. Film/TV representation: Lesley Thorne, Aitken Alexander Associates. Particular focus on literary and commercial debut novels, thrillers, topical fiction and quality women's fiction, biography, narrative non-fiction, memoir, history, popular culture and humour. *Commission* Home 15%, overseas 20%, film/TV 20%. Will suggest revision. Submit synopsis and three sample chapters (as a Word attachment by email) and an author biography. No postal submissions unless requested. No unsolicited MSS or telephone enquiries. Film/TV scripts for established clients only. No radio or theatre scripts, poetry, fantasy, self-help or short stories (unless full collections).

Authors include Matthew De Abaitua, Jeffrey Boakye, Kit Caless, Anne Charnock, Heather Cooper, Vina Jackson, Maxim Jakubowski, Antony Johnston, Louisa Leaman, Liliane Lijn, Vesna Maric, Caroline Sanderson, Nikhil Singh, Hazell Ward, Mike Wendling. *Founded* 2007.

The Susijn Agency

820 Harrow Road, London NW10 5JU
tel 020-8968 7435
email info@thesusijnagency.com
website www.thesusijnagency.com
Agent Laura Susijn

Specialises in world rights in English- and non-English-language literature: literary fiction and general non-fiction. *Commission* Home 15%, overseas 20%, theatre/film/TV/radio 15%. Send synopsis and three sample chapters.

Authors include Peter Ackroyd, Saud Alsanousi, Robin Baker, Ottavio Cappellani, Hwang Sok-yong, Radhika Jha, Uzma Aslam Khan, Parinoush Sainee, Darren Simpson, Sunny Singh, Bogdan-Alexandru Stanescu, Paul Sussman, Frank Westerman, David Whitehouse, Yan Lianke. *Founded* 1998.

Simon Trewin Creative

Soho Works, 2nd Floor, 180 Strand,
London WC2R 1EA
email newwriters@simontrewin.co.uk
website www.simontrewin.co.uk
X @simontrewin
Instagram @trewinagency
Agent Simon Trewin

Represents a broad range of titles and is also growing a list of consultancy client. Also a growing list of consultancy clients. Send a blank email to the email address listed above to receive a link to an online submissions form. Does not represent academic, cookery, picture books, sci-fi and fantasy.

Authors include Patience Agbabi, Charlotte Bradman, Sam Blake, John Boyne, Dr Harry Cliff, Chloe Esposito, Keith Lowe, Paul Lynch, Agnes Poirier, Dr Matthew Sweet. *Founded* 2019.

Jane Turnbull Agency*

Barn Cottage, Veryan Churchtown, Truro TR2 5QA
tel (01872) 501317
email jane@janeturnbull.co.uk
website www.janeturnbull.co.uk

Specialises in high quality non-fiction. Works in conjunction with Aitken Alexander Associates for sale of translation rights. Genres: biography, history, natural history, lifestyle, memoir, humour, TV tie-ins, cookery, some literary and YA fiction. *Commission* Home 15%, USA/translation 20%, performance rights 15%. See website for submission guidelines.

Authors include Kevin McCloud, Prue Leith, Penny Junor, David Lindo, Kate Bradbury, Kate Watson-Smyth, Lucy O'Brien, Andy Mulligan, Frederick Taylor, Lynne Murphy, Miki Berenyi, Jo Bradford, Richard Van Emden. *Founded* 1986.

Nick Turner Management†

tel 020-3723 8833
email nick@nickturnermanagement.com
website https://nickturnermanagement.com
X @nickturnermgmt
Agents Nick Turner, Phil Adie, *Agency Assistant* Andrew Allen

Represents writers and directors for film, TV and radio worldwide. Specialises in TV drama, comedy, continuing drama and children's. *Commission* Home 10%, overseas 15–20%. *Founded* 2016.

United Agents*†

12–26 Lexington Street, London W1F 0LE
tel 020-3214 0800
email info@unitedagents.co.uk
website www.unitedagents.co.uk
X @UA_Books
Bluesky @unitedagents.bsky.social
Instagram @unitedagentsbooks
Agents Olivia Davies, Caroline Dawnay, Ariella Feiner, Jodie Hodges, Millie Hoskins, Molly Jamieson, Caradoc King, Robert Kirby, Georgina Le Grice, Natalia Lucas, Laura Macdougall, Olivia Martin, Amy Mitchell, Becky Percival, Zoe Ross, Sophie Scard, Rosemary Scoular, Emily Talbot, Charles Walker

Fiction and non-fiction. *Commission* Home 15%, USA/translation 20%. See website for submission details. *Founded* 2008.

Suzann Wade Management

9 Wimpole Mews, London W1G 8PB
website www.suzannwade.com

Represents talent and writers globally. Possible options on novels with companies such as Channel 4, BBC, ITV, Amazon and Netflix. For TV/Film scripts, genres of particular interest are thrillers, crime and romcoms. Please submit via contact form on website and include your bio and a one-page synopsis of your writing. Responds only to those applicants that they are interested in. Do not send any scripts unless requested as any IP by default may lead to loss of ownership. No academic books. *Founded* 2006.

Watson, Little*

Suite 315, ScreenWorks, 22 Highbury Grove,
London N5 2ER
tel 020-7388 7529
email office@watsonlittle.com
website www.watsonlittle.com
X @watsonlittle
Managing Director James Wills, *Agents* Laetitia Rutherford, Donald Winchester, Megan Carroll, Ciara McEllin, Hannah Weatherill, *Rights Manager* Gabrielle Demblon

Offers a full service to its clients across all aspects of media. Handles a wide range of fiction and non-fiction for adults and children and works directly and in conjunction with US agents. Adult Fiction: literary, commercial women's, historical, reading group, crime and thriller. Non-fiction: history, science, popular psychology, memoir, humour, cookery and self-help. Children's: YA and middle-grade fiction, picture books and children's non-fiction in all genres. *Commission* Home 15%, USA/translation 20%. Email submissions@watsonlittle.com with an informative preliminary letter, synopsis and sample chapters. No poetry, TV, play or film scripts.

Authors include Freya Berry, Jenny Blackhurst, Sophie Claire, Robin Dunbar, Martin Edwards, Sarah Gristwood, Greg Jenner, Holan Liang, Alex Marwood, Alan Moore, Fiona O'Brien, Anika Scott, Ian Sinclair, Tom Wood. *Founded* 1970.

WGM Atlantic Talent and Literary Group

4 Bloomsbury Square, London WC1A 2RP
tel 020-3637 2064
email hello@wgmatlanticgroup.com
website www.wgmtalent.com
Facebook www.facebook.com/wgmtalent
Instagram @WGMAtlantictalent

Represents international and UK-based screenwriters, playwrights, authors and directors. The agency is recognised for developing a cross section of talent as well as having close relationships with industry partners. Email submissions only. Fiction: send a cover letter in body of the email, with a synopsis and first three chapters as separate attachments. Non-fiction: send a cover letter with a proposal and 20-page writing sample as attachments. *Founded* 2016.

Whispering Buffalo Literary Agency

97 Chesson Road, London W14 9QS
tel 020-7385 4655
email info@whisperingbuffalo.com
website www.whisperingbuffalo.com
Director Mariam Keen

Commercial and literary fiction, non-fiction, children's and YA fiction. Special interest in book-to-screen adaptations; TV and film rights in novels and non-fiction handled in-house. *Commission* Home 15%, overseas 20%. See website for current submission guidelines; only accepts submissions by email. *Founded* 2008.

Eve White Literary Agency*

15 Alderney Street, London SW1V 4ES
tel 020-7630 1155
email [firstname]@evewhite.co.uk
website www.evewhite.co.uk
Bluesky @evewhiteagency.bsky.social
Instagram @evewhiteliteraryagency
Contacts Eve White, Ludo Cinelli, Steven Evans

Boutique agency representing commercial and literary fiction and non-fiction, children's fiction and film/TV tie-ins. *Commission* Home 15%, overseas 20%. Will suggest revision where appropriate. See website for up-to-date submission requirements. No submissions by post.

Clients include Ruth Ware, James Norbury, Eloise Head, Len Pennie, Dr Kirren Schnack, Natalia Rudin, Rachel Wolf, Paul Cooper, Remi Idowu, Rae Earl, Rebecca Reid, Damian Le Bas, Luan Goldie, Sarah Ockwell-Smith, Han Smith. *Founded* 2003.

Dinah Wiener*

12 Cornwall Grove, London W4 2LB
tel 020-8994 6011
email dinah@dwla.co.uk
Director Dinah Wiener

Fiction and general non-fiction, film and TV in association. *Commission* Home 15%, overseas 20%, film/TV in association 15%. Not taking on new clients. No plays, scripts, poetry, short stories or children's books. *Founded* 1985.

Alice Williams Literary*

tel 020-7385 2118
email submissions@alicewilliamsliterary.co.uk
website www.alicewilliamsliterary.co.uk
Instagram @agentalicewilliams
Contact Alice Williams

Specialist literary agency representing writers and illustrators of picture books, children's fiction, teen/YA fiction and children's non-fiction. *Commission* Home 15%, USA/translation 20%, film/TV 20%. Submission by email only; attach full manuscript and synopsis, two picture book texts or illustration portfolio. See website for further guidelines and whether the agency is currently open or closed to submissions.

Clients include Zeshan Akhter, Fiona Barker, Lauren Beard, Ruby Clyde, Rachel Delahaye, Meg McLaren, Natelle Quek, Matt Ralphs, Santiago, Suzy Senior, Ciara Smyth, Hannah Tolson, Cat Weldon, Clare Helen Welsh, Pete Williamson. *Founded* 2018.

WME*

(William Morris Endeavour, UK)
100 New Oxford Street, London WC1A 1HB
tel 020-8929 8400
email hogden.assistant@wmeagency.com
website www.wmebookdepartment.com
X @WMEBooksUK, @WMEBooks
Books Matilda Forbes Watson, Hellie Ogden, Fiona Baird, Lucy Balfour, Suzannah Ball, Karolina Kaim, Francesca Ali, *Translation Rights* James Munro, Florence Dodd, Cody Siler, *Book to Film* Sanjana Seelam

Worldwide talent and literary agency with offices in London, New York, Beverly Hills, Nashville, Washington and Sydney. Handles translation rights directly in most territories. US rights handled by one of the US-based WME offices. Represents bestselling authors, critically acclaimed literary writers, award-winning thought leaders and up-and-coming talent. Sponsors the Lucy Cavendish Fiction Prize. Literary and commercial fiction, crime, thrillers, YA fiction, middle-grade fiction, memoir, self-help, lifestyle, sci-fi, fantasy, women's fiction, serious non-fiction and popular culture. *Commission* UK 15%, USA/translation 20%, film/TV 10%. Submit via the website following the indivdual guidelines set out by each agent.

Clients include Mohsin Hamid, Kiley Reid, Akala, Amor Towles, Jhumpa Lahiri, Glennon Doyle, Laura Dave, Brené Brown, Terry Hayes, Kiran Millwood Hargrave, M.J. Arlidge, Jessa Hastings, Annie Zimmerman, Anoushka Warden, Sarah A. Parker. *Founded* 1898.

The Writers' Practice

tel 07940 533243
email jemima@thewriterspractice.com
website https://thewriterspractice.com
Bluesky @writerspractice.bsky.social
Literary Agent Jemima Hunt

A boutique literary agency and editorial consultancy that specialises in author management, working closely with writers on all aspects of book development. Specialises in issue-led non-fiction and memoir; interested in crime and commercial fiction, and book-to-screen deals. *Commission* Home 15%, overseas 20%. For fiction, submit a brief synopsis and three chapters; for non-fiction, submit a pitch, book outline and sample chapter.

Clients include H.B. Lyle, Jenny Evans, Mikey Cuddihy, Henry Sanderson, Hannah Swanston. *Founded* 2012.

Susan Yearwood Agency*

2 Knebworth House, Londesborough Road, London N16 8RL
tel 020-7503 0954
email submissions@susanyearwoodagency.com
website https://susanyearwoodagency.com
Facebook www.facebook.com/susanyearwoodagency
X @sya_susan
Instagram @susanyearwoodagency
Contact Susan Yearwood

Book club fiction, commercial fiction and non-fiction; children's fiction, middle grade and teen/YA. *Commission* Home 15%, overseas 20%. Send submission with covering letter and brief synopsis via email. Submissions not accepted by hand or post. Tends not to read sci-fi and fantasy in adult fiction, short stories or poetry.

Authors include Fil Reid, Selina Flavius, Sarupa Shah. *Founded* 2007.

YMU Literary*

180 Great Portland Street, London W1W 5QZ
tel 020-8742 4950
email ymuLiterarySubmissions@ymugroup.com
website www.ymugroup.com
X @YMULiterary
Instagram @YMULiterary
Global Managing Director Briony Gowlett, *UK Managing Director* Anna Dixon, *Literary Executive* Elise Middleton

A bespoke literary agency within the UK's largest talent management agency, YMU Management, represents a broad range of writers of fiction and non-fiction across all genres. *Commission* Home 15%, USA 20%. Submissions should include an introductory email, detailed synopsis, and sample chapter. See website for further details.

Clients include Nathan Anthony (Bored of Lunch), Dr Whitney Bauman, Francis Bourgeois, Poppy Cooks, Fearne Cotton, Tom Daley, Jake Humphrey, Matt Lucas, Davina McCall, Ant McPartlin and Dec Donnelly, Rob Rinder, Stephen Mulhern, Dr Julie Smith, Stacey Solomon. *Founded* 2021.

Zeno Agency*

Primrose Hill Business Centre, 110 Gloucester Avenue, London NW1 8HX
tel 020-7096 0927
email info@zenoagency.com
website www.zenoagency.com
X @zenoagency
Bluesky @zenoagency.bsky.social
Instagram @zenoagency
Director John Berlyne, *Agent* Stevie Finegan, *Associate Agent* Bianca Gillam

Most adult fiction genres represented (commercial, crime/thriller, romance) with a specialism in sci-fi, fantasy and horror. Children's fiction from picture books through to YA. Non-fiction from specialists in their fields and authors with strong personal stories to tell (narrative, memoir, biography). Some illustrated non-fiction considered. *Commission* Home 15%, overseas 15% (via sub-agents 20%). Refer to the website for current submission guidelines. Does not consider poetry, plays or filmscripts.

Authors include Ben Aaronovitch, Aliette de Bodard, Travis Baldree, Jonathan Carroll, Charlaine Harris, Elizabeth Helen, Grady Hendrix, William Gibson, Emily Rath, Brandon Sanderson, Lavie Tidhar, M. A. Wardell, the estate of Roger Zelazny. *Founded* 2008.

Literary agents overseas

This list includes only a selection of agents across Australia and New Zealand (below), Canada (page 485) and the USA (page 487). Additional agency listings can be found at www.writersandartists.co.uk/resources/listings. Before submitting material, writers are advised to visit agents' websites for detailed submission guidelines.

The international dialling codes for phone numbers have been included in the listings below (+61 for Australia; +64 for New Zealand; and +1 for the USA and Canada). Remove the dialling code if calling from within that country.

sase = self-addressed stamped envelope

AUSTRALIA AND NEW ZEALAND

a4 Literary

email submissions@a4literary.com
website www.a4literary.com
Instagram @a4literary
Agents Grace Heifetz, Michaela McGuire, Tom Gilliatt, Rebecca Slater

Seeking smart and original fiction, non-fiction, poetry and writing for the screen and stage by Australian authors and creators. Email submission only. Include author bio and any writing credits and/or qualifications in body of email. For fiction (novels and short stories), attach a synopsis with first three chapters (or approx. 50 pages). For narrative non-fiction, attach a short overview and up to 10,000 words of sample writing. For subject-led non-fiction, attach a comprehensive overview together with no less than 5,000 words of sample writing. Not currently accepting submissions for illustrated children's books or purely academic works. *Founded* 2024.

Alex Adsett Literary

PO Box 694, Tugun, QLD 4224
email agent@alexadsett.com.au
website https://alexadsett.com.au
Principal Alex Adsett, *Agents* Rochelle Fernandez, Abigail Nathan, Lisa Fuller

Full-service agency, representing works of fiction and non-fiction for children, teens and adults. Fiction: literary and commercial fiction, crime, mystery, romance, sci-fi and fantasy. Children's: chapter book, middle grade and YA fiction (chapter or genre). Non-fiction: narrative non-fiction with a hook. Submission by invitation only; no unsolicited submissions. *Founded* 2008.

ALM: Australian Literary Management

Suite 1, 2A Booth Street, Balmain, NSW 2041
tel +61 (0)2 9818 8557
email alphaalm8@gmail.com
website http://austlit.com
Proprietor Lyn Tranter

For full details of genres represented, see website. Unsolicited submissions welcome from Australian writers. Not currently accepting submissions. Does not consider TV or film scripts of any kind, poetry, self-help, sci-fi and fantasy or books for children by unpublished authors. Does not accept self-published work or previously published works, including ebooks. *Founded* 1980.

Cameron's Management

Level 7, 61 Marlborough Street, Surry Hills, NSW 2010
tel +61 (0)2 9319 7199
email info@cameronsmanagement.com.au
website www.cameronsmanagement.com.au
Agents Anthony Blair, Needeya Islam, Sue Muggleton, Jonah Klein, Joel Pettersson, *Associate Agent* Stevie Answerth

Represents writers, directors, actors, presenters, designers, cinematographers, editors, composers and book authors across the full range of the film, television, live performance and publishing industries. Only accepts submissions in accordance with guidelines on website. *Founded* 1976.

Margaret Connolly & Associates

PO Box 945, Wahroonga, NSW 2076
tel +61 (0)2 9449 6342
email contact@margaretconnolly.com
website https://margaretconnolly.com
Proprietor Margaret Connolly

Represents novelists and non-fiction adult writers, children's writers and illustrators. Works closely with co-agents and sub-agents around the world. Consult website for submission information. *Founded* 1992.

Curtis Brown (Australia)

email submission@curtisbrown.com.au
website www.curtisbrown.com.au
X @curtisbrownaus
Managing Director Fiona Inglis, *Head of Agents* Pippa Masson, *Agents* Alexandra Christie, Tara Wynne, *Associate Agent* Caitlin Cooper-Trent

Australia's oldest and largest literary agency representing a diverse range of Australian and New Zealander authors. Submissions open in the months of March and August. Send cover email, synopsis and first three chapters. Not currently seeking stage/screenplays, poetry, self-help, children's picture books, early reader books, middle-grade fiction, comics, short stories, cookery books, educational, corporate, translated or comedy books.
Founded 1967.

Jenny Darling & Associates

PO Box 5328, South Melbourne, VIC 3205
email office@jennydarling.com.au
website www.jennydarling.com.au
Contact Jenny Darling

Adult fiction and non-fiction. *Commission* Home 15%, international/translation 20%, film/TV 20%.
Authors include Garry Disher, Mem Fox, Lian Hearn, Tim Winton, Charlotte Wood. *Founded* 1998.

Jacinta di Mase Management

website www.jacintadimase.com.au
Facebook www.facebook.com/jacintadimasemanagement
X @Jacinta_DiMase
Instagram @jacintadimase
Director Jacinta di Mase, *Agent* Danielle Binks

Commercial fiction and non-fiction for adults. Not currently accepting submissions. Consult website for updates from mid-2025.
Clients include Prof. Clare Wright, Jane Caro, Josh Bornstein, Katherine Collette, Aaron Fa'Aoso, Yves Rees, Briony Stewart, Tess Woods. *Founded* 2004.

Drummond Agency

PO Box 572, Woodend, VIC 3442
tel +61 (0)3 5427 3644
email info@drummondagency.com.au
website www.drummondagency.com.au/index.htm

Considers both fiction and non-fiction for adults and YA fiction. Query by telephone, email or letter. Do not send attachments unless requested. Represents Australian and New Zealander authors. Currently closed to submissions. No sci-fi or fantasy. Does not represent educational materials, poetry, plays, film scripts or children's picture books.
Authors include Randa Abdel-Fattah, Vikki Wakefield, Claire Zorn, Deborah Burrows, Margareta Osborn, Yvette Walker. *Founded* 1997.

Golvan Arts Management

website www.golvanarts.com.au
Facebook www.facebook.com/Golvan-Arts-Management-153871021304383

Represents a wide range of writers including writers of both adult and children's fiction and non-fiction, poetry, screenwriters and writers of plays. Also represents visual artists and composers. See the General Information section on the website before making contact via online form. *Commission* Home 16.5%. Send a brief introductory letter about your work in first instance. Do not send any sample material unless requested.

High Spot Literary

email [firstname]@highspotlit.com
website www.highspotlit.com
Facebook www.facebook.com/highspotlit
X @HighSpotLit
Instagram @Highspotlit
Founders Vicki Marsdon, Nadine Rubin Nathan, *Agent* Catherine Wallace

A full-service agency that provides traditional literary agent services with a marketing and social media eye. Guides authors through working with publishing partners for book publishing and/or book to film. Provides creative guidance and support to manage a successful literary career. See website for full submissions guidelines. Does not represent erotica, poetry or visual coffee table books at this time. Considers very few short story collections.

Margaret Kennedy Agency

PO Box 1433, Toowong, Brisbane, QLD 4066
tel +61 (0)7 3870 9996
email info@margaretkennedyagency.com
website www.margaretkennedyagency.com
X @mkliterary
Agent Hannah Douglas, *Consultant* Margaret Kennedy

A full-service agency representing adult fiction and literary non-fiction. Areas of special interest include non-fiction written by experts for general readers, food writing with a story, and essays and genre-defying short-form pieces. Submissions are open in January and July only. Send a brief query letter with the first 50 pages (fiction) or a letter and proposal (non-fiction). Does not consider genre fiction, self-help books, children's books or illustrations.
Founded 1996.

Sarah McKenzie Literary Management

tel +61 (0)4 1603 5061
email submissions@smlm.com.au
website www.smlm.com.au
Contact Sarah McKenzie

Representation for Australian and New Zealander authors. Actively seeks established and emerging authors of commercial, literary and genre fiction, non-fiction and children's fiction (including picture books, middle grade, YA and graphic novels). Submissions via email only. For fiction and memoir, include a covering letter, one- to two-page synopsis and 20 consecutive pages of the MS. For non-fiction, include a covering letter, one-page summary, author bio, one or two sample chapters and a table of contents. Does not represent works that have been previously self-published in any form, academic and spirituality titles, sci-fi fiction, novellas or poetry collections.

The Naher Agency

website www.naher.com.au
Founder Gaby Naher

Seeking intelligent and high concept fiction and non-fiction for adult by writers based in Australia and New Zealand (including Australian expats). Submit a pitch using the form found on the website. Writing sample on request. Does not represent sci-fi, romance, fantasy, poetry, YA fiction and children's or self-help books.

Clients include Nadia Mahjouri, Fleur McDonald, David Dyer, Dr Norman Swan, Minnie Darke, Heather Rose, Candice Fox, Kirsten Alexander, Joanna Jenkins. *Founded* 2024.

Jane Novak Literary Agency

PO Box 774, Five Dock, Sydney, NSW 2046
tel +61 (0)2 9281 8648
email jane@janenovak.com
website www.janenovak.com

Represents writers across all genres as well as a number of literary estates. Submissions are currently closed for fiction and children's/YA. Non-fiction submissions will be considered in digital form only. Inform the agency if submitting work to a publisher or another agency.

Authors include Helen Garner, Kate Grenville, Suzie Miller, David Malouf, Gerald Murnane, Behrouz Boochani, Patrick White.

Playmarket

PO Box 9767, Wellington 6141
email info@playmarket.org.nz
website www.playmarket.org.nz
Director Murray Lynch

Playwrights' agent, adviser and bookshop. Representation, licensing and script development of New Zealand plays and playwrights. Licenses productions of New Zealand plays nationally and around the world. *Founded* 1973.

Zeitgeist Agency

Level 1, 142 Smith Street, Summer Hill, NSW 2130
email query_sydney@zeitgeistagency.com
75 Rue E. Van Driessche, 1050 Brussels, Belgium
email query_brussels@zeitgeistagency.com
website www.zeitgeistagency.com
Instagram @zeitgeistwriters
Principal Agents Benython Oldfield, Sharon Galant, Thomasin Chinnery, Samuel Bernard

International literary, screen, theatre and talent management agency representing writers (fiction, non-fiction, memoir, children's and YA) and illustrators. Submit query or submission via email with 'Query' in the subject line. Specific submission guidelines for each genre can be found on the website.

Clients include Holly Ringland, Yumi Stynes, Vivian Pham, Susan Johnson, Benjamin Law, Mawunyo Gbogbo, Megan Rogers, Murong Xuecun, Annabel Abbs, Daria Desombre, Haska Shyyan, A.J. Betts, Gabriela Larios, Alison Edwards. *Founded* 2009.

CANADA

Acacia House Publishing Services

687 Oliver Street, Victoria, BC V8S 4W2
tel +1 226-387-4757
email bhanna.acacia@rogers.com
Managing Director Bill Hanna

Literary fiction/non-fiction, quality commercial fiction and most non-fiction. *Commission* English worldwide 15%, translation 25%, performance 20%. Works with overseas agents. Query first by email with sample of 50 pages max. No horror or occult.

Authors include Ron Base, Prudence Emery, Grit Laskin, Crispin Keith, Jill Downie, Mark Leier, John de Goey, Vlasta Van Kampen, Erin Ruddy, John Stephenson, Janet Turpin Myers, John Cooper, Noel Rae, the estates of Andre Gerolymatos and Alexis Troubetzkoy. *Founded* 1985.

Rick Broadhead & Associates

47 St. Clair Avenue West, Suite 501, Toronto, ON M4V 3A5
tel +1 416-929-0516
email info@rbaliterary.com
website https://rbaliterary.com

Interested in non-fiction, especially in the following categories: history, politics, business, true crime, investigative journalism, natural history/environment, national security/intelligence, current affairs, biography, science, pop culture, self-help, health, medicine and humour. Email queries preferred to submissions@rbaliterary.com. Writing sample on request. Not currently accepting fiction novels, screenplays, poetry or children's books.

Clients include Timothy Winegard, Chris Hadfield, Sam Kean, Jay Bahadur, Alex Hutchinson, William Davis MD. *Founded* 2002.

The Bukowski Agency

20 Prince Arthur Avenue, Suite 12-I, Toronto, ON M5R 1B1
tel +1 416-928-6728
email info@bukowskiagency.com
website www.bukowskiagency.com
Agent Denise Bukowski

Specialises in international literary fiction and up-market non-fiction for adults. See website for submission guidelines. Currently closed to unsolicited submissions. Does not represent children's literature, plays, poetry or screenplays. *Founded* 1986.

CookeMcDermid

219 Dufferin Street, Unit 208B, Toronto,
ON M6K 3J1
tel +1 647-788-4010
email admin@cookemcdermid.com
website https://cookemcdermid.com
Facebook www.facebook.com/CookeMcDermid
X @CookeMcDermid
Instagram @cookemcdermid
Agents Martha Webb, Suzanne Brandreth, Ron Eckel, Paige Sisley, Cody Caetano, Hana El Niwairi, Amy Moore-Benson

Represents authors of literary, commercial, sci-fi and fantasy fiction; a broad range of narrative non-fiction; health and wellness resources; middle-grade and YA books. Sells Canadian and American rights directly. The in-house rights team sells UK and translation rights, in conjunction with a network of co-agents around the world. CMD also sells film and TV rights directly, in addition to working with associates in New York and LA. Submission via QueryManager.

Clients include John Irving, Geddy Lee, Alicia Elliot, Paul Sun-Hyung Lee, Billy-Ray Belcourt, Michael Crummey, Claudia Dey, Elamin Abdelmahmoud, Robyn Doolittle, Scaachi Koul, Jen Agg, Robert Munsch, Carol Off, Sonya Lalli, Rick Mofina
Founded 2017.

Donaghy Literary Group

tel +1 647-527-4353
email [firstname]@donaghyliterary.com
website www.donaghyliterary.com
X @DonaghyLiterary
Agents Stacey Donaghy, Valerie Noble

Provides full-service literary representation to clients at all stages of their publishing career. Specialises in commercial fiction and seeking YA and adult novels. Genres represented include romance, psychological and domestic thriller, suspense, LGBTQ+, diverse stories, sci-fi, fantasy, historical fantasy and historical fiction. Visit agent pages on the website for information on each agent and what they are currently looking for. Only accepts submissions via QueryManager accessed via website through a link button on each agents' page. Do not query by phone or email. Welcomes both established and new writers.

Clients include K.A. Tucker, Jay Crownover, Jamie Shaw, Diana Gardin, Gustavo Florentin, Annika Sharma, Christopher Francis, Ara Grigorian, Kate L. Mary, Valerie Noble, Anita Kushwaha, Joe Bright, Desmond McLean, Shira Shiloah, Lisa Kusel.

P.S. Literary Agency

2nd Floor, 2010 Winston Park Drive, Oakville,
ON L6H 5R7
email info@psliterary.com
website www.psliterary.com
Threads @psliteraryagency
President & Principal Agent Curtis Russell, *Senior Literary Agents* Carly Watters (Senior Advisor), Maria Vicente (Advisor), *Literary Agents* Eric Smith, Claire Harris, Cecilia Lyra, *Associate Agents* Rose Ferrao, Nour Sallam

Represents both fiction and non-fiction works to publishers in North America, Europe and throughout the world. Categories include commercial, upmarket, literary, women's fiction, mystery, thriller, romance, sci-fi, fantasy, historical, LGBTQ+, YA, middle grade, picture books, graphic novels, memoir, history, politics, current affairs, business, wellness, cookery books, sports, humour, popular science, popular psychology, popular culture, design and lifestyle. Send queries to query@psliterary.com. Do not send email attachments unless specifically requested. Does not accept submissions via mail or telephone.
Founded 2005.

Seventh Avenue Literary Management

16708–20th Avenue, Surrey, BC V3Z 9R4
email info@seventhavenuelit.com
website www.seventhavenuelit.com
Director & Principal Agent Robert Mackwood

One of Canada's largest non-fiction and personal management agencies. Helps authors develop proposals and manuscripts for submission and negotiates on their behalf with publishing houses in Canada, the USA and worldwide. Authors' books are published by a range of publishers including international houses, independents and specialist presses. Send short query via email including a short description of the project and a brief bio. See the website for specific guidelines. Postal submissions accepted.

Transatlantic Agency

68 Claremont Street, Suite 100, Toronto,
ON M6J 2M5
tel +1 416-488-9214
website www.transatlanticagency.com
Facebook www.facebook.com/TransLitAgency
Instagram @transatlantic_agency

Represents more than 800 American, Canadian and internationally bestselling and award-winning clients, with a team of 20 experienced agents based in cities across North America. Offers a full spectrum of career representation to authors (adult, children's and YA, and illustrators) and storytellers (speakers, industry leaders and influencers) across all genres and formats for book, content development, speaking, TV and film. *Founded* 1993.

Westwood Creative Artists

386 Huron Street, Toronto, ON M5S 2G6
tel +1 416-964-3302
email wca_office@wcaltd.com
website https://wcaltd.com
X @WCA_LitAgency
Instagram @westwoodcreativeartists
President Jackie Kaiser, *Executive Vice President* Hilary McMahon, *Agents* Chris Casuccio, Sara Harowitz,

Bridgette Kam, John Pearce, Meg Wheeler, *Associate Agent* Briar Heckman

Represents Canadian authors. Interested in literary fiction, quality commercial fiction for adults and YA, including mysteries and thrillers, and non-fiction in the areas of memoir, history, biography, science, journalism and current affairs. Considers graphic novels and illustrated works. Email submissions to submissions@wcaltd.com. Send a covering letter and 10–20 pages of MS in body of email. See website for full submission guidelines. Does not represent screenwriters, playwrights or poets.

USA

**Agency includes agents who are members of the Association of American Literary Agents*

Adams Literary*

7845 Colony Road, C4 Suite 215, Charlotte, NC 28226
tel +1 704-542-1440
email info@adamsliterary.com
website www.adamsliterary.com
X @adamsliterary
Instagram @adamsliterary
Agents Tracey Adams, Josh Adams

Selectively children's through to adult fiction. Submissions currently closed; check website for updates.

Authors include John David Anderson, Hafsah Faizal, Margaret Peterson Haddix, Amie Kaufman, Jay Kristoff, Cynthia Lord, Vaunda Micheaux Nelson, C.S. Pacat, Wendy Shang, Tom Taylor.
Founded 2004.

Aevitas Creative Management*

19 West 21st Street, Suite 501, New York, NY 10010
tel +1 212-765-6900
website www.aevitascreative.com
Facebook www.facebook.com/AevitasCreative
X @AevitasCreative
Instagram @aevitas_creative

A full-service literary agency with offices in New York, Boston, Washington DC, Los Angeles, Detroit, Nashville, London and Barcelona, representing scores of award-winning authors, performers, thinkers, artists and public figures. Agents take submissions through the website; full submission guidelines can be found there.

Clients include Cheryl Strayed, Charles Blow, Safiya Sinclair, Grace Byers, Mercury Stardust.
Founded 2016.

The Axelrod Agency*

55 Main Street, PO Box 357, Chatham, NY 12037
tel +1 518-392-2100
email steve@axelrodagency.com
email lori@axelrodagency.com
website https://axelrodagency.com
President Steven Axelrod, *Foreign Rights Director* Lori Antonson

Works with overseas agents. *Commission* Fiction: home 15%, overseas 20%, film/TV rights 15%. Submit full-length MSS. Will suggest revision where appropriate. *Founded* 1983.

The Bent Agency*

PO Box 55772, Birmingham, AL 35205
email info@thebentagency.com
website www.thebentagency.com
Instagram @thebentagency
Agents Jenny Bent, Victoria Cappello, James Mustelier, John Silbersack

Represents a diverse range of genres including history, humour, lifestyle, inspiration, memoir, literary fiction, children's and commercial fiction. Only accepts email queries. See website for detailed query and submission guidelines. *Founded* 2009.

The Bindery Agency*

email info@thebinderyagency.com
website www.thebinderyagency.com
X @binderyagency
Instagram @thebindery.agency
Founder Alexander Field, *Managing Director* Ingrid Beck, *Agents* Trinity McFadden, Andrea Heinecke, *Associate Agents* John Blase, Morgan Strehlow

In addition to literary representation, the agency also consults with businesses and organisations on publishing strategy and develops highly specialised book projects offering a variety of boutique publishing options. Currently represents authors of general non-fiction, religion, literary fiction, sci-fi and fantasy, biography and memoir, pop culture, leadership, spiritual growth, Christian spirituality and more. Email book proposal along with a cover letter. Include a summary of the book concept, author bio and at least two sample chapters plus either a table of contents (for non-fiction) or one-page synopsis (fiction). Currently does not represent screenplays, plays or illustrators. *Founded* 2017.

David Black Agency*

335 Adams Street, Suite 2707, Brooklyn, NY 11201
tel +1 718-852-5500
email dblack@dblackagency.com
website www.davidblackagency.com
X @dblackagency
Instagram @davidblackagency
Contacts David Black, Rica Allannic, Jennifer Herrera, Gary Morris, Susan Raihofer, Sarah Smith, Mark Tavani, Joy Tutela, Anna Zinchuk, Ellen Scott

Represents an extensive list of both prescriptive and narrative non-fiction including business, memoir, history, politics, fitness and sport. Also represents both commercial and literary fiction, middle grade and YA. Queries to be addressed to specific agent and by email, unless otherwise specified. For most up-to-date submission guidelines and agent preferences see website.

Clients include Mitch Albom, Billie Jean King, Jonathan Eig, Julia Cameron, Bruce Feiler, Deborah Lipstadt, Lev Rosen, Emily Timberlake, Jessie Damuck, Devon Price, Joshua David Stein, Matt Laney, Ryan Pote, Osita Nwanevu, Gregg Olsen. *Founded* 1989.

The Booker Albert Literary Agency

PO Box 20931, York, PA 17402
email bookeralbertinfo@gmail.com
website www.thebookeralbertagency.com
X @BookerAlbertLit
Co-Founders Jordy Albert, Brittany Booker, *Junior Agents* Rebecca Lawrence, A.J. Van Belle

Full-service agency representing adult, New Adult, YA and middle-grade fiction. Particularly interested in sci-fi, fantasy, horror and romance (including contemporary and paranormal). Non-fiction interests include science, popular science, self-help and health/wellness. Welcomes writers with expertise links with evolution, ecology, statistics, microbiology and biogeoscience. Submission via QueryManager only. See agents' individual profiles on website for specific guidelines and areas of interest. No picture books, memoirs or screenplays at this time.

Clients include Charlotte Barnes, C.L. Bleek, Roberto Cofresí Hopgood, Jayne Denker, Lee A. Everett, Suzanne Feldman, Patrick Hurley, Zachary Long, Nicole Luiken, Ziah Miller, Rachel Reddick, Chris Scheina, Eva Siedler, Temma Thomas, Sheri Yutzy. *Founded* 2013.

Georges Borchardt*

228 East 45th Street, Suite 14S, New York, NY 10017
tel +1 212-753-5785
website www.gbagency.com
Founders Georges Borchardt, Anne Borchardt, *President* Valerie Borchardt, *Vice President* Samantha Shea, *Agents* Cora Markowitz, Pronoy Sarker

Full-length and short MSS. *Commission* Home/performance 15%, UK/translations 20%. Agents in most foreign countries. No unsolicited MSS. Closed to submissions.

Authors include Lesley Nneka Arimah, Nona Aronowitz, Chelsea Bieker, Anna Bruno, Amy Butcher, Jane Delury, Camille Dungy, Lydia Fitzpatrick, Simon Han, Greg Jackson, Andrew Moore, Adam O'Fallon Price, Willa Richards, Charlotte Shane, Shruti Swamy. *Founded* 1967.

Bradford Literary Agency*

5694 Mission Center Road, Suite 347, San Diego, CA 92108
email queries@bradfordlit.com
website www.bradfordlit.com
X @bradford_agents
Bluesky @bradfordagents.bsky.social
Instagram @bradfordlitagency

Currently looking for a wide array of genres. Fiction: romance, speculative, women's, sci-fi and fantasy, mystery, thrillers, historical, horror and magical realism. This includes children's picture books, chapter books, and middle grade, YA and New Adult fiction. Non-fiction: biography, memoir, narrative humour, pop culture, illustrated/graphic design, food and cooking, history and social issues. Queries accepted only via QueryManager. See website for detailed submission guidelines and for links to each agent's QueryManager form. Not currently looking for poetry, screenplays, short stories, Westerns, inspirational/spiritual, New Age, religion, inspirational, business, self-help, lifestyle, parenting, crafts or gift books. *Founded* 2001.

Brandt & Hochman Literary Agents*

1501 Broadway, Suite 2605, New York, NY 10036
tel +1 212-840-5760
website https://brandthochman.com
Agents Gail Hochman, Marianne Merola, Emily Forland, Emma Patterson, Jody Kahn, Henry Thayer, Mitchell Waters

Fiction and non-fiction for the general trade market including children's books. See website for full list of agents, the genres represented by each and individual email addresses. *Commission* Home 15%, overseas 20%, performance rights 15%. Queries by email or post (include a sase). Send a one- to two-page query letter with a book project and writing credentials. No screenplays or textbooks. *Founded* 1913.

The Brattle Agency

PO Box 380537, Cambridge, MA 02238
tel +1 617-721-5375
email submissions@thebrattleagency.com
website https://thebrattleagency.com

A full-service agency providing assistance to clients in all areas related to their work. Annual reading period for open submissions; see website for details. Queries should include a formal cover letter, brief synopsis and a CV (if submitting an academic manuscript).

Authors include Chris Amenta, Carlos Bauer, Joan Chase, Paul Griffiths, Minsoo Kang, Joanna Luloff, Luke Salisbury, Gilmore Tamny, Evelyn Maguire. *Founded* 2008.

Browne & Miller Literary Associates*

52 Village Place, Hinsdale, IL 60521
tel +1 312-922-3063
email mail@browneandmiller.com
website www.browneandmiller.com
X @BrowneandMiller
Contact Danielle Egan-Miller

General adult fiction and non-fiction. *Commission* Home 15%, overseas 20%. Works in conjunction with foreign agents. Query by email in first instance. Will suggest revision. No children's (including YA), fantasy, short stories, poetry, memoirs, screenplays or academic work. *Founded* 1971.

Maria Carvainis Agency*

Rockefeller Center, 1270 Avenue of the Americas, Suite 2915, New York, NY 10020
tel +1 212-245-6365
email mca@mariacarvainisagency.com
website www.mariacarvainisagency.com
President & Literary Agent Maria Carvainis

Represents a wide range of fiction and non-fiction with special interest in literary and mainstream fiction, mystery and suspense, thrillers, historicals, contemporary women's fiction, YA and middle grade, memoir, biography, history, business, psychology, pop culture and popular science. *Commission* Home 15%, overseas 20%. Email and postal submissions are accepted. Send a query letter, a synopsis of the work, first five to ten pages and a note of any writing credentials. See website for full submission guidelines. Does not represent screenplays, children's picture books, sci-fi or poetry. *Founded* 1977.

Wm. Clark Associates*

54 West 21st Street, Suite 809, New York, NY 10010
tel +1 212-675-2784
website www.wmclark.com
X @william_m_clark

Represents a wide range of titles across all formats for publishing, film, television and digital fields. Non-fiction areas of interest cover art, architecture, biography and memoir, business, current affairs and politics, cookery, history, music and popular culture such as the arts, religion and spirituality, science, technology and travel. Sells directly in global English language markets and to several other major foreign markets, whilst also working with co-agents. Query by online form only.

Clients ranging from authors of award-winning narrative and illustrated non-fiction books, to authors in translation, chefs, musicians and artists. *Founded* 1997.

Don Congdon Associates*

88 Pine Street, Suite 730, New York, NY 10005
tel +1 212-645-1229
email dca@doncongdon.com
website https://doncongdon.com
Agents Cristina Concepcion, Michael Congdon, Katie Kotchman, Maura Kye-Casella, Susan Ramer

Full-length and short MSS. General fiction and non-fiction. *Commission* Home 15%, overseas 20%, performance rights 15%. Works with co-agents overseas. No unsolicited MSS. Query/submissions by email or QueryManager only, in line with agent preference; submit synopsis and first chapter. Full submission guidelines can be found on the website. *Founded* 1983.

The Doe Coover Agency

PO Box 668, Winchester, MA 01890
tel +1 781-721-6000
email info@doecooveragency.com
website www.doecooveragency.com
Agents Doe Coover, Colleen Mohyde

Specialises in non-fiction: business, history, popular science, biography, social issues, cooking, food writing, gardening; also literary and commercial fiction. *Commission* Home 15%, overseas 10%. Email queries only. No poetry or screenplays.
Founded 1986.

Corvisiero Literary Agency

125 Park Avenue, 25th Floor, New York, NY 10017
119 Maple Avenue, Suite 204, Red Bank, NJ 07701
email info@corvisieroagency.com
website www.corvisieroagency.com
X @CorvisieroLit
Instagram @corvisierolit
Founder Marisa A. Corvisiero, *Vice President* Tessa Shaffer, *Associate Agents* Maggie Sadler, Kendyll Drilling, Catherine Ross, Alexandra Grana, Micah Brocker, Mira Landry, Lisa Gouldy, Gabrielle Harbowy, Ciara Smith, *Film & TV Agent* Ken Boxer

Offers international literary representation, management, and coaching services to fiction and non-fiction for all ages, in a wide spectrum of genres including screenplays. Only submit to one agent at a time via QueryManager. For fiction, send a query letter, one- to two-page synopsis and first five pages. For graphic novels, include 20 pages of the work along with illustration samples, query letter and synopsis. For non-fiction, include a full proposal and sample chapter. For screenplays, include a logline, genre, and upload the first 20 pages of the script. Not currently representing collections of short stories, novellas, essays or poetry. *Founded* 2012.

Creative Media Agency*

tel +1 212-812-1494
email paige@cmalit.com
website www.cmalit.com
Facebook www.facebook.com/PaigeWheelerAgent
X @pwheeler_agent
Instagram @cma_lit
Contact Paige Wheeler, *Associate Agents* Haley Casey, Shannon Snow, Megan Frayser, Laurie Dennison, Liv Ivanov, Vicky Weber

Represents mainly commercial fiction, both historical and contemporary, but list also features women's fiction and psychological thrillers such as mystery and crime novels. Non-fiction areas of interest include both narrative and prescriptive works. Query through QueryManager. For full submission guidelines see website. *Founded* 1997.

Curtis Brown*

228 East 45th Street, Suite 310, New York, NY 10017
tel +1 212-473-5400
email info@cbltd.com
website www.curtisbrown.com
X @CurtisBrownLtd

Instagram @curtisbrown.ltd
Ceo Timothy Knowlton, *President* Peter Ginsberg (at CA branch office), *Vice Presidents* Katherine Fausset, Holly Frederick, Jonathan Lyons, Laura Blake Peterson, *Contact* Kerry D'Agostino, James Farrell, Alexandra Franklin, *Film & TV Rights* Holly Frederick, *Film & TV Rights Associate* Alexandra Franklin, *Translation Rights* Karin Schulze

Fiction and non-fiction, juvenile, film and TV rights. *Commission* 15% Home, 20% overseas. No unsolicited MSS. See individual agents' entries on the Agents page of the website for specific query and submission information. No screenplays. *Founded* 1914.

Laura Dail Literary Agency*

30 Vandam Street, Suite 5A, New York, NY 10013
website www.ldlainc.com
X @LDLAInc
Bluesky @ldlainc.bsky.social
Instagram @LDLAInc
Contacts Laura Dail, Elana Roth Parker, Carrie Pestritto, Katie Gisondi, Aiden Siobhan, Jennifer Udden

Represents a wide range of both commercial and literary fiction, with an emphasis on novels with great characters and page-turning plots. Also represents middle grade and YA works of fiction including graphic novels and some non-fiction. Works with agents in a number of foreign territories. Accepts queries via QueryManager only. For full submission guidelines see website. No screenplays or poetry.

Clients include Marie Benedict, Lily Chu, Kiera Cass, Robyn Gigl, George Motz, Sarah Mlynowski, Debbie Rigaud, Natalia Sylvester. *Founded* 1996.

Liza Dawson Associates*

121 West 27th Street, Suite 1201, New York, NY 10001
website www.lizadawsonassociates.com
X @LizaDawsonAssoc
Founder Liza Dawson, *Agents* Caitlin Blasdel, Hannah Bowman, Tom Miller, Rachel Beck, Lauren Bajek

A full-service agency which draws on expertise as former publishers. Commercial and literary fiction and non-fiction. See website for full details of genres represented by individual agents, submission guidelines and email contacts.

Clients include Annie Barrows, Bob Brier, Pierce Brown, Zen Cho, David Santos Donaldson, Britt Frank, Ross Gay, R.F. Kuang, Victoria Law, Julia Lee, Victoria Christopher Murray, Charles Stross, the estate of Eleanor Roosevelt. *Founded* 1996.

Sandra Dijkstra & Associates*

1155 Camino Del Mar, PMB 515, Del Mar, CA 92014
tel +1 858-755-3115
website www.dijkstraagency.com
Contacts Sandra Dijkstra, Elise Capron, Jill Marr, Thao Le, Andrea Cavallaro, Jessica Watterson, Jennifer Kim, Jake Lovell, Nick Van Orden

Fiction: literary, contemporary, women's, romance, suspense, thrillers and sci-fi. Non-fiction: narrative, history, journalism, business, psychology, self-help, science and memoir/biography. Works in conjunction with foreign and film agents. *Commission* Home 15%, overseas 20%. Email submissions only. See website for the most up-to-date guidelines.

Clients include Amy Tan, Maxine Hong Kingston, Lisa See, Chitra Divakaruni, Jasmin Darznik, Eric Foner, Ian Morris, Walter Johnson, Erika Lee, Mae Ngai, Lillian Faderman, Elena Armas, Jessie Sima, Ali Hazelwood. *Founded* 1981.

Dunham Literary*

email query@dunhamlit.com
website www.dunhamlit.com
Contact Jennie Dunham, Anjanette Barr

Literary fiction and non-fiction, children's books. *Commission* Home 15%, overseas 20%. Send query by email including a synopsis and first five pages in the body of the email. *Founded* 2000.

Dunow, Carlson & Lerner*

27 West 20th Street, Suite 1103, New York, NY 10011
email mail@dclagency.com
website www.dclagency.com
Agents Henry Dunlow, Jennifer Carlson, Betsy Lerner, Arielle Datz, Stacia Decker, Susanna Einstein, Susan Graham, Erin Hosier, Eleanor Jackson, Julia Kenny, Edward Necarsulmer, Nicki Richesin, Chris Rogers, Rachel Vogel

Represents literary and commercial fiction, a wide range of non-fiction and children's literature for all ages. Query letters with first ten pages of your work preferred by email (no attachments). For query letters by post, include sase. *Founded* 2005.

Dystel, Goderich & Bourret*

1 Union Square West, Suite 904, New York, NY 10003
tel +1 212-627-9100
website www.dystel.com
Facebook www.facebook.com/DGandB
Threads @dystelgoderichbourret
Contacts Jane Dystel, Miriam Goderich, Michael Bourret, Jim McCarthy, Lauren Abramo, Stacey Glick, Ann Leslie Tuttle, Jessica Papin, John Rudolph, Sharon Pelletier, Michaela Whatnall, Leslie Meredith, Kendell Berdinsky

General fiction and non-fiction: literary and commercial fiction, narrative non-fiction, self-help, cookery books, parenting, sci-fi and fantasy, children's and YA including graphic novels. *Commission* Home 15%, overseas 19%, film/TV/radio 15%. Electronic submission by either email or QueryManager. Include a query letter and 25 pages of MS or proposal sample chapters. Does not represent poetry, plays or screenplays. *Founded* 1994.

The Ethan Ellenberg Literary Agency*

548 Broadway, 5C, New York, NY 10012
tel +1 212-431-4554
email agent@ethanellenberg.com
website www.ethanellenberg.com
President & Agent Ethan Ellenberg, *Senior Agent* Evan Gregory, *Agents* Bibi Lewis, Ezra Ellenberg

Fiction and non-fiction. Commercial fiction: sci-fi, fantasy, romance, thrillers, mysteries, women's and general fiction; also literary fiction with a strong narrative. Non-fiction: current affairs, history, adventure, true crime, science, health, psychology, cookery and spirituality. Children's fiction: interested in YA, middle grade and younger, of all types. Will consider picture books and other illustrated works. *Commission* Home 15%, overseas 20%. Accepts unsolicited MSS by email and seriously considers all submissions, including first-time writers. For fiction, submit query letter, one- to two-page synopsis and first 50 pages. For non-fiction, send a query letter and proposal (outline, sample material up to 50 pages, author CV). Illustrators should send four to five sample illustrations along with query letter. Unable to return any material from overseas. No poetry, short stories or screenplays. *Founded* 1984.

Fairbank Literary Representation*

21 Lyman Street, Waltham, MA 02452
tel +1 617-576-0030
email queries@fairbankliterary.com
website https://fairbankliterary.com
X @FairbankLit
Instagram @FairbankLit
Contacts Sorche Elizabeth Fairbank

Represents literary fiction than commercial. Fiction: literary, international voices, and voice-y novels with a strong sense of place. Non-fiction: books that tackle current events and topical and societal issues with a narrative treatment. Untold histories. Women's voices, class and race issues, quality lifestyle books (food, craft, design), and the rare memoir. Keen on signing more gift and pop culture books and impulse buys, especially with a humour angle. Seeking children's works (picture books and middle grade) by author-illustrators, as well as diverse illustrators of any type. Query by email preferred but accepted by mail as well. For full submission guidelines see website. No genre romance, sci-fi, fantasy, sports fiction, YA, screenplays or childrens unless by an author-illustrator. *Founded* 2002.

Diana Finch Literary Agency*

116 West 23rd Street, 5th Floor, New York, NY 10011
tel +1 917-544-4470
email dianafinchagent@gmail.com
website https://dianafinchliteraryagency.blogspot.com
X @DianaFinch
Owner & Agent Diana Finch

Memoirs, narrative non-fiction, science, history, environment, business, literary fiction, current affairs, health and how-to, sci-fi and fantasy, YA and middle-grade fiction. *Commission* Home 15%, overseas 20%. Queries through website; for fiction, include the first ten pages; for non-fiction, include full proposal and sample chapters. Not currently open for fiction submissions.

Clients include Noliwe Rooks, Azadeh Moaveni, Antonia Juhasz, Loretta Napoleoni, Owen Matthews, Greg Palast, Thaisa Frank, Eric Simons, Thomas Goltz, Mark Schapiro, Christopher Leonard, Robert Marion MD, the estate of Joanna Russ. *Founded* 2003.

FinePrint Literary Management*

207 West 106th Street, Suite 1D, New York, NY 10025
email submissions@fineprint.com
website www.fineprintlit.com
Ceo & Senior Agent Peter Rubie, *Agents* Laura Wood, Lauren Bieker, Zachary Honey, Morgan Hughes, Christine Goss, Bonnie Swanson, Arianna Siffiqui

Represents fiction and non-fiction, adult and children. Also handles book-to-film, TV dramatic rights, and worldwide subsidiary rights for agency authors. Each agent has specific interests and detailed likes and dislikes can be found on the website or agent's page on QueryManager. Query specific named agent by email only. For fiction, include a query letter, synopsis, short author bio of the author and the first two chapters. For non-fiction, include a query letter and a proposal. No longer accepting printed submissions unless specifically asked to send one. No original poetry, plays or screenplays. *Founded* 2007.

Folio Literary Management*

The Film Center Building, 630 9th Avenue, Suite 1009, New York, NY 10036
tel +1 212-400-1494
website www.foliolit.com, www.foliojr.com
X @FolioLiterary, @FolioJr
Instagram @folioliterary, @foliojr

Represents both first-time and established authors. Seeks upmarket adult fiction, literary fiction, commercial fiction that features fresh voices and/or memorable characters, and narrative non-fiction. Folio Jr is devoted exclusively to representing children's book authors and artists. Consult individual agents' pages on the website for current wish lists and submission guidelines. Submission by email or QueryManager only. Does not represent poetry, plays or screenplays. *Founded* 2006.

The Friedrich Agency*

281 McLain Street, Bedford Hills, NY 10507
email [initialsurname]@friedrichagency.com
website www.friedrichagency.com
Agents Molly Friedrich, Lucy Carson, Heather Carr

Represents literary and commercial fiction for adults, plus narrative non-fiction and memoir. Accepts queries by email and QueryManager. Query only one agent. No unsolicited MSS. No attachments to query emails unless invited. See website for detailed submission guidelines.

Clients include Elizabeth Strout, Karen Joy Fowler, Ruth Ozeki, Laurie Frankel, Jane Smiley, Esmeralda Santiago, Sy Montgomery, Terry McMillan, Cathleen Schine, Eileen Garvin, Leila Mottley, Rachel Harrison, John Verdon, Florence Williams, Archer Mayor. *Founded* 2006.

Gelfman Schneider Literary Agents*

850 Seventh Avenue, Suite 903, New York, NY 10019
email mail@gelfmanschneider.com
website www.gelfmanschneider.com
Agents Jane Gelfman, Deborah Schneider, Heather Mitchell, Penelope Burns

General commercial and literary adult fiction, non-fiction, and YA fiction in all genres. *Commission* Home 15%, overseas 20%. See website for detailed submission guidelines and information on which agents are accepting queries/submissions. *Founded* 1992.

Global Lion Intellectual Property Management

PO Box 669238, Pompano Beach, FL 33066
tel +1 754-222-6948
email queriesgloballionmgt@gmail.com
website https://globallionmanagement.com
Facebook www.facebook.com/GlobalLionMgt
X @globallionmgt
Instagram @globallionmgt
President & Ceo Liseanne Miller, *Literary Agent* Charlie Serabian

Specialises in commercial fiction (including thrillers, sci-fi and fantasy) and non-fiction covering education, self-help, business and technology, as well as books with film, TV or global publishing potential. Works in conjunction with agents worldwide. Initial submissions should include a synopsis, author bio, manuscript sample and details of personal social media and self-promotion.

Barry Goldblatt Literary

c/o Industrious – Brooklyn, 594 Dean Street, Brooklyn, NY 11238
tel +1 718-832-8787
website http://bgliterary.com
Contact Barry Goldblatt

Represents YA and middle-grade fiction, as well as adult sci-fi and fantasy. Has a preference for quirky, off-beat work. Submission via QueryManager only. No non-fiction. *Founded* 2000.

Frances Goldin Literary Agency*

47 East 19th Street, #3, New York, NY 10003
tel +1 212-777-0047
email agency@goldinlit.com
website www.goldinlit.com
X @GoldinAgency
Bluesky @goldinagency.bsky.social
Agents Sam Stoloff, Ellen Geiger, Matt McGowan, Caroline Eisenmann, Roz Foster, Jade Wong-Baxter, Ayla Zuraw-Friedland, Alison Lewis, Tess Weitzner, Ria Julien

Fiction (literary and high-quality commercial) and non-fiction. Email submissions welcome. For fiction, memoir, essays, or narrative non-fiction, send a query letter and the first 10–15 pages in the body of your email. For all other non-fiction, send a query letter. Does not handle screenplays, romance, and hardly any poetry. *Founded* 1977.

Irene Goodman Literary Agency*

27 West 24th Street, Suite 804, New York, NY 10010
email irene.queries@irenegoodman.com
website www.irenegoodman.com
Facebook www.facebook.com/IreneGoodmanAgency
X @IGLAbooks
Instagram @iglabooks
Agent Irene Goodman, *Foreign Rights Agents* Danny Baror, Heather Baror-Shapiro

Principally represents commercial fiction with an emphasis on women's voices, romantic novels, historical fiction, mystery, crime and suspense novels. Also represents middle-grade and YA books, including fantasy. Non-fiction areas of interest include health, business, anything French, Judaica, cookery books and pop culture. Works in collaboration with the foreign rights agency Baror International who deal with foreign publishers directly. Query by email. For fiction, send query letter and first ten pages of a manuscript. For non-ficton, send a proposal that includes an overview, descriptions of each chapter and comparison titles. Does not represent picture books, poetry or screenplays. *Founded* 1989.

Sanford J. Greenburger Associates*

55 Fifth Avenue, New York, NY 10003
tel +1 212-206-5600
website www.greenburger.com
X @GreenburgerLit
Instagram @greenburger_associates
President Heide Lange, *Agents* Dan Mandel, Faith Hamlin, Matt Bialer, Rachael Dillon Fried, Phair, Alexander Slater, Zoe Sandler, Clare Mao, *Associate Agents* Abigail Frank, Iwalani Kim, Bailey Tamayo, Madeline Wallace, Hannah Strouth

Full-service agency. Fiction and non-fiction for adults and children. Only accepts queries by email. See website for submission guidelines. No screenplays. *Founded* 1932.

The Joy Harris Literary Agency*

1501 Broadway, Suite 2605, New York, NY 10036
tel +1 212-924-6269
email contact@joyharrisliterary.com
website www.joyharrisliterary.com
X @JoyHarrisAgency
Instagram @joyharrisliterary
Agents Joy Harris, Adam Reed

Represents literary and commercial fiction and non-fiction including narrative non-fiction, biography and memoir. Submissions should be emailed, comprising of a query letter and an outline or sample letter. See website for detailed submission guidelines. No unsolicited manuscripts at this time. Does not currently accept poetry, screenplays, genre fiction or self-help. *Founded* 1990.

John Hawkins & Associates*

80 Maiden Lane, Suite 1005, New York, NY 10038
tel +1 212-807-7040
email jha@jhalit.com
website www.jhalit.com
President Moses Cardona, *Agents* Warren Frazier, Anne Hawkins

Fiction and non-fiction; YA. *Founded* 1893.

The Jeff Herman Agency

PO Box 1522, Stockbridge, MA 01262
tel +1 413-298-0077
email jeff@jeffherman.com
website www.jeffherman.com

Business, reference, popular psychology, technology, health, spirituality and general non-fiction. *Commission* Home/overseas 15%. Works with overseas agents. Will suggest revision where appropriate. *Founded* 1986.

HG Literary*

6 West 18th Street, Suite 7R, New York NY 10011
email [firstname]@hgliterary.com
website www.hgliterary.com
X @HGLiterary
Instagram @hgliterary
Partners Carrie Hannigan, Josh Getzler, *Agents* Victoria Wells-Arms, Soumeya Bendimerad Roberts, Wedni Gu, Julia Kardon, Bri Johnson, Jon Cobb, Ellen Goff, Alex Reubert

Represents a variety of both commercial and literary fiction, including women's literature, crime and mystery novels, historical fiction and thrillers. Also children's picture books, middle grade and YA fiction. Non-fiction areas of interest include memoir and narrative non-fiction relating to business, current affairs, popular psychology, science, food and select works of photography. Query one agent only by email or QueryManager. For full submission guidelines and agent preferences see website. Does not represent screenplays, romance or religious fiction. *Founded* 2011.

Hill Nadell Literary Agency

1728 1/2 Whitley Avenue, Los Angeles, CA 90028
tel +1 310-860-9605
email queries@hillnadell.com
website www.hillnadell.com
X @HillNadell
Instagram @hillnadell
Agents Bonnie Nadell, Dara Hyde

Literary and commercial fiction, narrative non-fiction, current affairs, memoirs, popular culture, cookery books, graphic novels and select children's books. *Commission* Home 15%, overseas 20%. Works in conjunction with agents in Scandinavia, France, Germany, Holland, Japan, Spain and more. QueryManager preferred and see website for agents' current interests. Include query letter and first ten pages. Hard copy submissions must include a sase. No scripts or screenplays. *Founded* 1979.

InkWell Management

521 Fifth Avenue, Suite 2600, New York, NY 10175
tel +1 212-922-3500
email info@inkwellmanagement.com
website https://inkwellmanagement.com
X @inkwellmgmt

Fiction and non-fiction. *Commission* Home/overseas 15%. Send a query letter and one or two chapters (authors) or link to portfolio (illustrators) to submissions@inkwellmanagement.com. No screenplays. *Founded* 2004.

JABberwocky Literary Agency*

49 West 45th Street, 5th Floor, New York, NY 10036-4603
website www.awfulagent.com
X @awfulagent
Bluesky @awfulagent.bsky.social
President Joshua Bilmes, *Vice President* Eddie Schneider, *Coo* Brady McReynolds, *Agents* Lisa Rodgers, Bridget Smith, Jordan Hamessley, Valentina Sainato, James Farner, *Subsidiary Rights Director* Susan Velazquez Colmant

Agency specialising in sci-fi and fantasy. There are nine acquiring agents; for their individual submission and query guidelines, visit the website. *Founded* 1994.

Heather Jackson Literary Agent*

email query@hjlit.com
website www.hjlit.com

Specialises in practical and narrative commercial non-fiction and 'can't put it down, must read now' fiction. Represents novelists and authors in personal health and wellbeing, history, popular science and psychology, politics and current affairs, business, memoir and self-help. Does not accept unsolicited proposals or manuscripts. Send a query email with a brief description of the book, its uniqueness in the marketplace and why you, and only you, can write it. Do not send attachments. Can only respond to projects of interest. *Founded* 2017.

Janklow & Nesbit Associates

285 Madison, 21st Floor, New York, NY 10017
tel +1 212-421-1700
email info@janklow.com
website www.janklowandnesbit.com
Instagram @janklownesbit
President Luke Nesbit

Commercial and literary fiction, and non-fiction. Works in conjunction with Janklow & Nesbit (UK). Submissions: send an informative cover letter, synopsis/outline and the first ten pages. For picture book submissions, include a dummy and at least one full-colour sample. For graphic novels, send ten illustrated pages with text and a synopsis. Address submissions to an individual agent, including your email address to submissions@janklow.com. For postal submissions, a return envelope with sufficient postage for material must be included for your work to be returned. *Founded* 1989.

Keller Media

578 Washington Boulevard, Suite 745,
Marina Del Rey, CA 90292
tel +1 800-278-8706
email help@kellermedia.com
website https://kellermedia.com
Founder Wendy Keller

Non-fiction for adults: business, self-help, psychology, health, history, science and nature, popular culture, current affairs, politics, how-to, inspirational and spirituality titles. Submission via form on website. Include brief summary of title and author credentials. Writing sample on request. Does not represent fiction of any kind, poetry, memoirs, autobiographies, true crime or screenplays. *Founded* 1989.

Harvey Klinger*

300 West 55th Street, #8J, New York, NY 10019
email queries@harveyklinger.com
website www.harveyklinger.com
X @HKLiterary
Agents Harvey Klinger, David Dunton, Andrea Somberg, Wendy Levinson, Rachel Ridout, Cate Hart

Commercial and literary adult and children's fiction and non-fiction – serious narrative through to self-help psychology books by authors who have already established strong credentials in their respective field. *Commission* Home 15%, overseas 25%. See website for submission guidelines and submission form. *Founded* 1977.

The Knight Agency*

232 West Washington Street, Madison, GA 30650
email admin@knightagency.net
website https://knightagency.net
Facebook www.facebook.com/knightagency
X @KnightAgency
Agents Deidre Knight, Pamela Harty, Elaine Spencer, Lucienne Diver, Nephele Tempest, Melissa Jeglinski, Kristy Hunter

Represents both first-time and established authors across a wide range of genres. For the genre interests of individual agents and detailed submission guidelines, see website. All queries should be sent via QueryManager. Not currently accepting screenplays. *Founded* 1996.

Stuart Krichevsky Literary Agency*

118 East 28th Street, Suite 908, New York, NY 10016
tel +1 212-725-5288
email query@skagency.com
website http://skagency.com/home
X @skagency
Contacts Stuart Krichevsky, David Patterson, Mackenzie Brady Watson, Melissa Danaczko, Laura Usselman, Aemilia Phillips, Barbara Jones, Chandler Wickers

Represents both fiction and non-fiction, focusing in particular on narrative non-fiction and literary journalism. Fiction areas of interest cover works of both a literary and commercial nature. Also represents YA fiction. Non-fiction list includes adventure, biography, culture, business, current affairs and politics, memoir, natural history, science and technology. Works with sub-agents in several major overseas territories. Query by email to one agent only; send first ten pages of a manuscript or a proposal. For agent preferences and emails, see website.

Authors include Mary Kay Andrews, Pamela Colloff, Jessica Goudeau, Elon Green, Gabino Iglesias, Michio Kaku, Piper Kerman, Sebastian Junger, José Olivarez, Nathaniel Philbrick, Prisca Dorcas Mojica Rodriguez, Margot Lee Shetterly, John Vaillant, Ashlee Vance.

kt literary*

9249 South Broadway, 200–543, Highlands Ranch, CO 80129
tel +1 720-344-4728
email contact@ktliterary.com
website https://ktliterary.com
Instagram @ktliterary
Agents Kate Testerman, Adria Goetz, Renee Nyen, Kelly Van Sant, Kari Sutherland, Savannah Brooks, Tara Gilbert, Laurel Symonds, Arley Sorg, Maria Napolitano

Representing all ages and genres of fiction, from picture books through adult, and some select non-fiction. Queries are accepted via QueryManager. No postal submissions.

Clients include Maureen Johnson, Stephanie Perkins, Trish Doller, Amy Spalding, Christy Mandin, Saadia Faruqi, S.T. Gibson, Isabel Canas, Jamie Pacton. *Founded* 2008.

Susanna Lea Associates

331 West 20th Street, New York, NY 10011
tel +1 646-638-1435
email ny@susannalea.com
website www.susannalea.com
X @SLANYC
Agents Susanna Lea, Stephanie Cabot, Lauren Wendelken, Stephen Morrison

General fiction and non-fiction with international appeal. Send query letter, brief synopsis, the first three chapters and/or proposal via email. No plays, screenplays or poetry.

Clients include Marc Levy, Jessie Inchauspé, Ingrid Betancourt, V.V. Ganeshananthan, Nicola Griffith, Priya Parmar, Ayaan Hirsi Ali, Tracey Lange, Margareta Magnusson, Fiona McFarlane, Mindy Mejia, Tom Mustill, Dolen Perkins-Valdez, Adam Ross. *Founded* 2004.

Levine Greenberg Rostan Literary Agency*

307 Seventh Avenue, Suite 2407, New York, NY 10001
tel +1 212-337-0934
email submit@lgrliterary.com
website https://lgrliterary.com
X @LGRLiterary
Instagram @lgrlit
Principals Jim Levine, Daniel Greenberg, Stephanie Rostan, *Agents* Sarah Bedingfield, Lindsay Edgecombe, Victoria Skurnick, Kerry Sparks, Danielle Svetcov, Monika Verma, Courtney Paganelli, *Associate Agent* Rebecca Rodd, *Agents-At-Large* Arielle Eckstut

Represents literary and commercial fiction, non-fiction and books for young readers across a diverse range of genres. Submissions via online form.

Julia Lord Literary Management*

38 West 9th Street, New York, NY 10011
email query@julialordliterarymgt.com
website www.julialordliterarymgt.com
Contacts Julia Lord, Ginger Curwen

Currently looking for submissions in the following genres: narrative non-fiction, reference, biography, history, lifestyle, sports, humour, science, adventure, general fiction, historical fiction, thrillers, mysteries and graphic fiction. Email and postal queries accepted. See website for submission guidelines. *Founded* 1999.

Donald Maass Literary Agency*

121 West 27th Street, Suite 1201, New York, NY 10001
tel +1 212-727-8383
email info@maassagency.com
website https://maassagency.com
Agents Donald Maass, Jennifer Jackson, Cameron McClure, Katie Shea Boutillier, Michael Curry, Caitlin McDonald, Jennifer Goloboy, Kiana Nguyen, Kat Kerr, Anne Tibbets, Jolene Haley, Kesia Lupo

Specialises in fiction of all genres. *Commission* Home 15%, overseas 20%. Query a specific agent by email and include a query letter, first five pages of the MS and a short one- to two-page synopsis. Paste all content into the body of the email. See individual agent profiles on website for email addresses and what they represent. Does not represent poetry, picture books or screenplays. *Founded* 1980.

Margret McBride Literary Agency*

PO Box 9128, La Jolla, CA 92038
tel +1 858-454-1550
email mmla@mcbridelit.com
website www.mcbrideliterary.com
President Margret McBride, *Associate Agent* Faye Atchison

Non-fiction including business, personal finance, health and wellness, history, psychology, true crime, politics and culture. Occasionally represents commercial fiction. *Commission* Home 15%, overseas 25%. All submissions to be sent via QueryManager. Include a one- to two-page overview of the book, author bio, a promotion/marketing plan, a comparative works section, chapter summaries and at least two sample chapters. No poetry or children's books.

Clients include John David Mann, Bob Burg, Colin Cowie, Tom Morris, Chin Ning Chu, Spencer Johnson, Sheldon Bowles, Ken Blanchard. *Founded* 1981.

Gina Maccoby Literary Agency*

PO Box 60, Chappaqua, NY 10514
tel +1 914-238-5630
email query@maccobylit.com
website www.publishersmarketplace.com/members/GinaMaccoby
Contact Gina Maccoby

Looking for high-quality upmarket fiction and non-fiction for adults and children. An engaging narrative voice and strong premise are most important; across all forms the agency is looking for compelling stories and fresh perspectives. Children's: YA and middle grade. Picture books of writer/illustrators only. Non-fiction areas of interest include history, biography, popular science and narrative journalism. No unsolicited submissions. Query first via email. Due to the volume of submissions received, will only reply if interested. *Founded* 1986.

McIntosh & Otis*

235 Main Street, Suite 318, White Plains, NY 10601
tel +1 212-687-7400
email info@mcintoshandotis.com
website https://mcintoshandotis.com
X @McIntoshAndOtis
Agents Elizabeth Winick Rubinstein, Christa Heschke, Daniele Hunter, Adam Muhlig

Adult and children's literary fiction and non-fiction. Electronic submission only, either by email or QueryManager. For fiction, send query letter, synopsis, author bio and first three chapters. For non-fiction, send query letter, proposal, outline, author bio and three sample chapters. For children and YA submissions, send a query letter, author bio, synopsis, the first three chapters and any relevant illustrations. Does not represent poetry, screenplays, and original theatrical or dramatic works of any kind. *Founded 1928.*

Carol Mann Agency*

55 Fifth Avenue, #1800, New York, NY 10003
tel +1 212-206-5635
email info@carolmannagency.com
website www.carolmannagency.com
X @carolmannagency
Instagram @carolmannagency
Contacts Carol Mann, Gareth Esersky, Joanne Wyckoff

Interested in fiction and non-fiction on the following subjects: business, food, health, history and politics, humour and popular culture, memoir, relationships and parenting, science and technology, spirituality and religion. *Commission* Home 15%, overseas 20%. Works in conjunction with foreign and film agents. Submission by email only with no attachments to submissions@carolmannagency.com. For fiction, send a query letter including a brief bio, and the first 25 pages of the MS. For non-fiction, send a query letter including a brief bio, a synopsis/proposal and the first 25 pages of the MS. *Founded* 1977.

The Evan Marshall Agency

1 Pacio Court, Roseland, NJ 07068-1121
tel +1 973-287-6216
email evan@evanmarshallagency.com
website www.evanmarshallagency.com
President Evan Marshall

General fiction. Works in conjunction with overseas agents. *Commission* Home 15%, overseas 20%. Not currently accepting new clients. *Founded* 1987.

Scott Meredith Literary Agency

PO Box 3090, Grand Central Post Office, New York, NY 10163-3090
email aklebanoff@scottmeredith.com
website www.scottmeredith.com
President Arthur Klebanoff

General fiction and non-fiction. *Founded* 1946.

Jean V. Naggar Literary Agency*

216 East 75th Street, Suite 1E, New York, NY 10021
tel +1 212-794-1082
email jvnla@jvnla.com
website www.jvnla.com
X @JVNLA
Instagram @jvnlainc
President Jennifer Weltz, *Partners* Alice Tasman, Ariana Philips, *Junior Agent* Cole Hildebrand, *Senior Agent and Head of Culinary Division* Sally Ekus

Works in conjunction with foreign and film agents. Commercial and literary fiction, non-fiction (narrative, memoir, journalism, psychology, history, pop culture, humour and culinary), and young readers (picture, middle grade, YA) and illustrators. Submit queries via form on website. *Founded* 1978.

Ayesha Pande Literary

tel +1 212-283-5825
email queries@pandeliterary.com
website www.pandeliterary.com
Facebook www.facebook.com/AyeshaPandeLiterary
X @pande_literary
Instagram @pandeliterary
Agents Ayesha Pande, Serene Hakim, Annie Hwang, Kayla Lightner, Paloma Hernando, *Affiliate Agents* Stephany Evans, Madison Smartt Bell, Luba Ostashevsky, Anne Edelstein

Represents writers and illustrators across fiction and non-fiction, children's and graphic novels. Interested in literary, upmarket and genre fiction. Non-fiction interests include narrative, popular science, health and history. Complete query form on website.

Clients include Danielle Evans, Patricia Engel, Ibram X. Kendi, Peter Rostovsky, Giaae Kwon, Tiffany Jewll, Lisa Ko, Shilip Somaya Gowda, Minda Honey, Russell Shorto. *Founded* 2007.

Park, Fine & Brower Literary Management*

55 Broadway, Suite 1601, New York, NY 10006
tel +1 212-691-3500
email info@parkfinebrower.com
website https://parkfinebrower.com
X @parkfinebrower
Instagram @parkfinebrower
Founding Partner Theresa Park, Celeste Fine, Kimberly Brower, *Partner* Andrea Mai, Abigail Koons, Emily Sweet, John Maas, Peter Knapp, Sarah Passick, *Literary Agents* Kathryn Toolan, Mia Vitale, *Associate Literary Agents* Stuti Telidevara, Ben Kaslow-Zieve, Charlotte Sunderland, Melissa Rodman

Boutique agency for both fiction and non-fiction. Fiction areas of interest lean more towards the commercial, including women's literature, mystery, historical fiction and plot-driven novels. Non-fiction list features biography, memoir, current affairs, politics, art, popular science and history. Also represents middle-grade and YA fiction. Works with a number of co-agents covering the major foreign territories. Send your query letter and accompanying material to queries@parkfinebrower.com, targeting one agent only. For adult fiction submissions, approx. the first 25 pages of your work. For YA and children's fiction submissions, include the first chapter or approx. the first ten pages of your work. For graphic novels, attach a low-res sample and link to portfolio. For agent preferences, see website. Does not represent poetry or screenplays.

Alison Picard, Literary Agent

PO Box 2000, Cotuit, MA 02635
tel +1 508-477-7192
email ajpicard@aol.com

Adult fiction and non-fiction, children's and YA. *Commission* Home 15%. Send query via email (no attachments). No short stories, poetry, plays, screenplays or sci-fi and fantasy.

Clients include David Housewright, Caryl Rivers, Jessica Fisher, David Alan Johnson, Susan Froetschel. *Founded* 1985.

Pippin Properties

110 West 40th Street, Suite 1704, New York, NY 10018
tel +1 212-338-9310
email info@pippinproperties.com
website www.pippinproperties.com
Facebook www.facebook.com/pippinproperties
X @LovethePippins
Instagram @pippinproperties
Contacts Holly McGhee

Focuses on children's book authors and artists, including picture books, middle grade, graphic novels and YA novels, and adult trade books on occasion. *Commission* Home 15%, overseas 25%. Query specific agent by email. For authors, include the first chapter and short synopsis, or entire picture book. For illustrators, send a query letter detailing your background in illustration and links to website with a dummy or other examples of your work.

Clients includes Kate DiCamillo, Peter H. Reynolds, Jandy Nelson, Doreen Cronin, Jon Agee, LeUyen Pham, Edel Rodriguez. *Founded* 1998.

Rees Literary Agency

One Westinghouse Plaza, Suite A203, Boston, MA 02136-2075
tel +1 617-227-9014
email [firstname]@reesagency.com
website www.reesagency.com
Instagram @reesagency
Agents Ann Collette, Lorin Rees, Rebecca Podos

Represents literary and commercial fiction, memoirs, history, biography, business, YA and middle grade, self-help, psychology and science. *Commission* Home 15%. See the website for individual agents' submission guidelines. *Founded* 1983.

The Angela Rinaldi Literary Agency*

email info@rinaldiliterary.com
website www.rinaldiliterary.com

Mainstream and literary fiction: women's, multicultural, mysteries, suspense, historical thrillers; non-fiction: memoir, biography, relationships, psychology, health/medical/wellness, business, parenting, cookery, lifestyle and personal finance. *Commission* Home 15%, overseas 25%. Email submissions only. For fiction, send a brief synopsis and the first ten pages. Non-fiction queries should include a detailed cover letter, your credentials and any publishing history. *Founded* 1994.

Root Literary*

email info@rootliterary.com
website www.rootliterary.com
Instagram @rootliterary
Owner Holly Root, *Agents* Kurestin Armada, Samantha Fabien, Melanie Figueroa, Taylor Haggerty, Alyssa Maltese, Molly O'Neill, Jessica Saint Jean

Represents authors, author-illustrators, graphic novelists and illustrators. Submissions via email or QueryManager. See individual agent pages for preferences. No screenplays or poetry, no authors of picture book texts only.

Rita Rosenkranz Literary Agency*

440 West End Avenue, Apartment 15D, New York, NY 10024
tel +1 212-873-6333
email rrosenkranz@mindspring.com
website www.ritarosenkranzliteraryagency.com
Founder Rita Rosenkranz

Dedicated to representing adult non-fiction in a diverse range of subject areas, including biography, business, food and health, history, music and popular culture, parenting, sport, spirituality, science, writing and how-to guides. Works with both major and regional publishers dealing with more select markets. Query by email or post. For full submission guidelines see website. *Founded* 1990.

Jane Rotrosen Agency*

318 East 51st Street, New York, NY 10022
tel +1 212-593-4330
email info@janerotrosen.com
website www.janerotrosen.com
X @Jane_Rotrosen
Instagram @jra_janerotrosenagency
Founding Partner Jane Rotrosen Berkey, *Managing Partner* Chris Prestia, *Agents* Andrea Cirillo, Meg Ruley, Annelise Robey, Amy Tannenbaum, Christina Hogrebe, Rebecca Scherer, Kathy Schneider, Jessica Errera, Logan Harper, Danielle Marshall, Casey Conniff

Represents authors of fiction and non-fiction. Genres represented in fiction include women's, suspense, thrillers, mysteries, crime fiction, historical novels, YA, romantasy, psychological suspense and romantic comedy. For non-fiction, represents current affairs, pop culture, platform-driven books in the business, wellness and personal growth categories. Visit the agent page on the website for agents' specific interests and contact details. Submissions by email. For fiction, include a synopsis and first three chapters. For non-fiction, include a proposal and sample chapters. Does not currently accept plays, screenplays or children's picture books.

Clients have produced over 1,000 international and domestic bestsellers in all formats. *Founded* 1974.

Regina Ryan Publishing Enterprises*

251 Central Park West, 7D, New York, NY 10024
email queries@reginaryanbooks.com
website www.reginaryanbooks.com
Facebook www.facebook.com/reginaryanbooks
Instagram @ReginaRyanBooks
Threads @ReginaRyanBooks
President Regina Ryan

Primarily represents adult non-fiction in the following areas: architecture, arts, gardening, popular culture, food, wellness, diet and lifestyle, the environment and sustainability, history, natural history (particularly in relation to birds), psychology and science, parenting, women's issues and sports. Well-written narrative non-fiction is also of great interest, including biography. Query by email only; send a proposal and, if possible, at least two sample chapters. We only rarely represent memoir or illustrated books.

Clients include Donald J. Kroodsma, Anita Sanchez, Edmund Stump, Hillel Zaltzman, Jackie Haskins, J. Craig Wheeler, Robert Smith MD, Thomas Helling, Andrea Lyon, David Deardorff, Kathryn Wadsworth, Suzi Eszterhas, Hillel Zaltzman, Dawn Kingston, Abby Eblen MD.

Susan Schulman Literary Agency*

454 West 44th Street, New York, NY 10036
tel +1 212-713-1633
email susan@schulmanagency.com
website www.schulmanagency.com
X @SusanSchulman
Agents Susan Schulman, Emelie Burl, *Foreign Rights* Linda Migalti

Agents for negotiation in all markets (with co-agents) of fiction and general non-fiction, children's books, academic and professional works, and associated subsidiary rights including plays, television and film. *Commission* Home 15%, UK 7.5%, overseas 20%. Return postage required. Email enquiries to queries@schulmanagency.com.

Wendy Sherman Associates*

138 West 25th Street, Suite 1018, New York, NY 10001
tel +1 212-279-9027
email submissions@wsherman.com
website www.wsherman.com
Contacts Wendy Sherman, Cherise Fisher, Laura Mazer, Callie Deitrick

Represents a variety of mainstream fiction and non-fiction, with a passion for character-driven literature. Fiction areas of interest include contemporary, historical, romance and women's literature, Southern voices and suspense. Non-fiction list features works of both a narrative and prescriptive nature. Popular categories include memoir, journalism, lifestyle (especially food), relationships, parenting and self-help books. Illustrated non-fiction in the areas of fashion, food and home décor is also accepted. Works with a number of co-agents covering the major foreign territories. Also has connections with film and television agents in Los Angeles. Query by email; for fiction send a query letter and the first ten pages of the MS, for non-fiction send a query letter and author bio. For full submission guidelines see website. *Founded* 1999.

Philip G. Spitzer Literary Agency*

50 Talmage Farm Lane, East Hampton, NY 11937
tel +1 631-329-3650
email kim.lombardini@spitzeragency.com
website www.spitzeragency.com
Agents Anne-Lise Spitzer, Lukas Ortiz, *Office* Kim Lombardini

General fiction and non-fiction; specialises in mystery, suspense/thriller, biography and memoir, history, politics and current affairs. Send proposal by email, including the first chapter. Client list currently full. *Founded* 1969.

Cullen Stanley International*

745 Fifth Avenue, Suite 500, New York, NY 10151
tel +1 917-677-4074
email submissions@cullenstanleyinternational.com
website www.cullenstanleyinternational.com
Contacts Cullen Stanley

Specialises in international rights representation on behalf of authors, agencies and publishers. Represents books with international appeal that will find readers in many languages around the world including narrative non-fiction, historical memoir, biography, books on design and mind, body & spirit. Send a query via email. Query letters should contain publication history, biographical information and a brief synopsis of your work; attach the first ten pages of the MS. Does not accept hard copy submissions. *Founded* 2017.

Sterling Lord Literistic*

594 Broadway, New York, NY 10012
tel +1 212-780-6050
email info@sll.com
website www.sll.com
X @SterlingLordLit
Instagram @sterlinglordlit
President Philippa Brophy, *Executive Vice President* Laurie Liss, *Chief Operating Officer* Nadyne Pike, *Vice Presidents* Doug Stewart, Robert Guinsler, Jim Rutman, *Senior Agents* Neeti Madan, Sarah Landis, *Agents* Elizabeth Bewley, Danielle Bukowski, Jessica Friedman, Mary Krienke, Jenny Stephens, *Associate Agents* Christopher Combemale, Lily Dolin, *Foreign rights* Szilvia Molnar, Amanda Price

Works with a number of co-agents in all major foreign territories. Also has connections in TV and film development and production. Represents a range of fiction and non-fiction in a variety of subject areas. Fiction list features books for both the commercial and literary market, including thrillers, gentle fantasy and sci-fi, and novels of cultural or geographical reference. Picture books, children's, middle grade and YA fiction are also strongly represented. Non-fiction areas of interest cover everything from biography and memoir to current affairs, journalism and science. More commercial subject areas such as food, lifestyle, self-help and travel are also covered. Query via online form including a query letter, synopsis and proposal (non-fiction) or three chapters (fiction). For agent preferences, see website. Does not represent screenplays.

Clients James McBride, Chanel Miller, William Gibson, Rachel Maddow, Hannah Gadsby, Gabrielle Zevin, Jason Rekulak, Phoebe Robinson, Alejandro Varela, Jenny Lawson, Stan and Jan Berenstain, Sheila Heti, Raquel Vasquez Gilliland, Shelby Mahurin, Bryan Washington. *Founded* 1952.

Stimola Literary Studio*

tel +1 508-696-9351
website www.stimolaliterarystudio.com
President & Founder Rosemary B. Stimola, *Vice President* Peter K Ryan, *Senior Agent* Erica Rand Silverman, *Agents* Adriana Stimola, Allison Hellegers, Allison Remcheck, *Literary Assistant* Hillary Godwin

Children's fiction and non-fiction, from preschool to YA; adult fiction, non-fiction, cookery books, lifestyle and mind, body & spirit. *Commission* Home 15%, overseas 20%. Most clients come via referral. Please refer to website for agent interests and submission guidelines *Founded* 1997.

3 Seas Literary Agency*

PO Box 444, Sun Prairie, WI 53590
tel +1 608-332-3430
website www.threeseasagency.com
Facebook www.facebook.com/people/3-Seas-Literary-Agency/100057827492698
X @threeseaslit
Agents Michelle Grajkowski, Cori Deyoe, Stacey Graham, Kara Grajkowski, Wynter Graham (sub-rights)

A full-service literary agency representing authors who write romance, women's fiction, sci-fi and fantasy, thrillers, YA and middle-grade fiction, as well as select non-fiction titles and picture books. Submission through QueryManager only. See individual agent pages for preferences. Will only reply if interested in your work. *Founded* 2000.

Trident Media Group

355 Lexington Avenue, 12th Floor, New York, NY 10017
tel +1 212-333-1511
email info@tridentmediagroup.com
website www.tridentmediagroup.com
Facebook www.facebook.com/TridentMediaGroup
X @Trident_Media
Instagram @trident_media

Adult and children's fiction and non-fiction across a variety of genres. *Commission* Home 15%, overseas 20-25%, in conjunction with co-agents/theatre/films/TV 15%. Will suggest revision. Query one agent via online form. Writing sample on request. *Founded* 2000.

Upstart Crow Literary

594 Dean Street, Office 47, Brooklyn, NY 11238
website www.upstartcrowliterary.com
Instagram @upstartcrowliterary
Agents Danielle Chiotti, Kayla Cichello, Susan Hawk, Ted Malawer, Alexandra Penfold, Michael Stearns

Adult fiction, non-fiction and children's books (picture books, chapter books, middle grade and YA). Currently seeking adult upmarket commercial and literary fiction, and non-fiction which covers narrative, memoir, lifestyle, relationships, humour, current events, food, wine and cookery. For children's, all genres are welcome. Submissions vary by agent; consult website for details. Not currently seeking romance, political thriller, sci-fi, horror or erotica for adult fiction. *Founded* 2009.

Watkins/Loomis Agency

PO Box 20925, New York, NY 10025
tel +1 212-532-0080
email assistant@watkinsloomis.com
website www.watkinsloomis.com
President Gloria Loomis, *Vice President* Julia Masnik

Specialises in literary fiction, biography, memoir and political journalism. No unsolicited MSS. Representatives Abner Stein (UK) and The Marsh Agency (overseas). No unsolicited MSS. *Founded* 1908.

WME

11 Madison Avenue, 18th Floor, New York, NY 10010
tel +1 212-586-5100
website https://wmebookdepartment.com
X @wmebooks
Instagram @wmebooks

Worldwide talent and literary agency with offices in New York, Beverly Hills, Nashville, Washington, Sydney and London. Represents bestselling authors, critically acclaimed literary writers, award-winning thought leaders and up-and-coming talent. *Founded* 1898.

Wolf Literary Services*

135 West 29th Street, Suite 603, New York, NY 10001
email queries@wolflit.com
website https://wolflit.com
X @WolfLiterary
Contacts Kirsten Wolf, Kate Johnson, Rach Crawford, Leigh Eisenman, Laura Southern

Represents fiction, non-fiction and illustrated books. Send a query letter and sample MS pages (for fiction) or full proposal (for non-fiction). Submission by email or QueryManager, as applicable. Does not accept mailed queries. Does not represent screenplays. *Founded* 2008.

WordLink Incorporated

PO Box 395, Enola, PA 17025
tel +1 631-882-3462
website www.wordlink.us
Facebook www.facebook.com/wordlink.us

Represents works of fiction and non-fiction as well as TV and film internationally. Send a query letter or use online form. See website for detailed submission guidelines. *Founded* 1998.

Writers House*

120 Broadway, 22nd floor, New York, NY 10271
tel +1 212-685-2400
7660 Fay Avenue, #338H, La Jolla, CA 92037
email info@writershouse.com
website www.writershouse.com
President Simon Lipskar

Fiction and non-fiction for adults and children, including illustrators and film/TV rights. Represents literary and commercial fiction, women's fiction, sci-fi and fantasy, narrative non-fiction, history, memoirs, biographies, psychology, science, parenting, cookery books, how-to, self-help, business, finance, YA and juvenile fiction/non-fiction and picture books. Send a query letter, a synopsis and ten pages of the MS addressed to one agent; email preferred. Does not represent original screenplays. *Founded* 1973.

The Wylie Agency

250 West 57th Street, Suite 2114, New York, NY 10107
tel +1 212-246-0069
email mail@wylieagency.com
website www.wylieagency.com

Literary fiction and non-fiction. Offices in New York and London. No unsolicited MSS accepted.

Art and illustration
Introduction

To establish yourself as an artist a decade ago, there was really only one credible route: secure representation through an agent or forge a connection with a gallery. This is no longer the case. Mirroring the democratisation of the book industry over the last ten years, the art and illustration industry has opened up significantly and diversified. You do not need representation to reach your audience. However, as for writers, this doesn't mean that the traditional routes to becoming an artist are no longer possible, it just means that artists and creatives have more choice and more control over how their work is distributed than they ever had before. They can mix and match how they work and who they work with. The relationship artists have with agents and art venues is now more commercial, collaborative and symbiotic. They can create art in more ways than before. It is no longer confined to the white walls of a gallery or the smooth pages of print.

The most successful creatives are those who embrace the hybrid model, utilising the strengths of not just galleries and agencies but also their own direct-to-audience platforms to build careers they themselves can dictate. The lines between high and commercial art is blurring. There are more shades of grey than ever before and that can only be a good thing.

Listings in this section:

- *Art agents and commercial art studios*, page 516

Being a book cover illustrator

While great writing is at the heart of most successful books, a wonderful cover plays a key role too. In this article, Laura Barrett explains the importance of book covers and how she goes about creating ones that entice and engage book-buyers.

We all know that we're not supposed to judge a book by its cover, but there's a whole industry of passionate people dedicated to proving that we most definitely should. A book's cover is our first impression of any given text; a gateway into the narrative, mood or visual world that the story populates. Whether for a work of fiction or non-fiction, a cover has to work effectively both physically as a printed book in a shop, and digitally as a tiny low-res jpeg on a screen. Personally, I find book covers are a real joy to illustrate; the challenge of trying to get that balance just right whilst exploring my visual style gives me creative purpose.

I always knew that I wanted to be an artist of some kind: as a child I'd watch my grandad create beautiful watercolour paintings and thought that I'd like to do something similar. I spent many an hour copying and reimagining 80s' VHS covers for my favourite Disney films. So it seems fitting that I now illustrate and design books, book covers, packaging (and more) for a living!

I studied for a degree in Graphic Design at Camberwell College of Arts, and was incredibly lucky that my freelance illustration career grew quite organically from there. An art director from the *Guardian* happened to see my illustrations at my degree show exhibition and commissioned me for a couple of editorial pieces. I was then thrilled when an editor from the publisher Taschen saw my work for the *Guardian*, and asked me to create several illustrations for an anthology, *The Fairy Tales of the Brothers Grimm*.

My first book cover actually came through a short stint selling my illustrated prints and cards at Camden Market. An editor at Oneworld Publications picked up one of my business cards from my stall and later got in touch to commission me for a new edition of *The Bhagavad Gita*. I loved the process of creating artwork for a scene from the Hindu epic, along with a paisley-inspired patterned frame.

From there, I've been fortunate enough that one piece of work has continued to lead to the next. I'm proud to have created covers for Penguin Random House (a personal ambition!), Simon & Schuster, Headline and HarperCollins, to name just a few. I've also worked on book interiors for Macmillan and Scholastic, and picture books for Andersen Press, Vintage Books and Hachette.

My absolute favourite book covers to illustrate have been for *Bookworm* by Lucy Mangan, *The Beloved Girls* by Harriet Evans and *The Amazing Mr Blunden* by Antonia Barber. I particularly love working with a narrative that has dark, folkloric or mysterious themes to delve into. For some insights into the journey of illustrating a book cover, from start to finish, read on …

The process

A commission usually starts with an email from someone at the publisher; either the art director, designer or occasionally the editor. In most cases, this email will arrive via my lovely agents at The Artworks, or Mendola Art if the client is in the US. Included in this digital box of delights will be the details of the commission (timings, a basic synopsis, territories the book will be published in, etc.), and the exciting part: the brief. The brief can sometimes be loose, with lots of creative freedom, or more prescriptive, with exact concept suggestions – or somewhere inbetween! Luckily I enjoy both extremes and the variety it brings.

The brief will often be a text-based document, but occasionally will include some reference images, such as other successful covers within that genre, or examples of my own artwork that the publisher likes. The text will state considerations such as the target audience, the overall feel and artwork specifications, such as dimensions and bleed. It will also include any space needed on the front cover, such as for quotes, a shout line, awards, etc.

It's not always necessary, or feasible, within the timeframe or my workload, but, if possible, I very much enjoy reading the text before responding to a brief and starting on the illustration. This often gives me a much richer idea of elements that could be included in the cover art; whether that's small decorative flourishes in a larger frame, or key background scenery and objects. One of my favourite parts of the process is hiding small details within the cover – little 'Easter eggs' from the story for the reader to spot.

Roughs and sketches

Once the brief, timings and fee have been agreed, we're good to get started. This is the part where lots of ideas start bouncing around, just waiting to be put to paper. First, I'll often make a list of possible elements I could include on the cover. I'll then come up with a series of very rough sketches on paper, before scanning and reworking them in Adobe Illustrator; drawing digitally with a graphics tablet. I'll draw all of the elements – characters, scenery, decorative detailing – and start to layer them up and play around with the best composition.

I think some illustrators will work up their roughs to more detailed pencil sketches, and move on to final artwork only after the roughs have been approved by the publisher. Other illustrators will work exclusively digitally, right from the outset. I like to work my roughs up to a standard that I'm happy with digitally, before laying them out in a pdf presentation, with lots of notes about what I'd refine and develop at the next stage. I'll often include a few options for the publisher to choose from. Then I hit 'send' …

Feedback and amendments

The roughs will make their way to the design team, the sales team and, sometimes at this stage, the author. Ideally, there will be unanimous and positive feedback most of the time, asking me to move straight to the next stage of continuing to develop the artwork to finals. Perhaps there'll be some minor amendments to make along the way.

Sometimes there's a little more back and forth, for example, asking me to push an idea further, scale something up or down, add in or remove a certain element, etc. Very occasionally there might be a number of different voices and ideas from the various teams involved in publishing a book, and it will take a couple of rounds to make sure that everyone is happy with the direction the cover is taking. This can be tricky but it's a worthwhile process and can make for a good creative challenge.

Once the team and I have agreed on how to move forward, I'll work on any amendments and refine the artwork to a stage that we're all on board with. There will sometimes then be a couple of other tiny tweaks, such as a quote that has changed length and needs more space, or another small illustrated element that needs a little more work. Sometimes it'll be feedback such as 'can we please add a bird here?'! I tend to send my roughs in greyscale and then work on colour options once I feel that the artwork is mostly complete. There might be a few email conversations around this. For years I worked purely in black and white, so I still don't feel like colour is my strongest skill, though I've grown more confident in this over the past few years.

Finals

When everyone at the publisher is happy with the artwork and the cover has been approved, I'll make sure that extra artwork (the bleed) is in place, along with any other printing specifications. Once that's done, it's time to go ahead and send the final high-res illustrated artwork.

Often I'll be asked to create illustrations for just the front cover, and depending on the licence agreement and fee, the designer might then (with my permission) use some small elements on the back cover. Other times, I'll work on the back cover and spine myself. If it's a hardback, there may even be some flaps to extend the artwork across. I particularly love creating a whole cohesive and tactile product, especially when the budget allows for some special finishes, such as some beautiful metallic foil or embossing. It really can be the icing on the cake.

Occasionally a publisher will also commission some chapter headers for the book's interiors. This can be a nice touch and a chance to either expand on some small elements from the cover, or to create some extra illustrations that also hint at the story.

The joy of seeing a book cover that you've worked on sitting on a shelf or table in a bookshop, or even in the window, is a real thrill. For a long time at the beginning of my freelance career, I worked part time in a bookshop. It was rather surreal seeing a customer browse and purchase a book that I'd had the pleasure of working on!

Design and illustration considerations

• It's worth thinking about whether you'd like to capture the atmosphere and theme of a novel, or to illustrate a key scene from the text instead. What will draw the reader in the most?

• A decorative frame or pattern can be a really nice visual way of containing a cover design. Layering can also add lots of depth and mystery.

• Sometimes the illustrator will be asked to work on the cover type; other times this is designed in-house or by a freelance designer. If this is something you'll be creating, will you be hand-drawing the lettering to give a tactile feel, or using digital type to convey a certain mood or place in time? If someone else is working on this, can you create space within your design in a playful way?

• One of my favourite aspects of illustrating book covers is the research stage. Taking inspiration from a particular time period can be good fun. I loved researching Victorian shopfronts for *The Toymakers*, and intricate ironwork for *The Beloved Girls*. What subjects will you suddenly become an armchair expert in?

• Working directly with the art director or designer can be really collaborative and they can provide invaluable input. I've regularly found myself pushed slightly outside of my comfort zone and it's made my artwork and style grow over the years, not to mention elevated the final delivered result.

Tips to get started

• Visit a bookshop and get a feel for different genres; what you think works well and what doesn't. There can be some homogeny and trends within particular genres, especially crime novels. It's useful to know what's popular but don't let that stop you creating your own unique style. The book industry runs anywhere from four months to a year or two ahead from commissioning the artwork to publication, so what's in fashion now won't necessarily still be in vogue by the time the cover you're working on hits the shelves.

• Equally, take inspiration from outside of the publishing world. Personally, most of my ideas come from nature, galleries and architecture.

• I'd definitely recommend creating self-initiated pieces and, depending on if you have the budget, sending them to art directors. You can either do this digitally or by mailing out physical printed examples. Choose your favourite book, a well-known classic or even a series to show your cohesive style and visual language. I was lucky enough to be commissioned by Orchard Books for three classic picture books after sending them a miniature *Alice in Wonderland*-themed concertina book that I illustrated. I designed and printed them so that they were small enough to post cheaply.

• Commissions can come months or even years after a piece of promotional work, or contact with an art director. If someone in the industry likes your work, they will hang on to your artwork and information, just waiting for the right project to commission you for.

Laura Barrett is an experienced designer and illustrator. She has created artwork for many leading international brands, including publishing's biggest names, from Penguin Random House to Vintage, Bonnier and Little, Brown. Alongside book covers, she creates animation, branding material, illustrations for package design and large-scale museum and exhibition graphics. See www.laurabarrett.co.uk for more information.

Illustrating non-fiction books

Freelance illustrator Frances Moffatt describes her route into professional non-fiction illustration and gives practical advice for aspiring illustrators on finding that first commission and the process from contract through to publication and beyond.

The world of non-fiction books provides a wealth of illustration opportunities for the freelance illustrator, but is often overlooked by illustration graduates in favour of children's middle-grade fiction and picture books. Non-fiction is an exciting, diverse sector of publishing to work in and can range from commissions for cookery books and instructional guides on exercise and fashion to adult colouring books.

My own journey to illustrating non-fiction began after I graduated from my MA in Illustration and, fittingly, consulted the *Writers' & Artists' Yearbook* to identify potential clients. I had come to the conclusion that my portfolio was suited to the 'lifestyle' market, with a predominantly female focus, and subjects such as fashion, health and beauty. I duly combed the *Yearbook* to find appropriate publishers and then sent off small promotional packs containing a bundle of postcards, a business card and a covering letter. I put all this information in a spreadsheet so I could keep track of whom I had contacted and when, and whether I had followed that up with a phone call.

Illustrations by Frances Moffatt from *Fashion Exercise Book* (Batsford)

Around 18 months later, I received an exciting email from Pavilion Books asking me if I would like to illustrate a fashion-themed colouring and doodle book aimed at the young adult and adult markets, to which I swiftly replied a resounding 'Yes!'. It turned out that one of the designers in their art department had liked the promo package I sent and had pinned up one of my postcards on her desk to keep me in mind if any suitable projects came up. *Fashion Exercise Book* was published in 2014 by Batsford (a Pavilion imprint), and I went on to illustrate a further book, *Pick Up a Pen*, in 2018, for their Portico list.

It's a commonly held belief that if you want to work in any aspect of the creative industries it is important to have 'contacts', but I can honestly say that, in my own experience and that of many other illustrators I know, this has not been the case. If your work is good, you have a solid online portfolio, and knowledge of where your work sits in the publishing market, then you have every chance of seeing your work in print. Also keep in mind that building a sustainable career as an illustrator is a marathon, not a sprint, and not getting an immediate response from potential clients is not a failure. In my case, I had some positive and encouraging feedback from art directors at various publishing houses, but it took nearly two years to receive an actual commission.

Commission, ideas and initial meeting

So … you have been commissioned to illustrate a book, either following an approach by a publisher or your own pitch. The next step is to sign your contract. Publishing contracts are long and have many clauses, so it is essential to read them carefully and to seek advice if there are any sections you don't understand. If you are a member of the Association of Illustrators (AOI), the professional body for illustration within the UK (https://theaoi.com; see page 535), you can access free legal and contracts advice.

In a publishing contract for illustrating a book, you will generally get an advance and a percentage of royalties from any sales. Your advance will then be paid in three parts: the first instalment on signing the contract, the second on submitting the final illustrations and the third on publication. Therefore your full payment will be spread out over a long period of time, which means it's important to manage your time and budget accordingly, and to understand that your book project will inevitably run alongside other shorter projects.

After agreeing the contract, the next step is a meeting with your commissioning editor and the team working on the book. This can be done over Skype or Zoom or in person, which I prefer. The team can vary in size depending on the nature of the project. It's a great opportunity to visit your publisher's headquarters, have a face-to-face meeting with the people you will be working with and to discuss potential directions and possibilities. For the initial meeting, it's a good idea to prepare some rough sketches and ideas, any visual inspiration and some examples of similar successful titles on the market. This doesn't have to be anything elaborate or polished; for this stage I usually use a PowerPoint for images and a sketchbook for ideas and roughs.

Synopsis, layouts and pencil roughs

Your book concept may be taken to a book fair, such as London or Frankfurt, which is an opportunity for co-editions to be sold to foreign publishers. For this, your publisher will need a written synopsis of the book and around three finished spreads. This is a really helpful step for you as an illustrator, because it means you get a clear idea of the publisher's vision for the book and the feel and the tone that they, and you, are looking for.

Once the synopsis has been pinned down, it's time to do the roughs for each spread, and this can take different forms depending on the book. For example, when I was working on *Fashion Exercise Book*, a colouring book with brief slogans on each page rather than proper 'text', it was quite an organic process. We started off with a list of ideas for page content, and then I worked closely with the designer, sending work back and forth until we arrived at a consistent look and feel for the illustrations. As a result, after a couple of spreads we had established a routine of sending through the rough pencil spreads for any adjustment and approval, and then sending the inked-up finals as I completed them, until the book was finished.

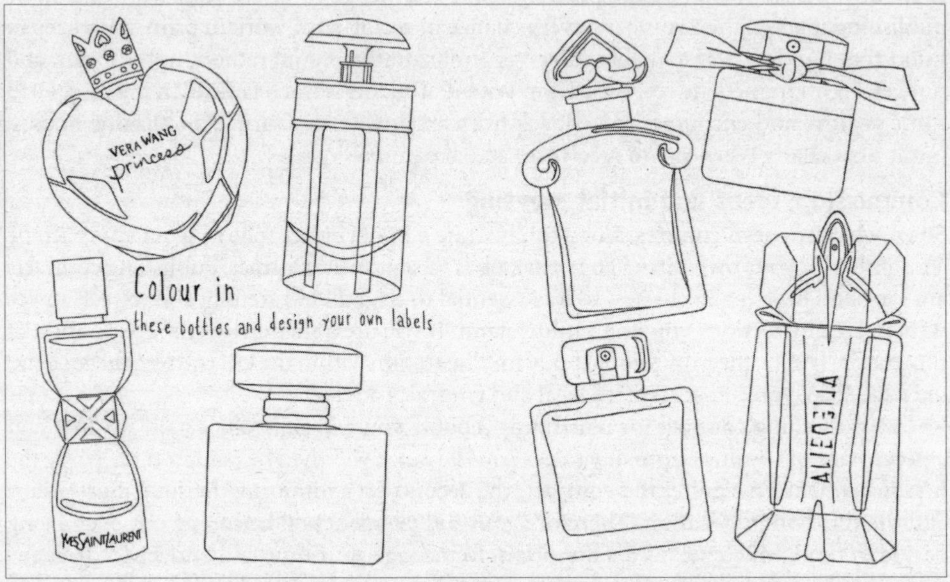

Illustrations by Frances Moffatt from *Fashion Exercise Book* (Batsford)

However, for *Pick Up a Pen*, because there was copy involved it required a bigger team, the process was slightly different and more formalised. I had input into the synopsis of the book, which was written up by a ghostwriter; I then submitted a pdf of pencil roughs of the whole book for approval, outlining what was going to be on each spread. Clearly at this point the text had not been written, but from the initial three spreads sent to book fairs I had an idea of the amount of text that would be on each page, which meant I could plan out the size and number of illustrations. As a result, my images for this book were a whole series of black-and-white 'spot' illustrations, which I submitted to the publisher in one batch at the end of the development stage; these were then sent to the book designer for page layout and the addition of limited accent colour.

So you will find that, when working on illustration for non-fiction books, there is commonality in the different stages of the project, but there is not just one set process or way of working. The main thing to remember is that clear and professional communication with the client and team at all times is paramount. It's likely that most of this communication will be conducted by email if you don't live near the publisher's offices (and they may well even be in a different time zone), so it's important to respond to all emails in a timely manner, and to just ask if you have questions or queries about any aspect of the brief or process. It's also really important to manage expectations; if you feel you are struggling with your deadline, it's best to speak up straightaway. It is much better to bring up any timing issues with as much notice as possible, and to negotiate an extension, than to struggle on and miss your deadline, as there is generally a little space in the schedule to allow for delays. And remember to *enjoy* the process! Freelance illustration can be a solitary profession at times, so illustrating a book allows you to be part of a creative team of experts in their field, which is an inspiring and rewarding experience.

Illustrations by Frances Moffatt from *Pick up a Pen* (Portico)

Proofs, publication, marketing and beyond

After you've submitted your final illustrations, what happens next? First, you will receive proofs to check. Proofs are prints of all the spreads of the book on loose sheets of paper; they will give you a pretty clear idea of what the final book will look like. After that you will receive a sample copy of the book, which for me is always a high point – the culmination of many months of hard work brought together in final form, ready to be sold.

The process of creating a book, from commission to publication, is a long one, usually around 12 months. Therefore you will have a long break between completing your illustrations and promoting the publication of your book, which involves a very different mindset and skills. You will need to work with your publisher on a marketing strategy, and you will also need to take responsibility for promoting the book yourself through social media, traditional media and in-person events.

In the weeks leading up to publication, you need to start building excitement and anticipation for your product across social media. You can start dropping 'teaser' images (small excerpts) from your book, along with a link to where people can pre-order; you can give your audience an insight into your development process, showing images of your pencil roughs or filming a short 'behind the scenes' video. In addition, you can work with your publisher to organise a book launch event – which is a great opportunity to both promote your book and to celebrate too! Venues for these can range from bookshops to restaurants to galleries.

At this stage you may also see your book published in co-editions across various countries with different publishers. In these cases, the front cover design may be amended or changed, and the book may be given a new title. For example, *Fashion Exercise Book* was published in France as *My Fashion Book – Coloriages Créatifs* (Éditions Marie Claire 2015) with a red and purple rather than an orange cover.

Once the process is over it's a great idea to keep in touch with your publishers, sending them updates on your new work, through further promotional packs or email links to your updated website, so they can keep you in mind for any future projects. When you have one book illustration project in your portfolio, you'll be in a strong position as you go back to your trusty *Writers' & Artists' Yearbook* for your next round of marketing. Potential clients will be more likely to commission you, as they have evidence you have already successfully handled illustrating a book from start to finish.

The good news is, if you're reading this, you are already on Step One of your journey towards being a published illustrator for non-fiction. If you have the passion and drive to continue to refine your illustrative practice, and have a considered and consistent marketing plan, you can move forward with confidence knowing that you are equipped with the knowledge and skills to make your publishing dreams a career reality. Good luck!

Frances Moffatt is a freelance illustrator and Programme Leader for BA (Hons) Illustration at the University of Lincoln. She has worked on a range of commissions for clients across editorial, publishing, fashion, beauty, product and live event illustration and is the author/illustrator of *Fashion Exercise Book, Pick Up a Pen* and *Fashion Colouring and Doodling,* all published by Pavilion Books. Frances has many years' experience of lecturing in illustration and design at degree level at a range of UK higher education institutions, and has spoken at design events and festivals, including TEDxBloomsbury and the Northern Festival of Illustration. See www.francesmoffatt.com for more information.

Creating comics

Hannah Berry describes how the creative world of comics, with its range and appeal, requires enthusiasm, resourcefulness and opportunism for success. She has advice on how to find an outlet and build a following for your work, as well as tips on how to seek out funding, get due remuneration for your work and protect its ownership.

The conversation goes like this: 'What do you do?' 'I work in comics!' 'Oh wow! What kind of comics do you make?' 'Well, you know the kind that are household names and get turned into nine-figure-budget blockbuster films?' 'Yeah?' 'Not those!'

The world of comics, behind its most visible popular image, is surprisingly wide-ranging, and I've managed to work in comics for nearly 20 years without penning a single superhero (I probably wouldn't turn it down if the opportunity arose, though. Give me a shout, Marvel.) I've made self-published zines, I've made literary graphic novels, I've made weekly cartoon strips. I've had comics in publications from *2000 AD* to the *New England Journal of Medicine*, and I've contributed to any number of anthologies in between. My career is nonsensical, total chaos, and I love it. Even when I hate it, I love it.

Making comics feels like the purest form of storytelling to me, with every aspect of the visuals and the text playing off each other in a delicious narrative alchemy. People unfamiliar with comics are surprised when I use the word 'subtle', but comics often are. They can be subtle, sincere and eloquent, or they can be surreal, discordant romps, or stark and abstract, or journalistic and impassioned … They can be anything, and they can be made by anyone. And the best thing about making comics is that, even when you're making them all alone at home, you're not totally alone. The community side of the scene is thriving and, with the existence of so many local groups, national organisations and collectives, it's a very accessible and extremely welcoming scene to get involved in.

From my experience, the UK comics scene is largely run on pervasive, infectious enthusiasm, rather than (unfortunately) actual money, which may explain why one tenth of professional creators who consider comics their primary job are still only able to make them in their spare time.[1] It's not all bad, though. Alongside its unfortunate hurdles – little-to-no career-supporting infrastructure, or money, or opportunities – this uniquely scrappy and independent ecosystem has many benefits: getting started is incredibly easy, the community support is strong, and there are very few gatekeepers. Still, if you've read this far then I'm assuming you're either my mother or you're seriously interested in getting involved with comics, so let's dive into a (non-exhaustive) overview.

In the very beginning, given that your career will be largely driven by that aforementioned enthusiasm, you need to ask yourself what kind of comics you enjoy reading and making. Are you drawn to certain characters? Specific genres? Are you funny, even if you do say so yourself? Do you have issues or themes you want to explore? Do you want to write, or draw, or both? What kind of stories do you like to read and/or tell? Do you see any of that reflected in the comics out there? If so, take a close look at those creators and see what they're doing: what festivals they go to; where they sell their comics; who (if anyone) publishes them; who their audiences are. If, on the other hand, you don't see it out there, you'll be forging your own path – so shine on, you beautiful diamond.

Webcomics

The outlet for your work depends entirely on the kind of comics you want to make, and how much time/energy/money you have to put towards it at that particular moment.

Webcomics are a financially low-stakes way of getting your work out into the world. These could be short, snappy gag cartoons or long-running sagas featuring a broad cast of characters but, in order to build up an audience, you'll need to be regular and consistent with your output. It's a real test of self-discipline, but the best and most prolific webcomic creators can amass huge followings across the entire Anglophone world, including highly comics-literate North America, and that leads to any number of opportunities. Your comics could be on your own dedicated website (which you can choose to monetise via advertising), on a dedicated webcomics platforms such as Webtoon or Tapas (who pay creators based on views), or simply on social media (no money, only prestige).

Self-publishing

And then there's paper. Sweet, sweet paper. Comics and graphic novels published by traditional publishers are very much in the minority; overwhelmingly the comics produced in the UK are self-published or small press comics. Publishers usually take care of the printing, packaging, shipping and promotion, but will take a bigger cut; going solo means you'll take on all the responsibility yourself but get all of the profit.

In self-publishing, the production values are entirely up to you. You can spend hundreds on a glossy full-colour print run, with spot varnish and French flaps, or get to work with a photocopier and a long arm stapler. If you're getting them printed, try not to go overboard with that first print run, no matter how appealing the economies of scale are; it's better to pay a little extra on a second print run after the first has sold out than to be sitting on boxes of unsold stock.

How many you print depends on where you're selling them. The best way to reach new audiences directly is to apply to be an exhibitor at a festival – essentially standing behind a table selling to passers-by. Thought Bubble (www.thoughtbubblefestival.com) and the Lakes International Comic Art Festival (www.comicartfestival.com) are two of the biggest festivals focusing solely on comics, and they attract hundreds of exhibitors and thousands of guests each year. But there are plenty of other festivals, zine fairs and conventions all over the UK – and around the world if you're feeling adventurous. There are some excellent guides online on 'tabling'; I'd recommend setting yourself up to take card payments, as cash has fallen extremely out of favour since the pandemic. And have fun – remember to leave your table occasionally so you can wander round, chat to others and look at their work. This is your best chance to explore what's out there, free from promoted content and algorithms.

You can keep the sales momentum going outside of festivals by selling your comic (physical or digital versions) through your own secured website, or through a retailing platform that gives you your own storefront, such as BigCartel (www.bigcartel.com) or Shopify (www.shopify.com/uk), or through online marketplaces like Comixology (www.amazon.co.uk/kindle-dbs/comics-store/home) or Etsy (www.etsy.com). If you want your comics to be sold by professionals, you can (and should!) also take your comics to bricks-and-mortar comic shops, many of which will have a healthy small press section, and ask nicely if they'll stock them. Finally, if your comic has connections to any special interest or any particular group, don't be afraid to approach organisations who share that interest. The Wellcome Collection (https://wellcomecollection.org) in London, for example, has an excellent health, medicine and science comics section in their bookshop.

Pricing your work is tough, as the urge to be competitive – and sometimes the feeling that your work is unworthy – can easily override making an actual profit. You'll need to calculate what you've already spent (on printing, paper, etc) and how much you *will* spend (on postage, packing, discount offered to a retailer, online payment fees, festival fees and expenses). The price you sell your work at will need to incorporate all of these *plus* make all the time you put into it worthwhile. Don't try to compete with bigger retailers or publishers; remind yourself that creative works everywhere have been devalued by outdated capitalist economic models which do not accurately reflect value. Whatever you choose, you'll still spend forever convincing yourself it was the wrong decision, so you might as well price your work up: you're worth it!

Self-publishing and webcomics both involve large amounts of self-promotion in order to get your work seen and drum up sales. For the love of God, don't sit back and wait to be 'discovered' or you'll be waiting a long time! The problem with comics in the UK is that the readership is still relatively small; convincing the wider public that comics are for *everyone*, by *anyone*, on any subject imaginable, is a perpetual struggle, though thankfully things are improving. Your biggest audience as a comics creator is likely to be other creators … there's a joke about the same fiver being passed around a convention as everyone buys each other's work (and it's funny because it's true). Promoting your work to your own friends and peers doesn't have to feel grubby, and it's actually easier if you've taken the time to help others spread the word on their work too. Comics websites like Broken Frontier (www.brokenfrontier.com) provide news and reviews on indie comics, and you can always politely submit your work for review to reach a wider audience and get some nice quotes.

Remember that it's a very, very small world, and that word can spread fast. Be kind, be respectful, help others wherever you can, and treat every job and every person professionally, even – especially – if you don't feel like a professional yet.

Funding

Increasingly, comics creators and publishers are funding their projects through crowdfunding. This is a great option if you've already built up an audience for your comics, and it can take a lot of the guesswork out of production. It takes a gargantuan effort to crowdfund a project, though, so this is a situation in which working as part of a collective could be advantageous – splitting the responsibilities and sharing the load. Remember to budget carefully, be realistic with the amount you need, and seek advice from other creators who have already crowdfunded their projects.

Many creators also receive regular donations from their readers, through sites like Patreon (www.patreon.com) and Ko-Fi (https://ko-fi.com), in exchange for access to exclusive content, work in progress, etc. It's a friendly but structured way to stay connected with and reward a loyal readership.

It's also possible to apply for public funding through the various Arts Councils. The application forms are long, but you can find a wealth of advice on how to tackle these online. Don't be deterred if you're unsuccessful on your first attempt! (I got an Arts Council England Project Grant on my fourth try.)

Being published by a publisher

Self-publishing isn't the only form of publishing, of course. Back in 2005 I sent a letter to Jonathan Cape, who I'd noticed were publishing graphic novels, asking if they'd be interested in looking at my graphic novel-in-progress. They looked, they liked, they made an offer. Absurd? Yes. But the point is they were looking for fresh new creators at the time, and this is still largely the case. I have it on good authority that most large publishers wait for submissions from agents, but most agents don't represent comics creators, so it seems that even now the best way in is to get in touch directly. Do your research, find out who is publishing the kind of stories you want to tell, use tact and precision, and submit your best letter outlining your story. There is excellent advice on this exact process elsewhere in this book, but, as an added note of optimism, I'd say that comics submissions seem to spend a lot less time waiting on that slush pile.

Work-for-hire

There are two modes of authorship when it comes to comics: the traditional author model and the work-for-hire model. In the former you're paid an advance and royalties and retain ownership of the copyright of your work. This is usually where you're doing all the writing and artwork yourself, although you can be co-author with another creator. It's worth noting that publishers using the traditional model don't usually match artists and writers in-house, so if you're an artist-only or writer-only who wants to work in this way you'll need to find someone to team up with first. (It's a good idea, if you're collaborating on something speculative with another creator, to get an agreement down in writing about who owns the copyright of the final product, and what can and can't be done with it; it may feel pre-emptively cynical, like a pre-nup, but you're protecting each other from future heartaches.)

The work-for-hire model is mostly used by publishers producing regular comic books and magazines, often involving licensed characters, in which the editor will put together a team of creators doing the writing, pencilling, inking, colouring and lettering. You're generally paid a one-off fee for the work but have no creative control over the finished product. In this situation, you might be pitching either the story as a writer or yourself as an artist. Most of these publishers will tell you how to submit work on their websites, but they do often visit festivals and conventions where they can be approached directly. This is a competitive area, so be prepared to knock on a few doors!

Sadly, in customary practice, comics creators' keenness to work in comics has too often been exploited. This is not so much the case any more, but there is still an unpleasant hangover to be aware of. Before you sign a contract with any publisher, commissioner or co-creator, be sure to run it past an organisation such as the Society of Authors (see page 746) or Association of Illustrators (see page 535), an agent or legal professional. No reputable publisher, commissioner or co-creator will be upset by you seeking out an informed opinion. If they are, I'd suggest they're not so reputable after all and you'll have saved yourself a lot of trouble down the line.

The other elephant in the room is the remuneration elephant. Technically, making comics is a skilled job and can (and should) be done in exchange for money, but realistically – as with most work in the arts – it's likely to be a while before you make a significant profit. You can put the work out first and hope to build up an audience (e.g. webcomics, self-publishing) or you can look around for paid work (e.g. freelancing, work-for-hire) for which you'll first need to build up a prerequisite skill set, and possibly contact list. Either way, you're playing the long game – we all are; 87% of creators supplement their income

with other work.[1] However, if you are not being paid, you should be working on what *you* want to work on, whether your own personal projects that fulfil your creative needs, work that you know you can use to promote yourself, or goodwill projects if you're in a position to do so. If you're being asked to do free work as a favour, think carefully before taking it on, and regard anything that's being promised in the future with a skeptical eye. Your work has value; many people know this but hope that *you* don't.

With comics being such a broad, informal church, the big question is: What does 'success' look like to you? Is it critical praise? Accolades? Financial stability? Being seen? Creative expression? All of these things are possible, even if some are harder to reach than others. One of the key differences between comics and other areas of the arts in the UK is that it's a huge grassroots community with not much of an establishment. Official opportunities are quite limited and extremely competitive, so most creators end up carving out their own opportunities.

Think of yourself as ivy, slowly but persistently climbing a wall. The ascent might feel inexorably slow, but the wall is erratic and peculiar and you'll find many surprising places to anchor your aerial roots, which is key. The single biggest thing I can impress on you is the need to be vigorously, ferociously opportunistic. The more proactive you are, both inside and outside of the comics scene, the more adventurous and resourceful you are, the further you will grow (and the more of the wall you will engulf with your leafy tendrils). Enjoy the ascent, remember that you're doing your best on a difficult surface, and celebrate that ridiculous, glorious wall every chance you get.

Hannah Berry is an award-winning comics creator, writer, cartoonist and illustrator; a Fellow of the Royal Society of Literature and UK Comics Laureate 2019–21. Her first graphic novel *Britten & Brülightly* was published by Jonathan Cape in 2008, with the French edition chosen for the Official Selection of the Festival International de la Bande Dessinée d'Angoulême. Her second graphic novel *Adamtine* was published in 2012 and her third, *Livestock*, in 2017, both by Jonathan Cape. *Livestock* won Berry a Best Writer Award at the 2017 Broken Frontier Awards and was nominated in the Best Graphic Novel category. She is a founding committee member of both the Society of Authors' Comics Creators Network and the Comics Cultural Impact Collective (CCIC), as well as a Trustee of the Cartoon Museum. For more information see https://hannahberry.co.uk. Follow her on Bluesky @streakofpith.bsky.social and Instagram @streakofpith.

1. *UK Comics Creators Survey* 2020. Survey funded by Arts Council England, British Council and the Scottish Centre for Comics Studies, University of Dundee, conducted by H. Berry and the Audience Agency; available on http://hannahberry.co.uk/survey.

Art agents and commercial art studios

Before submitting work, artists are advised to make preliminary enquiries and to ascertain terms of work. Commission varies but averages 25–30%. The Association of Illustrators (see page 535) provides a valuable service for illustrators, agents and clients. Note that the country code for phoning UK offices from overseas is +44.

sae = self-addressed envelope
*Member of the Society of Artists Agents
†Member of the Association of Illustrators

Advocate Art

27 Old Gloucester Street, London WC1N 3AX
tel 020-8390 6293
email mail@advocate-art.com
website www.advocate-art.com
Facebook www.facebook.com/advocateart
X @advocateart01
Instagram @advocateart01
Global Manager Amanda Hendon

Represents artists for children's, middle-grade and YA books, greeting cards and licensing, and advertising. Has 12 agents representing over 300 artists globally. For illustrators' submission guidelines see the website. Also has offices in New York City, Los Angeles and Seville, with agents located internationally. The website is in German, Spanish, Italian and French. Founded 1992.

Agency Rush

11 Vine Street, Brighton BN1 4AG
tel (01273) 675122
website https://agencyrush.com/
X @agencyrush
Instagram @agencyrush
Director Keeley Jay Fairwood

Represents nearly 30 artists and works with clients globally. Also offers help to non-represented artists on an ad hoc basis. Send up to six low-res examples of your work or a link to your website to join@agencyrush.com. Offices in Brighton and New York. Founded 2022.

Allied Artists/Artistic License

tel 07971 111256
email gary@allied-artists.net
website www.alliedartists-illustration.co.uk
Contact Gary Mills

Represents leading international illustrators specialising in children's books and magazines from pre-school to YA for fiction, non-fiction, picture books, novelty, graphic novels and educational books with a range of styles covering realistic, stylised, cute, sci-fi and cartoon and comic. Founded 1983.

Darley Anderson Illustration Agency

Unit 19, Matrix Studios, 91 Peterborough Road, London SW6 3BU
tel 020-3940 9012
website www.darleyandersonillustration.com
Instagram @darleyanderson_illustration
Managing Director Clare Wallace, *Agents* Lydia Silver, Becca Langton, Chloe Davis, *Head of International Rights* Kristina Egan

Represents bestselling and award-winning illustrators. Works across all areas of publishing: fiction and non-fiction, including picture books, gift titles and graphic novels. Collaborates with both adult and children's publishers. Actively looking for new talent, especially illustrators from under-represented backgrounds. Commission: 20%. Submission guidelines: send an email with portfolio attached as a pdf or in the email, along with information about yourself and links to social media channels. Author-illustrators should send texts as pdf or Word attachments, along with a brief synopsis and illustration samples. Submissions should be made directly to the agent of choice. Founded 1988.

Arena Illustration*†

31 Eleanor Road, London E15 4AB
tel 020-8555 9827
website www.arenaillustration.com
Facebook www.facebook.com/arena.illustration
X @arenatweet
Instagram @arenaillustration
Contact Tamlyn Francis

Represents 29 artists. Average commission: 25%. Founded 1970.

The Art Agency

21 Morris Street, Sheringham, Norfolk NR26 8JY
tel (01263) 823424
email artagency@me.com
website www.the-art-agency.co.uk
Facebook www.facebook.com/illustrationagency
Director Peter Kavanagh

Provides non-fiction, reference and children's book illustration. Specialises in non-fiction illustrations across a wide variety of subjects and age groups. Submit up to six samples by email along with a link to your website. Founded 1990.

Artist Partners*†

22 Albion Hill, Ramsgate, Kent CT11 8HG
tel 020-7401 7904
email christine@artistpartners.com
website www.artistpartners.com
X @ArtistPartners
Instagram @artistpartners
Managing Director Christine Isteed

Represents artists, including specialists, producing artwork in every genre for advertising campaigns, storyboards, children's and adult book covers, newspaper and magazine features and album covers. New artists are considered if their work is of high standard. Submission should be by email only. Founded 1951.

Artistique International

27 Old Gloucester Street, London WC1N 3AX
tel 020-7046 9525
email mail@artistique-int.com
website www.artistique-int.com
Contact Harry Burns

Specialises in editorial and advertising. Offices in London, Marbella, New York and Singapore. Founded 2016.

The Artworks*

4th Floor, 107 Charterhouse Street,
London EC1M 6HW
email submissions@theartworksinc.com
website www.theartworksinc.com
Facebook www.facebook.com/artworksillustration
X @ArtworksIllos
Instagram @theartworks_inc
Contacts Stephanie Alexander-Jinks, Alex Hadlow, Lucy Scherer

Represents 35 illustrators for design and advertising work as well as for non-fiction children's books, book jackets, illustrated gift books and children's picture books. Commission: 30% design and advertising, 25% publishing advances, 15% royalties, 25% book jackets. Founded 1983.

Beehive Illustration

42A Cricklade Street, Cirencester, Glos. GL7 1JH
email enquiries@beehiveillustration.co.uk
website www.beehiveillustration.co.uk
X @beehive_illus
Instagram @beehive_illustration
Contact Paul Beebee

Represents 200 artists specialising in ELT, education and general children's publishing illustration. Commission: 25%. Founded 1989.

Bernstein & Andriulli

72–74 Paul Street, London EC2A 4NA
website www.ba-reps.com
Instagram @barepsau
Global Managing Director Gregg Lhotsky

Represents photographers, illustrators, animators, design studios, CGI artists, mural artists, hair and makeup artists, stylists, immersive technologists and full service production. Please send work samples as a portfolio link; samples sent as external attachments will not be reviewed for security purposes. Do not send submissions to the info box. Send samples and explain why you are a good fit for the agency to: submissions@ba-reps.com. Founded 2015.

The Big Red Illustration Agency

29 Marlborough Ave, Cheadle Hulme,
Cheadle SK8 7AP
tel 0808 120 0996
email enquiries@bigredillustrationagency.com
website www.bigredillustrationagency.com
Facebook www.facebook.com/thebigredillustrationagency
X @big_red_author
Director Adam Rushton

Represents a number of professional illustrators. Works with a variety of clients including children's book publishers, design agencies, greetings card companies and toy manufacturers. Founded 2012.

The Bright Agency*

103–105 St John's Hill, London SW11 1SY
tel 020-7326 9140
US Office 50 West Street, C12, New York, NY 10006
tel +1 646-604-0992
email mail@thebrightagency.com
website www.thebrightagency.com
X @bright_agency
Instagram @bright_agency
Global Managing Director James Burns

Areas of representation include: children's illustration, greeting and gift (cards, social stationery and giftwrap), design and advertising (editorial, branding, adult publishing, packaging, web, digital and typography), animation, literary (children's fiction and non-fiction, adult fiction and non-fiction, and graphic novels) and licensing (toys and games, digital gaming, fabric and apparel, and homewares). For illustration, writing and animation submissions guidelines see website. No submissions by post. Clients include: Benji Davies, David Litchfield, Yasmeen Ismail, Chris Chatterton, Diane Ewen, Laura Hughes, Galia Bernstein, Mechal Roe, Aura Lewis, Karl James Mountford, Jane Newland, Brenna Nation and Hannah Peck. Founded 2002.

Central Illustration Agency

9 Perseverance Works, 38 Kingsland Road,
London E2 8DD

tel 020-3222 0007
email info@centralillustration.com
website www.centralillustration.com
Facebook www.facebook.com/centralillustrationagencyblog
X @ciablog
Contacts Ben Cox, Jules Beazley

An international resource for commercial art and motion graphics for the advertising, design and publishing industries. Commission: 30%. Founded 1983.

Collaborate Agency

Unit 7, Hove Business Centre, Fonthill Road, Hove, Brighton BN3 6HA
tel (01273) 251700
email hello@collaborate.agency
website https://collaborate.agency/
Facebook www.facebook.com/collaborate
X @c0llab0rate
Instagram @collaborateagency
Directors Caroline Burns, Edward Burns

Works on books for all ages and in all genres. Artists are skilled across all creative disciplines. Illustrators, editors, photographers, designers, web developers and animators. Offices in Brighton, London, New York, Gibraltar, Singapore and Seville. Founded 2008.

The Coningsby Gallery

30 Tottenham Street, London W1T 4RJ
tel 020-7636 7478
email info@coningsbygallery.com
website www.coningsbygallery.com
Directors Andrew Coningsby, Jonathan Hedley, Osian England, Larisa Kline, Raquel Leis Allio

Gallery located in Fitzrovia, London, available for exhibitions by fine artists and communication artists on a hire or fully represented basis. Has mounted successful exhibitions from highly established as well as up-and-coming fine artists and illustrators. Offers fine artists and illustrators highly specialist marketing support services. Email submissions from artists are welcome. See also Début Art for the agency side of the business (below). Founded 1994.

Creative Coverage

49 Church Close, Locks Heath, Southampton, Hants. SO31 6LR
tel (01489) 808261
email info@creativecoverage.co.uk
website www.creativecoverage.co.uk
Facebook www.facebook.com/CreativeCoverage
X @CreativeCov
Instagram @creativecov
Co-founders Tim Saunders, Caroline Saunders

Fine art book publisher and artists' agent. Marketing for selected professional artists. Founded 2013.

Creative Sparrow

12 Conqueror Court, Sittingbourne, Kent ME10 5BH
email contact@creativesparrow.co.uk
website https://creativesparrow.co.uk/
Instagram @creativesparrowart
Managing Director Hannah Curtis

An agency representing creatives across all industries. Working with clients and artists globally, facilitates collaborations for the art licensing, branding, advertising and publishing sectors. Founded 2021.

Début Art*†

30 Tottenham Street, London W1T 4RJ
tel 020-7636 7478
email info@coningsbygallery.com
website www.coningsbygallery.com
Directors Andrew Coningsby, Jonathan Hedley, Osian England, Raquel Leis Allion

A leading agency, with offices in London and New York, appointed by illustrators and animators to market and represent them. Has its own art gallery The Coningsby Gallery (above) in central London. Represents highly established illustrators and animators and also has a specialty in nurturing up-and-coming talent. Email submissions from artists are welcome. Founded 1985.

Dutch Uncle

13 Camden Passage, Angel, Islington, London N1 8EA
tel 020-7336 7696
email info@dutchuncle.co.uk
website www.dutchuncle.co.uk
Facebook www.facebook.com/dutchuncle
X @AgencyDU
Instagram @agencydu

Represents and seeks out creative talent for clients looking to commission content such as animation, illustration, book design and data visualisations. Offices also in New York and Tokyo. Founded 2006.

Eye Candy Illustration

Field Cottage, Saintbury WR12 7PX
tel 020-8291 0729
email info@eyecandyillustration.com
website www.eyecandyillustration.com
X @eyecandyillus
Managing Director Mark Wilson

Represents 50+ artists producing work for advertising campaigns, packaging, publishing, editorials, greeting cards, merchandising and a variety of design projects. Submit printed samples with sae or email low-res jpg files via website. Founded 2002.

Folio Illustration Agency†

10 Gate Street, London WC2A 3HP
tel 020-7242 9562
email info@folioart.co.uk
website www.folioart.co.uk
Facebook www.facebook.com/folioart

X @folioart
Instagram @folioart

All areas of illustration and animation. Founded 1976.

Good Illustration

40 Bowling Green Lane, London EC1R 0NE
tel 020-8123 0243 (UK), +1 347-627-0243 (US)
email draw@goodillustration.com
website www.goodillustration.com
Facebook www.facebook.com/goodillustration
X @gillustration
Instagram @goodillus
Directors Doreen Thorogood, Kate Webber, Tom Thorogood

Represents 50+ artists for advertising, design, publishing and animation. Send sae and samples. Commission: 25% publishing, 30% advertising. Founded 1977.

Handsome Frank

email hello@handsomefrank.com
website www.handsomefrank.com
X @Handsome_Frank
Founders Jon Cockley, Tom Robinson

Represents 40+ creatives, across five continents. Predominantly working with clients across advertising, design and publishing. Ranging from global brands to bold start-ups. Artists interested in being represented should email nine low-res jpgs to submissions@handsomefrank.com. Founded 2010.

Holroyde Cartey

email claire@holroydecartey.com
website www.holroydecartey.com
Directors Claire Cartey, Penelope Holroyde

Represents high-quality illustrators. Welcomes submissions from debut and established illustrators. Only accepts submissions via email. Aims to respond to every submission within about six weeks. Please send a portfolio of a dozen or so images in either jpg or pdf format of up to 5MB in size. Founded 2015.

IllustrationX*†

4th Floor, Silverstream House, 45 Fitzroy Street, London W1T 6EB
tel 020-7720 5202
email hello@illustrationx.com
website www.illustrationx.com/uk
Facebook www.facebook.com/weareillustrationx
X @illustrationx
Contact Juliette Lott

Welcomes submissions from illustrators and animators whose work is distinctive and innovative. Only accepts applications from artists through submissions page: www.illustrationx.com/applications. Founded 1929.

Image by Design Art Licensing

Suite 3, 107 Bancroft, Hitchin, Herts. SG5 1NB
tel (01462) 451190
email hello@ibd-licensing.co.uk
website www.ibd-licensing.co.uk
Facebook www.facebook.com/IBDArtLicensing
Instagram @ibdartlicensing
Contact Hugh Brenham

Art licensing agency representing talented creatives. Artwork for greeting cards, stationery, home decor, wall art, tableware, textiles, puzzles, giftware and more. Accepting submissions from artists and illustrators, please see website for details. Founded 1987.

Inky Illustration

Kemp House, 152–160 City Road, London EC1V 2NX
tel 0121 270 5828
email info@inkyillustration.com
website https://inkyillustration.com/
Facebook www.facebook.com/inkyillustration
X @inkyillo

Illustrators have experience working with clients on international advertising campaigns, publications and editorials, as well as commissions for smaller companies. Always happy to receive new work. Fill out the application form on the website or email to: submissions@inkyillustration.com. Hard copies of work are accepted with an sae if the work is to be returned. Founded 2009.

JSR

Studio 14–18, 2nd Floor, Old Street, London EC1V 9BH
tel 020-7228 6667
email illustration@jsragency.com
website www.jsragency.com
Facebook www.facebook.com/jsragency
X @jsragency
Founder & Director Jamie Stephen

Before submitting work for consideration artists should take a look at roster and make sure their work does not overlap with the artists currently represented. Please provide a pdf of your best work and website details in your submission: submissions@jsragency.com. Founded 2005.

B.L. Kearley Art & Antiques

Glebe House, Bakers Wood, Denham, Bucks. UB9 4LG
tel (01895) 832145
email christine.kearley@kearley.co.uk
website www.kearley.co.uk
Agent C. R. Kearley

Represents 30+ artists. Mainly specialises in children's book and educational illustration for the domestic market and overseas. Known for realistic figurative work. Also specialises in the sale of original book illustration artwork. Commission: 25%. Founded 1948.

Kids Corner

1 Mailing Street, West Street, Lewes BN7 2NZ
tel 020-7593 0506
email claire@meiklejohn.co.uk
website www.kidscornerillustration.co.uk
X @KidsCornerIllos
Instagram @kidscornerillustration_
Managing Director Claire Meiklejohn

Represents illustrators, from award-winning to emerging artists for children's publishing. Styles include fun, cute, stylised, picture book, young fiction, reference, graphic, traditional, painterly and digital. See also Meiklejohn Illustration (page 520). Founded 2015.

Lemonade Illustration Agency

167–169 Great Portland Street, 5th Floor, London W1W 5PF
tel 07891 390750
email studio@lemonadeillustration.com
US office 347 Fifth Ave, Suite 1402, New York, NY 10016, USA
website www.lemonadeillustration.com
Instagram @lemonadeillustrationagency

Represents 190+ award-winning illustrators working across all media from branding to children's picture books. Works with leading children's book publishers and educational publishers globally. Any submissions from artists by email must contain a website link and a cover letter. Unfortunately unable to reply to all submissions. Serves clients in all global markets with offices in London, New York, Sydney and Wakefield. Founded 2001.

David Lewis Illustration Agency

3 Somali Road, London NW2 3RN
tel 020-7435 7762, 07931 824674
email info@davidlewisillustration.com
website https://davidlewisillustration.com/
Director David Lewis, *Associate* Lisa Britton

Considers all types of illustration for a variety of applications suitable for book and magazine publishers, design groups, recording companies and corporate institutions. Also offers a comprehensive selection of images suitable for subsidiary rights purposes. Send sae with samples. Commission: 30%. Founded 1974.

Lipstick of London*

78 Clarendon Drive, London SW15 1AH
tel 07966 176989
email mc@lipstickillustration.com
website www.lipstickillustration.com
X @LipstickAgency
Instagram @lipstick_agency
Founder Marie-Claire Westover

Agency with artists who have experience spanning advertising, design, fashion, packaging, publishing, editorial, digital and motion and live events. Founded 2012.

Frances McKay Illustration

17 Church Road, West Mersea, Essex CO5 8QH
tel 07703 344334
email frances@francesmckay.com
website www.francesmckay.com
Proprietor Frances McKay

Represents 10–15 artists for illustration and writing children's books. For information on submissions please look at the website. Submit email with low-res scans or colour copies of recent work. Sae essential for return of all unsolicited samples sent by post. Commission: 25%. Founded 1999.

Meiklejohn Illustration*†

1 Mailing Street, West Street, Lewes BN7 2NZ
tel 020-7593 0506
email claire@meiklejohn.co.uk
website www.meiklejohn.co.uk
Facebook www.facebook.com/meiklejohnillustration
X @meiklejohn_
Instagram @meiklejohn_
Managing Director Claire Meiklejohn

Represents illustrators, covering a wide range of styles, from traditional, children's publishing, photorealistic, cartoon to contemporary. See also Kids Corner (page 520). Founded 1973.

NB Illustration*

Home Farm, East Horrington, Somerset BA5 3EA
tel 07720 827328
email info@nbillustration.co.uk
website www.nbillustration.co.uk
Facebook www.facebook.com/nbillustrationltd
X @nb_illustration
Instagram @nb.illustration
Directors Joe Najman, Charlotte Dowson

Represents 50+ artists and will consider all material for the commercial illustration market. For submission details see website. Submissions by email only. Commission: 30%. Founded 2000.

Outline Artists

90 The Avenue, London NW6 7NN
tel 07595 920113
email camilla@outlineartists.com
website www.outlineartists.com
Contacts Camilla Parsons, Ellie Phillips

An illustration and animation agency. Represents a diverse roster of talented image-makers from around the world. Founded 2015.

Phosphor Art*†

40 High West Street, Dorchester, Dorset DT1 1UR
tel 020-7064 4666

email info@phosphorart.com
website www.phosphorart.com
Director Catriona Wydmanski

Represents 45+ artists and specialises in innovative graphic digital illustration with artists working in watercolour, oil and gouache as well as pen and ink, scraper, charcoal and engraving styles. Also animation. Incorporates Ian Fleming Associates and The Black and White Line. Commission: 33.3%. Founded 1988.

The Plum Agency

Chapel House, St Lawrences Way, Reigate, Surrey RH2 7AF
tel (01737) 244095
email letterbox@theplumagency.com
website https://theplumagency.com/
Directors Mark Mills, Hannah Whitty

Represents 100+ artists and authors, producing texts and illustrations for children's publishing, advertising, editorial, greeting cards and packaging. See website for submission procedure. Commission: 30%. Founded 2006.

Sylvie Poggio Artists Agency

62 Ainsdale Road, London W5 1JX
tel 07775 894870
email sylvie-p@sylviepoggio.com
website www.sylviepoggio.com
Facebook www.facebook.com/Sylvie-Poggio-Artists-agency-700285410097943
X @sylviepoggioart
Directors Sylvie Poggio, Bruno Caurat

Represents 40 artists producing illustrations for publishing and advertising. Founded 1996.

RCW

20 Powis Mews, London W11 1JN
tel 020-7221 3717
email info@rcwlitagency.com
website www.rcwlitagency.com
Instagram @rcwliteraryagency
Contact Millie van Grutten

Represents leading illustrators of children's books, selling their work throughout the world in all media. Welcomes a broad range of styles across all genres of children's publishing including preschool, picture book, educational, gift, fiction, non-fiction, graphic novel and activity. Founded 1967.

Tallbean

tel (01728) 454921
email heather@tallbean.co.uk
website www.tallbean.co.uk
Founder Heather Richards

Provides specialist illustrators offering a range of styles. The team of well-established and creative illustrators is kept small to ensure a close working relationship. Founded 1996.

Vicki Thomas Associates

195 Tollgate Road, London E6 5JY
tel 020-7511 5767
email contact@vickithomasassociates.com
website www.vickithomasassociates.com
X @VickiThomasA
Instagram @vickithomasa
Consultant Vicki Thomas

Considers the work of illustrators and designers working in greetings/gift industries, and promotes work to gift, toy, publishing, licensing and related industries. Email sample images, covering letter and CV. Commission: 30%. Founded 1985.

Societies, prizes and festivals

Introduction

There is some circularity to our societies, prizes and festivals section: societies and festivals administer prizes, and prizes offer their winners memberships to societies, a place on a writing course or tickets to festivals. There are threads connecting this section to the others within the *Yearbook* too: literary agents and publishers administer prizes, seeking writers and artists they would like to represent and publish, as do magazines and newspapers; and there are initiatives dedicated to poetry, art and illustration, and screen and audio.

The benefits of joining a society, submitting to a prize, or attending a festival or writing retreat cannot be overstated. At the heart of them all is a commitment to championing creatives and sustaining communities in which they can thrive. There exists a society for every need a writer or an artist might have, whether that be protecting creators' rights in the age of AI, forging stronger links between libraries and the people they serve, or providing opportunities to support writers and artists of a specific genre or demographic.

Similarly, there is a prize for almost every literary or artistic endeavour, no matter how niche; from environmental photography to travel writing, comedy television scripts to graphic novels and poetry in translation. While many of the prizes provide financial rewards, they also offer feedback, mentoring and career support in various forms (recognising that being a writer or an artist requires more than putting pen to paper). Prizes, alongside societies and festivals, continue to be a vehicle for reaffirming a commitment to tackling inequality in the publishing industry, through inviting a specific demographic to enter or offering support tailored to help overcome barriers to accessibility.

Promoting accessibility is also one of the goals that drives the festivals landscape, which continues to thrive both nationally and locally. Festivals offer the perfect opportunity to meet fellow readers, writers and artists, and to be inspired by those further along on their publishing journey. Some festivals are broad, welcoming creatives of all kinds working in all forms, whilst others are more focused, inviting creators dedicated to a specific medium or audience. As with societies and prizes, they reinforce that creative pursuits do not have to be carried out in isolation; there is a community ready to embrace and support you.

Listings in this section:

- *Societies, associations and clubs*, page 535
- *Prizes and awards*, page 570
- *Grants, bursaries and fellowships*, page 623
- *Festivals and conferences for writers, artists and readers*, page 630
- *Writers' retreats and creative writing courses*, page 646
- *Postgraduate courses*, page 653
- *Libraries*, page 660

The winning touch: the impact of winning an award

Ingrid Persaud traces the zigzag route, via law, art and parenting, that led to the discovery of her writing voice. She describes the powerful life-changing effect award-winning success had on her fledgling writing career, and encourages others to pursue their own writing passion at whatever stage of life.

Writing is one of the few careers that you can start at any time – and the later in life the better. But I am bound to say that, given that I took the scenic route myself. Writing is my third (and final) act. If you were born into a lower-middle-class Trinidadian family like mine, particularly one with East Indian roots, there were only three career options: a young person with academic leanings could become a doctor, a lawyer or a failure. Keen to please, I read law at the LSE with every intention of returning home to practise as a barrister, have children and die. But it didn't take long to discover that practising law wasn't for me. I was horrified, but I couldn't lie; I just preferred hanging out at university. So I stayed on at LSE, only leaving when I got a job teaching law across the Aldwych at King's College. I was living my dream.

And yet ... deep within myself I knew something was missing. I was desperate for some form of self-expression which aligned my head, heart and hands. But I couldn't articulate the unease – I took time off to reflect. That's when I stumbled across the Slade Art Foundation Course. I had no background in art, and arrived at the entrance interview with my two hands swinging. They politely asked for my portfolio. Unfazed, I said I didn't have one; I was enthusiastic though, and would that be enough? I don't know why, but they decided to take a chance on me. At the end of a few intense months of immersion in art and art history, I had decided that I wanted to be an artist. That crazy decision took me back to university – this time to Goldsmiths College as an art undergraduate, and then to Central Saint Martins for a Masters in Fine Art. Oh, and along the way I gave birth to gorgeous identical twin boys. As is my wont, I stuck around institutions of higher education, picking up bits of teaching at Saint Martins and occasionally exhibiting work.

I might have made this mix of teaching, art practice and parenting work, but my then partner decided the twin babies deserved a childhood away from the confines of city life. We had ties to Barbados, and with reluctance I packed us in boxes and shipped us there, all the while grieving for the London art scene I would no longer inhabit. Writing a weekly essay became my way of interrogating this new life on a small rock. I discovered classified ads for Boss Fix, Uncrossing and Come to Me magical oils and went to the fish market with a bar full of ballroom dancers. Somewhere during the writing of that blog, I fell in love with the act of writing. When I tried to express myself on the page, I found the logic of law meeting the play of art, and melding. What I was discovering was the beginnings of a writing voice.

When I am introduced now, people often mention that I won both the Commonwealth Short Story Prize and the BBC National Short Story Award (NSSA) for my first short story, 'The Sweet Sop'. But I'm not a genius who opened her laptop and immediately wrote an award-worthy text. 'The Sweet Sop' flowed out of years spent grappling with language, with meaning, and with finding a way to express my *self*. I felt immensely lucky and honoured to win those two awards. But in the wake of the ceremonies and celebrations, I quickly found out just how much of an impact winning awards could have on a fledgling writing career. Agents are the first gatekeepers in the publishing world and I, of course, didn't have one; but on the night I won the BBC NSSA I let slip that I wasn't yet represented. Agents who a day before would not have read my emails, much less the unfinished novel manuscript I was working on, queued up to offer their services. Add serendipity to the mix and I signed with Zoë Waldie of RCW Literary Agency, and a few years on I know I've chosen well. She is a fierce critic and my loyal champion. Her integrity and expertise means I can entrust the management of my writing life to her hands.

Right this minute, if industry surveys are correct, about one million people are writing a novel. A goodly proportion will not finish what they started. But that still leaves a lot of competition. As Zoë helped me realise, the awards I had won meant that – for a moment at least – I had name recognition. If ever there was an opportunity to sell my novel manuscript, it was then. But Zoë was hampered by one slight problem – although I could hand over 20,000 words, the other 80,000 were as-yet unwritten. So I sat down at my desk and for the next three months wrote with back-breaking intensity, leaving off only for the most essential bodily needs: eating, sleeping and going to the bathroom. The work paid off. With Zoë's light editing, the MS was sent off to all the major UK-based publishing houses.

Love After Love was bought by Faber after a seven-way auction. And what a great publisher: I worked with a super-bright editor, Louisa Joyner, who took a decent manuscript and transformed it into an excellent novel. But then something happened that none of us could have predicted … Almost overnight, the world shut down. Borders closed and nations retreated as Covid-19 raged. It was in this scary, precarious atmosphere that *Love After Love* was published in April 2020. And here is where I understood the value of a small, nimble publisher like Faber: marketing and sales changed tack and pushed all their resources online; they lined up Zoom events to promote the book; and somehow, the book managed to gain visibility.

No spin can change the fact that 2020 was a ghastly year – on top of the pandemic, my long marriage was ending. Bookstores shuttered their doors just as my novel came out. I would have continued crying into my breakfast cereal except for the amazing good fortune of winning another life-changing award: the Costa First Novel Award. And let's be clear that prizes are simply what a particular panel of judges on a particular day decide about a particular book. Chance is a huge component. When I was told I'd won, it took me a good 20 minutes to speak. All the anxiety, hard work and sacrifice were vindicated. Positive reviews from publications such as the *Economist*, the *Guardian* and the *New York Times* were now independently justified. Zoë's faith as my agent and the Faber publishing team's trust had paid off. I exhaled.

My writing life post-Costa has shifted. The prize is now my calling card. Invitations to bookish events, never in short supply, now overwhelm and threaten my productivity. Commissions to write articles, short stories and essays arrive with increasing regularity. Foreign rights to *Love After Love* are being sold. The Italian iteration of the novel published earlier than planned to catch the wave of publicity that has accompanied the prize. Sales have increased. I can let go – because *Love After Love* has found its way in the world. But the real shifts have been internal. More than anything else, my long bouts of self-doubt have shortened. I sit a little straighter at my desk, and I am relishing this third act of my life. Not only am I doing what I love, but I'm making a modest living. Every morning I wake up ready to work. It doesn't mean I don't have unproductive, uninspired days; but I know now that I can get past these dips because I am doing what I love and I've been lucky enough to have some recognition.

In a crowded field, prizes and awards help to give our work a platform – a fighting chance of finding the readership it deserves. I hope my zigzag path and inability to qualify as a best young thing to hit the writing scene give you hope and courage. Now, get back to your desk, open that blank page and write. The muse will come, but she's often stuck in traffic. Meanwhile your passion awaits you.

Ingrid Persaud was born in Trinidad. Her debut novel, *Love After Love*, won the Costa First Novel Award 2020, the Author's Club First Novel Award 2021 and the Indie Book Award for Fiction 2021. Her latest novel, *The Lost Love Songs of Boysie Singh*, was published by Faber & Faber in April 2024. She also won the BBC National Short Story Award in 2018 and the Commonwealth Short Story Prize in 2017.

Festival fun: your guide to why, how and what

Author and screenwriter Adam Hamdy, co-founder of crime and thriller festival Capital Crime, sings the praises of literary festivals. He has tips on how to find, prepare for, enjoy and reap rewards from the festival experience and all it has to offer both authors and readers.

Why go to a literary festival?

Whether you're an aspiring or established author, or reader, if you've never been to a literary festival I'd highly recommend going. I went to my first literary festival in 2016, shortly before my debut novel, *Pendulum* (Headline 2016), hit the shelves. My publisher sent me to the Theakston Old Peculier Crime Writing Festival (see page 643) to promote the book and build relationships with bloggers, journalists and other authors. Unsure of what to expect, I was nervous on the drive up, but within an hour of arriving my only regret was that I hadn't been to a festival sooner.

I've been to the Cannes Film Festival, but I can't imagine walking up to Martin Scorsese or Steven Spielberg and managing to say anything more than, 'It's lovely to meet ...' before suited bouncers whisked me away. Literary festivals are nothing like that. I soon found myself chatting to new, established and downright legendary authors. Perhaps it's because we spend so much time alone, with nothing but our imaginations and the tyranny of a daily word count, but most writers are a gregarious bunch, always up for a chat and a laugh. And, because every writer you ever meet has their own horror story of rejections and knockbacks, you will find that, as a group, we're very accessible and happy to share our thoughts and experiences of the industry. If you want to learn about publishing a book, finding an agent, or the craft of writing – hang out at a festival bar.

In addition to informal opportunities to forge new relationships and learn from the pros, most festivals offer a structured programme of events designed to interest everyone from the general reader to the most established author. In our first year at Capital Crime, we had Ian Rankin and Don Winslow in conversation, an industry panel on how to become published, a creative masterclass with Anthony Horowitz, an interview with Kate Atkinson and so much more. There were heavyweight discussions about true-life crime and fun sessions; the role-play and banter of the Capital Crime debut novelists quiz – 'Whose Crime Is It Anyway?' – had the audience in stitches. After a pandemic hiatus, Capital Crime 2022 was an even bigger event.

While they're fun and entertaining experiences for readers, I would advise aspiring authors to go to festivals as soon as they can. Most festivals feature discussion about the craft and business of writing, so authors can learn a lot. I wish I'd gone to festivals when I was starting out as a writer because I think I could have saved myself a lot of heartache. They're great places to meet agents, hear what the industry is looking for and learn what life as an author is really like. A number of aspiring authors who attended Capital Crime went on to be signed with agents; it really can be a springboard for your career.

How to prepare for your first festival

If the idea of going to a festival has piqued your interest, you might want to start with a local event. Most UK towns and cities host a literary event, and if it's local it's likely to be a less costly experience than a distant, travel-and-hotel festival. If you belong to a writers' group, book club or have bookish friends, you might be able to convince others to attend with you, reducing potential angst. You might also want to check your local bookshops, as many run regular events that are good warm-ups for the full-blown festival experience. Even in deepest, darkest Shropshire, I have been to some amazing events run by independent bookshops – Booka in Oswestry is brilliant at attracting big-name authors as well as showcasing debut writers – which can give you a taste of the live experience.

When you're ready for one of the big festivals – Cheltenham, Hay, Harrogate, Capital Crime – make sure you plan ahead to get the most from the experience. Research the travel and accommodation available and ask around on social media for hints and tips on where to stay and how to reduce costs. Most festivals offer an 'early bird' discount for people who buy their tickets well in advance so, if you're sure you're going, save money by booking early.

Some festivals offer tickets to individual events, others sell 'rover' passes. Check the programme and make sure your ticket allows you to get into the events you're keen to attend. Capital Crime and a few other festivals offer concession prices for people on low incomes or specific groups, such as librarians. Make sure you check to see what discounts might be available before booking.

Once you've booked and sorted out travel and accommodation, take time to plan your schedule. When you're there, it's all too easy to get drawn into conversation at the bar, lose track of time and miss events. Allow yourself enough time to rest and grab tea, coffee or a bite to eat. If you're planning to go to author signings, make sure you know when they are and don't dawdle! Some big-name authors limit how many books they'll sign and will rarely be seen in the bar, so their signing appearance is the only time you'll be able to grab them.

Dress code is whatever you feel comfortable in. It helps to know a bit about the festival you're attending. At the Theakston Old Peculier Crime Writing Festival in Harrogate, for example, a lot of time is spent outside socialising in the beer tent and on the lawns of the famous Old Swan Hotel – so take clothes that reflect the vagaries of the British summer! Many festival sessions are held in large conference venues, and some can be chilly if the air-conditioning is too high or overwarm if there's no AC at all, which means layers are a good idea – so you can cool down or wrap up, depending on your internal climate control.

Most festivals provide tote bags and goodies. These are much sought-after and hugely helpful to stow all the books you may end up buying at the festival bookshop. You may not go *intending* to add to your reading pile but, believe me, you will.

Every festival is different

Do your research. Find out which festivals fit your personality and interests. Bloggers and journalists review festivals and talk about their experiences, which means you can get a good sense of a festival's ethos and atmosphere by reading what's been written about them online.

Some festivals run competitions or host special events. Capital Crime runs its Fingerprint Awards, where crime and thriller fans get to choose the winner in a selection of categories. Harrogate hosts an author dinner, where guests are able to spend a couple of hours with published authors over a meal. ThrillerFest in New York runs a best first-sentence competition in addition to its more widely publicised awards. Scour the festival's website and check on social media to ensure you know exactly what your chosen festival offers.

Attending as a panellist

As an author, you might be eligible to appear at the festival as a panellist. The right time to introduce yourself to a festival organiser is when you have a debut novel heading towards publication. If your book is going to be traditionally published, your publisher will usually make the festival organiser aware of the debut, but it doesn't hurt to connect with them directly as well. Check the festival website for information on being a panellist and how to get in touch.

If you are fortunate enough to be invited to appear at a festival, have a think about the panel topic the organisers give you and prepare some thoughts on interesting angles or subjects for discussion. Festivals are a live event, and you're there to entertain and engage the audience, not to sell your book. Selling your book is a happy by-product of an appreciative audience. If the audience feels you're an interesting or entertaining person, they will expect those qualities to be found in your work.

Perhaps you're nervous about speaking in public – I think most people are – but remember the audience is there because they're interested in what you have to say. Book-lovers tend to be a friendly crowd and will be sympathetic to the fact that you're out of your comfort zone. Take some deep breaths (it really does help) and speak a little slower and a little louder than normal, so your audience can hear you.

Although this may not sound very 'artist-in-a-garret', do think about your author brand. Hopefully, you've taken time to find your author voice and to discover who you are as a storyteller. Do the same with your public persona. What makes you stand out as a person? What do you bring to an event that no one else can? Once you've understood who you are, practise – take the opportunity to appear at as many events as possible, large or small. Hone your public speaking. It's like anything else in life – practice makes perfect, and the more preparation you do, the better the experience should be for you and your audience.

Also, given the times we live in, be sure to promote your appearance on social media. Sometimes, amid the buzz and busyness of the festival, it can be easy to forget to take photos and the obligatory selfie. Do try to record these moments – it's not only a useful tool for connecting with other authors and promoting your book, but it's also a lovely way to remember the experience. Writing brings plenty of lows, so it's always important

Festival dos and don'ts

- Do network with authors and other readers. Festival-goers are a friendly bunch and are generally happy to chat and provide advice.
- Dress code is whatever you feel comfortable in.
- Do have fun. Festivals are supposed to engage and entertain. Make the most of your time.
- Do read as many books by attending authors as possible. This will help you get more out of their events and to ask informed questions. Which brings us to the next point...
- Do ask questions. Authors love to be challenged and engaged. But...
- Don't hog the microphone. Keep your question short and to the point. If you have something you'd like to discuss with an author in more detail, save it for the signing.
- Don't be rude. Publishing is a polite world and rudeness doesn't generally get results.
- Don't be afraid to ask for help. Festivals employ staff and volunteers who are there to help you. Don't be afraid to approach them with any issue, no matter how big or small.

to celebrate the highs; I certainly count all my festival experiences as among the highs. In fact, it was while I was in New York, buzzing with the excitement of ThrillerFest (https://thrillerfest.com), that I joined forces with bookseller and agent extraordinaire David Headley to set up Capital Crime.

Adam Hamdy is an author and screenwriter, and co-founder of the crime and thriller festival Capital Crime (www.capitalcrime.org). Adam has a law degree from Oxford University and worked as a strategy consultant before taking up his writing career. He is the author of *The Other Side of Night* (Pan Macmillan 2022), and the *Scott Pearce* series (Pan Macmillan) – *Black 13* (2020), *Red Wolves* (2021) and *White Fire* (2023). His latest book is *Deadbeat* (Simon & Schuster 2025). He has co-written five books in the *Private* series with James Patterson. For more information see www.adamhamdy.com.

See also...

• *Festivals and conferences for writers, artists and readers*, page 630

At a crossroads? How to choose the best writer development initiative

Writing is often regarded as a solitary vocation, but the good news is that there is support available to help authors achieve their goals. Read on to find out more about Julia Forster's own journey to publication, and her excellent tips for accessing the right writers' development initiative.

If you could pick the perfect intervention for your development as a writer, what would it be? Writers are often brilliant at imagining big plot twists or perfecting a poem's line break, but many find it hard to know what support to seek out during a life-long career. Over the past 25 years of being a writer published across multiple genres, I've also maintained a career in publishing, specialising latterly in writer development and I now work as a writer retreat host and an author coach at Write Within. To help you to consider what you might try next, I'm going to share my experience of how I made writer development a cornerstone of my creative practice, followed by some suggestions around how you might engage with the myriad writer development schemes now on offer.

When I took an undergraduate module in creative writing at university in 1998, there were few literature development initiatives around. The good news is that the provision has expanded massively since then. Due partly to the lack of opportunities at the time, the route I chose was to study for a master's in creative writing. While on that course, I began to review poetry collections for a magazine; reviewing was a great way to attune my critical reading skills and to learn about writing to deadline, but also provided the bedrock of my publication track record.

While still in academia, I applied for a subsidised place on a residential Arvon poetry course; feedback from the tutors was crucial in developing my confidence. I lost my way a little after graduating, however, as the realities of working full-time set in. Completing Julia Cameron's 12-week workbook *The Artist's Way* got me back on track. The chapter on budgeting motivated me to rein in my outgoings and to go down to a four-day working week in order to free up time to write.

I composed a memoir of 80,000 words over the course of one year and asked a university friend whose judgement I trusted to critique it. Her reflections were that, because I wasn't well known, nobody would be interested in publishing the memoir, but moreover nothing happened of much substance in my childhood – ouch! While feedback can be bruising, sitting with it over several years enabled me to see there was still scope for the project to morph into fiction – but that development would come many years later. The lesson? Never throw anything away.

At the Frankfurt Book Fair in 2005, I negotiated my first book deal to write a short non-fiction work. Publication coincided with the birth of my first child and I took an extended maternity leave of five years, during which time I moved to Wales and had another baby. Attending a life-writing course at Tŷ Newydd Writing Centre (see page 651) provided me with the time and space to finally conceptualise my first novel. When both of my children were preschool, I applied for a 'Buying Time' bursary from my regional literature development agency, Literature Wales, and I used the sum awarded to pay for nursery fees so that I had the time to turn my memoir into a novel. It took me about a year to do that, and I used Robert McKee's book *Story* to help me to fine-tune the plot.

The *Writers' & Artists' Yearbook*, as well as its website (www.writersandartists.co.uk), was vital in guiding me through the process of submitting to literary agents and, once I had secured one, the agent helped me to finesse the manuscript. Most agents are editorially-minded; if you choose the 'traditional' publishing route, they are likely to help to polish your manuscript before it goes out on submission to publishers.

My third book, a collection of poetry, began while attending my local Stanza group; the Poetry Society publish online a listing of the UK Stanzas. These are brilliant environments to workshop your poetry, to network and to mutually support one another. I also developed some work by participating in a 'writing for beginners' community course run at my local arts centre: I like adopting a beginner's mindset in my practice. Over several years, my poems were published in anthologies and magazines and my work was also placed in competitions, all of which helped to build my case when I submitted the manuscript. I entered my work into competitions only where I felt there was congruence between my work and that of the judges', to better assist my chances.

Over the years, I've received two grants from the Society of Authors and – once my track record was substantial – I have also applied for writer residencies, with mixed success. For example, while I didn't make the final cut for the writer-in-residence at Gladstone's Library, I did receive an invitation to appear at their literary festival; what I took from this is that applying is often worth a punt, but that a large part of this job is about developing resilience skills and adopting a positive mindset.

Of course, my account reveals just one way to pave a path to publication. With that in mind, I've designed some author coaching-style questions for you to consider, and then given a brief overview of what options there might be for you to seek out.

- Reading my account, what stood out to you as relevant for your practice?
- What support do you currently feel you need to support your development?
- What's your very next step in taking action to seek out this support?

Some options for you to consider might include:

- **Manuscript assessment:** page-based editorial critique, ideally offered by a writer expert in your genre.
- **Mentoring:** one-to-one service with a writer who is a good fit editorially to help direct and advise you.
- **Coaching:** less directive than mentoring, coaching brings an attitude of curiosity to your creative practice so you can better understand your unique process.
- **Writing groups:** a great option if you need group accountability and social contact.
- **Short course (online or residential):** a fantastic way to hothouse your manuscript, receive tutoring and feedback within a like-minded group.
- **Higher education qualification (e.g. MA or PhD in creative writing):** a pricey option, but you can access world-class teaching in academia.
- **Performing at open mics:** get live feedback in real-time from a (you hope) supportive audience.
- **Writers' retreats:** craft your own, or find an organised one to focus on your work-in-progress, if funds allow.
- **Writer-in-residence:** competitive, but worth applying for once you have a track record.

• **Competitions:** either winning; being highly commended, shortlisted or longlisted builds reputation.
• **Writers' conferences and festivals:** a sociable means to network, gain tips and insights.

The best place to start your research is to discover what your regional writer or literature development agency offers. Many of these organisations run writers' conferences which can include workshops, seminars and even opportunities for you to present your work in 'agent hotseat' sessions. Most literature development agencies run writer development schemes and fellowships, some of which are focused on assisting writers from under-represented backgrounds.

Regional literature development agencies

Find full contact details in the *Societies, associations and clubs* section on page 535.

• Irish Writers Centre (also runs a scheme to support NI writers) https://irishwriterscentre.ie
• Literature Wales www.literaturewales.org
• Literature Works (south west England) https://literatureworks.org.uk
• National Centre for Writing https://nationalcentreforwriting.org.uk
• New Writing North https://newwritingnorth.com
• New Writing South https://newwritingsouth.com
• Writing East Midlands https://writingeastmidlands.co.uk
• Writing West Midlands https://writingwestmidlands.org
• Scottish Book Trust www.scottishbooktrust.com
• Spread The Word (London) www.spreadtheword.org.uk

On New Writing North's website, you can learn more about their Good Practice Guide for writer development programmes, research they conducted with Northumbria University; this is a fantastic repository of information on what to look out for when applying to schemes. Meanwhile, The Literary Consultancy (TLC; https://literaryconsultancy.co.uk) works with many of the literature development agencies to offer their Arts Council England-supported 'Free Reads' scheme for writers who might not be able to afford to access their editorial services under normal circumstances. There is a wide range of editorial services on offer elsewhere: check out the *Writers' retreats and creative writing courses* section of the *Yearbook* to find out more (see page 646).

Publishing houses large and small run writer development initiatives, such as the Penguin Random House WriteNow scheme, the Faber Academy and Nine Arches Press's Dynamo scheme. Some of the larger literary agencies also support development initiatives, such as the Curtis Brown Creative Breakthrough Writers' Programme, while some of the large literary festivals run initiatives for writers: Hay Festival, for example, has run the Writers at Work opportunity for Welsh writers for years.

Each spring, the London Book Fair (LBF) runs Authors HQ and the Writers' Summit. LBF is worth visiting to find out about the publishing industry, but do wear comfortable shoes as it's held in a vast conference centre. Some writer membership organisations, such as the Society of Authors and Byte the Book, offer discounted entry tickets to the LBF.

Writers, storytellers and performers can apply to the Arts Council England for Developing Your Creative Practice (DYCP) grants and Writing West Midlands runs popular online workshops on how to maximise your chances of success when applying to this fund. The Arts Council of Northern Ireland and the Scottish Book Trust distribute grants to support writers in developing their craft. Make sure you don't miss call-outs for opportunities such as this by joining the National Association of Writers in order to receive their e-bulletin, *The Writer's Compass*, and joining the Society of Authors to get their magazine, *The Author*; both are indispensable sources of information. Meanwhile, a cursory glance at the Societies section of this *Yearbook* reveals a huge variety of special-interest writer groups that may also assist you in scoping out opportunities, whether you're writing about beer, wine, haikus, horror or crime – you name it.

Some individual writers at the grassroots generously compile and share resources and opportunities via e-newsletters. They include Robin Houghton, whose quarterly spreadsheet gathers together poetry-related opportunities (https://robinhoughtonpoetry.co.uk), and Sian Meades-Williams' e-newsletter, *Freelance Writers' Job* (www.sianmeadeswilliams.com). Sian's book *The Pyjama Myth* (Unbound 2022) is a first-class guide to carving out a freelance writing career. At the other end of the spectrum there are behemoths such as the BBC-run 'BBC Writers', where opportunities geared towards writing for stage, screen or radio are advertised (www.bbc.co.uk/writers).

There is a growing array of residential writer's retreats on offer. However, if a residential isn't a viable option for you, Arvon run two-hour 'At Home' masterclasses that are good value for money. If you are based near a university, their life-long learning programmes often include affordable creative writing modules and, while many municipal libraries are strapped for cash, they do sometimes run community courses in creative writing.

If you are inspired to submit your work to competitions or want to get a piece published online or in a magazine, then take a look at the publications listed on page 36 onwards. If you want to map out micro-presses, you might also invest in the *Indie Press Guide* (Mslexia). There are umpteen other books which can help to guide the development of your practice, far too many to mention here. However, I will conclude by saying that Neil Astley's article on how to complete a poetry collection *Getting your poetry out there*, on page 334, was all I needed to read to understand how to put together a collection. I followed his advice to the letter in order to get my manuscript onto a poetry publisher's editorial desk. Dive into the other essays alongside this one in the *Yearbook*, and you'll be in very safe hands indeed.

Julia Forster runs Write Within, an author coaching service and a self-led writer's retreat with a sauna called the Writers' Cabin in mid Wales. The Writers' Cabin was picked by *The Sunday Times* as one of the UK's top writers' retreats just a few months after opening. Julia is a writer development specialist, an independent press book publicist, the in-house coach for the Poetry Pharmacy and also works freelance for The Literary Consultancy. She is the author of *What a Way to Go* (Atlantic 2016) and *Muses: Revealing the Nature of Inspiration* (Oldcastle Books 2007); her poetry collection, *Invisible Sisterhood*, is on submission at the time of writing. Visit www.writewithin.wales or see @_writewithin on Instagram.

Societies, associations and clubs

This list is divided into the following sections: Art, illustration and photography; Arts councils, royal societies and funding; Bibliographical and academic; Copyright and licensing; Editorial, journalism and broadcasting; Film, theatre and television; Libraries and information; Literacy; Members' clubs; Music; Representation and publishing; Translation; and Writers' organisations. Some also offer prizes and awards (see page 570).

ART, ILLUSTRATION AND PHOTOGRAPHY

Association of Illustrators

Somerset House, Strand, London WC2R 1LA
tel 020-7759 1010
email info@theaoi.com
website www.theaoi.com
Facebook www.facebook.com/theaoi
X @theaoi
Instagram @theaoi

Trade association that supports illustrators throughout their careers with business, licensing and contract advice, promotes illustration and encourages professional standards in the industry. Presents an annual programme of events and holds an annual competition, the World Illustration Awards, in partnership with the *Directory of Illustration*. Founded 1973.

The Association of Photographers

2nd Floor, 201 Haverstock Hill, London NW3 4QG
tel 020-7739 6669
website www.the-aop.org
Facebook www.facebook.com/AssociationOfPhotographers
Bluesky @assocphoto.bsky.social
Instagram @assocphoto

Exists to protect and promote the worth and standing of its members, and to vigorously defend, educate and lobby for the interests and rights of all photographers, especially in the commercial photographic industry. Founded 1968.

Axis

The Art House, Drury Lane, Wakefield WF1 2TE
email hello@axisweb.org
website www.axisweb.org
Facebook www.facebook.com/axisweb.org
X @axisweb
Instagram @axisweb

Supports visual artists' needs and creates a future where art is universally accessible. Facilitates engagement through events, artists talks and curated showcases, and provides artists with resources, opportunities, commissions, bursaries and insurance.

BAPLA (British Association of Picture Libraries and Agencies)

52 High Street, Pinner, Middlesex HA5 5PW
tel 020-8297 1198
email admin@bapla.org.uk
website https://bapla.org.uk
X @baplaUK

Trade association for picture libraries in the UK. Members include the major news, stock and production agencies as well as sole traders and cultural heritage institutions. Founded 1975.

The Blackpool Art Society

The Studio, Wilkinson Avenue, Blackpool FY3 9HB
tel (01253) 768297
email enquiries@blackpoolartsociety.co.uk
website www.blackpoolartsociety.co.uk/index.html
Membership £55 p.a.

Hosts various exhibitions (members' work only). Studio meetings, demonstrations, workshops and lectures. Founded 1884.

British Institute of Professional Photography

The Artistry House, 16 Winckley Square, Preston PR1 3JJ
tel (01772) 367968
email admin@bipp.com
website www.bipp.com
Facebook www.facebook.com/theBIPP
X @thebipp
Instagram @thebipp

An internationally recognised qualifying organisation with over 100 years' experience in supporting and networking opportunities for photographers. Delivers education, qualifications and professional development to photographers through a challenging qualifications structure alongside a full programme of training courses and events. Founded 1901.

British Interactive Media Association

tel 020-3538 6607
email web@bima.co.uk
website https://bima.co.uk
Facebook www.facebook.com/bimahq/
X @BIMA
Instagram @bima_hq_

BIMA is Britain's digital community that connects, develops and champions the industry. It facilitates professional networks, career development, business growth and the establishment of best practice standards. It also gives members a voice on issues affecting the industry. Open to any organisation or individual with an interest in multimedia. Founded 1985.

Cartoonists Club of Great Britain

website www.ccgb.org.uk
Facebook www.facebook.com/TheCartoonistsClub
X @CartoonistsGB
Instagram @cartoonistsclub

The UK's largest cartoonists' organisation. Provides a social base for cartoonists wherever they may live or work. Includes many different types of cartoonists. Social gatherings are held several times a year at different places around the country, and occasionally members also attend events abroad. Has a thriving online presence, forums for members and non-members, and a members' portfolio allowing them to promote their work. Publishes the monthly magazine *The Jester*. Founded 1960.

The Chartered Society of Designers

1 Cedar Court, Royal Oak Yard, Bermondsey Street, London SE1 3GA
tel 020-7101 0685
email membership@csd.org.uk
website www.csd.org.uk
Facebook www.facebook.com/charteredsocietyofdesigners
X @csdminerva
Instagram @csdminerva

The internationally recognised body for the design profession, providing support and guidance for designers at every stage of their career. Works to promote and regulate standards of competence, professional conduct and integrity, including working with government and official bodies, providing design education and administering awards. Provides members with general information, publications and guidance on copyright and other professional issues.

Event & Visual Communication Association

email info@evcom.org.uk
website www.evcom.org.uk
Facebook www.facebook.com/EVCOMUK1
X @EVCOMUK
Instagram @evcomuk

EVCOM is the only membership association that represents the corporate events and corporate film industries. Champions and supports the industry, hosting events, facilitating knowledge sharing and setting standards.

Federation of British Artists

17 Carlton House Terrace, London SW1Y 5BD
tel 020-7930 6844
email info@mallgalleries.com
website www.mallgalleries.org.uk/federation-british-artists
Facebook www.facebook.com/mallgalleries
X @mallgalleries
Instagram @mallgalleries

Administers nine major National Art Societies at Mall Galleries, The Mall, London SW1: the Royal Society of British Artists, the Royal Institute of Painters in Water Colours, the Royal Institute of Oil Painters, the New English Art Club, the Royal Society of Portrait Painters, the Pastel Society, the Hesketh Hubbard Art Society, the Royal Society of Marine Artists and the Society of Wildlife Artists. Founded 1961.

Fine Art Trade Guild

2 Wye House, 6 Enterprise Way, London SW18 1FZ
tel 020-7381 6616
email info@fineart.co.uk
website www.fineart.co.uk
Facebook www.facebook.com/FineArtTradeGuild
Instagram @fineartradeguild

Promotes the sale of fine art prints and picture framing in the UK and overseas markets; establishes and raises standards amongst members and communicates these to the buying public. Publishes *Art + Framing Today*, the trade's longest established magazine, and various specialist books. Founded 1910.

FOCAL (Federation of Commercial AudioVisual Libraries International Ltd)

27 Mortimer Street, London W1T 3BL
tel 07789 056661
email info@focalint.org
website www.focalint.org
Facebook www.facebook.com/focalinternational
X @FOCALint
Instagram @focal_international

A specialist, professional, not-for-profit trade association that represents the footage and content libraries in over 30 countries, as well as archive producers, researchers, consultants and facility companies. Runs the FOCAL International Awards. Founded 1985.

Free Painters & Sculptors London

email info@freepaintersandsculptors.co.uk
website www.freepaintersandsculptors.co.uk
Facebook www.facebook.com/fpsartistgroup/
Membership £60 p.a.

An established, artist-led organisation that promotes and exhibits a membership of painters, sculptors, printmakers and photographers. With over 70 years of experience, FPS helps artists build long-term networks that develop artistic sustainability, exposure and sales, while also encouraging artists to create work on their own terms. Welcomes applications from talented artists at all stages of their career. Founded 1952.

Greeting Card Association

PO Box, Teddington TW11 1EL
tel 020-7619 9266
email hello@gca.cards
website www.gca.cards
Facebook www.facebook.com/GreetingCardAssociation
X @GCAUK
Instagram @gca_uk
Chief Executive Amanda Fergusson

The GCA is an independent, not-for-profit trade organisation operating for the benefit of members, who include greeting card publishers, retailers and suppliers, and individuals working in the card industry. Supports members by providing a forum to promote their businesses, sharing specialist information, and organising events and networking opportunities. Founded 1919.

The Guild of Aviation Artists

tel 0333 130 2223
email admin@gava.org.uk
website www.gava.org.uk
President Chris French
Membership £80 p.a. full; £65 p.a. associates; £40 p.a. friends; £15 p.a. young friends (under 25 years of age and in continuing education)

Formed to promote aviation art through the organisation of exhibitions and meetings. Holds an annual exhibition and publishes a quarterly members' newsletter. Founded 1971.

Guild of Railway Artists

website www.railart.co.uk
Facebook www.facebook.com/The-Guild-of-Railway-Artists-520306528057416

Aims to forge a link between artists depicting railway subjects and give members a corporate identity. Stages railway art exhibitions and members' meetings and produces books of members' works. Founded 1979.

Hesketh Hubbard Art Society

17 Carlton House Terrace, London SW1Y 5BD
tel 020-7930 6844
email info@mallgalleries.com
website www.mallgalleries.org.uk/about-us/hesketh-hubbard-art-society
Membership £340 p.a.

Offers both amateur and professional artists the opportunity to work from life models in untutored sessions. Membership includes 44 drawing sessions and no cover charge. Prospective members are invited to attend one session free before deciding if they wish to apply for membership. Offers membership bursaries to artists aged between 18 and 30. Founded 1930.

The Hilliard Society of Miniaturists

tel 07910 504882
email info@hilliardsociety.org
website www.hilliardsociety.org
President Peter Hayton
Membership £65 p.a. artist member; £28 p.a. friend member

Increases knowledge and promotes the art of miniature painting. Annual exhibition held in June at Wells Town Hall; showcases members' work and produces a newsletter. Founded 1982.

Imaginative Book Illustration Society

email ibissec@martinsteenson.co.uk
website www.bookillustration.org
Membership Secretary Martin Steenson

Established to encourage research into, and to facilitate, the exchange of information on book and periodical illustrations, the artists and their publishers. The Society has a worldwide membership including artists, collectors, bibliographers, writers and general enthusiasts. Whilst IBIS embraces all aspects of illustrative art, the main emphasis is on the illustration of texts in English since the 1830s. Founded 1995.

Institute of Designers in Ireland

WeWork, 2 Dublin Landings, North Dock, Dublin D01 V4A3
email info@idi-design.ie
website www.idi-design.ie
Facebook www.facebook.com/idiireland
X @IDIIreland
President Mary Doherty
Membership €197 p.a.

IDI is the Irish design profession's representative body, covering every field of design. Promotes and advocates for Irish design as well as for the value of design more broadly. Founded 1972.

International Society of Typographic Designers

email mail@istd.org.uk
website www.istd.org.uk

Working closely with graphic design educationalists and the professional community, it establishes, maintains and promotes typographic standards through the forum of debate and design practice. Membership is awarded to practising designers, educators, writers, critics, theorists of design and students who demonstrate their commitment to achieving the highest possible quality of visual communication. Publishes a journal, *TypoGraphic*. Students of typography and graphic design are encouraged to gain membership by entering the annual student assessment scheme. Membership is also available to anyone who has an interest in typography and graphic design. Founded 1928.

National Acrylic Painters' Association

email contact@napauk.com
website www.napauk.com
Facebook www.facebook.com/napauk
Instagram @natacrylicpaintersassociation
Membership £45 p.a.

Promotes interest, excellence and innovation in the work of painters in acrylic. Holds an annual exhibition and administers awards. Founded 1985.

National Society for Education in Art and Design

3 Masons Wharf, Potley Lane, Corsham, Wilts. SN13 9FY
tel (01225) 810134
email info@nsead.org
website www.nsead.org
Facebook www.facebook.com/NationalSocietyforEducationinArtandDesign
Instagram @nsead1
General Secretary Michele Gregson

The leading national authority concerned with art, craft and design across all phases of education in the UK. Offers the benefits of membership of a professional association, a learned society and a trade union. Has representatives on national and regional committees concerned with art and design education. Publishes *International Journal of Art and Design Education* online and *AD* magazine for teachers. Founded 1888.

The Pastel Society

email info@thepastelsociety.org.uk
website www.thepastelsociety.org.uk
Facebook www.facebook.com/thepastelsociety
X @PastelSociety
Instagram @pastelsociety.uk

Pastel and drawings in all dry media. Annual Exhibition open to all artists working in dry media held at Mall Galleries, The Mall, London SW1. Administers awards for the best works exhibited. See website for submission and membership application guidelines. Founded 1898.

Printmakers Council

Ground Floor, Unit 23, Blue Anchor Lane, London SE16 3UL
tel 07531 883250
email printpmc@gmail.com
website www.printmakerscouncil.com
Facebook www.facebook.com/PrintmakersCouncil
X @PmCouncil
Instagram @printmakerscouncil
Membership £80 p.a.; £35 p.a. students

Artist-led group that promotes the use of both traditional and innovative printmaking techniques. Holds exhibitions of prints, provides information on prints and printmaking to both its membership and the public, and encourages cooperation and exchanges between members, other associations and interested individuals. Founded 1965.

Professional Cartoonists' Organisation

email info@procartoonists.org
website www.procartoonists.org
Facebook www.facebook.com/UKProfessionalCartoonists
X @procartoonists
Bluesky @procartoonists.bsky.social
Instagram @procartoonists
Membership £80 p.a.

Showcases UK cartoonists through its portfolio pages, a cartoon news blog and public events such as The Herne Bay Cartoon Festival. Founded 2006.

SAA (Supporting All Artists)

tel 0800 980 1123
email hello@saa.co.uk
website www.saa.co.uk
Facebook www.facebook.com/SupportingAllArtists
Instagram @supportingallartists
Membership From £49.95 p.a.

Art community with 30,000 members. Welcomes new members, from complete beginners and enthusiasts to professionals. Membership includes access to hundreds of member-only inspirational videos, *Paint & Create* magazine (four p.a.), exclusive discounts and offers on materials, paintings insurance for exhibitions and third-party public liability. Founded 1992.

The Society of Botanical Artists

Tennyson House, Cambridge Business Park, Cowley Park, Cambridge CB4 0WZ
email info@soc-botanical-artists.org
website www.soc-botanical-artists.org
Presidents Shevaun Doherty, Claire Ward
Membership £145 p.a.

Encourages the art of botanical painting. Entry details for the open exhibitions are available on the website. Founded 1985.

Society of Graphic Fine Art

email enquiries@sgfa.org.uk
website www.sgfa.org.uk
Facebook www.facebook.com/SocietyofGraphicFineArt
X @SGFADrawing
Instagram @drawingsocietyuk
President Susan Poole

Promotes and exhibits works of high quality in colour or black and white, with an emphasis on good drawing and draughtsmanship, in pencil, pen, brush, charcoal or any forms of original printmaking. Holds events throughout the year and an annual Open Exhibition with prizes and awards. Founded 1919.

Society of Heraldic Arts

8 Abbot Close, Ottery St Mary, Devon EX11 1FH
email k.arkinstall@tiscali.co.uk
website www.heraldic-arts.com
President Anthony Wood, *Chairman of the Appointments Board* Kevin Arkinstall

Serves the interests of heraldic artists, craftsmen, designers and writers, to provide a 'shop window' for their work, to obtain commissions on their behalf and to act as a forum for the exchange of information and ideas. Candidates for admission as craft members should be artists or craftsmen whose work comprises a substantial element of heraldry and is of a sufficiently high standard to satisfy the requirements of the society's advisory council. Founded 1987.

Society of Scribes and Illuminators

6 Queen Square, London WC1N 3AT
email honsec@calligraphyonline.org
website www.calligraphyonline.org
Facebook www.facebook.com/societyofscribesuk
X @ssi_uk
Instagram @ssi_uk
Membership £46 p.a. fellows; £37 p.a. lay members; £30 p.a. friends

Promotes and preserves the art of calligraphy and runs an education programme that includes a correspondence course, a creative development course, mentorship towards fellowship, a programme of study days, a series of masterclasses and recommendations for local learning opportunities. An archive/library and a bi-annual journal, *The Scribe*, are available to members. Founded 1921.

Society of Wildlife Artists

17 Carlton House Terrace, London SW1Y 5BD
tel 020-7930 6844
email info@mallgalleries.com
website www.swla.co.uk
Facebook www.facebook.com/people/Society-of-Wildlife-Artists/100066420164558/#
X @swlanaturaleye
Instagram @societyofwildlifeartists
President Harriet Mead
Membership £250 p.a. full; £85 p.a. associate

Promotes and encourages the art of wildlife painting and sculpture. Open Annual Exhibition at Mall Galleries, The Mall, London SW1, for any artist whose work depicts wildlife subjects (botanical and domestic animals are not admissible). Runs a bursary scheme for young artists to cover the costs of education, travel and materials.

The Society of Women Artists

email info@society-women-artists.org.uk
website www.society-women-artists.org.uk
Facebook www.facebook.com/SWABritain
X @SWAinfo
Instagram @swainfo
President Helen Sinclair, *Executive Secretary* Rebecca Cotton

Dedicated to promoting women artists. Members and non-members exhibit annually at the Mall Galleries. Successfully selected work should be handed in to Mall Galleries, The Mall, London SW1 (see website for deadline). Membership is by election and based on six works submitted. Founded 1855.

ARTS COUNCILS, ROYAL SOCIETIES AND FUNDING

Arts Council/An Chomhairle Ealaíon

70 Merrion Square, Dublin D02 NY52, Republic of Ireland
tel +353 (0)1 618 0200
website www.artscouncil.ie/home
Facebook www.facebook.com/artscouncilireland
X @artscouncil_ie
Instagram @artscouncilireland

The national development agency for the arts in Ireland. Promotes the arts through funding, research, information sharing, setting standards and encouraging appreciation. Founded 1951.

Arts Council England

tel 0161 934 4317
website www.artscouncil.org.uk
Facebook www.facebook.com/artscouncilofengland
X @ace_national
Instagram @aceagrams

The national development agency for arts and culture in England, distributing public money from the government and the National Lottery. Organisations, artists, events and initiatives can receive funding to help achieve the Council's mission of providing art and culture for everyone. There are five area councils: London, Midlands, North, South East and South West. Visit the website for information on funding support and advice, an online funding finder and funding FAQs. Founded 1946.

Arts Council of Northern Ireland

The MAC, 10 Exchange Street West, Belfast BT1 2NB
tel 028-9262 3555
email info@artscouncil-ni.org
website www.artscouncil-ni.org
Chief Executive Roisín McDonough

Promotes and encourages the arts throughout Northern Ireland. Artists in drama, dance, music and jazz, literature, visual arts, traditional arts and community arts can apply for support for specific schemes and projects. The value of the grant will be set according to the aims of the programme. Artists of all disciplines and in all types of working practice, who have made a contribution to artistic activities in

Northern Ireland for a minimum period of one year within the last five years, are eligible.

Books Council of Wales/Cyngor Llyfrau Cymru

Castell Brychan, Aberystwyth, Ceredigion SY23 2JB
tel (01970) 624151
email castellbrychan@books.wales
website https://llyfrau.cymru/en, www.gwales.com
Ceo Helgard Krause

Supports and develops the publishing industry in Wales. Promotes literacy and reading for pleasure through a range of public campaigns, activities and events across Wales, often working in partnership with schools, libraries and other literary organisations. Works with publishers to nurture new talent and content in Welsh and English, and offers specialist editing, design, marketing and distribution services. Administers grants to publishers and independent booksellers. Partly funded by the Welsh Government through Creative Wales and from the commercial operations of its wholesale book distribution centre. Founded 1961.

British Academy

10–11 Carlton House Terrace, London SW1Y 5AH
tel 020-7969 5200
website www.thebritishacademy.ac.uk
Facebook www.facebook.com/TheBritishAcademy
X @BritishAcademy_
Instagram @britishacademy_
Ceo Hetan Shah

The UK's national academy for humanities and social sciences. An independent fellowship of world-leading scholars and researchers; a funding body for research, nationally and internationally; and a forum for debate and engagement. It produces a wide range of publications, for academic and more general readerships.

The British Council

Bridgewater House, 58 Whitworth Street, Manchester M1 6BB
tel 0161 884 0291
website www.britishcouncil.org
Facebook www.facebook.com/britishcouncil
X @BritishCouncil
Instagram @britishcouncil
Chief Executive Scott McDonald, *Director of Cultural Engagement* Mark Stephens

The UK's international organisation for cultural relations and educational opportunities. Builds connections, understanding and trust between people in the UK and other countries through arts and culture, education and the English language. Working in close collaboration with book trade associations, the Literature team participates in major international book fairs.

Collaborates with offices overseas to broker relationships and create activities that link artists and cultural institutions around the world. Works with writers, publishers, producers, translators and other sector professionals across literature, publishing and education. The Visual Arts team connects professionals internationally through collaborative exhibition programmes, digital networking, training and development, and delegations. Manages and develops the British Council Collection and the British Pavilion at the Venice Biennale.

Creative Australia

PO Box 576, Pyrmont, NSW 2009, Australia
tel +61 (0)2 9215 9000
email enquiries@creative.gov.au
website www.creative.gov.au
Facebook www.facebook.com/creative.gov.au
X @creative_gov_au
Instagram @creative.australia
Ceo Adrian Collette

Provides a broad range of support for the arts, embracing music, theatre, literature, visual arts and crafts, dance, First Nations arts, and community and experimental arts.

Creative Scotland

Waverley Place, 2–4 Waterloo Gate, Edinburgh EH1 3EG
email enquiries@creativescotland.com
website www.creativescotland.com
Facebook www.facebook.com/CreativeScotland
Instagram @creativescots

The public body that supports the arts, screen and creative industries across all parts of Scotland on behalf of everyone who lives, works or visits there. Through distributing funding from the Scottish government and the National Lottery, Creative Scotland enables people to experience the arts and bring creative ideas to life. Supports writers and publishers based in Scotland through a range of funds and initiatives.

The Gaelic Books Council/Comhairle nan Leabhraichean

32 Mansfield Street, Glasgow G11 5QP
tel 0141 337 6211
email alison@gaelicbooks.org
website www.gaelicbooks.org
Director Alison Lang

Stimulates Scottish Gaelic publishing by awarding publication grants for commissioning new works from established and emerging authors and providing editorial advice and guidance to Gaelic writers and publishers. Has a bookshop in Glasgow that stocks all Gaelic and Gaelic-related books in print. All stock is listed on the website. Founded 1968.

Literature Wales

Tŷ Newydd Writing Centre, Llanystumdwy, Criccieth, Gwynedd LL52 0LW

tel 029-2047 2266, (01766) 522811
email post@literaturewales.org
website www.literaturewales.org
Facebook www.facebook.com/LlenCymruLitWales
X @LitWales
Instagram @llencymru_litwales
Executive Director Claire Furlong, *Artistic Director* Leusa Llewelyn

The national company for the development of literature in Wales. Works to inspire communities, develop writers and celebrate Wales' literary culture. Activities include the Wales Book of the Year Award; the Children's Laureate Wales and Bardd Plant Cymru schemes; creative writing courses at Tŷ Newydd Writing Centre; the professional development scheme Representing Wales; and the National Poet of Wales initiative. A member of the Arts Council of Wales' Arts Portfolio Wales.

Literature Works

Griffin Chartered Accountants, Courtenay House, Pynes Hill, Exeter, Devon EX2 5AZ
email info@literatureworks.org.uk
website www.literatureworks.org.uk, www.quaywords.org.uk
X @LitWorks
Bluesky @literatureworks.bsky.social
Instagram @literature_works

A charity and Arts Council England National Portfolio organisation in South West England. Champions words and storytelling to support creativity and wellbeing, connect people and communities and break down access barriers. Hosts a thriving online community of emerging and established writers, nurtures talent and provides resources for writers in the region.

Royal Academy of Arts

Burlington House, Piccadilly, London W1J 0BD
tel 020-7300 8090
website www.royalacademy.org.uk
Facebook www.facebook.com/royalacademy
Instagram @royalacademyarts
Threads @royalacademyarts
President Rebecca Salter

An independent, privately funded institution led by eminent artists and architects. Holds major loan exhibitions throughout the year, as well as the annual Summer Exhibition, and runs the Royal Academy Schools, a free fine art postgraduate programme for early career artists. Also holds a permanent collection, part of which is free to view. Founded 1768.

Royal Birmingham Society of Artists

RBSA Gallery, 4 Brook Street, St Paul's Square, Birmingham B3 1SA
tel 0121 236 4353
email rbsagallery@rbsa.org.uk
website www.rbsa.org.uk
Facebook www.facebook.com/rbsagallery
X @rbsagallery
Instagram @rbsagallery
Membership £45 p.a. Friends

RBSA is an artist-led charity that supports artists and promotes engagement with the visual arts through a range of exhibitions, events and workshops. The Society is comprised of almost 200 artists (new Associates are elected each April), 300 Friends and a small team of staff. Runs its own exhibition venue, the RBSA Gallery. Founded 1814.

Royal Institute of Oil Painters

17 Carlton House Terrace, London SW1Y 5BD
tel 020-7930 6844
website https://theroi.org.uk
Facebook www.facebook.com/The-Royal-Institute-of-Oil-Painters
X @InstituteRoi
Instagram @royalinstituteofoilpainters

Promotes and encourages the art of painting in oils. Open Annual Exhibition at the Mall Galleries, The Mall, London SW1. Founded 1882.

Royal Institute of Painters in Water Colours

17 Carlton House Terrace, London SW1Y 5BD
tel 020-7930 6844
email info@mallgalleries.com
website www.royalinstituteofpaintersinwatercolours.org
Facebook www.facebook.com/RIwatercolours
X @RIwatercolours
Instagram @royal_institute_watercolours
President Chris Myers

Promotes the appreciation of watercolour painting in its traditional and contemporary forms, primarily by means of an annual exhibition at the Mall Galleries, The Mall, London SW1, of members' and non-members' work. Also runs workshops and administers prizes. One of the oldest watercolour societies in the world. Founded 1831.

The Royal Musical Association

9 Patterson Avenue, Chorlton-cum-Hardy, Manchester M21 9NB
email exec@rma.ac.uk
website www.rma.ac.uk
Facebook www.facebook.com/RoyalMusicalAssociation
X @RoyalMusical
Executive Officer Amanda Babington

Promotes the investigation and discussion of subjects connected with the art and science of music. Sponsors conferences, study days and research/training events. Publishes the *Journal of the Royal Musical Association*, *RMA Research Chronicle* and the RMA Monographs series. Founded 1874.

The Royal Photographic Society

RPS House, 337 Paintworks, Arnos Vale, Bristol BS4 3AR
tel 0117 316 4450
email info@rps.org
website www.rps.org
Facebook www.facebook.com/royalphotographicsociety
X @The_RPS
Instagram @royalphotographicsociety
Membership £122 p.a. UK; £110 p.a. overseas; £92 p.a. over-65s; £56 p.a. under-25s, students and concessions

A world-leading photographic community with a membership of over 10,000 photographers worldwide. Inspires people through exhibitions, an award-winning journal, awards and events; helps photographers create images through its educational programmes and public initiatives; recognises skill and creativity and connects photographers. Membership is open to anyone with an interest in photography. Founded 1853.

The Royal Scottish Academy of Art and Architecture

The Mound, Edinburgh EH2 2EL
tel 0131 624 6110
email info@royalscottishacademy.org
website www.royalscottishacademy.org
Facebook www.facebook.com/RoyalScotAcad/
Instagram @royal_scottish_academy
Director Colin Greenslade

An independent membership-led organisation that supports arts and architecture in Scotland. Comprised of 120 Academicians elected by their peers in the disciplines of art and architecture. Elections take place every September. Also elects Honorary Academicians who are eminent in the arts or distinguished in the promotion of art and architecture. Runs a year-round programme of exhibitions, artist opportunities and events, and supports artists and architects through awards, residencies, scholarships and bursaries. Founded 1826.

The Royal Society

6–9 Carlton House Terrace, London SW1Y 5AG
tel 020-7451 2500
email library@royalsociety.org
website https://royalsociety.org
Facebook www.facebook.com/theroyalsociety
X @royalsociety
President Sir Adrian Smith PRS, *Treasurer* Prof. Jonathan Keating FRS, *Biological Secretary* Sir David Baulcombe FRS, *Physical Secretary* Prof. Sheila Rowan FRS, *Foreign Secretaries* Prof. Alison Noble FRS, Sir Mark Walport FRS, *Executive Director* Dame Julie Maxton

The independent scientific academy of the UK and the Commonwealth, dedicated to promoting excellence in science and science writing.

Royal Society of Arts

8 John Adam Street, London WC2N 6EZ
tel 020-7930 5115
email general@rsa.org.uk
website www.thersa.org
Facebook www.facebook.com/theRSAorg
X @theRSAorg
Instagram @thersaorg

The RSA is a social impact charity for the arts, manufacturing and commerce, which is committed to a world where everyone can fulfil their potential and contribute to more resilient, rebalanced and regenerative futures. Central to its work is a global network of over 31,000 Fellows. Welcomes people of all backgrounds. Founded 1754.

Royal Society of British Artists

email homesec@therba.org
website www.therba.org
Facebook www.facebook.com/RoyalSocietyBritishArtists
X @RoyalSocBritArt
Instagram @royalsocietybritishartists
Honorary Secretary Cheryl Culver

The RBA has supported contemporary artists through promoting the arts of painting, sculpture, drawing and printmaking. Activities include scholarships and exhibitions. Membership by election. Founded 1823.

Royal Society of Literature

Somerset House, Strand, London WC2R 1LA
tel 020-7845 4679
email info@rsliterature.org
website www.rsliterature.org
Facebook www.facebook.com/RoyalSocietyLiterature
X @RSLiterature
Instagram @royalsocietyofliterature
President Bernardine Evaristo
Membership £60 p.a.; £40 p.a. for those aged 18–30 years (fees decrease by £10 after the first year)

The RSL is the UK's charity for the advancement of literature. It acts as a voice for the value of literature and encourages and honours writers through its events programme, awards, prizes and outreach programme. Founded 1820.

Royal Society of Marine Artists

17 Carlton House Terrace, London SW1Y 5BD
tel 020-7930 6844
email rsma.contact@gmail.com
website www.rsma.org

Promotes and encourages the highest standards of marine art. Welcomes submissions for their Annual Open Exhibition at the Mall Galleries, The Mall, London SW1, usually held from late September (more information at www.mallgalleries.org.uk). Membership is achieved by a consistent record of success in having work selected and hung at this event and ultimately by election by the members.

The Royal Society of Miniature Painters, Sculptors and Gravers

email info@royal-miniature-society.org.uk
website www.royal-miniature-society.org.uk
Facebook www.facebook.com/RoyalMiniatureSociety
X @royalminiature
Instagram @royalminiature
Executive Secretary Claire Hucker
Membership By selection and standard of work over a period of years (SRMS student, ARMS associate, RMS full member)

An open Exhibition is held annually in June at the Bankside Gallery, Thames Riverside, 48 Hopton Street, London SE1 9JH. For online submission details see the website. Applications and enquiries to the Executive Secretary. Non-members welcome. Granted Royal Charter in 1905. Founded 1896.

Royal Society of Painter-Printmakers

Bankside Gallery, 48 Hopton Street, London SE1 9JH
tel 020-7928 7521
email info@re-printmakers.com
website www.re-printmakers.com
Instagram @re_printmakers
President Prof. David Ferry

Promotes all forms of printmaking. Election of Associates is held annually; for details check the website. New members are elected by the council based on the quality of their work alone, in a tradition reaching back over 100 years. Three members' exhibitions per year are held at Bankside Gallery, plus open submission printmaking exhibitions. Founded 1880.

Royal Society of Portrait Painters

17 Carlton House Terrace, London SW1Y 5BD
tel 020-7930 6844
email info@mallgalleries.com
website www.therp.co.uk, www.mallgalleries.org.uk
Facebook www.facebook.com/RoyalSocietyofPortraitPainters
X @RP_portraits
Instagram @royalsocietyportraitpainters

Upholds the values and practices of the discipline, and seeks to explore and develop new artistic models and perspectives. Annual Exhibition, at Mall Galleries, The Mall, London SW1, of members' work and work drawn from an open selection. Runs a programme of annual awards. Provides consultancy to those wishing to commission a portrait. Founded 1891.

Royal Society of Sculptors

Dora House, 108 Old Brompton Road, South Kensington, London SW7 3RA
tel 020-7373 8615
email info@sculptors.org.uk
website www.sculptors.org.uk
Facebook www.facebook.com/royalsocietyofsculptors
X @Royal_Sculptors
Instagram @royal_sculptors

An artist-led membership organisation that support and connect sculptors throughout their careers and offers exhibitions, creative workshops and events.

Royal Watercolour Society

Bankside Gallery, 48 Hopton Street, London SE1 9JH
tel 020-7928 7521
RWS Gallery, 3–5 Whitcomb Street, London WC2H 7HA
tel 020-8050 9425
email info@royalwatercoloursociety.com
website www.royalwatercoloursociety.co.uk
Facebook www.facebook.com/RoyalWatercolourSociety
Instagram @royalwatercoloursociety

An artist-led society whose members work in a variety of water-based media including gouache, acrylic, pen and ink, pigment, collage and mixed media as well as traditional watercolour. Promotes, by example and education, the understanding, appreciation and enjoyment of these media. Delivers regular exhibitions of members' work, as well as an annual open exhibition (the RWS Open) and a programme of events. Membership by election. Founded 1804.

Royal West of England Academy

Queen's Road, Clifton, Bristol BS8 1PX
tel 0117 973 5129
email info@rwa.org.uk
website www.rwa.org.uk
Director Ren Renwick

The RWA is an art gallery that promotes the visual arts through exhibitions, education and collaboration. Showcases innovative and thought-provoking works by emerging and established artists. Founded 1844.

BIBLIOGRAPHICAL AND ACADEMIC

The Association of Learned and Professional Society Publishers

Egale 1, 80 St Albans Road, Watford, Herts. WD17 1DL
email admin@alpsp.org
website www.alpsp.org
Facebook www.facebook.com/alpsp
X @alpsp

ALPSP is the international membership trade body that supports and represents not-for-profit organisations, both those that publish scholarly and professional content and those that partner with and provide services to not-for-profit publishers. ALPSP has 320 members in 35 countries. Its mission is to connect, inform, develop and represent the international scholarly and professional publishing community.

Bibliographical Society

Institute of English Studies, University of London, Senate House, Malet Street, London WC1E 7HU
email secretary@bibsoc.org.uk
website www.bibsoc.org.uk
Facebook www.facebook.com/BibSoc
X @BibSoc

The senior learned society dealing with the study of books and their history. Promotes and encourages study and research in the fields of historical, analytical, descriptive and textual bibliography as well as the history of printing, publishing, bookselling, bookbinding and collecting. Publishes the journal *The Library*. Founded 1892.

Cambridge Bibliographical Society

University Library, West Road, Cambridge CB3 9DR
email cbs@lib.cam.ac.uk
website www.lib.cam.ac.uk/collections/cambridge-bibliographical-society
Membership £12 p.a. individual; £25 p.a. institutions

Encourages the study of bibliography, including book and MSS production, book collecting and the history of libraries. Publishes *Transactions* (annual) and a series of monographs, and arranges a programme of lectures and visits. Founded 1949.

Classical Association

email office@classicalassociation.org
website www.classicalassociation.org
X @Classical_Assoc
Instagram @classicalassociation
Chair of Council Prof. J Mossman
Membership £27 p.a. standard; £19 p.a. concessions

An educational charity dedicated to making classical subjects widely accessible. Membership includes the general public and academic specialists. Provides financial support for outreach and engagement projects, produces academic and pedagogy journals, organises competitions and events including the UK's largest annual classics conference, and publishes podcasts and resources.

Early English Text Society

Faculty of English, St Cross Building, Manor Road, Oxford OX1 3UL
email eets@ell.ox.ac.uk
website www.eets.org.uk
X @EEngTextSoc
Honorary Director Dr H.L. Spencer, *Executive Secretary* Prof. D. Wakelin, *Treasurer & Membership Secretary* Dr Daniel Orton
Membership £30 p.a.

Aims to bring unprinted early English literature within the reach of students in sound texts. Founded 1864.

Edinburgh Bibliographical Society

c/o McNaughtan's Bookshop, 3A–4A Haddington Place, Edinburgh EH7 4AE
email secretary@edbibsoc.org
website www.edbibsoc.org
Secretary Derek Taylor
Membership £18 p.a.; £25 p.a. corporate; £12 p.a. full-time students

Encourages bibliographical activity through organising talks for members, particularly on bibliographical topics relating to Scotland, and visits to libraries. Publishes a journal (annual, free to members) and other occasional publications. Founded 1890.

Oxford Bibliographical Society

The Bodleian Library, Broad Street, Oxford OX1 3BG
email secretary@oxbibsoc.org.uk
website www.oxbibsoc.org.uk
Membership Individual: £30 p.a. UK; £35 p.a. Europe; £45 p.a R.O.W; Student: £15 p.a. UK; £20 p.a. Europe; £30 p.a R.O.W

Exists to encourage bibliographical research relating to MSS, printed books, libraries and the wider booktrade. Publishes monographs, offers grants and hosts talks, events and visits. Founded 1922.

COPYRIGHT AND LICENSING

Australian Copyright Council

PO Box 1986, Strawberry Hills, NSW 2012, Australia
tel +61 (0)2 9101 2377
email info@copyright.org.au
website www.copyright.org.au
Facebook www.facebook.com/AusCopyrightCouncil
X @AusCopyright
Instagram @auscopyrightcouncil
Ceo Eileen Camilleri

Provides easily accessible and affordable practical information, legal advice, education and forums on Australian copyright law for content creators and consumers. Represents the peak bodies for professional artists and content creators working in Australia's creative industries and Australia's major copyright collecting societies, including the Australian Society of Authors, the Australian Writers' Guild and the Australian Publishers Association.

Advocates for the contribution of creators to Australia's culture and economy and the importance of copyright for the common good. Works to promote understanding of copyright law and its application, supports appropriate law reform and fosters collaboration between content creators and consumers. Founded 1968.

Authors' Licensing and Collecting Society Ltd – see page 716

British Copyright Council
1st Floor, Goldings House, 2 Hayes Lane, London SE1 2BH
email info@britishcopyright.org
website www.britishcopyright.org
X @BritCopyright
President of Honour Maureen Duffy, *Vice-President* Geoffrey Adams, *Chairman* Trevor Cook

Represents those who create, hold interests or manage rights in literary, dramatic, musical and artistic works; provides an effective authoritative and representative voice for the copyright community; and encourages greater understanding and acceptance of copyright in the UK and around the world.

Copyright Clearance Center Inc.
Ivory House, St Katherine Docks, East Smithfield, London EW1 1AT
email info@copyright.com
website www.copyright.com
Facebook www.facebook.com/CopyrightClear

Removes the complexity from copyright issues and makes it easy for businesses and academic institutions to use copyright-protected materials while compensating publishers and content creators for their work.

The Copyright Licensing Agency Ltd – see page 714

DACS (Design and Artists Copyright Society) – see page 718

FACT (Federation Against Copyright Theft)
Regal House, 70 London Road, Twickenham, Middlesex TW1 3QS
tel 020-8891 1217
email contact@fact-uk.org.uk
website www.fact-uk.org.uk
X @factuk

Protects the content, product and interests of the film and television broadcasting industries and is regarded as the leader in intellectual property protection. Founded 1983.

The Irish Copyright Licensing Agency
63 Patrick Street, Dun Laoghaire, Dublin A96 WF25, Republic of Ireland
tel +353 (0)1 662 4211
email info@icla.ie
website www.icla.ie
Executive Director Samantha Holman

Licenses schools, higher education institutions and other users of copyright material to copy, reuse and share extracts of text- and image-based material, and distributes the monies collected to the authors and publishers whose works have been copied. Founded 1992.

PICSEL (Picture Industry Collecting Society for Effective Licensing)
112 Western Road, Brighton, East Sussex BN1 2AB
tel 07377 535095
email info@picsel.org.uk
website www.picsel.org.uk

A not-for-profit collecting society. Ensures that all visual artists, creators and representative rights holders of images receive fair payment for various secondary uses of their works following the initial publication, such as copying pages from books and magazines for use in schools and universities. Works to ensure all licence fees collected are distributed equitably, efficiently and in a transparent manner. Founded 2016.

EDITORIAL, JOURNALISM AND BROADCASTING

American Society for Indexing
1628 East Southern Avenue, 9–223, Tempe, AZ 85282, USA
tel +1 480-245-6750
email info@asindexing.org
website www.asindexing.org
Facebook www.facebook.com/asindexing
X @ASIndexing
Instagram @asindexing
Executive Director Gwen Henson

Increases awareness of the value of high-quality indexes and indexing; offers members access to educational resources that enable them to strengthen their indexing performance; keeps members up to date on indexing technology; and advocates for the professional interests of indexers.

Association of Freelance Editors, Proofreaders and Indexers of Ireland
email info@afepi-ireland.com
website www.afepi-ireland.com
Facebook www.facebook.com/AFEPI.Ireland
X @AFEPI_Ireland
Membership €100 p.a. full; €55 p.a. associate

AFEPI Ireland is an organisation for publishing and editorial freelancers in Ireland. Fosters high standards in editing, proofreading and indexing; protects the interests of its members; and helps to match authors, indie writers, publishers, businesses, public bodies and charitable organisations with suitable editorial freelancers. Membership is available to experienced professional editors, proofreaders and indexers.

For services for publishers and authors, see the online directory of freelance professional editors, proofreaders and indexers based in Ireland and Northern Ireland. Founded 1985.

British Association of Journalists

PO Box 79790, London NW11 1QT
tel 020-7353 3003
email office@bajunion.org.uk
website www.bajunion.org.uk
General Secretary Nigel Howard

Non-political trade union for professional journalists. Aims to protect and promote the industrial and professional interests of journalists. Founded 1992.

British Guild of Agricultural Journalists

The Farmers Club, 3 Whitehall Court, London SW1A 2EL
tel 07584 022909
email secretary@gaj.org.uk
website www.gaj.org.uk
X @GAJinfo
Chairman Ben Pike, *General Secretary* Nikki Robertson
Membership £78 p.a. full; £39 retired/student

Promotes high standards amongst journalists, photographers and communicators who specialise in agriculture, horticulture, food production and other rural affairs, and contributes towards a better understanding of agriculture. Founded 1944.

British Society of Magazine Editors

4 Conway Road, London N14 7BA
tel 020-8906 4664
email admin@bsme.com
website www.bsme.com
X @bsmeinfo
Instagram @_bsme

The only society in the UK exclusively for magazine and digital editors. Represents the needs and views of editors and acts as a voice for the industry.

CIEP (Chartered Institute of Editing and Proofreading)

Studio 651, Milton Keynes Business Centre, Foxhunter Drive, Linford Wood, Milton Keynes, Bucks. MK14 6GD
tel 020-8785 6155
email office@ciep.uk
website www.ciep.uk
Facebook www.facebook.com/EditProof
X @The_CIEP

A membership organisation promoting excellence in English language editing, setting and demonstrating editorial standards, and providing a community, training hub and support network for editorial professionals. Runs online courses and workshops in copy-editing, proofreading and related skills, for people starting an editorial career and those wishing to broaden their competence, and maintains an online directory of experienced editorial professionals. Also publishes factsheets and guides on various aspects of editing and business skills for the self-employed. Previously the Society for Editors and Proofreaders before being awarded its Royal Charter in 2019.

The Chartered Institute of Journalists

PO Box 765, Waltham Abbey EN8 1NT
tel 020-7252 1187
email memberservices@cioj.org
website https://cioj.org
Facebook www.facebook.com/CharteredInstituteofJournalists/EditProof
X @CIoJournalist

The senior organisation of journalists that promotes standards and ethics. Their work combines that of a professional society and a trade union. Founded 1884.

Editors' and Proofreaders' Alliance of Northern Ireland

email info@epani.org.uk
website www.epani.org.uk
Bluesky @epani.bsky.social
Coordinator Averill Buchanan

Establishes and maintains high professional standards in editorial skills in Northern Ireland. For services for authors, see the directory of freelance professional editors, proofreaders and indexers.

European Broadcasting Union

L'Ancienne Route 17A, Postal Box 45, 1218 Grand-Saconnex, Geneva, Switzerland
tel +41 (0)22 717 2111
email info@ebu.ch
website www.ebu.ch
Facebook www.facebook.com/EBU.HQ
X @EBU_HQ
Instagram @ebu_hq
Director General Noel Curran

EBU is the world's foremost alliance of public service media (PSM). Members represent 113 organisations in 56 countries, and an additional 31 associates in Asia, Africa, Australasia and the Americas. Members operate nearly 2,000 television, radio and online channels and services, broadcasting in more than 160 different languages. Together they reach audiences of more than one billion people around the world. EBU's television and radio services operate under the trademarks of Eurovision and Euroradio.

Foreign Press Association in London

8 St James's Square, London SW1Y 4JU
tel 020-7792 4565
email accreditation@fpalondon.org
website www.fpalondon.org
Facebook www.facebook.com/foreignpressassociation
X @FPALondon
Director Deborah Bonetti

The oldest and largest association of foreign journalists in the world. All major international news outlets are represented. Provides access and accreditation to a wide variety of events in the UK, and provides access to Parliament, N10 and the Royal Palaces. Organises press trips and briefings with ministers and leading figures in all departments. The FPA is one of the gatekeepers of the UK Press Card Authority (PCA) and provides UK Press Cards to bona fide international journalists. Founded 1888.

Independent Press Standards Organisation

10 Eastcheap, London EC3M 1AJ
tel 0300 123 2220
email inquiries@ipso.co.uk
website www.ipso.co.uk
Facebook www.facebook.com/ipsonews
X @IpsoNews

IPSO is the independent regulator of the newspaper and magazine industry. Exists to promote and uphold the highest professional standards of journalism in the UK and to support members of the public in seeking redress where they believe that the Editors' Code of Practice has been breached.

Journalists' Charity

11 Ribblesdale, Roman Road, Dorking, Surrey RH4 3EX
tel (01306) 887511
email enquiries@journalistscharity.org.uk
website https://journalistscharity.org.uk
Facebook www.facebook.com/journalistscharity
X @JournoCharity
Instagram @journalistscharity
Ceo James Brindle

For the relief of hardship amongst journalists, their widows/widowers and dependants. Financial assistance and retirement housing are provided. Founded 1864.

The Media Society

1 Blossom Yard, 4th Floor, London E1 6RS
email admin@themediasociety.com
website www.themediasociety.com/index.php
Honorary President Nigel Dacre
Membership £45 p.a., £10 p.a. students

Exists to promote and encourage collective and independent research into the standards, performance, organisation and economics of the media and to hold regular discussions and debates on subjects of topical or special interest and concern to print and broadcast journalists and others working in or with the media. Up to 22 evening debates and events organised throughout the year. In-person events are interspersed with online events, which are subsequently made available in video format online. Also publishes up to six newsletters each year. Founded 1973.

National Council for the Training of Journalists

The New Granary, Station Road, Newport, Saffron Walden, Essex CB11 3PL
tel (01799) 544014
email info@nctj.com
website www.nctj.com
Facebook www.facebook.com/TheNCTJ
X @NCTJ_news
Instagram @nctj_news

The NCTJ is a registered charity and awarding body that provides multimedia journalism training. Full-time accredited courses run at various colleges, universities and independent providers in the UK. Distance learning programmes and short courses are also available. Founded 1951.

National Union of Journalists

72 Acton Street, London WC1X 9NB
tel 020-7843 3700
email info@nuj.org.uk
website www.nuj.org.uk
Facebook www.facebook.com/groups/nujournalists, www.facebook.com/official.nuj
X @NUJofficial

Trade union for journalists and photographers, including freelancers. It covers the newspaper press, news agencies, magazines, broadcasting, periodical and book publishing, public relations departments and consultancies, information services and new media. The NUJ mediates disputes, organises campaigns, provides training and general and legal advice. Official publications: *The Journalist* (bi-monthly), the online *Freelance Directory* and *Freelance Fees Guide*, the *NUJ Ethical Code of Conduct* and policy pamphlets and submissions.

News Media Association

c/o Crowe LLP, 2nd Floor, 55 Ludgate Hill, London EC4M 7JW
email nma@newsmediauk.org
website www.newsmediauk.org
X @newsmediaorg

Promotes the interests of news media publishers to government, regulatory authorities, industry bodies and other organisations whose work affects the industry.

Newsbrands Scotland

17 Polwarth Grove, Edinburgh EH11 1LY
email john@newsbrandsscotland.com
website www.newsbrandsscotland.com
Director John McLellan

Formerly the Scottish Newspaper Society. Represents and safeguards the interests of the Scottish newspaper industry, maintains press freedom and improves the industry's profile. Founded 2009.

Reporters Without Borders

CS 90247, 75083 Paris Cedex 02, France
tel +33 (0)1 4483 8484
email secretariat@rsf.org
website https://rsf.org/en
Facebook www.facebook.com/Reporterssansfrontieres

Provides information on media freedom worldwide and issues regular press releases about abuses against journalists and censorship. Also protects journalists and bloggers in danger, acts as a pressure group and publishes the World Press Freedom Index. Its main activities are advocacy, awareness campaigns, assistance and legal aid, and cyber-security. Founded 2014.

Society of Editors

Stationers Hall, Ave Maria Lane, London EC4M 7DD
tel 07599 954636
email office@societyofeditors.org
website www.societyofeditors.org
President Sarah Whitehead

Formed from the merger of the Guild of Editors and the Association of British Editors, it has members in national, regional and local newspapers, magazines, broadcasting and digital media, journalism, education and media law. Campaigns for media freedom, self-regulation, the public's right to know and the maintenance of standards in journalism.

Society of Indexers – see page 692

Society of Women Writers & Journalists

42 Brookside Avenue, Polegate, Eastbourne, East Sussex BN26 6DH
email swwjviv@btinternet.com
website www.swwj.co.uk
Facebook www.facebook.com/societyofwomenwriters
X @SWWJ
Instagram @swwj_official
President Baroness Floella Benjamin OM DBE DL

The SWWJ aims to encourage literary achievement, uphold professional standards, promote social contact with fellow writers and defend the dignity and prestige of the writing profession. Membership is open to professionals of all genders; if accepted they will qualify for a Press card and post-nominals. New Writer and Friend membership categories also available. See website for a full list of benefits and information. Founded 1894.

Sports Journalists' Association

tel 020-8916 2234
email info@sportsjournalists.co.uk
website www.sportsjournalists.co.uk
Facebook www.facebook.com/sportsjournalistsGB/
X @SportSJA
Bluesky @sportsjournalists.co.uk

The SJA represents sports journalists across the country and is Britain's voice in international sporting affairs. Offers advice to members covering major events and acts as a consultant to organisers of major sporting events on media requirements. Founded 1948.

Voice of the Listener & Viewer

The Old Rectory Business Centre, Springhead Road, Northfleet DA11 8HN
tel (01474) 338716
email info@vlv.org.uk
website www.vlv.org.uk
Facebook www.facebook.com/VLVUK
X @vlvuk
Administrator Sarah Stapylton-Smith
Membership From £30 p.a.; academic, corporate and student rates available

VLV campaigns for accountability, diversity and excellence in UK broadcasting, seeking to sustain and strengthen public service broadcasting to the benefit of civil society and democracy in the UK. It holds regular conferences and seminars and publishes a bulletin and an e-newsletter. Founded 1983.

The Worshipful Company of Stationers and Newspaper Makers

Stationers' Hall, Ave Maria Lane, London EC4M 7DD
tel 020-7246 0982
email admin@stationers.org
website www.stationers.org
Facebook www.facebook.com/thestationerscompany
X @stationerscomms
Instagram @the.stationers.company
Membership Manager Karyn Keating

A Livery Company of the City of London, with over 1,000 members. Supports the communication and content industries through fellowship, education and training. Connected with the writing, printing, publishing, bookselling, newspaper and allied trades. Founded 1403.

Yachting Journalists' Association

tel 07770 021491
email chair@yja.world
website www.yja.world
Chairman Katy Stickland
Membership £50 p.a. (£45 p.a. if paid by Standing Order)

Promotes greater awareness of all aspects of leisure boating through the professional services offered by its members. Represents hundreds of specialist marine journalists, photographers, TV and radio presenters, and web editors across all major sailing and boating regions in the world. Members vote annually for the Yachtsman of the Year and the Young Sailor of the Year Award. Founded 1955.

FILM, THEATRE AND TELEVISION

AITA/IATA (International Amateur Theatre Association)

email secretariat@aitaiata.net
website www.aitaiata.net
Facebook www.facebook.com/aitaiata
X @aita_iata
Instagram @aita_iata
President & Councillor Aled Rhys-Jones (UK), *Vice President & Councillor* Sofia Wegelius (Finland), *Treasurer & Councillor* Patrick Schoenstein (France), *Councillors* Kelli McLoud Schingen (USA), Ksenia Nesterova (Russian Republic), Heidi Troi (Italy), Carlos Taberneiro (Spain), Stephen Tobias (Canada)
Membership €30–90 p.a. associate; €60–595 p.a. National Centres

Encourages, fosters and promotes non-professional theatre organisations and student, educational and adult theatre activities at international level. Organises international seminars, workshops, courses and conferences, and collates information of all types for national and international dissemination. Holds a programme of festivals celebrating adult and children's theatre.

BAFTA (British Academy of Film and Television Arts)

195 Piccadilly, London W1J 9LN
tel 020-7734 0022
email reception@bafta.org
website www.bafta.org
Facebook www.facebook.com/bafta
X @BAFTA
Instagram @bafta
Threads @bafta
Chief Executive Jane Millichip

A world-leading independent arts charity that brings work in film, games and television to public attention and supports the growth of creative talent in the UK and internationally. Through its Awards ceremonies and year-round programme of learning events and initiatives (which include workshops, masterclasses, scholarships, lectures and mentoring schemes) BAFTA identifies and celebrates excellence, inspires and nurtures new talent, and enables learning and creative collaboration. Founded 1947.

BECTU (Broadcasting Entertainment Communications and Theatre Union)

100 Rochester Row, London SW1P 1JP
email membership@bectu.org.uk
website https://bectu.org.uk/
Facebook www.facebook.com/BECTUOfficial
X @bectu
Bluesky @bectu.bsky.social
Instagram @bectuunion
General Secretary Mike Clancy

A sector of the trade union Prospect that defends the interests of writers in film, TV and radio. By virtue of its industrial strength, the union is able to help its writer members to secure favourable terms and conditions. In cases of disputes with employers, the union can intervene in order to ensure an equitable settlement. Its production agreement with Pact lays down minimum terms for writers working in the documentary area. Founded 1991.

BFI (British Film Institute)

21 Stephen Street, London W1T 1LN
tel 020-7255 1444
website www.bfi.org.uk
Facebook www.facebook.com/BritishFilmInstitute
X @BFI
Instagram @britishfilminstitute

Supports, nurtures and promotes the arts of film, television and the moving image. A registered charity, funded by government and earned income, and a distributor of National Lottery funds, the BFI is at the heart of the UK's fast-growing screen industries, protecting their legacy and advocating for their future. Works in partnership with cultural organisations, government and industry to make this happen. Founded 1933.

Independent Theatre Council

The Albany, Douglas Way, London SE8 4AG
tel 020-7403 1727
email admin@itc-arts.org
website www.itc-arts.org
Facebook www.facebook.com/independenttheatrecouncil
X @itc_arts
Membership £200 p.a.

Enables the creation of high-quality professional performing arts by supporting, representing and developing the people who manage and produce it. Has over 450 members from a wide range of companies, venues and individuals in the fields of drama, dance, opera, musical theatre, puppetry, mixed media, mime, physical theatre and circus. Founded 1974.

Little Theatre Guild of Great Britain

tel 07971 474721
email secretary@littletheatreguild.org
website www.littletheatreguild.org
National Secretary Anne Gilmour

Promotes closer cooperation amongst the 122 amateur theatres that constitute its membership (all based in the UK), acts as a coordinating and representative body on behalf of its members, and maintains and advances the highest standards in the art of theatre.

Pact (Producers Alliance for Cinema and Television)

3rd Floor, Fitzrovia House,
153–157 Cleveland Street, London W1T 6QW

tel 020-7380 8230
website www.pact.co.uk
X @PactUK
Chief Executive John McVay

The UK trade association that represents and promotes the commercial interests of independent feature film, television, animation and interactive media companies. Headquartered in London, it has regional representation throughout the UK in order to support its members, including an office in Leeds. An effective lobbying organisation, it has regular dialogues with government, regulators, public agencies and opinion-formers on all issues affecting its members, and contributes to key public policy debates on the media industry. It negotiates terms of trade with all public service broadcasters in the UK and supports members in their business dealings with cable and satellite channels and streaming services. It also lobbies for a properly structured and funded UK film industry and maintains close contact with other relevant film organisations and government departments.

Player–Playwrights

email pplaywrights@gmail.com
website www.playerplaywrights.co.uk
Facebook www.facebook.com/groups/playerplaywrights
Secretary Lynne O'Sullivan
Membership £15 in first year and £10 p.a. thereafter (plus £3 per attendance); guests and audience welcome (non-members £4 entrance)

Reads, performs and discusses plays and scripts submitted by members. Assists writers in improving and marketing their work and enabling actors to showcase their talents. New writers and new acting members are always welcome. Check website for details of group meets. Founded 1948.

The Society for Theatre Research

Savile House, 4 Mansfield Road, Oxford OX1 3TA
email contact@str.org.uk
website www.str.org.uk
X @TheSTR
Honorary Secretary Brianna Robertson-Kirkland

Supports and promotes theatre research. Publishes the journal *Theatre Notebook* along with at least one major book per year, holds public lectures and makes annual research grants. Also awards an annual prize for best book published in English on British Theatre. Founded 1948.

LIBRARIES AND INFORMATION

Campaign for Freedom of Information

email admin@cfoi.org.uk
website www.cfoi.org.uk
Facebook www.facebook.com/CampaignFOI
X @CampaignFOI

A non-profit organisation working to defend and improve public access to official information and to ensure that the Freedom of Information Act is implemented effectively. Advises members of the public about their rights to information under FOI and related laws, helps people challenge unreasonable refusals to disclose information, encourages good practice by public authorities and provides FOI training.

CILIP (The Library and Information Association)

Room 150, British Library, 96 Euston Road, London NW1 2DB
tel 020-8159 4925
website www.cilip.org.uk
Facebook www.facebook.com/CILIPinfo
X @CILIPinfo
Instagram @cilip_uk
Membership Varies according to level and income

The leading voice for the information, knowledge management and library profession. CILIP's goal is to put information and library skills and professional values at the heart of society.

English Association

Senate House, Malet Street, London WC1E 7HU
email hello@englishassociation.ac.uk
website www.englishassociation.ac.uk
X @englishassoc
Ceo Dr Rebecca Fisher
Membership From £55 p.a.

A membership association and a learned society for people passionate about English language, literature and creative writing. Brings together individuals and organisations from all sectors of education and English studies, and has a long history of engagement with national and international bodies. The elective Fellowship recognises outstanding achievement in English studies, and Officers and Committee members are leaders in their field. Through a portfolio of publications, an events programme, networking and campaigning, the association has shaped the discipline and continues to connect English teachers in schools, colleges and universities. Founded 1906.

English Speaking Board (International)

tel (01695) 573439
email business@esbuk.org
website https://esbuk.org/web/
Facebook www.facebook.com/EnglishSpeakingBoardUK/
X @ESBUK

Offers an extensive portfolio of qualifications in English language and oracy, including a new speech pathways qualification that gives greater flexibility to learners. These qualifications are designed for schools who wish to use spoken language to raise pupil achievement and develop enrichment programmes. ESOL Skills for Life and ESOL international qualifications are also accessible for individuals for whom English is not a first language. Centres may be eligible for financial support through its Christabel Burniston Fund.

The English-Speaking Union

Dartmouth House, 37 Charles Street,
London W1J 5ED
tel 020-7529 1550
email esu@esu.org
website www.esu.org
Facebook www.facebook.com/theesu/
Instagram @the.esu_

An educational charity and membership organisation that promotes international understanding and cooperation by widening the use of the English language throughout the world. Runs programmes, competitions and exchanges to give young people the speaking and listening skills and the cross-cultural understanding they need to thrive. Founded 1918.

Private Libraries Association

Ravelston, South View Road, Pinner,
Middlesex HA5 3YD
email info@plabooks.org
website www.plabooks.org
X @PLABooks
Instagram @pla_books
President Matthew Haley, *Honorary Secretary* Jim Maslen
Membership £30 p.a.

International society of book collectors and lovers of books. Made up of 450 individual members and 100 institutional members across the USA, Canada, Australia and Europe. Interests include private presses, illustration, binding, restoration, book history and bibliography. Founded 1956.

LITERACY

BookTrust

BookTrust HQ: 1 Aire Street, Leeds LS1 4PR
London Office: BookTrust, 29 Clerkenwell Road, Farringdon, London EC1M 5RN
tel 020-7801 8826
email query@booktrust.org.uk
website www.booktrust.org.uk
Facebook www.facebook.com/booktrust
X @Booktrust
Instagram @booktrust
Ceo Diana Gerald, *Chair of Trustees* John Coughlan

The UK's largest children's reading charity, dedicated to getting children reading. Supports parents and carers to share stories and books with children from a young age, with especial focus on disadvantaged children who need reading the most.

BookTrust reviews at least one children's book each day and runs the Waterstones Children's Laureate, BookTrust Storytime Prize and BookTrust Represents.

Children's Books Ireland

17 North Great George's Street, Dublin D01 R2F1, Republic of Ireland
tel +353 (0)1 872 7475
email info@childrensbooksireland.com
website www.childrensbooksireland.ie
Ceo Elaina Ryan, *Deputy Ceo* Jenny Murray, *Programme & Events Manager* Aoife Murray

Champions every child's right to develop a love of reading. Engages young people in reading, fosters a greater understanding of books for young people and acts as a core resource for those with an interest in books for children in Ireland. Celebrates the importance of authors and illustrators and works in partnership with the people and organisations who enhance children's lives through books.

Forward Arts Foundation

Somerset House Exchange, The Strand,
London WC2R 1LA
tel 020-8187 9861
email info@forwardartsfoundation.org
website www.forwardartsfoundation.org

Promotes appreciation and engagement with poetry through programmes and initiatives that run throughout the year. As well as advocating for the positive social impact of poetry and growing poetry audiences, the foundation supports and celebrates poets, works closely with schools and libraries, organises National Poetry Day each year and runs the Forward Prizes for Poetry.

Free Books Campaign

8A Gloucester Circus, Greenwich SE10 8RX
website https://freebookscampaign.co.uk/
X @bookscampaign
Founder Sofia Akel, *Head of Community* Princess Adenrele, *Head of Book Curation* Fatima Saleh

A social enterprise dedicated to ensuring that books are accessible to everyone, regardless of financial barriers. The Campaign's mission is to increase book ownership among underrepresented communities; to foster literacy, inspire creativity and provide a sense of escapism, particularly for those affected by austerity; and to amplify the voices of authors of colour.

LoveReading4Kids

157 Shooters Hill, London SE18 3HP
tel 020-3004 7204
website www.lovereading4kids.co.uk
Facebook www.facebook.com/lovereading4kids
X @lovereading4kids

A book recommendation site and online bookstore for children's books ranging from board books to YA.

Supports parents, teachers and school librarians in helping children find books that they will love and engendering a lifelong love of reading. Offers a variety of free services alongside the ability to read and write reviews. The website features Kids' Zone, an area designed specifically for children, with competitions, quizzes and book-related material. The LoveReading4Schools portal offers educational resources, recommended reading lists for all ages, topics and curriculum, and funding benefits.

National Literacy Trust

68 South Lambeth Road, London SW8 1RL
tel 020-7587 1842
email contact@literacytrust.org.uk
website https://literacytrust.org.uk
Facebook www.facebook.com/nationalliteracytrust
X @Literacy_Trust
Instagram @literacy_trust

An independent charity that helps change lives through literacy. Campaigns to improve public understanding of the importance of literacy; and delivers projects and works in partnership to reach those most in need of support.

The Queen's Reading Room

email info@thequeensreadingroom.co.uk
website https://thequeensreadingsroom.co.uk
Facebook www.facebook.com/TheQueensReadingRoom/
Instagram @thequeensreadingroom

Champions reading and its wellbeing benefits to individuals and communities. Through neuroscientific research the charity proves the benefits of reading to brain health, mental health and social connection; and through partnering with other organisations, sharing educational content and organising events and festivals makes reading more accessible. Founded 2023.

Read for Good

26 Nailsworth Mills, Nailsworth, Glos. GL6 0BS
tel (01453) 839005
email reading@readforgood.org
website www.readforgood.org
Facebook www.facebook.com/readforgood
X @ReadforGoodUK
Bluesky @readforgood.bsky.social
Instagram @readforgood

A charity that wants all children and young people in the UK to be able to develop a lifelong love of reading, positively shaping their futures and creating a more equal society. Runs Readathon, Track My Read and Read for Good in Hospitals. Founded 1984.

The Reading Agency

24 Bedford Row, London WC1R 4EH
tel 07933 181889
email info@readingagency.org.uk
website www.readingagency.org.uk
Facebook www.facebook.com/readingagency
X @readingagency
Instagram @readingagency
Ceo Karen Napier

A charity whose mission is to tackle life's big challenges through the proven power of reading. Works closely with public libraries, publishers, health partners and volunteers to bring reading programmes to adults and young people across the UK. Funded by Arts Council England, it supports a wide range of reading initiatives for adults and young people including Reading Ahead, World Book Night and the Reading Friends programme.

Scottish Book Trust

Sandeman House, Trunk's Close, 55 High Street, Edinburgh EH1 1SR
tel 0131 524 0160
email info@scottishbooktrust.com
website www.scottishbooktrust.com
Facebook www.facebook.com/scottishbktrust
X @ScottishBkTrust
Instagram @scottishbooktrust

Scotland's national agency for the promotion of reading, writing and literature. Offers mentoring and professional development for emerging and established writers. Programmes include Bookbug, a free universal book-gifting programme that encourages families to read with their children from birth; an ambitious schools programme including national tours; Authors Live, the virtual events programme; the Live Literature funding programme, a national initiative enabling Scottish citizens to engage with authors, playwrights, poets, storytellers and illustrators; and Book Week Scotland, held during the last week in November. Founded 1998.

Seven Stories – The National Centre for Children's Books

30 Lime Street, Ouseburn, Newcastle upon Tyne NE1 2PQ
tel 0300 330 1095
email info@sevenstories.org.uk
website www.sevenstories.org.uk
Facebook www.facebook.com/7stories
X @7stories
Instagram @7stories

Champions the art of children's books as an integral part of childhood and national cultural life through unique exhibitions, events for all ages and a national archive. The work of over 250 authors and illustrators, including Judith Kerr, Enid Blyton, Michael Morpurgo and David Almond is cared for in the archive collection. Operates as a charity – money earned and raised is used to save, celebrate and share children's books so future generations can enjoy Britain's rich literary heritage. Founded 1996.

Story Therapy

1 Sugworth Lane, Radley, Abingdon-on-Thames, Oxon OX14 2HZ
email admin@storytherapyresources.co.uk
website www.storytherapyresources.co.uk
Facebook www.facebook.com/storytherapy
X @StoryTherapy
Contact Hilary Hawkes

A non-profit social enterprise creating stories and resources, especially story-themed resources, that support children's emotional health and mental wellbeing. Founded 2016.

MEMBERS' CLUBS

The Arts Club

40 Dover Street, London W1S 4NP
tel 020-7499 8581
email membership@theartsclub.co.uk
website www.theartsclub.co.uk
Instagram @the_arts_club

A private members' club for all those connected with or interested in the arts, literature and science. Founded 1863.

Authors' Club

Whitehall Place, London SW1A 2HE
email info@authorsclub.co.uk
website www.authorsclub.co.uk
Facebook www.facebook.com/authorsclub1891
X @AuthorsClub
President John Walsh, *Chairperson* Lucy Popescu
Membership £100 p.a. associate

A club for all those professionally engaged with literature. Welcomes writers, publishers, critics, journalists and academics. Administers the Best First Novel Award and the Art Book Awards. Founded 1891.

New English Art Club (NEAC)

email info@neac.co.uk
website www.newenglishartclub.co.uk

An elected society of contemporary painters focused on art informed by the visual world and personal interpretation. Its Annual Exhibition, held at Mall Galleries, The Mall, London SW1, showcases work by its members and aspiring artists selected from an open submission.

Scottish Arts Club

24 Rutland Square, Edinburgh EH1 2BW
tel 0131 229 8157
email administrator@scottishartsclub.com
website www.scottishartsclub.com
Facebook www.facebook.com/scottishartsclub
Instagram @thescottishartsclub

A social hub for artists and those interested in the arts. Professional members include painters, sculptors, filmmakers, actors, musicians, playwrights, poets, novelists, journalists, architects, designers, dancers and diplomats. Also welcomes lay members and anyone interested in the arts. Events include performances, lectures and workshops. Founded 1873.

MUSIC

American Society of Composers, Authors and Publishers

250 West 57th Street, New York, NY 10107, USA
tel +1 212-621-6000
website www.ascap.com
Facebook www.facebook.com/ascap
X @ASCAP
Instagram @ascap
Threads @ascap

An organisation founded and governed by its members, it is the leading performance rights organisation representing more than one million songwriters, composers and music publishers.

The Guild of International Songwriters & Composers

30 Brantwood, Chester-le-Street DH2 2UL
tel 0330 202 0760
email gisc@songwriters-guild.co.uk
website www.songwriters-guild.co.uk
Membership £75 p.a.

Provides a copyright registration service, song assessment and international collaboration register to members; assists with protection of members' rights; and outlines requirements of record companies, publishers and artists.

Independent Society of Musicians

4–5 Inverness Mews, London W2 3JQ
tel 020-7221 3499
email membership@ism.org
website www.ism.org
Facebook www.facebook.com/ISMusicians
X @ISM_music
Bluesky @ism-music.bsky.social
Instagram @ism_music
Threads @ism_music
Chief Executive Deborah Annetts
Membership £190 p.a. standard; £57 p.a. early career rate; £17 p.a. students

Professional body for musicians. Promotes and supports the art of music and protects the interests of professionals within the music profession. Provides expert advice for its members. Publishes a quarterly magazine, *Music Journal*, and an annual Handbook. Founded 1882.

The Ivors Academy

1 Upper James Street, London W1F 9DE
tel 020-7636 2929

email contact@ivorsacademy.com
website www.ivorsacademy.com
X @ivorsacademy
Instagram @ivorsacademy
Membership £95 p.a. standard; £52 p.a. under-25s

A not-for-profit organisation dedicated to supporting songwriters and composers across all genres by advocating for and protecting their rights, providing tools and knowledge, and championing their achievements. Runs a programme of educational events offering members opportunities to share their insights and expertise, develop industry knowledge and collaborate with others. Also presents the Ivor Novello Awards, which are judged by fellow music creators.

Music Publishers Association

3rd Floor, 107 Grays Inn Road, London WC1X 8TX
tel 020-3848 7410
email info@mpagroup.com
website https://mpaonline.org.uk
Facebook www.facebook.com/MusicPublishersAssociation
X @the_MPA
Instagram @thempaonline

Trade organisation representing 165 UK music publishers. Promotes and safeguards its members' interests in copyright, trade and related matters. Sub-committees and groups deal with particular interests. Founded 1881.

PRS for Music

1st Floor Goldings House, 2 Hay's Lane, London SE1 2HB
tel 020-7580 5544
website www.prsformusic.com
X @PRSforMusic

Represents the rights of songwriters, composers and music publishers around the globe. Headquartered in the UK, it works on behalf of its members to grow and protect the value of their rights. Lobbies for a global standard for music royalties to ensure creators are paid whenever their musical compositions and songs are streamed, downloaded, broadcast, performed and played in public. Founded 1914.

REPRESENTATION AND PUBLISHING

Alliance of Independent Authors

7 Bell Yard, City of Westminster, London WC2A 2JR
email info@allianceindependentauthors.org
website www.allianceindependentauthors.org, https://selfpublishingadvice.org
X @IndieAuthorALLi
Instagram @indieauthoralli
Membership £69 p.a. Associate; £89 p.a. Author; £119 p.a. Authorpreneur

A global collaborative collective of self-publishing writers. Founded in 2012 at the London Book Fair by former author and former literary agent, Orna Ross, in response to her personal experience of self-publishing. Supports and advocates for the interests of independent, self-publishing authors everywhere and promotes the interests of indie authors within the literary and publishing industries; engages with booksellers, festivals, prize-giving committees, libraries, book clubs and the media.

It issues a directory of publishing services vetted for quality, value and ethical behaviour and maintains an active Watchdog desk which rates self-publishing providers and provides community alerts.

ALLi commissions original research as well as compiling facts and figures across the industry, making it the best source of data on self-publishing in the world: www.allianceindependentauthors.org/facts. Benefits for members include self-publishing advice, guidance and community; vetted services, service ratings and watchdog desk; legal and contract appraisal; discounts and deals; professional and business development; campaigns and advocacy.

Alliance of Literary Societies

email allianceoflitsocs@gmail.com
website www.allianceofliterarysocieties.wordpress.com
President James Naughtie, *Chair* Marty Ross, *Secretary* Anita Fernandez-Young

An umbrella organisation comprised of 120 literary societies (based in the UK and Republic of Ireland) that acts as a valuable liaison body between member societies to share knowledge, skills and expertise. Assists in the preservation of buildings, places and objects that have literary associations. Its publications include a twice-yearly newsletter. The ALS holds an annual literary weekend hosted by a different member society each year.

American Booksellers Association

tel +1 800-637-0037
email info@bookweb.org
website www.bookweb.org
Facebook www.facebook.com/americanbooksellers
Instagram @americanbooksellers

A national non-profit trade organisation that works with booksellers and industry partners to ensure the success and profitability of independently owned book retailers and to assist in expanding the book community. Provides education and information dissemination, offers business products and services, creates relevant awareness programmes and engages in public policy. Founded 1900.

Association for Scottish Literature

c/o Department of Scottish Literature, University of Glasgow, 7 University Gardens, Glasgow G12 8QH
tel 0141 330 5309

email office@asls.org.uk
website www.asls.org.uk
Facebook www.facebook.com/groups/scotlit
Bluesky @asls.org.uk.bsky.social
Instagram @associationforscotlit
President David Goldie, *Secretary* Moira Hansen, *Director* Duncan Jones
Membership £70 p.a. individuals; £20 p.a. UK students; £100 p.a. corporate

Promotes the study, teaching and writing of Scottish literature and furthers the study of Scottish languages. Publishes annually an anthology of new Scottish writing, *New Writing Scotland*; an edited text of Scottish literature; a series of academic journals; and the eZine *The Bottle Imp*. Also publishes *Scotnotes* (comprehensive study guides for major Scottish writers), literary texts and commentaries designed to assist the classroom teacher, and a series of occasional papers. Organises two conferences a year. Founded 1970.

Association of American Literary Agents

302A West 12th Street, Suite 122, New York, NY 10014, USA
email info@aalitagents.org
website https://aalitagents.org

A professional organisation of over 500 agents who work with authors and illustrators. Founded 1991.

Association of American Publishers

1730 Pennsylvania Avenue NW, Washington, DC 20006, USA
tel +1 202-347-3375
email info@publishers.org
website https://publishers.org
X @AmericanPublish

AAP is the trade association for US books, journals and education publishers, providing advocacy and communications on behalf of the industry and its priorities nationally and worldwide. Founded 1970.

The Association of Authors' Agents

The Society of Authors, 24 Bedford Row, London WC1R 4EH
tel 020-3880 2230
website www.agentsassoc.co.uk
President Claire Wilson, *Secretary* John Baker

Exists to provide a forum that allows member agencies to discuss issues arising in the profession; a collective voice for UK literary agencies in public affairs and the media; and a code of conduct to which all members commit themselves. Please note that the AAA is not able to offer advice on finding representation by an agent or getting published. Founded 1974.

Association of Canadian Publishers

401 Richmond Street West, Studio 258, Toronto, ON M5V 3A8, Canada
tel +1 416-487-6116
email admin@canbook.org
website https://publishers.ca
Executive Director Jack Illingworth

Represents approximately 115 Canadian-owned and controlled book publishers from across the country. Activities include government and public relations, marketing initiatives, research and communications, and professional development. Founded 1976.

Australian Crime Writers Association

tel +61 419-721-350
email info@austcrimewriters.com
website www.austcrimewriters.com
Facebook www.facebook.com/austcrimewriters
X @auscrimewriters
Instagram @auscrimewriters
Chairman Karina Kilmore

Represents Australian crime writers and readers. The Society is dedicated to promoting greater recognition for crime, thriller and mystery writing in Australia and to protecting the general professional interests of all creators of crime and mystery works.

Australian Publishers Association

60/89 Jones Street, Ultimo, NSW 2007, Australia
tel +61 (0)2 9281 9788
website www.publishers.asn.au
X @AusPublish
President Julie Burland

The APA is the national representative body for the Australian publishing industry. Founded 1948.

The Australian Society of Authors

Gadigal Country, Suite C1.06, 22–36 Mountain Street, Ultimo, NSW 2007, Australia
tel +61 (0)2 9211 1004
email asa@asauthors.org
website www.asauthors.org.au
Facebook www.facebook.com/asauthors
Instagram @asauthors
Threads @asauthors

The ASA is the national association for Australia's authors and illustrators. Provides advocacy, support and advice for authors and illustrators in matters relating to professional practice, as well as awards, scholarships, fellowships and mentorships. Founded 1963.

Australian Writers' Guild

Level 4, 70 Pitt Street, Sydney, NSW 2000, Australia
tel +61 (0)2 9319 0339
email admin@awg.com.au
website www.awg.com.au

The professional association representing writers for stage, screen, radio and online. Protects and promotes creative and professional interests. Founded 1962.

Book Marketing Society

email admin@bookmarketingsociety.co.uk
website www.bookmarketingsociety.co.uk
X @BMSoc
Membership £84 p.a. standard; £120 p.a. freelancer

Launched with the objective of becoming the representative body of marketing within the book industry. Provides a forum for sharing best practice, inspiration and creativity through regular awards and a lively programme of member meetings, development workshops, masterclasses and social events. Anyone who works for a book publisher, book retailer or book wholesaler is eligible for membership, including those working in associated areas.

The Booksellers Association

6 Bell Yard, London WC2A 2JR
tel 020-7421 4640
email mail@booksellers.org.uk
website www.booksellers.org.uk
Facebook www.facebook.com/thebooksellersassociation
X @BAbooksellers
President Fleur Sinclair

A membership organisation for all booksellers in the UK and Ireland, representing over 95% of bookshops. Key services include National Book Tokens, Batch Payment Services and BatchLine. Founded 1895.

Canadian Authors Association

Aurora, ON L4G 2R6, Canada
tel +1 877-905-1921 (ext. 800)
email office@canadianauthors.org
website www.canadianauthors.org
Facebook www.facebook.com/canadianauthorsassociation
X @canauthors
Administrative Director Brandi Tanner

A membership-based organisation for writers in all areas of the profession. Has chapters across Canada that provide writers with a wide variety of programmes, services and resources to help them develop skills in the craft and business of writing. Founded 1921.

Canadian Publishers' Council

Suite 6060, 3080 Yonge Street, Toronto, ON M4N 3N1, Canada
tel +1 647-255-8880
email dswail@pubcouncil.ca
website https://pubcouncil.ca
Facebook www.facebook.com/people/Canadian-Publishers-Council/100089305355472/
X @pubcouncil_ca
Instagram @pubcouncil_ca
President David Swail

Represents the interests of Canadian publishing companies that publish books and other media for schools, colleges and universities, professional and reference markets, and the retail and library sectors. Founded 1910.

Canadian Society of Children's Authors, Illustrators & Performers

720 Bathurst Street, Suite 412, Toronto, ON M5S 2R4, Canada
tel +1 416-515-1559
email office@canscaip.org
website www.canscaip.org
X @CANSCAIP
Administrative Director Helena Aalto
Membership $90 p.a. member; $50 p.a. friend

CANSCAIP is a membership-based non-profit organisation that supports the professional development of Canada's community of authors, illustrators and performers for children and teens. Founded 1977.

The Comics Cultural Impact Collective (CCIC)

email helloccic@gmail.com
website www.thecomicsculturalimpactcollective.org
Instagram @comicsculturalimpact

Established to raise the profile of comics and help establish viable careers in the industry. CCIC collaborates with institutions, organisations and individuals who work in and with comics to campaign for increased funding and support, and for greater awareness of the cultural, educational, artistic and economic value of the medium.

Creative Rights in AI Coalition

website www.creativerightsinai.co.uk

An umbrella group advocating for the protection of the rights of content creators in response to AI. Members include a diverse range of businesses and organisations from the creative industries. The three pillars of their policy are allowing intellectual property owners control over their own work, transparency in how AI developers are using content and how they are held responsible for infringing copyright, and support for growth and innovation in the creative industries. Founded 2024.

Creative UK

Tomorrow Building, 130 Broadway, 2nd Floor, Suite 7, MediaCityUK, Salford M50 2UW
tel 0333 023 5240
email info@wearecreative.uk
website www.wearecreative.uk
Facebook www.facebook.com/WeAreCreativeUK
Instagram @wearecreativeuk

The national network for the creative industries. Champions the social and economic value of the creative industries by connecting and supporting talent, businesses and organisations; providing development opportunities at a local and national level through a network of partners; and offering tailor-made resources and financial expertise.

Federation of European Publishers

Chaussee d'Ixelles, 29/35 Box 4, 1050 Brussels, Belgium
tel +32 2770 1110
email info@fep-fee.eu
website www.fep-fee.eu
X @FEP_EU
Director Anne Bergman-Tahon

Represents the interests of European publishers on EU affairs and informs members on the development of EU policies that could affect the publishing industry. Founded 1967.

Independent Publishers Guild

PO Box 12, Llain, Login SA34 0WU
tel (01437) 563335
email info@independentpublishersguild.com
website www.independentpublishersguild.com
Facebook www.facebook.com/independentpublishersguild
Bluesky @ipghq.bsky.social
Chief Executive Bridget Shine

The IPG is the UK's largest network of publishers, open to independent publishers from all sectors and of all sizes, plus suppliers and providers. Their events, resources and services are intended to help independent publishers and their teams. Events include the Spring and Autumn Conferences and the Independent Publishing Awards. Learning and development support is delivered via the online Skills Hub, mentoring schemes and training in AI tailored to the needs of publishers. Other benefits include weekly ebulletins, discounts on products and services, collective stands at book fairs, industry briefings and reports, and special interest groups focused on DEI, sustainability and various publishing sectors. Founded 1962.

Indie Press Network

website https://indiepressnetwork.com
X @IndiePressNet
Instagram @indiepressnetwork
Membership £20 p.a.

Connects independent book publishers with each other, with the aim of supporting independent presses writers. Provides guidance for those wishing to set up an independent press, information for booksellers and opportunities for presses to promote books and authors to readers.

International Authors Forum

6th Floor, International House, 1 St Katherine's Way, London E1W 1UN
tel 020-7264 5707
email luke.alcott@internationalauthors.org
website www.internationalauthors.org
X @IntAuthors
Instagram @internationalauthorsforum
Executive Administrator Luke Alcott

Represents over 700,000 authors around the world and has a membership made up of authors' organisations from every continent. Campaigns for authors' rights at national and international levels. Organises events, publications and opportunities to promote the importance of creative work financially, socially and culturally, and keeps members up to date with international developments in copyright law.

International Publishers Association

23 Avenue de France, 1202 Geneva, Switzerland
tel +41 (0)22 704 1820
email info@internationalpublishers.org
website www.internationalpublishers.org
Facebook www.facebook.com/InternationalPublishersAssociation
X @IntPublishers
Instagram @intpublishers
President Gvantsa Jobava, *Secretary-General* José Borghino

The IPA is a federation of national, regional and international publishers' associations. Promotes and protects publishing worldwide with a focus on copyright and freedom to publish. Membership comprises 105 organisations from 84 countries worldwide. Founded 1896.

Irish Writers Centre

19 Parnell Square, Dublin D01 E102, Republic of Ireland
tel +353 (0)1 872 1302
email info@irishwriterscentre.ie
website https://irishwriterscentre.ie
Facebook www.facebook.com/irishwritersctr
X @IrishWritersCtr
Instagram @irishwriterscentre
Ceo Mags McLoughlin

Leading resource and development organisation for writers in Ireland. Year-round programme (online and in person) provides creative writing courses, resources, mentoring opportunities and literary events. Each September the centre welcomes submissions to its international Novel Fair competition for aspiring novelists. Also supports the careers of writers through a series of free development programmes for writers resident on the island of Ireland. Founded 1991.

Irish Writers' Union/Comhar na Scríbhneoirí

Irish Writers Centre, 19 Parnell Square, Dublin 1, Republic of Ireland

email info@irishwritersunion.org
website https://irishwritersunion.org
Facebook www.facebook.com/IrishWritersUnion
X @WritersUnion_ie
Chairperson Lindsay J Sedgwick
Membership €50 p.a. full; €10 p.a. associate

Advances the cause of writing as a profession, to achieve better remuneration and more favourable conditions for writers. Provides a means for expressing the collective opinion of writers on matters affecting the profession. Negotiates on behalf of writers with national bodies, hosts events to advance writers' careers and publishes a monthly newsletter, *Final Draft*. Founded 1986.

Literature Alliance Scotland

email admin@literaturealliancescotland.co.uk
website https://literaturealliancescotland.co.uk/membership/
X @LitScotland

Scotland's largest literary network, LAS is a collective voice dedicated to advancing the interests of Scotland's literature and languages locally, nationally and internationally. Brings together a network of writers, publishers, educators, librarians, literature organisations and national cultural bodies.

National Book Critics Circle

email membership@bookcritics.org
website www.bookcritics.org
Facebook www.facebook.com/nationalbookcriticscircle
Bluesky @bookcritics.bsky.social
Instagram @bookcritics
Membership $15 p.a. student; $50 p.a. freelance critic; from $70 p.a. staff critic

Advocates for reading, criticism and literature, bringing together reviewers, authors, bloggers and publishing professionals. Through their website and newsletter they share news, features and criticism; host free public events; and administer a programme of awards annually. Members receive access to book reviewing advice, information on publications that accept freelance pitches for reviews and a variety of discounts on literary magazines. Founded 1974.

New Zealand Writers Guild

525 Rosebank Road, Avondale, Auckland 1026
tel +64 (0)9 360 1408
email guildhq@nzwg.org.nz
website www.nzwg.org.nz

Represents the interests of New Zealand writers (TV, film, radio and theatre); establishes and improves minimum conditions of work and rates of compensation for writers; and provides professional services for members. Founded 1975.

The Personal Managers' Association Ltd

email info@thepma.com
website www.thepma.com

Professional body for talent agencies in the UK. Membership comprises agencies who represent artists, writers, directors and creatives, working in screen, theatre and radio. Founded 1950.

Professional Publishers Association

Chancery House, 53–64 Chancery Lane, London WC2A 1QS
tel 020-7404 4166
email info@ppa.co.uk
website www.ppa.co.uk
X @PPA_Live

The PPA represents, champions and supports trusted editorial brands and specialist media businesses. Members range from large multinational companies to smaller independent publishers and from consumer magazine media to B2B news, data and information providers. Founded 1913.

Publishers Association (PA)

1st Floor, 50 Southwark Street, London SE1 1UN
email mail@publishers.org.uk
website www.publishers.org.uk
X @PublishersAssoc
Instagram @publishersassoc
President Mandy Hill, *Ceo* Dan Conway

A member organisation for UK publishing, representing companies of all sizes and specialisms. Members produce digital and print books, research journals and educational resources across genres and subjects. Exists to champion publishing to the wider world and has helped change laws, improve business conditions and inspire people to become publishers. Founded 1896.

Publishers Association of New Zealand (Te Rau o Tākupu)

Level 6, 19–21 Como Street, Takapuna, Auckland 0622, New Zealand
tel +64 (0)9 242 3820
email admin@publishers.org.nz
website www.publishers.org.nz
X @Publishers_NZ

PANZ represents book, educational and digital publishers in New Zealand. Members include the largest international publishers and companies in the independent publishing community.

Publishers' Association of South Africa

House Cloete, Wynberg Mews Brodie Road, Wynberg 7800, South Africa
tel +27 (0)21 762 9083
email pasa@publishsa.co.za
website www.publishsa.co.za
Facebook www.facebook.com/publishsa
Executive Director Mpuka Radinku

PASA is the largest publishing industry body in South Africa and is committed to creativity, literacy and encouraging a culture of reading. Promotes and protects the rights and responsibilities of the publishing sector in South Africa.

Publishers' Publicity Circle

email publisherspublicitycircle@gmail.com
website www.publisherspublicitycircle.co.uk
X @publicitycircle
Secretary/Treasurer Liz Scott

Enables all book publicists to meet and share information regularly. Monthly meetings provide a forum for press journalists, TV and radio researchers and producers to meet publicists collectively. Awards are presented for the best PR campaigns. Monthly newsletter includes recruitment advertising.

Publishing Ireland/Foilsiú Éireann

63 Patrick Street, Dun Laoghaire, Dublin A96 WF25, Republic of Ireland
email info@publishingireland.com
website www.publishingireland.com
Facebook www.facebook.com/PublishingIreland
X @PublishingIRL
Instagram @publishing_ireland
General Manager Orla McLoughlin

Enables publishers to share expertise and resources in order to benefit from opportunities and solve problems that are of common concern to all. Comprises most of the major publishing houses in Ireland, including trade, general and academic. Founded 1970.

Publishing Scotland

Scott House, 10 South St Andrew Street, Edinburgh EH2 2AZ
tel 0131 228 6866
email enquiries@publishingscotland.org
website www.publishingscotland.org
Facebook www.facebook.com/publishingscotland
X @PublishScotland
Bluesky @publishingscotland.bsky.social

A network for trade, training and development in the Scottish publishing industry. Runs events throughout the year, including workshops and courses, spotlights opportunities and supports the Scottish publishing industry. Founded 1974.

Scottish BPOC Writers Network (SBWN)

email scottishbpocwriters@gmail.com
website https://scottishbpocwritersnetwork.org/
Facebook www.facebook.com/groups/ScottishBPOCWriters/
Bluesky @scotbpocwriters.bsky.social
Instagram @scotbpocwriters
Threads @scotbpocwriters

SBWN is an advocacy and profession development group for Black and POC writers and literary professionals who are Scottish, based in Scotland or with strong connections to Scotland. Inclusive programming includes workshops, masterclasses, seminars and industry panels; curatorial roles; feedback and mentoring; and partnerships with literary and arts organisations.

Society of Artists Agents

website https://saahub.com
X @SaaAgents

Formed to promote professionalism in the illustration industry and to forge closer links between clients and artists through proper terms and conditions that protect the interests of both. Actively campaigns to protect copyright and intellectual property. Founded 1992.

Society of Authors

– see page 746

Society of Young Publishers

The Publishers Association, 1st Floor, 50 Southwark Street, London SE1 1UN
email sypchair@thesyp.org.uk
website www.thesyp.org.uk
X @SYP_UK, @SYPIreland, @SYP_LDN, @SYPNorth, @SYP_Oxford, @SYPScotland, @SYP_SouthWest, @SYP_Wales
Instagram @syp_uk, @syp_london, @syp.north, @oxford_syp, @sypscotland, @syp_southwest, @syp_wales
Membership £30 p.a. employed standard; £24 p.a. student/unemployed; £18 p.a. digital membership

Supports those of any age looking to get into publishing, or those within the first ten years of a career who are looking to get ahead. It is made up of seven regional committees (Ireland, Scotland, Wales, North, South West, London and Oxford), and a UK team responsible for the organisation's oversight. Runs a mentorship scheme for current and aspiring publishers based in the UK and Ireland. Two conferences are held each year, as well as numerous in-person and digital events; also shares a range of digital content and a quarterly magazine for members. Hosts the First Chapter Award alongside *The Publishing Post*. Founded 1949.

Theatre Writers' Union – see page 750

Trans Publishing Network

email thetranspublishingnetwork@gmail.com
Instagram @transpublishingnetwork
Founder Harry Nicholas

Created to provide a space for transgender and non-binary publishing professionals to collaborate and support each another, advocate for better representation across the publishing industry (from writers and editors to policy and decision-makers) and champion books by transgender and non-binary authors. Founded 2023.

Writers Guild of America, East

250 Hudson Street, Suite 700, New York, NY 10013, USA
tel +1 212-767-7800
website www.wgaeast.org
Facebook www.facebook.com/WGAEast
X @WGAEast
Instagram @wgaeast

WGAE represents writers in screen, TV and new media for collective bargaining. Provides member services including pension and health, as well as educational and professional activities. Runs regular events and administers annual awards. Founded 1954.

Writers Guild of America, West

7000 West 3rd Street, Los Angeles, CA 90048, USA
tel +1 323-951-4000
website www.wga.org
Facebook www.facebook.com/WGAWest
X @wgawest
Instagram @wgawest

WGAW represents and services writers in film, broadcast, cable and multimedia industries for the purposes of collective bargaining, contract administration and other services. Protects and advances the economic, professional and creative interests of writers through involvement with other writer organisations and engagement with public policy and legislation. Founded 1933.

Writers Guild of Canada

366 Adelaide Street West, Suite 401, Toronto, ON M5V 1R9, Canada
tel +1 416-979-7907
email info@wgc.ca
website www.wgc.ca
Facebook www.facebook.com/writers.guild.12
X @WGCtweet
Instagram @writers_guild_of_canada

Represents more than 2,500 professional screenwriters. Raises the profile of screenwriters, negotiates and administers collective agreements with independent producers and broadcasters, and hosts live events and awards.

WGGB (Writers' Guild of Great Britain) – see page 749

Writers Guild of Ireland

Art House, Curved Street, Temple Bar, Dublin 2, Republic of Ireland
tel +353 (0)1 670 9970
email info@script.ie
website https://script.ie/
Ceo Sharon McGarry, *Chairperson* Jennifer Davidson

Represents writers' interests in theatre, radio and screen. Founded 1969.

The Writers' Union of Canada

600–460 Richmond Street West, Suite 600, Toronto, ON M5V 1Y1, Canada
tel +1 416-703-8982
email info@writersunion.ca
website www.writersunion.ca

National organisation of professionally published writers. Founded 1973.

TRANSLATION

American Literary Translators Association

email info@literarytranslators.org
website www.literarytranslators.org
Interim Executive Director Sean Gasper Bye

ALTA is a broad-based professional association dedicated to the promotion of literary translation through services to literary translators, forums on the theory and practice of translation, and collaboration with the international literary community. Hosts an annual conference, offers fellowships and mentorship for emerging translators and bestows six translation awards. Founded 1978.

British Centre for Literary Translation

School of Literature, Drama and Creative Writing, University of East Anglia, Norwich Research Park, Norwich NR4 7TJ
tel (01603) 592785
email bclt@uea.ac.uk
website www.bclt.org.uk
Facebook www.facebook.com/bcltuea
X @bcltuea

A research centre within the School of Literature at the University of East Anglia in Norwich. Supports an MA in Literary Translation at the University of East Anglia and an extensive programme of PhD research. BCLT works in close partnership with the National Centre for Writing and a wide range of other national and international organisations to deliver a programme of activities that support the professional development and recognition of literary translation. These include the annual Sebald Lecture, held at the British Library in London, and the International Literary Translation and Creative Writing Summer School. Founded 1989.

Chartered Institute of Linguists

Star House, Star Hill, Rochester, Kent ME1 1UX
tel 020-7940 3100
website www.ciol.org.uk
Facebook www.facebook.com/charteredinstituteoflinguists
X @CIOL_Linguists
Bluesky @ciol-linguists.bsky.social
Instagram @ciolinguists
Threads @ciolinguists

CIOL is the foremost international membership organisation for all language professionals and is the only one offering a pathway to Chartership. Its diverse membership includes translators and interpreters, language teachers, university lecturers and linguists who use their foreign language skills in business, professions and government.

CIOL's associated charity, CIOL Qualifications, is an Ofqual-accredited awarding body offering professional qualifications in translation and public service interpreting. CIOL publishes a quarterly magazine, *The Linguist*, free to members and available to all online. Founded 1910.

The Institute of Translation and Interpreting

Milton Keynes Business Centre, Foxhunter Drive, Linford Wood, Milton Keynes MK14 6GD
tel (01908) 325250
email info@iti.org.uk
website www.iti.org.uk
Instagram @iti.uk
Membership From £99 p.a. professional; £49 p.a. student

The ITI is the independent professional association of practising translators and interpreters, with over 3,000 members based in the UK and internationally. Promotes the highest standards in the profession and serves as a focal point for all those who understand the importance of translating and interpreting to the economy and community. Provides guidance to those entering the profession and advice to both people offering their language services and their potential customers. Founded 1986.

Translators Association

24 Bedford Row, London WC1R 4EH
tel 020-3880 2230
email info@societyofauthors.org
website https://societyofauthors.org/groups/translators-association/

Specialist group within the Society of Authors (see page 746). Advocates for the rights and interests of emerging and established literary translators in all genres. Offers unlimited contract vetting and industry advice to members, co-programmes the Literary Translation Centre at the London Book Fair and actively engages with the sector through campaigns, events and resources.

WRITERS' ORGANISATIONS

All Party Parliamentary Writers Group

tel 020-7264 5700
email allpartywritersgroup@alcs.co.uk
website www.allpartywritersgroup.co.uk

Has Members from both the House of Commons and House of Lords. Seeks to represent the interests of all writers; to safeguard their intellectual property rights; and ensure they receive a fair level of recognition and remuneration for their contribution to the economy and society as a whole.
Founded 2007.

Association of British Science Writers

email info@absw.org.uk
website www.absw.org.uk
Facebook www.facebook.com/BritishScienceWriters
X @absw
Bluesky @absw.bsky.social
Chair Andy Extance, *Honorary President* Roger Highfield

A membership organisation for media professionals who cover science, medicine, environment, mathematics, engineering and technology. Champions independence and excellence in the reporting of science, medicine, engineering and technology. Trains and supports journalists and writers at all stages of their careers through conferences, summer schools and awards, in addition to a range of networking, training and debating events. Membership details/application through website only. Founded 1947.

Association of Christian Writers

email admin@christianwriters.co.uk
website www.christianwriters.co.uk
Facebook www.facebook.com/groups/24831838019
Membership £32 p.a.

ACW inspires excellence in writing from a Christian perspective, across every genre. Equips Christian writers through face-to-face and online conferences and workshops and a programme of writing competitions. Members encourage each other online and in affiliated local groups. Publishes a daily blog, *More Than Writers*, and a magazine, *Christian Writer*. Please note that ACW is not a publisher.
Founded 1971.

Authors Aloud UK

72 Castle Road, St Albans, Herts. AL1 5DG
tel (01727) 893992
email info@authorsalouduk.co.uk
website www.authorsalouduk.co.uk
Facebook www.facebook.com/Authors-Aloud-UK-497942623573822
X @AuthorsAloudUK
Instagram @authorsalouduk
Directors Naomi Cooper, Annie Everall

An author booking agency that brings together authors, illustrators, poets, storytellers and trainers with schools, libraries and festivals, in the UK and internationally, to promote enthusiasm for reading. Works with children's authors who wish to visit schools and libraries, in person and virtually, and who are published by mainstream children's publishers. Also arranges author tours and book-related events for publishers and other organisations.

Authors in Oundle

email info@authorsinoundle.co.uk
website www.authorsinoundle.co.uk
Facebook www.facebook.com/authorsinoundle
X @authorsinoundle
Instagram @authorsinoundle
Threads @authorsinoundle

Hosts year-round events in the historic town of Oundle and the surrounding villages. Fiction and non-fiction events feature novelists, poets, biographers and historians. Supports newly published books and both local and international authors, with the goal of fostering a respect for literature within the community. Founded 2024.

Black Writers' Guild

email hello@theblackwritersguild.com
website www.theblackwritersguild.com

Established to address the under-representation of Black writers and publishers within Britain's publishing industry, and the inequalities they experience. Alongside increasing representation, the Guild promotes fairness and equality within workplace cultures and equitable pay. Holds an annual conference. Founded 2020.

Book Aid International

39–41 Coldharbour Lane, London SE5 9NR
tel 020-7733 3577
email info@bookaid.org
website www.bookaid.org
X @Book_Aid

Book Aid International is a UK registered charity that promotes the power of books to help create a more equal world. Every year it provides over one-million carefully selected books to thousands of communities who have limited opportunities to read, and works with partners to support and establish libraries and reading spaces.

BookTrust Represents

BookTrust HQ: 1 Aire Street, Leeds LS1 4PR
London Office: 29 Clerkenwell Road, Farringdon, London EC1M 5RN
tel 020-7801 8826
email booktrust.represents@booktrust.org.uk
website www.booktrust.org.uk/booktrustrepresents
X @Booktrust

A project to support and promote authors and illustrators of colour and to reach more readers through school visits, special events and festivals. Also supports aspiring and new authors and illustrators of colour with training, mentoring, events and an online community. Find out more about the project and the associated research on the website. Founded 2019.

The British Fantasy Society

email secretary@britishfantasysociety.org
website www.britishfantasysociety.org
Facebook www.facebook.com/britishfantasysociety
Bluesky @britfantasysoc.bsky.social
Instagram @britishfantasysociety
Membership Concessions: £20 p.a.; Digital: £20 p.a.; Print: £35 p.a. single, £40 p.a. joint (UK); £45 p.a. single, £50 p.a joint (Europe); £60 p.a. single, £65 p.a. joint (R.O.W)

For readers, writers and publishers of fantasy, horror and related fields, in literature, art and cinema. Hosts an annual convention, FantasyCon, and sponsors the British Fantasy Awards. Publishes the *BFS Journal* and *BFS Horizons*. Founded 1971.

British Guild of Beer Writers

46 West Grange Green, Leeds LS10 3BB
email secretary@beerguild.co.uk
website www.beerguild.co.uk
Facebook www.facebook.com/BritBeerWriters/
X @Britbeerwriters
Bluesky @britbeerwriters.bsky.social
Instagram @britbeerwriters
Threads @britbeerwriters
Secretary Mike Hampshire
Membership £55 p.a.

Aims to improve standards in beer, cider and pub writing. Awards are given annually to writers, broadcasters and other communicators. Publishes an online directory of members with details of their publications and their particular areas of interest. Founded 1988.

The British Guild of Travel Writers

Larking Gowen, 1 Clayton Business Park, Great Blakenham, Ipswich IP6 0NL
tel 020-8144 8713
email hello@bgtw.org
website www.bgtw.org
Facebook www.facebook.com/TravWriters
X @TravWriters
Instagram @travwriters

Arranges meetings, discussions and visits for its members (who are all professional travel journalists) to promote and encourage the public's interest in travel. Annual awards for journalism (members only) and the travel trade. Founded 1960.

The British Haiku Society

16 Croft Gardens, Andover, Hampshire SP10 2RH
email britishhaiku@gmail.com
website www.britishhaikusociety.org.uk
Facebook www.facebook.com/thebritishhaikusociety
Instagram @britishhaikusociety
President Iliyana Stoyanova, *General Secretary & Treasurer* Paul Hickey, *Membership Secretary* Julie Williamson, *Editor, Blithe Spirit* Iliyana Stoyanova, *Editor, the brief* Maya Daneva, *Communications Officer* Jenny Shepherd

Pioneers the appreciation and writing of haiku and kindred forms of verse in the UK. Currently there are around 400 BHS members from 27 countries.

Members receive a quarterly journal, *Blithe Spirit*, an annual members' anthology and a newsletter. Runs the annual British Haiku Society Awards in three categories: haiku, tanka and haibun; publishes books concerning haiku and related matters; and is active in promoting the teaching of haiku in schools and colleges. Founded 1990.

British Science Fiction Association Ltd

19 Beech Green, Dunstable, Bedfordshire LU6 1EB
email membership@bsfa.co.uk
website www.bsfa.co.uk
Facebook www.facebook.com/groups/BritishScienceFictionAssociation
X @BSFA
Instagram @bsfa_vector
Membership £31 p.a. standard; £20 p.a. concession; £33 p.a. joint; £20 p.a. digital

A membership organisation for authors, publishers, booksellers and readers of sci-fi, fantasy and allied genres. Currently publishes *The BSFA Review*, a free digital magazine reviewing recent sci-fi and fantasy releases across all media, and *Fission*, an annual short story anthology. Runs regular events with authors that are free and open to the public.

Exclusively for members, BSFA publishes *Focus*, aimed at writers of all levels, as well as *Vector*, a critical journal featuring interviews, essays, reviews and other features, including peer-reviewed academic articles.

Has historically had strong ties with Eastercon, the UK's largest annual sci-fi convention; Eastercon is home to the annual BSFA Awards. Founded 1958.

Circle of Wine Writers

tel (01753) 882320
email administrator@circleofwinewriters.org
website www.circleofwinewriters.org
Facebook www.facebook.com/CircleofWineWriters
X @CircleofWine
Instagram @circleofwine

An association for those engaged in communicating about wines and spirits. Produces *The Circular* (monthly online newsletter) and organises tasting sessions as well as a programme of meetings, talks and trips. Founded 1960.

Crime Writers' Association

email secretary@thecwa.co.uk
website www.thecwa.co.uk
Facebook www.facebook.com/CrimeWritersAssociation
X @The_CWA
Bluesky @thecwa.bsky.social
Instagram @crimewritersassoc
Threads @crimewritersassoc
Secretary Vickie Goldie

The CWA represents writers of all kinds of crime fiction and non-fiction and at all stages of their careers. Membership is open to both traditionally published and self-published writers who can prove their professionalism, from anywhere in the world, plus anyone whose business is closely connected with crime writing. Membership benefits include book promotional platforms, monthly members' magazine *Red Herrings*, local chapters for social events, an annual conference and a free tax helpline from H.W. Fisher. Also runs the Dagger Awards. Founded 1953.

The Critics' Circle

email criticscircleallsections@gmail.com
website https://criticscircle.org.uk
President Corinne Julius, *Honorary General Secretary* Rick Jones

Established to promote the art of criticism, uphold its integrity, foster and safeguard the professional interests of its members, provide opportunities for socialising and networking, and support the advancement of the arts. Membership is by invitation only and granted only to persons engaged regularly and substantially in the writing or broadcasting of criticism of dance, drama, film, literature, music and the visual arts. Founded 1913.

dif

email difwriters@gmail.com
website www.bedif.org
Bluesky @difwriters.bsky.social
Instagram @difwriters
Threads @difwriters

An LGBTQ+ focused network of writers and artists who produce work that exists outside the mainstream. Offers opportunities including networking and residencies. Based in Bristol but operating across the UK and internationally. Founded 2024.

ESEA (East Asian and Southeast Asian) Publishing Network

email eseapublishingnetwork@gmail.com
X @eseapn
Instagram @eseapn

Brings together writers and publishing professionals from East and Southeast Asian backgrounds to support each other, collaborate and increase visibility and opportunities for the community within publishing. Members include writers, editors, agents, journalists and publishers across editorial, marketing, sales, design and production. Runs the ESEA Literary Festival. Founded 2022.

The Garden Media Guild

Katepwa House, Ashfield Park Avenue, Ross-on-Wye, Herefordshire HR9 5AX
tel (01989) 567393
email admin@gardenmediaguild.co.uk
website www.gardenmediaguild.co.uk
Facebook www.facebook.com/gdnmediaguild

X @GdnMediaGuild
Vice President Mike Howes
Membership £85 p.a.; associate membership £125 p.a.; probationary membership £63.75 p.a.

Raises the quality of garden writing, photography and broadcasting, helps members operate efficiently and profitably, improves communication between members and promotes liaison between members and the broader horticultural industry. Administers annual awards to encourage excellence in garden writing, photography, trade and consumer press journalism, TV and radio broadcasting, online media and blogging. Founded 1991.

Guild of Food Writers

email admin@gfw.co.uk
website www.gfw.co.uk
Facebook www.facebook.com/TheGFW
X @GuildFoodWriter
Instagram @thegfw
President Ruth Watson
Membership £92 p.a.

Brings together professional food writers including journalists, broadcasters and authors to compile a comprehensive and detailed directory of members. Extends the range of members' knowledge and experience by arranging discussions, tastings and visits, and encourages the development of new writers through competitions, awards, bursaries and mentorship. Awards entry is not restricted to members. Founded 1984.

Guild of Health Writers

Dale Lodge, 88 Wensleydale Road, Hampton, Middlesex TW12 2LX
tel 020-8941 2977
email admin@healthwriters.com
website www.healthwriters.com
X @HealthWritersUK
Membership £50 p.a.

A national, independent membership organisation representing Britain's leading health journalists and writers. Founded to encourage the provision of readable and accurate health information to the public. Members write on every aspect of health and wellbeing, from innovative medical science to complementary therapies and lifestyle issues. Provides training and networking opportunities. Founded 1994.

The Guild of Motoring Writers

Argyll House, 1 River Road, Littlehampton, West Sussex BN17 5BN
tel (01903) 386423
email generalsec@gomw.co.uk
website www.gomw.co.uk
Facebook www.facebook.com/gomwuk
X @gomw_uk
General Secretary Melissa Chadderton

The largest organisation of its kind in the world representing automotive journalists, photographers, broadcasters and artists. Based in the UK, it represents more than 500 members. Raises the standard of motoring journalism, encourages motoring, motorsport and road safety, and promotes professional training of journalists. Works closely with the motor industry and provides a link between fellow members around the world. Safeguards the interests of members in relation to the aims of the Guild. Founded 1944.

Hakluyt Society

The Map Library, The British Library, 96 Euston Road, London NW1 2DB
tel 07568 468066
email office@hakluyt.com
website www.hakluyt.com
Facebook www.facebook.com/HakluytSociety/
X @HakluytSociety
Membership £75 p.a. full; £37.50 p.a. student

Publishes original narratives of voyages, travels, naval expeditions and other geographical records. Hosts conferences and events, and administers awards. Founded 1846.

Harleian Society

College of Arms, 130 Queen Victoria Street, London EC4V 4BT
tel 020-7248 2762
email info@harleian.org.uk
website https://harleian.org.uk
Chairman Sir Thomas Woodcock KCVO DL FSA, *Honorary Secretary* Dominic C.D. Ingram, CHESTER HERALD OF ARMS

Institute for transcribing, printing and publishing the heraldic visitations of Counties, Parish Registers and any manuscripts relating to genealogy, family history and heraldry. Founded 1869.

Historical Novel Society

website https://historicalnovelsociety.org/
Facebook www.facebook.com/historicalnovelsociety
X @histnovsoc
Chairman Richard Lee
Membership £50 p.a.

Promotes the enjoyment of historical fiction. Based in the US and UK but welcomes members (who can be readers or writers) from all over the world. Publishes magazines, organises conferences and runs local chapters. Founded 1997.

Historical Writers' Association

email admin@historicalwriters.org
website https://historicalwriters.org
Facebook www.facebook.com/HistoriaHWA
X @HistoriaHWA
Membership £65 p.a. full, £40 p.a. associate (UK); £50 p.a. (overseas)

Association created by authors, publishers and agents of historical writing, both fiction and non-fiction. Creates opportunities online and in person for members to meet with fellow writers and enthusiasts of all things historical. Organises a range of regional events, publishes an online magazine and runs writing awards.

Horror Writers Association

PO Box 14387, Columbus, OH 43214, USA
email admin@horror.org
website https://horror.org
Facebook www.facebook.com/groups/Horrorwritersassoc
X @HorrorWriters
President Angela Yuriko Smith
Membership From $59 p.a.

The HWA is a worldwide organisation of writers and publishing professionals dedicated to promoting the interests of horror and dark fantasy writers. There are various levels of membership including writers, editors and academics. The HWA administers the annual Bram Stoker Awards, hosts horror conventions, and provides a range of services to its horror writer, editor and publisher membership base. Founded 1987.

I Am in Print

Kingfisher House, Rownhams, North Baddesley, Southampton SO52 9LP
email agent121@iaminprint.co.uk
website www.iaminprint.co.uk
Facebook www.facebook.com/iaminprint
X @IAminPrint
Instagram @iaminprint
Co-founders Elane Retford and Sarah Snook

Creates opportunities to support writers on their publishing journey. Writers can improve their pitch (cover letter, synopsis and opening chapters) through the online Agent121 feedback service, where writers meet literary agents and publishers for advice. Also runs the annual I Am Writing competitions. Founded 2018.

International Thriller Writers

PO Box 1402, Medina, OH 44258, USA
email KimberleyHowe@thrillerwriters.org
website https://thrillerwriters.org/
Facebook www.facebook.com/ThrillerWritersOrganization
X @thrillerwriters
Instagram @internationalthrillerwriters
Executive Director Kimberley Howe

An honorary society of authors who write thrillers, which covers subjects such as murder mystery, detective, suspense, horror, supernatural, action, espionage, true crime, war and adventure. Facilitates events and programmes that allow successful authors to help debut authors develop their careers; promotes literacy; supports libraries and other organisations; and furthers the interests of the genre. Hosts an annual conference, ThrillerFest.

The Munster Literature Centre

Frank O'Connor House, 84 Douglas Street, Cork T12 X70A, Republic of Ireland
email info@munsterlit.ie
website www.munsterlit.ie
Facebook www.facebook.com/munsterliteraturecentre
X @MunLitCentre

Promotes and celebrates literature and writers, especially within Munster. As well as organising The Cork International Poetry Festival and The Cork International Short Story Festival each year, the centre runs workshops, readings and competitions to support new and established writers. Founded 1993.

The Mythopoeic Society

PO Box 6707, Altadena, CA 91003–6707, USA
website www.mythsoc.org
Facebook www.facebook.com/MythSoc/
X @mythsoc

A non-profit international literary and educational organisation for the study, discussion and enjoyment of fantastic and mythic literature, especially the works of Tolkien, C.S. Lewis and Charles Williams. 'Mythopoeic' (myth-oh-PAY-ik or myth-oh-PEE-ik) means 'mythmaking' or 'productive of myth'. Membership is open to all scholars, writers and readers of these literatures. Sponsors three periodicals: *Mythprint* (a bulletin of book reviews, articles and events), *Mythlore* (scholarly articles on mythic and fantastic literature) and *Mythic Circle* (a literary annual of original poetry and short stories). Each summer the society holds an annual conference, Mythcon. Founded 1967.

National Association of Writers and Groups

Old Vicarage, Scammonden, Huddersfield HD3 3FT
email chairman@nawg.co.uk
website www.nawg.co.uk
Facebook www.facebook.com/NAWGNews
Chairman Chris Huck
Membership £50 p.a. group, £25 p.a. individual (UK); £56 p.a. group, £32 p.a. individual (EU); £62 p.a. group, £39 p.a. individual (R.O.W)

Advances the education of the general public throughout the UK, including the Channel Islands, by promoting the study and art of writing in all its aspects. Publishes *LINK*, a bi-monthly magazine; holds annual festivals and events; and runs competitions with cash prizes (some open to all). Founded 1995.

National Centre for Writing

Dragon Hall, 115–123 King Street, Norwich NR1 1QE

email info@nationalcentreforwriting.org.uk
website https://nationalcentreforwriting.org.uk
Facebook www.facebook.com/NationalCentreforWriting
X @WritersCentre
Bluesky @WritersCentre.bsky.social
Instagram @writerscentre

Celebrates and explores the artistic and social power of creative writing and literary translation. An ongoing programme of innovative collaborations engages writers, literary translators and readers in projects that support new voices and stories and respond to the rapidly changing world of writing. Workshops and mentoring available for writers at all levels, both face-to-face and online. Projects range from the Emerging Translator Mentorships to festivals such as the City of Literature strand of Norfolk & Norwich Festival. Founded 2018.

New Writing North

New Writing North, 120 Squires Building, Northumbria University, Sandyford Road, Newcastle upon Tyne NE1 8ST
tel 0191 204 8850
email office@newwritingnorth.com
website https://newwritingnorth.com
Facebook www.facebook.com/newwritingnorth
X @NewWritingNorth
Instagram @nwnnewwritingnorth

Supports writing and reading in the North of England. Commissions new work, creates development opportunities and nurtures talent. Founded 1996.

New Writing South

email hello@newwritingsouth.com
website www.newwritingsouth.com
Facebook www.facebook.com/newwritingsouth
Instagram @newwritingsouth

NWS champions all kinds of new creative writing in the South East and beyond. Develops writers' careers and helps fresh talent to flourish by providing development opportunities and commissioning new work. Committed to nurturing an inclusive community of writers, regardless of background or previous experience.

Norwich Writers' Circle

email membership@norwichwriters.com
website https://norwichwriters.wordpress.com
Facebook www.facebook.com/CircleWritersNorwich
X @norwichwriters
Instagram @norwichwriters
Membership Secretary Kathy Joy
Membership £39 p.a. full; £20 p.a online

A members group for writers based in Norwich. Holds bi-monthly meetings, online workshops and a year-round programme of competitions and awards. Meetings feature guest speakers and the opportunity to share and critique writing projects. Founded 1943.

Nothing in the Rulebook

email nothingintherulebook@gmail.com
website www.nothingintherulebook.com
Facebook www.facebook.com/nitrb/
X @NITRB_Tweets

A collective of creative writers dedicated to creative expression and celebrating and supporting artists. Contributors include both new and aspiring artists alongside established and award-winning voices. Publishes new writing (non-fiction, fiction and poetry), as well as feature pieces, reviews and interviews with artists and writers. Also seeks to bring people together through collective projects and events. Founded 2015.

PEN International

167–169 Great Portland Street, London W1W 5PF
email info@pen-international.org
website https://pen-international.org
Facebook www.facebook.com/peninternational/
X @pen_int
Instagram @peninternational

A world association of writers. Founded to promote friendship and understanding between writers and to defend freedom of expression within and between all nations. The initials PEN stand for Poets, Playwrights, Editors, Essayists, Novelists – but membership is open to all writers of standing (including translators). Founded 1921.

English PEN Centre

24 Bedford Row, London WC1R 4EH
tel 020-7046 7046
email enquiries@englishpen.org
website https://englishpen.org

Scottish PEN Centre

The Writers' Museum, Lady Stair's Close, Lawnmarket, Edinburgh EH1 2PA
tel 0131 226 5590
email info@scottishpen.org
website https://scottishpen.org

Irish PEN Centre

Irish Writer's Centre, 19 Parnell Square, Rotunda, Dublin 1, D01 E102
email irishpen20@gmail.com
website https://irishpen.com

Pen to Print

tel 020-8227 2267
email pentoprint@lbbd.gov.uk
website https://pentoprint.org
Facebook www.facebook.com/OfficialPentoPrint
X @Pen_to_Print
Instagram @officialpentoprint

An Arts Council funded library organisation providing a safe, collaborative environment to develop storytellers' authentic voices. Aspiring writers, especially those from backgrounds that are under-represented in publishing, are encouraged to reach communities with their stories and inspire potential in others. Runs writing classes and workshops; competitions including The Book Challenge; author talks; and ReadFest literary festival. Publishes *Write On!* magazine (print), *Write On! Extra* magazine (online) and *Write On! Audio* podcast.

The Poetry Book Society – see page 349

The Poetry Society – see page 349

The Romantic Novelists' Association

email info@romanticwriters.co.uk
website https://romanticnovelistsassociation.org
Facebook www.facebook.com/Romantic.Novelists.Association
X @RNAtweets
Instagram @romanticnovelists
Membership £70 p.a. full; £210 p.a. New Writers' Scheme

Promotes romantic fiction and encourages good writing within the genre. Inclusive of all forms of romantic fiction and welcomes authors from all backgrounds. Represents around 1,000 writers, agents, editors and other publishing professionals.

Unpublished writers are able to join through the New Writers' Scheme which includes full membership and the opportunity to submit one book-length MSS for critique each year. Any MSS which is subsequently published is eligible for the Joan Hessayon Award. Founded 1960.

Scattered Authors' Society

email scatteredauthorssociety@gmail.com
website www.scatteredauthors.org

Provides a forum for informal discussion, contact and support for professional writers in children's fiction. Founded 1998.

Scottish Association of Writers

27 Windsor Avenue, Newton Mearns, East Renfrewshire, Glasgow G77 5NX
email secretary@scottishassociationofwriters.com
website www.scottishassociationofwriters.com
Facebook www.facebook.com/groups/Sawriters
Secretary Anjina Sen

Promotes writing in Scotland. Runs its own writing groups and competitions, and organises outreach visits to writing clubs to promote good practice, offer workshops and advise on the current writing market. Hosts an annual conference attended by writers who are members of affiliated clubs. Founded 1969.

Scottish Fellowship of Christian Writers

website www.sfcw.info
Facebook www.facebook.com/Scottish-Fellowship-of-Christian-Writers-393556520670479
Membership £12 p.a.

To inspire, encourage and support Christians living in Scotland to make use of their creative writing talents. Publishes members' writing and a regular e-newsletter, and runs day conferences in May and November each year. Over 100 members. Founded 1980.

Sherborne Literary Society

email info@sherborneliterarysociety.com
website www.sherborneliterarysociety.com
Facebook www.facebook.com/SherborneLiterarySociety
Instagram @sherbornetravelwritingfestival
Membership £10 p.a.

Open to anyone who is interested in literature. Runs a year-round programme of events, as well as the Sherborne Prize for Travel Writing and Sherborne Travel Writing Festival. Members reviews of books are published on the website and in the *Sherborne Times*. Founded 2012.

SCBWI (Society of Children's Book Writers and Illustrators)

email britishisles-ra@scbwi.org
website www.scbwi.org/regions/british-isles
Facebook www.facebook.com/groups/122794234418913
X @SCBWI_bi
Bluesky @scbwi.bsky.social
Instagram @scbwi_british_isles
Threads @scbwi_british_isles
Co-Regional Advisers Natascha Biebow, Alison Gardiner

A global community of writers, illustrators, translators, publishers, librarians and advocates who support the creation of quality books for children and young adults. Provides resources, professional networking, and community-building opportunities that support writers, illustrators and translators throughout their careers, including marketing and publicity training, and writing and illustrating masterclasses. Also hosts in-person and online professional development events, retreats and conferences; administers prizes and grants; and publishes a bi-weekly blog, *Words & Pictures*, a monthly member newsletter, *Insight*, and a quarterly newsletter for published creators, *Pro Insider*. Founded 1971.

The Society of Civil and Public Service Writers

tel 020-8656 3891
email ecorduff@hotmail.com
website www.scpsw.org
Chair Ethel Corduff

Welcomes serving and retired members of the civil service, armed forces, police, local government, NHS and other public servants. Members can be aspiring or published writers. Holds meetings, workshops and monthly competitions for short stories, flash fiction and poetry, mostly with a cash prize. Founded 1935.

The Society of Medical Writers

SoMW, Acre-Rise Cottage, Upper Ludstone, Claverley, Wolverhampton WV5 7DH
email moldywarp@doctors.org.uk
website https://somw.org.uk

Recruits members from all branches of the medical profession, together with all professions allied to medicine, to foster interest in literature and in writing – not solely about medicine but also about art, history, music, theatre, etc. Members are encouraged to write fiction, poetry, plays, book reviews and non-fiction articles. Runs competitions, publishes *The Writer* (two p.a.) and holds annual conferences and workshops. Founded 1989.

Speaking Volumes

email sharmilla.beezmohun@speaking-volumes.org.uk
website https://speaking-volumes.org.uk
Facebook www.facebook.com/SpeakingVolumesLiveLiteratureProductions
Bluesky @speaking-volumes.bsky.social
Instagram @speaking.volumes

A live literature organisation that brings together diverse audiences and under-represented writers. Projects include live events, tours, workshops, festival appearances, readings and talks. Also publishes anthologies and resources, and are a source of information about Britain's diverse literary scene past and present. Founded 2010.

Spread the Word

The Albany, Douglas Way, London SE8 4AG
email hello@spreadtheword.org.uk
website www.spreadtheword.org.uk
Facebook www.facebook.com/spreadthewordwriters
X @STWevents
Bluesky @spread-the-word.bsky.social
Instagram @spreadthewordwriters

London's literature development agency, a charity and a National Portfolio client of Arts Council England. Develops the careers and creative talents of London's under-represented writers. Initiates change-making research and developmental programmes that prioritise equity and access. Partners with people and organisations to diversify storytelling and enrich the UK's literature ecology. Founded by Bernardine Evaristo and Ruth Borthwick.

The TV Foundation

117 Farringdon Road, London EC1R 3BX
email tvfoundation@thetvfestival.com
website www.thetvfestival.com/tv-foundation/new-talent/
Instagram @thetvfoundation

Offers support and access to opportunities for beginners and those looking to develop their career in television. Runs The Network, which provides masterclasses, workshops and networking for entrants to the industry, particularly those who are under-represented, and the New Writers' Collective, which offers free access to events for undiscovered writers. Also runs events throughout the year, including those focused on targeting inequality and climate change. Founded 1976.

Women Poets' Network from the Rebecca Swift Foundation

Rebecca Swift Foundation, 5 St Johns Lane, London EC1M 4BH
email info@rebeccaswiftfoundation.org
website www.rebeccaswiftfoundation.org
X @FoundationSwift

The UK's only charity dedicated to advancing the craft, creativity and wellbeing of women poets. The Network offers access to events, writing opportunities and professional development for women poets at all stages of their careers.

WritersMosaic

3 Johnson's Court, Fleet Street, London EC4A 3EA
tel 020-7353 7150
email contact@writersmosaic.org.uk
website https://writersmosaic.org.uk
Facebook www.facebook.com/writersmosaic
X @writersmosaic
Instagram @writersmosaic

A division of the Royal Literary Fund. A developmental resource and online magazine, celebrating and showcasing UK writers of the global majority to reflect the changing reality of contemporary Britain. Provides a platform for writers through authored talks, podcasts, creative exchanges and interviews. Shares cultural knowledge, critical engagement and in-depth insight into the lives and practices of contemporary writers and the modern literary landcape through images, illustrations and films commissioned by the wider editorial team of RLF writers.

Writing East Midlands

The Garage Studios, Unit 4, 41-43 St Mary's Gate, Notts. NG1 1PU
tel (01157) 934110
email info@writingeastmidlands.co.uk
website https://writingeastmidlands.co.uk
Facebook www.facebook.com/WritingEM
Bluesky @writingeastmidlands.com.bsky.social
Instagram @writingeastmidlands
Threads @writingeastmidlands

Supports writers of all ages, from all communities, at all stages in their careers. Services include writing masterclasses, workshops, mentorship programmes and internship schemes. Facilitates writing projects with communities that face barriers to the publishing industry, including Beyond the Spectrum for Autistic writers. Also runs The Writers' Conference, the Aurora Prize for Writing and *Pulse* magazine for writers.

Writing West Midlands

Studio 130, Zellig, Gibb Street, Birmingham B9 4AT
tel 0121 246 2770
website https://writingwestmidlands.org/
Facebook www.facebook.com/writingwestmidlands/
X @writingwestmidlands
Instagram @writingwestmids

A literature development agency that aims to improve access to creative opportunities for both readers and writers through support, resources and events. The Room 204 development programme provides mentoring, networking, workshops and other opportunities; applications must be submitted via the website. Also runs the Birmingham Literature Festival, the National Writers Conference, Spark Young Writers and the West Midlands Readers' Network. Founded 1999.

Prizes and awards

Prizes are divided into sections by prize category or format – for example, there are lists for 'Art, illustration and photography' prizes and for writing for the 'Children's' market. New writers might be particularly interested in consulting the 'Debut and emerging writers' list on page 580 and prizes for 'Self-published and unagented' authors on page 595.

The Fiction (page 608) and Non-fiction (page 615) lists, are broken-down by genre. There are separate sections for 'Short stories and flash fiction' (page 598) and 'Life writing' (page 583).

Many of the prizes seek entries from specific writers or artists based on, for example, their cultural background, the stage of their career or their country or region of residence. Some of the prizes are free to enter, and many more offer free or subsidised entries for writers on low income.

For a list of prizes that are open for specific groups of writers (based on their age, gender, race or sexuality), please see the Subject indexes that start on page 753.

NEW denotes new prizes for 2025/26.

ART, ILLUSTRATION AND PHOTOGRAPHY

Academy of British Cover Design: Annual Cover Design Competition

Underbelly, 11 Hoxton Square, London N1 6NU
website https://abcoverd.co.uk
X @ABCoverD

Recognises covers produced for any book published between 1 January and 31 December in the preceding year, by any designer in the UK, for a UK or overseas publisher. Designers may enter their own work or the work of other designers. There are ten categories: Children's 0–5, Children's 6–12, YA, Mass Market, Literary Fiction, Crime/Thriller, Sci-Fi/Fantasy, Non-Fiction, Series Design and Classic/Reissue. A cover can only be submitted in one category unless it is entered as an individual cover and again as part of a series design. Voting takes place during the awards ceremony. Founded 2014.

Aesthetica Art Prize

email art-prize@aestheticamagazine.com
website https://aestheticamagazine.com/artprize/
Facebook www.facebook.com/aestheticamagazine
X @AestheticaMag
Instagram @aestheticamag

Administered by *Aesthetica* Magazine. Recognises emerging, mid-career and established artists across a range of disciplines in contemporary art. Work should reflect key themes from our changing world and the role that contemporary art plays in understanding our life and times. Entries can be any of the following: painting, drawing, video, installation, sculpture, performance, photography and film. There are two prize categories: the Main Prize open to all creatives (£10,000) and the Emerging Prize open to students and recent graduates (£1,000). The Prize also includes an exhibition at a public gallery for the shortlisted artists and finalists. Selected longlisted artists are published in a digital profile showcase. Previous winners have exhibited across the UK and around the world. Founded 2007.

British Book Design and Production Awards

email heena.bulsara@bpif.org.uk
website www.britishbookawards.org/
X @BPIF
Instagram @bpifofficial

Recognises beautiful books across 18 categories: Best British Book, Best Student Book, Fine Binding & Limited Edition, Brand/Series Identity, Self-Published Books, Exhibition Catalogues, Photographic Books, Art & Architecture Monographs, Trade Illustrated, Lifestyle Illustrated, Literature, Educational Books, Scholarly, Academic & Reference Books, Children's Trade, Best Jacket/Cover Design, Graphic Novels, Sustainable Books and Book of the Year. Winners are announced at a ceremony each year.

Carnegie Medal for Illustration – see page 575

Cheltenham Illustration Awards

email pittvillepress@gmail.com
website www.cheltenham-illustration-awards.com

The awards are divided into two sections: Student (aged 18 and over), and Emerging and Established Illustrators. Entries must relate to that year's theme. The selected work is showcased in an exhibition and published in the *Cheltenham Illustration Awards Annual*, which is distributed to education institutions and publishers.

Coppercoat Brian Black Memorial Award

email yachtingmonthly@futurenet.com
website www.yachtingmonthly.com/tag/brian-black-memorial-award
Facebook www.facebook.com/yachtingmonthlymag
X @yachtingmonthly

Celebrates the best storytelling on the subject of marine environmental issues explored by boat. There are two categories: written (1,800-word article and accompanying images; 1st prize: £2,000) and photography (one photograph inspired by that year's theme and accompanying text of no more than 300 words; 1st prize: £1,000 and a Canon camera kit). Founded 2020.

Deutsche Börse Photography Foundation Prize

Börsenplatz 4, 60313, Frankfurt, Germany
email foundation@deutsche-boerse.com
email info@tpg.org.uk
website www.deutscheboersephotographyfoundation.org/en/support/photography-prize.php, https://thephotographersgallery.org.uk/

Initiated by the Photographers' Gallery and awarded together with the Deutsche Börse Photography Foundation. Rewards a living photographer, of any nationality, who has made the most significant contribution to the medium of photography in Europe during the previous year (1st prize: £30,000). Photography experts nominate candidates; a jury selects finalists and a winner. Founded 1996.

The Faber/Observer/Comica Graphic Short Story Prize – see page 601

First Graphic Novel Award

The Cartoon Museum, 63 Wells Street, London W1A 3AE
tel 020-7580 8155
email info@firstgraphicnovel.co.uk
website www.firstgraphicnovel.co.uk
X @1stgraphicnovel
Instagram @firstgraphicnovel
Director Corinne Pearlman

Open to individual creators or teams of writers and illustrators who are not represented by an agent and have not previously had a full-length graphic novel published. Entrants should submit a 15–20 page extract of a full-length work-in-progress (at least ten pages must be finished, the rest can be readable roughs); work can be fiction or non-fiction, with or without words, and in black and white or colour. 1st prize: £500 and creative and editorial support to develop work for publication by SelfMadeHero; longlisted authors' work is reviewed and receives feedback. Entry fee: £10 (£5 concessions). Founded 2012.

Folio Book Illustration Award

Clove Building, 4 Maguire Street, London SE1 2NQ
email foliobia@foliosociety.com
website www.foliosociety.com/folio-book-illustration-award
Facebook www.facebook.com/TheFolioSociety
X @foliosociety
Instagram @foliosociety

Open to both emerging and professional illustrators who have not previously been commissioned by the Folio Society. Entrants are asked to submit an illustration inspired by that year's chosen text, accompanied by a quotation (maximum 20 words) indicating which part of the text has been illustrated. 1st prize: £2,000; the overall winner and five runners-up also receive a £500 Folio gift voucher and a portfolio review by the Folio Art Directors. Founded 2022.

Fortnum and Mason Food and Drink Awards – see page 618

The Hugo Awards – see page 614

The Kitschies – see page 614

Kraszna–Krausz Book Awards

email info@kraszna-krausz.org.uk
website www.kraszna-krausz.org.uk
Facebook www.facebook.com/KrasznaKrausz
X @kraszna_krausz

Recognise individuals or groups who have made an outstanding original or lasting contribution to the literature of photography or the moving image. Two winning titles are selected; one in the field of photography and one in the field of the moving image (including film, television and new media). Each winning book receives a £5,000 cash prize. Founded 1985.

The Macmillan Prize for Illustration

Macmillan Children's Books, 6 Briset Street, London EC1M 5NR
email macmillanprize@macmillan.co.uk
website www.panmacmillan.com/mac-prize-entry-page

Seeks picture books from non-professional illustrators in the UK over the age of 18. Submitted books should be between 24–32 pages, the text can be fiction or non-fiction and the artwork must meet the specifications given on the website. 1st prize: £1,000; 2nd prize: £500; 3rd prize: £250. Founded 1985.

RBA Annual Exhibition

email honsec@therba.org
website www.therba.org
Facebook www.facebook.com/RoyalSocietyBritishArtists

X @RoyalSocBritArt
Instagram @royalsocietybritishartists
Honorary Secretary Cheryl Culver

Held at the Mall Galleries, The Mall, London SW1. The Grand Prize of £10,000 is divided into two Awards: £5,000 for a work by a non-member and £5,000 for a work by a member. The annual RBA Rising Stars exhibition, held at the Royal Over-Seas League in Mayfair, London, features work from artists aged 18–35 years and offers a scholarship for a month-long trip to Rome and cash prizes totalling £7,000.

The Royal Photographic Society Awards

RPS House, 337 Paintworks, Arnos Vale, Bristol BS4 3AR
tel 0117 316 4450
email info@rps.org
website https://rps.org/opportunities/
Facebook www.facebook.com/royalphotographicsociety
X @The_RPS
Instagram @royalphotographicsociety

A year-round programme of competitions, awards and bursaries for photographers and filmmakers in a range of mediums and genres. Recognises the contributions of established artists and provides opportunities for emerging creators. The RPS International Photography Exhibition (IPE) is the world's longest-running photography exhibition and invites submissions from photographers at all stages of their careers.

Royal Society of Portrait Painters Awards

17 Carlton House Terrace, London SW1Y 5BD
tel 020-7930 6844
email info@mallgalleries.com
website www.therp.co.uk, www.mallgalleries.org.uk
Facebook www.facebook.com/RoyalSocietyofPortraitPainters
X @RP_portraits
Instagram @royalsocietyportraitpainters

Runs an annual programme of awards, including: the Ondaatje Prize for Portraiture (£10,000), the de Laszlo Award Foundation Award for young artists (£3,000), the Smallwood Architect's Prize (£1,000), the William Lock Portrait Prize (£20,000), the Raw Umber Studios Award for technical excellence and creative expression (£2,000) and the RP Prize for the Best Small Portrait (£2,000).

The Jill Smythies Award

The Linnean Society of London, Burlington House, Piccadilly, London W1J 0BF
tel 020-7434 4479
email nominations@linnean.org
website www.linnean.org
Facebook www.facebook.com/linneansociety
Bluesky @linneansociety.bsky.social
Instagram @linneansociety

A prize of £1,000 is given to a botanical artist for outstanding, diagnostically relevant illustrations. Established in honour of Jill Smythies whose career as a botanical artist was cut short by an accident to her right hand. Seeks published illustrations, such as drawings and paintings, in aid of plant identification, with the emphasis on botanical accuracy and the accurate portrayal of diagnostic characteristics. Illustrations of cultivars of garden origin are not eligible. Closing date for nominations: 30 September. Founded 1988.

The V&A Illustration Awards

Victoria & Albert Museum, London SW7 2RL
email villa@vam.ac.uk
website www.vam.ac.uk/info/va-illustration-awards

Biennial awards open to illustrators living or publishing in the UK and students who have attended a course in the UK over the last two years. Categories: Adult Fiction, Adult Non-Fiction, Advertising and Commercial, Illustration for Children and Unpublished Emerging Illustrator. One winner in each category receives £3,000 and a runner-up in each category receives £750. One overall winner is named the Moira Gemmill Illustrator of the Year; they receive an additional £5,000 and their artwork becomes part of the V&A's collection.

Wildlife Photographer of the Year

The Natural History Museum, Cromwell Road, London SW7 5BD
website www.nhm.ac.uk/visit/wpy/competition.html

Open to photographers of all experience levels, aged 18 and over. There are 16 categories, ranging from Animal Portraits to Photojournalism and Urban Wildlife to Underwater Photography. The Grand Title award (£10,000) is given to the photographer whose individual image is judged to be the most striking and memorable. Prizes range in value depending on the category. The Young Wildlife Photographer of the Year recognises photographers aged 17 and under.

World Illustration Awards

Association of Illustrators, Somerset House, Strand, London WC2R 1LA
tel 020-7759 1010
email awards@theaoi.com
website https://worldillustrationawards.com
Facebook www.facebook.com/theaoi
X @theaoi
Instagram @worldillustrationawards

Presented by the Association of Illustrators in partnership with the *Directory of Illustration*, the awards programme celebrates contemporary illustration across the globe. A panel of international judges create a 500–strong longlist and shortlists 200 projects across 10 categories, which are celebrated in an online showcase with an industry events programme. For submission guidelines, categories and prizes, see the website.

BOOK INDUSTRY

An Post Irish Book Awards

137 Hillside, Dalkey, County Dublin A96 DP86, Republic of Ireland
tel +353 (0)85 144 9574
email bert@agile-ideas.com
website www.irishbookawards.ie
Administrator Bert Wright

A set of industry-recognition awards set up by a coalition of Irish booksellers to celebrate the extraordinary quality of Irish writing, to help bring the best books to a wider readership annually, and to promote an industry under competitive pressures. The awards include 18 categories spanning the entire spectrum of literary genres. Thousands of readers vote to select the winners every year and the awards are presented at a Gala Dinner and Awards Ceremony in late November each year.

The current headline sponsor is An Post, the state-owned provider of postal services in the Republic of Ireland. Submissions open 1 June; shortlist announced late October. Founded 2007.

The Bestseller Awards

NielsenIQ BookData, 3rd Floor, Station Place, Argyle Way, Stevenage, Herts. SG1 2AD
tel (01483) 712200
email marketing.book@nielseniq.com
website https://nielsenbestsellerawards.com
X @BestsellerAwrds
Instagram @bestsellerawrds

Administered by NielsenIQ in partnership with BolognaBookPlus. Presented to publishers and authors of books that achieve outstanding sales through the UK retail book trade. Any title that sells more than 250,000 copies (Silver), 500,000 copies (Gold) or 1,000,000 copies (Platinum) is recognised.

Both print and ebook sales are counted and all sales from publication (or from when NielsenIQ UK TCM records began: 1998 for print books and 2014 for ebooks) are included. The awards are a continual scheme with an annual review ceremony held every January when multiple awards are given out to various successful authors. Founded 2001.

Books Are My Bag Readers Awards

website www.nationalbooktokens.com/vote
Facebook www.facebook.com/nationalbooktokens
X @book_tokens
Bluesky @nationalbooktokens.bsky.social
Instagram @book_tokens
Threads @book_tokens

Curated by bookshops and chosen by readers across seven categories: Fiction, Non-Fiction, Poetry, Young Adult Fiction, Children's Fiction, Breakthrough Author and Readers' Choice, which is nominated exclusively by readers.

The British Book Awards

The Bookseller, The Stage Media Company Ltd., 47 Bermondsey Street, London SE1 3XT
email awards@thebookseller.com
website www.thebookseller.com/awards

Also known as The Nibbies, showcase and honour the books that have had the biggest impact on readers, and the publishers and booksellers who supported them. There are 12 categories recognising authors, illustrators, fiction, non-fiction, children's fiction, children's non-fiction and audiobooks. In 2024 a new category was introduced in association with The Reading Agency: Library of the Year. Founded 1990.

Diagram Prize for Oddest Book Title

The Bookseller, The Stage Media Company Ltd., 47 Bermondsey Street, London SE1 3X
email bent@thebookseller.com
website www.thebookseller.com
Administrator Horace Bent

Awarded annually to the book with the strangest title. Anyone can nominate titles for the award, a shortlist is compiled by *The Bookseller* magazine and the winner is decided by a public vote. The winning book is featured in the magazine and the nominator of that title has traditionally received a 'passable bottle of claret'. Founded 1978.

Indie Book Awards

6 Bell Yard, London WC2A 2JR
tel 020-7421 4694
email katie.connor@booksellers.org.uk
website www.booksaremybag.com/IndieBookAwards/About
Facebook www.facebook.com/booksaremybag
X @booksaremybag
Instagram @booksaremybag

The only awards given to an author or illustrator on behalf of independent bookshops and booksellers. Showcase the best paperback reads for the summer. Awards are given in four categories: Fiction, Non-Fiction, Children's Fiction and Picture Book.

Indie Champions Awards

website https://uk.bookshop.org/lists/annual-indie-champions-awards
Facebook www.facebook.com/BookshopOrgUK
X @bookshop_org_uk
Instagram @bookshop_org_uk

Celebrate writers, industry professionals, publishers and organisations who have taken concrete steps to financially support independent bookshops through Bookshop.org sales, alongside using the platform in innovative ways. Founded 2022.

The K&IM Information Resources Awards

CILIP, The British Library, 96 Euston Road, London NW1 2DB
tel 020-4513 2831
email jdburntoak@virginmedia.com
website www.cilip.org.uk

Information Resources Award

Awarded annually for outstanding information resources that are available and relevant to the knowledge, information management and library sector. Awards are made to both print and electronic resources. Recommendations are invited from Members of CILIP (the Chartered Institute of Library and Information Professionals), publishers and others, who are asked to submit nominations via the website. Winners receive a certificate.

The Walford Award

Awarded annually to an individual for an outstanding contribution to the knowledge and information management services.

National Book Critics Circle Awards

email membership@bookcritics.org
website www.bookcritics.org/awards/
Facebook www.facebook.com/nationalbookcriticscircle/
Instagram @bookcritics

Awards the best book published in English in the USA in the preceding year in six categories: Fiction, Non-Fiction, Biography, Autobiography, Poetry and Criticism. Also awards the John Leonard Prize for the best first book in any genre; the Gregg Barrios Book in Translation Prize for the best book of any genre translated into English; and the Ivan Sandrof Lifetime Achievement Award (for an individual) and Toni Morrison Achievement Award (for a literary organisation) for contributions to book culture. Submissions are not accepted but publishers can send copies of books to the committee for their consideration.

Next Generation Indie Book Awards

167 Midland Place, South East Calgary, Alberta T2X 1N1, Canada
email info@indiebookawards.com
website https://indiebookawards.com/
Facebook www.facebook.com/NextGenerationIndieBookAwards/
X @IndieBookAwards
Instagram @indiebookawards
Director Shelley Anderson

An international awards programme for independent authors and publishers. Prizes are awarded in over 80 categories spotlighting different genres, topics, formats, lengths and types of writer. Winners receive cash prizes, trophies and medals, and exposure. Entry deadline: February. Entry fee: $75.

Republic of Consciousness Prize for Small Presses

email rofcprize@gmail.com
website www.republicofconsciousness.com
X @PrizeRofc
Instagram @republicofconsciousness

Supports, promotes and celebrates small presses in the UK and Ireland. Rewards the best fiction published by small presses publishing fewer than eight books a year. The prize money is split between shortlisted and longlisted presses and shortlisted authors. Presses may only submit one title each year. Submission deadline: August. Founded 2017.

The Selfies Book Awards

email selfies@bookbrunch.co.uk
website https://theselfies.co.uk/

Established to discover and recognise self-published authors, the Awards are judged on the following criteria: an entertaining story, a well-produced book, an engaging cover and blurb, and a creative marketing and publicity plan. Entries must have been self-published in the preceding year. There are three categories: Adult Fiction, Children's Fiction (including YA) and General Non-Fiction. 1st prize in each category: £750 and a package of support including a profile in BookBrunch, advertising and PR. Shortlisted authors receive free entry to the London Book Fair and the Author HQ. Entry deadline: January. Entry fee: £34.50. Founded 2018.

CHILDREN'S

ALCS Educational Writers' Award

The Society of Authors, 24 Bedford Row, London WC1R 4EH
tel 020-3880 2230
email prizes@societyofauthors.org
website https://societyofauthors.org/prizes/other-prizes/alcs-educational-writers-award
Facebook www.facebook.com/TheSocietyofAuthors
X @Soc_of_Authors
Instagram @thesocietyofauthors
Grants & Prizes Manager Aine Pullan, *Grants & Prizes Design Manager* Natalie Thorpe, *Head of Fundraising, Grants & Prizes* Robyn Law

A collaboration between the Society of Authors and the Author's Licensing and Collecting Society. Alternates each year between books for ages 5–11 years and 11–18 years. Given to an outstanding example of traditionally published non-fiction (with or without illustrations) that stimulates and enhances learning. The work must have been first published in the UK, in the English language, within the previous two calendar years. Prize fund: £2,000. Founded 2008.

The Hans Christian Andersen Awards

International Board on Books for Young People, Nonnenweg 12, 4055, Basel, Switzerland
tel +41 (0)61 272 2917
email ibby@ibby.org
website www.ibby.org
Facebook www.facebook.com/ibby.international
Instagram @ibby.international

Given every other year by IBBY, they recognise lifelong achievement and are presented to an author and an illustrator whose complete works have made an important, lasting contribution to children's literature. The selection criteria include the aesthetic and literary qualities of writing and illustrating, as well as the ability to see things from the child's point of view and stretch the child's curiosity and imagination. The complete works of the author and of the illustrator are taken into consideration. Nominations are presented to IBBY by its Member Sections, which can put forward one candidate in each category. The Sections also recommend judges, ten of whom are picked by the Jury President to form the Jury that decides the winners. The Author's Award has been given since 1956 and the Illustrator's Award since 1966.

BookTrust Storytime Prize

BookTrust, 29 Clerkenwell Road, Farringdon, London EC1M 5RN
tel 020-7801 8800
email queries@booktrust.org.uk
website www.booktrust.org.uk/what-we-do/awards-and-prizes/current-prizes/booktrust-storytime-prize/

Celebrates the best books for sharing with young children between 0–5 years, with a particular focus on books that have a wide appeal to parents and carers and stories that can be read and enjoyed over and over again. The Prize is run in collaboration with public libraries who receive copies of the shortlisted books and are invited to vote on the shortlist alongside children and families. 1st prize: £5,000.

The Branford Boase Award

30 Winton Avenue, London N11 2AT
tel 020-8889 1292
email branford.boase@gmail.com
website www.branfordboaseaward.org.uk
Facebook www.facebook.com/branfordboaseaward
X @BranfordBoase

An annual award of £1,000 is made to a first-time writer of a full-length children's novel (seven years and older) published in the preceding year; the editor is also recognised. Encourages new writers for children and highlights the role of perceptive editors in developing new talent. The award was set up in memory of the outstanding children's writer Henrietta Branford and the gifted editor and publisher Wendy Boase who both died in 1999. Closing date for nominations: end of December. Founded 2000.

The Carnegies

Room 150 British Library, 96 Euston Road, London NW1 2DB
email carnegies@cilip.org.uk
website https://carnegies.co.uk
Facebook www.facebook.com/CarnegieMedals
X @CarnegieMedals
Bluesky @carnegiemedals.bsky.social
Instagram @carnegiemedals
Threads @carnegiemedals

Nominations for the following two awards are invited from members of CILIP (the library and information association), who are asked to submit one title per Medal, accompanied by an explanation of how the book they have selected meets the medal criteria. Submissions must have been first published in the UK during the preceding year or co-published elsewhere within a three-month time lapse. The awards are selected by librarian judges from the Youth Libraries Group of CILIP. Prizes are given from the Colin Mears Award fund.

As part of the Medals scheme, children read, review and vote on the shortlists; their favourite books receive the Shadowers' Choice Awards.

Carnegie Medal for Writing

Awarded annually for an outstanding book for children (fiction or non-fiction) written in English. 1st prize: £5,000.

Carnegie Medal for Illustration

Awarded annually for an outstanding illustrated book for children. Books intended for older as well as younger children are eligible. 1st prize: £5,000.

The Children's Book Award

email childrensbookaward@fcbg.org.uk
website https://fcbg.org.uk/cba-home
Facebook www.facebook.com/fcbgnews
X @FCBGNews
Instagram @fcbg_news
Administrator Sarah Stuffins

Awarded annually to authors and illustrators of children's fiction published in the UK. The only national award voted for solely by children. Awards are made in the following categories: Books for Younger Children, Books for Younger Readers and Books for Older Readers. The overall winner receives a silver acorn and holds the Oak Tree trophy for a year. Contact the administrator by email for submission criteria. Founded 1980.

English Association English 4–11 Children's Picture Book Awards

The English Association, Senate House, Malet Street, London WC1E 7HU

email awards@englishassociation.ac.uk
website https://englishassociation.ac.uk/english-4-11-picture-book-awards

Presented by the English Association to the best children's picture books of the year, both fiction and non-fiction, in the age ranges 4–7 years and 7–11 years. The winning books are chosen by the editorial board of *English 4–11*, the magazine for primary teachers, from a shortlist selected by a panel of teachers and primary specialists. Each year, one of the books submitted is selected as the recipient of the Margaret Mallett Prize for Children's Non-Fiction. Founded 1995.

Entente Littéraire Prize

Royal Society of Literature, Somerset House, London WC2R 1LA
tel 020-7845 4679
website https://rsliterature.org/entente-litteraire-prize
Facebook www.facebook.com/RoyalSocietyLiterature
X @RSLiterature
Instagram @royalsocietyofliterature

Established by the UK and French governments to celebrate the links between the two countries; administered by the Royal Society of Literature and the Institut Français du Royaume-Uni. The Prize promotes writing and translation from both countries, focusing on a different genre each year. Two winning books – one translated from English into French, the other from French into English – receive a prize of €8,000, shared between author and translator. Only accepts submissions from publishers. Founded 2023.

The Goldfinch Novel Award

24 High Street, Alton GU34 1BN
tel 07810 122426
email gary@goldfinch-books.com
website www.goldfinch-books.com
Facebook www.facebook.com/goldfinchbooks
X @GoldfinchBooks_
Instagram @goldfinchbooks
Director Gary Clark

Administered by Goldfinch Books in association with the Alton Arts Festival. The prize is for emerging authors (aged 16 years and older) who have completed a YA or adult novel that is at least 50,000 words in length. Entrants should submit the first 3,000 words of a novel and a one-page synopsis. The winning novel is chosen by a literary agent. 1st prize: £500 and a place on a creative writing course. Entry fee: £10. Entry deadline: May. Founded 2022.

The KPMG Children's Books Ireland Awards

17 North Great George's Street, Dublin 1 D01 R2F1, Republic of Ireland
tel +353 (0)1 872 7475
email info@childrensbooksireland.ie
website www.childrensbooksireland.ie

Leading annual children's book awards in Ireland. The awards are: Book of the Year, Eilís Dillon Award (for a first children's book), Honour Award for Fiction, Honour Award for Illustration, Judges' Special Award and Junior Juries Award. Schools and reading groups nationwide take part in the Junior Juries programme: participating groups make their own selection of suitable titles from the books shortlisted for the awards in March, using a specially devised activity pack to guide them in their reading; each group then votes for their favourite book. Entries close in November; shortlist announced in February; winners announced in May. Founded 1990.

The London Writers Awards – see page 609

New Zealand Book Awards for Children and Young Adults

NZ Book Awards for Children and Young Adults, 72 Te Wharepōuri Street, Wellington 6023, New Zealand
tel +64 (0)2 7773 9855
email childrensawards@nzbookawards.org.nz
website www.nzbookawards.nz/new-zealand-book-awards-for-children-and-young-adults
Facebook www.facebook.com/NewZealandCYABookAwards
X @nzcya
Instagram @nzcya_awards
Trust Manager Belinda Cooke, *Awards Administrator* Joy Sellen

Celebrates excellence in, and provides recognition for, the best children's books published in New Zealand. Awards are presented in six categories: Picture Book, Junior Fiction (the Wright Family Foundation Esther Glen Award), Young Adult Fiction, Non-Fiction (the Elsie Locke Award), Illustration (the Russell Clark Award) and te reo Māori (the Wright Family Foundation Te Kura Pounamu Award). Each of these awards carries prize money of $8,500. The overall prize, the Margaret Mahy Book of the Year award, carries a further prize of $8,500. A $2,500 prize (The NZSA Best First Book Award) is awarded to a previously unpublished author or illustrator. Eligible books must have been published in New Zealand between April and March in the period preceding the awards' August ceremony date. Governed by the New Zealand Book Awards Trust Te Ohu Tiaki i Te Rau Hiringa. Founded 1945.

PFD Queer Fiction Prizes – see page 597

Ruth Rendell Award

68 South Lambeth Road, London SW8 1RL
tel 020-7587 1842
email contact@literacytrust.org.uk
website https://literacytrust.org.uk/about-us/ruth-rendell-award/
Facebook www.facebook.com/nationalliteracytrust/

X @Literacy_Trust
Instagram @literacy_trust

Named after the author Ruth Rendell who championed literacy throughout her life. Recognises authors who exert special effort to promote literacy development. Authors can be traditionally or self-published but must have demonstrated a commitment to furthering literacy through working with charities, schools, adult education settings, or communities; using their platform to highlight literacy issues; and participating in events, workshops, awards, festivals and initiatives dedicated to reading and writing. Nominations can be made by publishers, libraries, booksellers, schools, charities and individuals through the website. Founded 2016.

The Times/Chicken House Children's Fiction Competition

Chicken House, 2 Palmer Street, Frome, Somerset BA11 1DS
tel (01373) 454488
email competitions@chickenhousebooks.com
website www.chickenhousebooks.com
Facebook www.facebook.com/chickenhousebooks
X @timeschprize
Instagram @timeschprize
Contact Jazz Bartlett Love

Open to unpublished writers of a full-length children's novel (7–18 years). Entrants must be over 18 and novels must be between 30,000 and 80,000 words in length. 1st prize: a worldwide publishing contract with Chicken House with a royalty advance of £10,000. The winner is selected by a panel of judges that includes children's authors, journalists, publishers, librarians and other key figures from the world of children's literature.

A second prize, The Lime Pictures New Storyteller Prize, runs alongside the main prize and seeks completed fiction manuscripts for TV and film for children aged seven years and older or young adults. 1st prize: £7,000, representation and consideration for TV or film development.

Entrants to both prizes should submit the full MSS, a one-page cover letter and a one-page synopsis. Entry deadline: June. Entry fee: £20.

Tir na n-Og Awards

Books Council of Wales, Castell Brychan, Aberystwyth, Ceredigion SY23 2JB
tel (01970) 624151
email wbc.children@books.wales
website https://llyfrau.cymru/en/gwobrau/tir-na-nog
Facebook www.facebook.com/LlyfrDaFabBooks
X @LlyfrDaFabBooks

Established to promote and raise the standard of children's and young people's books in Wales. Three awards (prize: £1,000 each) are presented annually by the Books Council of Wales and are sponsored by the Chartered Institute of Library and Information Professionals Cymru/Wales. Awards the best English-language book of the year with an authentic Welsh background (fiction and factual books originally in English are eligible, translations from Welsh or any other language are not eligible); the best original Welsh-language book aimed at the primary school sector; and the best original Welsh-language book aimed at the secondary school sector. Founded 1976.

CULTURAL AND INTERNATIONAL PERSPECTIVES

The Anglo-Hellenic League Runciman Award

The Hellenic Centre, 16–18 Paddington Street, London W1U 5AS
email runciman@anglohellenicleague.org
website www.anglohellenicleague.org/runciman-award
Facebook www.facebook.com/theanglohellenicleague
X @AngHellenLeague

An annual award, given by the Anglo-Hellenic League, to promote Anglo-Greek understanding and friendship. Entries must cover Greece or Hellenism and have been published in English in the previous years. Entries span history, archaeology, antiquity, biography, literature, philosophy, myth, novels, poetry, travel writing and literary translations. Entries must be nominated by publishers. The value of the award is £10,000. Founded 1986.

The Australian Fiction Prize

Level 19, 201 Elizabeth Street, Sydney, NSW 2000, Australia
website https://www.harpercollins.com.au/theaustraliafictionprize/

Previously the Australian/Vogel's Literary Award. An annual award of $20,000 for an unpublished work of fiction. Entrants must be under 30 years of age on the closing date and must normally be residents of Australia. The MSS cannot be under consideration by any publisher or award. 1st prize: $20,000 and an advance on publication of $15,000. Founded 1980.

Berman Literature Prize

website www.bermanliteratureprize.com

An annual prize awarded to a writer whose work explores Jewish culture and embodies the spirit of the Jewish tradition but also achieves universality. Entrants can be from any background and write in any genre. The prize is valued at SEK 750,000 Swedish kronor and the winner is named that year's Laureate at a ceremony in Stockholm. Founded 2020.

British Czech and Slovak Association Writing Competition

24 Ferndale, Tunbridge Wells, Kent TN2 3NS
tel (01892) 543206
email prize@bcsa.co.uk
website www.bcsa.co.uk

Recognises fiction and non-fiction on the links between Britain and the Czech and Slovak Republics, at any time in their history, or society in those republics since the Velvet Revolution in 1989. There is an optional theme each year; entries should not exceed 2,000 words. 1st prize: £400; 2nd prize: £150. Winning entries are published in the *British Czech & Slovak Review*. Closing date: end of June each year. Founded 2002.

The Caine Prize for African Writing – see page 599

Dayton Literary Peace Prize

PO Box 461, Wright Brothers Branch, Dayton, OH 45409-0461, USA
website www.daytonliterarypeaceprize.org
Facebook www.facebook.com/DaytonLiteraryPeacePrize
Instagram @daytonliterarypeaceprize

Pays tribute to books that promote peace and encourage empathy through a better understanding of other people, cultures, religions and political identities. There are two categories: Fiction and Non-Fiction, and a Distinguished Achievement Award. Authors from around the world are eligible. 1st prize: $10,000 in each category. Founded 1999.

The Eccles Institute & Hay Festival Writer's Award

The Drill Hall, 25 Lion Street, Hay-on-Wye HR3 5AD
tel (01497) 822620
email admin@hayfestival.org
website www.hayfestival.com/eccles-centre-hay-festival-writers-award
Facebook www.facebook.com/hayfestival
X @hayfestival
Instagram @hayfestival

Supports writers in the creative stage of a new fiction or non-fiction project on a theme central to the Eccles Institute's Americas collection. Celebrated globally through a series of events profiling winners at Hay Festival editions in Colombia, Peru, Mexico and Wales. Two winners receive £20,000 in four quarterly grants, access to the expertise of the British Library's curatorial staff and the opportunity to work with the Eccles Institute and Hay Festival.

Christopher Ewart-Biggs Memorial Prize

email clairemcauley@hotmail.com
website www.ewartbiggsprize.org
Administrator Claire McAuley

A biennial prize given to work that promotes and encourages peace and reconciliation in Ireland, understanding between Britain and Ireland, or closer co-operation between European countries. Open to writers, academics, filmmakers and creatives; entries must have been published or performed in the previous two years. 1st prize: £7,500. Entry deadline: 25 December 2025. Founded 1977.

The Franco-British Society's Literary Award

Franco-British Council, 5th Floor, 167–169 Great Portland Street, London W1W 5PF
email info@franco-british-society.org
website www.franco-british-society.org
X @FrancoBritSoc
Contact David Mackintosh

Recognises a full-length work of literature that contributes to Franco–British understanding. It must be first published in the UK between 1 January and 31 December, and written in English by a citizen of the UK, British Commonwealth or the Republic of Ireland. 1st prize: £100. No entry fee. Entry deadline: 31 December.

The Giller Prize

email info@gillerprize.ca
website https://gillerprize.ca
Facebook www.facebook.com/gillerprize
X @GillerPrize
Instagram @gillerprize
Executive Director Elana Rabinovitch, *Digital Manager* Emma Truax, *Director of Submissions* Daphna Rabinovitch, *Executive Assistant* Jacob Alvarado

Established by Jack Rabinovitch in honour of his late wife, literary journalist Doris Giller. Awarded to the best Canadian novel, graphic novel or short story collection published in English. Entries must be scheduled for publication before 30 September in the awarding year. 1st prize: $100,000; finalists each receive $10,000. To date, the Prize has awarded more than two million dollars to Canadian writers. Submissions only accepted from publishers.

International Prize for Arabic Fiction

28 St James Walk, London EC1R OAP
email fleurmontanaro@yahoo.co.uk
website https://arabicfiction.org
Facebook www.facebook.com/InternationalPrizeArabicFiction
X @Arabic_Fiction
Instagram @arabicfictionprize
Prize Administrator Fleur Montanaro

Rewards excellence in contemporary Arabic creative writing and increases the international reach of Arabic fiction through the translation of its winners into English and other languages. Six shortlisted finalists receive $10,000, with a further $50,000 going to the winner. Founded 2007.

Island Prize

tel 07751 864120
email contact@hhousebooks.com
website www.hhousebooks.com
X @HhouseBooks

Created to address the barriers to publication for African people and to create closer ties between Britain and Africa, the Prize is open to anyone born in or resident of an African country who has not previously had a novel published. The Prize is for a completed novel in English of between 35,000 and 100,000 words in any fiction genre; non-fiction, short stories and poetry are not eligible. Entrants should submit the first three chapters or 10,000 words of their novel, a one-page synopsis and a covering letter. 1st prize: £500; two runners-up also receive £200; all three winners are considered for representation and publication. Founded 2021.

The London Hellenic Prize

email enquiries@londonhellenicprize.org
website www.londonhellenicprize.eu
X @LHellenicPrize
Bluesky @lhellenicprize.bsky.social

Awarded to authors of original works written in (or translated into) English on a subject relating to, or inspired by, Hellenic civilisation, culture, history or literature, from ancient to modern times. Recognises works of excellence and originality that appeal to a general reader. The value of the prize is £10,000. Founded 1996.

Ockham New Zealand Book Awards

c/o Auckland Writers Festival,
Darby Building Level 2, 8 Darby Street,
Auckland 1010, New Zealand
tel +64 (0)9 376 8074
email awards@nzbookawards.org.nz
website www.nzbookawards.nz/new-zealand-book-awards
Facebook www.facebook.com/NewZealandBookAwards
X @theockhams
Instagram @newzealandbookawards
Awards Administrator Christina Chan, *Trust Manager* Belinda Cooke

Celebrates excellence in, and provides recognition for, the best books published annually in New Zealand. Awards are presented in four categories: Fiction (the Jann Medlicott Acorn Prize, 1st prize: $65,000), Poetry (the Mary and Peter Biggs Award, 1st prize: $12,000), Illustrated Non-Fiction (the BookHub Award, 1st prize: $12,000) and General Non-Fiction (1st prize: $12,000). There are also four awards for debut authors (the Mātātuhi Foundation Best First Book Awards, 1st prize in each category: $3,000) and a Māori language award (Te Mūrau o te Tuhi, 1st prize: $12,000). Eligible books must have been published in New Zealand in the calendar year preceding the awards ceremony date. Governed by The New Zealand Book Awards Trust Te Ohu Tiaki i Te Rau Hiringa. Founded 1968.

OCM Bocas Prize for Caribbean Literature

email info@bocaslitfest.com
website www.bocaslitfest.com
Facebook www.facebook.com/bocaslitfest
X @bocaslitfest
Instagram @bocaslitfest

Recognises literary books by Caribbean writers (writers must have been born in the Caribbean or hold Caribbean citizenship). Books published in the calendar year 2025 are eligible for the 2026 prize. There are two deadline dates for entries: books published before November 2025 (which should be received by the prize administrators by mid-November) and books published between 1 November and 31 December 2025 (which should be received by the prize administrators by the first week of January 2026). Books are judged in three categories: Poetry; Fiction (including novels and short stories); and Literary Non-Fiction (including books of essays, biography, autobiography, history, current affairs, travel and other genres that demonstrate literary qualities and use literary techniques, regardless of subject matter). Textbooks, technical books, coffee-table books, specialist publications and reference works are not eligible. The overall winner receives an award of $10,000. Entry fee: $45.

Pushkin House Book Prize

5A Bloomsbury Square, London WC1A 2TA
email bookprize@pushkinhouse.org.uk
website https://pushkin-house.vercel.app/projects/book-prize
Facebook www.facebook.com/PushkinHouseLondon
X @Pushkin_House
Instagram @pushkinhouselondon

Recognises non-fiction books on the subject of Russian culture, history and society that are both well-written and accessible. Entries can be submitted by authors or publishers, but must have been published in the previous year. Entrants should submit an entry form, an ebook copy of the book and a cover image. 1st prize: £10,000. Entry deadline: December. Entry fee: £25. Founded 2013.

Wingate Literary Prize

email admin@wingate.org.uk
website www.wingatefoundation.org.uk/literary_prize
Bluesky @thewingateprize.bsky.social
Instagram @the_wingate_prize

An annual prize of £4,000 is awarded, in association with the Jewish Literary Foundation, for a work of fiction or non-fiction that best translates the idea of Jewishness to the general reader. Founded 1977.

Sheikh Zayed Book Award

Department of Culture & Tourism, PO Box 7050, Abu Dhabi, UAE

email info@zayedaward.ae
website www.zayedaward.ae/en
Facebook www.facebook.com/ZayedBookAward
X @ZayedBookAward
Instagram @zayedbookaward

Celebrates writers and publishers whose work contributes to Arab literature and culture. Awards are divided into nine categories including Literature, Children's Literature, Literary and Art Criticism and Young Author. Entries must be in Arabic unless being submitted to the Arab Culture in Other Languages, Editing of Arabic Manuscripts or Translation categories, which accept work in any language. Winners in each category receive a gold medal and 750,000 UAE dirhams. See website for specific entry requirements for each category. Founded 2006.

DEBUT AND EMERGING WRITERS

Authors' Club Best First Novel

Whitehall Place, London SW1A 2HE
email info@authorsclub.co.uk
website www.authorsclub.co.uk/prizes
Facebook www.facebook.com/authorsclub1891
X @AuthorsClub

For the most promising debut novel first published in the UK in the previous year. Open to British, Irish or UK-based authors; there is no age limit. 1st prize: £2,500.

The Bath Novel Award

PO Box 5223, Bath BA1 0UR
email info@bathnovelaward.co.uk
website www.bathnovelaward.co.uk
Facebook www.facebook.com/bathnovelaward
X @bathnovelaward
Bluesky @bathnovelaward.bsky.social
Instagram @bathnovelaward

Celebrates unagented emerging writers of novels for adults or young adults. Submissions: first 5,000 words of a novel plus a one-page synopsis. Prize: £5,000. Entries open December until May. Entry fee: £29.99 per novel; sponsored places available for low-income writers. Founded 2013.

The Bloody Scotland Crime Debut of the Year – see page 612

The Bridport Prize

Bridport Arts Centre, South Street, Bridport, Dorset DT6 3NR
email kate@bridportprize.org.uk
website www.bridportprize.org.uk
Facebook www.facebook.com/bridportprize
X @BridportPrize
Instagram @bridportprize

Administers three prizes specifically for debut writers.

The Bridport Prize: Peggy Chapman-Andrews First Novel Award

Run in association with A.M. Heath Literary Agency, The Literary Consultancy and Headline Publishing. Enter first chapter(s) of a novel, up to 8,000 words, plus a 300-word synopsis. 1st prize: £1,500 plus mentoring through the The Literary Consultancy's Chapter & Verse scheme; 2nd prize: £750; three runners-up each receive £150. All runners-up also receive ongoing support. Extracts from the longlisted novels are published in an annual anthology in October. Enter by post or online. Entry deadline: 31 May. Entry fee: £24 per novel. Founded 2014.

The Bridport Prize: Young Writer Award

Established to encourage young writers taking the first steps on their writing journey. Awarded to the highest placed entry to the Bridport prize by a writer aged 16–25. Categories include Novel, Short Story, Poetry and Flash Fiction. 1st prize: £500. Entry deadline: May. Founded 2025.

The Bridport Prize: Never Too Late Award

Established to celebrate the hidden talent of older writers who often struggle to be seen despite a wealth of experience, creativity and stories to tell. Championed by bestselling author Kit de Waal and literary agent AM Heath. Awarded to the highest placed entry to the Bridport prize by a writer over the age of 60. Categories include Novel, Short Story, Poetry and Flash Fiction. 1st prize: £500. Entry deadline: May.

The Lucy Cavendish Fiction Prize

Lucy Cavendish College, University of Cambridge, Lady Margaret Road, Cambridge CB3 0BU
email comms@lucy.cam.ac.uk
website www.lucy.cam.ac.uk/fictionprize
Facebook www.facebook.com/lucycavcollege
X @LCFictionPrize
Instagram @lcfictionprize
Founder Prof. Janet Todd OBE

Helps undiscovered women and non-binary writers launch their literary careers. Seeks entries that combine literary merit with 'unputdownability'. Submissions must be unpublished and anyone who has previously had a full-length novel accepted for publication is not eligible to enter. Entrants must be resident in the UK or Ireland. 1st prize: £1,500. All shortlisted entrants receive a half-hour one-to-one consultation with the competition sponsor WME (a literary and talent agency). Founded 2010.

Comedy Women in Print Awards – see page 613

The Emerging Author Dagger

email comps@thecwa.co.uk
website www.thecwa.co.uk/awards-and-competitions/the-daggers/emerging-author-dagger/

Facebook www.facebook.com/groups/TheCrimeWritersAssociation/

Sponsored by Fiction Feedback. A crime writing competition for unpublished and unagented writers. Shortlisted writers have their entries shown to agents and publishers. The winner also receives £500. Entrants should submit the opening of a crime novel (3,000 words maximum; the novel does not need to be completed) and a 1,500-word synopsis via the website portal. The competition opens 1 October and closes at 6pm on the last working day of February.

Fish Publishing Writing Prizes

Fish Publishing, Durrus, Bantry, Co. Cork, Republic of Ireland
email info@fishpublishing.com
website www.fishpublishing.com/writing-contests
Facebook www.facebook.com/FishPublishingIreland
X @fishpublishing

International writing prizes set up to publish and encourage new writers. There are four prizes available: the Fish Short Story Prize, the Fish Short Memoir Prize, the Fish Flash Fiction Prize and the Fish Poetry Prize. Ten winners from each prize are published in the annual Fish Anthology and each competition has cash and other prizes including residencies and courses. Founded 1994.

The Somerset Maugham Awards

The Society of Authors, 24 Bedford Row, London WC1R 4EH
tel 020-3880 2230
email prizes@societyofauthors.org
website https://societyofauthors.org/prizes/the-soa-awards/somerset-maugham-awards
Facebook www.facebook.com/TheSocietyofAuthors
X @Soc_of_Authors
Instagram @thesocietyofauthors
Grants & Prizes Manager Aine Pullan, *Grants & Prizes Design Manager* Natalie Thorpe, *Head of Fundraising, Grants & Prizes* Robyn Law

Awards for writers under the age of 30. The prize money should be used for foreign travel that will enrich their work. Candidates must be a British national, or resident in Great Britain and Northern Ireland for three years prior to the date of submission. Poetry, fiction, non-fiction, *belles lettres* or philosophy, but not dramatic works, are eligible. Entries should be full length and submitted by the publisher. Founded in 1947 by W. Somerset Maugham.

McDermid Debut Award

32 Cheltenham Parade, Harrogate HG1 1DB
tel (01423) 562303
email info@harrogate-festival.org.uk
website https://harrogatetheakstoncrimeaward.com/
Facebook www.facebook.com/HarrogateInternationalFestivals
X @HarrogateFest
Bluesky @harrogatefestivals.bsky.social
Instagram @harrogatefestivals

Launched by Harrogate International Festivals to find new voices in crime fiction and named in recognition of world-famous crime writer Val McDermid. Entrants must be from the UK or Ireland and submissions should be debut novels published between May and April in the year preceeding the award. The winner is chosen by a judging panel of industry experts, including literary, broadcasting and media figures. 1st prize: £500; six shortlisted authors receive weekend passes to Theakston Old Peculiar Crime Writing Festival. Entry deadline: March. Founded 2024.

The McKitterick Prize

The Society of Authors, 24 Bedford Row, London WC1R 4EH
tel 020-3880 2230
email prizes@societyofauthors.org
website https://societyofauthors.org/prizes/the-soa-awards/mckitterick-prize
Facebook www.facebook.com/TheSocietyofAuthors
X @Soc_of_Authors
Instagram @thesocietyofauthors
Grants & Prizes Manager Aine Pullan, *Grants & Prize Design Manager* Natalie Thorpe, *Head of Fundraising, Grants & Prizes* Robyn Law

Established with an endowment from former *Political Quarterly* editor, Tom McKitterick. Open to debut novels published in the UK, in the previous year, and unpublished submissions (excluding works for children) by authors aged 40 years and older. The work must be in English. Founded 1990.

New Chapter NEW

1st Floor, 222 Gray's Inn Road, London WC1X 8HB
tel 020-7316 0332
email newchapter@simonandschuster.co.uk
website www.simonandschuster.co.uk/p/new-chapter
Facebook www.facebook.com/simonschusterUK
X @simonschusterUK

Open to fiction writers of colour who are unpublished and unagented. Entrants should submit three chapters of a commercial fiction novel accompanied by a synopsis; longlisted entrants must have an idea for a second book, which they will be expected to discuss. 1st prize: a two-book publishing contract and a £100,000 advance. Entry deadline: 31 July 2025. Founded 2025.

Queen Mary Wasafiri New Writing Prize

School of English and Drama, Queen Mary, University of London, Mile End Road, London E1 4NS
tel 020-7882 2686
email wasafirinewwritingprize@qmul.ac.uk
website www.wasafiri.org/new-writing-prize

Awarded in three categories: Fiction, Life Writing and Poetry, and open to anyone worldwide who has not published a complete book in the category they wish to enter. The Prize supports new writers, with no limits on age, gender, nationality or background. Entries should not exceed 3,000 words; Fiction and Life Writing entries may be an extract from a longer work, but should stand alone; Poetry entries should include no more than three poems. The three category winners are published by *Wasafiri* magazine and receive a cash prize of £1,000 each. They are also offered mentoring with Chapter and Verse or Free Reads and the opportunity to discuss their career plans with The Good Literary Agency. Entry deadline: June. Entry fee: £12; some subsidised entry fees are available. Founded 2009.

Rooney Prize for Irish Literature

Trinity Oscar Wilde Centre for Irish Writing, School of English, 21 Westland Row, Trinity College Dublin, Dublin 2, Republic of Ireland
tel +353 (1) 896 2885
email wilde@tcd.ie
website www.tcd.ie/OWC/the-rooney-prize-for-literature/

Awarded to an outstanding body of work by an emerging Irish writer under forty years of age. Fiction, non-fiction, short stories, poetry, children's fiction and plays are all eligible. The winner receives €10,000. Publishers must submit six copies of each work published by the author. Entry deadline: May. Founded 1976.

RSL Christopher Bland Prize

Royal Society of Literature, Somerset House, Strand, London WC2R 1LA
tel 020-7845 4679
email info@rsliterature.org
website www.rsliterature.org/rsl-christopher-bland-prize

Encourages and celebrates older writers. The Prize is given annually to a debut novelist or popular non-fiction writer, first published at the age of 50 or over. The writer must be a citizen of, or resident in, the UK or Republic of Ireland. 1st prize: £10,000. Founded 2019.

The Sunday Times Charlotte Aitken Young Writer of the Year Award

email Rlaw@societyofauthors.org
website www.youngwriteraward.com
Facebook www.facebook.com/YoungWriterAward
X @YoungWriterYear

A prize of £10,000 is awarded for a full-length published or self-published (in book or ebook format) work of fiction, non-fiction or poetry, by a British or Irish author aged 18–35 years. The winning book will be a work of outstanding literary merit. Runners-up receive £1,000 each. Submission deadline: September. Founded 1991.

The Times/Chicken House Children's Fiction Competition – see page 577

The Betty Trask Prize

The Society of Authors, 24 Bedford Row, London WC1R 4EH
tel 020-3880 2230
email prizes@societyofauthors.org
website https://societyofauthors.org/betty-trask
Facebook www.facebook.com/TheSocietyofAuthors
X @Soc_of_Authors
Instagram @thesocietyofauthors
Grants & Prizes Manager Aine Pullan, *Grants & Prizes Design Manager* Natalie Thorpe, *Head of Fundraising, Grants & Prizes* Robyn Law

Established at the bequest of Betty Trask. Celebrates debut novels in English (published or unpublished), of a traditional or romantic nature. Authors must be under the age of 35 and a resident of Great Britain, Northern Ireland or the Commonwealth for three years prior to the date of submission or a British national. Free to enter. Founded 1983.

Waterstones Debut Fiction Prize

203–206 Piccadilly, London W1J 9HD
website www.waterstones.com

Recognises debut fiction of all forms, including genre fiction, and fiction in translation. Voted for by Waterstones booksellers, the Prize is an extension and catalyst of the power of word-of-mouth recommendations. The winner receives £5,000 and future support for their career from Waterstones.

Zooker Award

Arkbound, Backfields House, Upper York Street, Bristol BS2 8QJ
email editorial@arkbound.com
website https://arkbound.com/zooker-award/

Awarded to first-time authors from disadvantaged backgrounds. Principally concerned with work that touches upon the themes of environmental sustainability and social inclusion, encouraging positive changes in behaviour or attitude for readers. Submitted work must have been published (not self-published) in the last four years. 1st prize: £1,000; three runners-up receive £100. Entry fee: £5.

JOURNALISM

ABSW Awards

email info@absw.org.uk
website www.absw.org.uk/pages/18-awards
Facebook www.facebook.com/BritishScienceWriters
X @absw
Bluesky @absw.bsky.social
Linkedin www.linkedin.com/company/association-of-british-science-writers/

Administered by the Association of British Science Writers. Recognise excellence in science journalism over ten categories including Editor, Feature, Audio, Video, News Analysis and Newcomer. 1st prize in each category: £500. Entry: free for members; £55 per category for non-members. Submissions open in January and winners announced in June/July.

The Burlington Contemporary Art Writing Prize

email burlingtoncontemporary@burlington.org.uk
website https://contemporary.burlington.org.uk/writing_prize
X @BurlContemp
Instagram @burlingtoncontemporary
Editor Christopher Baker

Run by *The Burlington Magazine* to discover new writers on the subject of contemporary art. Entrants should submit one review of a contemporary art show of between 800 and 1,000 words; the exhibition should be current or have closed less than six months prior to submission. Entrants should not previously have published more than six pieces of writing in print or online. 1st prize: £1,000, publication in the online magazine and a future publication in the print magazine. Entry deadline: July. Founded 2012.

Fortnum and Mason Food and Drink Awards – see page 618

London Press Club Awards

Stationer's Hall, Ave Maria Lane, London EC4M 7DD
tel 020-3026 0278
email info@londonpressclub.co.uk
website https://londonpressclub.co.uk/
X @londonpressclub

Celebrate excellence in journalism. Categories include: Print Journalist, Broadcaster, Scoop, Young Journalist, Daily Newspaper and Sunday Newspaper. Judges are invited to put forward suggestions for each category and editors are invited to make submissions to the judges.

The Media Freedom Awards

Stationers Hall, Ave Maria Lane, London EC4M 7DD
tel 07599 954636
email office@societyofeditors.org
website www.societyofeditors.org
X @PressAwardsuk

Annual awards celebrating excellence in campaigning and investigative journalism.

New Media Writing Prize

website https://newmediawritingprize.co.uk
Facebook www.facebook.com/newmediawritingprize
X @NMWPrize

Showcases exciting and inventive stories that integrate a variety of formats, platforms and digital media. Encourages the best in new media writing and promotes the future of the 'written' word and storytelling. There are five prizes: the Chris Meade Memorial Main Prize, the Writers Online Student Prize, the Social Good Prize, the Opening Up Prize and the FIPP Media Journalism Prize. Founded 2010.

The Orwell Prizes

The Institute of Advanced Studies, South Wing, Wilkins Building, University College London, Gower Street, London WC1E 6BT
tel 020-3108 1618
email info@orwellfoundation.co.uk
website www.orwellfoundation.com

Awarded annually for books and journalism that come closest to George Orwell's ambition to 'make political writing into art'. Four prizes are awarded annually: Political Fiction, Political Writing, Journalism and Reporting Homelessness. Work published between June and May of the subsequent year is eligible; books must be published in the UK or Ireland. Each prize is worth £3,000. Founded 1994.

Scottish Press Awards

17 Polwarth Grove, Edinburgh EH11 1LY
email scottishpressawards@eventconsultants.com
website www.newsbrandsscotland.com/to-enter

Promote journalistic excellence across print and digital. Open to journalists and photographers who work for newsbrands published in Scotland or cover Scottish affairs. There are 27 categories including Journalist, Photographer, Reporter, Columnist, Journalism Team, Campaign, Front Page and Podcast of the Year, as well as special categories for Sports, Food and Drink, Politics, Finance and Business, and Regional coverage. Submission deadline: January. Entry fee: £25. Founded 1979.

LIFE WRITING: AUTOBIOGRAPHY, BIOGRAPHY AND MEMOIR

The Ackerley Prize for Autobiography and Memoir

website www.jrackerley.com/the-ackerley-prize

An annual prize of £4,000 given for an outstanding work of literary autobiography written in English and published during the previous year by an author of British nationality. No submissions; books are nominated by the judges. Founded 1982.

The Biographers' Club Elizabeth Buccleuch Prize

E6 Albany, Piccadilly, London W1J 0AR
tel 07985 920341
email ariane.bankes@gmail.com
website www.biographersclub.co.uk
Prize Administrator Ariane Bankes

Sponsored by the Duke of Buccleuch in memory of his late wife Elizabeth, Duchess of Buccleuch, the Prize supports uncommissioned first-time writers working on a biography. Applicants should submit a proposal of no more than 20 pages including a synopsis and ten-page sample chapter (double-spaced, numbered pages, unstapled), a CV and a note on the market for the book and competing literature, to the prize administrator. 1st prize: £2,000. Entry fee: £15.

The Biographers' Club Hatchards Best First Biography Prize

E6 Albany, Piccadilly, London W1J 0AR
tel 07985 920341
email ariane.bankes@gmail.com
website www.biographersclub.co.uk
Prize Administrator Ariane Bankes

Awarded to the best book written by a first-time biographer. The Prize, worth £2,500, is sponsored by Hatchards Booksellers. Only entries submitted by publishers are accepted for consideration. Literary memoirs are also eligible but celebrity autobiographies and ghostwritten books are not.

Books must have a publication date between 1 January and 31 December in the preceeding year (proofs are acceptable). Three copies of each book should be submitted no later than 31 October (enclose a press release to confirm publication date) along with an entry form (downloadable from the website). Entry fee: £25 per title.

The Bridport Prize Memoir Award

Bridport Arts Centre, South Street, Bridport, Dorset DT8 3NR
email kate@bridportprize.org.uk
website https://bridportprize.org.uk/the-competition/memoir-award/
Facebook www.facebook.com/bridportprize
X @BridportPrize
Instagram @bridportprize

Offers support to new memoir writers. Entrants must not have traditionally published a memoir before or have a contract with a publisher and must not be represented by a literary agent. Entrants should submit the first chapters of a memoir (up to 8,000 words) and a 300-word overview. 1st prize: £1,500 plus mentoring from the Literary Consultancy; 2nd prize: £750 plus a full MSS appraisal; three highly commended entries: £150 plus a 50-page appraisal. Entry fee: £24. Closing date: 30 September. Founded 2022.

Fish Publishing Writing Prizes – see page 581

The Elizabeth Longford Prize for Historical Biography

32 Brunswick Gardens, London W8 4AL
tel 07875 088371
email katie.hambly1@btinternet.com
website www.elhb.uk
X @katiehamblypr

A prize of £5,000 is awarded annually for a biography published in the year preceding the prize, in memory of acclaimed biographer Elizabeth Longford and sponsored by Flora Fraser and Peter Soros. Judged by a panel of distinguished biographers and historians. No unsolicited submissions are accepted and works in translation are not eligible. Founded 2003.

Queen Mary Wasafiri New Writing Prize – see page 581

The James Tait Black Prizes

School of Literatures, Languages, and Cultures, The University of Edinburgh, 50 George Square, Edinburgh EH8 9LH
tel 0131 650 3619
email s.strathdee@ed.ac.uk
website www.ed.ac.uk/events/james-tait-black
Contact Sheila Strathdee

Two prizes of £10,000 are awarded annually: one for the best biography or work of that nature, the other for the best work of fiction, published during the calendar year 1 January to 31 December. The adjudicators are lecturers in English Literature at the University of Edinburgh, with the assistance of teams of postgraduate readers. Entries should be in English and published in the year of the award. Works in translation are eligible.

Publishers should submit two copies of any appropriate biography, or work of fiction, as early as possible with a note of the date of publication, marked 'James Tait Black Prize'. Closing date for submissions: 15 December. Founded 1918.

NATIONAL AND REGIONAL PRIZES UK AND IRELAND

The Aurora Prize

The Garage Studios, Unit 4, 41–43 St Mary's Gate, Nottingham NG1 1PU
tel 0115 793 4110
email info@writingeastmidlands.co.uk
website https://writingeastmidlands.co.uk/for-writers/aurora-prize-for-writing/

National competition seeking outstanding writing in two categories: Short Fiction (2,000 words) and Poetry (60 lines). Prizes in each category: 1st prize: £500, feedback from a literary agent or editor and a one-year membership to the Society of Authors; 2nd prize: £150; 3rd prize: a ticket to Writing East Midlands' Writers' Conference. The best writer from the East Midlands in each category receives £100. Entry deadline: August. Entry fee: £9 (subsequent entries £7). Founded 2016.

The Booker Prize

Somerset House, Strand, London WC2R 1LA
email contactus@bookerprizefoundation.org
website www.thebookerprizes.com
Facebook www.facebook.com/TheBookerPrizes
X @TheBookerPrizes
Instagram @thebookerprizes

Awarded by the Booker Prize Foundation to the author of the best eligible novel. Any novel in print or electronic format, written originally in English and published in the UK and Ireland by an imprint formally established in the UK or Ireland is eligible. Entries are accepted only from UK and Irish publishers. 1st prize: £50,000; six shortlisted authors: £2,500. Founded 1969.

Gordon Burn Prize

email office@newwritingnorth.com
website https://newwritingnorth.com/gordon-burn-prize/

Run by New Writing North, in partnership with the Gordon Burn Trust, Faber & Faber and Newcastle University. Celebrates fiction and non-fiction in the style of Gordon Burns. Entries should be experimental in style, push boundaries, cross genres and challenge reader's expectations. 1st prize: £10,000 and a three-month writing retreat. Founded 2012.

The David Cohen Prize for Literature

New Writing North, 120 Squires Building, Northumbria University, Sandyford Road, Newcastle upon Tyne NE1 8ST
tel 0191 204 8850
email office@newwritingnorth.com
website https://newwritingnorth.com/the-david-cohen-prize-for-literature/

Recognises writers who use the English language and are citizens of the UK or the Republic of Ireland, encompassing dramatists as well as novelists, poets and essayists. The biennial prize, of £40,000, is for a lifetime's achievement and is donated by the John S. Cohen Foundation. The David Cohen Prize for Literature is not open to applications but is awarded by an independent judging panel. Founded 1993.

The Curae Prize

email thecuraeprize@gmail.com
website https://thecuraeprize.uk/

A writing competition for carers across three categories: Short Fiction (4,000 words), Non-Fiction (4,000 words) and Poetry (40 lines). Entries should not previously have been published, including online or on a personal website/blog; entrants should be current, unpaid carers (volunteers for organisations do not count). 1st prize in each category: £250, book tokens, publication in a prize anthology, mentoring session, one year of support and a six-month subscription to Bookbrunch. Entry deadline: March. Founded 2023.

The Diverse Book Awards

email hello@thediversebookawards.co.uk
website www.thediversebookawards.co.uk

Administered by author Abiola Bello and publicist Helen Lewis to celebrate diversity in book publishing in the UK and Ireland. There are four fiction award categories: Adult, YA, Children's and Picture Books. Entries can be traditionally or self-published but must have been published in the preceding year. 1st prize: £500. Entry deadline: March. Founded 2020.

DUBLIN Literary Award

Dublin City Library and Archive, 139–144 Pearse Street, Dublin 2, D02 HE37, Republic of Ireland
tel +353 (0)1 222 4802
email literaryaward@dublincity.ie
website https://dublinliteraryaward.ie
Facebook www.facebook.com/DubLitAward
X @DublinLitAward
Instagram @dublinlitaward

Sponsored by Dublin City Council and managed by Dublin City Libraries, nominations are made by public libraries in capital and major cities throughout the world. Novels are nominated solely on the basis of 'high literary merit', and must be written in or translated into English. 1st prize: €100,000; if translated, the author receives €75,000 and the translator €25,000. The Award celebrates its 30th year in 2025. Founded 1996.

East Anglian Book Awards

email info@nationalcentreforwriting.org.uk
website https://nationalcentreforwriting.org.uk/get-involved/writers/eaba
Facebook www.facebook.com/NationalCentreforWriting
Bluesky @writerscentre.bsky.social
Instagram @writerscentre

Comprised of six categories: Fiction, General Non-Fiction, Poetry, Children's, History & Tradition, and Biography & Memoir, with the £1,000 prize money going to the overall winner: the East Anglian Book of the Year. Books must be largely set in East Anglia or be written by an author living in the region and have been published within the previous calendar year (August to August). Submissions open in July and close in September.

The Hawthornden Prize

Hawthornden Castle, Lasswade, Midlothian EH18 1EG
email office@hawthornden.org
website www.hawthornden.org/hawthornden-prize

A £25,000 prize awarded annually to the author of the book the judges consider the best work of imaginative literature published during the preceding calendar year by a British, Irish or British-based author. Poetry, novels, history, biography and creative non-fiction are all eligible, translations are not. Books are chosen rather than received by submission. Founded 1919.

Hay Festival Book of the Year

The Drill Hall, 25 Lion Street,
Hay-on-Wye HR3 5AD
tel (01497) 822620
email admin@hayfestival.org
website www.hayfestival.com/projects
Facebook www.facebook.com/hayfestival
X @hayfestival
Instagram @hayfestival

Nominations for the award can be made by publishers, authors and members of the public; the winner is chose from the submitted titles by the Festival team. The winner is announced on the eve of the Hay Festival Winter Weekend in late November and publicised on the festival website and social media.

Highland Book Prize

email highlandbookprize@moniackmhor.org.uk
website www.highlandbookprize.org.uk
Facebook www.facebook.com/highlandbookprize
X @HighlandBkPrize
Instagram @highlandbkprize

Recognises works of fiction, non-fiction and poetry that celebrate the landscape and culture of the Scottish Highlands, are set in the Highlands, or whose author was born in or lives in the Highlands. 1st prize: £2,000 and a retreat at Moniack Mhor Creative Writing Centre. Submissions are accepted from publishers only. Founded 2017.

The International Booker Prize

Somerset House, Strand, London WC2R 1LA
email contactus@bookerprizefoundation.org
website www.thebookerprizes.com
Facebook www.facebook.com/TheBookerPrize
X @TheBookerPrizes
Instagram @thebookerprizes

Awarded annually for a single work of fiction, translated into English and published in the UK and Ireland. Both novels and collections of short stories are eligible. As an acknowledgement of the importance of translation, the £50,000 prize is divided equally between the author and the translator. Each shortlisted author and translator receives £2,500. Entries only from UK and Irish publishers.

Kerry Group Irish Novel of the Year Award

24 The Square, Listowel, Co. Kerry V31 RD93, Republic of Ireland
tel +353 (0)68 21074
email info@writersweek.ie
website https://writersweek.ie/kerry-group-irish-novel-of-the-year/

An annual award for a work of literary fiction by an Irish author. Novels must have been published in the previous year; six copies of each book must be submitted. 1st prize: €20,000; four runners-up receive €500. Submission deadline: March.

Jhalak Prose Prize

email info@jhalakprize.com
website www.jhalakprize.com
X @jhalakprize
Instagram @jhalakprize

Seeks out the best books by British/British resident BAME writers. Entries can be in any genre of fiction or non-fiction, including short stories and graphic novels. 1st prize: £1,000 and a unique work of art created by artists of colour as part of the annual Jhalak Art Residency. Submissions open in September and close in December. Founded 2016.

Nilsson Local Heritage Writing Award

Listowel Writers' Week, 24 The Square, Listowel, Co. Kerry V31 RD93, Republic of Ireland
tel +353 (0)68 21074
email info@writersweek.ie
website https://writersweek.ie/nilsson-local-heritage-writing-award/

Awarded to the best book on local heritage and history by an Irish author. The work must have been published in the previous year. Two hard copies must be submitted. 1st prize: €1,000; 2nd prize: €400. Submission deadline: March.

MinK

email mklitfest@gmail.com
website www.mklitfest.org/mink2025
Facebook www.facebook.com/MKLitFest
X @MKlitfest
Instagram @mklitfest

Administered by Milton Keynes Literary Festival, the annual competition seeks flash fiction (500 words), creative non-fiction (500 words) and poetry (40 lines). Entries must respond to that year's chosen theme; the theme for 2025 was 'Home'. There are two categories: 14–19 and 20+. 1st prize in each category: £25; all shortlisted entries are published in an anthology.

Nero Book Awards

c/o The Booksellers Association, 6 Bell Yard, London WC2A 2JR
email info@nerobookawards.com
website https://nerobookawards.com
Facebook www.facebook.com/NeroBookAwards
X @nerobookawards
Instagram @nerobookawards

Administered by the Booksellers Association and in partnership with Brunel University London and Right to Dream. Recognises books that the judges most want to recommend across four categories:

Fiction, Debut Fiction, Non-Fiction and Children's Books. Judging panel includes publishing professionals, authors, booksellers and influencers. Shortlist announced in December, category winners in January and overall winner in March. 1st prize: £5,000 in each category; one overall winner receives the Nero Gold Prize and £30,000. Submissions accepted from publishers only. Founded 2023.

New Angle Prize for East Anglian Literature

Ipswich Institute, Reading Room and Library,
15 Tavern Street, Ipswich IP1 3AA
tel (01473) 253992
email library@ipswichinstitute.org.uk
website www.ipswichinstitute.org.uk/NAP.html
X @PrizeNewAngle
Prize Coordinator Jo Rooks

A biennial award for a recently published book of literary merit, associated with or influenced by the UK region of East Anglia (defined as Norfolk, Suffolk, north Essex, Cambridgeshire and the Fens).

The 2025 award is open to works of fiction or poetry, first published between 1 January 2023 and 31 December 2024. Past winners include Mark Cocker, Jim Kelly, Jules Pretty, Kate Worsley, Julia Blackburn and Anna Mackmin. 1st prize: £3,000; £500 for one runner-up.

Northern Writers' Awards

New Writing North, 120 Squires Building,
Northumbria University, Sandyford Road,
Newcastle upon Tyne NE1 8ST
email awards@newwritingnorth.com
website http://northernwritersawards.com/
Facebook www.facebook.com/newwritingnorth
X @NewWritingNorth
Instagram @newwritingnorth

Established by New Writing North, the Northern Writers' Awards support work-in-progress by new, emerging and established writers across the North of England. The Awards support writers creatively as they develop their work and professionally as they enter the publishing industry. There are three categories: Fiction, Narrative Non-Fiction and Poetry. Prizes range from £2,000 to £5,000.

The Northern Debut Awards recognise writers who have not been published and are in the midst of a work-in-progress. There are four categories: Fiction, Narrative Non-Fiction, Poetry and YA fiction. Five writers receive £2,000 each and mentoring.

Also runs the Tempest Prize for poetry, fiction and narrative non-fiction by a LGBTQ+ writer (£1,000 and mentoring); The Finchale Award for Short Fiction (£1,000); the Sid Chaplin Award for fiction and narrative non-fiction by a working-class writer (£2,000 and writing support); the Great Northern Read Award for debut writers of commercial, genre and book club fiction (£2,500 and mentoring from Johnson & Alcock literary agent); the Northern Promise TLC Awards for writers who have faced financial barriers or are under-represented in the publishing industry (three writers receive £500); and the Channel Four Writing for Television Awards (£3,000, mentoring and work placements).

See the website for individual entry requirements and deadlines.

The People's Book Prize

website www.peoplesbookprize.com
Facebook www.facebook.com/pages/The-Peoples-Book-Prize/200637717319384
X @PeoplesBkPrize
Founder & Prize Administrator Tatiana Wilson, *Director* Julie Hyde Mew, *Patron Emeritus* Frederick Forsyth CBE, *Founding Patron* Dame Beryl Bainbridge DBE

Awards are given in six categories. Publishers are invited to submit up to three titles for each of the first three categories: the Frederick Forsyth Fiction Award, Non-Fiction and Children's. The winners of the next three categories are chosen from the same pool of submissions: the Beryl Bainbridge First-Time Author Award, Best Publisher and Best Achievement.

Polari Book Prize

email paulburston@btinternet.com
website www.polarisalon.com
Facebook www.facebook.com/groups/36989183143
X @polarisalon

Established by Paul Burston, the Prize recognises emerging and established LGBTQ+ literary talent in three categories: the Book Prize, the First Book Prize, and the Children's and YA Prize. Any full-length novel, novella, short story collection, memoir, book of poetry or published play text written in English by a writer born or based in the UK or Ireland is eligible. Writers must identify as LGBTQ+ or explore LGBTQ+ characters in the work submitted. The winners of the First Book Prize and the Children's and YA Prize receive £1,000 each; and the winner of the Book Prize receives £2,000. Full eligibility and submission guidelines can be found on the website. Founded 2011.

The Queen's Reading Room Medal

email info@thequeensreadingroom.co.uk
website https://thequeensreadingroom.co.uk
Facebook www.facebook.com/TheQueensReadingRoom
Instagram @thequeensreadingroom

Celebrates individuals who promote reading and its benefits in their communities. Nominees may have championed reading in a variety of ways, including increasing access to books, encouraging non-readers to pick up books, creating literary events and volunteering for reading organisations. The winner receives a specially designed medal. Nomination deadline: December. Founded 2025.

RSL Ondaatje Prize

Royal Society of Literature, Somerset House, Strand, London WC2R 1LA
tel 020-7845 4679
email info@rsliterature.org
website www.rsliterature.org/rsl-ondaatje-prize

Endowed by Sir Christopher Ondaatje. An annual award for a distinguished work of fiction, non-fiction or poetry, evoking the spirit of a place. Entrants must be a citizen of the UK, RoI or Commonwealth, or have been resident in the UK for three years. 1st prize: £10,000. Founded 2004.

Rubery Book Award

2 Weights Drive, Worcestershire B97 6DZ
email enquiries@ruberybookaward.com
website www.ruberybookaward.com
Facebook www.facebook.com/ruberybookaward
X @RuberyBookAward
Instagram @ruberybookaward

Celebrates books on any subject in the following categories: Fiction, Non-Fiction, Short Fiction, Poetry, and Children and YA. Category winners receive £200 each and one overall Book of the Year receives £2,000. Books published by independent presses and self-published books are eligible. Founded 2010.

The Saltires: Scotland's National Book Awards

The Saltire Society, 9 Fountain Close, 22 High Street, Edinburgh EH1 1TF
tel 0131 556 1836
email literary@saltiresociety.org.uk
website www.saltiresociety.org.uk
X @saltire_society
Instagram @saltiresociety

Administered by the Saltire Society, the Awards recognise debut and established writers in the following categories: Fiction, Non-Fiction and Poetry. Authors from or living in Scotland are eligible. Entry fee: £30 per title. Also runs a Research award for work concerned with Scotland. Founded 1937.

Swansea University Dylan Thomas Prize

Keir Hardie Building, Swansea University, Singleton Park, Swansea SA2 8PP
tel (01792) 513025
email DTPrize@swansea.ac.uk
website www.swansea.ac.uk/dylan-thomas-prize
Facebook www.facebook.com/dylanthomasprize
X @dylanthomasprize
Instagram @dylanthomasprize
Director Elaine Canning

Awarded for the best published literary work in the English language, written by an author aged 39 or under. Celebrates the international world of fiction in all its forms including poetry, novels, short stories and drama. The Prize is named after Swansea-born writer, Dylan Thomas, and celebrates his 39-year career. 1st prize: £20,000. Founded 2006.

Wales Book of the Year Award

Literature Wales, Tŷ Newydd Writing Centre, Llanystumdwy, Cricieth, Gwynedd LL52 0LW
tel 029-2047 2266, (01766) 522811
email post@literaturewales.org
website www.literaturewales.org/our-projects/wales-book-year
Facebook www.facebook.com/LlenCymruLitWales
X @LitWales
Instagram @llencymru_litwales
Executive Director Claire Furlong, *Artistic Director* Leusa Llewelyn

Administered by Literature Wales. Presented to the best Welsh and English-language works first published in the year preceding the ceremony. Given to work in the fields of creative writing and literary criticism in four categories: Poetry, Fiction, Creative Non-Fiction, and Children and Young People. There are six awards each for work in Welsh and English (four category winners, one People's Choice winner and one overall winner each) with a total prize fund of £14,000. Entry to the prize is free for Welsh writers.

Wells Festival of Literature Competitions

email competitions@wellsfestivalofliterature.org.uk
website www.wellsfestivalofliterature.org.uk
Facebook www.facebook.com/Wellslitfest
X @wellslitfest
Instagram @wellsfestivalofliterature

Administers awards throughout the year in four categories: Poetry, Short Story, Books for Children and Young Poet. Prizes are awarded to the top three entries in each category and an additional prize for the best local writer in each category. All winners are recognised at the Festival each year.

POETRY

Aesthetica Creative Writing Award

email writing@aestheticamagazine.com
website https://aestheticamagazine.com/creative-writing-award/
Facebook www.facebook.com/aestheticamagazine
X @AestheticaMag
Instagram @aestheticamag

Administered by *Aesthetica* magazine. Celebrates the most innovative emerging, mid-career and established writers. Entries can be on any subject, but the prize is particularly interested in work that explores our changing world. There are two categories: Poetry and Short Fiction. The winner of each category receives £2,500, publication and a range of writing courses, masterclasses and subscriptions. Poetry submissions must be 40 lines or less and short fiction can be up to 2,000 words. The winner of each category receives £2,500 and a package of other prizes and benefits. Submission deadline: 31 August. Entry fee: £12 (poetry); £18 (short fiction).

Binsted Prize

email southdownspf@gmail.com
website https://www.sdpf.org.uk/competition/
X @SDPFestival

The South Downs Poetry Festival welcomes poems on any theme. Poems should be no longer than 40 lines and should not have been published. Prizes: 1st: £300; 2nd: £150; 3rd: £50. Winning and commended poems are published in an anthology; the winning poems also appear in the South Downs Poetry Festival magazine, *Poetry & All That Jazz*. Prize winners and commended poets are invited to read their entry at the festival. Entry fee: £5 for the first poem, £4 for subsequent poems; poets aged 16–25 years can enter for £3 per poem.

The Bournemouth Writing Prize – see page 599

The Bridport Prize: Poetry

Bridport Arts Centre, South Street, Bridport, Dorset DT6 3NR
email kate@bridportprize.org.uk
website https://bridportprize.org.uk/the-competition/poetry/
Facebook www.facebook.com/bridportprize
X @BridportPrize
Instagram @bridportprize

Supports poets on their journey to publication. Poems must not have been published or self-published and must not exceed 42 lines. 1st prize: £5,000; 2nd prize: £2,000; 3rd prize: £1,000; ten highly-commended entries each receive £100. Entry fee: £12 per poem. Closing date each year: 31 May.

British Haiku Society Awards

email bhsawardsadmin@fastmail.co.uk
website www.britishhaikusociety.org.uk/bhsawards/
Facebook www.facebook.com/thebritishhaikusociety
Instagram @britishhaikusociety

Awards prizes in three categories: Haiku, Tanka and Haibun. Submissions must be in English, unpublished and not under consideration for any other prizes. Prizes in each category: 1st: £125; runner-up: £50. All winners are published on the BHS website and in the May issue of the BHS journal, *Blithe Spirit*.

Canterbury Festival Poet of the Year

Festival House, 8 Orange Street, Canterbury, Kent CT1 2JA
tel (01227) 452853
email tina@canterburyfestival.co.uk
website https://canterburyfestival.co.uk
Facebook www.facebook.com/canterburyfest
X @canterburyfest
Instagram @canterburyfest

Managed by the Festival Friends, the competition attracts entries locally, nationally and internationally. Open from March to June. Entries that make the longlist are published in an anthology. Winners are announced on National Poetry Day. 1st prize: £300; 2nd prize: £150; 3rd prize: £75. Submission fee: £5. Founded 2007.

Cheltenham Poetry Festival International Poetry Prize

Flat 5, 19 Pittville Lawn, Cheltenham, Gloucestershire GL52 2BE
email cheltpoetrycomp25@gmail.com
website https://cheltenhampoetryfestival.co.uk/
Facebook www.facebook.com/Cheltpoetryfest
X @Cheltpoetfest
Instagram @cheltenhampoetryfestival

Accepts poems of no more than 50 lines; entries must be in English and must not previously have been published. 1st prize: £300 and an opportunity to read their work at the Cheltenham Poetry Festival; 2nd prize: £100; 3rd prize: £50. Entry deadline: October. Entry fee: £4 per poem; £10 for 3 poems; £15 for 5 poems.

Cholmondeley Awards

The Society of Authors, 24 Bedford Row, London WC1R 4EH
tel 020-3880 2230
email prizes@societyofauthors.org
website https://societyofauthors.org/prizes/the-soa-awards/cholmondeley-awards
Facebook www.facebook.com/TheSocietyofAuthors
X @Soc_of_Authors
Instagram @thesocietyofauthors
Grants & Prizes Manager Aine Pullan, *Grants & Prizes Design Manager* Natalie Thorpe, *Head of Fundraising, Grants & Prizes* Robyn Law

Honorary awards recognising the achievement and distinction of individual poets. Submissions are not accepted. Founded in 1966 by the late Dowager Marchioness of Cholmondeley.

The Curae Prize – see page 585

Disabled Poets Prize

email hello@disabledpoetsprize.org.uk
website https://disabledpoetsprize.org.uk
X @DisabledPoets

The UK's first poetry prize specifically for disabled poets, launched in collaboration with Spread the Word, Verve Poetry Press and CRIPtic Arts. Rewards the best poetry created by d/Deaf and disabled poets in two categories. Single Poem and Unpublished

Pamphlet: Prizes in each category: 1st: £500; 2nd: £250; 3rd: £100; three highly commended entries: £50 and creative development opportunities; the winning entry in the unpublished pamphlet category also receives a publication deal with Verve Poetry Press. Founded 2023.

The T.S. Eliot Prize

c/o T.S. Eliot Foundation,
3 Kensington Court Gardens,
Kensington Court Place, London W8 5QE
website https://tseliot.com/prize/
Facebook www.facebook.com/tseliotprize
X @tseliotprize
Instagram @tseliotprize
Director Michael Sims

An annual prize awarded by the T.S. Eliot Foundation to the best collection of new poetry published in the UK or the Republic of Ireland. 1st prize: £25,000; ten shortlisted poets receive £1,500 each. Submissions are invited from publishers in June with a closing date at the end of July. The shortlist is announced in October and the winner in January, the day after the T.S. Eliot Prize Readings in the Royal Festival Hall.

Erbacce Prize

5 Farrell Close, Melling, Merseyside L31 1BU
tel 07957 928671
email editor@erbacce-press.co.uk
website https://erbacce-press.co.uk
Prize Administrators Dr A. Taylor, Dr A. Corkish

Supports budding poets taking the next step in their career by giving them their first experience of publishing a collection. Seeks poems that are radical in form and/or content. Entrants should submit five pages of poetry via the website. Submissions may previously have been published individually. Entries are judged anonymously by a panel of poets and academics based in England, Wales and Belgium. One winner receives a publishing contract with Erbacce press, including editorial support, collaboration on a cover design, publication of a full-length poetry collection and a 20% royalty rate on copies sold through their online store. Eight or more runners-up are included in a bi-annual journal of the best new poetry. Submissions open January to April.

Fool for Poetry Chapbook Competition

The Munster Literature Centre,
Frank O'Connor House, 84 Douglas Street,
Cork T12 X704, Republic of Ireland
email foolforpoetry@munsterlit.ie
website https://www.munsterlit.ie/fool-for-poetry/

Run by the Munster Literature Centre. Open to new, emerging and established poets from any country, but at least one of the winners will not have previously been published. 1st prize: €1,000; 2nd prize: €500. Both winners receive a chapbook publication and 25 complimentary copies. The winning poets are also offered a reading and three nights' accommodation at the Cork International Poetry Festival. Entry fee: €25.

Forward Prizes for Poetry

Forward Arts Foundation,
Somerset House Exchange, Strand,
London WC2R 1LA
tel 020-8187 9861
email prizes@forwardartsfoundation.org
website www.forwardartsfoundation.org
X @ForwardPrizes
Bluesky @forwardprizes.bsky.social
Instagram @forwardprizes

Established by William Sieghart, four prizes are awarded annually: the Best Collection published in the UK and Republic of Ireland (£10,000); the Felix Dennis Prize for Best First Collection (£5,000); the Best Single Poem – Written (published but not as part of a collection, pamphlet or anthology; £1,000); and the Best Single Poem – Performed or Produced (£1,000).

All poems entered are also considered for inclusion in the *Forward Book of Poetry*, an annual anthology. Entries for the Best Collection and Best First Collection must be submitted by book publishers; entries for Best Single Poem – Written, by editors of newspapers, periodicals, magazines or online journals, or by competition organisers; Best Single Poem – Performed or produced, is the only category that allows self-submission. There are no submission fees. Founded 1992.

The Griffin Poetry Prize

The Griffin Trust for Excellence in Poetry,
363 Parkridge Crescent, Oakville, ON L6M 1A8, Canada
tel +1 905-618-0420
email info@griffinpoetryprize.com
website www.griffinpoetryprize.com
Facebook www.facebook.com/GriffinPoetryPrize
X @griffinpoetry
Instagram @griffinpoetry

Awarded annually to the best collection of poetry written in, or translated into, English. The winner receives $130,000 and shortlisted poets each receive $10,000. Additionally, the Canadian First Book Prize winner receives $10,000 and a six-week residency in Italy in partnership with the Civitella Ranieri Foundation. Submissions are accepted from publishers only. Founded 2000.

Hastings Book Festival Competition

99 Cambridge Road, Hastings, East Sussex TN34 1EP
email info@hastingsbookfest.org
website www.hastingsbookfest.org
Facebook www.facebook.com/HastingsBookFest/
Instagram @hastingsbookfestival

An annual competition for poetry (maximum 40 lines) and short stories (maximum 3,000 words). Prizes in each category: 1st prize: £250; 2nd prize: £100; 3rd prize: £50. Two further prizes are offered: The Sussex prize for the best entry in each category from an author living in Sussex and the LGBT+ Prize for the overall best entry from a UK-based LGBTQ+ writer. Entry fee: £8.25 per entry. Free entries are available for writers on low income. Submission deadline: July.

The International Poetry Business Book & Pamphlet Competition

The Poetry Business, Campo House,
54 Campo Lane, Sheffield S1 2EG
tel 0114 438 4074
email office@poetrybusiness.co.uk
website www.poetrybusiness.co.uk
Facebook www.facebook.com/thepoetrybusiness
Instagram @poetrybusiness
Directors Ann Sansom, Peter Sansom

Entrants are invited to submit a collection of 20 pages of poetry. Two winners are published by Smith|Doorstop books and receive £500 and a place on a residential writing course. Two runners-up receive £500 each and publication in *The North* magazine. There is also an opportunity to submit a full-length manuscript, which, where the judges feel it is appropriate, is published as a book in the following year. Entry fee: £29; free entries available for those who cannot afford the entry fee. Entry deadline: March. Founded 1986.

Iota Shot Pamphlet Awards

Templar Poetry & Iota Magazine, 58 Dale Road, Matlock, Derbyshire DE4 3NB
tel 07582 219078
email info@templarpoetry.com
website https://templarpoetry.com/pages/submissions-and-awards
Facebook www.facebook.com/templarpoetry/
X @TemplarPoetry

Administered by Templar Poetry. Offers poets the opportunity to publish their first pamphlet-length manuscript. Entrants should submit between 16 and 25 pages of poetry. Up to three poets are published; shortlisted poets have their work published in Iota magazine and are invited to submit a collection for publication. Entry deadline: October. Entry fee: £20.

Jhalak Poetry Prize

email info@jhalakprize.com
website www.jhalakprize.com
X @jhalakprize
Instagram @jhalakprize

Administered by the Jhalak Foundation, the Prize celebrates poetry by writers of colour in the UK and Ireland. Accepts entries of poetry aimed at adults as well as children and young adults, and both traditionally published and self-published entries. 1st prize: £1000 and a unique work of art created by artists of colour as part of the annual Jhalak Art Residency. Submissions open in September and close in December.

Keats-Shelley Prize – see page 616

Kent and Sussex Poetry Society Open Poetry Competition

email kentandsussexpoetry@gmail.com
website www.kentandsussexpoetry.com
Facebook www.facebook.com/kentandsussexpoetrysoc
X @KentSusXPoetry

Open to all unpublished poems, no longer than 40 lines. 1st prize: £1,000; 2nd prize: £300; 3rd prize: £100; 4th prize: four at £50. Entry fee £5 per poem (£4 per poem if submitting more than three poems). Entry deadline: January. Founded 1985.

The Laurel Prize

Poetrty School, 1 City Square, Leeds LS1 2ES
website https://laurelprize.com/
Instagram @thelaurelprize

Established by Poet Laureate Simon Armitage in association with the Poetry School. Awarded to the best collection of nature or environmental poetry that highlights the challenges of and potential solutions to the climate crisis. Entrants should submit published poetry collections of over 40 pages written in English. 1st prize: £5,000. Founded 2020.

Ledbury Poetry Competition

Ledbury Poetry, Barrett Browning Institute, Homend, Ledbury HR8 2AA
tel (01531) 634156
email director@ledburypoetry.org.uk
website https://ledburypoetry.org.uk
Facebook www.facebook.com/ledburypoetry
X @LedburyPoetry
Instagram @ledburypoetry
Director Amy Howard

Supports the work of emerging poets. Entrants should submit up to ten poems of no more than 40 lines each that have not previously been published. 1st prize: £1,000 and a place on a week-long poetry course; 2nd prize: £500; 3rd prize: £250. All winners are invited to perform their winning poem at the Ledbury Poetry Festival. Entry deadline: July. Entry fee: £6.

Listowel Writers' Week Poetry Competitions

Listowel Writers' Week, 24 The Square, Listowel, Co. Kerry V31 RD93, Republic of Ireland
tel +353 (0)1 682 1074
email info@writersweek.ie
website www.writersweek.ie/comp-2025/

Holds three poetry competitions: the Pigott Poetry Prize for the best collection of new poetry (€12,000 prize); the Poetry Collection Award for a collection of 6–12 poems or one long poem of comparable length (€2,500 prize); and the Single Poem Award for a poem of no more than 70 lines (€700 prize).

The London Magazine Poetry Prize

11 Queen's Gate, London SW7 5EL
tel 020-7584 5977
email info@thelondonmagazine.org
website www.thelondonmagazine.org/the-london-magazine-poetry-prize-2025/
X @TheLondonMag
Bluesky @thelondonmagazine.bsky.social
Instagram @thelondonmagazine
Editor Steven O'Brien, *Managing Editor* Jamie Cameron, *Editorial Assistant* Zadie Loft

Annual prize offering a chance to be published in the UK's oldest literary magazine, established in 1732. Poems submitted must be previously unpublished and no longer than 40 lines. Previous judges include Joelle Taylor, Fiona Benson and Jason Allen-Paisant. 1st prize: £500; 2nd prize: £300; 3rd prize: £200, plus publication in the magazine. Entry fee: first entry £10; subsequent entries £5 each; low-income writers can submit up to three poems for £5.

The Manchester Poetry Prize

The Manchester Writing School at Manchester Metropolitan University, Grosvenor East Building, Cavendish Street, Manchester M15 6BG
tel 0161 247 2000
email writingschool@mmu.ac.uk
website www.mmu.ac.uk/writingcompetition/
X @McrWritingSchl

Part of the Manchester Writing Competition run by The Manchester Writing School. Created by UK Poet Laureate (2009–19) Carol Ann Duffy, the competition is designed to celebrate Manchester as an international city of writers, find diverse new voices and create opportunities for writer development.

Entrants are asked to submit a portfolio of three to five poems. An award of £10,000 is made to the overall winner or winners. Entry fee: £18.

The Michael Marks Awards for Poetry Pamphlets

email admin@michaelmarksawards.org
website www.michaelmarksawards.org
Facebook www.facebook.com/michaelmarksawards
X @MarksAwards
Instagram @michaelmarksawards

Supported by the Michael Marks Charitable Trust, the Awards raise the profile of poetry pamphlets. Include prizes for pamphlet (£5,000), illustrations (£1,000) and publisher (£5,000). Pamphlets must have been published in the preceding year and can be submitted by poets and illustrators themselves or by publishers on their behalf. A separate award, The Environmental Poet of the Year (£1,000), is awarded for a portfolio of new poetry, which is published as a pamphlet as part of the prize. Founded 2009.

MinK – see page 586

The Moth Poetry Prize

Ardan Grange, Milltown, Belturbet, Co. Cavan, Ireland H14 K768, Republic of Ireland
tel +1 872-657-251
email enquiries@themothmagazine.com
website www.themothmagazine.com
Facebook www.facebook.com/themothmagazine
X @themothmagazine
Instagram @themothmagazine
Director Rebecca O'Connor

Awarded annually to 12 unpublished poems, chosen by a different judge each year. Previous judges include Fiona Benson, Nick Laird and Louise Gluck. 1st prize: €6,000; three runners-up receive €1,000; eight commended poems receive €250. Anyone over 16 can enter. All four poems appear in the *Irish Times* online. Entry deadline: 31 December. Entry fee: €16. Founded 2011.

Mslexia Competitions: Poetry

PO Box 656, Newcastle upon Tyne NE99 1PZ
tel 0191 204 8860
email competitions@mslexia.co.uk
website https://mslexia.co.uk/competitions/single-poem-poetry/,
https://mslexia.co.uk/competitions/pamphlet-poetry/
Facebook www.facebook.com/Mslexia/
X @mslexia
Instagram @mslexia

Two annual prizes for poets who identify as women. Poems should not previously have been published. Entry deadline: December.

Single poem: Entrants should submit a single poem; there is no word count. 1st prize: £2,000; 2nd prize: £500; 3rd prize: £250; the best entry from a poet who has not previously had their work published also receives £250. All of the winners and 16 runners-up are published in *Mslexia* magazine. Entry fee: £10.

Pamphlet: Entrants should submit one word document with no more than 40 lines of poetry on each page. 1st prize: £250 and publication with Bloodaxe Books. Entry fee: £20.

Michael Murphy Memorial Poetry Prize

The English Association, Room 244, Senate House, Malet Street, London WC1E 7HU
email awards@englishassociation.ac.uk
website https://englishassociation.ac.uk/michael-murphy-memorial-prize-poetry-competition/

A biennial prize celebrating a distinctive first book of poetry in honour of the eponymous poet. The winner receives £1,000 and a review of their collection appears in a selection of the English Association's publications. Submissions open again in January 2027.

National Poetry Competition

The Poetry Society, 22 Betterton Street, London WC2H 9BX
tel 020-7420 9880
email info@poetrysociety.org.uk
website https://poetrysociety.org.uk/competitions/national-poetry-competition/
Facebook www.facebook.com/thepoetrysociety
X @PoetrySociety
Bluesky @poetrysociety.bsky.social
Instagram @thepoetrysociety
Threads @thepoetrysociety

Accepts poems up to 40 lines long on any theme (previously unpublished and written in English). Judged by a panel of three leading poets. Entrants to the National Poetry Competition can opt in to be considered for the Peggy Poole Award, which provides a year of mentorship. Winning entries receive cash prizes. Founded 1978.

The New Poets Prize

The Poetry Business, Campo House, 54 Campo Lane, Sheffield S1 2EG
tel 0114 346 3037
email office@poetrybusiness.co.uk
website www.poetrybusiness.co.uk
Facebook www.facebook.com/thepoetrybusiness
Instagram @poetrybusiness
Directors Peter Sansom, Ann Sansom

A pamphlet competition for writers aged 17–24 years. Entrants are invited to submit short poetry collections of 12 pages. Two outstanding collections are published as pamphlets. Founded 1986.

PEN Heaney Prize

English Pen, 24 Bedford Row, London WC1R 4EH
tel 020-7250 8382
email events@englishpen.org
website www.englishpen.org/prizes/pen-heaney-prize

In collaboration with the estate of Seamus Heaney, the Prize seeks single-author volumes of poetry that reflect Heaney's values and interests and respond to the impact of cultural or political events on people and relationships. Collections published in the UK or Ireland in the year preceeding the Prize, in English or translated into English, are eligible. 1st prize: £5,000 for the author (and a further £5,000 for the translator where applicable). Entry deadline: June. Founded 2024.

The Plough Prize

The Plough Arts Centre, 9–11 Fore Street, Great Torrington, Devon EX38 8HQ
tel (01805) 622552
website www.theploughartscentre.org.uk/poetry-prize-2025
Facebook www.facebook.com/ThePloughArtsCentre
X @PloughArts
Instagram @plougharts

Open to poems on any subject, up to 40 lines long. 1st prize: £1,000; 2nd prize; £500; 3rd prize: £250. Entry deadline: March. Entry fee: £5.

Poems on the Move

Guernsey Literary Festival, PO Box 174, St Peter Port, Guernsey GY1 3LG
email poetry@guernseyliteraryfestival.com
website https://poemsonthemove.com
Facebook www.facebook.com/GuernseyLiteraryFestival
Instagram @guernseylitfest
Director Livia Bluecher

International poetry competition administered by the Guernsey Literary Festival. There are three categories: Young People (anybody aged 11–18 years old), Channel Islands (Channel Islands residents aged 18+), and Open (anybody aged 11–17 years old). Entries must not have previously been published and must be no longer than 14 lines and fit on a single A4 page. The top three poets in each category receive cash prizes and are invited to read their poems at the Festival; the top nine poems are exhibited at Guernsey Airport and across the island; the top 21 poems are displayed on Guernsey buses. Entry fee: £4 per poem or £10 for three (entries to the Young People category is free). Founded 2014.

The Poetry London Prize

Goldsmiths, University of London, New Cross, London SE14 6NW
email admin@poetrylondon.co.uk
website https://poetrylondon.co.uk/opportunities/#the-poetry-london-prize
Facebook www.facebook.com/poetrylondon
X @Poetry_London
Instagram @poetry_london

Awarded to a single poem of no more than 80 lines; poems should not previously have been published. 1st prize £5,000; 2nd prize £2,000; 3rd prize £1,000. Entry deadline: June. Entry fee: £5 per poem for subscribers; £10 per poem for non-subscribers; free entries are available for writers from disadvantaged backgrounds.

The John Pollard Foundation International Poetry Prize

Trinity Oscar Wilde Centre for Irish Writing, School of English, 21 Westland Row, Trinity College, Dublin, Dublin 2, Ireland
tel +353 (0)1 896 2885
email wilde@tcd.ie
website www.tcd.ie/OWC/john-pollard-prize

Administered by Trinity College Dublin's Oscar Wilde Centre, the Prize recognises exceptional debut collections of poetry. Submissions of poetry books, of at least 48 pages in length and published in the preceding year, are accepted from publishers only. 1st prize: €10,000. Founded 2019.

Queen Mary Wasafiri New Writing Prize – see page 581

The Rialto Nature and Place Poetry Competition

74 Britannia Road, Norwich NR1 4HS
email matt.howard@therialto.co.uk
website www.therialto.co.uk/pages/nature-poetry-competition

The Rialto, working in association with the RSPB, Birdlife International, The University of Leeds Poetry Centre and the Cambridge Conservation Initiative, invites poems that deal with any aspect of nature and place. Poems must be unpublished, written in English and not exceed 40 lines. 1st prize: £1,000; 2nd prize: £500; 3rd prize: £250. Entry deadline: April. Entry fee: £7; subsequent entries cost £4 each.

RSL Jerwood Poetry Awards

Royal Society of Literature, Somerset House, London WC2R 1LA
tel 020-7845 4679
email info@rsliterature.org
website https://rsliterature.org/rsl-jerwood-poetry-awards
Facebook www.facebook.com/RoyalSocietyLiterature
X @RSLiterature
Instagram @royalsocietyofliterature

The Awards provide mentoring and financial support annually for one poet from each UK nation. Nominations are accepted from selected literary and poetry organisations; nominees must be permanently resident in the UK. Each poet receives £10,000, as well as mentoring from an RSL Fellow poet and the opportunity to take part in networking sessions and put on their own events and performances. Founded 2024.

Society of Medical Writers Competitions – see page 621

The Somerset Maugham Awards – see page 581

Straid Collection Awards

Templar Poetry & Iota Magazine, 58 Dale Road, Matlock, Derbyshire DE4 3NB
tel 07582 219078
email info@templarpoetry.com
website https://templarpoetry.com/pages/submissions-and-awards
Facebook www.facebook.com/templarpoetry/
X @TemplarPoetry

Administered by Templar Poetry. Entrants should submit a full-length collection of poetry. Winning poets have their collections published and receive promotional support. Entry deadline: November. Entry fee: £25.

Ver Poets Open Competition

website www.verpoets.co.uk

Open to poems of up to 30 lines on any genre or subject matter, which must not have been previously published. 1st prize: £600; 2nd prize: £300; 3rd prize: £100. Shortlisted poems are published in an anthology. Entry deadline: April. Entry fee: £4 per poem, three poems for £10 (£3 per poem thereafter); free entries are available for low-income writers.

Welsh Poetry Competition

email info@welshpoetry.co.uk
website https://welshpoetry.co.uk/

Awarded to a single poem. 1st prize: £500; 2nd prize: £250; 3rd prize: £100. Winners and 17 runners-up are published in an anthology. Entry deadline: June. Entry fee: £6 per poem.

Wigtown Poetry Prizes

11 North Main Street, Wigtown, Dumfries and Galloway DG8 8HN
tel (01988) 402036
email mail@wigtownbookfestival.com
website www.wigtownpoetryprize.com
Facebook www.facebook.com/WigtownBookFestival
X @WigtownBookFest
Instagram @wigtownbookfest

Scotland's International Poetry Prizes recognise poetry across five categories.

There are three main categories: Wigtown International Poetry Prize (entries must be in English, Gaelic or Scots; 1st prize: £1,500); Wigtown Gaelic Poetry Prize (entries must be in Scottish Gaelic; 1st prize: £500); Wigtown Scots Poetry Prize (entries must be in Scots; 1st prize: £500). Runner-up in each main category: £200. Entry fee: £8–10; entries into the Gaelic and Scots Prizes are eligible for free entry into the International Prize.

Alastair Reid Pamphlet Prize: 1st prize: publication of a pamphlet of poetry. Entry fee: £25.

Dumfries and Galloway Fresh Voice Award: Exclusively for poets who have not published a full-length collection and live in the Dumfries and Galloway region. 1st prize: professional mentoring and a retreat at Moniack Mhor Creative Writing Centre. Entry fee: £10.

Poems should not exceed 40 lines and pamphlets should not exceed 12 pages. Entries open in November and close in May. Founded 2005.

Winchester Poetry Prize

University of Winchester, Sparkford Road, Winchester, Hampshire SO22 4NR
email hello@winchesterpoetryfestival.org
website www.winchesterpoetryfestival.org/prize

Awarded to poetry of up to 40 lines. Entries should be in English, typed and never before published. 1st prize: £1,000; 2nd prize: £500; 3rd prize: £250. An anthology of longlisted entries is published annually. Entry deadline: 31 July each year. Entry fee: £6 for first poem; £5 for subsequent poems. Founded 2016.

Writing Magazine: Swanwick Summer School Competition – see page 604

SELF-PUBLISHED AND UNAGENTED WRITERS

Blue Pencil Agency First Novel Award

email info@bluepencilagency.com
website https://bluepencilagency.com/
Facebook www.facebook.com/bluepencilagency
X @bluepencil_edit
Instagram @bluepencilagency

Open to unrepresented authors for a novel in any adult fiction genre. Offers cash prizes and agent introductions for the winner and runners-up. Entrants should submit their opening 5,000 words, a 300-word synopsis and a cover letter. Entries open in January and close in May. Founded 2017.

Blue Pencil Agency Pitch Prize

Open to unrepresented authors for a novel opening in any adult fiction genre. Up to ten winners are given the opportunity to pitch their novel to the literary agent judge. Entrants should submit the first 500 words of their opening chapter, a 300-word synopsis and a cover letter. Entries open in August and close in November. Founded 2019.

Book Edit Writers' Prize

email writersprize@thebookedit.co.uk
website www.thebookedit.co.uk/writers-prize
X @EmilyJPedder
Instagram @bookeditors
Founder Emily Pedder

Supports British- and UK-based unpublished novelists who are from backgrounds and communities currently under-represented in publishing. Eight winners are invited to read their work at a showcase in front of key literary agents; an anthology of the readings is published online. All entrants receive career advice. Entrants should submit the first 1,000 words of an adult or YA novel, a synopsis of the novel and details of their writing experience to date. Free to enter. Founded 2021.

Caledonia Novel Award

email caledoniaaward@gmail.com
website https://thecaledonianovelaward.com
Facebook www.facebook.com/caledoniaaward
X @caledoniaaward
Instagram @caledonianovelaward

International competition for unpublished and self-published novelists. Novels can be of any genre for adults or young adults. The award is open to writers of any nationality, aged 18 years and older. Entrants should submit the first 20 pages of a completed novel and a 200-word synopsis. 1st prize: £1,500; highly commended prize: £500; the author of the best novel from the UK and Ireland wins a free place on a writing course at Moniack Mhor Creative Writing Centre. Entry fee: £28. The award provides a number of sponsored places to low-income writers who are unable to afford the fee.

The Cheshire Novel Prize

website https://cheshirenovelprize.com
Facebook www.facebook.com/cheshirenovelprize
X @prize_novel
Instagram @cheshirenovelprize

Only accepts entries from unagented writers; self-published writers may apply. Every unsuccessful entrant receives at least one paragraph of feedback explaining why they were not longlisted. Submit a one-page synopsis and the first 5,000 words of a novel for adults or young adults (not children). 1st prize: £1,500; 2nd prize: £500. Entry fee £29; sponsored entries are available for writers who are under-represented in publishing. Founded 2021.

Comedy Women in Print Awards – see page 613

Creative Future Writers' Award

Community Base, 113 Queens Road,
Brighton BN1 3XG
tel (01273) 234780
email info@creativefuture.org.uk
website www.creativefuture.org.uk
Facebook www.facebook.com/creativefuture
X @CreativeF_uture
Instagram @creativefutureuk

An annual award for talented writers who lack opportunities due to mental health, disability or social circumstances. Entrants should submit 50 lines of poetry or 2,000 words of fiction or creative non-fiction. Prizes, including cash and professional and creative development support, are awarded to the top five writers in each category. Entry deadline: May. Founded 2013.

FAB Prize for Undiscovered Talent

email prize@fabfaber.co.uk
website www.fabprize.org
Facebook www.facebook.com/faberchildrensbooks
X @FaberChildrens
Instagram @faberchildrens

An annual competition for unagented and unpublished writers and illustrators from Black, Asian and/or non-white minority ethnic backgrounds. The Prize provides a unique opportunity to kickstart a writing or illustrating career. There are two categories: Text and Illustration. Entries must be text or artwork for children aged 1–18 years; writers should submit no more that 5,000 words of text (or the entirety of a picture book text); illustrators should submit a portfolio of their work. 1st prize in each category: £1,500 and access to mentoring and development opportunities. Founded 2017.

First Novel Prize

The Literary Studio Ltd, Gridiron Building,
One Pancras Square, London N1C 4AG
email hello@theliterarystudio.co.uk
website www.firstnovel.co.uk

Organised by The Literary Studio. Open to previously unpublished and independently published novelists. Entrants should submit an extract of up to 5,000 words from a novel of any adult genre. Judges include a leading literary agent and an adult fiction commissioning editor. 1st prize: £1,000; shortlist prize: £500. Entry fee: £25. Entries are open February to May every year.

Future Worlds Prize for Fantasy & Science Fiction Writers of Colour – see page 614

I AM Writing Competitions

Kingfisher House, Rownhams Lane,
North Baddesley, Southampton SO52 9LP
email competitions@iaminprint.co.uk
website www.iaminprint.co.uk
Facebook www.facebook.com/iaminprint
X @IAminPrint
Instagram @iaminprint

Awards are given in the following genres: Action/Adventure, Cosy Crime, Crime/Thriller, Historical, Horror, Literary, Romance, Sci-Fi/Fantasy, Chapter Books, Middle Grade/YA and Picture Books. Prizes include cash, feedback from literary agents and online meetings with publishing professionals.

The JBA Over 50 Debut Award

42 The Causeway, Edinburgh EH15 3PZ
email debut@jennybrownassociates.com
website https://jennybrownassociates.com/debut-writers-over-50-award
Facebook www.facebook.com/JennyBrownAssociates/
Instagram @jennybrownassociates

The biennial Award from Jenny Brown Associates recognises debut authors aged 50 or older, who are both unpublished and unrepresented. Entrants should submit the first 5,000 words of a novel. Winners are chosen by a panel of judges. 1st prize: £1,000 and a place on a residential writing course at Moniack Mhor Creative Writing Centre; runners-up receive mentoring sessions tailored to their work. Founded 2023.

Kindle Storyteller Award

website www.amazon.co.uk/b?node=12061299031

Open to submissions of new English-language books in any genre. Titles must be previously unpublished and be available as an ebook and in print via Kindle Direct Publishing. The award shortlist is decided by reader feedback and a panel of industry judges. The winning author receives £20,000 and promotional support for their title. Competition entry period runs from 1 May to 31 August.

Leapfrog Global Fiction Prize

Can of Worms Press, 7 Peacock Yard, Iliffe Street,
London SE17 3LH
email prize@leapfrogpress.com
website www.leapfrogprize.org,
www.canofworms.net/prize
Facebook www.facebook.com/Leapfrogpress
X @LeapfrogPress1
Instagram @leapfrogpress

Aimed at writers of literary and commercial fiction in two categories: the Adult Fiction category includes novels, novellas and short story collections; the YA and Middle-Grade Fiction category includes novels only. For both categories the minimum word count is 22,000 and work must be unpublished (individual stories in a collection may have already been published and self-published work that sold less than 200 copies is considered unpublished). 1st prize: publication with Leapfrog Press in the USA and Can of Worms Press outside the USA. Finalists receive $150 and a manuscript critique from one or more of the judges. Founded 2009.

#Merky Books New Writers' Prize

1 Embassy Gardens, 8 Viaduct Gardens,
London SW11 7BW
tel 020-7840 8400
email merkybooksnwp@penguinrandomhouse.co.uk
website www.penguin.co.uk/merky-new-writers-prize
X @MerkyBooks
Instagram @merkybooks

A competition for unpublished and unagented writers of fiction, aged between 18 and 35. Entrants should submit a 200-word synopsis and a 1,500-word extract. One winner receives a publishing contract; all shortlisted authors are invited to an in-person writers' camp that includes workshops, panel talks and one-to-one editorial feedback. Founded 2021.

The Moth Nature Writing Prize

Ardan Grange, Milltown, Belturbet, Co. Cavan,
Ireland H14 K768, Republic of Ireland
tel +1 872-657-251
email enquiries@themothmagazine.com
website www.themothmagazine.com
Facebook www.facebook.com/themothmagazine
X @themothmagazine
Instagram @themothmagazine
Director Rebecca O'Connor

Awarded to three unpublished pieces of prose or poetry (maximum 4,000 words) that best combine exceptional literary merit with an exploration of the writer's relationship with the natural world. The winners are chosen by a different judge each year. Previous judges include Richard Mabey, Helen Macdonald and Max Porter. 1st prize: €1,000 plus a week-long retreat at Circle of Misse in France; 2nd prize: €500; 3rd prize: €250. The winning pieces are published in the *Irish Times* online. Entry fee: €16. Entry deadline: 30 September. Founded 2020.

New Writers Award

Scottish Book Trust, Sandeman House,
Trunk's Close, 55 High Street, Edinburgh EH1 1SR
tel 0131 524 0160
email info@scottishbooktrust.com
website www.scottishbooktrust.com/writing-and-authors/new-writers-awards/
Facebook www.facebook.com/scottishbktrust/
X @scottishbktrust

An annual awards programme supporting individuals committed to developing their writing. There are five categories: Fiction, Narrative Non-Fiction, Poetry, Children's and YA. In association with Gaelic Books Council the Gaelic New Writing Awards are given to two writers working in Gaelic; The Callan Gordon Award is an additional award given every two years for a writer of poetry or short stories by a writer aged 18–35; The Next Chapter Award is given to a writer over the age of 40. Applicants should supply a personal statement, details of their writing experience, a description of the project they plan to work on and a sample of their writing. Award winners receive a tailored package of support, including £2,500; mentoring from writers and industry professionals; PR, performance and presentation training; the opportunity to showcase work to publishers and agents; and a week-long writing retreat. Applications close July.

PFD Queer Fiction Prizes

55 New Oxford Street, London WC1A 1BS
tel 020-7344 1000
email prize@pfd.co.uk
website https://petersfraserdunlop.com/about-us/pfd-queer-fiction-prize
X @PFDAgents
Instagram @pfdagents

Established by Peters, Fraser & Dunlop to discover new LGBTQ+ writing talent. There are two categories: Adult Fiction, and YA and Children's Fiction. Entrants should submit a three-chapter sample of their work, a two-page synopsis and a covering letter. Entrants must be unagented and not have previously published a novel or picture book; submitted work does not need to be complete. One winner in each category receives representation with PFD and support completing their novel. Founded 2022.

RatedWriters.com Book Awards

tel 07948 392634
email info@ratedwriters.com
website www.ratedwriters.com

Developed with Arts Council funding, the review site is free to join and offers writers an opportunity to share extracts of their work for others to review. This allows writers to develop their craft and view which audiences enjoy their work. Writers can also submit their extracts to the annual competition. Two winning extracts receive £500 and a full book or script critique; runners-up also receive full critiques. Entry fee: £12. Founded 2024.

Deborah Rogers Foundation Writers Award

email admin@deborahrogersfoundation.org
website www.deborahrogersfoundation.org
X @DRFWritersAward
Instagram @deborah_rogers_org/
Administrator Alison Menzies

Set up in memory of Deborah Rogers, a literary agent, who died in 2014. A biennial award that gives £10,000 to an unpublished author to enable them to complete a first book. Entrants should submit between 15,000 and 20,000 words of a work of fiction, non-fiction or short stories, for adults, young adults or children. Two shortlisted authors also receive £1,000 each. Submissions open in January 2027 and the winner is announced in November.

Saveas Writers' International Writing Competition

35 Spillett Close, Faversham, Kent ME13 8QP
email saveas@hotmail.co.uk
website https://saveaswriters.co.uk/competitions

Given in two categories: Poetry (The Canterbury Christchurch Poetry Prize) and Prose (The University of Kent Fiction Prize). Entries must be unpublished and should respond or relate to that year's theme; poems should be 60 lines or less, short stories should be 3,500 words or less. 1st prize: £200; 2nd prize: £100; 3rd prize: £50. Entry fee: £4 for one poem or £10 for three; £5 for one short story or £12 for three.

Selfies Book Awards

email selfies@bookbrunch.co.uk
website https://theselfies.co.uk
X @SelfiesAwards

Established by BookBrunch with sponsorship from IngramSpark and support from London Book Fair and Nielsen Book, the Awards recognise the best self-published books from the previous year in three categories: Adult Fiction, Children's Fiction and General Non-Fiction. Entries should combine an entertaining story, a well-produced book, a cover and blurb that are appealing to the target audience, and an effective marketing and publicity campaign.

Authors are invited to submit their own books (usually during November and December), a shortlist is announced in February and winners are announced in March. 1st prize in each category: £750. Founded 2018.

Mo Siewcharran Prize

email mosiewcharranprize@hachette.co.uk
website www.thefuturebookshelf.co.uk/landing-page/the-mo-siewcharran-prize-2025/
X @MoPrize

Nurtures unpublished writers from Black, Asian, mixed heritage and minority ethnic backgrounds, writing in English. Previous categories have included non-fiction, picture books, literary fiction, crime and thrillers; criteria for the 2026 prize are not yet available. The winner receives £2,500 prize money and consideration for publication. A package of prizes is also available for two runners-up. Entrants should submit a proposal of up to 10,000 words. Founded 2019.

The Sunday Times Charlotte Aitken Young Writer of the Year Award – see page 582

Writers' & Artists' Working-Class Writers' Prize

Bloomsbury Publishing, 50 Bedford Square, London WC1B 3DP
tel 020-7631 5985
email writersandartists@bloomsbury.com
website www.writersandartists.co.uk/competitions

Open to unpublished writers who consider themselves to be from a working-class background. Entrants should submit 2,000 words from a work-in-progress and a 200-word piece of writing about themselves and why the prize speaks to them. The winner receives mentoring support, a £200 cash prize, one year's subscription to the Society of Authors, access to Writers' & Artists' writing and publishing events, and a writing guide bundle including the latest edition of the *Writers' & Artists' Yearbook* or the *Children's Writers' & Artists' Yearbook*.

SHORT STORIES AND FLASH FICTION

Aesthetica Creative Writing Award – see page 588

The ALCS Tom-Gallon Trust Award

The Society of Authors, 24 Bedford Row, London WC1R 4EH
tel 020-3880 2230
email prizes@societyofauthors.org
website https://societyofauthors.org/prizes/the-soa-awards/alcs-tom-gallon-trust-award
Facebook www.facebook.com/TheSocietyofAuthors
X @Soc_of_Authors
Instagram @thesocietyofauthors
Grants & Prizes Manager Aine Pullan, *Grants & Prizes Design Manager* Natalie Thorpe, *Head of Fundraising, Grants & Prizes* Robyn Law

Funded by a bequest from Nellie Tom-Gallon in memory of her brother. An annual award for a short story, open to writers who have had at least one short story accepted for publication and are ordinarily resident in the United Kingdom, Commonwealth or the Republic of Ireland. The submission should not exceed 5,000 words. 1st prize: £1,000; one runner-up receives £500.

Dinesh Allirajah Prize for Short Fiction

email ra.page@commapress.co.uk
website https://commapress.co.uk/resources/prizes
Founder Ra Page

Hosted by Comma Press and the University of Central Lancashire. The submitted story must not have been published anywhere previously in print or online. One entry per author. 1st prize: £500.

Bath Flash Fiction Awards

website https://bathflashfictionaward.com
Facebook www.facebook.com/bathflashaward
X @BathFlashAward

Hosts two international flash fiction writing competitions: the Bath Flash Fiction Award and the Bath Novella-in-Flash Award. Entrants have the opportunity to appear in print and digital anthology collections, published by Ad Hoc Fiction, with overall winners receiving cash prizes.

Bath Flash Fiction Award

Has three rounds per year: March to June, July to October, and November to February. Entries should not exceed 300 words. 1st prize £1,000; 2nd prize £300; 3rd prize £100; 50 longlisted entrants are published in an anthology. Entry fee: from £9.

Bath Novella-in-Flash Award

Runs once per year, with a 6,000–18,000 word limit; each flash that makes up the novella should not be more than 1,000 words. Entries can be on any theme or subject but must be original, written in English and for adult or young adult readers; non-fiction and fiction written for children are not permitted. 1st prize: £300; two runners-up receive £100 each; all three winners are published individually. Entry fee: £16.

BBC National Short Story Award

BBC Broadcasting House, Portland Place, London W1A 1AA
email bbcnssa@bbc.co.uk
website www.bbc.co.uk/nssa

In partnership with Cambridge University, for a single short story (maximum 8,000 words). Expands opportunities for British writers, readers and publishers of the short story, and honours the UK's finest exponents of the form. The winner receives £15,000 and their story is broadcast on Radio 4; four runners-up receive £600. Submission deadline: March. Founded 2005.

The Bournemouth Writing Prize

Fern Barrow, Poole BH12 5BB
tel 0120 252 4111
email bournemouthwritingprize@bournemouth.ac.uk
website https://thebournemouthjournal.com/bournemouth-writing-prize/
Facebook www.facebook.com/groups/1138780447831925
X @TBJournalX
Instagram @thebournemouthjournal

An annual international short story and poetry competition. Entrants should submit either one short story of no more than 3,000 words or up to three poems of no more than 30 lines each. Three prizes are awarded in each category. 1st prize: £1,000; 2nd prize: £300; 3rd prize: £200. The winners also receive a ten-minute open mic slot at the Saturday Night Showcase at the Bournemouth Writing Festival (the short story winner will need to truncate their entry to fit into the timeframe), two tickets to the Showcase and two tickets to a talk or workshop at the Festival's Pavilion Dance. Entry fee: £10 per story or three poems. Entry deadline: January. Founded 2014.

Brick Lane Bookshop Short Story Prize

Brick Lane Bookshop, 166 Brick Lane, London E1 6RU
tel 020-7247 0216
email enquiries@bricklanebookshop.org
website https://bricklanebookshop.org/short-story-prize/
Facebook www.facebook.com/bricklanebookshop
X @BrickLaneBooks
Instagram @bricklanebookshop

A competition for short fiction between 1,000 and 5,000 words, in partnership with Spread the Word, Prototype, *The London Magazine* and Scratch Books. 1st prize: £1,000; 2nd prize: £500; 3rd prize: £250. Additional prizes provided by the partners include publication in an anthology and magazine, editorial feedback, workshops and courses. Entry deadline: March. Entry fee: £10; 50 free spaces are available for low-income writers.

The Bridport Prize: Short Story and Flash Fiction

Bridport Arts Centre, South Street, Bridport, Dorset DT6 3NR
email kate@bridportprize.org.uk
website https://bridportprize.org.uk/the-competition/short-story/, https://bridportprize.org.uk/the-competition/flash-fiction/

Two annual prizes for writers of short fiction. Entries must not have been published or self-published; stories written for children are not eligible.

Short story: Stories should not exceed 5,000 words. 1st prize: £5,000; 2nd prize: £2,000; 3rd prize: £1,000. Entry fee: £14.

Flash fiction: Stories should not exceed 250 words. 1st prize: £1,000; 2nd prize: £500; 3rd prize: £250. Entry fee: £11.

Entry deadline: 31 May.

The Caine Prize for African Writing

9 Hare & Billet Road, London SE3 0RB
email info@caineprize.com
website www.caineprize.com
Facebook www.facebook.com/caineprize
X @caineprize
Chair Ellah Wakatama OBE

Awarded to an African writer of a short story published in English. The prize, worth £10,000, was launched to encourage and highlight the richness and diversity of African writing by bringing it to a wider audience internationally. The focus on the short story form reflects the contemporary development of the African storytelling tradition. Publishers should submit short stories of between 3,000 and 10,000 words; stories must have been published in the previous five years. Founded 1999.

Commonwealth Short Story Prize

Commonwealth Foundation, Marlborough House, Pall Mall, London SW1Y 5HY
tel 020-7930 3783
email creatives@commonwealthfoundation.com
website www.commonwealthwriters.org/short-story-prize
Facebook www.facebook.com/cwfcreatives
X @cwfcreatives
Instagram @cwfcreatives

Administered by the Commonwealth Foundation, it is awarded for the best piece of unpublished short fiction (2,000–5,000 words) by a resident of the Commonwealth. Regional winners receive £2,500 and the overall winner receives £5,000. Translated entries are also eligible, as are stories written in selected languages other than English. The competition is open to any citizen of a Commonwealth country, aged 18 years and older.

The Curae Prize – see page 585

CWA Margery Allingham Short Mystery Prize – see page 611

CYMERA Prize for Speculative Short Fiction

email info@cymerafestival.co.uk
website www.cymerafestival.co.uk

Recognises the best Scottish writers of sci-fi, fantasy and horror writing. Entry is open to anyone living in Scotland or who identifies as Scottish either by birth or inclination. Entries should be unpublished stories containing elements of speculative writing, must be written in English, Scots, Gaelic or another Scottish language (with translation in English), and should not exceed 2,500 words. 1st prize: £150, a weekend pass to the CYMERA Festival and publication in *Shoreline of Infinity* Magazine (CYMERA Special).

The Rhys Davies Short Story Competition

Cultural Institute, Swansea University, Singleton Park, Swansea SA2 8PP
email rdshortstory@swansea.ac.uk
website www.swansea.ac.uk/cultural-institute/rhys-davies-short-story-competition/
Facebook www.facebook.com/CultureSwanUni
X @Culture_SwanUni
Instagram @culture_swanuni

Recognises unpublished short stories in any style and on any subject written by writers living in or from Wales. Entries must be written in English and should not exceed 5,000 words; entries must not have been previously published in print or online, including personal blogs or social media, or been broadcast or placed in a competition. 1st prize: £1,000; 11 runners-up receive £100 each; all 12 winners are published in an anthology by Parthian Books. Entry fee: £8; free entries are available for low-income writers. Founded 1991.

Desperate Literature Short Fiction Prize

tel +34 911 888 089
email prize@desperateliterature.com
website https://desperateliterature.com/prize/
X @DesperateLit

Celebrates the best new short fiction. Entries should be under 2,000 words; translations are eligible. The overall winner receives a €2,000 cash prize, a week's residency at the Civitella Ranieri Foundation and a manuscript assessment and a consultation with a literary agent. Two runners-up receive €1,000 each, two shortlisted writers receive travel opportunities, all shortlisted writers are published in an anthology and a journal. Entry fee: €20 first entry; €10 subsequent entries; sponsored entries are available for writers who cannot afford the fee. Founded 2018.

Edge Hill Short Story Prize

Edge Hill University, Department of English and Creative Arts, St Helens Road, Ormskirk, Lancs. L39 4QP
email cowanb@edgehill.ac.uk
website www.edgehill.ac.uk/shortstory
X @EHUShortStory
Instagram @edgehillprize
Contact Billy Cowan

Awarded annually by Edge Hill University for excellence in a published single-authored short story collection. Entrants must be normally resident in the UK or Ireland; collections must have been published in the previous year. The winner receives £10,000. There is also a prize of £1,000 for the best debut collection. Publishers are entitled to submit collections published during the preceding year. Authors must be normally resident in the UK or Ireland. Founded 2006.

Edinburgh Flash Fiction Award

email info@scottishartstrust.org
website www.scottishartstrust.org
Facebook www.facebook.com/edinburghwritingawards
Instagram @edinburghwritingawards

Open to stories on any topic up to 250 words. 1st prize: £2,000. The Write Mango Short Story Award is awarded to the most amusing, pleasantly bizarre or surreal story. The top 20 stories are published in an anthology and their writers are offered a free ticket to the annual Edinburgh Writing Awards dinner and awards event. Entry fee: £10. Free entries are available for writers in need of support. All entries open 1 May; free entry applications close 30 June; paid entries close 31 August.

Edinburgh Short Story Award

email info@scottishartstrust.org
website www.scottishartstrust.org
Facebook www.facebook.com/edinburghwritingawards
Instagram @scotstoryawards

Open to short stories on any subject up to 2,000 words. 1st prize: £3,000; the First Writer Award for the top story by an unpublished writer: £300; the Write Mango Short Story Award for the most amusing, pleasantly bizarre or surreal story: £300. Shortlisted writers are offered a free ticket to the annual Edinburgh Writing Awards dinner and event. The top 20 stories are published in an annual anthology. Entry fee: £11; free entries are available for writers in need of support. All entries open 1 November; free entry applications close 31 December; paid entries close 28 February.

Edinburgh True Flash Award

email info@scottishartstrust.org
website www.scottishartstrust.org
Facebook www.facebook.com/edinburghwritingawards
Instagram @edinburghwritingawards

Open to writers of flash memoir and creative non-fiction flash stories on any topic, up to 250 words.

The Award seeks true stories told in artful, original ways that entertain and amaze, make readers laugh out loud, bring them to tears or leave them outraged. 1st prize: £500; shortlisted entries are published in an anthology and their writers are offered a free ticket to the annual Flash Bash dinner and awards event. Entry fee: £10; free entries are available for writers in need of support. Entries open 1 May; free entry applications close 30 June; paid entries close 31 August.

The Faber/Observer/Comica Graphic Short Story Prize

Faber & Faber, The Bindery, 51 Hatton Garden, London EC1N 8HN
website www.faber.co.uk/about-faber/graphic-short-story-prize/

An award for graphic short stories. Offers a £1,000 cash prize and publication in the *Observer New Review*. One runner-up receives £250 and publication on theguardian.co.uk. Entries must be in English and unpublished; the layout should be four pages across a double-page spread and be able to be scaled up and down as necessary. Founded 2007.

Fish Publishing Writing Prizes – see page 581

Granite Noir Short Story Competition

His Majesty's Theatre, Rosemount Viaduct, Aberdeen AB25 1GL
tel (01224) 641122
email gncomp@aberdeenperformingarts.com
website www.aberdeenperformingarts.com/granite-noir/granite-noir-short-story-competition-tcs/
Facebook www.facebook.com/GraniteNoirFest
X @GraniteNoirFest

Administered by Granite Noir Festival. Accepts crime fiction short stories (including mystery and thrillers) of between 1,500 and 2,000 words. The winning writer is announced at the Festival and the winning story is published in a newspaper. Entry deadline: January.

Hastings Book Festival Competition – see page 590

Henshaw Press Short Story Competition

Hobeck Books, 4 Norbury Manor Barns, Manor Drive, Norbury, Staffs. ST20 0RL
email hobeckbooks@gmail.com
website www.henshawpress.co.uk, www.hobeck.net/henshaw-press-competition

Runs four times a year: March, June, September and December. Open worldwide to writers over 16 years. Entries should be unpublished short stories, can be on any subject and should be no more than 2,000 words. Judging panel consists of academic and professional writers. Also offers a free critique service for short stories written by people under 16. 1st prize: £200; 2nd prize: £100; 3rd prize: £50. Winning stories published bi-annually in an anthology by Hobeck Books. Entry fee: £6; all profits donated to charity.

The HWA Dorothy Dunnett Short Story Competition

The Union Building, 51–59 Rose Lane, Norwich NR1 1BY
email chair@historicalwriters.org
website https://historicalwriters.org/awards
Facebook www.facebook.com/HistoriaHWA/
X @HistoriaHWA

Celebrates the work of writer Dorothy Dunnett and the value of historical fiction. Entrants should submit a short story of no more that 3,500 words, set at least 35 years in the past. 1st prize: £500 and mentoring with an author and agent; two highly commended authors also receive mentoring; all shortlisted authors are published in an anthology and receive £25 compensation. Entry fee: £5.

London Independent Story Prize

email entry@londonindependentstoryprize.co.uk
website www.londonindependentstoryprize.co.uk
Facebook www.facebook.com/LIStoryPrize
X @LondonISP
Instagram @londonisp

Facilitates a networking opportunity for writers and a community that embraces multicultural differences and unique approaches to story writing. Competition categories: Flash Fiction, Short Story and Poetry. 1st prize in each category: £100; all finalists' work is published in an anthology. Entry fee: from £8.50.

The London Magazine Short Story Prize

11 Queen's Gate, London SW7 5EL
tel 020-7584 5977
email info@thelondonmagazine.org
website www.thelondonmagazine.org/category/tlm-competition
X @TheLondonMag
Bluesky @thelondonmagazine.bsky.social
Instagram @thelondonmagazine
Editor Steven O'Brien, *Managing Editor* Jamie Cameron, *Editorial Assistant* Zadie Loft

An annual prize offering a chance to be published in the UK's oldest literary magazine, established in 1732. Submitted short stories should not exceed 2,500 words and must not previously have been published. Previous judges include Max Porter, Susan Hill and Brandon Taylor. 1st prize: £500; 2nd prize: £300; 3rd prize: £200. All winners are published in the magazine. Entry fee: first entry £10 (£5 for low-income writers); subsequent entries £5 each.

The Louie Award

email info@austcrimewriters.com
facebook www.facebook.com/austcrimewriters/
X @auscrimewriters

Awarded to a crime fiction story of less than 500 words. Each year there is a different theme that entrants must incorporate into their story. 1st prize: $500; two highly commended writers receive $125 each. Entry deadline: March. Entry fee: $5.

Macavity Awards – see page 612

Bryan MacMahon Short Story Award

Listowel Writers' Week, 24 The Square, Listowel, Co. Kerry V31 RD93, Republic of Ireland
tel +353 (0)1 682 1074
email info@writersweek.ie
website https://writersweek.ie/competitions-2025/
Facebook www.facebook.com/writersweek

Administered by Listowel Writers' Week and awarded to the best short story (up to 3,000 words) on any subject. Prize: €1,000. Entry fee: €10. Submission deadline: March.

The Manchester Fiction Prize

The Manchester Writing School at Manchester Metropolitan University, Grosvenor East Building, Cavendish Street, Manchester M15 6BG
tel 0161 247 2000
email writingschool@mmu.ac.uk
website www.mmu.ac.uk/writingcompetition/
X @McrWritingSchl

Part of of the Manchester Writing Competition run by The Manchester Writing School. Created by UK Poet Laureate (2009–19) Carol Ann Duffy, the competition is designed to celebrate Manchester as an international city of writers, find diverse new voices and create opportunities for writer development.

Entrants are asked to submit a short story of up to 2,500 words. An award of £10,000 is made to the overall winner or winners. Entry fee £18.

The Moth Short Story Prize

Ardan Grange, Milltown, Belturbet, Co. Cavan, Ireland H14 K768, Republic of Ireland
tel +1 872-657-251
email enquiries@themothmagazine.com
website www.themothmagazine.com
Facebook www.facebook.com/themothmagazine
X @themothmagazine
Instagram @themothmagazine
Director Rebecca O'Connor

Awarded annually to three unpublished stories, chosen by a different judge each year. Previous judges include Sarah Hall, Ali Smith and Mark Haddon. 1st prize: €3,000 and publication in the *Irish Times* summer reading series; 2nd prize: a week-long retreat at Circle of Misse in France plus a travel stipend; 3rd prize: €1,000. Open to writers aged 16 years and older. Entry deadline: 30 June. Entry fee: €16. For full entry details and guidelines, see the website. Founded 2013.

Mslexia Competitions: Short Story and Flash Fiction

PO Box 656, Newcastle upon Tyne NE99 1PZ
tel 0191 204 8860
email competitions@mslexia.co.uk
website https://mslexia.co.uk/competitions/short-story/, https://mslexia.co.uk/competitions/flash-fiction/
Facebook www.facebook.com/Mslexia/
X @Mslexia
Instagram @mslexia

Two annual prizes for short story and flash fiction writers who identify as women.

Short story: Entrants should submit a story of no more than 3,000 words. Stories can be in any genre and written for adults or young adults. 1st prize: £3,000; three finalists receive £100 each. Entry fee: £12.

Flash fiction: Entrants should submit a story of no more than 300 words. 1st prize: £500; three finalists receive £50 each. Entry fee: £6.

All winners are published in Mslexia magazine. Submissions open in September.

New Welsh Writing Awards: Rheidol Prize for Prose with a Welsh Theme or Setting

PO Box/Blwch Post 170, Aberystwyth, Ceredigion SY23 1WZ
tel (01970) 628410
website https://newwelshreview.com/awards

Recognises the best writing in short form (5,000–30,000 words) with the winner receiving £1,000 cash as an advance against publication and a critique by a leading literary agent. Other prizes include writing retreats, publication in and subscription to the magazine. Entry fee: £12; some free entries available for low-income writers. Founded 2015.

The Seán Ó Faoláin International Short Story Competition

The Munster Literature Centre, Frank O'Connor House, 84 Douglas Street, Cork T12 X704, Republic of Ireland
email info@munsterlit.ie
website www.munsterlit.ie/ofaolain-competition
Facebook www.facebook.com/OFaolainCompetition
X @MunLitCentre

Sponsored by the Munster Literature Festival and dedicated to the Irish writer and theorist, Seán Ó Faoláin. The winner receives €2,000 and a featured reading at the Cork International Short Story Festival (including a four-night hotel stay and full board).

Parracombe Prize

Parracombe Community Trust, The Village Hall, Church Lane, Parracombe, Devon EX31 4RJ
website https://prize.parracombe.org.uk

A short story competition where the word count corresponds to the year – in 2026 the maximum word count is 2,026. Open to published, self-published and unpublished writers, but entries must not have been published elsewhere. 1st prize: £150; 2nd prize: £50; 3rd prize: £25. There is also a Local Writer's Prize of £50 for the best entry from a writer from North Devon. The top 35 entries are published in an anthology. Entry deadline: 31 January. Entry fee: £5.

V.S. Pritchett Short Story Prize

Royal Society of Literature, Somerset House, Strand, London WC2R 1LA
tel 020-7845 4679
email info@rsliterature.org
website https://rsliterature.org/v-s-pritchett-short-story-prize/

An annual prize awarded to a previously unpublished short story of between 2,000 and 4,000 words. Entrants must be permanently resident in the UK, RoI or the Commonwealth. The winner receives £1,000 and publication in *RSL Review*. Entry fee: £8 per entry; free entries are available for low-income writers. Founded 1999.

Prototype Prize

71 Oriel Road, London E9 5SG
email admin@prototypepublishing.co.uk
website https://prototypepublishing.co.uk/category/opportunities/
Facebook www.facebook.com/prototypepubs
X @prototypepubs
Instagram @prototypepubs

A biennial prize for published or unpublished writers and artists whose work sits at the intersections of different literary and artistic forms. Includes two categories; book-length project (1st prize: £3,000 and publication with Prototype) and short-form work (1st prize: £3,000 and publication with Monitor Books). Submissions can be in any style or form and on any subject matter; entrants must be resident in the UK and Ireland. Founded 2024.

QuietManDave

Manchester Writing School, Grosvenor East Building, Cavendish Street, Manchester M15 6BG
email writingschool@mmu.ac.uk
website www.mmu.ac.uk/qmdprize/

Named in honour of the writer Dave Murray, the prize is awarded to exciting examples of flash fiction and flash non-fiction, which can include anything from creative non-fiction to blog posts and reviews. Writers must be aged 16 or over; the award is eager to celebrate older writers who found writing later in life. Submissions should not exceed 500 words. Prizes in each category: 1st: £1,000; 2nd: £200; 3rd: £50. Entry fee: £5; sponsored entry is available for those on a low income.

Reedsy Short Story Contest

email prompts@reedsy.com
website https://blog.reedsy.com/creative-writing-prompts/contests/

A weekly short story competition. Every Friday a new batch of prompts is released around a common theme. Stories should be 1,000–3,000 words. 1st prize: $250 and potential publication in Reedsy's literary magazine, *Prompted*. Entry fee: $5.

Ringwood Short Story Competition

0/1 314 Meadowside Quay Walk, Glasgow, Scotland G11 6AY
email mail@ringwoodpublishing.com
website www.ringwoodpublishing.com
X @RingwoodPublish
Instagram @ringwoodpublishing

Established to discover over-looked talent regardless of background. Entrants must be resident in Scotland; submissions from writers from under-represented backgrounds are encouraged. Entrants should submit an unpublished short story and a cover letter. 1st prize: £100 and online publication; two runners-up are also published online. Submission deadline: December. Entry fee: £2. Founded 2020.

RTÉ Radio 1 Short Story Competition in Honour of Francis MacManus

RTÉ Radio Centre, Donnybrook, Dublin 4, Republic of Ireland
email fmacmanusstories@rte.ie
website www.rte.ie/radio/radio1/rte-short-story-competition/

Open to writers who hold an Irish passport or are resident on the island of Ireland. Seeks short stories in Irish or English that have not previously been published or broadcast. 1st prize: €5,000; 2nd prize: €4,000; 3rd prize: €3,000; winning entries are broadcast on RTÉ Radio and published online. Submissions open in February/March and close in May. Founded 1986.

The Olga Sinclair Prize

email competitions@norwichwriters.com
website https://norwichwriters.wordpress.com/olga-sinclair-prize-short-story-competition-2025/
Facebook www.facebook.com/CircleWritersNorwich
X @norwichwriters
Instagram @norwichwriters
Membership Secretary Kathy Joy

Run by the Norwich Writer's Circle to encourage short-story writing inspired by the city of Norwich. Stories do not have to be about or set in Norwich and entrants do not have to be based in Norwich, but stories must be based on that year's chosen theme, which is always related to the city. Previous themes have included the sea, mustard and markets. Stories should not exceed 2,000 words. 1st prize: £200; 2nd prize: £150; 3rd prize: £100. Entry deadline: July. Entry fee: £5 per entry. Founded 2016.

Stinging Fly/FBA Fiction Prize

The Stinging Fly, PO Box 6016, Dublin 1, Republic of Ireland
email info@stingingfly.org
website https://stingingfly.org
Facebook www.facebook.com/StingingFly
X @StingingFly

An annual award given to a story published in *The Stinging Fly* literary magazine in the previous year, whose author shows literary promise. The award is sponsored by Felicity Bryan Associates. 1st prize: €2,000. Founded 2022.

Weatherglass Books Novella Award

email novellaprize@weatherglassbooks.com
website https://weatherglassbooks.com
X @weatherglassbks
Founders Neil Griffiths, Damian Langian

A literary award for novellas of between 20,000 and 40,000 words, but no more than 200 pages. A shortlist is created by the Weatherglass editorial team, which is then judged by author Ali Smith. 1st prize: a £500 advance and publication with Weatherglass Books. Entry fee: £20. Founded 2023.

Writers' & Artists' Yearbook 2026 Short Story Competition

website www.writersandartists.co.uk/competitions

See information panel on page vii of this edition or visit the website for details.

Writing Magazine: Grand Prize

website www.writers-online.co.uk/writing-competitions/open-competitions/
Facebook www.facebook.com/WritingMagazine
X @WritingMagazine

Open to short stories in any form and on any topic. Stories must not exceed 2,000 words. 1st prize: £1,000 and publication in Writing Magazine; 2nd prize: £250; 3rd prize: £100; 4th prize: a mini-critique of the work; 5th prize: twelve-month Writers Online membership. Entry fee: £17.50 for non-members, £12.50 for members.

Writing Magazine: Swanwick Summer School Competition

website www.writers-online.co.uk/writing-competitions/open-competitions/
Facebook www.facebook.com/WritingMagazine
X @WritingMagazine

Run in collaboration with Swanwick Writers' Summer School, a programme for writers of all ages, abilities and genres. There is one shared theme each year and three categories: short stories of up to 1,000 words, poems of up to 40 lines and pieces of writing for children of up to 1,000 words. 1st prize: a fully inclusive stay at Swanwick Writers' Summer School; 2nd prize: £100 gift voucher; 3rd prize: a copy of the *Writers' & Artists' Yearbook*. Entry fee: £7.50 for non-members, £6 for members.

STAGE, SCREEN AND AUDIO

ARIAS (Audio & Radio Industry Awards)

email info@radioacademy.org
website www.radioacademy.org/arias

Run by The Radio Academy. Recognise the best in the UK audio and radio industry. The awards offer stations, podcasters, publishers, presenters and production companies an annual opportunity to enter work in a range of categories that reflect today's UK audio and radio landscape. Submissions open in January and close in February. Entry fee: from £45; free entries are available for producers of colour and LGBTQ+ producers of podcasts through the Podcasting, Seriously Awards Fund. Founded 1982.

BAFTA Rocliffe New Writing Competition

email office@rocliffe.com
website www.rocliffe.com
Facebook www.facebook.com/BAFTARocliffe
X @rocliffeforum
Instagram @rocliffeproductions

Established to champion emerging writing and directing talent and develop diverse stories with an international outlook. Run in partnership with BAFTA, there are three categories, of which only one is open each year: Children & Young Adult Media and TV Drama for 2025; Comedy for 2026; Film for 2027. All categories are judged by readers, a script selection panel and an industry jury, selected for their proven expertise in that medium. Three winners receive access to an industry showcase with professional actors and directors, industry introductions, bespoke masterclasses and a tailored career planning and profile building session to provide support navigating the industry. Bursaries are available for applicants who cannot afford the admission fee. Founded 2000.

Verity Bargate Award

Soho Theatre, 21 Dean Street, London W1D 3NE
email general@sohotheatre.com
website www.sohotheatre.com/projects/verity-bargate-award

A biennial award established to honour Soho Theatre's co-founder, Verity Bargate. It is open to artists resident in the UK or Ireland with fewer than three professional productions. The winner receives a full commission fee in respect of an exclusive option to produce the winning play at Soho Theatre. Free to enter. Founded 1982.

Bruntwood Prize for Playwriting

email bruntwood.prize@royalexchange.co.uk
website www.writeaplay.co.uk
Facebook www.facebook.com/bruntwoodprize
X @bruntwoodprize
Instagram @bruntwoodprize

Recognises playwriters regardless of background or experience. Unperformed plays are judged anonymously and read by a team of over 100 directors, producers, actors, managers, critics, agents and other industry professionals. There are four prize categories: The Bruntwood Prize (£20,000), The Judges Award (£10,000), The Bruntwood Prize International Award (£10,000) and The North West Original New Voice Award and Residency (£10,000 plus an additional £10,000 fund for professional development). Each winner is entered into a development process with the Royal Exchange Theatre in an endeavour to bring their work to production. Submissions open September 2025 and close January 2026. Founded 2006.

The Channel Four Writing for Television Awards – see page 587

The Alfred Fagon Award

email info@alfredfagonaward.co.uk
website www.alfredfagonaward.co.uk
Facebook www.facebook.com/alfredfagonaward
X @AlfredFagonAwrd
Instagram @Alfred_Fagon_Award
Creative Producer Pauline Walker, *Administrator* Hannah Rose Caton

An annual award of £6,000 for the Best New Play of the Year (which need not have been produced) for the theatre in English. TV and radio plays and film scripts are not eligible. Only writers of Caribbean and African descent resident in the UK are eligible. Applicants should apply online. Closing date: end July. Founded 1997.

The Imison Award

The Broadcasting Committee,
The Society of Authors, 24 Bedford Row, London WC1R 4EH
tel 020-3880 2230
email info@societyofauthors.org
website https://societyofauthors.org/prizes/audio-drama/imison
Facebook www.facebook.com/TheSocietyofAuthors
X @Soc_of_Authors
Instagram @thesocietyofauthors
Grants & Prizes Manager Aine Pullan, *Grants & Prizes Design Manager* Natalie Thorpe, *Head of Fundraising, Grants & Prizes* Robyn Law

Sponsored by the Peggy Ramsay Foundation and the Authors Awards and Advancement charity. Awarded to an audio drama script by a writer new to the medium. Submissions are accepted from any party, e.g., producer, broadcasting organisation, writer, agent. Prize fund: £3,000. Free to enter. Founded 1994.

Listening Books Members' Choice Award

tel 020-7407 9417
email info@listening-books.org.uk
website www.listening-books.org.uk/extra/members-choice-award
Facebook www.facebook.com/ListeningBooks12/
X @ListeningBooks
Instagram @listeningbooks

Recognises readers' favourite audiobooks. Audiobooks with the highest number of listens amongst Listening Books members form the shortlist; the winner is decided by a member vote and recognised in an online presentation hosted by patron Stephen Fry.

Mustapha Matura Award and Mentoring Programme

email info@alfredfagonaward.co.uk
website www.alfredfagonaward.co.uk/mustapha-matura-award
X @MustaphaMatura
Creative Producer Pauline Walker, *Administrator* Hannah Rose Caton

An annual award of £3,000 for newly emerging playwrights aged 25 years and younger. Winners also receive nine months of mentoring. Only writers of Caribbean and African descent resident in the UK are eligible. Submitted plays must be new and original; plays do not need to have been produced. Television, radio and film scripts are not eligible. Founded 2021.

Oxford/42 New Writing Prize NEW

Faculty of English Language and Literature, St Cross Building, Manor Road, Oxford OX1 3UL
tel (01865) 271055
email oxfordwritingprize@42mp.com
website www.english.ox.ac.uk/article/launch-of-new-writing-prize-now-open-for-submissions

Administered by the Faculty of English at the University of Oxford and the management and production company, 42, the Prize seeks novelists, playwrights and screenwriters. Entrants should submit a 300-word synopsis. 1st prize: £1,500 and professional representation from 42. Entrants should submit a 300-word synopsis, a two-sentence elevator pitch and one of the following: the first 10,000 to 15,000 words of a novel, a complete stage or radio play of between 30 and 90 pages, a script of between 30 and 60 pages for episode one of a TV show or a complete feature-length film script of 90 pages. Entry deadline: April. Founded 2025.

The Popcorn Writing Award

email development@popcorngroup.co.uk
website https://popcorngroup.co.uk/awards/popcorn-writing-award-in-edinburgh/
X @ThePopcornGroup
Instagram @thepopcorngroup

Recognises imaginative, new playwriting being performed at the Edinburgh Festival Fringe. Submitted plays must not have had a significant run before the festival and must be performed at one of the festival's partnering venues. Applicants should submit their play, a 10–15 word tagline and a summary of no more than 50 words to their venue. The winning writers share a £6,000 prize fund and receive production support. Founded 2019.

RTÉ Radio, Drama On One, P.J. O'Connor Radio Drama Awards

RTÉ Radio, Drama on One, Radio Centre, Donnybrook, Dublin 4, Republic of Ireland
email pjoconnorscripts@rte.ie
website www.rte.ie/dramaonone

Celebrate the best in new Irish writing. Candidates should submit plays written specifically for radio, of no more than 40 minutes in duration. 1st prize: €5,000; 2nd prize: €4,000; 3rd prize: €3,000.

The Tinniswood Award

Society of Authors, 24 Bedford Row, London WC1R 4EH
tel 020-3880 2230
email info@societyofauthors.org
website https://societyofauthors.org/prizes/audio-drama/the-tinniswood-award
Facebook www.facebook.com/TheSocietyofAuthors
X @Soc_of_Authors
Instagram @thesocietyofauthors
Grants & Prizes Manager Aine Pullan, *Grants & Prizes Design Manager* Natalie Thorpe, *Head of Fundraising, Grants & Prizes* Robyn Law

Presented annually for the best original audio drama script of the year. The Society of Authors honour the memory of radio and TV comedy scriptwriter Peter Tinniswood through the award, which celebrates and encourages high standards in radio drama. Submissions are accepted from any party (producer, broadcasting organisation, writer, agent, etc). The award is sponsored by the ALCS.

TRANSLATION

ALTA Awards

The University of Arizona, Esquire Building #205, 1230 North Park Avenue, Tucson, AZ 85721, USA
email rachaeldaum@literarytranslators.org
website https://literarytranslators.org/awards
Facebook www.facebook.com/LitTranslate
X @LitTranslate
Instagram @littranslate

The American Literary Translators Association awards prizes in six categories at their annual conference: The National Translation Awards in Poetry and Prose ($4,000 each), the only translation prizes to include a full evaluation of the source language text; The Lucien Stryk Asian Translation Prize ($10,000) for a translation from Chinese, Hindi, Japanese, Kannada, Korean, Sanskrit, Tamil, Thai or Vietnamese into English of either poetry or source texts from Zen Buddhism; The Italian Prose in Translation Award (IPTA) ($5,000) for a translation of fiction or literary non-fiction from Italian into English; The Spain-USA Foundation Translation Award (SUFTA) ($5,000) for a translation of literary prose by authors of Spanish nationality from Spanish, Catalan, Basque or Galician into English; The ALTA First Translation Prize ($3,000) for a debut literary translation from any other language into English; and the ALTA Travel Fellowships ($1,000), awarded to between four and six emerging translators to fund their attendance at the ALTA conference.

The John Calder Translation Prize

Society of Authors, 24 Bedford Row, London WC1R 4EH
tel 020-3880 2230
email prizes@societyofauthors.org
website https://societyofauthors.org/prizes/translation-prizes/john-calder-translation-prize/
Facebook www.facebook.com/TheSocietyofAuthors
X @soc_of_authors
Instagram @societyofauthors
Grants & Prizes Manager Aine Pullan, *Grants & Prizes Design Manager* Natalie Thorpe, *Head of Fundraising, Grants & Prizes* Robyn Law

Celebrates new and ambitious translations into English of full-length works (fiction, non-fiction and poetry) that are distinguished by the highly personal and imaginative approach of the authors to their subject. Entries can be from any language into English and must have been published in the UK in the year preceeding the submission deadline. 1st prize: £3,000; 2nd prize: £1,000. Submission deadline: March. Submissions are only accepted from UK publishers.

EBRD Literature Prize

EBRD, Five Bank Street, London E14 4BG
tel 020-7338 6000
email literatureprize@ebrd.com
website www.ebrd.com/ebrd-literature-prize.html

Administered by the European Bank for Reconstruction and Development (EBRD). Awarded to literary fiction translated into English that was originally written in any language of the regions in which the Bank currently invests. Books must have been published by a European or North American publisher in the previous year; submission accepted from publishers only. 1st prize: €20,000 divided equally between the winning author and translator; two finalists also receive €4,000 divided equally between authors and translators. Submission deadline: December.

European Union Prize for Literature

FEP, Chaussée d'Ixelles 29/35 (Galerie Toison d'Or), Box 4 B-1050, Brussels
email info@euprizeliterature.eu
website www.euprizeliterature.eu
Facebook www.facebook.com/euplprize
X @EUPLPrize
Instagram @euplprize

Supported by the Creative Europe programme of the European Union, this award is an annual initiative to recognise the best emerging fiction writers in Europe. National organisations nominate one book for each participating country. An overall winner and special mentions are collectively announced and later celebrated at an EUPL award ceremony. Founded 2008.

The Goethe-Institut Award for New Translation

The Society of Authors, 24 Bedford Row, London WC1R 4EH
tel 020-3380 2230
email prizes@societyofauthors.org
website https://societyofauthors.org/prizes/translation-prizes/german-goethe-institut-award
Facebook www.facebook.com/TheSocietyofAuthors
X @Soc_of_Authors
Instagram @thesocietyofauthors
Grants & Prizes Manager Aine Pullan, *Grants & Prizes Design Manager* Natalie Thorpe, *Head of Fundraising, Grants & Prizes* Robyn Law

A biennial prize for translation of a chosen extract from German into English. Open to emerging translators based in the UK and Ireland, whose literary translation work has not yet been published in print. 1st prize: €1,000 and a place at the International Translator's meeting, including a visit to the Leipzig Book Fair. Founded 2010.

International Prize for Arabic Fiction – see page 578

The Sarah Maguire Prize

Poetry Translation Centre, The Albany, Douglas Way, Deptford SE8 4AG
email prizes@poetrytranslation.org
website www.poetrytranslation.org/sarah-maguire-prize

Biennial prize in the memory of Sarah Maguire (1957–2017), the founder of the Poetry Translation Centre and champion of international poetry. Awarded to the best book of poetry from a living poet from beyond Europe in English translation, published anywhere in the world. Winning poets and translators share a prize of £3,000. Founded 2019.

NCW Emerging Translators Mentorships

National Centre for Writing, Dragon Hall, 115–123 King Street, Norwich NR1 1QE
email translation@nationalcentreforwriting.org.uk
website https://nationalcentreforwriting.org.uk/get-involved/translators/etm
Facebook www.facebook.com/NationalCentreforWriting
X @WritersCentre
Bluesky @writerscentre.bsky.social
Instagram @writerscentre

Administered by the National Centre for Writing. Pairs emerging translators with established translators for six months of mentoring. The mentee receives guidance while working on a specific translation project, support developing professional skills, access to talks and workshops, exposure to publishers and a bursary. Entrants must not have published more than one full-length literary translation and must translate into English. The scheme especially seeks translators from backgrounds or working in languages that are under-represented in translation. Entrants should submit a covering letter, a sample book proposal and a sample translation of no more that 2,000 words of prose or 100 lines of poetry. Entry deadline: August. Founded 2010.

Oxford Weidenfeld-Translation Prize

Oxford Comparative Criticism and Translation (OCCT), St Anne's College, Woodstock Road, Oxford OX2 6HS
email comparative.criticism@st-annes.ox.ac.uk
website https://occt.web.ox.ac.uk/the-oxford-weidenfeld-prize
Facebook www.facebook.com/CompCritOxford

Administered by the Oxford Comparative Criticism and Translation research centre in recognition of a book translated into English from any European language. The book can be a work of fiction, poetry or drama and must have been published in English in the UK within the previous year. One winner receives £2,000 at a prize-giving ceremony on Oxford Translation Day. Entry deadline: January. Founded 1999.

Stevns Translation Prize

email info@twolinepress.com
website www.stevnstranslationprize.com/

Offers emerging translators an opportunity to translate their first full-length work of fiction.

Each year a different language and book are chosen and applicants are asked to translate an extract. Entrants should submit the translated sample and a 500-word translators note. 1st prize: a contract to translate the whole book for publication in the UK and USA, mentorship with an experienced translator, and a six-week retreat and travel expenses. Entry fee: $18. Founded 2018.

TA First Translation Prize

Prizes Department, The Society of Authors, 24 Bedford Row, London WC1R 4EH
email prizes@societyofauthors.org
website https://societyofauthors.org/prizes/translation-prizes/ta-first-translation-prize
Facebook www.facebook.com/TheSocietyofAuthors
X @Soc_of_Authors
Instagram @thesocietyofauthors
Grants & Prizes Manager Aine Pullan, *Grants & Prizes Design Manager* Natalie Thorpe, *Head of Fundraising, Grants & Prizes* Robyn Law

Endowed by Daniel Hahn and Jo Heinrich. Given to debut literary translations into English published in the UK and Ireland. The work must be the first solo book-length project by the entrant; co-translators are not accepted; self-published, ebook only and poetry titles are not accepted. The winner is awarded £3,000 and a runner-up is awarded £1,000; the prize is shared between the translator and their editor. Founded 2017.

The Translation Prizes

The Society of Authors, 24 Bedford Row, London WC1R 4EH
tel 020-3880 2230
email prizes@societyofauthors.org
website https://societyofauthors.org/prizes/translation-prizes
Facebook www.facebook.com/TheSocietyofAuthors
X @Soc_of_Authors
Instagram @thesocietyofauthors
Grants & Prizes Manager Aine Pullan, *Grants & Prizes Design Manager* Natalie Thorpe, *Head of Fundraising, Grants & Prizes* Robyn Law

The Society of Authors offers a number of prizes for published translations into English from Arabic, Dutch, French, German, Hebrew, Italian, Spanish, Swedish and Japanese.

The Warwick Prize for Women in Translation

email womenintranslation@warwick.ac.uk
website https://warwick.ac.uk/fac/cross_fac/womenintranslation
Coordinator Holly Langstaff

Addresses the gender imbalance in translated literature and increases the number of international women's voices accessible to a British and Irish readership. Awarded annually to the best eligible work of fiction, poetry, literary non-fiction, work of fiction for children or young adults, graphic novel or play text; entries must be written by a woman, translated into English by a translator (or translators) of any gender, and published by a UK or Irish publisher. The £1,000 prize is divided between writer and translator. Entry deadline: May. Founded 2017.

Fiction

General fiction prizes are listed first, with prizes categorised by genre following under headings, e.g. 'Crime, mystery, thriller and horror'.

ACDI Literary Prize

The Society of Authors, 24 Bedford Road, London WC1R 4EH
tel 020-3880 2230
email prizes@societyofauthors.org
website https://societyofauthors.org/prizes/the-soa-awards/the-adci-literary-prize
Facebook www.facebook.com/TheSocietyofAuthors
X @Soc_of_Authors
Instagram @thesocietyofauthors
Grants & Prizes Manager Aine Pullan, *Grants & Prizes Design Manager* Natalie Thorpe, *Head of Fundraising, Grants & Prizes* Robyn Law

Established to celebrate and encourage positive representation of disabilities in literature, the Authors with Disabilities and Chronic Illnesses Literary Prize is open to authors with a disability or chronic illness and novels which include a disabled or chronically ill character or characters. Prize fund: £2,000. Founded 2022.

The Boardman Tasker Award for Mountain Literature – see page 619

The Sid Chaplin Award – see page 587

Climate Fiction Prize

email hello@climatefictionprize.com
website www.climatefictionprize.com
X @climate_fiction
Bluesky @climate-fiction.bsky.social
Instagram @climatefictionprize

Supported by Climate Spring, the Prize promotes innovative novels of literary merit that explore the climate crisis. 1st prize: £10,000. Founded 2024.

Edinburgh Novel Award

email info@scottishartstrust.org
website www.scottishartstrust.org

Facebook www.facebook.com/edinburghwritingawards
Instagram @edinburghwritingawards

Open to writers and illustrators working in traditional novel or graphic novel formats. Novels may be in any style, including comedy, romance, drama, horror, queer, contemporary, romantasy and speculative fiction. Writers should initially submit a short extract of a novel or graphic novel suitable for adults (5,000 words or 6–8 pages with finished art and text) plus a 300-word synopsis. Longlisted and shortlisted authors will be asked for more material but at no stage are writers asked to submit a completed novel. 1st prize: £1,500; all shortlisted entries are reviewed by a literary agency. Entry fee: £15; free entries are available for writers in need of support. Entries open 1 November; free entry applications close 31 December; paid entries close 28 February.

Encore Award

Royal Society of Literature, Somerset House, London WC2R 1LA
tel 020-7845 4679
email info@rsliterature.org
website https://rsliterature.org/the-encore-award/

Celebrates the best second novel of the year. The award fills a niche in the catalogue of literary prizes by celebrating the achievement of outstanding second novels. Entrants must have been resident in the UK, RoI or Commonwealth for the previous three years. 1st prize: £10,000; the other shortlisted titles also receive £1,000.

Goldsboro Books Glass Bell Award

23–27 Cecil Street, London WC2N 4EZ
tel 020-7497 9230
email enquiries@goldsborobooks.com
website www.goldsborobooks.com/
Facebook www.facebook.com/GoldsboroBooks
X @GoldsboroBooks
Instagram @goldsborobooks

Awarded annually to an outstanding work of contemporary fiction, rewarding quality storytelling in any genre. The winner of the Glass Bell receives £2,000 in prize money and a handmade glass bell. The jury of ten consists of team members from Goldsboro Books; books are selected in-house rather than through a submission process. Founded 2017.

The Goldsmiths Prize

Department of English & Creative Writing, Goldsmiths University of London, New Cross, London SE14 6NW
email goldsmithsprize@gold.ac.uk
website www.gold.ac.uk/goldsmiths-prize/
X @GoldsmithsPrize
Bluesky @goldsmithsprize.bsky.social
Instagram @goldsmithsprize
Prize Coordinator Livia Franchini, *Literary Director* Tim Parnell

Celebrates the qualities of creative daring and rewards fiction that breaks the mould or extends the possibilities of the novel form. 1st prize: £10,000. Prize opens for submissions late January; closing date for submission of entry forms late March; closing date for submission of books early July; shortlist announced late September/early October; winner announced November. Founded 2013.

The InWords Literary Award (TILA)

website https://tila.ink

An annual award that recognises a book or a body of work of exceptional literary merit. The winner is announced at Cheltenham Literary Festival and receives £10,000.

Lambda Literary Awards

PO Box 20186, New York, NY 10014
tel +1 213-277-5755
email awards@lambdaliterary.org
website https://lambdaliterary.org/awards/
Facebook www.facebook.com/LambdaLiterary
X @LambdaLiterary
Instagram @lambdaliterary

Established to increase the visibility of LGBTQ+ storytelling in all of its forms across 26 categories including Fiction, Non-Fiction, Poetry, Memoir/Biography, Romance, Anthology, Children's, Middle Grade, YA, Comics, Drama, Erotica, Mystery, Speculative Fiction and LGBTQ+ Studies. Special awards are also given to individual writers for their contribution to LGBTQ+ storytelling. Entries must have been published, distributed or performed in the US in the preceding year. Winners are announced at an online ceremony each year. Submission deadline: March. Founded 1989.

The London Writers Awards

The Albany Centre, Douglas Way, London SE8 4AG
email bobby@spreadtheword.org.uk
website www.spreadtheword.org.uk/projects/london-writers-awards

Set up by Spread the Word for London-based prose writers who identify as being from a background currently under-represented in publishing. The awards are given across three genres: literary fiction (including short stories), commercial fiction and children's (including middle-grade and YA fiction, excluding picture books). Recipients of the award receive a place on a programme that includes feedback, masterclasses and professional development. Founded 2018.

Mslexia Competitions: Novel (Adult)

PO Box 656, Newcastle upon Tyne NE99 1PZ
tel 0191 204 8860

email competitions@mslexia.co.uk
website https://mslexia.co.uk/competitions/adult-novel
Facebook www.facebook.com/Mslexia/
X @Mslexia
Instagram @mslexia

A biennial prize for novelists who identify as women. Entrants should not have traditionally published a novel before; self-published novels are eligible if they have sold less than 500 copies. Entrants should submit the first 5,000 words of a novel of at least 50,000 words. 1st prize: £5,000; the winner and three finalists also receive MSS feedback from the Literary Consultancy, and pitch training and introductions to agents and editors from New Writing North. Submissions open in June 2027. Entry fee: £26.

New Adult Book Prize NEW

The Stage Media Company Ltd,
47 Bermondsey Street, London SE1 3XT
email katie.fraser@thebookseller.com
website www.thebookseller.com/awards/new-adult-book-prize
X @thebookseller
Chair Katie Fraser

Administrated by *The Bookseller* in collaboration with Cheltenham Literature Festival. Open to all fiction genres, the prize showcases exceptional writing that explores the lives and challenges of people aged 19–29, with the winner announced at the Cheltenham Literature Festival. Eligible titles must be first published in print in the UK or Ireland, between 1 March 2024 and 28 February 2025. Self-published titles, non-fiction, anthologies and graphic novels are not eligible. Entry deadline: April. Founded 2025.

The Next Big Story NEW

25 Eccleston Place, London SW1W 9NF
tel 07700 153560
email hello@thenovelry.com
website www.thenovelry.com/prize
Facebook www.facebook.com/thenovelry
X @thenovelry
Instagram @thenovelry

Seeks works of fiction that showcase a gripping story and a unique voice. Entrants should submit the first three pages (maximum 1,500 words) of a novel for children or adults. Entries will be judged on the following five criteria: person, problem, place, plot and prose. The winner will be decided by a panel of judges and a public vote. 1st prize: £75,000; eight shortlisted entrants will receive a place on The Finished Novel Course. Entry deadline: 31 July 2025. Entry fee: £15. Founded 2025.

Nota Bene Prize

email notabeneprize@agile-ideas.com
website www.notabeneprize.com
X @notabeneprize
Instagram @notabeneprize

Dedicated to recognising influential fiction publicised by reader's word-of-mouth recommendations. Specifically seeks fiction with an original concept or style that is engaging, inclusive and gets people talking. Publishers must submit books written or translated into English and published in the preceeding year; a shortlist is created by a team of readers, authors, booksellers and content creators and voted on by readers and industry professionals. 1st prize: £1,500. Submission deadline: April. Founded 2003.

Oxford/42 New Writing Prize – see page 605

Page Turner Awards

tel 020-8133 6375
email paula@pageturnerawards.com
website https://pageturnerawards.com/
Facebook www.facebook.com/PageTurnerAwards
X @PageTurnerAward
Founders Ken Sheridan, Paula Sheridan

An inclusive series of awards designed for writers from any background, age, race or interest. The awards open each year in January and close at the end of June. Following the judging, longlists, shortlists and finalists are announced across August/September, followed by an award winners' and prize winners' online ceremony in November. The awards are made up of three literary awards, one each for published books, unpublished books and screenplays; awards for young writers and golden writers; awards dedicated to encouraging equality and diversity (the Challenged Writer Award and the Culture Award); and a mentorship programme. Founded 2020.

Prototype Prize – see page 603

Wilbur Smith Adventure Writing Prize

The Wilbur & Niso Smith Foundation, Unit 9,
5–7 Wells Terrace, London N4 3JU
email submissions@wilbur-niso-smithfoundation.org
website www.wilbur-niso-smithfoundation.org/
Facebook www.facebook.com/WNSmithFoundation
X @Wilbur_Niso_Fdn
Instagram @adventurewritingprize

Supports and celebrates today's best adventure writing. Open to writers of any nationality, writing in English. The Best Published Novel (1st prize: £10,000) is for full-length novels for adults or young adults. The New Voices Award (1st prize: one year of editorial support and one-to-one mentoring for five aspiring writers) is for a novel-in-progress, intended for adult readers. Entrants should submit the first three chapters (no more than 10,000 words) and a plot outline of no more than 1,000 words.

The Author of Tomorrow award seeks the adventure writers of the future and is open to young people across the world who have completed a short piece of adventure writing in English. There are three categories: 11 years and under, 12–15 years and 16–21 years.

Sustainable Story Award – see page 621

TikTok Book Awards

6th Floor, One London Wall, London EC2Y 5EB
website www.tiktok.com
Facebook www.facebook.com/tiktok
X @tiktok_uk
Instagram @tiktok_uk

Celebrates the best books and authors discussed on TikTok and the most popular creators who post videos about them. Judged by a panel of authors and publishing professionals, TikTok users vote on a shortlist and winners are announced in summer. Founded 2023.

The Virginia Prize for Fiction

80 Hill Rise, Richmond TW10 6UB
email vp@aurorametro.com
website www.aurorametro.com/virginia-prize-for-fiction-writing-contest/
Facebook www.facebook.com/AuroraMetroBooks

Named after Virginia Woolf, the biennial prize seeks novels for adult or YA readers. Entries should be unpublished novels of at least 45,000 words and entrants should identify as female or non-binary. 1st prize: editorial support and a publishing contract with Aurora Metro Books. Entry deadline: October 31st 2025. Entry fee: £15.

Women's Prize for Fiction

email info@womensprize.co.uk
website https://womensprizeforfiction.com
Facebook www.facebook.com/womensprize
X @WomensPrize
Instagram @womensprize
Threads @womensprize

Awarded to the best full-length novel of the year. Sponsored by Audible and Baileys, the prize champions excellence, originality and accessibility in women's writing. Novels must have been written in English and published in the UK between April and March for each year's prize cycle. 1st prize: £30,000 and a bronze statuette known as the 'Bessie', created and donated by the artist Grizel Niven.
Founded 1996.

CRIME, MYSTERY, THRILLER AND HORROR

Criminal Lines

6 Warwick Court, Holborn, London WC1R 5DJ
tel 020-7242 2811
email criminallines@amheath.com
website https://amheath.com/criminal-lines

Launched as a collaboration between literary agent A.M. Heath, publisher Orion and magazine *Crime Monthly*, the competition is open to crime writers across all subgenres who have not previously been published. Entrants should submit the first 5,000 words of a novel and a 1,000-word synopsis. 1st prize: £3,500 and representation with A.M. Heath; one runner-up will receive one year of mentoring from Orion. Entry deadline: December. Founded 2023.

CWA Dagger Awards

email comp@thecwa.co.uk
website https://thecwa.co.uk/awards-and-competitions/the-daggers
Contacts Vicki Goldie (CWA Secretary), Mike Stotter (Daggers Liaison)

Administered by the Crime Writers' Association. The Diamond Dagger is nominated by CWA members. The Gold Dagger, the Ian Fleming Steel Dagger, the John Creasey Dagger, the Dagger for Crime Fiction in Translation, the ALCS Gold Dagger for Non-Fiction, the Short Story Dagger, the Historical Dagger, the Twisted Dagger (psychological thrillers) and the Whodunnit Dagger (cosy crime) are nominated by publishers via the CWA website. The Dagger in the Library is nominated by library visitors and voted for by library staff.

CWA Margery Allingham Short Mystery Prize

email info@thecwa.co.uk
website www.thecwa.co.uk/ma

An annual competition for a short story of up to 3,500 words that follows Margery Allingham's definition of a mystery (see website). The international competition is open to all writers, published or unpublished. The story itself must not previously have been published in any form. 1st prize: £500. The competition opens on 1 October and closes at 6pm on the last working day of February.

The Emerging Author Dagger – see page 580

Joffe Books Prize for Crime Writers of Colour

email prize@joffebooks.com
website www.joffebooks.com
Facebook www.facebook.com/joffebooks
X @JoffeBooks
Instagram @joffebooks

Established to find new crime fiction writers of colour. Entrants must be from Black, Asian, Indigenous and minority ethnic backgrounds writing in any crime fiction genre, including psychological thrillers, cosy mysteries, police procedurals, suspense mysteries and domestic noirs. Entrants must be UK residents or British citizens and must be writing in English. 1st prize: £1,000, a two-book publishing deal with Joffe Books and a £25,000 audiobook offer from Audible for the first book. Entrants should submit a full-length MSS, a synopsis of the book and a biography. Founded 2021.

Ned Kelly Awards

email info@austcrimewriters.com
website www.austcrimewriters.com/ned-kelly-awards
Facebook www.facebook.com/austcrimewriters/
X @auscrimewriters

Honour crime fiction and true crime writing in four categories: Best Crime Fiction, Best Debut Crime Fiction, Best True Crime and Best International Crime Fiction. Authors must be citizens of or resident in Australia and books must have been published in the preceding year. Also gives Lifetime Achievement Awards to writers, publishers, reviewers and fans who have made a significant contribution to Australian crime writing. Entry deadline: April. Entry fee: $55. Founded 1995.

Macavity Awards

email janet@mysteryreaders.org
website https://mysteryreaders.org/macavity-awards/

Named after T.S. Eliot's Macavity the Mystery Cat, the awards recognise the best mystery books of the year as nominated and voted by Mystery Readers International Members. There are five categories: Mystery Novel, First Mystery, Mystery Short Story, Non-fiction/Critical and the Sue Feder Memorial Award for Best Historical Mystery. Founded 1987.

McDermid Debut Award – see page 581

McIlvanney Prize for the Scottish Crime Novel of the Year

Bloody Scotland, 19A Canning Street,
Edinburgh EH3 8HE
website https://bloodyscotland.com/prizes/
Facebook www.facebook.com/bloodyscotland
X @BloodyScotland
Bluesky @bloodyscotland.bsky.social

A crime book is eligible if the author was born or raised in Scotland, is a permanent resident of Scotland or has a strong and enduring connection to Scotland. 1st prize: £1,000. Entry fee: £40 plus VAT per entry.

The Bloody Scotland Crime Debut of the Year

The award recognises new talent in crime writing, with the same criteria as the McIlvanney Prize. 1st prize: £500. Entry fee: £40 plus VAT per title. Founded 2019.

Petrona Award

email admin@petronaaward.co.uk
website www.petronaaward.co.uk

Celebrates the best Scandinavian Crime Novel translated into English and published in the UK in the previous year. Either the original author must have been born in Scandinavia or the novel must be set in Scandinavia. Publishers must enter on the behalf of an author. 1st prize: the original author receives a trophy; both author and translator receive a cash prize. Entry deadline: February. Free to enter. Founded 2013.

Bram Stoker Awards

PO Box 14387, Columbus, OH 43214, USA
email stokerchair@horror.org
website www.thebramstokerawards.com

Administered by the Horror Writers Association, they recognise superior achievement in horror writing. There are 13 categories: Novel, First Novel, Short Fiction, Long Fiction, Middle Grade, YA, Fiction Collection, Poetry Collection, Anthology, Screenplay, Graphic Novel, Non-Fiction and Short Non-Fiction. Longlisted works are nominated by society members and the jury; authors can submit their own work to the jury. Submission deadline: 30 November. Awards are presented each year as part of an association banquet. Founded 1988.

Theakston Old Peculier Crime Novel of the Year Award

32 Cheltenham Parade, Harrogate HG1 1DB
tel (01423) 562303
email info@harrogate-festival.org.uk
website https://harrogatetheakstoncrimeaward.com/
Facebook www.facebook.com/HarrogateInternationalFestivals/
X @HarrogateFest
Instagram @harrogatefestivals

Voted for by members of the public and a jury-panel, celebrating excellence and originality in British and Irish crime fiction. The winner is announced at Harrogate International Festivals' Theakston Old Peculier Crime Writing Festival and receives £3,000. Previous winners include Mick Heron, Val McDermid, Denise Mina, Lee Child, Clare Mackintosh, M.W. Craven and Jo Callaghan. An award recognising an Outstanding Contribution to Crime Fiction is also delivered.

Thriller Awards

PO Box 1402, Medina, OH 44258, USA
email AwardsVP@thrillerwriters.org
website https://thrillerwriters.org
Facebook www.facebook.com/ThrillerWritersOrganization
X @thrillerwriters
Instagram @internationalthrillerwriters

Recognises the best thrillers of the year in seven categories: Standalone Thriller, Standalone Mystery, Series Novel, First Novel, YA Novel, Short Story and Audiobook. Submissions must have been written in English and published in the preceding year.

COMEDY

The Bollinger Everyman Wodehouse Prize for Comic Fiction

Everyman's Library, 50 Albemarle Street, London W1S 4BD
tel 020-7493 4361
X @EverymansLib
Instagram @everymanslibrary

The UK's leading prize dedicated to comic fiction. Awarded to the most original comic novel of the previous 12 months. The winner receives a jeroboam of Bollinger Special Cuvée, a case of Bollinger La Grande Année and a complete set of the Everyman Wodehouse collection; a rare-breed pig is named after the winning novel for a year. Eligible novels must have been published in the UK and Ireland between 1 June and 31 May. Closing date: end of June; shortlist announced in October; winner announced in December. Launched in 2000 on the 25th anniversary of the death of P.G. Wodehouse.

Comedy Women in Print Awards

email hello@comedywomeninprint.co.uk
website www.comedywomeninprint.co.uk
X @CWIPprize
Instagram @cwipprize

The UK and Ireland's first comedy literary prize dedicated to celebrating witty women's writing. There are three categories: Self-Published Comedy Novel, Published Comedy Novel and Unpublished Comedy Novel. Prizes include access to courses, publicity packages and cash prizes. Entry forms, terms and conditions and submission guidelines can be found on the website. Founded 2019.

HISTORICAL

Winston Graham Historical Prize

Royal Cornwall Museum, River Street, Truro, Cornwall TR1 2SJ
email winstongraham@royalcornwallmuseum.org.uk
website www.royalcornwallmuseum.org.uk/home/awards
Facebook www.facebook.com/RoyalCornwallMuseum
X @Cornwall_Museum
Instagram @cornwall_museum

Established with a legacy from Poldark author Winston Graham and managed by the Royal Institution of Cornwall. Celebrates historical fiction that features a strong sense of place. Open to writers across the UK and Ireland. 1st prize: £3,000. Entry deadline: December. Founded 2008.

The HWA Crown Awards

The Union Building, 51–59 Rose Lane, Norwich NR1 1BY
email admin@historicalwriters.org
website https://historicalwriters.org/awards
Facebook www.facebook.com/HistoriaHWA/
X @HistoriaHWA

Recognises full-length works of fiction and non-fiction in three categories: Debut, Non-Fiction and Gold (for novelists who have published more than one book). Books must have been published in the UK, in English, in the previous year; the key events within the book must take place at least 35 years in the past. Submissions must be made by publishers and close in April. Entry fee: £35.

The HWA Dorothy Dunnett Short Story Competition – see page 601

Walter Scott Prize for Historical Fiction

10 Brewery Park Business Centre, Haddington EH41 3HA
website www.walterscottprize.co.uk
Facebook www.facebook.com/walterscottprize
X @waltscottprize
Instagram @walterscottprize

Founded by the Duke and Duchess of Buccleuch and administered by the Abbotsford Trust, home of Sir Walter Scott. Rewards fiction of exceptional quality that is set in the past (according to Walter Scott's subtitle for Waverley, at least 60 years ago). Books must be written in English and have been published in the UK, Eire or the Commonwealth during the previous calendar year. Books must be submitted by publishers; self-published authors are not eligible. The winner receives £25,000 and shortlisted authors receive £1,500 each. The Prize is usually awarded at the Borders Book Festival in Melrose each June. Submission deadline: October. Founded 2009.

ROMANCE

The Romantic Novel of the Year Awards

email info@romanticwriters.co.uk
website www.romanticnovelistsassociation.org
Facebook www.facebook.com/Romantic.Novelists.Association
X @RNAtweets
Instagram @romanticnovelists
Chair Seana Talbot

Reader-judged awards presented in the following categories: Debut, Contemporary, Popular, Romantic Comedy, Fantasy, Thriller, Historical, Shorter Novel, Saga and Christmas/Festive. In addition, the Joan Hessayon Award is open to members of the Romantic Novelists' Association's New Writers' Scheme who submit a MSS for critique between January and August and whose MSS is subsequently accepted for publication.

Awards are open to both members and non-members of the RNA. Novels must be first published between 1 January and 31 December of the year of entry. Submission deadline: September.

The Betty Trask Prize – see page 582

SCI-FI AND FANTASY

British Science Fiction Association Awards

19 Beech Green, Dunstable, Bedfordshire LU6 1EB
email chair@bsfa.co.uk
website https://bsfa.co.uk/
Facebook www.facebook.com/groups/BritishScienceFictionAssociation
X @bsfa

Honours sci-fi writing and promotes the genre. Awards are made in the following categories: Short Fiction, Shorter Fiction, Artwork, Novel, Short Non-Fiction, Long Non-Fiction, Younger Readers, Collection and Audio Fiction. There are three rounds: longlist (September to December), shortlist (January) and final vote (opens February and closes at noon on the day of the awards ceremony). Founded 1970.

Arthur C. Clarke Award

website www.clarkeaward.com

An annual prize of a number of pounds sterling equal to the current year (e.g. £2,026 in 2026) plus an engraved bookend is given for the best sci-fi novel with first UK publication during the previous calendar year. Titles are submitted by publishers. Founded 1985.

CYMERA Prize for Speculative Short Fiction – see page 600

Future Worlds Prize for Fantasy & Science Fiction Writers of Colour

email info@futureworldsprize.co.uk
website www.futureworldsprize.co.uk
X @FutureWorldsPrz
Instagram @futureworldsprize

Uncovers unpublished fantasy and sci-fi writers of colour. Entrants must not be published, under contract with a publisher or have won another writing competition. Entrants should submit an extract from a short story or the opening chapters of a novel (5,000–10,000 words), a synopsis of their work (1,000 words) and a covering letter. Prizes: 1st: £4,500; 2nd: £2,500; up to six runners-up: £850. All shortlisted writers receive four mentoring sessions over a one-year period. Submission window opens from October to January. Founded 2020.

The Hugo Awards

PO Box 242, Fernley, NV 89408-0242, USA
email info@thehugoawards.org
website www.thehugoawards.org

The most prestigious sci-fi awards, nominated and voted for by members of the World Science Fiction Society (WSFS). There are 17 categories recognising writers, illustrators and editors across formats including novels, novellas, short stories, graphic novels, comics, films, television, radio, theatre and computer games. There are two additional awards presented alongside the Hugo Awards: The Lodestar Award for Best Young Adult Book and the Astounding Award for Best New Writer. Winners are announced at an annual ceremony at Worldcon and each receive a trophy. Founded 1953.

The Kitschies

email submissions@thekitschies.com
website https://thekitschies.com
Facebook www.facebook.com/Kitschies
X @TheKitschies

Awards the year's most progressive, intelligent and entertaining works that contain elements of the speculative or fantastic. There are three categories: Red Tentacle (Novel), Golden Tentacle (Debut Novel) and Inky Tentacle (Cover Art). Novels must have been published in the previous year. Prizes total £2,500. Entry deadline: February. Founded 2009.

The Mythopoeic Fantasy Award for Adult Literature

PO Box 6707, Altadena, CA 91003–6707, USA
email awards@mythsoc.org
website www.mythsoc.org
Facebook www.facebook.com/MythSoc/

Given to the fantasy novel, multi-volume novel or single-author story collection for adults published during the previous year that best exemplifies the spirit of the Inklings.

The Mythopoeic Awards are chosen from books nominated by individual members of the Mythopoeic Society and selected by a committee of Society members. Authors, publishers and their representatives may not nominate their own books for any of the awards.

The Mythopoeic Scholarship Award in Myth and Fantasy Studies

PO Box 6707, Altadena, CA 91003–6707, USA
email awards@mythsoc.org
website www.mythsoc.org
Facebook www.facebook.com/MythSoc/

Given to scholarly books on specific authors in the Inklings tradition, or to more general works on the genres of myth and fantasy.

The Mythopoeic Scholarship Award in Inklings Studies

Given to books on J.R.R. Tolkien, C.S. Lewis and/or Charles Williams that make significant contributions to Inklings scholarship.

Non-fiction

General non-fiction prizes are listed first, with prizes categorised by type of non-fiction following under headings, e.g. 'Academic writing and essays'.

ALCS Educational Writers' Award – see page 574

The Baillie Gifford Prize for Non-Fiction

website www.thebailliegiffordprize.co.uk
Facebook www.facebook.com/BGPrize/
X @BGPrize

Rewards the best of non-fiction and is open to authors of any nationality. Covers all non-fiction in the areas of current affairs, history, politics, science, sport, travel, biography, autobiography and the arts. Formerly known as The Samuel Johnson Prize (1999–2015). 1st prize: £50,000; shortlisted authors receive £5,000 each. Submissions must be made by publishers, not individual authors.

The Curae Prize – see page 585

The Pol Roger Duff Cooper Prize

email DuffCooperPrize@gmail.com
website www.duffcooperprize.org
X @DuffCooperPrize
Instagram @duffcooperprize

An annual prize for a work of non-fiction published in the UK. The prize of £5,000 comes from a fund established by the friends and admirers of Duff Cooper, 1st Viscount Norwich (1890–1954) after his death. Accepts submissions from publishers only.

Financial Times and Schroders Business Book of the Year Award

email bookaward@ft.com
website www.ft.com/bookaward

Identifies the book that provides the most compelling and enjoyable insight into modern business issues including management, finance and economics. Submissions should be made via a publisher. The winner receives £30,000 and runners-up each receive £10,000. Founded 2005.

Prototype Prize – see page 603

Women's Prize for Non-Fiction

email info@womensprize.com
website https://womensprize.com
X @WomensPrize
Instagram @womensprize
Threads @womensprize

Awarded to the best work of narrative non-fiction written in English and published in the UK in the preceding year. Sponsored by Findmypast, the prize celebrates excellence in writing and research, strong and original narrative voices, and accessibility. 1st prize: £30,000 and an artwork known as 'The Charlotte', created by sculptor Ann Christopher; the prize is funded by the Charlotte Aitken Trust. Founded 2023.

ACADEMIC WRITING AND ESSAYS

British Academy Medals and Prizes

The British Academy, 10–11 Carlton House Terrace, London SW1Y 5AH
tel 020-7969 5200
email prizes@thebritishacademy.ac.uk
website www.thebritishacademy.ac.uk/prizes-medals

Prizes and medals are awarded by the British Academy for outstanding work in various fields of the humanities and social sciences on the recommendation of Fellows and specialist committees. Prizes and medals include: the Burkitt Medal for Biblical Studies; the Derek Allen Prize (made annually in turn for Musicology, Numismatics and Celtic studies); the Edward Ullendorff Medal (Semitic languages and Ethiopian studies); the Grahame Clark Medal (Prehistoric Archaeology); the Sir Israel Gollancz Prize (English studies); the Kenyon Medal (Classical Studies and Archaeology); the Serena Medal (Italian studies); the Leverhulme Medal and Prize (awarded every three years, alternating between the humanities and social sciences); and the Landscape Archaeology Medal. Nominations open for all prizes and medals on the 1 December. Presentations are made in Autumn.

Also runs two competitions open for public submissions: the Peter Townsend Prize (Social Policy), 1st prize: £1,000; and the Brian Barry Prize in Political Science, 1st prize: £1,500 and publication in the *British Journal of Political Science.*

The British Academy Book Prize

The Prize, worth £25,000, celebrates the best work of non-fiction, based on exceptional research and written for the general reader, in the fields of the humanities and social services. It is part of a wider programme of year-round public events supporting the Academy's purpose – to deepen understanding of people, societies and cultures. The Prize is open to writers of any nationality. There is no fee to nominate and anyone may make a nomination. Nominations for the 2026 prize are open from mid-January to the end of February; judges select a shortlist of up to six books, announced in September; the winner is announced in October. Previous winners include:

Ross Perlin, Nandini Das, Alia Trabucco Zeran, Sujit Sivasundaram, Hazel V. Carby and Toby Green. Founded 2013.

The Rose Mary Crawshay Prize

Awarded each year for an historical or critical book by a woman, on any subject connected with literature. Eligible nominations must be for books published within the last three years. Nominations open in December and close in January, and are invited from Fellows of the British Academy. Prize: £500. Founded 1888.

Anne Brown Essay Prize

11 North Main Street, Wigtown, Dumfries and Galloway DG8 9HN
tel (01988) 402036
email annebrownessayprize@wigtownbookfestival.com
website www.wigtownbookfestival.com/our-projects/the-anne-brown-essay-prize
Facebook www.facebook.com/WigtownBookFestival
X @WigtownBookFest
Instagram @wigtownbookfest

Awarded by Wigtown Book Festival to promote intelligent and thought-provoking literary essays. Established in memory of former festival trustee and radio journalist, Anne Brown. Essays can be published or unpublished, must not exceed 4,000 words and can be on any subject, but entrants are encouraged to explore 'aspects of our shared social, cultural or emotional lives'. Writers must be born or living in Scotland. 1st prize: £1,500.

The Conversation Prize

email uk-support@theconversation.com
website https://theconversation.com/uk
Facebook www.facebook.com/ConversationUK
X @ConversationUK
Instagram @theconversationdotcom

Run in partnership with Faber and Curtis Brown, the Prize is open to academic authors in the UK, Europe and Commonwealth. Entrants should submit a long-form article accompanied by a non-fiction book pitch. The winning entry is published on *The Conversation* website. Submissions open in Autumn.

Edinburgh Essay Award

email info@scottishartstrust.org
website www.scottishartstrust.org
Facebook www.facebook.com/edinburghwritingawards
Instagram @edinburghwritingawards

Open to essays and creative non-fiction, up to 2,000 words. Accepts cultural, political, environmental, historical and philosophical topics, travel narratives and memoir. 1st prize: £1,000; the top fifteen stories are published in an anthology. Entry fee: £10; free entries are available for writers in need of support. Entries open 1 November; free entry applications close 31 December; paid entries close 28 February.

Fitzcarraldo Edition/Mahler & Lewitt Studios Essay Prize

email essayprize@fitzcarraldoeditions.com
website https://fitzcarraldoeditions.com/prizes/essay-prize

Gives the best emerging essay writers a chance to develop their talent and provides the winner with their first experience of publishing a book, from planning, research and writing through to editing, production and publicity. Entrants should submit a 5,000-word proposal for a book-length essay (minimum 25,000 words) and a 5,000-word writing sample. Essay proposals should explore and expand the possibilities of the essay form, there is no restriction on theme or subject matter. Entrants should be unpublished and reside in Great Britain or Ireland. The winner receives £4,000, a residency at the Mahler & LeWitt Studios in Spoleto, Italy, and their book is published by Fitzcarraldo Editions. Submission deadline: March. Founded 2016.

The Calvin and Rose G. Hoffman Memorial Prize

The King's School, 25 The Precincts, Canterbury, Kent CT1 2ES
email bursar@kings-school.co.uk

Awarded to the writer of the best distinguished scholarly essay on Christopher Marlowe and his relationship to William Shakespeare. Entries should be no longer than 20,000 words and must be accompanied by an entry form. Closing date: 1 September.

Keats–Shelley Prize

KSMA Registered Office, 11 Staple Inn, London WC1V 7QH
email hello@keats-shelley.org
website www.keats-shelley.org
Facebook www.facebook.com/keatsshelleyhouse
X @Keats_Shelley

Encourages poets and essayists to respond to the work of the Romantics. Entrants should submit poems (30 lines) inspired by that year's theme or essays (3,000 words) on any aspect. 1st prize: £1,000; two highly-commended entries also receive £500 each. Entry deadline: January. Entry fee: £10 (poetry), free (essays). Also runs the Young Romantics Prize for poets and essayists aged 16–18. Founded 1988.

The Juliet McLauchlan Prize

The Polish Social and Cultural Association, 238–246 King Street, London W6 0RF
email hughepstein@hotmail.co.uk
website www.josephconradsociety.org/prizes_study_grants.htm

Awarded by the Joseph Conrad Society for an essay on any aspect of the work and life of Joseph Conrad. Fosters new interest in and study of the writer.

Dedicated to the memory of the society's first Chair, Juliet McLauchlan. Essays must be between 5,000 and 7,000 words, written in English and cannot previously have been published. 1st prize: £200.

Nine Dots Prize

email questions@ninedotsprize.org
website https://ninedotsprize.org/
X @NineDotsPrize

A biennial award that recognises innovative thinking in response to contemporary social issues. Entrants are asked to submit a 3,000-word response to a question posed about the problems facing the modern world. The author can agree or disagree, critique or reject, but must address the question fully and insightfully. The winner receives $100,000 to fund a short book on the same subject. The next award cycle commences in October 2026. Founded 2016.

OUP First Book Prize NEW

Oxford University Press Distribution Services, North Kettering Business Park, Hipwell Road, Kettering, Northants NN14 1UA
email first.bookprize@oup.com
website https://academic.oup.com/pages/early-career-researcher-first-book-prize/%20
Facebook www.facebook.com/OUPAcademic
X @OUPAcademic

Gives up to ten applicants the opportunity to publish their first academic book fully open access, making the work widely available and thus increasing its potential reach. Applicants must be early career researchers working in the humanities or social sciences, within six years of their first academic appointment or the award of their PhD. Especially welcomes applications from academics from under-represented backgrounds and those working on diverse subjects. Applicants should submit a proposal and two sample chapters. Entry deadline: March. Founded 2025.

The Samuel Pepys Award

Paul Gray, Haremoor House, Faringdon, Oxon SN7 8PN
tel 07802 301297
email plgray@btinternet.com
website www.pepys-club.org.uk

A biennial prize for a book published in English that makes the greatest contribution to the understanding of Samuel Pepys, his times or his contemporaries. The winner receives £2,000 and the Robert Latham Medal. Closing date: 30 June 2027 (for publication between 1 July 2025 and 30 June 2027). Founded by the Samuel Pepys Award Trust in 2003 on the tercentenary of the death of Pepys.

The RP Critical Writing Prize

17 Carlton House Terrace, London SW1Y 5BD
tel 020-7930 6844
email luke@therp.co.uk
website www.therp.co.uk/the-rp-writing-prize
Facebook www.facebook.com/RoyalSocietyofPortraitPainters
X @RP_portraits
Instagram @royalsocietyportraitpainters

Promotes new writing on any aspect of contemporary portrait painting. Entrants should submit a 250-word proposal for a piece of writing of between 1,000 and 1,500 words. The work could be a review of an individual artwork or exhibition, or something more experimental. 1st prize: £500; two Special Mention Awards: £250; all three pieces of writing are published in the RP Annual Exhibition Catalogue. Entry deadline: 30 June. Founded 2023.

STR Theatre Book Prize

email theatrebookprize@str.org.uk
website www.str.org.uk/grants-prizes/theatre-book-prize/

Established to mark the Society's Golden Jubilee. Given to the best book on the subject of British theatre. All new works of original research first published in English are eligible except for play text and studies of drama as literature. The Society for Theatre Research also awards research grants and administers the New Scholars Prize. Founded 1998.

Reginald Taylor and Lord Fletcher Essay Competition

British Archaeological Association, 18 Stanley Road, Oxford OX4 1QZ
email editor@thebaa.org
website https://thebaa.org/scholarships-awards/reginald-taylor-lord-fletcher-essay-prize/
Editor John Munns

A medal and £500 are awarded biennially to the best unpublished essay of high scholarly standard, which shows original research on a subject of archaeological, art-historical or architectural interest within the period from the Roman era to the Middle Ages. The winning essay may be published in the Association's journal. Next awards: Winter 2025 and Winter 2027. The essay should not exceed 8,000 words. Founded in memory of E. Reginald Taylor FSA and Lord Fletcher FSA.

Wasafiri Essay Prize

c/o School of Arts, Queen Mary, University of London, Mile End Road, London E1 4NS
tel 020-7882 2686
email wasafiri-editorial-assistant@qmul.ac.uk
website www.wasafiri.org/wasafiri-essay-prize/
X @WasafiriMag
Bluesky @wasafirimag.bsky.social
Instagram @wasafirimag

Established to recognise and support contemporary literature researchers and academics who are at the start of their career. The judging panel are looking for critical essays that are innovative, engaging, nuanced and pay close attention to both style and content. Entrants must have received a PhD in the previous eight years; essays must be between 6,000 and 9,000 words and on the subject of international contemporary literature. The winner receives £250, publication in *Wasafiri* and a mentoring session. Entry deadline: May. Founded 2022.

LIFESTYLE, FOOD AND DRINK

The British Guild of Beer Writers Awards

46 West Grange Green, Leeds LS10 3BB
email secretary@beerguild.co.uk
website www.beerguild.co.uk/awards
Facebook www.facebook.com/BritBeerWriters
X @Britbeerwriters
Bluesky @britbeerwriters.bsky.social
Instagram @britbeerwriters
Threads @britbeerwriters

Open to anyone who makes content related to or communicates about beer, cider, pubs or breweries, including journalists, authors, bloggers, poets, illustrators, filmmakers, broadcasters and photographers. Categories vary each year but focus on writing, audio and video on related subjects. Winners are chosen by an independent judging panel. Category winners and runners-up receive cash prizes.

Fortnum and Mason Food and Drink Awards

181 Piccadilly, London W1A 1ER
website www.fortnumandmason.com/awards/food-and-drink-awards

Celebrates writers, photographers and broadcasters on the subject of food and drink across 13 categories: Food Book, Debut Food Book, Cookery Book, Debut Cookery Book, Drink Book, Debut Drink Book, Food Writer, Drink Writer, Cookery Writer, Restaurant Writer, Photographer, Programme and Audio (Radio or Podcast). Each category has its own entry guidelines but all entries must have been published or transmitted in the previous year. 1st prize in each category: a trophy and a Fortnum & Mason Hamper. Founded 2012.

Garden Media Guild Awards

Katepwa House, Ashfield Park Avenue, Ross-on-Wye, Herts. HR9 5AX
tel (01989) 567393
email admin@gardenmediaguild.co.uk
website www.gardenmediaguild.co.uk/awards
Facebook www.facebook.com/gdnmediaguild
X @GdnMediaGuild
Instagram @gdnmediagld

Celebrate gardening communication across 18 categories, including books, journalism, radio, TV, blogs and social media. Awards are presented at a ceremony each year.

Jane Grigson Trust Sous Chef Award

email award@janegrigsontrust.org.uk
website https://janegrigsontrust.org.uk/the-award/
X @JGrigsonTrust
Instagram @janegrigsontrust

Award for first-time food and drink writers who have been commissioned but not yet published. The Award is open to non-fiction books on food and drink including cookbooks, memoir, travel and history, so long as the primary subject is food and/or drink. 1st prize: £2,000. Founded 2016.

Guild of Food Writers Awards

51 High Street, Welford, Northampton NN6 6HT
tel 07565 192477
email awards@gfw.co.uk
website www.gfw.co.uk/guild-of-food-writers-awards
Facebook www.facebook.com/TheGFW
X @GuildFoodWriter
Instagram @thegfw

Recognises achievements in food writing and broadcasting. There are 15 categories across books, magazines and self-published content, on subjects including food, drinks, restaurants, recipes and investigative journalism. Founded 1996.

The André Simon Memorial Fund Book Awards

email katie@andresimon.co.uk
website www.andresimon.co.uk
X @AndreSimonAward
Instagram @andresimonawards

Celebrates excellent new writing in the fields of food and drink. Presents two awards of £2,000, one each for the best new books on food and on drink, and two further awards of £1,500, a Special Commendation award and the John Avery award. All works first published in the calendar year of the award are eligible. Entries are accepted from publishers only. Founded 1978.

HISTORY

Cundill History Prize

840 Dr Penfield Avenue, Room 233, Montreal, QC H3A 1A4, Canada
email cundill.prize@mcgill.ca
website www.cundillprize.com
Facebook www.facebook.com/cundillprizemcgill
X @CundillPrize
Instagram @cundill.prize

Awarded each year to an individual who has published a book in English determined to have had, or likely to have, a profound literary, social and intellectual impact. Established by Peter Cundill and administered by Montreal's McGill University, the Cundill Prize recognises outstanding works of non-fiction that are grounded in scholarly research while retaining wide appeal and interest to the general public. The Prize is the largest non-fiction history prize in the world and welcomes submissions on any historical period or subject, regardless of the nationality or place of residence of the author. 1st prize: $75,000; two runners-up receive $10,000 each.

Templer Medal Book Prize

email templermedal@sahr.org.uk
website www.sahr.org.uk

Awarded annually to the book that has made the most significant contribution to the history of the British Army. The winner is announced at an award ceremony every April and receives a cash prize. An additional prize for the best debut is awarded to encourage new military writers. Founded 1981.

The Wolfson History Prize

email wolfsonhistoryprize@wolfson.org.uk
website www.wolfsonhistoryprize.org.uk
X @wolfsonhistory

Awarded annually for over 50 years to promote and recognise outstanding history written for a general audience. Books are judged on the extent to which they are carefully researched, well-written and accessible to the non-specialist reader. Books must be published in the UK in the calendar year preceding the year of the prize. The subject matter of the book may cover any aspect of history, including historical biography. The author must be normally resident in the UK during the year of publication and not be a previous winner of the prize. Previously shortlisted authors are eligible. The winning author is awarded £50,000. The five remaining shortlisted authors are awarded £5,000 each. All submissions must come via the publisher. Full details on the process are available online.

NATURE WRITING

The Boardman Tasker Award for Mountain Literature

8 Bank View Road, Darley Abbey, Derby DE22 1EJ
tel (01332) 342246
website www.boardmantasker.com
X @BoardmanTasker

Given for a work of fiction, non-fiction, drama or poetry, the central theme of which is concerned with the mountain environment. The prize of £3,000 commemorates the lives of mountaineers Peter Boardman and Joe Tasker. Authors of any nationality are eligible but the work must have been published or distributed in the UK in the preceding year. Entries from publishers only. Founded 1983.

Richard Jefferies Award

email award@richardjefferiessociety.org
website www.richardjefferiesaward.org

Recognises the best nature writing of the year that reflects the heritage and spirit of Richard Jefferies' countryside books. Nominations can be made by anyone. Sponsored by the White Horse Bookshop, the winner receives £1,000. Founded 2015.

Marsh Ecology Book of the Year

British Ecological Society, 42 Wharf Road, London N17GS
tel 020-3994 8282
email hello@britishecologicalsociety.org
website https://www.britishecologicalsociety.org/membership-community/honours-awards-and-prizes/marsh-book-of-the-year-award/
Facebook www.facebook.com/BritishEcolSoc
X @BritishEcolSoc
Instagram @britishecolsoc

Recognises the contribution of book authors to ecology and the development of the subject and the lack of financial reward that academic writing brings compared to other forms of publishing. Open to authors anywhere in the world. 1st prize: £1,000.

The Moth Nature Writing Prize – see page 596

Nature Chronicles Prize

email emma@naturechroniclesprize.com
website https://naturechroniclesprize.com
Facebook www.facebook.com/naturechroniclesprize
X @NaturePrize

A biennial literary award for unique, essay-length (2,000–8,000 words) non-fiction that responds to the current time and state of the world, challenging established notions of nature writing where necessary. The winner receives £10,000 and five runners-up £1,000 each. All six winning entries are published in an anthology. Submissions open in September 2025. Entry fee: £15.

The Wainwright Prize

email danielle@agile-ideas.com
website https://wainwrightprize.com/
Facebook www.facebook.com/WainwrightPrize
X @wainwrightprize
Instagram @wainwrightprize

Awarded annually to the books that most successfully encourage their readers to explore the outdoors and nurture a respect for the natural world. The Prize celebrates nature and our environment and informs readers of the threats the earth currently faces. There are three categories: Nature Writing, Writing on Conservation and Children's Writing on Nature and Conservation. A prize fund of £7,500 is shared between three winners. Founded 2014.

POLITICS AND CURRENT AFFAIRS

Airey Neave Book Prize

PO Box 111, Leominster HR6 6BP
email aireyneavetrust@gmail.com
website www.aireyneavetrust.org.uk/airey-neave-book-prize

Awarded to the non-fiction book that the judges believe has made the most significant, original, relevant and valuable contribution to the understanding of terrorism. Entries must have been published in English in the previous year. 1st prize: £5,000. Founded 2017.

Moore Prize for Human Rights Writing

email submissions@cgmoorefoundation.org
website www.cgmoorefoundation.org/prize
Facebook www.facebook.com/cgmoorefoundation.org
X @cgmoorefoundat1
Instagram @cgmooreprize

Awarded to a work of non-fiction that promotes values consistent with the advancement of human rights and dignity. Submitted works must achieve this through narratives that incorporate one of the following: illustrates abuses and violations of human rights; contributes to a greater understanding of the way human rights are administered; focuses on monitoring and enforcement of human rights legislation; generates awareness of human rights issues related to privacy, freedom of expression and dissemination of information. Authors and publishers can submit work, readers can nominate work through the website. Submissions must be at least 80,000 words long, published in the previous year, in English and if co-authored there must not be more than three authors. Open to authors worldwide. 1st prize: £1,000.

The Orwell Prizes – see page 583

The Unwin Award

1st Floor, 50 Southwark Street, London SE1 1UN
email mail@publishers.org.uk
website www.publishers.org.uk
X @PublishersAssoc
Instagram @publishersassoc

Administered by the Publishers Association and funded by a grant from the Unwin Charitable Trust, the Award recognises up-and-coming non-fiction authors who have made significant contributions to the way readers understand society and the world. The Unwin Award Lecture runs alongside the Award. The Award is for a body of work rather than a single title. 1st prize: £10,000. Founded 2024.

Westminster Book Awards

6 Bell Yard, London WC2A 2JR
email mail@booksellers.org.uk
website www.booksellers.org.uk/industryinfo/eventsandawards/WestminsterBookAwards
X @BAbooksellers

Administered each year by the Publishers Association and the Booksellers' Association. Champion the best political writing and recognise the important link between politics and the book industry. Each year publishers nominate books in three categories: Best Biography by a Parliamentarian; Best Fiction or Non-Fiction Book by a Parliamentarian; and Best Political Book by a Non-Parliamentarian. Booksellers select the shortlists and parliamentarians vote for the winner in each category. Founded 2016.

SCIENCE

British Psychological Society Book Awards

The British Pyschological Society,
30 Tabernacle Street, London EC2A 4UE
tel 020-7330 0890
email awardsandgrants@bps.org.uk
website www.bps.org.uk/book-award
Facebook www.facebook.com/OfficialBPS
X @bpsofficial

Recognises high-quality psychology books across four categories: Popular Science, Text Book, Practitioner Text and Academic Monograph. Nominations can be made by individuals, authors, agents or publishers. 1st prize in each category: £500. Entry deadline: June.

The Royal Society Trivedi Science Book Prize

The Royal Society, 6–9 Carlton House Terrace, London SW1Y 5AG
tel 020-7451 2500
email sciencebooks@royalsociety.org
website https://royalsociety.org/awards/medals-and-prizes/science-book-prize/
Facebook www.facebook.com/theroyalsociety
X @royalsociety
Bluesky @royalsociety.org.bsky.social
Instagram @theroyalsociety
Threads @theroyalsociety

Sponsored by the Trivedi Family Foundation. Open to authors of science books written for a non-specialist audience. The winner receives £25,000 and each shortlisted author receives £2,500. Publishers may submit any number of books. Entries may cover any aspect of science and technology but educational textbooks published for professional or specialist audiences are not eligible. Entry deadline: March. Founded 1988.

The Royal Society Young People's Book Prize

The Royal Society, 6–9 Carlton House Terrace, London SW1Y 5AG
tel 020-7451 2500

email sciencebooks@royalsociety.org
website https://royalsociety.org/medals-and-prizes/young-peoples-book-prize/
Facebook www.facebook.com/theroyalsociety
X @royalsociety
Bluesky @royalsociety.org.bsky.social
Instagram @theroyalsociety
Threads @theroyalsociety

Open to books for children aged 14 years and younger that have science as a substantial part of their content, narrative or theme. An expert adult panel chooses the shortlist, but the winner is chosen by groups of young people in judging panels across the UK. Pure reference works including encyclopedias, educational textbooks and descriptive books are not eligible. The winning entry receives £10,000 and shortlisted entries receive £2,500. Entries open in February each year. Founded 1988.

Society of Medical Writers Competitions

SoMW, Acre-Rise Cottage,
Upper Ludstone Claverley,
Wolverhampton WV5 7DH
email moldywarp@doctors.org.uk
website http://somw.org.uk/competitions-and-awards/

Bi-annual awards in three categories: Fiction (2,500 words), Non-Fiction (2,500 words) and Poetry (40 lines). Entries must not have been previously published. Results are published in the society magazine, *The Writer*. All winning entries are eligible for the Wilfred Hopkins Award, given for the best piece across all categories over the entire year. Also runs the Roger Bacon Biography Award for medical students.

Sustainable Story Award NEW

website www.worldofbooks.com/en-gb/pages/sustainable-story-award
Facebook www.facebook.com/WobGroup
Instagram @worldofbooksofficial

Administered by World of Books to support authors who advocate for environmental, social and economic sustainability in their work. Open to writers of fiction, non-fiction and children's literature who have already published at least one book. Entrants should submit a book proposal including the first three chapters and a statement explaining how their entry promotes sustainability. 1st prize: £15,000; two runners-up receive £5,000 each; winners also receive mentorship from the judges. Entry deadline: July. Founded 2025.

SPORT

William Hill Sports Book of the Year Award

William Hill, St John's Centre, Leeds LS2 8JF
email whsboty@williamhill.co.uk
website https://news.williamhill.com/sport/sports-book-of-the-year/
X @BookiePrize
Instagram @bookieprize

The world's most valuable and longest-established literary sports writing prize. Previous winners include Jeremy Wilson, Duncan Hamilton and Donald McRae. The winner receives £30,000 and a trophy. Shortlisted authors receive a leather-bound copy of their book and £3,000. Founded 1989.

The Sports Book Awards

Studio 106, Leather Factory Studios, Brook Lane, Holt BA14 6RL
email danielle@agile-ideas.com
website https://sportsbookawards.com
X @sportsbookaward

Highlight the most outstanding sports books of the previous calendar year, to showcase their merits and to enhance their reputation and profile. There are 14 categories to reflect every sport and genre sub-category in sports writing, including children's sports writing. The winners are announced at an annual award ceremony. Entry deadline: January.

TRAVEL

British Guild of Travel Writers Members' Excellence Awards

Larking Garden, 1 Clayton Business Park,
Great Blakenham, Ipswich IP6 0NL
tel 020-8144 8713
email hello@bgtw.org
website https://bgtw.org/awards/
Facebook www.facebook.com/TravWriters
X @TravWriters

Celebrates the best travel writing, photography, blogging and broadcasting. The 16 categories include: Feature, Book, Blogger and Photographer. Awards are presented at an annual gala.

The Ilse Schwepcke Prize

Society of Authors, 24 Bedford Row,
London WC1R 4EH
tel 020-3880 2230
email prizes@societyofauthors.org
website https://societyofauthors.org/prizes/other-prizes/ilse-schwepcke-prize/
Facebook www.facebook.com/TheSocietyofAuthors
X @soc_of_authors
Instagram @thesocietyofauthors
Grants & Prizes Manager Aine Pullan, *Grants & Prizes Design Manager* Natalie Thorpe, *Head of Fundraising, Grants & Prizes* Robyn Law

An annual award for women's travel writing in English. An independent jury selects a shortlist and the winning book is announced at the International Frankfurt Book Fair. Entries must have been published in the UK in the year preceeding the submission deadline. 1st prize: £5,000. Submission deadline: March. Submissions are only accepted from established publishers.

Sherborne Prize for Travel Writing NEW

email prize@sherbornetravelwritingfestival.com
website www.sherbornetravelwritingprize.com
Facebook www.facebook.com/SherborneLiterarySociety
Instagram @sherbornetravelwritingfestival

Awarded to a British or European travel writer who bridges gaps between people and societies through their work. Entries should be fiction or non-fiction (including creative non-fiction) published in the previous two years. Seeks work that is high quality, ambitious and promotes understanding in an increasingly divided world. Entries accepted from publishers and literary agents only. Entry deadline: September; winner announced at the Sherborne Travel Writing Festival. 1st prize: £10,000. Founded 2025.

The Edward Stanford Travel Writing Awards

Stanfords, 7 Mercer Walk, Covent Garden, London WC2H 9FA
tel 020-7836 1321
email press@stanfords.co.uk
website www.stanfords.co.uk
Facebook www.facebook.com/stanfordstravel
X @StanfordsTravel
Instagram @standfordstravel

Administered by Stanfords and sponsored by Viking. Recognise exceptional travel writing published in the previous year. The categories include: Travel Book of the Year, Children's Travel Book of the Year, Bradt New Travel Writer of the Year, and The Viking Award for Fiction with a Sense of Place. The winner in each category receives a personalised handmade globe trophy.

Grants, bursaries and fellowships

This section lists grants, bursaries and fellowships, and the organisations that award them. They support writers and artists, and promote access to, and engagement with, literature and the arts. They offer financial aid (to fund research, travel or time to dedicate to a project), feedback on work, development courses, writing retreats, residencies, career advice, mentoring, and networking opportunities with editors and agents.

Arts Council England

tel 0161 934 4317
website www.artscouncil.org.uk
Facebook www.facebook.com/artscouncilofengland
X @ace_national
Instagram @aceagrams

The national development agency for the arts in England, providing funding for a range of arts and cultural activities. Provides organisations, artists, events and initiatives funding to help them achieve the Council's mission of providing art and culture for everyone. Visit the website for information on funding support and advice.

The Arts Council/An Chomhairle Ealaíon

70 Merrion Square, Dublin D02 NY52, Republic of Ireland
tel +353 (0)1 618 0200
website www.artscouncil.ie/home
Facebook www.facebook.com/artscouncilireland
X @artscouncil_ie

Outlines all of its funding opportunities for individuals, groups and organisations on its website. Covers writing, art, theatre, film, music and more. Also publishes regular information on grants and awards, news and events, and arts policy.

The Authors' Contingency Fund

Grants Department, The Society of Authors, 24 Bedford Row, London WC1R 4EH
tel 020-3880 2230
email grants@societyofauthors.org
website https://societyofauthors.org/grants-writers-in-need/
Facebook www.facebook.com/TheSocietyofAuthors
X @Soc_of_Authors
Instagram @thesocietyofauthors
Grants & Prizes Manager Aine Pullan, *Grants & Prizes Design Manager* Natalie Thorpe, *Head of Fundraising, Grants & Prizes* Robyn Law

Offers hardship grants to established writers, illustrators and translators, whose writing-related activity makes up a significant amount of their overall income, and find themselves in sudden financial difficulty. Guidelines and application form available via the website.

The Authors' Foundation

The Society of Authors, 24 Bedford Row, London WC1R 4EH
tel 020-3880 2230
email grants@societyofauthors.org
website https://societyofauthors.org/grants/grants-for-work-in-progress
Facebook www.facebook.com/TheSocietyofAuthors
X @Soc_of_Authors
Instagram @thesocietyofauthors
Grants & Prizes Manager Aine Pullan, *Grants & Prizes Design Manager* Natalie Thorpe, *Head of Fundraising, Grants & Prizes* Robyn Law

Provides grants for professional writers to help develop a work-in-progress. Applications are open on a rolling basis, awarding funding for research, travel or other necessary expenditure.

Open to applications from authors commissioned by a commercial British publisher to write a full-length work of fiction, poetry or non-fiction, or those without a publishing contract, who have had one previous book published commercially and where there is a strong likelihood that a further book will be published in the UK. Also open to applications from writers who have previously had a work, of which they are the sole author, professionally performed on stage, screen or radio or who are currently under contract to write a script that will be professionally performed. Founded 1984.

The Malorie Blackman Scholarships for Unheard Voices

email writing@citylit.ac.uk
website www.citylit.ac.uk/malorie-blackman-scholarships

Offers three annual awards, worth up to £1,000 each, to fund one year's study within the Creative Writing department at City Lit. The awards especially welcome entries from 'Unheard Voices'. Open for submissions from December to the end of January. Founded 2020.

Bloomsbury Academic Writing Fellowship

Bloomsbury Publishing, 50 Bedford Square, London WC1B 3DP
tel 020-7631 5985

email academicfellowship@bloomsbury.com
website www.writersandartists.co.uk/bloomsbury-fellowship
Facebook www.facebook.com/WritersArtistsYearbook
X @Writers_Artists

Established to support a UK-based writer from an under-represented ethnic background with the development of an academic book project into a completed manuscript that is ready to be sent to publishers. Entrants should submit a 200-word synopsis and a 1,000–1,500 word sample extract. One recipient receives one year of editorial support, mentorship and networking opportunities, plus a £1,000 grant. Entry deadline: September. Founded 2023.

Bloomsbury Mentorship Programme

50 Bedford Square, London WC1B 3DP
tel 020-7631 5600
email bloomsburymentorship@bloomsbury.com
website www.bloomsbury.com/uk/connect/bloomsbury-mentorship-programme-2025
Facebook www.facebook.com/BloomsburyPublishing
X @BloomsburyBooks
Instagram @bloomsburypublishing

Established to address systemic barriers within publishing for those who are under-represented within the industry. The year-long mentorship with the Bloomsbury editorial team is an opportunity for the recipient to develop their writing. One writer receives the mentorship; longlisted writers are invited to a publishing workshop and networking event, and offered a place on a writing course. Entrants should not have previously published a full-length fiction book; entries should include the first 2,000 words of a work of fiction (which does not need to be completed) and a synopsis. Entry deadline: October. Founded 2023.

The K. Blundell Trust

The Society of Authors, 24 Bedford Row, London WC1R 4EH
tel 020-3380 2230
email grants@societyofauthors.org
website https://societyofauthors.org/grants/grants-for-work-in-progress
Facebook www.facebook.com/TheSocietyofAuthors
X @Soc_of_Authors
Instagram @thesocietyofauthors
Grants & Prizes Manager Aine Pullan, *Grants & Prizes Design Manager* Natalie Thorpe, *Head of Fundraising, Grants & Prizes* Robyn Law

Grants are given to published writers under 40 years who are British by birth and ordinarily resident in the UK to assist with the development of their next book. The work must increase social awareness and may be fiction or non-fiction. The fund is open for applications on a rolling basis. Applicants must have had a previous book published by a commercial UK or Irish publisher. See website for application form and guidelines; apply by email.

Stern Bryan Fellowship

c/o Dr Glenda Cooper, Department of Journalism, City, University of London, Northampton Square, London EC1V 0HB
email Stern.fellowship@gmail.com
website www.city.ac.uk/prospective-students/finance/funding/stern-bryan-fellowship

Established in memory of *Washington Post* editor Laurence Stern, it offers a three-month residency at the *Washington Post* for a British journalist working in print, digital, radio or television. Previous winners have gone on to work for Channel 4, the *Guardian* and the *Daily Mail*. Applicants should submit a CV, two references and three samples of recent work. Submissions deadline: March.

Creative Access

ITV, Westworks, 195 Wood Lane, London W12 7FQ
email info@creativeaccess.org.uk
website www.creativeaccess.org.uk
Facebook www.facebook.com/CreativeAccessUK
X @_CreativeAccess
Instagram @_creativeaccess

One of the UK's leading diversity, equity and inclusion organisations providing career support and development for those from under-represented communities. Works with hundreds of creative organisations across the UK to create inclusive workspaces, providing services such as recruitment, mentoring, research-driven consultancy and training. Founded 2012.

Creative Scotland

Waverley Gate, 2–4 Waterloo Place, Edinburgh EH1 3EG
email enquiries@creativescotland.com
website www.creativescotland.com/funding
Facebook www.facebook.com/CreativeScotland
Instagram @creativescots

The public body that supports the arts, screen and creative industries across all parts of Scotland on behalf of everyone who lives, works or visits there. Through distributing funding from the Scottish Government and the National Lottery, Creative Scotland enables people to experience the arts and bring creative ideas to life. Supports writers and publishers based in Scotland through a range of funds and initiatives.

Design. Publishing. Inclusivity.

email contact@dpi.org.uk
website www.dpi.org.uk
X @dpi_org
Instagram @dpi_org

The mentorship scheme runs annually and offers ten applicants an opportunity to develop skills to pursue a career in book design. No prior education or experience is required; existing designers are eligible to apply. Each successful applicant is matched with a mentor for a period of six months. Applicants must be from a group that is under-represented in publishing. Founded 2022.

Discoveries

email discoveriesprize@curtisbrown.co.uk
website www.womensprize.com/discoveries

Run in partnership with Audible and Curtis Brown, the programme offers practical tools and encouragement to aspiring female novelists of all backgrounds.

Invites entries from writers who identify as women, are unpublished and unagented, and reside in the UK or Ireland; entrants should submit the opening of a novel (up to 10,000 words) in any adult fiction genre. 1st prize: £5,000, a bespoke creative writing course, a personalised mentoring package and an offer of literary agent representation.

A toolkit of resources is available online, including writing tips and insights into the agenting and publishing process, and advice from Women's Prize judges and winners. Founded 2020.

Emerging Writers Programme

tel 020-7766 4765
email emergingwriters@londonlibrary.co.uk
website www.londonlibrary.co.uk/about-us/ll-emerging-writers

Open to all writers above the age of 16, the programme offers writers, in all genres, one year's free membership to The London Library, writing development masterclasses and peer support. The programme runs from July to June each year and sessions take place in the evening. The Emerging Writers Programme Access Bursary assists writers who require financial assistance to take part in the scheme. The Virago Participation Bursary is awarded to Black women and Black non-binary writers to assist with any financial issues that might prevent them from accessing the full programme. Applicants should be working on a project that is intended for publication and must submit a personal statement and a sample of their writing. Founded 2019.

Escalator New Writing Fellowships for Emerging Writers

National Centre for Writing, Dragon Hall, 115–123 King Street, Norwich NR1 1QE
email info@nationalcentreforwriting.org.uk
website https://nationalcentreforwriting.org.uk/escalator
Facebook www.facebook.com/NationalCentreforWriting
X @WritersCentre
Bluesky @writerscentre.bsky.social
Instagram @writerscentre

A scheme for unpublished fiction writers based in the East of England who do not yet have an agent, in particular those who identify as LGBTQ+ or whose ethnicity is under-represented in publishing. Successful participants receive eight months of mentoring, which includes feedback, discussion and goal-setting; networking with fellow participants; an opportunity to showcase work to agents, publishers and other industry professionals; subsidised places on workshops, courses and masterclasses; and resources to help promote their writing in the future. Founded 2004.

Genesis Emerging Writers Programme

email emergingwriters@jewishliteraryfoundation.co.uk
website https://jewishliteraryfoundation.co.uk/genesis-emerging-writers-programme/applying-to-the-programme
Facebook www.facebook.com/jewishbookweek
X @jewishbookweek

Provides ten writers in the early stages of their careers with mentoring, peer support, access to seminars and workshops, and a bursary to allow them to focus on their writing. Applicants should have no more than three years publishing experience and must have a pre-existing project that they are working on and intend to publish. Entry deadline: May. Founded 2001.

GLL Literary Foundation Author Placements

Greenwich Leisure Limited, Middlegate House, The Royal Arsenal, London SE18 6SX
tel 0330 123 1500
email library.foundation@gll.org
website www.better.org.uk/library/gll-literary-foundation
Facebook www.facebook.com/GLLLiteraryFoundation
Instagram @gll_literaryfoundation
Ceo Peter Bundey, *Head of Libraries* Rebecca Gediking, *Children's Librarian* Jenny Hawke, *Patron* Joseph Coelho

The GLL Literary Foundation offers children's authors placements to improve their promotional skills and ability to deliver events, recognising the importance of these skills to an author's career. Authors must write for children in any of the following genres: picture books, early readers, chapter books, YA, poetry, non-fiction, novels, graphic and verse novels; must reside in an area where Greenwich Leisure Limited (GLL) manage public libraries (see website for a list); and must have published between one and three books in the previous five years. The one-year in-person placements include bursaries, access to business courses, opportunities to attend networking events with publishers and authors, and support and training to deliver literary events. Authors must be nominated by their publishing house;

self-published authors are not eligible. Applications open in November and close in January; successful recipients are announced in February. Founded 2024.

The Greene Door Project

T18 West Wing, Somerset House, Strand, London WC2R 1LA
website https://greeneheaton.co.uk/the-greene-door
X @greeneandheaton

Run by Greene & Heaton Literary Agency. Offers online MSS feedback sessions to writers who are under-represented in publishing; especially seeks own-voice authors. Open to writers of all genres of fiction, non-fiction and YA. Applicants should submit a cover letter, a synopsis of their work and no more than the first 5,000 words of a novel. Founded 2018.

The Eric Gregory Awards

The Society of Authors, 24 Bedford Row, London WC1R 4EH
tel 020-3380 2230
email prizes@societyofauthors.org
website https://societyofauthors.org/prizes/the-soa-awards/eric-gregory-awards
Facebook www.facebook.com/TheSocietyofAuthors
X @Soc_of_Authors
Instagram @thesocietyofauthors
Grants & Prizes Manager Aine Pullan, *Grants & Prizes Design Manager* Natalie Thorpe, *Head of Fundraising, Grants & Prizes* Robyn Law

Recognises a collection of poetry by authors under 30 years. Founded by the late Dr Eric Gregory, it encourages young poets to devote more time to writing. Candidates must be a British National or resident in Great Britain, Northern Ireland or the Commonwealth for three years prior to the date of submission; candidates must be under the age of 30 on 31 March in the year of the award (i.e. the year following submission). The work submitted may be a published or unpublished volume of poetry, drama-poems or *belles lettres*; and no more than 30 poems should be submitted.

Hawthornden Fellowships

Hawthornden Literary Retreat, Hawthornden Castle, Lasswade, Midlothian EH18 1EG
email grants@hawthornden.org
website www.hawthorndenliteraryretreat.org

Applications are invited from novelists, poets, playwrights, biographers, essayists and other creative writers who require time and space to work on current projects. The Fellowships provide four-week residencies in Hawthornden Castle, Scotland, Casa Ecco, Italy and Ditmas Park, Brooklyn, USA. Application forms are available from January for Fellowships awarded in the following year.

Francis Head Bequest

Grants Department, Society of Authors, 24 Bedford Row, London WC1R 4EH
tel 020-3880 2230
email grants@societyofauthors.org
website https://societyofauthors.org/grants/grants-writers-in-need/
Facebook www.facebook.com/TheSocietyofAuthors
X @Soc_of_Authors
Instagram @thesocietyofauthors
Grants & Prizes Manager Aine Pullan, *Grants & Prizes Design Manager* Natalie Thorpe, *Head of Fundraising, Grants & Prizes* Robyn Law

Provides grants to published British authors over the age of 35 who need financial help during a period of illness, disablement or temporary financial crisis.

Ignite Fellowship

Scottish Book Trust, Sandeman House, Trunk's Close, 55 High Street, Edinburgh EH1 1SR
tel 0131 524 0160
email applications@scottishbooktrust.com
website www.scottishbooktrust.com/writing-and-authors/ignite-fellowship
Facebook www.facebook.com/scottishbktrust/
X @scottishbktrust
Instagram @scottishbooktrust

Supports established writers who are embarking on or working through a significant project. Writers can apply whether the project is in the early stages or already a work-in-progress. There are three awards available. In partnership with the Gaelic Books council one of the awards is given to a writer working in Gaelic; writers working in Scots are also encouraged. All fellows receive support tailored to their project, including £5,000 to allow them to focus on their work; press and PR training; personal development opportunities; and a week-long writing retreat.

The P.D. James Memorial Fund

Society of Authors, 24 Bedford Row, London WC1R 4EH
tel 020-3380 2230
email grants@societyofauthors.org
website https://societyofauthors.org/grants/p-d-james-memorial-fund
Facebook www.facebook.com/TheSocietyofAuthors
X @Soc_of_Authors
Instagram @thesocietyofauthors
Grants & Prizes Manager Aine Pullan, *Grants & Prizes Design Manager* Natalie Thorpe, *Head of Fundraising, Grants & Prizes* Robyn Law

Offers regular payments to a small number of Society of Authors members who find themselves in financial hardship. To be eligible, applicants must have been a SoA member for at least ten years (this does not have to be continuous). Awards are given by committee to long-term members who are either over the age of 60 or who are completely incapacitated for work. The fund currently distributes £2,200 per annum to each recipient.

Megaphone Writer Development Scheme

email megaphone.write@gmail.com
website https://megaphonewrite.com
X @MegaphoneWrite

An Arts Council England funded project that offers a year of one-to-one mentoring and masterclasses for writers of colour based in England who are writing a novel for children or teenagers. Bursaries are available for writers who cannot afford the fees.

David Miller Internship Programme

email admin@deborahrogersfoundation.org
website www.deborahrogersfoundation.org
X @DRFWritersAward
Instagram @deborah_rogers_org/
Administrator Alison Menzies

Set up in memory of David Miller, a literary agent, who died in 2016. In partnership with Creative Access, the Deborah Rogers Foundation offers six-week paid internships in rights and agenting to candidates from backgrounds that are under-represented in the publishing industry. Applications are accepted in April and May, interviews take place in June, and internships run from September to October. Companies who have previously provided placements as part of the programme include Aitken Alexander Associates, David Higham Associates, ILA, Penguin Random House, Faber, Profile Books, PEW Literary, Greyhound Literary and Eccles Fisher Associates.

New Writers Collective

117 Farringdon Road, London EC1R 3BX
email tvfoundation@thetvfestival.com
website www.thetvfestival.com/tv-foundation/new-talent/
Instagram @thetvfoundation

Administered by the TV foundation, ten aspiring television writers take part in a programme of opportunities and support. Entrants must not be represented by an agent, must not have any paid TV writing experience or credits, and must be usually resident in the UK. Entrants should submit 20 pages of a completed script alongside a 100-word biography, a logline for the script and a one-page summary of the idea. Co-written entries are accepted. Winning writers receive access to the Edinburgh TV Festival, screenwriting events and scripted executives at All3Media. Entry deadline: January. Entry fee: £24. Founded 2020.

Prototype Development Programme

71 Oriel Road, London E9 5SG
email admin@prototypepublishing.co.uk
website https://prototypepublishing.co.uk/category/opportunities/
Facebook www.facebook.com/prototypepubs
X @prototypepubs
Instagram @prototypepubs

Offers career support and development opportunities to eight emerging writers and artists whose work sits between traditional publishing categories and conventional literary forms. The six-month programme includes group workshops, feedback sessions, and a series of seminars led by writers, publishers, editors and literary agents. All sessions are remote to make them as accessible as possible. Entrants should submit a summary of their experience, a statement explaining why they are interested in the programme and a 20-page sample of work (poetry, fiction, non-fiction or visual). Founded 2024.

The Peggy Ramsay Foundation

7 Savoy Court, London WC2R 0EX
email prf@harbottle.com
website www.peggyramsayfoundation.org

Grants are made to writers of stage plays in accordance with the criteria on the Foundation's website. Awards are made at intervals during each year. A total of approx. £200,000 is expended annually. Founded 1992.

The Royal Literary Fund

3 Johnson's Court, Fleet Street, London EC4A 3EA
tel 020-7353 7150
email help@rlf.org.uk
website www.rlf.org.uk
Facebook www.facebook.com/royalliteraryfund
X @royallitfund
Instagram @royalliteraryfund

A UK charity that supports writers in financial need. Annually delivers over £5 million in grants, education and outreach programmes. Offers a range of grants to professional writers needing short- to long-term financial support who are in debt, facing reduced income or unable to write due to a change in circumstances, sickness, disability or age. RLF Education creates earning opportunities for over 650 professional writers who work as RLF Fellows at over 90 institutions across the UK. Writers continue their work through local reading groups, expressive writing sessions and helping to develop writing skills in workplaces. Founded 1790.

RSL Giles St Aubyn Awards for Non-Fiction

Royal Society of Literature, Somerset House, Strand, London WC2R 1LA
tel 020-7845 4679
email info@rsliterature.org
website www.rsliterature.org/rsl-giles-st-aubyn-awards-for-non-fiction

Awards offering financial assistance to authors engaged in writing their first major commissioned work of non-fiction. Entrants must be permanently resident in the UK or the RoI. There are three awards valued at £10,000, £5,000 and £2,500. Founded 2017.

RSL Literature Matters Awards

Royal Society of Literature, Somerset House, London WC2R 1LA
tel 020-7845 4679
email info@rsliterature.org
website https://rsliterature.org/award/rsl-literature-matters-awards/
Facebook www.facebook.com/RoyalSocietyLiterature
X @RSLiterature
Instagram @royalsocietyofliterature

Annual project awards that recognise and enable literary excellence and innovation. Priority is given to proposals that will help connect with audiences or topics outside the usual reach of literature, and/or help generate public discussion about why literature matters. Applicants must be permanently resident in the UK. The total value of the available awards is £20,000, awarded across a number of projects.

Tees Valley Artists of the Year

tel (01325) 792600
email creativeplace@teesvalley-ca.gov.uk
website https://teesvalley-ca.gov.uk/business/tees-valley-artists-of-the-year-2025/

Highlights and supports local talent by providing a package of support to five artists. The programme gives each artist £28,000 (intended to serve as a year's wage to allow the artists to focus on their projects), a professional development budget to improve their skills and practice, industry mentoring and career support. Applicants can work in any discipline, including visual arts, performance, digital media and writing. Entry deadline: February. Founded 2024.

TLC ACE Free Reads Scheme

East Side, Platform 1, King's Cross Station, London N1C 4AX
tel 020-3751 0757 (ext. 800)
email info@literaryconsultancy.co.uk
website www.literaryconsultancy.co.uk/editorial/ace-free-reads-scheme
Director Aki Schilz

TLC receives funding from Arts Council England to enable the provision of bursaried MSS assessments for writers from low-income households. The scheme is known as the Free Reads Scheme and offers access to TLC's core services to writers who might not be able to afford them. Free Reads are selected by a range of literature development bodies from across the UK. For detailed submission guidelines and eligibility information, see the website.
Founded 2001.

The Travelling Scholarships

The Society of Authors, 24 Bedford Row, London WC1R 4EH
tel 020-3880 2230
email prizes@societyofauthors.org
website https://societyofauthors.org/prizes/the-soa-awards/travelling-scholarships
Facebook www.facebook.com/TheSocietyofAuthors
X @Soc_of_Authors
Instagram @thesocietyofauthors
Grants & Prizes Manager Aine Pullan, *Grants & Prizes Design Manager* Natalie Thorpe, *Head of Fundraising, Grants & Prizes* Robyn Law

Established by an anonymous benefactor to enable British creative writers to keep in touch with their colleagues abroad. Scholarships are nominated by assessors; applications are not accepted.
Founded 1944.

Wellcome Collection Non-Fiction Awards

email bobby@spreadtheword.org.uk
website www.spreadtheword.org.uk/projects/wellcome-collection-non-fiction-awards/
Bluesky @spread-the-word.bsky.social
Instagram @spreadthewordwriters
Threads @spreadthewordwriters

A writer development programme for under-represented non-fiction writers that offers them opportunities to turn their ideas into full-length book proposals. Applicants should be writing on the subjects of health and being human, should be unagented and should not previously have published a work of non-fiction. Under-represented writers includes writers who are disabled, neurodivergent, D/deaf or of the Global Majority. As part of the programme winners will receive a £2,000 bursary, mentoring, masterclasses, feedback group sessions and a meeting with an agent. Entry deadline: November. Founded 2022.

Windham-Campbell Prizes

Beinecke Rare Book & Manuscript Library, 121 Wall Street, New Haven, CT 06510-1242, USA
website https://windhamcampbell.org
Facebook www.facebook.com/WindhamCampbellPrizes
X @WindhamCampbell
Instagram @windhamcampbell

Administered by the University of Yale, each year eight writers are awarded $175,000 each to support their writing. Writers are recognised for their merit or potential and can come from anywhere in the world. Founded 2013.

David T.K. Wong Fellowship

School of Literature, Drama and Creative Writing, University of East Anglia, Norwich NR4 7TJ
email davidtkwongfellowship@uea.ac.uk

website www.uea.ac.uk/about/school-of-literature-drama-and-creative-writing/creative-writing/writing-fellowship/david-tk-wong-fellowship

An annual award of £26,000 to enable a fiction writer who wants to write in English about East and Southeast Asia to spend a year in the UK, at the University of East Anglia. The Fellowship is named after its sponsor David T.K. Wong, a retired Hong Kong businessman, who has also been a teacher, journalist and senior civil servant, and is a writer of short stories. Entrants should submit an unpublished piece of prose of no more than 2,500 words. The 2024/25 Fellow is Doua Thao. Entry deadline: February. Entry fee: £10.

WriteNow Programme

One Embassy Gardens, 8 Viaduct Gardens, London SW11 7BW
email writenow@penguinrandomhouse.co.uk
website www.penguin.co.uk/company/creative-responsibility/writenow/whats-on-offer.html
Facebook www.facebook.com/PenguinRandomHouse
X @PenguinUKBooks

A writer development programme that nurtures and publishes new, unpublished writers from under-represented communities. Each year the genre of writing that entrants must submit changes; previous genres have included romance, crime, thrillers, sci-fi, fantasy and horror. Writing for middle-grade, young adult and adult readers is accepted. All applicants should submit 1,000 words from a book they are working on and shortlisted writers will be required to submit a further 40,000 words. Shortlisted applicants receive feedback from an editor. Successful applicants receive one year of mentoring with a Penguin editor to develop their writing and career, as well as drop-in sessions with partner organisations.

Writers & Artists: Accessible to All

Bloomsbury Publishing, 50 Bedford Square, London WC1B 3DP
tel 020-7631 5985
email AccessWA@bloomsbury.com
website www.writersandartists.co.uk/accessible-to-all

Financial assistance to a combined value of £4,000 has been made available to help ensure that everything W&A offers – events, writing courses and editing services – is accessible to all. See the website for more details and eligibility.

Festivals and conferences for writers, artists and readers

There are hundreds of arts festivals in the UK each year. We list a selection of literature, writing, and general arts festivals that include literary events. Some of these festivals celebrate a specific genre or type of writing, whilst others feature a variety of different authors and events. See festival websites for dates and full programmes of events.

AIM Literary Festival

tel (01494) 265002
email events@authorinme.com
website https://aimliteraryfestival.com
Facebook www.facebook.com/authorinmepublishing
X @AuthorInMeUK
Instagram @authorinme_publishing
Takes place October

Developed by Author In Me Publishing. A week-long celebration of the power of storytelling and cultural diversity to connect and inspire. Brings together readers, authors and publishers for a range of events including panel discussions, workshops and book launches. Founded 2019.

The Aldeburgh Literary Festival

Aldeburgh Book Shop, 42 High Street, Aldeburgh IP15 5AB
tel (01728) 452389
email johnandmary@aldeburghbookshop.co.uk
website www.aldeburghbookshop.co.uk/aldelitfest
Takes place March

Organised by John and Mary James of The Aldeburgh Bookshop, the festival aims to unite the local with the global. Tickets can be obtained by returning a physical booking form to the bookshop either in person or by mail. Founded 2002.

Aldeburgh Poetry Festival

email poetryalde@gmail.com
website www.poetryinaldeburgh.org
Facebook www.facebook.com/AldeburghPoetry
X @PoetryAldeburgh
Instagram @poetryinaldeburgh
Takes place November

Annual festival of contemporary poetry based in East Anglia. In-person events take place over one weekend; online and other live events take place throughout the year. Founded 1989.

Alton Arts Festival

email info@altonartsfestival.com
website www.altonartsfestival.com
Facebook www.facebook.com/people/Alton-Arts-Festival/61550842865597
Instagram @altonartsfestival
Chair Annie Lancaster
Takes place 3–12 July 2026

A not-for-profit festival featuring a programme of literary, music, theatre and visual arts events. Run entirely by volunteers for the benefit of the local community. Founded 2024.

Appledore Book Festival

18 Windmill Lane, Northam, Bideford, Devon EX39 1BZ
email director@appledorebookfestival.co.uk
website www.appledorebookfestival.co.uk
Facebook www.facebook.com/appledorebookfestival
X @AppledoreBkFest
Instagram @appledorebookfestival
Festival Director Jane Beaton
Takes place 12–21 September 2025

Founded by children's author Nick Arnold, this annual festival aims to entertain, inform and inspire a love of reading and creative writing with events on a diverse range of subjects. Features fiction and non-fiction authors for both adults and children. An extensive programme of events in schools follows the main festival. Founded 2006.

Aspects Irish Literature Festival

City Hall, The Castle, Bangor BT20 4BT
website www.aspectsfestival.com
Facebook www.facebook.com/CultureArdsandNorthDown
X @aspectsfestival
Instagram @cultureardsandnorthdown
Takes place September–October

An annual celebration of contemporary Irish writing, based in Bangor, featuring novelists, poets and playwrights. Includes readings, children's events and exhibitions.

Barnsley Book Festival

Barnsley Libraries, The Glassworks, Barnsley S70 1GW
tel (01226) 770770
email barnsleylibraryenquiries@barnsley.gov.uk
website https://visitbarnsley.co.uk/barnsleybookfestival
Facebook www.facebook.com/barnsleylibraries
X @BarnsleyLibs

Instagram @barnsleylibs
Takes place February

Featuring a diverse line-up of authors, poets, artists and performers, events include book launches, performances, workshops and talks for all ages. Founded 2024.

The Bath Festival

tel (01225) 463362
email info@bathfestivals.org.uk
website https://bathfestivals.org.uk/the-bath-festival
Facebook www.facebook.com/thebathfestival
X @TheBathFestival
Instagram @thebathfestival
Takes place May

An annual festival with leading guest writers. Includes readings, debates, discussions, workshops and events. Runs a year-round programme of outreach events to inspire and engage local communities.

Bay Tales Live

website https://baytales.com
Facebook www.facebook.com/BayTales
X @bay_tales
Bluesky @baytales.bsky.social
Instagram @bay_tales
Threads @bay_tales
Takes place February/March

A crime fiction festival based in the north east of England. The Festival takes place at the Whitley Bay Playhouse and includes panel discussions, interviews and signings and an onsite bookshop. Has received support from publishers including Pan Macmillan and Orion. Previous speakers include patron Ann Cleeves, Vaseem Khan, Val McDermid, Ruth Ware and Nicci French. Founded 2020.

Birmingham Literature Festival

Studio 130, Zellig, Gibb Street, Birmingham B9 4AT
tel 0121 246 2770
email programming@writingwestmidlands.org
website www.birminghamliteraturefestival.org
Facebook www.facebook.com/BhamLitFest
X @BhamLitFest
Instagram @bhamlitfest
Programmes Director Shantel Edwards
Takes place October

A project of Writing West Midlands. Showcases the very best writers, speakers, thinkers, activists and artists from the UK and across the world.

Black British Book Festival

Moseley Exchange, 149–153 Alcester Road, Birmingham B13 8JP
email info@blackbritishbookfestival.com
website https://blackbritishbookfestival.com
X @BBBookFestival
Instagram @bbbookfestival
Founder & Ceo Selina Brown
Takes place October

Europe's largest Black Literature Festival, dedicated to highlighting Black writers across genres and career levels, improving the accessibility of the publishing process for Black writers and generating valuable opportunities for them. Also promotes literacy, nurturing a passion for reading in both children and adults through year-round projects within local communities and national campaigns and collaborations. Founded 2021.

Bloody Scotland Festival

Caledonia Exchange, 19A Canning Street, Edinburgh EH3 8HE
email info@bloodyscotland.com
website www.bloodyscotland.com
Facebook www.facebook.com/bloodyscotland
X @BloodyScotland
Instagram @bloodyscotland
Takes place 12–14 September 2025

Based in Stirling, this international crime writing festival has brought hundreds of crime writers, both new and established, to the stage. Events cover a range of criminal subjects including fictional forensics, psychological thrillers, tartan noir, cosy crime and many more; 'Pitch Perfect' is an opportunity for eight aspiring authors to pitch their novel in front of literary agents and industry professionals and receive constructive feedback; the 'Crime in the Spotlight' programme invites new authors to read an excerpt of their work before main events. Has an international focus; crime writing talent from outside of Scotland is always welcome. Founded 2012.

Borders Book Festival

Harmony House, St Mary's Road, Melrose TD6 9LJ
email info@bordersbookfestival.org
website www.bordersbookfestival.org
Facebook www.facebook.com/bordersbookfestival
X @BordersBookFest
Instagram @bordersbookfest
Takes place June

An annual festival with a programme of events featuring high-profile and bestselling writers, including a Family Festival programme. The winner of the Walter Scott Prize for Historical Fiction is announced during the festival. Founded 2004.

Borris House Festival of Writing and Ideas

email info@festivalofwritingandideas.com
website https://festivalofwritingandideas.com
Facebook www.facebook.com/writingandideas
X @Writingandideas
Instagram @writingandideas
Takes place June

Brings together speakers, including international novelists, poets, musicians, academics and journalists, for a weekend of stimulating conversation. Events are spread across the grounds of Borris House. Founded 2011.

Boswell Book Festival

website www.boswellbookfestival.co.uk
Facebook www.facebook.com/boswellbookfestival
X @bozzyfest
Instagram @boswellbookfest
Takes place May

The world's only festival of biography and memoir, named after Ayrshire biographer James Boswell. Programmed around stories taken from the inspirational lives of people past and present, shared through writing, drama, art and music. Features discussions with authors and personalities and writing workshops. Previous attendees include Judi Dench, Maggie O'Farrell, James Naughtie and Andrew O'Hagan.

Bournemouth Writing Festival

6 Wilfred Road, Bournemouth BH5 1NB
email info@bournemouthwritingfestival.co.uk
website www.bournemouthwritingfestival.co.uk
Facebook www.facebook.com/BournemouthWritingFestival
Instagram @bournemouthwritingfestival
Festival Director Dominic Wong
Takes place April

A variety of self-published, published and writing professionals impart their knowledge and advice to writers of all ages, backgrounds, abilities and genres, regardless of where they are on their writing journey. Free and ticketed events include workshops, talks, walks, writing competitions and networking opportunities. Founded 2023.

Bradford Literature Festival

Horton Building, University of Bradford, Richmond Road, Bradford BD7 1DP
tel (01274) 044140
email info@bradfordlitfest.co.uk
website www.bradfordlitfest.co.uk
Facebook www.facebook.com/bradfordlitfest
X @BradfordLitFest
Instagram @bradfordlitfest
Ceo & Artistic Director Syima Aslam
Takes place June–July

An annual arts event, and year-round cultural outreach programme, that hosts a diverse range of authors, poets, speakers, musicians and artists from Bradford, the UK and around the world. Taking place over ten days, the programme includes over 400 events with a mix of topic-led events, author talks, poetry line-ups, live music, film, theatre and more. Operates an extensive ethical ticketing policy, offering free or discounted tickets to those who might otherwise be unable to attend the festival. Founded 2014.

Bread and Roses

c/o Five Leaves Bookshop, 14A Long Row, Nottingham NG1 2DH
email bookshop@fiveleaves.co.uk
website www.fiveleavesbookshop.co.uk

An annual weekend of radical politics, music and literature held at various venues in Nottingham. The only book festival supported by trade unions.

Brighton Festival

Church Street, Brighton BN1 1UE
tel (01273) 709709
email info@brightonfestival.org
website www.brightonfestival.org
Facebook www.facebook.com/brightonfestival
X @brightfest
Takes place May

An annual arts festival with an extensive national and international programme featuring theatre, dance, classical and contemporary music, books, outdoor and family events. Founded 1967.

Budleigh Salterton Literary Festival

10 Fairfield Close, Exmouth EX8 2BN
tel (01395) 262635
email festival@budlitfest.org.uk
website https://budlitfest.org.uk
Facebook www.facebook.com/BudleighSaltertonLiteraryFestival
Instagram @budlitfest
Chair Sue Briggs
Takes place 17–21 September 2025

Held beside the sea on the Jurassic Coast, the festival features leading writers and celebrities, events for families and workshops for writers. Includes an outreach programme in schools. Founded 2009.

Buxton International Festival

3 The Square, Buxton, Derbyshire SK17 6AZ
tel (01298) 70395
website https://buxtonfestival.co.uk
Facebook www.facebook.com/buxtonfestival
X @BuxtonFestival
Instagram @buxtonfestival
Takes place July

A celebration of opera, music and literature. Features distinguished authors mainly, but not exclusively, in the spheres of history, biography, music and politics. Founded 1979.

Cambridge Literary Festival

Unit 7, Hope Street Yard, Hope Street, Cambridge CB1 3NA
tel (01223) 515335
email hello@cambridgeliteraryfestival.com
website https://cambridgeliteraryfestival.com
Facebook www.facebook.com/CamLitFest
X @camlitfest
Takes place April and November

Brings together an eclectic mix of writers, thinkers and speakers, covering poetry, politics, fiction, finance, history, hip-hop, comedy and current affairs. Founded 2003.

Canterbury Festival

Festival House, 8 Orange Street, Canterbury, Kent CT1 2JA
tel (01227) 452853
email info@canterburyfestival.co.uk
website https://canterburyfestival.co.uk
Takes place 17 October–1 November 2025, 16–30 October 2026

Showcases the best in performing arts, including classical and contemporary music, theatre, circus, comedy, talks and family events. Also runs year-round public engagement projects to inspire creativity in people of all ages.

Capital Crime Festival

Leonardo Royal Hotel (St Paul's), 10 Godliman Street, London EC4V 5AJ
email info@capitalcrime.org
website www.capitalcrime.org
Facebook www.facebook.com/CapitalCrimeLondon
X @CapitalCrime1
Instagram @capitalcrime1
Takes place Summer

One of the largest celebrations of crime and thriller fiction featuring leading crime and thriller creatives. Welcomes international authors and filmmakers to London and brings the best of everything crime and thriller-related to fans through entertaining and thought-provoking events. Founded 2019.

Charleston Festival

Charleston, Firle, Lewes, East Sussex BN8 6LL
tel (01323) 811626
email events@charleston.org.uk
website www.charleston.org.uk/festival
Facebook www.facebook.com/CharlestonTrust
Instagram @charlestontrust
Takes place May

Charleston, the modernist home and studio of painters Vanessa Bell and Duncan Grant, hosts an annual literary festival that attracts artists, writers, performers and changemakers, and celebrates the best in art, literature, ideas and politics.

Chiswick Book Festival

email admin@chiswickbookfestival.net
website www.chiswickbookfestival.net
Facebook www.facebook.com/chiswickbookfestival
X @W4BookFest
Instagram @chiswickbookfest
Takes place 10–15 September 2025

Brings writers and readers together to support reading-related charities. Since its inception it has raised over £140,000. Hosts a range of literary events, covering history, poetry, biography, fiction, thrillers, gardening, food, wine, politics, creative writing and self-help. Children's book events are also central to the festival, encouraging a love of both reading and writing. Founded 2009.

Cliveden Literary Festival

tel 020-3488 3401
email info@clivedenliteraryfestival.org
website www.clivedenliteraryfestival.org
Facebook www.facebook.com/clivedenlitfest
X @clivedenlitfest
Instagram @clivedenlitfest
Takes place September

Set in Cliveden. Since 1666 its literary salon has helped inspire writers such as Alexander Pope, George Bernard Shaw, Jonathan Swift, Alfred Lord Tennyson and Sir Winston Churchill. The programme of events, including talks and panel discussions, is announced each summer. Founded 2017.

The Coast Is Queer

website https://coastisqueer.com
Facebook www.facebook.com/CoastIsQueerFest
Instagram @coastisqueerfest
Takes place October

Brings together authors and poets, performers, scriptwriters, activists and audiences to celebrate queer writing, lives and communities. Events include writing workshops publishing advice, panel discussions, book launches and performances.

Cork International Short Story Festival and Poetry Festival

Frank O'Connor House, 84 Douglas Street, Cork T12 X70A, Republic of Ireland
tel +353 (0)21 432 2396
email info@munsterlit.ie
website www.munsterlit.ie, www.corkpoetryfest.net, www.corkshortstory.net
X @MunLitCentre
Takes place May (Poetry Festival), October (Short Story Festival)

Run by the Munster Literature Centre, these festivals include readings, workshops, seminars and public interviews involving some of the world's best writers and poets. Founded 2000.

Creative Folkestone Book Festival

Quarterhouse, Mill Bay, Folkestone, Kent CT20 1BN
tel (01303) 760740
email info@creativefolkestone.org.uk
website www.creativefolkestone.org.uk/folkestone-book-festival
Facebook www.facebook.com/FolkestoneBookFestival
Instagram @fstonebookfest
Takes place 13–23 November 2025

Invites writers and authors to take part in talks and debates on a unique range of topics. Founded 2002.

Cuckfield Book Festival

email info@cuckfieldbookfest.co.uk
website https://cuckfieldbookfest.co.uk
Facebook www.facebook.com/cuckfieldbookfest
X @CuckfieldBF
Instagram @cuckfieldbookfest
Takes place 3–5 October 2025

Includes talks and workshops featuring authors from a wide range of genres across fiction, non-fiction and poetry. Also runs a programme of events for young people. Founded 2016.

Cúirt International Festival of Literature

Galway Arts Centre, 47 Dominick Street, Galway H91 X0AP, Republic of Ireland
email info@cuirt.ie
website www.cuirt.ie
Facebook www.facebook.com/CuirtFestival
X @CuirtFestival
Instagram @cuirtfestival
Takes place April

Through a festival every April and a year-round programme of engagement, Cúirt brings readers and writers together to tell stories, share new perspectives, and celebrate writing, books and reading in all forms. Provides a platform for new writers and development opportunities. Founded 1985.

Curious Minds

4 Chapel Row, Bath BA1 3DR
email bathartscollective@gmail.com
website www.batharts.co.uk/curious-minds
Facebook www.facebook.com/bathartscollective
Instagram @curiousmindsfest
Takes place March

A diverse arts festival featuring book talks and writing workshops, alongside live performances, film screenings and walking tours around the city of Bath. Features local, emerging and established names with events designed to entertain, challenge and inspire. Founded 2024.

CYMERA

email programme@cymerafestival.co.uk
website www.cymerafestival.co.uk
Facebook www.facebook.com/cymerafest
X @CymeraF
Instagram @cymerafestival
Takes place June

Scotland's festival of sci-fi, fantasy and horror writing, provides a blend of in-person and online events, featuring writer panels, workshops, quizzes and games. Also runs a year-round programme of events. The Brave New Words scheme offers a platform for emerging and newly published writers to read their work in front of an audience, just before some of the main events. A limited number of tickets are available for those who are on low income or unemployed.

The Daunt Books Festival

83–84 Marylebone High Street, London W1U 4QW
tel 020-7224 2295
email enquiries@dauntbooks.co.uk
website https://dauntbooks.co.uk/festival
Takes place Spring

This annual celebration of literature proves that a bookshop is not just a place to buy books but a space to bring readers together, to foster a literary community and to have a great deal of fun in the process.

Deptford Literature Festival

email festival@spreadtheword.org.uk
website https://deptfordlitfest.com
Producer Tom MacAndrew
Takes place March

Celebrates the diversity and creativity of Deptford and Lewisham through words, stories and performance. Features writers, artists and arts organisations based in the area, and hosts creative writing workshops and a programme of events for children and families. Events are free to attend.

Derby Book Festival

13 Lavender Row, Darley Abbey, Derby DE22 1DF
website www.derbybookfestival.co.uk
Facebook www.facebook.com/DerbyBookFestival
X @DerbyBookFest
Instagram @derby_book_festival
Takes place May/June

Celebrates the joy of books and reading for all ages and interests, with a programme featuring writers, poets, historians, politicians, illustrators, storytellers and musicians. Each year the festival welcomes internationally celebrated bestselling authors as well as a broad range of local writing talent. In addition, runs a small Autumn festival and a year-round community and schools programme. Founded 2015.

DESIBlitz

Spaces Crossway, 156 Great Oxford Charles St, Queensway, Birmingham B3 3HN
tel 0121 285 5288
email arts@desiblitz.com
website www.desiblitz.com/literaturefestival/
Facebook www.facebook.com/desiblitz
X @desiblitz
Instagram @desiblitz
Managing Director Indi Deol
Takes place October

Dedicated to celebrating British South Asian writing and storytelling, supporting, inspiring and amplifying diverse voices, and providing a platform for emerging and established authors to connect with readers and the wider literary community. Features a programme of book launches, panel discussions, author interviews, creative writing and publishing workshops, and live performances. Also provides opportunities for unpublished writers to share their work, engage with publishers and gain valuable insights from experienced authors. 90% of events are free to attend, making literature available to all.

Dublin Book Festival

email info@dublinbookfestival.com
website www.dublinbookfestival.com
Facebook www.facebook.com/DublinBookFestival
X @DublinBookFest
Instagram @dublinbookfest
Director Julianne Mooney, *Marketing Manager* Róisín Russel
Takes place 5–9 November 2025

Brings together the best of Irish writing and publishing, offering a chance for the voices of both established and emerging authors and poets to be heard. Events include book launches, interviews, panel discussions, workshops and a children's and schools programme. Founded 2006.

Durham Book Festival

New Writing North, 120 Squires Building, Northumbria University, Sandyford Road, Newcastle upon Tyne NE1 8ST
email office@newwritingnorth.com
website https://durhambookfestival.com
Facebook www.facebook.com/DurhamBookFestival
X @durhambookfest
Instagram @durhambookfest
Takes place October

A book festival for both readers and writers, taking place in the city of Durham. Events explore a variety of diverse topics and include author talks, writer workshops and a programme for children and families. Founded 1990.

Ealing Book Festival

email info@ealingbookfestival.com
website https://ealingbookfestival.com
X @EalingBkFest
Instagram @ealingbookfestival
Takes place April

Spotlights writers from the London borough of Ealing and beyond. Events include panel discussions, book signings and activities that aim to connect the writing community and literary scene within Ealing with readers of all ages. Founded 2024.

East Riding Festival of Words

email lama.admin@eastriding.gov.uk
website www.festivalofwords.co.uk
Facebook www.facebook.com/ERLibraries
X @ERLibraries
Takes place March

Includes authors' events, readings, panel events and workshops, as well as children's activities and performances. Also features opportunities for writers to network, learn career skills and work on their writing. Founded 2000.

Edinburgh Comic Art Fair

website https://ecaf.uk
Takes place November

ECAF is a gathering of artists, comic authors, fans and readers that expands the reach and creativity of the genre and offers unique events, from writing poetry graphic novels to illustrating folk tales to publishing zines. Comic creators take part in panels, talks, workshops and portfolio reviews.

Edinburgh International Book Festival

121 George Street, Edinburgh EH2 4YN
tel 0131 718 5666
email admin@edbookfest.co.uk
website www.edbookfest.co.uk
Facebook www.facebook.com/edbookfest/
X @edbookfest
Instagram @edbookfest
Takes place 9–24 August 2025 / 8–23 August 2026

A key event in Edinburgh's annual August festival season and one of the largest public celebrations of words and ideas in the world. Around 600 UK and international writers appear in over 500 events for adults, children and schools. Programme details available in June. Founded 1983.

Edinburgh Women's Fiction Festival

email info@edwomensficfest.co.uk
website www.edwomensficfest.co.uk
Facebook www.facebook.com/EdWomensFicFest
X @EdWomensFicFest
Instagram @edwomensficfest
Takes place 26–27 September 2025

Celebrates fiction for, by and about women and welcomes anyone who enjoys reading and writing women's fiction. Features both writing and publishing events – each year a dedicated team of publishing professionals supports the Festival.

Ennis Book Club Festival

tel +353 86 152 2169
email info@ennisbookclubfestival.com
website www.ennisbookclubfestival.com
Takes place First weekend in March

An annual literary weekend that brings together book club members, book lovers, writers and other artists. Includes lectures, readings, discussions, theatre, music and more. Founded 2007.

ESEA Literary Festival

email eseapublishingnetwork@gmail.com
X @eseapn

Instagram @eseapn
Co-founders Maria Garbutt-Lucero, Joanna Lee
Takes place July and September

Established by the East and Southeast Asian Publishing Network to celebrate writers and publishers from these backgrounds and increase the visibility of their work and their contributions to Britain's literary landscape. Also runs events throughout the year. Founded 2023.

Falmouth Book Festival

The Poly, 24 Church Street, Falmouth TR11 3EG
tel (01326) 319461
email colin@falmouthbookfestival.com
website www.falmouthbookfestival.com
Facebook www.facebook.com/FalmouthBookFestival
X @BookFalmouth
Instagram @falmouthbookfestival
Takes place 14–20 October 2025

Brings people together to engage with and share a love of literature in all its forms. Includes author talks, performances and activities for children and families. In association with Falmouth University. Founded 2021.

Fleet Street Quarter Festival of Words

Unit 411, 160 Fleet Street, London EC4A 2DQ
email info@fleetstreetquarter.co.uk
website www.fleetstreetquarter.co.uk/news/festival-of-words
X @fleetstquarter
Instagram @fleetstquarter
Takes place May

Recognises the power of words to change the world. Features authors of fiction, non-fiction and poetry, broadcasters, journalists, screenwriters and spoken word artists. Events are diverse in nature and topic and include a programme for children.
Founded 2024.

Free Books Festival

8A Greenwich Circus, Greenwich SE10 8RX
website https://freebookscampaign.co.uk/
X @bookscampaign
Founder Sofia Akel, *Head of Community* Princess Adenrele, *Head of Book Curation* Fatima Saleh
Takes place July

Established by The Free Books Campaign, the annual Festival is a celebration of diverse literature that brings together authors, readers and communities. By centring authors of colour, the Festival challenges the lack of representation in publishing and ensures that everyone sees themselves reflected in the stories they read. Events include panel discussions, author readings, workshops and interactive activities designed to ignite a passion for reading.

Granite Noir

His Majesty's Theatre, Rosemount Viaduct, Aberdeen AB25 1GL
tel (01224) 641122
website www.aberdeenperformingarts.com/granite-noir/
Facebook www.facebook.com/GraniteNoirFest
X @GraniteNoirFest
Takes place February

Inspired by the contribution that Scottish writers make to crime fiction and the city of Aberdeen, the line-up each year features authors and publishing representatives. Events include talks, workshops, walking tours and exhibitions. Some events are live-streamed online.

Guernsey Literary Festival

PO Box 174, St Peter Port, Guernsey GY1 3LG
tel 07781 136328
email poetry@guernseyliteraryfestival.com
website https://poemsonthemove.com
Facebook www.facebook.com/GuernseyLiteraryFestival
Instagram @guernseylitfest
Director Claire Allen
Takes place April/May

Attracts speakers from a wide range of disciplines, from literature to politics, history to sport, the environment to food, and biography to travel. Features workshops with visiting authors, runs writing competitions and organises an education and community programme. Founded 2014.

Guildford Book Festival

2 Hindmoor Manor, Hindhead Road, Hindhead, Surrey GU26 6AX
tel (01483) 444334
email alexandrews@guildfordbookfestival.co.uk
email volunteers@guildfordbookfestival.co.uk
website www.guildfordbookfestival.co.uk
X @gfordbookfest
Instagram @guildfordbookfestival
Director Alex Andrews, *Volunteer Co-ordinator* Jane Purnell, *Social Media Co-ordinator* Priya Attapatto
Takes place 27 September–20 October 2025

An annual festival with a diverse programme of outstanding conversation and lively debate to further an interest and love of literature. Hosts author events, workshops and a schools programme, plus selected online events. Founded 1989.

Hastings Book Festival

99 Cambridge Road, Hastings, East Sussex TN34 1EP
email info@hastingsbookfest.org
website www.hastingsbookfest.org
Facebook www.facebook.com/HastingsBookFest/
Instagram @hastingsbookfestival
Directors Helen Drake, Tola Dabiri, Julie Allen, Chris Connelly
Takes place Over two weekends in September

Annual book festival featuring author events, writing workshops, a book fair, an open mic poetry evening, competitions for short story and poetry, and writing workshops in various genres. Also includes events for children. Founded 2018.

Hay Festival

The Drill Hall, 25 Lion Street,
Hay-on-Wye HR3 5AD
tel (01497) 822620
email submissions@hayfestival.org
website www.hayfestival.com
Facebook www.facebook.com/hayfestival
X @hayfestival
Instagram @hayfestival
Takes place Late May–early June; Hay Festival Winter Weekend takes place late November

Brings together writers, comedians, musicians, filmmakers, historians, politicians, environmentalists and scientists from around the world to communicate challenging ideas. Hundreds of events take place over 11 days. Within the annual festival is a festival for families and children, HAYDAYS, which introduces young people, from toddlers to teenagers, to their favourite authors. Programme published April. Founded 1987.

Henley Literary Festival

Kings Arms Barn, Kings Road,
Henley-on-Thames RG9 2DG
tel (01491) 575948
email info@henleyliteraryfestival.co.uk
website www.henleyliteraryfestival.co.uk
Facebook www.facebook.com/HenleyLitFest
X @HenleyLitFest
Instagram @henleylitfest
Takes place 4–12 October 2025

A week of talks, panel discussions and workshops featuring well-known authors and personalities. Events for adults and children take place in venues across Henley-on-Thames and online. Also runs a festival schools programme and year-round pop-up events. Founded 2007.

Huddersfield Literature Festival

email info@huddlitfest.org.uk
website www.huddlitfest.org.uk
Festival Director Michelle Hodgson
Takes place Spring

Showcasing new, emerging and established writers and artists, the diverse programme includes in-person, online and hybrid author talks, creative workshops, multi-arts performances, innovative special projects, spoken word events and family-friendly events. Includes many free and low-cost events, and several with live subtitling.
Founded 2006.

Ilkley Literature Festival

Word Up North, 2nd Floor, Fairfax House,
38 The Grove Promenade, Ilkley LS29 9LW
tel (01943) 601210
email info@ilkleylitfest.org.uk
website www.ilkleyliteraturefestival.org.uk
Facebook www.facebook.com/ilkleylitfest
X @ilkleylitfest
Instagram @ilkleylitfest
Director Erica Morris, *Programme Manager* Becky Wholley
Takes place October

One of the UK's longest-running and widest-ranging literature festivals, delivered by arts charity Word Up North. Features author discussions, workshops, readings, literary walks and children's events. Founded 1973.

Independent Bookshop Week

6 Bell Yard, London WC2A 2JR
tel 020-7421 4656
email emma.bradshaw@booksellers.org.uk
website www.booksaremybag.com/IndependentBookshopWeek
Facebook www.facebook.com/booksaremybag
X @booksaremybag
Instagram @booksaremybag
Takes place June

An annual celebration of independent bookshops. Part of the Books Are My Bag campaign to promote high-street bookshops and shopping locally and sustainably. Founded 2006.

International Literature Festival Dublin

13 Adelaide Road, Dublin D02 P950,
Republic of Ireland
email info@ilfdublin.com
website https://ilfdublin.com
X @ILFDublin
Takes place May

ILFD takes place over ten days and features discussions, performances and cross-cultural conversations. Focuses on diverse literary themes, offers engaging events for all ages, and celebrates global voices and creative insights. Founded 1998.

Jewish Book Week

email info@jewishliteraryfoundation.co.uk
website https://jewishliteraryfoundation.co.uk/
X @jlfbookweek
Instagram @jewishliteraryfoundation, @jewishbookweek
Festival Director Claudia Rubenstein
Takes place February–March

A festival of writing, arts and culture, with sessions at King's Place, London and online. Explores Jewish themes and writers, and is open to everyone. Includes events for children and teenagers. Founded 1952.

King's Lynn Festival

3 Thoresby College, Queen Street, King's Lynn,
Norfolk PE30 1HX

tel (01553) 767557
email info@kingslynnfestival.org.uk
website www.kingslynnfestival.org.uk
Facebook www.facebook.com/kingslynnfestival
X @KLFestival
Takes place July

An annual arts festival with a music focus. Includes literature events featuring local and leading writers. Founded 1951.

King's Lynn Literature Festivals

email enquiries@lynnlitfests.com
website www.lynnlitfests.com
X @lynnlitfests
Chairman Sherie Naidoo
Takes place 26–28 September 2025

Brings together national and international writers of fiction, non-fiction and poetry for readings and discussions with an East Anglian audience.

Ledbury Poetry Festival

Ledbury Poetry House, Barrett Browning Institute, Homend, Ledbury HR8 2AA
tel (01531) 634156
email director@ledburypoetry.org.uk
website www.poetry-festival.co.uk
Facebook www.facebook.com/ledburypoetry
X @ledburypoetry
Instagram @ledburypoetry
Director Amy Howard
Takes place June–July

Features nationally and internationally renowned poets, together with a poet-in-residence programme, slams, competitions, workshops, community events and exhibitions. Also runs poetry events for children, hosts an annual Poetry Competition and works to increase the visibility of poets and critics of colour.

Leeds Lit Fest

email enquiries@leedslitfest.co.uk
website www.leedslitfest.co.uk
Facebook www.facebook.com/LeedsLitFest
X @LeedsLit
Instagram @leeds_lit_fest
Takes place June

Celebrates the literature scene in Leeds with local writers and performers showcasing their talents alongside national and international artists. Hosts a programme of author talks, workshops, panels, performances and poetry and spoken word events. Founded 2019.

Listowel Writers' Week

24 The Square, Listowel, Co. Kerry V31 RD93, Republic of Ireland
tel +353 (0)1 682 1074
email info@writersweek.ie
website https://writersweek.ie
Facebook www.facebook.com/writersweek
X @WritersWeek
Instagram @writersweek
Takes place May–June

Ireland's oldest literary festival, covering all genres of writing and supporting both established and new writers. Events include panel discussions, moderated talks, poetry readings, interviews, writing workshops and opportunities to meet authors. Founded 1970.

Litfest

The Storey, Meeting House Lane, Lancaster LA1 1TH
tel (01524) 509005
email marketing@litfest.org
website www.litfest.org
Facebook www.facebook.com/LitfestLancaster
X @Litfest
Instagram @litfestlancaster
Takes place March

Celebrates and promotes contemporary literature, illustration and ideas. Features local, national and international writers, poets and performers. Litfest is the literature development agency for Lancashire. Founded 1978.

London Literature Festival

email literatureandspokenword@southbankcentre.co.uk
website www.southbankcentre.co.uk/whats-on/festivals-series/london-literature-festival
Facebook www.facebook.com/southbankcentre
X @southbankcentre
Takes place 21 October–2 November 2025

Combines year-round literature events with an engaging festival programme, encompassing free public programming, thematically focused talks and debates, newly commissioned performances and a family offer to coincide with the half-term school holiday. Founded 1967.

London Screenwriters' Festival

email info@londonswf.com
website https://londonscreenwritersfestival.com/
X @londonswf
Instagram @londonswf
Takes place April

A gathering of filmmakers, producers, practitioners, actors and executives. A programme of structured seminars, lessons, workshops, and networking opportunities allow attendees to develop their understanding of the practice and business of screenwriting. Includes the Great British Pitchfest, Mentoring Script Labs, Actors Table Read, The Script Surgery and The Legal Clinic.

Love Stories etc...

HarperNorth, Windmill Green, 24 Mount Street, Manchester M2 3NX
email hello@harpernorth.co.uk
website https://librarylive.co.uk

Instagram @bookminxsjv
Festival Co-directors Alice Murphy-Pyle, Sara-Jade Virtue

Manchester's first romance festival, created to celebrate modern romance fiction and encourage romance readers to discover new authors. Features panels, workshops and book signings. Founded 2024.

Lyra Bristol Poetry Festival

website www.lyrafest.com
Facebook www.facebook.com/lyrabristol/
Bluesky @lyrafest.com.bsky.social
Instagram @lyrafest

Annual festival in Bristol celebrating all forms of poetry. Events include readings, slam competitions, film screenings, walking tours, panels and lectures. Prioritises diversity, accessibility and bringing together communities. Also runs the Bristol City Poet and Young City Poet initiatives, both of which appoint a poet to speak on behalf of the Bristol community and the issues that matter most to them.

Manchester Literature Festival

The Department Store, 5 Oak Street,
Manchester M4 5JD
email office@manchesterliteraturefestival.co.uk
website www.manchesterliteraturefestival.co.uk
Instagram @mcrlitfest
Co-directors Cathy Bolton and Sarah-Jane Roberts
Takes place October

An annual two-week festival showcasing new commissions and celebrating the best literature and imaginative writing from around the world. Note that MLF only accepts a small number of submissions each year, with the majority of the festival being curated by the team.

Margate Bookie Festival

email info@margatebookie.com
website www.margatebookie.com
Facebook www.facebook.com/MargateBookie
X @MargateBookie
Instagram @margatebookie
Takes place October

Brings together well-known writers and local authors across a weekend of events for both adults and children. Celebrates literature, comedy and music with over 4,000 visitors every year. Also runs a year-round programme of creative writing workshops and courses. Founded 2015.

Marlborough Literature Festival

email general@marlboroughlitfest.org
website www.marlboroughlitfest.org
Facebook www.facebook.com/MarlboroughLitFest
X @MarlbLitFest
Instagram @marlboroughlitfest
Festival Patron Sir Simon Russell Beale
Takes place 25–28 September 2025

An annual literary festival in the market town of Marlborough, celebrating the best in writing and reflecting the legacy of writers linked to the town such as Siegfried Sassoon, John Betjeman and William Golding. Champions new and upcoming writers as well as established names and offers a varied programme of events for all ages, including fiction, non-fiction, poetry, children's events and creative writing workshops in local venues in and around Marlborough. Has a strong outreach programme, delivering free author talks to local schools. Founded 2010.

Milton Keynes Literary Festival

Milton Keynes Central Library,
555 Silbury Boulevard MK9 3HL
email mklitfest@gmail.com
website www.mklitfest.org
Facebook www.facebook.com/MKLitFest
X @MKlitfest
Instagram @mklitfest
Threads @mklitfest
Takes place April

An annual Spring festival for writers and readers, including author events and writing workshops. Runs a year-round programme of online and in-person events and a writing competition. Founded 2017.

Monty Lit Fest

Montgomery Town Hall, Broad Street, Montgomery, Powys SY15 6PH
email enquiries@montylitfest.com
website https://montylitfest.com
Facebook www.facebook.com/montylitfest
X @montylitfest
Instagram @montylitfest
Takes place June

A diverse programme of events brings together a wide range of audiences to celebrate writers who live in or write about Wales. Founded 2016.

National Eisteddfod of Wales

40 Parc Ty Glas, Llanishen, Cardiff CF14 5DU
tel 0845 409 0900
email gwyb@eisteddfod.cymru
website https://eisteddfod.wales
Facebook www.facebook.com/eisteddfod
X @eisteddfod
Instagram @eisteddfod
Takes place 2–9 August 2025

Wales's largest cultural festival. Includes a literary pavilion, an arts exhibition and music events, alongside a programme of competitions. The event is held in a different part of Wales every year; the 2025 festival will be held in Wrexham and the 2026 festival in Pembrokeshire. Founded 1861.

National Poetry Day

Forward Arts Foundation,
Somerset House Exchange, The Strand,
London WC2R 1LA

tel 020-8187 9861
email info@forwardartsfoundation.org
website https://nationalpoetryday.co.uk
Facebook www.facebook.com/PoetryDayUK
X @PoetryDayUK
Instagram @nationalpoetryday
Takes place 2 October 2025

Organised by the Forward Arts Foundation to encourage poetry reading and writing. Combines poetry recommendations and teaching resources with nationwide events to highlight the artistic and social value of poetry. Each year it takes place on the first Thursday in October and explores a different theme. Founded 1999.

Ness Book Fest

email nbfinverness@gmail.com
website https://nessbookfest.com
Facebook www.facebook.com/NessBookFest
Takes place October

Organised and run by the community, for the community. Events are free to attend and held in accessible, central locations throughout the city; recordings are shared online. Aims to encourage regular book festival demographics to attend, as well as those who have never visited a book festival before. Guest authors write in a wide range of genres, from crime and thriller to poetry, and events include author talks, panel discussions, workshops and a full children's programme brought to local schools.

New Delhi World Book Fair

National Book Trust, Ministry of Education, Government of India, Nehru Bhawan, 5 Institutional Area, Phase-II, Vasant Kunj, New Delhi-110070, India
email ndwbf.nbt@gmail.com
website www.nbtindia.gov.in
Facebook www.facebook.com/nationalbooktrustindia
X @nbt_india
Instagram @nbt_india
Takes place February

Organised by India's National Book Trust. Facilitates the sale of rights and cultural exchanges, and features book launches, panel discussions, mentorship opportunities for emerging writers, a designated Children's pavilion and a themed pavilion (the theme for 2025 was the 75th anniversary of India as a Republic). Founded 1972.

Newcastle Noir

website www.newcastlenoir.co.uk
Facebook www.facebook.com/NewcastleNoir
X @NewcastleNoir
Takes place 1–6 December

An annual crime fiction festival established to promote top-class crime writing in the region and to celebrate an intriguing and increasingly diverse genre. Founded 2014.

Norfolk & Norwich Festival

Norwich Guildhall, Gaol Hill, Norwich NR2 1JS
tel (01603) 877750
email info@nnfestival.org.uk
website https://nnfestival.org.uk
Facebook www.facebook.com/NNFestival
X @NNFest
Takes place May

Transforms public spaces, city streets, performance venues, parks, forests and beaches, bringing people together to experience a variety of events spanning music, theatre, literature, visual arts, circus, dance and free outdoor events. Founded 1988.

Norwich Book Festival

The Forum, Millenium Plain, Norwich NR2 1TF
email norwichbookfestival@theforumnorwich.co.uk
website www.norwichbookfestival.org.uk
Facebook www.facebook.com/norwichbookfest/
X @BookFestNorwich
Instagram @bookfestnorwich
Ceo Chris Gribble, *Event Producer* Aisla McKay
Takes place October

A city-wide festival celebrating stories and their readers. Brings together readers, writers, bookshops, literary organisations and other key Norwich institutions. Founded 2024.

Off the Shelf Festival of Words Sheffield

tel 0114 222 3895
email offtheshelf@sheffield.ac.uk
website www.offtheshelf.org.uk
Facebook www.facebook.com/OffTheShelf/
X @otsfestival
Instagram @offtheshelffestival
Takes place 10–26 October 2025

Brings together writers, historians, poets, artists, scientists, journalists and musicians to celebrate books, words and ideas.

Oundle Festival of Literature

tel (01832) 270312
email hello@oundlefestivalofliterature.co.uk
website www.oundlelitfest.org.uk
Facebook www.facebook.com/OundleFestivalofLit/
Bluesky @oundlefestoflit.bsky.social
Instagram @oundlefestivaloflit
Threads @oundlefestivaloflit
Festival Secretary Sue Pearson

Runs a programme of year-round author events aimed at exciting, informing, entertaining and educating through talks, discussions and workshops. Founded 2002.

Oxford Literary Festival

c/o Gravita, 40–41 Park End Street, Oxford OX1 1JD
tel 07931 560223
email info@oxfordliteraryfestival.org

website https://oxfordliteraryfestival.org
Takes place March/April

An annual festival held in venues across the city and university, in partnership with the *Telegraph*. Presents topical debates and discussion panels, and a programme of children's events. Topics range from contemporary fiction to discussions on politics, history, science, gardening, food, poetry, philosophy and art. Founded 1998.

Paisley Book Fest

email bookfest@renfrewshire.gov.uk
website https://paisleybookfestival.com
Facebook www.facebook.com/BookPaisley
Instagram @paisleybookfest
Takes place April

Celebrates Scottish arts and culture. Events include author talks, writing workshops and publishing advice, covering a range of genres, from flash fiction to memoir. Also runs a schools programme and facilitates the Janet Coats Memorial Prize.

Primadonna Festival

Food Museum, Stowmarket, Suffolk IP14 1DL
email hello@primadonnafestival.com
website https://primadonnafestival.com
Facebook www.facebook.com/primadonnafest
X @primadonnafest
Instagram @primadonnafestival
Director Alice Hardaker
Takes place 18–20 July 2025

A female-led literary festival that nurtures a community of people of all genders and backgrounds, including those who are under-represented in the arts and have both seen and unseen disabilities. The programme of events promotes inclusivity and demonstrates diversity; it features local and international talent, household names and under-the-radar writers. Founded 2019.

Push the Boat Out Festival

email info@pushtheboatout.org
website https://pushtheboatout.org
Facebook www.facebook.com/PTBOpoetry
X @PTBOpoetry
Bluesky @ptbopoetry.bsky.social
Instagram @ptbopoetry
Festival Director Emma Collins
Takes place November

Edinburgh's international poetry festival. Increases the diversity of poetry in Scotland – in form, cross-art-form pollination, voices performed and those who feel welcomed to become members of its audiences and participants. Founded 2020.

Rainham Poetry Festival

tel 07801 522901
email goatstarbooks@gmail.com
website www.rainhampoetry.org
Takes place April

A two-day festival of poetry that brings together local, national and international poets, both new and established, to celebrate the power of poetry to change the world.

Raworths Harrogate Literature Festival

tel (01423) 562303
email info@harrogate-festival.org.uk
website https://harrogateinternationalfestivals.com/raworths-literature-festival
Facebook www.facebook.com/HarrogateInternationalFestivals
X @HarrogateFest
Bluesky @harrogatefestivals.bsky.social
Instagram @harrogatefestivals
Takes place 9–19 October 2025

A celebration of great writing and leading thinkers. Champions up-and-coming talent and established writers, featuring politicians, historians, journalists, comedians, and film and television makers. Founded 2013.

Romance Writing Festival

6 Wilfred Road, Bournemouth BH5 1NB
email info@bournemouthwritingfestival.co.uk
website www.romancewritingfestival.co.uk
Facebook www.facebook.com/people/Romance-Writing-Bournemouth/61568271561436/
Instagram @romancewritingfestival
Festival Director Dominic Wong
Takes place October

A celebration of the romance genre, featuring authors, publishers, editors and literary agents across talks, panels, workshops and networking opportunities. The festival welcomes both aspiring and experienced writers and explores all aspects of romance writing, from crafting compelling characters to navigating the publishing industry. Founded 2025.

Rye Arts Festival

email box-office@ryeartsfestival.org.uk
website https://ryeartsfestival.org.uk
Facebook www.facebook.com/RyeArtsFestival
X @Ryearts
Takes place September

Set in the historic town of Rye. Presents a programme of literary events, talks, panel discussions and workshops featuring leading writers of fiction, non-fiction, poetry, music and drama. Founded 1971.

Salisbury International Arts Festival

Wiltshire Creative, Malthouse Lane, Salisbury SP2 7RA
tel (01722) 320117
email info@wiltshirecreative.co.uk
website www.wiltshirecreative.co.uk/salisbury-international-arts-festival
Facebook www.facebook.com/wiltscreative

X @WiltsCreative
Takes place May–June

A thriving, annual multi-arts festival that delivers a variety of different arts events each year, including concerts, comedy, poetry, dance, outdoor spectacles and commissioned works. Founded 1974.

The SE London Book Fest

98 Braidwood Road, London SE6 1QZ
email selbookfest@gmail.com
X @selbookfest
Instagram @selbookfest
Takes place Autumn

A month-long festival that celebrates local talent and new writers. Events take place in independent bookshops and other venues across South East London. All proceeds from the Festival go towards supporting local food banks. Founded 2024.

The Self-Publishing Conference

Troubador Publishing Ltd, Unit E2,
Airfield Business Park,
Market Harborough LE16 7UL
tel 0116 279 2299
email conference@troubador.co.uk
website www.conference.troubador.co.uk
Facebook www.facebook.com/troubadorpublishing
X @matadorbooks
Instagram @troubador_publishing

Designed to educate, inform and inspire authors who are self-publishing or considering it as a publication route. Offers insight into diverse publishing options, opportunities to learn from and engage with industry experts, and the chance to network with experienced self-publishers. Fiction, non-fiction, business and children's writing are all represented. Tickets include access to workshops, keynote speakers, lunch, refreshments and an evening drinks reception.

Sevenoaks Literary Festival

email info@sevlitfest.com
website https://sevlitfest.com/
Facebook www.facebook.com/SevenoaksLitFest
X @Sevenoakslit
Instagram @sevenoaks_literary_festival
Takes place September

An eclectic festival featuring novelists, biographers, historians, poets and musicians talking about and performing their work. Also features a school's day for local children. Founded 2001.

Sherborne Travel Writing Festival

email info@sherborneliterarysociety.com
website www.sherbornetravelwritingfestival.com
Facebook www.facebook.com/SherborneLiterarySociety
Instagram @sherbornetravelwritingfestival
Takes place April

A weekend-long event featuring travel writers discussing work that spans the globe. Events cover fiction and non-fiction, and include events for aspiring travel writers.

The Stanfords Travel Writers Festival

Stanfords, 7 Mercer Walk,
Covent Garden WC2H 9FA
tel 020-7836 1321
email press@stanfords.co.uk
website www.stanfords.co.uk/stanfords-travel-writers-festival
Facebook www.facebook.com/standfordstravel
X @StanfordsTravel
Instagram @stanfordstravel
Takes place January/February

Held at Destinations: The Holiday & Travel Show in Manchester (January) and London (February), it hosts book signings and live author events. Founded 2014.

StAnza: Scotland's International Poetry Festival

tel (01334) 475000 (box office)
email stanza@stanzapoetry.org
website www.stanzapoetry.org
Facebook www.facebook.com/stanzapoetry
X @StAnzaPoetry
Instagram @stanzapoetry
Executive Producer Suzie Kirk Dumitru
Takes place March

Dedicated to programming a wide diversity of poetries and poets, alongside other art forms such as music and visual art. International in focus and has a hybrid format, including both live and digital events. Founded 1998.

States of Independence

DeMontfort University, Hugh Aston Atrium,
The Newarke, Leicester LE2 7BY
email statesofindie@gmail.com
website http://leicestercentreforcreativewriting.our.dmu.ac.uk
Facebook www.facebook.com/StatesOfIndependence
X @StatesofIndie

An annual one-day festival celebrating independent publishing, held at De Montfort University in Leicester. Involves independent publishers and presses, independent authors, zine makers, artist collectives, writing clubs and literature organisations. Founded 2010.

Stratford-upon-Avon Literary Festival

email info@stratfordliteraryfestival.co.uk
website www.stratlitfest.co.uk
Facebook www.facebook.com/stratfordlitfest
X @StratLitFest
Instagram @stratfordlitfest
Festival Director Annie Ashworth
Takes place May and October

A feast of workshops, panel discussions, celebrity and author events. Also runs a year-round programme of events and projects for families and regional schools aimed at entertaining and inspiring children and encouraging literacy, as well as events in the community and writing workshops in prisons. Founded 2008.

Swindon Festival of Literature

Lower Shaw Farm, Shaw, Swindon, Wilts. SN5 5PJ
tel (01793) 771080
email swindonlitfest@lowershawfarm.co.uk
website www.swindonfestivalofliterature.co.uk
Festival Director Matt Holland
Takes place May

A festival of ideas and entertainment with leading authors, speakers and performers across prose, poetry, drama, dance, music, circus skills and storytelling. Readings, discussions, performances and talks take place in theatres, arts centres, parks and pubs. Founded 1994.

Theakston Old Peculier Crime Writing Festival

Old Swan Hotel, Swan Road, Harrogate HG1 2SR
tel (01423) 562303
email info@harrogate-festival.org.uk
website www.harrogateinternationalfestivals.com/crime-writing-festival
Facebook www.facebook.com/HarrogateInternationalFestivals
X @HarrogateFest
Bluesky @harrogatefestivals.bsky.social
Instagram @harrogatefestivals
Takes place July

The world's largest and most prestigious celebration of crime fiction, featuring over 100 authors and 30 author events. Founded 2003.

The Times and Sunday Times Cheltenham Literature Festival

53–57 Rodney Road, Cheltenham GL50 1HX
email literature@cheltenhamfestivals.com
website www.cheltenhamfestivals.com/literature
Facebook www.facebook.com/cheltenhamfestivals
X @cheltfestivals
Takes place 10–19 October 2025

An annual festival and one of the oldest literary events in the world. Events include debates, talks and lectures, poetry readings, novelists in conversation, exhibitions, discussions, workshops and a Lit Crawl. Also runs a family programme, with events for toddlers to teenagers. Founded 1949.

Tottenham Literature Festival

website www.berniegrantcentre.co.uk/whats-on/tottenham-literature-festival-2025
Facebook www.facebook.com/BGArtsCentre
X @BGArtsCentre
Instagram @bgartscentre
Takes place November

Brings together Black writers, poets, journalists and artists across a series of events including performances, panel discussions, workshops and film screenings. Also runs a family programme that aims to inspire and engage children and celebrate the diversity of children's publishing. Founded 2019.

Tring Book Festival

Our Bookshop, 87 High Street, Tring, Herts. HP23 4AB
tel (01442) 827653
website www.tringbookfestival.co.uk
Facebook www.facebook.com/tringbookfest
X @tringbookfest
Takes place November

Features interviews, debates and workshops across a wide range of genres, as well as events for children. Also runs year-round events, a schools programme and an independent bookshop in Tring. Founded 2023.

UEA Live

UEA Live, Public Engagement, CAP 3.17, University of East Anglia, Norwich NR4 7TJ
tel (01603) 592286
email uealive@uea.ac.uk
website www.uealive.com
Facebook www.facebook.com/uealitfest
X @UEALitfest
Instagram @uealitfest

Based at the University of East Anglia, where some of the greatest writers of today have studied and worked, including Kazuo Ishiguro, Ian McEwan and Anne Enright. Previously known as the UEA Literary Festival. Events take place throughout the year. Founded 1991.

Warwick Words History Festival

The Court House, Jury Street, Warwick CV34 4EW
tel 07944 768607
email info@warwickwords.co.uk
website https://warwickwords.co.uk
X @WarwickWords
Takes place 29 September–5 October 2025

Celebrates historical writing, both fact and fiction. Provides an opportunity to meet authors and discuss their work. Founded 1999.

WayWORD Festival

website www.waywordfestival.com
Facebook www.facebook.com/waywordabdn
X @waywordabdn
Instagram @waywordabdn
Takes place 1–5 October 2025

A student and youth-led cross-arts festival exploring unconventional forms of expression in collaboration with the University of Aberdeen and the WORD Centre for Creative Writing. Events take place in-person and online, feature a diverse line-up of poets, authors and artists, and include panel discussions, readings and workshops.

Wells Festival of Literature

email admin@wellsfestivalofliterature.org.uk
website www.wellsfestivalofliterature.org.uk
Facebook www.facebook.com/Wellslitfest
X @wellslitfest
Instagram @wellsfestivalofliterature
Takes place 17–25 October 2025

Features leading writers of fiction and non-fiction, poets, politicians, performers and more. Administers four competitions. Festival run entirely by volunteers with all profits going to help fund educational projects in local schools and colleges to encourage young people to love literature and to celebrate the written word. Founded 1992.

Wigtown Book Festival

11 North Main Street, Wigtown,
Dumfries and Galloway DG8 9HN
tel (01988) 402306
email mail@wigtownbookfestival.com
website https://wigtownbookfestival.com
Facebook www.facebook.com/WigtownBookFestival
X @WigtownBookFest
Instagram @wigtownbookfest
Takes place 26 September–5 October 2025

Annual festival in Scotland's National Book Town, bringing readers, aspiring writers and published authors together across 200 events. Big Wig (for children) and Wigtown YA (for young people) run alongside the main festival. Also runs outreach events throughout the year, facilitates a mentorship programme for writers and administers two prizes. Founded 1999.

Wimbledon Book Fest

35 Wimbledon Hill Road, London SW19 7NB
email boxoffice@wimbledonbookfest.org
website www.wimbledonbookfest.org
Facebook www.facebook.com/Wimbledonbookfest/
Instagram @wimbookfest
Takes place 16–26 October 2025

Fosters a space for art and culture within the community. Guest speakers include writers from all genres, with a focus on inspiring stories, diversity and inclusion. Runs educational workshops and projects for young people during the festival and throughout the year. Founded 2006.

Winchester Books Festival

Avebury House, 6 St Peter Street,
Winchester SO23 8BN
email info@winchesterbooksfestival.com
website https://winchesterbooksfestival.com
Instagram @winchester_books_festival
Co-founders Sophie Liardet, Sian Searles
Takes place April

Hosts a well-rounded programme of talks, panel discussions and workshops covering fiction and non-fiction, aimed at both children and adults. Celebrates regional authors and local history and culture. Founded 2023.

Winchester Poetry Festival

c/o University of Winchester, Sparkford Road,
Winchester, Hampshire SO22 4NR
email hello@winchesterpoetryfestival.org
website www.winchesterpoetryfestival.org
Facebook www.facebook.com/WinchesterPoetryFestival
X @WinPoetryFest
Instagram @winchesterpoetry
Contact Amy Juliet Brown
Takes place October 2025/27

A biennial festival dedicated to celebrating the power of poetry to connect people and enrich lives. Founded 2013.

Worldcon

World Science Fiction Society, PO Box 61363,
Sunnyvale, CA 94088, USA
website www.worldcon.org
Takes place August

The annual convention of the World Science Fiction Society (WSFS), known as the World Science Fiction Convention (Worldcon), takes place in a different location each year. Groups of members can bid to host the convention in their area. Features creators, publishers and producers of sci-fi and fantasy in all of its forms, including writers and illustrators in various genres and formats; awards the Hugo Awards each year. The 2025 convention took place in Seattle and the 2026 convention will take place in Los Angeles. Founded 1939.

WOW London Festival

The HKX Building, 3 Pancras Square,
London N1C 4AG
email hello@thewowfoundation.com
website https://thewowfoundation.com
Facebook www.facebook.com/womenoftheworldfestival
X @WOWisglobal
Instagram @wowglobal
Takes place May

Established by the Women of the World (WOW) Foundation to celebrate women, girls and non-binary people and facilitate conversations around gender discrimination. Includes authors across a range of genres discussing the potential for literature and other forms of media to combat discrimination and promote positive representation. Events take place across the UK and internationally all year round. Founded 2010.

YALC (Young Adult Literature Convention)

email yalc@showmastersevents.com
website https://londoncomicconwinter.com/YALC
Facebook www.facebook.com/ukYALC
X @yalc_uk
Instagram @yalc_uk
Takes place 15–16 November 2025

A celebration of the best YA books and authors. An interactive event where YA fiction fans can meet their favourite authors, listen to panel discussions and take part in workshops. Founded 2014.

Writers' retreats and creative writing courses

The following list of creative writing courses and writers' retreats is not exhaustive but is intended to give readers a flavour of the many options available. Some offer bursaries. Details of postgraduate courses are on page 653.

Arvon

Lumb Bank – The Ted Hughes Arvon Centre,
Heptonstall, Hebden Bridge,
West Yorkshire HX7 6DF
tel (01422) 843714
email national@arvon.org
website www.arvon.org
Facebook www.facebook.com/arvonfoundation
Instagram @arvon__
Chief Executive Andrew Kidd

See individual entries for Arvon's writing houses: The Hurst – The John Osborne Arvon Centre (see page 649), Lumb Bank – The Ted Hughes Arvon Centre (see page 650), Totleigh Barton (see page 651) and Writers Retreat at The Clockhouse (below).

Leading creative writing charity, known for its diverse creative writing courses and author-led events. An online programme, 'Arvon at Home', offers virtual writing weeks, masterclasses and readings. Residential five-day courses are set in historic writing houses in rural locations. Week-long courses, both in-person and at-home, include workshops and one-to-one tutorials. Courses cover a range of genres including fiction, poetry, theatre, creative non-fiction and writing for children. Grants and concessions are available. Founded 1968.

Arvon Writers Retreat at the Clockhouse

Clunton, Craven Arms, Shrops. SY7 0JA
tel (01588) 640658
email thehurst@arvon.org
website www.arvon.org/centres/clockhouse/

Four apartments, each with a bedroom, study and en suite bathroom, and all food provided, for six-day and four-day writing retreats.

Anne Aylor Creative Writing Courses

46 Beversbrook Road, London N19 4QH
tel 020-7263 0669
email enquiries@anneaylor.co.uk
website www.anneaylor.co.uk
Facebook www.facebook.com/AnneAylorCreativeWritingCourses/
Contact Anne Aylor

Weekend and overseas courses, as well as customised courses for all levels of ability. See website for forthcoming events.

Blue Pencil Agency Events

email online@bluepencilagency.com
website www.bluepencilagency.com
Facebook www.facebook.com/Bluepencilagency.com
X @bluepencil_edit
Instagram @bluepencilagency
Contact Emma Haynes

Online craft tutorials, masterclasses and Q & A sessions with creative writing tutors, authors and literary agents. Suitable for fiction writers across all genres as well as non-fiction writers. See website for full list of events and dates. Recordings with handouts may be purchased by writers unable to attend the live events. Costs vary; all events offer a free place for writers on limited incomes.

Casa Ana Creative Writing Retreats

Calle Artesa 7, Ferreirola, 18414 La Taha, Granada, Spain
tel +34 678 298 497
email info@casa-ana.com
website www.casa-ana.com/creative-writing-retreats

Mentored writing retreats and courses in a 400-year-old house in Andalusia. Offers four residential writers' retreats each year in spring, summer and autumn. Nine places available in each retreat, which lasts for two weeks and includes a one-to-one mentoring service and optional reading/critiquing sessions. Also hosts week-long novel writing retreat. All retreats and courses conducted in English.

Château de Lavigny International Writers' Residence

Route d'Etoy 10, 1175 Lavigny, Switzerland
tel +41 (0)21 808 6143
email chlavigny@hotmail.com
website www.chateaudelavigny.ch
Residence and Programme Director Sophie Kandaouroff

International residence for writers in the Swiss canton of Vaud, which hosts 20 or more writers from around the world. Writers come for four weeks, in groups of up to six, from May to October. They are housed in an 18th-century manor house overlooking Lake Geneva. There is a fee for full board during four weeks; lodging for the duration is free. Sessions are in

English or French and writers must be published. A small number of full-grant fellowships, including full bed and board, are offered each year.

City Lit

1–10 Keeley Street, London WC2B 4BA
tel 020-7831 3111
email writing@citylit.ac.uk
website www.citylit.ac.uk/courses/history-culture-and-writing/writing

Affordable courses on a wide range of creative-writing topics, including writing fiction, non-fiction, journalism, children's writing and writing for both the stage and screen.

The Complete Creative Writing Course

Groucho Club, 45 Dean Street, London W1D 4QB
email jamie@writingcourses.org.uk
website www.writingcourses.org.uk
Contact Jamie Winter

Friendly creative writing courses held at Central London venues and online, with a solid focus on authors developing their own work. Tutor Alice Adams is a published author and experienced teacher. Suitable for both fiction and memoir writers; topics covered include creating complex characters, dialogue, writer psychology, procrastination and goal-setting, and getting published. Costs range from £125 to £450.

Cove Park

Peaton Hill, Cove, Argyll and Bute G84 0PE
tel (01436) 850500
email information@covepark.org
website www.covepark.org
Director Alexia Holt

International artist residency centre. Offers a year-round programme of residencies for writers, translators and artists from all disciplines. See website for details of the funded residency programme and to subscribe to newsletter.

The Creative Writer's Workshop

Kinvara, Co. Galway, Republic of Ireland
tel +353 (0)86 252 3428
email office@thecreativewritersworkshop.com
website www.thecreativewritersworkshop.com
Founder Irene Graham

Fiction and memoir-writing retreats in the West of Ireland; six-month Memoir Masterclass; 12-week memoir-writing course online with workbook. The workshops are accredited by George Mason University in the USA as part of its undergraduate and graduate degree programmes.

Curtis Brown Creative

Cunard House, 15 Regent Street, London SW1Y 4LR
tel 020-7393 4266
email help@curtisbrowncreative.co.uk
website www.curtisbrowncreative.co.uk
Facebook www.facebook.com/CurtisBrownCreative
X @cbcreative
Bluesky @cbcreative.bsky.social
Instagram @curtisbrowncreative

The only creative writing school run by a major literary and talent agency (The Curtis Brown Group). Offers courses in London and online. Over 250 students to date have subsequently signed publishing deals; alumni include Bonnie Garmus, Julia Armfield, Lucy Rose and Sean Lusk. Subjects covered include fiction, short stories, children's fiction (YA, middle grade and picture books), memoir and screenwriting. Curtis Brown Creative also runs the Breakthrough Writers' Programme, which offers free courses, mentoring and scholarships for under-represented writer

Deià Writers' Camps

email info@muswell-press.co.uk
website www.deiawriterscamps.com
Instagram @deiawriterscamps
Contacts Kate Beal and Sarah Beal, Muswell Press

Boutique writing retreats based in Deià, Mallorca. Aimed at writers of all levels, who can develop their skills under the guidance of industry experts. Price includes a full programme of tuition, workshops and one-to-one sessions, individual rooms with bathrooms, airport transfers and six nights' full-board accommodation, with food prepared by a local chef. Travel to extra activities also included; and optional wellness activities include yoga, hiking and the use of the swimming pool. See website for full information and costs.

Faber Academy

The Bindery, 51 Hatton Garden, London EC1N 8HN
tel 020-7927 3827
email academy@faber.co.uk
website www.faberacademy.com
Facebook www.facebook.com/faberacademy
X @faberacademy
Bluesky @faberacademy.bsky.social
Instagram @faber_academy
Threads @faber_academy
Director Joey Connolly

Expert guidance from first line to final draft. Online and in-person writing courses, as well as mentoring programmes and manuscript assessments from industry experts.

Fictionfire Literary Consultancy

110 Oxford Road, Old Marston, Oxford OX3 0RD
tel 07827 455723
email info@fictionfire.co.uk
website www.fictionfire.co.uk
Facebook www.facebook.com/FictionfireLiteraryConsultancy

X @LornaFergusson
Contact Lorna Fergusson

In-person and online creative writing courses, retreats and workshops. Guest talks and workshops can be arranged for writers' groups, libraries, educational establishments, conferences and festivals. Manuscript appraisal, editing, mentoring and consultation services also available. Founded 2009.

Foxes' Retreat Tailored Writing Retreats

The Old Kennels, Birdsgrove Lane,
Ashbourne DE6 2BP
tel 07734 328762
email myszka@foxesretreat.com
website www.foxesretreat.com
Facebook www.facebook.com/retreatfoxes
Director, Writer and Therapist Myszka Fox

Bespoke writing retreats in the Peak District focusing on creativity and wellbeing, hosted by novelists Myszka and Adam Fox. Fully catered accommodation available with private study bedrooms, wifi, armchairs and writing desks. Separate entrance to The Hayloft, ensuring privacy and solitude, if required. Optional add-on workshops: Character Building & Development, Flash Fiction and Short Story Writing. Therapeutic Writing sessions, safely led by BACP-registered Psychotherapeutic Counsellor, Myszka.

Online one-to-one coaching for writing and workshops available on request.

Maria Frankland Creative Writing Courses

email maria@mariafrankland.co.uk
website www.mariafrankland.co.uk
Contact Maria Frankland

Write a Novel, Write a Collection of Poetry, Write your Life Story and Write a Collection of Short Stories courses. All stages of writing are supported, from planning to publication, and follow a progressive 26-session online programme over a year. Visit the website to receive a free booklet: *The 7 S.E.C.R.E.T.S. to Achieving your Writing Dreams.*

The French House Party, Carcassonne

Domaine St Raymond, 11150 Pexiora, France
tel 07900 322791 (admin)
email hello@frenchhouseparty.eu
email frenchhouseparty@gmail.com
website www.frenchhouseparty.eu
website www.thefrenchhouseparty.com
Facebook www.facebook.com/p/French-House-Party-Carcassonne
X @FrenchHousePart
Instagram @frenchhouseparty
Director Dr Moira Martingale

Creative residential all-inclusive holiday courses in south-west France held between April and October. Creative writing, song-writing, Michelin-star cookery, art. Homeschool learning family groups also hosted. Founded 2007.

Gaia Partnership

email gaiapartnership@gmail.com
website www.gaiapartnership.net
Contact Jay Aspen

Eco-venue on the Welsh Borders, close to Hay-on-Wye. Offers fully catered creative writing weekends for aspiring and published authors alike. Friendly ethos cultivated, with opportunities for sharing work (if desired). See website for more details.

Gale & Co

144 Liverpool Rd, London N1 1LA
tel 07944 137248
email kathy.gale@galeandco.co.uk
website www.galeandco.co.uk
Facebook www.facebook.com/kathygaleandco
X @KathyGaleAndCo

Professional coaching consultancy for authors. Experienced team of writing coaches with decades of senior publishing experience focuses on supporting writers to achieve success. Many of those authors have gone on to be signed by publishers such as Bloomsbury, Canongate and Nosy Crow, and are represented by agencies including Curtis Brown and David Higham.

Garsdale Retreat

Clough View, Garsdale Head, Sedbergh,
Cumbria LA10 5PW
tel (01539) 234184
email garsdaleretreat@gmail.com
website www.thegarsdaleretreat.co.uk
Contact Rebecca Nouchette

Creative writing centre in the Yorkshire Dales National Park. Provides untutored retreats and residential courses tutored by professional writers, enabling participants to develop their individual creativity. All abilities welcomed and a high level of individual tuition is offered in classes with a maximum number of eight students. All courses and retreats are fully catered, allowing participants to focus on their writing.

The Good Ship Illustration

17 Walkergate, Berwick-upon-Tweed TD15 1DJ
email ahoy@thegoodshipillustration.com
website www.thegoodshipillustration.com
Facebook www.facebook.com/goodshipillo
Instagram @thegoodshipillustration
Staff Helen Stephens, Katie Chappell, Tania Willis, Alice Wood

Training and courses for illustrators and image-makers. Currently offers three eight-week courses. Find Your Creative Voice offers illustrators powerful strategies to unleash their creativity, build their creative confidence and find their unique voice. The Picture Book Course helps attendees learn how to make picture books from a place of playful curiosity, offering structure and guidance along the way. The Business Course covers all aspects of working professionally as an illustrator, including key issues such as marketing, branding, fees, contracts and self care. Prices start from £495.

The Grange

9 Eastcliff Road, Shanklin, Isle of Wight PO37 6AA
tel (01983) 867644
email stay@thegrangebythesea.com
website www.thegrangebythesea.com

Hosts weekend residential creative writing workshops. Secluded but close to local amenities and the beach.

Green Ink Writers' Gym

tel 07870 630788
email thewritersgym@rachelknightley.com
website www.writersgym.com
Instagram @jointhewritersgym
Contact Dr Rachel Knightley

Writing workouts, courses and coaching for life, work and art via a membership platform and podcast. Personal trainer: fiction and non-fiction author, qualified business and personal coach and creative writing lecturer Dr Rachel Knightley.

The Hurst – The John Osborne Arvon Centre

Clunton, Craven Arms, Shrops. SY7 0JA
tel (01588) 640658
email thehurst@arvon.org
website www.arvon.org

Offers residential writing courses from April to December. Grants available. The Hurst is situated in the Clun Valley in Shropshire, 12 miles from Ludlow, and is set in 30 acres of woodland, with gardens and a lake.

Irish Writers Centre – Áras Scríbhneoirí na hÉireann

19 Parnell Square, Dublin D01 E102, Republic of Ireland
tel +353 (0)1 872 1302
email info@writerscentre.ie
website https://irishwriterscentre.ie
Facebook www.facebook.com/IrishWritersCtr
X @IrishWritersCtr
Instagram @irishwriterscentre
Ceo Mags McLoughlin

Support and development organisation for Irish writers. Carries out its work online and in person on an all-island basis. Works with writers of all types and talents, and actively encourages writers from all communities to engage in creative writing. Also a membership organisation that looks for new opportunities for members to grow as writers and to connect with each other through IWC programmes and support. Founded 1991.

Isle of Wight Writing Courses and Workshops

Wright Diamond Press, 39 Ranelagh Road, Sandown, Isle of Wight PO36 8NT
tel (01983) 407772
email ffair77@btinternet.com
website www.felicityfairthompson.co.uk
website www.wightdiamondpress.com/learn-writing
Facebook www.facebook.com/felicityfair.thompson1
X @ffair77
Contact Felicity Fair Thompson

Email and postal MS critiques and editing, and one-to-one advice on film scripts, travel writing, poetry, novels and children's stories. In-person options also available for beginners and for experienced writers, including workshops, detailed online discussion, professional guidance and individual editorial advice.

Jericho Writers

Box 321, 266 Banbury Road, Oxford OX2 7DL
tel 0345 459 9560, +1 646-974-9060 (US)
email info@jerichowriters.com
website https://jerichowriters.com
Instagram @jerichowriters
Founder Harry Bingham

Inclusive online writing organisation offering editorial services and events for all genres, including writing for children, and tutored courses. Also available: guidance for self-publishers, masterclasses, agent one-to-ones, a free community for writers to connect, and expert guides to writing and publishing. See website for information on Festival of Writing.

Le Verger

Savignac-Lédrier, Dordogne 24270, France
email info@retreatfrance.co.uk
website www.retreatfrance.co.uk
Contact David Lambert

Residential writers' retreats and tutored courses in the French countryside. Literary and speculative fiction, screenwriting, poetry, writing for the stage, life writing and academic writing from June to September with experienced tutors. Shared or individual accommodation in the main house, the Piggery or a writer's cabin; full board (includes local wines) for up to seven writers. Also welcomes translators, illustrators, photographers and anyone working on a creative project (see new Creative Arts retreat). French courses available at all levels. Prices include group transfers to/from Limoges airport or train station. Scholarships available. Founded 2010.

Limnisa Writing Retreats By the Sea

Agios Georgios, Methana 18030, Greece
tel +31 681 027701
email info@limnisa.com
website www.limnisa.com
Instagram @limnisa_greece

International retreats for writers and readers. Single rooms, studios and tents. Vegetarian meals. Yoga. Yearly competitions in English and Dutch.

Lumb Bank – The Ted Hughes Arvon Centre

Heptonstall, Hebden Bridge,
West Yorkshire HX7 6DF
tel (01422) 843714
email lumbbank@arvon.org
website www.arvon.org

Offers online and residential writing courses. Grants available. Lumb Bank is an 18th-century former mill-owner's house set in 20 acres of steep pasture land.

Missenden School of Creative Arts

Jessamine House, King Street, Tring HP23 6BE
tel 07955 484605
email info@missendenschoolofcreativearts.co.uk
website www.missendenschoolofcreativearts.co.uk
Instagram @missendenschoolofcreativearts

Weekend and summer school art, craft and general interest courses for all abilities.

Moniack Mhor

Teavarran, Kiltarlity, Beauly,
Inverness-shire IV4 7HT
tel (01463) 741675
email info@moniackmhor.org.uk
website www.moniackmhor.org.uk
Centre Director Rachel Humphries

Year-round residential creative writing courses, retreats and residencies. Also offers online courses, a programme of awards, residencies and retreats for writing groups and organisations. Tuition is by established writers, and the range of courses designed to suit writers at all stages. Grants available on all courses. Founded 1993.

Morley College

61 Westminster Bridge Road, London SE1 7HT
tel 020-7450 1889
email enquiries@morleycollege.ac.uk
website www.morleycollege.ac.uk
Facebook www.facebook.com/morleycollegelondon
X @morleycollege
Instagram @morley_college
Creative Writing Course Leader Dr Florence Marfo

Offers a number of creative writing courses throughout the year, including a memoir-writing course.

National Centre for Writing (NCW Academy)

Dragon Hall, 115–123 King Street, Norwich, Norfolk NR1 1QE
tel (01603) 877177
email academy@nationalcentreforwriting.org.uk
website https://nationalcentreforwriting.org.uk/academy
Facebook www.facebook.com/NationalCentreforWriting
Instagram @writerscentre

Offers a wide range of online tutored courses for writers, including: writing historical fiction; an introduction to scriptwriting; kickstarting poetry; and beginner and intermediate courses in writing fiction, creative non-fiction and crime fiction. See website for forthcoming courses and pricing information.

The Novelry

25 Eccleston Place, London SW1W 9NF
tel 0770 015 3560
email hello@thenovelry.com
website www.thenovelry.com
Facebook www.facebook.com/thenovelry
X @thenovelry
Founder Louise Dean

Online novel writing school aimed at writers seeking to complete a novel or memoir to publishing standard. Submits graduates' work directly to literary agency partners in the US and UK. Also offers writing courses for novelists as well as one-to-one coaching from a team of published authors and professional editors. Prospective students can book a free online chat for more information. Founded 2017.

Open College of the Arts

The Michael Young Arts Centre, Room 201, DMC02, County Way, Barnsley S70 2JW
email enquiries@oca.ac.uk
website www.oca.ac.uk
Facebook www.facebook.com/openartscollege

Distance learning arts courses. Students can undertake part-time foundation, degree or master's courses from home, at their own pace, on a variety of topics, including creative writing.

Oxford University Summer Schools

Department for Continuing Education,
1 Wellington Square, Oxford OX1 2JA
tel (01865) 270360
website www.conted.ox.ac.uk/summer-schools

Offers a range of options, including:

Creative Writing Summer School: intensive three-week summer school in July/August at Exeter College. *Email*: writingsummer@conted.ox.ac.uk

Oxford University Summer School for Adults (OUSSA): a choice of more than 60 one-week accredited courses in a variety of subjects, including creative writing. *Email*: oussa@conted.ox.ac.uk

Inspiring Oxford and The Oxford Experience: Introductory one-week summer courses held at Brasenose College and Christ Church. *Email*: summerschools@conted.ox.ac.uk

Also short online courses and virtual classes in creative writing and literature – multiple intakes per year. *Email*: onlinecourses@conted.ox.ac.uk

The Ruppin Agency Writers' Studio

tel 01490 419787
email studio@ruppinagency.com
website www.ruppinagency.com
Facebook www.facebook.com/ruppinagency
X @ruppinagency
Instagram @ruppinagencywritersstudio

Former literary agent Jonathan Ruppin and author/creative writing academic Dr Emma Claire Sweeney head a team of 40 published writers offering bespoke in-person or online mentoring packages, manuscript and submission-package assessment, line-editing for authors of adult and YA fiction and trade non-fiction, and community project support. Writing retreats in UK and France, including Little Goat Barn residential retreats in north Wales.

SCBWI-BI Writers' Events

email araevents@britishscbwi.org
website www.scbwi.org/regions/british-isles
Instagram @scbwi_british_isles

Online listings of retreats and other writing and literary events across the UK organised by the Society of Children's Book Writers and Illustrators.

Scottish Universities' International Summer School

21 Buccleuch Place, Edinburgh EH8 9LN
tel 0131 650 4369
email suiss@ed.ac.uk
website www.suiss.ed.ac.uk
Facebook www.facebook.com/ScottishUniversitiesInternationalSummerSchool/
X @suiss_EDI

Creative writing, theatre and performance programmes offered as part of a broader range of summer activities. The four-week Creative Writing course is aimed at developing writers; the two-week Theatre and Performance course offers an introduction to British and Irish theatre.

Skyros Writers' Lab

9 Eastcliff Road, Shanklin,
Isle of Wight PO37 6AA (admin)
tel (01983) 865566
email holidays@skyros.com
website www.skyros.com
Facebook www.facebook.com/skyroshols

Support and guidance for writers at all stages of the creative process. Visiting authors have included Sophie Hannah, Sue Townsend, Marina Warner and Hilary Mantel. Courses are held on the Greek island of Skyros.

Stiwdio Maelor

Maelor, Corris, Machynlleth SY20 9SP
tel 07480 231003
email stiwdiomaelor@gmail.com
website https://stiwdiomaelor.com
Facebook www.facebook.com/StiwdioMaelor
Instagram @stiwdiomaelor
Contact Veronica Calarco

Offers writers, artists and creatives time and space out of their normal life and time to focus on the development of their work and explore the scenic Snowdonia National Park.

Totleigh Barton

Sheepwash, Beaworthy, Devon EX21 5NS
tel (01409) 231338
email totleighbarton@arvon.org
website www.arvon.org
Facebook www.facebook.com/Arvon
X @TotleighBarton
Instagram @arvon__
Director Kerensa Wilton, *Deputy Director* Sarah Beverley, *Administrator* Heather Cosgrove Chubb

Offers residential writing courses all year round in a rural setting. Grants available. An Arvon writing house. Full online programme available at: www.arvon.org/arvon-at-home/

Travellers' Tales

58 Summerlee Avenue, London N2 9QH
email info@travellerstales.org
website www.travellerstales.org
X @jonathanlorie
Director Jonathan Lorie

Training agency for travel writers at all levels. Offers vocational courses with top travel writers in London, including beginners' weekends, masterclasses and creative retreats. Online tuition also available. Founded 2004.

Tŷ Newydd Writing Centre

Tŷ Newydd, Llanystumdwy, Cricieth,
Gwynedd LL52 0LW
tel (01766) 522811
email tynewydd@literaturewales.org
website www.tynewydd.wales
Instagram @canolfantynewydd

Residential creative writing courses for writers of all abilities over the age of 16. Course topics range from poetry and popular fiction to writing for the theatre and developing a novel for young adults. No qualifications are necessary; staff can advise on the suitability of courses. Also offers courses for schools, corporate courses and awaydays for companies. Tŷ

Newydd is home to Nant, the writers' retreat cottage located on site. Run by Literature Wales, the national organisation for the development of literature in Wales.

UAL (University of the Arts, London) Short Course Office

Granary Square, 1 Granary Building, King's Cross, London N1C 4AA
email ualshortcourses@arts.ac.uk
website www.arts.ac.uk/colleges/central-saint-martins/courses/short-courses
Facebook www.facebook.com/UALShortCourses/
X @CSMShortCourses

Annual programme of courses in a variety of subjects taught by expert practitioners.

Urban Writers' Retreat

email hello@urbanwritersretreat.co.uk
website www.urbanwritersretreat.co.uk
Facebook www.facebook.com/UrbanWritersRetreat
X @urbanwriters
Contact Charlie Haynes

Courses and residential retreats for writers, giving them the time and space they need to concentrate on their work. Retreats are held in Newton Abbot, Devon; all food included. Each writer has their own private room. Online courses also available.

Writers & Artists

Bloomsbury Publishing plc, 50 Bedford Square, London WC1B 3DP
tel 020-7631 5985
email writersandartists@bloomsbury.com
website www.writersandartists.co.uk
Facebook www.facebook.com/WritersArtistsYearbook
X @Writers_Artists
Instagram @writers_artists_
Contacts James Rennoldson, Clare Povey, Amelia Brown

Hosts online and offline masterclasses, conferences and writing courses throughout the year. Masterclasses and conferences are run independently or in collaboration with literary festivals, universities and charities such as Book Aid International, Literature Works and the Open University. A series of events dedicated to writing and illustrating books for children and young adults is held in March each year. Online writing courses – which cover a variety of genres – take place on weekday evenings. Also offers a range of editing services, and works regularly with literary agents to provide guidance on the submission process. The W&A platform is free to join, contains hundreds of writing and publishing advice articles, and offers a lively community area and personalisation features. Financial assistance on selected events and services made available each year.

The Writers Bureau

tel 0161 819 9922
email studentservices@writersbureau.com
website www.writersbureaucourse.com
Facebook www.facebook.com/thewritersbureau
X @writersbureau

Provides a range of writing-related distance-learning courses, Zoom workshops, mentoring and reviews. Also has a Writers' Community for people to share information related to writing and make writing friends, as well as a monthly writing group and a poetry club where people can share and comment on each other's work. All services are designed to provide support to writers so they can develop their skills and achieve their writing goals. Writers of all levels are welcome, including beginners.
Founded 1989.

Writers' Cabin at Write Within

Nant Y Filltir, Penegoes, Machynlleth, Powys SY20 8UW
tel 07866 384359
email julia@writewithin.wales
website www.writewithin.wales
X @WriterForster
Contact Julia Forster

Self-led rural writer's retreat three miles outside Machynlleth, mid-Wales, which sleeps up to two people with a separate shower room and large sauna. Writers' Cabin was picked in 2024 by *The Sunday Times* as one of the top seven UK writer's retreats.

Self-catered stays last either three, four or seven days and include a complimentary sauna session and a bottle of Poetry Pharmacy 'pills' (poetry extracts on a piece of paper). Secluded cabin includes one double bed. with one single pull-out sofa also available. Satellite WiFi, heritage writing desk, comfortable office chair and well-appointed kitchenette (no oven). Price per night starts at £117.

During week-day retreats, one-to-one author coaching sessions are available with experienced author coach, novelist and poet Julia Forster, who has worked in publishing for over 25 years.

The Writers' Summer School at Swanwick, Derbyshire

c/o Old Farmhouse, Station Road, Ulceby, N. Lincs DN39 6TT
tel 07827 671735
email secretary@swanwickwritersschool.org.uk
website www.swanwickwritersschool.org.uk
Facebook www.facebook.com/SwanwickWriters
X @swanwickwriters

Extensive choice of courses, talks and workshops. Offers several highly subsidised places for writers aged between 18 and 30, and assistance for writers unable to afford the full course fee. Full details of the programme and information on how to apply for the TopWrite Programme and Assisted Places Scheme are available on the website.

POSTGRADUATE COURSES

Aberystwyth University
Department of English and Creative Writing, Hugh Owen Building, Penglais Campus, Aberystwyth, Ceredigion SY23 3DY
tel (01970) 621537
email english@aber.ac.uk
website www.aber.ac.uk/en/english

Courses offered include MA Creative Writing, MA Literary Studies, PhD Creative Writing and PhD English.

Anglia Ruskin University
East Road, Cambridge CB1 1PT
email jon.stone@aru.ac.uk
website https://aru.ac.uk/study/postgraduate/creative-writing
website www.aru.ac.uk/study/postgraduate/creative-writing-and-publishing
Facebook www.facebook.com/angliaruskin
Bluesky @aruwriting.bsky.social
Course Leader MA Creative Writing Jon Stone, *Course Leader MA Creative Writing and Publishing* Katharine Reeve

Offers full or part-time creative writing course options, with a January or September start (MA Creative Writing only), as well as a further research programme in the form of a PhD. Alumni scholarships (£400) are available for the latter. Opportunities to be involved in Cambridge Writing Centre events. Taught by a team of published writers, with guest workshops. Consists of Cambridge-based in-person seminars, four hours a week full-time.

The Cambridge School of Art, based at Anglia Ruskin, also offers an MA in Children's Book Illustration.

Bangor University
Bangor, Gwynedd LL57 2DG
tel (01248) 351151
email postgraduate@bangor.ac.uk
website www.bangor.ac.uk/study/postgraduate/creative-writing
Facebook www.facebook.com/BangorUniversity
Instagram @bangor_university/

Offers MA Creative Writing in English and Welsh medium.

Bath Spa University
Newton Park, Newton St Loe, Bath BA2 9BN
tel (01225) 875875
email admissions@bathspa.ac.uk
website www.bathspa.ac.uk/schools/school-of-writing-publishing-and-the-humanities/

Offers a variety of postgraduate courses on subjects including Creative Writing, Writing for Young People, Nature and Travel Writing, Scriptwriting, and Children's Publishing.

Birkbeck College, University of London
Malet Street, London WC1E 7HX
tel 020-7631 6000
website www.bbk.ac.uk/schools/arts
Facebook www.facebook.com/BirkbeckUniversityofLondon
X @BirkbeckUoL

Courses offered include MA Creative Writing, MFA Creative Writing, MA Journalism, MA Film and Screen Media and MA Screenwriting.

Bournemouth University
Fern Barrow, Poole, Dorset BH12 5BB
tel (01202) 961916
email futurestudents@bournemouth.ac.uk
website www.bournemouth.ac.uk/study/courses/ma-creative-writing-publishing
website https://thebournemouthjournal.com
Facebook www.facebook.com/JoinBournemouthUni/
X @bournemouthuni
Programme Leader Dr Bradford Gyori

Offers MA Creative Writing and Publishing, which combines creative support with industry-relevant knowledge. Students can work on publishing projects with the university's own literary review, the *Bournemouth Journal*. Students and staff run the annual Bournemouth Writing Prize, and produce outreach anthologies celebrating the work of various writing communities.

University of Brighton
School of Humanities, Village Way, Falmer, Brighton BN1 9PH
tel (01273) 643359
email jsm@brighton.ac.uk
website www.brighton.ac.uk/courses/study/Creative-Writing-MA-PGCert-PGDip.aspx
Contact Dr Jess Moriarty

Offers MA Creative Writing (PGCert PGDip). Working with professional writers, students develop skills to produce and share stories in a variety of genres. Provides links with local publishers, writers and creative companies and offers a unique artist in residency module where students work with organisations on a specific creative brief linked to their individual writing practice. Students have the opportunity to share their work through established student-led anthologies and open mic nights.

Brunel University London
Uxbridge, Middlesex UB8 3PH
tel (01895) 274000
website www.brunel.ac.uk/creative-writing
X @Bruneluni

Offers MA Creative Writing: can be completed in one year full-time or over two years part-time.

University of Cambridge Institute of Continuing Education
Madingley Hall, Madingley, Cambridge CB23 8AQ
tel (01223) 746222

email enquiries@ice.cam.ac.uk
website www.ice.cam.ac.uk/courses/courses-subject/visual-culture
Facebook www.facebook.com/CambridgeICE
X @litandcw_ice

Home to the University of Cambridge Centre for Creative Writing. Offers a wide range of short and part-time courses at introductory and advanced levels on creative writing, literature, art history and visual culture.

Cardiff University

Cardiff School of English,
Communication and Philosophy,
John Percival Building, Colum Drive,
Cardiff CF10 3EU
tel 029-2087 6049
email encap@cardiff.ac.uk
website www.cardiff.ac.uk/study/postgraduate

Courses offered include MA Creative Writing, MA News Journalism, and PhD Creative and Critical Writing (English and Welsh).

University of Central Lancashire

Preston, Lancs. PR1 2HE
tel (01772) 201201
email pgapplications@uclan.ac.uk
website www.uclan.ac.uk/postgraduate/courses/publishing-ma
Facebook www.facebook.com/OfficialUCLan/
X @UCLan
Instagram @uclanuni

Offers MA Publishing affiliated with the in-house press, UCLan Publishing. This close link offers students the opportunity to draw on the press's resources and to gain valuable experience.

University of Chester

Parkgate Road, Chester CH1 4BJ
email a.chantler@chester.ac.uk
website www.chester.ac.uk/study/course-search/creative-writing-writing-and-publishing-fiction-m
Course Leader Dr Ashley Chantler

Offers an MA in Creative Writing: Writing and Publishing Fiction. The course has four modules: Writing Short Fiction for Publication; Writing Novels for Publication; Getting Your Fiction Published; and The Major Fiction Writing Project.

University of Chichester

Bishop Otter Campus, College Lane, Chichester, West Sussex PO19 6PE
tel (01243) 816000
email h.frey@chi.ac.uk
email h.dunkerley@chi.ac.uk
website www.chi.ac.uk
Contacts Professor Hugo Frey (Head of Department), Professor Hugh Dunkerley (MA Creative Writing Programme Coordinator)

Offers BA, MA and PhD Creative Writing. Students work with practising writers. Specialisms include: novels, short stories, creative non-fiction, YA fiction, writing for children, fantasy and poetry.

Hosts regular visits by high-profile writers, editors and agents. Many students go on to publish and win prizes. Second in the country for Creative Writing Courses (*Guardian* University Guide 2023). Part-time or full-time study. MA begins 29 September 2025.

City University of London

School of Arts and Social Sciences,
Northampton Square, London EC1V 0HB
website www.city.ac.uk
Facebook www.facebook.com/cityuniversitylondon
X @CityUniLondon

Postgraduate courses in creative writing, English and publishing.

University of Cumbria

Fusehill Street, Carlisle CA1 2HH
tel 0808 291 6578
email enquirycentre@cumbria.ac.uk
website www.cumbria.ac.uk/study/courses/postgraduate/literature-romanticism-and-the-english-lake-district
Facebook www.facebook.com/universityofcumbria
X @CumbriaUni
Course Leader Dr Penny Bradshaw

Courses offered include MA Literature, Romanticism and the English Lake District.

De Montfort University

The Gateway, Leicester LE1 9BH
tel 0116 255 1551
email enquiry@dmu.ac.uk
website www.dmu.ac.uk

Courses offered include MA Creative Writing and MA English Language Teaching.

University of Derby

email askadmissions@derby.ac.uk
website www.derby.ac.uk/postgraduate/english-creative-writing-publishing-courses/creative-writing-ma
Facebook www.facebook.com/derbyuni
X @uni_writing
Instagram @derbyuni
Course Leaders Dr Christos Callow, Jr and Dr Simon Heyward

Offers a practice-taught MA Creative Writing for full- and part-time students. Covers a wide range of genres, including fiction, poetry, script-writing and creative non-fiction. Alongside the creative and critical main programme, three career pathways have been developed to help students find future employment: Creative Writing pathway with an additional module, What is the Imagination For?; Creative Writing with Publishing, which is centred around book production, taking modules from MA in Publishing; and Creative Writing for Gaming, which focuses on digital and tabletop games.

Graduates have worked with Writing East Midlands, the Derby Poetry Festival and other local and national organisations, in addition to publishing fiction, performing at spoken word events and finding internships with arts venues and game companies. Scholarship information is available online.

University of East Anglia

Admissions Office, School of Literature,
Drama and Creative Writing,
Faculty of Arts and Humanities,
Norwich Research Park, Norwich NR4 7TJ
tel (01603) 591515
email admissions@uea.ac.uk
website www.uea.ac.uk/about/school-of-literature-drama-and-creative-writing

Offers a well-regarded MA Creative Writing. Students may specialise in prose, poetry, scriptwriting, biography and creative non-fiction or crime fiction, and have the opportunity to learn from published writers and peers in workshops and one-to-one supervisions; and benefit from industry links. Other options include studying literature of interest as a critic, or creative critic, focusing on the modern and contemporary or medieval and early modern periods.

Edge Hill University

Department of English,History and Creative Writing,
St Helens Road, Ormskirk L39 4QP
tel (01695) 579997
email cowanb@edgehill.ac.uk
website www.edgehill.ac.uk/course/creative-writing-ma

Courses offered include MRes and PhD programmes in creative writing.

University of Edinburgh

Old College, South Bridge, Edinburgh EH8 9YL
tel 0131 650 1000
website www.ed.ac.uk
X @UniofEdinburgh

Postgraduate courses include Creative Writing, Film Studies, and Illustration.

Edinburgh Napier University

Merchiston Campus, 10 Colin Road,
Edinburgh EH10 5DT
tel 0333 900 6040
email studentrecruitment@napier.ac.uk
website www.napier.ac.uk/courses/ma-writing-genre-fiction-postgraduate-online-learning
Facebook www.facebook.com/EdinburghNapierUniversity/
X @EdinburghNapier
Instagram @edinburghnapier/
Tutors David Bishop, Elizabeth Dearnley, Nicholas Binge and Noelle Harrison

Part-time online MA Writing Genre Fiction or full- and part-time MA Creative Writing. Strong focus on genre fiction. Also offers modules on graphic novels and screenwriting.

University of Essex

Wivenhoe Park, Colchester CO4 3SQ
tel (01206) 872626
email pgadmit@essex.ac.uk
website www.essex.ac.uk/literature-film-and-theatre-studies
Facebook www.facebook.com/LiFTS.UoE/
X @LiFTS_at_essex

Postgraduate courses include Creative Writing, Film and Literature, Theatre Practice and Scriptwriting.

University of Exeter

Stocker Road, Exeter EX4 4PY
website www.exeter.ac.uk/postgraduate/courses/english/creative-ma/
Facebook www.facebook.com/exeteruni
X @UniofExeter
Instagram @uniofexeter

Offers MA Creative Writing, delivered by a team of internationally recognised writers. Also regularly hosts visiting speakers: writers, agents and publishers.

Falmouth University

Falmouth Campus, Woodlane, Falmouth,
Cornwall TR11 4RH
tel (01326) 211077
website www.falmouth.ac.uk/study/postgraduate

Courses offered include MA Film & Television, MA Fine Art (online), MA Comedy Writing (online) MA Game Design, MA Illustration (online), MA Illustration: Authorial Practice, MA Professional Writing, MA Writing for Script & Screen (online) and MA Journalism (online).

University of Glasgow

Creative Writing, School of Critical Studies,
5 Lilybank Gardens, Glasgow G12 8QQ
tel 0141 330 8372
email critstudies-pgenquiries@glasglow.ac.uk
website www.gla.ac.uk/subjects/creativewriting
X @UoGWriting

Courses include MLitt, MFA and DFA in Creative Writing, and MLitt by distance learning.

University of Hull

Cottingham Road, Hull HU6 7RX
tel (01482) 346311
website www.hull.ac.uk/faculties/subjects/english
Facebook www.facebook.com/UniversityOfHull
X @UniOfHull

Postgraduate courses include MA Creative Writing (online), MA Creative Writing and English Literature and MA English Literature.

Kingston University

Penrhyn Road, Kingston upon Thames, Surrey KT1 2EE
tel 020-3510 0106
website www.kingston.ac.uk
Facebook www.facebook.com/kingstonuni
X @KingstonUni

Postgraduate courses in Creative Writing (MA), Journalism (PgDip/MA) and Publishing (MA). The MA Creative Writing can be completed in one year (full-time), two years (part-time) or two years full-time including a professional placement.

Lancaster University

Department of English Literature and Creative Writing, The County College, Lancaster University, Lancaster LA1 4YD
tel (01524) 593089
email elcwteaching@lancaster.ac.uk
website www.lancaster.ac.uk/english-literature-and-creative-writing
Contact The Teaching Office

Courses offered include MA Creative Writing by Distance Learning, MA Creative Writing (Modular), MA Creative Writing with English Literary Studies, MA English Literary Studies with Creative Writing, MA English Literary Studies, PhD Creative Writing and PhD English Literature and Creative Writing.

University of Leeds

Faculty of Arts, Humanities and Cultures, University of Leeds, Leeds LS2 9JJ
website https://ahc.leeds.ac.uk/
Facebook www.facebook.com/universityofleeds

Postgraduate courses include MA Writing for Performance and Digital Media, Creative Writing, Media Industries, and Film, Photography and Media.

University of Lincoln

Brayford Pool, Lincoln LN6 7TS
tel (01522) 882000
email enquiries@lincoln.ac.uk
website www.lincoln.ac.uk/course/crtvwtma
Facebook www.facebook.com/universityoflincoln/
X @unilincoln
Instagram @unilincoln
Staff Daniele Pantano, Chris Dows, Amy Lilwall, Robert Weston, Sherezade García Rangel, Jason Whittaker

Offers MA Creative Writing. Strong focus on employability: aims to prepare student writers for a professional writing or publishing career. Students also gain practical experience working as editors on *The Lincoln Review*, an international literary journal. Opportunities to work across different genres and formats, including fiction, poetry, scriptwriting, non-fiction, the graphic novel, writing for video games and roleplaying games, conceptual and visual literatures, and writing for performance. A wide range of visits from professional authors, editors, producers, agents and directors, including Patience Agbabi, Robert Shearman, Andrew Graham-Dixon and Carol Ann Duffy. Available scholarships include those aimed at alumni and international students. Founded 2008.

Liverpool John Moores University

Tithebarn Street, Liverpool L2 2QP
tel 0151 231 2121
email APSadmissions@ljmu.ac.uk
website www.ljmu.ac.uk/study/courses/postgraduates/screenwriting
Programme Leader Screenwriting Richard Monks

Offers MA Screenwriting (based at Liverpool Screen School) and MA Writing.

University of London, Goldsmiths

Goldsmiths, University of London, London SE14 6NW
tel 020-7919 7171
website www.gold.ac.uk
Facebook www.facebook.com/GoldsmithsUoL
Instagram @goldsmithsuol

Postgraduate courses include Artists' Film and Moving Image, Art Psychotherapy, Art and Ecology, Arts and Learning, Black British Literature, Children's Literature, Children's Book Illustration, Computational Arts, Computer Games Art and Design, Creative and Life Writing, Creative Writing and Education, Curating, Digital Media, Dramaturgy and Writing for Performance, Film and Screen Studies, Filmmaking, Fine Art, Journalism, Performance Making, Audio, Radio and Podcasting, Script Writing and Translation.

University of London, Royal Holloway

Egham, Surrey TW20 0EX
tel (01784) 434455
website www.royalholloway.ac.uk
Facebook www.facebook.com/royalholloway
X @RoyalHolloway

Postgraduate courses include Creative Writing, Writing for Theatre, Screen and Radio, Producing Film and Television.

London College of Communication

277 High Holborn, London WC1V 7EY
tel 020-7514 6500
website www.arts.ac.uk/colleges/london-college-of-communication
Facebook www.facebook.com/londoncollegeofcommunication
X @LCCLondon

Postgraduate courses include MAs in Publishing, Screenwriting, Television, Photography, Games Design, Virtual Reality, Illustration and Visual Media, Film.

The London Film School

24 Shelton Street, London WC2H 9UB
tel 020-7836 9642
email info@lfs.org.uk
website https://lfs.org.uk

Offers two-year MA Filmmaking, one-year MA Screenwriting programmes. Also offers a one-year MA International Film Business course in association with the University of Exeter.

University of Manchester

University of Manchester, Oxford Road, Manchester M13 9PL
tel 0161 275 3107
website www.alc.manchester.ac.uk/centrefornewwriting
X @ECW_UoM

Courses offered include MA Creative Writing, MA Playwriting and MA Screenwriting.

The Manchester Writing School at Manchester Metropolitan University

Grosvenor East Building, Cavendish Street, Manchester M15 6BG
tel 0161 247 2000
email writingschool@mmu.ac.uk
website www.mmu.ac.uk/writingschool
X @McrWritingSchl
Creative Director Professor Carol Ann Duffy, *Contact and Senior Lecturer (admission and general enquiries)* James Draper

Courses offered include Master of Fine Arts (MFA) and Master of Arts (MA) in Creative Writing with specialist routes in Novel, Poetry, Writing for Children & Young Adults, Scriptwriting and Creative Non-Fiction. Campus-based and international online distance learning, available to study full-time (MA: one year, MFA: two years) or part-time (MA: two years; MFA: three years). September and January enrolment. Scholarships available (including Joyce Nield Fund for non-UK Commonwealth students). Evening taught, with strong industry links. MFA students complete a full-length book/script. MA in Publishing presented in collaboration with industry partners. PhD in Creative Writing, including PhD by practice, and BA programmes also available.

Middlesex University

The Burroughs, Hendon, London NW4 4BT
tel 020-8411 5555
website www.mdx.ac.uk/courses/
Facebook www.facebook.com/MiddlesexUniversity
X @MiddlesexUni

Post-graduate courses include: MA Media Management, MA Fine Art, MA Photography and MA Professional Arts Practice (Distance education).

National Film and Television School

Beaconsfield Studios, Station Road, Beaconsfield, Bucks. HP9 1LG
tel (01494) 671234
email info@nfts.co.uk
website https://nfts.co.uk
Facebook www.facebook.comNFTSFilmTV
Instagram @NFTSFilmTV

MA, diploma, certificate and short courses covering a wide range of disciplines relating to film, television and games.

Newcastle University

Newcastle upon Tyne NE1 7RU
tel 0191 208 6000
website www.ncl.ac.uk
Facebook www.facebook.com/newcastleuniversity
X @UniofNewcastle

Courses include MAs in Creative Writing and Writing Poetry, MPhil and PhD in Creative Writing; students benefit from close links to local partners such as Bloodaxe Books and Northern Stage. MA International Multimedia Journalism also available.

Northumbria University

Faculty of Arts, Design and Social Sciences, Lipman Building, Newcastle upon Tyne NE1 8ST
tel 0191 227 4444
website www.northumbria.ac.uk
Instagram @northumbriauni

Offers one- or two-year MA Creative Writing. Good links to regional literary organisations, such as New Writing North. One of the course's core modules, Professional Practice, offers students important insights into the world of literary publishing.

Nottingham Trent University

School of Social Sciences, Clarendon Street, Nottingham NG1 4FQ
tel 0115 848 4200
email rory.waterman@ntu.ac.uk
email hum.enquiries@ntu.ac.uk
website www.ntu.ac.uk/course/english-linguistics-creative-writing
X @ntuhum
Programme Leader Dr Rory Waterman

Offers a long-established and practice-based MA Creative Writing. Close links to the writing industry, an annual anthology, a programme of guest talks and workshops and many successful graduate writers. Diverse module options include: Fiction, Poetry, Writing for Stage, Radio and Screen, all taught by leading practitioners.

Oxford Brookes University

Headington Campus, Oxford OX3 0BP
email query@brookes.ac.uk
website www.brookes.ac.uk/courses/postgraduate/creative-writing/
Facebook www.facebook.com/oxfordbrookes
X @oxford_brookes
Instagram @oxfordbrookes

Offers three courses in creative writing: MA, PGDip or PGCert. Tutors are published writers. Creative Writing Fellows and visiting lecturers meet students, who will have the opportunity to meet literary agents from Felicity Bryan Associates. Applications for the MA must be accompanied by a portfolio of recent creative work: this should be either five poems, 2,000 words of prose or a proportional mixture of the two.

Oxford University

Department for Continuing Education,
Rewley House, 1 Wellington Square,
Oxford OX1 2JA
tel (01865) 270360
website www.conted.ox.ac.uk

MSt in Creative Writing: a two-year part-time master's degree covering prose fiction, narrative non-fiction, poetry, radio and TV drama, stage drama and screenwriting. Offers high contact hours, genre specialization and critical and creative breadth. *Email*: mstcreativewriting@conted.ox.ac.uk.

Short courses in Oxford and online including day schools, weekly learning programmes and advanced summer schools. *Email*: enquiries@conted.ox.ac.u

University of Plymouth

Drake Circus, Plymouth PL4 8AA
tel (01752) 585858
email admissions@plymouth.ac.uk
website www.plymouth.ac.uk
Facebook www.facebook.com/plymouthuni
Instagram @plymuni

MA courses include Creative Writing, English Literature and Screenwriting.

Queen's University, Belfast

University Road, Belfast BT7 1NN
tel 028-9024 5133
website www.qub.ac.uk
Facebook www.facebook.com/QueensUniversityBelfast
X @QueensUBelfast

Offers MA/Postgraduate Diploma Creative Writing.

University of Roehampton

Grove House, Roehampton Lane, London SW15 5PJ
tel 020-8392 3000
website www.roehampton.ac.uk/postgraduate-courses/childrens-literature-distance-learning
Facebook www.facebook.com/roehamptonuni
X @RoehamptonUni
Instagram @uni_roehampton

Postgraduate courses include Children's Literature.

The Royal Central School of Speech and Drama

Embassy Theatre, Eton Avenue, London NW3 3HY
tel 020-7722 8183
email sarah.grochala@cssd.ac.uk
website www.cssd.ac.uk/courses/writing-theatre-film-radio-television-mamfa
X @CSSDLondon

Offers MA/MFA Writing for Theatre, Film, Radio and Television. MA can be done in one year full-time or part-time over two years; MFA is two years, full-time.

University of St Andrews

School of English, St Andrews, Fife KY16 9AR
tel (01334) 462668
email pgeng@st-andrews.ac.uk
website www.st-andrews.ac.uk/english/postgraduate

Courses offered include PhD, MFA or MLitt Creative Writing; MFA or MLitt Playwriting and Screenwriting.

University of Salford

The Crescent, Salford M5 4WT
tel 0161 295 5000
website www.salford.ac.uk
Facebook www.facebook.com/salforduni
Instagram @salforduni

Postgraduate courses include MA/PgDip Journalism, MA Literature and Culture and MA Creative Writing: Innovation and Experiment.

Sheffield Hallam University

City Campus, Howard Street, Sheffield S1 1WB
tel 0114 225 5555
email enquiries@shu.ac.uk
website www.shu.ac.uk
Facebook www.facebook.com/sheffieldhallamuniversity
X @sheffhallumuni

Postgraduate courses include Creative Writing and Sports Journalism.

University of Stirling

Stirling, FK9 4LA
tel (01786) 473171
email liam.bell@stir.ac.uk
website www.stir.ac.uk/courses/pg-taught/creative-writing/
Facebook www.facebook.com/universityofstirling/
X @StirUni
Instagram @universityofstirling

Offers MLitt Creative Writing, focusing on creative non-fiction, fiction and poetry. A sample of creative work is required to support all applications.

Workshops, seminars and talks from visiting lecturers are available, as is one-to-one tuition.

University of Wales Trinity Saint David

Carmarthen Campus, Carmarthenshire SA31 3EP
tel (01570) 422351
email info@uwtsd.ac.uk
website www.uwtsd.ac.uk/ma-creative-writing
Facebook www.facebook.com/trinitysaintdavid
X @UWTSD

Offers MA Creative Writing; can be completed in person or through blended (mixed online and on campus) delivery.

Warwick Writing Programme

School of Creative Arts,
Performance and Visual Cultures,
Faculty of Arts Building, University of Warwick,
Coventry CV4 7EQ
tel 024-7652 3665
email SCAPVCenquiries@warwick.ac.uk
website https://warwick.ac.uk/fac/arts/scapvc/wwp/
Programme Director Dragan Todorović

Courses offered include MA Writing, MA Writing for Media, MA Literary Translation Studies, PhD Literary Practice and MPhil/PhD Literary Translation Studies.

Libraries

Libraries are not just repositories for books and a source of reference, they provide an increasing range of different services, using a multitude of media to reach more diverse audiences. Countless writers attest to the importance of libraries in shaping and helping develop their creative ambitions. Local libraries are a good source of information about the writing process and how to get published. They often hold author events, reading groups and creative writing classes. Note that the code needed for phoning UK libraries from overseas is +44.

TYPES OF LIBRARIES

• **Public libraries** are accessible to the general population and are usually funded by a local or district council. They typically offer a mix of lending and reference facilities. Public libraries are distinct from research libraries, subscription libraries and other specialist libraries in terms of their funding and access, but may offer some of the same facilities to visitors. Public library services are facing financial challenges and cuts to funding, so many library authorities are looking for new approaches to working with communities in order to build sustainable library services for the future.
• Most **community libraries** are part of the local public library network and many are considered part of the statutory library provision. Most authorities have found ways to ensure that community libraries can remain part of their network, often including the library management system. A list of community libraries in the UK can be found at www.publiclibrariesnews.com. Consult this website to find your nearest and local UK public and community libraries: www.gov.uk/local-library-services.
• An **academic library** is usually affiliated to an educational institution and primarily serves the students and faculty of that institution. Many are accessible to the public.
• A **subscription library** is one that is funded via membership or endowments. Access is often restricted to members but membership is sometimes extended to groups who are non-members, such as students.
• Many libraries belong to the Association of Independent Libraries and a list of members can be found on the Association's website (see below).

SOME OF THE BEST

Britain has such a wealth of comprehensive and historic libraries that a full list of them is not possible in this publication. Here is just a small selection of public libraries with outstanding collections in the UK.

Barbican Library

Barbican Centre, Silk Street, London EC2Y 8DS
tel 020-7638 0569
email barbicanlib@cityoflondon.gov.uk
website www.barbican.org.uk/your-visit/during-your-visit/library
Facebook www.facebook.com/Barbicanlibrary
X @barbicanlib

The largest of London's lending libraries with a strong arts and music section, a children's library, a London collection, literature events programme and reading groups.

Belfast Central Library

Royal Avenue, Belfast BT1 1EA
tel 028-9050 9150
email belfast.central@librariesni.org.uk
website www.librariesni.org.uk/libraries/greater-belfast/belfast-central-library
Facebook www.facebook.com/BelfastCentralLibrary
X @BelfastCentLib

The library holds the greatest number of titles in Northern Ireland. The library houses a number of special collections including a digital film archive and the Northern Ireland Music Archive.

Library of Birmingham

Centenary Square, Broad Street, Birmingham B1 2ND
tel 0121 242 4242
email enquiries@libraryofbirmingham.com
website www.birmingham.gov.uk/info/50132/visiting_the_library_of_birmingham
Facebook www.facebook.com/libraryofbirmingham
X @LibraryofBham
Instagram @the_library_of_birmingham

The largest public library in the UK and the largest regional library in Europe. Houses locally relevant collections of archives, photography and rare books. Facilities include an art gallery space. It is also home to the BFI Mediatheque, providing free access to the National Film Archive.

Bristol Central Library

Deanery Road, City Centre, Bristol BS1 5TL
tel 0117 903 7250
email bristol.library.service@bristol.gov.uk
website www.bristol.gov.uk/libraries-archives/central-library
Instagram @thelibrarybrisol

Includes collections related to Bristol's slave trade, 19th-century travel and art. An appointment must be made by email or phone five working days in advance to view rare items.

Canterbury Library

18 High Street, Canterbury, Kent CT1 2RA
tel 03000 413131
email canterburylibrary@kent.gov.uk
website www.kent.gov.uk/libs
Facebook www.facebook.com/KentLibrariesArchives
Instagram @canterburylibrary

The main library for the city of Canterbury. Canterbury Library was the first publicly funded library in Great Britain, through innovative interpretation of the Museums Act 1845 for provision of a museum of arts and science. It is now part of a large network of public libraries managed by Kent County Council. For services see website.

Cardiff Central Library

The Hayes, Cardiff CF10 1FL
tel 029-2038 2116
email centrallibrary@cardiff.gov.uk
website https://cardiffhubs.co.uk/hub/central-library-hub/
Facebook www.facebook.com/cardifflibraryservice
X @cdflibraries
Instagram @central_library_hub

The largest public library in Wales, opened in 2009, houses 90,000 books, 10,000 of which are in Welsh.

Leeds Library

18 Commercial Street, Leeds LS1 6AL
tel 0113 245 3071
email enquiries@theleedslibrary.org.uk
website www.theleedslibrary.org.uk
Facebook www.facebook.com/leedslibrary
X @theleedslibrary
Instagram @theleedslibrary

Founded in 1768 as a proprietary subscription library, it is now the oldest surviving example of this sort of library in the UK. It includes specialist collections in travel, topography, biography, history and literature. There are long runs of periodicals, popular novels, children's books, and Civil War pamphlets and Reformation Tracts. About 1,500 new books and audio/visual items are added every year.

Liverpool Central Library

William Brown Street, Liverpool L3 8EW
tel 0151 233 3069
email refbt.central.library@liverpool.gov.uk
website https://liverpool.gov.uk/libraries/explore-central-library/central-library/

The collection includes 15,000 rare books, some of which date back to the 13th century.

London Library

14 St James's Square, London SW1Y 4LG
tel 020-7766 4700
email reception@londonlibrary.co.uk
website www.londonlibrary.co.uk
Facebook www.facebook.com/thelondonlibrary
X @thelondonlib
Bluesky @thelondonlibrary.bsky.social
Instagram @thelondonlibrary

A subscription lending library containing over one million books and periodicals in over 50 languages, the collection includes works from 1700 to the latest publications in print and electronic form. Over 6,000 new books are added each year. Membership is open to all. The library's emerging writers' programme offers writers, in all genres, one year's free membership of The London Library and includes writing development masterclasses, literary networking opportunities, peer support and guidance in use of the Library's resources. For details: www.londonlibrary.co.uk/about-us/ll-emerging-writers.

Manchester Central Library

St Peter's Square, Manchester M2 5PD
tel 0161 234 1983
email libraries@manchester.gov.uk
website www.manchester.gov.uk/centrallibrary
Instagram @manchestercentrallibrary

Manchester's main library, the second biggest public lending library in the UK, houses a number of specialist collections such as Elizabeth Gaskell, Bellot Chinese and Thomas Penson De Quincey collections.

Mitchell Library

North Street, Glasgow G3 7DN
tel 0141 287 2999
email libraries@glasgowlife.org.uk
website www.glasgowlife.org.uk/libraries/venues/the-mitchell-library
Facebook www.facebook.com/GlasgowLibraries
X @GlasgowLib

One of the largest public reference library in Europe housing over one million items. Holds an unrivalled collection of material relating to the city of Glasgow. To contact the special collections team, email specialcollections@glasgowlife.org.uk or phone 0141 287 2988.

Newcastle City Library

Charles Avison Building, 33 Newbridge Street West, Newcastle upon Tyne NE1 8AX
tel 0191 277 4100
email information@newcastle.gov.uk
website https://new.newcastle.gov.uk/libraries/find-library/city-library
Facebook www.facebook.com/NewcastleLibraries
X @ToonLibraries

Newcastle's main public library includes a café, exhibition spaces, a rare books and watercolours collection, a viewing deck and six floors of books.

Norfolk and Norwich Millennium Library

The Forum, Millennium Plain, Norwich NR2 1AW
email libraries@norfolk.gov.uk
website www.norfolk.gov.uk/libraries-local-history-and-archives/libraries/visit/locations-and-opening-times/norfolk-and-norwich-millennium-library
Facebook www.facebook.com/MillenniumLibrary
X @MillenniumLib

As well as holding tens of thousands of books, the Norfolk and Norwich Millennium Library hosts regular events with the aim of engaging the local community, including board game afternoons and expert advice sessions. It is also home to the American Library, Memorial to the 2nd Air Division 8th Air Force, United States Army Air Forces.

Westminster Reference Library

35 St Martin's Street, London WC2H 7HP
tel 020-7641 6200 (press 2)
email referencelibrarywc2@westminster.gov.uk
website www.westminster.gov.uk/library-opening-times-and-contact-details/westminster-reference-library
X @WCClibraries

Specialist public reference library with collections in performing arts and art and design. Hosts regular and varied events, includes an exhibition space and a Business Information Point. Also has a range of business resources including market research, company and legal databases. Includes collection from Westminster Music Library.

LIBRARIES OF LEGAL DEPOSIT IN THE UK AND IRELAND

A library of legal deposit is a library that has the power to request (at no charge) a copy of anything published in the UK. There are six legal deposit libraries in the UK and Ireland. To obtain a copy of a book, five out of the six legal deposit libraries must make a request in writing to a publisher within one year of publication of a book, newspaper or journal. This request comes via the Agency for the Legal Deposit Libraries and they distribute the five books to the individual locations. Different rules apply to the British Library in that all UK libraries and Republic of Ireland publishers have a legal responsibility to send a copy of each of their publications to the library, without a written request being made (although they may receive an electronic notification). The British Library is the only legal deposit library with its own Legal Deposit Office. Since April 2013, legal deposit also covers material published digitally and online, so that the legal deposit libraries can provide a national archive of the UK's non-print published material, such as websites, blogs, e-journals and CDs.

The Agency for the Legal Deposit Libraries (ALDL)

21 Marnin Way, Edinburgh EH12 9GD
tel 0131 334 2833
email publisher.enquiries@legaldeposit.org.uk
website www.legaldeposit.org.uk

The ALDL requests and receives copies of publications for distribution to five major libraries (not the British Library). It is maintained by five legal deposit libraries and ensures that they receive legal deposit copies of British and Irish publications. The agency must request copies on behalf of the libraries within 12 months of the date of publication. On receiving such a request, a publisher must supply a copy for each of the requesting libraries under the terms of the Legal Deposit Libraries Act 2003 (UK) and the Copyright and Related Rights Act 2000 (Ireland).

Bodleian Libraries of the University of Oxford

Broad Street, Oxford OX1 3BG
tel (01865) 277162
email reader.services@bodleian.ox.ac.uk
website www.bodleian.ox.ac.uk
Facebook www.facebook.com/bodleianlibraries
X @bodleianlibs
Instagram @bodleianlibrary

With over 13 million items, the Bodleian Libraries together form the second-largest library in the UK after the British Library, and is the main reference library of Oxford University. It is one of the oldest libraries in Europe. It holds special collections in classics and ancient history, English, history, history of science, local history, philosophy, reference, theology and patristics.

The British Library

St Pancras Building, 96 Euston Road, London NW1 2DB
Legal Deposit Office: The British Library, Boston Spa, Wetherby, West Yorkshire LS23 7BQ
email legal-deposit-books@bl.uk
website www.bl.uk
Facebook www.facebook.com/britishlibrary
X @BritishLibrary
Instagram @britishlibrary

The British Library holds books, journals, newspapers, sound recordings, patents, original manuscripts, maps, online images and texts, plays, digital books, and poet and author recordings. The collection holds over 170 million published items from across the globe. The special collections and rare items include Shakespeare's first folio, the Magna Carta dated 1215, Lindisfarne Gospels from circa 700 and Charles Darwin's Natural Selection letter.

Cambridge University Library

West Road, Cambridge CB3 9DR
tel (01223) 333000
email library@lib.cam.ac.uk
website www.lib.cam.ac.uk
Instagram @cambridgeuniversitylibrary

Cambridge University Library houses its own collection and also comprises four other libraries within the university. The library dates back to the 15th century and now has a collection of over ten million items in electronic and physical formats. It is the only legal deposit library that keeps a large percentage of its books on Open Access. To visit the rare books collection email: rarebooks@lib.cam.ac.uk.

National Library of Scotland

Edinburgh (main location): George IV Bridge, Edinburgh EH1 1EW
tel 0131 623 3700
email enquiries@nls.uk
Glasgow (Kelvin Hall): 1445 Argyle Street, Glasgow G3 8AW
tel 0141 880 2329
website www.nls.uk
Facebook www.facebook.com/NationalLibraryOfScotland
X @natlibscot
Instagram @natlibscot

The National Library of Scotland holds over 34 million items. It is the world's central source for research relating to Scotland and the Scots. The library also holds a copy of the Gutenberg Bible, a First Folio of Shakespeare and the last letter written by Mary Queen of Scots. It contains important items relating to Jane Austen, Lord Byron and Sir Arthur Conan Doyle. The library is based in both Edinburgh and Glasgow. The George IV Bridge site in Edinburgh houses the main reading rooms, events centre and registration. The map rooms are at the Causewayside site (33 Salisbury Place, Edinburgh, EH9 1SL). The moving image archive can be found at the Kelvin Hall, Glasgow site.

National Library of Wales

Aberystwyth, Ceredigion SY23 3BU
tel (01970) 632800
email gofyn@llgc.org.uk
website www.library.wales
Facebook www.facebook.com/llgcymranlwales
X @nlwales

The National Library of Wales was established in 1907 and holds over 6 million books and newspapers, including many important works such as the first book printed in Welsh and the first Welsh translation of the Bible.

Trinity College Library Dublin

College Green, Dublin 2, Republic of Ireland
tel +353 (0)1 896 1127
email library@tcd.ie
website www.tcd.ie/library
Facebook www.facebook.com/tcdlibrary
X @tcdlibrary
Instagram @tcdlibrary

Trinity College Library is the largest library in Ireland and is home to the *Book of Kells* – two of the four volumes are on permanent public display. The library houses sound recordings, maps, databases, and a digital collection. Currently it has over seven million printed volumes with extensive collections of journals, manuscripts, maps and music reflecting over 400 years of academic development.

DESIGNATED OUTSTANDING COLLECTIONS

The Designated Outstanding Collections scheme was established in 1997 by the Museums and Galleries Commission to identify collections of national and international importance in non-national museums and galleries. In 2005 the scheme was extended to include libraries and archives. The scheme is now administered by Arts Council England and there are currently 163 Designated Outstanding Collections in England. To find out if there is a Designated Outstanding Collection library near you: www.artscouncil.org.uk/designated-collections.

SPECIALIST LIBRARIES IN THE UK

Writers often need access to specialised information sources in order to research their work. The following are a sample of specialist libraries in the UK. In addition to the libraries listed below, many university libraries hold special collections which are accessible to the public, usually by appointment. Check individual university library websites for details.

BBC Written Archives Centre

Peppard Road, Caversham Park, Reading RG4 8TS
email heritage@bbc.co.uk
website www.bbc.co.uk/archiveservices/written-archives-centre

Home of the BBC's written records. Holds thousands of files, scripts and working papers, dating from the BBC's formation in 1922, together with information about past programmes and the history of broadcasting. Does not have recordings or information about current programmes.

BFI National Archive and Reuben Library

Belvedere Road, South Bank, London SE1 8XT
tel 020-7255 1444

email library@bfi.org.uk
website www.bfi.org.uk/archive-collections
Facebook www.facebook.com/BritishFilmInstitute
X @BFI
Bluesky @britishfilminstitute.bsky.social
Instagram @britishfilminstitute

Established in 1933, the BFI National Archive is one of the largest film and television collections anywhere. Dating from the earliest days of film to the 21st century, it contains nearly a million titles. The archive holds over 800,000 items of film – including television programmes, documentaries, newsreels, as well as educational and training films – and is updated daily. The majority of the collection is British material but it also features internationally significant holdings. The Archive also collects films which feature key British actors and the work of British directors. Using the latest preservation methods, the BFI cares for a variety of often obsolete formats. The BFI Reuben Library at BFI Southbank is home to a huge collection of books, journals, documents and audio recordings about the world of film and television.

British Library for Development Studies (BLDS)

Institute of Development Studies at the University of Sussex, Brighton BN1 9RE
tel (01273) 678163
email blds@ids.ac.uk
website https://bldslegacycollection.uk/

Europe's largest research collection on economic and social change in developing countries.

British Newspaper Archive

tel (01382) 210100
website www.britishnewspaperarchive.co.uk
Facebook www.facebook.com/TheBritishNewspaperArchive
X @BNArchive
Instagram @thebritishnewspaperarchive

The British Newspaper Archive gives access to over three million historical local, national and regional newspaper pages from across the UK and Ireland. The Archive is currently in partnership with the British Library and findmypast.co.uk to digitise up to nearly 63 million newspaper pages from the British Library's vast collection.

The Brontë Parsonage Museum Collection

The Library, Brontë Parsonage Museum, Church Street, Haworth BD22 8DR
tel (01535) 642323
website www.bronte.org.uk/museum-and-library/library-new
Facebook www.facebook.com/BronteParsonageMuseum
X @BronteParsonage
Instagram @bronteparsonagemuseum

Anyone can use the Parsonage Library but to view original materials they must provide an academic reference in advance of their visit (see website for details on how to arrange a visit).

Caird Library and Archive

Greenwich, London SE10 9NF
tel 020-8312 6516
email library@rmg.co.uk
website www.rmg.co.uk/collections/caird-library

Specialist maritime research library at the National Maritime Museum in Greenwich.

Catholic National Library

Centre for Catholic Studies, Department of Theology and Religion, University of Durham, Abbey House, Palace Green, Durham DH1 3RS
tel 0191 334 1656
email ccs.admin@durham.ac.uk
website www.dur.ac.uk/theology.religion/ccs

Holds over 70,000 books, pamphlets and periodicals on theology, spirituality and related subjects, biography and history.

Chained Library

Hereford Cathedral Library and Archives, Hereford Cathedral, 5 College Cloisters, Cathedral Close, Hereford HR1 2NG
tel (01432) 374200
email library@herefordcatherdral.org
website www.herefordcathedral.org/chained-library

Hereford Cathedral has housed a collection of books accessible to the public from the 12th century. The chaining of books was a widespread security system in European libraries from the Middle Ages to the 18th century; this is the largest to survive with all its chains, rods and locks intact. The library is open Monday to Saturday 10.30am to 5pm.

Chawton House Library

Chawton, Alton, Hants. GU34 1SJ
tel (01420) 541010
email info@chawton.net
website https://chawtonhouse.org/the-library/using-the-library/
Facebook www.facebook.com/ChawtonHouse
X @ChawtonHouse

The collection, numbering over 4,500 items, focuses on women's writing in English from 1600 to 1830 and includes some manuscripts. The library also houses the Knight Collection, which is the private library belonging to the Knight family, the owners of Chawton House for over 400 years.

Chetham's Library

Long Milgate, Manchester M3 1SB
tel 0161 834 7961

email fwilde@chethams.org.uk
website https://library.chethams.com/
Facebook www.facebook.com/chelthamslibrary
X @chelthamslibrary

Founded in 1653, this is the oldest public library in the English-speaking world. In addition to a collection of early printed books, it includes manuscript diaries, letters and deeds, prints, paintings and glass lantern slides. Use of the library is free, no membership or reader's ticket is required. Researchers need a prior appointment by phone or email (above) at least one working day in advance to consult library material.

Commonwealth Library and Archives

Commonwealth Secretariat, Marlborough House, Pall Mall, London SW1Y 5HX
tel 020-7747 6164 (librarian), 020-7747 6167 (archivist)
email library@commonwealth.int
website https://thecommonwealth.org/library-and-archives/
Facebook www.facebook.com/commonwealthsec
X @commonwealthsec

Collection covers politics and international relations, economics, education, health, gender, environment and management. Holds a comprehensive collection of Commonwealth Secretariat publications and its archives. Opening hours are Monday to Friday from 10am to 4.45pm.

Crafts Council Research Library

Crafts Council, 44A Pentonville Road, London N1 9BY
tel 020-7806 2500
email reception@craftscouncil.org.uk
website www.craftscouncil.org.uk/insight-and-advocacy/research-library
Facebook www.facebook.com/CraftsCouncilUK/
X @CraftsCouncilUK

Houses a large collection of contemporary craft books and catalogues as well as journals. Covers ceramics, textiles, jewellery, fashion accessories and paper.

The Dana Research Centre and Library

165 Queens Gate, London SW7 5HD
tel 020-7942 4242
email smlinfo@sciencemuseum.ac.uk
website www.sciencemuseum.org.uk/researchers/dana-research-centre-and-library
Facebook www.facebook.com/sciencemuseumlondon
X @sciencemuseum

Allows access to around 500,000 items covering museum studies, the history and biography of science technology and medicine and the philosophical and social aspects of these subjects. It is advisable to book ahead of a visit.

University of Exeter Library, Special Collections

Old Library, Prince of Wales Road, Exeter EX4 4SB
tel (01392) 263867
email libspc@exeter.ac.uk
website www.exeter.ac.uk/departments/library/special-collections

The Bill Douglas Cinema Museum is home to one of the largest collections of material relating to the moving image in Britain. It holds a collection of over 85,000 items. Special collections include the Agatha Christie archive, which houses correspondence between Agatha Christie and Edmund Cork, between Cork and American literary agent, Harold Ober, and other interested parties. There are between 5,000-6,000 letters in the collection.

Feminist Library

The Sojourner Truth Community Centre, 161 Sumner Road, Peckham, London SE15 6JL
tel 020-7261 0879
email admin@feministlibrary.co.uk
website https://feministlibrary.co.uk/
Facebook www.facebook.co/feministlibrary
X @feministlibrary
Instagram @feministlibrary

The Feminist Library holds a large archive collection of women's liberation movement literature, particularly second-wave materials dating from the late 1960s to the 1990s.

Gladstone's Library

Church Lane, Hawarden, Flintshire CH5 3DF
tel (01244) 532350
email enquiries@gladlib.org
website www.gladstoneslibrary.org
Facebook www.facebook.com/gladstoneslibrary
X @gladlib
Instagram @gladstonelibrary

Britain's first residential library, the building houses 20,000 of Gladstone's books. Since the library opened in 1902, it has continued to acquire books specialising in those subjects that were of most interest to Gladstone: theology, history, philosophy, classics, art and literature. Researchers seeking an extended period of quiet study can stay in one of 26 rooms in the Gothic stone building.

Goethe-Institut London Library

50 Princes Gate, Exhibition Road, London SW7 2PH
tel 020-7596 4040
email library@london.goethe.org
email info-london@goethe.org
website www.goethe.de/ins/gb/en/sta/lon/bi2.html
Facebook www.facebook.com/goethe.institut.london
X @GI_London1

Specialises in German literature, especially contemporary fiction and drama, film DVDs and books/audiovisual material on German culture and recent history. The e-library gives access to Goethe Institut libraries in the UK, Ireland and the Netherlands and allows electronic downloading of ebooks and electronic newspapers for a predetermined period of time.

Guildhall Library

Aldermanbury, London EC2V 7HH
tel 020-7332 1868/1870
email guildhall.library@cityoflondon.gov.uk
website www.cityoflondon.gov.uk/things-to-do/history-and-heritage/guildhall-library
X @GuildhallLib

Books collection comprises over 200,000 titles dating from the 15th century to the 21st century and includes books, pamphlets, periodicals, trade directories and poll books. Covers all aspects of life in London, past and present.

Imperial War Museum Archive and Reading Room

IWM London, Lambeth Road, London SE1 6HZ
email researchroom@iwm.org.uk
website www.iwm.org.uk/research/research-facilities
Facebook www.facebook.com/iwm.london
X @I_W_M

Responsible for a unique national reference library with over 150,000 items on 20th- and 21st-century conflict involving British and Commonwealth countries. Along with material on military units and campaign histories, contains biographies, manuals, items relating to the economic, social and cultural aspects of war, journals, newspapers, ephemera, propaganda and digital resources. The Archive and Research Room is open four days a week (Tuesdays, Wednesdays, Thursdays and Fridays 10am until 4.30pm) to fifteen researchers who can order up to ten items at a time per day. Pre-booking is essential.

Lambeth Palace Library

15 Lambeth Palace Road, London SE1 7JT
tel 020-7898 1400
email archives@churchofengland.org
website www.lambethpalacelibrary.info
Facebook www.facebook.com/LambethPalaceLibrary
X @lampallib

The historic library of the Archbishops of Canterbury and the principal library and record office for the Church of England. Check website for details or future changes to opening times. To book a spot in the reading room please fill out the contact form on the website.

The Library of the Society of Friends

Friends House, 173–177 Euston Road, London NW1 2BJ
tel 020-7663 1135
email library@quaker.org.uk
website www.quaker.org.uk/resources/library/visit-the-library
Facebook www.facebook.com/BritishQuakers/
Instagram @britishquakers

The library has over 80,000 books and pamphlets, including a unique collection of 17th-century Quaker and anti-Quaker material. Open to researchers Tuesdays, Wednesdays and Thursdays 10am to 5pm (with a lunch break 1pm to 2pm). To be able to use a desk space and work with collection material you need to register and book an appointment.

Linen Hall Library

17 Donegall Square North, Belfast BT1 5GB
tel 028-9032 1707
email info@linenhall.com
website www.linenhall.com
Facebook www.facebook.com/LinenHallLibraryBelfast
X @thelinenhall
Instagram @linen_hall

Renowned for its Irish and Local Studies Collection, including early Belfast and Ulster printed books and 350,000 items in the Northern Ireland Political Collection (NIPC). Also large General Lending Collection. Open Monday to Friday, 9.30am to 5.30pm.

National Art Library

Victoria & Albert Museum, Cromwell Road, London SW7 2RL
tel 020-7942 2000
email hello@vam.ac.uk
website www.vam.ac.uk/info/national-art-library
Facebook www.facebook.com/victoriaandalbertmuseum
X @V_and_A

Houses around one million books but also holds prints, drawings, paintings, photographs, ceramics and glass, textiles and fashion, furniture, design, metalwork and sculpture. The collections range from medieval manuscripts to contemporary artists' books and armorial bindings to comics and graphic novels. Anyone can register to visit its collection, which focuses on the decorative arts in the museum's collection. Currently open Tuesdays, Wednesdays and Thursdays from 11am until 5pm.

Natural History Museum Library and Information Services

Cromwell Road, London SW7 5BD
tel 020-7942 5000 (switchboard), 020-7942 5460 (archives/general library), 020-7942 6156 (Ornithology library, Tring)
email library@nhm.ac.uk
website www.nhm.ac.uk/research-curation/science-facilities/library
Facebook www.facebook.com/naturalhistorymuseum
X @NHM_Library

Online catalogue contains all library material acquired since 1989 and about 80% of earlier items. The library collection contains more than one million items. For contact and opening times before a planned visit, see website.

RNIB National Library Service

PO Box 173, Peterborough PE2 6WS
tel 0303 123 9999 (library), 0300 303 8313 (bookshare)
email library@rnib.org.uk
website www.rniblibrary.com, www.rnibbookshare.org/cms
Facebook www.facebook.com/rnibuk
X @RNIB

The largest specialist library for readers with sight loss in the UK. It offers a comprehensive range of books and accessible information for children and adults in braille and Talking Books. Audiobooks are also available for download. RNIB Bookshare opens up the world of reading in education for learners with a print-disability, including those with dyslexia or who are blind or partially sighted.

Royal College of Music, Museum and Library Collections

Royal College of Music, Prince Consort Road, London SW7 2BS
tel 020-7591 4325
email library@rcm.ac.uk
website www.rcm.ac.uk/library

The Library's collections include over 500,000 items including manuscripts, early printed editions, personal archives and concert and opera programmes. Researchers and members of the public are welcome to visit during normal opening hours. See website for opening times.

John Rylands Research Institute and Library

150 Deansgate, Manchester M3 3EH
tel 0161 306 0555
email uml.special-collections@manchester.ac.uk
website www.library.manchester.ac.uk/rylands/
Facebook www.facebook.com/JohnRylandsLibrary
X @UoMLibrary
Instagram @thejohnrylands

The library is part of the University of Manchester but is open to the public. Home to 1.4 million items, including books, manuscripts, maps, artworks and objects.

Tate Library & Archive

Tate Britain, Millbank, London SW1P 4RG
tel 020-7887 8838
email reading.rooms@tate.org.uk
website www.tate.org.uk/visit/tate-britain/library-archive-reading-rooms/library

Located at Tate Britain, broadly covers those areas in which the Tate collects. Tate Library collections include over 115,000 books and monographs, 175,000 recent and historic exhibition catalogues, more than 10,000 artists' books, zines and serials, 3,000 print and online journals, printed ephemera, audio and video recordings, as well as microfilm and microfiche collections and half a million press cuttings.

Wales Broadcast Library

The National Library of Wales, Aberystwyth, Ceredigion SY23 3BU
tel (01970) 32800
email gofyn@library.wales
website www.library.wales/national-broadcast-archive

The National Library of Wales is home to the Wales Broadcast Library. The library has around 400,000 items available. To use the Wales Broadcast Library, visitors must register first and then they will be able to view or listen to the broadcasts at the Library's Broadcast Archive Centre.

Wellcome Library

Wellcome Collection, 183 Euston Road, London NW1 2BE
tel 020-7611 8722
email library@wellcome.ac.uk
website http://wellcomelibrary.org/
Facebook www.facebook.com/Wellcomelibrary/
X @WellcomeLibrary

One of the world's major resources for the study of medical history. Also houses an expanding collection of material relating to contemporary medicine and biomedical science in society. In terms of visual culture, the collection includes over 250,000 prints, paintings, drawings, photographs and digital images from the 14th century to the present. The audio-visual collections include 20th- and 21st-century public health information films, surgical training films, interviews, oral histories and broadcast radio and television programmes. Finally, there is an extensive collection of books on the history of modern health and medicine, as well as historical textbooks in fields such as anatomy, herbal medicine, surgery and subjects allied to health and medicine.

Westminster Music Library and Archives

35 St Martin's Street, London WC2H 7HP
tel 020-7641 6200
email musiclibrary@westminster.gov.uk
website www.westminster.gov.uk/leisure-libraries-and-community/library-opening-times-and-contact-details/westminster-music-library

Holds a wide range of scores, orchestral sets, books on music, music journals and a collection of Mozart sound recordings, formerly the GLASS collection.

Women's Library @ LSE

School of Economics and Political Science, Houghton St, London WC2A 2AE
tel 020-7955 7229
email library.enquiries@lse.ac.uk
website www.lse.ac.uk/library/collection-highlights/the-womens-library
X @LSELibrary

Houses the most extensive collection of women's history in the UK. Part of the London School of Economics. Open Monday to Friday, 10am to 4pm.

Wordsworth Library

Dove Cottage, Grasmere, Cumbria LA22 9SH
tel (01539) 435544
email enquiries@wordsworth.org.uk
website https://wordsworth.org.uk/
Facebook www.facebook.com/WordsworthTrust/

William Wordsworth's home, Dove Cottage, houses a small library which is situated in a two-storey converted coach house adjacent to the cottage museum. It contains treasures of all kinds related to the Romantic movement, from books to paintings and Wordsworth's manuscripts.

Working Class Movement Library

Jubilee House, 51 The Crescent, Salford M5 4WX
tel 0161 736 3601
email enquiries@wcml.org.uk
website www.wcml.org.uk
Facebook www.facebook.com/wcmlibrary
X @wcmlibrary

Records over 200 years of organising and campaigning by ordinary men and women. The collection provides an insight into working people's daily lives. Collection contains: books, pamphlets, archives, photographs, plays, poetry, songs, banners, posters, badges, cartoons, journals, biographies, reports.

Wren Library

Trinity College Cambridge, Cambridge CB2 1TQ
email wren.library@trin.cam.ac.uk
email archives@trin.cam.ac.uk
website www.trin.cam.ac.uk/library/wren-library

This library houses the manuscript of Winnie-the-Pooh and the papers of philosopher Ludwig Wittgenstein. As an academic library it's only open to the public for two hours each day during term time. To view rare books and manuscripts use the first email above. To view the college archive and modern manuscripts use the second email above.

Zoological Society of London Library

Outer Circle, Regent's Park, London NW1 4RY
tel 020-7449 6293
email library@zsl.org
website www.zsl.org/about-us/library
Facebook www.facebook.com/officialzsl
X @officialzsl

Contains a unique collection of journals and books on zoology and animal conservation.

ORGANISATIONS THAT SUPPORT LIBRARIES

There are many organisations which are affiliated to, and champion the use of libraries in the UK. These include:

APPG for Libraries Information & Knowledge in Parliament

tel 020-4513 2831
website www.cilip.org.uk/page/APPGLInK
Facebook www.facebook.com/CILIPinfo/wall
X @CILIPinfo
Instagram @clip_uk

The goal is to provide information and opportunities for debate about the important role libraries play in society and their future; to highlight the contribution that a wide variety of library and information services make, including those in public, school, government, health sector, colleges, private companies and university libraries; and to promote and discuss themes in the wider information and knowledge sector including the impact of technology, skills and training, professional standards and broader issues. There are separate divisions for Cymru Wales, Ireland and Scotland so please see website for divisional contact details.

Arts Council England

tel 0161 934 4317
website www.artscouncil.org.uk
X @ace_national
Instagram @aceagrams

The developmental agency for libraries in England and has responsibility for supporting and developing libraries. See also page 350.

Association of Independent Libraries

Church Lane, Doncaster DN5 7AU
email info@independentlibraries.co.uk
website http://independentlibraries.co.uk
Facebook www.facebook.com/IndependentLibraries
X @indielibraries

Develops the conservation, restoration and public awareness of independent libraries in the UK. Together, its members possess over two million books and have many listed buildings in their care.

Association of Senior and Children's Education Librarians (ASCEL)

Wolverhampton Central Library, Snow Hill, Wolverhampton WV1 3AX

email info@ascel.org.uk
website www.ascel.org.uk
X @ASCELUK

A national membership network of Senior Children's and Education Librarians. It aims to stimulate innovation and share initiatives relating to children and young people using public libraries and educational services.

BookTrust

No. 1 Aire Street, Leeds LS1 4PR
email queries@booktrust.org.uk
website www.booktrust.org.uk
Facebook www.facebook.com/booktrust
X @Booktrust
Instagram @booktrust

Charitable organisation that aims to give everyone access to books from an early age and the chance to benefit from reading. The focus is on children from birth to the first years of primary school, particularly children from low-income or vulnerable backgrounds. As well as the Leeds office, there are offices in London, Cardiff and Belfast. See also page 551.

Chartered Institute of Library and Information Professionals (CILIP)

7 Ridgmount Street, London WC1E 7AE
tel 020-7255 0500
email info@cilip.org.uk
website www.cilip.org.uk
Facebook www.facebook.com/CILIPinfo
X @CILIPinfo
Instagram @cilip_uk

The leading professional body for librarians, information specialists and knowledge managers. Aims for a fair and economically prosperous society underpinned by literacy, access to information and the transfer of knowledge. A registered charity. Offices in London, Wales, Scotland and Northern Ireland.

Friends of Libraries

Many libraries in the UK have Friends of Libraries organisations affiliated to them that support library use through charitable means. Sometimes Friends groups are set up to campaign against a potential council closure or reduction in budget. They have been known to set up their own community libraries.

Friends of National Libraries

email info@fnlmail.org.uk
website www.fnl.org.uk
X @FNL313
Bluesky @thefnl.bsky.social

Has awarded thousands of grants to regional, specialist and national libraries that have acquired rare books, manuscripts archives and fine bindings which are now accessible to all.

Internet Library for Librarians

email info@itcompany.com
website www.itcompany.com/inforetriever/index.htm

One of the most popular information resource sites for librarians since 1994, an information portal specifically designed for librarians to locate internet resources related to their profession.

Libraries Connected

email info@librariesconnected.org.uk
website www.librariesconnected.org.uk
X @libsconnected
Bluesky @librariesconnected.bsky.social
Instagram @librariesconnected

A charity, previously known as the Society of Chief Librarians (SCL). Partly funded by Arts Council England as the Sector Support Organisation for libraries. This funding provides increased capacity with a new team of staff and trustees to work alongside members. Remains a membership organisation, made up of every library service in England, Wales and Northern Ireland.

Libraries Week

website www.librariesweek.org.uk

The first Libraries Day took place in February 2012 and is now a week-long annual event in the UK dedicated to the celebration of libraries and librarians. Green Libraries Week, which took place in October 2024 led by CILIP, was the first national celebration of libraries, across all sectors, from public libraries on the high street to national, health and academic libraries, where the focus was on the climate and sustainability. Each year, author talks and competitions are arranged by local authorities, universities, library services and local community groups.

The Library Campaign

email thelibrarycampaign@gmail.com
website www.librarycampaign.com

Aims to advance the lifelong education of the public by the promotion, support, assistance and improvement of libraries through the activities of Friends of Library groups and user groups.

Library Planet

website https://libraryplanet.net/
Instagram @library_planet

A crowdsourced travel guide for the libraries of the world. The intention is to inspire library travellers. To contribute to Library Planet, please send an email to: booksofkells@live.com.au. See website for details on how to contribute and what to write.

National Literacy Trust

tel 020-7587 1842
email contact@literarytrust.org.uk
website www.literacytrust.org.uk
Facebook www.facebook.com/nationalliteracytrust

X @literacy_trust
Instagram @literacy_trust

Aims to improve reading, writing, speaking and listening skills in disadvantaged communities, in part through access to libraries. See also page 552.

Private Libraries Association

email info@plabooks.org
website www.plabooks.org
X @PLAbooks
Instagram @pla_books

An international society of book collectors and lovers of books. Publications include *The Private Library* (quarterly), annual *Private Press Books*, and other books on book collecting.

Public Library News

website www.publiclibrariesnews.com

Promotes knowledge about libraries in the UK.

The Reading Agency

website https://readingagency.org.uk
Facebook www.facebook.com/readingagency
X @readingagency
Instagram @readingagency

Aims to give everyone an equal chance in life by helping people become confident and enthusiastic readers, and that includes supporting library use.

School Library Association (SLA)

1 Pine Court, Kembrey Park, Swindon SN2 8AD
tel (01793) 530166
email info@sla.org.uk
website www.sla.org.uk
Facebook www.facebook.com/schoollibraryassociation
X @uksla
Instagram @uksla

The main goal is to support people involved with school libraries, promoting high-quality reading and learning opportunities for all. Founded 1937.

Self-publishing and indie authors

Introduction

There is no single, definitive way to publish a book. Many good and successful strategies are available to writers, giving them a choice as to whether they pursue traditional or self-publishing routes. These two strands of publishing are not in opposition to one another, so often perceived as a binary-pairing of a good and a bad publishing practice; in reality, they run in parallel. Both require the same steps, the same preparations, with the only key difference being who undertakes the individual tasks and who finances them.

If you are to self-publish successfully, you need to familiarise yourself with traditional publishing processes. Knowing what is involved at each stage of the editorial and production process, who is making the decisions, why these decisions are made, is important. Publishing traditionally comes with security, contracts and contacts but usually the trade-off is receiving only a percentage of the money made through book sales by way of author royalties, which will need to be shared with an agent, if you have one. This can make self-publishing look financially appealing on paper.

An author could go from earning a small percentage of the profits if published traditionally, up to around 70% through Amazon Kindle Direct Publishing. The difference is dizzying, but in practice, the return depends on your market reach, how much the book is sold for and how many books you can sell without a big-name publishing house's logo printed on the book's spine or access to its marketing channels.

Self-publishing is certainly not the easier option, but it is potentially the most rewarding emotionally due to the control offered to the individual author. You are author-driven, not industry-led. The 'self' in self-publishing does not mean you have to go it alone if you don't want to (though this is, of course, an option to someone with enough skill and entrepreneurial spirit). Rather, the 'self' gives you the freedom to be your own project manager and build up a team of professionals of your choosing. Many freelancers offering services to independent authors have worked in-house at publishing houses. As an indie author you have access to that talent pool.

Knowing what you want to achieve comes only second to what you can afford. Independent publishing can go from very minimal start-up costs to thousands of pounds very quickly, so spend some time before you begin the process of publishing your book looking at costs. Treat self-publishing like buying a new kitchen or organising an event; approach different individuals who you have researched, vetted, and think are suitable and ask for written quotations. Put simply, you are a client looking for a vendor.

Listings in this section:

- *Publishing services for independent authors*, page 694

Paid-for publishing services: *Is it a steal?*

The UK writers' unions, the Society of Authors (SoA) and the Writers' Guild of Great Britain (WGGB), investigated the practices of companies that charge writers to publish their work while taking rights. The findings were published in their 2022 report *Is it a steal?* Their investigation into 'hybrid'/paid-for publishing services raises awareness and work for change in what is a growing section of the writer services sector. Authors are advised to read the report and heed its advice.

Below are key extracts from this report. The full version can be found at: https://writersguild.org.uk/wp-content/uploads/2022/05/REPORT-Is-it-a-steal.pdf

As part of an investigation into practices in the sector, the SoA and the WGGB carried out a survey of authors who had used 'hybrid'/paid-for publishing services. 240 writers responded to the survey which ran online between 28 February and 25 April 2021.

The findings of that survey have informed our in-depth assessment of the relationship between writers and companies who often refer to themselves as 'hybrid', 'partnership' or 'contributory' publishers (among other terms) but which have much in common with what have historically been described as 'vanity' publishers.

Summary findings:

- 94% of respondents lost money, typically in the thousands.
- The average loss was £1,861 with some writers reporting losses as high as £9,900.
- The median cost of publication was £2,000.
- A median of only 67 books were sold per deal, resulting in royalties of only £68.
- 59% of writers said their book was not available to buy in retail outlets.

We received reports of aggressive marketing tactics by 'hybrid'/paid-for publishers in their approaches to writers, their manipulative sales approaches, unclear contracts, obscure publishing processes and services that fell far short of expectations and value.

Recommendations

1. We have identified an urgent need to educate writers about all models of publishing and to support them through any publishing process they choose. We have made five recommendations for writers to follow.
2. We strongly urge all publishers to commit to 15 key publishing principles, including offering clarity about their business models, production and book-marketing capacity, as well as notifying people who enter into 'hybrid'/paid-for agreements about their Consumer Rights.
3. We are working with third parties – including the Publishers Association, the Independent Publishers Guild, and various advertising platforms – who in various ways give these 'hybrid'/paid-for companies credibility, to ensure that they are not helping to promote or validate companies whose operations are based on poor practice and the exploitation of writers.

What is 'hybrid'/paid-for publishing?

In a traditional or conventional trade publishing contract, a publisher provides everything from editing and printing to marketing, publicity and distribution. It takes a licence of rights and pays writers a fee or an advance, and royalties. It does not ask for payments from a writer. It funds its operation by sales of books and is therefore investing cash and resources, and taking a risk on the book's success.

'Hybrid'/paid-for publishing deals should also not be confused with self-publishing. Writers can self-publish at very little cost to themselves, but even if they pay a **self-publishing service provider** to edit, design, produce and market their book, the rights will remain with the writer. The writer receives all profits after the sales platform or distributor takes its cut and can extract themselves from the agreement at any time. Such service providers are funded by payments agreed, and preferably negotiated, with the author.

Defining 'hybrid'/paid-for publishing services

If a writer pays money for publication and grants the company a licence of rights or if the company takes a share of any profits, the writer is dealing with a 'hybrid'/paid-for publishing service.

The companies in question sometimes describe themselves as 'contributory', 'subsidy' or 'partnership' publishers, but they have much in common with what used to be called 'vanity' publishers. In their marketing approaches to writers, they often suggest that they operate as traditional publishing houses. In fact, some are run as imprints of major publishers, gaining legitimacy from their parent brands.

At first glance, 'hybrid'/paid-for publishing deals can look much like traditional publishing agreements, but they are very different. There is rarely any sign of expenditure by the 'hybrid'/paid-for publisher except what is funded by the author. As such, terms like 'hybrid', 'contributory' and 'partnership' can appear deliberately misleading. Writers pay the publisher. They are offered no advance, and there is usually no undertaking or intention by the 'hybrid'/paid-for publisher to publish the work other than as an ebook and/or as Print on demand ('POD'), or in an ultra-short print run. The writer does not own any of the books produced except for limited initial copies.

Anyone can set themselves up as such a publisher, regardless of their financial stability, publishing knowledge and experience, or commercial expertise. Start-up and overhead costs are minimal, and expenses are funded by writers, not by income from book sales.

At the point of submitting a work for publication, writers are vulnerable. They have invested a great deal of time, work, energy and creativity in their manuscript. Now they want to be read, and for their work to be legitimised.

'Hybrid'/paid-for publishing services often exploit this desire, sending excessive praise about manuscripts and telling writers what they want to hear. They might claim their approach is better than traditional publishing or self-publishing, without ever explaining what that means. They will stress how excited they are to be working with the writer. Of course, at the point of hearing a 'publisher' express interest in their work like this, it can be difficult for a writer to step back and see it for what it is: a sales approach, designed to take advantage of writers' hopes, their passion for their work and their desire for validation – not to mention their lack of knowledge about the complexities of the publishing industry.

In our view, of all the publishing approaches available, a 'hybrid'/paid-for deal is the worst option a writer can take. In our direct experience of working with SoA and WGGB members, and as our research bears out, 'hybrid'/paid-for publishing deals do not result in enough sales or exposure to justify the payment by the author. For many years, even before researching for this report, we have seen how such services fall short of expectations, with writers unnecessarily handing over rights and control over their manuscripts, along with large sums of money. We have seen the impact this has on writers' careers and confidence in their work, and on their finances. We have seen too many cases where the 'hybrid'/paid-for model amounts to a counterfeit approach to publishing. We invariably advise writers against it.

If you are a writer considering a 'hybrid'/paid-for deal, we recommend taking the following five steps before you commit:

1. Educate yourself.

The publishing industry is complex. Do your research to get a broad understanding of how it works and the options available before you commit to any publishing deal. For starters, download the free SoA guide *What type of deal is that?* for a no-nonsense introduction to the pros, cons and gotchas of five publishing approaches.

2. Consider carefully what you want from publication and whether a 'hybrid'/paid-for deal is the best way to achieve it.

Is a 'hybrid'/paid-for publishing deal a better option than self-publishing, with its substantial investment from you as well as surrendering rights in your work? To commission self-publishing services will probably cost you less and you will retain all rights in your work.

3. Look closely at the detail of the deal.

How much will you have to pay? What is covered for that payment? Are there guarantees on the number of books to be printed? And will you own any of them, or will you have to pay more to get hold of copies yourself ('author copies')? What rights are you giving away? Will you have to make further payments later? Can you terminate the deal, when and how?

4. Research the company offering the deal.

Ask the SoA and WGGB what we know about them. Ask others who have used the company. Look for online reviews (though be mindful of paid-for positive reviews) and check their history at Companies House. Check the Watchdog Advisory Ratings on the Alliance of Independent Authors' (ALLi) website. In short, don't sign with a company unless you are confident about what you can expect if you work with them.

5. Have your contract vetted.

Remember that all contracts are negotiable. If you are an SoA or WGGB member, get your contract vetted as part of your membership. We recommend that you always do this regardless of the type of deal or contract you are being offered.

Is it a steal? is supported by the Authors' Licensing and Collecting Society (ALCS).

See also...

- *Society of Authors*, page 746
- *Writers' Guild of Great Britain (WGGB)*, page 749

Understanding book design

Freelance designer Catherine Lutman guides you through the purpose and process of book design, and the numerous elements that must work together to suit a book's specific requirements, with the useful terminology and details you need to know about typography and layout, briefing a designer, and the use of imagery and illustrations.

The cover of a book typically draws a consumer to pick it up, glance at the back cover, and then scan a few pages at random from inside. And then it's essential to make sure the pages are legible, professionally designed, and appropriate for the genre. No matter how strong the cover or the content, if the *internal* pages are poorly laid out the reader will be put off. Many design decisions influence how a reader experiences your content – and the more complex the content, the more involved is the work of the designer.

Typography and layout

The design of the internal pages is a delicate balancing act between many factors:

- **Typography** – the art and technique of arranging type. The designer will decide the style and organisation of all the words in the book, including titles, headings, sub-headings, body text, quotes, featured text, tables, captions, indents, footnotes, running heads and/or footers and page numbers.
- **Hierarchy** – the organisation of elements on the page according to their importance or the order in which they should be read. Hierarchy helps us navigate the book and process the content. It can be achieved through the use of scale, weight, colour and spacing.
- **Margins** – these perform several functions in the book. Margins provide space for the reader to hold the book; they keep the text block or content away from the gutter (the inner margin of a book); they make the book visually appealing and reserve space for running heads, footers and page numbers. A larger margin is usually found at the inner edge than at the outer, as the binding means the book does not lay completely flat.
- **Grid** – a structure of lines that aid the designer in organising and aligning the page elements.
- **Baseline grid** – designers can choose to align some or all of the text to a baseline grid (see the diagram on page 676). When text is aligned in this way, subconsciously readers perceive pages as neater and more harmonious.
- **Leading (line spacing)** – the vertical space between lines of text. It should feel comfortable to the eye.
- **White space** – a well-balanced page layout will include generous white space. Resist the temptation to overcrowd the page in order to keep the extent down.
- **Measure (line width)** – the designer takes care that the width of the text blocks, and therefore number of words on a line, is comfortable for the reader to scan. Where a single block would be too wide, columns of text can be used.
- **Imagery** – the scale, position and type of imagery is fundamental to how the content is experienced. If an image is placed across a double-page spread, care must be taken that important details (such as one or more people in the image) are not lost in the gutter.
- **Tables, charts and graphs** – these need to display information effectively and accurately and can add interest to the layout.

• **Colour scheme** – the choice of colours in two- and four-colour books is integral to the design. Choosing to publish a book in colour has cost implications but, in a children's picture book for example, it is usually a matter of necessity.
• **Extent** – the total number of pages in the book. The extent is made up of *signatures* or *sections*; each of these is a sheet of paper folded into eight, 16 or 32 pages. Therefore, the extent of the book will jump up in these increments. Designers bear this in mind as they work with the layouts to make sure the layout fills the sections.
• **Paper** – the choice of coated or uncoated paper and the weight and colour of the paper are all design decisions. A bulky, non-reflective, uncoated paper may be preferable for a novel, whereas a full-colour photography book may print best on a bright white, coated paper.

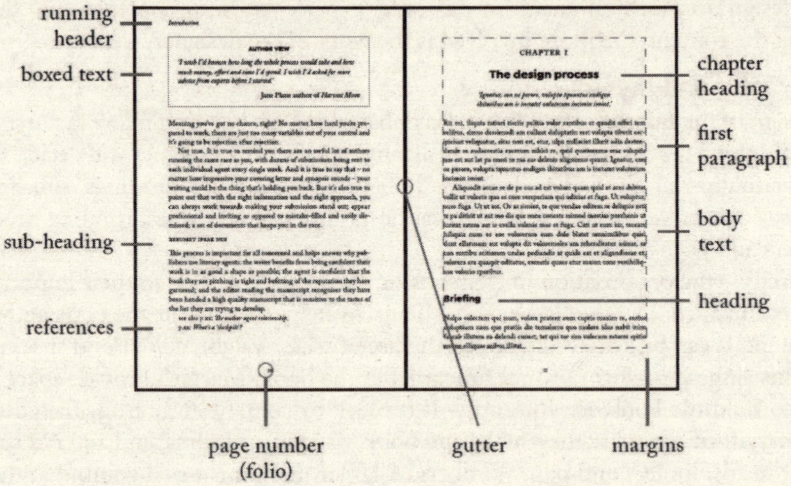

Layout and hierarchy

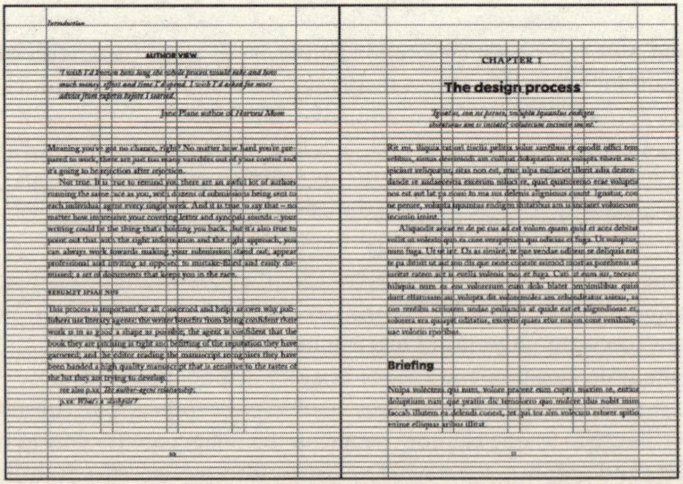

Grid and baseline grid

Choice of fonts

There are hundreds of fonts with many classifications, but for the purposes of book layout design the two main types are *serif* and *sans serif*. A serif is a small stroke at the end of the larger stroke in a letter; a sans serif font does not have these. Broadly speaking, sans serif fonts are considered more modern and serif fonts more traditional. However, it is generally accepted that serif fonts are easier and more comfortable to read for long passages of text; this is why the majority of novels are set in serif fonts, whether they are historical or contemporary. In a text-based book, sans serif fonts can be useful for headings, subheadings and extra material that you may want to give more emphasis to, as they can provide contrast to the body copy and help distinguish the page hierarchy or create interest in the layout.

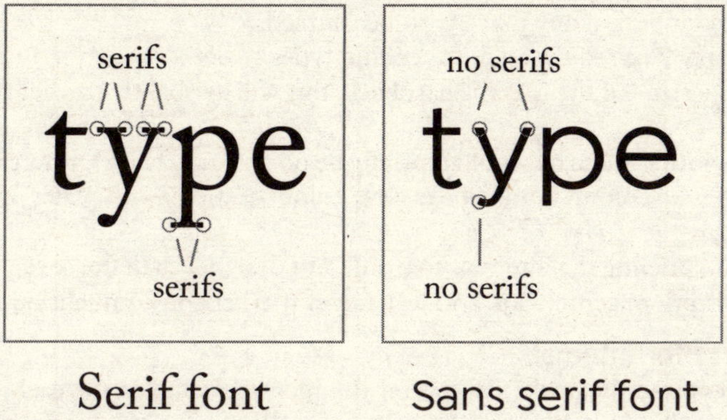

Font licensing

Any fonts you install on your computer need to be licensed. There are certain fonts called *system fonts* that are already installed on every computer (including Arial, Times New Roman, Courier and Georgia) but, for any other fonts, you need to have a licence for each machine they are used on. An experienced designer will have built up a library of licensed fonts and, if they have a Creative Cloud (www.adobe.com/uk/creativecloud.html) subscription for design applications such as InDesign and Photoshop, they will have a licence to use any fonts from the Adobe Typekit library. Some fonts are only available from particular type foundries and can be expensive; some companies even commission fonts and hold their exclusive licence. Free font sites such as Dafont (www.dafont.com) are popular, but always check the licence as some 'free' fonts are only free for personal use, which means that you cannot use them in any material you intend to sell or distribute commercially.

Typesetters

For certain types of publication, it is common practice for the designer to design a sample chapter and pages from the prelims and endmatter; after these are approved, they then hand the layout of the complete book over to a typesetter. This approach is appropriate for a lengthy book in which each chapter or section is similar or is very text-heavy in content, such as a novel or reference book. A heavily illustrated book, such as a children's book, cookery book or an art book, or one that is not lengthy would be laid out entirely by a designer. Your designer can advise you on what is appropriate for your book and may be able to find a typesetter for you if needed.

Briefing the 'internals'

Depending on the type of book and the skill set of the designer, you may wish to treat the design of the cover and internals (internal content) separately and brief different designers to do each part. Obviously, a cover design is often highly creative whereas a page layout may require a very precise and detailed mindset, but many book designers are experienced in working in either discipline. Fees for the design of the internals can vary widely depending on complexity and extent: some designers quote per page and others quote for a sample chapter, expecting the layout of the whole book to be undertaken by a typesetter. The brief for the internals may include the following elements:

- **Sample** – a representative sample of the content.
- **Summary of content** – chapter titles, content of prelims and endmatter.
- **Imagery** – description of any imagery to be sourced.
- **Page plan** – may be a requirement for certain types of book.
- **Trimmed page size** – if the cover is hardback, this will be slightly smaller than the cover size.
- **Number of colours** – a novel would typically be one colour (black), whereas a children's book would be four-colour. Some books have colour sections with plates of photographs and other images.

NB If you are briefing the internals to a different designer than the cover, you will need to add the description, genre, look and feel, target market and competition to the brief.

Design process for internals

The designer commonly works up several double-page spreads for each initial design option, based on the sample you provided, giving fewer options than for a cover. The layouts try to include all the key elements from the content: chapter headings, introduction, body text, imagery, any text features, running heads or footers and page numbers. The designer may suggest additional elements to add interest, such as ornaments (small decorative symbols that separate sections) or boxed text.

The aim of the first round is to pick the option that will be carried forward and perfected. Once the sample chapter has been designed, the prelims and endmatter can be designed and, if the services of a typesetter are being used, the book can be handed over to be typeset. If the designer is laying out the book from beginning to end, there can be a lengthy process of building up the layouts as the content is finalised, culminating in rounds of proofing.

Imagery and illustration

If you intend to use graphic elements in your book, there are some important technical and legal aspects to bear in mind, particularly if you plan to source the images yourself. Design, illustration and photography are seen as distinct disciplines. Although some creatives provide some or all of these services, you may need to engage a different person as designer, illustrator or photographer. Your designer may be able to suggest illustrators or photographers, or they may suggest sourcing images from an image library.

Copyright

It is vital that you have permission to use any imagery in your book: you cannot simply pull an image from the internet and use it. Firstly, an image dragged from a website is unlikely to be of print quality and, secondly, it is illegal to use intellectual property in your book without acquiring the explicit right to do so. You could commission an illustrator or photographer to create original work for your publication or purchase a licence to use an image.

Commissioning an illustrator or photographer

If you have decided to commission original imagery, the process of selecting an illustrator or photographer is much the same as finding a designer. Ask to see their portfolio to get an idea of their style and experience. As with design, some areas of photography or illustration are highly specialised, and some people may work in a specific area such as technical illustrations or food photography. Most illustrators or photographers do not automatically grant you a licence to own the artwork outright; instead, they retain the copyright and would expect a further fee for a reprint or repurpose. Clarify this point when you commission them to do the work.

When briefing the illustrator or photographer, you can make good use of mood boards. Some illustrations need to be extremely specific and briefed individually; you may need them to fit a designated space in the layout and supply requested dimensions for each one. A photographer might require the collaboration of additional people for the shoot: an art director, stylist and assistant commonly form the team. The book designer often takes the role of art director. Post-production work such as retouching and colour correction might be needed, although some photographers undertake these tasks themselves.

Royalty-free images

A royalty-free image is one you can buy a simple licence to use right away, without negotiating the fee and usage with an agent. Libraries such as Shutterstock (www.shutterstock.com), iStock (www.istockphoto.com) or Adobe Stock (https://stock.adobe.com/uk) have many hundreds of thousands of royalty-free photographs, illustrations and graphics you can purchase. You need to make sure the licence you purchase covers the usage you need; for example, some licences have a restriction on the number of times the image can be printed (and in which territories) and where they can be reproduced. Generally, though, a standard licence will suffice for use in your book.

Rights-managed images

Rights-managed images, found on sites like Getty Images (www.gettyimages.co.uk), are sold on a one-time-use basis for reproduction in a specific way. These can be of a very high quality by a well-known artist or photographer, or they may cover a specialised subject. A rights-managed image is usually considerably more expensive than a royalty-free image.

Summary

Many elements come together to make up the design of your book and determine its success. At every stage, effective communication and collaboration with experienced professionals will give you the best chance of achieving your goal – to create a memorable and appropriate design that showcases your work and puts it in the hands of your intended audience.

Catherine Lutman is an award-winning freelance designer, art director and design manager based in London. She has 20 years' experience in the publishing industry and has worked with many of the world's leading publishers. Catherine specialises in the design of non-fiction, reference and illustrated books on a wide range of subjects from artist's monographs to children's reference. A selection of her work can be seen at www.catherinelutman.com.

This article is an extract from Chapter 3 'Design: from manuscript to finished book' by Catherine Lutman in the *Writers' & Artists' Guide to Self-Publishing* (Bloomsbury 2020)

In praise of fanfic

Hari Patience-Davies uncovers the rich field of fanfiction, a world full of creative opportunities and possibilities, where prequels, sequels, crossovers, alternate universes and viewpoints, 'fix-its' and 'what ifs' provide fertile ground for writers to practise and enjoy their craft.

Recently I read an amazing reimagining of Jane Austen's *Pride and Prejudice* (1813). Unlike other versions that have appeared over the years, this one featured no zombies and no murders in need of solving at Pemberley Hall – instead it was an exquisitely plotted alternative life of Elizabeth Bennet that unfurled over about 500,000 words (the original novel is only around 120,000 words long), wherein our heroine followed the drum to the Peninsula War with her first husband. Such was the scope of the story that it had several alternate endings and an impressive cameo from the Duke of Wellington.

I'd love to recommend it to everyone I've ever met, but I suspect that more than a few of them would turn their noses up at it. You see, it wasn't a published novel but a story written by a fan, something generally referred to as fanfic or fanfiction.

What is fanfic?

There are many ways of describing fanfiction – some call it theft, others 'unoriginal drivel', still more have mocked it for being full of badly spelled porn written by teenagers. But if we're looking for a basic description, a fanfic is a story (or comic or video edit) that is based on an original work by someone else. That work could be a novel, a comic book, a television show or film – it could even be based on a podcast or cartoon strip. A particularly 'Marmite' (you love it or you hate it) area of fanfic is Real Person Fiction or RPF, in which the author conjures a story where their favourite pop star is in love with them, or possibly in love with their bandmate, or maybe just running a coffee shop somewhere in the Lower East Side. You would be hard-pressed to describe RPF as being based on an original work by another creative though. Some could possibly be claimed by the public relations experts who feed stories to the tabloids.

It might be easier to say what fanfic is not. It is not profitable. It is not sellable. It is not something that any fan can claim is entirely theirs, even if the particular creative interpretation is their own, as it is grown from the seed of someone else's idea. Fanfiction is written without authorisation or permission. Sometimes an author may be approached by a copyright owner (the original author, their estate or publisher) to write an official prequel or sequel, such as Geraldine McCaughrean's *Peter Pan in Scarlet* (OUP 2006). Commissioned work is not fanfiction; it may have been written by a fan but, because that fan had permission, it doesn't meet the criteria.

So why, in this *Yearbook* designed to help struggling writers and artists find their way into paid creative work, are we talking about fanfic? Because, while we may all dream of *Sunday Times* bestseller lists, Hollywood three-picture-deals, or writing the Great British Novel, we shouldn't lose sight of what brought us here in the first place – the sheer joy of creation. Historically, fanfiction has fallen into something of a grey area. In the early days of the internet, author and publishers pushed back hard by sending 'cease and desist' letters, in some cases to children. Entire fanfiction archive websites disappeared overnight when faced with the wrath of a major studio or publisher. It was standard operating practice for years for fanfiction writers to include a disclaimer at the top of every chapter saying something like: 'I do not own these characters and am writing this story for my own amusement and not for any profit'.

In 2014, UK copyright law was amended to include: 'Fair dealing with a work for the purposes of caricature, parody or pastiche does not infringe copyright in the work'.[1] Many have taken this to mean that fanfiction – so long as it is not generating any money – is legal. As with many questions of legality, the enforcement of this depends upon the creativity of your legal counsel and the flexibility of the judge hearing the case. We are not legal experts here at the *Yearbook* and, should you wish to write something that could be classed as fanfiction for the purposes of profitable publication, we would advise speaking to a lawyer with expertise in copyright law first.

Fanfiction websites

The website Archive of Our Own (AO3; https://archiveofourown.org) looks to US copyright law for protection. On their website AO3 state: '... fanworks are creative and transformative, core fair uses, and [we] will therefore be proactive in protecting and defending fanworks from commercial exploitation and legal challenge.' AO3 is an entirely non-profit, non-commercial endeavour, funded by regular donation drives that ensure the servers stay on and the site stays live; they also maintain a legal support service for fans.

Now, instead of cracking down on fanfic writers, authors are advised by publishers and lawyers not to read any of the fanfiction associated with their works. The fear is that, if an author is known to read fanfic, and if an idea first explored by a fan should surface in a future novel by the original author, then the author could be sued by the fan-writer. I've seen several tweets and blogs by content creators asking people not to send them character musings or sequel ideas, as even reading someone else's take could prevent them from writing a potential sequel.

So, the legal threat to fanfiction is gone but the social stigma remains. Fanfiction is regarded as derivative, lesser, a juvenile pursuit – a reputation that I feel is entirely undeserved. It's time for us to re-evaluate the worth of fanfiction, both as readers and writers.

Why write fanfic?

Do you remember when you were a child? If your toy box was anything like mine,

Fanfiction websites

Archive of Our Own (AO3)

https://archiveofourown.org

The largest fanfiction website in the world, which hosts over 14 million fanworks across over 71,460 fandoms. Established in 2007, this is the main home for fanfic online – especially as it has its own lawyers who work to ensure that fanfic authors are protected from legal threats. Perhaps as a result of this legal protection, AO3 has no formal restrictions on content for publication, though it does ask that all users tag any sexually explicit or potentially problematic work. Any story published with no warning tags in place is automatically placed behind a disclaimer, to prevent people from stumbling across it accidentally. In 2019 AO3 won the Hugo Award for Best Related Work.

Fanfiction.net (FF.net)

www.fanfiction.net

The second largest fanfiction website, started in 1998, has over 12 million registered users and hosts stories in over 40 languages. In comparison to AO3, FF.net has stricter publishing guidelines in terms of what is allowed to be published; no explicit adult fiction is permitted (though some can still be found that has yet to be removed) and anything related to works published by Anne Rice, Laurel K. Hamilton, Robin Hobb and several other authors are also banned at each author's request.

[1] The Copyright and Rights in Performances (Quotation and Parody) Regulations 2014; www.legislation.gov.uk/uksi/2014/2356/regulation/5/made

you never had a full set of everything … a few My Little Ponies, a He-Man, some Barbies and one random Care Bear. Short of the full cast needed to recreate a favourite movie or story, I was forced to create crossover mash-ups: a My Little Pony might rescue Barbie from a kidnapping to thwart the evil plans of He-Man; the next day He-Man might need rescuing from the nefarious clutches of the Care Bear. Fanfic can be like that – take all your favourite characters, throw them into a scenario, and munch some popcorn while they figure it out.

There's a huge amount of freedom in not writing for publication. You get to experiment – to try out new genres or new styles. If you're someone who over-writes, you could hone your short-form writing by taking on the challenge of writing 100-word 'drabbles' or three-sentence stories. If you want to work on your dialogue, you could attempt to tell a story using only speech and see if you can still make it clear who is saying what.

Fanfiction offers many opportunities for writing and style exercises. When you're writing a story set in an established universe some of the heavy lifting is already done – you don't need to describe characters or establish the rules of the world, as your audience already knows them. That leaves you the freedom to focus in on the type of story you want to write. Fanfiction is a great way to practise your writing craft, and it is certainly true that being able to write in someone else's universe – where your audience already knows the rules and you don't have to explain them – is a comforting place to start.

What could I write?

Have you ever wondered what Irene Adler's internal narrative might have been in *Sherlock*? Or Darth Vader's thoughts at the end of *The Empire Strikes Back*? Considering how certain events might have been seen from someone else's point of view is a standard fanfiction trope. Twisting the narrative like this can reveal hidden motivations and may even make sense of some of the apparent plot holes. This is not an approach unique to fanfiction, as many authors have revisited the stories of out-of-copyright characters, as in the reimagining of Mrs Rochester from Charlotte Brontë's *Jane Eyre* (1847) in *Wide Sargasso Sea* (André Deutsch 1966) by Jean Rhys.

Rather than a different point of view, you could try a different universe – or rather an alternate universe (AU). Again, this is a wide-ranging trope, found in well-known creative works such as the film *Apocalypse Now*, an alternate universe retelling of Joseph Conrad's *Heart of Darkness*, or *10 Things I Hate About You*, which brings Shakespeare's *The Taming of the Shrew* into an American high school. In an AU you might find superheroes teaming up as food truck chefs in Manhattan or facing off as coaches of rival sports teams. AUs cover a wide array of possibilities; popular recurring themes include placing all the characters in high school or running a coffee shop together. It's well known now that *Fifty Shades of Grey* (Vintage Books 2011) started life as an AU fanfic of Stephanie Meyer's *Twilight* series (Little, Brown 2005–08).

Another approach to alternate universes is to take a 'what if' approach to a canon moment … What if Sam and Dean Winchester of *Supernatural* were African American? What if Aragorn was female? What if Veronica Mars became an FBI agent? … What changes would this make to the existing canon? Would the Winchesters have had a different reaction from the law-enforcement officers they worked with to kill monsters? Would Aragorn have still been well received as the returning king? Would Veronica have found happiness solving federal crimes? Fanfic gives the writer, and their audience, a way of exploring these possibilities. It's something that Marvel comics have done for years with their *What If ...?* special issues and short runs like *1602* and *Powerless*, so it's not too surprising to find their fans exploring similar ideas in 'fic'.

A type of story which fits within alternate universes but is so common as to have its own label is the crossover. What if Buffy Summers was a Jaeger pilot (*Pacific Rim*) – who would her co-pilot be? Or what would Bilbo Baggins' daemon be? Was Eliot Spencer from *Leverage* ever a member of a Stargate team (the showrunners say he was, but they couldn't get permission to mention it on screen)? It's fun to see fictional universes collide, and the copyright owners have used this to great effect with team-up games such as *Super Smash Bros* or *Kingdom Hearts*, the occasional visit by Mulder and Scully to *The Simpsons*' Springfield, and the massive multi-show crossovers run each year for *Arrow*, *The Flash*, *Legends of Tomorrow* and more.

It's not unusual for fans to be dissatisfied with the twists and turns that the official narrative has taken. Marvel Cinematic Universe fans rebelled en masse, with the #CoulsonLives hashtag, after Coulson's apparent death in *The Avengers*. In time, he was resurrected to lead *Marvel's Agents of SHIELD* television show, but before that happened fanfiction writers had provided myriad examples of how Agent Coulson miraculously survived or mysteriously came back to life, as 'fix-it fics'. Sometimes fix-its are also crossovers, in which characters from one show or book turn up to help solve a problem in another. *Leverage*, featuring Robin-Hood-like criminals, is so popular as a fix-it crossover partner that its characters have helped fix fandoms from *The Avengers* to *The Walking Dead*.

These five tropes barely scratch the surface of the ocean of possibilities there are in fanfiction – it's a very open field and all contributions are welcome.

A final thought

Some people might ask why they should waste their time writing fanfiction when they could be working on an original work for publication. To that I offer three responses:

1. Any form of regular writing practice can make you a better writer.
2. Even if you never get published, writing and sharing fanfic online can connect you to a community of readers, who will generally offer incredibly positive commentary on your work (in over 20 years of writing fanfic I have received a grand total of two negative comments out of thousands). That audience can help you feel pride and delight in your writing on even the most difficult day.
3. Creative hobbies are proven to make people happier[2] – and even better at their day jobs – with a 15–30% increase in positive performance reviews tracked in one study.[3] Happy people are also 12% more productive at work.[4]

[2] 'New research published by the Society for Personality and Social Psychology (and not the Institute of the Completely Obvious, as you may have expected), says that valuing your time more than the pursuit of money leads to feelings of greater wellbeing. And by valuing your time, they mean spending it wisely on hobbies, exercising or being with your family.' Hobbies make us happier – so ignore the mockery, and enjoy,' Fay Schopen; www.theguardian.com/commentisfree/2016/jan/11/hobbies-happier-gardening-bird-watching-stroking-cat

[3] 'One study from San Francisco State University found that people who often engaged in a creative activity scored 15–30% higher on performance rankings. They were also more likely to come up with creative solutions to on-the-job problems." How hobbies can improve your happiness and productivity at work,' Aytekin Tank; https://www.fastcompany.com/90389174/how-hobbies-benefit-your-productivity

[4] 'Economists carried out a number of experiments to test the idea that happy employees work harder. In the laboratory, they found happiness made people around 12% more productive.' https://warwick.ac.uk/newsandevents/pressreleases/new_study_shows

Nobody writes fanfiction to get famous; though some people have made it through the glass ceiling between fan-writer and professional author due to their fanfiction works, they are the exception, not the rule. No, we write fanfiction because it's a creative outlet, and because as fanfic writers we may even develop fans of our own who leave positive feedback on our work and increase our kudos. We write for the joy of creation, the excitement of receiving glowing comments and the accomplishment of finishing a story. We write because we have to, and we write because – although not all of us get to be published – with fanfiction we can all get to be read.

Hari Patience-Davies has been finding joy and fulfilment writing fanfiction for over 20 years, but she won't tell you her AO3 username. Hari is co-founder and Storytelling Coach for Patience Davies Consulting, www.patiencedavies.com.

Harnessing the power of BookTok and social media to promote your writing

Social media has transformed publishing over the past few years, particularly in the way readers and authors 'find' each other. In this article, author Rosie Hewlett explains how she uses BookTok and other platforms to build and maintain a thriving online community.

Until recently, the books that dominated the bestseller lists were exclusively those backed by the largest publishers with costly and carefully curated marketing campaigns. With the recent meteoric rise of BookTok and Bookstagram, however, there has been an exciting shift in the world of book marketing. Due to the power of social media, we can now see readers steering market trends through organic word-of-mouth, catapulting even the smallest indie books into the bestseller charts. Just look at recent successes such as *When the Moon Hatched* by Sarah A. Parker and *Quicksilver* by Callie Hart, both of which were self-published. *When the Moon Hatched* was an 'instant viral sensation' and described as the 'fantasy phenomenon of the year'; it would subsequently be acquired by HarperVoyager in a nine-way auction. Similarly, *Quicksilver* dominated TikTok feeds, topped worldwide bestseller lists and was acquired by Hodderscape in a ten-way auction; film rights were sold recently to Netflix. As indie authors, neither Parker nor Hart had a marketing team or a large-scale budget at their disposal. But just by having social media accounts, these writers had all the resources they needed for success. Through sparking the interest of readers online, both Parker and Hart managed to light the match that would set all of BookTok ablaze. This is a pattern we are seeing more and more frequently; books that have been rejected by publishers are embraced by BookTok and Bookstagram. As an author who self-published her first book, I personally find it very encouraging to see the book market being driven by readers, creating opportunities for all kinds of authors irrespective of the size of the publishing campaign behind them.

But how can you utilise social media to market your book? I know this can seem a daunting prospect for many, especially for those self-publishing or unversed in TikTok and Instagram. There's so much noise generated online that it's hard to know how to cut through and make yourself heard over the chaos. In this article, I am going to outline my advice for authors wishing to traverse the world of social media marketing. I'll start by telling you a little about myself and my experience.

After being unsuccessful in securing a literary agent for my first book, *Medusa*, I decided to self-publish. It is no exaggeration to say I was massively out of my depth here, as I was totally new to the book world and knew next to nothing about publishing. However, in my day job I worked in a creative marketing agency (specifically for Film and TV), so I knew a thing or two about grabbing people's attention online. Even so, it was still a huge undertaking to market a book entirely by myself, and when I started out, I had a grand total of zero followers on Instagram and TikTok. It didn't help that there is great deal of negative 'advice' surrounding self-publishing. I was warned I would be lucky to sell 50 copies in my book's lifetime, and that self-publishing would ruin any future chances of being traditionally published. I am happy to report that both warnings were entirely false. Since publication, *Medusa* has sold over 10,000 copies and has garnered such a great following that it has now been picked up by Penguin Random House to be re-released in September 2025. Additionally, I signed a two-book deal with Penguin Random House and my second book, *Medea*, became an instant *Sunday Times* bestseller in Spring 2024. I firmly believe that the online community I managed to build when self-publishing *Medusa* is one of the main reasons why *Medea* was able to hit number three on that chart.

Whilst I do not claim to be an expert in social media marketing, I feel I have learnt a great deal through publishing *Medusa* and *Medea*. But here are my top tips for making the most of social media to promote your writing.

Word-of-mouth

The most powerful tool social media offers authors is word-of-mouth. You can shout endlessly about your book on your own account, but unless you're an established author with a loyal following, people are far more likely to listen to recommendations from other readers. Whilst you still want to be posting your own content (which I will discuss below), it is important to also encourage readers to post about your book. The key ways authors can achieve this are:

• **Advanced reader copies (ARCs)** – this was the main way I built a buzz for *Medusa*, by reaching out to readers on BookTok and Bookstagram and offering them a free ARC in exchange for an honest review. Positive reader reviews are invaluable for authors, especially if they share them on their social channels and have a decent following of fellow book-lovers. My main advice here is not to send your book to everyone and anyone, though. Take the time to do your research, make sure you are connecting with readers you know are fans of your genre and who have enjoyed similar books; that way, they are much more likely to accept your ARC and, most importantly, actually enjoy and post about it! I spent many, many hours scrolling through readers' Instagrams and TikToks, narrowing my search down to those who expressed a particular love for Greek mythology. By being selective about the readers I approached, I was able to have a far higher success rate in those who actually ended up sharing a positive review. I would also advise sending hard copies over ebooks, as this gives readers something tangible to photograph and share. In total, I sent ARCs of Medusa to approximately 40 readers, which generated enough of an online buzz on the build-up to publication to allow me to earn a promising number of pre-orders.

• **Giveaways** – these are another way you can encourage readers to post about your book whilst also growing your following. For both *Medusa* and *Medea*, I ran several giveaways on my social channels, offering readers the chance to win a signed ARC. To enter the giveaway, all readers had to do was follow me, comment on the post, and share it on their stories. This is an easy way to generate engagement that will boost the algorithm in your favour, bringing more eyes to your page and, hopefully, more followers, whilst also generating shareable content for your book.

Creating content

As well as encouraging readers to post, you need to ensure you are also sharing your own content on a regular basis. People with large followings on TikTok often post daily, if not twice a day! I know it can seem overwhelming having to create so much content, but here are some things to consider that will hopefully help generate ideas:

• **Have a clear, concise hook** – people's attention spans are extremely short, especially when scrolling through TikTok. You have mere seconds to work with, so it's imperative you have a short, snappy hook for your book that succinctly captures its essence. A recent example of this is Laura Steven's one-line sell for her latest book *Our Infinite Fates*: 'they've loved each other in a thousand lifetimes, they've killed each other in every one.' This is a brilliantly impactful hook; it immediately grabs your attention, giving you a clear idea of what the book is about whilst also making you want to know more. If you look on Steven's socials, you can see she repeatedly shared this line, often accompanied with just a video of the book's beautiful cover. These posts generated fantastic engagement and ultimately proved very successful as *Our Infinite Fates* became a number one *New York Times* bestseller. Being able to distil your book down into a single line is an incredibly effective way of leaving a quick yet memorable mark on readers, which suits the fast-paced landscape of TikTok and Instagram.

• **Lean into trends** – Though TikTok's algorithm can seem a mystery, the best way to gain views is to utilise trending audio. If the term has you immediately feeling out of your depth, my advice would be to firstly download TikTok and simply start scrolling. You'll quickly find there are certain audio clips or song snippets that appear repeatedly on your feed, often being used in similar contexts – this is what we call a 'trending audio'. When this happens, the TikTok algorithm will automatically push all videos using that sound onto people's feeds, making it a great way to maximise views. However, you cannot simply slap music onto a video of your book and expect strong engagement – you must first understand the context of the trend and play into it. This is where you need to be creative – how can you harness a trend to suit your book, what elements can you manipulate to crossover? All marketing requires imagination: that's part of the challenge and the fun. If you still feel overwhelmed, I advise following other authors on TikTok. There are lots of clever and innovative ways authors are marketing themselves online, so go out there, start scrolling and find some inspiration!

• **Visuals are important** – I know we authors are drawn to the written word, but don't forget that TikTok and Instagram are primarily focused on visual content. Personally, I have found 'mood reels' are an impactful marketing strategy, using a montage of images to convey my book's vibe and tone, accompanied with a quote or the 'hook' I talked about earlier. Additionally, character art has recently proven popular on Instagram. Finding an artist to capture a scene from your story is a great way to entice readers, especially if you can pair it with trending audio as mentioned above. Lastly, don't ever underestimate the power of a pretty photo. Some of my most popular posts on Instagram are just aesthetic photos of *Medea* and *Medusa* – because let's face it, we definitely do judge books by their covers, so make sure you give your book a worthy photoshoot!

Market yourself

It's important to remember that you are not just marketing your book, but also yourself. You want to build an audience that you can grow and cultivate throughout your career and your future books. As writers, I know many of us are far more comfortable hiding behind our laptops, but you'll find the authors with the largest followings on social media are those who are willing to share themselves as well as their books. I have a few suggestions below on how you can start doing this:

- **A Day in the Life** – my most successful video on TikTok (with over 100k views to date) was me filming a normal day in my life as an author. It may be surprising to some, but these types of videos are very popular on TikTok. You might think your day-to-day is too mundane to share, but don't forget that readers are always fascinated to see the magic behind a book's creation. By sharing your daily life and writing process, you will start building an audience that is invested in both you and your work.
- **Sharing your experience** – I have found that both readers and aspiring writers love to hear about author's experiences. My second most successful video on TikTok is one where I shared my struggles with publishing *Medusa* and my ultimate success when landing a deal with Penguin Random House. So, don't be afraid to be vulnerable. People will find you more authentic if you are willing to talk about the lows of writing and publishing as well as the highs. Sharing your experiences is also a great way to generate content for those who haven't yet finished writing their books. People love to follow the author process, and if you can start building a large following early on, it can be a great incentive when pitching to agents and publishers down the line.
- **Building relationships** – You shouldn't view social media as just a tool for generating sales, but rather a platform to build a community and connect with readers. As I said above, you want to cultivate a readership that will support you throughout your career. Thankfully, this is very easy to do. Just take the time to engage with your readers – reply to their comments, like their pictures, share their posts. The community I've built through publishing *Medusa* and *Medea* has been the most rewarding part of my author experience, and I know I owe everything to my lovely readers who have continued to support me! Social media is also a great way to connect with other authors, creating a network of writers who support and celebrate each other's work.

I know the likes of Booktok and Bookstagram can seem daunting from the outset, but these platforms offer incredibly exciting opportunities for authors. I truly hope the tips I have shared here will help you feel confident when it comes to online marketing, allowing you to build your readership and see your book soar into the bestseller lists.

Rosie Hewlett is a *Sunday Times* bestselling writer. Passionate about showcasing strong female voices from the ancient world, she is the author of *Medusa* (initially self-published but re-releasing in September 2025 by Penguin Random House) and *Medea* (Penguin Random House 2024). Follow her on Instagram @rosiehewlett.author.

ISBNs: what you need to know

The BookData ISBN Agency for UK & Ireland receives a large number of enquiries about the ISBN system. The most frequently asked questions are answered here; for more information visit www.nielsenisbnstore.com.

Contact details

BookData ISBN Agency for UK and Ireland
3rd Floor, Station Place, Argyle Way,
Stevenage SG1 2AD
tel (01483) 712215
email isbn.agency@nielseniq.com
website www.nielsenisbnstore.com

What is an ISBN?

An ISBN is an International Standard Book Number and is 13 digits long.

What is the purpose of an ISBN?

An ISBN is a product number, used by publishers, booksellers and libraries for ordering, listing and stock control purposes. It enables them to identify a particular publisher and allows the publisher to identify a specific edition of a specific title in a specific format within their output.

Does an ISBN protect copyright?

A widely held misconception is that an ISBN protects copyright. The copyright belongs to the author and in the UK authors are protected by the Berne Convention, more information available here: *Berne Convention for the Protection of Literary and Artistic Works* (www.wipo.int/treaties/en/ip/berne). In general, publishers don't tend to buy copyrights for books. They license the copyrights, which the author retains.

What is a publisher?

The publisher is generally the person or organisation taking the financial and other risks in making a product available. For example, if a product goes on sale and sells no copies at all, the publisher loses money. If you get paid anyway, you are likely to be a designer, printer, author or consultant of some kind.

What is the format of an ISBN?

The ISBN is 13 digits long and is divided into five parts separated by spaces or hyphens.

- Prefix element: for the foreseeable future this will be 978 or 979.
- Registration group element: identifies a geographic or national grouping. It shows where the publisher is based.
- Registrant element: identifies a specific publisher or imprint.
- Publication element: identifies a specific edition of a specific title in a specific format.
- Check digit: the final digit which mathematically validates the rest of the number.

The four parts following the prefix element can be of varying length. Prior to 1 January 2007, ISBNs were ten digits long; any existing ten-digit ISBNs must be converted by prefixing them with '978' and the check digit must be recalculated using a Modulus 10 system with alternate weights of 1 and 3. The ISBN Agency can help you with this.

Do I *have* to have an ISBN?

There is no legal requirement in the UK and Ireland for an ISBN and it conveys no form of legal or copyright protection. It is simply a product identification number.

Why should I use an ISBN?

If you wish to sell your publication through major bookselling chains, independent bookshops or internet retailers, they will require you to have an ISBN to assist their internal processing and ordering systems.

The ISBN also provides access to bibliographic databases, such as the Nielsen BookData Database, which use ISBNs as references. These databases help booksellers and libraries to provide information for customers. Nielsen BookData has a range of bibliographic metadata and retail sales monitoring services which use ISBNs and are vital for the dissemination, trading and monitoring of books in the supply chain. The ISBN therefore provides access to additional marketing opportunities which could help sales of your product.

Where can I get an ISBN?

ISBNs are assigned to publishers in the country where the publisher's main office is based. This is irrespective of the language of the publication or the intended market for the book. ISBNs are geo-specific and must be acquired from the ISBN Agency in the country where you are based and publishing from. Each country has a National ISBN Agency that supplies ISBNs only to publishers within their territories.

The BookData ISBN Agency is the national agency for the UK, Republic of Ireland, and British Overseas Territories. If you are based in the UK and Ireland, you can purchase ISBNs online from the BookData ISBN Store: www.nielsenisbnstore.com.

A publisher based elsewhere will not be able to get ISBNs from the UK Agency (even if you are a British Citizen) but you can contact the International ISBN Agency for further information via their website www.isbn-international.org/agencies. Having a non-UK ISBN does not preclude you from registering your book for the UK trade with BookData or to sell your book through UK bookshops.

How long does it take to get an ISBN?

If you purchase your ISBNs online from the BookData ISBN Store you will receive your ISBN allocation within minutes. If you are purchasing ISBNs direct from the ISBN Agency via an off-line application, it can take up to five days. The processing period begins when a correctly completed application is received in the ISBN Agency and payment is received.

How much does it cost to get an ISBN?

ISBNs can be bought individually or in blocks of ten or more. Refer to www.nielsenisbnstore.com or email the ISBN Agency: isbn.agency@nielseniq.com.

Who is eligible for ISBNs?

Any individual or organisation who is publishing a qualifying product for general sale or distribution to the market. By publishing we mean making a work available to the public.

Which products do NOT qualify for ISBNs?

Any publication that is without a defined end should not be assigned an ISBN. For example, publications that are regularly updated and intended to continue indefinitely are not eligible for an ISBN.

Some examples of products that do not qualify for an ISBN are:

- Journals, periodicals, serials, newspapers in their entirety (single issues or articles, where these are made available separately, may qualify for ISBN);
- Abstract entities such as textual works and other abstract creations of intellectual or artistic content;
- Ephemeral printed materials such as advertising matter and the like;

• Customised print-on-demand publications (Publications that are available only on a limited basis, such as customised print-on-demand publications with content specifically tailored to a user's request shall not be assigned an ISBN. If a customised publication is being made available for wider sale, e.g. as a college course pack available through a college book store, then an ISBN may be assigned);
• Printed music;
• Art prints and art folders without title page and text;
• Personal documents (such as a curriculum vitae or personal profile);
• Greetings cards;
• Music sound recordings;
• Software that is intended for any purpose other than educational or instructional;
• Electronic bulletin boards;
• Emails and other digital correspondence;
• Updating websites;
• Games.

Following a review of the UK market, it is now permissible for ISBNs to be assigned to calendars and diaries, provided that they are not intended for purely time-management purposes and that a substantial proportion of their content is textual or graphic.

What is an ISSN?

An International Standard Serial Number. This is the numbering system for journals, magazines, periodicals, newspapers and newsletters. It is administered by the British Library, contact *tel* (01937) 546959 or *email* issn-uk@bl.uk.

Where do I put the ISBN?

The ISBN should appear on the reverse of the title page, sometimes called the copyright page or the imprint page, and on the outside back cover of the book. If the book has a dust jacket, the ISBN should also appear on the back of this. If the publication is not a book, the ISBN should appear on the product, and on the packaging or inlay card. If the publication is a map, the ISBN should be visible when the map is folded and should also appear near the publisher statement if this is elsewhere.

I am reprinting a book with no changes – do I need a new ISBN?

No.

I am reprinting a book but adding a new chapter – do I need a new ISBN?

Yes. You are adding a significant amount of additional material and altering the content of the book.

I am reprinting a book with a new cover design – should I change the ISBN?

No. A change of cover design with no changes to the title, author name, or content of the book does not need to have a new ISBN.

I am changing the binding from hardback to paperback. Do I need a new ISBN?

Yes. Changes in binding always require new ISBNs even if there are no changes to the content of the book.

I am changing the price – do I need a new ISBN?

No. Price changes with no other changes do not require new ISBNs and in fact must not change the ISBN.

Indexing

A good index is essential to the user of a non-fiction book; a bad index will let down an otherwise excellent book. The functions of indexes, and the skills needed to compile them, are explained here by the Society of Indexers.

An index is a detailed key to the contents of a document, unlike a contents list, which shows only the sections into which the document is divided (e.g. chapters). An index guides readers to information by providing a systematic arrangement of entries (single words, phrases, acronyms, names and so on) in a suitably organised list (usually alphabetical) that refers them to specific locations using page, column, section, frame, figure, table, paragraph, line or other appropriate numbers or hyperlinks.

Professional indexing

A well-crafted index produced by a skilled professional with appropriate subject expertise is an essential feature of almost every non-fiction book. A professional indexer has subject knowledge and considers the text from the readers' perspective, anticipating how they will approach the subject and what language they will use. The indexer analyses the content of the text and provides a carefully structured index to guide readers efficiently into the main text of the book.

A detailed, comprehensive and regularly updated Directory of Professional Indexers is on the Society of Indexers' website. Professional competence is recognised in three stages by the Society. Professional Members (MSocInd) have successfully completed initial training (see below) or have many years' continuous experience. Advanced Professional Members (MSocInd(Adv)) have demonstrated skills and experience gained since their initial training, while Fellows of the Society of Indexers (FSocInd) have undergone a rigorous Fellowship pathway, revised in 2022, to demonstrate both continuing professional development and evaluation of their index quality.

Indexing fees depend on many factors, particularly the complexity of the text, but for a straightforward text the Society recommends (as of 2025) £32.70 an hour, £3.65 per page, or £9.90 per 1,000 words. Indexing should normally be organised by the publisher, but may be left to the author to do or to arrange. It is rarely a popular task with authors, and they are often not well suited to the task, which takes objectivity, perspective, speed, patience, attention to detail and, above all, training, experience and specialist software. Moreover, authors are generally too close to the text by this stage.

Ebooks and other electronic material

An index is necessary for ebooks and other electronic material. It is a complete myth that users of ebooks can rely solely on keyword-based retrieval systems; these pick out far too much information to be usable and far too little to be reliable. Only careful analysis by the human brain creates suitable index terms for non-fiction ebooks. There are no shortcuts for judging relevance, for extracting meaning and significance from the text, for identifying complex concepts, or for recognising different ways of expressing similar ideas. Index entries must also be properly linked to the text when a printed book is converted into an ebook. Linked indexes can be achieved via the technique of embedded indexing, where index entries are anchored within the text at their precise location.

The Society of Indexers

The Society of Indexers was founded in 1957 and is the only autonomous professional body for indexers in the UK. The main objectives of the Society are to promote high standards in all types of indexing and highlight the role of indexers in the organisation of knowledge; to provide, promote and recognise facilities for both the initial and the further training of indexers; to establish criteria for assessing conformity to indexing standards; and to conduct research and publish guidance, ideas and information about indexing.

The Society holds an annual conference and publishes *The Indexer* journal, the *SIdelights* member newsletter and other occasional publications, with further resources on its website. It runs several local groups and ongoing CPD sessions, both in person and online, including a mentoring scheme for new professionals, to foster member-to-member communications, professional development and mutual support. The Society also instigated a National Indexing Day (#IndexDay), which takes place each March, to commemorate its founding date, to celebrate indexes and indexers and to provide events for publishers to learn more about indexing.

Further information

Society of Indexers
Woodbourn Business Centre, 10 Jessell Street, Sheffield S9 3HY
tel 0114 453 4928
email admin@indexers.org.uk
website www.indexers.org.uk
X @indexers
Membership (2025) new member £127.50 p.a. (including 25% discount valid for first year of membership); standard membership £170 p.a.

Indexing as a career

Indexing is often taken up as a second career, frequently drawing on expertise developed in some other field. Both intellectually demanding and creative, it requires considerable and sustained mental effort. Indexers need to be well-organised, flexible, disciplined and self-motivated, and resilient enough to cope with the uncertainties of freelance work. The Society of Indexers' long-established training course, which has received the CILIP Seal of Recognition (see CILIP page 550), gives a thorough grounding in indexing principles and practice on real documents. Based on the principle of open learning, it enables students to learn in their own way and at their own pace. There is access to study materials, practice exercises and quizzes, and links to a wide range of useful resources. Online tutorials are undertaken at various stages during the course. After completing the four assessed modules, which cover the core indexing skills, students undertake a book-length practical indexing assignment. Successful completion of the course leads to Accreditation, designation as a Professional Indexer (MSocInd), and entry in the Society's online *Directory of Professional Indexers*.

Further reading

Booth, P.F., *Indexing: The Manual of Good Practice* (K.G. Saur 2001)

British Standards Institution, *British Standard Recommendations for Examining Documents, Determining their Subjects and Selecting Indexing Terms* (BS6529:1984)

'Indexes' (chapter from *The Chicago Manual of Style*, 18th edn; University of Chicago Press 2024)

International Organization for Standardization, *Information and Documentation – Guidelines for the Content, Organization and Presentation of Indexes* (ISO 999:1996)

Mulvany, N.C., *Indexing Books* (University of Chicago Press, 2nd edn 2005)

Stauber, D.M., *Facing the Text: Content and Structure in Book Indexing* (Cedar Row Press 2004)

Publishing services for independent authors

This is a selection of the expanding list of companies that offer editorial, production, marketing and distribution support predominantly (but not exclusively) for authors who want to publish independently. As with all the organisations mentioned in the *Yearbook*, we recommend that you check carefully what companies offer and their fees; also be aware of any minimum commitment requirements. A longer list of companies and individuals who provide similar services is included in our subscription service: www.writersandartists.co.uk/shop/subscriptions.

POD = print on demand

AESOP (All Editorial Services Online for Publishers & Writers)

28A Abberbury Road, Iffley, Oxford OX4 4ES
tel 07933 331977
email aesop@copyedit.co.uk
website www.copyedit.co.uk
Contact Martin Noble

Services include copy-editing, rewriting, proofreading, indexing and editorial reports and reviews. Advice to publishers, authors and literary agents also available, as is support with ghostwriting, novelisation, research and fact-checking. Extensive range of topics and genres covered. Founded 1979.

Aimée Hill | AJ Editorial Services

email aimee@ajeditorialservices.com
website www.ajeditorialservices.com
X @AjEditorial
Bluesky @aimeehill.bsky.social

Developmental editing and copy-editing for fantasy, sci-fi and contemporary fiction. Works with UK and US English using New Hart's and CMOS. Intermediate member of the Chartered Institute of Editing and Proofreading and rated Excellent as a partner member of the Alliance of Independent Authors.

A1 Book Publishing UK

Room 1, 48 Park Road, Birmingham B13 8AH
tel 0800 002 911
email a1help@qualityservice.com
website https://a1proofreading.co.uk/a1-book-publishing-uk
Facebook www.facebook.com/A1-Book-Publishing-UK-240624720597580/
Contact Ian Melling

Editorial services for self-publishing authors, including proofreading manuscripts (£9.99 per 1,000 words), book covers, book design and eBook conversion. KDP/Amazon publishing service available for £245. Distribution and marketing support also available. Founded 2012.

Suzanne Arnold

email suzanne@suzannearnold.com
website www.suzannearnold.com
Facebook www.facebook.com/suzannearnoldeditor
Bluesky @suzannearnold.com.bsky.social
Instagram @suzanne_arnold_editor

Non-fiction for adults: manuscript assessments, developmental editing (big picture, structure), copy-editing (spelling, grammar and consistency) and proofreading. Advanced Professional Member of the Chartered Institute of Editing and Proofreading with over 25 years' experience working for publishers and businesses.

Betterwrite

107A Maas Road, Birmingham B31 2PP
tel 0121 475 5876
email robertmatthews_edit@yahoo.co.uk
website https://betterwrite.com
Contact Rob Matthews

Experienced team of handpicked editors, all members of the Chartered Institute of Editing and Proofreading, working across multiple fiction genres: crime/thriller/mystery, adventure/fantasy/romance, sci-fi, historical, children's books, YA fiction and commercial women's fiction. Offers a straightforward personal service by email for independent fiction writers: authors are matched with the most appropriate editor and their text prepared for publication or self-publication. Structural, developmental, copy-editing and line-editing available. See website for full details; payment by instalment available. Founded 2015.

Bookblast® CIC

PO Box 20184, London W10 5AU
tel 020-8968 3089
email mss@bookblast.com
website www.bookblast.com
Instagram @bookblastoffical
Founder Georgia de Chamberet

Writing agency offering editorial, translation (French to English), promotional and consultancy services to the book trade and writing professionals. Also manages literary estates and promotes cultural diversity by breaking or relaunching quality writing and a multitude of voices from around the world into the mainstream. Founded 1997.

BookPrinting UK

Remus House, Coltsfoot Drive, Woodston, Peterborough PE2 9BF
tel (01733) 898102
email info@bookprintinguk.com
website www.bookprintinguk.com
X @BookPrintingUK

Colour and b&w printing and POD books in a range of bindings. Can provide custom illustration and interior layout options, as well as typesetting. Supplies templates for formatting manuscript files before sending. Can also distribute print books direct to customers. Prints bookmarks, posters and flyers.

Janey Burton

email janey@janeyburton.com
website https://janeyburton.com/
Facebook www.facebook.com/JaneyBurtonEditor/

Experienced publishing consultant, editor and contracts negotiator. Services offered include: mini consultation (fiction and non-fiction), contracts consultation and negotiation, manuscript assessment. Prices and booking information available on the website. Also see online for a blog for authors and to sign up for the monthly newsletter, *The Inbox Edition*.

Cameron Publicity and Marketing Ltd

4th Floor, 49 St James's Street, London SW1A 1AH
tel 020-7917 9812
email info@cameronpm.co.uk
website www.cameronpm.co.uk
Facebook www.facebook.com/CameronPublicity
X @CameronPMtweets
Director Ben Cameron

Publicity and marketing campaigns for publishers and independent authors including media awareness, websites and social media. Founded 2006.

The Choir Press

132 Bristol Road, Gloucester GL1 5SR
tel (01452) 500016
email enquiries@thechoirpress.co.uk
website www.selfpublishingbooks.co.uk
Contact Rachel Woodman

Self-publishing services, including print-on-demand distribution, copy-editing, book design and layout, and preparation of print-ready files. See website for fee information. Author visits by arrangement. Founded 1982.

The Conrad Press Ltd

43 Nunnery Fields, Canterbury, Kent CT1 3JT
tel (01227) 472874, 07831 259889
email writingandeditingoffice@theconradpress.com
website www.theconradpress.com
Facebook www.facebook.com/theconradpress
X @theconradpress
Instagram @theconradpressltd_
Managing Director James Essinger, *Deputy Managing Director* Zoe Verner

Subsidy publisher: authors make a contribution to the publishing costs but these are refunded from book sales revenue. All genres covered, including novels, children's books (no picture books), YA fiction and non-fiction, memoirs, short stories and collections of poetry. Founded 2015.

Consulting Cops for Writers

2 Rose Cottages, Boreham, Essex CM3 3HR
tel 07968 582423
email enquiries@consultingcops.com
website www.consultingcops.com
X @ConsultingCops
Instagram @consultingcops
Owner & Founder Lyndon Smith

Experienced team of serving and former police officers/staff, offering to match writers' crime-related work with the relevant expert and supply them with the information needed to ensure projects read authentically. Services include: scene/chapter/whole project review; research; consultation. Website contains a variety of useful author aids, including police ranks, acronyms, phonetic alphabet and websites to assist with further research.

Cornerstones

5th Floor, 167–169 Great Portland Street, London W1W 5PF
email helen@cornerstones.co.uk
website https://cornerstones.co.uk
Facebook www.facebook.com/CornerstonesUK
X @CornerstonesLit
Instagram @cornerstoneslit
Founder Helen Bryant, *Managing Editor* Kate Padiachy

Transatlantic literary consultancy. Editorial packages include industry-style reader's reports, one-to-one mentoring, final-stage copy-editing and proofreading, as well as the intensive Edit Your Novel online course. Founded 1998.

Ingrid Cranfield

16 Myddelton Gardens, London N21 2PA
tel 020-8360 2433, 07708 608787
email ingrid@ingridcranfield.co.uk
website https://ingridcranfield.co.uk
Facebook www.facebook.com/ingrid.cranfield

Advisory and editorial services for authors, publishers and media, including critical assessment and

appraisal, developmental editing, copy-editing, rewriting, proofreading, research, interviews; also training in editing and proofreading, creation of guidelines for authors. Special interests: geography, travel, exploration, adventure; language and literacy; government and politics; education; art and architecture (including Japanese); family histories. Translations from German and French.
Founded 1972.

Andrew Crofts

email CroftsA@aol.com
website https://andrewcrofts.com

Experienced and bestselling ghostwriter and author; more than 80 books published. Also guides clients through independent publishing processes.

eBookPartnership.com

7 Bell Yard, London WC2A 2JR
email helpdesk@ebookpartnership.com
website www.ebookpartnership.com
X @ebookpartners

Ebook conversion service, producing digital files for authors, publishers and content owners worldwide. Also POD and worldwide distribution for clients, who can access daily reports and submit changes 24/7. Network includes retailers, subscription services and e-libraries. Founded 2010.

Editegrity

email kelly@editegrity.com
Facebook www.facebook.com/kellyeurgan
X @editegrity
Instagram @editegrity
Contact Kelly Urgan

Offers proofreading, developmental and copy-editing for both traditionally published and self-publishing authors. Non-fiction topics include history, travel, creative non-fiction. Fiction genre specialisms include YA, historical fiction, fantasy, romance and sci-fi. Proficient in both US and UK English. Member of the Chartered Institute of Editing and Proofreading and the Historical Novel Society.

Finish Your Novel

email info@finishyournovel.org
website www.finishyournovel.org
Mentors Clare Allan, Alexandra Benedict, Jonathan Myerson

Bespoke mentoring service from the former directors of the Novel Writing MA at City University London, all of whom have extensive experience in guiding writers from first idea to finished manuscript. Taster sessions available. Also offered: full draft readings; specialist webinars; and a range of support tailored to specific needs. See website for pricing information.

Fuzzy Flamingo

23 Haddonian Way, Market Harborough LE16 9GD
tel 07588 966425
email contact@fuzzyflamingo.co.uk
website https://fuzzyflamingo.co.uk/
Facebook www.facebook.com/FuzzyFlamingoDesign
X @FlamingoFuzzy
Editor Jen Parker

Design and editing services as well as self-publishing packages for children's and YA authors and multi-author collaborations.

Gecko Edit

email kath@geckoedit.com
website www.geckoedit.com
Facebook www.facebook.com/GeckoEdit/
Contact Katherine Kirk

Offers professional line editing, copy-editing, typesetting, and proofreading services for self-published and traditionally published authors of adult and young adult science fiction, fantasy, speculative fiction, romance, romantasy, book club fiction and historical fiction. Specializes in US English (CMOS). Advanced Professional member of the Chartered Institute of Editing and Proofreading. Fees listed on website. Founded 2020.

Glassboxx

Oxford House, 12–20 Oxford Street, Newbury RG14 1JB
tel (01635) 581185
email info@glassboxx.com
website https://glassboxx.com
X @glassboxx
Instagram @glassboxxbooks

Ecommerce solution that enables publishers and retailers to sell digital and print books directly to readers with flexible DRM. Also offers merchant services and end-user support and has been awarded a Stationers' Warrant for excellence in innovation.

Grammar Factory Publishing

3906–25 Telegram Mews, Toronto, ON M5V 3Z1, Canada
email info@grammarfactory.com
website https://grammarfactory.com
Executive Publisher Scott MacMillan

Professional service publisher offering ghostwriting, editing and publishing services; customers include speakers, business leaders and entrepreneurs.

Grosvenor House Publishing

Link House, 140 The Broadway, Tolworth, Surrey KT6 7HT
tel 020-8339 6060
website www.grosvenorhousepublishing.co.uk
Facebook www.facebook.com/GrosvenorHousePublishing
Founder Kim Cross

Publishes across a range of genres including children's and non-fiction in colour, b&w, POD, paperback, hardback and ebook formats. Offers a

£795 publishing package which includes typesetting and five free print copies as well as an ISBN, and print and ebook distribution via online retailers. Marketing services include producing posters and postcards, and website set-up from template with two years' hosting. Ebook publishing costs £195 if the print edition of the book has been produced by the company and £495 otherwise. Print costs and royalties depend on book specification. A proofreading service is offered at a rate of £5 per 1,000 words. See website for full list of costs.

HelpMePublish Consultancy

61a Great Titchfield St, London W1W 7PP
tel 07710 523591
email info@helpmepublish.co.uk
website www.helpmepublish.co.uk
Contacts Brian Jarman, Annabel Hughes

Offers ghostwriting, proofreading and editing services, as well as advice for authors on how to get their work published, from finding an agent to self-publishing. See website for information on rates and how to book an initial consultation.

Indexing Specialists (UK) Ltd

29 Norway Street, Portslade BN41 1GN
email indexers@indexing.co.uk
website www.indexing.co.uk
Contact Milla Hills

Experienced indexers for all types of books and encyclopedias, on professional, scientific and general subjects. Large projects involving multiple indexers can be arranged. Founded 1965.

The Inkwell Group

The Old Post Office, Kilmacanogue,
Co. Wicklow A98 V215, Republic of Ireland
tel +353 (0)1 276 5921, +353 (0)87 283 5382
email vanessa@inkwellwriters.ie
website www.inkwellwriters.ie
Contact Vanessa Fox O'Loughlin

Literary consultancy providing industry-led critique, readers reports and editing services, plus career-strategy consultancy. Also offers a full range of 'Getting Published' events and workshops for festivals and organisations. Founded 2006.

Jelly Bean Self-Publishing

Candy Jar Ltd, Mackintosh House,
136 Newport Road, Cardiff CF24 1DJ
tel 029-211 5702
email submissions@jellybeanselfpublishing.co.uk
website www.jellybeanselfpublishing.co.uk
Director Shaun Russell

Self-publishing imprint of Candy Jar Books. Bespoke services including editing, typesetting, illustration, cover design, audiobook production and marketing support. Can accommodate authors of various genres, budgets and timetables. Welsh Self-Publisher of the Year 2020. Founded 2012.

Journey Books

Bradt Guides, 31a High Street, Chesham,
Bucks. HP5 1BW
tel (01753) 893444
email journeybooks@bradtguides.com
website www.bradtguides.com/journeybooks/

Contract publishing imprint from travel publisher, Bradt Guides. Offers a range of publishing services, from an initial editorial report to full trade publication with professional editing, typesetting, design and worldwide distribution for print and ebooks. A particular expertise in travel-related books but will consider all proposals. Suitable for both first-timers and previously published authors looking to publish independently. See website for full range of packages and pricing.

The JQ Ghostwriting Agency

17 Carlton House Terrace, London SW1Y 5AH
tel 07396 344505
email joey@jq-agency.co.uk
website www.jq-agency.co.uk
Editor Joey Quince

Specialist ghostwriter of memoir, sports memoir and historical fiction, taking authors from seed concept to final draft.

Kindle Direct Publishing

website https://kdp.amazon.com
Facebook www.facebook.com/KindleDirectPublishing
X @AmazonKDP

Ebook self-publishing and distribution platform for Kindle and Kindle Apps. Its business model offers up to a 70% royalty (on certain retail prices between $2.99–$9.99) in many countries and availability in Amazon stores worldwide. POD options are also available. Books are made exclusive to Amazon (which means they cannot be sold through an author's personal website, for example), but authors can share in the KDP every time the book is borrowed from the Kindle Owners' Lending Library.

Kobo Writing Life

email writinglife@kobo.com
website www.kobo.com/p/writinglife
Facebook www.facebook.com/KoboWritingLife
X @kobowritinglife
Instagram @kobo.writing.life

Ebook self-publishing platform where authors can upload manuscripts and cover images. These files are then converted into ebooks before being distributed through the Kobo Store. Authors are able to set pricing and DRM territories, as well as track sales. Royalty rates vary depending on price or territory; enquire directly. Free to join. Owned by Rakuten.

Bryony Leah Editorial

email bryony@bryonyleah.com
website www.bryonyleah.com
Instagram @bryony_leah

Professional fiction editor offering line editing, copy-editing, and proofreading services for self-publishing and independent authors. Over ten years' experience writing and editing fiction in UK and US English. Preferred genres include: romance (all sub-genres and heat levels), contemporary, new adult, women's fiction, YA, romantasy, and any form of love story. Manuscript assessments and additional editorial services also available (see website). Professional Member of the Chartered Institute of Editing and Proofreading, the Editorial Freelancers Association, and ACES: The Society For Editing.

Liminal Pages

3rd Floor, 86–90 Paul Street, London EC2A 4NE
email sophie@liminalpages.com
website https://liminalpages.com
Facebook www.facebook.com/liminalpages
Contact Sophie Playle

Online training for freelance editors to run their own business, including skills such as copy-editing, developmental fiction editing and more. Founded 2013.

The Literary Consultancy (TLC)

East Side, Kings Cross Station, London N1C 4AX
tel 020-3751 0757 (ext. 800)
email info@literaryconsultancy.co.uk
website https://literaryconsultancy.co.uk
Instagram @theliteraryconsultancy
Director Aki Schilz, *Head of Writing Services* Joe Sedgwick

Supports writers of fiction, non-fiction, poetry, scripts and children's books. Offers a range of services for writers at all levels, including manuscript assessment, developmental editing, and editor one-to-ones. Also online and in-person mentoring, and a membership programme, 'Being A Writer'. Fees vary depending on service. Industry links with agents and publishers. Approved by Arts Council England. Founded 1996.

Local Legend

email peace@local-legend.co.uk
website https://local-legend.co.uk
Facebook www.facebook.com/locallegendpublishing
Instagram @locallegendpublishing
Contact Nigel Peace

Independent, not-for-profit company publishing paperbacks and eBooks in the Mind, Body & Spirit genre. Finished books are distributed for sale worldwide through physical and online book stores and on all digital platforms. A biannual Spiritual Writing Competition is offered and titles have won several other national prizes. Email synopsis and sample chapters to the address above. Fiction and non-fiction accepted. Note that a publishing fee is charged to cover costs, as is an annual market distribution fee; royalties are paid half-yearly.

The London Ghostwriting Company

3rd Floor, 207 Regent Street, London W1B 3HH
tel 020 7193 8257
email enquiries@londonghostwriting.com
website https://londonghostwriting.com/
X @LGC_ghost
Founder Luke Shipman

Editorial and ghostwriting services for authors, agents, publishers and new writers. Provides clients with print-ready, ghostwritten manuscripts, screenplays and story solutions across genre, story type and format. Fiction and non-fiction. Full list of writing and consultancy services can be found on the website. Founded 2016.

Nicky Lovick

tel 07971 829252
email nickylovick@gmail.com
website https://nickylovick.com
X @LovickNicky

Book editor with more than 20 years' experience in structural editing, copy-editing and proofreading. Specialises in women's commercial fiction, crime and thrillers. Works for both top five and independent publishers.

Mereo Books

2nd Floor, 6–8 Dyer Street, Cirencester, Glos. GL7 2PF
tel 020-3286 8686
email info@mereobooks.co.uk
website www.mereobooks.com
X @MereoBooks
Director Antonia Tingle, *Editor-in-Chief* Chris Newton

Publishes in hardback, paperback, audio and ebook formats. Also offers ghostwriting services. Allocates ISBNs and distributes to online retailers including Amazon and Barnes & Noble, as ebooks or POD and from stock for trade distribution or through their international sales network of agents. Additional services include editing, typesetting, interior layout design, cover design, ebook production, book promotion and book marketing for both fiction and non-fiction titles, all using in-house expertise.

MiblArt

email team@miblart.com
website https://miblart.com/
Facebook www.facebook.com/miblart/
Instagram @miblart

Cover design company for self-published authors. Services offered include ebook and print cover design, illustrated book cover design, and ebook and print formatting. Also creates marketing materials for authors (banners for social media, logos, bookmarks, brochures, websites). Author benefits include unlimited number of revisions and quick turnround times. No upfront payment required. Authors retain all copyrights. Founded 2015.

Novel editing services
tel 07801 055556
email suzyscreen@hotmail.com
Contact Susan Wallace

High-level, thorough edit by senior journalist experienced in writing 'real-life stories' in women's magazines and qualified in psychology and screenwriting. Email full manuscript with a phone number in confidence, or call first. Fixed fee and turnaround deadline provided. Founded 2008.

Otherwise Publishing
tel (01424) 718297
email info@otherwise-publishing.co.uk
website www.otherwise-publishing.co.uk
Facebook www.facebook.com/otherwisepublishing
Co-founders Angela Young, Simon Daley

Self-publishing services for new and experienced authors. Provides advice and full project management, from initial idea through to delivery of printed books. Services include concept development, copywriting and ghostwriting, structural editing, proofreading, indexing, cover design, page design and typesetting, photography, illustration, printing, binding, shipping and options for warehousing, distribution, sales and publicity.

Paragon Publishing
4 North Street, Rothersthorpe, Northants NN7 3JB
tel (01604) 832149
email intoprint@live.com
website www.intoprint.net
Proprietor Mark Webb

Packagers of non-fiction and fiction books for independent authors, working regularly with novelists, poets, academics, businesses, associations and writers' groups. Provides a range of editorial services, such as writing, editing and proofing, alongside book and cover design, and page layout, to create print-ready PDFs in b&w or colour as well as print-on-demand options. Publishes Kindle, and ePub on Play and Kobo, and multilingual editions. Experienced at working with new writers to help them to publish, providing ISBN, marketing consultancy and distribution to booksellers worldwide. Ghostwriting and illustration services also available. Founded 1992.

Pomegranate PA
Clavering House, Clavering Place,
Newcastle upon Tyne NE1 3NG
email karen@pomegranatepa.co.uk
website www.pomegranatepa.co.uk
X @pomegranatepa
Freelance Proofreader Karen Stubbs

Proofreading and editorial services. All subjects considered. Quotes available on request. Founded 2013.

Prepare to Publish Ltd
tel (01865) 922923
email mail@preparetopublish.com
website www.preparetopublish.com
Editor Andrew Chapman

Editorial and typesetting agency for book production. Services include copy-editing and proofreading services (non-fiction, with particular specialisms in British history, business and the history of ideas), plus print and digital formatting. Free advice on self-publishing. Clients typically include independent publishers, business leaders planning publications and authors who have completed a first draft.

David Price
tel 07528 756124
email david@d-price.co.uk
website https://d-price.co.uk

Copy-editing, proofreading, research, writing, rewriting. Special interests: operettas and musicals, travel guides, art and art history, modern European history (including the former Soviet Union). Founded 1995.

PublishNation
Suite 544, Kemp House, 152 City Road,
London EC1V 2NX
email david@publishnation.co.uk
website www.publishnation.co.uk
Publisher David Morrison

Offers POD paperback and Kindle format ebooks, available through Amazon. Publication in both print and digital formats costs £495 or £215 for Kindle format. Images may be included from £3.95 each. A range of book sizes is available, as are free template book covers. Enhanced cover design costs £40. Marketing services include creation of a press release, social media accounts and author website. Standard proofreading is £8 per 1,000 words, while an 'express' option from £125 focuses on the beginning of the manuscript. Editorial critique reports range in price from £99 for manuscripts of up to 15,000 words to £219 for manuscripts of up to 120,000 words.

Reedsy
email service@reedsy.com
website https://reedsy.com
X @ReedsyHQ
Founders Emmanuel Nataf, Matt Cobb, Ricardo Fayet, Vincent Durand

Provides authors with the tools and resources needed to bring their book to life, and connects them with a curated community of publishing professionals (including editors, designers, marketers and ghostwriters). Also offers an online novel-writing course (https://reedsy.com/learning), featuring over 20 hours of video lessons, live webinars and access to a community of like-minded writers. Founded 2014.

Rethink Press

Ivy House, Beccles Road, Fritton, Norfolk NR31 9HB
email info@rethinkpress.com
website www.rethinkpress.com
Facebook www.facebook.com/RethinkPress
X @RethinkPress
Instagram @rethinkpress
Founders Lucy McCarraher, Joe Gregory

Independent hybrid publisher of business and self-development books, offering professional writing, coaching and publishing packages for print, ebook and audiobook titles. Specialises in books by entrepreneurs, experts and business leaders.

The Right Book Company

c/o SRA Books, Studio 6, 9 Marsh Street, Bristol BS1 4AA
tel 0117 422 5540
email info@therightbookcompany.com
website http://therightbookcompany.com
Facebook www.facebook.com/therightbookcompany
X @therightbookco
Founder, Director and Publisher Sue Richardson

Brings business and personal development books to local and international markets, working with experts, thought leaders and business owners. Aims to help authors to build their authority and brand, leverage opportunity and have their message heard by their target audience.

Rowanvale Books Ltd

The Gate, Keppoch Street, Roath, Cardiff CF24 3JW
tel 029-2128 0895
email info@rowanvalebooks.com
website www.rowanvalebooks.com
X @RowanvaleBooks
Managing Director Cat Charlton

Hybrid publishers, offering authors the entire range of publishing services, tailored to suit individual authors' requirements and budget. These range from stand-alone self-publishing services and customised self-publishing packages to full global sales representation and distribution to bookstores. Accredited with Excellent partner status with the Alliance of Independent Authors. Founded 2012.

The Self-Publishing Partnership Ltd

10B Greenway Farm, Bath Road, Wick, nr. Bath BS30 5RL
tel (01225) 478444
email enquiries@selfpublishingpartnership.co.uk
website www.selfpublishingpartnership.co.uk
X @SelfPublishBath
Contacts Douglas Walker, Garry Manning

Independent self-publishing provider. Services offered include proofreading / copy-editing, page design / typesetting, cover design, print and e-book management. ISBNs, as well as subsequent sales listings & order fulfilment service, also available. Cost estimates available following a discussion of authors' requirements. Founded 2014.

Self-Publishing Review

email editor@selfpublishingreview.com
website www.selfpublishingreview.com
Facebook www.facebook.com/selfpublishingreview
X @selfpubreview
Instagram @selfpubreview

Professional editorial reviews, Amazon ebook promotions, marketing services and book editing for independent titles. US based. Founded 2008.

SilverWood Books

14 Small Street, Bristol BS1 1DE
tel 0117 910 5829
email enquiries@silverwoodbooks.co.uk
website www.silverwoodbooks.co.uk
X @SilverWoodBooks
Publishing Director Helen Hart

Complete self-publishing service for adult and children's books (including picture books), from manuscript feedback to editing and proofreading, professional cover and page design, typesetting, ebook hand-formatting and conversion, b&w and colour POD, short-run and lithographic printing, one-to-one support and coaching. Distributes to bookshops via wholesalers and to online retailers including Amazon. See website for price information.

Socciones Literary Consultancy

tel (01792) 687867
email info@socciones.co.uk
website www.socciones.co.uk/contact

Offers design, editing, and publishing services centred around the Amazon publishing ecosystem, with packages for fiction, non-fiction and children's books.

Softwood Books

Office 2, Wharfside House, Prentice Rd, Stowmarket, Suffolk IP14 1RD
email hello@softwoodbooks.com
website www.softwoodbooks.com
Facebook www.facebook.com/softwoodbooks
X @softwoodbooks
Instagram @softwoodbooks
Managing Director Maddy Glenn, *Creative Director* Nathan James, *Project Manager* Holly Nicoll, *Designer* Jasmine Higgins

Bespoke, 'pick n' mix' range of award-winning publishing services. including editing, book & eBook design, illustration, translation, printing, POD and distribution services (GPSR compliant). Social media management and marketing for authors also available. Free publishing consultations offered over Zoom. Founded 2017.

Spiffing Publishing

6 Jolliffe's Court, 51–57 High Street, Wivenhoe, Colchester, Essex CO7 9AZ
tel (01206) 585200
email enquiries@spiffingpublishing.com
website https://spiffingpublishing.com
Instagram @spiffingpublishing
Managing Director Stefan Proudfoot

Independent publishing agency specialising in fully bespoke services and one-to-one free consultation with clients. Offers a range of services, from award-winning cover design to editing and proofreading, typesetting, printing, international multi-channel distribution, websites and book marketing. Also assists authors with brand-building for their own independent publishing. Authors retain their own copyright and all royalties. Founded 2013.

Tantamount

tel 024-7722 0299
email hello@tantamount.com
website www.tantamount.com

Specialists in print, standard reflowable and enhanced rich-media digital publications, as well as branding for authors. Offers a range of editorial, design and publishing services to individual authors and publishing houses. Integrated online presence and self-publishing services allow writers to deal with a single supplier for all digital, design and publishing requirements and to achieve a coherent brand image for their work. Specialist support for first-time professional writers through 'From Authority to Authorship' mentoring programme. Founded 2002.

Michael Terence Publishing

Two Brewers House, 2A Wellington Street, Thame OX9 3BN
tel 020-3582 2002
email admin@mtp.agency
website www.mtp.agency/submissions
Facebook www.facebook.com/mtp.agency
Founders Karolina Robinson, Keith Abbott

Supports self-publishing authors across a range of genres: fiction (including crime, science fiction, historical, children's, poetry) and non-fiction (including biography, true stories). Special consideration given to new and little-published authors. Open for submissions from authors worldwide: see website for full details, including costs. Founded 2016.

Tim Saunders Publications

49 Church Close, Locks Heath, Southampton, Hampshire SO31 6LR
tel (01489) 808621
email tsaunderspubs@gmail.com
website https://tsaunderspubs.weebly.com/

Offers a range of publishing services, including editorial and marketing support for adult and children's titles. Also monthly flash fiction, poetry and short story writing challenges: Four Words, Idea, Proverbs, Title and Writing Prompt (accepted submissions published on website and in anthologies). Ongoing opportunities to contribute poetry and short stories to anthologies on various subjects.

Troubador

Troubador Publishing Ltd, Unit E2, Airfield Business Park, Market Harborough, LE16 7UL
tel 0116 279 2299
email books@troubador.co.uk
website www.troubador.co.uk
Facebook www.facebook.com/matadorbooks
X @matadorbooks
Instagram @troubador_publishing
Managing Director Alex Thompson, *Operations Director* Chloe May

Publishing services for independent authors. Offers support with editorial, marketing and sales and distribution activities. See website for pricing examples. Founded 1999.

Try Writing

tel 07773 797817
email traceyiceton@hotmail.co.uk
website www.trywriting.co.uk
Contact Tracey Iceton

Provides a full range of manuscript appraisal/critiquing services, editorial guidance and one-to-one mentoring programmes for emerging creative writers across all genres/forms of writing but specialises in fiction (short stories and novels). Services are tailored to authors' individual needs and offer constructive advice designed to help manuscripts achieve publishable standard. Try Writing is run by Tracey Iceton PhD, author of the *Celtic Colours Trilogy* (Cinnamon Press) and creative writing tutor.

User Design, Illustration and Typesetting

tel 07790 924159
email info@userdesignillustrationandtypesetting.com
website www.userdesignillustrationandtypesetting.com
Director Thomas Bohm

Book design, book cover design, graphic communication design, illustration, proofreading and typesetting service. Other services include information design, website design, accessibility and usability. Founded 2003.

White Magic Studios

Fairbourne Drive, Atterbury, Milton Keynes MK10 9RG
tel 020-3475 0507

email info@whitemagicstudios.co.uk
website www.whitemagicstudios.co.uk
Facebook www.facebook.com/whitemagicstudiosuk

Offers a range of services to authors, including book cover design, text layout and formatting, illustrations for children's books, author website set-up, book trailers and ebook conversion. Editorial support also available: see website for full range of options.

Whitefox Publishing

25 Horsell Road, London N5 1XL
email info@wearewhitefox.com
website www.wearewhitefox.com
Facebook www.facebook.com/wearewhitefox
X @wearewhitefox
Instagram @whitefox_publishing
Partners Annabel Wright, John Bond

Full-service and completely bespoke publishing solutions for writers, industry specialists, creators and brands. Authors are guided through the entire process, overseeing each stage from editorial and design through to print, sales, distribution and marketing. Founded 2012.

Claire Wingfield Editorial & Literary Services

email contact@clairewingfield.co.uk
website www.clairewingfield.co.uk
Contact Claire Wingfield

Full range of editing and proofreading services, plus a made-to-measure literary consultancy service for writers of fiction and non-fiction. The consultancy service includes a detailed report that identifies the strengths and weaknesses of a MS/proposal, giving suggestions for improvement. Full book-production services available. Founded 2006.

The Word Tank

2 Rosendale, Gill's Green, Cranbrook TN18 5EN
email enquiries@thewordtank.com
website www.thewordtank.com
X @thewordtank
Contacts Chris Brock, Victoria Brock

Professional editing and publishing services from an experienced team, including proofreading, copy-editing, copywriting, cover design and interior formatting. Also independent publishing and marketing support. Partner members of Alliance of Independent Authors; professional members of Chartered Institute of Editors and Proofreaders.

Wrate's Editing Services

14C Woodland Road, London SE19 1NT
tel 020-8670 0660
email danielle@wrateseditingservices.co.uk
website http://wrateseditingservices.co.uk
X @WratesEditing
Instagram @wrates_editing
Contact Danielle Wrate

Helps authors with all aspects of the self-publishing process, from draft manuscript to publication. Primary services include proofreading, copy-editing, manuscript assessment, cover design, interior layout, ebook conversion, printing, ISBN registration and marketing. Works with both novelists and non-fiction authors; free, no-obligation sample edit and publishing guide available. Founded 2013.

The Writing Hall

33 Mount Pleasant, Ackworth, Pontefract, West Yorkshire, WF7 7HU
tel 07983 089621
email diane@thewritinghall.co.uk
website www.thewritinghall.co.uk
Facebook www.facebook.com/thewritinghall
X @thewritinghall
Contact Diane Hall

Services include developmental editing and copy-editing, proofreading, typesetting, cover design, small run printing, ebook formatting, writing workshops, book launches and literary events, and marketing and social media coaching. Also available: writing coaching/mentoring, manuscript critique, ghostwriting and literary consultancy and advice. Submissions are welcome in most genres, particularly contemporary fiction, business titles, romance, comedy. Founded 2007.

@YouCaxton

23 High Street, Bishops Castle, Shrops. SY9 5BE
email newbooks@youcaxton.co.uk
website www.youcaxton.co.uk
Partners Robert Fowke, Robert Branton

Specialises in memoir and general non-fiction, selected fiction and full-colour productions and art books. Support for self-publishers includes structural editing, copy-editing, proofreading, cover design and interior layout, print and ebook production and a full distribution service. Additional services comprise a range of marketing tools for self-publishing, author websites and web pages, a book packaging and design service for publishers and a publication project-management service for academic and corporate clients. Also provides a fine-art printing service for photographers and artists.

Law and copyright

UK copyright law and publishing rights

Publisher Lynette Owen outlines the basic principles of copyright and how UK copyright law provides a framework for the protection of creative works, with particular reference to publishing.

Creators including writers and artists are dependent on copyright to protect their works and to underpin the arrangements they make with the publishers who bring their works to market. The United Kingdom has the oldest tradition of copyright legislation, starting with the Statute of Anne which came into force in 1710. The last full revision of UK copyright law resulted in the Copyright, Designs and Patents Act 1988 (CPDA); this replaced the 1956 Copyright Act, which in turn replaced the 1911 Copyright Act. Since the 1988 Act, there have been a number of revisions, usually undertaken via Statutory Instruments.

What is copyright?

Copyright is one aspect of intellectual property rights (IPR), which are often defined as relating to 'works of the mind'. Other aspects include design and patent rights. Copyright has both positive and negative aspects – it enables rightsholders to authorise the use of their work in a variety of ways and also to take action against unauthorised use. It is worth flagging here that there are different philosophies of copyright; the UK, in common with other Anglophone countries, operates under common law, based on factual case law, and views copyright works as property which can be traded and transferred. By contrast, countries which operate under civil law, based on civil codes, (e.g. the countries of mainland Europe) view copyright (referred to as *droit d'auteur*) more as a human right belonging to the creator, with far more restrictive regulations on how it can be exploited.

How does it work?

Each country has its own national copyright legislation which normally covers works created by citizens of that country, creators normally resident in that country and works first published in that country. There is also normally an obligation to respect the creative works originating in other countries which belong to the same international copyright conventions; this is normally undertaken in the form of 'national treatment', i.e. each member country provides to the creative works from other member states the same standard of protection it would grant to the works of its own citizens. This means that there may be varying standards of protection from country to country, for example in terms of the duration of copyright protection; there may also be differing exceptions to copyright from country to country. Most countries in the world now belong to one or more of the international copyright conventions: the Berne Convention (1886), the Universal Copyright Convention (1952) and the World Intellectual Property Organization (WIPO) Copyright Treaty (1996, but in force from 2002 – this convention reinforces the concept of copyright in the digital age). Membership of a convention requires member states to observe certain minimum standards of copyright protection.

What types of work are protected by copyright?

The CDPA (Copyright, Designs and Patents Act 1988) provides copyright protection to three main categories of creative works:

1. Original literary, dramatic, musical and artistic works

'Literary works' includes any work which is written, including tables, graphs, compilations and computer programs. It also includes databases which involve creativity in terms of selection by the compiler. Dramatic and musical works include performable works such as plays and dances, with the lyrics of musical works protected separately. Artistic works include graphic works (paintings, drawings, maps, engravings or similar works), sculptures, collages, works of architecture and works of artistic craftsmanship (although these can also be protected under design rights). All works must be original and in written or other fixed form.

2. Sound recordings, films and broadcasts

These are also protected and may involve the many different copyrights of performers, producers and broadcasters. Broadcasts traditionally covered transmission by radio and television, but now include satellite broadcasts and transmissions via the internet.

3. Copyright in typographical arrangements

This is a specific right under UK copyright law which does not appear in the legislation of many other countries. This right covers the design and layout of text and, as such, is a right quite separate from that of the creative content of the text; it belongs to the publisher in recognition of their skill and investment in the layout of a work and lasts for 25 years from the date of first publication of that version of the text.

Who owns the copyright?

Copyright subsists in a work as soon as it is created; there is no requirement for any formal registration to achieve protection. The first owner of copyright is normally the creator, e.g. the writer, artist, composer, etc. The major exception to this, in UK copyright law, is if a work is created as part of the creator's regular employment, in which case copyright belongs to the employer. A good example of this would be when a publisher employs a team of lexicographers in-house to compile dictionary entries. US copyright law has a provision for 'works for hire' where content (text, illustrations, etc) may be commissioned by a publisher, usually on the basis of an outright fee, with copyright then belonging to the commissioning entity.

In the case of copyright controlled by the creator, he or she will then have a choice on how to deal with the question of copyright when dealing with a publisher. For an author or illustrator seeking a contract with a publisher, there are two possibilities:

i) They may retain ownership of the copyright and grant an exclusive licence or licences to one or more publishers for publication of the work in an agreed language, in agreed format/s, within agreed sales territories and for an agreed period of time. For example, an author could grant an exclusive licence to a UK publisher for the UK and Commonwealth markets, and a separate licence to a US publisher for the American market. This is a common scenario in trade (general) publishing.

ii) In educational, academic and professional publishing, the scenario may be different. The author may be asked to assign copyright to the publishing house – this is often a requirement for academic journal articles but may also be requested for books, even when the author is receiving an advance and ongoing royalties; it is particularly logical for multi-author works where individual contributors may each be paid an outright fee. There is often much misunderstanding of copyright assignment and publishers should always be prepared to explain to authors and illustrators their reasons for requesting it. One particularly powerful reason is that it is often much simpler to take action against piracy if copyright is in the name of the publishing house.

With the rise of the internet, there is a need for protection of internet transmissions and for user-generated works; these are covered under provisions for 'communication to the public' and 'making available to the public'. However, the question of copyright ownership in user-generated works is complex, given the scale of material which is uploaded to social media sites such as YouTube, Facebook, X, Instagram, TikTok and others. If the material uploaded is original to the person undertaking the uploading, then copyright will belong to them, but a lot of such material may belong to other parties and may have been uploaded without their knowledge or consent.

What are moral rights?

Moral rights are personal to the creator and were introduced into UK copyright legislation for the first time in the CDPA 1988; they had long been a feature of civil law. They are quite separate from the economic rights of the creator and in the UK they last for the same period as copyright protection; in some other legislations they are inalienable and perpetual. They include the right of paternity (the right to be recognised as the creator), the right of integrity (the right to object to derogatory or damaging treatment of the work) and the right to object to false attribution of a work. UK legislation is unusual in that it requires the creator to assert his or her right of paternity (this is often done via a notice on the title verso page of a book); it also allows for the creator to waive his or her moral rights, something which may be necessary for certain forms of publication or when a book is used as the basis for film or television exploitation.

How long does copyright last?

In the case of the UK, the period of protection is now 70 years from the end of the year in which the creator dies – in the case of works of collaborative authorship, from the end of the year in which the last author dies. The term of protection was extended from 50 to 70 years for all works still in copyright as at 1 July 1995, as a result of an EU directive to harmonise the term of copyright within the European Union. Works published in the USA since 1 January 1978 also now have a similar period of protection. However, many countries in the world still have a shorter period of protection (e.g. China has a period of 50 years *post mortem auctoris*).

What does copyright enable the owner to do?

It enables the owner to undertake or authorise reproduction and distribution of the work to the public, as well as a range of other methods of exploiting the work, including performance, broadcasting and adaptations (which would include translations). It is normally an infringement of copyright for anyone to undertake any of these activities without authorisation from the copyright holder.

What action can be taken against copyright infringement?

UK copyright legislation permits action to be taken under civil or criminal law, depending on the nature of the infringement; penalties are decided by the courts. By contrast, the legislation of some countries defines the penalties in terms of maximum financial fines or terms of imprisonment. There are many possible categories of infringement – these could include unauthorised reproduction, unauthorised adaptation, plagiarism and passing off. In the digital age, unauthorised use of copyright content has increased; some is undertaken for commercial purposes via torrent sites, whilst other cases may be file sharing (e.g. of textbooks amongst students). The Publishers Association has a website which enables its members to issue 'notice and takedown' to infringing sites (see www.copyrightinfringementportal.com).

Are there exceptions to copyright?

Most national copyright laws list a number of uses of copyright material which can be undertaken without permission from or payment to the copyright owner, subject to certain conditions. The CDPA 1988 provides for a number of these:

- Fair dealing with a literary, dramatic, musical or artistic work for the purposes of research or study;
- Fair dealing for the purposes of criticism or review;
- Fair dealing with a work (other than a photograph) for the purpose or reporting current events.

These uses are permitted subject to due acknowledgement to the creator and the source, provided they do not adversely affect the normal interests of the copyright holder. There is no statutory definition of *fair dealing*, but most publishers would consider that fair dealing does not apply to use in the context of a commercial publication, so an author wishing to include copyright text or illustrations from outside sources in his or her own book should not assume that this is covered by fair dealing, however short the material may be.

The CDPA also provides for the copying of material for educational purposes, provided this is not undertaken by a reprographic process; thus, for example, displaying a passage of text on an interactive whiteboard is permitted. Large-scale copying of limited amounts of copyright material via photocopying or scanning (e.g. for course-packs for schools or universities, or on a company intranet) is covered under collective licences issued by the Copyright Licensing Agency (CLA) which negotiates licences to schools, colleges, universities, government departments and private businesses for such use; a share of licence revenue is paid to authors via the Authors Licensing and Collecting Society (ALCS), to visual artists via the

Useful websites

Authors Licensing and Collecting Society (ALCS): www.alcs.co.uk

Copyright Licensing Agency (CLA): www.cla.co.uk

Design and Artists Copyright Society (DACS): www.dacs.org.uk

Intellectual Property Office (IPO): www.gov.uk/government/organisations/intellectual-property-office

Picture Industry Collecting Society for Effective Licensing (PICSEL): https://picsel.org.uk

Publishers' Licensing Services (PLS): www.pls.org.uk

Publishers Association: www.publishers.org.uk

Society of Authors: https://societyofauthors.org

World Intellectual Property Organisation (WIPO): www.wipo.int/portal/en/index.html

Design and Artists Collecting Society (DACS) or the Picture Industry Collecting Society for Effective Licensing (PICSEL), and to publishers via Publishers' Licensing Services (PLS). Organisations similar to CLA exist in many overseas countries and revenue from the copying of extracts from UK copyright works abroad is channelled to CLA via bilateral agreements with those organisations.

There are also provisions for the inclusion of short passages of published literary and dramatic works in educational anthologies, provided this does not affect the interests of the copyright holders and that such material does not represent the majority of the anthology.

The CDPA 1988 permits the making of a single copy of a copyright work by a library on behalf of a person undertaking research or private study, and it also permits libraries to make copies for the purposes of preservation or replacement of a damaged item.

There has been a copyright exception for visually impaired people since the Copyright (Visually Impaired Persons) Act 2002, giving them the right to accessible versions of copyright content (e.g. in Braille, audio or text-to-speech versions).

2014 saw the introduction of a number of amendments to existing copyright exceptions and some new exceptions, introduced via statutory instruments. Among them was an exception for copying for private use; fair dealing for non-commercial research or private study; a fair dealing exception for criticism or review or otherwise (the latter term undefined); a new exception for caricature, parody or pastiche; a new exception for text and data analysis for non-commercial research; and an extension of the exception for visually impaired persons to cover persons whose ability to read is affected by their disability (either physical or e.g. dyslexia). It remains the case that any fair dealing use must acknowledge the source and must not affect the normal interests of the rightsholder.

Copyright acts

- Copyright, Designs and Patents Act 1988 (but it is vital to use an up-to-date amended version). See www.gov.uk/government/organisations/intellectual-property-office.
- Duration of Copyright and Rights in Performances Regulations 1995 (SI 1995 No. 3297)
- Copyright and Rights in Database Regulations 1997 (SI 1997/3032) amended by the Copyright and Rights in Databases (Amendment) Regulations 2003 (SI 2003/2501)
- Copyright and Related Rights Regulations 2003 (SI 2003 No. 2498)
- Intellectual Property (Enforcement, etc) Regulations 2006 (SI 2006 No. 1028)
- Performances (Moral Rights, etc) Regulations 2006 (SI 2006 No. 18)
- Copyright and Rights in Performances (Quotation and Parody) Regulations 2014
- Copyright and Rights in Performances (Personal Copies for Private Use) Regulations 2014

How has UK copyright law changed?

In particular, UK copyright law has been influenced by a number of EU directives over the years, which have normally been implemented via statutory instruments. The most significant have been: the 1993 Directive on the Duration of Copyright and Authors' Rights (93/98/EEC), implemented via the Duration of Copyright and Rights in Performance Regulations 1995 (SI 1995 No 3297); the EC Database Directive 96/9 EC which was implemented via the Copyright and Rights in Databases Regulations 1997; and the EU Directive 2001/29/EC on the Harmonisation of Certain Aspects of Copyright and Related Rights in the Information Society, which included a transmission right and the right for copyright holders to use encryption and identifier systems to protect their works (implemented by SI 2003 No. 2498, the Copyright and Related Rights Regulations).

After two and a half years of high-profile negotiations and public debate, the European Union undertook a major copyright review. This led to the Directive on Copyright in the Digital Single Market, adopted in 2019 and to be implemented by EU member states by June 2021. In the meantime, following the outcome of the Brexit referendum of 23 June 2016, the UK left the EU on 31 January 2020, with a transition period running until 31 December 2020. From 1 January 2021 the UK was therefore free to set its own copyright agenda. The majority of the provisions of EU copyright legislation have been retained for the time being, but the UK has not implemented the 2019 DSM/Copyright Directive; it could however choose to implement similar provisions. Some key elements of the Directive (Article 17, the liability regime and monitoring/filtering obligations for online content sharing platforms, and Articles 19–21, the so-called 'bestseller' provisions for remuneration for authors and performers) will not be included in UK law.

In 2021 the UK Intellectual Property Office (IPO) undertook a consultation on a possible change to the current regime on exhaustion of intellectual property rights. A move from the regional exhaustion regime which applied whilst the UK was a member of the EU to an international exhaustion regime would open up the UK market to parallel importation of competing editions of books, in particular from the USA and from developing countries where publishers have been granted licences for local low-price editions. Following strong lobbying from the creative industries, and in particular from the book trade and authors, on 18 January 2022 the UK government announced that no changes would be made at the moment, but that the matter may be subject to future review. At the time of writing, no formal decision has been reached.

Copyright under the microscope?

The last 25 years have seen a plethora of reviews of copyright – at international, multinational and national level – raising the question of the balance of interest between rightsholders and users, and questioning whether copyright remains fit for purpose. The rise of the internet has raised expectations amongst many users that content should be instantly available and preferably free of charge. The dangers of this have been seen all too clearly, in particular with the adverse impact on the music, film and computer software industries and their creators. On the other hand, some creators have been happy to make their work available under a range of Creative Commons licences, some more restrictive than others (see https://creativecommons.org/licenses). There is an ongoing move towards Open Access in the academic sector, with its impact being felt particularly in the area of academic journals, but later extended to academic monographs.

Copyright has had a long history of adapting to developments in technology and to changing market needs; hence it remains fit for purpose and is a necessary framework that enables creators to receive a just reward for the use of their work and to recognise the skills and investment of those who, like publishers, bring their works to market. *At Risk: Our Creative Future*, a report from the House of Lords Communications Committee published on 17 January 2023, voiced concern about any government moves which would weaken copyright law and impact negatively on UK creative industries. In the same month, publishers welcomed the UK government's decision not to broaden the copyright exception for text and data mining (TDM) to include commercial use.

Perhaps the most pressing concern on the copyright front is the rise of generative AI (Artificial Intelligence) in the form of programmes which, when prompted, can generate images, music and text. Such programmes have been trained on large bodies of existing content, much of it covered by copyright but without permission from or payment to the rightsholders. Quite apart from the legal and economic issues, there are moral and security concerns about the integrity and reliability of AI-generated output, which is capable of producing fake news and obscene material. Examples of image programmes include MidJourney, Stable Diffusion and OpenAI's Dall-E2. For music, programmes include Vall-E, Google Research's MusicLM and OpenAI's Jukebox. Human images and voices can also be utilised and this was a key reason behind the SAG-AFTRA actors' strike in 2023.

The production of text via generative AI continues to be of major concern to authors, literary agents and publishers. Large Language Models (LLMs) include ChatGPT (owned by OpenAI, with Microsoft as a major investor), Google's Gemini (formerly Bard), Microsoft's BingAI and Meta's LlaMa. Launched on 30 November 2022, ChatGPT was trained on a large body of existing content, much of it in copyright, without permission from rightsholders; it attracted more than 100 million users within the first two months. Its broad appeal led in March 2023 to an open letter from more than 3000 signatories, including Yoshua Bengio and Steve Wozniak, calling for the tech companies to pause the training of AI systems and citing possible harms to society. In July 2023, the US Authors Guild on behalf of over 10,000 authors sent an open letter to the Ceos of Alphabet (Google's parent company), Meta, OpenAI, Stability AI and IBTI, calling for them to seek consent from rightsholders and to credit and pay for the use of copyright material for training purposes. In September 2023, the Authors Guild on behalf of 17 authors lodged a class action suit against OpenAI for copyright infringement; this was followed in December 2023 by a suit from the *New York Times*. Numerous lawsuits against AI companies are currently in train. The stance of the tech companies is that LLMs do not copy material, rather read and learn from it, and that the US concept of fair use should then apply. Whilst the majority of AI companies are US-based, January 2025 saw the launch of China's DeepSeekR1, with substantially lower development costs.

In terms of legislation, in the USA, June 2023 saw an AI Bill of Rights from the White House Office of Science and Technology. In November 2023, President Biden issued an Executive Order on Safe, Secure and Trustworthy AI, including a requirement for the protection of rights of creators. The European Union has introduced the AI Act to regulate AI; it came into force on 1 August 2024 with provisions which will come into operation gradually over the next six to 36 months. In the UK, in January 2023, the House of Lords Communications and Digital Committee issued a report, *AI Risk: Our Creative Future*, expressing concerns about any proposed legislation which might weaken copyright protection. A White Paper entitled *A Pro-innovation Approach to AI Regulation* was published in March 2023. The UK hosted an AI Safety Summit at Bletchley Park on 1–2 November 2023, although this focused more on security concerns than on intellectual property issues. The AI (Regulation) Bill was submitted to Parliament in November 2023 but was dropped due to the General Election in July 2024; the new Labour government has announced plans to introduce legislation in 2025 to address AI risks. The Paris AI Action Summit was held on 10–11 February 2025; intellectual property was mentioned as an area for global reflection but many in the creative industries felt that it had not been highlighted as an urgent priority.

2024 saw announcements of a number of multi-million dollar licensing deals between AI companies and major academic and professional publishers including Taylor & Francis, Wiley and Oxford University Press. Policy regarding consent from and/or payment to authors has varied between publishers and has caused controversy.

Many authors, agents and publishers remain concerned that no copyright content should be used for AI training purposes without permission from and appropriate compensation to rightsholders, with ongoing efforts by the Creative Rights in AI Coalition seeking to ensure appropriate recognition for creators. One solution might be a collective licensing scheme via the CLA; PLS are consulting publishers and ALCS consulting authors about this possibility. In January 2024, there was some indication that the government is considering a copyright exception for AI, but with a controversial opt-out provision for rightsholders which would pose practical difficulties. On 17 December 2024, the government launched a consultation on AI and copyright, running until 25 February 2025; over 2500 responses were received by the Intellectual Property Office with results to be reviewed and published in line with Cabinet Office guidelines. In late January 2025 the House of Lords voted to add provisions to a Data Bill which would make the existing copyright framework enforceable.

In the meantime, many authors have been seeking contractual assurances from publishers that their work will not be made available for AI training and that AI will not be employed for exploitation of their work (e.g. for foreign language translations or audiobook narration). In turn, many publishers are requiring contractual assurances from authors that the work they submit has not been created by AI; this raises questions of the extent to which some use of AI might be considered permissible, e.g. for content checking, spelling and grammar checking and the creation of indexes.

Lynette Owen OBE has worked at Cambridge University Press, Pitman Publishing, Marshall Cavendish and Pearson Education, and is now a freelance copyright and rights consultant at Lynette Owen Consulting. Her book, *Selling Rights*, is published by Routledge (9th edition published July 2024). She is the General Editor of *Clark's Publishing Agreements: A Book of Precedents* (Bloomsbury Professional, 11th edition 2022; 12th edition due 2026).

Further reading

Cornish, William et al., *Intellectual Property, Patents, Copyrights, Trademarks and Allied Rights* (Sweet & Maxwell, 9th edn 2019)

Bently, Lionel and Sherman, Brad, *Intellectual Property Law* (OUP, 6th edn 2022)

Caddick, Nicholas et al., *Copinger and Skone James on Copyright* (Sweet & Maxwell, 18th edn and Second Supplement 2022)

Jones, Hugh and Benson, Christopher, *Publishing Law* (Routledge, 5th edn 2016)

Owen, Lynette (Gen. Ed.), *Clark's Publishing Agreements: A Book of Precedents* (Bloomsbury Professional, 11th edn 2022; 12th edition due 2026)

For a view of copyright from the US perspective:

Netanel, Neil Weinstock, *Copyright: What Everyone Needs to Know* (OUP New York 2018)

A legal lexicon

data protection

The duty to protect the privacy of individuals if they share their personal information with a company (name, date of birth, gender, email or home address, etc.). This might be through a newsletter sign up, survey or book order on a website. The Data Protection Act 2018 insists that recipients of this kind of personal information must store it safely, use it only for the purpose communicated to the individual and only store data for as long as is necessary.

defamation

To defame someone is to damage their reputation and can result in legal action taken against the author or publisher if the case is serious enough. Defamatory content might include mocking and ridicule or making a false statement about a person or company. In fiction a character could be considered defamatory if they bear resemblance to a real person or body of people. Defamation court cases can be extremely expensive, meaning that publishers will often cease publication if there is even a possibility of being sued and will include clauses in their contracts stating the author is responsible (legally and financially) for any defamatory content found in their work.

intellectual property (IP)

An idea or creation which is not tangible or material but is sellable and ownable. This includes trademarks, copyrights and patents of character names, plot devices and fictional places; text, photographs and illustrations; databases and software.

libel

Defamatory statements which are written or published. This can now include social media posts and comments – the authors of which have been successfully sued in court.

moral rights

There are two key moral rights which an author should be aware of and they apply even after an author has assigned their copyright to another party. The right to paternity gives an author the right to assert themselves as the creator of a work and prevents false attribution. The right to integrity prevents a work being edited or changed without the author's permission.

permissions

If someone wants to use part or the whole of another writer's work, they must first receive their permission to do so (or the permission of the copyright or licence holder). An author must do the same if they want to use someone else's work, for example an illustration or quotation. Permissions are granted in a contract and usually in return for payment. Permissions must be cleared before publication to avoid contravening copyright.

privacy and confidentiality

A breach of privacy occurs when confidential information is shared beyond the person or people for whom it was intended and can be met with legal action. A duty of confidence exists between an author and their publisher which prevents confidential information, such as ideas and manuscripts as well as commercial information about the publisher, from being shared. An author must also respect the right to privacy – in both fiction and non-fiction – if their work is inspired by real people or events. For example, if writing about a former line of work, avoid sharing confidential or sensitive information, or if writing a romance novel, avoid basing the lead character on an ex.

slander

Defamatory statements which are spoken aloud. For an author this could include statements made during a book tour or promotional interview.

subsidiary rights

Also known as ancillary rights, i.e. secondary to **volume rights** (see below), these are rights which are licensed to a publisher which then licenses them to a third party. These might be a foreign publisher with whom a translation is negotiated or a newspaper or magazine that wishes to print an extract from a book. A literary agent will often not assign copyright in some subsidiary rights to a publisher and will manage them for an author. These include those rights that might be exploited in areas beyond the page, such as film or TV and merchandising rights.

trademark

A sign, design or expression that is legally protected which identifies the individuality of these symbols and their distinction from those used by others in a similar business and protects them from copying. For example, J.K. Rowling has copyrighted various character names and features of her *Harry Potter* series, such as Hogwarts School of Witchcraft and Wizardry and Gryffindor House.

volume rights

The rights for a publisher to publish a book in its main editions: print, audio and ebook.

Protecting your content: piracy and IP

Given the marked increase in piracy in the publishing industry since the introduction of digital technology, what steps can authors take to combat IP theft and protect their work, to avoid significant financial and reputational loss? Content protection solutions provider MUSO explains the threat and provides valuable advice for self-published and ebook authors.

Protecting your intellectual property: combating piracy in the world of self-publishing

For self-published authors, intellectual property (IP) protection is a crucial aspect of success in the digital age. With the rise of digital technologies, book publishing has undergone a significant transformation. While this has made books easier to publish and more accessible, it has also exposed them to rampant piracy. The ease of sharing and distributing digital content has led to a rise in IP theft. The consequences of piracy can be severe, causing financial loss, damaging reputations, and undermining the value of an author's work. However, there are steps that self-published authors and authors of ebooks can take to protect their IP and prevent piracy.

Understanding the threat

Piracy is the unauthorised use or reproduction of someone else's work. In the context of self-publishing, piracy can occur when someone illegally downloads and distributes an author's ebook without their permission. Piracy is a widespread problem, and it can be challenging to detect and prevent.

The impact of piracy

The cost of piracy to the publishing industry is immense. According to a study by the International Intellectual Property Alliance (IIPA), the global book-publishing industry loses over $20 billion annually to piracy. Moreover, the increase in piracy is likely to continue. Piracy in the publishing industry has seen a marked rise in the last few years, with a notable uptick following the first lockdowns of the pandemic. Significantly, in May 2020, publishing overtook film as the second most in-demand media sector for digital piracy, behind TV. And publishing continues to over-index in total piracy demand. MUSO's own data showed 215 billion visits to piracy websites across all media industries in 2022, an 18% increase compared with 2021. However, looking at publishing specifically, there were 59.2 billion visits to publishing piracy sites in 2022 … a *37.1% increase* on the 2021 figure.

Piracy can have severe consequences for self-published authors. Financial loss is a significant concern. Piracy can cause authors to lose out on royalties and revenue from sales. Moreover, the proliferation of pirated copies can result in a decrease in demand for an author's work, reducing the value of their intellectual property. Piracy can also harm an author's reputation. Illegally distributed copies can be of poor quality, damaging the author's reputation as a writer. Additionally, pirated copies may be accompanied by negative reviews or comments, further undermining an author's reputation.

Steps to protect your IP

Fortunately, there are steps that self-published authors can take to protect their intellectual property and combat piracy.

1. Protect all of your content as early as possible

Don't just protect your most popular titles – ensure that *all* your books are protected. And don't wait until you find pirated copies of your content – be proactive and protect your content *before* you experience piracy. As unlicensed content is often well hidden, they are likely to have been on the internet for some time before you discover pirated copies. It's important that you get ahead of the issue.

2. Register your work with the appropriate authorities.

Registering your work with the appropriate authorities can help protect your IP rights. In the US, the Copyright Office offers copyright registration for authors (www.copyright.gov/registration). Similar services are offered by national government bodies including the Intellectual Property Office in the UK (www.gov.uk/government/organisations/intellectual-property-office). Registration can help establish evidence of ownership, making it easier to enforce IP rights in the event of piracy.

3. Monitor your work online.

Monitoring your work online can help you detect and respond to piracy. There are several tools available that can help you track your ebooks' distribution, such as the Digital Millennium Copyright Act (DMCA) Takedown Notice process. These tools can help you identify and respond to pirated copies of your work. For details, see some useful information on the Copyright Alliance's site: https://copyrightalliance.org/faqs/what-is-dmca-takedown-notice-process.

4. Understanding the nature of piracy.

Piracy in publishing is a complex and multi-faceted issue. There are many reasons for pirating content, many types of piracy, and a huge number of channels dedicated to distributing illegal ebook copies. The better you understand the contributing factors and the main sources of your pirated content, the more equipped you will be to tackle them.

5. Take legal action if necessary.

In the event of piracy, taking legal action may be necessary. This can involve sending cease-and-desist letters, filing copyright infringement lawsuits, or working with law enforcement to investigate and prosecute offenders. It is essential to seek legal advice before taking any legal action.

All of the above measures can help to reduce the piracy of your content. However, for a self-published or debut author, this can be quite daunting and take up a huge amount of time and carry a huge admin and cost burden. Anti-piracy vendors do exist that can help reduce this burden and can automate this process of trawling the internet, issuing takedown notices and getting infringing content removed at scale. Vendors should also be able to remove content from eBay, Amazon, Google and other 'grey' market sites.

Who are MUSO?

MUSO are a leading content protection solutions provider for the publishing industry. We work with all sizes of businesses across the publishing sector, from enterprise-size global publishers to thousands of independent and self-published authors. Our founding vision was to empower creative people to be more creative by taking away the time-consuming problem of piracy with best-in-class technology.

Our automated anti-piracy services are designed specifically for independent publishers and authors. Our affordable and flexible pricing enables the protection of an entire catalogue or a single book. We automatically monitor for illegal links and infringements and issues takedown notices, which remove piracy at scale across a wide range of piracy websites and search listings.

Copyright Licensing Agency

The Copyright Licensing Agency (CLA) is a not-for-profit company, recognised by the UK government as the collective management organisation for published material (www.gov.uk/copyright-licensing-agency-licence). CLA provides content users with access to millions of titles worldwide, and in return ensures that creators, artists, photographers and writers, along with publishers, are paid royalties for the copying, sharing and re-use of limited extracts of their published work.

CLA was established in 1983 as a joint venture between Publishers' Licensing Services (PLS) (see page 719) and Authors' Licensing and Collecting Society (ALCS) (see page 716). It was placed in an unique position of representing authors and publishers by licensing the copying of their work and promoting the role and value of copyright. CLA later expanded its licensing agreement to include the Design and Artists Copyright Society (DACS) (page 718) and the Picture Industry Collective Society for Effective Licensing (PICSEL), meaning that visual artists and photographers could receive licence fee distributions, and licensees were covered to copy images and artistic works found in content being copied. The allocation of fees is based on subscriptions, library holdings and detailed surveys of copying activity (see link.cla.co.uk/about-us and read the 'Distribution Model Report').

Further information

Copyright Licensing Agency
3rd Floor, 6 Hays Lane, London SE1 2HB
tel 020-7400 3100
email cla@cla.co.uk
website www.cla.co.uk

Helping organisations Copy, Right

CLA provides lawful access to over eight million print and online publications, and for over 40 years, has helped organisations to research, create and collaborate with a range of simple licensing solutions whilst ensuring creators' rights are respected.

With over 20 licences covering the UK's education, public and commercial sectors, CLA facilitates the efficient reuse of content by 12.7 million students and over 9.5 million employees in over 40,000 schools, universities, and organisations across the UK. These licences are tailored to each sector, taking into account the specific needs of those who rely on copying and reusing content as part of their day-to-day work.

Further to this, with 42 reciprocal agreements with countries around the world, CLA's licences allow content users to copy from publications published in more than 39 international territories. Visit link.cla.co.uk/copyright for further information.

CLA's role in the creative ecosystem

CLA's unique position in the creative ecosystem perfectly positions it to act as a trusted intermediary between rightsholders and content users and efficiently distribute the revenues generated to content creators. Through its licences, CLA has generated over £1.5 billion in collective licensing revenues that have been distributed to over 200,000 authors, publishers and visual artists. This helps to ensure that creators are incentivised to create more content in the future, ultimately contributing to the UK's world-leading creative sector.

Looking forward

CLA has demonstrated over the last forty years that copyright licensing is able to adapt to technological change, support innovation and play a vital role in connecting content users to content creators in an efficient and fair way. CLA has developed digital tools such as Check Permissions, Digital Content Store, and Education Platform to keep their licences and services relevant in a fast-changing environment while ensuring fair returns for copyright owners.

In 2023, the CLA set out to develop licensing solutions to help ensure this is the case for both Generative AI and Text and Data Mining (TDM). They published a research report looking into the dynamic relationship between UK creatives and generative AI. The aim was to spark further discussion and develop tools that protect and value human creative endeavour (https://cla.co.uk/ai-research). From 1 May 2025, CLA will be updating and extending their licences to cover Workplace Generative AI use - for corporate and public sector organisations. The launch of a groundbreaking new Generative AI Training Licence is set to launch in Q3 2025. This will provide a collective licensing solution that gives the rightsholder the opportunity to receive remuneration for the use of their works in generative AI models, whilst ensuring copyright and content protection. This initiative is a significant step forward and is the first of its kind to be developed in the UK. More information can be found at https://cla.co.uk/ai-and-copyright.

Authors' Licensing and Collecting Society

ALCS is the rights management society for UK writers.

ALCS is the largest writers' organisation in the UK with over 125,000 members. In 2024, ALCS paid their eligible members over £44 million. Once you've paid your £36 lifetime membership fee (which is simply deducted from the first payment you receive), whatever you've earned in secondary royalties is paid into your bank account during twice yearly distributions.

If you are a published writer, you can be part of this organisation committed to ensuring that writers' intellectual and moral rights are fully respected and fairly rewarded. ALCS represents all types of writer and includes educational, research and academic authors drawn from the professions, scriptwriters, adapters, playwrights, poets, novelists, editors and freelance journalists.

Membership

Authors' Licensing and Collecting Society
6th Floor, International House, 1 St Katharine's Way, London E1W 1UN
tel 020-7264 5700
email alcs@alcs.co.uk
website www.alcs.co.uk
X @ALCS_UK
Chief Executive Barbara Hayes

Membership is open to all writers and successors to their estates at a one-off fee of £36 deducted from your first payment. Members of the Society of Authors, the Writers' Guild of Great Britain, National Union of Journalists, Chartered Institute of Journalists and British Association of Journalists can join for free. ALCS charges a 10% commission rate on all payments to fund its operations.

Established in 1977, ALCS is a non-profit that was set up in the wake of the campaign to establish a Public Lending Right (see page 741) to help writers protect and exploit their collective rights. The organisation now represents the interests of all UK writers and aims to ensure that they are fairly compensated for any works that are copied, broadcast or recorded.

Internationally recognised as a leading authority on copyright matters and authors' interests, ALCS is committed to campaigning on behalf of writers to ensure their intellectual property rights are respected and that they are fairly compensated for their invaluable work. It closely monitors all matters affecting copyright, both in the UK and internationally, and makes regular representations to the UK government and the European Union.

ALCS collects fees that are difficult, time-consuming or legally impossible for writers and their representatives to claim on an individual basis, money that is nonetheless due to them. To date, it has distributed over £700 million in secondary royalties to writers. Over the years, ALCS has developed highly specialised knowledge and sophisticated systems that can track writers and their works against any secondary use for which they are due payment. A network of international contacts and reciprocal agreements with foreign collecting societies also ensures that UK writers are compensated for any similar use overseas.

The primary sources of fees due to writers are secondary royalties from the following:

Photocopying, scanning and the digital reuse of electronic and online publications

This income is from licences issued by the Copyright Licensing Agency (CLA; see page 714), originally set up by ALCS and the Publishers' Licensing Services (PLS) to license reproduction rights on behalf of its member organisations. The CLA offers a number of licensing options for businesses, educational institutions and government agencies to ensure writers are paid fairly when their works are copied or scanned.

Overseas Public Lending Right (PLR)

PLR schemes are typically set up to pay authors when libraries lend their books (to compensate them for the lack of sales). Whilst UK PLR is administered by the British Library (see page 741), ALCS collects money due to UK writers from international PLR systems.

Retransmission of all types of scripted works broadcast on TV and radio

This is the simultaneous showing of one country's broadcasting in another country through a cable network. ALCS receives fees for the cable transmission of British programmes, and then distribute that money to the relevant writers.

Educational recording

The Copyright, Designs and Patents Act 1988 gave schools, colleges and other educational establishments the right to record any radio or TV broadcast for educational purposes without infringing copyright. The Educational Recording Agency (ERA), which was established in 1989, licenses this activity and collects fees to compensate the authors and other owners of rights in the broadcast works. ALCS pays writers their share of these fees.

Tracing authors

ALCS is dedicated to protecting and promoting authors' rights and enabling writers to maximise their income. It is committed to ensuring that royalties due to writers are efficiently collected and speedily distributed to them. One of its greatest challenges is finding those writers for whom it holds funds and ensuring that they claim the money that is owed to them. Any published writer could have funds held by ALCS for them. The amount may be nominal, or it could run into several thousand pounds. Either call or visit the ALCS website – see the **Membership** box for contact details.

DACS (Design and Artists Copyright Society)

A non-for-profit organisation, DACS is the UK's leading visual artists' rights management organisation.

Established by artists for artists in 1984, DACS is the flagship rights management organisation for visual artists in the UK. Passionate about transforming the financial landscape for visual artists, DACS acts as a trusted broker for 102,500 artists worldwide.

Contact details

DACS
33 Old Bethnal Green Road, London E2 6AA
tel 020-7336 8811
email info@dacs.org.uk
website www.dacs.org.uk
Membership Free to join

DACS is a leading voice in campaigning for artists' rights, championing their sustained and vital contribution to the creative economy. Through its services, DACS collects and distributes royalties to visual artists and their estates through Payback, Artist's Resale Right, Copyright Licensing and Artimage.

Payback

Every year, DACS pays artists for the use of artworks that are published in UK books, magazines and shown on TV. If their artwork has been published or broadcast on television, artists could be entitled to a share of millions in royalties. DACS' 2024 distribution saw the annual Payback scheme pay thousands of artists and their representatives a share of over £5.6 million.

Artist's Resale Right

The Artist's Resale Right is a royalty that is due when a work is resold by an art market professional for over £1,000 or the equivalent in pounds sterling. DACS collect resale royalties and provide a quick, efficient payment service trusted by thousands of UK artists and estates. Artists can sign up as a member and DACS will monitor sales of artwork by auction houses, galleries and dealers and collect royalties on their behalf.

Copyright Licensing and Artimage

DACS has 40 years of experience helping artists generate income through the licensed use of their work. Its dedicated team collaborate with artists and leading brands to facilitate partnerships that both parties can be proud of, while making sure artists' rights are always protected. Artimage (www.artimage.org.uk) is DACS' curated image platform, which makes available over 30,000 hi-res, artist or estate-approved images to a wide range of clients. Through Artimage DACS offers a wraparound service: putting licences in place, collecting royalty fees, and releasing quality image files.

Additional Benefits for Members

DACS' Artist's Resale Right, Copyright licensing and Artimage members can all access DACS' Copyright Advice Service free of charge. This service includes advice and guidance about copyright matters and reviews of relevant sections in agreements. DACS also have a copyright enforcement service for licensing members, which aims to protect artists' rights and artistic integrity by pursuing action when work is misused.

Publishers' Licensing Services

Publishers' Licensing Services' (PLS) mission is to provide efficient and effective copyright and licensing services, and support publishers in providing access to their content.

Contact details

PLS
1 St Katharine's Way, London E1W 1UN
tel 020-7079 5930
email pls@pls.org.uk
website www.pls.org.uk

PLS manages the interests of publishers in licensing the copying of extracts from books, journals, magazines and websites. PLS provides various other services, including the award-winning PLSclear, which streamlines the process of seeking and managing permissions, and Access to Research, which enables free access in public libraries to academic journal articles.

A not-for-profit organisation, PLS has been serving the collective interests of publishers since 1981. It is owned and governed by four publisher trade associations.

Key activities

• Collective licensing

Collective licensing offers a simple and cost-effective solution for those who wish to copy from published materials without breaking the law, and for rights-holders where direct licensing is inefficient and not cost-effective.

PLS licenses the rights granted to it by publishers through two licensing organisations. The Copyright Licensing Agency (CLA) licenses organisations in the education, public and business sectors, allowing them to copy extracts from a broad range of titles in return for a licence fee. CLA also has reciprocal agreements with equivalent organisations around the world. CLA is able, therefore, to collect licensing revenue for the use of UK publications abroad. PLS licenses some magazine publishers' rights to businesses and government through NLA media access. PLS distributes the resulting licensing revenue to publishers according to the usage data collected from users. PLS distributed over £48 million of collective licensing revenue to publishers in 2024/25.

• Permissions

PLSclear is an award-winning free service that makes it quick and easy to request permission to reuse content from books, journals, magazines and websites. With hundreds of publishers using PLSclear to manage their permissions, increasing numbers of permissions-seekers are bookmarking PLSclear as their first port of call to reuse published content. Find out more at https://plsclear.com/Home/Index.

• Rights and Licensing Hub

The Rights and Licensing Hub is an initiative supported by PLS to share knowledge and encourage best practice in rights and licensing in all areas of the publishing industry and to raise awareness of the importance of good rights management. The resource offers publisher case studies, free online training courses, and careers advice for rights professionals. Find out more at www.rightsandlicensing.co.uk.

• Access to research

The Access to Research service provides free access to approximately 40 million academic articles in public libraries across the UK. 95% of UK local authorities are currently signed up, with approximately 3,000 libraries using the service. Articles are provided directly from publishers' websites and are accessed from library computers via a discovery service called Summon, generously provided by ProQuest.

Access to Research is a unique collaboration between Publishers' Licensing Services, who administer the service, publishers, and UK public libraries. It was launched in September 2015 in response to a key recommendation of the Finch Group, namely that major journal publishers should grant public libraries a licence to provide free access to their academic articles. Find out more at www.accesstoresearch.org.uk.

See also...

- *Authors' Licensing and Collecting Society*, page 716
- *Copyright Licensing Agency*, page 714
- *UK copyright law and publishing rights*, page 703

Financial advice and support

Managing your finances: a guide for writers

Chartered accountants Jonathan and Louise Ford of Writers Tax Limited set out a clear view of the various financial issues that a writer needs to understand and consider at each stage of their writing career, with helpful links and valuable advice.

In some ways the financial issues of being a writer are no different to pursuing any other occupation. You earn money for your skill, you deduct the costs you have incurred earning your money, and you pay tax on what's left. However, there are several factors that, in combination, make the situation of a writer unique; many writers have income from multiple sources, as well as overseas tax issues and matters concerning copyright.

We'll look at the different stages of a writer's career and the financial aspects you may need to consider as your career develops: 1) getting started – unpaid writing done for love not money; 2) paid writing often running alongside traditional employed income; 3) paid writing as main source of income; and 4) lifelong considerations.

Do I need an accountant?

If your financial situation is straightforward, there may be no need for you to appoint an accountant. If you are employed, then PAYE usually does a reasonable job of collecting the right amount of tax. Your writing income may be quite modest so it should be straightforward to deal with and – if the numbers are not very big – it may not cause too many issues if you get things a little wrong. To help you as your career develops, a good accountant can do the following:

- Deal with HMRC on your behalf;
- Submit your tax returns on time, so you don't get penalties for being late;
- Make sure you are claiming for the things you can claim for (and not claiming for things you shouldn't);
- Advise you on ways of saving tax legitimately;
- Help you to keep your records accurately;
- Help you to avoid nasty surprises and unexpected tax bills;
- Be on hand for all your tax-related questions.

Anybody can call themselves an accountant, even if they have no qualifications or experience. Try to choose someone who is a member of a professional accountancy body, such as ICAEW, ICAS, AAT, ACCA or CIOT. It is also worth getting recommendations from other writers. Social media groups can be a useful source when looking for accountants who act for lots of writers and understand their needs.

Stage 1: getting started

When you're at an early stage of your writing career and not earning any money from it, there is little you need to do to stay compliant. However, there are still some important things you can consider.

Setting up a dormant limited company

If you are planning to write a book and you would like the royalty income of that book to be held in a limited company, then consider setting up a company even before you start writing. This will allow you to write the book on behalf of your company. If you wait to set the company up until the book is complete, and publishers are interested, then you would have to transfer the copyright of the book to the company at market value; this could cause issues in terms of valuing the copyright and can create a tax problem that could have been avoided. To decide whether this is right for you, you need to weigh up the cost and hassle of having a dormant limited company against the possible future advantages.

Creative averaging

There are a number of conditions you need to satisfy to be eligible for creative averaging; more details are available on HMRC Helpsheet HS234. One such condition is that you cannot use your first year of trading as part of any creative averaging calculation. Using the example given in the box, Theo would need to be submitting information to HMRC about his writing business from the 2021/22 tax year to be able to claim creative averaging in 2023/24.

Loss relief against other income

It is possible for a sole trader to make a loss and to set that loss against other income. This can be beneficial for tax reasons. For example, if an author makes a loss of £5,000 and they also have *employed income* of £30,000, they could offset the £5,000 loss against their employed income so that they only have to pay tax on £25,000. To be able to offset losses against other income, you need to be able to show HMRC that the loss has been incurred on a commercial basis with a view to making a profit. A vague idea that one day you might write a book on Greece would not be sufficient evidence to get a tax deduction on the costs of your holiday.

Creative averaging example

Theo earns nothing in the tax year 2023/24 while he is writing his novel.

In 2024/25 his book is published and he makes a profit of £30,000. Without creative averaging his tax bill in 2023/24 would be nothing, but in 2024/25 he would owe £3,486 in income tax and £1,045.80 in National Insurance – a total of £4,531.80.

If he elects to use creative averaging, his £30,000 profit would be split across both tax years, giving him a total tax bill of £704.70 in 2023/24 and of £631.80 in 2024/25. By choosing to use creative averaging, Theo would have saved £3195.30 over the two tax years.

Pre-trading expenses

If you haven't been reporting expenditure to HMRC as losses, then it is still possible to get tax relief for 'pre-trading expenditure'. The relief allows you to claim for expenditure incurred within seven years of starting to trade and, in effect, gives tax relief as if it was incurred on the first day of trading. The 'wholly and exclusive' rule will still apply, so it is important to be able to link the expenditure you are claiming to the income you are receiving. The stronger the link, the more likely HMRC are to accept it. In order to maximise any possible pre-trading expenditure claim, it is important to try and keep records and receipts *just in case* you might need them in the future.

Stage 2: paid writing as additional income

Most writers at this stage will still be running their writing business as a sole trader (or freelancer – there is no difference in terms of tax). Legally you don't need to do anything to set up as a sole trader. As soon as you start writing with a view to making a profit, you've become a sole trader. The tax system is very flexible. You can have a part-time employed job, be a partner in a bookshop and be a published author, all at the same time. Important things to consider at this stage are:

Registering with HMRC

If you earn more than £1,000 from self-employment you need to register as a sole trader with HMRC. You can do this at www.gov.uk/register-for-self-assessment. You need to register by 5 October in your second tax year (tax years run from 6 April to 5 April).

For example, if you started on 20 November 2024 (tax year 2024/25) then you would need to register with HMRC by 5 October 2025 (tax year 2025/26). You would then get sent a tax return to complete by 31 January 2026 if filing online or 31 October 2025 if filing by paper.

Two or more writers working together may also need to consider if they are in partnership with each other. A partnership has to be registered in its own right with HMRC and submit a tax return each year.

Submitting a tax return

The tax system is called Self Assessment and this means that it is necessary for you to assess what rules and regulations apply to your tax position. There are a range of penalties that HMRC levy and, although it is possible in certain circumstances to appeal the penalties, it is well worth doing all you can to avoid them in the first place.

Keeping records

A self-employed person needs to keep records for at least five years from 31 January following the tax year they relate to. For example, if you have transactions in the tax year to 5 April 2025, you need to keep your records until 31 January 2031. You can keep records digitally or on paper. You should keep copies of bank statements, contracts, receipts for expenditure you are claiming for and any invoices you have raised. It is also worth keeping a note of any unusual non-business transactions. If you win £1,000 at the races or get a generous gift from Aunt Ethel, you want to be able to prove this wasn't undeclared income from writing.

It is usually a good idea to have a separate business bank account that you use just for your writing income. This will help to keep things organised and could give you a little more privacy, as your accountant – and possibly HMRC – don't have to look through all your private outgoings.

Making Tax Digital for Income Tax

From 6 April 2026 there is a new system for reporting income to HMRC called Making Tax Digital for Income Tax (MTD for IT). This will affect landlords and sole traders. Those with qualifying income of £50,000 or more will have to join from April 2026 and those with qualifying income of more than £30,000 will join from April 2027. It is sales or turnover that matters rather than profit. Under the new system taxpayers will have to do the following:

- keep their records digitally
- provide a quarterly return to HMRC through compatible software
- provide an annual tax return

If you think you will be affected and you aren't currently keeping your records on cloud bookkeeping software then it would be worth exploring this further.

There is more information available at www.gov.uk/guidance/check-if-youre-eligible-for-making-tax-digital-for-income-tax.

Claiming expenses

A writer pays tax on their profit. Profit is income minus allowable costs, often referred to as 'expenses'. Sometimes people talk about things being 'tax deductible', which means they can be deducted from your profit before calculating the tax bill, rather than being deducted from your tax bill. For example, if a higher-rate tax payer spends £100 on stationery, this is tax deductible and so it will reduce her profits by £100 and save income tax at 40%, i.e. £40.

Trading allowance

You can claim a £1,000 trading allowance against your self-employed income instead of claiming for expenses you have incurred. You cannot claim the trading allowance and expenses at the same time. Claiming the trading allowance would be suitable when the trading allowance is more than the expenses incurred. However, you can't use the trading allowance to turn your profit into a loss. There are also restrictions to prevent you from using the trading allowance if the income is received from a business controlled by you, or by someone connected to you.

What can you claim for?

The rule is that an expense must be 'wholly and exclusively' for the purpose of your business. Typical costs are:

- Accountancy
- Advertising
- Agent commission
- Bank charges
- Computing and IT
- Printing, postage and stationery
- Professional subscriptions
- Internet and telephone
- Software subscriptions
- Research
- Travel

Some costs may have an element of private use. In this case, HMRC will allow the cost to be apportioned provided you can justify the calculation. For example:

- Motor expenses – may be apportioned according to business use.
- Home as office – apportioned according to rooms and time spent in use.

Alternatively, you may be able to use HMRC Simplified Expenses. You can find more details at www.gov.uk/simpler-income-tax-simplified-expenses.

HMRC Self Assessment penalties

Late filing

Up to 3 months late £100, plus

after 3 months £10 per day for 90 days (max £900), plus

after 6 months penalties accrue at regular intervals based on 5% of the tax due or £300 – whichever is the greater.

You can estimate your penalty at www.gov.uk/estimate-self-assessment-penalties.

Late payment of tax

5% of tax due if not paid within 30 days with further 5% penalties every 6 months.

Interest is also charged (at the bank base rate plus 2.5%).

Incorrect returns

Penalties are charged for tax returns that HMRC consider to be incorrect. There is an appeals process. The penalties are all behaviour based and are as follows:

- Careless errors – 0% to 30% of the additional tax due.
- Deliberate errors – 20% to 70% of the additional tax due.
- Deliberate and concealed errors – 30% to 100% of the additional tax due.

Prizes and bursaries

There are many prizes and awards open to authors and other creatives, and entering competitions or seeking awards is a normal part of these professions and a good way for them to obtain extra income from their work. Such prizes are usually taxable. However, there are exceptions. When a prize is unsolicited, and awarded as a mark of honour, distinction or public esteem in recognition of outstanding achievement in a particular field, it won't be taxable. For example, if your publisher or agent enters you for a competition without your knowledge or consent, any prize money received should not be taxable.

Cloud bookkeeping

Recent years have seen the development of relatively cheap, simple bookkeeping packages like Xero and Quickbooks. These allow you to link up your business bank account to your accounting records, so you can quickly and accurately keep track of your income and expenditure. They have the advantage of being regularly backed up, less prone to error, and easy to use. You can also store your receipts and paperwork digitally.

Payments on account

For self-employed people the tax system can require payments on account of tax to be made every six months. Each payment on account is half of the previous year's tax bill.

For example: Jo's first year of trading is the tax year 2024/25; she owes tax of £4,000 for the 2024/25 tax year which is due for payment by 31 January 2026. Also, on 31 January 2026 she'll need to pay a payment on account of £2,000 towards her 2026/27 tax bill. She'll have to make a further payment of £2,000 in July 2026. Her actual tax bill for 2025/26 is £5,000. In January 2027 her payments will be:

	£
Tax due for tax year 2025/26	5,000
Less:	
Payment on account - paid 31 January 2026	2,000
Payment on account - paid 31 July 2026	2,000
Balance for 2025/26	1,000
Add:	
Payment on account for 2026/27 (50% of £5,000)	2,500
Total due 31 January 2027	3,500

When income is rising, payments on account can catch out the unwary, as each January there is both a shortfall of tax and a new, higher payment on account to pay. A sensible approach is to save for your tax throughout the year and to complete your tax return early in the tax year, so you have plenty of notice if the bill is higher than expected.

When income is falling (or ceasing) then it is possible to make a claim to HMRC to reduce payments on account so that you don't pay tax in advance that is more than necessary. If the payments on account you make are more than your tax bill, these will be offset against your next payments on account or refunded to you.

Setting up a limited company as a 'money box'

If you already have a paid job, then it's possible that your additional income from writing may take your total income into a higher tax band. If you don't need the money now, setting up a limited company could mean that the company pays corporation tax at a lower rate.

For example, Jamie earns £60,000 through his employment; he also receives £2,212 in Child Benefit in respect of his two children. He earns a further £20,000 in profit as a writer. He doesn't need to access the additional money now and is happy to leave it in his company. His tax liability as a sole trader can be compared with that of the limited company as follows:

Sole trader	**£**
Income tax on £20,000 @ 40%	8,000
High Income Child Benefit Tax Charge	2,212
Total due	10,212

Limited company	**£**
Corporation tax on £20,000 @ 19%	3,800
Total due	3,800

Although this is an extreme example, it shows that through using a limited company Jamie has saved £6,412 of tax on £20,000 of income. Once Jamie wants to take the money out of the company, it will be taxable on him personally, but he can control the amount paid so that it might be covered by his personal allowance entirely or subject to a lower rate of tax than he is paying now. If Jamie's plans are to build up a savings buffer, so that one day he can take the plunge and become a full-time writer, then this could be of real benefit.

Corporation tax is payable on the profit earned by a company. The first £50,000 of profit is taxed at 19%. Profits between £50,000 and £250,000 are taxed at a marginal rate of 26.5% and profits over £250,000 at 25%. There are also special rules that reduce the tax bands where more than one company is controlled by the same people.

Stage 3: writing as main source of income

Typically, a writer at this stage will either be self-employed or trade through a limited company. A limited company has to be 'incorporated' at Companies House and, once it is set up, it exists as a legal entity. It can enter into contracts, have a bank account, and exist without you. It is possible to trade both as a sole trader and through a limited company. It may even be the case that an author has some of their books taxed as a sole trader and other titles taxed within a limited company.

Issues on incorporation

If you do trade through a limited company, it is important to ensure that the underlying paperwork is correct. Here are some issues to bear in mind:

- For a company to receive copyright income, it must be legally entitled to the income. This can be achieved by ensuring the company exists before the book has been written and a service contract is in place between the director (i.e. the author) and the company.
- It isn't sufficient to simply 'bank' any proceeds into your company. All contracts need to be properly drawn up in the company's name.
- If you simply give your copyright to your company, it can create a tax issue; HMRC will expect you to pay income tax on the market value of the gift and will also expect the company to pay tax on the income it receives. In effect, the same income could be taxed twice.

• It is possible to sell the copyright to the company. This results in a better tax position, as the company would be able to get some tax relief for the cost of the copyright, but it will require a valuation of the copyright which brings with it costs and some uncertainty.
• Once your company owns the copyright, royalty income is 'locked' into being paid to the company. If you wished to own the copyright personally, it would need to be transferred out of the company at a fair value. You may find you have a company for a much longer time than you first anticipate, because it may not be practical to close it down until the copyright has a negligible value.

VAT

VAT (Value Added Tax) is a tax that businesses are required to charge their customers for goods or services. A writer is no different from any other business and therefore must charge VAT when supplying writing services. The standard UK rate of VAT is currently 20%. VAT is a complicated subject and much of it is beyond the scope of this book. However, there are some key things a writer should be aware of.

A VAT-registered business usually submits a quarterly VAT return within one month and seven days of the end of the VAT quarter. Any VAT due is then paid by the same deadline. Being VAT-registered is not entirely bad news; a VAT-registered business has to charge VAT on their relevant services, but they can also claim back VAT on things they buy for their business. For example, in the VAT quarter ending 31 December 2024 a writer gets a publishing deal for £10,000 plus £2,000 of VAT. Their agent charges them £1,500 plus £300 VAT, and they buy a computer for writing for £500 plus £100 VAT. They would submit a VAT return to HMRC by 7 February 2025 and pay over £1,600, as follows:

	£
VAT charged	2,000
Less:	
VAT on agent's fees	300
VAT on computer	100
Paid to HMRC	1,600

Although this may make you feel worse off, especially when you are paying £1,600 to HMRC, you are in fact better off by £400 – this being the difference between the VAT you have been paid and the VAT you have paid out.

IR35

IR35 was introduced in April 2000 to stop the practice of employees setting up a limited company (a 'personal service company') and invoicing their employer for their work rather than being paid as an employee. This practice led to a large tax saving for both the employer and the employee.

IR35 only applies to limited companies, so a writer who is trading as a sole trader can ignore it. From April 2021 both public entities and larger private companies have to look at the status of people working through personal service companies and, if necessary, deduct tax and National Insurance.

For most writers operating through a personal service company, it will be clear that they are not working for anyone as disguised employment. For other writers the situation may be more uncertain. For example, a copywriter with their own company providing weekly content for a client who describes them as their 'Content Manager', pays them a regular salary, expects them to attend meetings on site and doesn't allow a substitute, may be caught by the IR35 rules.

The IR35 rules are complex and, if caught by the rules, your limited company has to pay out most of the money it receives as a salary to the employee – together with Employers National Insurance.

Specialist help should be sought if you think your company may be affected by IR35.

Sole trader or limited company – the key differences

Sole trader	Limited company
Starting up	
Nothing legal required	Must be incorporated at Companies House
Closing down	
Nothing legal required	Must be formally struck off at Companies House
Legal protection	
None – you and the business are one and the same	Limited liability (but watch out for contracts that pass on liabilities to directors)
If you are sued, then all your assets are at stake	If the company is sued, then only the assets of the company are at stake
Tax on profits	
Income tax paid depending on total earnings from all sources in the year; rates may be 0%, 20%, 40% or 45% depending on income	Corporation tax paid; rates are between 19% and 26.5%
Tax on profits extracted	
Not applicable – you pay tax on profit whether extracted or not	Dividend tax due at rates of 0%, 8.75%, 33.75% or 39.35% depending on income
National Insurance	
Pay Class 4 National Insurance	Only pay National Insurance on salaries paid to employees if they earn over the limit
Reporting	
Must tell HMRC you are trading and must complete an individual Self Assessment tax return each year (and comply with MTD for IT form 6 April 2026)	Must file accounts each year with Companies House Must submit a Confirmation Statement each year to Companies House Must file a corporation tax return each year with HMRC May have to run a payroll and report to HMRC Likely that director/shareholder will have to complete an individual Self Assessment tax return each year
Separate business bank account	
Advisable	Essential
VAT	
Can be VAT registered; it is a person that is VAT registered, not a business, which may have unintended consequences	Can be VAT registered
Creative averaging	
Can be used	Cannot be used
Why choose this one?	
Simple; cheap; you want to take all the money out of business when it's earned, not concerned about legal liability	Possible to save tax if you don't require all the money or are able to take advantage of splitting income; provides legal liability protection

VAT registration threshold

A business needs to register for VAT when the level of sales exceeds the VAT threshold. The VAT threshold is currently £90,000 and it applies to the last 12 months. To know whether you need to register or not, you have to look back at your cumulative sales over the last 12 months and, if these exceed the VAT threshold, you must register. You are also required to register if you believe your sales in the next 30 days alone will be more than the VAT threshold – for example if you bag a big publishing deal.

Some writers will make an early 'protective' VAT registration, so that they know they are registered and don't have to worry about tripping over the VAT threshold. It is important to remember that the turnover figure is not necessarily the amount you receive. For example, a writer gets an advance of £10,000; their agent deducts 15% plus their VAT and so the writer only receives £8,200. The figure that counts towards the VAT threshold is £10,000.

You do not need to include employment income in your turnover calculation or non-UK income (such as royalties from Amazon).

Finally, you need to include services you buy that are subject to the 'reverse charge' rules in your turnover calculation. For example, a writer who uses Facebook and Amazon advertising and spends, on average, more than £7,500 per month on this type of service would be required to register for VAT even if they are not making any sales themselves that are subject to VAT.

Voluntary registration

You can voluntarily register for VAT even if your sales are under the VAT registration threshold. The reason you may want to do this is to recover the VAT you are being charged – typically by your agent. For example, a writer gets a publishing deal for £25,000; their agent charges 15% commission plus VAT. If they are not VAT-registered, they'll lose the agent VAT of £750 but, if they are VAT-registered, they'd be able to recover this.

Being in the 'VAT club' will allow you to recover VAT on all your other business expenditure, such as computer costs and accountancy fees. Whether it is a good idea to register early depends on your circumstances. If you're not incurring much VAT, then it may not be worth the hassle.

What to include in your sales for VAT

You need to include all your UK sales and any foreign sales collected by your UK publisher. You can exclude any direct foreign sales (such as Amazon self-publishing or sales you or your agent have agreed with a foreign publisher). If you're a sole trader, you can exclude any employed income. But, if you are self-employed as something else too (e.g. you're both a plumber and a writer), you need to aggregate both sets of income. The VAT registration belongs to the *person*, not the *business*.

Claiming back VAT

When you first register for VAT, you can reclaim VAT on goods purchased up to four years prior to registration provided those goods are still held when registration takes place. VAT on services supplied in the six months prior to registration may also be reclaimed. To claim VAT you'll need a valid VAT receipt; a credit card receipt isn't enough, and a VAT inspector will disallow any expenditure that you can't produce a valid VAT receipt for – even if it's obvious that you would have paid VAT.

Not all expenditure has VAT charged on it:

Usually has VAT	Usually has no VAT
Agent commission	Trains, planes and taxis
Accountancy fees	Software subscriptions from overseas
Stationery	Postage
Computers and UK software	Entertainment
Internet and mobile phone	Insurance

Withholding tax and double taxation relief

Writers will often receive some or, in the case of an author selling via Amazon Kindle Direct Publishing (KDP), most of their income from an overseas source. Many foreign countries will charge a 'withholding tax' on such royalty payments, for example 30% in the case of the USA. Once withholding tax is paid, it is often not cost effective to try to recover it from the country in question, as doing so may require local professional advice and tax returns to be submitted to the country in question.

It is often possible to avoid any withholding tax being deducted in the first instance by completing the information required by the overseas publisher, so they don't have to apply withholding tax. Amazon KDP has an online tax interview to make it as easy as possible for you to comply. Other publishers in other countries will have to follow their own rules and will often ask for a Certificate of Residence to prove you are a UK tax payer. There are more details on applying for a Certificate of Residence at www.gov.uk/guidance/get-a-certificate-of-residence.

If you do suffer withholding tax, then it may be possible to use the foreign tax you have paid to offset against your tax liability on the same income when you complete your tax return. A word of warning though: you may not get back the full amount of foreign tax paid and relief is restricted to the amount of UK tax you would have to pay on the same income or the amount of foreign tax you would have paid had you complied with the requirements to avoid withholding tax.

Stage 4: Lifelong considerations

As a writer's career becomes more established, there are other financial considerations.

Pensions

State Pension

To qualify for the new State Pension, you need a minimum of ten qualifying years and at least 35 qualifying years to receive the maximum payments. You can check your pension entitlement online at www.gov.uk/check-state-pension. If you have gaps in your pension contribution history, then you can consider making voluntary contributions.

Private pensions

If you have been employed, you may have an occupational pension from your employment in place. Most writers who have been self-employed will depend upon their own pension arrangements using 'defined contribution' schemes. Contributions to a private pension by

Writers' Guild Pension Scheme

For their members writing for TV, radio and film, WGGB (Writers' Guild of Great Britain) have negotiated agreements with the BBC, ITV and PACT so that pension contributions are made to the Writers' Guild Pension Scheme. In return for the writer making a contribution to the scheme, the production company will also make a contribution, in addition to the writer's fee. More details are available from WGGB (see page 749 for contact details).

an individual are made net of basic rate income tax. This means that a contribution of £80 actually means the amount invested is £100, with £20 being claimed by the pension company from the government. A higher-rate tax payer would save another £20 in income tax, making the cost of putting £100 into a pension just £60. There are rules regarding how much you can invest each year and many people will need professional advice as to what scheme they invest in.

Insurances

Being a self-employed writer does mean that you don't have the same safety net that many employees may have. It is sensible to think about how you and your family would manage if you died or, through injury or illness, were unable to continue to earn a living. There are insurance policies that are available to help.

- **Life insurance** can provide a lump sum or a monthly income for a period of time if you die.
- **Critical illness insurance** can provide a lump sum or a monthly income for a period of time if you are diagnosed with a critical illness.
- **Income protection insurance** can provide a monthly income if you are unable to work due to ill health.

Wills

Making a will is important for a number of reasons. Amongst other things, you can specify who inherits your assets, make tax efficient choices and provide instructions as to who looks after your minor children. A writer also needs to consider what happens with any copyright they hold as part of their estate. Copyright can last up to 70 years after death, so it may represent a valuable asset. You may also have particular instructions as to what happens to your personal papers and unpublished works. It is also worth thinking about what happens with digital assets such as blogs, social media accounts, online videos, and access to cloud storage services like Dropbox. A bit of forward planning may save a lot of trouble for the people dealing with your estate.

Further advice: useful websites

HMRC
www.gov.uk/government/organisations/hm-revenue-customs

Institute of Chartered Accountants in England and Wales
www.icaew.com

Institute of Chartered Accountants of Scotland
www.icas.com

These author associations offer support and advice on financial matters to their members:

National Union of Journalists
www.nuj.org.uk (see page 547)

Society of Authors
https://societyofauthors.org (see page 746)

WGGB (Writers' Guild of Great Britain)
https://writersguild.org.uk (see page 749)

Accountancy and business software tools include:

Sage
www.sage.com/en-gb/sage-business-cloud/accounting

Quickbooks
https://quickbooks.intuit.com/uk

Xero
www.xero.com/uk

Jonathan Ford BSC FCA and **Louise Ford** BA FCA are the directors of Writers Tax Ltd, a firm of chartered accountants that specialises in helping authors, scriptwriters and other professional writers with their tax and accountancy needs, which they established in 2020. They both qualified as chartered accountants with Price Waterhouse in Liverpool. Jonathan worked at Grant Thornton and later as Financial Controller at Mersey TV before setting up his own company. See their website https://writers.tax for more information.

National Insurance contributions

Sarah Bradford sets out the facts about National Insurance, explaining the contributory principle that underlies it, the various classes of contribution payable by workers (both employed and self-employed), the related benefit entitlements and information on current rates and earnings thresholds.

Nature of National Insurance contributions

The payment of primary Class 1 and Class 4 National Insurance contributions secures access to the state pension and to contributory benefits. This is the contributory principle of National Insurance. National Insurance contributions are payable by employed earners and their employers and also by self-employed earners. People who do not have any earnings or whose earnings are not sufficient to trigger a liability to pay National Insurance contributions and who do not receive National Insurance credits can choose to pay Class 3 or Class 2 National Insurance contributions voluntarily to maintain their contribution record.

If sufficient National Insurance contributions of the right type are paid or credited for a tax year, the year will be a qualifying year for National Insurance purposes. A person needs 35 qualifying years in order to receive the full state pension when they reach state pension age. Where a person has at least ten qualifying years, they will receive a reduced state pension.

Classes of National Insurance

There are various different classes of National Insurance contribution. The class (or classes) that you pay will depend on whether you are an employed earner, a self-employed earner, an employer or a voluntary contributor. Contributions may be earnings-related, payable on profits or payable at a flat rate, depending on the class.

The different classes of contribution are shown in the box below. Class 1 and 4 contributions are only payable once earnings exceed certain thresholds and limits. The rates and thresholds applying to 2025/26 are set out in the box on page 738.

Classes of National Insurance

Nature of contribution	Payable by
Class 1 Earnings-related	Employed earners (primary Class 1 contributions) Employer (secondary Class 1 contributions)
Class 1A Earnings-related	Employer on taxable benefits in kind and taxable termination payments and sporting testimonials
Class 1B Earnings-related	Employer on items included within a PAYE Settlement Agreement and on the tax due under that agreement
Class 2 Flat rate	Voluntary contributions payable by self-employed earners with low profits
Class 3 Flat rate	Voluntary contributions
Class 3A Variable amount	Payable between 12 October 2015 and 5 April 2017 voluntarily by those who reached state pension age before 6 April 2016 to boost their state pension
Class 4 Profit-related	Self-employed earners

Contributions payable by writers and artists

As for other earners, the class of National Insurance payable by writers and artists depends on whether they are a self-employed earner or an employed earner. This is not something that they can choose – it will depend on the facts of the engagement. It is important that the employment status of the writer or artist is categorised correctly as this will affect not only what class (and therefore how) they pay, but also what benefits they are entitled to.

Categorisation – employed earner *v* self-employed earner

To ensure that writers and artists pay the right class of National Insurance contributions, it is important they are correctly categorised. Employed earners with sufficient earnings will pay Class 1 National Insurance contributions, whereas self-employed earners with sufficient profits will pay Class 4 contributions. Employed earners with low earnings and self-employed earners with low profits will receive a National Insurance credit if their earnings/profits exceed a minimum level. Self-employed earners whose profits are too low to benefit from the National Insurance credit can choose to pay Class 2 contributions voluntarily.

A worker's categorisation depends on the characteristics of the engagement. In many cases, it will be clear whether a worker is an employed earner or a self-employed earner. For example, a writer who is employed by a publishing firm and has a contract of employment will be an employed earner and will pay Class 1 National Insurance contributions on their earnings, whereas a freelance writer who undertakes commissions for a variety of people and is paid a fee for each commission will be a self-employed earner and will pay Class 4 contributions if their profits exceed the Class 4 lower profits limit.

Characteristics of employment

The following characteristics apply to an engagement where the worker is an employed earner:

- they are required to work regularly unless they are unwell or on leave;
- they are expected to work a minimum number of hours a week and expect to be paid for the time that they work;
- a manager or supervisor is responsible for their workload and will say when a job should be finished or how it should be done;
- they must do the work themselves – they can't send someone else to do it instead;
- the business deducts tax and National Insurance from their pay;
- they are entitled to paid holiday;
- they are entitled to statutory payments;
- they can join the business's pensions scheme;
- they are subject to grievance and disciplinary procedures;
- the contract sets out the procedure applying in the event of redundancy;
- they work at the business premises or at a location specified by the business;
- they work for only that business or, if they have another job, it is completely separate;
- the offer letter and contract refer to the 'employee' and the 'employer'.

For example, a staff writer who is paid a salary and contracted to work 35 hours a week would be an employed earner.

Characteristics of self-employment

The following characteristics indicate that the writer or artist is a self-employed earner:

- they are in business for themselves and are responsible for the success or failure of the business and can make a profit or a loss;
- they decide what work they take on and where and how they do it;
- they can hire someone else to do the work;
- they are responsible for fixing unsatisfactory work in their own time;
- they agree a fixed price for a job – the fee is the same regardless of how long it takes them to do the work;
- they use their own money to buy any equipment needed and to cover the running costs of the business;
- they work for more than one client.

For example, a writer who is commissioned to write specific articles for different publications and who works for a number of publishers, being paid a fee for each article, would be a self-employed earner.

Marginal cases

It will not always be clear whether a writer or artist is an employed earner or a self-employed earner. In this situation, it is necessary to look at the overall picture and see whether, on balance, the writer or artist is employed or self-employed. It should be noted that there is not one single definitive test, rather a question of seeing what characteristics of employment and what characteristics of self-employment are present.

In reaching a decision, the following factors need to be considered:

- The nature of the contract and the written terms – a contract for *services* indicates employment and a contract of *service* indicates self-employment.
- The nature of the engager's business and the nature of the job.
- Right of substitution – a right to send a substitute indicates self-employment.
- Mutuality of obligation – for a contract for services there must be minimum mutual obligations; the employer is obliged to offer work and the employee is obliged to do that work.
- Right of control – a high degree of control (on the part of the employer) over how and where the worker performs the work suggests employment.
- Provision of equipment – the provision by the worker of their own equipment suggests self-employment.
- Financial risk – a person who is self-employed bears a higher degree of financial risk than an employee.
- Opportunity to profit – a person who is self-employed has the opportunity to profit if they do the job quicker or under-budget.
- Length of engagement – while this is not a decisive factor, an open-ended contract is more likely to indicate employment.
- Part and parcel of the organisation – a worker who is seen as 'part and parcel' of the organisation is likely to be an employee.
- Entitlement to benefits – a worker who is entitled to employee-type benefits, such as a pension, is more likely to be an employee.
- Personal factors – a highly skilled worker may not need supervising but may still be an employee.

• Intention – while intention alone cannot determine status, it can be useful in forming an opinion on whether the worker is employed or self-employed.

Check Employment Status for Tax (CEST) tool

HMRC have produced a tool – the Check Employment Status for Tax (CEST) tool – which can be used to reach a decision on whether a writer or artist is employed or self-employed. The tool asks a series of questions on the engagement, which must be answered honestly, in order to reach a decision. As long as the information provided is accurate and represents the reality of the engagement, HMRC will stand by the decision that is reached. The CEST tool is available on the government website at www.gov.uk/guidance/check-employment-status-for-tax.

Workers providing their services through a personal service company

Anti-avoidance rules apply where services are provided through a personal limited company or another intermediary to an end client. There are two sets of rules to consider – the off-payroll working rules and the IR35 rules. The rules that apply depend on the nature of the end client.

• Off-payroll working rules

The off-payroll working rules were introduced from 6 April 2017. They applied from the date when services were provided through an intermediary to a private sector body. The rules were extended from 6 April 2021, and from that date they also apply when the end client is a medium or large private sector organisation.

The end client must carry out a status determination to ascertain whether the worker would be an employee of the end client if they provided their services to them directly. Where this is the case, the end client must deduct tax and National Insurance from payments made to the worker's personal company (after adjusting the bill for VAT and the cost of any materials), and report this to HMRC. The worker receives credit for the tax and National Insurance on payment made to them by their personal limited company. They do not need to consider the IR35 rules because the off-payroll working rules apply instead.

• IR35

From 6 April 2021 onwards, the IR35 rules only apply where a worker provides their services to a small private sector organisation through an intermediary, such as a personal service company. The worker's personal service company must determine whether the worker would be an employee of the small private sector organisation if they provided their services directly. If the answer is 'yes' the IR35 rules apply. The intermediary must calculate the deemed employment payment at the end of the tax year, and account for tax and National Insurance on that payment to HMRC.

Employed earners – Class 1 National Insurance

Class 1 National Insurance is payable on the earnings of an employed earner. The employed earner pays primary contributions and the secondary contributor (which is generally the employer) pays secondary contributions. The payment of primary Class 1 National Insurance contributions by the employed earner is the mechanism by which the employed earner earns the right to the state pension and contributory benefits. Secondary Class 1 contributions, payable by the employer, do not earn benefit entitlement – they are akin to a tax on the employee's earnings.

Contributions are calculated by reference to earnings for the earnings period on a non-cumulative basis; no account is taken of earnings previously in the tax year, only those for the earnings period. The earnings period will normally correspond to the pay interval. However, directors have an annual earnings period, regardless of their actual pay frequency. The employer must deduct primary contributions from the employee's pay and pay them over to HMRC together with tax deducted under PAYE and the employer's secondary contributions.

• Primary Class 1 National Insurance

Primary Class 1 National Insurance contributions are payable by employees aged 16 and over until they reach state pension age (which depends on their date of birth). No contributions are payable until earnings reach the *lower earnings limit* (set at £125 per week, £542 per month, £6,500 per year for 2025/26). They are then payable at a notional zero rate until earnings reach the *primary threshold*. This is important as it secures the year as a qualifying year for National Insurance purposes (as long as earnings are paid above the lower earnings limit for each earnings period in the tax year). Where earnings are below the lower earnings limit, the year is not a qualifying year (although may become one if the worker receives National Insurance credits or pays voluntary contributions).

Contributions are payable on earnings above the *primary threshold* at the main primary rate of 8% (2025/26 rate) until earnings reach the upper earnings limit and at the additional primary rate of 2% (2025/26) on earnings in excess of the *upper earnings limit* and at the additional primary rate of 2% (2025/26) on earnings in excess of the *upper earnings limit*

The *primary threshold* is set at £242 per week (£1,048 per month, £12,570 per year) for 2025/26 and is aligned with the personal allowance applying for tax purposes. The *upper earnings* limit is set at £967 per week, £4,189 per month and £50,270 per year for 2025/26.

• Secondary Class 1 contributions

Secondary contributions are payable by the secondary contributor, which in most cases is the employed earner's employer. They are payable on the earnings of an employee aged 16 and above; unlike primary contributions, the secondary liability does not stop when the employed earner reaches state pension age.

Contributions are payable at the secondary rate of 15% on earnings in excess of the *secondary threshold* (set at £96 per week, £417 per month, £5,000 per year for 2025/26).

A higher secondary threshold applies to the earnings of employees under the age of 21 (the upper secondary threshold for under 21s), to those of apprentices under the age of 25 (the apprentice upper secondary threshold) and to armed forces veterans in the first year of their first civilian employment since leaving the armed forces. Each of these thresholds are aligned with the upper earnings limit for primary Class 1 purposes (set at £967 per week, £4,189 per month and £50,270 per year for 2025/26).

A separate secondary threshold applies to the earnings of a new employee in the first 36 months of their employment with an employer with physical premises in a special tax site, such as a Freeport or an investment zone. For 2025/26, this threshold is set at £481 per week, £2,083 per month and £25,000 per year.

These upper thresholds only apply for secondary Class 1 purposes; the employee or apprentice pays the primary contributions at the usual rates.

Eligible employers can claim the Employment Allowance which is offset against their secondary Class 1 National Insurance liability. The Employment Allowance is set at £10,500 for 2025/26 (capped at the employer's secondary Class 1 liability where this is lower).

For 2025/26, employers whose secondary Class 1 liability exceeded £100,000 in 2024/25 are able to benefit from the Employment Allowance as the previous condition restricting the allowance to employers whose secondary Class 1 liability for the previous year was less than £100,000 has been lifted. Companies where the sole employee is also a director do not qualify for the allowance.

The Employment Allowance is not given automatically and must be claimed. This can be done through the employer's payroll software.

• Earnings for Class 1 purposes

Class 1 contributions are calculated on the earnings for the earnings period. The definition of 'earnings' includes any remuneration or profits derived from the employment. This will include payments of wages and salary, but will also include other items such as statutory sick pay, statutory payments, and certain share-based remuneration. Comprehensive guidance on what to include in earnings for National Insurance purposes can be found in the HMRC guidance CWG2 *Employer further guide to PAYE and National Insurance contributions*. The 2025/26 edition is available at www.gov.uk/government/publications/cwg2-further-guide-to-paye-and-national-insurance-contributions.

• Class 1A National Insurance contributions

Class 1A National Insurance contributions are employer-only contributions payable on taxable benefits in kind and also on taxable termination payments in excess of the £30,000 tax-free threshold and taxable sporting testimonials in excess of the £100,000 tax-free threshold. They are payable at the Class 1A rate, which for 2025/26 is set at 15%. The Class 1A rate is aligned with the secondary rate of Class 1 contributions.

• Class 1B National Insurance

Class 1B National Insurance contributions are employer-only contributions payable in place of the Class 1 or Class 1A liability that would otherwise arise on items included within a PAYE Settlement Agreement (PSA), and also on the tax due under the PSA. The Class 1B rate is aligned with the secondary Class 1 rate and is set at 15% for 2025/26.

Self-employed earners – Class 4 National Insurance contributions

Where a writer or artist is a self-employed earner, if their profits are high enough, they will pay Class 4 contributions on their profits. These are payable via the Self Assessment system and must be paid by 31 January after the end of the tax year to which they relate (i.e. by 31 January 2027 for 2025/26 contributions).

Self-employed earners whose profits are too low to pay Class 4 National Insurance contributions or receive a Class 4 National Insurance credit can choose to pay voluntary Class 2 contributions.

Class 4 National Insurance contributions are payable by self-employed earners on their profits if these are high enough. No contributions are payable on profits below the lower

National Insurance rates and thresholds 2025/26

National Insurance class	Rate or threshold
Class 1	
Lower earnings limit	£125 per week
	£542 per month
	£6,500 per year
Primary threshold	£242 per week
	£1,048 per week
	£12,570 per year
Secondary threshold	£96 per week
	£417 per month
	£5,000 per year
Upper earnings limit	£967 per week
	£4,189 per month
	£50,270 per year
Upper secondary threshold for under 21s	£967 per week
	£4,189 per month
	£50,270 per year
Apprentice upper secondary threshold	£967 per week
	£4,189 per month
	£50,270 per year
Veterans upper secondary threshold	£967 per week
	£4,189 per month
	£50,270 per year
Upper secondary threshold for special tax sites	£481 per week
	£2,083 per month
	£25,000 per year
Primary (employee) contributions	
On earnings between the primary threshold and the upper earnings limit	8%
On earnings above the upper earnings limit	2%
Secondary (employer) contributions	
On earnings above the relevant secondary threshold	15%
Class 1A and Class 1B	
Contribution rate (employer only)	15%
Class 2 (voluntary: self employed)	
Flat rate contribution	£3.50 per week
Small profits threshold	£6,845 a year
Class 3 (voluntary)	
Flat rate contribution	£17.75 per week
Class 4	
Lower profits limit	£12,570 a year
Upper profits limit	£50,270 a year
Main rate on earnings between the lower profits limit and the upper profits limit	6%
Additional rate on profits in excess of the upper profits limit	2%

profits limit, set at £12,570 for 2025/26. Class 4 contributions are payable at the main rate, set at 6% for 2025/26, on profits between the lower profits limit and the upper profits limit, set at £50,270 for 2025/26, and on profits in excess of the upper profits limit, at the additional Class 4 rate, set at 2% for 2025/26.

A self-employed earner whose profits are between the small profits threshold (set at £6,845 for 2025/26) and the lower profits limit (set at £12,570 for 2025/26) is awarded a National Insurance credit. This provides them with a qualifying year for state pension purposes for zero contribution cost. Self-employed earnings whose profits are below the lower profits threshold do not receive a National Insurance credit.

• Voluntary Class 2 National Insurance contributions

Self-employed earners whose earnings are below the small profits threshold (set at £6,845 for 2025/26), and who so not have sufficiently high profits to receive a National Insurance credit, can opt to pay voluntary Class 2 contributions to secure a qualifying year for state pension purposes. For 2025/26, voluntary Class 2 contributions are payable at £3.50 per week. Contributions for 2025/26 must be paid by 31 January 2027. Paying voluntary Class 2 contributions is a much cheaper option that paying voluntary Class 3 contributions.

Voluntary contributions – Class 3

A person can pay voluntary Class 3 contributions to plug gaps in their contributions record. Class 3 contributions are payable at the rate of £17.75 per week for 2025/26. Where a person has profits from self-employment below the *small profits threshold* (set at £6,845 for 2025/26), they can instead pay voluntary Class 2 contributions; at £3.50 per week for 2025/26 this is a much cheaper option.

Maximum contributions

Where a person has more than one job, or is both employed and self-employed, there is a cap on the contributions that are payable for the year. The calculations are complex.

National Insurance credits

National Insurance credits are available in certain circumstances where people are unable to work or because they are ill. There are two types of credit. Class 1 credits count towards state pension and contributory benefits, while Class 3 credits only count towards the state pension. Further detail on National Insurance credits can be found on the government website at www.gov.uk/national-insurance-credits.

Benefit entitlement

Class of contributions	Benefit entitlement
Primary Class 1 (employed earner)	State Pension, contribution-based Jobseeker's Allowance, contribution-based Employment and Support Allowance, Maternity Allowance and Bereavement Payment, Bereavement Allowance, Bereavement Support Payment.
Class 2 (voluntary: self-employed earners)	State Pension, contribution-based Employment and Support Allowance, Maternity Allowance and Bereavement Allowance.
Class 3 (voluntary contributions)	State Pension and Bereavement Payment, Bereavement Allowance, Widowed Parent's Allowance.

Benefit entitlement

The payment of National Insurance contributions (and the award of National Insurance credits) earns entitlement to the state pension and certain contributory benefits. The payment of primary Class 1, Class 2, Class 3 and Class 4 contributions confers benefit entitlement. Benefit entitlement depends on the class of contribution paid.

Sarah Bradford BA (Hons), FCA CTA (Fellow) is the director of WriteTax Ltd and the author of *National Insurance Contributions 2025/26* (and earlier editions) published by Bloomsbury Professional. She writes widely on tax and National Insurance contributions.

Public Lending Right

Under the PLR system, payment is made from public funds to authors and other contributors (writers, illustrators/photographers, translators, adapters/retellers, ghostwriters, editors/compilers/abridgers/revisers, narrators and producers) whose books (print, audiobook and ebook) are lent from public libraries. Payment is annual; the amount authors receive is proportionate to the number of times that their books were borrowed during the previous year (July to June).

How the system works

From the applications received, the PLR office compiles a database of authors and books (the PLR Register). A representative sample of book issues is recorded, consisting of all loans from selected public libraries. This is then multiplied in proportion to total library lending to produce, for each book, an estimate of its total annual loans throughout the country. The estimated loans are matched against the database of registered authors and titles to discover how many loans are credited to each registered book for the calculation of PLR payments, using the ISBN printed in the book (see below).

Parliament allocates a sum each year (£6.6 million for 2023/24) for PLR. This fund pays the administrative costs of PLR and reimburses local authorities for recording loans in the sample libraries (see below). The remaining money is divided by the total estimated national loan figure for all registered books in order to work out how much can be paid for each estimated loan of every registered ISBN.

Further information

Public Lending Right – British Library
Boston Spa, Wetherby, West Yorkshire LS23 7BQ
tel (01937) 546030
website www.bl.uk/plr, www.plrinternational.com
Contact Head of PLR Operations

The UK PLR scheme is administered by the British Library from its offices in Boston Spa. The UK PLR office also provides registration for the Irish PLR scheme on behalf of the Irish Public Lending Remuneration office.

Application forms, information and publications are all obtainable from the PLR Office. See website for further information on eligibility for PLR, loans statistics and forthcoming developments.

British Library Advisory Committee for Public Lending Right

Advises the British Library Board, the PLR Head of Policy and Engagement and Head of PLR Operations on the operation and future development of the PLR scheme.

Limits on payments

If all the registered interests in an author's books score so few loans that they would earn less than £1 in a year, no payment is due. However, if the books of one registered author score so high that the author's PLR earnings for the year would exceed £6,600, then only £6,600 is paid. (No author can earn more than £6,600 in PLR in any one year.) Money that is not paid out because of these limits belongs to the fund and increases the amounts paid that year to other authors.

The sample

Currently a statistical sampling method is employed to collect loans data. The sample represents only public lending libraries – academic, school, private and commercial libraries are not included. Only books which are loaned from public libraries can earn PLR; consultations of books on library premises are excluded.

The sample consists of the entire loans records for a year from libraries in more than 72 public library authorities spread through England, Scotland and Wales, and whole data is collected from Northern Ireland. In 2023/24, sample loans represent around 37% of the national total. All the computerised sampling points in an authority contribute loans data ('multi-site' sampling). An amendment to PLR legislation came into force in October 2023, allowing a gradual increase in the number of public libraries in the sample, with an aim to transition to full loans data collection over the next few years. Therefore the need to replace seven libraries every year, the removal of a library after four years is no longer required. Loans are totalled every 12 months for the period 1 July–30 June.

An author's entitlement to PLR depends on the loans accrued by his or her books in the sample. This figure is averaged up to produce first regional and then finally national estimated loans.

ISBNs

The PLR system uses ISBNs (International Standard Book Numbers) to identify books lent and correlate loans with entries on the PLR Register so that payments can be made. ISBNs are required for all registrations. Different editions (e.g. 1st, 2nd, hardback, paperback, large print) of the same book have different ISBNs. See *ISBNs: what you need to know* on page 689.

Authorship

In the PLR system the author of a printed book or ebook is any contributor such as the writer, illustrator, translator, compiler, editor or reviser. Authors must be named on the book's title page, or be able to prove authorship by some other means (e.g. receipt of royalties). The ownership of copyright has no bearing on PLR eligibility. Narrators, producers and abridgers are also eligible to apply for PLR shares in audiobooks and e-audiobooks.

Summary of the 42nd year's results

Registration: authors. When registration closed for the 42nd year (30 June 2024) there were 63,583 authors and assignees.

Eligible loans. The loans from UK libraries credited to registered books – approximately 33% of all library borrowings – qualify for payment. The remaining loans relate to books that are ineligible for various reasons, to books written by dead or foreign authors, and to books that have simply not been applied for.

Money and payments. PLR's administrative costs are deducted from the fund allocated to the British Library Board annually by Parliament. Total government funding for 2023/24 was £6.6 million. The amount distributed to authors was just over £6.4 million. The Rate per Loan for 2023/24 was 11.76 pence.

The numbers of authors in various payment categories are as follows:

*298	payments at	£5,000–6,600
375	payments between	£2,500–4,999.99
911	payments between	£1,000–2,499.99
939	payments between	£500–999.99
3,369	payments between	£100–499.99
18,383	payments between	£1–99.99
24,275	TOTAL	

* Includes 206 authors whose book loans reached the maximum threshold

Co-authorship/illustrators. In the PLR system the authors of a book are those writers, translators, editors, compilers and illustrators as defined above. Authors must apply for registration before their books can earn PLR and this can be done via the PLR website. There is no restriction on the number of authors who can register shares in any one book as long as they satisfy the eligibility criteria.

Writers and/or illustrators. At least one contributor must be eligible and they must jointly agree what share of PLR each will take based on contribution. This agreement is necessary even if one or two are ineligible or do not wish to register for PLR. The eligible authors will receive the share(s) specified in the application.

Translators. Translators may apply for a 30% fixed share (to be shared equally between joint translators).

Editors and compilers. An editor or compiler may apply to register a 20% share if they have written at least 10% of the book's content or more than ten pages of text in addition to normal editorial work and are named on the title page. Alternatively, editors may register 20% if they have a royalty agreement with the publisher. In the case of joint editors/compilers, the total editor's share should be divided equally.

Audiobooks. PLR shares in audiobooks are fixed by the UK scheme and may not be varied. *Writers* may register a fixed 60% share in an audiobook, providing that it has not been abridged or translated. In cases where the writer has made an additional contribution (e.g. as narrator), she/he may claim both shares. *Narrators* may register a fixed 20% PLR share in an audiobook. *Producers* may register a fixed 20% share in an audiobook. *Abridgers* (in cases where the writer's original text has been abridged prior to recording as an audiobook) qualify for 12% (20% of the writer's share). *Translators* (in cases where the writer's original text has been translated from another language) qualify for 18% (30% of the writer's share). If there is more than one writer, narrator, etc the appropriate shares should be divided equally.

Dead or missing co-authors. Where it is impossible to agree shares with a co-author because that person is dead or untraceable, then the surviving co-author or co-authors may submit an application to register a share which reflects their individual contribution to the book.

Transferring PLR after death. First applications may not be made by the estate of a deceased author. However, if an author registers during their lifetime the PLR in their books can be transferred to a new owner and continues for up to 70 years after the date of their death. The new owner can apply to register new titles if first published one year before, or up to ten years after, the date of the author's death. New editions of existing registered titles can also be registered posthumously.

Residential qualifications. To register for the UK PLR scheme, at the time of application authors must have their only home or principal home in the UK or in any of the other countries within the European Economic Area (i.e. EC member states plus Iceland, Norway and Liechtenstein).

Eligible books

In the PLR system each edition of a book is registered and treated as a separate book. A book is eligible for PLR registration provided that:

- it has an eligible author (or co-author);
- it is printed and bound (paperbacks count as bound);

- it has already been published;
- copies of it have been put on sale, i.e. it is not a free handout;
- the authorship is personal, i.e. not a company or association, and the book is not crown copyright;
- it has an ISBN;
- it is not wholly or mainly a musical score;
- it is not a newspaper, magazine, journal or periodical.

Audiobooks. An audiobook is defined as an 'authored text' or 'a work recorded as a sound recording and consisting mainly of spoken words'. Applications can therefore only be accepted to register audiobooks which meet these requirements and are the equivalent of a printed book. Music, dramatisations and live recordings do not qualify for registration. To qualify for UK PLR in an audiobook contributors should be named on the case in which the audiobook is held; or be able to refer to a contract with the publisher; or be named within the audiobook recording.

Ebooks. Previously only ebooks downloaded to fixed terminals in library premises and then taken away on loan on portable devices to be read elsewhere qualified for PLR payment. Information provided by libraries suggested that the vast majority of ebook and digital audio lending was carried out 'remotely' to home PCs and mobile devices, which meant the loan did not qualify for PLR.

On 27 April 2017 the Digital Economy Bill, which included provision to extend the UK PLR legislation to include remote loans of ebooks from public libraries, received Royal Assent. The new arrangements took effect officially from 1 July 2018, and remote ebook loans data is now collected, and the first payments arising from the newly eligible loans were made in February 2020. The PLR website provides updated information on this legislation.

Statements and payment

Authors who have registered their email address may view their statement online. Only registered authors with an offline account and no registered email address receive a statement posted to their address, if a payment is due.

Sampling arrangements

To help minimise the unfairness that arises inevitably from a sampling system, the scheme specifies the eight regions within which authorities and sampling points have to be designated and includes libraries of varying size. Prior to an amendment to legislation that came into force October 2024, part of the sample drops out by rotation each year to allow fresh libraries to be included. Since the amendment, once included in the sample a library will stay in the sample. The aim is to slowly transition to full public library loans data collection over the next few years. The following library authorities were designated for the year 1 July 2024–30 June 2025 (all are multi-site authorities). This list is based on the nine government regions for England plus Northern Ireland, Scotland and Wales. The composition of the PLR library authority sample changes annually and not all regions have to be represented each year.

- East – Bedford, Cambridgeshire, Central Bedfordshire, Lincolnshire, Norfolk, Peterborough, Suffolk, Southend-on-Sea

• East Midlands – Derbyshire, Leicester City, Leicestershire, North Northamptonshire, Nottinghamshire, West Northamptonshire
• London – Bexley, Brent, Bromley, Camden, City of London, Croydon, Ealing, Enfield, Hammersmith and Fulham, Haringey, Harrow, Havering, Hillingdon, Hounslow, Islington, The Royal Borough of Kensington and Chelsea (RBKC), Lambeth, Merton, Newham, Redbridge, Richmond Upon Thames, Southwark, Sutton, Tower Hamlets, Waltham Forest, Wandsworth, Westminster
• North East – Darlington, Durham, Gateshead, Hartlepool, Middlesborough, Newcastle, North Tyneside, South Tyneside, Stockton-on-Tees
• North West & Merseyside – Blackburn & Darwen, Blackpool, Bolton, Cheshire West, East and Chester, Cumberland, Halton, Knowsley, Liverpool, Manchester, Oldham, Rochdale, Sefton, St Helens, Stockport, Tameside, Warrington, Westmoreland and Furness, Wigan, Wirral
• South East – Brighton and Hove, Buckinghamshire, East Sussex, Kent, Luton, Medway, Oxfordshire, Portsmouth, Southampton, Surrey, West Berkshire, Windsor and Maidenhead
• South West – Cornwall, Devon, Gloucestershire, Hampshire, Isle of Wight, Plymouth, Swindon, Torbay, Wiltshire, Worcestershire
• West Midlands – Coventry, Sandwell, Shropshire, Solihull, Staffordshire, Stoke on Trent, Warwickshire, Wolverhampton
• Yorkshire & The Humber – Barnsley, Bradford, Doncaster, Kingston Upon Hull, Kirklees, Leeds, North Lincolnshire, North Yorkshire, Rotherham, Sheffield, Wakefield
• Northern Ireland – The Northern Ireland Library Authority
• Scotland – Aberdeen, Angus, Clackmannanshire, Dumfries & Galloway, Dundee, East Ayrshire, East Dumbartonshire, East Lothian, East Renfrewshire, Glasgow, Highland, Inverclyde, Moray, North Ayrshire, North Lanarkshire, Orkney, Perth & Kinross, Shetland, South Ayrshire, South Lanarkshire, Stirling, West Dumbartonshire, West Lothian
• Wales – Bridgend, Caerphilly, Cardiff, Carmarthenshire, Ceredigion, Conwy, Denbighshire, Gwynedd, Methyr Tydfil, Monmouthshire, Neath Port Talbot, Pembrokeshire, Powys, Rhondda Cynon Taf, Swansea, Torfaen, Wrexham.

Participating local authorities are reimbursed on an actual cost basis for additional expenditure incurred in providing loans data to the PLR Office. The extra PLR work mostly consists of modifications to computer programs to accumulate loans data in the local authority computer and to transmit the data to the PLR Office.

Reciprocal arrangements

Reciprocal PLR arrangements now exist with the German, Dutch, Austrian and other European PLR schemes. Authors can apply for overseas PLR for most of these countries through the ALCS (Authors' Licensing and Collecting Society; see page 716). The exception to this rule is Ireland. Authors should now register for Irish PLR through the UK PLR Office. Further information on PLR schemes internationally and recent developments within the EC towards wider recognition of PLR is available from the PLR Office or on the international PLR website.

Society of Authors

The Society of Authors (SoA) is the UK trade union for all types of writers, illustrators and literary translators at every stage of their careers.

Founded in 1884, the Society of Authors now has over 12,000 members. Members receive unlimited free advice on all aspects of the profession, including confidential clause-by-clause contract vetting, access to professional and geographic author communities and a wide range of exclusive offers. It campaigns and lobbies on the issues that affect authors and holds hundreds of events online and across the UK each year, offering opportunities for authors to network and learn from each other. It manages more than 58 literary estates, the income from which helps to fund the organisation's work.

Members

SoA members include household names, such as Malorie Blackman, Stephen Fry, Lemn Sissay and Kate Mosse, but they also include authors right at the start of their careers. Amongst the SoA membership are academic writers, biographers, broadcasters, children's writers, crime writers, dramatists, educational writers, ELT writers, health writers, ghostwriters, graphic novelists, historians, illustrators, journalists, medical writers, non-fiction writers, novelists, poets, playwrights, radio writers, scriptwriters, short story writers, translators, spoken word artists, YA writers and more.

The benefits available to all SoA members include the following:

- assistance with contracts, from negotiation and assessment of terms to clause-by-clause, confidential vetting;
- unlimited advice on queries, covering any aspect of the business of authorship;
- taking up complaints on behalf of members on any issue concerned with the business of authorship;

Membership

The Society of Authors
24 Bedford Row, London WC1R 4EH
tel 020-3880 2230
email info@societyofauthors.org
website https://societyofauthors.org
Chief Executive Anna Ganley

There are two membership options: Regular and Plus membership.

Full membership is available to professional writers, poets, translators and illustrators working in any genre or medium. This includes those who have had a full-length work traditionally published, broadcast or performed commercially; self-published or been published on a print-on-demand or ebook-only basis and who meet sales criteria; published or had broadcast or performed an equivalent body of professional work; or administrators of a deceased author's estate. Authors at the start of their careers are invited to join as Associates.

Associate membership is available to anyone actively working to launch a career as an author. This includes authors who are starting out in self-publishing but who are not yet making a profit; authors who have been offered a contract for publication or agent representation but who are not yet published; students engaged on a course of at least one academic year's duration that will help them develop a career as an author, as well as other activities that mark the early stages of an author's career. Associate members enjoy all the same services and benefits as Full members.

Membership is subject to election and payment of subscription fees.

The subscription fee (tax deductible) starts at £32.50 per quarter, or £22.75 for those aged 35 or under. A concessionary rate for over 65s is available on request. Joint membership is also available for £48.75.

• pursuing legal actions for breach of contract, copyright infringement and the non-payment of royalties and fees, when the risk and cost preclude individual action by a member and issues of general concern to the profession are at stake;
• conferences, seminars, meetings and other opportunities to network and learn from other authors;
• regular communications and a comprehensive range of publications, including the SoA's quarterly journal, *The Author*;
• discounts on books, exclusive rates on specialist insurance, special offers on products and services and free membership of the Authors' Licensing and Collecting Society (ALCS; see page 716).

Networks and groups for members include:
• Authors with Disabilities and Chronic Illnesses – a peer support network for authors living and working with health challenges;
• Comics Creators Network – a professional support network for all types of comics creators;
• Children's Writers and Illustrators Group – a professional community of writers and illustrators who create content for the children's publishing market;
• Educational Writers Group – protecting the interests of educational authors in professional matters, especially contracts, rates of pay, digitalisation and copyright;
• Poetry and Spoken Word Group – a new, increasingly active group to which all new member poets are subscribed on joining SoA;
• Scriptwriters Group – representing members working in radio, TV, film and games development;
• Translators Association – a source of expert advice for individual literary translators and a collective voice representing the profession (see page 561);
• Carers Network – a new group designed to help keep writers writing when they take on caring responsibilities for someone with an illness or disability;
• The SoA also coordinates a growing network of over 49 local author communities across the UK.

Campaigning and lobbying

The SoA is a voice for authors and works at a national and international level to improve terms and treatment of authors, negotiating with all parties including publishers, broadcasters, agents and governments. Current areas of campaigning include contract terms, copyright, freedom of expression, tax and benefits arrangements and Public Lending Right (PLR; see page 741) – which the SoA played a key role in establishing.

In the UK the SoA lobbies parliament, ministers and departments and makes submissions on relevant issues, working closely with the Department for Culture, Media and Sport and the All Party Parliamentary Writers Group. The SoA is a member of the British Copyright Council and was instrumental in setting up ALCS. They chair the Creators for Rights Alliance (CRA), a partnership of unions and member organisations from across the creative industries, working together on common interests such as copyright, payment and credit, and in 2022 launched the cross-industry 'Pay the Creator' campaign. It is recognised by the BBC in the negotiation of rates for authors' contributions to radio drama, as well as for the broadcasting of published material.

The SoA is a member of the European Writers' Council and applies pressure globally, working with sister organisations as part of the International Authors' Foundation.

It also works closely with other professional bodies, including the Association of Authors' Agents, the Booksellers Association, the Publishers Association, the Independent Publishers Guild, the British Council, the National Union of Journalists and the Writers' Guild of Great Britain. (See the societies listings that start on page 535.)

Awards and grants

The SoA supports authors through a wide range of awards and grants. Over £900,000 in awards and grant are given annually. The following prizes and awards are administered:

- the annual SoA Awards – ten prizes for poetry, fiction and non-fiction, and illustration, awarding authors at the beginning of their careers as well as those well established;
- two audio drama prizes: the Imison Award for a writer new to radio drama and the Tinniswood Award for best original audio drama;
- awards for translations from Arabic, Dutch/Flemish, French, German, Hebrew, Italian, Japanese, Spanish and Swedish into English;
- *The Sunday Times* Charlotte Aitken Young Writer of the Year Award;
- the ALCS Educational Writers' Awards;
- the Ilse Schwepcke Prize for Women's Travel Writing;
- the Authors' Foundation and K. Blundell Trust, which give grants to assist authors working on their next book;
- the Authors' Contingency Fund, which offers hardship grants to authors in financial difficulty;
- the SoA Access Fund;
- Strachey Trust Grant.

Writers' Guild of Great Britain (WGGB)

The WGGB is the TUC-affiliated trade union for writers.

WGGB represents writers working in film, television, audio, theatre, books, poetry, animation, comedy and videogames. Formed in 1959 as the Screenwriters' Guild, the union gradually extended into all areas of freelance writing activity and copyright protection. It comprises professional writers in all media, united in common concern for one another and regulating the conditions under which they work.

Apart from necessary dealings with government and policies on legislative matters affecting writers, the WGGB is, by constitution, non-political, has no involvement with any political party and members pay no political levy.

WGGB employs a permanent general secretary and other permanent staff and is administered by an Executive Council of around 20 members.

Membership

Writers' Guild of Great Britain
1st Floor, 134 Tooley Street, London SE1 2TU
tel 020-7833 0777
email admin@writersguild.org.uk
website https://writersguild.org.uk
Facebook www.facebook.com/thewritersguild
X @The WritersGuild
General Secretary Ellie Peers

WGGB has a range of membership options, and welcomes writers at all stages of their careers – whether they are professional writers with credits and an agent, or just starting out. There is also a membership level for students and for those who work professionally with writers, for example agents. Find out about eligibility criteria, subscription amounts and join online via the WGGB website: www.writersguild.org.uk/join-renew

Members receive a weekly email newsletter. The WGGB website contains full details of collective agreements and WGGB activities, plus a 'Find a Writer' service and a dedicated members' area; information is also made available on X, Facebook, Instagram and other social media channels. Other benefits include legal advice and contract vetting; free training; member events, discounts and special offers (subject to membership tier).

WGGB agreements

WGGB's core function is to negotiate minimum terms in areas in which its members work. Agreements form the basis of the individual contracts signed by members. It also gives individual advice to its members on contracts and other matters and maintains a welfare fund to help writers in financial trouble. Details of negotiations outlined below represent just some of the union's work in this area.

Television

WGGB negotiates minimum terms agreements with the BBC, ITV, Netflix, Pact (Producers' Alliance for Cinema and Television; see page 549) and TAC (representing Welsh-language television producers).

WGGB TV agreements regulate minimum fees, residuals and royalties, copyright, credits and general conditions for television plays, series and serials, dramatisations and adaptations, soaps, sitcoms and sketch shows. One of the WGGB's most important achievements has been the establishment of pension rights for members. The BBC, ITV and independent producers pay a pension contribution on top of the standard writer's fee on the understanding that the WGGB member also pays a contribution.

The switch to digital television, subscription-video-on-demand and download-to-own services, mobile phone technology and the expansion of the BBC's commercial arm have seen WGGB in constant negotiation over the past two decades. WGGB now has agreements for all of the BBC's digital channels and for its joint venture channels. In May 2012 it signed new agreements with the BBC extending minimum terms over online services such as iPlayer. From April 2015 the first payments under the Writers Digital Payments scheme (a not-for-profit company) were paid out to writers whose work had been broadcast on BBC iPlayer and ITV Player. In 2016 WGGB negotiated a 75% fee increase for writers working under its 2003 Pact agreement, and also started work on rewriting the agreement. In 2017 it negotiated a new script agreement for television and online with the BBC, which was renegotiated in 2024 to provide additional compensation for writers' work across a number of new platforms.

Film

In 1985 an agreement was signed with two producer organisations: the British Film and Television Producers' Association and the Independent Programme Producers' Association (now known as Pact). Since then there has been an industrial agreement covering UK film productions and pension fund contributions have been negotiated for WGGB members. The agreement was renegotiated in February 1992 and consultations on an updated arrangement are in progress.

Audio

WGGB has a standard agreement for Radio Drama with the BBC, establishing a fee structure that is reviewed annually. It was comprehensively renegotiated in 2005 resulting in an agreement covering digital radio. In 1985 the BBC agreed to extend the pension scheme already established for television writers to include radio writers. WGGB has special agreements for Radio 4's *The Archers* and for BBC iPlayer. A separate agreement covers the reuse of old comedy and drama material on digital BBC Radio 4 Extra. It has also negotiated rates for podcasts.

Books

WGGB fought for the loans-based Public Lending Right (PLR, see page 741) to reimburse authors for books lent in libraries. The scheme is now administered by the British Library; WGGB is represented on its advisory committee. WGGB has a Books Committee, which works on behalf of book writers and poets. Issues affecting members include authors' earnings, self-publishing, print-on-demand services and ebooks, and in 2022 the union launched the *Is It A Steal?* (see page 672) joint campaign with the Society of Authors to tackle bad practice in the hybrid/paid-for publishing sector.

Theatre

In 1979 WGGB, together with the Theatre Writers' Union, negotiated the first industrial agreement for theatre writers. The Theatres National Committee Agreement (TNC) covers the Royal Shakespeare Company, the Royal National Theatre Company and the English Stage Company at the Royal Court. When their agreement was renegotiated in 2007, WGGB achieved a long-standing ambition of a minimum fee of £10,000 for a new play; for current minimum rates see the WGGB website.

In June 1986, a new agreement was signed with the Theatrical Management Association (now UK Theatre), which covers 95 provincial theatres. In 1993, this agreement was comprehensively revised and included a provision for a year-on-year increase in fees in line with the Retail Price Index. The agreement was renegotiated in 2015, and in 2024 (following a deal struck by WGGB and the Scottish Society of Playwrights), playwrights working under the agreement received landmark new terms for the digital exploitation of their work).

After many years of negotiation, an agreement was concluded in 1991 between WGGB and the Independent Theatre Council (ITC), which represents 200 of the smaller and fringe theatres as well as educational and touring companies. This agreement was revised in 2002 and the minimum fees are reviewed annually. WGGB is currently talking to the ITC about updating the agreement. The WGGB Theatre Committee runs the Olwen Wymark Theatre Encouragement Award scheme. In 2022 the union launched a landmark New Play Commission Scheme to address the severe impact Covid-19 had on playwrights and new writing in the theatre sector, resulting in commissions for 18 new plays, which have now started to be performed at theatres across the UK.

Videogames

WGGB counts games writers amongst its members and holds regular networking events for them. The union publishes guidelines for games writers and those who work with them, outlining best practice in this growing area.

Other activities

WGGB is in touch with government and national institutions wherever and whenever the interests of writers are in question or are being discussed, for example submitting evidence to a Parliamentary inquiries and responding to consultations, for example on copyright and AI. It holds cross-party Parliamentary lobbies with Equity and the Musicians' Union to ensure that the various artforms they represent are properly cared for and writers' voices are heard during, for instance, the Brexit transition and the Covid-19 pandemic. In the run up to the 2024 General Election the union launched a manifesto, 'Putting writers at the heart of the story', calling for the next government to take urgent action around fair pay, fair treatment, a sustainable sector and copyright and AI. Working with the Federation of Entertainment Unions, WGGB makes its views known to bodies, such as Arts Council England and Ofcom on a broader basis.

WGGB is an active affiliate of the British Copyright Council, Creators' Rights Alliance and other organisations whose activities are relevant to professional writers. Internationally, it plays a leading role in the International Affiliation of Writers Guilds, which includes the American Guilds East and West, the Canadian Guilds (French and English) and the Irish, Mexican, French, Israeli, South African and New Zealand Guilds. When it is possible to make common cause, the guilds act accordingly. WGGB takes a leading role in the Fédération des Scénaristes d'Europe.

On a day-to-day basis, WGGB gives advice on contracts and takes up issues that affect the lives of its members as professional writers. Other benefits include access to free and discounted training, exclusive events and discounts and a dedicated online members' area. Full members are entitled to submit a profile for inclusion in the WGGB online *Find A Writer* directory; pay no joining fee for membership to Writers Guild of America East or

West (if they meet joining criteria); and are eligible for Cannes accreditation. Regular committee meetings are held by specialist WGGB Craft Committees, and its active branches across the UK organise panel discussions, talks and social events. WGGB also has an Equality & Diversity Committee where activists have been involved in many initiatives, including an access rider to reduce access barriers for freelance writers and a new series of member networks for under-represented writing groups.

Campaigns include Save Audio Drama at the BBC and sustained campaigning and lobbying around Artificial Intelligence and threats to writers' copyright and remuneration. In 2018 the union's Equality Writers campaign was launched following Equality Writes, following an independent report commissioned by WGGB which revealed the lack of gender equality in the UK screen industries. The union has also campaigned against the privatisation of Channel 4. It has spoken out on arts funding cuts and the impact of the cost-of-living crisis.

Subject indexes
Magazines by subject area

These lists provide a broad classification and pointer to possible markets. Contacts for *Magazines UK and Ireland* start on page 36.

Advertising, design, printing and publishing

BFS Journal 42
Campaign 45
PR Week 72
Press Gazette 73
Slightly Foxed 79

Agriculture, farming and horticulture

Country Life 48
Farmers Weekly 53
The Field 53
Irish Farmers Journal 61
The Scottish Farmer 77

Architecture and building

The Architects' Journal 38
The Architectural Review 38
Architecture Today 38
Building 44
Building Design 44
Country Homes and Interiors 48
Country Life 48
Homes & Gardens 59
Wallpaper* 83

Art and collecting

Apollo 38
Art Monthly 38
The Art Newspaper 38
Art Quarterly 38
ArtReview and ArtReview Asia 38
Artists & Illustrators 39
The Book Collector 43
The Burlington Magazine 44
Ceramic Review 46
Coin News 47
Country Life 48
Embroidery magazine 52
Gibbons Stamp Monthly 56
Irish Arts Review 61
Leisure Painter & The Artist 63
Medal News 65
RA Magazine 74
Stamp Magazine 80
Tate Etc 81

Aviation

Aeroplane Monthly 36
AIR International 37
Aviation News 39

Business, industry and management

Fishing News 53
Management Today 65
MoneyWeek 66

Cinema and films

Campaign 45
Empire 52
The Face 53
Little White Lies 64
Screen Daily 78
Sight and Sound 79

Economics, accountancy and finance

Accountancy Age 36
Accounting & Business 36
Africa Confidential 37
African Business 37
The Banker 40
Business & Accountancy Daily 44
Economica 51
The Economist 51
FT Adviser 55
Insurance Age 61
Investors' Chronicle 61
MoneyWeek 66
Taxation 81

Education

Educate 51
The Linguist 63
Music Teacher 67
Nursery World 69

Engineering and mechanics

Car Mechanics 45
Electrical Review 52
Energy Engineering 52
The Engineer 52
Engineering in Miniature 52
Model Engineer & Workshop 66

RAIL 75
Railway Gazette International 75
The Railway Magazine 75

Fiction

Aesthetica Magazine 36
Andromeda Magazine 37
BFS Horizons 41
Briefly Write 43
Chat 46
C&otildeingō Magazine 47
Crannóg 48
Critical Quarterly 49
Crow & Cross Keys 49
Crystal Magazine 49
Cyphers 49
DIVA 50
Dream Catcher 51
The Dublin Review 51
Erotic Review 53
Fictive Dream 53
Firewords 53
Flash: The International Short-Short Story Magazine 54
Folding Rock 54
Granta 57
Gutter 57
Inkfish Magazine 60
Ireland's Own 61
Irish Pages: A Journal of Contemporary Writing 62
The Lincoln Review 63
Litro 64
The London Magazine: A Review of Literature and the Arts 64
Magma Poetry 65
Mslexia 66
My Weekly 67
The North 68
Northern Gravy 69
oranges journal 70
Orbis International Literary Journal 70
Panorama: The Journal of Travel, Place and Nature 70
The Passionfruit Review 71
The People's Friend 71
Pride 73
Prospect Magazine 74
The Scots Magazine 77
Shooter Literary Magazine 78
Shoreline of Infinity 79
Spellbinder Magazine 79
Stand Magazine 80
The Stinging Fly 80
Streetcake Magazine 80
Take a Break 81
Tears in the Fence 82
walk 83
Wasafiri 84
woman&home 84
Woman's Own 85
Woman's Weekly 85

Food and drink

Bella 41
The Caterer 45
Condé Nast Traveller 47
Decanter 50
delicious. 50
Good Food 56
Good Housekeeping 56
House & Garden 59
LandScape Magazine 63
Living Plantfully 64
The National Trust Magazine 67
Olive 69
Prima 73
Sainsbury's magazine 77
Scottish Field 77
The Vegan 83
Vegan Food & Living 83
Waitrose Food 83

Gardening

BBC Gardeners' World Magazine 40
Country Life 48
The English Garden 52
The Field 53
Flora 54
Garden Answers 55
Garden News 55
Grow Your Own 57
Hortus 59
House & Garden 59
Kitchen Garden 62
woman&home 84

Health and home

Asylum 39
Black Beauty & Hair 42
Breathe 43
Country Homes and Interiors 48
Country Living 48
H&E naturist 58
Homes & Gardens 59
House & Garden 59
Ideal Home 60
Period Living 71
Saga Magazine 77
Sainsbury's magazine 77
Style at Home 81
The Vegan 83
The World of Interiors 85

History and archaeology

BBC History Magazine 40
Coin News 47
Geographical 56
History Today 59
The National Trust Magazine 67

Leisure interests, pets

Astronomy Now 39
BBC Sky at Night Magazine 41
Bird Watching 42
Birdwatch 42
Caravan Magazine 45
Climber 47
Country Walking 48
Dogs Today 51
Family Tree 53
The Field 53
Flora 54
Gibbons Stamp Monthly 56
The Great Outdoors Magazine 57
i-D 60
MMM (The Motorhomers' Magazine) 65
Our Dogs 70
Practical Caravan 72
Practical Fishkeeping 72
Rouleur 76
Scottish Field 77
The Sewing Directory 78
Stamp Magazine 80
Wasafiri 84
Your Dog Magazine 86
Your Horse Magazine 86

Literary (see also Poetry)

Acumen Literary Journal 36
Aesthetica Magazine 36
Andromeda Magazine 37
Atrium 39
The Author 39
Blithe Spirit 42
The Book Collector 43
Booklaunch 43
Books Ireland 43
The Bookseller 43
Briefly Write 43
Crannóg 48
Critical Quarterly 49
Crow & Cross Keys 49
Crystal Magazine 49
The Dickensian 50
Dream Catcher 51
The Dublin Review 51
Fictive Dream 53
Firewords 53
Flash: The International Short-Short Story Magazine 54
Folding Rock 54
fourteen poems 55
The Frogmore Papers 55
The Ghastling 56
Granta 57
Gutter 57
Here Comes Everyone 58
Hinterland 58
Index on Censorship 60
Ink Sweat & Tears 60
Inkfish Magazine 60
International Affairs 61
Irish Pages: A Journal of Contemporary Writing 62
The Lake 62
The Lincoln Review 63
Literary Review 63
Litro 64
London Grip 64
The London Magazine: A Review of Literature and the Arts 64
London Review of Books 64
Magma Poetry 65
Modern Poetry in Translation 66
Mslexia 66
New Welsh Review 68
The North 68
Northern Gravy 69
The Oldie 69
oranges journal 70
Orbis International Literary Journal 70
Oxford Poetry 70
Oxford Review of Books 70
Panorama: The Journal of Travel, Place and Nature 70
The Passionfruit Review 71
Pennine Platform 71
Prole 73
Propel Magazine 73
Prospect Magazine 74
Pushing Out the Boat 74
Shooter Literary Magazine 78
Slightly Foxed 79
Snowflake Magazine 79
The Spectator 79
Spellbinder Magazine 79
Stand Magazine 80
The Stinging Fly 80
Strong Words 80
Tears in the Fence 82
Wasafiri 84
Writing Magazine 85

Marketing and retailing

Business & Accountancy Daily 44
Campaign 45
Drapers 51
The Grocer 57
Marketing Week 65
Retail Week 76

Medicine and nursing

British Medical Journal 43
Irish Medical Times 61
The Lancet 63
Nursery World 69
Nursing Times 69
The Practising Midwife 73
Pulse 74

Motor transport and cycling

BBC Top Gear 41
Bike 42
Buses 44
Car 45
Car Mechanics 45
Classic Cars 46
Commercial Motor 47
Custom Car 49
Cycling Weekly 49
MCN (Motor Cycle News) 65
MMM (The Motorhomers' Magazine) 65
Truck & Driver 82

Music and recording

BBC Music Magazine 41
Classical Music 47
Early Music 51
The Face 53
Hi-Fi News 58
Kerrang! 62
Mojo 66
Music Teacher 67
Music Week 67
Musical Opinion 67
NME (New Musical Express) 68
Opera 69
Opera Now 70
Record Collector 75
Songwriting and Composing 79
The Strad 80
Tempo 82

Natural history

BBC Wildlife Magazine 41
Bird Watching 42
Birdwatch 42
British Birds 43
Geographical 56
LandScape Magazine 63
The National Trust Magazine 67
Nature 67
Our Dogs 70
Resurgence & Ecologist 76

Nautical and marine

Boat International 42
Classic Boat Magazine 46
Motor Boat and Yachting 66
The Motorship 66
Practical Boat Owner 72
Sailing Today with Yachts & Yachting 77
Sea Breezes 78
Ships Monthly 78
Waterways World 84
Yachting Monthly 85
Yachting World 85

Poetry

Abridged 36
Acumen Literary Journal 36
Aesthetica Magazine 36
The Alchemy Spoon 37
Allegro Poetry 37
And Other Poems 37
Atrium 39
Bad Lilies 40
BFS Horizons 41
Blithe Spirit 42
Briefly Write 43
Butcher's Dog 45
Cõnfingō Magazine 47
Crannóg 48
Critical Quarterly 49
Crow & Cross Keys 49
Crystal Magazine 49
Cumbria and Lakeland Walker 49
Cyphers 49
The Dawntreader 49
Dream Catcher 51
Firewords 53
fourteen poems 55
The Frogmore Papers 55
Gutter 57
hedgerow: a journal of small poems 58
Here Comes Everyone 58
Ink Sweat & Tears 60
Inkfish Magazine 60
Irish Pages: A Journal of Contemporary Writing 62
The Lake 62
The Lincoln Review 63
Literary Review 63
London Grip 64
The London Magazine: A Review of Literature and the Arts 64
London Review of Books 64
Long Poem Magazine 64
Magma Poetry 65
Modern Poetry in Translation 66
Mslexia 66
New Welsh Review 68
The North 68
Northern Gravy 69
Orbis International Literary Journal 70
Oxford Poetry 70
Oxford Review of Books 70
Panorama: The Journal of Travel, Place and Nature 70
The Passionfruit Review 71
Pennine Platform 71
PN Review 71
Poetry Ireland Review/Iris Éigse Éireann 71
Poetry London 72
The Poetry Review 72
Poetry Wales 72
Pride 73
Prole 73
Propel Magazine 73

Pulsar Poetry Webzine 74
Pushing Out the Boat 74
Reach Poetry 75
The Rialto 76
Shooter Literary Magazine 78
Shoreline of Infinity 79
Snowflake Magazine 79
Spellbinder Magazine 79
Stand Magazine 80
The Stinging Fly 80
Streetcake Magazine 80
Tears in the Fence 82
Wasafiri 84
Wet Grain 84

Politics

Africa Confidential 37
Delayed Gratification 50
Hot Press 59
International Affairs 61
MoneyWeek 66
New Internationalist 67
New Statesman 68
The Political Quarterly 72
Prospect Magazine 74
Red Pepper 75
The Spectator 79
The Week 84
The World Today 85

Radio and TV

Broadcast 44
Campaign 45
Empire 52
Hi-Fi News 58
InterMedia 61
Opera Now 70
Radio Times 74
The Stage 80
Television 82
TV Times Magazine 83
What's On TV 84

Religion, philosophy and New Age

Africa: St Patrick's Missions 36
Baptist Times 40
The Catholic Herald 45
Catholic Pictorial 46
Church of England Newspaper 46
Church Times 46
The Dawntreader 49
Fortean Times 54
The Friend 55
The Furrow 55
Jewish Chronicle 62
Jewish Telegraph 62
Life and Work: The Magazine of the Church of Scotland 63
Methodist Recorder 65
New Humanist 67
Premier Woman Alive 73
Reform 76
The Tablet 81
The War Cry 84

Rural life and country

BBC Countryfile Magazine 40
Cotswold Life 48
Country Life 48
Cumbria and Lakeland Walker 49
Devon Life 50
The Field 53
The National Trust Magazine 67
The Scots Magazine 77
Scottish Field 77
The Yorkshire Dalesman 86

Sciences

BBC Science Focus 41
BBC Sky at Night Magazine 41
Nature 67
New Scientist 68
Scientific Computing World 77

Sports and games

Angling Times 37
AW (Athletics Weekly) 40
Darts World 49
Descent: The magazine of underground exploration 50
The Field 53
Fly Fishing & Fly Tying 54
Forty20 54
FourFourTwo 54
Golf Monthly 56
The Great Outdoors Magazine 57
Horse & Hound 59
Horse & Rider 59
MBUK (Mountain Biking UK) 65
Our Dogs 70
Rouleur 76
Rugby World 76
Runner's World 76
Sea Angler 78
Today's Golfer 82
Trail 82
Trout & Salmon 82
World Soccer 85

Travel and geography

Caravan Magazine 45
Condé Nast Traveller 47
Geographical 56
Panorama: The Journal of Travel, Place and Nature 70
Wallpaper* 83
Wanderlust 83

Publishers of fiction (UK)

Contacts for *Book publishers UK and Ireland* start on page 118.

Adventure/westerns

Birlinn 123
Bloomsbury Publishing 124
Burning Chair Publishing 127
The Canelo Group 128
Faber & Faber 139
Hachette UK 145
Harlequin UK 146
Headline Publishing Group 149
Little, Brown Book Group 156
The Orion Publishing Group 165
Pan Macmillan 167
Penguin Random House UK 169
SmashBear Publishing 178
Transworld 183
Vintage 186
Wildthought Books 187

Comedy/humour

Allison & Busby 119
Duckworth Books 136
Everyman's Library 138
Korero Press 154
Little, Brown Book Group 156
Michael O'Mara Books 165
The Orion Publishing Group 165
P&H Books 166
Piccadilly Press 170
Quartet Books 171
Rymour Books 174
Scholastic 175
Transworld 183

Crime/detective/mystery

Allison & Busby 119
Amazon Publishing 119
Angry Robot Books 120
Atlantic Books 121
Bad Press Ink 121
Bedford Square Publishers 122
Bitter Lemon Press 123
Black & White Publishing 123
Bloodhound Books 124
Bloomsbury Publishing 124
Boldwood Books 125
Bonnier Books UK 125
Bookouture 126
British Library Publishing 127
Burning Chair Publishing 127
The Canelo Group 128
Cornerstone 132
Cranthorpe Millner Publishers 133
Diamond Books 135
dp books 136
Duckworth Books 136
Everyman's Library 138
Faber & Faber 139
Fahrenheit Press 139
Gallic Books 142
Hachette UK 145
Hamish Hamilton 146
HarperCollins Publishers 146
Hera Books 149
Hobeck Books 150
Holland House Books 150
Ignite Books 152
Inspired Quill 152
Joffe Books 153
Leamington Books 155
Legend Press 155
Little, Brown Book Group 156
Loudhailer Books 157
McNidder & Grace 158
Mango Books 159
Moonflower 160
Muswell Press 161
Northodox Press 163
Michael O'Mara Books 165
Oneworld Publications 165
Orenda Books 165
The Orion Publishing Group 165
Pan Macmillan 167
Penguin Michael Joseph 169
Penguin Random House UK 169
Pushkin Press 171
Quadrant Books 171
Quartet Books 171
Ringwood Publishing 173
Rymour Books 174
Sapere Books 175
Seren 176
Severn House 177
SRL Publishing 179
Transworld 183
Vintage 186
Wildthought Books 187
Zaffre 188

Diverse ethnicities

Allison & Busby 119
Arkbound 120
Cassava Republic Press 128
Chapman Publishing 129
Ayebia Clarke Publishing Ltd 130
Dialogue 135
Honno (Welsh Women's Press) 150

HopeRoad 150
Jacaranda Books 153
Lantana Publishing 155
Neem Tree Press 162
Oneworld Publications 165
Peepal Tree Press 167
Quartet Books 171

General

Abacus 118
Afsana Press 118
Allison & Busby 119
Amazon Publishing 119
Aurora Metro 121
Authentic Media 121
Bearded Badger Publishing 122
Bedford Square Publishers 122
Bloomsbury Publishing 124
Bonnier Books UK 125
The Book Guild 125
Bookouture 126
Canongate Books 128
Century 129
Chapman Publishing 129
Cicada Books 130
Cló Iar-Chonnacht Teo 130
Collective Ink 131
Cornerstone 132
Crescent Moon Publishing 133
Crowdbound 133
Dahlia Books 133
Faber & Faber 139
The Gallery Press 142
Garnet Publishing 142
Guppy Publishing 145
Halban Publishers 146
Hamish Hamilton 146
Harlequin UK 146
HarperCollins Publishers 146
Head of Zeus 149
Hera Books 149
Hodder & Stoughton 150
Honno (Welsh Women's Press) 150
Inkandescent 152
Jacaranda Books 153
Legend Press 155
Lightning Books 155
Little, Brown Book Group 156
Loudhailer Books 157
Luath Press 157
Mango Books 159
Manilla Press 159
Maverick House 159
Mirror Books 160
John Murray Group 161
Myriad Editions 162
New Island Books 162
Ockham Publishing Group 163
Old Barn Books 164
The Oleander Press 164
Michael O'Mara Books 165
The Orion Publishing Group 165
Pan Macmillan 167
Peepal Tree Press 167
Penguin Michael Joseph 169
Perspective Books 169
Poolbeg Press 170
Quartet Books 171
Route 173
Scorpius Books 175
Scribe 176
Seren 176
Severn House 177
Silvertail Books 177
Simon & Schuster UK 177
Studio Press 180
Sweet Cherry Publishing 180
Thistle Publishing 182
ThunderPoint Publishing 182
Tippermuir Books 183
Transworld 183
Valley Press 185
Velocity Press 185
Wildthought Books 187

Graphic/cartoons

Amazon Publishing 119
Avery Hill Publishing 121
Bloomsbury Publishing 124
Breakdown Press 126
Cornerstone 132
Faber & Faber 139
David Fickling Books 140
Flying Eye Books 141
Granta Books 144
Guppy Publishing 145
The Irish Pages Press/Cló An Mhíl Bhuī 153
Knight Errant Press 154
Korero Press 154
Luna Press Publishing 157
Myriad Editions 162
Pushkin Press 171
SelfMadeHero 176
Strange Region 180
Titan Books 183
Valley Press 185
Vintage 186

Historical

Allison & Busby 119
Amazon Publishing 119
Birlinn 123
Black & White Publishing 123
Bloodhound Books 124
Boldwood Books 125
Bonnier Books UK 125
Bookouture 126
Chapman Publishing 129
Cranthorpe Millner Publishers 133
Darf Publishers 134
Deixis Press 134
dp books 136
Duckworth Books 136

Everyman's Library 138
Gallic Books 142
Hachette UK 145
Harlequin UK 146
HarperCollins Publishers 146
Henningham Family Press 149
Hobeck Books 150
Holland House Books 150
Honno (Welsh Women's Press) 150
Indigo Dreams Publishing 152
IWM (Imperial War Museums) Publishing 153
The Lilliput Press 155
Little, Brown Book Group 156
Pan Macmillan 167
Penguin Michael Joseph 169
Penguin Random House UK 169
Quartet Books 171
Romaunce Books 173
Rymour Books 174
Sapere Books 175
Severn House 177
Sparsile Books 179
Storm Publishing 180
Ta-Ha Publishers 181
Transworld 183
Vintage 186
Wildthought Books 187

Horror

Amazon Publishing 119
Bad Press Ink 121
Deixis Press 134
Elsewhen Press 138
Flame Tree Publishing 140
Ghost Orchid Press 143
Haunt Publishing 148
Knight Errant Press 154
Korero Press 154
Loudhailer Books 157
The Orion Publishing Group 165
Pan Macmillan 167
Scorpius Books 175
SelfMadeHero 176
Severn House 177
SmashBear Publishing 178
Snowbooks 178
Tartarus Press 181
Titan Books 183
Transworld 183

LGBTQ+

Afsana Press 118
Arachne Press 120
Arkbound 120
Black Bee Books 123
Chapman Publishing 129
Cipher Press 130
Dialogue 135
Ghost Orchid Press 143
Hamish Hamilton 146
HarperCollins Publishers 146
Henningham Family Press 149
Hodder & Stoughton 150
Inspired Quill 152
Knight Errant Press 154
Little, Brown Book Group 156
Loudhailer Books 157
Lurid Editions 158
Muswell Press 161
Michael O'Mara Books 165
Pan Macmillan 167
Penguin Random House UK 169
Quartet Books 171
Strange Region 180
Vintage 186

Literary

Abacus 118
Afsana Press 118
Allison & Busby 119
Alma Books 119
And Other Stories 119
Arkbound 120
Atlantic Books 121
Authentic Media 121
Bad Press Ink 121
Banshee Press 122
Bearded Badger Publishing 122
Bedford Square Publishers 122
Betimes Books 122
Bloomsbury Publishing 124
Bluemoose Books 125
Bonnier Books UK 125
Chapman Publishing 129
Cinnamon Press 130
Ayebia Clarke Publishing Ltd 130
Cōnfingō Publishing 131
Cranthorpe Millner Publishers 133
Crescent Moon Publishing 133
Darf Publishers 134
Daunt Books 134
Dead Ink Books 134
Dedalus 134
Deixis Press 134
Dialect Press 135
Dialogue 135
Dodo Ink 136
Duckworth Books 136
Enitharmon Editions 138
Everyman's Library 138
Faber & Faber 139
Fairlight Books 139
Fitzcarraldo Editions 140
Flipped Eye Publishing 141
Fly on the Wall Press 141
Footnote Press 141
Galley Beggar Press 142
Garnet Publishing 142
Ghost Orchid Press 143
Granta Books 144
Hachette UK 145
Halban Publishers 146
Hamish Hamilton 146

HarperCollins Publishers 146
Head of Zeus 149
Headline Publishing Group 149
Héloïse Press 149
Henningham Family Press 149
Hodder & Stoughton 150
Holland House Books 150
Honno (Welsh Women's Press) 150
Indigo Dreams Publishing 152
Influx Press 152
Inspired Quill 152
Jacaranda Books 153
Legend Press 155
Lightning Books 155
The Lilliput Press 155
Little, Brown Book Group 156
Loudhailer Books 157
Lurid Editions 158
The Mercier Press 160
John Murray Group 161
Muswell Press 161
Myriad Editions 162
Neem Tree Press 162
The New Menard Press 162
New Welsh Rarebyte 162
Nordisk Books 162
Northodox Press 163
The Oleander Press 164
Orenda Books 165
Ortac Press 166
P&H Books 166
Pan Macmillan 167
Penguin Random House UK 169
Quadrant Books 171
Quercus Publishing 172
Renard Press 173
Revenge Ink 173
Rymour Books 174
Saqi Books 175
Saraband 175
Scotland Street Press 176
Scottish Mountaineering Press 176
Seren 176
Simon & Schuster UK 177
Sincere Corkscrew 178
Skein Press 178
Sparsile Books 179
Stairwell Books 179
Stewed Rhubarb Press 180
Strange Region 180
Swift Press 180
Ta-Ha Publishers 181
Taproot Books 181
Tartarus Press 181
Templar Poetry 182
Thinkwell Books 182
3TimesRebel 182
Tippermuir Books 183
Tramp Press 183
Transworld 183
Turas Press 183
UEA Publishing Project 184
Vintage 186
The Waywiser Press 187
Weatherglass Press 187
Wild Hunt Books 187
Wildthought Books 187
Wrecking Ball Press 188

New/experimental

Bad Press Ink 121
Canongate Books 128
Chapman Publishing 129
Crescent Moon Publishing 133
Deixis Press 134
Faber & Faber 139
Fahrenheit Press 139
Honno (Welsh Women's Press) 150
Influx Press 152
Loudhailer Books 157
Prototype 171
Revenge Ink 173
Seren 176
Sincere Corkscrew 178
Weatherglass Press 187
Wild Hunt Books 187

Romantic

Allison & Busby 119
Amazon Publishing 119
Black & White Publishing 123
Bloodhound Books 124
Boldwood Books 125
Bonnier Books UK 125
Bookouture 126
British Library Publishing 127
The Canelo Group 128
dp books 136
Hachette UK 145
Harlequin UK 146
HarperCollins Publishers 146
Hera Books 149
Joffe Books 153
Little, Brown Book Group 156
Pan Macmillan 167
Penguin Michael Joseph 169
Quadrant Books 171
Romaunce Books 173
Sapere Books 175
Severn House 177
SmashBear Publishing 178
Storm Publishing 180
Transworld 183
Zaffre 188

Sci-fi/fantasy

Allison & Busby 119
Amazon Publishing 119
Angry Robot Books 120
Bad Press Ink 121
Bookouture 126
British Library Publishing 127
Burning Chair Publishing 127

Cranthorpe Millner Publishers 133
Deixis Press 134
dp books 136
Duckworth Books 136
Elsewhen Press 138
Flame Tree Publishing 140
Galley Beggar Press 142
Hachette UK 145
HarperCollins Publishers 146
Inspired Quill 152
Knight Errant Press 154
Little, Brown Book Group 156
Luna Press Publishing 157
Moonflower 160
Orbit 165
The Orion Publishing Group 165
Pan Macmillan 167
Penguin Random House UK 169
Quadrant Books 171
Quartet Books 171
Scorpius Books 175
Simon & Schuster UK 177
SmashBear Publishing 178
Snowbooks 178
Storm Publishing 180
Transworld 183

Short stories

Ad Hoc Fiction 118
Bradt Travel Guides 126
Chapman Publishing 129
Ayebia Clarke Publishing Ltd 130
Cló Iar-Chonnacht Teo 130
Comma Press 131
Dahlia Books 133
Daunt Books 134
Dead Ink Books 134
Dialect Press 135
Eglantyne Books 137
The Emma Press 138
Everyman's Library 138
Faber & Faber 139
Fairlight Books 139
Fincham Press 140
Flame Tree Publishing 140
Floris Books 141
Fly on the Wall Press 141
Galley Beggar Press 142
Ghost Orchid Press 143
Granta Books 144
Guillemot Press 145
Hamish Hamilton 146
Hobeck Books 150
Honno (Welsh Women's Press) 150
Indigo Dreams Publishing 152
Inspired Quill 152
ISF Publishing 153
Leamington Books 155
The Lilliput Press 155
Lucent Dreaming 157
Luna Press Publishing 157
Neem Tree Press 162
Pan Macmillan 167
Penguin Random House UK 169
Prototype 171
Salt Publishing 174
Sans. PRESS 174
Scratch Books 176
Seren 176
SmashBear Publishing 178
Strange Region 180
ThunderPoint Publishing 182
Transworld 183
UEA Publishing Project 184
Valley Press 185
Weatherglass Press 187
Wrecking Ball Press 188

Teen/YA

Andersen Press 119
Aurora Metro 121
Barbican Press 122
Burning Chair Publishing 127
Candy Jar Books 128
Chicken House 129
Claret Press 130
Cornerstone 132
Cranthorpe Millner Publishers 133
Dref Wen 136
Elsewhen Press 138
Everything with Words 138
Faber & Faber 139
Farshore Books 139
David Fickling Books 140
Floris Books 141
Guppy Publishing 145
Hachette Children's Trade 145
Hachette UK 145
HarperCollins Publishers 146
Hashtag Press 148
Henningham Family Press 149
HopeRoad 150
Hot Key Books 151
Little Tiger Press 156
Mantra Lingua 159
Moonflower 160
Neem Tree Press 162
Northodox Press 163
The O'Brien Press 163
Oneworld Publications 165
Piccadilly Press 170
Poolbeg Press 170
Simon & Schuster UK 177
SRL Publishing 179
Sweet Cherry Publishing 180
ThunderPoint Publishing 182
Tippermuir Books 183
Titan Books 183
Troika 183
UCLan Publishing 184
Usborne Publishing 185
Walker Books 186

Translation/international

Alma Books 119
Amazon Publishing 119
Aurora Metro 121
Barbican Press 122
Canongate Books 128
Carcanet Press 128
Chapman Publishing 129
Charco Press 129
Cló Iar-Chonnacht Teo 130
Darf Publishers 134
Daunt Books 134
Dedalus 134
Dedalus Press 134
Eglantyne Books 137
Enitharmon Editions 138
Everyman's Library 138
Faber & Faber 139
Fitzcarraldo Editions 140
Gallic Books 142
Goat Star Books 143
Halban Publishers 146
Haus Publishing 148
Héloïse Press 149
Honno (Welsh Women's Press) 150
HopeRoad 150
Jantar Publishing 153
Major Books 158
Neem Tree Press 162
The New Menard Press 162
Nordisk Books 162
The Oleander Press 164
Oneworld Publications 165
Orenda Books 165
The Orion Publishing Group 165
Parthian Books 167
Peirene Press 168
Profile Books 171
Pushkin Press 171
Quartet Books 171
Saqi Books 175
Saraband 175
Seren 176
Shearsman Books 177
Skein Press 178
Tilted Axis Press 182
Vintage 186

War

Little, Brown Book Group 156
The Orion Publishing Group 165
Sapere Books 175
Severn House 177
Transworld 183
Ulric Publishing 184

Publishers of non-fiction (UK)

Contacts for *Book publishers UK and Ireland* start on page 118.

Academic and professional

Bennion Kearny 122
Birlinn 123
Bloomsbury Publishing 124
Brilliant Publications 126
Cambridge University Press & Assessment 128
Cengage Learning 129
CGI Publishing 129
James Clarke & Co. 130
Cork University Press 132
Council for British Archaeology 132
Duckworth Books 136
Edinburgh University Press 137
The Educational Company of Ireland 137
Elsevier 138
Equinox Publishing 138
University of Exeter Press 139
Four Courts Press 142
Garnet Publishing 142
Gingko 143
Goldsmiths Press 143
Hachette UK 145
Hadean Press 145
HarperCollins Publishers 146
Hurst Publishers 151
Imprint Academic 152
Institute of Public Administration 152
Irish Academic Press 153
Jacaranda Books 153
Jane's 153
Peter Lang 155
Liverpool University Press 157
Luna Press Publishing 157
The Lutterworth Press 158
McGraw-Hill Education 158
Management Books 2000 158
Manchester University Press 159
Medina Publishing 159
The Mercier Press 160
On Stream Publications 165
Oxford University Press 166
Penguin Press 169
Polity Press 170
Portland Press 170
Royal Collection Trust 173
Rymour Books 174
SAGE Publishing 174
Saqi Books 175
Silvertail Books 177
Siri Scientific Press 178
Society for Promoting Christian Knowledge (SPCK) 178

Taylor & Francis Group 181
Thinkwell Books 182
TSO (The Stationery Office) 183
UCL Press 184
University College Dublin Press 185
University of Wales Press 186
Welsh Academic Press 187
John Wiley & Sons 188
Yale University Press London 188

Archaeology

Ashmolean Museum Publications 120
Berghahn Books 122
Birlinn 123
Bloomsbury Publishing 124
Boydell & Brewer 126
The British Museum Press 127
Cambridge University Press & Assessment 128
Council for British Archaeology 132
University of Exeter Press 139
Fonthill Media 141
Logaston Press 157
Manchester University Press 159
Pen & Sword Books 168
Taylor & Francis Group 181
Thames & Hudson 182

Architecture and building

ACC Art Books 118
Bloomsbury Publishing 124
Blue Guides 125
Country Books 132
The Crowood Press 133
The Dovecote Press 136
Fircone Books 140
5mBooks 140
Garnet Publishing 142
Graffeg 144
Laurence King Publishing 154
Frances Lincoln 156
Lund Humphries 158
MACK 158
Manchester University Press 159
Merrell Publishers 160
Old Pond Publishing 164
Oxford University Press 166
Prestel Publishing 171
Quarto Group Publishing UK 172
Reaktion Books 172
Sheldrake Press 177
Taschen UK 181
Taylor & Francis Group 181
Thames & Hudson 182
University College Dublin Press 185
Philip Wilson Publishers 188
Yale University Press London 188

Art and craft

Anness Publishing Ltd 120
Black Dog Press 123
Bloomsbury Publishing 124
The Bright Press 126
The Crowood Press 133
David & Charles 134
Fircone Books 140
Floris Books 141
Graffeg 144
Guild of Master Craftsman Publications 144
Halsgrove Publishing 146
Hardie Grant UK 146
Korero Press 154
Frances Lincoln 156
Luath Press 157
Lund Humphries 158
MACK 158
Murdoch Books 161
Octopus Publishing Group 164
Ortac Press 166
Quarto Group Publishing UK 172
Quiller Publishing 172
Search Press 176
September Publishing 176
Stanley/Barker 179
Strange Region 180
Taschen UK 181
Tate Enterprises 181
Thames & Hudson 182
3dtotal Publishing 182
Two Rivers Press 184
Valley Press 185
Vintage 186
Philip Wilson Publishers 188

Aviation

The Crowood Press 133
Fighting High 140
Fonthill Media 141
Grub Street Publishing 144
Haynes Publishing 148
Jane's 153
Osprey Publishing 166
Pen & Sword Books 168

Biography, autobiography and memoir

Allison & Busby 119
Alma Books 119
Amazon Publishing 119
Amberley Publishing 119
Atlantic Books 121
Aureus Publishing 121
Barbican Press 122
Black & White Publishing 123
Black Bee Books 123
Blackstaff Press 123
John Blake Publishing 124
Blink Publishing 124
Bonnier Books UK 125
Canbury Press 128
Candy Jar Books 128
Canongate Books 128
Cinnamon Press 130
Ayebia Clarke Publishing Ltd 130
James Clarke & Co. 130

Cornerstone 132
Country Books 132
Cranthorpe Millner Publishers 133
Darton, Longman and Todd 134
Daunt Books 134
Duckworth Books 136
Dynasty Press 136
Ebury Publishing 136
Fleming Publications 141
Fonthill Media 141
Gallic Books 142
Garnet Publishing 142
Gibson Square 143
Gill 143
Granta Books 144
Guild of Master Craftsman Publications 144
Hachette UK 145
Halban Publishers 146
HarperCollins Publishers 146
Haus Publishing 148
Headline Publishing Group 149
Henley Hall Press 149
Hodder & Stoughton 150
Ignite Books 152
Imprint Academic 152
Indigo Dreams Publishing 152
Irish Academic Press 153
The Irish Pages Press/Cló An Mhíl Bhuī 153
The Lilliput Press 155
Little, Brown Book Group 156
The Lutterworth Press 158
McNidder & Grace 158
Mandrake of Oxford 159
Manilla Press 159
Maverick House 159
Mensch Publishing 160
Mentor Books 160
Mirror Books 160
Morrigan Book Company/City of Dublin Press 161
Murdoch Books 161
John Murray Group 161
Muswell Press 161
New Island Books 162
The O'Brien Press 163
Michael O'Mara Books 165
Omnibus Press/Wise Music Group 165
The Orion Publishing Group 165
Orphans Publishing 166
Oxford University Press 166
Pan Macmillan 167
Penguin General 168
Penguin Michael Joseph 169
Penguin Press 169
Perspective Books 169
Plexus Publishing 170
Profile Books 171
Quartet Books 171
Quarto Group Publishing UK 172
Quiller Publishing 172
Route 173
St Pauls Publishing 174
Salt Publishing 174
Saraband 175
SelfMadeHero 176
September Publishing 176
Seren 176
Shepheard-Walwyn (Publishers) 177
Sigma Press 177
Simon & Schuster UK 177
Colin Smythe 178
Society for Promoting Christian Knowledge (SPCK) 178
Sparsile Books 179
SRL Publishing 179
3TimesRebel 182
Tippermuir Books 183
Transworld 183
Vallentine Mitchell 185
The Waywiser Press 187
Welsh Academic Press 187
Yale University Press London 188

Business, industry and management

Bennion Kearny 122
Bloomsbury Publishing 124
Bristol University Press/Policy Press 126
Cengage Learning 129
Collective Ink 131
Cornerstone 132
Crown House Publishing 133
Do Books 136
Ebury Publishing 136
Edward Elgar Publishing 137
Eye Books 139
Globe Law and Business 143
Harriman House 148
Hay House Publishers 148
The History Press 150
Jordan Publishing 154
Kogan Page 154
McGraw-Hill Education 158
McNidder & Grace 158
Management Books 2000 158
Manchester University Press 159
Mensch Publishing 160
Mentor Books 160
John Murray Group 161
Oak Tree Press 163
The Orion Publishing Group 165
Pan Macmillan 167
P8tech 168
Profile Books 171
Simon & Schuster UK 177
TSO (The Stationery Office) 183

Cartography/maps

AA Publishing 118
Bodleian Library Publishing 125
British Library Publishing 127
Discovery Walking Guides 135
HarperCollins Publishers 146
Myriad Editions 162
Octopus Publishing Group 164

Comedy, humour

Amazon Publishing 119
Amber Books 119
Birlinn 123
Black & White Publishing 123
Blackstaff Press 123
John Blake Publishing 124
Blink Publishing 124
Canongate Books 128
Ebury Publishing 136
The Gresham Publishing Company 144
Hachette UK 145
Hardie Grant UK 146
HarperCollins Publishers 146
Hodder & Stoughton 150
Icon Books 151
Little, Brown Book Group 156
Loudhailer Books 157
Luath Press 157
Mentor Books 160
The Mercier Press 160
New Island Books 162
The O'Brien Press 163
Octopus Publishing Group 164
Michael O'Mara Books 165
The Orion Publishing Group 165
Pan Macmillan 167
Profile Books 171
Quiller Publishing 172
September Publishing 176
Sheldrake Press 177
Studio Press 180
Summersdale Publishers 180
Ta-Ha Publishers 181
Tippermuir Books 183
Transworld 183

Cookery, food and drink

Anness Publishing Ltd 120
Aurora Metro 121
Black & White Publishing 123
Blink Publishing 124
Bloomsbury Publishing 124
DK 135
Ebury Publishing 136
Elliott & Thompson 137
Equinox Publishing 138
Flame Tree Publishing 140
W. Foulsham & Co. 142
Garnet Publishing 142
Gill 143
Graffeg 144
Grub Street Publishing 144
Hardie Grant UK 146
HarperCollins Publishers 146
Headline Publishing Group 149
Hodder & Stoughton 150
Igloo Books 151
Kitchen Press 154
Kyle Books 154
Little, Brown Book Group 156
Lucent Dreaming 157
Murdoch Books 161
Nourish Books 163
Octopus Publishing Group 164
On Stream Publications 165
The Orion Publishing Group 165
Pan Macmillan 167
Penguin Michael Joseph 169
Quiller Publishing 172
Revenge Ink 173
Ryland Peters & Small 174
Sheldrake Press 177

Crime

Allison & Busby 119
Amazon Publishing 119
Biteback Publishing 123
Black & White Publishing 123
John Blake Publishing 124
Bristol University Press/Policy Press 126
Cornerstone 132
Headpress 149
Mandrake of Oxford 159
Maverick House 159
Mentor Books 160
Milo Books 160
Mirror Books 160
The O'Brien Press 163
Ringwood Publishing 173
Tippermuir Books 183

Cultural studies

Arkbound 120
Berghahn Books 122
Bitter Lemon Press 123
Bloomsbury Publishing 124
Boydell & Brewer 126
The British Museum Press 127
Calon Books 127
Claret Press 130
Ayebia Clarke Publishing Ltd 130
Collective Ink 131
Cork University Press 132
Cornerstone 132
Crescent Moon Publishing 133
Dialogue 135
Edinburgh University Press 137
Free Association Books 142
Gibson Square 143
Gingko 143
Graffeg 144
Granta Books 144
Hachette UK 145
Hurst Publishers 151
Imprint Academic 152
Jacaranda Books 153
Lawrence & Wishart 155
Loudhailer Books 157
Lucent Dreaming 157
Manchester University Press 159
Medina Publishing 159
Ortac Press 166

Phaidon Press 170
Pluto Press 170
Polity Press 170
Prestel Publishing 171
Reaktion Books 172
Repeater Books 173
Route 173
Ta-Ha Publishers 181
Thames & Hudson 182
Unicorn Publishing Group 184
Verso 185
Vintage 186

Current affairs

Atlantic Books 121
Biteback Publishing 123
Bloomsbury Publishing 124
Cornerstone 132
Ebury Publishing 136
Fabian Society 139
Footnote Press 141
Garnet Publishing 142
Gibson Square 143
Gill 143
Hachette UK 145
HarperCollins Publishers 146
Haus Publishing 148
Icon Books 151
Irish Academic Press 153
Lawrence & Wishart 155
Maverick House 159
The Mercier Press 160
Milo Books 160
New Island Books 162
Octopus Publishing Group 164
Oneworld Publications 165
Oxford University Press 166
Penguin General 168
Penguin Press 169
Poolbeg Press 170
Profile Books 171
Repeater Books 173
Transworld 183
TSO (The Stationery Office) 183
Verso 185
Yale University Press London 188

Design

ACC Art Books 118
Black Dog Press 123
Bloomsbury Publishing 124
The Bright Press 126
Brilliant Publications 126
Do Books 136
Flame Tree Publishing 140
Laurence King Publishing 154
Korero Press 154
Kyle Books 154
Frances Lincoln 156
Manchester University Press 159
Merrell Publishers 160
Octopus Publishing Group 164
Prestel Publishing 171
Quarto Group Publishing UK 172
Reaktion Books 172
Taschen UK 181
Thames & Hudson 182
Vintage 186

Economics, accountancy and finance

Agenda Publishing 119
Bloomsbury Publishing 124
Bristol University Press/Policy Press 126
Cambridge University Press & Assessment 128
Cengage Learning 129
Cornerstone 132
Edward Elgar Publishing 137
Elliott & Thompson 137
Fabian Society 139
Harriman House 148
Icon Books 151
Inspired Quill 152
Institute of Public Administration 152
Kogan Page 154
LexisNexis 155
McGraw-Hill Education 158
John Murray Group 161
W.W. Norton & Co. 163
Oak Tree Press 163
Oxford University Press 166
Penguin Press 169
Pluto Press 170
Princeton University Press – Europe 171
Reaktion Books 172
Taylor & Francis Group 181
Verso 185
Vintage 186
Yale University Press London 188

Education

Amgueddfa Cymru – Museum Wales 119
Bloomsbury Publishing 124
Brilliant Publications 126
Cambridge University Press & Assessment 128
Cengage Learning 129
Christian Education 130
Colourpoint Creative 131
Crown House Publishing 133
DK 135
Dref Wen 136
The Educational Company of Ireland 137
Encyclopaedia Britannica (UK) 138
Fabian Society 139
CJ Fallon 139
Flame Tree Publishing 140
Folens Publishers 141
Gill 143
Goldsmiths Press 143
Hachette Learning 145
Hachette UK 145
HarperCollins Publishers 146
Hopscotch 150

Howgate Publishing 151
Igloo Books 151
Institute of Public Administration 152
IOP Publishing 152
Kogan Page 154
McGraw-Hill Education 158
Kevin Mayhew 159
Mentor Books 160
Oxford University Press 166
Pearson UK 167
Ruby Tuesday Books 174
St Pauls Publishing 174
Scholastic 175
Springer Nature 179
Taylor & Francis Group 181
Trotman Indigo Publishing 183
Welsh Academic Press 187
ZigZag Education 188

Environment and development

Agenda Publishing 119
Arkbound 120
Bloomsbury Publishing 124
Boydell & Brewer 126
Canbury Press 128
Fabian Society 139
5mBooks 140
Footnote Press 141
Hazel Press 149
Henley Hall Press 149
The Lilliput Press 155
Frances Lincoln 156
Maverick House 159
Merlin Press 160
Murdoch Books 161
Oneworld Publications 165
Pan Macmillan 167
Pelagic 168
Pluto Press 170
Quarto Group Publishing UK 172
Springer Nature 179
Taylor & Francis Group 181

Fashion

ACC Art Books 118
Bloomsbury Publishing 124
Cengage Learning 129
Laurence King Publishing 154
Kyle Books 154
Merrell Publishers 160
Octopus Publishing Group 164
Plexus Publishing 170
Prestel Publishing 171
Quarto Group Publishing UK 172
Thames & Hudson 182
Vintage 186

Film and cinema

Berghahn Books 122
Bloomsbury Publishing 124
Crescent Moon Publishing 133
DK 135
Edinburgh University Press 137
University of Exeter Press 139
Faber & Faber 139
HarperCollins Publishers 146
Headpress 149
Laurence King Publishing 154
MACK 158
McNidder & Grace 158
Manchester University Press 159
Pan Macmillan 167
Plexus Publishing 170
Quarto Group Publishing UK 172
Reaktion Books 172
Scholastic 175
Studio Press 180
Taschen UK 181
Taylor & Francis Group 181
Titan Books 183

Fine art and antiques

ACC Art Books 118
Alma Books 119
Ashmolean Museum Publications 120
Black Dog Press 123
Bloomsbury Publishing 124
Blue Guides 125
Bodleian Library Publishing 125
Boydell & Brewer 126
Brilliant Publications 126
British Library Publishing 127
The British Museum Press 127
Cambridge University Press & Assessment 128
Cōnfingō Publishing 131
The Crowood Press 133
Richard Dennis Publications 135
Edinburgh University Press 137
Fircone Books 140
Flame Tree Publishing 140
Flapjack Press 140
Four Courts Press 142
Garnet Publishing 142
Gibson Square 143
Gingko 143
Graffeg 144
Halsgrove Publishing 146
HarperCollins Publishers 146
Laurence King Publishing 154
Korero Press 154
Frances Lincoln 156
Liverpool University Press 157
LOM ART 157
Luath Press 157
Lund Humphries 158
The Lutterworth Press 158
McNidder & Grace 158
Manchester University Press 159
Mandrake of Oxford 159
Kevin Mayhew 159
Merrell Publishers 160

Natural History Museum Publishing 162
Octopus Publishing Group 164
Ortac Press 166
Oxford University Press 166
Phaidon Press 170
Prestel Publishing 171
Quarto Group Publishing UK 172
Quiller Publishing 172
Reaktion Books 172
Royal Collection Trust 173
September Publishing 176
Seren 176
Sheldrake Press 177
Taschen UK 181
Tate Enterprises 181
Taylor & Francis Group 181
Thames & Hudson 182
3dtotal Publishing 182
Two Rivers Press 184
Unicorn Publishing Group 184
Valley Press 185
Vintage 186
Philip Wilson Publishers 188
Yale University Press London 188

Gardening

ACC Art Books 118
Anness Publishing Ltd 120
The Crowood Press 133
David & Charles 134
DK 135
W. Foulsham & Co. 142
Graffeg 144
Hardie Grant UK 146
Headline Publishing Group 149
Henley Hall Press 149
Kyle Books 154
Frances Lincoln 156
Merrell Publishers 160
Murdoch Books 161
Octopus Publishing Group 164
Orphans Publishing 166
Pan Macmillan 167
Pen & Sword Books 168
Quiller Publishing 172
Ryland Peters & Small 174
Thames & Hudson 182
Tippermuir Books 183

Gender studies, gay and lesbian, LGBTQ+

Arkbound 120
Bloomsbury Publishing 124
Crescent Moon Publishing 133
Hazel Press 149
Headpress 149
The Indigo Press 152
Inspired Quill 152
Jacaranda Books 153
Lucent Dreaming 157
Pan Macmillan 167
Polity Press 170
Quartet Books 171

Health

Anness Publishing Ltd 120
Bedford Square Publishers 122
Bloomsbury Publishing 124
Bonnier Books UK 125
Bookouture 126
Canbury Press 128
Crown House Publishing 133
DK 135
Ebury Publishing 136
Findhorn Press 140
Floris Books 141
W. Foulsham & Co. 142
Free Association Books 142
The Gresham Publishing Company 144
Hardie Grant UK 146
HarperCollins Publishers 146
Hay House Publishers 148
Institute of Public Administration 152
Kyle Books 154
McNidder & Grace 158
The Mercier Press 160
John Murray Group 161
Nourish Books 163
Octopus Publishing Group 164
The Orion Publishing Group 165
Pan Macmillan 167
Penguin General 168
Perspective Books 169
Phoenix Publishing House 170
Quartet Books 171
Ryland Peters & Small 174
Springer Nature 179
Studio Press 180
Summersdale Publishers 180
Taylor & Francis Group 181
Transworld 183
Watkins Publishing 186

Heritage

Afsana Press 118
Bloomsbury Publishing 124
Calon Books 127
Ayebia Clarke Publishing Ltd 130
Country Books 132
Countryside Books 132
DB Publishing 134
Eglantyne Books 137
Graffeg 144
Irish Academic Press 153
McNidder & Grace 158
Manchester University Press 159
Neem Tree Press 162
Profile Books 171
Quiller Publishing 172
Sigma Press 177
Two Rivers Press 184

History

Amazon Publishing 119
Amber Books 119
Amberley Publishing 119
Amgueddfa Cymru – Museum Wales 119
Appletree Press 120
Ashmolean Museum Publications 120
Atlantic Books 121
Authentic Media 121
Berghahn Books 122
Birlinn 123
Biteback Publishing 123
Blackstaff Press 123
Bloomsbury Publishing 124
Bodleian Library Publishing 125
Boydell & Brewer 126
British Library Publishing 127
The British Museum Press 127
Calon Books 127
Cambridge University Press & Assessment 128
Candy Jar Books 128
Canongate Books 128
James Clarke & Co. 130
Cló Iar-Chonnacht Teo 130
Collective Ink 131
Cork University Press 132
Cornerstone 132
Country Books 132
Cranthorpe Millner Publishers 133
The Crowood Press 133
DB Publishing 134
DK 135
The Dovecote Press 136
Duckworth Books 136
Ebury Publishing 136
Edinburgh University Press 137
Eglantyne Books 137
Elliott & Thompson 137
University of Exeter Press 139
Fighting High 140
Fleming Publications 141
Fonthill Media 141
Footnote Press 141
Four Courts Press 142
Garnet Publishing 142
Gibson Square 143
Gill 143
Gingko 143
Goldsmiths Press 143
Grub Street Publishing 144
Guild of Master Craftsman Publications 144
Hachette UK 145
Halban Publishers 146
HarperCollins Publishers 146
Headline Publishing Group 149
Henley Hall Press 149
The History Press 150
Hodder & Stoughton 150
Icon Books 151
Institute of Public Administration 152
Irish Academic Press 153
IWM (Imperial War Museums) Publishing 153
Lawrence & Wishart 155
The Lilliput Press 155
Frances Lincoln 156
Liverpool University Press 157
Logaston Press 157
Luath Press 157
The Lutterworth Press 158
McNidder & Grace 158
Manchester University Press 159
Mensch Publishing 160
Mentor Books 160
The Mercier Press 160
Merlin Press 160
Morrigan Book Company/City of Dublin Press 161
Murdoch Books 161
John Murray Group 161
Natural History Museum Publishing 162
New Island Books 162
The O'Brien Press 163
Octopus Publishing Group 164
The Oleander Press 164
Michael O'Mara Books 165
On Stream Publications 165
Oneworld Publications 165
The Orion Publishing Group 165
Osprey Publishing 166
Oxford University Press 166
Pan Macmillan 167
Pelagic 168
Pen & Sword Books 168
Penguin General 168
Penguin Press 169
Pluto Press 170
Polity Press 170
Profile Books 171
Quarto Group Publishing UK 172
Quiller Publishing 172
Reaktion Books 172
Revenge Ink 173
Rymour Books 174
Saraband 175
Sheldrake Press 177
Shepheard-Walwyn (Publishers) 177
Simon & Schuster UK 177
Colin Smythe 178
Society of Genealogists 178
Sparsile Books 179
Taylor & Francis Group 181
Thames & Hudson 182
Transworld 183
Unicorn Publishing Group 184
University College Dublin Press 185
Vallentine Mitchell 185
Verso 185
Vintage 186
Welsh Academic Press 187

Illustrated books

Amber Books 119
Amberley Publishing 119
Anness Publishing Ltd 120

Birlinn 123
Bloomsbury Publishing 124
Bodleian Library Publishing 125
The Bright Press 126
The British Museum Press 127
DK 135
Fircone Books 140
From You To Me 142
Gemini Books Group 143
Graffeg 144
Guild of Master Craftsman Publications 144
Hachette Children's Trade 145
Halsgrove Publishing 146
Happy Yak 146
Hardie Grant UK 146
Laurence King Publishing 154
Frances Lincoln 156
LOM ART 157
McNidder & Grace 158
Merrell Publishers 160
Myriad Editions 162
Octopus Publishing Group 164
Omnibus Press/Wise Music Group 165
Orphans Publishing 166
Osprey Publishing 166
Pan Macmillan 167
Penguin Random House UK 169
Quarto Group Publishing UK 172
Ryland Peters & Small 174
Scholastic 175
September Publishing 176
Simon & Schuster UK 177
Taschen UK 181
Thames & Hudson 182
Watkins Publishing 186

International issues

Afsana Press 118
Bloomsbury Publishing 124
Boydell & Brewer 126
Bristol University Press/Policy Press 126
Edinburgh University Press 137
University of Exeter Press 139
Fabian Society 139
Halban Publishers 146
Hurst Publishers 151
Manchester University Press 159
The Oleander Press 164
Oneworld Publications 165
Pluto Press 170
Saqi Books 175
Ta-Ha Publishers 181
Taylor & Francis Group 181
University of Wales Press 186

Irish interest

Appletree Press 120
Cló Iar-Chonnacht Teo 130
Colourpoint Creative 131
Cork University Press 132
The Educational Company of Ireland 137
Folens Publishers 141
Four Courts Press 142
Gill 143
Irish Academic Press 153
The Irish Pages Press/Cló An Mhíl Bhuī 153
The Lilliput Press 155
The Mercier Press 160
Morrigan Book Company/City of Dublin Press 161
On Stream Publications 165
Pluto Press 170
Colin Smythe 178
Somerville Press 178
University College Dublin Press 185

Law

Bloomsbury Publishing 124
Bristol University Press/Policy Press 126
Cambridge University Press & Assessment 128
Edinburgh University Press 137
Edward Elgar Publishing 137
Globe Law and Business 143
Institute of Public Administration 152
Jordan Publishing 154
LexisNexis 155
Manchester University Press 159
Oak Tree Press 163
Oxford University Press 166
Taylor & Francis Group 181
Thomson Reuters – Round Hall 182

Leisure interests and hobbies

AA Publishing 118
Amazon Publishing 119
Amberley Publishing 119
Bennion Kearny 122
The Bright Press 126
Cicerone 130
Countryside Books 132
The Crowood Press 133
David & Charles 134
Fernhurst Books 139
W. Foulsham & Co. 142
Guild of Master Craftsman Publications 144
Haynes Publishing 148
Pen & Sword Books 168
Royal National Institute of Blind People (RNIB) 173
Search Press 176
Taylor & Francis Group 181
Wild Things Publishing 187

Lifestyle, home and DIY

Amazon Publishing 119
Anness Publishing Ltd 120
Black & White Publishing 123
Blink Publishing 124
The Bright Press 126
The Crowood Press 133
David & Charles 134
Elliott & Thompson 137

W. Foulsham & Co. 142
Graffeg 144
Harriman House 148
Haynes Publishing 148
Igloo Books 151
Murdoch Books 161
Octopus Publishing Group 164
Quarto Group Publishing UK 172
Ryland Peters & Small 174

Literary criticism and essays

Alma Books 119
Bloomsbury Publishing 124
Bodleian Library Publishing 125
Boydell & Brewer 126
British Library Publishing 127
Ayebia Clarke Publishing Ltd 130
James Clarke & Co. 130
Daunt Books 134
Edinburgh University Press 137
The Emma Press 138
Enitharmon Editions 138
Fincham Press 140
HarperCollins Publishers 146
Hazel Press 149
Imprint Academic 152
The Irish Pages Press/Cló An Mhíl Bhuī 153
The Lilliput Press 155
Liverpool University Press 157
Loudhailer Books 157
Manchester University Press 159
Oxford University Press 166
Polity Press 170
Pushkin Press 171
Quartet Books 171
Salt Publishing 174
Seren 176
Colin Smythe 178
Strange Region 180
University College Dublin Press 185
University of Wales Press 186
The Waywiser Press 187

Local interest

Amberley Publishing 119
Birlinn 123
Blackstaff Press 123
Calon Books 127
Colourpoint Creative 131
Country Books 132
Countryside Books 132
DB Publishing 134
The Dovecote Press 136
University of Exeter Press 139
Fonthill Media 141
Four Courts Press 142
Halsgrove Publishing 146
Logaston Press 157
Lonely Planet Publications 157
Mabecron Books 158
Medina Publishing 159
Metro Publications 160
On Stream Publications 165
Pen & Sword Books 168
Scottish Mountaineering Press 176
Society of Genealogists 178
Stenlake Publishing 179
ThunderPoint Publishing 182
Two Rivers Press 184

Medicine and nursing

Cambridge University Press & Assessment 128
DK 135
Elsevier 138
5mBooks 140
Hachette Learning 145
McGraw-Hill Education 158
Oxford University Press 166
SAGE Publishing 174
Science Museum Group 175
Springer Nature 179
Taylor & Francis Group 181
John Wiley & Sons 188

Military

Amber Books 119
Amberley Publishing 119
Birlinn 123
Blink Publishing 124
Candy Jar Books 128
The Crowood Press 133
Eglantyne Books 137
Fighting High 140
Fonthill Media 141
Grub Street Publishing 144
Haynes Publishing 148
Howgate Publishing 151
Hurst Publishers 151
IWM (Imperial War Museums) Publishing 153
Jane's 153
Osprey Publishing 166
Pen & Sword Books 168
Penguin Michael Joseph 169
Quarto Group Publishing UK 172
Transworld 183
Ulric Publishing 184

Mind, body & spirit (MBS)

Amazon Publishing 119
Bedford Square Publishers 122
Bonnier Books UK 125
Collective Ink 131
Cornerstone 132
Crown House Publishing 133
Darton, Longman and Todd 134
Findhorn Press 140
Floris Books 141
W. Foulsham & Co. 142
Free Association Books 142
Hachette UK 145
Hardie Grant UK 146

Hawthorn Press 148
Hay House Publishers 148
Hodder & Stoughton 150
Kyle Books 154
Loudhailer Books 157
McNidder & Grace 158
The Mercier Press 160
John Murray Group 161
Octopus Publishing Group 164
Penguin General 168
Perspective Books 169
Phoenix Publishing House 170
Ryland Peters & Small 174
Watkins Publishing 186
Zambezi Publishing 188

Music

Alma Books 119
Amber Books 119
Arc Publications 120
Aureus Publishing 121
Birlinn 123
Black Dog Press 123
Boydell & Brewer 126
British Library Publishing 127
Cambridge University Press & Assessment 128
Cork University Press 132
Elliott & Thompson 137
Equinox Publishing 138
Faber & Faber 139
Flame Tree Publishing 140
Graffeg 144
HarperCollins Publishers 146
Headpress 149
Icon Books 151
The Lutterworth Press 158
McNidder & Grace 158
Manchester University Press 159
Kevin Mayhew 159
W.W. Norton & Co. 163
Octopus Publishing Group 164
Omnibus Press/Wise Music Group 165
The Orion Publishing Group 165
Ortac Press 166
Oxford University Press 166
Plexus Publishing 170
Reaktion Books 172
Red Planet Books 172
Repeater Books 173
St David's Press 174
Sheldrake Press 177
Stainer & Bell 179
Strange Region 180
Tangerine Press 181
Taylor & Francis Group 181
Transworld 183
University College Dublin Press 185
Valley Press 185
Velocity Press 185
Vintage 186
Yale University Press London 188

Natural history

Amber Books 119
Blackstaff Press 123
Bodleian Library Publishing 125
Calon Books 127
The Crowood Press 133
DK 135
The Dovecote Press 136
Ebury Publishing 136
Findhorn Press 140
Graffeg 144
Granta Books 144
HarperCollins Publishers 146
Little Toller Books 157
Natural History Museum Publishing 162
Pan Macmillan 167
Pelagic 168
Quiller Publishing 172
Saraband 175
Scottish Mountaineering Press 176
Siri Scientific Press 178
Taylor & Francis Group 181
Transworld 183
Vertebrate Publishing 185
Vintage 186
Whittet Books 187
Wildthought Books 187

Nautical and marine

Amberley Publishing 119
Boydell & Brewer 126
Brown, Son & Ferguson 127
University of Exeter Press 139
Fernhurst Books 139
Fonthill Media 141
Jane's 153
Pen & Sword Books 168

Novelty, gift books

Allison & Busby 119
Amber Books 119
Appletree Press 120
John Blake Publishing 124
Crowdbound 133
Ebury Publishing 136
Elliott & Thompson 137
Helen Exley 139
From You To Me 142
Gemini Books Group 143
Guild of Master Craftsman Publications 144
Hachette Children's Trade 145
Hachette UK 145
HarperCollins Publishers 146
Igloo Books 151
Frances Lincoln 156
Octopus Publishing Group 164
Old Barn Books 164
The Orion Publishing Group 165
Pan Macmillan 167
Penguin Random House UK 169
Profile Books 171

Quarto Group Publishing UK 172
Quiller Publishing 172
Ryland Peters & Small 174
Shepheard-Walwyn (Publishers) 177
Summersdale Publishers 180
Two Windmills 184

Performing arts

Aurora Metro 121
Bloomsbury Publishing 124
The Bright Press 126
The Crowood Press 133
University of Exeter Press 139
Faber & Faber 139
Oxford University Press 166
Strange Region 180

Photography

ACC Art Books 118
Amber Books 119
Appletree Press 120
Black Dog Press 123
Bloomsbury Publishing 124
The Bright Press 126
Cōnfingō Publishing 131
David & Charles 134
DK 135
Fleming Publications 141
Garnet Publishing 142
Graffeg 144
Guild of Master Craftsman Publications 144
Laurence King Publishing 154
McNidder & Grace 158
Merrell Publishers 160
Natural History Museum Publishing 162
Octopus Publishing Group 164
Prestel Publishing 171
Quiller Publishing 172
Reaktion Books 172
Stanley/Barker 179
Strange Region 180
Taschen UK 181
Taylor & Francis Group 181
Thames & Hudson 182

Politics

Agenda Publishing 119
Atlantic Books 121
Biteback Publishing 123
Blackstaff Press 123
Bloomsbury Publishing 124
Bristol University Press/Policy Press 126
Cambridge University Press & Assessment 128
Canbury Press 128
Canongate Books 128
Cornerstone 132
Ebury Publishing 136
Edinburgh University Press 137
Elliott & Thompson 137
Gibson Square 143
Gill 143
Goldsmiths Press 143
HarperCollins Publishers 146
Henley Hall Press 149
Hurst Publishers 151
Icon Books 151
Imprint Academic 152
Institute of Public Administration 152
Irish Academic Press 153
Lawrence & Wishart 155
Little, Brown Book Group 156
Luath Press 157
Manchester University Press 159
Mensch Publishing 160
Mentor Books 160
The Mercier Press 160
The O'Brien Press 163
Oneworld Publications 165
Oxford University Press 166
Pan Macmillan 167
Penguin General 168
Penguin Press 169
Pluto Press 170
Polity Press 170
Princeton University Press – Europe 171
Profile Books 171
Quartet Books 171
Reaktion Books 172
Repeater Books 173
Ringwood Publishing 173
St David's Press 174
September Publishing 176
Shepheard-Walwyn (Publishers) 177
Simon & Schuster UK 177
Taylor & Francis Group 181
University College Dublin Press 185
Verso 185
Vintage 186
Welsh Academic Press 187

Popular culture

Afsana Press 118
Amazon Publishing 119
Blink Publishing 124
Bloomsbury Publishing 124
Bonnier Books UK 125
Canongate Books 128
Ebury Publishing 136
Hachette UK 145
HarperCollins Publishers 146
Henley Hall Press 149
Laurence King Publishing 154
Korero Press 154
Lawrence & Wishart 155
McNidder & Grace 158
Manchester University Press 159
Mensch Publishing 160
Muswell Press 161
Octopus Publishing Group 164
P&H Books 166
Penguin General 168
Penguin Michael Joseph 169
Penguin Random House UK 169

Plexus Publishing 170
Repeater Books 173
Taschen UK 181
Thames & Hudson 182
ThunderPoint Publishing 182
Titan Books 183
Vintage 186
Weatherglass Press 187

Reference

Amber Books 119
Anness Publishing Ltd 120
Atlantic Books 121
Bloomsbury Publishing 124
Bonnier Books UK 125
British Library Publishing 127
Cambridge University Press & Assessment 128
James Clarke & Co. 130
Cornerstone 132
DK 135
Elsevier 138
Encyclopaedia Britannica (UK) 138
Flame Tree Publishing 140
Fly on the Wall Press 141
Gill 143
The Gresham Publishing Company 144
Guild of Master Craftsman Publications 144
Guinness World Records 145
Hachette Learning 145
HarperCollins Publishers 146
Hymns Ancient and Modern 151
Jordan Publishing 154
Kyle Books 154
John Murray Group 161
The O'Brien Press 163
Octopus Publishing Group 164
The Oleander Press 164
Oxford University Press 166
Pan Macmillan 167
Penguin General 168
Radio Society of Great Britain 172
Taylor & Francis Group 181
TSO (The Stationery Office) 183
Two Windmills 184
Unicorn Publishing Group 184
Vallentine Mitchell 185

Religion, philosophy and New Age

Afsana Press 118
Agenda Publishing 119
Authentic Media 121
Bloomsbury Publishing 124
Bryntirion Press 127
Cambridge University Press & Assessment 128
Canbury Press 128
Catholic Truth Society 129
Christian Education 130
Churchwarden Publications 130
James Clarke & Co. 130
Collective Ink 131
Columba Books 131
Darton, Longman and Todd 134
Ebury Publishing 136
Edinburgh University Press 137
Floris Books 141
W. Foulsham & Co. 142
Four Courts Press 142
Garnet Publishing 142
Gibson Square 143
Gingko 143
Gresham Books 144
Hadean Press 145
HarperCollins Publishers 146
Hymns Ancient and Modern 151
Icon Books 151
Imprint Academic 152
ISF Publishing 153
Kube Publishing 154
Lawrence & Wishart 155
The Lilliput Press 155
The Lutterworth Press 158
Manchester University Press 159
Mandrake of Oxford 159
Kevin Mayhew 159
Mud Pie 161
Muddy Pearl 161
John Murray Group 161
Ockham Publishing Group 163
Oneworld Publications 165
Oxford University Press 166
Pan Macmillan 167
Penguin Press 169
Reaktion Books 172
Revenge Ink 173
Ringwood Publishing 173
George Ronald 173
St Pauls Publishing 174
Scripture Union 176
Stainer & Bell 179
Ta-Ha Publishers 181
Thames & Hudson 182
Vallentine Mitchell 185
Verso 185
Wooden Books 188

Rural life and country

Amberley Publishing 119
The Crowood Press 133
Logaston Press 157
Quiller Publishing 172
Merlin Unwin Books 185
Whittet Books 187
Wild Things Publishing 187
Wildthought Books 187

Science

Bloomsbury Publishing 124
The Bright Press 126
Cambridge University Press & Assessment 128
Cornerstone 132
Elliott & Thompson 137
Elsevier 138

Floris Books 141
Garnet Publishing 142
Goldsmiths Press 143
HarperCollins Publishers 146
IOP Publishing 152
Frances Lincoln 156
McGraw-Hill Education 158
John Murray Group 161
Natural History Museum Publishing 162
W.W. Norton & Co. 163
Ockham Publishing Group 163
Oneworld Publications 165
Oxford University Press 166
Portland Press 170
Princeton University Press – Europe 171
Profile Books 171
SAGE Publishing 174
Science Museum Group 175
Sparsile Books 179
Springer Nature 179
Transworld 183
Vintage 186
John Wiley & Sons 188
Yale University Press London 188

Scottish interest

Acair 118
Appletree Press 120
Birlinn 123
Edinburgh University Press 137
Floris Books 141
The Gresham Publishing Company 144
Luath Press 157
Rymour Books 174
Scottish Mountaineering Press 176
Shepheard-Walwyn (Publishers) 177
Stewed Rhubarb Press 180
ThunderPoint Publishing 182
Tippermuir Books 183
The Wee Book Company 187

Social sciences

Afsana Press 118
Alma Books 119
Arkbound 120
Berghahn Books 122
Bloomsbury Publishing 124
Bristol University Press/Policy Press 126
Cambridge University Press & Assessment 128
Equinox Publishing 138
Fonthill Media 141
Free Association Books 142
Goldsmiths Press 143
The Indigo Press 152
Peter Lang 155
Liverpool University Press 157
McGraw-Hill Education 158
Merlin Press 160
W.W. Norton & Co. 163
Ortac Press 166
Oxford University Press 166
Polity Press 170
Princeton University Press – Europe 171
SAGE Publishing 174
University College Dublin Press 185
University of Wales Press 186

Sports and games

Appletree Press 120
Atlantic Books 121
Aureus Publishing 121
Bennion Kearny 122
Birlinn 123
Black & White Publishing 123
Blackstaff Press 123
Bloomsbury Publishing 124
The Crowood Press 133
DB Publishing 134
Ebury Publishing 136
Elliott & Thompson 137
Fonthill Media 141
W. Foulsham & Co. 142
Graffeg 144
Halcyon Publishing 146
HarperCollins Publishers 146
Maverick House 159
Milo Books 160
The O'Brien Press 163
Quarto Group Publishing UK 172
Quiller Publishing 172
Ringwood Publishing 173
St David's Press 174
Sigma Press 177
Thinkwell Books 182

Transport, including cycling

AA Publishing 118
Amberley Publishing 119
Colourpoint Creative 131
The Crowood Press 133
Fonthill Media 141
Haynes Publishing 148
McNidder & Grace 158
Stenlake Publishing 179
Ulric Publishing 184

Travel and geography

AA Publishing 118
Amber Books 119
Amberley Publishing 119
Apa Publications 120
Appletree Press 120
Bennion Kearny 122
Blackstaff Press 123
Blue Guides 125
Bradt Travel Guides 126
Canongate Books 128
Cicerone 130
Colourpoint Creative 131
Countryside Books 132
Discovery Walking Guides 135
DK 135

Duckworth Books 136
Ebury Publishing 136
Eland Publishing 137
Eye Books 139
W. Foulsham & Co. 142
Garnet Publishing 142
Gibson Square 143
Granta Books 144
Hodder & Stoughton 150
ISF Publishing 153
Lonely Planet Publications 157
Luath Press 157
Murdoch Books 161
John Murray Group 161
Muswell Press 161
Octopus Publishing Group 164
The Oleander Press 164
On Stream Publications 165
Penguin General 168
Penguin Random House UK 169
Prestel Publishing 171
Quarto Group Publishing UK 172
Reaktion Books 172
September Publishing 176
Sheldrake Press 177
Summersdale Publishers 180
Sunflower Books 180
ThunderPoint Publishing 182
Vertebrate Publishing 185

Welsh interest

Amgueddfa Cymru – Museum Wales 119
Calon Books 127
Dref Wen 136
Honno (Welsh Women's Press) 150
Seren 176
University of Wales Press 186
Welsh Academic Press 187

Publishers of plays (UK)

Playwrights are reminded that it is unusual for a publisher of trade editions of plays to publish plays which have not had at least reasonably successful, usually professional, productions on stage first. See listings starting on page 118 for contacts.

Alma Books 119
Barbican Press 122
Bloomsbury Publishing 124
Brown, Son & Ferguson 127
Chapman Publishing 129
Cló Iar-Chonnacht Teo 130
Concord Theatricals 131
Cressrelles Publishing 133
Everyman's Library 138
Faber & Faber 139
Flapjack Press 140
The Gallery Press 142
Nick Hern Books 149
The Lilliput Press 155
Kevin Mayhew 159
Renard Press 173
Seren 176
Colin Smythe 178
Strange Region 180
Josef Weinberger Plays 187

Publishers of poetry (UK)

See listings starting on page 118 for contacts.

Alma Books 119
Arachne Press 120
Arc Publications 120
Bad Betty Press 121
Barbican Press 122
Birlinn 123
Black Cat Poetry Press 123
Bloodaxe Books 124
Blue Diode Publishing 125
Broken Sleep Books 127
Burning Eye Books 127
Canongate Books 128
Carcanet Press 128
CB Editions 129
Chapman Publishing 129
Cinnamon Press 130
Cló Iar-Chonnacht Teo 130
Cōnfingō Publishing 131
Cornerstone 132
Crescent Moon Publishing 133
Dedalus Press 134
Dialogue 135
Eglantyne Books 137
Elephant Press 137
The Emma Press 138
Enitharmon Editions 138

Everyman's Library 138
Faber & Faber 139
Flapjack Press 140
Flipped Eye Publishing 141
Fly on the Wall Press 141
The Gallery Press 142
Goat Star Books 143
Guillemot Press 145
Guppy Publishing 145
Haunt Publishing 148
Hazel Press 149
Honno (Welsh Women's Press) 150
Indigo Dreams Publishing 152
Inkandescent 152
The Irish Pages Press/Cló An Mhíl Bhuī 153
Jantar Publishing 153
Knight Errant Press 154
Leamington Books 155
The Lilliput Press 155
Liverpool University Press 157
Luath Press 157
Lucent Dreaming 157
New Island Books 162
The New Menard Press 162
Nine Arches Press 162
Offord Books 164
Out-Spoken Press 166
Oversteps Books 166
Parthian Books 167
Pavilion Poetry 167
Penguin Press 169
Penguin Random House UK 169
Prototype 171
Renard Press 173
Revenge Ink 173
Route 173
Salmon Poetry 174
Salt Publishing 174
Scotland Street Press 176
Scottish Mountaineering Press 176
Seren 176
Shearsman Books 177
Stairwell Books 179
Stewed Rhubarb Press 180
Strange Region 180
tall-lighthouse 181
Taproot Books 181
Templar Poetry 182
Tippermuir Books 183
Turas Press 183
Two Rivers Press 184
UEA Publishing Project 184
Valley Press 185
Verve Poetry Press 185
Vintage 186
The Waywiser Press 187
Wrecking Ball Press 188

Literary agents for children's books

The following literary agents will consider work suitable for children's books, from authors and/or illustrators of children's books. Listings start on page 452. See also *Art agents and commercial art studios* on page 516.

The Agency (London) 452
Aitken Alexander Associates 453
Darley Anderson and Associates 453
ASH Literary 454
Bath Literary Agency 454
Bell Lomax Moreton Agency 454
The Bent Agency 455
The Blair Partnership 455
Jenny Brown Associates 456
Felicity Bryan Associates 456
C&W Agency 456
Georgina Capel Associates 457
The Catchpole Agency 457
Anne Clark Literary Agency 457
Colwill & Peddle 458
Gemma Cooper Literary 458
Creative Authors 459
Rupert Crew 459
Curtis Brown 459
Dark House Literary & Screen Agency 460
DHH Literary Agency 460
Diamond Kahn & Woods Literary Agency 460
Eddison Pearson 461
Fraser Ross Associates 462
Greene & Heaton 463
The Greenhouse Literary Agency 464
Marianne Gunn O'Connor Literary, Film/TV Agency 464
Hardman & Swainson 465
Antony Harwood 465
A.M. Heath & Co. 465
Sophie Hicks Agency 466
David Higham Associates 466
Holroyde Cartey 466
Oscar Janson Smith Agency 467
Kane Literary Agency 468
LBA Books 469
Lindsay Literary Agency 470
Luithlen Agency 470
Eunice McMullen 471
Marjacq Scripts 471
MBA Literary and Script Agents 471
Madeleine Milburn Literary, TV & Film Agency 472
MMBcreative 472
Morgan Green Creatives 473
Kate Nash Literary Agency 473

Andrew Nurnberg Associates 474
Paper Lion 474
Peters Fraser & Dunlop 475
RCW 476
Redhammer Management 476
Seventh Agency 477
The Shaw Agency 477
Caroline Sheldon Literary Agency 478
Hannah Sheppard Literary Agency 478
Dorie Simmonds Agency 478
The Soho Agency 478
Spring Literary 478
Abner Stein 479
Sarah Such Literary Agency 479
United Agents 480
Watson, Little 480
Whispering Buffalo Literary Agency 481
Eve White Literary Agency 481
Alice Williams Literary 481
Susan Yearwood Agency 482
YMU Literary 482

Literary agents for television, film, radio and theatre

Listings for these and other literary agents start on page 452.

The Agency (London) 452
Aitken Alexander Associates 453
Berlin Associates 455
Blake Friedmann Literary Agency 455
Alan Brodie Representation 456
Georgina Capel Associates 457
Casarotto Ramsay & Associates 457
Jonathan Clowes 458
Curtis Brown 459
Felix de Wolfe 460
Fillingham Weston Associates 461
Film Rights 461
FRA 462
Jüri Gabriel 462
Bill Goodall Literary Agency 463
The Haworth Agency 465
David Higham Associates 466
Valerie Hoskins Associates 466
Independent Talent Group 467
JFL Agency 467
Michelle Kass Associates 468
Ki Agency 468
Knight Hall Agency 468
LBA Books 469
Limelight Celebrity Management 469
The Literary Office 470
MBA Literary and Script Agents 471
Madeleine Milburn Literary, TV & Film Agency 472
Morgan Green Creatives 473
PBJ Management 474
Peters Fraser & Dunlop 475
Sayle Screen 477
Linda Seifert Management 477
Sheil Land Associates 477
Elaine Steel Writers' Agent 479
Micheline Steinberg Associates 479
Rochelle Stevens & Co 479
Sarah Such Literary Agency 479
Nick Turner Management 480
WGM Atlantic Talent and Literary Group 481
Eve White Literary Agency 481
WME 481

Prizes and awards

The listings for Prizes begin on page 570, where they are sorted by genre. Below Prizes are grouped by age, ethnicity, sexuality, gender, disability, and class.

Age

Under 25: The Bridport Prize: Young Writer Award 580
Under 25: The New Poets Prize 593
Under 25: Mustapha Matura Award and Mentoring Programme 605
Under 30: The Eric Gregory Awards 626
Under 30: The Somerset Maugham Awards 581
Under 30: The Australian Fiction Prize 577
Under 35: The Betty Trask Prize 582
Under 35: The Sunday Times Charlotte Aitken Young Writer of the Year Award 582
Under 35: #Merky Books New Writers' Prize 596
Under 35: New Writers Award 597
Under 39: Swansea University Dylan Thomas Prize 588
Under 40: Rooney Prize for Irish Literature 582
Over 40: The McKitterick Prize 581
Over 50: The JBA Over 50 Debut Award 596

Over 50: RSL Christopher Bland Prize 582
Over 60: The Bridport Prize: Never Too Late Award 580

Disabled people

ACDI Literary Prize 608
Book Edit Writers' Prize 595
Creative Future Writers' Award 595
Disabled Poets Prize 589
The London Writers Awards 609
Wellcome Collection Non-Fiction Awards 628

Ethnicity

The Diverse Book Awards 585
FAB Prize for Undiscovered Talent 595
Future Worlds Prize for Fantasy & Science Fiction Writers of Colour 614
Jhalak Prose Prize 586
Joffe Books Prize for Crime Writers of Colour 611
The London Writers Awards 609
#Merky Books New Writers' Prize 596
Mo Siewcharran Prize 598

LGBTQ+

Book Edit Writers' Prize 595
Escalator New Writing Fellowships for Emerging Writers 625
Hastings Book Festival Competition 590
Lambda Literary Awards 609
The London Writers Awards 609
PFD Queer Fiction Prizes 597
Polari Book Prize 587
Northern Writers' Awards 587

Women

The Lucy Cavendish Fiction Prize 580
Comedy Women in Print Awards 613
Creative Future Writers' Award 595
Mslexia Competitions: Novel (Adult) 609
Mslexia Competitions: Short Story and Flash Fiction 602
Mslexia Competitions: Poetry 592
The Ilse Schwepcke Prize 621
The Warwick Prize for Women in Translation 608
Women's Prize for Fiction 611
Women's Prize for Non-Fiction 615

Working class

Creative Future Writers' Award 595
Northern Writers' Awards 587
Writers' & Artists' Working-Class Writers' Prizes 598

Listings index

All companies, public and commercial organisations, societies, festivals and prize-giving bodies, that have a listing in the *Yearbook* are included in this index.

A for Authors 452
a4 Literary 483
AA Publishing 118
Abacus *see* Little, Brown Book Group
Abbey Theatre Amharclann na Mainistreach 415
ABC-CLIO 203
Aberystwyth University 653
Abingdon Press 203
Harry N. Abrams 203
Abridged 36
ABSW Awards 582
Acacia House Publishing Services 485
Academy of British Cover Design: Annual Cover Design Competition 570
Acair 118
ACC Art Books 118
Accidental Agency, The 452
Accountancy Age 36
Accounting & Business 36
ACDI Literary Prize 608
ACER Press 190
Ackerley Prize for Autobiography and Memoir, The 583
Actors Touring Company 421
Acumen Literary Journal 36
Adams Literary 487
Ad Hoc Fiction 118
Alex Adsett Literary 483
Advertising Standards Authority 391
Advocate Art 516
Aeroplane Monthly 36
AESOP (All Editorial Services Online for Publishers & Writers) 694
Aesthetica Art Prize 570
Aesthetica Creative Writing Award 588
Aesthetica Magazine 36
Aevitas Creative Management 487
Aevitas Creative Management UK 452
Affirm Press 190
Africa Confidential 37
Africa: St Patrick's Missions 36
African Business 37
Afsana Press 118
Agency for the Legal Deposit Libraries (ALDL), The 662
Agency (London), The 452
Agency Rush 516
Agenda Publishing 119
AIM Literary Festival 630
Aimée Hill | AJ Editorial Services 694
AIR International 37
Airey Neave Book Prize 620
AITA/IATA (International Amateur Theatre Association) 549
Aitken Alexander Associates 453
Akashic Books 203
University of Alabama Press, The 203
Alchemy Spoon, The 37
ALCS Educational Writers' Award 574
ALCS Tom-Gallon Trust Award, The 598
Aldeburgh Literary Festival, The 630
Aldeburgh Poetry Festival 630
All Party Parliamentary Writers Group 561
Allegro Poetry 37
Allen & Unwin 190
Alliance of Independent Authors 554
Alliance of Literary Societies 554
Allied Artists/Artistic License 516
Dinesh Allirajah Prize for Short Fiction 598
Allison & Busby 119
Allographic 352
ALM: Australian Literary Management 483
Alma Books 119
Almeida Theatre 412
ALTA Awards 606
Alton Arts Festival 630
Amazon Prime 395
Amazon Publishing 119
Amber Books 119
Amberley Publishing 119
American Booksellers Association 554
American Literary Translators Association 560
American Society for Indexing 545
American Society of Composers, Authors and Publishers 553
Amgueddfa Cymru – Museum Wales 119
AMP Literary 453
Ampersand Agency, The 453
An Post Irish Book Awards 573
And Other Stories 119
Hans Christian Andersen Awards, The 575
Andersen Press 119
Darley Anderson and Associates 453
Darley Anderson Illustration Agency 516
And Other Poems 37
Andromeda Magazine 37
Anglia Ruskin University 653
Angling Times 37
Anglo-Hellenic League Runciman Award, The 577
Angry Gable Press 203
Angry Robot Books 120
Anness Publishing Ltd 120
Annick Press 194
Anthropocene 37

Anvil Press 194
A1 Book Publishing UK 694
Apa Publications 120
Apollo 38
APPG for Libraries Information & Knowledge in Parliament 668
Applause Theatre and Cinema Book Publishers 204
Apple Tree Literary 453
Apple TV+ 395
Appledore Book Festival 630
Apples and Snakes 352
Appletree Press 120
Arachne Press 120
Arc Publications 120
Arcade Publishing 204
Architects' Journal, The 38
Architectural Review, The 38
Architecture Today 38
Arena Illustration 516
Argus, The 30
ARIAS (Audio & Radio Industry Awards) 604
University of Arkansas Press, The 204
Arkbound 120
Yvonne Arnaud Theatre Management Ltd 415
Suzanne Arnold 694
ARP Books 194
Arsenal Pulp Press 194
Art Agency, The 516
Art Monthly 38
Art Newspaper, The 38
Art Quarterly 38
ArtReview and ArtReview Asia 38
Artellus 453
Artist Partners 517
Artistique International 517
Artists & Illustrators 39
Arts Club, The 553
Arts Council/An Chomhairle Ealaíon 539
Arts Council England 350, 539, 623, 668
Arts Council/An Chomhairle Ealaíon, The 623
Arts Council of Northern Ireland 539
Arts Council of Wales 350
Artworks, The 517
Arvon 354, 646
Arvon Writers Retreat at the Clockhouse 646
ASH Literary 454
Ashmolean Museum Publications 120
Asian Today, The 34
Aspects Irish Literature Festival 630
Association for Scottish Literature 554
Association of American Literary Agents 555
Association of American Publishers 555
Association of Authors' Agents, The 555
Association of British Science Writers 561
Association of Canadian Publishers 555
Association of Christian Writers 561
Association of Freelance Editors, Proofreaders and Indexers of Ireland 545
Association of Illustrators 535
Association of Independent Libraries 668
Association of Learned and Professional Society Publishers, The 543
Association of Photographers, The 535
Association of Senior and Children's Education Librarians (ASCEL) 668
Astra Publishing House 204
Astronomy Now 39
Asylum 39
Atlantic Books 121
Atrium 39
Attitude 39
Auckland University Press 199
Audible 223
Audio Factory 223
Audiobook Creation Exchange (ACX) 223
Audiobooks.com 223
Aureus Publishing 121
Aurora Metro 121
Aurora Prize, The 584
Australian Copyright Council 544
Australian Crime Writers Association 555
Australian Fiction Prize, The 577
Australian Publishers Association 555
Australian Society of Authors, The 555
Australian Writers' Guild 555
Authentic Media 121
Author, The 39
Authors Aloud UK 561
Authors' Club 553
Authors' Club Best First Novel 580
Authors' Contingency Fund, The 623
Authors' Foundation, The 623
Authors in Oundle 562
Author's Republic 223
Avery *see* Penguin Publishing Group
Avery Hill Publishing 121
Aviation News 39
Avon *see* HarperCollins Publishers
AW (Athletics Weekly) 40
Award Publications 121
Axelrod Agency, The 487
Axis 535
Anne Aylor Creative Writing Courses 646

BackTrack 40
Bad Apple Press 190
Bad Betty Press 121
Bad Lilies 40
Bad Press Ink 121
BAFTA (British Academy of Film and Television Arts) 549
BAFTA Rocliffe New Writing Competition 604
Baillie Gifford Prize for Non-Fiction, The 615
Jonathan Ball Publishers 201
Banbury Guardian 30
Bangor University 653
Banker, The 40
Banshee Press 122
BAPLA (British Association of Picture Libraries and Agencies) 535
Baptist Times 40
BARB 396
Barbican Library 660
Barbican Press 122

Barefoot Books 204
Verity Bargate Award 604
Kate Barker Literary Agency 454
Barnsley Book Festival 630
Barrington Stoke 122
Basic Books Group 204
David Bateman Ltd 199
Bath Festival, The 631
Bath Flash Fiction Awards 598
Bath Literary Agency 454
Bath Novel Award, The 580
Bath Spa University 653
Bay Tales Live 631
Bayeux Arts 194
BBC, The 391
BBC Books *see* Ebury Publishing
BBC Countryfile Magazine 40
BBC Gardeners' World Magazine 40
BBC History Magazine 40
BBC Music Magazine 41
BBC National Short Story Award 598
BBC News 15
BBC Radio 397
BBC Science Focus 41
BBC Sky at Night Magazine 41
BBC Top Gear 41
BBC Wildlife Magazine 41
BBC Written Archives Centre 663
Beacon Press 204
Bearded Badger Publishing 122
BECTU (Broadcasting Entertainment Communications and Theatre Union) 549
Bedford Square Publishers 122
Betimes Books 122
Beehive Illustration 517
Belfast Central Library 660
Belfast Telegraph 24
Belgrade Theatre, The 415
Bell Lomax Moreton Agency 454
Bella 41
Bella Books 204
Bellevue Literary Press 204
Lorella Belli Literary Agency (LBLA) 454
Bennion Kearny 122
Bent Agency, The 455, 487
Berghahn Books 122
Berlin Associates 455
Berman Literature Prize 577
Bernstein & Andriulli 517
Berwick Advertiser 26
Best 41
Bestseller Awards, The 573
Betterwrite 694
Between the Lines 194
BFI (British Film Institute) 549
BFI National Archive and Reuben Library 663
BFS Horizons 41
BFS Journal 42
British Guild of Travel Writers Members' Excellence Awards 621
Bibliographical Society 544
Big Issue, The 42
Big Red Illustration Agency, The 517
Bike 42
Bindery Agency, The 487
Binsted Prize 589
Biographers' Club Elizabeth Buccleuch Prize, The 583
Biographers' Club Hatchards Best First Biography Prize, The 584
Bird Watching 42
Birdwatch 42
Birkbeck College, University of London 653
Birlinn 123
Library of Birmingham 660
Birmingham Literature Festival 631
Birmingham Repertory Theatre Ltd 415
Biteback Publishing 123
Bitter Lemon Press 123
bks Agency, The 455
Black & White Publishing 123
Black Beauty & Hair 42
Black Bee Books 123
Black British Book Festival 631
Black Cat Poetry Press 123
David Black Agency 487
Black Dog Press 123
Black Inc Books 190
Black Writers' Guild 562
Blackbird Books 201
Malorie Blackman Scholarships for Unheard Voices, The 623
Blackpool Art Society, The 535
Blackpool Gazette 28
Blackstaff Press 123
Blair Partnership, The 455
Blake Friedmann Literary Agency 455
John Blake Publishing 124
Blink Publishing 124
Blithe Spirit 42
Bloodaxe Books 124
Bloodhound Books 124
Bloody Scotland Festival 631
Bloomsbury Academic Writing Fellowship 623
Bloomsbury Mentorship Programme 624
Bloomsbury Publishing 124, 190
Bloomsbury Publishing USA 205
Blue Diode Publishing 125
Blue Guides 125
Blue Pencil Agency Events 646
Blue Pencil Agency First Novel Award 595
Bluemoose Books 125
K. Blundell Trust, The 624
Boardman Tasker Award for Mountain Literature, The 619
Boat International 42
Bodleian Libraries of the University of Oxford 662
Bodleian Library Publishing 125
Bodley Head, The *see* Vintage
Bold Strokes Books 205
Boldwood Books 125
Bollinger Everyman Wodehouse Prize for Comic Fiction, The 613
Bolton News 28

Bonnier Books UK 125
Book Aid International 562
Book Bureau Literary Agency, The 456
Book Collector, The 43
Book Edit Writers' Prize 595
Book Guild, The 125
Book Marketing Society 556
Book Slam 353
BookBeat 223
Bookblast® CIC 694
Booker Albert Literary Agency, The 488
Booker Prize, The 585
Book*hug Press 194
Booklaunch 43
Bookouture 126
BookPrinting UK 695
Books Are My Bag Readers Awards 573
Books Council of Wales/Cyngor Llyfrau Cymru 540
Books Ireland 43
Books on the Hill Press 126
Bookseller, The 43
Booksellers Association, The 556
BookTrust 551, 669
BookTrust Represents 562
BookTrust Storytime Prize 575
Bootleg Theatre Company, The 415
Georges Borchardt 488
Borders Book Festival 631
Borris House Festival of Writing and Ideas 631
Boswell Book Festival 632
Boundless Theatre 421
Bournemouth Daily Echo 31
Bournemouth University 653
Bournemouth Writing Festival 632
Bournemouth Writing Prize, The 599
Boydell & Brewer 126
Bradford Literary Agency 488
Bradford Literature Festival 632
Neil Bradley Studio 87
Bradt Travel Guides 126
Brandt & Hochman Literary Agents 488
Branford Boase Award, The 575
Brattle Agency, The 488
George Braziller 205
Bread and Roses 632
Breakdown Press 126
Breakwater Books 194
Breathe 43
Brick Books 194
Brick Lane Bookshop Short Story Prize 599
Bridge Theatre, The 412
Bridport Prize, The 580
Bridport Prize Memoir Award, The 584
Bridport Prize: Poetry, The 589
Bridport Prize: Short Story and Flash Fiction, The 599
Briefly Write 43
Bright Agency, The 517
Bright Press, The 126
Brighton Festival 632
University of Brighton 653
Brilliant Publications 126
Bristol Cable, The 32
Bristol Central Library 660
Bristol Old Vic 415
Bristol Post 32
Bristol University Press/Policy Press 126
British Academy 540
British Academy Medals and Prizes 615
British Association of Journalists 546
British Birds 43
British Book Awards, The 573
British Book Design and Production Awards 570
British Centre for Literary Translation 560
British Chess Magazine 43
British Copyright Council 545
British Council, The 352, 540
British Czech and Slovak Association Writing Competition 577
British Fantasy Society, The 562
British Film Institute 127
British Guild of Agricultural Journalists 546
British Guild of Beer Writers 562
British Guild of Beer Writers Awards, The 618
British Guild of Travel Writers, The 562
British Haiku Society, The 349, 562
British Haiku Society Awards 589
British Institute of Professional Photography 535
British Interactive Media Association 535
British Library, The 662
British Library for Development Studies (BLDS) 664
British Library Publishing 127
British Medical Journal 43
British Museum Press, The 127
British Newspaper Archive 664
British Psychological Society Book Awards 620
British Science Fiction Association Awards 614
British Science Fiction Association Ltd 563
British Society of Magazine Editors 546
Broadcast 44
Rick Broadhead & Associates 485
Alan Brodie Representation 456
Broken Sleep Books 127
Brontë Parsonage Museum Collection, The 664
Jenny Brown Associates 456
Brown Bear Books 225
Anne Brown Essay Prize 616
Brown, Son & Ferguson 127
Browne & Miller Literary Associates 488
Brunel University London 653
Bruntwood Prize for Playwriting 605
Felicity Bryan Associates 456
Stern Bryan Fellowship 624
Bryntirion Press 127
Budleigh Salterton Literary Festival 632
Building 44
Building Design 44
Bukowski Agency, The 485
Bulletin 44
Bulls Presstjänst AB 87
Burford Books 205

Burlington Contemporary Art Writing Prize, The 583
Burlington Magazine, The 44
Gordon Burn Prize 585
Burnet Media 201
Burning Chair Publishing 127
Burning Eye Books 127
Janey Burton 695
Burton Mail 25
Buses 44
Bush Theatre 412
Business & Accountancy Daily 44
Business Post 15
Business Traveller 45
Buster Books *see* Michael O'Mara Books
Butcher's Dog 45
Buxton International Festival 632

Café Writers Norwich 353
Caine Prize for African Writing, The 599
Caird Library and Archive 664
Caitlin Press 195
John Calder Translation Prize, The 606
Caledonia Novel Award 595
Calon Books 127
Cambrian News 33
Cambridge Bibliographical Society 544
Cambridge Independent 25
Cambridge Literary Festival 632
Cambridge News 25
Cambridge University Library 663
University of Cambridge Institute of Continuing Education 653
Cambridge University Press & Assessment, Africa 201
Cambridge University Press & Assessment 128, 205
Cambridge University Press & Assessment Education Australia 190
Cameron Publicity and Marketing Ltd 695
Cameron's Management 483
Campaign 45
Campaign for Freedom of Information 550
Campbell *see* Pan Macmillan
Canadian Authors Association 556
Canadian Publishers' Council 556
Canadian Society of Children's Authors, Illustrators & Performers 556
Canbury Press 128
Candlewick Press 205
C&R Press 205
C&W Agency 456
Candy Jar Books 128
Canelo Group, The 128
Cannon Poets 354
Canongate Books 128
Canopus Publishing 225
Canterbury Festival 352, 633
Canterbury Festival Poet of the Year 589
Canterbury Library 661
Canterbury Press *see* Hymns Ancient and Modern
Jonathan Cape *see* Vintage
Georgina Capel Associates 457
Capital Crime Festival 633
Car 45
Car Mechanics 45
Caravan Magazine 45
Carcanet Press 128
Cardiff Central Library 661
Cardiff University 654
Carnegies, The 575
Rebecca Carter Literary 457
Cartoonists Club of Great Britain 536
Maria Carvainis Agency 489
Casa Ana Creative Writing Retreats 646
Casarotto Ramsay & Associates 457
Robert Caskie 457
Cassava Republic Press 128
Catapult Book Group 205
Catchpole Agency, The 457
Caterer, The 45
Catholic Herald, The 45
Catholic National Library 664
Catholic Pictorial 46
Catholic Truth Society 129
Lucy Cavendish Fiction Prize, The 580
Caxton Press, The 199
CB Editions 129
Cengage Learning 129
Cengage Learning Australia 190
Center Street 205
Central Illustration Agency 517
University of Central Lancashire 654
Century *see* Cornerstone
Ceramic Review 46
CGI Publishing 129
Château de Lavigny International Writers' Residence 646
Chained Library 664
Channel 4 393
Channel 5 393
Chapman Publishing 129
Charco Press 129
Charleston Festival 633
Charlton Press, The 195
CIEP (Chartered Institute of Editing and Proofreading) 546
Chartered Institute of Journalists, The 546
Chartered Institute of Library and Information Professionals (CILIP) 669
Chartered Institute of Linguists 560
Chartered Society of Designers, The 536
Chat 46
Chatto & Windus/Hogarth *see* Vintage
Chawton House Library 664
Cheltenham Illustration Awards 570
Cheltenham Poetry Festival International Poetry Prize 589
Cheshire Novel Prize, The 595
Chester Chronicle, The 28
University of Chester 654
Chetham's Library 664
University of Chicago Press 206
Chichester Festival Theatre 416
University of Chichester 654

Chicken House 129
Children's Book Award, The 575
Children's Books Ireland 551
Child's Play (International) 129
Chiswick Book Festival 633
Choc Lit *see* Joffe Books
Choir Press, The 695
Cholmondeley Awards 589
Teresa Chris Literary Agency 457
Christian Education 130
Chronicle, The 26
Chronicle & Echo, Northampton 25
Chronicle Books 206
Church of England Newspaper 46
Church Times 46
Churchwarden Publications 130
Cicada Books 130
Cicerone 130
Cico Books *see* Ryland Peters & Small
CILIP (The Library and Information Association) 550
Cinnamon Press 130
Cipher Press 130
Circle of Wine Writers 563
City Lights Publishers 206
City Lit 354, 647
City University of London 654
City AM 15
Clan Destine Press 191
Claret Press 130
Wm. Clark Associates 489
Anne Clark Literary Agency 457
Arthur C. Clarke Award 614
Ayebia Clarke Publishing Ltd 130
James Clarke & Co. 130
Classic Boat Magazine 46
Classic Cars 46
Classical Association 544
Classical Music 47
Mary Clemmey Literary Agency 458
Climate Fiction Prize 608
Climber 47
Cliveden Literary Festival 633
Cló Iar-Chonnacht Teo 130
Closer 47
Cloudscape Comics 195
Jonathan Clowes 458
Coast Is Queer, The 633
Coffee House Poetry 353
Coffee House Press 206
David Cohen Prize for Literature, The 585
Coin News 47
Collaborate Agency 518
Collective Ink 131
Colourpoint Creative 131
Columba Books 131
Columbia University Press 206
Colwill & Peddle 458
Comedy Women in Print Awards 613
Comics Cultural Impact Collective (CCIC), The 556
Comma Press 131
Commercial Motor 47
Commercial radio 397
Commonwealth Library and Archives 665
Commonwealth Short Story Prize 599
Community Care 47
Complete Creative Writing Course, The 647
Computer Weekly 47
Computeractive 47
Concord Theatricals 131
Concordia Publishing House 206
Condé Nast Traveller 47
Cōnfingō Magazine 47
Cōnfingō Publishing 131
Don Congdon Associates 489
Coningsby Gallery, The 518
Margaret Connolly & Associates 483
Conrad Press Ltd, The 695
Constable & Robinson *see* Little, Brown Book Group
Consulting Cops for Writers 695
Contact Theatre Company 416
Conversation, The 15
Conversation Prize, The 616
CookeMcDermid 486
Coombs Moylett Maclean Literary Agency 458
Gemma Cooper Literary 458
Doe Coover Agency, The 489
Coppercoat Brian Black Memorial Award 571
Copyright Clearance Center Inc. 545
Cordite Books 191
Cork International Short Story Festival and Poetry Festival 633
Cork University Press 132
Cornell University Press 206
Cornerstone 132
Cornerstones 695
Cornish Guardian 32
Cornishman 32
Corvisiero Literary Agency 489
Cosmopolitan 48
Cotswold Life 48
Council for British Archaeology 132
Country Books 132
Country Homes and Interiors 48
Country Life 48
Country Living 48
Country Walking 48
Countryman Press, The 206
Countryside Books 132
Courier, The 29
Cove Park 647
Coventry Telegraph 34
Crafts Council Research Library 665
Ingrid Cranfield 695
Crank, The 48
Crannóg 48
Cranthorpe Millner Publishers 133
CRC Press *see* Taylor & Francis Group
Creation Theatre Company 416
Creative Access 624
Creative Australia 540
Creative Authors 459
Creative Content Ltd 223

Creative Coverage 518
Creative Folkestone Book Festival 633
Creative Future Writers' Award 595
Creative Media Agency 489
Creative Rights in AI Coalition 556
Creative Scotland 540, 624
Creative Sparrow 518
Creative UK 556
Creative Writer's Workshop, The 647
Crescent Moon Publishing 133
Cressrelles Publishing 133
Rupert Crew 459
Crime Writers' Association 563
Criminal Lines 611
Julie Crisp Literary Agency 459
Critical Quarterly 49
Critics' Circle, The 563
Andrew Crofts 696
Crow & Cross Keys 49
Crowdbound 133
Crown House Publishing 133
Crown Publishing Group 206
Crowood Press, The 133
Crystal Magazine 49
Cuba Press, The 199
Cuckfield Book Festival 634
Cúirt International Festival of Literature 634
Cull & Co. 459
Cumbria and Lakeland Walker 49
University of Cumbria 654
Cundill History Prize 618
Curae Prize, The 585
Curious Minds 634
Curtis Brown 459, 489
Curtis Brown (Australia) 483
Curtis Brown Creative 647
Curve 416
Custom Car 49
CWA Dagger Awards 611
Cycling Weekly 49
CYMERA 634
CYMERA Prize for Speculative Short Fiction 600
Cyphers 49

Dahlia Books 133
Laura Dail Literary Agency 490
Daily Express 15
Daily Mail 15
Daily Mirror 16
Daily Post 33
Daily Record 16
Daily Star 16
Daily Star Sunday 16
Daily Telegraph 16
Dana Research Centre and Library, The 665
Darf Publishers 134
Dark House Literary & Screen Agency 460
Jenny Darling & Associates 484
Darlington and Stockton Times 26
Darton, Longman and Todd 134
Darts World 49
Daunt Books 134
Daunt Books Festival, The 634
David & Charles 134
Caroline Davidson Literary Agency 460
Rhys Davies Short Story Competition, The 600
DAW Books 207
Dawntreader, The 49
Liza Dawson Associates 490
Dayton Literary Peace Prize 578
DB Publishing 134
De Montfort University 654
Felix de Wolfe 460
Dead Ink Books 134
Début Art 518
Decanter 50
Dedalus 134
Dedalus Press 134
Deià Writers' Camps 647
Deixis Press 134
Delayed Gratification 50
delicious. 50
Delta Books *see* Jonathan Ball Publishers
Richard Dennis Publications 135
Deptford Literature Festival 634
Derby Book Festival 634
Derby Telegraph 25
Derby Theatre 416
University of Derby 654
Descent: The magazine of underground exploration 50
DESIBlitz 634
Design. Publishing. Inclusivity. 624
Desperate Literature Short Fiction Prize 600
Deutsche Börse Photography Foundation Prize 571
Devon Life 50
DHH Literary Agency 460
Jacinta di Mase Management 484
Diagram Prize for Oddest Book Title 573
Diagram Visual Information 225
Dialect Press 135
Dialogue 135
Diamond Books 135
Diamond Kahn & Woods Literary Agency 460
Dickensian, The 50
dif 563
Digital Camera 50
Sandra Dijkstra & Associates 490
Elise Dillsworth Agency 460
Disabled Poets Prize 589
Discoveries 625
Discovery Walking Guides 135
Disney+ 395
DIVA 50
Diverse Book Awards, The 585
DK 135
DMG Media Licensing 87
Do Books 136
Dodo Ink 136
Dogs Today 51
Donaghy Literary Group 486
Donmar Warehouse 412
Dorset Echo 32
Douglas & McIntyre 195

Dovecote Press, The 136
Dover Publications 207
dp books 136
Drapers 51
Dream Catcher 51
Dref Wen 136
Druid 416
Drummond Agency 484
Dublin Book Festival 635
Dublin Gazette 24
DUBLIN Literary Award 585
Dublin Review, The 51
Duckworth Books 136
Robert Dudley Agency 461
Pol Roger Duff Cooper Prize, The 615
Dukes, The 416
Dundee Evening Telegraph 29
Dundee Rep and Scottish Dance Theatre Limited 416
Dundurn Press 195
Dunham Literary 490
Dunmore Publishing 199
DunnFogg 461
Dunow, Carlson & Lerner 490
Durham Advertiser 27
Durham Book Festival 635
Dutch Uncle 518
Dynasty Press 136
Dystel, Goderich & Bourret 490

Ealing Book Festival 635
Early English Text Society 544
Early Music 51
University of East Anglia 655
East Anglian Book Awards 585
East Anglian Daily Times 25
East Riding Festival of Words 635
Eastern Angles Theatre Company 421
Eastern Daily Press 25
eBookPartnership.com 696
EBRD Literature Prize 606
Ebury Publishing 136
Eccles Institute & Hay Festival Writer's Award, The 578
Echo 24, 30
Echo Publishing 191
Economica 51
Economist, The 51
ECW Press 195
Eddison Pearson 461
Edge Hill Short Story Prize 600
Edge Hill University 655
Edify 199
Edinburgh Bibliographical Society 544
Edinburgh Comic Art Fair 635
Edinburgh Essay Award 616
Edinburgh Flash Fiction Award 600
Edinburgh International Book Festival 635
Edinburgh Napier University 655
Edinburgh Novel Award 608
Edinburgh Short Story Award 600
Edinburgh True Flash Award 600
University of Edinburgh 655
Edinburgh University Press 137
Edinburgh Women's Fiction Festival 635
Editegrity 696
Editors' and Proofreaders' Alliance of Northern Ireland 546
Educate 51
Educational Company of Ireland, The 137
Edwards Fuglewicz Literary Agency 461
EE TV 396
Eglantyne Books 137
Eland Publishing 137
Electrical Review 52
Elephant Press 137
Edward Elgar Publishing 137
T.S. Eliot Prize, The 590
ELK Publishing 191
ELLE (UK) 52
Ethan Ellenberg Literary Agency, The 491
Elliott & Thompson 137
Elsevier 138
Elsevier Australia 191
Elsevier (Clinical Solutions) 207
Elsewhen Press 138
Elwin Street Productions 225
Embroidery magazine 52
Emerging Author Dagger, The 580
Emerging Writers Programme 625
Emma Press, The 138
Empire 52
Encore Award 609
Encyclopaedia Britannica (UK) 138
Energy Engineering 52
Engineer, The 52
Engineering in Miniature 52
English Association 550
English Association English 4–11 Children's Picture Book Awards 575
English Garden, The 52
English Speaking Board (International) 550
English-Speaking Union, The 551
Enitharmon Editions 138
Ennis Book Club Festival 635
Entente Littéraire Prize 576
Equinox Publishing 138
Erbacce Prize 590
Erotic Review 53
Escalator New Writing Fellowships for Emerging Writers 625
ESEA Literary Festival 635
ESEA (East Asian and Southeast Asian) Publishing Network 563
Esquire 53
Essex Chronicle 30
University of Essex 655
Europa Editions 207
European Broadcasting Union 546
European Union Prize for Literature 607
Europress Features (UK) 87
Evening Express (Aberdeen) 29
Evening News (Edinburgh) 29
Event & Visual Communication Association 536

Everyman Theatre Cheltenham 417
Everyman's Library 138
Everything with Words 138
Christopher Ewart-Biggs Memorial Prize 578
University of Exeter Library, Special Collections 665
Exeter Northcott Theatre 417
University of Exeter Press 139
University of Exeter 655
Exisle Publishing 191
Helen Exley 139
Express & Echo 32
Express & Star 34
Eye Books 139
Eye Candy Illustration 518

FAB Prize for Undiscovered Talent 595
Faber Academy 647
Faber & Faber 139
Faber/Observer/Comica Graphic Short Story Prize, The 601
Fabian Society 139
Face, The 53
FACT (Federation Against Copyright Theft) 545
Alfred Fagon Award, The 605
Fahrenheit Press 139
Fairbank Literary Representation 491
Fairlight Books 139
CJ Fallon 139
Falmouth Book Festival 636
Falmouth University 655
Family Tree 53
Farmers Weekly 53
Farrar, Straus and Giroux 207
Farshore Books *see* HarperCollins Publishers
Feather Proof Books 207
Featherstone Cairns 461
Federation of British Artists 536
Federation of European Publishers 557
Feminist Library 665
Feminist Press, The 207
Fernhurst Books 139
Fernwood Publishing 195
David Fickling Books 140
Fictionfire Literary Consultancy 647
Fictive Dream 53
Field, The 53
Fig Tree *see* Penguin General
Fighting High 140
Fillingham Weston Associates 461
Film Rights 461
Financial Times 17
Financial Times and Schroders Business Book of the Year Award 615
Finborough Theatre 412
Diana Finch Literary Agency 491
Fincham Press 140
Findhorn Press 140
Fine Art Trade Guild 536
FinePrint Literary Management 491
Finish Your Novel 696
Fircone Books 140
Firefly Press 140
Firewords 53
First Graphic Novel Award 571
First Novel Prize 596
Fish Publishing Writing Prizes 581
Fishing News 53
Fitzcarraldo Edition/Mahler & Lewitt Studios Essay Prize 616
Fitzcarraldo Editions 140
Fitzhenry & Whiteside 195
5mBooks 140
Flame Tree Publishing 140
Flapjack Press 140
Flash: The International Short-Short Story Magazine 54
Fleet Street Quarter Festival of Words 636
Fleming Publications 141
Flipped Eye Publishing 141
Flora 54
Floris Books 141
Fly Fishing & Fly Tying 54
Flyaway Books 207
Flying Eye Books 141
Fly on the Wall Press 141
FOCAL (Federation of Commercial AudioVisual Libraries International Ltd) 536
Folding Rock 54
Folens Publishers 141
Folio Book Illustration Award 571
Folio Illustration Agency 518
Folio Literary Management 491
Fonthill Media 141, 207
Fool for Poetry Chapbook Competition 590
Footnote Press 141
Foreign Press Association in London 546
Foresight News 87
Forest Avenue Press 207
Forge *see* Tor Publishing Group
Fortean Times 54
Fortnum and Mason Food and Drink Awards 618
42 462
Forty20 54
Forward Arts Foundation 551
Forward Prizes for Poetry 590
W. Foulsham & Co. 142
Four Courts Press 142
FourFourTwo 54
fourteen poems 55
Foxes' Retreat Tailored Writing Retreats 648
Foyle Young Poets of the Year Award 356
FRA 462
Franco-British Society's Literary Award, The 578
Maria Frankland Creative Writing Courses 648
Fraser Ross Associates 462
Free Association Books 142
Free Books Campaign 551
Free Books Festival 636
Free Painters & Sculptors London 536
Freemantle Press 191
Freesat 396
French House Party, Carcassonne, The 648
Friedrich Agency, The 491

Friend, The 55
Friends of Libraries 669
Friends of National Libraries 669
Frieze 55
Frog Literary Agency 462
Frogmore Papers, The 55
From You To Me 142
FT Adviser 55
Fulcrum Publishing 208
Furrow, The 55
Future Tense Books 208
Future Worlds Prize for Fantasy & Science Fiction Writers of Colour 614
Fuzzy Flamingo 696

Jüri Gabriel 462
Gaelic Books Council/Comhairle nan Leabhraichean, The 540
Gaia Books *see* Octopus Publishing Group
Gaia Partnership 648
Gale & Co 648
Gallery Press, The 142
Galley Beggar Press 142
Gallic Books *see* Pushkin Press
Garden Answers 55
Garden Media Guild, The 563
Garden Media Guild Awards 618
Garden News 55
J. Garnet Miller *see* Cressrelles Publishing
Garnet Publishing 142
Garsdale Retreat 648
Gay Times 55
Gecko Edit 696
Gelfman Schneider Literary Agents 492
Gemini Books Group 143
Genesis Emerging Writers Programme 625
Genesis Poetry Slam 353
Geographical 56
Getty Publications 208
Ghastling, The 56
Ghost Orchid Press 143
Gibbons Stamp Monthly 56
Gibbs Smith 208
Gibson Square 143
Gill 143
Giller Prize, The 578
Gingko 143
Gladstone's Library 665
Glamour 56
Glasgow Evening Times 29
University of Glasgow 655
Glassboxx 696
GLL Literary Foundation Author Placements 625
Global Blended Learning 225
Global Lion Intellectual Property Management 492
Globe Law and Business 143
Gloucester Citizen 32
Gloucestershire Echo 32
Goat Star Books 143
David R. Godine, Publisher 208
Godsfield Press *see* Octopus Publishing Group
David Godwin Associates (DGA) 462
Goethe-Institut Award for New Translation, The 607
Goethe-Institut London Library 665
Barry Goldblatt Literary 492
Goldfinch Novel Award, The 576
Frances Goldin Literary Agency 492
Goldsboro Books Glass Bell Award 609
Goldsmiths Press 143
Goldsmiths Prize, The 609
Golf Monthly 56
Golvan Arts Management 484
Good Food 56
Good Housekeeping 56
Good Illustration 519
Good Ship Illustration, The 648
Bill Goodall Literary Agency 463
Irene Goodman Literary Agency 492
Goose Lane Editions 196
Gordon Hill Press 196
GQ 56
Graeae Theatre Company 421
Graffeg 144
Winston Graham Historical Prize 613
Graham Maw Christie 463
Grammar Factory Publishing 696
Grand Central Publishing 208
Grange, The 649
Granite Noir 636
Granite Noir Short Story Competition 601
Granta 57
Granta Books 144
Graywolf Press 208
Grazia 57
Great Outdoors Magazine, The 57
Annette Green Authors' Agency 463
Christine Green Authors' Agent 463
Green Ink Writers' Gym 649
Green Print *see* Merlin Press
Louise Greenberg Books 463
Sanford J. Greenburger Associates 492
Greene & Heaton 463
Greene Door Project, The 626
Greenhouse Literary Agency, The 464
Greenock Telegraph 29
Greenstone Literary 464
Greeting Card Association 537
Eric Gregory Awards, The 626
Gresham Books 144
Gresham Publishing Company, The 144
Greyhound Literary 464
Griffin Poetry Prize, The 590
Jane Grigson Trust Sous Chef Award 618
Grimsby Telegraph 34
Grocer, The 57
David Grossman Literary Agency 464
Grosvenor House Publishing 696
Grove Atlantic, Inc. 208
Grow Your Own 57
Grub Street Publishing 144
Guardian 17
Guardian Licensing 87
Guernica Editions 196

Guernsey Literary Festival 636
Guild of Aviation Artists, The 537
Guild of Food Writers 564
Guild of Food Writers Awards 618
Guild of Health Writers 564
Guild of International Songwriters & Composers, The 553
Guild of Master Craftsman Publications 144
Guild of Motoring Writers, The 564
Guild of Railway Artists 537
Guildford Book Festival 636
Guildhall Library 666
Guillemot Press 145
Guinness World Records 145
Guitarist 57
Marianne Gunn O'Connor Literary, Film/TV Agency 464
Guppy Publishing 145
Gutter 57
Gwyn Palmer Associates (Literary Agents) 464

Hachette Aotearoa New Zealand 199
Hachette Australia 191
Hachette Book Group 208
Hachette Children's Trade 145
Hachette Learning 145
Hachette UK 145
Hadean Press 145
Hakluyt Society 564
Halban Publishers 146
Halcyon Publishing 146
Halifax Courier 35
Halsgrove Publishing 146
Hamilton Agency, The 464
Hamish Hamilton *see* Penguin General
Hamlyn *see* Octopus Publishing Group
Hampshire Chronicle 30
Hampstead Theatre 412
Hanbury Agency, Literary Agents, The 465
H&E naturist 58
Handsome Frank 519
Happy Yak 146
Hardie Grant UK 146
Hardman & Swainson 465
Harleian Society 564
Harlequin Enterprises 196
Harlequin UK 146
HarperCollins Publishers 146, 209
HarperCollins Publishers (Australia) 191
HarperCollins Publishers (Canada) 196
HarperCollins Publishers (New Zealand) 199
Harper's Bazaar 58
Harpeth Road Press 209
Harriman House 148
Joy Harris Literary Agency, The 492
Harrogate Theatre 417
Hart Publishing *see* Bloomsbury Publishing
Hartlepool Mail 27
Harvard University Press 209
Harvill Secker *see* Vintage
Antony Harwood 465
Hashtag Press 148
Hastings Book Festival 636
Hastings Book Festival Competition 590
Haunt Publishing 148
Haus Publishing 148
John Hawkins & Associates 493
Haworth Agency, The 465
Hawthorn Press 148
Hawthornden Fellowships 626
Hawthornden Prize, The 585
Hay Festival 637
Hay Festival Book of the Year 586
Hay House Publishers 148
Haynes Publishing 148
Hayters Teamwork 87
Hazel Press 149
Francis Head Bequest 626
Head of Zeus *see* Bloomsbury Publishing
Headline Publishing Group 149
Headliners 87
Headlong Theatre 422
Headpress 149
Heart of Albion 225
Heat 58
A.M. Heath & Co. 465
hedgerow: a journal of small poems 58
Hello! 58
Héloïse Press 149
HelpMePublish Consultancy 697
Henley Literary Festival 637
Henley Hall Press 149
Henningham Family Press 149
Henshaw Press Short Story Competition 601
Hera Books 149
Herald 17, 32
Herald Express 33
Herald on Sunday 17
Here Comes Everyone 58
Hereford Times 33
Jeff Herman Agency, The 493
Nick Hern Books 149
Hesketh Hubbard Art Society 537
Hesperus Press 150
HG Literary 493
HHB Agency 465
Hi-Fi News 58
Sophie Hicks Agency 466
High Life 58
High Spot Literary 484
David Higham Associates 466
Highland Book Prize 586
Hill Nadell Literary Agency 493
William Hill Sports Book of the Year Award 621
Hilliard Society of Miniaturists, The 537
Hinterland 58
Hippocrene Books 209
Historical Novel Society 564
Historical Writers' Association 564
History Press, The 150
History Today 59
Histria Books 209
Hobeck Books 150
Hodder & Stoughton 150

Calvin and Rose G. Hoffman Memorial Prize, The 616
Holiday House 209
Holland House Books 150
Holroyde Cartey 466
Henry Holt and Company 209
Vanessa Holt 466
Holroyde Cartey 519
HOME 417
Homes & Gardens 59
Honno (Welsh Women's Press) 150
HopeRoad 150
Johns Hopkins University Press 210
Hopscotch 150
Kate Hordern Literary Agency 466
Horror Writers Association 565
Horse & Hound 59
Horse & Rider 59
Hortus 59
Valerie Hoskins Associates 466
Hot Key Books 151
Hot Press 59
Houghton Mifflin Harcourt 210
House & Garden 59
House of Anansi Press and Groundwood Books 196
House of Riviera 151
W. F. Howes Ltd 224
Howgate Publishing 151
Huddersfield Daily Examiner 35
Huddersfield Literature Festival 637
Hugo Awards, The 614
Huia Publishing 199
Hull Daily Mail 35
Hull Truck Theatre Co. Ltd 422
University of Hull 655
Clare Hulton Literary Agency 466
Hulu 396
Hurst – The John Osborne Arvon Centre, The 649
Hurst Publishers 151
Hutchinson Heinemann *see* Cornerstone
HWA Crown Awards, The 613
HWA Dorothy Dunnett Short Story Competition, The 601
Hymns Ancient and Modern 151

I Am in Print 565
I AM Writing Competitions 596
i Paper 18
i Weekend 18
Icon Books 151
Icon Magazine 60
i-D 60
Ideal Home 60
Idler, The 60
Ig Publishing 210
Igloo Books 151
Ignite Books 152
Ignite Fellowship 626
Ilkley Literature Festival 637
University of Illinois Press 210
IllustrationX 519
Image by Design Art Licensing 519
Imaginative Book Illustration Society 537
Imison Award, The 605
Imperial War Museum Archive and Reading Room 666
Imprint Academic 152
Inanna Publications and Education 196
Independent 18
Independent Bookshop Week 637
Independent Press Standards Organisation 547
Independent Publishers Guild 557
Independent Radio News (IRN) 87
Independent Society of Musicians 553
Independent Talent Group 467
Independent Theatre Council 549
Index on Censorship 60
Indexing Specialists (UK) Ltd 697
Indiana University Press 210
Indie Book Awards 573
Indie Champions Awards 573
Indie Press Network 557
Indiegogo 189
Indigo Dreams Publishing 152
Indigo Press, The 152
Influx Press 152
Infobase Publishing 210
K&IM Information Resources Awards, The 574
Ink Sweat & Tears 60
Inkandescent 152
Inkfish Magazine 60
Inkshares 210
Inkwell Group, The 697
InkWell Management 493
Inky Illustration 519
Inner Traditions Bear & Company 211
Inside Soap 60
Inspired Quill 152
Institute of Designers in Ireland 537
Institute of Public Administration 152
Institute of Translation and Interpreting, The 561
Insurance Age 61
InterMedia 61
International Affairs 61
International Authors Forum 557
International Booker Prize, The 586
International Literature Festival Dublin 637
International Poetry Business Book & Pamphlet Competition, The 591
International Prize for Arabic Fiction 578
International Publishers Association 557
International Society of Typographic Designers 537
International Thriller Writers 565
Internet Library for Librarians 669
Inverness Courier 29
Investors' Chronicle 61
Invisible Publishing 196
InWords Literary Award (TILA), The 609
IOP Publishing 152
Iota Shot Pamphlet Awards 591
Ipsos MORI 397
Ipswich Star 25
Ireland's Own 61

Irish Academic Press 153
Irish Arts Review 61
Irish Copyright Licensing Agency, The 545
Irish Examiner 18
Irish Farmers Journal 61
Irish Independent 18
Irish Medical Times 61
Irish News 24
Kerry Group Irish Novel of the Year Award 586
Irish Pages: A Journal of Contemporary Writing 62
Irish Pages Press/Cló An Mhíl Bhuī, The 153
Irish Times 18
Irish Writers Centre 557
Irish Writers Centre – Áras Scríbhneoirí na hÉireann 649
Irish Writers' Union/Comhar na Scríbhneoirí 557
ISF Publishing 153
Isis Audio 224
Island Prize 578
Isle of Wight Writing Courses and Workshops 649
Isle of Wight County Press 30
Ithaca Press *see* Garnet Publishing
ITV Plc 394
Ivors Academy, The 553
Ivy Press 225
IWM (Imperial War Museums) Publishing 153

JABberwocky Literary Agency 493
Jacaranda Books 153
Heather Jackson Literary Agent 493
P.D. James Memorial Fund, The 626
Jane's 153
Jane's Defence Weekly 62
Janklow & Nesbit Associates 493
Janklow & Nesbit (UK) 467
Oscar Janson Smith Agency 467
Jantar Publishing 153
Jawdance 353
JBA Over 50 Debut Award, The 596
Richard Jefferies Award 619
Jelly Bean Self-Publishing 697
Jericho Writers 649
Jermyn Street Theatre 412
Jersey Evening Post 24
Jewish Book Week 637
Jewish Chronicle 62
Jewish Telegraph 62
JewishGen Press 211
JFL Agency 467
Jhalak Poetry Prize 591
Jhalak Prose Prize 586
Joffe Books 153
Joffe Books Prize for Crime Writers of Colour 611
Johnson & Alcock 467
Jolly Fish Press 211
Tibor Jones & Associates 467
Jordan Publishing 154
Journal, The 27
Journalists' Charity 547
Journey Books 697
JQ Ghostwriting Agency, The 697
JSR 519
Jane Judd Literary Agency 467
Juta and Company 201

Kane Literary Agency 468
University Press of Kansas 211
Michelle Kass Associates 468
Keane Kataria Literary Agency 468
B.L. Kearley Art & Antiques 519
Keats–Shelley Prize 616
Keller Media 494
Ned Kelly Awards 612
Kelpies *see* Floris Books
Kenilworth Press *see* Quiller Publishing
Margaret Kennedy Agency 484
Kensington Publishing 211
Kent and Sussex Courier 30
Kent & Sussex Poetry Society 353
Kent and Sussex Poetry Society Open Poetry Competition 591
Bill Kenwright Ltd 413
Kerrang! 62
Ki Agency 468
Kickstarter 189
Kids Can Press 196
Kids Corner 520
Kiln Theatre 413
Kindle Direct Publishing 697
Kindle Storyteller Award 596
Laurence King Publishing 154
King's Head Theatre 413
King's Lynn Festival 637
King's Lynn Literature Festivals 638
Jessica Kingsley Publishers *see* John Murray Group
Kingston University 656
Kitchen Garden 62
Kitchen Press 154
Kitschies, The 614
Harvey Klinger 494
Knight Agency, The 494
Knight Errant Press 154
Knight Hall Agency 468
Knopf Canada *see* Penguin Random House Canada
Knopf Doubleday Publishing Group 211
Koa Press 200
Kobo 224
Kobo Writing Life 697
Kogan Page 154
Korero Press 154
KPMG Children's Books Ireland Awards, The 576
Kraszna–Krausz Book Awards 571
Krause Publications 211
Stuart Krichevsky Literary Agency 494
kt literary 494
Kube Publishing 154
University of KwaZulu-Natal Press 201
Kyle Books 154

Lake, The 62
Lambda Literary Awards 609
Lambeth Palace Library 666
Lancashire Post 28
Lancashire Telegraph 28

Lancaster University 656
Lancet, The 63
LandScape Magazine 63
Peter Lang 155
Lantana Publishing 155
Laurel Prize, The 591
Lawbook 191
Lawrence & Wishart 155
Lawyer, The 63
Laxfield Literary Associates 468
LBA Books 469
Le Verger 649
Susanna Lea Associates 469, 494
Leader, The 33
Bryony Leah Editorial 697
Leamington Books 155
Leapfrog Global Fiction Prize 596
Ledbury Poetry Competition 591
Ledbury Poetry Festival 352, 638
Leeds Library 661
Leeds Lit Fest 638
Leeds Playhouse 417
University of Leeds 656
Legend Press 155
Leicester Mercury 26
Leisure Painter & The Artist 63
Lemonade Illustration Agency 520
Levine Greenberg Rostan Literary Agency 495
Barbara Levy Literary Agency 469
Lewinsohn Literary Agency 469
David Lewis Illustration Agency 520
Lexington Literary 469
LexisNexis 155
LexisNexis Australia 192
LexisNexis Canada 197
LexisNexis NZ 200
LGC (Local Government Chronicle) 63
Libraries Connected 669
Libraries Week 669
Library Campaign, The 669
Library of the Society of Friends, The 666
Library Planet 669
Life and Work: The Magazine of the Church of Scotland 63
Lightning Books 155
Lilliput Press, The 155
Limelight Celebrity Management 469
Liminal Pages 698
Limnisa Writing Retreats By the Sea 650
Frances Lincoln 156
Lincoln Review, The 63
University of Lincoln 656
Lincolnshire Echo 35
Lindsay Literary Agency 470
Linen Hall Library 666
Linguist, The 63
Lipstick of London 520
Listening Books Members' Choice Award 605
Listowel Writers' Week 638
Listowel Writers' Week Poetry Competitions 591
Literary Consultancy (TLC), The 698
Literary Office, The 470
Literary Review 63
Literature Alliance Scotland 558
Literature Wales 349, 540
Literature Works 541
Litfest 638
Litro 64
Little, Brown and Company 211
Little, Brown Book Group 156
Little People Books 225
Little Theatre Guild of Great Britain 549
Little Tiger Press 156
Little Toller Books 157
Little White Lies 64
Live Theatre 417
Liverpool Central Library 661
Liverpool Echo 28
Liverpool Everyman and Playhouse 417
Liverpool John Moores University 656
Liverpool Literary Agency, The 470
Liverpool University Press 157
Living Plantfully 64
Llewellyn Worldwide 212
Nilsson Local Heritage Writing Award 586
Local Legend 698
James Lockhart Agency 470
Logaston Press 157
LOM ART 157
London Bubble, The 422
London College of Communication 656
London Film School, The 657
The London Ghostwriting Company 698
University of London, Goldsmiths 656
London Grip 64
London Hellenic Prize, The 579
London Independent Story Prize 601
London Library 661
London Literature Festival 638
London Magazine Poetry Prize, The 592
London Magazine: A Review of Literature and the Arts, The 64
London Magazine Short Story Prize, The 601
London Press Club Awards 583
London Review of Books 64
University of London, Royal Holloway 656
London Screenwriters' Festival 638
London Standard 26
London Writers Awards, The 609
Lonely Planet 212
Lonely Planet Publications 157
Long Poem Magazine 64
Elizabeth Longford Prize for Historical Biography, The 584
Julia Lord Literary Management 495
Loud Poets (I Am Loud CIC) 353
Loudhailer Books 157
Louie Award, The 602
Love Stories etc... 638
LoveReading4Kids 551
Nicky Lovick 698
Andrew Lownie Literary Agency 470
Luath Press 157
Lucent Dreaming 157

Luithlen Agency 470
Lumb Bank – The Ted Hughes Arvon Centre 650
Lume Books *see* Joffe Books
Luna Press Publishing 157
Lund Humphries 158
Lurid Editions 158
Lutterworth Press, The 158
Lutyens & Rubinstein 471
David Luxton Associates 471
Lyons Press, The 212
Lyra Bristol Poetry Festival 639
Lyric Hammersmith 413

M6 Theatre Company 422
Donald Maass Literary Agency 495
Mabecron Books 158
Macavity Awards 612
Margret McBride Literary Agency 495
Gina Maccoby Literary Agency 495
McGill-Queen's University Press 197
McGraw-Hill Canada 197
McGraw-Hill Education 158, 192
McGraw-Hill Professional 212
McIntosh & Otis 495
MACK 158
Frances McKay Illustration 520
Bryan MacMahon Short Story Award 602
Macmillan Education *see* Springer Nature
Macmillan Education South Africa 201
Macmillan Prize for Illustration, The 571
Macmillan Publishers 212
Eunice McMullen 471
McNidder & Grace 158
McPherson & Company 212
McSweeney's Books 213
Magma Poetry 65
Sarah Maguire Prize, The 607
Mail, The 28
Mail on Sunday 18
Major Books 158
Major Street Publishing 192
Mākaro Press 200
Management Books 2000 158
Management Today 65
Manchester Central Library 661
Manchester Evening News 28
Manchester Fiction Prize, The 602
Manchester Literature Festival 639
Manchester Poetry Library 351
Manchester Poetry Prize, The 592
University of Manchester 657
Manchester University Press 159
Manchester Writing School at Manchester Metropolitan University, The 657
Mandrake of Oxford 159
Mango Books 159
Manilla Press 159
Carol Mann Agency 496
Mantra Lingua 159
Margate Bookie Festival 639
Marjacq Scripts 471
Market House Books 225
Marketing Week 65
Michael Marks Awards for Poetry Pamphlets, The 592
Marlborough Literature Festival 639
Marsh Agency, The 471
Marsh Ecology Book of the Year 619
Evan Marshall Agency, The 496
Maskew Miller Learning 202
University of Massachusetts Press, The 213
Massey University Press 200
Somerset Maugham Awards, The 581
Maven Literary Management 471
Maverick House 159
May Literary Agency 471
Kevin Mayhew 159
MBA Literary and Script Agents 471
MBUK (Mountain Biking UK) 65
McDermid Debut Award 581
Jemma McDonagh Agency 472
McIlvanney Prize for the Scottish Crime Novel of the Year 612
Sarah McKenzie Literary Management 484
McKitterick Prize, The 581
Juliet McLauchlan Prize, The 616
MCN (Motor Cycle News) 65
Medal News 65
Media Freedom Awards, The 583
Media Music Now 224
Media Society, The 547
Media.info 398
Medina Publishing 159
Medway Messenger 31
Megaphone Writer Development Scheme 627
Meiklejohn Illustration 520
Melbourne University Press 192
Melville House 213
Men's Health 65
Mensch Publishing 160
Mentor Books 160
Mercier Press, The 160
Mercury Theatre Colchester 418
Scott Meredith Literary Agency 496
Mereo Books 698
#Merky Books New Writers' Prize 596
Merlin Press 160
Merrell Publishers 160
Methodist Recorder 65
Metonymy Press 197
Metro 19
Metro Publications 160
MiblArt 698
University of Michigan Press, The 213
Microsoft Press Books 213
Middlesex University 657
Madeleine Milburn Literary, TV & Film Agency 472
Milkweed Editions 213
David Miller Internship Programme 627
Mills & Boon *see* Harlequin UK
Rachel Mills Literary 472
Mill, The 28
Milo Books 160

Milton Keynes Literary Festival 639
MinK 586
Mirror Books 160
Missenden School of Creative Arts 650
University of Missouri Press 213
MIT Press, The 213
Mitchell Beazley *see* Octopus Publishing Group
Mitchell Library 661
MMBcreative 472
MMM (The Motorhomers' Magazine) 65
Model Engineer & Workshop 66
Modern Poetry in Translation 66
Mojo 66
MoneyWeek 66
Moniack Mhor 650
Monty Lit Fest 639
Moonflower 160
Moore Prize for Human Rights Writing 620
Morgan Green Creatives 473
Morley College 650
Morning Star 19
Morrigan Book Company/City of Dublin Press 161
Moth Nature Writing Prize, The 596
Moth Poetry Prize, The 592
Moth Short Story Prize, The 602
Motor Boat and Yachting 66
Motorship, The 66
Mslexia 66
Mslexia Competitions: Novel (Adult) 609
Mslexia Competitions: Poetry 592
Mslexia Competitions: Short Story and Flash Fiction 602
Mud Pie 161
Muddy Pearl 161
Munster Literature Centre, The 565
Murdoch Books 161
Judith Murdoch Literary Agency 473
Michael Murphy Memorial Poetry Prize 592
John Murray Group 161
Mushens Entertainment 473
Music Publishers Association 554
Music Teacher 67
Music Week 67
Musical Opinion 67
Mustapha Matura Award and Mentoring Programme 605
Muswell Press 161
My Weekly 67
Myriad Editions 162
Mythopoeic Fantasy Award for Adult Literature, The 614
Mythopoeic Scholarship Award in Myth and Fantasy Studies, The 614
Mythopoeic Society, The 565

Nagle Agency, The 473
Jean V. Naggar Literary Agency 496
Naher Agency, The 485
Kate Nash Literary Agency 473
National, The 19
National Acrylic Painters' Association 538
National Art Library 666
National Association of Writers and Groups 565
National Association of Writers' Groups 351
National Association of Writers in Education (NAWE) 355
National Book Critics Circle 558
National Book Critics Circle Awards 574
National Centre for Writing 565, 650
National Council for the Training of Journalists 547
National Eisteddfod of Wales 639
National Film and Television School 657
National Library of Scotland 663
National Library of Wales 663
National Literacy Trust 552, 669
National Poetry Competition 593
National Poetry Day 639
National Poetry Library 351
National Society for Education in Art and Design 538
National Trust Magazine, The 67
National Union of Journalists 547
Natural History Museum Library and Information Services 666
Natural History Museum Publishing 162
Nature 67
Nature Chronicles Prize 619
Naxos AudioBooks 224
NB Illustration 520
NB Magazine 67
NB Publishers 202
NCW Emerging Translators Mentorships 607
Neal Street Productions Ltd 413
University of Nebraska Press 214
Neem Tree Press 162
Nelson Education 197
Thomas Nelson Publisher 214
Nero Book Awards 586
Ness Book Fest 640
Netflix 396
New Adult Book Prize 610
New Africa Books 202
New Angle Prize for East Anglian Literature 587
New Chapter 581
New Delhi World Book Fair 640
New Directions 214
New English Art Club (NEAC) 553
New European, The 19
New Harbinger Publications 214
New Holland Publishers 192
New Humanist 67
New Internationalist 67
New Island Books 162
New Law Journal 68
New Media Writing Prize 583
New Menard Press, The 162
University of New Mexico Press 214
New Perspectives Theatre Company 422
New Poets Prize, The 593
New Scientist 68
New Statesman 68
New Theatre: Dublin, The 418
New Theatre Quarterly 68

New Vic Theatre 418
New Welsh Review 68
New Welsh Rarebyte 162
New Welsh Writing Awards: Rheidol Prize for Prose with a Welsh Theme or Setting 602
New Wolsey Theatre, The 418
New Writers Award 597
New Writers Collective 627
New Writing North 566
New Writing South 566
New Zealand Book Awards for Children and Young Adults 576
New Zealand Council for Educational Research 200
New Zealand Writers Guild 558
Newcastle City Library 661
Newcastle Noir 640
Newcastle University 657
NeWest Press 197
News and Star (Carlisle) 29
News Letter 24
News Media Association 547
News, Portsmouth, The 31
Newsbrands Scotland 547
Next Big Story, The 610
Next Generation Indie Book Awards 574
Nimbus Publishing 197
Nine Arches Press 162
Nine Dots Prize 617
Nine Pens 162
NME (New Musical Express) 68
Nobrow *see* Flying Eye Books
Noemi Press 214
No Exit Press *see* Bedford Square Publishers
Nordisk Books 162
Norfolk & Norwich Festival 640
Norfolk and Norwich Millennium Library 662
North, The 68
University of North Carolina Press, The 214
North Literary Agency, The 473
North Point Press *see* Farrar, Straus and Giroux
Northbank Talent Management 473
Northern Echo, The 27
Northern Gravy 69
Northern Poetry Library 351
Northern Stage (Theatrical Productions) Ltd 418
Northern Writers' Awards 587
Northodox Press 163
Northumbria University 657
W.W. Norton & Co. 163, 214
Norwich Book Festival 640
Norwich Evening News 25
Norwich Writers' Circle 566
Nosy Crow 163
Nota Bene Prize 610
Nothing in the Rulebook 566
Nottingham Playhouse 418
Nottingham Post 26
Nottingham Trent University 657
Nourish Books 163
Jane Novak Literary Agency 485
Novel editing services 699
Novelry, The 650
Andrew Nurnberg Associates 474
Nursery World 69
Nursing Times 69

Seán Ó Faoláin International Short Story Competition, The 602
Oak Tree Press 163
Oberon Press 197
O'Brien Press, The 163
Observer, The 19
Ockham New Zealand Book Awards 579
Ockham Publishing Group 163
OCM Bocas Prize for Caribbean Literature 579
Octagon Theatre 418
Octopus Publishing Group 164
Odyssey Books 200
Ofcom 391
Off the Shelf Festival of Words Sheffield 640
Offord Books 164
OK! 69
University of Oklahoma Press 214
Old Barn Books 164
Old Pond Publishing 164
Old Red Lion Theatre, The 413
Oldie, The 69
Oleander Press, The 164
Olive 69
Michael O'Mara Books 165
Omnibus Press/Wise Music Group 165
On Stream Publications 165
Oneworld Publications 165
Open College of the Arts 650
Opera 69
Opera Now 70
OR Books 214
Orange Tree Theatre 413
oranges journal 70
Orbis International Literary Journal 70
Orbit *see* Little, Brown Book Group
Orenda Books 165
Originate Literary Agency 474
Orion Publishing Group, The 165
Orphans Publishing 166
Orpheus Books Ltd 226
Ortac Press 166
Orwell Prizes, The 583
Osprey Publishing 166
Otago University Press 200
Otherwise Publishing 699
Oundle Festival of Literature 640
OUP First Book Prize 617
Our Dogs 70
Out-Spoken 353
Out-Spoken Press 166
Outline Artists 520
Oversteps Books 166
Oxford Bibliographical Society 544
Oxford Brookes University 658
Oxford Literary Festival 640
Oxford Mail 31
Oxford Poetry 70
Oxford Review of Books 70

Listings index

Oxford Times, The 31
Oxford University 658
Oxford University Press 166, 215
Oxford University Press, Canada 197
Oxford University Press Southern Africa 202
Oxford University Summer Schools 650
Oxford Weidenfeld-Translation Prize 607
Oxford/42 New Writing Prize 605

P&H Books 166
PA Media 88
Pact (Producers Alliance for Cinema and Television) 549
Page Turner Awards 610
Paines Plough 422
Paisley Book Fest 641
Paisley Daily Express 30
Palgrave Macmillan *see* Springer Nature
Palimpsest Press 197
Pan Macmillan 167
Pan Macmillan Australia 192
Pan Macmillan SA 202
Ayesha Pande Literary 496
Panorama: The Journal of Travel, Place and Nature 70
Paper Lion 474
Paper Literary 474
Paragon Publishing 699
Paramount+ 396
Park, Fine & Brower Literary Management 496
Parracombe Prize 603
Parthian Books 167
Passionfruit Review, The 71
Pastel Society, The 538
Pavilion Books *see* HarperCollins Publishers
Pavilion Poetry 167
PBJ Management 474
PC Pro 71
Pearson Canada 197
Pearson UK 167
Peepal Tree Press 167
Jonathan Pegg Literary Agency 475
P8tech 168
Peirene Press 168
Pelagic 168
Pelican Publishing 215
Pen & Sword Books 168
PEN Heaney Prize 593
PEN International 566
Pen to Print 566
Penguin General 168
Penguin Michael Joseph 169
Penguin Press 169
Penguin Publishing Group 215
Penguin Random House 215
Penguin Random House Australia 192
Penguin Random House Canada 198
Penguin Random House Children's UK 169
Penguin Random House New Zealand 200
Penguin Random House South Africa 202
Penguin Random House UK 169
Penguin Random House UK Audio 169
Penguin Young Readers 215
Pennine Platform 71
University of Pennsylvania Press 215
Pennsylvania State University Press 215
People's Book Prize, The 587
People's Friend, The 71
Samuel Pepys Award, The 617
Pérez Literary & Entertainment 475
Period Living 71
Permanent Press, The 215
Persephone Books 169
Personal Managers' Association Ltd, The 558
Perspective Books 169
Peterborough Telegraph 26
Peters Fraser & Dunlop 475
Petrona Award 612
PEW Literary 475
PFD Queer Fiction Prizes 597
Phaidon Press 170
Philip's *see* Octopus Publishing Group
Phoenix Publishing House 170
Phosphor Art 520
Photographer, The 71
Piatkus Constable & Robinson *see* Little, Brown Book Group
Alison Picard, Literary Agent 496
Piccadilly Press 170
PICSEL (Picture Industry Collecting Society for Effective Licensing) 545
Pimlico *see* Vintage
Pink News 19
Pippin Properties 497
Player–Playwrights 550
Playmarket 485
Plexus Publishing 170
Plot Agency, The 475
Plough Prize, The 593
Plum Agency, The 521
Pluto Press 170
University of Plymouth 658
PN Review 71
Poems on the Move 593
Poetry Archive, The 351
Poetry Book Society, The 349
Poetry Business, The 349
Poetry Ireland 349
Poetry Ireland Review/Iris Éigse Éireann 71
Poetry Kit, The 351
Poetry London 72
Poetry London Prize, The 593
Poetry Review, The 72
Poetry School, The 355
Poetry Society, The 349
Poetry Society Education 355
Poetry Space 352
Poetry Wales 72
Poets and Writers 352
Poets' Café 353
Sylvie Poggio Artists Agency 521
Poke, The 20
Polari 353
Polari Book Prize 587

Policy Press *see* Bristol University Press/Policy Press
Political Quarterly, The 72
politics.co.uk 20
Polity Press 170
John Pollard Foundation International Poetry Prize, The 593
Pomegranate PA 699
Poolbeg Press 170
Popcorn Writing Award, The 606
Portland Press 170
Portobello Literary 475
Potomac Books 216
powerHouse Books 216
Shelley Power Literary Agency 476
PR Week 72
Practical Boat Owner 72
Practical Caravan 72
Practical Fishkeeping 72
Practising Midwife, The 73
Premier Woman Alive 73
Prepare to Publish Ltd 699
Press, The 35
Press and Journal 30
Press 53 216
Press Gazette 73
Prestel Publishing 171
David Price 699
Pride 73
Prima 73
Primadonna Festival 641
Princeton University Press 216
Princeton University Press – Europe 171
Printmakers Council 538
V.S. Pritchett Short Story Prize 603
Private Eye 73
Private Libraries Association 551, 670
Professional Cartoonists' Organisation 538
Professional Publishers Association 558
Profile Books 171
Prole 73
Propel Magazine 73
Prospect Magazine 74
Proteus Theatre Company 422
Prototype 171
Prototype Development Programme 627
Prototype Prize 603
PRS for Music 554
P.S. Literary Agency 486
Psychologies 74
Public Library News 670
Public Media Alliance 397
Publishers Association (PA) 558
Publishers Association of New Zealand (Te Rau o Tākupu) 558
Publishers' Association of South Africa 558
Publishers' Publicity Circle 559
Publishing Ireland/Foilsiú Éireann 559
Publishing Scotland 559
Publishizer 189
PublishNation 699
Puffin *see* Penguin Young Readers
Pulsar Poetry Webzine 74
Pulse 74
Pure Indigo 171
Push the Boat Out Festival 641
Pushing Out the Boat 74
Pushkin House Book Prize 579
Pushkin Press 171
Puzzle House, The 88
Pyramid *see* Octopus Publishing Group

Quadrant Books 171
Quantum *see* W. Foulsham & Co.
Quartet Books 171
Quarto Group Publishing UK 172
Quarto Publishing Group USA 216
Queen Mary Wasafiri New Writing Prize 581
Queen's Reading Room, The 552
Queen's Reading Room Medal, The 587
Queen's Theatre, Hornchurch 419
Queen's University, Belfast 658
University of Queensland Press 192
Quercus Publishing 172
Questors Theatre, The 413
QuietManDave 603
Quiller Publishing 172
Quirk Books 216

RA Magazine 74
Radiant Press 198
Radio Academy, The 398
Radio Society of Great Britain 172
Radio Times 74
Radiocentre 398
RAIL 75
Railway Gazette International 75
Railway Magazine, The 75
Rainbow Poetry Recitals 354
Rainham Poetry Festival 641
RAJAR 398
Peggy Ramsay Foundation, The 627
Rand McNally 216
Random House Children's Books 216
Random House Publishing Group 217
Rann Media 88
Ransom Publishing 172
RatedWriters.com Book Awards 597
Raworths Harrogate Literature Festival 641
Razorbill *see* Penguin Young Readers
RBA Annual Exhibition 571
RCW 476, 521
Reach Poetry 75
Read for Good 552
Reading Agency, The 552, 670
Reading Chronicle 31
Reaktion Books 172
Record Collector 75
Red 75
Red Ladder Theatre Company 422
Red Pepper 75
Red Planet Books 172
Redhammer Management 476
Reedsy 699
Reedsy Short Story Contest 603

Rees Literary Agency 497
Reform 76
Renard Press 173
Ruth Rendell Award 576
Repeater Books 173
Reporters Without Borders 548
Republic of Consciousness Prize for Small Presses 574
Resurgence & Ecologist 76
Retail Week 76
Rethink Press 700
Revenge Ink 173
Rhiza Edge 192
Rialto, The 76
Rialto Nature and Place Poetry Competition, The 594
Lisa Richards Agency, The 476
Richford Becklow Agency 476
Right Book Company, The 700
Angela Rinaldi Literary Agency, The 497
Ringwood Publishing 173
Ringwood Short Story Competition 603
Rizzoli International Publications 217
RNIB National Library Service 667
Rocking Chair Books Literary Agency 476
Rocky Nook 217
Rodale Book Group 217
University of Roehampton 658
Deborah Rogers Foundation Writers Award 597
Romance Writing Festival 641
Romantic Novel of the Year Awards, The 613
Romantic Novelists' Association, The 567
Romaunce Books 173
George Ronald 173
Ronsdale Press 198
Rooney Prize for Irish Literature 582
Root Literary 497
Rita Rosenkranz Literary Agency 497
Jane Rotrosen Agency 497
Rouleur 76
Route 173
Routledge 217
Routledge *see* Taylor & Francis Group
Rowanvale Books Ltd 700
Rowman & Littlefield *see* Bloomsbury Publishing
Royal Academy of Arts 541
Royal Birmingham Society of Artists 541
Royal Central School of Speech and Drama, The 658
Royal Collection Trust 173
Royal College of Music, Museum and Library Collections 667
Royal Court Theatre 414
Royal Exchange Theatre Company Ltd 419
Royal Institute of Oil Painters 541
Royal Institute of Painters in Water Colours 541
Royal Literary Fund, The 627
Royal Lyceum Theatre Company 419
Royal Musical Association, The 541
Royal National Institute of Blind People (RNIB) 173 76
Royal National Theatre 414
Royal Photographic Society, The 542
Royal Photographic Society Awards, The 572
Royal Scottish Academy of Art and Architecture, The 542
Royal Shakespeare Company 419
Royal Society, The 542
Royal Society of Arts 542
Royal Society of British Artists 542
Royal Society of Literature 542
RSL Christopher Bland Prize 582
RSL Giles St Aubyn Awards for Non-Fiction 627
RSL Ondaatje Prize 588
Royal Society of Marine Artists 542
Royal Society of Miniature Painters, Sculptors and Gravers, The 543
Royal Society of Painter-Printmakers 543
Royal Society of Portrait Painters 543
Royal Society of Portrait Painters Awards 572
Royal Society of Sculptors 543
Royal Society Trivedi Science Book Prize, The 620
Royal Society Young People's Book Prize, The 620
Royal Television Society 397
Royal Watercolour Society 543
Royal West of England Academy 543
RP Critical Writing Prize, The 617
RSL Jerwood Poetry Awards 594
RSL Literature Matters Awards 628
RTÉ 395
RTÉ Radio 1 Short Story Competition in Honour of Francis MacManus 603
RTÉ Radio, Drama On One, P.J. O'Connor Radio Drama Awards 606
Rubery Book Award 588
Ruby Tuesday Books 174
Rugby World 76
Runner's World 76
Running Press Group 217
Ruppin Agency Writers' Studio, The 651
Rutgers University Press 217
Regina Ryan Publishing Enterprises 497
Rye Arts Festival 641
Ryland Peters & Small 174
John Rylands Research Institute and Library 667
Rymour Books 174

S4C 395
SAA (Supporting All Artists) 538
Saga Magazine 77
SAGE Publishing 174
Sailing Today with Yachts & Yachting 77
Sainsbury's magazine 77
University of St Andrews 658
St David's Press 174
St Martin's Press 217
St Pauls Publishing 174
University of Salford 658
Salisbury International Arts Festival 641
Salisbury Playhouse 419
Salmon Poetry 174
Salt Publishing 174
Saltires: Scotland's National Book Awards, The 588
Sans. PRESS 174

Santa Monica Press 217
Sapere Books 175
Saqi Books 175
Saraband 175
Sasquatch Books 218
Saveas Writers' International Writing Competition 597
Sayle Literary Agency, The 477
Sayle Screen 477
Scarborough News, The 35
Scattered Authors' Society 567
SCBWI-BI Writers' Events 651
Schofield & Sims 175
Scholastic 175, 218
Scholastic Australia 193
School Libraries in View/SLG Newsletter 77
School Library Association (SLA) 670
Susan Schulman Literary Agency 498
Ilse Schwepcke Prize, The 621
Science Museum Group 175
Scientific Computing World 77
SCM Press *see* Hymns Ancient and Modern
Scorpius Books 175
Scotland on Sunday 20
Scotland Street Press 176
Scots Magazine, The 77
Scotsman 20
Walter Scott Prize for Historical Fiction 613
Scottish Arts Club 553
Scottish Association of Writers 567
Scottish Book Trust 552
Scottish BPOC Writers Network (SBWN) 559
Scottish Farmer, The 77
Scottish Fellowship of Christian Writers 567
Scottish Field 77
Scottish Mountaineering Press 176
Scottish Poetry Library 351
Scottish Press Awards 583
Scottish Sun 20
Scottish Universities' International Summer School 651
Scratch Books 176
Screen Daily 78
Scribe 176
Scripture Union 176
Scunthorpe Telegraph 35
SE London Book Fest, The 642
Sea Angler 78
Sea Breezes 78
Seal Press 218
Seamus Heaney Centre at Queen's, The 350
Search Press 176
Second Story Press 198
Seen and Heard 78
Linda Seifert Management 477
Self-Publishing Conference, The 642
Self-Publishing Partnership Ltd, The 700
Selfies Book Awards, The 574, 597
SelfMadeHero 176
Self-Publishing Review 700
Sentinel 34
September Publishing 176
Seren 176
Seven Stories – The National Centre for Children's Books 552
Sevenoaks Literary Festival 642
Seventh Agency 477
Seventh Avenue Literary Management 486
Severn House 177
Sewing Directory, The 78
SFX Magazine 78
Shakespeare North Playhouse 419
Shaw Agency, The 477
Shearsman Books 177
Sheffield Hallam University 658
Sheffield Theatres 420
Sheil Land Associates 477
Caroline Sheldon Literary Agency *see* RCW
Sheldon Press *see* John Murray Group
Sheldrake Press 177
Shepheard-Walwyn (Publishers) 177
Hannah Sheppard Literary Agency 478
Sherborne Literary Society 567
Sherborne Prize for Travel Writing 622
Sherborne Travel Writing Festival 642
Wendy Sherman Associates 498
Sherman Theatre 420
Shields Gazette, The 27
Ships Monthly 78
Shooter Literary Magazine 78
Shoreline of Infinity 79
Short Books *see* Octopus Publishing Group
Shortlands Poetry Circle 354
Show of Strength Theatre Company Ltd 420
Shropshire Star 34
Shuter and Shooter Publishers 202
Mo Siewcharran Prize 598
Sight and Sound 79
Sigma Press 177
Silvertail Books 177
SilverWood Books 700
Dorie Simmonds Agency 478
Simon & Schuster 218
Simon & Schuster (Australia) 193
Simon & Schuster Children's Publishing Division 219
Simon & Schuster UK 177
André Simon Memorial Fund Book Awards, The 618
Sincere Corkscrew 178
Olga Sinclair Prize, The 603
Siri Scientific Press 178
Sirius Media Services Ltd 88
Philippa Sitters Associates 478
Skein Press 178
Sky 396
Skyhorse Publishing 219
Skyros Writers' Lab 651
Slightly Foxed 79
SmashBear Publishing 178
Wilbur Smith Adventure Writing Prize 610
Colin Smythe 178
Jill Smythies Award, The 572
Snowbooks 178

Snowflake Magazine 79
SoapBox Spoken Word CIC 354
Socciones Literary Consultancy 700
Socialist Worker 20
Social Spider 26
Society for Promoting Christian Knowledge (SPCK) 178
Society for Theatre Research, The 550
Society of Artists Agents 559
Society of Authors 559
Society of Botanical Artists, The 538
SCBWI (Society of Children's Book Writers and Illustrators) 567
Society of Civil and Public Service Writers, The 567
Society of Editors 548
Society of Genealogists 178
Society of Graphic Fine Art 538
Society of Heraldic Arts 539
Society of Medical Writers, The 568
Society of Medical Writers Competitions 621
Society of Scribes and Illuminators 539
Society of Wildlife Artists 539
Society of Women Artists, The 539
Society of Women Writers & Journalists 548
Society of Young Publishers 559
Softwood Books 700
Soho Agency, The 478
@sohoplace 414
Soho Press 219
Soho Theatre 414
Somerville Press 178
Songwriting and Composing 79
Sourcebooks 219
South Wales Argus 33
South Wales Echo 33
South Wales Evening Post 34
Southern Daily Echo 31
Southport Reporter 29
Sparsile Books 179
Speaking Volumes 568
Spectator, The 79
Spellbinder Magazine 79
Sphere *see* Little, Brown Book Group
Sphinx Theatre Company 423
Spiffing Publishing 701
Spinifex Press 193
Philip G. Spitzer Literary Agency 498
Sports Book Awards, The 621
Sports Journalists' Association 548
Spread the Word 568
Spring Literary 478
Springer Nature 179
Square Mile 80
SRL Publishing 179
Stage, The 80
Stainer & Bell 179
Stairway Press 219
Stairwell Books 179
Stamp Magazine 80
Stand Magazine 80
Edward Stanford Travel Writing Awards, The 622
Stanford University Press 220
Stanfords Travel Writers Festival, The 642
Stanley/Barker 179
Cullen Stanley International 498
StAnza: Scotland's International Poetry Festival 642
States of Independence 642
Elaine Steel Writers' Agent 479
Abner Stein 479
Micheline Steinberg Associates 479
Stenlake Publishing 179
Stephen Joseph Theatre 420
Sterling Lord Literistic 498
Rochelle Stevens & Co 479
Stevns Translation Prize 607
Stewed Rhubarb Press 180
Stimola Literary Studio 499
Stinging Fly, The 80
Stinging Fly/FBA Fiction Prize 604
University of Stirling 658
Stiwdio Maelor 651
Bram Stoker Awards 612
Storm Publishing 180
Story Therapy 553
Storymix 226
STR Theatre Book Prize 617
Strad, The 80
Straid Collection Awards 594
Strange Region 180
Stratford Herald 31
Stratford-upon-Avon Literary Festival 642
Streetcake Magazine 80
Strong Words 80
Studio Press 180
Stuff 81
Style at Home 81
Stylist 81
Sarah Such Literary Agency 479
Summersdale Publishers 180
Sun 20
Sun on Sunday 20
Sunday Express 21
Sunday Independent 21
Sunday Life 24
Sunday Mail 21
Sunday Mercury 34
Sunday Mirror 21
Sunday National 21
Sunday People 21
Sunday Post 21
Sunday Sun 27
Sunday Telegraph 22
Sunday Times, The 22
Sunday Times Charlotte Aitken Young Writer of the Year Award, The 582
Sunderland Echo 27
Sunflower Books 180
Survivors' Poetry 350
Susijn Agency, The 479
Sustainable Story Award 621
Swansea Grand Theatre 420
Swansea University Dylan Thomas Prize 588
Sweet Cherry Publishing 180
Swift Press 180

Swindon Advertiser 31
Swindon Festival of Literature 643
Syndey University Press 193

TA First Translation Prize 608
Tablet, The 81
Tachyon Publications 220
Ta-Ha Publishers 181
James Tait Black Prizes, The 584
Take a Break 81
Take a Break's Take a Puzzle 81
Talawa Theatre Company 423
Tale Publishing 193
Tallbean 521
tall-lighthouse 181
Tangerine Press 181
Tantamount 701
Taproot Books 181
Tarquin Publications 181
Tartarus Press 181
Taschen UK 181
Tate Enterprises 181
Tate Etc 81
Tate Library & Archive 667
Tatler 81
I.B. Tauris *see* Bloomsbury Publishing
Taxation 81
Taylor & Francis Group 181
Reginald Taylor and Lord Fletcher Essay Competition 617
Te Herenga Waka University Press 200
Tears in the Fence 82
Tees Valley Artists of the Year 628
Teeside Gazette 27
Telegraph & Argus 35
Telegraph – Content Licensing & Syndication, The 88
Television 82
Templar Books 182
Templar Poetry 182
Templer Medal Book Prize 619
Tempo 82
Ten Speed Press 220
University of Tennessee Press 220
Michael Terence Publishing 701
Tes (The Times Educational Supplement) 22
Tess (The Times Educational Supplement Scotland) 22
University of Texas Press 220
Thames & Hudson 182
THE (Times Higher Education) 22
Theakston Old Peculier Crime Novel of the Year Award 612
Theakston Old Peculier Crime Writing Festival 643
Theatr Clwyd 420
Theatre Centre 423
Theatre Royal Bath 420
Theatre Royal Plymouth 420
Theatre Royal, Stratford East 414
Theatre Royal Windsor 421
Thinkwell Books 182
Thistle Publishing 182
Vicki Thomas Associates 521
Thompson Educational Publishing 198
Thomson Reuters 22
Thomson Reuters – Round Hall 182
Thornapple Press 198
3 Seas Literary Agency 499
3dtotal Publishing 182
3TimesRebel 182
Thriller Awards 612
ThunderPoint Publishing 182
TikTok Book Awards 611
Tilted Axis Press 182
Tim Saunders Publications 701
Times, The 22
Times and Sunday Times Cheltenham Literature Festival, The 643
Times/Chicken House Children's Fiction Competition, The 577
Tin House 220
Tinniswood Award, The 606
Tiny Owl Publishing 183
Tippermuir Books 183
Tir na n-Og Awards 577
Titan Books 183
TLC ACE Free Reads Scheme 628
TLS (The Times Literary Supplement) 23
Today's Golfer 82
Top Santé 82
Tor Publishing Group 220
University of Toronto Press 198
Tortoise 23
Totleigh Barton 651
Tottenham Literature Festival 643
Toucan Books 226
Tower Poetry 350
Christopher Tower Poetry Competition 356
Trail 82
Tramp Press 183
Trans Publishing Network 559
Transatlantic Agency 486
Translation Prizes, The 608
Translators Association 561
Transworld 183
Betty Trask Prize, The 582
Travellers' Tales 651
Travelling Scholarships, The 628
Traverse Theatre 421
Simon Trewin Creative 480
Trident Media Group 499
Tring Book Festival 643
Trinity College Library Dublin 663
Troika 183
Trotman Indigo Publishing 183
Troubador 701
Trout & Salmon 82
Truck & Driver 82
Try Writing 701
TSO (The Stationery Office) 183
Tundra Books 198
Tupelo Press 221
Turas Press 183
Jane Turnbull Agency 480

Nick Turner Management 480
Tuttle Publishing/Periplus Editions 221
TV Foundation, The 568
TV Times Magazine 83
Two Rivers Press 184
Two Windmills 184
Tŷ Newydd Writing Centre 651 355

UAL (University of the Arts, London) Short Course Office 652
UCLan Publishing 184
UCL Press 184
UEA Live 643
UEA Publishing Project 184
Ugly Hill Press 201
Ulric Publishing 184
Ulverscroft 184
Unicorn Publishing Group 184
Unicorn Theatre 414
Union Square & Co. 221
Unisa Press 203
United Agents 480
University College Dublin Press 185
Unnamed Press | Smith & Taylor Classics 221
UNSW Press 193
Unwin Award, The 620
Merlin Unwin Books 185
Upstart Crow Literary 499
Urban Writers' Retreat 652
Usborne Publishing 185
User Design, Illustration and Typesetting 701
UWA Publishing 193

Vallentine Mitchell 185
Valley Press 185
Van Schaik Publishers 203
V&A Illustration Awards, The 572
Vegan, The 83
Vegan Food & Living 83
Velocity Press 185
Ver Poets 354
Ver Poets Open Competition 594
Verso 185
Vertebrate Publishing 185
Verve Poetry Press 185
Viking *see* Penguin General
Viking Sevenseas NZ 201
Vintage 186
Virgin Media 396
Virginia Prize for Fiction, The 611
Visible Fictions 421
Viz 83
Vogue 83
Voice, The 23, 33
Voice of the Listener & Viewer 548

Suzann Wade Management 480
Wainwright Prize, The 619
Waitrose Food 83
Wales Book of the Year Award 588
Wales Broadcast Library 667
Wales on Sunday 23
University of Wales Press 186
University of Wales Trinity Saint David 659
walk 83
Walker Books 186
Wallpaper* 83
Wanderlust 83
War Cry, The 84
Warwick Prize for Women in Translation, The 608
Warwick Words History Festival 643
Warwick Writing Programme 659
Wasafiri 84
Wasafiri Essay Prize 617
University of Washington Press 221
WaterBrook Multnomah Publishing Group 221
Waterstones Debut Fiction Prize 582
Waterways World 84
Watford Palace Theatre 421
Watkins Publishing 186
Watkins/Loomis Agency 499
Watson, Little 480
Waywiser Press, The 187
WayWORD Festival 643
Weatherglass Books Novella Award 604
Weatherglass Press 187
Wee Book Company, The 187
Week, The 84
Weekly Gleaner 23
Josef Weinberger Plays 187
Welbeck Publishing Group 187
Wellcome Collection Non-Fiction Awards 628
Wellcome Library 667
Wells Festival of Literature 644
Wells Festival of Literature Competitions 588
Welsh Academic Press 187
Welsh Poetry Competition 594
WENN 88
Western Daily Press 33
Western Morning News 33
Westminster Book Awards 620
Westminster Music Library and Archives 667
Westminster Reference Library 662
Westwood Creative Artists 486
Wet Grain 84
Wey Poets (Surrey Poetry Centre) 355
WGM Atlantic Talent and Literary Group 481
What's On TV 84
Whispering Buffalo Literary Agency 481
White Bear Theatre Club 415
Eve White Literary Agency 481
White Magic Studios 701
Whitecap Books 198
Whitefox Publishing 702
Whittet Books 187
Wide Eyed Editions 187
Dinah Wiener 481
Wigtown Book Festival 644
Wigtown Poetry Prizes 594
Wild Hunt Books 187
Wildlife Photographer of the Year 572
Wild Things Publishing 187
Wildthought Books 187
John Wiley & Sons Australia 193
John Wiley & Sons 188 221

Wilkinson Publishing 193
Alice Williams Literary 481
Philip Wilson Publishers 188
Wimbledon Book Fest 644
Winchester Books Festival 644
Winchester Poetry Festival 644
Winchester Poetry Prize 594
Windham-Campbell Prizes 628
Windmill Books 226
Wingate Literary Prize 579
Claire Wingfield Editorial & Literary Services 702
Wisdom Publications 222
Wits University Press 203
WME 481, 499
Wolf Literary Services 499
Wolfson History Prize, The 619
Woman 84
woman&home 84
Woman's Own 85
Woman's Weekly 85
Wombat Books 193
Women Poets' Network from the Rebecca Swift Foundation 568
Women's Library @ LSE 668
Women's Prize for Fiction 611
Women's Prize for Non-Fiction 615
David T.K. Wong Fellowship 628
Wooden Books 188
Worcester News 34
Word Tank, The 702
WordLink Incorporated 500
Wordsworth Library 668
Working Class Movement Library 668
Working Partners 226
Workman Publishing Company 222
World Illustration Awards 572
World of Interiors, The 85
World Soccer 85
World Today, The 85
Worldcon 644
Worshipful Company of Stationers and Newspaper Makers, The 548
WOW London Festival 644
Wrate's Editing Services 702
Wrecking Ball Press 188
Wren Library 668
Write Out Loud 352
Write-on Group, The 350
WriteNow Programme 629
Writers & Artists 652
Writers & Artists: Access to All 629
Writers' & Artists' Working-Class Writers' Prize 598
Writers' & Artists' Yearbook 2026 Short Story Competition 604
Writers Bureau, The 652
Writers' Cabin at Write Within 652
Writer's Digest Books 222
Writers Guild of America, East 560
Writers Guild of America, West 560
Writers Guild of Canada 560
WGGB (Writers' Guild of Great Britain) 560
Writers Guild of Ireland 560
Writers House 500
Writers' Practice, The 482
Writers' Summer School at Swanwick, Derbyshire, The 652
Writers' Union of Canada, The 560
WritersMosaic 568
Writing East Midlands 568
Writing Hall, The 702
Writing Magazine 85
Writing Magazine: Grand Prize 604
Writing Magazine: Swanwick Summer School Competition 604
Writing West Midlands 569
Wylie Agency, The 500

Yachting Journalists' Association 548
Yachting Monthly 85
Yachting World 85
YALC (Young Adult Literature Convention) 645
Yale University Press 222
Yale University Press London 188
Susan Yearwood Agency 482
Yellow Jersey Press *see* Vintage
Yen Press 222
YMU Literary 482
York Theatre Royal 421
Yorkshire Dalesman, The 86
Yorkshire Post 35
@YouCaxton 702
Young Poets Network 356
Young Vic Theatre Company 415
Your Dog Magazine 86
Your Horse Magazine 86
YouView 396

Zaffre 188
Zambezi Publishing 188
Sheikh Zayed Book Award 579
Zed Books *see* Bloomsbury Publishing
Zeitgeist Agency 485
Zeno Agency 482
ZigZag Education 188
Zooker Award 582
Zoological Society of London Library 668

Listings index